Introduction to Information Science

Introduction
to
Information
Science

compiled
& edited
by
Tefko Saracevic

R. R. BOWKER COMPANY
New York & London
1970

Published by R. R. Bowker Company
(A Xerox Company)
1180 Avenue of the Americas
New York, N.Y. 10036

Copyright © 1970 Xerox Corporation
All rights reserved.

ISBN: 0-8352-0313-1
Library of Congress Catalog Card
Number: 77-108783

Manufactured in the United States
of America

TO BLANKA, AIDA, ALAN
AND
TO MY PARENTS

Contents

PART THREE—EVALUATION OF INFORMATION SYSTEMS

Preface

In selecting and organizing material for this source-book, the compiler hopes to find an audience which shares some of his professional interests, outlook, and educational problems — an audience to whom the book may be of value in two respects: as an indication of an overall framework, structure, connections and directions in the field of information science, and as an educational text for learning and teaching.

On the most general level this book is based on the question, "What was and what is the work in information science all about?" It is intended for the student of the "information problem" working in disciplines that are directly and primarily devoted to that problem — disciplines such as information science, information retrieval, librarianship, documentation, and computer science — as well as for the student from any of the disciplines that are in part devoted to investigating the behavior of information and the processes of communication — disciplines such as psychology, linguistics, logic, systems engineering, electrical engineering, cybernetics, etc.

The main emphasis of this book is on work of a theoretical and experimental nature rather than on practical applications. However, the articles selected are viewed as having a considerable potential in two major respects: they have important implications for the practice of information handling, but even more important, they contain aspects of generalization. The book is oriented toward basic and experimental work, such as that performed by traditional sciences, with the hope that a reader may find much relevant to his own interests, educational level and background, a bridge toward generalizations, a feeling of interconnection between seemingly unrelated works either presented in the book or found in the literature, an awareness of apparent gaps in knowledge, and even ideas for practical solutions or further theoretical or experimental work. Since this is a book of readings, these things may be pointed out but cannot be elaborated upon — the reader is left to his own elaborations.

From a personal standpoint this book is a result of lacks, wants, and needs. In the past, my education and research efforts have been hampered by the lack of an overall structure (i.e., an order of parts) of the field of information science, in terms of which some generalizations and relations may be expressed. Numerous perfectly acceptable, clear, and concise definitions of the subject matter of information science have been offered, but still lacking is an intellectual framework into which a variety of theoretical, experimental, philosophical and practical works from various fields on the general subject of information behavior and communication processes may be fitted so that their interconnections are clear.

For teaching purposes, we have also desperately needed texts summarizing, synthesizing, interpreting, and connecting the results of investigations widely dispersed over time, over fields, over approaches and over several literatures. Although in general we have sensed that there is a unity, the unifying structure has yet to be explicitly stated. Although we also have felt that there are significant relationships among a number of philosophical statements, theories, and experiments and a variety of practical information systems, such relationships have not been formally or practically worked out. I am not the first person to whom the idea of a synthesizing textbook in information science (not information retrieval) has appealed. In the absence of such a textbook other teachers in my school and I have selected a limited number of readings for class discussion in some depth. From the selection of these readings has evolved the structure and context exhibited in this sourcebook. Over the years the students in our school were very receptive to our selections and their enthusiasm was actually the prime impetus for the publication of this book. Thus, the organization of and selections in the book have been successfully applied and tested in an educational situation.

The difficulties in discerning a structure, a wholeness, interrelations, and organization are not solely a property of information science. Like many other modern fields, information science has a number of built-in contradictions which prevent us from seeing the forest for the trees; for example:

. . . information science encompasses work by people from a variety of disciplines bringing their own points-of-view, approaches and interpretations;

. . . the interrelationships are not apparent, and the workers often are unaware of others working on similar problems;

. . . a semantic chaos exists, very effectively preventing communication;

. . . a tension leading to noncommunication exists among basic scientists, applied scientists, technologists, and practitioners, each claiming the field as being solely his area while ignoring (or at times downgrading) the work of others;

. . . basic, commonly accepted and thus unifying theories are nonexistent;

. . . the methodological problems are overwhelming;

. . . much of the work is centered in very few areas, which have become over-populated in both people and literature, and the whole field tends to be identified as consisting of those areas only.

In trying to resolve these contradictions, my colleagues, students and I have often heatedly and always enthusiastically discussed the nature and structure of information science. In those discussions we have often turned into home-spun philosophers, sociologists, psychologists and historians of science. These discussions were instrumental in the birth of this book. A random selection from the questions we have discussed may further illuminate and clarify the need to resolve the problem of structuring the field of information science:

. . . what are the relationships between work on the general subject of communication in psychology, sociology, linguistics, information theory, computer hardware and software, librarianship, information retrieval, logic, mathematics, biomedicine, physics, systems engineering, general systems theory, cybernetics, information science?

. . . specifically, what is the relationship between the physical, semantic and behavioral theories about the nature of "information" as a basic phenomenon?

. . . what is the relation among various communication phenomena, all of which have similar or closely related distribution patterns expressed by empirical laws such as: growth, dispersion, utilization and obsolescence of literatures and knowledge in general, citation networks, frequency of words in texts, dispersion of authors over literature, utilization of information collections, etc?

. . . what is the relation between any and all of the studies on the distribution patterns of these phenomena and user and uses studies? Communication theories?

. . . how can all these studies be utilized to discern structures and behavior of literatures which could be of practical use to information systems?

. . . what are the differences in processing "data," "information," "facts," "documents," "records?" At what level are all of these actually the same?

. . . what do libraries, information retrieval systems, inventory systems, data processing systems and other kinds of information and communication systems have in common? How do they differ?

. . . how can acquisitions and deletions in information systems be made on a formal (or at least on quasiformal) basis, instead of relying completely on intention and skill?

. . . what do various kinds of information representations have in common? — e.g., what is the relation between linguistic studies on syntax and the development of programming languages? Among the myriad indexing, coding and classification schemes? Between texts of documents and indexes, or texts and every other kind of representation?

. . . what is the relation between information representation and file structuring? — e.g., what does work on classification have to do with the organization of associative list and chain files?

. . . isn't the basic problem in dealing with the computer a special case of the general "library problem," namely a problem of acquiring, representing, organizing, storing, searching, disseminating, and/or displaying of information?

. . . what is the relation between studies on human behavior in communication and studies, models and theories on the behavior, structure and performance of information systems?

. . . how are studies in performance testing of information systems related to user studies or system studies in general?

. . . finally, and most importantly, how does theoretical work relate to experimental studies, or either to practical development, application and operation — or vice versa? Why is there very little communication between the world of practice in information handling on one hand and the world of theory and experimentation in information science on the other hand?

It is obvious that the answers to most of these questions will not be forthcoming for a long, long time. Yet it is perhaps not overly ambitious to hope that this book may provide some clues as to how some of these relations may be better understood, and possibly suggest how some of the answers may be approached.

Let us now turn to the shortcomings of this book. Any sourcebook — and this one is no exception — contains serious restrictions, limitations and handicaps. First, the organization of and selections in this book represent one man's view of a fluid and highly complex field. The limitations of the compiler's environment, background, knowledge, interests, and prior work cannot help but color, predispose, prejudice and bias his views. Although advice, help, and counsel was sought and every attempt was made to be objective, the book still remains one man's interpretation.

Second, because each article was written as a single contribution inevitably there exists among articles a number of repetitions. Being a new field, authors were forced to elaborate on even the most basic concepts and definitions in a number of articles. For instance, a number of authors were forced to elaborately discuss their view of the "information problem" in order that their subsequent work may have a framework. Such repetition may be tiresome, but on the positive side some repetitions may be actually helpful in that they reinforce views and illuminate a problem from different angles.

Third, articles are written in different styles peculiar to each author, and thus, the reader will have to make adjustments from article to article. Some styles are more personable to some readers than others; some are more and some are less difficult to read. The elements of style had no effect on the selection of articles.

Fourth and last, a semantic problem is inevitably present in any sourcebook. In information science the problem of inconsistency in terminology is a serious one, as can be easily seen from perusing the articles. Different names are used in different articles for the same concepts, and different concepts are sometimes labeled with the same names. Unfortunately, the reader himself must act as his own translator. For numerous reasons — the most important being to preserve the faithfulness of the sources — no attempt has been made to edit style or vocabulary.

Mindful of the problems in dealing with information science literature, I should like to extend to the reader two suggestions. A point of caution and encouragement should be made in relation to the approach used in a number of articles. Many are mathematical or statistical in nature, involving symbolism of various kinds and many readers may not be trained for or have an inclination to follow the symbolic reasoning. However, for intelligent comprehension of what is being said, a background in symbolic reasoning or mathematics and statistics is not necessary. Most (if not all) of the articles presented here have texts surrounding the symbolism, explaining the approach, meaning and conclusions. With a little practice, considerable comprehension can be gained by reading around the symbols. Furthermore, the reader's attention is called to the citations in many of the articles, as a source of further educational and historical information, as well as an indicator of relationships among various kinds of work being done both inside and outside of the field of information science.

It is clear that no adequate synthesis of the contents of information science can be made here, but it is my hope that these selections may form a backbone, suggest a direction, for the badly needed unifying synthesis of work in and around information science.

Acknowledgments

This book is an outgrowth of the educational and research activity in which I have been engaged since 1962 at the Center for Documentation and Communication Research of the School of Library Science, Case Western Reserve University, Cleveland, Ohio, under the leadership of Dean Jesse H. Shera. Thanks are due to my institution for providing me with help, time and assistance.

No book of this nature can be organized and compiled without help from many people, unfortunately too numerous to mention. I acknowledge my indebtedness to all my colleagues at the School and the Center, who as a group and individually provided stimulus, encouragement and assistance in many small and in many big ways, but most importantly, who provided an atmosphere conducive to free exchange of ideas and to thought.

Especially welcome encouragement, as well as most helpful suggestions in the organization and selection of material, has been gratefully received from Dr. William Goffman; as a matter of fact, in many respects this is really his book. A number of other colleagues encouraged this work and helped in the selection of articles: Alvin J. Goldwyn, Alan M. Rees, Joseph C. Donohue and George J. Baumanis. My ideas have also been influenced by John S. Dillon and Richard C. Fahringer of the American Management Association in New York, for whom I have designed and conducted several short courses in fundamentals of information retrieval. My thanks to the numerous participants at these courses for enlightening discussions in which they aided me in seeing the problems of many special applications and to the AMA for making possible this valuable exchange of ideas.

Any success this book may have I gladly share with those whose assistance I have acknowledged; however, if there is any criticism it should be directed to me, since all of the final decisions were mine.

The authors represented here are due my thanks; in the first place for doing the work, and secondly for granting me permission to include their articles. Also, thanks to the numerous publishers for permission to reprint.

Finally, I would like to recognize the people without whose dedicated work the book would not have been possible: Elaine Brown for helping in securing the material for selection and creation of the index, Barbara Denison and Edward Verhosek for suggestions and editing, Sophie Sobin and Dianne L. Wasdovich for typing, and Frank Delchin for many kinds of technical assistance.

I would like to end these acknowledgements with a very personal note. I came to these United States some eleven years ago, and this country has given me the most a country can give: a chance, an opportunity, a place. There are no words in the language to acknowledge that.

Tefko Saracevic
Cleveland, Ohio
January 1970

General Introduction

From the point of view of a student of man's communication processes and information systems — particularly as they relate to the communication of knowledge — this general introduction proffers a rationale for the organization of the material in this sourcebook and the criteria for selection. The particular choice of selections can, of course, only be taken as one man's sampling of a rapidly proliferating literature and widely scattered research in the field of information science. But the general organization of the book, which is intended to be largely introductory, suggests a structure for the field through an ordering of parts or a logic of relationships; in a sense, it presents an analysis of the subject matter of information science. This structure is discerned from both the subject content and the problem-orientation of existing information science literature.

Subject Considerations

At the base of information science is a concern about man's communication processes. Communication is a basic process which underlies and permeates all activity of people as social beings. Throughout history, the communication of man's knowledge and society has assumed a diversity of forms. At present, our preoccupation with communication is due largely to the extraordinary developments in communication technology. However, more basic is the realization that effective communication is vital to man's well-being and decision-making, to the functioning of man's social structures, and possibly even to his very existence. Clearly, information science shares the concern about communication with a number of other traditional and modern disciplines. Since the boundaries are by no means clear-cut, we may think of information science as one of the numerous, modern inter- or supra-disciplinary activities that have moved toward integrative efforts in viewing phenomena and problems. Thus, we can find in information science elements of all four cornerstones of contemporary knowledge: humanities, physical sciences, biological sciences and social sciences.

A communication process can be thought of as a sequence of events resulting in the transmission of something called information from one object (usually referred to as the source) to another (the destination). We may not know what information is, but we can study its various manifestations, properties and effects. Analogies for such an approach abound in the sciences; for example, man doesn't know what electricity and gravity are, but he is quite familiar with their behavior, properties, and effects. Thus, information may be viewed as a complex phenomenon with a variety of physical, biological, and behavioral properties which may be studied in isolation, as properties have been studied in other fields. However, the special interest of information science is to study a variety of properties of information and communication processes *not* in isolation, but in that dynamic and mutual interaction which shows their interrelation and interdependence. In other words, the basic subject matter of information science is study of the behavior, properties and effects of information in all of its facets and study of a variety of communication processes affecting and being affected by human beings.

Communication processes are carried out by means of systems, referred to here by the generic name, *information systems*. For a variety of communication processes, there are a variety of information systems that utilize various properties of information in isolation or in interaction; furthermore, it is well known that even for the same communication process there may be a variety of differently designed, constructed or conceived systems. Thus it is also of interest in information science to study the structure, objectives, functions, properties, behavior, and performance of information systems.

Information science, in this context, seems to be following the general patterns of development found in most nascent sciences and many traditional sciences as well. It is fundamental to information science to study the interaction of a large number of properties, processes and/or elements and to study their organization (e.g., "whole," "system," "structure," "organized complexity") rather than to stress the mechanistic one-way causality or to isolate individual causal strains. Warren Weaver pointed out that the classical sciences developed the theories of unorganized complexity; today the basic problem confronting all sciences is that of organized complexity. In approaching that problem, the sciences including information science are faced with an immensely complex and highly difficult task.

The selections in this book are organized in four parts: three reflect the basic subject areas of works in information science and one contains a theory that assimilates these areas. The first part relates to the basic phenomena under investigation in information science; namely, it relates to the nature and properties of information and of communication processes. The second part is devoted to works on aspects of internal organization of information systems. The third part presents studies on performance of information systems.

Orientation Considerations

Information science is viewed here as being interested basically in theory and experimentation, that is, in basic and applied aspects, rather than in development or operations. Although derived from art and practice and in great part oriented toward professional art and practice, information science is not directly a pragmatic discipline. The relation between information science investigations and the art and practical aspects of information handling is seen as being similar to the relation between biomedical research and medical practice. A persistent point of confusion is the relation between information science and information technology. Information science is not interested in information technology (hardware or software) per se, nor is a computer itself, for instance, of direct interest; however, the, utilization and effects of information technology, especially computers, pose a number of interesting and highly complex research problems for information scientists.

Thus, information science is viewed here as basically a science- and research-related discipline rather than a practice- or technology-related discipline. As in many other similar situations, this does not even remotely imply that a professional practitioner could not be a researcher or vice versa. To the contrary, when research and practice are blended into a feedback cycle, the benefits are greatest for both. Clearly, both the basic and applied approaches and their results can be (and have been) used as the foundation for practical and developmental work as well as for systems analysis and design and for management decision-making. In the other direction, practical problems have quite often been and should be even more the bases for investigation in information science.

The work in information science can and does exhibit various orientations toward different problem areas, for instance:

. . . problems associated with the dynamics and statics of knowledge in general and literature in particular, i.e., study of the patterns of general organization, creation, scatter, distribution, utilization and obsolescence of knowledge and literature;

. . . problems related to the multiple aspects of the communication behavior of man — the information creator and user;

. . . the problems of functioning of a variety of information systems — libraries, information retrieval systems, data processing systems, signal transmission systems, command and control systems, etc.;

. . . the problems of utilization of technology;

. . . the problems associated with information representation, such as structure of natural and artificial languages, indexing, classification, coding, etc.;

. . . recognition problems, such as pattern recognition and artificial intelligence.

Different orientations have also been exhibited by taking different approaches and using different methodological tools on any of the above approaches.

Even a superficial historical analysis of information

science literature will reveal that some of these problem orientations have attracted considerably more attention than others. By far, the largest proportion of information science literature is oriented toward problems associated with two areas: technology and information representation. In relation to system problems, some systems received more attention than others; for example, information retrieval systems received more attention than libraries; overall, computer-oriented systems have received more attention than the non-computer systems. In general, the work in information science has been characterized by a heavy orientation toward:

a) scientific and technical literature as a conveyor of information,
b) scientists and engineers as information users,
c) information retrieval systems,
d) computers as a technology,
e) information representation as one of the functions of information systems.

As with all new fields, information science did not escape the arguments over the "proper" orientation. Obviously, many orientations are present, many are valid; a heavy emphasis within a period of time on a limited number of orientations does not deny the importance and validity of the other sparsely populated, problem orientations. Since this book is a representation of information science literature, it is obvious that the selections had to follow the major problem orientations (outlined above) as found in the literature.

Basic Phenomena

The present status of views and insights concerning basic phenomena of concern to information science can be traced through the works presented in Part I. Chapter 1 is devoted to the present concepts of information as a phenomenon. Current work on the nature of information received its greatest impetus from Shannon's and Weaver's information theory; therefore, two articles about information theory appropriately start the selections. Since information theory is restricted basically to only one, the physical, property of information, other selections in Chapter 1 are devoted to semantic and behavioral properties. While the works on semantic properties formally treat the notions of meaning, the behavioral studies concentrate on the relations between information, communication processes and human behavior. The behavioral studies are further represented by selections in Chapters 2 and 3.

The selections in Chapter 2 reflect several approaches to the study of communication processes. As all processes, communication processes are time-dependent phenomena. Studies related to them have in common the transfer of information spanning various time-periods, even when these periods themselves are of no concern. In this sense we may talk about such studies as being concerned with communication patterns. Communication studies significant to information science are those which deal with communication of human knowledge, because this is (as far as human activities are concerned) the most important communication there is. In the realm of information science, the study of the communication of knowledge has been conducted from two different approaches: one is the study of the behavior of literature, using mostly statistical and mathematical approaches, and the other is the study of the behavior of users of information, using mostly psychological approaches. Appropriately, this Chapter is divided into two sections, in order to distinguish between the two orientations.

Finally, Chapter 3, the last chapter in the part on Basic Phenomena, deals with relevance, as a key concept and key problem in communication. Underlying the significance of relevance and the reason for treating it as a basic phenomena is the recognition that relevance was, is and always will be present in all communication, whether the communication is conducted among individuals or between information systems and individuals. Relevance is viewed here as a measure of the effectiveness of a contact between a source and a destination in a communication process.

In summary: Information is viewed as a phenomenon, communication as a process dealing with that phenomenon, and relevance is viewed as a measure reflecting the effectiveness of that process.

Information Systems

Part II offers works dealing with information systems, or some aspects thereof. The general orientation is obviously toward information retrieval systems and processes, because the overwhelming majority of the systems-related works in information science tend to go in that direction. However, it is clear that the theories, approaches, results, and conclusions need not be restricted to information retrieval systems. Many generalizations are valid for most, if not all, information systems; the overall structure of Part II is one of these generalizations. Actually, Part II could be divided into two parts: the first being Chapter 4, "Structure of Information Systems," and the second, Chapters 5-9, each devoted to a particular function of information systems. Chapter 4 presents works that investigate models (i.e., analogies) and that conceptually describe the elements (processes, components, functions, interactions) which are present in information systems. The works selected are representative of the modeling approaches taken to date. One is a mathematical and logic-oriented representation of some of the processes that are subject to such representation; the second is a behavioral model, describing the system in interaction with its environment; and the third is a technological one, flow charting the pattern of processes in information systems.

As mentioned, Chapters 5 and 9 are devoted to works on individual functions of information systems. Here, "functions" are taken as being the major classes of action or, more precisely, the order of processes. It is believed that all information systems share the following five basic functions (loosely defined):

(a) Acquisition — getting the material ("information," "data," "knowledge," "books," "commands," "signals," etc.) which at a minimum implies some selection process.

(b) Information Representation — conceptual handling of the acquired material in some representative form and structure, which at a minimum implies a language (natural, artificial, indexing, classification, coding, etc.) or some combination of languages.

(c) Organization of Files — storing of materials and/or storing of their representations, which at a minimum implies physical arrangement.

(d) Question Handling and Search Procedures — getting whatever is in the system out in some organized and delineated fashion, which at a minimum implies the ability to search on a restrictive basis; i.e., it implies an output selection process.

(e) Dissemination — distributing of the output, or displaying it in some organized form, which at a minimum implies arrangement of both a conceptual and a physical nature and distribution patterns.

A chapter is devoted to each of these five functions. It may be obvious that many, if not most, works are not and cannot be limited to any one function, because they deal with functions in systems. It is well known that the elements of systems interact not only within the system but also with the system's environment. Thus, the interactions prevent coherent isolations; that is, a given function can hardly be treated without taking other interacting elements (functional and/or environmental) into account. Often it was extremely difficult to assign individual works to individual functions, and the articles presented under given functions should not be viewed as pertaining only to those functions, since they may deal as well with other problem areas. However, the book is so structured as to suggest that the *emphasis* of the work presented in the article more closely relates it to the function or problem area under which it appears than to any other.

Evaluation of Information Systems

Part III presents selections which deal with still another large area of effort in information science. This area includes performance studies on the people involved with the system; on the development of measures and methodologies for testing; on test results illuminating the effects of variables in the system; and on the economics and growth of information systems. Ironically, the evaluation effort may be described as addressing itself to the question: "Well, the information systems work all very well in practice, but how do they work in theory and experimentation?"

The evolution of the evaluation effort in information science has an interesting history and current developments should be interpreted in the light of it. The high cost of designing, developing and operating information systems in general, and information retrieval systems in particular, and the claims of the designers and managers of such systems brought about a new class of investigations: test and evaluation. Encountering unexpected methodological difficulties, test studies were plagued with many experimental errors (a situation which happens in experimentation in any field); in turn, two new kinds of efforts arose—test criticism, and development of measures and methodologies for testing. All of these efforts pointed toward a still larger problem area, experimentation in information science in general. This includes the problem of relating experiments to appropriate theories; the problem of measures, methodologies, controls and identification of experimentally manipulative variables; the problem of deriving and generalizing conclusions and relating them to studies and to theory, etc. It seems fair to conclude that the activity of testing, more than any other effort, was responsible for attempts to introduce scientific method and rigor, and thereby to introduce science, into a field which basically had an overwhelming engineering-oriented, technological and practical tradition. In any case, testing raised more questions than it answered. It proved to be of little help to those for whom it was initially intended — the designers, developers and operators of information retrieval systems. However, it gave great impetus to the consolidation of information science.

The chapters in Part III reflect four types of effort: behavioral studies of people involved with information retrieval systems, the so-called "human factors," and the factors affecting them (Chapter 10); the development of measures which might influence the performance of information systems (Chapter 11-A); a selection of articles stemming from larger testing projects, incorporating results on performance of a series of variables found in information systems (Chapter 11-B); and finally, a selection of studies related to economics and the growth of information systems (Chapter 12). Most of the selections pertain to information retrieval systems, because these information systems drew most of the attention and effort. It is suggested here that many conclusions from these studies could be generalized for other information systems — especially libraries.

A Unifying Theory

Part IV of the book is devoted to a single, extensive study by Goffman that presents a general communication theory which in its own way unifies many of the concepts, theories, and ideas incorporated in other selections and in other works. It has been pointed out frequently that one of the basic problems of information science is lack of a theoretical base. Goffman's theory may be viewed as an attempt to create such a base, which is the principal reason for its inclusion in these selections. The approach taken is a formal, mathematical one which may limit the audience, but it may also increase the usefulness and generalizability of the theory — a likelihood which has often been demonstrated by mathematically-based theories throughout the history of science.

In order to illuminate further the structure of information science, the theory is summarized here. Communication processes can be represented as epidemic processes; i.e., the principles governing the spread of infectious diseases are among those underlying the process of the transmission of ideas. Consequently, the epidemic theory is applied to the study of processes in which information is transmitted within a population. The fundamental notion of stability of an epidemic process (diseases or ideas) is introduced, and a stability theorem is derived.

Information retrieval is considered as an instrumental process necessary for providing effective contact in the transmission of ideas. The mechanism of the information retrieval process (which instigates an epidemic process) is defined, certain general properties of the mechanism are established, and the means of controlling it are discussed.

Information retrieval systems are viewed as the means by which information retrieval processes are carried out. The theory is concerned with the aspects of retrieval systems that relate to their nature, their design, their components, and the evaluation of their performance.

Finally, the theory addresses itself to the problems of controlling the processes involved. Conditions for optimal control of an epidemic process are formally established. This result makes it possible to determine the conditions for stability without knowing the solution to the sets of differential equations which represent the process. The usefulness of the theory has been tested in a number of experiments, with encouraging results (see Article 8).

Criteria for Selection

The quality of the work presented in the articles selected was a major criterion, but by no means was an attempt made to select the "best" articles. Rather, it was attempted to select those articles representative of the work in the field in general, representative of different approaches to, viewpoints of, and attacks on given problem areas, and representative of a variety of backgrounds of workers in the field. In order to ensure some prejudged quality of the selections, the articles that appeared in journals which have well-known and high-quality editorial review procedures were given priority. This practice is reflected in the final choice of the articles. Of the 66 selections, 61 are from 15 different journals listed below; four are original articles, parts of which have appeared or are to appear in journals (Articles 14, 19, 61 and Chapter 13); and one is from a well-known and well-received book (Article 17). Technical report literature and papers from proceedings were considered, but because it was found that the editorial policies which govern their birth had no uniformity whatsoever, it was decided not to include any of them. This does not mean, in any sense, that the technical report and proceedings literature should be ignored, nor does it imply any judgment of the quality of such sources.

Another important criterion was recency. Since this book was not intended to be a historical collection, an effort was made to select works illustrating recent efforts, approaches, and trends. It should be mentioned that this criterion was easily achieved, since information science is such a new field that most of the work in it is fairly recent. Theoretical and experimental works were given priority over surveys, although some surveys are included economically to illuminate a whole area.

Still another criterion that was applied pertained to relationships. There was an attempt to select works that explicitly or implicitly exhibit relationships between different problem areas and other works both within and outside the field of information science. As mentioned above, it was intended that the selections themselves should show the structure and relationships of the field; therefore, articles exemplifying these relationships received priority.

Finally, an important but limiting criterion was the economics of book publishing. Although the number of articles selected is relatively large, there were still many articles that might have been selected but could not be included here because it was not economically feasible.

Some remarks about the mechanism of selection and the distribution of selected articles are in order. The selections were made by perusing journals, bibliographies, reviews, indexing and abstracting journals, citations, reading lists (public and private), and other books, and by seeking consultation and advice. The literature considered for selection covered a period from 1945 to January 1970.

Some 2,000 articles from some 40 different sources (journals, books, proceedings of conferences, sources of technical reports, etc.) were considered. These were reduced to some 450 journal articles as general candidates, which in turn were examined in depth and organized according to the overall structure of the book. This procedure was followed by a process of elimination and comparison which reduced the sample to some 120 articles, and this process was repeated until the final 66 selections were obtained. Obviously, the granting of permission of publishers to reprint played a role in the final selection; however, only a very few requests were denied.

With regard to the time distribution of the selections, the forties did not produce any selections (although it could be considered that the work on information theory (Articles 1 and 2) really dated from that period); the fifties have 3 selections; 1960-1964 have 9; 1965 has 5; 1966 has 6; 1967 has 10; 1968 has 13; 1969 (including the four original articles) has 19; and 1970 has 1. As mentioned, the selection was concluded with January 1970.

The following are the journals from which the selections were made, with the number of articles chosen from each:

American Documentation	19
Journal of the Association for Computing Machinery	8
Journal of Documentation	7
Information Storage and Retrieval	6
Nature	4
ASLIB Proceedings	3
Communications of the Association for Computing Machinery	3
Science	3
American Psychologist	2
American Economic Review	1
Behavioral Science	1
British Journal for the Philosophy of Science	1
College and Research Libraries	1
ETC: Review of General Semantics	1
Information and Control	1
From Books	1
Original Articles (parts have appeared or are to appear in journals)	4

Finally, for the student of information science, this concluding note: this book is intended to be representative of the structure and content of information science. If nothing else, it demonstrates that information science is complex and interdisciplinary in structure, and now that its content is quite developed, there is a considerable amount of knowledge to consider and to study.

Part One
Basic
Phenomena

To observe the backgrounds of the authors contributing to the first part strikes a keynote in the information science perspective. Their fields of major concentration throughout their professional lives run an interdisciplinary gamut from natural sciences to mathematics, from logic to linguistics, from engineering to librarianship, from humanities to philosophy, and from social and behavioral sciences to biomedicine.

Fundamental to information science are the notions of information as a phenomenon and communication as a process. Although intuitively quite well understood, these nuclei are just beginning to coalesce into formal knowledge. There are many isolated pieces scattered widely across times, disciplines, approaches, and literatures. No attempts to put the existing pieces together and fill the gaps have as yet caught universal attention. This is not surprising. In dealing with information, we are faced with a complex phenomenon which exhibits a staggering variety of physical, biological, and behavioral properties.

In dealing with communication processes, we are brought full-circle to people and to the most precious communication there is — the communication of knowledge — again, a process of the greatest complexity. The highest ambition of information science it to put together some of the pieces of knowledge from a number of disciplines regarding information and communication, and to add some pieces of its own.

The motivation for work in information science stems from the fact that man has communicated quite well without knowing formally how he is doing it, where "formally" is interpreted broadly as meaning precise understanding. In the complex world of today, and in the even more sophisticated world expected tomorrow, "quite well" is not good enough; the hope is that man might communicate better with the help of information science. And the problems of our society demand effective communication as the base for all rational solutions.

Chapter One
Notions
of
Information

Information theory dealing with transmission of signals, as introduced by Shannon and Weaver, received a fantastic amount of attention in fields where the term "information" was commonplace, probably because the theory has classic originality, simplicity, and elegance. A review and a critique of information theory by Rapaport is presented in Articles 1 and 2. It was realized (as is pointed out by all authors in the chapter) that the precise mathematical definitions of information theory, though it was hoped they would be sufficient, were not adequate for describing all properties of information which pertained to man and his behavior. Thus, additional theories covering other than physical properties of information are represented in the subsequent selections.

Bar Hillel and Carnap (Article 3) introduced a formal logical approach in formulating the semantic properties of information. Shreider (Article 4) used a mathematical approach in dealing with the transformational aspects of information, as related to knowledge. Fairthorne (Article 5) presents a paradigm of activities related to "information flow"; he comes closest to linking the theories pertaining to information to information systems. The terminology introduced by Shannon was adopted, used, and misused in several fields. Perhaps Fairthorne, by explicating this semantic chaos in his article, did a great terminological service to information science.

Information as a phenomenon has attracted a scientific audience only in the last two decades, which in scientific fields is a very short time. But it is obvious that much fundamental work lies ahead.

1. What Is Information?

ANATOL RAPOPORT

ETC: A Review of General Semantics
Vol. 10, No. 4, 1953

Suppose someone tosses a penny, and you try to guess "heads" or "tails." Every time you guess correctly you win the penny, and every time you guess wrong you pay your opponent a penny. You have a fifty-fifty chance to win on each throw. If you keep playing long enough, unless you are extremely lucky or unlucky, your winnings will about equal your losses.[1]

Now suppose some character comes along and tells you he has a crystal ball through which he can see how the penny falls, and that for a price, he will signal this information to you, so that you can win every time. You have no scruples about playing the game fairly (you are the "economic man" that classical theoreticians of economics keep talking about). What is the information offered worth to you?

A common sense argument shows that if the crystal ball really works, the information is worth to you anywhere up to a penny a reading. If you pay a whole penny, you will win all of your opponent's money and pay it all to the crystal ball reader. Then you can expect to be no better or no worse off than if you played the game trusting to your own guesses (or if you didn't play the game at all: the fun of playing the game doesn't count here, because the "economic man" doesn't have any fun anyway). It follows that if you pay your informant anything less than a penny a guess, you are sure to be ahead in the long run.

Now suppose the man with the crystal ball is a charlatan. He can't guess the throws any better than you can. He knows, of course, that very soon he will give you wrong information and that when he does, you may balk at paying him for further "tip offs." So he proposes what seems like a fair deal: you give him a percentage of your winnings *only* when you win and pay him nothing if his information proves false. Is it now worthwhile to employ him? This time a common sense argument says that it is worth nothing to have him around. If he is no better guesser than you are, you may as well make the guesses yourself and not pay anything.[2]

1. That is to say, the ratio of your winnings to your losses will be very close to one. In the long run, both the winnings and the losses will be so large that their *difference* may be considerable. However your winnings (or losses) *per game* will be very small.

2. The tendency to believe what we would like to be true often overrules common sense considerations. For an illuminating example, see the article on "Water Witching" by Evon Z. Vogt in *The Scientific Monthly*, Vol. LXXV, No. 3 (September 1952).

But now consider the intermediate case, where the crystal ball is good but not perfect. In other words, your informant can guess better than you, but he makes mistakes. Now is it worthwhile to pay him? Yes, it is worthwhile, and it is the more worthwhile the greater the *difference* between his guessing ability and yours. Certainly if you are as good as he is, there is no point in paying him. In other words, if your chances of guessing are as good as his, he is *giving you no information in the long run*. If he is better than you are, even if he is not a perfect guesser, your guessing record will be improved by the information he gives you, and the amount of improvement is, in a way, a measure of the information you receive from him. If he is a worse guesser than you are, you *lose* information if you follow his advice. This situation hints at a possibility of defining information *quantitatively* as the improvement of one's chances of making the right guess.

In *any* situation, information about something we already know is worthless as information. The keen competition among newspapers for "scoops" reflects this attitude. A "scoop" carries more information than a re-write story. Any kind of a message carries more or less information in it depending on the state of knowledge of the recipients. This much has been known ever since messages were invented. In our own day of precise formulation of problems, however, an altogether new way of measuring the amount of information in a message is being developed.

In the example just cited a measure of the amount of information contained in a message is indicated in terms of how much such information is worth in a gambling situation. It is not necessary, however, to measure information in terms of its monetary value any more than it is necessary to depict chance events in terms of gambling situations. Such examples are often chosen because gambling has long served as a link between commonplace situations and sophisticated probabilistic arguments. There is more to the mathematical theory of information than a computation of how much we are willing to pay for the privilege of cheating in games or how the novelty of stories is reflected in the circulation of the newspapers that print them.

1. The Mathematical Theory of Information

The mathematical theory of information was born among communication engineers and is commanding ever greater attention among mathematically inclined biologists and semanticists. The reason for this increasing interest lies, I think, in the fact that the mathematical theory of information has been recognized as another successful instance of making *precise* and *quantitative* an extremely important concept which had been talked about only vaguely before. I believe that the notion of the "quantity of information" is a Big Idea in science, similar in scope to the precise definition of "the amount

of matter" as registered on a balance or the "amount of energy" as derived from potentials, velocities, and heat, or the "amount of entropy" as derived from the probabilities of the states of a system. The vast importance of this new big idea is in its potential applications to the fundamental biological and general semantics problems. We will touch on some of these below. Let us first take a closer look at some basic notions contained in the definition of the "amount of information."

As Warren Weaver has remarked,[3] the amount of information in your message is related not to what you are saying but to what you *could* say. This relation links the amount of information in a message with the amount of *pre-conceived* knowledge about its content (recall the intuitive relation between the amount of information and how much we already know or can guess).

Let us suppose that all you can say is "yes" and "no" (in other words, you are as either-or-ish as you can possibly be). Then all you are ever *expected* to say is "yes" or "no," so that one already has a 50% "knowledge" of your potential pronouncements. Thus, if you are entirely two-valued, you cannot give as much information in your one-word speeches as you could if you were "multi-valued." If you selected your messages from *ten* possible ones, all equally likely, then one could hope to guess what you are going to say only once in ten times, instead of every other time, and your information giving capacity would be considerably increased.

The "canned" messages offered by Western Union (birthday greetings, etc.) carry far less information (and therefore are cheaper to send) than individually composed messages, because there are far fewer canned messages to choose from.

In order to define the amount of information in a message, then, we must know the total number of messages in the *repertoire of the source* from which the message is chosen. Let us take a concrete case.

For simplicity, we will assume that all messages are in code and consist of combinations of two signals "1" and "0" (just as all Morse Code messages are combinations of two signals "dit" and "dah"). We ask: how many different messages can we send? Obviously if the length of the message is unlimited, we can send an unlimited number of messages. Let us, therefore, consider only messages of a certain length, say n signals long. We can easily see that there can be exactly 2^n distinct messages n signals long. This follows, because we have 2 choices for the first signal ("1" or "0"), 2 for the second, which makes $2^2 = 4$ choices for a message of two signals. To each of these, we can again add either of two signals to make a message three signals long, etc., so that to make a message n signals long, we have $2 \times 2 \times 2 \ldots 2$ a product of n 2's or 2^n choices.

Therefore if you know that a certain message is n "bi-

3. Claude E. Shannon and Warren Weaver, *The Mathematical Theory of Communication* (Urbana 1949).

nary" signals long,[4] you know you have one chance in 2^n to guess its contents exactly, provided all the messages are equally likely. We could therefore take the number 2^n as a measure of the amount of information such a message carries. But we don't have to take 2^n. We can take some other number *derived* from 2^n, if it is more convenient to do so. The choice of a quantity with which we measure something is not unique. For example, to measure the "size" of a circle, we can take its diameter, but we are equally justified in taking its area, which is a quantity derived from the diameter in a certain way.[5] There is good reason for taking as the measure of the amount of information, carried by a message n binary signals long, not 2^n (which is the reciprocal of the probability of guessing it, or, if you like, the "unlikelihood" of guessing it) but the *logarithm* of that number.

If you remember your high school algebra, you will recall that the logarithm of a number is the power to which a certain fixed number, called the "base" must be raised to get that number. If we conveniently take 2 as our base, then $\log_2(2^n)$ (read "the logarithm to the base two of two to the n-th) is just n.[6] Thus, by the convention we have just established, a message n binary signals long contains n "binary units" of information, or one binary unit per signal. This binary unit is called a "bit" for short. Now we see the advantage of taking the logarithm of the unlikelihood of guessing (2^n) for our measure, since we can now say that a message twice as long (one $2n$ signals long) will contain just twice the amount of information. This is a very convenient way of talking.[7]

It may have occurred to the reader that we have gone around in a circle. Would it not have been simpler to skip the argument about "probabilities of guessing" altogether and start out by a "natural" definition of the amount of information as simply a number proportional to the length of the message?

It would, if we confined ourselves to messages from a single source. However the interesting part of information theory deals with determining the amount of infor-

4. That is, where each signal can take one of two possible values.

5. A mathematician would say, "The area is a certain *function* of the diameter."

6. Obviously n is the power to which 2 must be raised to get 2^n.

7. To resort to our analogy again, suppose we knew nothing about areas and described the sizes of circles by their diameters. If we had to paint circles for a living, we would soon discover that to paint a circle "twice the size" would require four times as much paint, one "thrice the size" would require nine times as much paint, etc. This would be somewhat confusing until some genius suggested to take the *square* of the diameter as the size measure (a semantic reform). Now the amount of paint would be strictly proportional to the (newly defined) size of the circle. Similarly, if we take the logarithm of the "unlikelihood of guessing" as a measure of the amount of information in a message, instead of the unlikelihood itself, the amount of information will be proportional to the length of the message.

mation in a message in terms of the character of its *source*, not merely in terms of its length (it isn't what you say; it's what you *could* say). It is the amount of information per *signal* that we are interested in, in other words, the rate at which information is coming at us as we are receiving the message. This rate is one bit per signal in the case of a source with two equally likely signals. Where there are more signals in the source, and especially where the signals are not equally likely or where they are not independent, the amount of information per signal is not nearly so easy to compute. For this purpose, the "round about" definition is necessary. Furthermore, the "round about" definition points up the connection between information theory and the possibility of mathematicizing psychological and semantic concepts, as we shall see.

Let us again suppose that we speak a language composed of two binary signals "1" and "0." But let us now suppose that the "1" occurs far more frequently than the "0." Such is actually the case with the symbols of the languages we ordinarily use. For example, good English can be written with some 30 symbols (the 26 letters, a "space" and some punctuation marks). We can say definitely that some signals occur in English far more frequently than others. Or suppose that "1" and "0" are signals given out by a machine which is inspecting mass-produced parts, where "1" means "O.K." and "0" means "reject." If on the average only one item in a hundred is defective, then the "1" will register ninety-nine times more frequently than the "0." How much information is now contained in a message n units long?

In view of what we said about the meaning of information, we must conclude that in this case the amount of information contained in a message n units long must be less than n bits, because we already have a good chance of guessing what a message will say. If n is, say, 10, we have better than nine chances out of ten to guess the message if we guess it to be all "1's." Since the message does not add as much to our knowledge as it would if the signals were equally likely, we must conclude that it carries less than n bits of information. But how much less?

Suppose a message n units long has n_1 "1's" and n_2 "0's," so that $n_1 + n_2 = n$. What is the probability of occurrence of such a message? If the occurrence of one signal does not influence that of another, it doesn't matter in what order the signals occur. Since in our example the probability of a "1" is .99, and that of a "0" is .01, the probability of n_1 "1's" and n_2 "0's" *arranged in a particular way* (that is, the probability of a particular message) will be $(.99)^{n_1} (.01)^{n_2}$. The logarithm of the reciprocal of this number to the base 2, as we have agreed, will be a measure of the amount of information in such a message. This logarithm is equal to $-n_1 \log_2(.99) - n_2 \log_2(.01)$.

Now we have the amount of information in a particular message with n_1 "1's" and n_2 "0's." But we don't want to measure the information of particular messages. We want to measure the information of an *average* message n signals long coming from the source we have described. We will get this average if we substitute for n_1 and n_2 their average values, averaged over a great many messages coming from the source. Since the frequencies of the "1's" and the "0's" are in the ratio of 99 to 1, it follows that the average value of n_1 will be 99 times that of n_2. Furthermore, $n_1 + n_2$ must equal n. Therefore $n_1 = .99n$ and $n_2 = .01n$ on the average. Then the amount of information in an average message n signals long will be $-.99n \log_2(.99) - .01n \log_2(.01)$. If we wish to express the amount of information per signal, we divide by n and get $-.99 \log (.99) - .01 \log (.01)$. If we calculate this number, we find it to be equal to about .11 bits or only one-ninth of what it would be if the "O.K." and "reject" signals were equally likely.

The method here described can be extended to compute the amount of information per signal from any source in which the occurrence of one signal does not influence the occurrence or non-occurrence of another. If the source has a repertoire of signals numbered 1 to N, and if they occur with relative frequencies (probabilities) $p_1, p_2 \ldots p_N$, then the amount of information per signal, usually denoted by H, is expressed in the following formula:

$$H = - p_1 \log p_1 - p_2 \log p_2 - p_3 \log p_3 \ldots - p_N \log p_N.$$

In the example we solved there were only two signals, whose p_1 and p_2 were respectively .99 and .01.

2. Applications to Technological Communication Theory

So far we really did nothing but define terms and draw consequences from our definitions. We said nothing concrete about why we should want to make these particular definitions or draw these particular consequences. We did mention the looming importance of the information concept in semantics, psychology, and biology, but to someone who encounters this concept for the first time, the connection between it and what is generally thought to be the subject matter of biology, etc., is anything but clear.

It is not easy to make such connections clear. In fact, the strenuous work of highly skilled specialists goes almost entirely into uncovering such connections. They cannot be therefore obvious or intuitively evident or even easy to understand when explained. All we can do within the scope of this article is give hints about the sort of reasoning which leads to uncovering the possibilities of applying the quantification of information to several scientific fields.

The first step in solving a problem is to state it. The statement usually involves a description of an existing state and a desirable state of affairs where the factors involved in the discrepancy are explicitly pointed out. The success with which any problem is solved depends to a great extent on the clarity with which it is stated. In fact, the solution of the problem is, in a sense, a clarification (or concretization) of the objectives. Take the problem of curing disease. For ages, it had been implicity stated thus:

> A is sick.
> This is bad.
> Let us find ways to make A well.

Vague statements lead to vague methods, where success is erratic and questionable. With the classification of diseases (as initiated, say, by Hippocrates), the problem is re-stated:

> A has a fever.
> This is bad.
> Let us look for ways to rid A of fever.

Here there is more promise of success, because the events which make up sickness are somewhat extensionalized. Still further extensionalization appears with the discovery of events *concomitant* with the symptoms, for example the presence of micro-organisms. Now the problem is

> A is infected with tuberculosis bacilli.
> They make A sick.
> Let us find ways to get rid of the bacilli.

Further extensionalization could be, for example, a description of the biochemical processes characteristic of the tuberculosis bacilli which interfere with A's biochemical processes, etc. The more a given problem is extensionalized, the greater promise there is in finding a solution.

The problems of communication hygiene are now assuming an importance equal to those of physiological hygiene. A naive statement of a communication problem dates back to antiquity.

> A talks to B.
> B does not understand A.
> Let us explain to B what A means.

However "attempts to explain" *themselves* depend on the proper functioning of the communication process. If this process is not understood, attempts to explain cannot be expected to have more success than the original attempt to communicate. The first steps in communication hygiene are therefore aimed at the understanding of the communication process. Hence the emergence of communication science.

In examining instances of "failure to understand," we see that it can occur on different levels. A most obvious cause of such failure can be laid to the imperfect transmission of signals. B can fail to understand A simply because A talks with a heavy accent, or is a small child who has not learned to pronounce the words clearly or is talking over a telephone with a bad connection or over a radio with too much static.

Communication problems on this level may deal with acoustics or electronics but also with physiological functions such as hearing and sight and their psychological correlates, the perception of "gestalts" and recognition. Obviously no transmission and no reception of any signal is perfect. An important class of questions in communication theory concerns with the *thresholds* of intelligibility. One wishes to know, for example, how bad static has to be before it begins seriously to interfere with the transmission of spoken information over a radio channel of given characteristics. Evidently both the characteristics of transmission and reception and those of the subject matter broadcast are important in the problem. Information theory provides a measure of these variables. It provides, for example, a measure of the complexity involved in "fidelity" of reproduction.[8] It provides a method of estimating quantitatively the effects of "noise" on reception, since the effects of noise are equivalent to loss of information. It provides theoretical limits for the performance of a channel of given characteristics, somewhat in the way thermodynamics indicates the limits of efficiency of a heat engine.

3. Applications to Semantics

The semanticist is usually unconcerned with these purely "technical" problems of communication and leaves them to the communication engineer. Division of labor is entirely proper in approaching any complicated set of problems; but it is a mistake to take too seriously the dichotomies we set up in parceling out the jobs. These dichotomies lead not only to the persistence of elementalistic notions but also delay the discovery of analogous *methods* fruitful in the various aspects of the problem. It may be true that the technical problems of long range communication (radio, television, etc.) can be treated entirely independently of the semantic content of the messages or the semantic reactions of the audience. But it may also be true that the methods involved in treating those problems (for example, the mathematical theory of information) can be applied in the seemingly different contexts of the events which interest general semanticists, psychologists, and others.

Such possibilities are already apparent. To point them out, we will examine a little more closely the formula given above which describes the amount of information in terms of the repertoire of the source and the relative frequencies of the signals employed. As we said, the formula holds if the signals are independent of each other.

8. If a musical tone has few overtones, it can be mathematically described by a few parameters (the relative intensities of its overtones) and thus carries less information and is easier to reproduce with fidelity than a tone which carries many overtones.

But what if this is not the case? What if the occurrence of one signal influences *the* chances of the occurrence of another? This is certainly true in the case where the source is the English alphabet, and the messages consist of English sentences. In this case, it is almost certain that the letter q will be followed by a u (barring comparatively rare words like Iraqi). It is practically impossible for the letter z to be followed by a consonant, etc.

Under these conditions, the formula for the amount of information per signal must be modified. We will not go into the details of this modification here. We will only point out that the problem of computing the amount of information under various conditions of communication has led to a number of important *concepts,* in terms of which the technical problems of communication are described. One important characteristic of thse concepts is that they are often stated in mathematical language *and therefore the techniques of mathematical deduction can be applied to them.* This circumstance makes the problems of communication much more explicit and the solutions to such problems easier to find.

Another important advantage of those concepts is that they give hints on how the precise methods of dealing with communication in the (comparatively) uncomplicated area of technology could be extended to the more complicated areas of psychology, semantics, and general semantics. For example, the modification of our formula on page 8 to take into account the interdependence of signals gives rise to the concept of "redundancy" of the source output, and if the source is an entire language, this concept can be extended to mean the "redundancy" of a language. In information theory, redundancy is a measure of the interdependence of the signals. But redundancy has also an intuitive component, and the precise definition makes possible the extensionalization of this intuitive component.

The connection between the precise and the intuitive notions of redundancy is dramatically illustrated in C. Shannon's monograph, *The Mathematical Theory of Communication.* Suppose we put all the letters of the English alphabet into a hat in equal amounts and pull them out one by one "at random." What would they spell? Here is a sample of such a "language."

XFOML RXKHRJFFJUJ ZLPWCFWKCYJ FFJ-EYVKCQSGHYD QPAAMKBZAACIBZLHJQD

In anyone's estimation this sample does not "make sense." Now suppose that instead of putting the letters into the hat in equal numbers, we put them in proportionally to the frequency with which they actually occur in English[9] and again pull them out at random. The resulting sample now looks like this.

9. The relative frequencies of letters in English has been made familiar by the printer's cliché, e t a o i n s h r d l u . . .

OCRO HLI RGWR NMIELWIS EU LL NBNES-
EBYA TH EEI ALHENHTTPA OOBTTVA NAH
BRL.

This still doesn't make "sense." But there is no question that it makes *somewhat* more "sense" than before.
It *looks* more like English. It does not bristle quite so
much with J's and Z's. Somehow we feel that a "grada-
tion" of sense can be established even among random
samples of letters. The feeling is strengthened when we
perform the next experiment. We now put into our hat
not single letters but *pairs*, taking care of keeping their
numbers proportional to their actual occurrence in English. Now we get the following sample.

ON IE ANTSOUTINYS ARE T INCTORE ST BE
S DEAMY ACHIN D ILONASIVE TUCOOWE
AT TEASONARE FUSO TIZIN ANDY TOBE
SEACE CTISBE.

Now there is no doubt that we are approaching "English." The sample contains two or three real English
words and several "near-words" like DEAMY and TEA-
SONARE. A sample of "triples" looks even better.

IN NO IST LAT WHEY CRATICT FROURE
BIRS GROCID PONDENOME OF DEMONST-
URES OF THE REPTAGIN IS REGOACTION
OF CRE.

Perhaps this sample reminds us of Jabberwocky. It
should, because Jabberwocky too is an "approximation"
to English, a very good approximation that almost makes
real sense.

What can be done with letters can be done with words.
Compare, for example, the sample of randomly selected
words,

REPRESENTING AND SPEEDILY IS AN GOOD
APT OR COME CAN DIFFERENT NATURAL
HERE HE THE A IN CAME THE TO OF TO
EXPERT GRAY COME TO FURNISHES THE
LINE MESSAGE HAD BE THESE

with a sample of randomly selected *pairs* of words,

THE HEAD AND IN FRONTAL ATTACK ON
AN ENGLISH WRITER THAT THE CHARAC-
TER OF THIS POINT IS THEREFORE AN-
OTHER METHOD FOR THE LETTERS THAT
THE TIME OF WHO EVER TOLD THE PROB-
LEM FOR AN UNEXPECTED,

and see how much more "sense" there is in the second,
although it still doesn't "mean" anything.[10]

10. All the foregoing samples have been taken from C.
Shannon, *op. cit.*

These "approximations" to English are examples of
how the intuitive feeling that one piece of gibberish is
somehow closer to the English language than another is a
reflection of a precisely and quantitatively defined situation.[11] The situation has to do with the characteristic
linkages used in English. The extent of these linkages is
also a measure of the *redundancy* of the English language.
Redundancy can also be taken as a measure of the fraction of letters which can be randomly deleted from a
reasonably long message without making the message
unintelligible. FR EXMPLE WENTYIVE PRCET OF
HE LTTERS I TIS SENTENCE HVEBEN DLETED
AT RANM. The redundancy of English is said to be
over 50%

Redundancy is thus both a linguistic and a mathematical term. The more redundancy there is in a source, the
more tolerance there is for noise and other imperfections
of transmission without serious interference with intelligibility. The importance of the redundancy concept in
cryptography is likewise apparent. The more redundant
the source of messages, the easier it is to break a code.
In stenography redundancy is a measure of the amount
of drastic abbreviation that can be introduced without
danger of confusion. All these linguistic matters are contiguous to the field of interest of semanticists and of
general semanticists. A manner of expression full of
clichés is, of course, high in redundancy. It turns out in
the mathematical theory of information that messages
from a cliché-ridden source (such as the oratorical repertoire of a run-of-the-mill politician) are also poor in
information. This is something semanticists have known
all along, but it is gratifying to have this knowledge formulated precisely. Precisely formulated knowledge is
valuable not only for its own sake but also as a jumping-
off place to new knowledge.

4. Connection with Physics

The mathematicians who derived the formula for the
amount of information soon noticed that it looks exactly
like the formula for *entropy* in statistical mechanics.
Mathematicians are often excited by such analogies.
There is an important difference between a mathematical
analogy and an ordinary "metaphorical" one. Arguments
based on ordinary analogies are seldom conclusive. For
example, just because it is true that natural selection
benefits the survival of a species, it does not follow that
economic competition is indispensable for the vigor of a
nation. Nor is the justification of capital punishment convincing on the basis of its analogy with surgery applied
to a diseased part of the body. A mathematical analogy,
however, is a quite different matter. Such analogy is evidence of similar *structure* in two or more classes of events,

11. Every one has experienced hearing a conversation in
which no words could be distinguished but where one could
be reasonably sure that the language spoken was or was not
English.

and a great deal can be deduced from such similarity. For example, because both electrical and mechanical oscillators can be described by the same kinds of equations, it follows that a great deal of reasoning which applies to one applies also to the other. Since the analogy between information and entropy is a mathematical analogy, it too may be symptomatic of a structure similarity in the events involved in the determination of physical entropy and those involved in the measurement of information. It seems worthwhile, therefore, to look at this analogy more closely.

The concept of entropy was first introduced into thermodynamics as a measure of the *unavailability* of heat energy for transformation into useful work. The principle of conservation of energy (the First Law of Thermodynamics) says that a given amount of heat is equivalent in terms of its energy content to a given amount of work. For example, the heat energy of a slice of bread (about 100 "large" calories) is theoretically convertible into about 300,000 foot pounds of work. But this equivalence of heat and work does not mean that we can take heat from any source and convert it all into work. If this were true, there would be no need of fuels. We could take the practically inexhaustible heat of the oceans and drive all our machinery with it, with only a slight cooling of the oceans as the result. But this cannot be done. In any engine, where heat is converted into work, this can be done only if heat is allowed to flow from a source at higher temperature to a sink at lower temperature. Thus a difference in temperature is indispensable for turning heat into work. The boiler and the cooler of a steam engine illustrate this principle. The less the difference in temperatures, the smaller is the fraction of the amount of heat which can be transformed into work, i.e., the smaller the efficiency of the engine.

Now entropy is, among other things, a measure of the equalization of temperature throughout a system. If the temperature is constant throughout a system, the entropy is greatest in it, and none of the heat is available for work.

In classical thermodynamics, entropy was expressed in terms of the heat and the temperature of the system. With the advent of the kinetic theory of matter, an entirely new approach to thermodynamics was developed. Temperature and heat are now pictured in terms of the kinetic energy of the molecules comprising the system, and entropy becomes a measure of the *probability* that the velocities of the molecules and other variables of a system are distributed in a certain way. The reason the entropy of a system is greatest when its temperature is constant throughout is because this distribution of temperature is the *most probable*. Increase of entropy was thus interpreted as the passage of a system from less probable to more probable states.

A similar process occurs when we shuffle a deck of cards. If we start with an orderly arrangement, say the cards of each suit following each other according to their value, the shuffling will tend to make the arrangement disorderly. But if we start with a disorderly arrangement, it is very unlikely that through shuffling the cards will come into an orderly one. This is so, because there are many more "disorderly" than orderly arrangements, and so the disorderly state of a deck of cards is more probable.

Thus, the "amount of order" is connected with probabilistic concepts and through them with entropy (the less order, the more entropy). But it is also connected with the "amount of information." For example, far less information is required to describe an orderly arrangement of the cards than a disorderly one. If I say "Starting with ace, deuce, etc., to king; hearts, diamonds, clubs, spades," I have determined the position of every card in the deck. But to describe an arbitrary random arrangement, I have to specify every one of the fifty-two cards.

It is through these notions of probability, order, and disorder that entropy is related to information. The formal equivalence of their mathematical expressions indicates that both concepts describe similiarly structured events.

5. Applications to Biology

Both entropy and information can be defined in terms of the same kinds of variables, namely probabilities of events. Now entropy plays an important part in chemistry and in biochemistry. For example, the knowledge of the entropies of two states of a system indicates whether the system can pass from one state to the other *spontaneously*, say whether a certain chemical reaction can take place *without outside interference*. The interesting thing about chemical reactions in living organisms is that many of them are such that they do not ordinarily take place without interference. Such are, for example, the synthesis of sugars from water and carbon dioxide by green plants and the synthesis of complicated proteins from amino-acids by animals. In these reactions, the ordinary processes (oxidation of sugars and the decomposition of proteins) are reversed. Therefore there must be interference. Early thinkers on this subject postulated the operations of "vital forces" within living things which made these "up-hill" reactions possible.

No evidence of any phenomenon explicitly violating known physical and chemical laws has ever been observed in any organism. True, "up-hill" reactions seem to contradict the law of thermodynamics which demands a continuous increase in entropy (the Second Law of Thermodynamics), but there is nothing in the laws that says that it cannot be circumvented *locally*. In other words, what living things seem to do is create little "islands of order" in themselves at the expense of increased disorder elsewhere. This is the meaning of Schroedinger's famous remark that "life feeds on negative entropy."[12]

12. E. Schroedinger, *What Is Life?* (Cambridge and New York 1945).

Life, therefore, depends essentially on an ordering process, on fighting off the general trend toward chaos, which is always present in the non-living world. But to increase the order of anything means to make it describable with less information (less effort). And is this process not the very essence of knowledge, of science itself? Or of any behavior where complex skills are involved? When a chess genius plays a dozen games simultaneously from memory, or when a musician masters the intricate complexity of muscular movements which go into the rendition of a musical creation, or when a scientist weaves a mass of seemingly unrelated data into a monolithic theory, they are all contributing to the process of decreasing the "entropy" of a portion of the world, of making it more comprehensible with less effort.

Organisms, geneticists tell us, evolve by suffering random genetic variations, which in the process of many generations are selected for their survival value. If these variations were independent of each other, nothing would ever come of evolution. God alone knows how many mutations it took to enable our prehuman ancestor to speak and to make him *want* to speak. Single mutations are improbable enough. But when many have to combine to give rise to some complex patterns of behavior, such as speech, the probability of their being so combined would be infinitesimally small, if the mutations were accumulated independently of each other. But they are not accumulated independently. Rather they seem to be "hoarded" like pieces of a jigsaw puzzle, so that in the process of accumulation *gaps* arise, which are later filled by the proper mutations.

Thus evolution itself is an ordering process. Gross changes of structure, of physiology, and of behavior are made possible because structures, physiological processes, and behavior patterns are always being organized into assemblies. The promise which information theory holds for biology is the same that it holds for linguistics and semantics — the promise to make possible a precise language for talking about the structure of assemblies and the fundamental processes involving the emergence of order from chaos and chaos from order.

Korzybski and others maintained that structure is the only content of knowledge. Korzybski also emphasized the "false-to-factness" of the two-valued orientation. It is therefore futile to suppose that a portion of the world either is or is not "structured." It may be *partially* structured. Therefore a measure of structure or of the amount of organization is required. We have seen how through the entropy concept "amount of information" can be equated to the "amount of disorder." That is not to say that information is a carrier of disorder. On the contrary, information is the carrier of order. What is meant by the equivalence is that the more disordered a portion of the world is, the more information is *required* to describe it completely, that is, to make it known. Thus the process of obtaining knowledge is quantitatively equated to the process of ordering portions of the world.

Significantly, attempts are made to define the life process itself in terms of the creation of order. It has been proposed, for example, to define the amount of entropy in an organism as equal to the amount of entropy it would have if it were completely disorganized minus the amount of information necessary to construct it from its disorganized state. It follows that the more complex an organism is, the more ordered it is, the less entropy it contains. One also suspects from this definition that it is easier to construct a dead organism than a live one. But one also conjectures that the only difficulty in constructing an actual living thing is that an immense amount of information is required to do so.

Living things, therefore, appear in the light of information theory as the carriers of knowledge (i.e., of structure). Man's unique place in the universe is in that he not only carries this "physiological knowledge" within him but has also developed a "second order knowledge," a knowledge of what knowledge consists of and has thus added a new dimension to the life process.

2 The Promise and Pitfalls of Information Theory

ANATOL RAPOPORT
Behavioral Science
Vol. 1, 1956

Information theory, repeatedly hailed as a "major breakthrough" came at a time when mathematical sciences had just become newsworthy — on the heels of nuclear fission. But while the impact of the suddenly publicized atomic physics has been on the entire population through the conventional channels of popular fancy — the awesome possibilities for good and evil of vast amounts of suddenly harnessed energy — the appeal of information theory has been largely confined to academic circles. Yet the nature of this appeal has been not unlike the other. It is felt that a new conceptualization has crystallized which will lead to momentous theoretical reconstructions in biology, psychology, and the social sciences. A vast proliferation of papers devoted to attempts to exploit the new conceptualization reflects this feeling. A 1953 bibliography of information theory[1] contains some 800 entries. Writings on the subject range from sophisticated analysis of radar systems and television circuits to crackpot speculations. Usually, there is a well-marked negative correlation between the scope and the soundness of the writings, so that it is not hard to understand the disappointment with "information theory" as a broad conceptual tool: the sound work is confined either to engineering or to rather trivial applications (rote learning, etc.); ambitious formulations remain vague.

The creators of information theory could, of course, point out that their discipline was conceived in the context of communication engineering, computing machinery, and automation, that they did not coin the phrase, "Life feeds on negative entropy"; that the parallel between entropy and information has been noted merely as a formal identity of mathematical expressions, and that those who wish to speculate about the effects of the Second Law of Thermodynamics on a "closed society" and similar matters should do so at their own risk, etc.

Yet the challenge of extending the concepts of information theory remains, and, as a matter of fact, is traceable to the writings of its founders.* It seems useful, therefore, to try to see what the problems of extension and generalization actually are, that is, to try to state the issues as "problèmes bien posés."

* Perhaps a historical analogy is found in the proliferation of speculations concerning the broader meanings of the "uncertainty principle" in quantum theory. Actually many of these speculations are found in the writings of Bohr himself, one of the fathers of quantum physics.

Given a set of configurations of any system with associated independent probabilities of occurrence p_i, the *uncertainty* of the set is defined in information theory as

$$H = -\sum_i p_i \log_2 p_i \qquad [1]$$

Thus if one selects a message from a source of n messages, each selection is a "configuration" characterized by a certain probability. Then H is the uncertainty (per message) associated with the source. The receipt of the message transmitted without error "destroys" the uncertainty of the recipient, with regard to which message will be chosen. Therefore H measures also the amount of information per message.

Now in statistical mechanics, the thermodynamic quantity *entropy* also appears as the same expression, where now the set of configurations comprises all the arrangements of positions and momenta of the particles comprising a system that correspond to the thermodynamic *state* of the system. It turns out that states described in thermodynamics as *equilibrium states* have corresponding to them the greatest number of such configurations and so are "most probable." The trend toward equilibrium observed in all systems "left to themselves" is interpreted in statistical mechanics as the predominance of occurrence of the more probable states over the less probable.

A homely example illustrates the principle. In a well-shuffled deck of cards the number of red cards among the first 26 cards will be not too far off from 13. At any rate with continued shuffling, numbers around 13 for reds among the first will appear far more frequently than numbers around 26 or 0. This is so because many more arrangements of the deck are possible where the reds are evenly distributed than when they are all in one half. It is justifiable to say that the "equilibrium condition" (where a red card has as much chance of passing from the first half of the deck to the second as vice versa) is the condition of the greatest "entropy" of the deck.

The condition "if the system is left to itself" is crucial. Nothing is easier than to lower the "entropy" of a deck of cards by deliberate re-arrangements. Once thermodynamic entropy was recognized as a measure of "disorder" in a system it was natural to raise the question of whether the Second Law could be circumvented by the intervention of an "intelligence." The seed of the idea relating information to entropy was sown. The idea first appears in the writings of none other than James Clerk Maxwell himself, one of the founders of statistical mechanics. He writes in *Theory of Heat* ". . . a being whose faculties are so sharpened that he can follow every molecule in his course . . . would be able to do what is at present impossible to us . . . Let us suppose that a vessel is divided into two portions, *A* and *B* by a division in which there is a small hole, and that a being who can see the individual molecules opens and closes this hole, so as to allow only the swifter molecules to pass from *A* to *B*,

and only the slower ones to pass from *B* to *A*. He will, thus, without expenditure of work raise the temperature of *B* and lower that of *A*, in contradiction to the second law of thermodynamics."[2]

Thus was born Maxwell's Demon, possibly a descendant of the Homunculus, to challenge by means of his phenomenal acuity and infinitesimal reaction time the the inexorable Second Law.

Maxwell's Demon, or Maxie, as we will call him for short, now 85 years old, is still a subject of serious theoretical discussion. A paper of historical significance for information theory was devoted entirely to him by L. Szilard.[3] Szilard has shown that in lowering the entropy of a gas by his "decisions" Maxie causes an increase of entropy *elsewhere* which, as calculations show, more than compensates for the decrease and thus vindicates the dictum of the Second Law that the entropy of a *closed* system (which in this case must include Maxie and his apparatus) can only increase. More recently, L. Brillouin[4] emphasized Maxwell's assumption that Maxie *can see* the molecules. Thus, he cannot be sitting in the total darkness of the enclosed gas (even if the gas is hot and radiates light, it does not help him to distinguish the molecules if the whole system is in equilibrium). To see the molecules Maxie must use a flashlight and thus, as, Brillouin shows, feeds "negative entropy" in the form of a light beam into the system. It is this negative entropy which is more than an ample source to account for the resulting decreased entropy of the gas alone.

Thus Maxie is shown to be cheating like any charlatan exhibiting a perpetual motion machine. These discussions are interesting, because they may lead to insight concerning the way enzymes work. It is the enzymes which are credited with the "local" contraventions of the Second Law which seem to be operating in living systems. On the other hand, it is known that eventually all enzymes become "denatured" and lose their function as "organizers" of living processes. ("For an enzyme to be in equilibrium is to be denatured." — Wiener) It has been remarked that besides counting the rise in entropy in the gadgets which Maxie must have for his entropy-lowering activity, one should take into account the rise in entropy within Maxie himself, perhaps the denaturation of his enzymes reflecting the "entropic costs" of his decisions. This, in turn, leads to speculations concerning similar processes in all "organizing" activity, the perfection of technology, accumulation of scientific knowledge, etc. Are we becoming "denatured" to the extent that we "order" the world to suit our needs? We mention this only to illustrate how easy it is to embark on metaphysical and even theological speculations once one becomes seriously concerned with the Second Law.

So much concerning the possible exploitation of the conjectured equivalence of information and physical entropy. Let us turn to the speculations revolving around the concept of information as a tool for quantifying the "amount of knowledge." Here, even more than in matters dealing with physical entropy the scope of attempted generalizations far outruns available tools of analysis. This is not surprising, since "knowledge" evokes strong intuitively felt similarity to information and since knowledge has been traditionally the subject matter of philosophic speculation. Accordingly, one finds a wealth of discussion about fighting the inexorable Second Law by increasing our knowledge (knowledge = information = negative entropy), about the inevitable collapse of totalitarian societies (totalitarian society = closed society = closed system, in which entropy is bound to increase) and similar matters much removed from the theory originally designed to inquire into conditions which make for efficient transmission of signals over a channel.

We must disavow in passing any suggestion that we consider such speculation as entirely idle. After all, the Copernican revolution had a profound effect much beyond astronomy, and the law of conservation of matter has implications much more far reaching than making for correct bookkeeping in the chemist's laboratory. However, the profound effect of celestial mechanics and the conservation laws on our world view operated, we think it is safe to say, through the resulting success of scientific method, and the latter depends for its operation on precise definitions of situations one deals with. Therefore it seems to us that the search for applications of information theory to communication in a broader sense than it is understood by those who think in terms of wires and tubes (i.e., broadly to problems of human communication), while commendable and attractive, must be tempered by a sober attempt to keep the universe of discourse well-defined.

A difficult transition is from the concept of information in the technical (communication engineering) sense to the semantic (theory of meaning) sense. This transition has been undertaken by Carnap, Bar-Hillel, and other workers. The difficulties involved become immediately apparent. Suppose we ask how much information is contained in an average English word. Has the question any meaning? This depends on to whom it is addressed. The telegraph engineer has a most definitive answer. He knows that the redundancy of English reduces the amount of information per letter from about 5 to 2 bits, and since the "average" word has about 5 letters, this makes 10 bits the information content of the average word. The telephone engineer's or the linguist's answer requires a more intricate analysis in terms of phonemes, distinctive features, etc., but his answer can, *in principle,* be equally direct.

Now what does 10 bits per word mean? It should mean that if I think of an English word and you try to guess it, you should be able to do it in about 10 guesses requiring yes or no answers. If you choose your guesses judiciously, you should be able to do it simply guessing letter by letter. But suppose letter guessing is disallowed. You are required to guess, as in the game of Twenty Questions, by narrowing down logical categories. As

people who play Twenty Questions know, extremely bizarre notions can be guessed within that limit; so it is possible that an experienced player can guess a single word in ten tries. It is remarkable, however, that while it would be rather simple to program a logical computer so as to guess any word letter by letter, to build a machine that would do so by "logical categories" would involve building into the machine the entire encyclopedia of human knowledge! Moreover, any eight-year-old can be taught to guess any word letter by letter (even unfamiliar words, if the question, "Is that all?" is included). But if the word is not in his repertoire, no amount of advance instruction will enable an eight-year-old to guess it by "logical categories."

This illustrates a cardinal feature of information theory. It is fundamentally a theory of *selection.* Something is selected from a well-defined set. To examine the selective process, it is essential to be able to examine the set.

The modest but, we think, significant applications of information theory to certain psychological experiments owe their success to the fact that in each situation the set in question was strictly defined: a list of syllables to be memorized, associations to be formed, responses selected from, etc. There was, therefore, no difficulty in quantifying the associated "amounts of information" and relating such accounts to certain aspects of performance.

To many these results appear somewhat trivial. We do not agree. If information theory is to break out of its original habitat of bandwidths and modulations, a proper beginning must be made, which usually means a modest beginning. Experimental psychology has made this beginning possible. However, one must admit that the gap between this sort of experimentation and questions concerning the "flow of information" through human communication channels is enormous. So far no theory exists, to our knowledge, which attributes any sort of unambiguous measure to this "flow." It is naive to take simply the flux in signals per second to multiply by bits per signals in the communication engineering sense and call the result "amount of communication" in the sense of transmission of knowledge (labeling everything one does not like "noise"). If there is such a thing as semantic information, it is based on an entirely different kind of "repertoire" which itself may be different for each recipient. To be defined as a quantity of information a signal must be selected from a set or matched with an element of a set. It is misleading in a crucial sense to view "information" as something that can be poured into an empty vessel, like a fluid or even like energy.

Yet some meaning lurks in the expression "to acquire information"! We feel, however vaguely, that as a race we have learned certain things as a result of which we can more effectively "order the universe" to our liking. We have learned to reverse the degradation of energy locally by putting heat to work. We like to think that in increasing our average life span, we are challenging (again only locally) the trend toward chaos (all living things seem to do so, but we think we do it better). At this point we could be accused of the same promiscuous speculation we have implicity warned against. We can only plead that such speculation is extremely difficult to avoid.

Let us try for a while to walk the tight rope between rigor and speculative abandon. It was probably the now famous remark of Schroedinger, "Life feeds on negative entropy," that has been responsible for speculations which are always tantalizing but which range from profound to irresponsible. A most prosaic interpretation is simply in terms of thermodynamic bookkeeping. The First Law having long been established, it is axiomatic that life feeds on energy: it converts chemical energy of ingested food and of sunlight into work necessary to pursue its activities. The energy equation must balance. However, with the advent of the Second Law in its classical, i.e., purely thermodynamic form, another bookkeeping appears necessary. The entropy inequality must hold. A living organism must ingest at least enough *free* energy, which contains a negative entropy term, to account for any local decrease of entropy concomitant to its *organizational* activity. All this would be perfectly clear if the "increment of organization" inherent in a process were as clearly defined as an increment of energy. One might argue as many do, that organization is simply the negative of entropy. True, entropy is unambiguously defined in classical thermodynamics, but this discipline confines itself only to processes which take place under continued equilibrium (reversible processes). The classical definition, therefore, is inappropriate for living processes ("For an organism to be in equilibrium is to be dead." — Wiener). The advent of statistical mechanics with its redefinition of entropy as the probability of an aggregate of states does make possible the extension of the entropy concept to non-equilibrium states, indeed in information-theoretical terms. Hence the excitement. One feels it may be possible to calculate the "amount of organization" of configurations arising in the living process and thus establish the bookkeeping demanded by the Second Law to deal with those aspects of life, which, it is felt, are much more crucial than those covered by energetics bookkeeping (First Law).

One such attempt, to give an example, is due to R. C. Raymond.[5] Raymond proposes to define the entropy of a configuration by the sum of two terms, a positive one, equal to the entropy the aggregate would finally attain if left to itself (i.e., its classical entropy) and a negative term equal to the amount of information necessary to reconstruct the original configuration from equilibrium (from complete chaos). This definition is attractive and indeed fits perfectly into the situation previously discussed where Maxie works with 100% efficiency pumping information (= negative entropy)

into a system which starts with positive entropy only.

We suspect, however, that there are grave difficulties associated with this definition when one tries to extend it to situations other than the simplest (ideal gas, etc.). The difficulty is the same conceptual one which governs the applications of information theory to semantic problems. What are the elements of a configuration? And what is the set from which messages describing the construction of a configuration from chaos are selected? That is not to say that it is impossible to define these elements, but only that it appears that the definition must be made anew in each instance. How then is one to agree on a definition once for all so as to make the entropy of a configuration unambiguous?

Let us take an example. How much "order" is contained in a particular arrangement of a deck of cards? According to one view, since each arrangement is equiprobable its probability being $(52!)^{-1}$, it follows that $\log_2 (52!)$ yes-no decisions are required to reconstruct a particular order from a thoroughly shuffled deck. Now although $(52!)$ is prodigiously large ($\sim 10^{68}$) its logarithm is not (~ 200), and it is perfectly feasible to guess the arrangement in about 200 guesses, provided one is allowed to guess card by card. But suppose one is to guess by arrangements only? *We simply do not have the language* to classify the card arrangements so as to be able to make judicious dichotomies for yes-no answers. Our knowledge of card arrangements is confined to very few, which we call "ordered" (e.g., arrangements by suits and face values), and we tend to lump all the other arrangements as "meaningless" chaos. Similarly, a dictionary is useful only because its entries are arranged in a *particular* order meaningful to us. It is no consolation to be told that any other arrangement is equally improbable and therefore should be considered as having an equally low "entropy." One suspects that similar considerations apply to biology and make Raymond's definition of order less useful than it appears. Only *certain* arrangements maintain life. It is misleading therefore to measure the amount of order simply by the amount of talking one has to do to give instructions for its reconstruction or by how improbable the configuration in question is. All *particular* configurations are a priori equally improbable. As for the amount of information arrangements which we tend to consider necessary for reconstruction of order, paradoxically the ordered are usually reconstructible with *fewer* instructions. To reconstruct the ordered card arrangement, we need only say, "arrange in descending order of values the spades, clubs, diamonds, and hearts," whereas to reconstruct an arbitrary arrangement from another arbitrary one, we will generally have to name the position of each card separately! So in biological situations one might think certain arrangements have to be first *singled out* as the significant ones. Then one can hope to quantify the degree to which an arrangement approaches the "proper" one. But the discovery of "proper" arrangements is not simply a matter of counting; it is a matter of understanding the life process. Hence much more than understanding the theoretical tool of information theory is required for a proper application of the tool.

With regard to the other proposed extension of the entropy concept (as it appears in information theory), i.e., to the study of human communication (intertwined with semantic problems), the task is at least as difficult. To answer the question, "How much does a man know?" or "How much has he learned?" is possible in the sense of the present state of information theory only if one can specify a set from which selections must be made. Information is measured by the extent to which it makes uncertain selection certain. An attempt to define such repertoires of selection often leads to conclusions which seem, to say the least, unsatisfactory. Suppose, for example, a person does not know whether ghosts exist. Then he reads a book which presents weighty evidence against the existence of ghosts, as a result of which he becomes convinced that ghosts do not exist. How much information has he acquired? One can "reason" as follows. Prior to reading the book he was equally uncertain about which answer is proper, "Yes" or "No." After reading the book, he is certain of the answer "No." Therefore he has acquired one bit of information. We submit, the conclusion is unsatisfactory. (We will refrain from raising the question about the case where the man is convinced by reading a book that ghosts do exist.) Or take another example. A child learns that $2 + 2 = 4$. How much has he learned? The formal argument could run thus. If the child is acquainted with the names of numbers $1, 2, \ldots . n$ and was equally uncertain about which was the right answer, then he has acquired $\log_2 n$ bits of information. This conclusion seems to be equally ludicrous. These examples are given solely to illustrate what pitfalls await those who wish to extend the formal aspects of information theory to applications with more human interest. It is tempting to suggest that the American Revolution was triggered by one bit of information ("One if by land; two if by sea"). In this case the contention is not wholly unjustified: it refers to the simplicity of the arrangement for implementing one of two alternative plans of resistance, depending on the choice of the British commander to move by land or by sea against the insurgents. The simplicity of the arrangement was made possible by previous elaborate organization (of Minutemen, etc.) which it served to trigger. But such reductions of complicated situations to well-specified alternatives are rare.

Lest we seem to pause on a pessimistic note, let us reiterate our faith in the future of information theory. It is sometimes instructive to learn from historical analogy. A precursor of information theory, of which the latter is an elaborate extension, was probability theory, which started from humble beginnings as an intellectual schematization of what happens in games of chance, and which has grown to become one of the fundamental tools of exact science, whose logical foundations are a challenge to most serious philosophers. We note that attempts to extend probability theory to epistemological problems, for example, were also studded with pitfalls. No less a figure than Laplace, starting with a plausible theory of induction, came to rather ridiculous conclusions concerning the probability that the sun would rise on the following day. The axiomatization of probability theory is of recent origin and rests squarely on the definition of a "sample space," i.e., an explicit listing of the range of events over which the probability measure is to be defined. The notion of sample space seemed to have given a *coup de grâce* to the hope of extending exact probabilistic notions to measure a "degree of belief," a subjective concept. (What is the probability that the Democrats will win in 1956?) Yet there were those who refused to give up hope of successful axiomatization of "personal probability," so as to extend the strictly objectivistic view adhered to by the majority. As a result we have, for example, the highly interesting formulation of L. J. Savage[6] in which this axiomatization is achieved, not without the use of rather sophisticated conceptual and mathematical machinery.

We believe that extensions of information theory and of the entropy concept, which is now riding on the coat tails of information theory, are entirely in order. We are afraid, however, that these extensions are no easy matter and cannot be achieved by "semantic suggestion," that is, a tendency to confuse invention of nomenclature with discovery of principles.

References

1. F. L. Stumpers, *A Bibliography of Information Theory*. Cambridge, Mass.: Research Laboratory of Electronics, Massachusetts Institute of Technology (1953).
2. Quoted by L. Brillouin, *Journal of Applied Physics*, **22**, p. 334 (1951).
3. L. Szilard, "Über die Entropieverminderung in einem Thermodynamischen System bei Eingriffen intelligenter Wesen," *Zeitschrift für Physik*, **53**, 840–856 (1929).
4. L. Brillouin, "Maxwell's Demon Cannot Operate: Information and Entropy I," *Journal of Applied Physics*, **22**, 334–337 (1951).
5. R. C. Raymond, "Communication, Entropy, and Life," *American Scientist*, **38**, 273–278 (1950).
6. L. J. Savage, *Foundations of Statistics*, New York: John Wiley & Sons (1954).

3 Semantic Information

YEHOSHUA BAR-HILLEL
RUDOLF CARNAP
The British Journal for the
Philosophy of Science
Vol. 4, No. 14, August, 1953

The Mathematical Theory of Communication, often referred to also as Theory (of Transmission) of Information, as practised nowadays, is not interested in the content of the symbols whose information it measures. The measures, as defined, for instance, by Shannon,[1] have nothing to do with what these symbols symbolise, but only with the frequency of their occurrence.[2] The prob-

1. See, e.g., C. E. Shannon and W. Weaver, *The Mathematical Theory of Communication*, University of Illinois Press, 1949. E. Colin Cherry's 'A History of the Theory of Information', *Proceedings of the Institution of Electrical Engineers*, 1951, 98, part iii, pp. 383–393, gives an excellent account of the development of this theory and contains also an extensive bibliography up to 1950.

2. A notable exception to this general trend of communication engineers is D. M. MacKay, who recognised as early as 1948 that the concept of information treated in Communication Theory, which he proposes to call 'selective information,' should be supplemented by a concept of 'scientific information.' It seems, however, that this concept does not coincide with what we call here 'semantic information'. A clarification of the exact relationship will be undertaken elsewhere.

The clearest presentation of MacKay's ideas may be found in his contribution to the *Transactions of the Eighth Conference on Cybernetics*, 'In Search of Basic Symbols',

abilities which occur in the definientia of the definitions of the various concepts in Communication Theory are just these frequencies, absolute or relative, sometimes perhaps estimates of these frequencies.

This deliberate restriction of the scope of Statistical Communication Theory was of great heuristic value and enabled this theory to reach important results in a short time. Unfortunately, however, it often turned out that impatient scientists in various fields applied the terminology and the theorems of Communication Theory to fields in which the term 'information' was used, pre-systematically, in a semantic sense, that is, one involving contents or designata of symbols, or even in a pragmatic sense, that is, one involving the users of these symbols. There can be no doubt that the clarification of these concepts of information is a very important task. However, the definitions of information and amount of information given in present Communication Theory do not constitute a solution of this task. To transfer these definitions to the fields in which those semantic or pragmatic con-

New York, 1952, pp. 181–235, where an earlier paper of his, 'The Nomenclature of Information Theory', is also reprinted.

cepts are used, may at best have some heuristic stimulating value but at worst be absolutely misleading.

In the following, the outlines of a Theory of Semantic Information will be presented. The contents of the symbols will be decisively involved in the definition of the basic concepts of this theory and an application of these concepts and of the theorems concerning them to fields involving semantics thereby warranted. But precaution will still have to be taken not to apply prematurely these concepts and theorems to fields like psychology and other social sciences, in which users of symbols play an essential role. It is expected, however, that the semantic concept of information will serve as a better approximation for some future explanation of a psychological concept of information than the concept dealt with in Communication Theory.

The fundamental concepts of the theory of semantic information can be defined in a straightforward way on the basis of the theory of inductive probability that has been recently developed by one of us.[3] Unfortunately, the space at our disposal does not permit us to develop the full terminological background on which our presentation is based. We have to refer once and for all to the extensive presentation of this background given in [Prob.] or to the more concise summary given in [Cont.]. (In the Appendix, an even more concise summary is offered for the convenience of the reader.) Let us state only that what follows refers to a fixed language system L_n^π, by which we mean, approximately, an applied first-order functional semantical system with n individuals, say $a_1, a_2 \ldots , a_n$, and π primitive properties, say $P_1, P_2, \ldots , P_\pi$. A disjunction which, for each of the πn atomic statements, contains either this statement or its negation (but not both) as a component, will be called a *content-element*. The content-elements are the weakest factual statements of L_n^π inasmuch as the only factual statement L-implied by a content-element is this content-element itself. One of the 64 content-elements in L_3^2, for instance, is

$$P_1a_1 v \sim P_2a_1 v \sim P_1a_2vP_2a_2vP_1a_3vP_2a_3.$$

The class of all content-elements L-implied by any statement i (in L_n^π) is called the *content* of this statement and denoted by 'Cont (i)'. It can be easily verified that the content of any atomic statement contains exactly half of all content-elements, that of an L-true statement none, and that of an L-false statement all of them. The last property may look slightly artificial but is no more so than the use of, say, the null-set in set-theory.

We offer Cont (i) as an explicatum for the ordinary concept 'the information conveyed by the statement i',

3. R. Carnap, *Logical Foundations of Probability*, University of Chicago Press, 1950, cited here after as [Prob.] and *The Continuum of Inductive Methods,* University of Chicago Press, 1952, cited hereafter as [Cont.].

taken in its semantic sense. We have no time to show at length that Cont (i) is an adequate explicatum. But it can be immediately verified that it fulfils at least the condition that Cont (i) includes Cont (j) if i L-implies j. This condition should be regarded as a necessary, though certainly not sufficient, condition of adequacy of any proposed explanation of the mentioned concept.

Since Cont (i) is equal to the class of the negations of the state-descriptions contained in the range of $\sim$ i, the properties of Cont (i) can be easily derived from the properties of the concept 'range of i' which has been treated at length in [Prob.]. We shall say nothing more here.

It is often important not only to know what is the information conveyed by some statement but also to attach a measure to this information. We need not start afresh looking for appropriate measure-functions ranging over contents since measure-functions over ranges have been extensively discussed in [Prob.]. For each of the latter m-functions, as they are called in [Prob.], a corresponding content-measure-function is defined simply by

$$\mathrm{cont}\ (i) = m\ (\sim i).$$

cont (i) (read : the content-measure of i) is offered as one (not *the*) explicatum of the ordinary concept 'amount of information conveyed by i' in its semantic sense. Among the most important properties of cont (i), immediately derivable from the corresponding properties of m(i) treated in [Prob.] we have

$$0 \leqq \mathrm{cont}\ (i) \leqq 1,$$

where the extremes are reserved for L-true and L-false statements, respectively, and

$$\mathrm{cont}\ (i \cdot j) = \mathrm{cont}\ (i) + \mathrm{cont}\ (j) - \mathrm{cont}\ (ivj).$$

From the last theorem follow immediately:

$$\mathrm{cont}\ (i \cdot j) \leqq \mathrm{cont}\ (i) + \mathrm{cont}\ (j),$$

and the interesting additivity theorem:

cont (i . j) = cont (i) + cont (j) if and only if i and j are L-disjunct.

Here, however, an inconsistency in the intuitions of many of us becomes apparent. Though it is indeed, after some reflection, quite plausible that the content of a conjunction should be equal to the sum of the contents of its components if and only if these components are L-disjunct or content-exclusive, in other words, if they have no factual consequences in common, it is also plausible, without much reflection, that the content of the conjunction of two basic statements, say 'P_1a_1' and '$\sim P_2a_3$'

should be equal to the sum of the contents of these statements since they are independent, and this not only in the weak deductive sense of this term, but even in the much stronger sense of initial irrelevance. But no two basic statements with different predicates are L-disjunct, since they have their disjunction, which is a factual statement, as a common consequence. Our intuitions here, as in so many other cases, are in conflict and it is best to solve this conflict by assuming that there is not *one* explicandum 'amount of information' but at least two, for one of which cont is a suitable explicatum, whereas the explicatum for the other has still to be found.

So far we have dealt with the information conveyed by some statement separately. At times, however, we are as much, or even more, interested in the information conveyed by a statement j in excess to that conveyed by some other statement i or a class of statements. We therefore define the concepts 'content of j relative to i' and 'content-measure of j relative to i' by

$$\text{Cont} (j/i) = \text{Cont} (i \cdot j) - \text{Cont} (i)$$

and

$$\text{cont} (j/i) = \text{cont} (i \cdot j) - \text{cont} (i)$$

respectively. (Notice that the ' — ' in the first of these definitions is the symbol of class-difference, in the second that of ordinary numerical difference.) The maximum value of cont (j/i) is obviously cont (j) and this value is obtained if and only if i and j are L-disjunct. The minimum value of cont (j/i) is o and this value is obtained if, and only if, i L-implies j. Of special interest is that

$$\text{cont} (j/t) = \text{cont} (j),$$

where t stands for any L-true statement (any 'tautology'), since this allows us to define cont (j) in terms of cont (j/i), thereby reversing the definition procedure followed by us before. Even more interesting is that

$$\text{cont} (j/i) = \text{cont} (i \supset j),$$

from which it follows that, given i, j conveys no more additional information than i $\supset$ j, by itself a much weaker statement.

If we stipulate now, for the second explicatum of 'amounts of information', that all basic statements shall convey the same amount of information, and this independently of whether these statements appear alone or as components in some non-contradictory conjunction, and if we stipulate, in addition, for the purpose of normalisation, that the amount of information conveyed by a basic statement shall be 1, it can easily be seen, along well-known lines of computation, that these stipulations

are fulfilled if we define this second function, to be called 'measure of information' and denoted by 'inf', as

$$\text{inf}(i) = \text{Log} \ \frac{1}{1\text{-cont} (i)}$$

(where 'Log' stands for $\log_2$), from which we obtain, by simple substitution,

$$\text{inf}(i) = \text{Log} \ \frac{1}{m (i)} = - \text{Log m} (i).$$

The last equation is analogous to a definition of amount of information in Communication Theory but with inductive probability instead of statistical probability.

Among the various theorems regarding inf let us mention

$$\text{o} \leqq \text{inf}(i) \leqq$$

and the theorem of additivity, which, however, involves now a quite different condition.

inf(i . j) = inf(i) + inf(j) if, and only if, i is initially irrelevant to j (with respect to that m-function on which inf is based).

Sometimes inf(i . j) is greater than inf(i) + inf(j). If anyone should find this strange that might be due to the fact that he has subconsciously switched to some other explicatum, such as cont, for which this can indeed not happen.

Another theorem of great importance deals with inf(j/i). It states that

$$\text{inf}(j/i) = \text{Log} \ \frac{1}{c (j, i)} = - \text{Log c} (j, i)$$

where c(j, i) is the degree of confirmation of (the hypothesis) j on (the evidence) i, defined in [Prob.] as $\dfrac{m(i \cdot j)}{m(i)}$.

The statistical correlate of inf has found a large field of application in communication engineering. Neither cont nor its statistical correlate have found any useful application so far. It is, however, to be expected that the facet of the amount of information which is measured by cont, should find its fields of application too, especially so since cont is a mathematically simpler function of m than inf.[4]

Among the various m-functions on which cont and inf may be based, there are two groups of special importance. The first group consists of just one member, to be designated here by 'm_D' — its symbol in [Prob.] is 'm†'

4. Indeed, in a paper by John G. Kemeny and Paul Oppenheim, 'Degree of Factual Support', *Philosophy of Science*, 1952, 19, 288–306 (published after the present paper was read in London), a concept of Strength of a statement was used whose definition corresponds closely to that of our cont$_D$.

— : the second group has infinitely many members denoted collectively by 'm_I'. m_D assigns to each content-element the same value. This makes the computations with this function especially easy, in general, and the preference given to it understandable. It suffers, however, from the great disadvantage that it does not allow us, roughly speaking, to learn from experience. 'P_1a_4', for instance, will have a c_D-value of $\frac{1}{2}$, on no evidence at all or, in other words, on the tautological evidence, and the same c_D-value on the evidence '$P_1a_1 . P_1a_2 . P_1a_3$'. In spite of this defect, there are situations in which m_D, c_D, and the information-functions based upon them may be of importance. Situations in which we intend to use only deductive reasoning are of this type, hence the subscript 'D' for 'deductive'.

In those situations in which inductive reasoning is to be applied, only such m-functions may be used which allow us to learn from experience, in other words, which fulfil the Requirement of Instantial Relevance.[5] These are the functions m_I; the 'I' stands for 'inductive'.

All the theorems that hold for cont and inf in general hold, of course, also for $cont_D$ and inf_D and all the $cont_I$ and inf_I functions. For these more specific functions, however, additional theorems can be proven. For lack of space, this will not be done here. Let us only remark that certain inconsistencies in our intuitive requirements with regard to information-functions may be due to a subconscious switching from D-type functions to I-type functions and vice versa.

Situations often arise in which we do not know whether a certain event has occurred or will occur, but only that exactly one event out of a class of mutually exclusive events has occurred or will occur. The statements describing these events convey each a certain amount of information on the available evidence. It makes therefore good sense to ask for some average of the amount of information conveyed by these statements. If these statements refer to future events, one talks about the amount of information that may be expected to be conveyed, on the average. In [Prob.] it is shown that in many similar situations the c-mean estimate of the function in question will be a satisfactory measure for this expected value. Confining ourselves here, for the sake of easy comparability with prevailing Communication Theory, to inf and using 'exhaustive system' to denote a class of statements of the above-mentioned character, we define *the (c-mean) estimate of the measure of information conveyed by (the members of the exhaustive system) H on (the evidence) e*, in symbols: est (inf, H, e), as follows:

$$\text{est}(\inf, H, e) = \sum_{p=1}^{n} c(h_p, e) \times \inf(h_p/e).$$

5. See R. Carnap, 'On the Comparative Concept of Confirmation', this *Journal*, 1953, 3, p. 314.

From this definition and from a prior theorem on inf (h_p/e) the theorem

$$\text{est}(\inf, H, e) = -\sum_{p} c(h_p, e) \times \text{Log } c(h_p, e)$$

immediately follows. The communicational correlate of this theorem is well-known. We see no reason, so far, to attach any special significance to the formal similarity of its right side to certain entropy-type expressions in statistical thermodynamics.

To give a simple illustration: If on the basis of available evidence, mainly prior observations, the c-value of the hypothesis, h_1, 'There will be warm weather in London on the 23rd of September 1953',[6] is $\frac{1}{2}$, the c-value of h_2, 'There will be temperate weather . . .', is $\frac{1}{4}$, and the c-value of h_3, 'There will be cold weather . . .', is $\frac{1}{4}$, then

$$\text{est}(\inf, H, e) = -\sum_{p} c(h_p, e) \times \text{Log } c(h_p, e)$$

$$= \tfrac{1}{2} \times 1 + \tfrac{1}{4} \times 2 + \tfrac{1}{4} \times 2 = 1.5$$

(where $H = \{h_1, h_2, h_3\}$).

If $H = \{h_1 \ldots h_n\}$ and $K = \{k_1 \ldots k_m\}$ are (deductively) independent exhaustive systems (on e) (i.e. no $h_p . k_q$ is L-false (on e)), then $H . K$, defined as $\{h_1 . k_1, h_1 . k_2 \ldots h_1 . k_m, h_2 . k_1 \ldots h_n . k_m\}$ is exhaustive too (on e), hence

$$\text{est}(\inf, H . K, e) = \sum_{p=1}^{n} \sum_{q=1}^{m} c(h_p . k_q, e) \times \inf(h_p . k_q/e).$$

We have

$$\text{est}\{\inf, H . K, e) \leqq \text{est}(\inf, H, e) + \text{est}(\inf, K, e),$$

with equality holding if, and only if, the h's and the k's are mutually irrelevant.

If the statement k is added to our evidence, *the posterior estimate of the measure of information conveyed by H on e and k will, in general, be different from the prior estimate of the measure of information conveyed by H on e alone*. This difference is often of great importance and will therefore receive a special name, *amount of specification of H through k on e* and be denoted by 'sp (inf, H, k, e)'. The formal definition is

$$\text{sp}(\inf, H, k, e) = \text{est}(\inf, H, e) - \text{est}(\inf, H, e . k).$$

It is easy to see that $\text{sp}(\inf, H, k, e) = 0$ if (but not only if) k is irrelevant to the h's on e. sp may have positive and negative values with its maximum obviously equal to the prior estimate itself. This value will be ob-

6. The formulation of this statement exceeds already the potentialities of the language-systems envisaged here. However, this is of no importance in this connection.

tained when e. k L-implies some h_n. In this case. H is completely specified through k (on e).

Let, to continue our previous illustration, k_1 be a certain report of weather-instrument-readings. Let $c(k_1, e . h_1) = \frac{1}{4}$, $c(k_1, e . h_2) = c(k_1, e . h_3) = \frac{1}{2}$. The following diagram will help to visualise the situation:

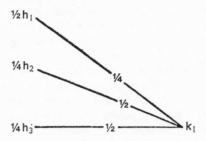

It is easy to compute, or to read from the diagram, that $c(h_1, e . k_1) = c(h_2, e . k_1) = c(h_3, e . k_1) = \frac{1}{3}$. Hence $\text{est}(\text{inf}, H, e . k_1) = \text{Log } 3 = 1.585$ and $\text{sp}(\text{inf}, H, k_1, e) = -0.085$.

Situations often arise in which the event stated in k has not yet occurred, or, at least, in which it is not known whether it has occurred but in which it is known that either it or some other event belonging to a certain class of events will occur or has occurred. In such circumstances, it makes sense to ask for some average of the posterior estimate of the measure of information conveyed by H on e and (some member of) K (the exhaustive system of the k's). We are led to *the (c-mean) estimate of this posterior estimate* denoted by '$\text{est}(\text{inf}, H/K, e)$' and defined as

$$\text{est}(\text{inf}, H/K, e) = \sum_{q=1}^{m} c(k_q, e) \times \text{est}(\text{inf}, H, e . k_q).$$

Let us complete our illustration in the following diagram:

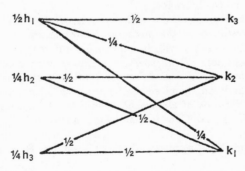

Then $\text{est}(\text{inf}, H/K, e) = \sum_q c(k_q, e) \times \text{est}(\text{inf}, H, e . k_q)$

$$= \tfrac{3}{8} \times \text{Log } 3 + \tfrac{3}{8} \times \text{Log } 3 = 1.189.$$

The estimate of the amount of specification of H through K on e is, of course, equal to the difference between the prior estimate of the measure of information conveyed by H on e and the estimate of the posterior estimate of the measure of information conveyed by H on e and K, in symbols:

$$\text{sp}(\text{inf}, H, K, e) = \text{est}(\text{inf}, H, e) - \text{est}(\text{inf}, H/K, e).$$

In our example, $\text{sp}(\text{inf}, H, K, e) = 1.5 - 1.189 = 0.311$.

Let us mention only three theorems in this connection, the communicational correlates of which are well-known:

$$\text{est}(\text{inf}, H/K, e) = \text{est}(\text{inf}, H . K, e) - \text{est}(\text{inf}, K, e),$$
$$\text{sp}(\text{inf}, H, K, e) = \text{sp}(\text{inf}, K, H, e),$$
$$\text{sp}(\text{inf}, H, K, e) \geqq 0.$$

Lack of space prevents us from going any deeper into the significance of the concepts and theorems indicated in the last section. It seems that the theory of semantic information might be fruitfully applied in various fields, for instance in the Theory of Design of Experiments[7] and in Test Theory.[8]

In view of the many misunderstandings and misapplications, in which Communication Theory has been involved, it would be desirable to undertake a clarification of its foundations. So would be a comparison between the theory outlined here and Communication Theory. These two tasks will be undertaken elsewhere by one of the authors (B.-H.).

Appendix

The language systems dealt with in this paper contain a finite number of *individual constants* which stand for *individuals* (things, events, or positions) and a finite number of *primitive one-place predicates* which designate primitive properties of the individuals. In an *atomic statement* e.g., '$P_1 a_1$' ('the individual a_1 has the property P_1'), a primitive property is asserted to hold for an individual. Atomic statements and statements formed out of one or more of them with the help of the customary connectives of negation, '$\sim$' ('not'), of disjunction, 'v' ('or'), of conjunction, '.' ('and'), of (material) implication, '$\supset$' ('if . . . then'), and of (material) equivalence, '$\equiv$' (if and only if), are *molecular statements*. All atomic statements and their negations are *basic statements*. It is known that with the help of these tools numerical statements can be formed. Hence absolute frequencies (cardinal num-

7. Indeed, R. A. Fisher defined in *The Design of Experiments,* Edinburgh and London, 1935 (in a less developed form already in papers dating back to 1922), a concept of Amount of Information which is, however, only distantly related to that developed here. Fisher's concept is certainly not a communicational one, but it is, like the communicational one, of a statistical, and not of a semantical, nature.

8. Recent work done by Lee J. Cronbach at the University of Illinois seems to point in this direction. See, e.g., his preliminary report 'A Generalised Psychometric Theory Based on Information Measure', mimeographed, March 1952.

bers of classes or properties) and relative frequencies can be expressed in them (but not measurable quantities like length and mass).

Any sentence is either *L-true* (logically true, analytic, e.g. '$P_1a_1 \vee \sim P_1a_1$') or *L-false* (logically false, self-contradictory, e.g. '$P_1a_1 . \sim P_1a_1$') or *factual* (logically indeterminate, synthetic, e.g. '$P_1a_1 \vee \sim P_2P_3$'). Logical relations can be defined, e.g. 'The statement i *L-implies* the statement j' for 'i $\supset$ j is L-true', 'i is *L-equivalent* to j' for 'i $\equiv$ j is L-true' 'i is *L-disjunct* with j' for 'ivj is L-true'.

A *state-description* is a conjunction containing as components for every atomic statement either this statement or its negation, but not both, and no other statements. Thus a state-description completely describes a possible state of the universe in question. For any statement j of the system the class of those state-descriptions in which j holds, i.e. each of which L-implies j, is called the *range* of j. The range of j is null if, and only if, j is L-false; in any other case j is L-equivalent to the disjunction of the state-descriptions in its range.

4 On the Semantic Characteristics of Information

Information Storage & Retrieval
Vol. 2, No. 4, August, 1965

1. The Inadequacy of the Classical Interpretation of the Term "Information"

The word "information" is usually applied in two senses. In the first place there is the intuitive conception of "information" in the widest sense. Secondly, there is the strict mathematical definition of the quantity of information. The latter concept is often identified with the word "information". The strict concept of information was defined by Shannon [1], and previously, in a more general form, by Hartley and others; it has a precise mathematical meaning.

Of course, where the amount of information is expressed by quantities of the entropy type, this strict concept is not sufficient for the description of all situations and does not cover all the properties of information with which one has to deal.

What is, in general, understood by the "information" and "information characteristics" of some process? Usually it is those properties of the physical world which in some sense are contrasted with energy or mass characteristics. If a communication in the form of a Russian text is given, it is not important whether this text is written on paper, transmitted by telegraph, broadcast on radio or recorded on stone tablets. In each of these cases the means of recording the energy used in the transfer of information and the mass of the material carriers are different. Nevertheless, the information contained in the message is the same in all cases.

There is no need to say more, since information is just as much an objective property of matter, as are mass and energy. The only difference is that the concepts of mass and energy are well established in science, whereas the concept of information has become an object of science only in the last 15–20 years, in connection with the development of cybernetics, computational technology and communication systems.

The definition of quantity of information according to Shannon (see [1]) was a result of the study of problems of communication theory and applies, first of all, to the theory of the transfer of messages.

Often, however, one meets the evaluation of quantity of information in altogether different situations. Let us consider, for example, solving problems by means of computers. In such a case we often describe as information a programme which is fed into a computer, as well as the initial data and the data which are stored in the memory of the computer. It would be very difficult, however, to evaluate the quantity of this information.

When the magnitude of the problem to be solved is to be characterized, the number of programme instructions, the number of punched cards used and the time necessary for the run of the programme are given. No statistical quantities of the entropy type are, however, considered. The characteristics given above (and some more complicated ones) are just the information characteristics of the process of resolution of the problem with the aid of the given computer.

The words in an alphabet, to which Markov's algorithm is applied, are also the information worked upon by the algorithm. Similarly, one may speak about information worked upon by Turing's machine, by a finite automaton, and so on.

There exists a whole series of situations for which it is obvious that in order to describe the information the characteristics of its contents are needed and not statistical properties connected with the transfer frequency of these or other signals.

In several works devoted to information theory, for example in [2], it is stressed that the meaning or semantic characteristics of information should be studied. A number of publications have since been devoted to this aspect of information theory. (See, for example, [3], [4], [5] and [6].)

Why are we often dissatisfied with the classical concept of information?

Let us consider an example. Someone tosses a coin and records the result on a board. This may be communicated as follows: either the actual words "heads" and "tails" are written in succession, depending on which side was turned up, or the person recording may, by convention, mark the symbols "1" for heads and "0" for tails.

From the viewpoint of classical theory, the quantity of information is the same in either case. This is obvious, since by referring to a conversion table in which "1" corresponds to "heads" and "0" to "tails" one may obtain all necessary information from the succession of ones and noughts.

From the viewpoint of statistical characteristics, the amount of information will be the same in both cases.

In other words, in the statistical theory of information what matters is only the potential ability to deduce from a given statement a certain quantity of information, not what information the receiver can deduce from the statement.

The existence of a conversion table is not essential in communication theory; it does not characterize the conducting ability of a channel, but only some properties of the receiver, which are inessential in this case. There exists, however, a great number of problems in which such conversion tables have primary importance and where the ability of the receiver to "understand" the communication is the most important characteristic of the process.

Thus, for example, in machine translation there is a statement in English. It is required to deduce from it all necessary information for the synthesis of the equivalent Russian sentence. In this case there is no simple transcoding, where a word corresponds to a word. The rules of translation of an English sentence into a Russian sentence are extremely complicated.

In order to achieve such a translation, a great store of preliminary information is necessary. The quantity of information needed for this translation is difficult to determine in the classical terms of Shannon's information theory. This example shows clearly that that quantitative characteristic of the ability of the receiver to understand the received information may be very important.

Shannon's determination of the amount of information is, in fact, probability-theoretic.

Let us consider, according to [2], Shannon's determination of quantity of information in the simplest case. Let some event A have an *a priori* probability of occurrence p. As a result of the reception of the statement it appears that the event has now a new probability of occurrence p_1. It is then assumed that the quantity of information contained in the given statement with regard to the given event is equal to the logarithm of the ratio:

$$\mathcal{I} = \log \frac{p_1}{p}$$

In particular, if as a result of the statement it appears that the event A has, in fact, occurred, this information will be equal to:

$$\mathcal{I} = \log \frac{1}{p}$$

In effect, Shannon's information theory is based on the above definition. Its mathematical form makes possible the application of this idea in more complex situations.

Such more complex situations are connected with the determination of the average information per event in the given statement, with the study of a continuous system of events, etc. For the study of such complex situations an orderly and very elegant mathematical theory of information, based on Shannon's work, has been constructed. One thing is important, that in such a system before even considering the information contained in a statement about a given event, it is necessary to consider the *a priori* probability of the event concerned. It is not enough to be able to determine such a probability. Often this probability is unknown and we have no way of determining it. Moreover, we often cannot in principle discuss the probability of such and such an event at all.

When it is not known whether a certain event occurred, the event is not necessarily a chance one in the meaning used in the theory of probability. An event may be completely determined, i.e. such that it is known for certain whether it occurred or not. Alternatively, it may not be determined.

In a number of situations concerning non-determined events we may speak about their probabilities. This means that a certain numerical characteristic with the necessary properties can be assigned to each of them. Nevertheless, in a number of situations such a characteristic cannot, on principle, be introduced. How, for instance, can we determine the probability of the appearance of an aeroplane over a given region? From which considerations could it be deduced? In some cases, where there are many flights having some regularity, these appearances may be described as a sequence of chance events.

In many works, however, the probabilistic scheme is applied to situations in which it would be meaningless to speak about the *a priori* probability of the events.

Let us imagine a (classical) process of obtaining information in the form of the following scheme. We assume that the events $A_1, A_2, \ldots, A_n$ are possible *a priori* with probabilities: $p_1, p_2, \ldots, p_n$.

In this way, the receiver has a kind of guide in the form of a table:

$$A_1 A_2 \ldots A_n$$
$$p_1, p_2 \ldots p_n$$

This guide characterizes, so to say, the "external world" of the receiver: it is *a priori* knowledge. On receiving statements the description of the external world will change, and new tables will be formed:

$$A_1 A_2 \ldots A_n$$
$$p'_1 p'_2 \ldots p'_n$$

where the lower row shows the probabilities obtained as a result of the receipt of the statement. This change of the receiver is characterized by the entropy type quantities in Shannon's theory. It is important for us that the quantity of information received is measured by the degree of change of the guide to the external world. On the other hand, the fact that the guide itself appears as a description of probability distribution, and the actual values of the degree of its changes, are less important.

Such a guide can also be infinite or even include a continuous series of events. For example, it can be a system of events characterized by $\xi < a$, where ξ is a continuous random quantity. In practice it is never necessary to consider an infinite guide because any quantity can be considered with accuracy to some threshold value.

The essential point is thus that information received is characterized by a change in the guide which expresses the knowledge of the receiver about the external world. From these considerations one can approach the meaning characteristics of information, which no longer have to correspond to any presupposed statistical model.

One more situation requires attention. We used to think (as follows from Shannon's first theorem) that, in the optimum method of coding, a statement containing more information requires more binary symbols (bits).

However, a statement on the discovery of a new chemical element, which can be coded in a small number of binary symbols and for which it would be meaningless to speak about an *a priori* probability, undoubtedly contains much information. At the same time, information about measurements of physico-chemical properties of some substance may be considerably less important, although it may need for its coding a much more extensive table.

This situation can easily be explained by the fact that information about the discovery of a new element will enter into a much bigger number of articles, books, etc. (changing our knowledge about the world considerably more) than a detailed table of physico-chemical properties of the substance concerned.

2. The Thesaurus and Its Transformations

We shall now proceed to some definitions. Let us assume that we have a guide, in which is recorded our knowledge (or, generally, the knowledge of some receiver of information) about the external world. We shall denote this guide by the letter θ and we shall call it a thesaurus. This term has been borrowed from lexicological practice. A thesaurus is a unilingual dictionary, showing all the semantic connections between the words. Thesauri contain some thematic descriptions, which are the semantic characteristics of the words. The first thesaurus, Roget's, was published as early as 1852.

Let us assume that a thesaurus is given, which can be in any one of a set of states. We shall denote a received statement by T and assume that each statement changes the state of the thesaurus, i.e. is equivalent to a transformation of it. Whether we shall call the result a new state of the thesaurus or a new thesaurus is not important.

In particular, when we refer to information in the classical meaning of the word, a thesaurus is equivalent to a list of events and their probabilities. Received statements, changing the probabilities of the events, act as transformations of this list.

In particular, some statements require the assignment of zero probability to some events. This means that the events in question should be dropped from the list. Of course, we could not enlarge the list, only reduce it. Generally speaking, however, a list of events can also be enlarged by the action of a statement. A new event, of which we were not previously aware, may become known.

We can give a definition of the amount of information, by analogy with the classical case, as follows: The amount of information $\mathcal{I}(\theta, T)$ will be defined as the degree of change of the thesaurus θ under the action of the given statement T. This means, in principle, that to each admissible text T (a statement expressed in a certain code) there corresponds a certain operator A_T which acts on the thesaurus θ.

We shall not discuss any definite quantitative characteristic. Various measures of change can be considered. If we take any characteristic in particular, we might also take its square, multiply it by some coefficient, etc.

The important point is that the amount of information contained in the statement T with respect to the thesaurus θ is characterized by the degree of change of the thesaurus under the action of the statement.

It should be mentioned that when, in the classical theory, it is asserted that the amount of information is equal to the logarithm of the probability ratio, a certain mathematical assumption is being made. It is connected with certain considerations of mathematical aesthetics, leading to an elegant mathematical theory. This is important since in this way we obtain a mathematical device which is a valuable tool.

Evidently, there are some statements that cannot be accepted by the given thesaurus at all. The information in such statements for the given thesaurus is zero.

Of course, if a thesaurus changes into itself under the action of a statement (its state remains unchanged), then $\mathcal{I}(\theta, T) = O$. This corresponds to the situation where a nonunderstood text does not contain any information. Obviously, the problem of the statistical properties of information recedes here into background. We could introduce statistical characteristics and obtain in a particular case a definition in which the change of thesaurus would be connected with a change in probability. We cannot, however, discuss any construct probability in general.

It would also be possible to introduce weightings characterizing the importance of a change in various parts of the thesaurus.

It may be noted that A. N. Kolmogorov, in his lecture to the Moscow Mathematical Society in December 1963, discussed the construction of a theory of probability from a new point of view, namely that the notion of probability is secondary to that of information. He proposed first to define information in some way, and then, proceeding from it, to construct a theory of probability.

Actually, to human intuition the concept of "probability" is more complex than that of "information". Consequently it is important to have a definition of information that is not based on an existing scheme of probability theory. From the viewpoint of the statistics of the appearance of a given symbol in a communication channel, the concept of probability is essential. But it is possible that even in this case it would be methodologically simpler to proceed from the notion of information.

We shall now introduce a second definition, using the concept of a thesaurus. We shall remember that to a statement (text) T there corresponds an operator A_T acting on the thesaurus θ.

Let there be two texts T and T_1. What does it mean for these two texts to carry the same information? Or, in other words, what does it mean for these two texts to be synonymous? The definition is, of course, that two texts T and T_1 are synonymous if they correspond to the same transformation operator of the thesaurus: $A_T = A_{T_1}$. We emphasize that we are concerned with the synonymity of the texts T and T_1, i.e. that those texts carry identical information with respect to the given thesaurus θ. Two texts T and T_1 can have identical amounts of information $\mathcal{I}(T_1, \theta) = \mathcal{I}(T_2, \theta)$, but the information may be different. In that case the texts are, of course, not synonymous.

We have, in fact, defined what it means to say that two statements T and T_1 have the same meaning with regard to the given receiver of information, viz., the thesaurus. It is clear that the equivalence of the two texts T and T_1 is considered with respect to the given thesaurus.

Evidently, if there are different thesauri, two texts synonymous with respect to one thesaurus may be found not synonymous with respect to the second. As an example let us consider two texts T and T_1. Let the first, T, be the full text of "Eugene Onegin", and the second T_1, a prose caricature of it: there lived two gentlemen, Lenski and Onegin, they courted Olga and Tatiana, they quarrelled, one of them killed the other, and so on. This second text has for most of us nothing in common with the title "Eugene Onegin". Nevertheless, it is easy to imagine someone for whom these texts T and T_1 carry the same information. Moreover, if we want to model in a machine the understanding of a text, it would be difficult to make a machine that would be able to discern the peculiarities of the poetical text, as contrasted with a good prose transcription. It is necessary to point out that the machine, which has to receive meaningful information, should be able not only to store the received information but also to make logical conclusions. Thus we can say that a machine understands the text of "Eugene Onegin" if, for instance, it can answer the question: "On what date did the duel between Onegin and Lenski take place?" True, there is no direct indication of it in the text but it is known that the duel took place immediately after the birthday of Tatiana, and this is 25th of January; hence the required answer may be deduced.

If we consider the rules of construction of the operator A_T as something outside the thesaurus θ, then the quantity $\mathcal{I}(T, \theta)$ depends on these rules. Otherwise it can be said that $\mathcal{I}(T, \theta)$ is determined by the text T and by the thesaurus in the wide meaning of the word.

Let us consider separately a thesaurus in the narrow sense, not including in it the rules of construction of the operator A_T. The important property of this concept is that the preliminary increase of the knowledge stored in the thesaurus θ (enlargement of thesaurus) can not only decrease, but can also increase, the quantity $\mathscr{I}(T, \theta)$. Implicitly this means that someone who has learned a branch of science will, generally speaking, derive more from a special text in this branch than he would have before he had learned it. We shall note that this peculiar property of the model of semantic information basically distinguishes it from the classical theory of information. In the latter an increase in the *a priori* information always decreases the amount of information extracted from the given statement. The point is that in communication theory there is no question of a degree of "understanding" of the statement by the receiver. It is taken for granted that the receiver is always correctly "tuned". In the semantic theory of information the essential role is played by the very possibility of correct "tuning" of the receiver.

Let us take as an example of a statement the text of a textbook of probability theory and give it to two people, receivers of information: a boy from the third form, who has not learned very much so far, and someone with considerable *a priori* knowledge, a student of mathematics, who is already familiar with mathematical analysis and the foundations of mathematics, but has not yet studied probability theory. Which will derive more information from the textbook? The answer is clear: it will be the student who will obtain more information from the given text, i.e. the one who knew more beforehand and was better prepared for the receipt of the information. Of course, the opposite is also possible, when the amount of received information falls with the increase of *a priori* knowledge. The information contained in the statement: "The Volga flows into the Caspian Sea" means nothing to us, as we do not learn anything new from it. But in more complex cases we are capable of understanding more with increase of our knowledge.

If the thesaurus becomes more complicated, it can change more under the action of a new text. A complicated thesaurus changes more intensely than a simple one.

The situation described can be summed up as follows. A primitive thesaurus can extract hardly anything from the given text T (it cannot comprehend it). A developed thesaurus comprehends text T well and obtains maximum information. A saturated thesaurus is unable to acquire new information, it knows everything already.

A similar reasoning, applied to the art of the theatre, was made by N. Akimov ([7], p. 20): ". . . the attention of the spectator to what happens on the stage is conditioned by two opposing factors: that which is common to the spectator and to the action on the stage, and that which differs between him and his experience on one side, and the staged impressions on the other. . . . If there is on Mars a life essentially different from ours, then we would probably have much difficulty in sitting through a Martian spectacle. If the spectator does not see on the stage anything new to himself, anything that would enrich his experience, then no matter how exactly it resembles his everyday life, he is wasting his time in the theatre. In the equilibrium of these two factors lies the secret of the "profitability of production".

3. The Formal Model

We shall now proceed with the formal description of the model. We begin with the construction of a thesaurus. We shall consider three sets: $\sqcap\{a, b, \ldots\}$, $M\{x, y, \ldots\}$, and $C\{\alpha, \beta \ldots\}$. The elements of the set $\sqcap$ we shall call predicates, those of M objects, and those of C events.

In the set $\sqcap$ there are given two relationships: consequence (denoted by $\supset$) and applicability (denoted by $\vdash$).

These relationships have the following properties:

1. $a \supset a$
2. If $a \supset b$ and $b \supset c$, then $a \supset c$
3. If $a \supset b$ then $b \vdash a$
4. If $a \vdash b$ and $b \vdash c$, then $a \vdash c$

From 3 and 4 is deduced:

5. If $a \supset b$ and $c \vdash b$, then $c \vdash a$.

Implicitly the relationship of applicability is understood in this way: $a \vdash b$ means that property a is applicable to all objects to which is applicable property b.

Note: In what follows many-placed predicates may be used. The relationship of applicability for them will be written in the form: $a_i \vdash b_j$. This notation means that the predicate a is applicable in the ith place to all objects (events) to which the predicate b is applicable in the jth place.

There may be need for a more general type of relationship: $a_{i1} \ldots i_l \vdash (b_{j1}, \ldots, b_{jl})$. It reads: predicate a is applicable in places $i_1, \ldots, i_l$ to groups of l objects (events), to which are applicable the predicates shown at the right-hand side of the expression, in respective places.

The relationship of applicability is used in the algorithm of the analysis of the text of the rule of construction of operator A_T, but it is not essential for the thesaurus in the narrow sense.

It is permissible to form from some pairs of elements of the sets $\sqcap$ and M pairs of the type ax (this reads: "object x possesses property a") and the type $7ax$ (this reads: "object x does not possess property a"). Such pairs are called atomic propositions. Moreover, if the first proposition is true, then the second is false and vice versa. If ax is admissible and $b \vdash a$, then bx is also admissible.

Similarly, for l-placed predicates $a\varepsilon\sqcap$ it is possible to form atomic propositions of the form $ax_1 \ldots x_l$ and $7ax_1 \ldots x_l$.

We shall require that the rules permitting the applica-

tion of an l-placed predicate a to the sequence of objects $(x_1, x_2, \ldots, x_l)$ may be represented in the following form. Let us introduce the ternary function $R(a, x, \kappa)$, $(a \varepsilon \sqcap, x \varepsilon M, (\kappa$ — an integer). The atomic proposition $ax_1, x_2, \ldots x_l$ should be admissible if and only if $(\forall_\kappa) R(a, x_\kappa, \kappa)$ is true.†
$1 \leqq \kappa \leqq l$

If A and B are propositions, then $A \vee B$, $A \wedge B$ and $7A$ are also propositions by definition.

Let us introduce now the following conditions:

1. If the atomic proposition $ax_1 \ldots x_l$ is admissible and $b_i \vdash a_{\kappa i}$ for $\kappa_i \varepsilon E \leqq [1, l]$, and i passes through all places of the predicate b, then the atomic proposition $bx_{\kappa 1}, x_{\kappa 2} \ldots$ is admissible.

2. The atomic propositions $ax_1 \ldots x_l$ and $7ax_1 \ldots x_l$ are admissible or not admissible together.

3. If $a \supset b$ and $ax_1 \ldots x_l$ is true, then $bx_1 \ldots x_l$ is true, and if $bx_1 \ldots x_l$ is false, $ax_1 \ldots x_l$ is false.

Before we define the set of events C, we shall introduce a list of quantors, with the aid of which these events will be determined.

The quantor of generation (rise, introduction) will be denoted by d. The expression $(dx)(ax)$ is read thus: "there arises x, which has the property a".

The quantor of description L in the expression $a(Lx)bx$ is read thus: "that x which has the property b, has the property a."

The quantor of set description ε permits us to introduce the expression $a(\varepsilon x)bx$, which is read thus: "those x, which have the property b, have the property a".

The quantor of general description a is used in expressions of the form $a(\mathrm{a}x)bx$: "all those x, which have the property b, have the property a".

The difference between the last two quantors consists in that the quantor ε acts only on objects belonging to the set M, but quantor a acts on all objects which may later belong to M.

In other words the proposition $a(\mathrm{a}x)bx$ is equivalent to the relationship $b \supset a$.

Furthermore, we shall denote by a symbol of the form $A(x_1, x_2, \ldots, x_l)$ a proposition formed out of atomic propositions containing objects $x_1, \ldots, x_l$.

Using the quantors introduced above we can form various quantor expressions with l-placed predicates. These expressions for $l = 2$ are shown in the following table. For $l > 2$ similar expressions can be easily formed by analogy.

We can now define an event. The definition of an event is recursive. 1. Any expression in Table I which includes quantors d, L and ε is an event. 2. A logical combination of events formed with the aid of symbols $\vee$, $\wedge$ and 7, is an event. 3. Any expression of the form shown in Table I with quantors d, L and ε where some (or all) objects are replaced by events, is an event.

† An analogous question arises concerning the rules of determination of applicability of expressions of the type aa, where a is an event.

TABLE I

Quantor	Types of propositions
d	$(dx_1)(dx_1)A(x_1, x_2)$
L	$B[(Lx_1)A_1(x_1),(Lx_2)A_2(x_2)]$
	$B[(Lx_1)(Lx_2)A(x_1, x_2)]$
ε	$B[(\varepsilon x_1)A_1(x_1),(\varepsilon x_2)A_2(x_2)]$
	$B[(\varepsilon x_1)(\varepsilon x_2)A(x_1, x_2)]$
a	$B[(\mathrm{a}x_1)A_1(x_1),(\mathrm{a}x_2)A_2(x_2)]$
	$B[(\mathrm{a}x_1)(\mathrm{a}x_2)A(x_1, x_2)]$
L, ε	$B[(Lx_1)A_1(x_1),(\varepsilon x_2)A_2(x_2)]$
	$B[(Lx_1)(\varepsilon x_2)A(x_1, x_2)]$

In this way the set of events C has been defined.

We shall impose on the sets M, $\sqcap$ and C an additional condition. We shall require, namely, that with each object $x \varepsilon M$ be connected a predicate $x^* \varepsilon \sqcap$, of the form "coincides with object x". Clearly x^*y is true when $y = x$, and it is false when $y \neq x$. The set of such one-place predicates we shall denote by $\sqcap_M$. Thus, the set $\sqcap$ changes with a change in the set of objects.

Analogically, we shall require that to each event α there corresponds a predicate $\alpha^* \varepsilon_1 \sqcap_\sigma C \sqcap$, reading: "participates in the event α". Generally speaking, the definition of this predicate consists in specifying how much any particular event, in virtue of the recursiveness of its definition, can be composed in different ways from simpler events and objects.

In particular, it would be possible to consider separately the predicate α^{**}: "coincides with the event α".

We are now in a position to give the definition of a thesaurus (in the narrow sense).

The thesaurus θ is the aggregate of the sets $\sqcap$, M and C, with the relationships $\supset$ and given in $\sqcap$.

We shall now consider elementary operators acting on the thesaurus. Expressions constructed in the forms shown in Table I will be called canonical.

1. To the canonical expression α containing quantors L and ε there corresponds an elementary operator on the thesaurus θ, transforming it as follows: event α is added to set C (if it was not already there), predicate α^* is added to set $\sqcap$, and the relationship of applicability is established between the external predicate participating in the statement of α, and the internal predicates (unless this relationship was established before).

2. To the canonical expression α containing quantor d there corresponds an elementary operator on thesaurus θ of the following form: event α is added to the set C; objects x_i, remaining in the field of action of quantor d, are added to set M; predicates x_i^* are added to the set $\sqcap$.

3. To the canonical expression α containing the quantor a there corresponds an elementary operator establishing new relationships of the type $\supset$ in the set $\sqcap$. (The expression $a(\mathrm{a}x)bx$ requires the establishment of the relationship $b \supset a$, if it was not there already).

A thesaurus in the wider sense is obtained from a thesaurus in the narrow sense by the addition of rules allowing texts T, which compose a class K_θ, to correspond with a set of elementary operators and to determine the order of their application. The production of these operators in due order determines the operator A_T of the transformation of thesaurus θ under the action of text T. It is evident from the above that in order to construct operator A_T it is sufficient to be able to represent text T in form of some structure of canonical expressions.

If it is not possible to distinguish any canonical expressions in text T, then this text cannot transform the thesaurus θ. In such a case it may be said that the text is "incomprehensible" to the thesaurus. If the text can be analysed into canonical expressions, but the operator A_T does not transform the thesaurus θ, we may say that the text T does not contain any new information for the given thesaurus.

Algorithm оı, which builds the operator A_T according to the text T, will be called the algorithm of text analysis with the aid of the thesaurus.

Thus, a thesaurus in the wider sense is a combination of a thesaurus in the narrow sense and a text analysis algorithm оı.

We shall now give examples of analysing Russian text into canonical expressions.

Example I. Let the following text be given.
"Today a new house was built." Let us assume that the following predicates had been given beforehand: a_1 — house (to be a house), a_2 — new, a_3 — to be built, a_4 — today.

The text written in canonical expressions is:

1. $(dx)(a_1x)$
2. $a_2(Lx)a_1x$
3. $a_3(Lx)a_2x \equiv \alpha_1$
4. $a_4\alpha_1$

We shall note that in order to produce this version of the text we needed only the predicates to be given beforehand. The sets M and C could have been empty initially. But as a result of the text analysis some elements appeared in them. The fact that the sets M and C are being filled in the process of text analysis is very important.

Example II. Let us consider the text:
"A numerical sequence is called regular, if it is monotonic and bounded."

The following predicates are used; a_1 — to follow (to be a sequence), a_2 — numerical (to consist of numbers), a_3 — to be called (two-placed predicate), a_4 — monotonic, a_5 — bounded, a_6 — regular.

The record of meaning is:

1. $(dx)a_1x$
2. $a_2(Lx)a_1x$
3. $a_4(Lx)a_1x \equiv \alpha_1$
4. $a_5(Lx)a_1x \equiv \alpha_2$
5. $\alpha_1 \wedge \alpha_2 \equiv \alpha_4$
6. $a_3(\exists x)\alpha_4^*x(\exists y)a_6y$

Here it is important that the predicate a_6 could not have belonged to the set ⊓ beforehand. The above record says that it should be introduced into that set. But even if it was already there, the relationships $a_6 \supset a_4$, $a_6 \supset a_5$, and $a_6 \vdash (a_1a_2)$, which are to be introduced into ⊓, appear to be new. (There is in such a case another predicate in ⊓, other than a_6, which corresponds to the word "regular" not referring to numerical sequence.) We shall note, in addition, that the object x in this case can be disregarded "after use" (that is, removed from the set M). Generally speaking, the problem of a quantor "converse" to d is not a simple one. Thus physical annihilation of the object x does not mean that it vanishes from M, since it may be mentioned again later. In what cases an object should be "forgotten", that is disregarded, we shall not decide here.

We would make one more remark. Text T may be analysable into canonical expressions, but the analysis algorithm may establish an order of the expressions which would not allow for the determination of the composition of the corresponding elementary operators.

In order that such a composition may be determined, several conditions must be fulfilled. All these conditions can be reduced in essence to the following. If either the operator $a(Lx)bx$ or $a(\varepsilon x)bx$ is used, then is should be supplemented by the operator $(dx)bx$. The only exception is the case where $b \, \varepsilon \sqcap_M$.

If a certain event a enters into the field of action of a quantor which forms part of a canonical expression singled out of the text T, then this event should be determined by one of the preceding operators or be included in the set C before the text analysis starts.

Since the algorithm of analysis оı sets up the order of the sequence of elementary operators singled out of the text, a modification of the description quantor L^* can be made, in the following way. The expression $a(L^*x)bx$ means: "that x, which was the last of those having property b, has property a".

In actual fact, in comprehending a text we use indeed the operator of description. For instance, let the word "house" be used somewhere in the text, e.g. "someone stopped in front of a nine-storey house". Then this phrase will, unless otherwise stated, be referring to a new object, which is a house.

The transformation operators of a thesaurus can also be interpreted in another way. (We shall assume further on that in M there is always a so-called "empty-object", denoted by #).

Let us consider multivalued functions f, given in ⊓ and assuming some values in the set E, which is a direct product $M \cup CxK$.

Here K is a set of two elements $K = \{*, 7\}$. The equation $f(a) = (x,*)$ means that ax is fulfilled; the equation $f(a) = (x, \backslash)$ means that there is a negation $7ax$. The equation $f(a) = (\#,*)$, or, correspondingly, $(\#,7)$, means that there is no object or no event, respectively, having the property a (property a is fulfilled only by the empty object $\#$).

In order to include here also the case of many-placed predicates it would be necessary to define the set E as follows

$$E = (M \cup C) \cup (M \cup C)^2 \cup \ldots \cup (M \cup C)^n \ldots xK,$$

where $(M \cup C)^n$ is a set of n-placed strings of objects and events.

It is easy to see that if the function f is given together with its field of determination, the thesaurus in the narrow sense can be determined accurately as regards the relationships $\supset$ and $\vdash$.

The operator A_T may be regarded as an operator transforming function f into function f'. True, this operator changes simultaneously the set of meanings and the field of determination of the function. Such an interpretation of thesaurus is considered in [3].

We do not consider here the problem of the actual construction of the algorithm of text analysis оI. It would be possible to show several methods of construction of this algorithm for texts with various limitations. The problem of construction of algorithm оI is closely connected with the problem of analysis in mechanical translation. The construction of an algorithm with sufficiently wide possibilities requires much experimental work in machine processing of texts.

4. Some Peculiarities of the Model

In the described model the analysis of information is reduced to the extraction of elementary events from the text. Analogical problems occur in any process of "comprehending" the meaning of a statement which is expressed in some code. Thus the problem of "comprehension" of a machine programme, encoded in the machine language ALGOL, also consists in interpreting the text elements in this language as events in the "machine thesaurus".

In the definition of the quantity of information which was given above, the pragmatic side is very important. This is the problem of how the information contained in the given text can be used. It has a fundamental significance. In actual fact, the evaluation of the quantity of information contained in the given statement is closely connected with the question of how it will be utilized by the receiver of the information. That is, the pragmatic aspect of information, namely the way of its interpretation by the receiver, should be reflected in the evaluation.

On the other hand, it would seem that the measure of information should characterize what was contained in this information, that is, the semantic characteristics of that information. Here, in reality, there is no contradiction, since the objective characteristic of the text should express all aspects of the system of signs. In particular, the syntax of the system influences considerably the

method of construction, according to the text, of the operator which will transform the thesaurus.

It is clear that we always obtain information from some transmitter which is in possession of it. This transmitter is, in fact, an analogical thesaurus, containing a store of information about the external world. From this viewpoint the transmission and the reception constitute an exchange of information between the two thesauri. The consideration of the transmitted text is pragmatism from the viewpoint of the receiver, and semantics from the viewpoint of the transmitter.

An essential problem arises here. It is evident that two thesauri must have the same order of complexity if they are to understand each other. If the transmitter is much more "intelligent" than the receiver, the latter will simply not understand the former. We shall not consider the fashionable problem of whether a machine can be more "intelligent" than man. So far there are no such machines; so far man is much more developed than any machine (although it is conceivable that a machine that will surpass man will be constructed in the future). As the matter stands now, man commands a much richer language and can put in his statements much more than machines can comprehend. Texts in human languages are "saturated", and for their comprehension there would be required thesauri incomparably more richly endowed than those possessed by contemporary machines. Man can generate in his language a much richer variety of shades of meaning than a machine can receive. It is not without reason that within recent years dozens of so-called "general" programming languages have been elaborated. Their inventors attempt to make them, on the one hand, sufficiently simple and formal for the machine to follow unambiguously the programmes encoded in them, and, on the other hand, to make them as near as possible to the natural language of man.

When man wants to converse with the machine in his own language, great difficulties arise. They are connected with the fact that the description of the world, i.e. the thesaurus of the machine, is simpler than and, what is more important, differently organized from that of man.

The opposite situation, when man does not understand the machine, is met by any programmer when he traces, with enormous effort, errors in a programme (written in the machine language) checked so many times before, or finds that it was simply an accidental slip of the machine.

That is why the problem of mutual correspondence of thesauri is not simple and attracts much interest. This problem is also specially important in the planning of further developments in computer technology, in order to make a machine to understand man.

Let us consider one more question. The determination of the synonymity of two texts T_I and T_2 with respect to the thesaurus θ is a natural development of the idea of Carnap's intensional equivalency and equal intensional structure [8]. According to Carnap, two texts have the same meaning (the same "intension") if they would retain the same meaning in any conceivable state of the world. This definition is applied to texts in a certain formal semantic system [8]. This definition in fact means that the two texts are synonymous with respect to any possible thesaurus. But it is of interest to consider cruder or local thesauri as well.

The problem of modelling the process of comprehension would be hopeless if there were no possibility of studying cruder models of this process. Moreover, the essence of the comprehending process is connected with various methods of extracting a small number of semantic characteristics, essential for the given situation, i.e. extracting the "main part" of the thesaurus, which is indispensable for the transformation of the given text (see [9]). Let us note that in complex processes of teaching, the process of the comprehension of the situation, consisting precisely in elucidating the essential characteristics of that situation, plays the fundamental role (see [10]). On the other hand, attempts to describe fully the "semantic portrait" of the words of the given language, independently of a concrete thesaurus, lead, it seems, to immensely complicated and badly formulated processes.

References

1. K. Shannon: Statistical theory of transmission of signals. In the symposium: *Theory of Transmission of Electric Signals in the Presence of Noise* [in Russian], pp. 7–85. Moscow, Foreign Literature Publishing House (1953).

2. S. Goldman: *Information Theory*. London (1953).

3. Y. Bar-Hillel and R. Carnap: Semantic information. *Brit. J. Philos. Sci.*, 1954, **9**, [*89*], 12–27.

4. C. J. Maloney: Semantic information. *Amer. Doc.*, 1962, **13**, 276–286.

5. C. F. Hockett: An approach to the quantification of semantic noise. *Philos. Sci.*, 1952, **19**, 257–260.

6. Yu. A. Shreĭder: On the quantitative characteristics of semantic information. *Nauch.-Tekh. Inform.*, 1963, [*10*], 33–38.

7. N. Akimov: *On the Theatre*. Moscow-Leningrad (1962).

8. R. Carnap: *Meaning and Necessity* [in Russian]. Moscow-Leningrad (1959).

9. Yu. A. Shreĭder: Machine translation on the basis of semantic coding of texts. *Nauch.-Tekh. Inform.*, 1963, [*1*], 34–38.

10. Yu. A. Shreĭder: *Models of Teaching and Control Systems*. A supplement to the translation of the book "Stochastic Models of Teaching" by R. Bush and F. Mosteller. Moscow, Fizmatgiz, 1962, pp. 465–479.

5 Morphology of "Information Flow"

ROBERT A. FAIRTHORNE
*Journal of the Association
for Computing Machinery
Vol. 14, No. 4, October, 1967*

1. Introduction

The word "information" and such phrases as "information flow" appear frequently in papers on topics ranging from data processing equipment to higher education, from psychology to the storage and retrieval of documents. Often their use is merely metaphorical, or they are convenient labels for an amorphous mass of ill-defined activities and phenomena. Sometimes context determines the meaning, e.g., whether transfer rates of marked objects (records), average power consumption required for signaling, sets of linguistic expressions, changes in the state of knowledge of recipients, structural change produced by stimuli on automata, number of natural language lexical units uttered or written per second, accession rate of new documents, or any other rates associated with any processes involved in message transfer.

Often the context does not determine the local meaning of the word "information," because it refers to something different each time it is used, even within the same passage.

Such ambiguity could be, and should be, avoided by stating in concrete terms what actually is being talked about: documents, messages, power, and so on. However,

this involves stylistic and ethical matters that do not concern this paper.

Its concern is to distinguish between the distinct activities shrouded by the blanket word "information," to investigate the conditions under which the phrase "information flow" has any useful meaning, and to indicate discrimination between distinct types of flow.

This is by no means a philosophical exercise. Engineering development of symbol manipulating systems demands that metaphorical expressions be replaced by names and verbs denoting observable, and controllable, entities. For instance, aeronautics would come to a halt if the flight of aircraft were explained in these terms:

". . . levitation is screened and perhaps condensed in the wings. The premise underlying nearly all aircraft is that levitation is selectively transmitted through the wings and engines. At various parts . . . some levitation is allowed to be continued through the engines, while some levitation is discarded."

This is a quotation from a published report on test and evaluation of document retrieval systems, but with "levitation" substituted for "information," "aircraft" for "document retrieval systems," and "wings and engines" for "system."

Again, diagrams purportedly displaying the workings of information retrieval systems often consist of arrows joining labeled boxes. This implies, and sometimes is actually labeled as, flow or something or other between boxes, and of the same something or other throughout the system. However, the boxes often have nothing in common. One labeled "ideas" (or even "facts") may be joined directly to one labeled "printed documents."

Inasmuch as the word "flow" has meaning here, it is purely metaphorical. Worse, it puts the mind in blinkers. That a system responds to a stimulus does not entail the existence of some conserved quantity that flows through it. When a finger pulls the trigger, nothing flows from finger to bullet. It is just a causal sequence. As MacKay [1] remarks, "'Amount of information' measures not a 'stuff' but a relation." Nevertheless, what I have called elsewhere [2] the Phlogiston Theory of Information is widely held, explicitly or implicitly. Reasons for this, pointed out by Gilbert [3], include superficial study and purely rhetorical extrapolation of Shannon's strictly delimited Information Theory beyond its valid scope.

2. Limitation of Scope

Any discipline must define its scope. That is, it must define what matters it will study explicitly. These matters must then be studied and talked about in their own terms, not in terms of their possible applications. The principles of the applications lie outside the scope of the discipline, and therefore of its own principles and its terminology. Terminology based on accidental features of applications, e.g., "fact retrieval," is a sure sign of noncoherent activities with neither clearly defined scope nor common principles.

To begin with the scope must include all those, but only those, phenomena that are essential to the nature of the study. Newton, developing mechanics, was ultimately concerned with motions of the moon, cannonballs, apples, and pendulum clocks. However, he first considered only the inertial properties of such objects. He did not bring in astronomical, military, horticultural, and horological aspects. It was for the astronomers, gunners, fruit pickers, and clockmakers to do that. In the same way, Shannon considered explicitly the most reduced activity that still retained the essentials of communication: the activity of devising patterns of signals appropriate to a particular physical mode of communication in order to indicate choices made from a particular set of messages. Clearly this involves informing, in the sense of telling or signaling, in its most simple form. The recipient is told which message has been chosen. He is not told what the message is or what it refers to, if anything. Nor is there any guarantee even if he is told, and even if he could interpret the code, that the recipient would be informed, in the sense of change of state of his knowledge. This depends on his personal history and psychology. However, he will not be informed at all unless he is told. Thus

the Shannon model is necessary, though not sufficient. In fact, it models certain aspects of Signaling.

As such it is a remarkable example of the power and value of two of the less advertised essentials of scientific progress: intellectual parsimony and intellectual humility.

Clearly the scope of Signaling is not sufficient for Information or Message Transfer systems. It is necessary, for we must assume that records of messages can be and have been typed, printed, signaled, reproduced, coded, and so forth by various methods and in various physical modes. But we are not concerned with performing such functions ourselves. They are performed by "black boxes" we are outside of.

We must now find the smallest black box that we are inside of.

To do this we first note some matters, essential to our wider interests, that Shannon's model omits. These are, who signals to whom about what. They enter into the Shannon model only implicity as statistical and physical characteristics of the channel, and the social statistics of choice and use of messages.

They enter explicitly into any activities that take signals or coded messages as a base. So, besides Channel, Code, and Message, which together form the floor of our new black box, we must take into account one or more of what in general terms we will call, following Seboek [4, 5], Source, Destination, and Designation. In 1934 Buhler [6] denoted them by *Kundgabe, Appell,* and *Darstellung.* In German these have wide ranges of particular meanings, but Seboek's equivalents reproduce their general senses. In special cases one can use specific terms such as, for instance, Author, Reader, and Topic.

As has been done here Seboek [4, 5] considers these three variables together with the Shannon Signaling triad. Thereafter his development diverges from that of this paper, being directed to other ends.

When considered by itself the triad, Source, Destination, Designation, constitutes Discourse as such. That is, it suffices for study of those aspects of communication that are independent of particular modes of representation on the one hand, and particular characteristics (including existence) of what is talked about on the other. Thus it forms the ceiling of our black box, because we cannot go beyond it without taking part in the discourse ourselves.

To do this is to change our scope and function completely, just as to change from typist to author is to change one's scope and function completely, even if one continues to type.

We are thus within the black box of Discourse and outside the black box of Signaling (including printing, reproduction, and so on.).

We use the latter; we are used by the former. That is, we are not authors or printers or telegraphists, nor do we use the discourse. We only mention it or deliver it to potential users. We are not concerned with the subjects of the discourse as such, only with how they are talked or written about, who writes and talks about them, how often they are asked for in what terms and by whom, and so on.

At all times we must keep distinct linguistic behavior (e.g., the utterance of words), linguistic events (e.g., spoken words, printed expressions,) mental linguistic events (e.g., recognition of a word as such), and what linguistic entities may refer to (e.g., what a word may be the name of, what an expression is said to be about). The last does not fall within our scope. If it does not manifest itself implicitly in observable characteristics of our six variables, we cannot deal wth it and should not attempt to do so. At best we are the tools of Discourse — not its authors, not its users.

Brief glimpses of life within the black box of Recorded Discourse have been given in earlier papers by the author [7, 8].

3. Variables

The scope of our activities and studies lie inside Discourse but outside Signaling, i.e., outside the scope of Shannon's Information Theory. The variables involved are, in general terms, Source, Destination, Designation, and Message, Channel, Code.

In the present context a Code is a symbol system used to indicate choices made from a set of Messages, and represented by patterns of physical events (signals or inscriptions) consistent with the physical mode and conditions of communication, the Channel, in the given social and physical environment.

Formally the Message set is adequately defined as an agreed finite set of distinct identifiable entites, from which choices are made by Sources. Here we regard it also as drawn from what can be told in a given recorded language.

The Sources are those within the given environment who tell it, in the sense of being agreed and identifiable publishers, distributors, organizations, or accepted authors. The latter need not be actual authors. From the present point of view the works of Shakespeare, or of anonymous authors, are those records that the local retrieval tools attribute to "Shakespeare," or to "anon."

The Destinations are those within the given environment who are to be told, or wish to be told. They must be identifiable, but otherwise may be organizations, functionaries, groups, or individuals.

A set of Designations is assigned to Messages, Sources, or Destinations to characterize them according to what is told, or is to be told. They are aspects of what the particular discourse is "about," in some operational sense. For example, Subject Indexing assigns topics to the messages; author indexes may be classified by subject matter; Selective Dissemination of Information designates executives according to what they should be told about. Clearly the same set of Designations can be assigned differently according to circumstances. A reader (Des-

tination) may well differ with the author (Source) as to the main interest (Designation) of an article (Message).

4. Notification

The next step is to isolate the simplest type of activity that properly belongs to all of documentation, informational activities or sciences, library work, record management, and the like, in their usually accepted senses.

The lowest level task common to all these, but above the level of file organization, reproduction, and other noninterpretative tasks, is what is here called "Notification," that is, the task of alleviating the situation where a reader has to receive messages not by direct communication or by personal inspection of documents (or other linguistic records), but by specifying to some delegate his requirements in terms of document characteristics such as author, bibliographical or textual description, physical format, or topic, subject matter, interest.

In other words, Notification covers techniques for relating Destination to Message in terms of one or more of Source, Code, Channel, or Designation. If the Notification service not only tells ("informs") the Destination (reader, user) of messages, but also supplies, reproduces, or utters them, the activity becomes, in Lea M. Bohnert's words, "Message Delivery."

5. Basic Activities

Notification is the lowest level complete documentary, or informational, activity. Experience, if nothing else, shows it to be a complex one, built up by coordinating subactivities. These subactivities are not self-sufficient, but are separable components of the main activity. That is, they can be studied or carried out apart from the others, provided that the others are allowed for implicitly. The Shannon Signaling model (Figure 1) discussed above illustrates clearly an activity that is not self-sufficient, but can be studied usefully in temporary isolation.

The same is true for Discourse (Figure 2). This cannot take place without a physical Channel, detectable and interpretable Codes, and sets of agreed Messages. Nevertheless it can be studied usefully in terms only of who is talking to whom about what, without explicit reference to the form or mechanics of communication, or the nature of the subject matter, apart from how it is talked about.

We now analyze Notification into its basic, separable activities by using a long-established observation: Linguistic relations are conveniently represented as ternary, involving three elements. Linguistic communication necessarily requires intermediaries, and "between-ness" is essentially a ternary relation.

By choosing three out of the six variables we can generate twenty distinct triads. Figure 3 represents these as the complete graph connecting six vertices. One can readily recognize some of the triads as basic communication activities. Naming them in general enough terms is another matter, because general terms or even specific terms may not yet exist. Until recently few have been required to discriminate between the activities, let alone to name them.

Without prejudice to future terminology, the following list loosely identifies some of the more common triads:

Channel, Source, Destination
Channel, Source, Code
Channel, Destination, Code
Channel, Message, Code
Channel, Message, Designation
Code, Message, Designation
Code, Message, Source
Code, Message, Destination
Source, Message, Destination
Designation, Message, Destination
Designation, Message, Source
Designation, Destination, Source
Routing, Delivery
Transmission
Reception
Signaling
Parking (e.g., arrangement by subject matter)
Marking (e.g., subject classification)
Attribution
Addressing
Linguistic Accord
Prescription (e.g., subject request: Selective Dissemination of Information)
Authorship
Discourse

6. Measure

Formally, any of these triads is equivalent to any other, if the sets that make up their elements and the statistics of their use are properly defined. When this is so, the methods of Shannon's Information Theory will be valid. So will be his entropic-type measure. But formal validity does not entail utility. Moreover, what is referred to and measured will not necessarily be information in any reasonable sense. If it should be, it will inform about different things. For instance, within the Routing triad (Channel, Source, Destination), this measure indicates average unpredictability of traffic. Within Discourse (Designation, Source, Destination) it indicates average complexity of the discourse, in the sense of variability of subject matter.

7. Binary Connections

Each basic activity involves exactly three elements. Therefore any connections or functional dependences between pairs of elements are undefined unless at least one other element is mentioned.

For example, Shannon's Information Theory is concerned with Coding the use of a given Message set to

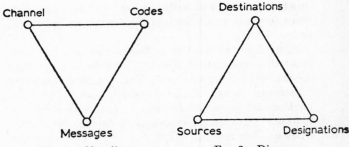

FIG. 1. Signaling.   FIG. 2. Discourse.

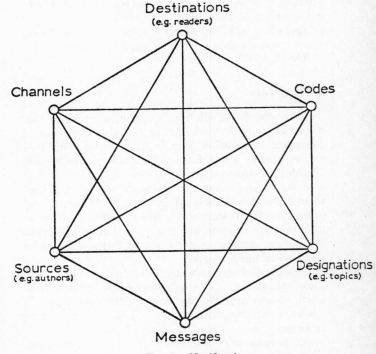

FIG. 3. Notification.

suit the characteristics of a physical Channel. This is an aspect of Signaling.

However, Coding the use of a given Message set to suit its Designations is not an aspect of Signaling, but of Subject Classification, that is, establishment of a code to link a set of messages with a set of topics, subject matter, or user interests.

It is important to note that a priori the Message set and the Designation set are arbitrary and independent, just as the Message set and the Channel are arbitrary and independent. They are what they are said to be, and the business of Coding, both in Signaling and Subject Classification, is to make the best of them. That is, the topic of a message is no more an intrinsic part of the message than the signaling channel is an intrinsic part of the message. There are many ways in which messages can be signaled; there are many ways in which they may interest readers. In any particular case these ways are fixed by the environment, physical and social. The system must accept them, not enforce them.

In Notification there are four types of connection, ranging from physical to interpretative, between Destination (reader) and Message. These arise according as the third member of the triad is Source (author), Designation (topic of interest), Code (script, language), or Channel (physical location, physical access or transport).

This holds good for all the fifteen possible pairs of elements. Each can be related in four distinct modes, according to which of the remaining four elements is involved.

8. Conditions for "Flow"

The third member of a triad defines the mode of connection between the other two. Indeed, it is itself the connection. However, this does not imply any valid notion of flow. Inasmuch as there is flow, its endpoints lie outside the triad.

Consider the familiar Shannon triad. A certain measure of Selective Information is valid within it. This measures what one can call, roughly, average complexity of signal. This again implies an average flow of power from Source to Designation. But neither of these appear explicitly in the triad, though they are implicit in the characteristics of the Channel.

However, explicit study of flow here demands explicit description of the particular Source, Channel, Designation triad. This may correspond to a physical communication or transport network, access to file locations, or the like.

But to establish such a triad, we have to establish others. Clearly both Source and Destination must have at least tacit agreement on the Message set; the Code must be compatible with the Channel and legible to the Destination; the Destination must be able to interpret the Code in terms of Message, and so on. Even without explicit reference to the Designations of the messages, we have here ten interrelated basic activities. Seven are identified in Figure 4. Each can be studied separately, but by itself is but a component of the total task.

Thus communication, even without consideration of what is talked about, involves ten basic activities.

However, these basic activities have, or should have, elements in common, not merely names in common. For example, a common error is to confuse two "reader interest" triads (Message, Designation, Destination) that have the same set of messages but different sets of readers and therefore in general different sets of subject interests (Designations).

The question arises, how many of these basic activities (triads) must be established in order to achieve a complex activity, in particular, to determine flow in some rational sense between two sets of elements? Clearly, if the elements are properly and consistently defined in some

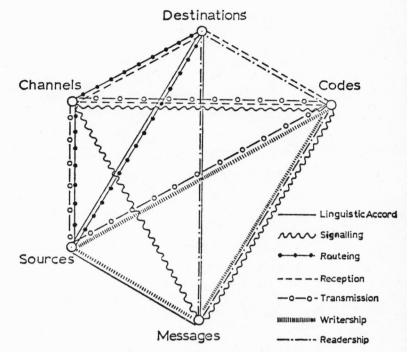

Fig. 4. Some interrelated activities.

basic activities, other basic activities will be carried out implicitly.

The answer is obvious enough. If two triads ABC, BCD, are established with two elements in common, the tetrad $ABCD$ is properly established. That is, all four of its basic activities will be carried out explicitly or implicitly, and A, D are legitimately connected.

They are not uniquely connected, because the pair B, C can be chosen in six ways.

To illustrate this, again consider Subject Classification, which codes messages according to their topics, a particular kind of Designation. Topics involve a particular set of users, but only implicitly. For the same set of Messages and the same set of Topics, we establish also the "subject arrangement" triad. This relates the same messages to sites, positions, or locations (the Channel) according to Topic (Figure 5). These two activities are the basic documentation operations which I have called Marking and Parking [9, 10].

Clearly there is now a dependence between Code and Site. The Code not only is the name of a topic, but also the address of messages on that topic. All four triads are properly defined. To all of them Shannon's entropic measure is applicable though, of course, in different triads it measures information about different things.

This Marking and Parking tetrad is completely defined, and represents a separable composite activity. However, it is not adequate in itself for Notification, because it omits the reader (Destination).

The readers are brought in by any activity associating them with any pair of the marking and parking variables.

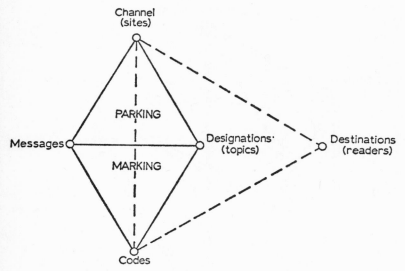

FIG. 5. Notification by topic.

For example, we can give them a Channel, such as access to the shelves or files, in terms of the Codes considered as addresses. This establishes directly a Destination, Channel, Code triad, and indirectly the corresponding Destination, Message, Designation triad together with the four others involving the Destination.

This particular pentad represents "notification and message delivery by topic." It is formally equivalent to any message management or transfer system that does not involve Sources explicitly.

Pentads are established by three matched basic activities. Which three are used is to some extent arbitrary, to be settled by environment and convenience. The illustration has used Topic Marking, Topic Parking, and Open Access — a common choice, but not inevitable.

This kind of Notification would not help readers seeking messages by known authors or other Sources. To superimpose this facility we would have to establish a fourth basic activity that related authors with two other variables. Whatever these two may be, they are already matched into existing activities. Unless the author's habits of discourse conform or are made to conform with these, we cannot establish a compatible fourth activity. For instance, only sets of abnormally repetitious authors and conservative readers would make possible parking by topic and by author simultaneously.

This consideration seriously restricts attempts to notify by mixed modes. They can succeed only in environments that rigidly discipline discourse toward narrow ends by dictating who tells whom about what in which manner, or who requests what in which manner, or both. This can reduce the universe of discourse to a mere echo chamber surrounding physical activities of signaling, storage, and transport. The more rigorous the constraints the less ambiguous is the term "flow" and the less appropriate the term "information."

In general, and in practice, one must provide distinct alternative modes of notification as tools for the system user, not as substitutes for him. Fundamentally there are six modes, according to which pair of basic activities is used to relate Destination with Message. Put in another way, each mode of notification involves a tetrad of variables, two of which are Destination and Message, the other two selected from Code, Designation, Channel, and Source.

Inasmuch as there is flow between Message and Destination, whatever it is that flows depends on the other conjugate pair of the tetrad. Thus six distinct flows are possible.

Any measures of such flow must depend on measures associated with the two basic triads which form the tetrad. For instance, under certain conditions Shannon entropic-type measures are valid. In each triad each measure measures different things. Therefore measures of the flow as such must have two components. Currently I am studying these problems.

To some extent one can talk meaningfully about "information flow" in relation to the six flows relating Destination to Message in notification activities. But even if meaningful, such talk is rarely useful or helpful. Inasmuch as each mode of notification informs, it informs differently about different things. At no time is it concerned, nor can it be concerned, with how the reader is informed by the messages. It can only tell him about them.

References

1. MACKAY, D. M. The informational analysis of questions and commands. In *Information Theory, 4th London Symposium, Sept. 1960.* Butterworth and Co., London, 1961, pp. 469–476.
2. FAIRTHORNE, R. A. "Use" and "mention" in the information sciences. In *Proc. Symposium on Education for Information Sciences, Sept. 1965.* Spartan Press, Washington, D.C., 1965, pp. 9–12.
3. GILBERT, E. N. Information theory after 18 years. *Science 152* (April 15, 1966), 320–326.
4. SEBOEK, T. A. Coding in the evolution of signalling behaviour. *Behavioral Science 7* (Oct. 1962), 430–432.
5. ———. The information model of language. In *Natural Language and the Computer*, Garvin, P. (Ed.), McGraw-Hill, New York, 1963, pp. 47–64.
6. BUHLER, M. *Sprachtheorie.* Fischer, Jena, Germany, 1934.
7. FAIRTHORNE, R. A. Basic postulates and common syntax. In Shera, J. H. (Ed.), *Advances in Documentation and Library Science, Vol. 3: Information Retrieval and Machine Translation*, Ed. by A. Kent. New York, Interscience, a Division of Wiley, 1961, Part 2, Chap. 44, pp. 1007–1020. (Reprinted in Fairthorne, R. A., *Towards Informa-*

tion Retrieval. Butterworth and Co., London, 1961, pp. 170–185.)

8. ———. Documentary classification as a self-organizing system. In *Information Theory, 4th London Symposium, Sept. 1960*. Butterworth and Co., London, 1961, pp. 426–436. (Reprinted in Fairthorne, R. A., *Towards Information Retrieval*. Butterworth and Co., London, 1961, pp. 186–199.)

9. ———. Essentials for document retrieval. *Special Libraries 46* (Oct. 1955), 340–353.

10. ———. The patterns of retrieval. *American Documentation 7* (April 1956), 65–70. (Reprinted in Fairthorne, R. A., *Towards Information Retrieval*. Butterworth and Co., London, 1961, pp. 83–93.)

Chapter Two
Communication
Processes

There are as many interpretations of the concept of "communication" as there are of "information." These are different but not quite separate concepts; the relation between the two is the same as that between energy and the flow of electricity. In other words, information is a fundamental phenomenon, comparable to energy and matter, and communication is comparable to processes which deal with energy and matter. When it comes to communication of knowledge, this complexity is compounded with all types of man's biological, behavioral, sociological, cultural, ecological, and even idiosyncratic features.

The chapter is divided into two sections, but the works are clearly overlapping. The first section (A) presents representative works which, although using different approaches, deal with the general question: "What are the patterns to be found in the growth of knowledge in general, and the behavior of literature containing and representing knowledge in particular?" The second section (B) is directly concerned with people—the behavior of information users.

The significance of Kochen's article (Article 6) is that he synthesizes a number of mathematical, statistical, behavioral and ethical approaches concerned with "lawful regularities governing the acquisition of information and its transformation into knowledge, the assimilation of knowledge into understanding, the fusion of understanding into wisdom." Even more importantly, Kochen provocatively raises the questions and takes the approaches which should be guidelines for future explorations. He points to the necessity of merging scientific method with ethical and qualitative values; in other words, he advocates and indicates means to achieve a fusion of sciences and humanities.

Price (Article 7), using a quantitative, statistical approach, investigates the nature of scientific literature as an interlocked, interrelated, living network. This network has some significant properties which may, to a great extent, explain the communication and cumulation of knowledge in science — properties such as "research front" (analogous to Kochen's "quality of knowledge"), "immediacy factor," and "half-life of literature."

Goffman (Article 8) and Goffman and Warren (Article 9) use mathematical approaches to study in great depth the structure of specific literatures in defined scientific areas. Regularities that allow predictions are uncovered (Article 8), and a general law governing the scatter of articles on a subject among journals as governed by authors is suggested (Article 9). Bradford's law of dispersion of literature was used on a variety of data; the regularity of behavior of literature as a whole and the literature of individual authors is striking.

Three articles in the second section are representative of some thousand or more works, generically known as "user studies." In the past, user studies have been characterized as being behaviorally or, more specifically, psychologically and sociologically oriented; as limiting the populations under study almost exclusively to scientists, technologists, and to those in science-based professions; as gathering enormous amounts of data; and as deriving relatively few generalizations, but specifying the problems of investigations.

The lead article in this section by Ziman (Article 10) actually is not a user study, but a provocative statement on the problems of communication in science, a critique of certain modern communication practices, and a series of highly important suggestions. In other words, this is a problem-statement article.

The Parker and Paisley article (Article 11) resembles Kochen's — reporting a retrospective and prospective type of investigation. They synthesize the approaches and representative findings from studies on scientists' use of information; they evaluate theories on use of information, and they suggest methodologies as well as research areas for future investigations.

Rosenberg (Article 12) uses an extremely interesting methodology in his study of industrial personnel, a group of users less researched than scientists.

Price and Beaver (Article 13) analyzed the communication patterns in a most interesting and quite important information system — the "invisible college." Every information user in any walk of life probably communicates within his "invisible college" to a much greater extent than he communicates with "visible" or formal information systems within his reach. How the formal and informal systems interact or supplement each other is an open question. Some answers to that question will be most significant in illuminating the area of human communication.

A. Behavior of Knowledge and Literature

6 Stability in the Growth of Knowledge

MANFRED KOCHEN
American Documentation
Vol. 20, No. 3, July, 1969

1 Introduction

A new intellectual discipline seems to be in the making. It is the study of processes by which knowledge grows. It seeks conditions under which such growth is stable. Knowledge grows in individuals by natural learning processes. Knowledge grows in communities by other natural processes, such as scientific advance and revolution.

What is the evidence for believing that this is an emerging new discipline? The main reason is the increase in the number of new-generation, creative, well-trained scholars likely to spur the vigorous development of this field. According to Hamblem (1), in 1964–5 there were 18 degree programs in information science (2 at the B.S. level, 12 at the M.A. level, 4 at the Ph.D. level) with 16 more being planned. These new

This was the first Distinguished Lecture of the American Society for Information Science. It was presented at ASIS chapters in Cleveland, Columbus, Dayton, Chicago, Los Angeles, Philadelphia, and Boston. The help of all these responsive audiences, which resulted in an improved version of the lecture after each presentation, is hereby gratefully acknowledged. Some of the ideas and results emerged from the author's still developing and maturing reflections about information science. This paper was prepared with partial support of grants NIH MH12977.03 (which sponsors the work on the simulation of learning processes) and NSF GN716 (which sponsors work on integrative mechanisms in literature growth).

scholars are searching for an intellectual nucleus in which to invest their best. Information Science is being created by them. This paper proposes to define the intellectual core of the new discipline.

Important conditions for the birth of a new discipline are present: We have a time-honored intellectual puzzle in the challenge of explicating learning processes; we have new concepts and methods from the computer arts and sciences; we have unprecedented opportunities for observing the birth and growth of new fields within the lifetimes of observers.

Perhaps it is useful, at the outset, to specify what the new field of study is not. It is not the analysis or design of computer-aided systems for retrospective search, current awareness, or bibliographic control. Not that the art and science underlying such novel systems is unimportant or irrelevant to information science. Far from it. What concerns us about these systems, however, is the search for conditions under which they are of value, in somewhat the spirit that medical science seeks such conditions for various drugs. Such a quest is seldom successful with an industrial engineering approach: a search for superficial performance criteria like labor displaced, time saved, etc. and optimization of benefit/cost ratio. Rather, the basic mechanisms of nature by which the growth processes in learning and the advance of science are regulated should be understood before proposed remedies can be evaluated reliably.

About the newer technological developments in libraries, information services, schools, publication enterprises, communication media, research institutes, etc.— both hardware and software—we need to understand the conditions under which their use is valuable or detrimental. It is entirely possible that automation of journal production—which could reduce costs by a factor of 10—may at best provide temporary relief, while opportunities to attack fundamental problems are missed. The growth of literature is well documented,[1] and is causing some scientists (2) to ask whether knowledge is growing too fast for man to adjust.

The knowledge industry (3) is ripe for innovations. Indeed its phenomenal size and growth (26% of the GNP or $136 billion in 1958 (4) and 33% of the GNP or $195 billion in 1963 (5) spread over education, communication media, information services, research and development and information machines) may be related to both the rate of innovation and the emerging need. About this industry, Clark Kerr stated his belief that it could affect the second half of the 20th century with a force comparable to the auto industry's impact on the first half, and the railroads' impact on the second half of the 19th century.

In this paper we trace some of the intellectual developments in theories of learning processes and theories of literature dynamics. By a learning process we mean the way an individual represents internally his relevant external world so that he can take increasingly effective actions (6). This means being able to assimilate newly arriving data into an increasingly organized, internal model rather than compiling and cataloging inputs for efficient storage and recall.

The growth of knowledge is a process which occurs naturally in society. The intellectual trials blazed by de Solla Price (7) and Kuhn (8), for example, are spurring current mathematical studies (9, 10). The growth of knowledge is a social process connected with learning. Since both are growth processes, a key problem is common to both: under what conditions is growth normal, stable? The confluence of these two lines of investigation and the application of tested mathematical methods and concepts seem to bring us closer to explicating the basic concept of *stability* and to answer this question usefully.

"Knowledge is power, knowledge is safety, knowledge is happiness," said Thomas Jefferson (13) (though some attribute the first phrase to F. Bacon). That science has increased man's control over nature is widely recog-

nized, but that this control always increases his happiness and well-being is under dispute. Bertrand Russell (14) pointed out that an animal species which survives achieves equilibrium between its passions and the conditions of its life. Changing the conditions upsets this equilibrium. Normally, passions readjust to restore equilibrium before too long. Deviations from equilibrium remain within bounds. Small perturbations in conditions do not, normally, set off violent and growing departures from equilibrium.

This is the general concept of stability. One leading modern scientist after another has begun to ask whether the continued growth of knowledge threatens our individual liberty, our civilization, or even the entire biosphere. "Science has not given men more self-control, more kindliness, or more power of discounting their passions in deciding upon a course of action," says Bertrand Russell (14). And to quote Theodore Roosevelt (15) "To educate a man in mind and not in morals is to educate a menace to society." The key problem is whether the growth of knowledge is paralleled, stably, by the growth of wisdom. Or, do growth of knowledge and growth of wisdom diverge?

We examine three levels of stability (1) in purely quantitative terms; we study how the number of workers in a specialty grows and stabilizes; (2) with more stress on the quality of growing knowledge, on how it leads to deeper understanding; we study how the paradigms of a field stabilize; and (3) with stress on basic values, such as ethical values, on how they lead to greater wisdom; we study mechanisms that stabilize the gap between knowledge and action.

2 The Emphasis on Quantity

What is the traditional picture of the growth of knowledge? Each contributor shapes his building blocks of data or theorems and adds it to a cumulating pile. Each specialty grows from its fixed core outward toward other specialties. "All areas of knowledge are growing by expansion from within and accretion from without, by internal subdivision and external overlappings with neighboring areas," says Bochner (16). This centrifugal tendency fosters cross-disciplinary work. It may fill gaps and may mesh knowledge into a pattern. At the same time, there is also a centripetal tendency toward more extensive specialization, toward theoretical and empirical refinement.

One of the first theoretical models for one aspect of the growth of knowledge—the research and development process—was created in 1959 by Hetrick and Kimball (17). Stimulated by the success of operations analysis in submarine detection during World War II— despite, or perhaps *because*, very complex real situations were oversimplified to make the formulation mathematically tractable—these pioneers undertook a similar

---

[1] Scientific findings are now being reported in over 60,000 (11) journals. Three new journals are being founded every day while one dies. The growth rate is fittingly illustrated by *Mathematics Reviews*, which contained about 2,000 reviews in 1940, 4,000 in 1950, and about 8,000 in 1960 (12).

approach. They treated Research and Development as a two-stage process, analogous to certain chemical processes. In the first stage, key facts as yet unknown are transformed at a rate r_1 into key facts which are known but not as yet applied. In the second sequential step, the latter facts are transformed into useful applications at a rate r_2. They showed that to maximize the overall production of useful applications, r_1 should be equal to r_2, a result which is well known to chemists who have studied reactions with two sequential steps. This result is not sensitive to numerous details and approximations.

Hetrick and Kimball showed that discovering basic facts requires about half as much effort (measured in dollars or man-hours required) as applying them. Hence, basic research should be about $\frac{1}{3}$ of the total Research and Development effort. In newly emerging fields, they compute a recommended level of 50% on basic research. In the rare case of an almost exhausted field, in which discovery is easy, it could drop below 20%, a figure below which it should never drop otherwise.

In a penetrating review, Platt (18) sees this work as a convincing first step in "research on research," which he says, "should be and will be . . . a major field of study." Though this prediction has not materialized, evidence is accumulating; the new field might well still coalesce into the theoretical nucleus of information science which we are discussing in this paper.

Another more recent attempt (19) to model the growth of a scientific specialty was to study the population of contributors, viewing the changes in their numbers as an epidemic process. Mathematically, the study of epidemic processes resembles the study of ecology initiated by Volterra and Lotka and also the study of the spread of rumors and influence (20). The spread of ideas in a population of scientists is assumed to be analogous to the spread of infection. In mathematical epidemiology (21), the primary quantity of interest is the number of infectives, and how this number, $I(t)$, varies with time t. The function, $I(t)$, is assumed to increase continuously with the real variable t at a continuous rate, $I'(t)$, which is proportional to both: (a) the number of infectives present in the population, and (b) the number of susceptibles in the population.

References 9, 10, and 19 are a straightforward application to modeling the growth of a specialty. There, $I(t)$, the number of infectives, is interpreted as the number of active contributors to that specialty. This is defined operationally as the number of people whose first paper in H. Selye's (22) collection of *2282 papers* by *2195 authors* on mast cells (the specialty chosen for study) was published *in or before year t* and whose *last paper* in that collection was dated *later than t − 1*. The number of susceptibles, $S(t)$, is here interpreted as the number of authors among the 2195 whose first paper in the Selye collection is published after year t.

We may visualize the 2282 papers strung out along a line according to their publication date. Picking t as a particular date, like 1945, $S(1945)$ is the number of authors whose first paper is to the right of 1945 and $I(t)$ is the number of authors who contributed papers lying to the left of 1945 (provided the last one is after 1944).

The basic assumption says that during a small time period from t to $t+\Delta t$ the number of newcomers to the specialty would double if the number of active old-timers were doubled, given that the number of potential newcomers—i.e., students or scientists switching specialties—stays fixed; also the number of newcomers doubles if the number of potential newcomers doubles, given that the number of old-timers stays fixed. Instead of doubling, with 2 as the constant of proportionality, it could be multiplied by a factor of a, which was, in fact, estimated at .014 persons per year for mast cell research. Thus, $I'(t) = aI(t)S(t)$. Furthermore, active contributors "retire." In the mast cell study, for example, a contributor is said to retire 1 year after the date of his last paper in the Selye collection, just as infectives are removed by death or immunity. Denote the rate of retirement by b. It is about 4.4 persons per year for mast cells. Also, a fresh supply of active contributors enters the population at a constant rate c, about nine people per year for mast cells. Thus

$$I'(t) = aI(t)S(t) - bI(t) + c.$$

A similar differential equation can be written for the rate of decrease in the number of potential contributors (susceptibles), $S(t)$, with d and e in place of b and c:

$$S'(t) = -aI(t)S(t) - dS(t) + e.$$

The rate at which the number of retired contributors grows is, therefore, $bI(t) + ds(t)$.

The concept of stability enters in its most superficial, though already very precise, form as the peak of the *growth-rate* curve $I'(t)$. The arrival rate of newcomers reaches a maximum; the process is self-limiting. Though the total number of active contributors, $I(t)$, may still grow, the epidemic is over, and "recovery"—in this case the decline of a specialty—has begun. The number of active contributors, $I(t_0)$ grows or declines at a constant rate at a time of stability t_0. A growth process starting (i.e. going through) at $I(t_0) + e$, where e is small fluctuation in the number of contributors, would differ only slightly from the growth process starting (i.e. going through) $I(t_0)$.

The requirement that $I(t_0)$ changes at time t_0 at a constant rate means, mathematically, that the first time derivative, $I'(t_0)$ at time t_0 is constant; it means also that the second time derivative at t_0, $I''(t_0)$—the rate at which $I'(t_0)$ changes at t_0—is zero. This implies that the growth curve of I versus t has an inflection point at $t = t_0$—the point in an S curve where the curvature switches from concavity to convexity. Of course, when $I''(t_0) = 0$, then $I'(t_0)$, which is constant, can in particular also be 0, as in the case of a growth curve which settles on an asymptote. The condition, $I'(t_0) =$ a constant, implies that the retirement rate is constant in that year of stability. For mast cell research, the predicted year is 1978, when this specialty will also be most active due largely to the introduction of the electron microscope.

More generally, suppose the entire society is composed of n pools of specialists. Let $I_i(t)$ and $S_i(t)$ be, as before, the number of active and potential contributors to specialty pool i, $i = 1, \ldots, n$. Included among these populations are not only pools of specialists on mast cells or lasers, but a pool of students, a pool of retired workers, a pool of users of all kinds, a pool of librarians, and—most important—a pool of scholars and theorists who evaluate [2] and synthesize. To characterize the interaction between one pool, say the ith, and another, say the jth, we consider:

a_{ij}, the rate at which active contributors defect from j to i

b_{ij}, the rate at which potential contributors defect from j to i

c_{ij}, the rate at which potential contributors to i are inspired by the number of active contributors in j to become active contributors in i. Then

$$I'_i(t) = S_i(t) \sum_{j=1}^{n} c_{ij} I_j(t) + \sum_{j=1}^{n} a_{ij} I_j(t) - \sum_{j=1}^{n} a_{ji} I_i(t).$$

Letting A, B, and C denote the $n \times n$ matrices with elements (a_{ij}), (b_{ij}), (c_{ij}) respectively, this is

$$I' = SCI + AI - IA^T 1$$

where: I and I' are n-component column vectors; the superscript T denotes the transpose of a matrix (or vector), so that, for example, $I^T = (I_1, I_2, \ldots, I_n)$; 1 is the column vector consisting of n 1's; and S denotes the matrix

$$\begin{pmatrix} S_1 0 \ldots 0 \\ 0 S_2 0 \ldots 0 \\ 0 0 S_3 \ldots 0 \\ \vdots \\ 0 0 0 \ldots S_n \end{pmatrix} \text{ and } I \text{ the matrix } \begin{pmatrix} I_1 0 0 \ldots 0 \\ 0 I_2 0 \ldots 0 \\ 0 0 I_3 \ldots 0 \\ \vdots \\ 0 0 0 \ldots I_n \end{pmatrix}$$

Similarly, we have

$$S' = -SCI + BS - SB^T 1$$

As before, S and S' denote the n-component column vectors. These represent $2n$ differential equations for the $2n$ functions summarized in $S(t)$ and $I(t)$. All these functions are assumed to be continuous in the real variable t.

To investigate stability, it is not necessary to solve this system of differential equations, which is quite difficult. Solving it means finding the two vector functions $S(t)$ and $I(t)$ which satisfy the system as well as a specified initial condition: at time $t = t_0$, $I(t_0) = u$ and $S(t_0) = v$. A solution $I(t)$, $S(t)$, is said to be stable at

time $t = t_0$ if a small change in u or v gives rise to another pair of vector functions which are also solutions and do not depart from $I(t)$ and $S(t)$ without bound. Much of the *theory* of differential equations (24) states such properties of solutions as deductions from the analytic form of the differential equation. One of the most important methods for such deductions is that of Liapounoff (25). This is based on a theorem stating that a process, like $[I(t), S(t)]$, is stable at $t = t_0$ if there exists, in some neighborhood of (u, v) a function $V(I,S)$ with the following properties:

(a) $V(I_1, \ldots, I_n, S_1, \ldots, S_n)$ and its $2n$ partial derivatives are continuous in the neighborhood N of $I = u, S = v$;
(b) $V(u,v) = 0$;
(c) $V(I,S) > 0$ everywhere in N except at $I = u, S = v$; and
(d) The time derivative, dV/dt, is 0 or negative.

In this case, it can be shown by methods similar to those used in 9, that the function $V(I,S) = |AI + BS - (IA^T + SB^T)1|$ satisfies the above 4 conditions in the neighborhood of any u, v for which $V(u, v) =$ a constant. This is easy to show for $(u, v) = (0, 0)$. Condition (a) is satisfied by the requirements of continuity in t. Condition (b), $V(0,0) = 0$ is evident from the form of $V(I,S)$, because I and S are matrices of all zeroes in this case. Condition (c) is guaranteed by the absolute value sign in the expression for $V(I,S)$. Condition (d), that $\frac{dV}{dt} = 0$, follows from the requirement that $V(0,0) =$ a constant.

Under certain mathematical conditions, $\frac{dV(I,S)}{dt} = |AI' + BS' - (I'A^T + S'B^T)1| \frac{d}{dt} |I' + S'| = \frac{d^2}{dt^2} |I + S|$, and this is 0 if $\frac{dV}{dt} = 0$. This implies, as in the nonvector case, that $I + S$ is at a generalized inflection point and $I' + S'$ is a constant vector: the net *rates* at which the numbers in the various contributor pools change at that time are constant. This concept of stability and the powerful mathematical machinery to determine the conditions of stability captures the intuitive notion of stability common to many physical, engineering, chemical, physiological, ecological, and economic problems (26, 27).

The simplest concrete example with familiar intuitive appeal is that of a cone on a flat surface. Equilibrium states exist with the cone standing on its base, lying on its side, or precariously balanced upside down on its apex (Fig. 1).

Equilibrium means that all forces acting on the cone are balanced, and the cone will not move. If it were to move, let us describe its motion by how the coordinates of its center, $c(t)$, vary with time t, given that they are at $c = u$ at $t = 0$ (Fig. 2). In the third case, a slight perturbation of $c(0)$ from u to $u + \Delta u$ results in rapid

---

[2] This is the first point at which we introduce, beyond the merely quantitative, the deeper qualitative aspects involved in describing the growth of knowledge (23).

FIG. 1. Three types of stability of a cone in equilibrium. *Left,* unstable; *center,* metastable; *right,* stable.

return to equilibrium. The potential energy as a function of c, which is cup-shaped, is a Liapounoff function, i.e., it satisfies the 4 conditions for $V(c)$ of Liapounoff's theorem. Thus $c(0)$ is a stable equilibrium state.

Rather than extend and analyze in detail the implications of such mathematical models, considerably more and deeper thought should go into: (1) critically reviewing the choice of basic variables and assumptions to check that they capture the most fundamental forces underlying the growth of knowledge; (2) relating a refined model to operational measures; and (3) assessing the ease with which some of the basic conjectures can be proved mathematically and verified by data.

The most serious omission, by far, is any variable describing the "quality" of knowledge. The variable $I_1(t)$ may encompass how many facts are known in specialty 1, but it does not distinguish key from peripheral facts. It may be proportional to the number of documents in specialty 1, but it says nothing about the number of documents which are *good,* either because they add to, or because they use, the facts of a field in a significant way. Extensions of such models could include variables like $I_{17}(t;1,5)$, the number of active workers in mission-oriented specialty #17 which uses facts from discipline-oriented specialties numbers 1 and 5, but this still takes no account of quality.

3 The Emphasis on Quality: Synthesis and Evaluation

Suppose that we could explicate the concept of a specialty "topic." Assume further that we can partition all knowledge into n topics (without ad hoc operational criteria, e.g., that mast cell research is defined by the

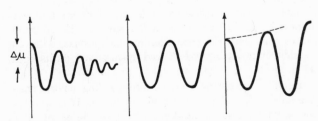

FIG. 2. Motion of cones due to slight deviations from equilibrium: $c(t)$, a one-dimensional case of $c(t)$. *Left,* third case; *center,* second case; *right,* first case.

Selye document collection). We could, perhaps, characterize the topic i at time t by the variables $I_i(t)$ and $S_i(t)$ and the constants in the matrices A, B, and C. Even after we worked all this out, we would still miss at least two other major characteristics of the knowledge system: the corpus of documents in a specialty and the paradigm which characterizes the field itself.

The active contributors to specialty i play a role far greater than merely that of authors and readers: they process data, ideas, and questions with the help of theories and methods learned from their mentors and colleagues, not only by reading their papers, but by talking to them, working for them, and studying under them. Both the active workers *and* their writings infect newcomers to a field. The process by which the active workers infect each other or newcomers, however, is not entirely, nor even perhaps most importantly, through their documented writings. These two sources of infection—stored documents and active workers—should be studied separately.

To document is not always to infect, nor vice-versa. When a newspaper editor recently deleted "former" from the sentence, "Mr. A, a former Michigan Democrat, is supporting Nixon," when in fact, Mr. A is now a very active Republican, the editor is, perhaps subconsciously, trying to infect, rather than document. He may, of course, succeed in inspiring letters to the editor that correct his error, thus contributing to the "growth" of knowledge about Mr. A's political activities. Actually, what grows is only the amount of paper [3] due to making and correcting errors while knowledge has temporarily decreased.

We might at this point note a possible distinction between information and knowledge. Information, though it may remove uncertainty about which of a well-defined number of possible outcomes has occurred—i.e., which letter follows next in a text—is essentially raw data. Knowledge, as suggested by C. W. Churchman (28), is interpreted data. It results from information by transforming the raw data through a point of view, a "Weltanschauung." Studying how active contributors to a field infect each other or newcomers should be sharply separated from growth of documented literature and its effects.

Documents can be modeled as devices for validating, preserving, and communicating (in the sense of public broadcasting to-whom-it-may-concern messages rather than private point-to-point messages) knowledge and decisions in a community (29). It was Descartes (15) who said, "Reading good books is like having a conversation with the highly worthy persons of the past who wrote them; indeed, it is like having a prepared conversation in which those persons disclose to us only their best thinking." The term "document" is here used as a verb.

---

[3] Perhaps the term "information explosion," understood as a proliferation of as yet uninterpreted signs being recorded, is appropriate. Or, perhaps, the term "information poisoning" introduced by Giuliano or *paper pollution* is even more apt.

In its more conventional sense as a noun, it is the physical medium which stores information, and this is not what is intended here.

The active contributors can be modeled as information processors for (1) question-asking, or recognizing what is known to be unknown in a field; (2) question-answering, or puzzle-solving; (3) fact-finding; (4) applications; and, most important, (5) theory-formation. As such they interact not only with each other and documents, but with the paradigm characterizing the field.

Let us define, after Kuhn (8), a paradigm as the totality of achievements which are recognized as such by an entire community of practitioners which, for a time, provide model problems and solutions. We can model a paradigm as a system of representation, in terms of a language or set of sentences which can be generated by a grammar. The set of sentences would be partitioned into three parts: (1) a finite subset representing what is known to be known. This comprises solutions, the answers, the salient documented facts characterizing the field and widely used by its practitioners. (2) Another finite subset representing what is known to be unknown. This comprises the outstanding questions and puzzles which also characterize the field. (3) The remainder. Both the first two sets—how much is known to be known and how much is known to be unknown—grow with time up to a point where the field splits into descendant fields that may cross-fertilize with other fields, and grow until it splits in its turn.

In setting up differential equations to relate the growth of these two quantities, a fundamental assumption is made. Every question answered engenders a number of questions no one would have thought of posing before. However, what is known to be known grows not only because information-processors pick problems and solve them. Only what P. Weiss (2) calls the curious mind does that, while most of the documented facts are contributed by an "infective" with an incurious mind, which "just amasses data that he hopes will provide him with questions."

In writing equations which relate the growth of literature to the growth of knowledge, and to the growth of the corps of active workers, the questions of author motivation and the system by which a community distributes credit to contributors cannot be ignored. These factors may well be the prime determinants of quality. A necessary, though by no means sufficient, condition for the healthy, normal growth of a field, in the sense that the gap between quantity and quality doesn't widen, is the production of enough and good enough theory capable of synthesizing cumulative knowledge. Knowledge does not grow according to the accumulation of observations but by the repeated overthrow of scientific theories. "Yet," says Karl Popper (30), "this growth is not merely a sequence of better and better deductive systems, but a progression from problems to problems, of ever increasing depth." Science starts from problems or puzzles, not

observations. Puzzles arise when experience disappoints our expectations, our paradigms. In time, puzzles may lead to crises, according to Kuhn (8). Their resolution requires the assimilation of a new theory, which means *reconstruction* of prior theory and *re-evaluation* of prior data. "This is an intrinsically revolutionary process that is seldom completed by a single man and never overnight."

If it is true, as asserted by de Solla Price—without *theoretical* foundation—that the number of good papers increases as the square root of the total number of papers, then obviously the *fraction* of papers that are good would become infinitesimally small were this to continue indefinitely. But the process does not proceed thus in a continuous way; it is characterized by discontinuities related to crises and revolutions.

For crises to arise, it is necessary for the current paradigm of a specialty to be questioned by the exhibition of anomalies and paradoxes. It is also necessary for a new and better paradigm to coexist which can resolve the paradoxes, and thus begin to compete very strongly with the old one. The new pattern of thought, according to Kuhn, is built of simple, new, powerful and unifying ideas like Newton's theory of universal gravity, about some connection about hitherto unconnected things. While the topic of apples was irrelevant to the topic of planets until the new theory, these two topics are now relevant from one point of view.

It is well known that today's revolutionaries are tomorrow's conservatives. The very scientists who create a new paradigm to replace the old tend to cling tenaciously to their paradigm when it is, in turn, threatened by the newer one. This gives a paradigm great stability. To quote R. B. Lindsay (31), "Every successful theory tends to become solidified as scientific dogma; there is a tendency to endeavor to fit all newly obtained experiences into its mold under the impression that the final pattern of understanding has been reached. This leads inevitably to inflexibility and ultimately to frustration."

Attempts to integrate knowledge are often embodied in works of synthesis like theory books, penetrating and critical survey-review articles, or good expository articles. Insofar as such works evaluate and use the hard, original results achieved by others, they are often received with indifference or even hostility, perhaps especially when they threaten the prevalent paradigms. As Kemeny (12) remarks about the author of a would-be survey paper, "A major expository article may scarcely raise his reputation but may help his natural competitors. So the article is not written." It might thus be reasonable to assume that the number of documents which are works of evaluation and synthesis grows at a rate inversely proportional to the number of active contributors (curious or noncurious) but directly proportional to the number of curious active contributors, because only a fraction of the curious minds would be attracted to this task.

If authors are predominantly influenced by the values

which give more credit to the hard, original research contributions—i.e., solving puzzles—than to the scholarly works of evaluating and synthesizing the original work of others, then the number of good works of synthesis will remain small. As a result, the number of topics increases, each becoming increasingly narrow, until the newcomers (students), users (mission-oriented actors who draw on many specialties), or other non-specialists can no longer choose efficiently among the great variety and quantity. The demand for guidance in this shallow maze of specialties, which a hierarchy of such works of synthesis could have met, will thus exceed supply. Then the number of good expository works will begin to increase, because the values will now be reversed, with more credit given to a good expository work than to original question-answering. In time, however, the cycle may repeat itself.

If it repeats, its oscillations may decrease in time, which is a condition of stability. In any case, by stressing the role of theory as a device for integrating, synthesizing, and evaluating what is known, we are led to criteria of quality for active contributors and the documented literature. Quality is here related to the elegance, the deductive and summarizing power, the simplicity, and the generalizing scope of the theories underlying a paradigm. The continual tug of war between forces that tend to uphold the current paradigm and revolutionary forces that tend to replace it is one of nature's self-regulatory mechanisms for maintaining quality.

Thus, despite revolutions, systems of representation into which new knowledge is continually assimilated and cumulated knowledge reassimilated seem to evolve without deterioration of quality. In the long run, our understanding seems to increase or at least not to decrease. And if there are temporary down-swings, when we seem to understand less than we did before, at least we understand with much greater precision just what and how much we do *not* know.

4 Stability and Values

Cassidy (*32*) draws a distinction between knowledge, understanding, and wisdom. He points out that, while *knowledge* results from analytic activity, *understanding* results from synthetic activity, such as the invention of a connection between apples and planets.[4] He then defines wisdom as knowledge and understanding of not only knowledge but of *experience* as well. He stresses that "fragmentation of knowledge and experience opposes wisdom; excessive specialization, while it may give deep understanding, does not confer wisdom."

---

[4] This refers, of course, to the story by which Newton may have hit upon the law of universal gravitation during that summer when, at age 21, because Cambridge University was closed due to the plague and he had to while away his time at home, he discovered the telescope, the law of gravitation and the use of fluxions (differential calculus). The association between an apple falling from a tree or from heights visible only by telescope, and the moon, is not so far-fetched.

The majority of people have some information about a great many topics and a little understanding about a few topics, but there seems to be a big gap between their wisdom and what they know. "An average man of 70," says B. Glass (*33*), "was educated in a world of 50 years ago, a world of unbelievable cultural antiquity in terms of all we do and prize today. Man has worked himself into an evolutionary dilemma of appalling dimensions." Such a man is not likely to have much appreciation of science, certainly not modern science, most of which was developed after his formal education was completed. To even the younger average man, a scientist is often only a special kind of mechanic, and science an esoteric specialty, far removed from his day-to-day experience.

It is possible that knowledge can grow without being recognizably more relevant to basic human values, such as happiness and well-being. But whose happiness and well-being (*3, 5, 34*)? Is the aesthetic value of a good theory, which certainly brings pleasure to the scientific community, enough? Or are other values pertaining to survival equally or more basic? The development of relativity and quantum theory was a triumph for science and made the study of physics as pleasurable as any artistic or humanistic subject. With the consequent emergence of atomic energy and its military uses, however, many intellectuals began to re-evaluate the growth of knowledge.

Some scientists question, by the ground-rules of science itself, whether their field can grow normally if the relevance to its use and its roots in human experience become more tenuous and far removed.

Von Neumann, for example, (*35*) warned of the danger of mathematical specialties developing along lines of least resistance, characterized by increasingly pure aestheticizing, art for art's sake, but *not* always in the hands of artists with exceptionally mature tastes. "Thus, the stream of mathematical knowledge," said he, "far from its empirical source, is in danger of separating into a multitude of *insignificant* specialties, a disorganized mass of details and complexities. While at the beginning, the style of the developing subject is usually classical, the danger signs are up when it begins to become baroque."

Bochner (*16*), on the other hand, points out that the word "mathematics" stems from a root which means "learnable knowledge." He claims that "the 'purer' mathematics is, the more it embodies the significant designs of the texture of knowledge; for this reason, significant applications to basic science came more from mathematics pursued for its own sake than from mathematics pursued to a purpose."

In a beautiful little book which is remarkable for its lucidity (*33*), Bentley Glass shows that purposes and basic values themselves may arise from natural, evolutionary processes. In search of criteria for the significance of a field—in the context of advising the government about support priorities in future days when funds are limited—Weinberg (*36*) suggests that topic as having merit which "contributes most heavily and illuminates most brightly its neighboring disciplines." Included among the neighboring disciplines of a field like nuclear physics, however, might well be emerging fields like those Platt called "research on research" or what Glass calls a science of ethical values. Symmetrically, if knowledge dynamics is indeed, as claimed in this paper, emerging as a new field, then its neighboring fields may include modern genetics, molecular biochemistry, cognitive psychology, the computer sciences, and other rapidly advancing fields likely to create many options of tremendous import for human values (e.g., controlling the sex of our children, behavior modification, weather modification). If knowledge dynamics is to become significant, then it will have to contribute and illuminate these neighboring disciplines, which it could and should do, precisely because of its central concern with the disparity between understanding and wisdom or values.

Quality of documented literature, like quality in a paradigm or in the performance of an active contributor, resides not only in intellectual depth; insofar as evaluation for quality involves reference to values, quality is intimately related to values. And not necessarily only individual human values. What is of value to an individual may not be of value to the species and vice-versa. The values of a species may not be compatible with the values of a larger ecological system. In the long-term course of evolutionary processes, despite instabilities relative to values at one level, there are stabilities at higher levels which keep in good operation the machinery of nature in its wisdom with all its self-regulating features and encompassing in its core the growth of knowledge.

5 Learning Processes

To explicate some of the concepts of the last two sections, consider an idealization of the way knowledge might be assimilated into wisdom by a hypothetical machine. In a sense, this is a more detailed model of the information-processing agent, or one of the $I(t)$ active contributors. One of his (its) functions is question-answering. Another is question-asking, which is much more fundamental; we measure learning by the number and quality of questions asked rather than answered. A third and most important function of the learner is that of model or theory-formation. This is closely related to program-formation by a computer.

Here learning means the capability of representing a relevant external environment so that increasingly effective actions can occur. This does not mean conditioning, amassing of indexed data, setting of thresholds, improving performance of a particular behavior, etc. At the heart of this definition is the concept of stability. If the learner has learned to play a board game like checkers (37)—including its having had to learn the rules—and the environment changes "slightly" so that it is now con-

fronted with having to learn a slight variant of checkers, then the learner can "transfer" some of its generalizations and abstractions. In other words, if the environment does not change much or too rapidly, the learner attains equilibrium in that it successfully "copes" with the tasks and opportunities this environment presents. Should this environment change suddenly or greatly, in that new tasks or opportunities appear, then the learner can readjust with sufficient rapidity to restore this kind of equilibrium. This is the same basic idea of stability again.

How can we make this precise? Imagine both the learner and its environment E as abstract automata. Suppose, as an example, that a state of the environment could be depicted, graphically, as illustrated in Figure 3. Here X and A are the labels of two objects, which also may have attributes like hardness, color, chemical composition, brightness, etc. Viewed abstractly, suppose that each object is characterized by m attributes x_1, x_2, x_3, . . . , x_m, the first two being position-coordinates and taking values from 1 to 8. The learner is presumed to have sensory meters capable of detecting these attributes when they change.

As E changes from one state to another, both the objects X and A might move. A second figure like Figure 1 would show them in their new positions, with X at coordinates (2,3) rather than (2,2). Assume now that E also specifies for the learner whether the new state is to be valued more, less, or the same as the old state. Here the value system is part of the environment, at least at this level. For example, the learner may be told, through examples, that any state in which A and X are in neighboring squares is preferred to a state in which they aren't. The learner's job is to form and use a statement such as the above.

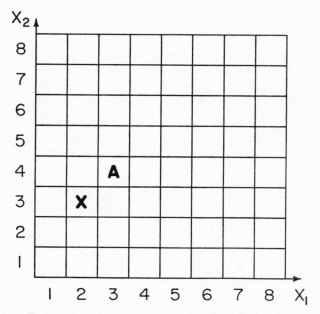

FIG. 3. State of the learner's simulated environment

The learner also has a repertoire of actions. This is most important, for otherwise his learning would be entirely in the form of predictions. Though predictions have intrinsic value, it seems better to incorporate this value into the weight of evidence for hypotheses than to make it a value in its own right, of equal stature to the value of changing environmental states.

Suppose that the action repertoire is [R, L, U, D, N], interpreted as movement to the right, left, up, down, and nowhere respectively (provided there are no conflicts), whenever the learner picks the corresponding output letter. Of course, this must be learned by the learner, including the hypothesis that it (the learner) is the causative agent of these changes and that it is capable of co-determining, together with E's current state, the next state of E.

The learner, as a computer program, functions as follows. On receipt of data input about what attributes of the E-state changed, together with a record of its own preceding action plus the value assigned by E to this state-change, the learner searches a cumulated, indexed store of hypotheses for one or more that might be useful in choosing the next action. If possible, the learner-actor selects that next action which, according to one of its hypotheses, is likely to drive E into a preferred state. If this is not possible or if there is insufficient data, the learner may select an action at random.

The learner also tests some of its stored hypotheses. The weight of evidence for those which are further confirmed by the data that just came in is increased. If they are also likely to be useful in action-selection, such hypotheses are made readily accessible, so that they are likely to be found early in future searches. Hypotheses which are refuted by input data are qualified. This could lead to very long, baroque sentences, with far more exceptions than rule. Occasionally, then, a clean-up process to condense several hypotheses into fewer and simpler ones is turned on.

Every now and then new hypotheses are generated by empirical induction from input data or by other less systematic means.[5] Thus, in time, a store of cross-referenced, hierarchized hypotheses is built up and begins to constitute a system of representation with an inferential structure. This system of representation can occasionally be replaced, in its entirety, by a revolutionary process somewhat analogous to that described by Kuhn (8). The

system of representation dealt with here, moreover, takes the value-structure imposed by E into account.

The question of stability can now arise in the following form. Suppose that the state transition-function for E is fixed, but the assignment of a value—i.e., whether the current state is more, less, or equally valued than the next state—can be varied. Suppose further that there is a way of specifying whether or not one way of assigning values to state-pairs is close to another way. If we now change E by switching from one such way to another that is close to it, will the learner be able to use what he has learned? Or will he have to start all over? If he can readjust quickly enough, the learning process is stable (40). "Nine-tenths of wisdom is being wise in time," said T. Roosevelt.

The environment E is assumed to be a *vastly* more complex automaton than the learner. Indeed, if E's next state is partly co-determined by E's current state and the learner's action, then it is also partly co-determined by the simultaneous actions of any other learner. In a certain sense every possible learner is part of an overall E. It is therefore conceivable that two learners capable of communication and cooperation can "cope" with a greater variety and higher levels of tasks and opportunities presented by E than could an isolated single learner. Moreover, from a practical viewpoint of experimentation and observation about existing (human) learners, requiring two of them (one might be a programmed computer) to communicate about their models, hypotheses, or plans allows us to eavesdrop on some of their cognitive processes. From an even more practical viewpoint of designing devices capable of training or teaching human learners, of amplifying a person's ability to answer and even ask questions, it is important that learners can operate on at least two levels of languge: (1) a private one, suitable for the internal system of representation involving the cross-referenced, indexed store of hypotheses with an inference structure; and (2) a public language, into which learners translate messages from the private language for communication to another and from which learners translate public-language messages they receive. The possibility of a useful public language is based on the assumption that the samples of E-states to which the two communicating learners have been exposed have enough overlap to enable them to have formed many hypotheses which would have the same translations in the public language.

Thus, if one learner detects a gap in its "knowledge" about E, he might observe or experiment, i.e., "interrogate" E; he might, however, also ask another learner who has acquired the needed data previously. Insofar as the question might be more penetrating than a mere request for missing data, one learner could complement another's task of summarizing large accumulations of data. Asking penetrating questions reflects, of course, the learner's knowledge that he does not know but needs to know.

[5] Here, the well-known two approaches to "thinking," *cognito* (derived etymologically from its ancient meaning "shaking together") and *intelligo*, appear side by side as supplementary processes. The interplay between the two has been studied by psychologists and by creative as well as knowledgeable scientists since Poincaré and Hadamard. The contrast between the two is most vividly sketched in a recent book by DeBono (38), as one between vertical or high-probability thinking, analogous to deepening a hole which has already been dug by many people for a long time (the prevailing paradigm or branches thereof) and lateral or low probability thinking, analogous to starting a new hole elsewhere.

Some of the ideas developed here relate to the approch of Piaget (39), particularly in his stress on "learning by doing." The problem of forming a "point of view" or "shift of representation," however, which seems to underlie the creative process, is most stressed here.

And that is in itself a great deal of understanding. It, too, could be shared.

If a learner can ask questions of another, it can also try to answer questions, if only to say, "I don't know." The questions are received as messages in the public language. Considerable progress has recently been made in the construction of computer programs that can process such questions, where the public language is a lightly constrained subset of English (41). There are numerous open and difficult questions of theoretical import. Such problems as the degree to which the data base must be well-structured, the nature of the inference mechanism, the reduction of search spaces, and the effectiveness and efficiency of algorithms for syntactic analysis, deduction, and search are all under investigation. Basically, the English-like query is parsed, much as a computer parses a program statement. Accompanying the parsing process is a translation process from the public to the private language, which in some cases is a simple, first-order applied predicate calculus. When translated into the private language, which is a processing language (42), the question has become a program that can search for the answer.

Question-answering is a simple form of instruction in that it reduces uncertainty in the questioner. In more advanced forms of instruction, the teacher is less passive; rather than responding only to questions, the teacher-learner incites the learner-learner to ask questions. In this way a learner can train other learners to become partners with which to continue communication and cooperation toward optimizing values.

But which values? The E-assignment of values to pairs of successive E-states may differ for two learners. Insofar as one learner A can change or influence this E-assignment of values for another learner B, A can modify B's behavior to further the attainment of A's own highest values, which might now also coincide with B's attainment of its own values. That learner most capable of influencing the E-assignment of values to other learners is the strongest, and its values may predominate, at least temporarily. But does that imply that might makes right? No, unless this most powerful learner is not only a benevolent despot but also one who can, all by itself, adjust very rapidly to the constantly changing rules of the game of an environment which becomes more complex just as fast as the learner has learned to cope with it—perhaps faster. No again, because one learner, with its fixed and limited capacities for information storage and processing of the types discussed—assimilation of knowledge into models and theories that reflect understanding and transforming such understanding into wisdom—cannot adjust without limit to an environment which is constantly growing more complex, without limit, due to the presence of so many other learners. The process by which the environment increases in complexity can, on the one hand, become self-limiting. There can be a stable equilibrium state, with the behavior of most learners modified so that their values are consonant with the value system of the most powerful. Alternately, there are enough checks and balances in a continually expanding environment of learners with diverse value systems to ensure long-term stability at higher levels.

6 Conclusion

I have tried to demonstrate that a new scientific discipline is emerging. We might call it epistemo-dynamics. It is concerned with lawful regularities governing the acquisition of information and its transformation into knowledge, the assimilation of knowledge into understanding, the fusion of understanding into wisdom. These dynamic processes are presumed to occur in nature, of which evolving man and his societies are part. Nature, in its wisdom to date, has always evolved enough self-regulating mechanisms to ensure stability at all levels. For example, man the hunter killed enough wolves in Yellowstone to permit its moose population to expand beyond its food supply; accordingly, man the conservator (the U.S. Park Service) tries to redistribute the moose population over other territories. To take another example, man the author, fearful of perishing lest he publish, injects erroneous or insignificant "facts" or ideas into the literature, thus swelling it and forcing man the reader and user to become more selective; as the poor author's credibility diminishes, so does his readership; and if institutionalized publishers, libraries and university departments persist in perpetuating the flood thus generated (perhaps even at an accelerated pace with computer aids) they, too, will in time lose support.

The new discipline cannot as yet be characterized by pointing to some fundamental papers and books, though references (43, 44, 33) are first approximations. The evidence that seeds for a discipline exist is threefold: (1) New concepts, or old concepts (45, 46, 47) reformulated in modern information-processing terms, such as "learning" and "stability," are being explicated by a young and intellectually vigorous new generation of students. (2) These students seem to find the puzzle of learning processes an exciting intellectual challenge, one to which larger numbers of better educated scientists are being attracted. (3) The existence of large data bases on citation patterns (48), indexed document collections, user profiles, plus the rapid emergence of new fields and professional organizations within the life-span of a research project make the gathering of empirical data—perhaps even under controlled experimental conditions—a definite possibility.

The new discipline could become the core of the information sciences. If it does emerge as a viable scientific discipline, then, by virtue of its central concern with stability, it will, as a significant branch of knowledge which has been evolved by nature's wisdom, ensure stability.

A necessary condition, however, for this new discipline to grow into a viable field is that it be developed in the hands of *both* scientists and humanists. The former without the latter may deepen our understanding by making this yet another specialty, fragmented like most others. Humanists without scientists may advance the field no further than has been the case for ethics, epistemology, and other non-specialized areas in which lack of deep understanding was the price for choosing very deep and relevant questions. The study of the growth of knowledge in a community is partly historical, partly humanistic, partly scientific. So is the study of learning in man.

The following quotation from Isidor Rabi supports this view: "What the world needs is a fusion of the sciences and the humanities. The humanities express the symbolic, poetic, and prophetic qualities of the human spirit. Without them we would not be conscious of our history; we would lose our aspirations and the graces of expression that move men's hearts. The sciences express the creative urge in man to construct a universe which is comprehensible in terms of the human intellect. Without them, mankind would find itself bewildered in a world of natural forces beyond comprehension, victims of ignorance, superstition and fear." And it was Einstein (*15*) who said: "Real human progress depends not so much on inventive ingenuity as on conscience."

In an excellent pamphlet by R. M. Hutchins, S. Buchanan, D. N. Michael, C. Sherwin, J. Real, and L. White, entitled "Science, Scientists, and Politics" (An Occasional Paper by the Center for the Study of Democratic Institutions, Sept. 1963), these authors repudiate C. P. Snow's idea of "two cultures." They argue for the overwhelming importance of research on research, of developing a scientific understanding of science itself. We argue, in this paper, that this is now becoming possible.

While there may be a useful analogy between learning in an individual brain and the growth of knowledge in the "world brain (*23*)," it is probably not fruitful to press it too far. An explication of learning viewed as reorganizing information (*49*) is essential in any explication of the growth of knowledge in a community. The continued survival of the biosphere may well depend on how well individuals in various species can learn to take timely actions on the basis of its collective and growing wisdom.

References

1. HAMBLEN, J., *Computers in Higher Education*, So. Reg. Educ. Bd., Atlanta, August 1967, p. 66.
2. WEISS, P., The Growth of Science: Its Liberating Force and Limitations, in Sweeney, *op. cit.*, p. 60.
3. BOULDING, K. E., Knowledge as a Commodity, *Series Studies in Social and Economic Sciences*, Symposia Studies Series No. 11, National Institute of Social and Behavioral Sciences, Washington, D.C., 1962.
4. MACHLUP, F., *The Production and Distribution of Knowledge in the United States*, Princeton University Press, Princeton, N.J., 1962.
5. BURCK, G., Knowledge: the Biggest Growth Industry of Them All," *Fortune*, November 1964, pp. 130–270.
6. KOCHEN, M., *Cognitive Mechanisms*, IBM Report RAP–16, Yorktown Heights, N.Y., April 1960.
7. DE SOLLA PRICE, D. J., *Science Since Babylon*, Yale University Press, New Haven, 1961.
8. KUHN, T., *The Structure of Scientific Revolutions*, University of Chicago Press, Chicago, 1962.
9. GOFFMAN, W., AND V. A. NEWILL, Communication and Epidemic Processes, *Proceedings of the Royal Society*, A 298:316–334 (1967).
10. GOFFMAN, W., Mathematical Approach to the Spread of Scientific Ideas—the History of Mast Cell Research, *Nature*, 212 (No. 5061):449–452 (October 1966).
11. JONES, H. M., Modern Scholarship and the Data of Greatness, in Sweeney, *op. cit.*, p. 29.
12. KEMENY, J., The Knowledge Explosion: A Mathematician's Point of View, in Sweeney, *op. cit.*, p. 89.
13. LAKOFF, S. A. (Ed.), *Knowledge and Power*, The Free Press, New York, 1966.
14. RUSSELL, B., *The Future of Science*, Philosophical Library, New York, 1959.
15. GREENBERG, S., *A Treasury of the Art of Living*, Wilshire Book Co., Hollywood, Calif. 1967. Quotes from Rabi, p. 256, Einstein, p. 257, Descartes, p. 234, and Roosevelt.
16. BOCHNER, S., *The Role of Mathematics in the Rise of Science*, Princeton University Press, Princeton, N.J., 1966.
17. HETRICK, J. C., AND G. E. KIMBALL, *Basic Research in the Navy*, Naval Res. Adv. Committee, OTS, Dept. of Commerce, Vol. I, 69 pp., and Vol. II, 102 pp., Washington, D.C., 1959.
18. PLATT, J. R., Research on Research, *Bulletin of the Atomic Scientists* 16:220–221 (June 1960).
19. GOFFMAN, W., AND V. A. NEWILL, Generalization of Epidemic Theory: an application to the transmission of ideas, *Nature*, 204:225–228 (1964).
20. POOL DE SOLA, I., AND M. KOCHEN, *Contact Nets*, in preparation.
21. BAILEY, N. T. J., *The Mathematical Theory of Epidemics*, Griffin, London, 1960.
22. SELYE, H., *The Mast Cells*, Butterworth, London, 1965.
23. KOCHEN, M., *The Growth of Knowledge*, Wiley, New York, 1967.
24. BELLMAN, R., *Stability Theory of Differential Equations*, McGraw-Hill, New York, 1953.
25. LIAPOUNOFF, A., *Problème Général de la Stabilité du Mouvement*, Annals of Mathematical Studies No. 17, Princeton University Press, Princeton, N.J., 1949.
26. ASHBY, W. R., *Introduction to Cybernetics*, Chapman and Hall, Ltd., London, 1961, pp. 73–85.
27. MORISHIMA, M., *Equilibrium, Stability and Growth: A Multi-sectoral Analysis*, Oxford University Press, New York, 1964.
28. CHURCHMAN, C. W., Problem of Representation in Problem Solving and Inquiry, to appear in *Proceedings of Fourth Systems Symposium: Formal Models and*

Non-Numerical Problem-Solving by Computers, M. Mesarovic (Ed.), Case-Western Reserve, Cleveland, 1969.

29. Kochen, M., *Information Retrieval Systems Theory*, Wiley, New York, in preparation.

30. Popper, K., *Conjectures and Refutations: The Growth of Scientific Knowledge*, Basic Books, New York, 1963, p. 222.

31. Lindsay, R. B., *The Role of Science in Civilization*, Harper & Row, New York, p. 21.

32. Cassidy, H. G., Liberation and Limitation, in *The Knowledge Explosion*, S. Sweeney · (Ed.), Farrar, Straus & Giroux, New York, 1966, p. 188.

33. Glass, B., *Science and Ethical Values*, University of North Carolina Press, Chapel Hill, 1965.

34. Lynd, R. S., *Knowledge for What?*, Princeton University Press, Princeton, 1939.

35. von Neumann, J., in Heywood, R. B. (Ed.), *The Works of the Mind*, Univ. of Chicago Press, 1947, p. 196.

36. Weinberg, A., *Criteria for Scientific Choice*, in Lakoff, *op. cit.*, p. 406.

37. Samuel, A. Some Studies in Machine Learning Using the Game of Checkers, *IBM Journal of Research & Development* 3 (No. 3): 211–229 (July 1959).

38. de Bono, E., *New Think: The Use of Lateral Thinking in the Generation of New Ideas*, Basic Books, New York, 1967.

39. Piaget, J., *Logic and Psychology*, Basic Books, New York, 1957.

40. Brillouin, L., *Science and Information Theory*, Academic Press, New York, 1956, chapters 18–20.

41. Kochen, M., Automatic Question-Answering of English-Like Questions about Simple Diagrams, *Journal of the Association for Compuuting Machinery*, January 1969.

42. Holt, Anatol, et al., Final Report for the Information System Theory Project, to RADC #AF30 (602)–4211 from Applied Data Research, Inc., Princeton, N.J., February 1968, pp. 1–342.

43. Garfield, E., Primordial Concepts, Citation Indexing and Historio-Bibliography, *Journal of Library History*, 2:235–249 (1967).

44. Knuth, D. E., *The Art of Computer Programming. Volume 1: Fundamental Algorithms*, Addison-Wesley, Reading, Mass., 1968.

45. Dessauer, F. E., *Stability*, The Macmillan Co., New York, 1949.

46. Jordan, D. S., *The Stability of Truth*, Henry Holt, New York, 1911.

47. Neisser, H., *On the Sociology of Knowledge*, J. H. Heineman, Inc., New York, 1965.

48. Garfield, E. et al., *The Use of Citation Data in Writing the History of Sciences*, Report from the Institute for Science Information, Philadelphia, 1964.

49. Deutsch, K. W., Communication Codes for Organizing Information, *Behavioral Science*, 11 (No. 1): 1 (January 1966).

Related Literature

Booth, W. C., *The Knowledge Most Worth Having*, University of Chicago Press, Chicago, 1967.

Bronowski, J., *Science and Human Values*, Harper, New York, 1956.

Kochen, M., Automatic Question-Answering of English-Like Questions about Arithmetic, Joint Conference on Artificial Intelligence, May 7–9, 1969, Washington, D.C.

Sweeney, F., *The Knowledge Explosion: Liberation and Limitation*, Farrar, Straus & Giroux, New York, 1966.

7 Networks of Scientific Papers

DEREK J. de SOLLA PRICE
Science
Vol. 149, July 30, 1965

This article is an attempt to describe in the broadest outline the nature of the total world network of scientific papers. We shall try to picture the network which is obtained by linking each published paper to the other papers directly associated with it. To do this, let us consider that special relationship which is given by the citation of one paper by another in its footnotes or bibliography. I should make it clear, however, that this broad picture tells us something about the papers themselves as well as something about the practice of citation. It seems likely that many of the conclusions we shall reach about the network of papers would still be essentially true even if citation became much more or much less frequent, and even if we considered links obtained by subject indexing rather than by citation. It happens, however, that we now have available machine-handled citation studies, of large and representative portions of literature, which are much more tractable for such analysis than any topical indexing known to me. It is from such studies, by Garfield (*1, 2*), Kessler (*3*), Tukey (*4*), Osgood (*5*), and others, that I have taken the source data of this study.

Incidence of References

First, let me say something of the incidence of references in papers in serial publications. On the average, there are about 15 references per paper and, of these, about 12 are to other serial publications rather than to books, theses, reports, and unpublished work. The average, of course, gives us only part of the picture. The distribution (see Fig. 1) is such that about 10 percent of the papers contain no references at all; this notwithstanding, 50 percent of the references come from the 85 percent of the papers that are of the "normal" research type and contain 25 or fewer references apiece. The distribution here is fairly flat; indeed about 5 percent of the papers fall in each of the categories of 3, 4, 5, 6, 7, 8, 9, and 10 references each. At the other end of the scale, there are review-type papers with many references each. About 25 percent of all references come from the 5 percent (of all papers) that contain 45 or more references each and average 75 to a paper, while 12 percent of the references come from the "fattest" category — the 1 percent (of all papers) that have 84 or more references each

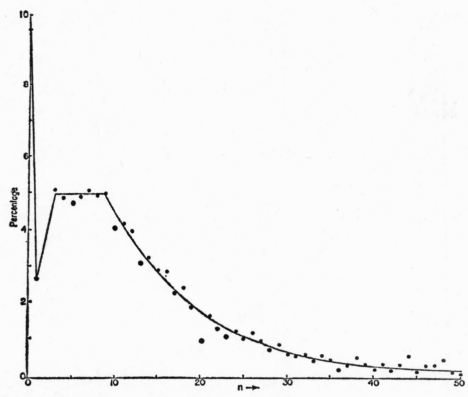

Fig. 1. Percentages (relative to total number of papers published in 1961) of papers published in 1961 which contain various numbers (n) of bibliographic references. The data, which represent a large sample, are from Garfield's 1961 *Index* (2).

and average about 170 to a paper. It is interesting to note that the number of papers with n references falls off in this "fattest" category as $1/n^2$, up to many hundreds per paper.

These references, of course, cover the entire previous body of literature. We can calculate roughly that, since the body of world literature has been growing exponentially for a few centuries (6), and probably will continue at its present rate of growth of about 7 percent per annum, there will be about 7 new papers each year for every 100 previously published papers in a given field. An average of about 15 references in each of these 7 new papers will therefore supply about 105 references back to the previous 100 pages, which will therefore be cited an average of a little more than once each during the year. Over the long run, and over the entire world literature, we should find that, on the average, *every scientific paper ever published is cited about once a year.*

Incidence of Citations

Now, although the total number of citations must exactly balance the total number of references, the distributions are very different. It seems that, in any given year, about 35 percent of all the existing papers are not cited at all, and another 49 percent are cited only once (n = 1) (see Fig. 2). This leaves about 16 percent of the papers to be cited an average of about 3.2 times each. About 9 percent are cited twice; 3 percent, three times; 2 percent, four times; 1 percent, five times; and a remaining 1 percent, six times or more. For large n, the number of papers cited appears to decrease as $n^{2.5}$ or $n^{3.0}$. This is rather more rapid than the decrease found for numbers of references in papers, and indeed the number of papers receiving many citations is smaller than the number carrying large bibliographies. Thus, only 1 percent of the cited papers are cited as many as six or more times each in a year (the average for this top 1 percent is 12 citations), and the maximum likely number of citations to a paper in a year is smaller by about an order of magnitude than the maximum likely number of references in the citing papers. There is, however, some parallelism in the findings that some 5 percent of all papers appear to be review papers, with many (25 or more) references, and some 4 percent of all papers appear to be "classics," cited four or more times in a year.

What has been said of references is true from year to year; the findings for individual cited papers, however, appear to vary from year to year. A paper not cited in

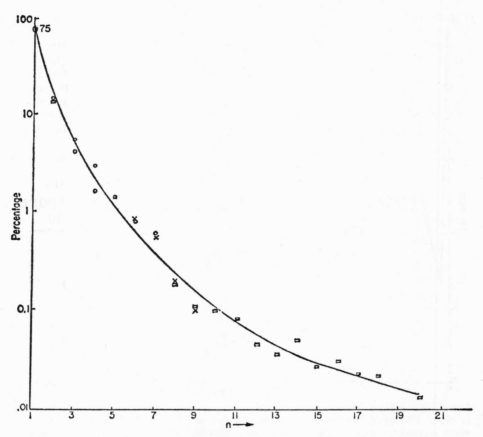

FIG. 2. Percentages (relative to total number of cited papers) of papers cited various numbers (n) of times, for a single year (1961). The data are from Garfield's 1961 *Index* (*2*), and the points represent four different samples conflated to show the consistency of the data. Because of the rapid decline in frequency of citation with increase in n, the percentages are plotted on a logarithmic scale.

one year may well be cited in the next, and one cited often in one year may or may not be heavily cited subsequently. Heavy citation appears to occur in rather capricious bursts, but in spite of that I suspect a strong statistical regularity. I would conjecture that results to date could be explained by the hypotheses that every year about 10 percent of all papers "die," not to be cited again, and that for the "live" papers the chance of being cited at least once in any year is about 60 percent. This would mean that the major work of a paper would be finished after 10 years. The process thus reaches a steady state, in which about 10 percent of all published papers have never been cited, about 10 percent have been cited once, about 9 percent twice, and so on, the percentages slowly decreasing, so that half of all papers will be cited eventually five times or more, and a quarter of all papers, ten times or more. More work is urgently needed on the problem of determining whether there is a probability that the more a paper is cited the more likely it is to be cited thereafter. It seems to me that further work in this area might well lead to the discovery that classic papers could be rapidly identified, and that perhaps even the "superclassics" would prove so distinctive that they could be picked automatically by means of citation-index-production procedures and published as a single *U.S.* (or *World*) *Journal of Really Important Papers.*

Unfortunately, we know little about any relationship between the number of times a paper is cited and the number of bibliographic references it contains. Since rough preliminary tests indicate that, for much-cited papers, there is a fairly standard pattern of distribution of numbers of bibliographic references, I conjecture that the correlation, if one exists, is very small. Certainly, there is no strong tendency for review papers to be cited unusually often. If my conjecture is valid, it is worth noting that, since 10 percent of all papers contain no bibliographic references and another, presumably almost independent, 10 percent of all papers are never cited, it follows that there is a lower bound of 1 percent of all papers on the number of papers that are totally disconnected in a pure citation network and could be found only by topical indexing or similar methods; this is a very small class, and probably a most unimportant one.

The balance of references and citations in a single year

indicates one very important attribute of the network (see Fig. 3). Although most papers produced in the year contain a near-average number of bibliographic references, half of these are references to about half of all the papers that have been published in previous years. The other half of the references tie these new papers to a quite small group of earlier ones, and generate a rather tight pattern of multiple relationships. Thus each group of new papers is "knitted" to a small, select part of the existing scientific literature but connected rather weakly and randomly to a much greater part. Since only a small part of the earlier literature is knitted together by the new year's crop of papers, we may look upon this small part as a sort of growing tip or epidermal layer, an active research front. I believe it is the existence of a research front, in this sense, that distinguishes the sciences from the rest of scholarship, and, because of it, I propose that one of the major tasks of statistical analysis is to determine the mechanism that enables science to cumulate so much faster than nonscience that it produces a literature crisis.

An analysis of the distribution of publication dates of

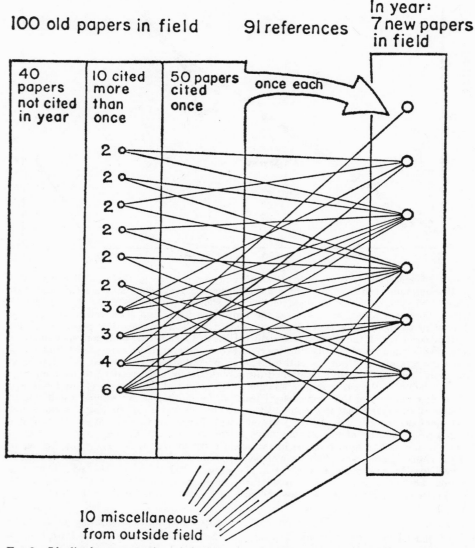

FIG. 3. Idealized representation of the balance of papers and citations for a given "almost closed" field in a single year. It is assumed that the field consists of 100 papers whose numbers have been growing exponentially at the normal rate. If we assume that each of the seven new papers contains about 13 references to journal papers and that about 11 percent of these 91 cited papers (or ten papers) are outside the field, we find that 50 of the old papers are connected by one citation each to the new papers (these links are not shown) and that 40 of the old papers are not cited at all during the year. The seven new papers, then, are linked to ten of the old ones by the complex networks shown here.

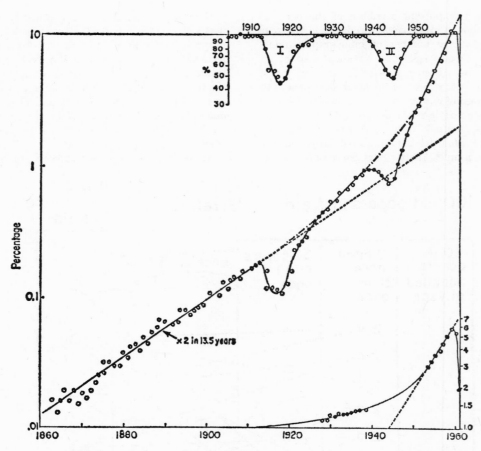

Fig. 4. Percentages (relative to total number of papers cited in 1961) of all papers cited in 1961 and published in each of the years 1862 through 1961 [data are from Garfield's 1961 *Index* (*2*)]. The curve for the data (solid line) shows dips during World Wars I and II. These dips are analyzed separately at the top of the figure and show remarkably similar reductions to about 50 percent of normal citation in the two cases. For papers published before World War I, the curve is a straight line on this logarithmic plot, corresponding to a doubling of numbers of citations for every 13.5-year interval. If we assume that this represents the rate of growth of the entire literature over the century covered, it follows that the more recent papers have been cited disproportionately often relative to their number. The deviation of the curve from a straight line is shown at the bottom of the figure and gives some measure of the "immediacy effect." If, for old papers, we assume a unit rate of citation, then we find that the recent papers are cited at first about six times as much, this factor of 6 declining to 3 in about 7 years, and to 2 after about 10 years. Since it is probable that some of the rise of the original curve above the straight line may be due to an increase in the pace of growth of the literature since World War I, it may be that the curve of the actual "immediacy effect" would be somewhat smaller and sharper than the curve shown here. It is probable, however, that the straight dashed line on the main plot gives approximately the slope of the initial falloff, which must therefore be a halving in the number of citations for every 6 years one goes backward from the date of the citing paper.

all papers cited in a single year (Fig. 4) sheds further light on the existence of such a research front. Taking [from Garfield (*2*)] data for 1961, the most numerous count available, I find that papers published in 1961 cite earlier papers at a rate that falls off by a factor of 2 for every 13.5-year interval measured backward from 1961; this rate of decrease must be approximately equal to the exponential growth of numbers of papers published in that interval. Thus, the chance of being cited by a 1961 paper was almost the same for all papers published more than about 15 years before 1961, the rate of citation presumably being the previously computed average rate of one citation per paper per year. It should be noted that, as time goes on, there are more and more papers available to cite each one previously published. Therefore, the chance that any one paper will be cited by any other, later paper decreases exponentially by about a factor of 2 every 13.5 years.

For papers less than 15 years old, the rate of citation is considerably greater than this standard value of one citation per paper per year. The rate increases steadily, from less than twice this value for papers 15 years old to 4 times for those 5 years old; it reaches a maximum of about 6 times the standard value for papers 2½ years old, and of course declines again for papers so recent that they have not had time to be noticed.

Incidentally, this curve enables one to see and dissect out the effect of the wartime declines in production of papers. It provides an excellent indication, in agreement with manpower indexes and other literature indexes, that production of papers began to drop from expected levels at the beginning of World Wars I and II, declining to a trough of about half the normal production in 1918 and mid-1944, respectively, and then recovering in a manner strikingly symmetrical with the decline, attaining the normal rate again by 1926 and 1950, respectively. Because of this decline, we must not take dates in the intervals 1914–25 and 1939–50 for comparison with normal years in determining growth indexes.

The "Immediacy Factor"

The "immediacy factor" — the "bunching," or more frequent citation, of recent papers relative to earlier ones — is, of course, responsible for the well-known phenomenon of papers being considered obsolescent after a decade. A numerical measure of this factor can be derived and is particularly useful. Calculation shows that about 70 percent of all cited papers would account for the normal growth curve, which shows a doubling every 13.5 years, and that about 30 percent would account for the hump of the immediacy curve. Hence, we may say that the 70 percent represents a random distribution of citations of all the scientific papers that have ever been published, regardless of date, and that the 30 percent are highly selective references to recent literature; the distribution of citations of the recent papers is defined by the shape of the curve, half of the 30 percent being papers between 1 and 6 years old.

I am surprised at the extent of this immediacy phenomenon and want to indicate its significance. If all papers followed a standard pattern with respect to the proportions of early and recent papers they cite, then it would follow that 30 percent of all references in all papers would be to the recent research front. If, instead, the papers cited by, say, half of all papers were evenly distributed through the literature with respect to publication date, then it must follow that 60 percent of the papers cited by the other half would be recent papers. I suggest, as a rough guess, that the truth lies somewhere between — that we have here an indication that about half the bibliographic references in papers represent tight links with rather recent papers, the other half representing a uniform and less tight linkage to all that has been published before.

That this is so is demonstrated by the time distribution: much-cited papers are much more recent than less-cited ones. Thus, only 7 percent of the papers listed in Garfield's 1961 *Index* (*2*) as having been cited four or more times in 1961 were published before 1953, as compared with 21 percent of all papers cited in 1961. This tendency for the most-cited papers to be also the most recent may also be seen in Fig. 5 (based on Garfield's data), where the number of citations per paper is shown as a function of the age of the cited paper.

It has come to my attention that R. E. Burton and R. W. Kebler (*7*) have already conjectured, though on somewhat tenuous evidence, that the periodical literature may be composed of two distinct types of literature with very different half-lives, the classic and the ephemeral parts. This conjecture is now confirmed by the present evidence. It is obviously desirable to explore further the other tentative finding of Burton and Kebler that the half-lives, and therefore the relative proportions of classic and ephemeral literature, vary considerably from field to field: mathematics, geology, and botany being strongly classic; chemical, mechanical, and metallurgical engineering and physics strongly ephemeral; and chemistry and physiology a much more even mixture.

Historical Examples

A striking confirmation of the proposed existence of this research front has been obtained from a series of historical examples, for which we have been able to set up a matrix (Fig. 6). The dots represent references within a set of chronologically arranged papers which constitute the entire literature in a particular field (the field happens to be very tight and closed over the interval under discussion). In such a matrix there is high probability of citation in a strip near the diagonal and extending over the 30 or 40 papers immediately preceding each paper in turn. Over the rest of the triangular matrix there is much less chance of citation; this remaining part provides, therefore, a sort of background noise. Thus, in the special circumstance of being able to isolate a "tight" subject field, we find that half the references are to a research front of recent papers and that the other half are to papers scattered uniformly through the literature. It also appears that after every 30 or 40 papers there is need of a review paper to replace those earlier papers that have been lost from sight behind the research front. Curiously enough, it appears that classical papers, distinguished by full rows rather than columns, are all cited with about the same frequency, making a rather symmetrical pattern that may have some theoretical significance.

Two Bibliographic Needs

From these two different types of connections it appears that the citation network shows the existence of

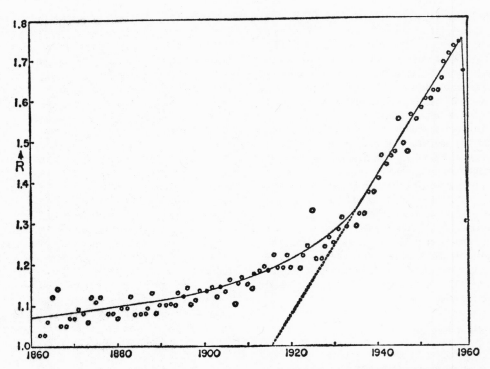

Fig. 5. Ratios of numbers of 1961 citations to numbers of individual cited papers published in each of the years 1860 through 1960 [data are from Garfield's 1961 *Index* (2)]. This ratio gives a measure of the multiplicity of citation and shows that there is a sharp falloff in this multiplicity with time. One would expect the measure of multiplicity to be also a measure of the proportion of available papers actually cited. Thus, recent papers cited must constitute a much larger fraction of the total available population than old papers cited.

two different literature practices and of two different needs on the part of the scientist. (i) The research front builds on recent work, and the network becomes very tight. To cope with this, the scientist (particularly, I presume, in physics and molecular biology) needs an alerting service that will keep him posted, probably by citation indexing, on the work of his peers and colleagues. (ii) The random scattering of Fig. 6 corresponds to a drawing upon the totality of previous work. In a sense, this is the portion of the network that treats each published item as if it were truly part of the eternal record of human knowledge. In subject fields that have been dominated by this second attitude, the traditional procedure has been to systematize the added knowledge from time to time in book form, topic by topic, or to make use of a system of classification optimistically considered more or less eternal, as in taxonomy and chemistry. If such classification holds over reasonably long periods, one may have an objective means of reducing the world total of knowledge to fairly small parcels in which the items are found to be in one-to-one correspondence with some natural order.

It seems clear that in any classification into research-front subjects and taxonomic subjects there will remain a large body of literature which is not completely the one or the other. The present discussion suggests that most papers, through citations, are knit together rather tightly. The total research front of science has never, however, been a single row of knitting. It is, instead, divided by dropped stitches into quite small segments and strips. From a study of the citations of journals by journals I come to the conclusion that most of these strips correspond to the work of, at most, a few hundred men at any one time. Such strips represent objectively defined subjects whose description may vary materially from year to year but which remain otherwise an intellectual whole. If one would work out the nature of such strips, it might lead to a method for delineating the topography of current scientific literature. With such a topography established, one could perhaps indicate the overlap and relative importance of journals and, indeed, of countries, authors, or individual papers by the place they occupied within the map, and by their degree of strategic centralness within a given strip.

Journal citations provide the most readily available data for a test of such methods. From a preliminary and very rough analysis of these data I am tempted to conclude that a very large fraction of the alleged 35,000

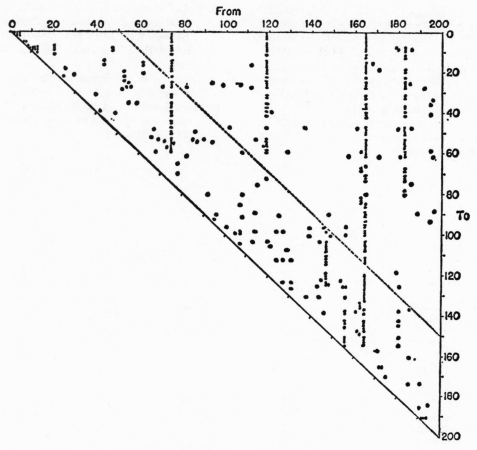

FIG. 6. Matrix showing the bibliographical references to each other in 200 papers that constitute the entire field from beginning to end of a peculiarly isolated subject group. The subject investigated was the spurious phenomenon of N-rays, about 1904. The papers are arranged chronologically, and each column of dots represents the references given in the paper of the indicated number rank in the series, these references being necessarily to previous papers in the series. The strong vertical lines therefore correspond to review papers. The dashed line indicates the boundary of a "research front" extending backward in the series about 50 papers behind the citing paper. With the exception of this research front and the review papers, little background noise is indicated in the figure. The tight linkage indicated by the high density of dots for the first dozen papers is typical of the beginning of a new field.

journals now current must be reckoned as merely a distant background noise, and as very far from central or strategic in any of the knitted strips from which the cloth of science is woven.

References and Notes

1. E. GARFIELD and I. H. SHER, "New factors in the evaluation of scientific literature through citation indexing," *Am. Doc.* **14,** 191 (1963); ———, *Genetics Citation Index* (Institute for Scientific Information, Philadelphia, 1963). For many of the results discussed in this article I have used statistical information drawn from E. Garfield and I. H. Sher, *Science Citation Index* (Institute for Scien-

tific Information, Philadelphia, 1963), pp. ix, xvii–xviii.

2. I wish to thank Dr. Eugene Garfield for making available to me several machine printouts of original data used in the preparation of the 1961 *Index* but not published in their entirety in the preamble to the index.

3. I am grateful to Dr. M. M. Kessler, Massachusetts Institute of Technology, for data for seven research reports of the following titles and dates: "An Experimental Study of Bibliographic Coupling Between Technical Papers" (November 1961); "Bibliographic Coupling Between Scientific Papers" (July 1962); "Analysis of Bibliographic Sources" in the *Physical Review* (vol. 77, 1950, to vol. 112,

1958), (July 1962); "Analysis of Bibliographic Sources in a Group of Physics-Related Journals" (August 1962); "Bibliographic Coupling Extended in Time: Ten Case Histories" (August 1962); "Concerning the Probability that a Given Paper will be Cited" (November 1962); "Comparison of the Results of Bibliographic Coupling and Analytic Subject Indexing" (January 1963).

4. J. W. TUKEY, "Keeping research in contact with the literature: Citation indices and beyond," *J. Chem. Doc.* **2,** 34 (1962).

5. C. E. OSGOOD and L. V. XHIGNESSE, *Characteristics of Bibliographical Coverage in Psychological Journals Published in 1950 and 1960* (Institute of Communications Research, Univ. of Illinois, Urbana, 1963).

6. D. J. DE SOLLA PRICE, *Little Science, Big Science* (Columbia Univ. Press, New York, 1963).

7. R. E. BURTON and R. W. KEBLER, "The 'half-life' of some scientific and technical literatures," *Am. Doc.* **11,** 18 (1960).

8 Mathematical Approach to the Spread of Scientific Ideas— the History of Mast Cell Research

WILLIAM GOFFMAN
Nature
Vol. 212, No. 5061, October, 1966

One of the most intriguing problems of modern science is the obscure nature of its own growth. Indeed, there are few notable scientists who have not, at one time or another, given serious thought to the questions of how their particular science has reached its present state and what will be the course of its future development. These questions seem to be of such importance to scientists that they have emerged as fundamental scientific problems in their own right.[1]

Goffman and Newill[2] have pointed out that the process by which ideas spread within a population of scientists possesses epidemiological properties and can therefore be investigated as an epidemic process. Consequently, a new set of mathematical tools can be applied to the problem of explaining the nature of scientific development. In particular, this approach makes it possible to establish the relative importance of past lines of inquiry within a given area of scientific research, and to predict the future behaviour of existing lines of investigation as well as the emergence of important new ones within the given area.

The purpose of this communication is to demonstrate this method by applying it to the development of knowledge about mast cells. In his recent comprehensive survey[3] of this subject, Prof. Hans Selye has assembled a "full bibliography" in which "every aspect of the mast cell is dealt with"[4]. This bibliography constitutes ideal data for the application of epidemic theory to the spread of scientific ideas, since it provides us with all the contributions to the subject area, from Ehrlich's discovery of the mast cell in 1877 until 1963.

1. The Mathematical Model

I shall treat the communication of knowledge about mast cells as an epidemic process. An epidemic process is a time dependent phenomenon. In general, it can be characterized in terms of a set N (a population) and a set of states E (susceptible, infective and removed) among which the population N is distributed at any given time. A transition from the susceptible to the infective state is caused by exposure to some phenomenon (infectious material) which is transmitted by an infective to a susceptible. A transition to the removed state results from the removal of an individual from circulation for any one of a number of reasons, for example, death. The process itself may be in one of two states at a given point in time: (1) stable: the change in the rate at which the number of infectives accrue with respect to time is equal to zero; (2) unstable: the change in the rate at which the number of infectives accrue with respect to time is not equal to zero. If the change in this rate is positive, then the process is said to be in an epidemic state.

For a population N consisting of S susceptibles, I infectives and R removals, the general epidemic process can be mathematically represented by the following system of differential equations:

$$\frac{dS}{dt} = -\beta SI - \delta S + \mu$$

$$\frac{dI}{dt} = \beta SI - \gamma I + \nu \qquad (1)$$

$$\frac{dR}{dt} = \delta S + \gamma I$$

where S, I and R are continuous functions of the real variable t, β is the rate of infection, $\delta(\gamma)$ is the rate at which susceptibles (infectives) are removed and $\mu(\nu)$ is the rate at which a new supply of susceptibles (infectives) enters the population. The population N is therefore increasing with time and the number of new infections occurring in a given time interval is proportional to the number of susceptibles and infectives in the population.

A necessary condition for the process to enter an epidemic state is that

$$\frac{dI}{dt} > 0.$$

Hence

$$S > \frac{\gamma - \nu/I}{\beta} = \rho$$

represents a threshold density of susceptibles, that is, no epidemic can develop from time t_0 unless S_0. the number of susceptibles at that time, exceeds the threshold

$$\rho = \frac{\gamma - \nu/a}{\beta}$$

where a is the number of infectives at t_0. Furthermore, the epidemic state cannot be maintained over a time interval $(t - t_0)$ unless the number of susceptibles is greater than ρ throughout that period of time. Clearly as I increases, ν/I converges rapidly to zero, and ρ therefore converges rapidly to γ/β. The size of the epidemic is the total number of infections occurring in the course of its development, and its intensity is the ratio of its size to the total population in which it has developed. The epidemic curve which traces the development of the process in time is given by the differential equation,

$$\frac{dI}{dt} = f(t).$$

The process reaches a peak and thus stabilizes itself when

$$\frac{d^2 I}{dt^2} = 0.$$

If this is the case, then

$$\frac{dR}{dt} = \varkappa$$

that is, the rate of change of removal is constant in a region of stability.[5]

The solution of the system of differential equations (1) which characterize the epidemic process is necessary for analysing and predicting its course. Unfortunately, the exact solution of such systems of equations is not always possible. An adequate approximation is, however, obtainable by use of the following recursive expression which is stated in vector form[6]:

$$\bar{x}_i = \bar{x}_{i-1} + [t - t_{i-1}]\bar{x}'_{i-1} \qquad (2)$$

2. The Mast Cell Study

In investigating the spread of knowledge relating to mast cells, I shall consider three classes of individuals. At any given point in time, I shall deal with those individuals who (1) are contributing to some specific aspect of mast cell research, (2) have contributed in the past to the specified area and (3) may contribute to it in the future. In epidemiological terms these mutually exclusive classes of individuals represent respectively the (1) infectives, (2) removals and (3) susceptibles of the population at that particular point in time.

The basic population with which we are concerned in the mast cell investigation is the total number of authors who appear in the Selye collection. This represents the total number of contributors to the subject and consists of 2,195 unique members.

The following general definitions will be used:

(1) An individual is said to have become a contributor (infective) to a specific aspect of mast cell research in the year of publication of his first paper in the Selye collection which deals with that aspect.

(2) An individual is said to be removed as a contributor (removal) to a specific aspect of mast cell research one year after the date of publication of his last paper in the Selye collection which deals with that aspect.

The total population of mast cell contributors represents the infective population. The instigator of this epidemic process is, of course, Ehrlich. The distribution of the change in the number of contributors (infectives) with respect to time, $\triangle I/\triangle t$, is given in Fig. 1. Intervals of five years were selected because of the radical fluctuation of the distribution within smaller time intervals. Fig. 1, therefore, represents the epidemic curve for the total world population of mast cell workers from 1878–1963.

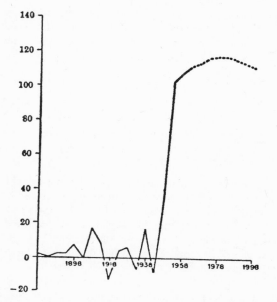

FIG. 1.   Rate of change in number of mast cell contributors.

It can be seen that mast cell research did not enter an epidemic state until the period immediately after World War II. This situation is also reflected in the literature on this subject. The total world literature from Ehrlich's first paper in 1877 until 1963 consists of 2,282 publications. The distribution of publications in five year intervals is given in Fig. 2. This shows that for about sixty years the state of mast cell research as shown by the number of workers and the number of publications in the field remained fairly stable.

It was shown that stability of an epidemic process described by the system of differential equations (1) implies that the rate of change of removal is constant. If this system of equations is a suitable mathematical representation of the growth of mast cell research, then the rate of change of removal, $\triangle R/\triangle t$, of mast cell contributors (Fig. 3) should rapidly converge to a constant in the time interval 1878–1943.

It would appear from Fig. 3 that the mathematical representation chosen is suitable for characterizing the growth of mast cell research.

The future behaviour of the epidemic, as indicated by the broken line in Fig. 1, was obtained as follows: the solution of the system of equations (1) is not possible,

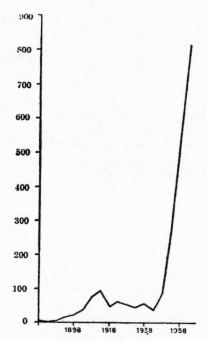

FIG. 2.   Rate of change of mast cell literature.

but it is known that $I = \mathrm{f}(t)$ is an exponential function. Hence, the approximate values of I can be obtained from the expansion of the exponential function into a power series of the form:

$$I = C_0 + C_1 t + C_2 t^2 + \ldots + C_n t^n + \ldots \qquad (3)$$

and the approximate values for $\triangle I/\triangle t$ were then obtained. Consequently, we can predict that mast cell research will reach a peak in 1978, approximately thirty years after the post-war outbreak.

As can be seen from Fig. 1, little progress was made in mast cell research for some sixty years after the initial discovery. This situation changed in 1937 when Scandi-

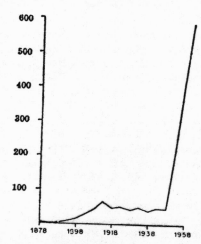

FIG. 3.   Rate of change of removal of mast cell contributors.

navian workers found that heparin was synthesized and stored in mast cells of higher vertebrates. Fifteen years later in Scotland, it was shown that the mast cell is as rich in histamine as it is heparin. American workers then demonstrated serotonin in the mast cells of the mouse and rat. These discoveries stimulated intensive interest in mast cells and played an important part in the post-war outbreak of mast cell research.

The relative importance of these discoveries can be estimated quantitatively by treating each of these aspects of mast cell research as an epidemic process. In accordance with the general definitions (1) and (2), the distributions of the change in the number of contributions to heparin-related, histamine-related and serotonin-related research on mast cells can be easily obtained. These distributions are given in Fig. 4. The future behaviour of each process was predicted in the same manner as for the total population.

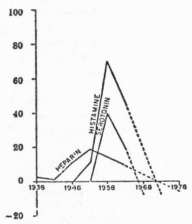

Fig. 4. Rate of change of the heparin, histamine and serotonin contributors.

All three lines of investigation have reached their peak points, and are now declining. It is interesting to note that the heparin curve reached its peak and started its descent at the time when the histamine curve was increasing at its greatest rate, and that the serotonin curve is completely embedded in the histamine curve.

This suggests a shift of activity from heparin to histamine in the 1953–1958 period, and that serotonin workers tend also to be histamine workers. The relationship of the three areas of research activity is further indicated in Tables 1 and 2.

From Table 1, it is clear that, despite the longer duration of the heparin line, the histamine "epidemic" is greatest in both size and intensity. Table 2 shows that 47 per cent of the heparin-involved investigators and 82 per cent of the serotonin-involved workers were also involved with histamine, while only 42 per cent and 36 per cent of the histamine workers were involved with heparin and serotonin respectively. Although 54 per cent of the serotonin investigators were involved with heparin, 93

TABLE I

SIZE AND INTENSITY OF HEPARIN, HISTAMINE AND SEROTONIN EPIDEMICS

	Heparin 1937–1963	Histamine 1953–1963	Serotonin 1958–1963
Size of population	397	443	196
Total population	1,702	1,392	903
Intensity	0·23	0·32	0·22

per cent of these were also involved with histamine. It would therefore seem that, of the three, the discovery that the mast cell is rich in histamine was of the greatest importance.

TABLE II

	Heparin + histamine	Heparin + serotonin	Histamine + serotonin	Heparin + histamine + serotonin
Size of population	187	107	161	100

Since 1953, the electron microscope has been used by an increasing number of workers in mast cell research. The slightly increasing increments (3 and 14 respectively in the five year spans from 1953–1963) suggest that a major outbreak in this area may be in the making. The epidemic theory can be applied, in order to predict the future importance of this tool in mast cell research.

(a) Assume that the susceptible population at any given point in time during the course of the epidemic process consists of all mast cell workers who are not at that moment using electron microscopy. (b) Assume that the initial point, t_0, of the process is 1953, at which time the population N consists of $I = 2$ infectives and $S = 168$ susceptibles. (c) The infective and removal populations are established in accordance with general definitions (1) and (2).

Substituting the observed values (Table 3) for $\Delta I / \Delta t$,

TABLE III

OBSERVATIONS OF ELECTRON MICROSCOPY ACTIVITY IN MAST CELL RESEARCH

	I	S	ΔI	ΔS	ΔRI
1953	2	168			
1958	5	273	3	105	10
1963	19	371	14	98	14

$\Delta R_I / \Delta t = \gamma I$, I and S into equation (1), we obtain the simultaneous equations

$$3 = 2.168\beta - 10 + \nu \qquad (4)$$
$$14 = 5.372\beta - 14 + \nu$$

the solution to which is $\beta = 0.014$ and $\nu = 9$. The solution for γ from the two observed values of $\Delta R_I / \Delta t$ gives values of 5 and 2.8 respectively. Estimating the value of I in 1968 by means of expression (3), and solving for γ, we obtain a value of $\gamma = 4.4$, which falls between the two observed values. We shall, therefore, take 4.4 as the estimated value for γ. Extrapolating the values for $\Delta I / \Delta t$ by means of expression (2) we obtain the predicted behaviour (Fig. 5) of the epidemic curve. (It should be

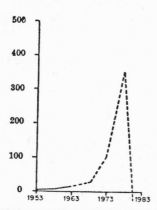

Fig. 5. Rate of change of electron microscope contributors.

noted that the threshold of $\rho = \gamma/\beta = 314$ is exceeded by every value of S throughout the epidemic except at the peak point where $S = 260$.) Thus, it is predicted that the use of the electron microscope will become "epidemic" in mast cell research and that this epidemic will reach its peak in 1978, which is precisely when mast cell research as a whole will attain a maximum.

3. Conclusion

I have attempted to demonstrate the application of the mathematical theory of epidemics to the investigation of the spread of scientific ideas. In particular, I have shown how this mathematical method can be used to establish the relative importance of existing lines of inquiry to the development of a given scientific topic, predict their future behaviour and predict the emergence of new important lines of investigation. For this purpose, the entire population of mast cell workers, as listed in Prof. Selye's recent monograph on the subject, was selected. This selection was made because the whole collection exists as a unit in Prof. Selye's own library in Montreal, and was made available for this investigation.

The results presented here do not exhaust the information which can be obtained from these data, since the total population can be dissected and investigated in a variety of ways, for example, by the discipline or geographical location of its members. These results, however, are sufficient to demonstrate the predictive value of the approach.

Clearly, the method is completely general and can be applied to any scientific area or sub-area. All that is needed is a well-defined subject field and a means of representing the total population of workers in that area. In fact, investigations similar to the one presented here are being carried out for symbolic logic and lasers, and will be reported in the near future.

References

1. PRICE, D. J., *Medical Opinion and Review* (July 1966).
2. GOFFMAN, W., and NEWILL, V. A., *Nature,* **204,** 225 (1964).
3. SELYE, H., *The Mast Cells* (Butterworth, 1965).
4. RILEY, J. F., *Nature,* **209,** 118 (1966).
5. GOFFMAN, W., *Nature,* **210,** 786 (1966).
6. HUREWICZ, W., *Lectures on Ordinary Differential Equations* (M. I. T. Press, 1958).

9 Dispersion of Papers Among Journals Based on a Mathematical Analysis of Two Diverse Medical Literatures

WILLIAM GOFFMAN
KENNETH S. WARREN
Nature
Vol. 221, No. 5187, March, 1969

We have analysed two diverse medical literatures — mast cell and schistosomiasis. Although the literatures were very different in size as well as content, the ratio of journals to authors was almost identical, suggesting that this parameter may be constant for all medical literatures. Furthermore, the average output of papers by the authors of each literature, as determined for each time interval of 5 years did not vary over a period of 80 years. Interestingly, this paper/author ratio was approximately equal to the minimal constant of Bradford's law of dispersion[1] which governs the division of a literature into a nucleus of periodicals more particularly about a subject, and succeeding zones containing the same number of articles as the nucleus. Finally, the factors governing the dispersion among journals of entire literatures also appear to be relevant to the distribution of the individual bibliographies of a representative set of medical researchers.

The literatures relating to research in schistosomiasis and mast cells constitute ideal sets of data for studying the dispersion of a medical literature. It would be difficult to find two literatures more dissimilar than these. One deals with a major disease, while the other is concerned with a single cell. Although each represents a well-defined developing area of medical research, they differ in size — the mast cell literature is about a quarter of the size of the schistosomiasis literature even though both have developed over a long period of time.

In his recent monograph on mast cells, Selye[2] assembled a full bibliography[3] containing all contributions to the subject from 1877, when the cell was discovered by Ehrlich, up to the early part of 1964. The bibliography of the world's schistosomiasis literature, by Warren and Newill[4], covers the total literature on the subject from 1852, when Bilharz discovered the parasitic worm responsible for this disease, up to 1962. The distributions of the mast cell and schistosomiasis literatures among their respective sets of journals are shown in Table I, and the numerical characteristics of these literatures are given in Table II.

On the basis of the data in Table II, it follows that

$$J_c/J_s \approx a_c/a_s \approx Z_c/Z_s = 587/1{,}738 \approx 2{,}195/6{,}511 \approx 328/908 \approx 1/3$$
$$\text{or} \quad J_c/a_c \approx J_s/a_s = 587/2{,}195 \approx 1{,}738/6{,}511 \approx 0.27 \quad (1)$$

That is, there were three times as many schistosomiasis authors as mast cell authors; three times as many

TABLE I

DISPERSION OF LITERATURES AMONG JOURNALS

Mast Cell		Schistosomiasis			
Journals	Articles	Journals	Articles	Journals	Articles
1	66	1	325	1	36
1	58	1	266	2	35
1	57	1	259	1	34
1	55	1	215	1	33
1	53	1	211	3	32
1	46	1	171	3	31
1	40	1	159	2	29
2	38	1	143	5	28
1	37	1	137	1	27
1	35	1	136	1	26
1	34	1	118	2	25
1	32	1	115	3	24
1	31	1	112	4	23
1	30	1	108	2	22
1	28	2	105	4	21
1	27	1	94	3	20
2	23	1	90	4	19
1	22	1	80	10	18
2	21	1	74	8	17
2	20	2	72	10	16
2	19	2	70	9	15
2	18	1	68	10	14
1	17	1	66	10	13
1	16	1	64	6	12
3	15	1	56	11	11
6	14	2	55	14	10
3	13	2	51	19	9
5	12	1	50	29	8
8	11	1	47	27	7
6	10	1	45	44	6
11	9	1	44	57	5
6	8	2	42	76	4
8	7	1	41	137	3
8	6	1	40	266	2
16	5	2	39	908	1
24	4	3	37		
35	3				
90	2				
328	1				

TABLE II

NUMERICAL CHARACTERISTICS AND NOTATION OF PARAMETERS OF TWO MEDICAL LITERATURES

	Mast cell		Schistosomiasis	
	Number	Notation	Number	Notation
Articles	2,378	A_c	9,914	A
Authors	2,195	a_c	6,511	a_s
Journals	587	J_c	1,738	J_s
Most articles in one journal	66	j_c	325	j_s
Journals with one article	328	Z_c	908	Z_s
Articles per author	1·1	$g_c = A_c/a_c$	1·5	$g = A_s/a_s$

journals containing schistosomiasis articles as mast cell articles; and three times as many journals containing one schistosomiasis paper as those containing one mast cell article. Thus, the ratio of journals to authors for each literature is a constant, $W \approx 0.27$. Clearly, this relation did not hold for the journal/paper ratios because there were four times as many schistosomiasis articles as mast cell articles, but only three times as many authors. This is because the average number of papers per author differs for the two literatures. Hence, in terms of papers, expression (1) becomes

$$J_c/J_s \approx A_c.g_s/A_s.g_c$$

or

$$A_c/A_s \approx J_c.g_c/J_s.g_s = (587)(1.1)/(1,738)(1.5) \approx 1/4$$

Thus it seems that the number of authors and not the number of papers determined the scatter of the schistosomiasis and mast cell articles among their respective sets of journals.

The most commonly cited work dealing with the dispersion of the literature of a given subject among a set of journals is that of S. C. Bradford, who in 1948 formulated the following law.[1] "If scientific journals are arranged in order of decreasing productivity of articles on a given subject, they may be divided into a nucleus of periodicals more particularly devoted to the subject, and several groups of zones containing the same number of articles as the nucleus, where the number of periodicals in the nucleus and succeding zones will be as $1 : n : n^2 : \ldots$." Bradford's law can be stated more precisely in the following manner[5]. Consider a collection of J periodicals containing all articles A on a given subject. If these periodicals are arranged in descending order of publication of articles in this subject area and divided into k groups containing numbers of periodicals $J_1, J_2, \ldots, J_\kappa$ such that each group contains the same number of articles on the subject, then according to Bradford's law:

$$J_i = b_k J_{i-1} = b_k^{i-1} J_1 \qquad \begin{array}{l} i = 1, 2, \ldots, k. \\ k = 2, 3, \ldots, m. \end{array}$$

where J_1 is the nucleus and $b_\kappa > 1$ is the so-called Bradford multiplier for k divisions of the J periodicals. In general, the Bradford multiplier b will decrease as the number of divisions k increases. Because both A and J are always finite, there exists, for any collection of articles and set of journals containing them, a maximal number of divisions, m, in the sense of Bradford. Clearly, for a maximal division the nucleus J_1 and the Bradford multiplier b_m are minimal. The minimal nucleus thus represents the most significant set of journals for a given literature because it is the smallest core of periodicals devoted to that subject. The smallest number of articles A/m which can possibly effect a maximal division of a

TABLE III

MAXIMAL DIVISIONS OF JOURNALS CONTAINING MAST CELL AND SCHISTOSOMIASIS LITERATURES

	Mast cell				Schistosomiasis		
Zone	Articles	Journals	bm_c	Zone	Articles	Journals	bm_s
1	181	3	—	1	591	2	—
2	194	4	1·3	2	685	3	1·5
3	182	5	1·2	3	610	4	1·3
4	171	6	1·2	4	694	6	1·5
5	165	8	1·3	5	657	8	1·3
6	170	11	1·3	6	678	12	1·5
7	171	14	1·2	7	667	18	1·5

set of journals containing the literature of a given subject is the number of relevant articles j belonging to the most productive journal on that subject. In this case, the minimal nucleus consists of a single periodical. This situation, however, may not always exist. Consider the set of Z journals, each of which contains only a single paper on the subject. The smallest number of articles, A/m, which can effect a division of the J journals in the sense of Bradford must be greater than $Z/2$, otherwise there would exist succeeding zones (the last two) with equal numbers of journals containing the same number of articles, contrary to Bradford's law. Thus the minimal nucleus can consist of a single periodical only if j, the number of relevant papers in the most productive journal, is greater than $Z/2$. If, on the other hand, j is less than or equal to $Z/2$, then the minimal nucleus will consist of the smallest number of journals at the top of the ordered list, the sum of whose publications on the subject of interest is greater than $Z/2$.

The first seven zones of the maximal divisions of the schistosomiasis and mast cell literatures are given in Table III. Because in both cases j was less than $Z/2$, the minimal nucleus for each literature contained more than one journal. For the mast cell the minimal nucleus included the three most productive journals whose 181 publications on the subject exceeded a $Z/2$ of 164. Simi-

larly, it was established that the minimal nucleus for the schistosomiasis literature consisted of two periodicals containing 591 papers on the subject with $Z/2$ equal to 454.

For collections where $Z > j$, such as the mast cell and schistosomiasis literatures, the maximal division can be more formally established as follows. Because, in such a division, each of the J_m journals in the mth zone will contain but a single relevant publication and because the number of relevant articles belonging to the journals of the mth zone must equal the number of relevant articles belonging to the journals of the $m-1$ zone,

$$A/m = J_m = Z - J_m + 2P \text{ or } P = (2J_m - Z)/2 \quad (2)$$

where P is the number of journals in the $m-1$ zone, each of which contains only two of the A articles. According to Bradford's law

$$J_m/(Z - J_m) + P = b_m$$

Hence,

$$A/m = J_m = B_m.Z/2 \quad (3)$$
$$\text{and } b_m \leqq 2.$$

In terms of the mast cell and schistosomiasis literatures, relation (1) can be expressed as

$$Z_c/Z_s \approx A_c.g_s/A_s.g_c = m_c.J_{mc}.g_s/m_s.J_{ms}.g_c$$

because $a = A/g$ and $A = mJ_m$. Substituting the values for J_m from expression (3) yields

$$Z_c/Z_s \approx m_c.b_{mc}.Z_c.g_s/m_s.b_{ms}.Z_s.g_c$$
$$\text{or} \qquad g_c/g_s \approx m_c.b_{mc}/m_s.b_{ms}$$
$$\text{and} \qquad b_{mc} \approx h.g_c/m_c; \quad b_{ms} \approx h.g_s/m_s$$

Hence, at its lower limit, that is, in the maximal division, the Bradford multiplier b converges to a multiple of the

TABLE IV

DISPERSION OF TEN INDIVIDUAL BIBLIOGRAPHIES AMONG JOURNALS

	I			II			III			IV			V		
Zone	Papers	Journals	b	Papers	Journals	b	Papers	Journals	b	Papers	Journals	b	Papers	Journals	b
1	28	1	—	16	1	—	13	1	—	14	1	—	17	2	—
2	32	2	2·0	22	2	2·0	15	2	2·0	15	2	2·0	17	3	1·5
3	30	3	1·5	24	3	1·5	17	3	1·5	12	5	2·5	16	5	1·7
4	29	6	2·0	19	5	1·6	15	4	1·3	14	9	1·8	13	9	1·8
5	20	13	2·2	16	9	1·8	15	8	2·0	14	14	1·5	12	12	1·3
6	20	20	1·5	17	17	1·9	18	18	2·2	0	0	0·0	0	0	0·0
	159	45 Av. 1·8		114	37 Av. 1·7		93	36 Av. 1·8		69	31 Av. 1·9		75	31 Av. 1·5	

$A = 159; a = 92$	$A = 114; a = 73$	$A = 93; a = 55$	$A = 69; a = 32$	$A = 75; a = 41$
$g \approx 1·7; J = 45$	$g \approx 1·5; J = 37$	$g \approx 1·7; J = 36$	$g \approx 2·1; J = 31$	$g \approx 1·8; J = 31$
$Z = 26; j = 28$	$Z = 19; j = 16$	$Z = 19; j = 13$	$Z = 18; j = 14$	$Z = 17; j = 9$
$A/m \approx 22$	$A/m \approx 15$	$A/m \approx 16$	$A/m \approx 18$	$A/m \approx 15$

average number of papers per author g. But from Table III it can be observed that in both cases b_m is approximately equal to g. Hence, $h \approx m_c \approx m_s$, that is, the number of zones in the maximal division of each set of journals is approximately equal. Thus expression (3) becomes

$$A/m = J_m = g.Z/2 \qquad (3')$$

Moreover, the value of g for each of the two literatures is invariant with respect to time, as shown in Fig. 1, which gives the average number of papers per author in each 5 year interval since 1882. Hence, the average rate of production, g, for the two medical literatures seemed to be a constant, independent of time, to which the Bradford multiplier converged. Consequently, the relation expressed by (1), that is, the constancy of the journal/author ratios of the two literatures, will not vary with respect to time.

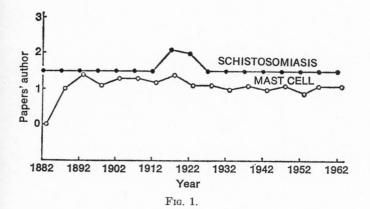

FIG. 1.

The minimal nucleus for each literature can be obtained analytically from the knowledge of its journal distribution and its production constant g, using expression (3'). Expression (3') yields values of $J_{ms} \approx (1\cdot5)(908)/2 \approx 681$ for schistosomiasis and $J_{mc} \approx (1\cdot1)(328)/2 \approx 180$ for mast cell. Thus the number of articles effecting the maximal division of the two literatures should be approximately 681 and 180 for schistosomiasis and mast cell respectively. The minimal nuclei should therefore contain approximately $J_{ms}/j_s \approx 681/325 \approx 2$ and $J_{mc}/j_c \approx 180/66 \approx 3$ periodicals. Both of these results are in agreement with the data in Table III. Moreover, the expected number of divisions m_c and m_s would equal 13 and 15 respectively, thus confirming the assertion that $m_c \approx m_s$ in the maximal divisions of the two literatures.

The bibliographies of ten medical researchers in various specialties were analysed in terms of the dispersion laws discussed in the previous section. Although each of these individuals has worked in more than one area of medical research, their major contributions represent the following specialties: infectious disease, parasitology, virology, anatomy, immunology, biochemistry, pharmacology, haematology and coagulation. Moreover, all of these individuals are still active and cover a range of experience from 10 to 35 years. Table IV shows the maximal divisions of these ten bibliographies.

Here A denotes the total number of papers authored or co-authored by each investigator; a, the number of collaborators producing these articles; J, the total number of journals among which these papers were scattered; Z, the number of journals containing only one of these papers; g, the average number of papers per author; j, the largest number of papers appearing in a single journal; A/m, the estimated number of papers effecting the maximal divisions; and Av., the average minimal Bradford multiplier b_m. In those cases where $j > Z$, $A/m = j$, while for $j \leqq Z$, A/m was obtained from expression (3').

In all but one instance, (V), $j > Z/2$, hence the minimal nucleus in nine cases consisted of a single journal. Of the ten sets of data, $j > Z$ in three cases (VIII, IX, X); $j \approx Z$ in two (VI, VII) and $j < Z$ in the other five. For the seven cases where $j \leqq Z$, the estimated number of articles effecting the maximal division as obtained analytically from expression (3') seemed to fit the data. The

Zone	VI			VII			VIII			IX			X		
	Papers	Journals	b	Papers	Journals	b	Papers	Journals	b	Papers	Journals	b	Papers	Journals	b
1	11	1	—	9	1	—	23	1	—	15	1	—	8	1	—
2	14	2	2·0	12	2	2·0	26	2	2·0	14	1	1·0	10	3	3·0
3	14	4	2·0	9	4	2·0	17	7	3·5	12	2	2·0	14	7	2·3
4	14	13	3·2	8	8	2·0	21	19	2·7	10	4	2·0	0	0	0·0
5	0	0	0·0	0	0	0·0	0	0	0·0	9	8	2·0	0	0	0·0
	53	20 Av. 2·4		38	15 Av. 2·0		87	29 Av. 2·7		60	16 Av. 1·7		32	11 Av. 2·6	

$A = 53; a = 25$ — $A = 38; a = 19$ — $A = 87; a = 36$ — $A = 60; a = 39$ — $A = 32; a = 9$
$g \approx 2\cdot1; J = 20$ — $g \approx 2\cdot0; J = 15$ — $g \approx 2\cdot4; J = 29$ — $g \approx 1\cdot5; J = 16$ — $g \approx 3\cdot5; J = 11$
$Z = 12; j = 11$ — $Z = 8; j = 9$ — $Z = 17; j = 23$ — $Z = 7; j = 15$ — $Z = 2; j = 8$
$A/m = 12$ — $A/m \approx 8$ — $A/m \approx 23$ — $A/m \approx 15$ — $A/m \approx 8$

number of zones was approximately the same and the average number of papers per author was less than or approximately equal to 2. In all ten cases the data seemed to confirm the assertion that Bradford's law of dispersion applied to the scatter of individual bibliographies and that the minimal Bradford multiplier b is approximately equal to the paper/author ratio g.

In conclusion, because the two entire literatures considered (mast cell and schistosomiasis) differ in almost every respect, it is possible that the relations expressed by equations (1) and (3') constitute general laws governing the dispersion of any medical literature. Moreover, the factors governing the journal distribution of entire literatures also seemed to be relevant to the distribution of the bibliographies of individual medical investigators.

References

1. Bradford, S. C., *Documentation* (Crosby Lockwood, London, 1948).
2. Selye, H., *The Mast Cells* (Butterworth, London, 1968).
3. Goffman, W., *Nature*, **212,** 449 (1966).
4. Warren, K. S., and Newill, V. A., *Schistosomiasis, a Bibliography of the World's Literature from 1852–1962* (Western Reserve University Press, Cleveland, 1967).
5. Leimkuhler, F. F., *J. Doc.*, **25,** 197.

B. Behavior of Information Users

10 Information, Communication, Knowledge

J. M. ZIMAN
Nature
Vol. 224, October 25, 1969

Of all the trendy, cliché words, "communicate" is about the squarest. When E. M. Forster invented the phrase "only connect" as the dedicating "quotation" for one of his novels, he was talking of the human heart, not about the spewed-forth products of the head-office duplicator, nor the glossy gaudiness of the Sunday supplement. The virtues of the hermit, the delights of silence, are not to be despised.

But, for scientific research, communication is essential. I will not spell out here my contention that science is to be characterized as "public knowledge"; in other words, that the aim of the scientist is to create, criticize, or contribute to a rational consensus of ideas and information[1]. If you accept this as a general notion, you will agree that the results of research only become completely scientific when they are published. All practising scientists know this, though they are often more careless with their grammar than they would dream of being with their galvanometers.

It keeps being said, generation after generation, that the then current system of scientific communication is in a dreadful mess, and that something ought to be done about it. Century after century, nothing much does get done about it, except that it swells to ever greater bulk.

Our present discontents were originally voiced by Bernal, 30 years ago[2], and although many other pundits have expressed support for his diagnosis of our ills, and for his proposed remedies, nothing much has been done about these either.

There are two simple interpretations of this state of affairs. Those of us who are radicals at heart will blame the innate conservatism of humanity, and say that we continue to put up with a grossly inefficient and cumbersome system because we are too lazy to make a change, or too unimaginative to appreciate the tremendous advantages that a new system would offer. The natural conservatives, on the other hand, will deny that the system is as bad as all that, and point to the good sense of the scientific community in not having been stampeded into some extravagent and newfangled scheme whose untried benefits exist only on paper.

It may be, however, that the situation is a little more complicated; the symptoms of disease may have been correctly noted by the radicals, but they may be advocating quite the wrong cure!

As a contribution to this debate, I shall attempt first to justify the present system — that is, to set out explicitly its unconscious rationale. A social institution that has existed for several centuries must have an intelligible function; when we understand that properly, we can ask how the present practice ought to be modified to continue to achieve the desired goals. Whether these modifications are judged as evolutionary or reactionary must depend on your own state of mind on the subject.

Our present system of scientific communication depends almost entirely on the "primary" literature. This has three basic characteristics: it is fragmentary, derivative, and edited. These characteristics are, however, quite essential.

The invention of a mechanism for the systematic publication of fragments of scientific work may well have been the key event in the history of modern science. A regular journal, such as the *Philosophical Transactions of the Royal Society*, carries from one research worker to another the various discoveries, deductions, speculations, and observations which are of common interest. It is no longer necessary to amass a vast quantity of material, or to conceive a complete new "world system", fully armed at all points, before going into print with a great thick book. Although the best and most famous scientific discoveries seem to open whole new windows of the mind, a typical scientific paper has never pretended to be more than another little piece in a larger jigsaw — not significant in itself but as an element in a grander scheme. This technique, of soliciting many modest contributions to the vast store of human knowledge, has been the secret of Western science since the seventeenth century, for it achieves a corporate, collective power that is far greater than any one individual can exert. Primary scientific papers are not meant to be final statements of indisputable truths; each is merely a tiny tentative step forward, through the jungles of ignorance.

1. Citations

Scientific papers are derivative, and very largely unoriginal, because they lean heavily on previous research. The evidence for this is plain to see, in the long list of citations that must always be published with every new contribution. These citations not only vouch for the authority and relevance of the statements that they are called upon to support; they embed the whole work in a context of previous achievements and current aspirations. It is very rare to find a reputable paper that contains no references to other research. Indeed, one relies on the citations to show its place in the whole scientific structure, just as one relies on a man's kinship affiliations to show his place in his tribe. All this becomes perfectly natural, and proper, once one has accepted that normal science is a highly cooperative activity, the corporate product of a vast social institution, rather than a series of individual forays into the unknown.

The editing — in fact, the censorship — of the scientific literature is a more delicate matter. It occurs in two stages. In the first place, the author presents an entirely

false picture of his actual procedure of discovery. All the false starts, the mistakes, the unnecessary complications, the difficulties and hesitations, are hidden; and a yarn, of preternatural prescience, precision, and profit, is spun. By the vision of hindsight, all is made easy, simple — and apparently inevitable. A scientific paper is not a candid autobiography, but a cunningly contrived piece of rhetoric. It has only one purpose; it must persuade the reader of the veracity of the observer, his disinterestedness, his logical infallibility, and the complete necessity of his conclusions.

Critics with literary sensibilities comment wittily on the outrageous style of so much scientific writing. But this is not a particularly important issue in the attack on our system of communications. Scientists use jargon because they are obsessed with the desire to show that their work really does belong within a reputable context; they feel that it must conform to the conventions of the particular audience to which it is directed, and that they must use the appropriate technical language of the subject, however clumsy and contrived this may seem to the outsider. They favour the passive voice, the impersonal gender, and the latinized circumlocution, because these would seem to permit, in the circumstances, a climate of opinion within which, as it were, one can express relatively positive assertions in a tentative tone to which one would not be utterly committed if it should happen that complete coincidence had not been achieved with objective reality. This sort of shyness is not just a trick for escaping when one turns out to be wrong; it is a device of "inverted rhetoric" by which an apparently modest and disinterested tone enhances the acceptability of one's utterances.

2. Referees Essential

External censorship of scientific papers is, of course, the function of the anonymous referees. Every professional scientist soon becomes aware of these mysterious deities, who must be appeased with all manner of absurd reformulations and sacrifices of beloved passages of text. In due course, he will be invited to take on this mask himself, and will roar like any ass in a lion's skin to frighten his junior colleagues. As you will learn at any laboratory coffee club, the editing and refereeing of journals is a fertile source of folklore, anecdotes, grumbling, and bad feeling.

I would argue, nevertheless, that this also is an essential element of our system of scientific publication. We must be able to rely on the basic accuracy and honesty of what we read in other people's papers, for we are always using their results in the construction of our own researches, and simply cannot find the time to repeat all their experiments, measurements, calculations or arguments for ourselves. Scientific authors are often wrong, but their errors are usually made in good faith. I cannot see how this innocence could be preserved, against careerist pressures to publish, if there were no scrutiny by expert referees. The communication problem would be ten times worse if we had to wade through tomes of irresponsible nonsense in a search for a few reputable papers. Even the most commercial of daily newspapers distinguishes in its layout between genuine news and mere advertising. It is true that an experienced scientist "internalizes" the critical standards of the referees, and can be relied on to be honest, accurate, and reasonably plausible, in all his writings; but that does not justify the abolition of the referees — any more than the habitual honesty of middle-aged bank clerks would justify the abolition of the fraud squad.

These are the characteristics of the primary system of scientific communication; it is not, perhaps, very elegant as literature, even when bound in red leather volumes with gold lettering, but it has a purpose which it serves well enough. What are the defects?

To some extent, they are contradictory. One demand is for greater speed of publication. It is argued that the strategy of the individual research worker is so strongly influenced by the information that he receives from his contemporaries and rivals, that a good deal of scientific effort is wasted by multiple discovery or by one scientist being unaware of relevant results that have already been obtained elsewhere because of the delays of publication.

Now, in the first place, I think that the supposed wastage from this cause is somewhat exaggerated. A simultaneous discovery by independent researchers is not necessarily such a bad thing; it is disappointing for those concerned, but it is an admirable form of confirmation of the supposed result. It is seldom that there is just a particular discovery to be made — like finding the very sixpence that one has just dropped — but rather a complex of ideas and phenomena which may be illuminated in different ways by different investigators. Nobody, surely, regrets that Heisenberg and Schrödinger should have simultaneously "discovered" what turned out to be the same quantum mechanics; they arrived by somewhat different routes, and alighted at different stations on the way, so they have somewhat different stories to tell us about their journey. Scientific experiments and calculations are often repeated, as serious "original" investigations, to demonstrate a new technique, or to improve the accuracy of the results. It is tiresome to be forestalled; but obsession with sheer immediacy and speed is a neurotic symptom, mainly to be observed in certain fashionable fields where too many people are chasing too few ideas. If this is how you feel, then I advise you to look for a more profitable field of study where your innate originality may be more fruitful!

I am talking here about "pure" science without an immediate application. The situation is rather different in applied research and development, where the best available solution to some particular problem is being sought, and where the rewards of success — or the cost of failure — may be measured in millons of pounds. The hindrances to the immediate spread of new knowledge are not then so much in the machinery of publications, but rather the barriers of secrecy deliberately raised around industrial and military research. The communication system of technology is quite different from that of pure science, having different ends, different norms, and altogether different standards of morality. Applied scientists and technologists do, indeed, seek a great deal of information from the literature of basic science, but my impression is that they are seldom sufficiently instructed to be able to benefit from the very latest, as yet unpublished, research findings.

3. Speed of Communication

What are the natural time constants of research? These have not been studied in great depth, and probably vary greatly from one discipline to another, and from one epoch to another. At the peak of a revolution, for example, as depicted by Watson[3] in *The Double Helix*, a few days or weeks may see the breaking of the wave; on the other hand, in the formulation of the question to be answered, a decade may not be too long for successful rumination and significant progress. In general, I would confirm the observations of Garvey[4], who found that the various stages of hypothesis, design of apparatus, experiment, testing, confirmation, critical analysis, informal discussion, writing up, and so on, take months or years to complete, so that the interval of about four months between the receipt of a typescript and its publication in a reputable journal is not a significant proportion of the time required to "make a discovery".

The conventional system does not lack the means of quick publication when this is called for. For nearly a century, *Nature* has published "letters" reporting important new discoveries within a few weeks of notification — for example, the first observation of a pulsar was announced on February 24, 1968, in a letter dated February 9. Given that word of the discovery had already been spread by telephone, teleprinter, daily newspaper, jet plane, and first class railway carriage, to everyone who had a professional interest in the subject, this seems quite fast enough for a definitive formal announcement. Let us also recall, more modestly, that only about one paper in ten thousand is so startling as to set the scientific world a-jangling, so that a very small number of quick-publication journals would be quite enough — provided that all the little shepherd boys can be taught not to cry "Wolf!" too often.

We find, nevertheless, that these neurotic, overcompetitive tendencies are being pandered to by the publishers and the scientific literature. It is now considered necessary to have a "letters" journal in every field — not only *Physics Letters*, but soon, perhaps, titles as absurdly specialized as, say, *III–V Semiconductor Letters* or

Gravitational Wave Letters. These are legitimate media for the publication of very small items of knowledge of the sort that often arise in the course of research or teaching — a better measurement of a standard parameter, a shorter proof of a well-known theorem, a correction to a conventional misunderstanding — but their claims to immediacy and importance are almost entirely misplaced.

Another development, which has been accorded almost official approval (see debate between M. Moravcsik and S. Pasternack[5]), is the systematic exchange of "preprints" of papers that are being submitted for publication. This procedure has two roots; it stems from the ancient courtesy of writing private letters to distant colleagues in advance of the official journals, and from the custom, developed during the Second World War, of circulating reports (often secret) of the results of researches to all interested parties, quite independently of the usual channels of publication.

In itself, there is no great harm in this custom, which can often serve a useful purpose. In the days of the unevenly cut stencil, smudged through on to a sort of feeble blotting paper, such preprints were, of course, impossible to read anyway; elegant electric typing, Xeroxed to look like the original, wrapped up in beautiful arty covers, does not nowadays make the contents any more plausible. Goodness knows how much money is spent on this form of self-advertisement — the airmail postage alone, on the material I receive, would pay my journal subscriptions.

What was wrong was the proposal to develop "preprint exchanges" that would attempt to make this haphazard custom truly efficient. Each author was to send his typescript to a central office where it would be duplicated and sent out to everybody else in the group. Membership of the group would be controlled by some procedure of authentication and introduction; no doubt after the sponsoring body had grown tired of subsidizing the duplicating and office costs, subscriptions would have been solicited from the various contributors. It is clear that a marvellous discovery had been made by the proponents of this scheme: they had invented, not the wheel, but the scientific journal of a learned society. Given another decade or so, they might even have rediscovered the referee!

4. Informal Exchange

To my mind, it is tragic that so many excellent and experienced scientists should have fallen into this trap, and encouraged vast expenditure on preprints and such like, instead of putting all their weight into the reform of the existing learned societies and the improvement of their journals. As I have said, the necessary delays occasioned by refereeing and decent printing are not really gross; a journal that gets a year behind in publication just needs a thorough kicking by its subscribers and con-

tributors: to supersede it by yet another machine liable to just the same faults is sheer folly.

At the heart of the matter is the fallacy of giving too much significance to the role of "informal" communication. Of course this is very important indeed — all those private letters, conversations over drinks, chatty seminars, conferences, meetings, lecture tours, and such like. It has always been understood that much scientific knowledge actually travels in this way — especially those key attitudes, techniques, and insights that can only be transferred by prolonged contagion. The conventional footnote: "Mephistopheles (private communication)", indicating the importance of a whisper in the ear at a crucial moment, is often more honorific than the citation of a printed paper, and a courtesy that should always be accorded.

But the informal cannot, by definition, be made specific and rigid. One of the major purposes of the whole scientific enterprise is to draw from the confused, vague, inchoate "stuff of experience" a few precise, clearly defined, "objective" (that is, if I may use the term, "consensible") concepts, principles, or observations. It is essential that scientific work should be "written up" in full, with all the details of technique, interpretation, and logical limitation necessary to persuade the reader of the truth of the conclusions — or at least sufficient for him to repeat the experiment or calculation for himself. The primary scientific literature is sometimes referred to, slightly deprecatingly, as "archival", as if it were a sort of antiquarian record of deeds done and now finished. That is very far from the case. There is a long period during which they are active documents, cited by other workers and relied on in detail for later developments. A paper is useless unless it has these qualities of precision, for it cannot otherwise be accorded the critical judgment of the scholarly community, and thus be accepted or rejected as part of the whole body of scientific knowledge. I am not denying the value of hints, intuitions, speculations, and other means of spreading new ideas; but it must always be clear, in the mind of the listener or reader, whether or not, so to speak, the witness is on oath. Any reputable scientist who allows his research work to be widely published in permanent form must take the consequences for any errors that it contains; he cannot repudiate the responsibility for misleading his colleagues by saying that of course it was only an "informal" communication, and hence to be understood only in a Pickwickian sense.

5. Information in Print

The other great objection to present procedures of scientific publication is the vast bulk of material that is printed and has to be stored on the library shelves. More serious than the cost of infinite numbers of new bookcases is the difficulty of finding out what each of these papers has to say, and deciding whether we ought to study it more closely. This is called the information explosion, and the problem is said to be that of information retrieval.

The conventional system is not without its resources against this suffocating foe. The standard weapon is the abstract journal, where short summaries of all the papers in the current primary journals are printed in classified order, so that they can be noticed when they first appear, or rediscovered through the index if they happen to be forgotten. The first charge on the foundation of a new scientific laboratory should be a subscription to the appropriate abstract periodical, which will need to be consulted daily by the scientific staff. This sort of publication is indispensable to the scholarly world, for it is the only overall index to the archives of a discipline.

A lot of mud gets slung at abstract journals, mainly by those who do not think at all about the difficulties of editing and publishing them. Consider, for example, the practical problems of getting an up to date, reliable, accurately printed summary in English of, say, the articles (in Mongolian) in the *Proceedings of the National Academy of Sciences of Outer Mongolia*, issued thrice yearly and sent by a slow boat from China. Or decide for yourself how you ought to classify a contribution entitled "Localization of electrons in ordered and disordered systems: I, Percolation of classical particles": does it belong under electron theory, or classical mechanics, or percolation theory, or ordered systems, or disordered systems — or actually under metals, liquid, or even semiconductors, amorphous? The tasks of abstracting, translating, classifying, and editing such publications demand a high degree of skill and scientific knowledge. The cost of such organizational skill is not negligible; there has been a tendency to take for granted that it can be done on a shoestring, in spite of the tremendous increase in the bulk and complexity of the material to be dealt with. Most scientific papers now carry abstracts prepared by their authors, very often with translations into the major scientific languages, so that some of the burdens have been eased, but it is still a big job that has to be done to the utmost of perfection.

It is not surprising that such systems have attracted the attention of the technicians of data storage — the computer engineers. "Why", they ask, "should one bother to have all this stuff printed in great fat books, when it could be stored so economically on magnetic tapes, and called up for instant perusal by pressing the appropriate buttons? Here is an activity ripe for electronic mechanization." This is a laudable aim; but the idealized system that they describe is still a long way from realization. It is instructive to look at the difficulties to be overcome.

The first obstacle is that the amount of "information" to be stored is very large and miscellaneous. What the searcher wants, eventually, is a chance to glance at the text of every scientific article relevant to his particular problem. Nobody is going to go to the tremendous expense of putting on to magnetic tape the full text, or

even the abstracts, of all the scientific journals that have ever been printed. The labour of setting them into type in the first place was expensive enough; who is going to press all the teletype keys those billions of times so that the words may eventually be reproduced once more, rather less elegantly, as computer print-out? The fact is that in a good scientific library, with the journals well bound, and properly classified, it is remarkably easy to collect together the actual volumes one needs, and lay them open on the table for this sort of perusal. The mechanical storage of documents by microfilming videotape, or other means cannot yet compete with the shelf of books for occasional access — if you know what you are looking for!

6. Mechanized Indexing

The emphasis then shifts to the indexing and classifying phases of the operation. Can a machine system be devised that will turn up the addresses of all scientific articles that are relevant to the problem in hand? This is an extremely interesting question, of which considerable study has been made (for example, ref. 6). It turns out to be only part of the general problem of the classification of information. A computer can certainly be used to search for complex combinations of topics described by a collection of key words — for example, electron, localized, disordered system — which could not easily be located with precision in an ordinary classified index. There are tricks that can be played, like going through a list of approximate synonyms of the topic names presented by the enquirer. It is even possible (though expensive and laborious) to have the computer scan through the texts of all the abstracts in its store, so as to throw up, say, all the articles that contain the word "percolation".

But all such procedures are subject to the fundamental law of information retrieval — as the recall ratio increases, the precision ratio decreases. In other words, if you try to get hold of nearly every paper that there is on your chosen subject, you will be faced with a collection in which a high proportion of the material is obviously irrelevant; in your attempt to find out all about the percolation of electrons in semiconductors, you will be inundated with papers about the percolation of water through the foundations of dams! As with the analogous problem of machine translation, the difficulties arise from the imprecision and metaphorical flexibility of language. The limitations of a particular system of automated retrieval will really depend on the nature of the scientific information being sought, and (as with the most elementary indexing operation) the fundamental skills of those who put the data on the tapes in the first place.

It is thus by no means certain that automatic information retrieval systems should immediately replace the conventional abstract journals with their comprehensive classified indexes. Computerized typesetting is playing an important part in the simultaneous compilation of primary journals, indexes, abstract journals, "title" journals, and their various author and subject indexes, but this is only a technical refinement of the conventional system. There are also very interesting possibilities for the retrieval of precise data in those branches of science where exact description and classification are rigorously prescribed, such as biological taxonomy and structural chemistry. The question of the identity of a particular chemical compound, as defined by one of those pretty pictures of interconnected hexagons that decorate the pages of the biochemical literature, is capable of strict formal analysis, so that a pharmaceutical company could make doubly sure that their new pet product had never previously been described or synthesized before they launched it on suffering humanity.

Another use to which computers have been put is in the preparation of citation indexes. This is a new device[7] where references are given for all papers that have cited a particular paper published previously. By revealing the interconnexions of the scientific literature so clearly, this sort of index is of great interest to those who study the scholarly community at work, and it can also be used to search for possible relevant material, as a supplement to the ordinary abstracts. Unfortunately, it is a very expensive publication, which is not yet worth its marginal utility except to the very largest institutions.

7. Inefficient Computers

The real reason why computer storage is not very efficient in these circumstances is that verbal information is a rather passive material, which can only be processed effectively by the human mind. There is so very little that one can really do to a classified index of abstracts on tape, except to run through it now and then looking for particular items. One cannot add together, or subtract, or logically collate, or Fourier transform, or determine the convexity of, or what you may call it, such a miscellaneous set. The specific technical advantages of a computer — the power to perform vast numbers of such operations at enormous speed — are seldom exploited. We can ask it to produce six different kinds of index — by name of author, by subject, by institution, by date, by journal, by country — and then what? Some of the writing on automatic information retrieval is really an attempt to invent more uses for it to justify the enormous initial cost.

Much effort, for example, has been expended on the idea that what everybody really has been waiting for is a daily alerting service that will tell each one of us about the latest papers in the topics which interest us. Thus, I shall have given instructions, on a punch card, to be kept up to date on "the theory of liquids", on "electron theory of metals", on the "structure of alloys" and on "lattice conduction in solids"; hey presto, the latest abstracts or papers on just these topics will be waiting on my desk each morning by courtesy of Electronic Alerting

Services for Yokels (EASY). But I don't really care that much about what everybody is doing in all these subjects; and anyway I have not the time to read through all this stuff carefully; and also I've got interested in spin waves again recently and have forgotten to inform EASY about this; and what I suddenly discovered last week was a paper published ten years ago which gave the solution to my problem in another form; and anyway I'm damned if I'm going to become the slave of this sort of guff, which is worse than the leaflets hopefully distributed by publishers; and I don't see why I should pay £100 a year for it out of my own pocket, when that would improve the lighting in the library, buy us decent blackboards, provide free tea for the whole research group, and could generally be spent more profitably. You see what I mean.

The cost of a powerful and efficient system of information retrieval is not negligible — and I believe that it can soon become uneconomic in basic research. But as I have already pointed out, when legal, military, and financial forces are in the field, as in many branches of technology, the failure to be aware of some small piece of published (or unpublished) knowledge may be very costly indeed. An industrial corporation, a government public health authority, a defence ministry, must invest heavily in this type of machinery — and must also try to buy the best men to run it. Within the realms of basic academic science the consequences of reduplication of published work are not so easily measurable, nor so gross. The conventional abstract journals provide more than enough material for effective searching. Indeed, one of the saddening impressions I brought back from a recent visit to physics laboratories in India and Pakistan was the inadequate use that was being made of the ordinary library facilities that were available. People were studying problems that had been posed in papers twenty years ago, and seemed not to have even looked at the more recent literature. We have many decades of progress to suffer before the conventional system of publication becomes obsolete in these surroundings.

8. Specialized Journals

The conventional system has another weapon up its sleeve: specialization. The bulk of science grows by a complex process in which old journals expand, and then subdivide, and new ones also arise in the interdisciplinary regions. It may even be claimed that the modern scientist need not read any more journals than his predecessors — he simply narrows his vision until he takes in about as much material as before, over a more limited and specialized range. This process seems to evolve with such statistical regularity that the dispersion of articles among the various journals can be described by an empirical mathematical law[8]. Goffman and Warren showed, for example, that about half the 10,000 articles in a bibliography on the disease schistosomiasis were to be found in less than fifty journals, even though there were nearly

1,000 other journals containing one article apiece on this particular topic. I suspect that the concentration of the really significant literature in this field is even more marked — that a dozen leading journals, with nearly a quarter of all the published papers, would contain most of the best work. In other words, a scientist active in this field would keep abreast of major current developments if he skimmed through the table of contents of these journals as they appeared, trusting to abstracts and review articles for news of cointributions in other media.

For it must be emphasized that the Matthew effect[9] is strongly at work here, as in all fields of social competition: "to him who hath, shall be given". A journal that begins to specialize in a particular topic attracts many papers on that topic, and is soon able to set a high standard that reinforces its prestige. One of the advantages of being an established expert in some branch of science is that one knows which are the most prestigious journals, and one has a ready entry, for oneself and one's pupils, to the most widely read publications with an international circulation.

Indeed, this can have most serious effects on the development of good scientific standards in many countries. The local journal of the national academy has too small a circulation, and is too diffuse in subject matter, to be an attractive vehicle of publication for the scientists of that country. They in their turn, by insisting on publishing their work in foreign or vaguely international journals, rob the local journal of its best material, thus depressing the apparent standard of research in that country.

Or is it now too late to save the general journals of the national academies and learned societies? Is it not more realistic to recognize that specialization of the organs of primary scientific publication serves a real purpose and should be encouraged rather than resisted? There are, for example, plans afoot to rationalize the spheres of intellectual interest of the various journals published by the various national physical societies of Europe, and thus give official recognition to the accomplished fact that the Italian journal specializes in elementary particle theory, that the Dutch journal is the leading international publication in statistical mechanics, and so on. Here is a way in which the conventional system of scientific publication can adapt and reform itself under pressure.

Of course, our friends the root and branch boys have not failed to put forward a "rationalized" scheme as the logical conclusion of this line of development. They would have us create a single centralized bureau of scientific publication, to which would be despatched typescripts (or would it be transcripts of telephone messages?) to be edited, refereed, classified, printed, and sent out in exactly pre-selected categories to licensed subscribers. I do not think I need to set out the objections to this modest proposal; it would be monopolistic, bureaucratic, fundamentally inefficient, blinkering and inflexible; scientific knowledge is not like bread, that can be manufactured by machines and distributed on a very large scale, provided that no one minds if it is as tasteless and formless as cotton wool; food for the mind requires to be prepared with a human touch. Indeed, the degree to which the publishing of primary papers in physics and chemistry in the United States is already centralized and mechanized deserves some critical thought.

9. Published Proceedings

Returning to the problem of finding one's way through the vast jungles of the literature, a continuing puzzle and offence to sensible scholars is the vogue for the publication of the papers presented at scientific conferences. One can understand the vanity of the organizers and participants, who love to see themselves in print, and the cost-benefit accountancy of administrators who feel they must have some tangible return for the expenses that have been incurred in getting everybody together for a few days — but why should anyone be willing to buy an expensive volume of short communications, inferior versions of proper papers, published several years after they were written and delivered? The answer is simple: a well planned conference, being a meeting of most of the "invisible college" of experts in a particular topic, is an occasion for general stocktaking, and the proceedings can be expected to give a fairly complete coverage of results achieved and work in progress at that epoch. In other words, a conference report, although inferior to conventional publications in speed, quality, and accessibility, can be used very effectively as a starting point for further search or research. Conceived apparently as a medium for quick, informal communication, it becomes a means of attack on the bulkiness of the literature.

But surely this need is much better met by review articles deliberately commissioned for this purpose. The growth of this class of secondary literature is an important feature of the conventional system of scientific communication in the past half century — a part of the machinery that is often ignored by the technocrats, but which really needs to be greatly strengthened.

In its narrow sense, a review article is little more than a classified bibliography — *a catalogue raisonné* of the primary literature, putting the results into order and commenting impartially on any obvious contradictions or controversies. The author is thought to have achieved his object if he has turned over every stone, and solemnly described every strange creature that he may have found thereunder. There are charming conventions of understatement that preserve the timid and pedantic writer from seeming to have offered any criticism of the nonsense he finds petrified in the sacred tablets of the primary journals. Fortunately, mild words like "discrepancy", "approximation", and "disagreement" are readily translated into "hopelessly inconsistent", "sadly erroneous", and "totally at loggerheads" by the experienced reader!

But a good review article, besides performing this archival function, should go much further. As I have emphasized, the primary literature is fragmentary, and only intelligible within the context of active research. It is a ridiculous, but commonly held, belief that the publication of the results of particular investigations is sufficient to create a body of knowledge. On the contrary; the information to be gleaned from a primary scientific paper is often about as meaningful as an entry in a telephone directory, or map reference in a military despatch; it only acquires significance by use, or by its place in a larger pattern, which must at some stage be made explicit. The job of the review writer is to sift and sort the primary observations and to delineate this larger pattern. He is neglecting his scientific duty if he does not offer criticism where it is justified, of if he fails to present a rational assessment of controversial matters within his province. It is only by such public re-appraisals that those who are not already expert in the subject can have any idea of the credibility of the innumerable results "reported in the literature".

10. Knowledge not Information

I cannot emphasize too strongly the importance of this activity of intellectual synthesis — a process of purification by recrystallization that must go through many stages, spread over many years, from the lecture by the chairman of a topical conference to the review article, monograph, textbook, encyclopaedia, and the *haute vulgarisation* of scientific journalism. Any notion that we may have about the nature of science includes the belief that something like an overall pattern is to be discovered and described. What we need is scientific knowledge — not more and more miscellaneous and unrelated information. The starting point for a search should not have to be an abstract journal or a computerized retrieval system — it should be an encyclopaedic treatise or textbook where the information has been transformed into an intelligible pattern of thought — if you like, a well-founded theory — from which can be deduced the characteristics of the particular datum, specimen, or phenomenon that we are studying.

Why is it so difficult to get this essential work done?[10] Why are most scientists so reluctant to spend time on the writing of reviews and monographs — to the extent that the American Physical Society, publishing tens of thousands of pages of primary science each year, has to fill many of the issues of *Reviews of Modern Physics* with conference reports, or with speculative articles masquerading as reviews? The collection and compilation of data are neglected. I am told that the prime task of biological taxonomy — the preparation of monographs summarizing the characteristics of, and reclassifying, large groups of related species — is now seriously undermanned. The treatises that do get written are often collective works, where each of a dozen experts spends a few months

on a review of what he considers his particular aspect of the subject, while the attempts of the editor to piece the material into a coherent whole are frustrated by the knowledge that the slightest criticism or attempted amendment of any one contribution will cost him endless controversy — and another year's delay before final publication.

It can be argued that the financial returns for such work are meagre, and indeed that scientific books will soon price themselves out of the market.[11] This is nonsense. Scientific books are as necessary to research as scientific instruments. What is the sum required to equip and maintain a laboratory; is it $10,000 per PhD per year? Five per cent of this would buy him most of the books that are published within his field, and would be regarded as lavish provision for a library. We must simply learn to spend this money, just as we have learned to buy cathode ray oscilloscopes, microscopes, cyclotrons, ultra-centrifuges, and secretarial assistance. Stinting on library costs is just silly! Anyway, according to the take-over panel, technical publishers are not doing so badly, thank you very much.

Nor do the royalties paid to authors have much significance. The amounts are not large, but nor are they trivial when considered as a supplement to a regular salary. The present situation is that a reasonably good monograph in a conventional scientific field sells 2,000 or more copies at about £5 each. At a rate of 10 per cent the author should get at least £1,000, on which he will, of course, have to pay tax. A very successful textbook writer could do much better than this, and make a good living from this profession alone. But this is not the point; for a university teacher, the writing of books is part of his legitimate duties, so that he may regard a royalty as a windfall, for which he has not had to slave additionally. I do not believe that reviews and treatises can really be bought for hard cash from those who should be writing them anyway, and I should be reluctant to make the financial returns so high as to prostitute what must be, in the end, a labour of love.

11. No Glory for Reviewers

Our present system of rewards and incentives in science does not encourage individuals to devote themselves for years on end to these critical synthesizing activities. "Recognition", by way of professional advancement and prestige, is given solely for primary research; has any citation for a scientific Nobel prize, or for election to a national academy, ever mentioned that the hero was the author of a valuable treatise or of the authoritative review that has since determined the course of research in his field? In a cold calculation of interest, the returns for bookwriting could never match the extra income to be won by getting promotion for successful research work. Who is prepared to spend four or five years learning the literature of a subject and trying to expound it intelligibly in 500 pages for the sake of only one more entry in his list of publications, of no greater apparent weight than a page and a half in *Physical Review Letters?*

But I am not going to propound some gimmicky scheme for prestigious prizes, review professorships, monographic fellowships of academies, and such like, to raise the status of the writing of treatises. The fact is that most professional scientists are willing enough to expound their ideas to suitably captive and ignorant audiences. Academics work hard at their lecture notes, and can be persuaded to expand these into university textbooks. The invitation to prepare a course for young research workers at a summer school is usually very acceptable; and although the notes, when eventually published, may lack polish and precision, they make up for this by freshness of style and lack of pedantry. I do not observe that *Scientific American* has any difficulty in coaxing material from active research workers of high standing, even though it must later be transformed by their editorial staff into the bland, uniform, strawberry-ice prose of a popular article.

Yet there is a coy reluctance to address oneself openly to other research workers in one's own, or neighboring, fields, for they are supposed to know it all already. I appreciate that such writing is often ephemeral, and may quickly be overtaken by new discoveries — but that applies to all original research. There is a strange avoidance of explicit statement of basic principles. It is somehow deemed improper to set out the evidence, boldly, for and against some speculative theory. We are supposed, each one of us, to be carrying on our own internal debates on all such matters — and it is assumed that we shall all, by some magical dispensation or providence, thereby arrive at the same goals of comprehension. There is no appreciation of the great range of expertise and learning even among fully fledged professionals, so that a whole system of fundamental principles may be held as self-evident by one group, and yet be quite unfamiliar to others. We greatly underestimate the degree to which a set of new ideas may develop, in the minds of other people, with the possibility of revolutionizing our

own point of view. At the research frontier, we are daunted by the very confusion and uncertainty of the knowledge we are to expound, instead of being challenged to make it clearer and more precise. Not only must we popularize our science to the layman; it is only by attempting to explain it to each other that we find out what we really know.

The trouble is, quite simply, a matter of philosophy. We are so obsessed with the notions of discovery and individual originality that we fail to realize that scientific research is essentially a corporate activity, in which the community achieves far more than the sum of the efforts of its members. It is not enough to observe, experiment, theorize, calculate, and communicate; we must also argue, criticize, debate, expound, summarize, and otherwise transform the information that we have obtained individually into reliable, well established, public knowledge.

References

1. ZIMAN, J. M., *Public Knowledge* (Cambridge University Press, London, 1968).
2. BERNAL, J. D., *The Social Function of Science* (Routledge, London, 1939).
3. WATSON, J., *The Double Helix* (Weidenfeld and Nicolson, London, 1968).
4. GARVEY, W. D., and GRIFFITH, B. C., *Science,* **146,** 1955 (1964).
5. *Physics Today,* **19,** 62 (1966).
6. *Communication in Science: Documentation and Automation* (edit. by de Reuck, A., and Knight, J.) (Churchill, London, 1967).
7. GARFIELD, E., and SCHER, I., *Science Citation Index* (1961) (Philadelphia Institute for Scientific Information, 1963).
8. GOFFMAN, W., and WARREN, K. S., *Nature,* **221,** 1205 (1969).
9. MERTON, R. K., *Science,* **159,** 56 (1968).
10. HERRING, C., *Physics Today,* **21,** 27 (1968).
11. BENJAMIN, C., *Sci. Res.,* **3,** No. 19, 32 (1968).

11 Research for Psychologists at the Interface of the Scientist and His Information System

EDWIN B. PARKER
WILLIAM J. PAISLEY
American Psychologist
Vol. 21, No. 11, November, 1966

How do scientists obtain the information they need? Since the Royal Society Scientific Information Conference (1948) first focused attention on it, this question has come to be asked by an increasing number of investigators. Directed as it is to the understanding and prediction of scientists' needs for information and to their information-seeking and information-processing behavior, it is clearly a question for psychological research.

At least until recently, research into this and related questions was better known to the documentation research community than to psychologists. An understanding of user needs and information-seeking habits is important to those who design and implement scientific information systems and services. The "literature notes" section of *American Documentation,* recently expanded into a separate quarterly journal, *Documentation Abstracts,* has for some time had a "use and user studies" section. Menzel's (1966) chapter in the forthcoming *Annual Review of Information Science and Technology* (Cuadra, 1966) is titled "Information Needs and Uses in Science and Technology."

In the next few pages we shall summarize representative findings on scientists' use of information, comment on conceptualization and theory concerning information use, discuss seven methodologies that promise continued utility for investigations in this area, and suggest further research that particularly needs the attention of psychologists.

1. Scientists' Use of Information: Some Representative Findings

Prior to the Royal Society Conference (1948), studies of the information system of science were studies of archives — reference counts of most-cited books and journals. Two papers delivered at the Conference shifted the emphasis by reporting patterns of archive *use*. Bernal (1948) collected data concerning use of journals from British scientists at several government, university, and private research institutes. Urquhart (1948) surveyed users of the London Science Museum Library to determine what references led them to request publications, whether the publications proved to contain needed information, and for what purposes the information was being sought.

Since both focused narrowly on the serial literature,

neither Bernal's nor Urquhart's study would be considered adequate today. Accumulating data have not been kind to normative assumptions of ways in which scientists *ought* to use information. We have been forced to broaden our investigations to include informal (chiefly interpersonal) systems, "accidental" acquisition of useful information, "inefficient" and "irrational" information-seeking, and so on.

Weak as these precedent studies were, they prepared the way for satisfactory efforts of the 1950s. In 1952 Herner (1954) obtained personal interviews with a large sample of scientists affiliated with Johns Hopkins University. His data suggest differences in information use among scientists in the various disciplines, between "pure" and "applied" scientists, and even between two equivalent groups of applied scientists (engineers) who differed only in departmental affiliation.

Herner's was the first substantial study in which the formal and informal communication systems of science were explored jointly. It was also the first study in which attributes of scientists were systematically examined in relation to information use. Unfortunately, as we continue to discover, a scientist's use of information is not explained by single attributes, and at the time of Herner's study the field had several years to wait for its first explicitly multivariate analysis. We still speculate on Herner's finding that pure scientists are literature dependent while applied scientists are colleague dependent in seeking information, and we still lack a fully controlled analysis to interpret this difference.

Shaw (1956) conducted two diary studies, one year apart, with the same group of United States Forest Service scientists and technologists. He found scientists' rank to be a further correlate of information use — higher ranked scientists spending more time with library materials and subscribing to more journals (an artifact of the number of association memberships?). Although archival sources were most often mentioned in the diaries, from 11% (in chemistry) to 22% (in engineering) of all print sources entered in diaries were bulletins, reports, and other nonarchival publications.

Publications sought by the diarists conformed to the "standard curve" of age almost invariably observed in this field (and systematically explored by Cole, 1963, and Bourne, 1963): Journal use decreases as journal age increases in an exponential function with parameters that change markedly from one field of science to another.

Urquhart (1948) had found that verbal recommendations accounted for only 16% of all references that led to information seeking, as against 33% of all references found in abstracts and digests. Shaw found that personal recommendations accounted for 24% of all references that led to information seeking, while only 8% came from abstracts and reviews. This difference, also observed in other studies involving British and American scientists, suggests that there might be British and American "styles of information seeking" in which print and interpersonal sources are valued differently. Many artifacts challenge these comparisons, however.

Ackoff and Halbert (1958) made approximately 25,000 observations of the daily activities of about 1,500 chemists in universities and industrial organizations. They found that the amount of time spent in scientific communication varied greatly (from 16% to 61%) in the sample. The mean percentage of total time spent in scientific communication, 33%, may be compared with means of 10% in business communication, 6% in thinking and planning alone, 6% in equipment setup, 23% in equipment use, 6% in data treatment, and 10% in personal and social activities. Therefore it may be said that scientific communication is the chemist's modal daily activity.

Oral communication occupied somewhat more time than written communication (19% to 14%). Of the latter, 9% involved unpublished materials.

The most significant correlation observed among activities links scientific communication to thinking and planning alone, suggesting that both activities occur during the same phase of a research project. A significant negative correlation between scientific communication and equipment use suggests that these activities dominate different phases of a project.

Several studies in the late 1950s began to emphasize the importance of interpersonal sources and the unplanned acquisition of useful information. Under the title, "How Scientists Actually Learn of Work Important to Them" (with implicit stress on the adverb), Glass and Norwood (1959) reported that casual conversation was the most-mentioned first source of information on items chosen by each scientist-respondent as "representing scientific concepts and research of major or crucial significance to the development of his own work."

Medical scientists studied by Herner (1959) mentioned colleagues second only to their own previous work in response to the question, "Do you recall where you got the idea (or inspiration) for your present or most recent project?" Herner summarizes his analysis: "The primary conclusion that can be drawn from the foregoing paragraphs is a reaffirmation of the significant role of personal contacts in the getting and transmitting of scientific and technical information [p. 283]."

It was left to Menzel (1958), however, to observe that individual accidents summed to a systemic regularity, that the scientist in a rich information environment might reasonably depend on accidents to keep up to date and even to learn answers to specific questions. Menzel's interviews with chemists, biochemists, and zoologists uncovered many instances in which an elaborate interpersonal network ultimately linked the scientist who had information and the scientist who needed it.

Menzel's study also provided the field with its first significant taxonomy of information functions, namely: (*a*) providing scientists with available answers to specific questions, (*b*) keeping scientists abreast of developments in their chosen areas of attention, (c) enabling scientists to review recent years' work in other areas (d) giving testimony to the reliability of a source of information, (e) broadening a scientist's area of attention, (f) furnishing the scientist with feedback to his own assertions, (g) helping the scientist to orient his work within the totality of research endeavors.

Although the function served by information had largely been ignored in precedent studies, Menzel found an intimate connection between function and source-turned-to. For instance, books are the modal source for reviewing recent work in other areas, and conversations are the modal source for feedback.

The thoughtfulness of Menzel's discussion in this study and in his review of the field (1960) signaled the end of the beginning of research on scientific information use. Investigators now are challenged to do justice to the full complexity of the scientific information system.

Well-conducted studies of the 1960s are impossible to summarize because of the range of variables they encompass. The American Psychological Association Project on Scientific Information Exchange in Psychology now includes about 20 studies and substudies, each exploring in depth one aspect of psychologists' use of information.

From the aggregate data of these studies, Garvey and Griffith (1963) have assembled an empirical "map" of the information system serving American psychologists. One dimension of the map is time — roughly 5 years from the inception of a typical research project to its mention in the *Annual Review of Psychology*, with oral dissemination occurring chiefly in the second year, formal publication and distribution of reprints in the third year, abstracting in the fourth year, etc. The second dimension of the map is proximity to the reporting scientist; an "ingroup" receives preprints and oral communications that others do not. The two dimensions interact: Those close to the reporting scientist learn of his work sooner.

Findings on information use in the research environment. There is a body of research on the interaction between situation factors, information inputs, and performance or productivity. The research environment, like other environments in which people live and work, seems definitely to affect information-processing behavior, although we have not dealt adequately with at least two artifacts: (a) scientists found in any research environment are a self-selected population; personal attributes may affect both the choice of environment and information-processing behavior; (b) an environment is structured partly by the tasks that are performed in it; tasks may affect both the environment and information-processing behavior.

Hertz and Rubenstein (1953) found that amount of communication varied with function in the research team (e.g., higher among those with administrative functions, lower among those with design functions), with institutional rank, with the duration of the research project, and with the size of the research team. They also found in-

triguing communication cycles throughout the work day and the work week.

Meltzer (1956) sought to account for differences in productivity on the basis of such factors as funds available for research, freedom in the choice of research topics, and type of research organization. His data indicate that type of research organization is not related to productivity by itself, but the "funds" and "freedom" factors are positively correlated with productivity and negatively correlated with each other. In combination the two factors interact: if either is low, productivity is relatively low; if both are high, productivity is very high.

In a study of medical scientists affiliated with a government research organization, Pelz (1956) found that performance (assessed by a panel of the scientist's peers) was correlated with two interacting factors: frequency of contact with colleagues and similarity of those colleagues and the scientist in terms of "science orientation" and "prestige orientation." Scientists who interacted daily with *dissimilar* colleagues were higher in rated performance than scientists who interacted daily with similar colleagues, but higher performance seemed to be associated with similarity in value orientation among scientists who were more isolated. This finding is nonetheless interesting for the variety of artifacts that challenge it (e.g., busy high-performance scientists may have won the prerogative of associating with whom they please; interaction patterns may be a consequence of performance, not vice versa).

A study of bioscientists by Shilling, Bernard, and Tyson (1964) focused on two personal attributes, age and sex, as copredictors with environment factors of communication patterns and productivity. Laboratory policies affecting communication received unusual attention, much to the benefit of the analysis. It was found, for instance, that unrestricted long-distance telephoning correlates highly with success in obtaining information but not with productivity, while unrestricted travel correlates highly both with information success and with productivity. A finding reminiscent of Pelz's analysis was the correlation of productivity with diversity of research interests in the laboratory. Again, the direction of causality (if any) is unclear.

If no coherent pattern of scientific information use emerges from these findings, the fault should be attributed to the complexity of the problem and not to the energy or ingenuity of the many investigators who have confronted it. The keys to progress, better theory and better methods, are slowly being shaped.

2. Toward a Theory of Information Use

The first 20 years of research on scientists' use of information concentrated on collecting better data. Imaginative development of methodology is still needed, as will be discussed below, and more data will be required. But special attention should be given to the explication of information use concepts and the formulation of testable propositions relating information use to antecedents and consequences. One example of the need for explication should suffice. If the "utility" of an information service is a function of the "relevance" of the information it brings to the scientist, and perhaps also of the "user satisfaction" and scientific productivity it generates, then we should agree on the meaning of these terms, both conceptually and operationally.

With the notable exception of Derek Price's work (see Price, 1963), the few propositions that have appeared in the literature of scientific information have not ventured far from the data that inspired them. Mote (1962), for instance, related amount of information requested to the diffuseness of the scientist's subject area (an intriguing variable for the study of information use in behavioral science). He was able to operationalize the number of information requests through one channel only, the corporation library, and his trichotomous "diffuseness" index was defined ad hoc, by subject areas within the corporation's research sphere. The functional relationship of diffuseness and information use was left largely unexplored (i.e., does a diffuse subject area require a larger volume of information to be processed by each scientist, or do scientists who enjoy working in such areas also enjoy processing a large volume of information?).

McLaughlin, Rosenbloom, and Wolek (1965) have made the most systematic effort thus far to bring behavioral theory to bear on the analysis of information use data. Summary statements such as the following may not yet represent a theory of information seeking, but they go beyond the "brute empiricism" of most analyses in the field:

> We believe that the behavior of engineers seeking information to meet specific needs is largely *programmed* in the sense that specific patterns of behavior, relatively stable over time, are invoked under such circumstances. . . . We believe that a major factor behind this implicit strategy is the perceived cost of information seeking. . . . [V]alue [in the sources] must be in line with the average cost of using them [p. 29].

Even so, their propositions are very close to their data. As an example, the proposition, "The incidence of 'oriented' search falls as job title rises," contains a simple variable (job title) instead of a concept (rank or function) that could be functionally related to the search mode. Surely it is not the scientist's job title per se that accounts for his mode of search.

An excessively critical examination of these propositions seems a bit unfair. The investigators could have followed precedent in the field, discussing isolated fragments of behavior, without reference to an integrative theory. The field benefits from their choice of the more vulnerable course.

3. Methods for Study of Information Use

The study of scientific information use has no methodology it can call uniquely its own. This is not surprising: Information use is a behavior, and data are collected on any behavior by asking people about it, by observing its occurrence, or by examining its artifacts (e.g., documents). The methodologies that now constitute the field's repertory are interesting, however, in their diversity and in their adaptation to the special problem of measuring some aspect of information use or communication.

Questionnaire, Interview, and Diary Studies

To guide the choice among these methods, a distinction has been made between typical or habitual information use and "critical-incident" information use. Typical behaviors prove to be reportable in a self-administered questionnaire (cf. Wuest, 1965) although we expect some normative bias when recall is less than perfect. Given a high level of response, the self-administered questionnaire technique is probably sounder than its critics have implied, even if individual questions have justifiably been challenged.

"Critical-incident" reports are better obtained through personal interviews, notwithstanding the successful use of a self-administered questionnaire for this purpose by McLaughlin, Rosenbloom, and Wolek (1965). The critical-incident approach first appeared prominently in this field in Herner's (1954, 1959) well-structured personal interviews and has since come to be regarded as a particularly useful focus for interviewer probing. A recent improvement in critical-incident methodology is the concept of an "information chunk," introduced by the Auerbach Corporation (1965) in its study of Department of Defense research personnel. Defined as "the smallest quantity of information required to answer a task-related question," the "information chunk" permits partitioning a critical-incident into a series of information-seeking behaviors.

If measurement of typical information use invites normative bias, the critical-incident approach is never more reliable than the chosen time sample. If, as in the McLaughlin, Rosenbloom, and Wolek (1965) study, a single corporation provides the entire sample of respondents, it is important to know of corporate activities that might create an atypical time sample. For instance, the corporation library may be undergoing reorganization, with disruption of services. If, as in the Auerbach (1965) study, a national sample of researchers is drawn, localized time sample anomalies merely contribute to error variance. Even in this case, however, it is not impossible that the *national* system is undergoing some perturbation, such as a security scare.

Two similar methods of study, the diary and the solution-development record (respectively among the oldest and the newest methods in the field), stand midway between the typical-behavior and the critical-incident approaches. If diary recording of activities continues for several days or weeks, then the obtained data are rich enough to reflect typical behavior. If each information use is related to part of an ongoing task, then data are obtained on a series of critical incidents. Unfortunately, scientists are not the most conscientious diary keepers we might wish to have. From the earliest much-cited diary study (Bernal, 1948) to recent ones (such as Garvey & Griffith, 1963), the level of noncooperation has been relatively high. Even among the cooperators, there has been evidence of disregarded instructions: Hogg and Smith (1959) reported that some scientists in their sample were neglecting the diary, filling in several days at a time, and that others were saving the entire project "until they were free to do some reading." Shaw (1965) examined library records to supplement his diaries; discrepancies between self-reports and recorded behavior were great enough to lead him to conclude that "the diary method, even with better than average cooperation and supervision, is not reliable enough to justify further studies over extended periods of time [p. 60]."

The solution-development record (Allen, 1965) is in effect a diary, but the basic entries are a scientist's estimates of the likelihood of various solutions to the problem on which he is working. A change in estimates over time implies information input, and an interviewer follows up such a change by questioning the scientist about his recent use of information.

The potential of these techniques — self-administered questionnaires, interviews, diaries — has by no means been exhausted. Nearly 20 years after the Royal Society Scientific Information Conference (1948), we still lack reliable base-line data on information use by field of science, by type of research, by location of research center, by personal attributes of the scientist, etc.

Participant-Observer Studies

Participant observers were effectively used by Ackoff and Halbert (1958) in the study cited above in which approximately 25,000 records of the daily activities of chemists were obtained. The behavior of each chemist at each observation was coded into categories of communication, equipment activity, data treatment, personal and social activities, etc. When the chemist was observed to be communicating, the activity was further coded according to channel, source person (or receiver), and phase (reading, writing, hearing, telling). Unlike the scientist, the participant observer has no reason to embellish the record (e.g., to show high use of a prestigious information source). Since participant observers can be trained collectively in record-keeping procedures, it is more justifiable to compare their records across several scientists than to compare self-kept records of the same scientists. The primary disadvantage of participant observation is

that the observer can collect data only when the scientist is within his range of observation. In the Ackoff and Halbert study, the range of observation was restricted to the scientist's laboratory.

There is one variant of the participant-observer technique that might be useful in determining scientists' needs for information. The provision of an "information assistant" for each scientist during the period of study would provide an expanded information service that the scientist could use. The assistant would presumably have some knowledge of the scientist's subject field and be trained to use all of the relevant information services available in the scientist's field. He could serve as an additional interface between the scientist and all of the available information services. The time and energy of the information assistant would substitute for the time and energy of the scientist in providing additional information or information in a more useful form. Such a technique, although obviously expensive, should permit the determination of information needs not being met by the present flow of information to the scientist.

Sociometric Analysis

Scientists talk to one another at conventions and cocktail parties. They learn of research related to their own through correspondence and telephone conversations. They visit other research centers and exchange preprints. The incidence and perceived utility of such information sources may be measured by questionnaire and interview techniques. In addition, there is a well-developed research methodology that has been relatively ignored in studies of scientific information flow: sociometric analysis. Studies of the influence of interpersonal relations among physicians on time of adoption of new drugs (Coleman, Katz, & Menzel, 1966; Coleman, Menzel, & Katz, 1958) provide an excellent precedent.

Price (1963) presents an insightful discussion of what he calls "invisible colleges" of scientists. Using historical records, he generates many ideas about scientific communication patterns that should be tested by examining the network of acquaintance patterns of individual scientists in relation to their communication to obtain scientific information. It would be useful to examine systematically the extent to which informal communication flows within groups of scientists in the same research specialty. The acquaintance patterns and the extent of social contact should be examined. The amount and kind of scientific communication (whether formal or informal) between individuals with similar research interests (i.e., in the same invisible college) could be compared with the amount and kind of communication between individuals with different research interests. Innovations such as formalized preprint distribution, suggested for physics by Moravcsik (1965) and debated by Moravcsik and Pasternack (1966), would be easier to evaluate if more data on informal communication networks were available.

Connections among documents, rather than people, have been studied by citation analysis (Garfield, Sher, & Torpie, 1964; Kessler, 1963; Price, 1965). Reciprocal citation patterns among psychological journals were examined by Xhignesse and Osgood (1963). The primary utility of such studies is historical description, although the method is also used to develop retrieval techniques and to measure the links between subfields of science.

Experiments and Quasi Experiments in Field Settings

Occasionally there are opportunities to go beyond passive observation to a design that qualifiess as an experiment or as a quasi experiment (cf. Campbell & Stanley, 1963), even when the scientists are take *in situ*. Allen (1964) took advantage of a unique situation in which many teams of scientists were competing to find the best solution to a common task: preparing research and development proposals in competition for a government contract. Although proposal teams were not randomly assigned to conditions, this strategy improves greatly upon survey methodology by controlling extraneous factors related to the task. The quality of each proposal was evaluated by the responsible government agency, and laboratory policies and information inputs were studied as predictors of quality.

In Allen's study the "request for proposal" was the experimental stimulus that set the proposal teams in motion. In other studies an innovation in the information system has served as the stimulus. Lipetz (1964) followed up the introduction of an experimental physics citation index, distributed only to a subsample of *Physical Review* and *Journal of Applied Physics* subscribers, with various measurements of the use of the index. Garvey and Griffith (1965) discuss "Theoretical and methodological considerations in undertaking innovations in scientific information exchange" in their Report No. 12. As new innovations are introduced into scientific information systems, many more opportunities for field experiments or quasi experiments will present themselves. Such opportunities should provide richer evidence than can be obtained from survey studies.

Laboratory Experiments

Two of the most puzzling topics in scientific information use, motivation and cognitive organization, are amenable to study in the psychological laboratory, and in fact psychologists have long been concerned with both.

Motivation of information seeking. An understanding of *why* information is sought might allow us to account for gross individual differences observed in this behavior among scientists. Interview questioning about the functions of information (cf. Menzel, 1958) has suggested that familiar motives are present: an achievement motive, a curiosity motive, a self-evaluation motive, an affiliation

motive. But introspection on motives is difficult to validate; induction of motives in the laboratory in the context of an information-seeking task provides unconfounded data to complement observations in natural settings.

Representative of much work by psychologists, the experimental procedures developed by Irwin and Smith (1957) and Lanzetta and Kanareff (1962) have great promise for the experimental study of information seeking. In each of these experiments subjects requested varying amounts of information in discrete units, allowing precise measurement of processed information that can only be approximated in natural settings.

Although both the Irwin-Smith and the Lanzetta-Kanareff experiments were tied to a straightforward utility motive (cash payoff), various "soft" motives could be introduced with appropriate conditions. For example, Paisley (1965a) found that ego involvement (induced as fear of failure) increased the amount of information seeking in a low-publicity condition but decreased it in a high-publicity condition, in comparison with information-seeking levels in the absence of ego involvement. It seems possible to make the psychologist's laboratory a microcosm of the scientist's own laboratory and to arouse there — perhaps in "games" — the many motives that lead to information seeking.

Cognitive organization of information. There is growing consensus that information files should be organized adaptively rather than prescriptively. That is, it should be possible for a user to locate desired information under many headings rather than the few prescribed by a "universal classification" scheme. The ideal adaptive system would regroup its holdings to match each user's habits of cognitive organization. The system would be an extension of the user's own memory, queried in the same idiom.

The study of patterns of association in users draws upon a strong tradition in psychological research. Well-tested procedures are available for collecting data on scientists' normative and idiosyncratic ways of organizing topics and concepts in their fields. When a substantial body of association data has been collected, one of several techniques for reducing the complexity of the data (such as Deese's — 1952 — factor analysis of association matrices) would serve to identify modal patterns of association among users. Richer data from individual subjects would permit analysis of idiosyncratic patterns, with emphasis on such factors as internal coherence, levels of superordinance and subordinance, stability over time, change as a result of transaction with information systems, etc.

Document Analysis

A scientific paper, article, or book is itself a rich source of data on scientists' communication patterns and cognitive processes. The use of citations to plot networks of papers has already been discussed. When more adequate sociometric data have been collected from scientists themselves, reciprocal citations will help to validate the pattern.

Computerized content analysis of text promises eventually to provide an objective and reliable means of indexing scientific documents. Doyle (1962) has developed a document-description program based on co-occurrence of significant terms. Salton and Lesk (1965) report a similar program that is already answering requests on an experimental basis. Other investigators are reporting initial successes in this intensely active research area (cf. Baxendale, 1966). It should not be overlooked that these document-description routines simultaneously yield data on authors' (scientists') patterns of verbal association.

Computer-Based Research

The use of time-shared computer systems as communication media for the flow of scientific information is opening up new and promising research possibilities. The on-line computer system can provide a setting in which information-seeking behavior is accurately and unobtrusively observed, the success of information searches can be directly and efficiently measured, and experiments of various kinds can be conducted.

Reference-retrieval systems on a time-shared computer are already in existence (Kessler, 1965) or planned for the near future (Overhage & Harmon, 1965). The basic idea of such systems is that users sitting at remote consoles can search the data base of references (books, journal articles, or whatever) maintained in computer storage. Because of the flexibility of computer processing, searches can be made in many ways not possible in traditional kinds of information storage. For example, Kessler's physics information system at MIT permits citation searches (finding journal article which include a specified article or articles in their reference lists) or bibliographic-coupling searches (finding articles that share references in common with specified other articles). Unlike traditional title indexes (e.g., as in card catalogues) it permits searches on title words other than the first word in the title. Files can be searched by corporate author (i.e., the institution with whom the author is affiliated) as well as standard author searches.

Because of the immediate feedback provided by the time-shared computer, searches can be modified while in progress. The search commands can be broadened if not enough material is being retrieved, or narrowed if too much material is being retrieved. The search order can be cancelled as soon as enough relevant information is obtained, or modified to try another search strategy if the first attempt is not successful. Most importantly, the process is under direct control of the user (cf. Paisley & Parker, 1965).

The psychological research potential in such systems is exciting. The psychologist can have the computer system unobtrusively monitor all user interaction with the system, providing either complete records or tabulated summaries of both the information-seeking behavior and the results of searches by all users of the system. Instead of depending almost entirely on questionnaire or interview techniques to reconstruct information-seeking behavior, complete records of information transactions would be available for content analysis, to study what information is sought and how it is sought.

The computer system can also serve as a perfectly trained, unbiased interviewer. Questionnaires can be administered by the computer to determine the characteristics of searchers and to obtain their evaluation of the success of the search. It can also serve as a general "feedback" communication channel from the users to either the system operators or the researchers, permitting the users to pass on their ideas, suggestions, and criticisms at the time when they are most salient.

Such a computer system can become the test vehicle for experiments on alternate indexing systems, search strategies, or kinds and sources of information. When alternate sources of information are made equally available, or alternate strategies for searching the same information source, then relative usage can become one criterion variable. User evaluation of the success of the search (as measured by a computer-administered questionnaire) is another. If users are paying to use the information system, then charges for different kinds of searches at different times could be experimentally manipulated.

4. Needed Psychological Research

Much of the previous research should be characterized as "applied research" because the data were collected for administrative purposes and because no innovation of methodology or theory was involved. Nevertheless, satisfactory answers to the question "How do scientists obtain the information they need?" require "basic research" into the nature of human information-seeking and information-processing behavior. This is true regardless of whether the motivation for the psychological research is understanding and prediction for its own sake or for the sake of devising better information systems.

It seems likely that the funds available for this kind of research will expand in the next few years. Such documents as the recent COSATI report (Committee on Scientific and Technical Information, 1965) are indicative of increased Federal interest in the problem. It also appears likely that many research sponsors will be primarily concerned with developing improved information systems. It might be more appropriate to describe such research as "mission-oriented" research — research intended to organize the flow of information to scientists in a way most efficient for the conduct of their research.

There are at least three ways in which psychological research is essential to the accomplishment of the mission to provide an efficient flow of information to scientists (including, of course, psychologists).

Criterion Measures. The first is the development of criterion measures for the design and evaluation of information systems. Many of the missions in our society have technological goals, such as sending a manned space vehicle to the moon or producing efficient thermonuclear power. The information science mission, however, is to facilitate a peculiarly human intellectual behavior, namely, research itself. Because of this essential difference, the criteria for evaluation of an information system cannot be specified as technological ones. They must be specified as behavioral ones. The development of criterion measures to instruct the designers and operators of information systems (whether journal editors, planners of computer-based reference-retrieval systems, or whomever) about what they should try to accomplish and how to measure their success thus becomes a task for psychological research. Without such explicit specification of goals and criteria for evaluation, the mission is likely to flounder. Some research has been devoted to this problem (Bourne, 1966; Bourne, Peterson, Lefkowitz, & Ford, 1961), but much more is needed.

Feedback. A second way in which psychological research is essential to the accomplishment of efficient information flow is in the provision of adequate "feedback loops" within the information system. Payment for information services, whether by journal subscription, membership in professional societies, institutional support for a library, registration for professional conventions, or in other ways, may not be an adequate index of the utility of such services for meeting information needs. Other motivations beside information seeking influence such an index. Support for libraries as well as support for other information services may be quite unresponsive to needs of users if no mechanism is introduced to determine those needs or to adequately measure relative usage of different kinds of services. The application of psychological research techniques, including sample survey research with questionnaires or interviews, is necessary to provide adequate flow of information to the system operators about how well (or badly) the system is serving intended goals. The bulk of previous information research probably falls in this category.

Constraints. A third way in which psychological research is needed for the accomplishment of efficient information flow is to provide explicit specification of constraints on the design or operation of information systems. To assume that an efficient flow of information among rational automatons could model an efficient flow of information among human scientists would be to deny much of what we know about human psychology. The system we are trying to make efficient will have to contend with a good deal of apparent irrationality and inefficiency on the part of scientists, if only because such apparent irrationality may be the source of the creativity that distinguishes the productive scientist from an automaton. The task of psychological research in this context is to test the behavioral assumptions of systems designers.

Such a task requires basic research into the nature of human information-processing behavior.

References

Ackoff, R. L., & Halbert, M. H. *An operations research study of the scientific activity of chemists.* Cleveland: Case Institute of Technology, 1958.

Allen, T. J. *The utilization of information sources during R&D proposal preparation.* Cambridge: M.I.T., Alfred P. Sloan School of Management, 1964.

Allen, T. J. Sources of ideas and their effectiveness in parallel R&D projects. (Report No. 130–65). Cambridge: M.I.T., Sloan School of Management, 1965.

Auerbach Corporation. DOD user needs study: Phase I. (Final Technical Report 1151-TR-3 to the Advanced Research Projects Agency, Department of Defense) Philadelphia: Auerbach Corporation, 1965.

Baxendale, P. Content analysis, specification and control. In C. Cuadra (Ed.), *Annual review of information science and technology.* New York: Wiley, 1966.

Bernal, J. D. Preliminary analysis of pilot questionnaire on the use of scientific literature. *The Royal Society Scientific Information Conference,* 1948, 589–637.

Bourne, C. P. Some user requirements stated quantitatively in the 90% Library. Menlo Park, California: Stanford Research Institute, 1963.

Bourne, C. P. Evaluation of indexing systems. In C. Cuadra (Ed.), *Annual review of information science and technology.* New York: Wiley, 1966.

Bourne, C. P., Peterson, G. D., Lefkowitz, B., & Ford, D. Requirements, criteria, and measures of performance of information storage and retrieval systems. (Final report to the office of Science Information Service, National Science Foundation) Menlo Park, Calif.: Stanford Research Institute, 1961.

Campbell, D. T., & Stanley, J. C. Experimental and quasi-experimental designs for research on teaching. In N. L. Gage (Ed.), *Handbook of research on teaching.* Chicago: Rand McNally, 1963.

Cole, P. F. Journal usage versus age of journal. *Journal of Documentation,* 1963, **19,** 1–11.

Coleman, J. S., Katz, E., & Menzel, H. *Doctors and new drugs.* Indianapolis: Bobbs-Merrill, 1966, in press.

Coleman, J., Menzel, H., & Katz, E. Social processes in physicians' adoption of a new drug. *Journal of Chronic Diseases,* 1958, **8,** 1–19.

Committee on Scientific and Technical Information (COSATI), Federal Council for Science and Technology. *Recommendations for National Document Handling Systems in Science and Technology.* Washington, D.C.: Clearinghouse for Federal Scientific and Technical Information, 1965.

Cuadra, C. (Ed.) *Annual review of information science and technology.* New York: Wiley, 1966.

Deese, J. On the structure of associative meaning. *Psychological Review,* 1952, **69,** 161–175.

DOYLE, L. B. Indexing and abstracting by association. *American Documentation*, 1962, **13**, 378–390.

GARFIELD, E., SHER, I. H., & TORPIE, R. J. *The use of citation data in writing the history of science*. Philadelphia: Institute for Scientific Information, 1964.

GARVEY, W. D., & GRIFFITH, B. C. *Reports of the American Psychological Association's Project on Scientific Information Exchange in Psychology*. Washington, D.C.: American Psychological Association, 1963.

GARVEY, W. D., & GRIFFITH, B. C. *Reports of the American Psychological Association's Project on Scientific Information Exchange in Psychology*. Washington, D.C.: American Psychological Association, 1965.

GLASS, B., & NORWOOD, S. H. How scientists actually learn of work important to them. In, *Proceedings of the International Conference on Scientific Information*. Washington, D.C.: National Academy of Science–National Research Council, 1959.

HERNER, S. Information-gathering habits of workers in pure and applied science. *Industrial and Engineering Chemistry*, 1954, **46**, 288–336.

HERNER, S. The information-gathering habits of American medical scientists. In, *Proceedings of the International Conference on Scientific Information*. Washington, D.C.: National Academy of Sciences–National Research Council, 1959.

HERTZ, D. B., & RUBENSTEIN, A. H. *Team research*. New York: Columbia University, Department of Industrial Engineering, 1953.

HOGG, I. H., & SMITH, J. R. Information and literature use in a research and development organization. In, *Proceedings of the International Conference on Scientific Information*. Washington, D.C.: National Academy of Science–National Research Council, 1959.

IRWIN, F. W., & SMITH, W. A. S. Value, cost, and information as determiners of decision. *Journal of Experimental Psychology*, 1957, **54**, 229–232.

KESSLER, M. M. Bibliographic coupling between scientific papers. *American Documentation*, 1963, **14**, 10–25.

KESSLER, M. M. The MIT technical information project. *Physics Today*, 1965, **18**(3), 28–36.

LANZETTA, J. T., & KANAREFF, V. Information cost, amount of payoff, and level of aspiration as determinants of information seeking in decision making. *Behavioral Science*, 1962, **7**, 459–473.

LIPETZ, B. *Evaluation of the impact of a citation index in physics, AIP/IRP CI-3 (1964)*. New York: American Institute of Physics, 1964.

MCLAUGHLIN, C. P., ROSENBLOOM, R. S., & WOLEK, F. W. *Technology transfer and the flow of technical information in a large industrial corporation*. Cambridge, Mass.: Harvard University, School of Business Administration, 1965.

MELTZER, L. Scientific productivity in organizational settings. *Journal of Social Issues*, 1956, **12**, 32–40.

MENZEL, H. *The flow of information among scientists: Problems, opportunities, and research questions*. New York: Columbia University, Bureau of Applied Social Research, 1958.

MENZEL, H. Planned and unplanned scientific communication. In, *Proceedings of the International Conference on Scientific Information*. Washington, D.C.: National Academy of Sciences–National Research Council, 1959.

MENZEL, H. *Review of studies in the flow of information among scientists*, New York: Columbia University, Bureau of Applied Social Research, 1960.

MENZEL, H. Information needs and uses in science and technology. In C. Cuadra (Ed.), *Annual review of information science and technology*. New York: Wiley, 1966.

MORAVCSIK, M. J. Private and public communications in physics. *Physics Today*, 1965, **18**(3), 23–26.

MORAVCSIK, M. J., & PASTERNACK, S. A debate on preprint exchange. *Physics Today*, 1966, **19**(6), 60–73.

MOTE, L. J. B. Reasons for the variations in the information needs of scientists. *Journal of Documentation*, 1962, **18**, 169–175.

NATIONAL ACADEMY OF SCIENCES–NATIONAL RESEARCH COUNCIL. *Proceedings of the International Conference on Scientific Information*. Washington, D.C.: National Academy of Sciences–National Research Council, 1959.

OVERHAGE, C. F. J., & HARMON, R. J. *Intrex: Report of a planning conference on information transfer experiments*. Cambridge: MIT Press, 1965.

PAISLEY, W. J. Extent of information-seeking as a function of subjective certainty and the utility of the information. Unpublished doctoral dissertation, Stanford University 1965. (a)

PAISLEY, W. J. The flow of (behavioral) science information: A review of the research literature. Stanford, Calif.: Institute for Communication Research, 1965. (b)

PAISLEY, W. J., & PARKER, E. B. Information retrieval as a receiver-controlled communication system. In L. B. Heilprin, B. E. Markuson, & F. L. Goodman (Eds.), *Proceedings of the Symposium on Education for Information Science*. Washington, D.C.: Spartan Books, 1965.

PELTZ, DONALD C. Social factors related to performance in a research organization. *Administrative Science Quarterly*, 1956, **1**, 310–325.

PRICE, D. J. DE S. *Little science, big science*. New York: Columbia University Press, 1963.

PRICE, D. J. DE S. Networks of scientific papers. *Science*, 1965, **149**, 510–515.

ROYAL SOCIETY [U. K.]. *Report and papers submitted to the Royal Society Scientific Information Conference*. London: Royal Society, 1948.

SALTON, G., & LESK, M. E. The SMART Automatic Document Retrieval System — an illustration. *Communications of the ACM*, 1965, **8**, 391–398.

SHAW, R. R. *Pilot study on the use of scientific literature by scientists*. Washington, D.C.: National Science Foundation, 1956.

SHILLING, C. W., BERNARD, J., & TYSON, J. W. *Informal communication among bioscientists*. Washington: George Washington University, Biological Sciences Communication Project, 1964.

URQUHART, D. J. The distribution and use of scientific and technical information. *The Royal Society Information Conference*, 1948, 408–419.

WUEST, F. J. *Studies in the methodology of measuring information requirements and use patterns*. Bethlehem: Lehigh University, Center for the Information Sciences, 1965.

XHIGNESSE, L. V., & OSGOOD, C. E. *Bibliographical citation characteristics of the psychological journal network in 1950 and in 1960*. Urbana: University of Illinois, Institute of Communications Research, 1963.

12 Factors Affecting the Preferences of Industrial Personnel for Information Gathering Methods

VICTOR ROSENBERG
Information Storage & Retrieval
Vol. 3, No. 3, July, 1967

1. Introduction

Many recent studies have attempted to investigate the behavioral aspects of the information gathering process. Generally, these studies have developed an insight into the ways by which scientists obtain information, and have developed the methodology for such studies. A number of studies have also sought to determine the actual information needs of scientists. Generally neglected, however, are attempts to discover (a) why individuals prefer certain methods, (b) what attributes of information gathering methods are important, and (c) if the study of the information seeking process should be restricted to research scientists. The purpose of this study is to investigate such questions, in an attempt to make the interpretation of results from information user studies more meaningful.

Most efforts in the actual development of information retrieval systems have been based, either explicitly or implicitly, on the assumption that the greatest need for improved availability of information exists among research scientists. Although differences exist in the types of information required by different professions, it is not at all clear that the basic principles underlying the development of retrieval systems should be different for different environments.

2. Method

To obtain the data for the investigation, a structured questionnaire was administered to a selected group of subjects. The questionnaire was designed to minimize the inconvenience of the subjects while extracting the necessary information.

The questionnaire first asked the subject to indicate whether he spent more than 50 per cent of his time in research or research related activities. This question separated the subjects into two groups: (a) "research" and (b) "nonresearch". All data were analyzed between the two groups.

Part I of the questionnaire presented the subject with three hypothetical situations which required information and which would be likely to be part of his general experience. The situations presented concerned research for a proposal, research for a journal article, and research on work being done in a particular field. The purpose of a given hypothetical situation was to establish a frame of reference within which the subject was asked to rank eight information gathering methods. The same eight methods were presented in each of the hypothetical situations, but in each case the methods were rearranged in a different, random order, minimizing the possibility of subsequent questions being influenced by previous ones (i.e., order effects).

The information gathering methods were selected from a group of methods which appeared in an earlier study [1]. From a list of twenty-three items, the most popular, on the basis of choice by the subjects of that study, were selected and modified. The methods were thus representative of generally used information seeking techniques.

Part IIA of the questionnaire, listing the same eight methods as in Part I, asked the subject to rate each method by the criterion of ease of use. The subject rated the method on a seven point scale ranging from "extremely simple" to "extremely difficult."

Similarly in Part IIB, the subject was asked to rate the methods by the criterion of amount of information expected, rating the methods from "very little" to "very much" information expected. As in Part I, the order of presentation was randomized. Part II was prepared in four sets, each set listing the methods in a different random order, to minimize any possibility of order effects.

3. Selection of Subjects

The population from which the sample was taken was professional personnel employed by scientific organizations. The sample was more specifically defined as persons holding at least a bachelors degree, employed in organizations with interests in scientific research.

An attempt was made to secure employee directories from which to draw a random sample. The cooperating organizations indicated, however, that the release of such directories was against corporate policy, so that an alternative sampling procedure was used. Six organizations cooperated in the project, and in each case a quantity of questionnaires was sent to a cooperating individual, who was instructed to distribute the questionnaire to professionals in his organization representing as many departments as possible. The questionnaires were returned by mail.

4. Results

The entire distribution of the questionnaire to the six cooperating organizations totalled 175. One hundred and eight questionnaires were completed and returned. Eleven per cent (12) of the returned questionnaires were rejected because certain parts of the questionnaire were incorrectly or incompletely filled out. Since no due date was given to the subjects, some of the questionnaires were returned after the completion of the analysis and therefore were not included in the sample.

The subjects were divided into the "research" and "nonresearch" categories on the basis of question number one which asked "Do you spend more than 50 per cent of your time in research or research related activities". The resulting set of usable questionnaires contained 52 (55 per cent) in the research category and 44 (45 per cent) in the nonresearch category.

The data resulting from Part I of the study consisted of sets of ranked items for each of the three hypothetical situations, listed in the data as questions (Table I).

TABLE I

HYPOTHETICAL SITUATIONS LISTED AS QUESTIONS

No. 1. You are working on a design for a procedure or experiment and wish to know if similar work has been done or is currently being done by someone else.

No. 2. You are preparing a proposal for a new project either to the management of your organization or to an outside agency. You wish to substantiate the proposal with a thorough bibliography. The proposal involves approximately $60,000.

No. 3. You wish to gather information in order to write an article in your area of specialization for a trade or research journal.

Thus for each group of subjects there were three sets of ranks and the degree of consistency in the ranking was measured within each group, for each question separately and averaged for the set of all three taken together.

To measure the consistency of ranking among subjects, the Kendall coefficient of concordance, W, was used. The test ascertains the overall agreement among k sets of rankings (i.e. the association among them). If there were perfect agreement among the subjects in their ranking, each method would have the same rank for each subject. The Kendall coefficient of concordance is an approximate index of the divergence of the actual agreement shown in the data from the maximum possible (perfect) agreement [2].

Computing W for each question in a given group,

$$W = s / [1/12 k^2 (N^3 - N)].$$

where

$s =$ sum of squares of the observed deviations from the mean of the totals R_j, thus

$$s = \Sigma [R_j - (R_j/N)]^2.$$

k number of sets of rankings, i.e. the number of subjects.

N number of items ranked

and the denominator, $1/12 \, k^2 (N^3 - N)$ is the maximum possible sum of squared deviations.

For the data of Part I, the resulting coefficients of concordance are shown in Table II.

TABLE II

KENDALL W FOR PART I

Group	k	Question			Average
		no. 1	no. 2	no. 3	
Research	52	0·452	0·511	0·539	0·501
Nonresearch	44	0·326	0·352	0·469	0·382

The statistic, W, is linearly related to the χ^2 (chi-square) by the formula:

$$\chi^2 = k(N-1)W.$$

The χ^2 statistic is used to test the statistical significance of W. In the resulting χ^2 table (Table III) all entries are significant at the 0·05 level.

TABLE III

χ^2 FOR PART I

Group	k	Question			$d.f.$
		no. 1	no. 2	no. 3	
Research	52	164·528	186·004	196·196	7
Nonresearch	44	100·408	108·416	144·452	7

The correlation between the rankings of the two groups was measured by applying the Spearman rank correlation coefficient: r_s to the ranks of the totals of each method for each question and for the totals over the three questions. Kendall [3] claims that the best estimate of the ranking of N items is the ranking of the sums of the various rankings, provided W is significant. The ranks of the various sums (Table IV) are used to find r_s.

TABLE IV

RANKS OF TOTALS

Methods	Questions						Totals	
	Q_1		Q_2		Q_3			
	R	NR	R	NR	R	NR	R	NR
1	1	4	2	3	1	1	1	1·5
2	2	2	1	1	2	2	2	1·5
3	8	8	8	8	8	8	8	8
4	6	6	4·5	6	5	6	5	6
5	5	5	3	4·5	4	4	4	5
6	3	1	4·5	2	3	3	3	3
7	7	7	7	7	7	7	7	7
8	4	3	6	4·5	6	5	6	4

Note: R = research; NR = nonresearch

The methods are listed by numbers which are interpreted in Table V. The fractional rankings represent ties which are averaged for the computation.

TABLE V

NUMBERING OF METHODS

The numbering of information gathering methods in the text corresponds to the following listing:
Methods:

No. 1. Search your personal library.

No. 2. Search material in the same building where you work, excluding your personal library.

No. 3. Visit a knowledgeable person—20 miles away or more.

No. 4. Use a library that is not within your organization.

No. 5. Consult a reference librarian.

No. 6. Visit a knowledgeable person nearby (within your organization).

No. 7. Write a letter requesting information from a knowledgeable person—20 miles away or more.

No. 8. Telephone a knowledgeable person who may be of help.

The statistic, r_s, is calculated by the formula:

$$r_s = 1 - (6 \sum_{i=1}^{n} d_i^2) / (N^3 - N)$$

where

d_i = the deviation between two ranks

and

N = number of items ranked.

For the data shown the r_s in each case is significant at the 0·05 level.

TABLE VI

r_s BETWEEN GROUPS

	Question			Totals
	no. 1	no. 2	no. 3	
$r_s =$	0·833	0·786	0·976	0·923

The statistic r_s is a one-tailed test showing that a significant relationship exists in the data. It is a nonparametric test having an efficiency of 91 per cent when compared to the Pearson r [4].

The data in Part II of the questionnaire were ratings given to each method on the criteria (a) ease of use and (b) amount of information.

For the data of the "ease of use" ratings the null hypothesis was that no difference existed in the mean ratings given for the methods by the two groups (i.e. $H_0 : \mu_R = \mu_{NR}$ for all methods). The null hypothesis was tested by means of standard t tests corrected by Sheffe's method, which is the most conservative of the generally used procedures for correcting critical values when a number of t tests are used [5]. The results of the t tests for the "ease of use" ratings are shown in Table VII. None of the results of the t test are significant at the 0·05 level.

A similar analysis was performed on the data from

TABLE VII

t TESTS FOR EASE OF USE RATINGS

	Methods							
	No. 1	No. 2	No. 3	No. 4	No. 5	No. 6	No. 7	No. 8
$t =$	0·780	0·434	0·752	0·419	0·362	0·275	0·507	0·792

Part IIB, the "amount of information" ratings. The results of the *t* test for these data (Table VIII) again show no significant difference at the 0·05 level.

TABLE VIII

t TESTS FOR AMOUNT OF INFORMATION RATINGS

	Methods							
	No. 1	No. 2	No. 3	No. 4	No. 5	No. 6	No. 7	No. 8
$t =$	0·718	0·989	0·754	1·007	0·587	0·548	0·398	0·596

The results from Parts I and II were then compared by finding correlation coefficients between the sets of ranks and the sets of ratings for each group. To find the correlation coefficients a ranking was derived from the average ratings of the methods in each case and compared to the ranks given by the subjects (Table IX).

TABLE X

SPEARMAN RANK CORRELATION COEFFICIENTS

	Subject rankings	
Derived rankings from	research	nonresearch
Ease of use	0·868	0·877
Amount of information	−0·166	−0·113

that the subjects applied essentially the same standard in ranking the eight methods [6]. The ranking of the totals for each group can be taken as the best estimate of the ranking based on the given data. The significance of the statistic, W, is not interpreted to mean that the estimated rankings are correct by an external criterion, but rather that they are the best estimate for the given data. The fact that W was significant in all cases was considered important because the subsequent analysis was based on the reliability of the rankings of the totals.

The comparison of the estimated rankings for the two groups using the Spearman test showed that there was no significant difference between the two groups in the rankings. The null hypothesis was, H_0: The ranks are identical. The net result of the first two tests was that the two groups used essentially the same criterion within

TABLE IX

	DERIVED RANKINGS							
	Method							
	No. 1	No. 2	No. 3	No. 4	No. 5	No. 6	No. 7	No. 8
	Research							
Subject ranking	1	2	8	5	4	3	7	6
Derived ease of use ranking	1	2	8	6	5	4	7	3
Derived amount of information ranking	3	7	6	8	4	5	1	2
	Nonresearch							
Subject ranking	1·5	1·5	8	6	5	3	7	4
Derived ease of use ranking	1	3	8	7	5	4	6	2
Derived amount of information ranking	1	7	5	6	3	8	2	4

The Spearman rank correlation coefficient was used for this test (Table X). The correlation of the ranks derived from the ease of use ratings to the subject rankings were significant for both research and nonresearch groups, whereas the correlation of the ranks derived from the amount of information ratings to the subject ranking were not significant for either group. Significance was determined at the 0·05 level in all cases.

5. Interpretation of Results

The initial test determining the degree of agreement among the subjects in the ranking of the methods showed

the groups for ranking the items and that, on the basis of the test, there was essentially no difference between the two groups in the resulting rankings.

For the data in Part II, *t* tests were applied to test for significant differences in the mean ratings on a given method between the two groups. The null hypothesis for comparison of the two means on a given rating of a method was $H_0: \mu_R = \mu_{NR}$. Since no difference was found to be significant on the basis of the data, it was inferred that no meaningful differences existed between the average ratings of the group (i.e. for each method, both groups gave the same average rating). This shows that, given a set of methods, both groups gave essentially the same response in each case when asked to rate the methods according to ease of use and amount of information expected.

To test the correlation between the results of Part I and the results of Part II, the ratings of Part II were converted to ranks by ranking the mean ratings. Since the rankings of Part I were on an ordinal scale, the inferences about the correlation of the data were kept at the ordinal level. Thus the inferences say nothing about the relative magnitude of the ratings, but only about their rank [7]. The results of this analysis showed a marked correlation between the ease of use ratings and the subject rankings for both research and nonresearch groups, and a marked lack of correlation between the amount of information ratings and the subject rankings.

The statistic used to test the correlation, r_s, ranges from -1 to $+1$. A value for r_s of $+1$ corresponds to perfect agreement, and a value of -1 corresponds to "perfect" inverse agreement (i.e. the highest subject ranked item has the lowest derived rank, etc.). Thus values close to $+1$ reflect a high degree of agreement between the two variables, whereas a value close to zero represents randomness or lack of agreement. On the basis of this statistic, it is clear that the subject's preference ranking was far more closely related to his evaluation of the method's ease of use than to his evaluation of amount of information expected. Alternatively, a subject's preference for a method of getting information is more likely to correspond to his estimation of the method's ease of use than his estimation of amount of information expected. This inference holds for both research and nonresearch personnel.

The actual methods listed in the questionnaire and the hypothetical situations which served as a framework for the rankings and in some sense for the rating also, played a relatively minor part in the study. No attempt was made to make inferences about the methods themselves except that one was ranked or rated above another. Thus the hypothetical situations and methods themselves served only to gather data about the relationships between the two groups of subjects and between the ratings and the rankings. The interest in the relationships between the sets of data exclusively served as a justification for the use of the structured questionnaire. No attempt was made to discover (a) what a subject felt he would actually do, or (b) what a subject actually does in the given situations. Such observations have been reported in what are generally known as information user studies.

A significant limitation of the procedure used in the investigation was that there was no way of validating the questionnaire to test its sensitivity to the variables to be measured. General procedure requires the test to be administered to samples where differences in the tested variable are known to exist to determine the sensitivity of the test to the variable in question. Since the experimental hypothesis was that no differences existed between the two groups tested, no population could be found where differences were known to exist. The consistency of the data and the significance of the tests, however, imply that the testing procedure was valid. The similarity of the results to the results of studies observing actual behaviour also provides support for the validity of the experimental procedure.

6. Discussion

Although much research has been done to study the information gathering behaviour of professional personnel, very little has been done to establish the reasons for the observed behaviour. The relative priority of the most frequently used channels has been established by almost all studies, and in almost every case the analysis has shown that one of the most significant factors in determining the priority is the availability of the source. The implication is that the information gathering behaviour of users is dictated primarily by the facilities available and changes to reflect a change in the availability of facilities. The importance of availability of information is consistent with the results of the present study and implies that the primary attribute of any information gathering method is its ease of use [8].

Although the methods listed in the study were only secondarily important, the overall preference listing of the methods shows an interesting correlation with a study where actual performance was measured. In a study investigating the utilization of information sources in research and development proposal preparation [9], information sources were divided into three categories: (a) literature search; (b) consulting with laboratory specialists; and (c) consulting with outside sources. The data from the study show, among other things, that the mean times spent in each activity were: (a) 28.4 man-hr; (b) 17.2 man-hr; and (c) 11.6 man-hr, respectively. If one divides the information gathering methods of the present study in a similar manner, there seems to be a one to one relationship between the preference rankings given and the results of Allen's study, if preference can be equated with time spent [10].

The comparison of the two studies shows that there is substantial agreement between the results of the present study giving the subject's opinion of preference and Allen's study showing actual performance. Such agreement combined with the general inference of user studies concerning the importance of availability can be considered a substantiation of the validity of the present study.

It may also be inferred from the agreement between the two studies that asking the subject for opinions concerning information gathering behaviour yields results as meaningful as the results from observation studies, provided the sample is sufficiently large. Since observation studies are more complex and difficult to control, the use of structured questionnaires requesting opinions could greatly simplify and thereby expand the scope of studies investigating information gathering behaviour.

7. Conclusions

From the results of the experiment, it is reasonable to conclude that: (a) research and nonresearch professional personnel in industry or government do not differ to any appreciable extent in their evaluation of information gathering methods; and (b) the preference for a given method reflects the estimated ease of use of the method rather than the amount of information expected. These conclusions in conjunction with the results of observation studies imply further that the basic parameter for the design of any industrial information system should be the system's ease of use, rather than the amount of information provided, and that if an organization desires to have a high quality of information used, it must make ease of access of primary importance.

Since the optimization of all variables has not yet become a practical reality, the design of an actual system usually permits the optimization of some parameters only at the expense of others. If all other variables such as cost, environment, etc., are held constant, a system can be designed to provide a maximum amount of information at the expense of effort, or it can be designed to minimize effort at the expense of information yield. Cast in the terms of information retrieval, one can maximize either recall or precision. In industrial environments, the design criteria should lean toward the minimization of effort (i.e. precision).

A secondary conclusion, supported by the correlation of the results with observation studies, is that user surveys can be accomplished by the use of a well-designed structured questionnaire technique, without resorting to direct observation, if the sample is large enough. The questionnaire technique is far more efficient and less expensive than observation surveys. However, additional research should be done to establish in more detail the relationship between observation and questionnaire techniques.

On the basis of the present study, it appears that further research using similar techniques could accurately identify the relationship of information system characteristics to the system environment. Such further research might, for example, examine the relationships between academic and industrial environments. A further examination of the factors involved in the concept "ease of use", (e.g. time, distance, or intellectual effort), should also prove useful in providing a more detailed description of the information gathering process and system environments.

References

1. V. ROSENBERG: *The attitudes of scientists toward information seeking activities*, Lehigh University, Bethlehem (1965). (Unpub.)
2. S. SIEGEL: *Nonparametric statistics for the behavioral sciences*, pp. 229–239, McGraw-Hill, New York (1956).
3. S. SIEGEL, *op. cit.*, p. 238.
4. S. SIEGEL, *op. cit.*, pp. 202–213.
5. B. J. WINER: *Statistical principles in experimental design*, pp. 85–89, McGraw-Hill, New York (1962).
6. S. SIEGEL, *op. cit.*, p. 238.
7. W. L. HAYS: *Statistics for psychologists*, pp. 68–76, Holt, Rinehart & Winston, New York (1963).
8. BUREAU OF APPLIED SOCIAL RESEARCH: *Review of studies in the flow of information among scientists*. Columbia University (1960).
9. THOMAS J. ALLEN: *The utilization of information sources during R & D proposal preparation*, Rept. no. 97–64, Alfred P. Sloan School of Management, Massachusetts Institute of Technology, Cambridge, Mass. (October, 1964).
10. C. W. HANSON: 'Research on users' needs: where is it getting us?' *Aslib Proc.*, 1964, **16,** 69.

13 Collaboration in an Invisible College

DEREK J. dE SOLLA PRICE
DONALD dEB. BEAVER
American Psychologist
Vol. 21, No. 11, November, 1966

Many studies of the sociology of modern science and the communication patterns of scientists now agree that one of the dominant characteristics is that form of organization which has become known as the "Invisible College." The name derives historically from a group of people in the midseventeenth century who later formally organized themselves into the Royal Society of London. Before that they had met informally, and distinct from the groups centered on Wadham College and Gresham College, the more visible colleges. They communicated by letter to gain an appreciative audience for their work, to secure priority, and to keep informed of work being done elsewhere by others. In its modern context of the organizational structure of Big Science, the term is not so specific and unfortunately the definition and understanding of the term have varied considerably from writer to writer.

The basic phenomenon seems to be that in each of the more actively pursued and highly competitive specialties in the sciences there seems to exist an "ingroup." The people in such a group claim to be reasonably in touch with everyone else who is contributing materially to research in this subject, not merely on a national scale, but usually including all other countries in which that specialty is strong. The body of people meet in select conferences (usually held in rather pleasant places), they commute between one center and another, and they circulate preprints and reprints to each other and they collaborate in research. Since they constitute a power group of everybody who is really somebody in a field, they might at the local and national level actually control the administration of research funds and laboratory space. They may also control personal prestige and the fate of new scientific ideas, and intentionally or unintentionally they may decide the general strategy of attack in an area.

These quite important phenomena are at present known only from personal histories and interviews, and so far as we know there has never been an objective analysis of an Invisible College structure by any other means. It is relatively easy to interview a known "somebody" in a chosen research field, but opportunities are few to select a group of people that constitutes the greater part of a single Invisible College. The basic difficulty of study is to capture and dissect out such a body. In what follows we present an outline and preliminary analysis of a likely specimen which was kind enough to agree to its capture and study, hoping that the information arising may be of value to those concerned with the analysis of scientific organization and communication and perhaps also to other groups of scientists. At this stage we have been at pains to preserve our primitive ignorance of the scientific content of the work of this group and also our lack of any personal knowledge of the participants in it; our hope is that some knowledge of the structure can be found first objectively and then checked later with the subjective data obtained from interviews.

The group investigated is Information Exchange Group No. 1 (IEG 1) or Oxidative Phosphorylation and Terminal Electron Transport, organized by the Division of Research Grants of the National Institutes of Health. The group was established in February 1961 with 32 members. By June 1965 it had grown to 592 members and another six information exchange groups in other specialties had been started by the same office.[1] Any scientist who is a bona fide researcher in the field in question may apply for membership in the group or may be nominated by other members. All members receive updated membership lists giving mailing addresses, and they all receive the numerous photocopied memos which are circulated. About 90% of these memos are preprints of papers which are eventually published, with or without change, and the remaining 10% are discussion of previous papers and an occasional technical or personal note intended for general circulation. Members may participate in this process which bills itself as a "continuing international congress by mail" by merely sending a fair typescript of their contribution to the central office. With no editorial intervention it is then photocopied and distributed so that scientist-to-scientist contact takes only a couple of weeks instead of the several months of delay attending the formal publication. The total cost of the operation works out at about $125 of subsidy per member per year, and at about $.40 for each single copy of a memo. Though there has been much discussion of such techniques of shortcutting the normal channels of publication, particularly amongst the physicists,[2] we are not at this point concerned with the advantages and disadvantages of the IEG as a practical communication system, but only with the accidental by-product of a corpus of data which enables one to see something of the structure of the group of people involved.

Our source data are a set of the membership lists and the memos which are circulated to all members. The membership list has been growing exponentially since its

foundation, with a doubling time of about 13 months, so that in November 1965 there were 517 members. The number of memos has also been increasing exponentially, but with a doubling every 7 months, so that there was at the time of study about one memo a day on the average. The group of members is international, about 62% from the United States, 9% from the United Kingdom, 5% from Japan, 3% each from Australia and Sweden, 2% each from Canada, France, Germany, and the USSR, and a remaining 10% from another 19 different countries. Compared with the average world state for all sciences, or even for the most active sciences, the growth rate is clearly an order of magnitude higher than one would expect, and the share of the US probably rather disproportionately large. It would seem therefore that the group is still in process of spreading out to a fair coverage of all workers in the field. Some recent decline in the growth curves may be due to this process becoming effectively complete, though stable conditions have not yet been reached.

Our present report is based upon 533 available memos,[3] each of which bears on its by-line the names of one or more authors. In all 555 different authors are named, and if we call each appearance of a name in a by-line an *authorship*, there were 1,239 such authorships. It follows that each author had, in the 5-year interval considered, about .96 papers and 2.23 authorships, there being overall about 2.32 authorships in the by-line to each paper. The actual distribution of this multiple authorship is shown in Table I. The mode is clearly

TABLE I

DISTRIBUTION OF MULTIPLE AUTHORSHIP

Authors per paper	Number of such papers	Number of such authorships
1	114	114
2	230	460
3	123	369
4	45	180
5	14	70
6	4	24
7	2	14
8	1	8
Total	533	1,239

that of the two-author paper, and a side investigation was able to show that the distribution has not changed significantly over the 5 years.

The trend in multiple authorship agrees closely with that cited by Beverly L. Clarke (1964, pp. 822–824,

1. For a history of IEG see Green (1964, 1965) and also two unpublished accounts by Errett C. Albritton: "The Information Exchange Group — an Experiment in Communication" (July 1965), and "The Information Exchange Group — an Experimental Program" (February 1966). Another account with bibliography is given by Moore (1965).

2. See, for example, Moravcsik (1966) and Pasternack (1966).

3. It consists of memos numbered 1 through 535 with the exception of the following 11 which were not circulated or were otherwise unavailable to us: 36, 77, 257, 263, 308, 321, 400, 412, 491, and with the addition of 9 papers numbered irregularly as X34, X35, X36, Y36, Sp. 1, Sp. 1a, 363A, X84, 278-II.

2.30 authorships/paper), but though similar in trend it is sensibly different from that found for chemistry (Price, 1963, p. 88) and for physics (Keenan, 1964, p. 5, 1.80 authorships/paper). It is quite clear that there are minor variations from field to field of science, and probably also variations in the national habits and conventions of who shall get his name on a paper, but on the whole the distribution in IEG 1 is in keeping with that expected. It has been shown by Hirsch and Singleton (1965) that the amount of multiple authorship in a field is closely related to the amount of financial support — government, foundation, or private — given to the research producing these papers. Presumably part of the origin of multiple authorship has a basis in the financial and economic as well as professional dependence of one author upon another. According to the data of Hirsch and Singleton the average number of authors per paper for nonsupported work in 1936–64 was 1.16, while for supported work it rose from 1.38 to values of circa 1.60 during the last 3 years of study when support had been most intense. The figure here of 2.32 would suggest that the field here studied must be highly subsidized. It is also worth noting that, as in other studies, the number of papers with n authors is proportional in the first approximation to $1/|n-1$ — except for the number of single-author papers (which should be twice as numerous). This law would hold for a random Poisson distribution of authorships with probability unity. If this, or anything like it were the cause of the distribution, it would point to the possibility that the group under study had systematically included too few single-author papers. Perhaps there is something in the nature of the subject matter or of the manner of organization that is prejudiced against a significant proportion of those who habitually publish without collaborators.

For a general analysis of the group of authors it is important to note that they are by no means coincident with the membership of the IEG 1. Though there were 555 different authors and IEG 1 had a membership of 517 scientists, only 231 names were common to both classes. There were therefore 324 authors who were not members of the group, and there were 286 members who had never helped to contribute a paper. Another side investigation showed that this breakdown, giving about 45% of the members as authors, was stable, it being the same in November 1964 as in November 1965, though presumably the founding fathers of the group were all considerable authors. The 324 authors who are not members of the group may reasonably be presumed to be the collaborators of authors who are members; in fact the ratio of all authors (555) to those who are also members (231) is 2.4 which is only slightly higher than the average number of authors per paper. The identity of the considerable number (286) of members who are not authors cannot be established with the means at present available; we shall hope that analysis of the references in the papers might indicate whether there are scientists in this field, and perhaps amongst this subgroup of non-contributing members, who are active in publication but opposed to this organization. Alternatively, members of this subgroup could be people who are interested but not active in the research front, or they could be people who are not now, nor perhaps have ever been interested in this topic.

Focusing our attention now on the 555 authors who between them contributed the 533 memos, we next give the results of an investigation into their productivities and the extent to which they collaborated with each other. An index card was made up for each author named,[4] and on it were listed the papers in which he was listed as an author and the names of those other authors with whom he was listed for each paper. From each card the total number of papers and the number of different persons with whom he had been involved as a collaborator could be read. The results of this analysis are listed in Figure 1, and also from this figure the marginal totals enable the distributions in productivity and amount of collaboration to be seen.

The distribution of productivity alone follows the normal pattern so far as one can tell with the rather small numbers involved (Price, 1963, pp. 42–51). A majority of the authors ($311/555 = 56\%$) are known only from a single authorship of a paper. Since the aggregate of their authorships is only a quarter of the total number ($311/1,239$) it follows that in general they must be names whose single occurrence has been on papers with several other authors. For larger productivities, the number of authors with their names on n papers is, in the first approximation, proportional to $1/n^2$ in the usual manner — a trend that has been constant for the last 3 centuries. At the other end of the productivity distribution there are as always a few very prolific authors. The top 30 authors who each contributed to six or more papers are responsible between them for another quarter ($306/1,239$) of the authorships.

The distribution of the number of collaborators per author has a well-marked maximum at two, corresponding to three-author papers; a skewing of the distribution to the left makes this agree with the average of 2.32 authors per paper which has been already noted. At the top end of the distribution there are, this time, 17 people who collaborate a great deal, the minimum being with 8 people and the maximum being with 34 other authors.

Going now from the marginals to the main matrix of Figure 1 it will be noted that there is a good correlation between the productivities and the amount of collaboration of the authors. The most prolific man is also by far the most collaborating, and three of the four next most prolific are also among the next most frequently collaborating. It is, of course, obvious that if multiple author-

4. To avoid personal issues we identify each author not by name but by a two-letter code acronym.

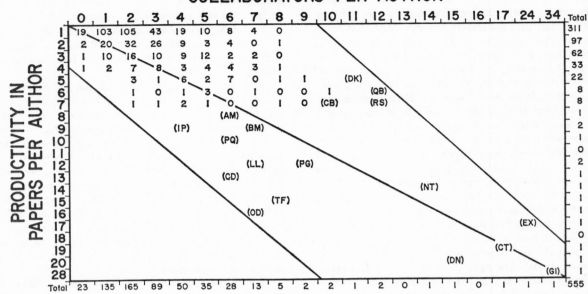

Fig. 1. Numbers of authors in all categories of productivity and collaborativeness, and code names of the most productive persons. (Productivity and collaboration are well correlated; no author has many collaborators and low productivity, or vice versa.)

ship is the rule a man will increase his number of collaborators with every paper he writes, but it is nevertheless surprising to find such a small scatter away from the main diagonal of the matrix. This implies that over the entire range of productivities there is little deviation from the main pattern of picking up about one new collaborator for each new paper written. There are in other words no people who display a marked tendency to stick to well-formed groups or to avoid previous colleagues. It is especially noteworthy that nobody who worked without collaborators or with only 1 coauthor succeeded in producing more than 4 papers in the 5-year period, whereas everybody with more than 12 collaborators produced 14 or more papers in the same time.

The natural inference from this is that there exists a core of extremely active researchers and around them there is a large floating population of people who appear to collaborate with them in one or two multiple-authorship papers and then disappear not to be heard from again. We investigate this phenomenon in two ways; first by the calculation of *fractional productivities,* and second by the investigation of the way in which authors are grouped by the sets of all people who have ever collaborated with each other.

We define fractional productivity as the score of an author when he is assigned $1/n$ of a point for the occurrence of his name among n authors on the by-line of a single paper. Thus a man with one paper of which he is the sole author, a second of which he is one of two authors, and a third in which he is one of five, will have a fractional productivity of 1.7 and a full productivity

of three papers. On the average it happens that the fractional productivities as so calculated are about half of the full productivities for most authors. More than two-thirds of the population of authors (380/555) had fractional productivities less than unity by this calculation, so confirming the existence of this large floating population of lightweights.

The use of fractional productivities provides a breakthrough in understanding the nature of the distribution law of productivity. For theoretical reasons (Price, 1963, pp. 49–50) it is to be expected that the logarithm of productivity should be normally distributed in a population. This is difficult to test with the integral values of full productivity, since the number of people with the minimum of unit productivity is already usually more than half the total population. Now, using fractional productivities it turns out that the expected law is quite well obeyed; a plot on logarithmic probability graph paper showing that those with less than a unit of fractional productivity are on a normal curve continuous with and a reasonable extension of that for people with fractional productivity greater than unity, the same people being in much the same rank order at the high end of the distribution. Interestingly, the median of the distribution is at a little less than a fractional score of .5 or half a paper per man and the standard deviation is the same as for full productivity. We suggest on this basis that part of the social function of collaboration is that it is a method for squeezing papers out of the rather large population of people who have less than a whole paper in them. Since the probability that a man can double his score of papers is known to be about one in four, it follows that for every person with a whole paper in him there may (if the curve can be legitimately extended) be 4 people with only half a paper each. If collaboration is forbidden one gets only one paper, but if half papers are permitted by society, as they now are, an extra two papers can be produced by suitable collaboration. If quarter papers are permitted another four extra papers will be forthcoming, and presumably the process might be continued indefinitely. A marked bending of the distribution line in Figure 2 however indicates that for the smallest fractional productivities there are less authors than one would expect, so that there seems some reluctance of society to accept its full quota of those with the present minimum of one-eighth of a paper each — there are only 4 such people in the sample and a normal distribution would contain about 60.

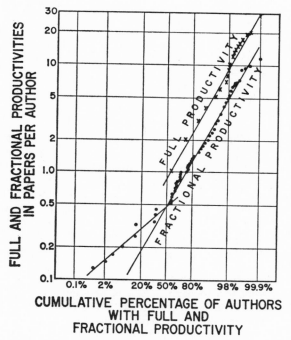

Fig. 2. A cumulative percentage distribution of authors on full and fractional productivity. (The use of fractional productivities shows that the distribution of productivity is in good agreement with the theoretical expectation that the logarithm of the productivity is normally distributed in the population.)

In some fields of science there is a strong convention, different from field to field, about the order of the names in the by-line of a paper. In theoretical physics it is invariably alphabetic, in some biosciences it is in order of seniority of the author or in the magnitude of his personal contribution to the collaboration. To test for this effect a preliminary investigation was made of the distribution of first-named authorships. Much more variation was found than with the comparison of frac-

tional and full productivities. The top three men were highest equally in all varieties of productivity, but below this level there were a number of high producers on full and fractional counts who rated lower in first authorships than those who were quite low on the other two counts. The convention seems to vary considerably, therefore, from man to man, and further investigation is needed.

Having now confirmed the existence of a core and a floating population, it remains to consider their relation to each other. To this end, the deck of index cards of authors was sorted manually so as to place together each author with those who had collaborated with him and also with those who had collaborated with his collaborators, etc. Thus, if two authors had collaborated on a paper, and then one of them had gone on to publish a second paper with three new additional collaborators, all five would be in a group that had produced two papers, one with two authors and another with four. The result of the investigation is shown in Table II. At the top of this table is a line indicating that 23 of the 122 groups consisted of a single individual each, an author who collaborated with nobody else, and that these authors produced a total of 30 papers. At the bottom of the table is a line showing that the largest group of all contained 77 authors who collaborated in many different combinations in producing 117 papers.

The five largest groups account in all for about a third of the total population of authors, and each group contains one or more individuals whose record is high in productivity score and in number of collaborators. Typically, each group contains a small number of very active people and a large number of individuals who have collaborated only on a few papers. For example, in the largest group of all there are 6 of the 77 authors whose names appear on 28, 15, 14, 12, 10, and 9 papers, respectively, for a total of 88 of the 271 authorships within this group. In this same group 55 of the authors (71%) have their names on 3 papers or less and produce a total of 99 authorships. Similarly, in the second largest group, the top authors have 19, 17, and 12 papers each for a total of 48 of the 161 authorships, while 30 of the 58 authors have their name on a single paper only.

Perhaps the most striking feature of this part of the investigation is the finding that separate groups exist in what would otherwise appear to be a single invisible college. One would naturally expect that authors who do not collaborate or those who have published a memo with only one or two other people would remain as isolated monads, pairs, and triads in such a study of groupings. One would, however, reasonably suppose that with authors who collaborate a great deal and with a constant flow of people each person would rapidly become connected, at some distance or other, with every other person. This does not happen, and there are at least five major noninterconnecting groups and probably several more of slightly smaller size.

TABLE II

CHARACTERISTICS OF GROUPS OF AUTHORS RELATED TO EACH OTHER BY COLLABORATION

Number of authors in group	Code name of big man	Number of such groups	Total authors in such groups	Number of papers from group	Number of authorships	Full productivity	Fractional productivity	Multiplicity of authorship
N		G	M = NG	P	A	P/M	A/M	A/P
1		23	23	30	30	1.30	1.30	1.00
2		30	60	45	85	.75	1.42	1.89
3		27	81	56	128	.69	1.58	2.29
4		13	52	35	86	.67	1.65	2.46
5		7	35	32	80	.91	2.29	2.50
6		7	42	28	82	.67	1.95	2.93
7		7	49	42	105	.86	2.14	2.50
8		3	24	30	72	1.20	3.00	2.40
9	BM	1	9	7	19	.78	2.11	2.71
14	RS	1	14	12	36	.86	2.58	3.00
31	DN	1	31	32	84	1.03	2.74	2.63
58	CT	1	58	67	161	1.16	2.78	2.40
77	GI	1	77	117	271	1.52	3.52	2.32
	Totals	122.	555	533	1,239			
					Average values	0.96	2.23	2.32

A preliminary check of the listed locations of authors shows that each group is centered on, but not confined to, the institution or working area of its leading members. The biggest group is gathered around the largest research institute for this field, directed by their most active producer and collaborator who is moreover the chairman of this IEG 1 and a founder of the whole IEG apparatus as well as an editor of an important journal in the area. Another group exists in several Japanese institutes and universities.

Another noteworthy result of this phase of the study is that although the number of authorships per paper does not seem to vary significantly with the size of group (except that it must be unity for single-author papers and far below average even for two-author papers) there is a striking variation of the productivities from group to group. In terms of the number of complete papers produced per man the value is much higher than average for the largest groups and also for those who work alone. It is smaller than average for all groups of sizes in between. The effect is even more striking for fractional productivities of the groups measured in terms of the number of authorships per man; in this case the productivities are seen to increase rather regularly with the size of the group, the largest groups having values much higher than the smallest groups. Though the effect is large, its interpretation is most difficult. If the good of science be measured in terms of papers produced, the gain can be maximized by having scientists work either singly and without collaboration, or in very large inter-related groups. Medium-sized groups lower the amount produced. If, on the other hand, the gain to the author be measured in terms of the number of authorships he collects, then he will increase his stock by moving to the largest available group and decrease it drastically by working on his own. Clearly both goods are well served only by the largest groups, and it is therefore for this reason that the invisible college group may exist. Exactly why this should be so is however a matter which is still dark to us.

Among the most interesting further problems which arise from this research is that of determining whether the palpable invisible college which has been studied is in fact several different, relatively unconnected, separate groups. Partly this could be determined by interviews, partly it could be checked automatically by seeing whether the references in papers of one group tended to cite that group exclusively or involved one or more of the other groups too. Further, this analysis of references might well reveal the existence of any body of notable contributors to the research front of the literature who were neither known authors from this study nor non-author members of the IEG 1 group. A very cursory preliminary investigation indicates that the amount of self-citation by a group is heavy — about a quarter of all references rather than the one-tenth that is normal to scientific papers — but that references to the other groups also occur. It also indicates that about one-third of the references are to authors outside the IEG 1 authorship rolls. The data are, however, far too fragmentary for even tentative conclusions beyond the fact that linking authors by their involvement in collaboration provides a technique which is likely to agree with citation linkages and with the subjective estimates of what may constitute an invisible college.

The implications of this study are considerable for analyzing the social life of science and the nature of collaboration and communication at the research front. Not only have we indicated that the research front is dominated by a small core of active workers and a large and weak transient population of their collaborators, but we point the way, in conclusion, to the possibility that it is by working together in collaboration that the greater part of research front communication occurs. Perhaps the recent acceleration in the amount of multiple authorship in several regions of science is due partly to the building of a new communication mechanism deriving from the increased mobility of scientists, and partly to an effort to utilize larger and larger quantities of lower-level research manpower. If this is so, then the conventional explanation of collaboration, as the utilization of many different skills and pairs of hands to do a single job otherwise impossible to perform, is woefully inadequate and misleading.

References

CLARKE, B. L. Multiple authorship trends in scientific papers. *Science*, 1964, **143**, 822–824.

GREEN, D. E. An experiment in communications: The information exchange group. *Science*, 1964, **143**, 308–309.

GREEN, D. E. Information exchange group number one. *Science*, 1965, **148**, 1543.

HIRSCH, W. & SINGLETON, J. F. Research support, multiple authorship and publication in sociological journals 1936–1964. Unpublished preprint, June 1965.

KEENAN, S., & ATHERTON, P. *The journal literature of physics*. New York: American Institute of Physics, AIP/DRP PA1, 1964.

MOORE, C. A. Preprints. An old information device with new outlooks. *Journal of Chemical Documentation*, 1965, **5**(3), 126–128.

MORAVCSIK, M. J. On improving communication. *Bulletin of the Atomic Scientists*, 1966, **22**(5), 31.

PASTERNACK, S. Is journal publication obsolescent? *Physics Today*, 1966, **19**(5), 38–43.

PRICE, D. J. DE S. *Little science, big science*. New York: Columbia University Press, 1963.

99

Chapter Three
The Concept
of
Relevance

If one were to pick the most controversial subject in information science, 'relevance' would undoubtedly be among the top contenders. 'Relevance' was denoted by many a name and connoted by many a definition, but regardless of the names or definitions, regardless of recognition or lack of it, relevance remains one of the basic properties related to information. It is also one of the basic aspects of communication processes. It is related to one of the basic objectives of all information systems, namely to the provision of relevant information. Thus, relevance is of fundamental concern to information science because it serves as a measure of the effectiveness of any and all communication processes.

The whole area of investigation of relevance is fairly new. Mere recognition of the fact that relevance — provision of 'relevant' information — was a problem of some magnitude dates back only ten to fifteen years. Instead of presenting a series of articles on relevance, it was decided to synthesize and critically evaluate the past views, trends, theories, definitions, hypotheses and experimental results related to relevance. The synthesis culminated in an exploration of relations between relevance and the known distributions of various communication processes. At the end, a hypothesis is suggested stating that relevant answers at a source and at a destination in a communication process are distributed in accordance with the Bradford law of literature scatter.

14 The Concept of "Relevance" in Information Science: A Historical Review

TEFKO SARACEVIC

1. Introduction

Underlying the significance of relevance as a fundamental concept in communication is the assertion or recognition that the phenomenon of relevance was, is, and always will be present in all communication, whether the communication is conducted among individuals or between information systems and individuals. Information has many associated properties, and relevance is one of the most important ones.

In the case of information systems in general, the basic purpose is to provide "relevant" information to a user or groups of users — a point made implicitly or explicitly so often that it requires no explication.

In the case of libraries, relevance was implicitly recognized in the very organization of classification schemes, subject headings, and catalogs. In the reference process, the interaction between the requester and a librarian is explicitly carried out in order to increase the relevance of materials or answers provided.

Today, even the social systems (e.g., universities) are being analyzed on the basis of "relevance" in their actions (e.g., curricula). Again, "relevance" is used exactly in the same sense as in the context of information systems in particular and cummunication processes in general.

In the case of direct communication among people, there is the same basic desire — to communicate information with some desired effect — that is, to communicate "relevant" information.

The notion and discussion of relevance can be traced to the earliest philosophical thought. However, the present concern about relevance, and the rise of relevance as one of the most significant research problems in information science, it not of philosophical origin. It stems from serious and critical practical problems encountered in the operations of information retrieval systems and of libraries, and in the applications of computers to information processing. The problems not only involve design and operation of systems with the ability to provide relevant answers to queries in a timely, orderly, effective, and efficient manner, but also, and even more so, with the ability to suppress and not to provide nonrelevant answers. In other words, the concern about relevance in modern times emanates mainly from the "amount" of existing nonrelevance, which is making communication increasingly difficult.

It can be stated that information communicated that

is not relevant is not information, but such an approach is limited and deficient, since it does not take into account a number of possible viewpoints on relevance of information in a communication process. For instance, relevance may be considered from the points of view of the source or a variety of sources of information, and from the points of view of the destination or a variety of destinations to which information is transmitted; in addition, a variety of representations of information as well as transmitting or processing aspects may have to be taken into account.

It is most important to state the restrictive framework within which relevance is being considered in this paper, and to stress that this restriction be kept in mind at all times. The notion of relevance of interest to information science is directly connected with the concept of communication as a process. A communication process is viewed here as a sequence of events where something called information is transmitted from one object (source) to another (destination), often in a series of reiterative or feedback-type sequences. The objects, sources, and destinations may be people, organisms, records, machines, or systems in general. This view of communication implies that both the source and the destination contain, among other factors, a store, file, or memory of knowledge and/or knowledge-based constructs. This important implication should always be taken into account.

We may not know what information is but we can study some of its properties and effects. Analogies of such an approach abound: Man doesn't know what electricity is, for instance, but he is quite familiar with its behavior, properties, and effects. Intuitively, it is well understood that relevance is a most important property of information, that relevance indicates a relation between a source and destination in a communication process; more specifically, *relevance is a measure of effective contact between a source and a destination.*

> . . . But what relations does relevance specify?
> . . . What is an "effective contact"?
> . . . How is an information system connected with relevance?
> . . . What is the role of a source in connection with relevance and what is the role of a destination?
> . . . How are people with their possible subjective characteristics involved in relevance, both as individuals or as various social groups?
> . . . What is the relation and difference between relevance and relevance judgments?
> . . . What are the connections between some aspects of the general organization, creation, scatter, distribution, utilization, and obsolescence of knowledge and relevance?

Concise explications do not exist. In information science these and similar questions were a subject of ex-tensive and at times vitriolic debates, as well as many axioms, numerous definitions, some fully stated hypotheses, a limited number of experiments, and a few formal theories. Thus, as a result, the views and understanding of relations specified by relevance during the last two decades have undergone convoluted transformations. Although there is a voluminous literature on relevance, our formal knowledge about it is admittedly quite inadequate. The formal knowledge that exists is hardly cumulative, based in part on the historical fact that many works and writings concerning relevance were done in isolation of one another. Efforts went in many independent directions, with little or no connection between theoretical and experimental work, or between dogmatic pronouncements and experimental observations.

The aim of this paper is to review, synthesize, summarize, and evaluate the activities related to the notion of relevance in information science. In a sense, the present review is a continuation of a similar but shorter review performed a few years ago (Rees and Saracevic, 1966). Two reasons for the need of such a review follow.

First, because of the fundamental nature of relevance, it seems important that students of the properties of information, students of communication processes, and especially students of man's communication of man's knowledge, along with designers, developers, operators, and students of information systems, be acquainted with the historical developments related to the notion of relevance.

Second, it is an unfortunate fact that although relevance has been subject of considerable theoretical and experimental research in information science in the sixties, at the start of the seventies there are no ongoing research projects (known to this reviewer) that deal directly with relevance. Relevance lends itself especially well to controlled experimentation, and it is modestly hoped that the synthesis presented here might enhance and encourage further research on relevance.

2. Approach and Organization

The approach taken in this study resembles the traditional approach of scientific treatises. A treatise implies: (a) a systematic, historic, and chronological exposé of a subject; (b) a correlation between various trends, viewpoints, and works; and (c) a critical synthesis of what is known, with suggestions as to the possible fruitful directions of future work. The organization of this study was dictated by two restrictions: consideration of the above approach and multiplicity of loosely connected or largely unconnected views, trends, and works on relevance. The study is divided into seven parts, each part representing an area or aspect within which relevance was studied or discussed. An attempt is made to maintain a chronology of views, works, and writings within each part. In addition, the parts (representing different areas) themselves are ordered chronologically, with regard to their appearance or prominence in connection with relevance. The seven parts of the study are summarized below to provide an overall view.

The first part identifies the beginning of the concern about relevance which resulted from the emergence of information retrieval systems in the early fifties. The operational or "systems view" on relevance was the outgrowth of the operational problems anticipated and encountered. This view considered relevance as being completely affected and determined by a system and its internal arrangements. Thus, relevance was considered solely a property of the source in a communication process. The first part also contains a review of the assumed connection between the logic used in retrieval of documents by a retrieval system and relevance. The assumption, which caused a great deal of confusion, was that the partitioning (dividing) of a file into retrieved and not retrieved sets was equivalent to partitioning a file into relevant and nonrelevant sets. These views and assumptions were first challenged at the International Conference for Scientific Information held in 1958, from which many new views on revelance emerged, views which affected relevance activity for a decade.

The second part is devoted to formal theoretical works on relevance starting in 1960 with the theory presented by Maron and Kuhns. Only four larger theoretical studies were found in the literature on relevance. Although the theoretical work had no noticeable connection with subsequent experimentation on relevance, it accomplished two important functions: First, it clarified and delimited the notion of relevance and of the relations involved, and second, it provided a potential framework for experimentation; a theory may serve as a starting point and/or as an ending explanation for experimental observations. Unfortunately, relevance theories were, at that point, not used in this capacity.

The third part deals with the connection between relevance and performance testing of information retrievel systems. By the early and mid-sixties, the problems and significance of relevance were brought into the limelight through the activity of testing. Relevance was chosen as the criterion for performance measures. Many methodological problems were uncovered, especially in using people and their relevance judgments as test instruments for recording relevance at the destination. Through this activity, a view of relevance emerged which considered relevance solely a property of a destination in a communication process. Another point of confusion was injected: Relevance judgment (which is actually only one of the possible responses at a destination) was incorrectly and almost totally equated with relevance (which is actually a property of information involving the whole of a communication process).

The fourth part summarizes the definitions, axioms, and hypotheses that emerged as a result of the debate about relevance, following the testing activity. Numerous definitions and hypothetical statements were offered, but only a few fully stated hypotheses are to be found in the literature. These are synthesized and contrasted. Chronologically, the period of definitions and hypotheses encompasses the mid-sixties.

The fifth and largest part of the study deals with experiments on relevance. It is believed that the experiments included accurately represent, but do not necessarily cover, the totality of all the conducted experiments on relevance. Each experiment is summarized in terms of the basic aims or variables observed, the methodology used, and the results obtained. The experiments were almost exclusively concerned with relevance judgments by people and were summarized in terms of the five major classes of variables investigated: documents and document representations, queries, judgmental situations, modes for expression, and people's characteristics. Chronologically, the experimental period started in 1960, but came to full bloom during the second half of the sixties.

The sixth part is devoted to the synthesis of what we have learned from experimentation. The conclusions and implications from all experiments are synthesized and enumerated in terms of the variables studied. These conclusions are made on the basis of the evaluation of the experimental results obtained by the reviewer rather than on the basis of the conclusions of the experimenters. It is pointed out that the experimental observations overall actually warrant only speculative conclusions. The second section in this part is devoted to critical reflections on the experiments. Serious conceptual, methodological, and environmental shortcomings are stated with the hope that they may be avoided in the future.

The seventh part deals with an area of investigation rarely if ever explicity linked to relevance. It is conjectured that some empirical distribution laws, describing observed regularities of patterns in some communication situations, are actually relevance-related distributions. Connected with relevance are the following observed distributions: (a) the frequency of utilization of periodicals from a library collection and the frequency of retrieval of documents as answers from a retrieval system file; (b) the productivity of authors in subject areas in science and relation of the number of authors to the number of journals in a field, i.e., Lotka's and Goffman/Warren's laws; (c) distribution of citation networks and practices in science; (d) frequency of appearance of words in a text, i.e., Zipf's law and its generalizations for many distributions of things ranked in order of size; and (e) in particular, the scatter-pattern of articles on a subject over journals, i.e., Bradford's law. The Bradford law is hypothetically considered as directly describing a distribution of relevant answers, selected by a source from its file, which transmits answers to destinations in response to a large number of queries; from those answers that they receive, the destinations select relevant answers — again those relevant answers at destinations (over a number of queries) are hypothetically considered to be distributed according to Bradford's law. A testable hypothesis to that effect is offered as a concluding part of this study, i.e., it is suggested that relevant answers are distributed by the sources and by the destinations according to Bradford's law; however, the zones at the sources' and destinations' ends may differ in size and order.

It may be of interest to observe that the activities related to relevance followed the pattern of activities exhibited in investigations of many other phenomena throughout the history of science. Thus, they were somewhat predictable, and possibly the general trend of the future activities may also be predictable. First, there is the recognition of the existence of phenomenon and a problem; second, a rather simplified view of the nature of the phenomenon and problem emerges; third, faults are found with the simplified view and corrections are suggested; fourth, the simplified view, together with corrections, is rejected and other views are offered; fifth, definitions and hypotheses are proposed; sixth, theories and experiments emerge; seventh, a new correction of views is undertaken; eighth, updated and new theories and experiments emerge, etc. This cycle repeats itself until one of two things happens: the phenomenon is clarified (positively or negatively) or an impasse is reached, which awaits a breakthrough at a later time (again either positive or negative, where negative means that the phenomenon is dismissed or exchanged with another phenomenon). It is suggested here that the general study of relevance in information science is, at the start of 1970, at an impasse. The impasse was reached right after point six in the cycle as described above. Theories and experiments had emerged but a new correction of views has not yet been undertaken (point seven), and as a result neither has a new cycle of updated theories and experiments taken place. The reasons for the impasse are suggested in Part Six on Synthesis. In a sense Part Seven of this study on Relevance-Related Ditribution is an attempt to bring a different approach to relevance, suggesting new experiments, thus, it is a modest attempt to start point seven of the cycle in the development of the understanding of a phenomenon as described above.

The approximate chronological development of various areas of relevance-related activities is graphically illustrated in Graph 1. The solid lines indicate periods of more vigorous activity in an area. The legend defines each area and provides some of the authors identified with the given area. It is hoped that this chronological graph will help the reader to obtain a general overview of all of the activities on relevance.

Part 1. Operations of Information Retrieval Systems and Relevance

The Systems View—The "False Drop"

Present concern over the concept of relevance can be traced to the beginnings of information retrieval systems in the early fifties. It was correctly recognized as early as information retrieval systems were practically conceived that not all of what will be retrieved will necessarily be relevant. Needless to say, the operational results manifoldly confirmed the suspicion.

The pioneers of information retrieval, Mooers (1950), Perry (1951), and Taube (1955) were the first to discuss relevance from the point of view of nonrelevance — that is, unwanted information provided by a retrieval system. In that sense, nonrelevance was conceived in terms of "false coordination," "noise," "extra tallies," "negative classes," etc., basically considering the phenomenon of nonrelevance as resulting from a malfunction of the system. Specifically, false drops were considered to be a result of inadequacy and ineffectiveness of information representations: coding schemes, indexing languages, description of syntactic and semantic relationships of terms, which led to mismatchings. In general, the views on relevance in information retrieval were greatly affected by the concept of "noise" in Shannon's information theory.

From such an approach relevance was viewed as the result of a match between the terms of a question and the terms of an index. This led to consideration of "relatedness" among documents, where "relatedness" was treated as a synonym of relevance. Relevance was solely conceived and considered to be a property of the internal organization of the system and of the documents included in the system. It appeared as if one could arrange a matching between questions and relevant answers solely by system manipulation. In other words, relevance was considered an exclusive property of the source in a communication process. However, it should be pointed out that recent experimental studies confirm that some of the internal system arrangements, i.e., arrangements by the source (e.g., type, order or number of documents presented, and especially the content of contained documents), may have a considerable effect on relevance judgments as variables, but they are by no means the only factors that enter into such judgments.

Relevance and the Formal Logic of Retrieval Operations

While the previously stated "systems view" associated relevance, or rather nonrelevance, with the effectiveness of system operations, it must be noted and understood that a notion of relevance is implied in the formal logic of retrieval operation, which is employed in a wide range of present information retrieval systems or even information systems in general. Since the actual formal logic is not of direct interest here, it is sufficient to say that underlying the retrieval operations are propositional calculus and its isomorphic relative Boolean algebra, in terms of which queries are stated and index terms manipulated. For example, one allowable operation is the creation of a union: documents or indexes are retrieved

Graph 1: Chronological Order of Various Areas in the Investigation of Relevance in Information Science with Identification of Some of the Authors Associated with Each Activity

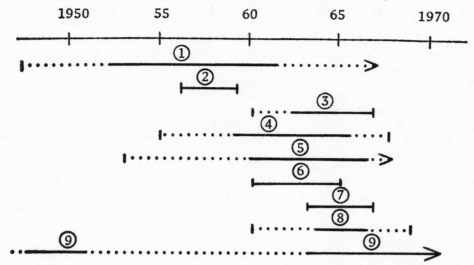

[solid lines represent periods of more vigorous activity]

Legend:	Activity	Authors
①	Operational concern with relevance, "systems view"	Mooers, Perry, Taube
②	First doubts and first debate (ICSI)	Vickery, Fairthorne, Bar-Hillel, Fano, etc.
③	Theories on relevance	Maron/Kuhns, Hillman, Goffman, Goffman/Newill
④	Performance measures using relevance as criteria	Perry, et al., Swets, Goffman/Newill, Salton, Pollock, etc.
⑤	Testing of IR systems	Cleverdon, Salton, etc.
⑥	Second debate; problems of relevance judgment	Doyle, Cuadra, Rees, Taube, O'Connor, etc.
⑦	Definitions and hypotheses	Rees/Saracevic, Rees/ Schultz, Cuadra/Katter, O'Connor
⑧	Relevance experiments	Resnick, Roth/Resnick/ Savage, Dym/Shirey/Kurfeest, Barhydt, Cuadra/Katter, Rees/ Schultz, Lesk/Salton, Gifford/ Baumanis, O'Connor, Saracevic
⑨	Relevance-related distributions	Lotka, Bradford, Zipf, Price, Goffman/Warren, Leimkuhler, Brookes, etc.

if either term A or B or C, etc., can be found in the document or index. Another operation is the creation of an intersection: documents or indexes are retrieved if they contain term A and B and C, etc., in the given document or index.

Thus, a file of documents (or indexes) is partitioned (divided) by these and other logical operations into two sets: one set that is retrieved and one set that is not retrieved. The retrieved set can be also ordered according to some criteria. There is a basic assumption that the logical operations have something to do with "relevance," that is, it is assumed that partitioning of the file into a retrieved and a not retrieved set is the same as partitioning the file into a relevant and a nonrelevant set. However, formally and strictly speaking, that "relevance" is only related to the system or source, or specifically to the partition of a source's file, according to some logic directly acceptable to that file. Thus, a system or source always performs perfectly in partitioning a file in two (or more) sets for retrieval: it provides "relevant" answers exactly as it is being asked. It is only our (at times reasonable) assumption that these partitioned sets are somewhat related to relevance as desired or acceptable at the destination not only in the retrieval process but also in the communication process as a whole. The relevance by a system or source is expressed by logical operations and the relevance at destination is often expressed by human judgment.

Thus, it is clear that one of the salient points of confusion in perceiving relevance stemmed from the inability to differentiate between the system's or source's assignment of relevance and the user's or destination's assignment of relevance. A system, to arrive at relevance is partitioning its files according to some criteria and logic and on the basis of some information representation while the user may employ an entirely different criteria and logic, as well as employing (most of the time) an entirely different information representation. The system's (source's) relevance attempts to be a representation of the user's (destination's) relevance and the "relevance problem" basically stems from the fact that no representation represents accurately at all times the object being represented. In a sense, a retrieval system is a user's relevance assessment delegate. From this point of view, we will also discuss later the system performance measures which attempt to measure the performance of a system as a delegate of a user.

The First Doubts and the First Relevance Debate

The first official recognition that relevance may not be just a simple system phenomenon related to the effectiveness of matching within a retrieval system, and the first extensive exploration of the relevance concept, came in 1958 at the International Conference for Scientific Information (ICSI) in Washington (National Academy of Sciences, 1959). A number of views on relevance were presented both in formal papers and discussions. Many of the present views on relevance can be traced to ICSI.

At ICSI, Vickery, in two papers, presented two separate views on relevance: one pertained to "user relevance" and the other, "relevance to a subject." Bar Hillel, as a critic, strongly suggested that a careful distinction be made between "relatedness" and "degree of relevance." Others pointed out that relevance is represented not by a dichotomy but by a continuum. Fairthorne insisted that the relevance of a document and the description of its "contents" (such as done by indexing) are not the same. Fano, presenting his dream of library service, hinted that much more is involved than judging relevance solely in relation to the subject content of a question. He was unwilling to phrase questions in any combination of prescribed words, but he was prepared to indicate which documents are "like" and which are "unlike" the ones he requested. In essence, Fano was arguing that he could judge relevance.

The implicit consensus of the ICSI debate was that:

1. relevance is more than the operation of relating, performed internally within systems;
2. relevance is not exclusively a property of document content or document relatedness;
3. relevance is not a dichotomous decision;
4. there *is* such a thing as "user relevance" which *can* be judged, thus, a notion of relevance as considered by a destination was born.

By way of comment, it has to be pointed out that there was, in 1958, no explicit discussion on the subjectivity of the human judgment of relevance or even of relevance in any judgmental situation.

The views held on relevance were based on logical or intuitive inferences unsupported by generalizable, theoretical, or experimental evidence. This fact reflects that in 1958 research and experimentation in information retrieval had barely started to emerge, while the developmental activity was already about ten years old.

Part 2. Theories

As the debate on relevance proceeded a number of workers in the field became interested in relevance from an abstract point of view; their interest concentrated on building theories, formulated in terms of mathematical, statistical, or logical language and constructs. The formal, abstract approach is best characterized by Hillman (1964):

". . . it is to describe a concept of relevance independent of, and logically prior to, any notion of relevance as determined by, and thus, restricted to, a particular system of storage and retrieval. In addition, this concept must not be defined with respect to index terms or the like . . . ."

Contrasted with the systems view, relevance was not viewed as a property of a system. Being abstract, the notions were not restricted to any one operational or even judgmental situation. In other words, although operations were implied, they were immaterial for the purpose of the theories.

Maron and Kuhns (1960) presented one of the first large and formal theoretical treatises in the field as a whole. Their theory was concerned with a derivation of a measure indicating the probability that a document will satisfy a given request; given a probability approximation, a set of documents satisfying a request may be ranked as to their relevance. The concept of relevance, which was considered a primitive notion, was explicated to provide a quantitative expression. "In some sense," to quote the authors, "the problem of explicating the notion of relevance (which is the basic concept in a theory of information retrieval) is similar to that of explicating the notion of amount of information (which is the basic concept of Shannon's communication theory) . . . we approach the notion of relevance also in a probabilistic sense." The quantity called a 'relevance number' was formulated in terms of conditional probabilities, indicating the relation between a user, his request, the subject area of the request, and a document supplied as an answer. Specifically, the 'relevance number' is the probability indicating that, given a user does request information on a subject (designated by some given representation), he will be satisfied with a given document provided by a system. Methods and problems of approximation of the probabilities were extensively elaborated. The significance of the Maron-Kuhns theory lies in the utilization of the concept of probabilities to describe complex relations indicated by relevance. The probabilistic approach was successfully used in many fields for describing complex phenomena and especially in expressing such phenomena as measures. Thus, Maron and Kuhns laid the groundwork for treating relevance as a measure, both theoretically and in terms of practical approximations. Also, through the experiments that followed, Maron and Kuhns demonstrated the power of the connection between a theory and subsequent experimentation.

In another theory, Hillman (1964) was concerned with the basic problem of defining the concept of relevance. He formally specified the relations indicated by relevance utilizing the constructs offered by formal logic in general and Carnap's concept-formation theory in particular. Starting from the basic point of view that the mutual relevances of queries and documents involve the problem of conceptual relatedness (i.e., relevance defined as conceptual relatedness), Hillman proceeded to examine the applicability of constructs in logic in describing such a relatedness. He critically analyzed the utility of the theory of concept-formation, which led him to the discussion of the problems in defining a 'concept'. An interpretation of 'concept' applicable to a description of

relevance-relations was suggested in terms of similarity-classes and the appropriate theorems concerned with the nature and properties of similarity-relations were stated. The shortcomings of the procedure were examined and the human relevance judgment (under defined restrictions) was suggested as one of the bases for establishing similarity-relations. The significance and strength of Hillman's work lies in the critical examination of the applicability of formal logical constructs to the definition of relevance and the relations it indicates.

In a third theory, Goffman (1964) dealt with relevance from a formalistic mathematical point of view. He defined relevance as a measure of information conveyed by a document relative to a query. Then he proceeded to examine conditions under which relevance will satisfy the properties required of a measure as stated in the mathematical theory of measures. The mathematical properties of a measure, in brief, are: (a) it is real-valued and non-negative (i.e., expressed by a positive real number); (b) it is completely additive (i.e., the sum of the measures is the measure of the sum; parts measured either independently or as a whole have to have the same measure); (c) it has guaranteed an order (e.g., a smaller set has a smaller measure over it); and (d) it has an absolute zero. Goffman established and proved a theorem which says in effect that if relevance is determined simply on the basis of the relationship between the query and the document (that is, from individual documents in isolation to each other), then relevance does not have one of the properties required of a measure; it does not satisfy the property of being completely additive, i.e., the sum of relevancies expressed over individual documents may be greater than the relevancy of all documents when taken together and in relation to each other. Goffman then proceeded to state and prove another theorem showing that when relevance is determined not only on the basis of the query-document relationship but also in terms of the documents' relationship to each other, relevance has the properties required of a measure as stated above. Thus, given that one wants to treat relevance as a measure, two relationships have to be taken into account: one between query and documents and one among documents. In general then, from that point of view relevance is a comparative relation.

The above notions and the theory of relevance as a measure were incorporated in a larger and general theory of communication by Goffman and Newill (1967) — where the communication processes were represented and treated as an analogy of epidemic processes. The process of the spread of ideas was treated in analogy with the process of the spread of diseases. Epidemic theory was applied to the study of communication processes in which information is transmitted within a population. A communication process was described as a sequence of events resulting in the transmission of information from one object (source) to another (destination). The process is carried out within a population which has distinct subpopulations (infectives, susceptibles, and removals) as well as being in one of three states (increasing, decreasing, stable). A stability theorem defined under what conditions the process is stable. Within a communication process there is a sub-process, called information retrieval, formally described as an instrument for providing effective contact between the source (infectives) and destination (susceptible). By "effective contact" it is meant that a process which, when properly carried out, assures that the information transmitted from the source(s) to a target(s) is relevant, i.e., the process results in the accumulation of knowledge at the destination. The conditions for such an effective contact were formally stated, using probability theory. The conditional probabilities associated with relevance were defined, using the dependency relations between documents and a query, and among the documents. A series of theorems provided a well-defined and original framework for these dependency relations. In other words, relevance was interpreted as a formal measure of the effectiveness of the transmission of information in an information retrieval process (or broadly, in a dissemination process) within a framework of a communication process. In the words of authors:

"... This notion reflected the fact that any measure of the effectiveness of information conveyed must depend upon what is already known. Therefore, it is necessary to introduce a dependency relation among the members of I (infectives), relative to a S (a susceptible), namely the notion of conditional probabilities of relevance."

The significance of the Goffman-Newill treatment of relevance lies in the fullest formal mathematical definition and treatment to date, and even more so in incorporation of relevance in a larger theory of communication, where its place in the communication processes was fully defined.

In conclusion, the theoretical points of view recognized relevance as a phenomenon indicating relations. As such, relevance may be viewed as a measure associated with conditional probabilities; it may have some statistical distribution properties, in other words. It was also recognized that it is a complex and comparative relation affected by properties of and interrelation between documents (or abstractly any conveyor of information) and their representations as well as properties of queries, the sources of queries, and their representations.

Part 3. Performance of Retrieval Systems and Relevance

Relevance as a Criterion for Performance Measures

As a result of extensive efforts and economic investments in the design, development, and operations of information retrieval system, and especially as a result of the utilization of sophisticated information technology,

demands were put forth to investigate the performance and claims of a variety of competing retrieval systems.

The testing of any system requires at least the following: a model, a prototype, or a set of hypotheses to be tested; a criterion or criteria reflecting the system's performance objectives; measures in terms of which performance criteria are quantified; instruments for recording the measures; and methodologies for measuring. Of interest here are the criteria, measures, and instruments used for the testing of effectiveness (as opposed to efficiency) of information retrieval systems.

The first quantifiable measures were proposed by Kent, Perry, and associates (1955), using "pertinency" (in a context synonymous with "relevance") as a criterion. The measures were the familiar "recall" and "relevance"; the latter was because of semantic confusion renamed "precision." Over the years a great number of measures were proposed, and few were utilized.

Swets (1963), reviewing the effectiveness related performance measures for retrieval systems proposed up to that time, found that from some ten different measures eight used relevance as the criterion and the other two could not be numerically expressed. In more recent work Pollock (1968) found much the same situation — regardless of the measure proposed or used, relevance was and is the criterion on which the measures are based. As a matter of fact, it seems that no other effectiveness criterion than relevance was or is being seriously contemplated, or at least none exists that has caught some general attention.

Since we are not concerned here with the review of the measures themselves, it is sufficient to say that all of the measures are attempting in some manner or other to measure, or rather approximate, the agreement or disagreement between a system's (source's) assignment of relevance and a user's or user's delegate (destination's) assignment of relevance. In other words, a user's relevance judgment over some set of records, documents or their representations is being used as a standard against which a set of system's answers is being compared, and the measures reflect the comparison.

After relevance was selected as a criterion for performance, but prior to actual testing, there still remained the probelm of what instruments were to be used to record the relevance of documents (or any other records) in relation to queries (or any other response-demanding mechanism). This problem is separate from other problems of methodology, such as what and how many documents or records should be used, how are they to be processed, how to obtain and deploy the queries, how to search, etc. Some of the early tests in the fifties used documents as instruments. To explain: From a test file certain documents called "source documents" were used to create a query and subsequently record as instruments their own retrieval; the measures reflected the success of a system in retrieval of the source documents.

But most often in tests people were used as instruments. They recorded the relevance of a document as it is supposed to be related to a query or to some other records or documents serving as a query. People are used as recording instruments in many situations besides retrieval systems tests. Such use has many problems associated with it, problems which were investigated in a number of fields, principally in psychology. But the problems associated with using people in recording relevance were not well known. For instance, it wasn't clear at all what type of people are appropriate to record relevance: the user, i.e., the one who asked the query, or a user delegate? If a delegate, should he be a subject expert, a system operator, or a group of any of these recording relevance by consensus? How stable are people as relevance recording instruments?

The recording of the relevance of documents in relation to queries eventually was considered to be a judgment — judgment in the sense of a preferential discriminatory response. Slowly, relevance and relevance judgment came to be considered one and the same; the terms were used interchangeably. In reality, they are quite different concepts, although a relation certainly exists between relevance as a relation between a source and destination in a communication process and relevance judgment as a certain response at a destination. The lack of distinction between the two was a most unfortunate development because it caused a considerable amount of confusion. This point will be elaborated later in the reflections on experimentation. To contrast two reviewed views of relevance: from the "systems point of view" relevance was considered to be solely a property of a source and from the "judgment or psychological point of view" relevance was considered to be solely a property of a destination in a communication process. By way of comment, it is suggested that neither view is entirely correct; relevance encompasses both, the source and the destination.

The Testing Activity and the "Relevance Problem"

The activity of testing of information retrieval systems, which started in the fifties and gained impetus in the early sixties, produced a whole corpus of critical literature. Many issues were raised which were related to testing methodologies; among them the problems of relevance, or more precisely of relevance judgments, came into sharp focus. By and large, the test experiments ignored the issues of relevance judgment, but the critics didn't. As Cuadra and Katter (1967) stated:

". . . Most of the workers engaged in system evaluation from 1953 to the present, have had relatively little interest in relevance judgments *per se*. They have been interested in them primarily as a criterion by which to evaluate manual or computer-based searches, or comparisons between them. These workers, of course, have been aware of disagreement

among judges, but they have tended to consider such disagreement largely as an irritant, to be stamped out or bypassed as quickly as possible, rather than as a phenomenon worthy of interest in its own right."

The great debate on relevance and relevance judgment that followed the testing activity (the "second relevance debate") began in the early sixties, and it still wasn't exhausted at their end. The most positive result of the debate was that it spurred relevance experimentation. The experimentation was especially affected by the conclusions made at a conference called by the National Science Foundation (NSF 1964). One of the conclusions stated:

". . . a major obstacle to progress in the area of (information retrieval systems) evaluation methodology is the lack of sufficient knowledge regarding the character and variability of human assessments of the relevance of retrieved documents . . . Such relevance assessments are fundamental to the development of reliable methods and techniques for measuring the effectiveness of document searching systems . . ."

It should be mentioned that regardless of the correctness or incorrectness of the above conclusion and of the rationale of the "second relevance debate" the inferences were (as in the first ICSI debate) logical, intuitive, and experience-based and not connected in general to experimental observations or defined theoretical constructs. If they were on occasion, it was rather a rare exception than a rule which, again, doesn't mean they were incorrect. The NSF conclusions and the statements in the "second debate" sound definite and positive, but it should be realized that in reality they were assumptions only.

The issues that were raised and examined, but not necessarily resolved in the debate and by the subsequent experimentation, may be categorized in these classes which are later elaborated in separate sections of this review:

1. The definition and concept of relevance; how can relevance be defined?
2. The hypothesis and assumptions about the variables affecting relevance judgments; what are the major classes of variables?
3. The experimental observations of the effects of major hypothesized variables on relevance judgments; how and to what extent they affect the judgment?
4. The objectivity/subjectivity of relevance and relevance judgments; to what extent do people's relevance judgments agree or disagree? Under what circumstances does the agreement increase or decrease? Given instability of relevance judg-

ments, how do they affect the reliability of results of test experiments?

5. The methodological problems associated with relevance experimentation; what are the appropriate experimental methodologies, designs, approaches, and analysis techniques? What are the methodologies for using relevance judgments?

Part 4. Definitions and Hypotheses

The Conceptions: Definitions Galore

One (and usually among the first) approach in the clarification of a phenomenon consists of attempts to define it. Definitions of relevance started to appear after it was seen that the first views were oversimplifications. The significance of definitions of relevance are manifold. First, they delineated, illuminated, and hypothesized about the subject area referred to; second, they served as instructions to the users of retrieval systems as to the framework for judgments; and third, by themselves, they were recognized as potential variables affecting results of experiments and tests. Thus, the review of relevance definitions seems to warrant attention.

Definitions of relevance were so numerous that Rees and Schultz (1967) found it almost impossible to identify the sources and authors; instead two lists were constructed that summarized the definitions. It is worthwhile to examine these and additional definitions because of the already enumerated reasons and also because they suggested experimentation and a more formal approach in the past and may do so in the future. Here is a sampling of definitions offered, arranged in a traditional form:

Relevance is:
. . . correspondence between a document and a question; a measure of informativeness of a document to a question;
. . . an indication of how good or satisfactory an answer document is to a question;
. . . the degree of relationship (relatedness, overlap, fit), existing between a document and a question;
. . . the degree of fit between document and prior knowledge of user;
. . . a property which assigns members of a file to the answer;
. . . appropriateness of a document to a question;
. . . a measure of surprise that something appearing in a document is connected with one's information need or question (i.e., that it is previously unknown information and/or previously unrelated information);
. . . relatedness of information to the question even if the information provided is known or outdated;
. . . a measure of usefulness of an answer;
. . . an indication of significance to an important purpose;
. . . a satisfactory answer;

Relevant materials or information are:
. . . documents from which answers to questions could be inferred;
. . . ideas or facts so closely related to the problem at hand that disregarding them would alter the problem;
. . . ideas or facts useful in considering the matter at hand;
. . . answers of use in current work;
. . . answers required for professional growth;

While the above provides a list of popularly accepted definitions of relevance, the approach below shows relevance as an algorithm, which displays certain relationships among parts while permitting a rather free manipulation of the parts. The algorithm takes the following form:

Relevance is the ___A___ of a ___B___ existing between a ___C___ and a ___D___ as judged by an ___E___ ;

where: A represents the gage of measure;
B represents the aspect of relevance;
C represents the object upon which relevance is measured;
D represents the context within which relevance is measured;
E represents the assessor.

A, B, C, D and E, which represent fillers for appropriate slots, are expanded in Figure 1 in order to show all parts whose relationship to each other seem meaningful to demonstrate almost every definition ever used for the concept of relevance.

Another approach used in defining relevance was to avoid the term altogether and substitute near synonyms, such as "satisfaction," "usefulness," "appropriateness," etc. By avoidance and substitutions, quite a few different connotations to the general concept of "relevance" may be given, but the basic problem is not avoided.

From Definitions to Hypotheses

Although the definitions of relevance and the debates provided a general consensus about the conception of relevance and overall a better understanding of the complexity of the problem, it was clear that, in order to answer the numerous questions asked and to enlarge knowledge, different work had to be done. As in many other fields where phenomena are investigated, the next step was the implicit or explicit proposal of hypotheses, followed by experimentation.

Some hypothetical statements about relevance that could be gleaned from the debate literature (1960-1966) include:

. . . only the user himself may judge the relevance of the documents to him and his uses, i.e., the judgment of relevance may be subjective;

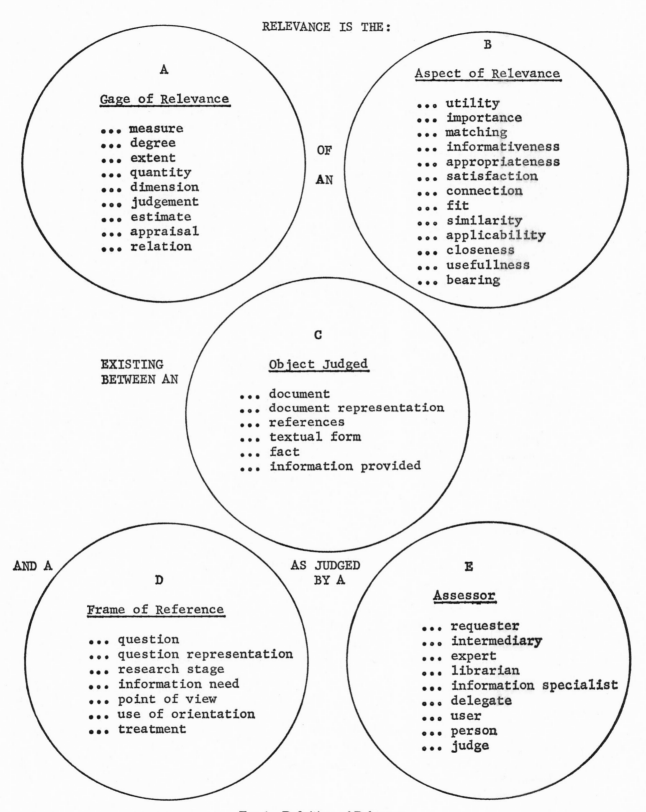

RELEVANCE IS THE:

A

<u>Gage of Relevance</u>

... measure
... degree
... extent
... quantity
... dimension
... judgement
... estimate
... appraisal
... relation

OF

AN

B

<u>Aspect of Relevance</u>

... utility
... importance
... matching
... informativeness
... appropriateness
... satisfaction
... connection
... fit
... similarity
... applicability
... closeness
... usefullness
... bearing

C

<u>Object Judged</u>

... document
... document representation
... references
... textual form
... fact
... information provided

EXISTING
BETWEEN AN

AND A

AS JUDGED
BY A

D

<u>Frame of Reference</u>

... question
... question representation
... research stage
... information need
... point of view
... use of orientation
... treatment

E

<u>Assessor</u>

... requester
... intermediary
... expert
... librarian
... information specialist
... delegate
... user
... person
... judge

FIG. 1. Definitions of Relevance.

... for the same user a relevance judgment may change over time, i.e., the changes in cognitive set may need to be accounted for in relevance judgments;

... various types of judgments may exist because of the different purposes for which information is required, i.e., the query itself, the environment of user, the intended usage may affect the judgment.

The debate concerned itself also with the objectivity/subjectivity of relevance. Two schools of thought were developed, best represented by Doyle (1963) and Cuadra (1964). In general, Doyle viewed relevance as a subjective and elusive property that cannot serve as a criterion for any measures. Cuadra, on the other hand, conceded that relevance may be subjective, but called for rigorous experimental observations upon which to base conclusions.

From a different point of view, and on the basis of operational experience, Rees and Saracevic (1963), and again Rees (1963), suggested that, in relation to answers from retrieval systems, there may exist two quite different aspects of relevance that must be distinguished. The question asking/answering process was hypothesized to consist of the following sequence:

Thus, relevance does not imply pertinence, nor does pertinence imply relevance. In other words, there may be answers that are relevant but not pertinent, or pertinent but not relevant.

The concept of information need, which was not a new concept (e.g., Maron and Kuhns (1960) used it in their theory in the same sense as above), was widely accepted from practical experience: ". . . what a person asks may not be the question he had in mind . . . ," or ". . . what is considered as an answer often has little connection with the question . . . ." However, the concept also had its fierce critics. O'Connor (1968) for instance asks numerous penetrating questions about ". . . the meaning of that sacred expression . . . information need . . . ," pointing out that there could be numerous explanations, all unclear, and that basically the "satisfaction of information need is a cover-up for question negotiation." Lancaster (1968), in answering O'Connor's charges, pointed out that he always regarded the meaning of "information need" as self-evident; given that a user looks through the entire collection himself, he can separate it into documents that he can and cannot make some use of in the current project. Those documents that he can make some use of satisfy the user's "information need." The distinction is made between a query and

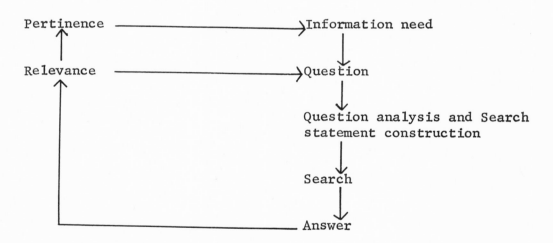

Information need was considered as underlying a question in the sense of a desire to be furnished with unknown knowledge for use in a problem-solving situation; the question was seen as the verbalized (oral or written) representation of the need. Since the question as a representation may or may not necessarily correspond to the need, it follows that documents relevant to the query may not necessarily be appropriate to the information need. Adopting this hypothesis and using it in a proposal for testing methodology Goffman and Newill (1966) called the property which assigned members of a file (e.g., documents) as answers to the question relevance; conversely, the property that assigned members of a file as answers to the information need was called pertinence.

information need, it was pointed out by Lancaster, because user's descriptions as to what documents will satisfy his need are often imperfect.

In any case, the significance of the concept of information need lies in considering the query as a representation; as such, the query may not be a representation of any one variable (i.e., "need") but of a whole complex of variables all related to and affecting the concept of relevance judgment. As a matter of fact, most if not all relevance judgment hypotheses began in one way or another by unravelling the concept of information need.

Three other hypotheses will be summarized here and all of them stem from experimental efforts. Their significance lies in the fact that they cumulated and classified the variables assumed to significantly affect relevance judgments by humans. The effects of some, but by no means of all, of the hypothesized variables were tested experimentally.

Cuadra and Katter (1967) in an experiment that will be summarized later, identified five major classes of "relevance-related variables as a working list of variables that may have impact on relevance judgment: The Document, the Information Requirement Statement, the Judge, the Judgment Conditions and the Available Mode of Expression." Within each class, subvariables were enumerated as shown in Figure 2; the ones carrying the asterisks were examined with varying degrees of emphasis in that study.

The second hypothesis stems from an experimental study reported by Rees, Schultz, et al. (1967), which was also formulated by Rees and Saracevic (1966). It started by viewing the relevance judgment as a decision by a request-formulator, the user, which specified the relationship between a document and the request. It was considered that one property of the decision is that it is a matter of degree. Furthermore, it should be taken for granted that, as far as a user is concerned, his decision over a given document set at a given point in time is objective and absolute. If this decision is delegated to someone other than the user, then it is considered to be an approximation, subject to a final decision by the user. The user, or his delegate, is considered to be a relevance judge. It was hypothesized that the relevance judgment is reliable and objective — that is, it has a high degree of agreement (compared with general human agreements in judgmental situations) when performed under well-defined restrictions. Specifically, it was hypothesized that the relevance judgment is an objective instrument when a specific ordered and finite number of systems *responses* to a fully defined *request* are related by and for specific kinds of *persons* (users), performing specified *functions* in specified *subject areas* for a specified *purpose*, within a specified *environment* and at a certain limited point in *time* (the italicized terms represent classes of variables which were fully elaborated). Relevance was then defined as a relation between system responses and the user request, established by a judgment made by the user or his delegate, a relation which incorporates all the above restrictions and possibly others. In the case of a delegated relevance judgment, it was hypothesized that such judgment will be a close approximation to that of the user's, given that the user and delegate have certain similarities in their background and that all the above variables are specified by the user and understood by the delegate.

The third hypothesis was formulated by O'Connor (1967). It started by defining as relevant to the request those documents which satisfy a subject retrieval request. O'Connor noted that in practice there sometimes is disagreement among people competent to judge whether a given document is relevant to a specified request. He hypothesized that relevance disagreements occur because of differences in interpretation of either requests or

documents. The reasons for which a retrieval request may be differently interpreted were linked to unclear requests, specifically listed as: expressions which are ambiguous in the situation (semantic ambiguity); syntactic ambiguity; vagueness of scope of what is requested; differences in interpretation of the subject of the request; uncertainties related to what the requestor knows; how he will evaluate and interpret papers; and what his background and circumstances are. The reasons for disagreements about whether a particular document is of the kind specified by the request were specified as: unclear document; difference in interpretation of the subject of the document; the judges having different scientific or subject intuition, background, and viewpoint; errors in interpretations; ignorance; differences on an inference basis. A difference was drawn between interpretations on documents about a subject and on documents satisfying a question. It was suggested by O'Connor that many of the disagreements among various judges may be resolved after discussions and clarifications about the interpretations of the request and reasons for inferences; in other words, even if there are initial disagreements a high degree of agreement on relevance of an answer may be reached after rational discussions and clarifications on either the request or the documents, or both.

In summary, let us contrast the three major experimental hypotheses on relevance judgments. The Cuadra/Katter hypothesis was concerned with detailed enumeration of variables which may affect relevance judgments and with classifying them into major classes. The Rees/Schultz/Saracevic hypothesis was more restrictive in that it concentrated on stressing the variables and conditions under which the judgment would achieve a high degree of agreement. O'Connor concentrated on the reasons for relevance judgment disagreements and on conditions under which agreement in relevance judgment may or may not coincide — relating those conditions to unclearness.

The Cuadra/Katter hypothesis was derived from a psychological approach and point of view by utilizing constructs similar to those used in psychological studies of judgmental situations. The Rees/Schultz hypothesis stemmed partially from psychological approaches, partially from retrieval systems operational experience, and partially from considerations of communication processes in science and technology. O'Connor's hypothesis was derived from practical retrieval system considerations (it is the most practically oriented and documented of the three hypotheses), from considerations of communication processes, and evidence from the history of science. All three hypotheses are conceptually quite similar, although quite different in style and argument. Even O'Connor's hypothesis, which seems on the surface most different, concentrated on the same variables. All stress, the importance of a variety of aspects of the background and actions of judges, the documents being judged, the query, and the situation (conditions) in relation to which the judgment is made.

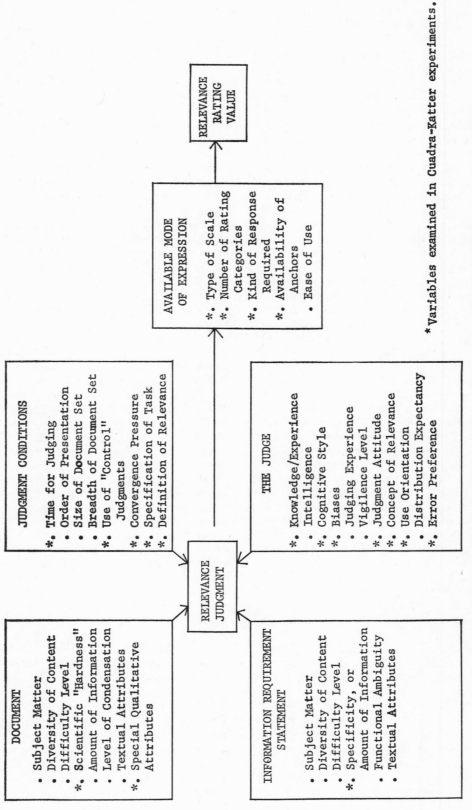

FIG. 2. Variables Related and Potentially Related to Relevance Judgments as Hypothesized by Cuadra and Katter (1967).

*Variables examined in Cuadra-Katter experiments.

The experiments, reviewed below, illuminated the effects of some of the variables hypothesized, but by no means to the extent that any of the hypotheses mentioned could be rejected or accepted, or even modified. Thus, in order to substantiate, repudiate, delineate, or modify any of these hypotheses a considerable amount of experimental work remains to be done.

Part 5. Experiments

Overview

One of the striking aspects of a concept as controversial and admittedly as significant and fundamental as relevance is that, although it produced voluminous literature, there were very few experimental studies. Furthermore, the experimental studies conducted did not produce even remotely conclusive observations. Clearly, a small number of experiments could not produce conclusive observations on any complex phenomenon, especially if they were non-repetitive, non-cumulative, and difficult to compare. However, the experimental studies were a step in the right direction; they promise, in conjunction with theory-building and theory-relating, the only way of creating formal knowledge on relevance.

On the positive side, the relevance experiments:

. . . identified a score of variables involved;
. . . produced some evidence on the extent of the involvement and effects of some variable;
. . . identified methodological problems, which led to refinements in experimentation;
. . . substantiated theories to some extent;
. . . raised the level of discussion;
. . . involved people from a number of sciences which brought in a variety of approaches.

On the negative side, the relevance experiments were characterized or criticized for:

. . . methodological omissions, crudeness, oversimplifications or overcomplications;
. . . inadequacy of controls;
. . . smallness and inadequacy of samples, either of documents, queries, answers, judges, etc.; (by way of comment, this is a most serious and quite valid criticism of all the experiments; e.g., if there were a large sample of judges, the number of items judged would be invalidly low or vice versa);
. . . often an unwarranted jump between actual observations and the conclusions, which tended to be overly optimistic and sweeping in generalizations;
. . . a preoccupation with and an exaggerated emphasis of the statistical methods of analysis at the expense of the overall experimental design; i.e., the quality and the sophistication of the statistical

analysis methods were equated to the sophistication in experimentation.

Below, the experiments are reviewed according to the classes of variables treated. The experiments pertain to the following five general classes of variables:

1. Documents and Document Representations,
2. Queries,
3. Judgmental Situations and Conditions,
4. Mode of Expression,
5. People (Judges).

Needless to say, all of the experiments should be treated as fixed-effect experiments, i.e., strictly speaking, the conclusions pertain to the conditions and range of effects operating in the given experiment only. Generalizations can be made to some extent, but with due caution. Many of the experiments too often claimed generalizations in a manner that it was concluded that some or other effect was "proven." Such generalizations should be rejected. However, this doesn't mean that the experiment itself and the direct results shouldn't be carefully considered. All experiments below were reviewed from this point of view.

The two largest and most comprehensive experiments were those reported by Rees and Schultz (1967) and Cuadra and Katter (1967), conducted at Case Western Reserve University and at System Development Corporation, respectively, and special attention will be given them.

The experiments reviewed represent the majority but not all of the experiments on relevance. Omitted for the sake of brevity were master's degree dissertations and small scale experiments. Also omitted were many important and interesting experiments where relevance was not the prime aspect and variable under consideration, but it was considered as a part of another experiment. Many retrieval system test experiments are an example of such omitted experiments. For example, experiments by Swanson (1960), Kuhns and Montgomery (1964), and Tague (1965) dealt in an extremely interesting way with relevance, but were not primarily devoted to that problem; instead they dealt primarily with processing aspects of information systems.

Documents and Document Representation

Documents and/or document representations (e.g., titles, citations, abstracts) were the first variables ever treated experimentally in relation to relevance judgments and, of all other variables, they were treated the most times experimentally. The reason for this early and continuous interest stems from the fact that documents and/or document representations are the items provided by retrieval systems to users; observations on how they affect the user and his judgment have direct implications for practical decisions in retrieval systems design and operations. It was the widely held view that documents, as represented by indexing languages and coding schemes are the only variables that mattered, especially since they are the only ones that can be effectively controlled by the system itself. Furthermore, in every major hypothesis or theory, documents were considered to be one of the major variables.

I.

One of the first published experiments dealing exclusively with relevance was conducted by Resnick (1961), with the purpose to:

"... compare the effectiveness of titles with that of abstracts when they were used for the purpose of notifying research workers of the availability of documents which might be relevant to their work interest."

The judges were regular users of a Selective Dissemination of Information (SDI) system. Of 400 answers sent to users as a notification in response to their questions, one half consisted of titles only sent to one group of users while abstracts in addition to the titles formed the other half sent to another group. Results indicated that there were no significant differences in the ordering rate for a "hard copy" (i.e., full text) of a document when either titles or titles plus abstracts were used for notification. Furthermore, it was found that once the full text was received, the percent of full text documents judged relevant to users' interests was not significantly different from the percent of users who ordered on the basis of titles alone and of those who ordered from titles plus abstracts. Once users received full text documents, they judged approximately sixty percent of them as being relevant. In other words, when receiving titles or titles plus abstracts, users tend to cautiously over-estimate the relevance; they also tend to scale it down once full texts are received. It seemed that in comparison to full texts, relevance may not be fully recognized by users from titles or abstracts.

II.

Rath, Resnick, and Savage (1961) conducted an experiment to determine which of the four types of "lexical indicators" (document representations) of content could be utilized best by subjects to distinguish relevant documents from irrelevant documents in answering 100 short questions. The lexical indicators were: titles, auto-abstracts (ten percent of sentences from the text, selected by machine), pseudo-auto abstracts (first and last five per cent of sentences from text), and full text. Questions were based on twenty-one documents taken from a ninety-two document population. There were fifty subjects (college students) divided into groups performing the judgment. The results indicated that there were no major differences in judgment among the groups using complete text and either of the two kinds of abstracts, but the title groups scored considerably lower, i.e., determining the "usefulness" of documents from titles

was low. Furthermore, the group using full text expressed the highest confidence in their judgment. In other words, inadequacy in using titles only to recognize the relevance of full texts of documents was again observed in this experiment.

III.

An experiment reported by Dym (1967) and Shirey and Kurfeerst (1967), among others, investigated the effects of five various "Intermediate Response Products" (document representations) on relevance judgments in comparison to judgments based on full texts of documents. Each of the seventy users in the medical field submitted a question in response to which (after the searching of various indexes) they received a total of 1,114 answers to judge. First, they judged a document representation and then the full text of the document. The answers submitted for judging were randomly divided into five groups, similar in size, according to five document representations, in order that each full text be judged in comparison to only one representation. It was found that the probability of a final full text judgment being identical (either relevant or not relevant) with a prior judgment on the basis of:

1. citations as .69,
2. citations plus abstracts as .73,
3. citation plus first paragraph as .74,
4. citation plus last paragraph as .74, and
5. citations plus first and last paragraph as .82.

Thus, titles (with bibliographic citations) had the lowest coincidence, and a combination of citations plus first and last paragraph of a document had the highest coincidence of equivalent relevance judgments in comparison to the judgment on full text.

IV.

Within their study, Cuadra and Katter (1967) performed fifteen experiments. One of the experiments examined the reactions of judges to stylistic characteristics of articles (documents) and the elements of style underlying those reactions. Forty-one librarians and library school students rated each of the twelve journal articles on library automation and information services for their relevance to each of the five information requirement statements (queries). They also rated each article on the extent to which each of twenty defined stylistic characteristics applied to it, e.g., fair/unbiased, dogmatic/opinionated, incomplete/sketchy, authorative/definite, etc. A factor analysis of stylistic phrases was correlated with ratings of articles. It was found that judges did not separate their relevance judgments from stylistic considerations. Factors of style in articles labeled "level of cognitive difficulty," "objectivity and fairness," and "lack of sustained focus" affected the judgments, either by reducing or increasing the relevance ratings. The conclusion was that not only the content but also the style of an article significantly effects relevance judgment.

In another experiment of the same study, the effects on relevance judgment of the degree of specificity of information contained in queries and documents were investigated. Two independent groups of twenty-three and twenty-five librarians and library school students judged the relevance of each of the twelve journal articles in library automation and information services for each of the five questions. For documents, information specificity was equated with rated scientific hardness, solidness, and objectivity of the articles. Six of the articles used were rated *a priori* as the scientifically hardest from a sample of forty documents, and the other six used were the softest rated. The analysis of results showed that the scientifically "harder" (more "information-specific") articles produced lower relevance ratings, i.e., they were less relevant. Articles that were less "information-specific" produced lower certainty of judgments, and the judges then tended to err on the side of leniency, i.e., the articles were judged as more relevant; they had a higher relevance score. "Harder" articles produced better interjudge agreement than the "softer" ones.

V.

Rees and Schultz (1967) investigated, among other variables, two variables that belong under this class: one is the effect of various documents and the other of various document representations on relevance ratings by various medically-oriented groups, differing in their medical expertise. Sixteen documents, full texts, and their representations, i.e., titles and titles plus bibliographic citations, were judged by: forty medical experts (M.D.'s — researchers and nonresearchers), twenty-nine medical scientists (Ph.D.'s), twenty-five M.D. residents, twenty-nine medical students, and sixty-one medical librarians. Judgments were made in relation to an elaborately described diabetes research project, presented in three research stages, each stage representing periods of: (1) research formulation; (2) research implementation; and (3) analysis of the experiments. Judgments were performed after each stage and recorded on an eleven-point relevance scale. The findings of interest to the variable documents and document representations were as follows: documents themselves, in the full text form, were the single most influential experimental variable in the experimental design; individual documents received significantly different ratings, both as a function of various groups of judges assigning ratings and as a function of the research stage at which the rating was assigned. In relation to document representations, it was found that librarians tended to increase the scale values of the relevance ratings from titles to citations to full texts, while other groups tended to decrease the ratings; i.e., on the average, titles and citations were less relevant to librarians in comparison to full texts, while to others, titles and citations were more relevant in comparison to full texts. Medical experts and scientists tended to judge titles and citations quite liberally, prob-

ably estimating that the full text of a document may reveal items of interest. Their judgment was much more stringent, when they received the full text. In other words, titles were again observed not to be the "best" conveyor of relevance of full texts. But the most important finding was that, although many variables affect the relevance judgment, the most significant effect is due to various documents — the items provided by a system. More than anything else, it seems that the variety of what is being provided will affect how it is being judged.

VI.

In another experiment, Saracevic (1968 and 1969) reported on the comparative changes in relevance judgments of users when three representations of the output of searchers were presented to the users in succession. Twenty-two users submitted 99 questions to experimental information retrieval systems and received 1,086 documents as answers, first receiving titles, then abstracts, and finally full texts. The ability of users to recognize relevance from shorter formats in comparison to full text judgment was observed. Of 1,086 answers evaluated, 843 or 78% had the same judgment on all three formats. Of 207 answers judged relevant from full text, 131 (61%) were judged so from titles and 160 (77%) from abstracts. Conversely, of 167 answers judged relevant from titles, only 131 were finaly considered so on full text; of 175 answers judged relevant from abstracts, 160 were judged so from full text. In other words, full text judgment provided the largest number of relevant answers. Titles seemed to be fairly inadequate for recognizing nonrelevant answers.

In contrasting the six studies reviewed, we may find that one study (Resnick — 1961) was conducted in connection with an operational retrieval system, two studies (Dym, Shirey and Kurfeerst — 1967 and Saracevic, 1969) were conducted in connection with laboratory or experimental retrieval systems, and the other three were specifically designed to simulate a relevance judgment situation.

The number of judges, documents, and queries varied greatly from study to study, and so did the methodologies. Although aims of all studies were similar, specific comparisons between studies are impossible. However, a general observation may be made: The trends exhibited in judging document representations versus full texts of documents were remarkably similar. General conclusions will be made later in this paper, together with conclusions on all other variables.

The Query

In the broadest sense, the query, used here as synonymous with a request, a question, or an information requirement statement, or more precisely a string of words requiring a response, is the variable in response to which documents (again broadly interpreted) are supplied for judgments. As to the form, queries may be interrogative questions, e.g., "What is . . . ?;" they may be imperative statements requiring a response, e.g., "Provide information on. . . .;" they may also be in the form of statements requiring responses containing similar linguistic or conceptual statements, e.g., "Provide documents similar to this document." In any case, a desire for a response is implied. It should be noted that, in the reviewed experiments, the effect of queries on relevance judgments was usually not investigated directly or in isolation; experimental observations were made on the relation between queries and documents (or their representations), judged as to their relevance.

I.

Caudra and Katter (1967), within the experiment previously described, explored the effects on relevance judgments of the degree of specificity of information contained in information-requirement statements (queries). For the queries, information specificity was equated with syntactic completeness. Each of five query statements was used in two versions — one, more specifically stated, was in ordinary prose, and the other was less specifically stated, in which all punctuation and function words had been deleted; the resulting words and phrases were then rearranged in alphabetical order, i.e., a form of an index was created. There were two groups of twenty-three and twenty-five judges, judging relevance of each of the twelve journal articles for each of the five queries. One group judged the more specific and the other the less specific queries. The findings were as follows: the more information-specific queries, i.e., queries with syntax, produced significantly higher inter-judge agreement in rating, but the ratings were generally lower. Thus, it seems that the more information in a query (even if that information is only syntactic in nature), more agreement may be expected. Perhaps the agreement is lower, because syntax is removed and, thus, less information is available.

II.

Rees and Schultz (1967), in their experiment, investigated the effect of each of the three stages of research on relevance judgments. The stages of research may be equated with queries. Judgments were performed after an elaborate statement about each research stage was presented to the judges. The first stage described the formulation of the research project for which the documents should be judged; the second stage was the implementation of the experimental approach and design; and the third stage was the evaluation and interpretation of data. Thus, stages, as a variable, may be viewed as an increase in information specificity given to the judges. The findings were as follows.

a. research stages were a significant factor affecting the mean rating of documents — that is, increased information concerning the course of the presented research affected the ratings significantly;
b. all of the major judgmental groups (Ph.D.'s,

M.D.'s, medical students, librarians) rated the documents, in general, as decreasingly relevant to the presented research as they were exposed to further stages of research. Here, the agreement was higher — that is, all groups, regardless of background, reacted similarly;
c. there was a relatively large drop in mean ratings from the first to second stage and a much smaller drop between the second and third stage.

The results suggest the following interpretation: as a judge is given more information about a query, e.g., as his knowledge about a research project more closely resembles that of the experimenter, he becomes more critical and demanding in rating articles as relevant. With a greater understanding of the goals and implementation of the query, e.g., experiment, a judge can be more specific about those items of information that may have a direct or indirect relationship with the query.

III.

Gifford and Baumanis (1969) were concerned with the relation between the texts (wording) of queries as stated and the texts of documents provided as answers. The purpose was to explore directly what makes a document relevant, particularly by determining whether meaningful, textual ("linguistic") differences can consistently be found between relevant and nonrelevant documents in relation to the text of the stated query. Sixty-one queries submitted by users, 858 abstracts retrieved as answers by experimental systems, and the users' relevance ratings on abstracts (as being either relevant, partially relevant or nonrelevant) were used in the investigation. For each query, the answers were grouped into three groups — those judged relevant, partially relevant, and nonrelevant; each group was inspected for common occurrence of words, phrases, and other textual properties which might account for the particular rating. The findings include: in relation to the text of the query, the documents judged relevant differed in direct, observable ways from the nonrelevant documents. These differences were of a textual nature, corresponding to rating difference; these textual differences were generally quite straightforward differences in word occurrences; a statement of these differences as properties to be required of relevant abstracts often constituted a meaningful, relatively unambiguous interpretation of the query.

In other words, texts of queries correspond with texts of relevant answers, but did not correspond with texts of nonrelevant answers. In a sense, this experiment, with a rather large sample, confirmed the significance of documents and of the direct relation between documents and queries in a communication process as a whole.

IV.

O'Connor (1969) performed an experiment resulting from his hypothesis (1967) about disagreements in relevance judgments based on either unclear queries and documents, or a familiar type of scientific disagreement about a passage's meaning, the statement's correctness, or an inference's correctness. Eighty-two documents and thirty questions in the subject area of information retrieval were compared independently by two judges to find answer-providing documents. In other words, those documents from which answers to queries could be inferred were considered as relevant. After independent judgments, the two judges compared their judgments and, in the case of disagreements, tried to resolve differences through rational discourse. Here are the findings: there were thirty-two independent agreements (by both judges) and thirty-four initial disagreements, which after discussion became agreements in that a document is an answer to a question. Thus, there were sixty-six agreements on answer-providing documents between both judges, one half of which were agreed upon independently; the other half were fully agreed upon only after a discussion. There were fourteen other instances of initial disagreement between the judges, i.e., one judge judged a document as an answer to a question, the other did not; each of these was resolved by agreement after a discussion that the document was not an answer. After the discussion, no disagreement remained; thus, a total of forty-eight disagreements were completely resolved by logical procedures. Although based on a small sample (two judges), this experiment is of a general interest, because it shows that one step "behind" the subjectivity of relevance judgment (which is by psychometric techniques demonstrated as a degree of disagreement) may be an area of non-subjective and logical agreement dependent on rational discussion. In other words, at least when relevance is viewed as inference of answers to questions from documents, there may be an extremely high degree of agreement after iterative comparisons of inferences.

In conclusion, by way of methodological comment, the last two experiments had interesting and innovative methodological techniques, which may be of promise, for the study of relevance as a phenomenon in communication and not only as a judgment.

As previously remarked, the methodologies differed so much that specific cumulation of experimental findings from experiment to experiment is impossible. However, after weighing all the findings, some general and more or less speculative conclusions are possible, which are brought forth later in this paper.

The Judgmental Situation and Condition

This variable refers to the situation defined and constructed for the judge for the relevance judging task. It was examined in only two, the Cuadra/Katter and Rees/Schultz studies. As examined in those experiments, this variable may be termed as an examination of the effects on relevance judgments of different experimental set-ups.

I.

The following was examined in three experiments by Cuadra and Katter:

a. Interaction among component aspects of relevance: Four different definitions of relevance were used: categorical, implied, and correlated relevance, and as control, the overall relevance. One group consisted of eight judges, two of nine judges, and one of thirteen judges, judging independently (each group using one definition only) five articles to four queries. The judges were attendees of the 1966 convention of the then American Documentation Institute (ADI). The articles were from the *1966 ADI Proceedings;*

b. Sensitivity of judgment to relevance definitions: Twelve judges received one definition and thirteen judges received a slightly different definition of relevance in judging five articles to four queries. The judges were attendees of the 1966 convention of ADI. The articles were from the *1966 ADI Proceedings;*

c. Time and stringency pressures in judgments: Three groups of eight or nine judges rated five articles to four queries; one group in four minutes for each rating, the second in two minutes, and the third in four minutes with added stringency instructions. The judges were seniors and graduate students in a library school. The articles were from the *1966 ADI Proceedings.*

Here are some of the more important findings in order of the experiments as above.

(a) narrowing the definition of relevance from correlated to implied to categorical made the rating task easier; the narrowed definition produced the highest agreement; there were somewhat different patterns of ratings for each definition;

(b) a small and subtle difference in the wording of the definition of relevance produced statistically significant changes in relevance ratings. A shorter definition produced lower interjudge agreement and generally higher ratings;

(c) when more time was allowed for each judgment, the mean of relevance ratings on two-thirds of the articles increased, and decreased on the remaining third; the stringency instructions designed to make the judge err on the side of stringency for relevance ratings increased the means of relevance ratings, i.e., the judgments were more lenient — a finding contrary to what was expected.

II.

Rees and Schultz, in the already described study, presented to each of the 184 judges at each of the three research stages at which judgment on sixteen articles was performed, four definitions of aspects of relevance to be judged and one definition of usefulness. The aspects of relevance were defined as:

(a) the overall relevance of an article;
(b) formulative relevance, arising in formulation of the specific research;
(c) methodological relevance, arising in selection of the experimental procedures; and
(d) interpretive relevance, arising in interpretation of the data.

Usefulness was defined as the degree to which the document may be able to be used by each judge, given that he is doing this research. The findings were as follows: the relevance aspect judged did, to some extent but not greatly, affect the rating; but, in general, the judges did not tend to differentiate much among different relevance aspects and usefulness. Aspects 1 (overall), 2 (formulative), and 4 (interpretive relevance) tended to produce similar results, while aspect 3 (methodological relevance) produced ratings different from other aspects, probably because judges were looking for a description of specific techniques which involved an understanding of some of the most complex material. Usefulness was highly correlated with overall relevance to such an extent that eventually no distinction was made between them, which was a surprising discovery in the investigation. But even where disagreement existed in rating, the judges agreed almost unanimously with respect to the relative ordering of the documents on all the rating aspects.

In conclusion, both studies merely touched upon the important aspect of the overall situation, the environment, within which relevance is considered. The findings were rather inconclusive. The two studies differed somewhat in findings. The first study found a difference in the ratings because of differences in the definitions of relevance; the second study found that the differently defined aspects of relevance were not affecting the ratings to any great extent. However, a closer examination of data of both studies shows that different relevance definitions produced only slight differences in ratings. Clearly, a great deal more experimental work remains to be done. It is suggested here that the most fruitful experiments may be those (not yet conducted) that will examine the relevance and relevance judgment within the environment of the communication processes of different classes of users.

Mode for Expression

In any experiment, in any field, instruments used for recording do affect, to some smaller or greater extent, what is being recorded. Thus, instruments themselves may be subjects of a study. In relation to relevance judgment experiments, the instruments studied as variables were the available modes for the judges on or by which they could record or express their judgments. The concern is identical to that for socio- and psychometric devices, with the scales and metrics for measurements. Measuring techniques from sociology and psychology were used to study the effects of a variety of scales on relevance judgments, as reviewed below. These were the only studies devoted to investigating this variable.

I.

Cuadra and Katter (1967), (reported also by Katter, 1968), in three experiments, examined the following:

a. the amount of difference in judgment results when judgment is recorded on a rating scale versus ranking of documents; two groups of psychology students judged twice nine psychology abstracts against eight short queries; one group did it twice on a nine-point rating scale, another once on the rating and the second time on a ranking scale;
b. the effects of the number and description of categories on a scale; eight groups of ten to thirteen judges judged five short articles to four short queries; each group used à different scale version: with either two, four, six or eight categories and one of the two caption descriptions, one more imperative than the other; judges were attendees of the 1966 American Documentation Institute convention and articles were from the Proceedings of the convention;
c. the sensitivity of two different scale forms: a nine-point category scale versus a magnitude-ratio procedure (where the judge selects an arbitrary number to express his judgment of the first document presented and expresses all other judgments as a ratio of the first number). Two sets of twelve articles, each related by a previous judgment to a query, were used for judgment; half of the articles were previously judged very relevant and half were judged to be of little relevance. Eight groups of ten to twelve library school students judged relevance, each using either a different set or a different scale form.

The findings were as follows:

(a) studied were the number of occurred reversals of judgments, where in one scale form document A was judged as more relevant than document B and in another B was judged more relevant than A. In the group where the nine-point rating scale was used twice, there was five percent of reversal and in the group where the second time a ranking was used, the reversals were 16.5 percent. Thus, the rating scale seems to affect a higher consistency and, thus, by itself may less distort the results;
(b) the judges, using the two and four category scales, felt more uncertain about their judgment and expressed more difficulty in making the judgment. The judges, using scales with six and eight categories, were more certain about their judgment. The stronger and noncomparative language,

by which categories were defined, to some extent affected the certainty of judgment. Thus, if high certainty in judgment may be desired, it seems that a rating scale with many categories (six or more) should be used; and

(c) the judges, using the category scale in judging documents (which were already judged once), had a much higher agreement with the original judgments. The utilization of the magnitude-ratio scale was confusing. Until better magnitude-ratio scales are found, they are not recommended by experimenters for usage in recording of relevance judgments.

II.

Rees and Schultz (1967) conducted a separate experiment within their study in which the usage of an eleven-point rating scale was compared with that of a ratio-type scale. The ratio-scale was one where to each pair of documents presented for judging, the judge assigned 100 points in accordance with his estimate of the ratio of the overall relevance of the two documents. In the same experiment, the re-testing reliability of both scales was investigated. Twelve abstracts were judged by twenty-one medical students in relation to the description of the first (formulative) stage of the research project used in their general experiment. Both scales were used for each document. The same session with the same judges was repeated two weeks later. After the sessions, a slight majority of judges felt that the ratio-scale gave a better reflection of their estimates of relevance; on the question of ease-of-use preference, the opinions were evenly divided. For individual documents, the distribution of judgments was different between the two scales. The rating scale tended to skew the distribution of judgments for the same document by different judges into one direction. The ratio-scale made the distribution more uniform, but neither of them produced a normal distribution of judgments. The rating scale tended to be concentrated around the end points for most documents, that is, judges tended to mark documents generally high or generally low; however, there was a small class of documents with the widest distribution of judgments which were characterized by a heavier use of middle points, which may be termed "moderately relevant." The reliability of judgments, when calculated as a mean over the twenty-one judges, was as follows: using the rating scale, judges agreed with themselves in two sessions on seventy-three per cent of the judgments, and using the ratio-scale, on eighty-eight per cent of the judgments. In general, as reliability results go, these are very high figures. The reaction of the judges in the experiment remained constant over a short period of time; thus, the judgment displayed stability.

In both studies the conclusion is made that a two-point rating scale (i.e., Relevant and Not Relevant) is inadequate for judgment, because it is not sensitive enough

to the complex interaction of factors influencing such judgments; that it is an oversimplification to telescope a variety of degrees of relevance into yes/no decisions; and that at times it may even be a distortion. However, these are deduced conclusions; no experiment actually directly compared a two-point scale with other scales. As a matter of fact, both studies noticed a heavy use of end points on the many-point scales. Both noticed that even if ratings of degree of relevance were scattered, the relative position of documents as to their relevance from highest to lowest was remarkably consistent among all kinds of groups of judges, especially on the documents of high relevance. These observations were more pronounced in the study by Rees and Schultz.

Similar observations on consistency of relative positioning were made by Lesk and Salton (1968) in an experiment reviewed in the next section.

If a high degree of consistency of relative positioning of documents as to their relevance among various groups of people is really a fact that could be expected generally, that is, if it is not only an observation from a limited number of experiments, then this is a most important and significant finding with far-reaching implications for practice, for development of services and future systems, and clearly, for future direction in theory-building and experimentation. Among others, this may substantiate the hypotheses and theories considering relevance as a comparative property. Thus, it may be more proper to ask people to compare a set of documents rather than to judge relevance of individual documents to a query. Furthermore, these findings suggest that an important area of investigation may be the possible regularity of distribution patterns of documents as to their relevance; do documents (or answers in general) as to relevance follow some already known distributions also associated with some known communication phenomena other than relevance; is relevance connected by behavior to other known communication behavior through its distributions? Is there a family of relevance-related distributions? These points will be discussed at the end of this review.

People

Finally, to review the experimental observation on the most important aspect: how people affect relevance judgments. The basic item studied in all experiments reviewed below was some aspect of the consistency of or agreement in judgment as affected by certain human characteristics: most had something to do with professional education or lack of it; e.g., as those belonging to a group of librarians, M.D.'s, psychologists, scientists, "experts," "nonexperts," etc. Other characteristics investigated related to perception of people on the utilization of answers. It is clear that the other four classes of variables investigated and reviewed above relate more or less to people in two respects: either how people (judges, users, user delegates, system operators, etc.) were affected by them in their judgment or how these variables fared from some action by people (e.g., relation between texts and answers, distribution of judgments over documents or document representations, etc.)

I.

Resnick and Savage (1964) compared the ability of people to consistently judge the relevance of documents to their general interest. Furthermore, the consistency of judgments was investigated when made on the basis of citations, abstracts, keywords, and full texts. Thirty-four documents were judged as either relevant or irrelevant by technical professionals of an IBM division in relation to their interest; fourteen people judged full texts of documents, eight judged citations, twelve abstracts, and twelve index terms. A month later, they repeated their judgments over the same sets. When combined over the forty-six judges, ninety per cent of the total judgments were the same, either relevant or irrelevant on both occasions, and ten per cent changed the second time from relevant to irrelevant or vice versa. The least consistent were the judgments on abstracts; the consistency of judgments on other representations and on full text was quite similar. On closer examination, it can be recalculated that of those documents (from all representations including full texts) identified as relevant in the first session, twenty-four percent were found as nonrelevant in the second session; or specifically twenty-six percent of those answers judged relevant the first time, were judged nonrelevant the second time from full texts, fourteen percent from citations, thirty percent from abstracts, and twenty-five percent from index terms. Thus, the incredibly high consistency was actually due more to consistently judging nonrelevance rather than relevance, which is an important and substantial difference. It seems that once something is recognized as not relevant that, by and large, it remains not relevant, while the items judged relevant may, the second time around, more frequently obtain a different judgment.

II.

Barhydt (1967) compared the relevance judgment of users (people posing questions to a retrieval system) with that of "experts" (non-user subject specialists, peers of the user) and retrieval system specialists. (Remark: It should be noted that from the report it isn't clear exactly how many persons were involved). Thirty-seven questions were posed by educational researchers to an experimental retrieval system in educational media. The findings were as follows: sixty-eight percent of the abstracts judged relevant by users were judged so by experts and fifty-nine percent by retrieval specialists. On the other hand, of the abstracts judged nonrelevant by the users, sixty-nine percent were judged so by experts and seventy-six percent by retrieval specialists. Thus, both groups, the experts and retrieval specialists,

had fairly similar overall agreements on relevance judgments among themselves in comparison to users' judgments. The retrieval specialists were much closer to user judgments in judging answers as nonrelevant than relevant. Again, this experiment observed in part the same phenomena as the previous experiment: There seems to be a higher agreement among people on nonrelevance than on relevance.

III.

Cuadra and Katter (1967 and 1967a) investigated whether the particular attitude taken by the judge about the intended use of documents ("implicit use orientation") affected the amount of relevance attributed to documents. Judges were psychology students. (Remark: It should be noted that it isn't clear from the reports exactly how many judges were used). They rated the relevance of each of nine psychology journal abstracts to eight short questions in two sessions. In the first session, judges rated the general overall relevance. In the second session, judges rated relevance of the same abstracts and questions in accordance to modified instructions as to use orientations. There were fourteen different modified instructions each stated to orient the judges to a different ultimate use of a document. For each of the fourteen use orientations, an independent sample of twelve or more judges was used (thus, there were at least some 150 judges). The fourteen implicit use orientations which were fully defined to judges were titled: one or more terms, combination of terms, concern with terminology, loose metaphor, selective review, exhaustive bibliography, student project exemplars, stimulative value, practically useful, overview of the results, hard factual, methodological interest, preparing new study, and writing up study.

In addition to judging relevance, the ease of judging each use orientation was indicated by the judges. The findings were as follows: all of the fourteen special instructions as to the intended use produced different relevance scores than were made under the initial instructions to judge overall relevance. In comparison to the values on overall relevance, the largest shifts in ratings were in the use orientations "concern with terminology" and "methodological interest." The smallest differences produced the intended uses for "selective review," "exhaustive bibliography," and "writing up study." It is interesting to note that the use orientations that produced largest shifts were considered by the judges the most difficult to judge, while those that produced smallest shifts were the easiest to judge. Thus, the relevance scores were observed to be sensitive to the assumptions a judge (in the case of a delegate to the user) made about the intended utilization of answers. However, by way of comment, the observations of that experiment may be interpreted differently: when each definition of "implicit use orientation" is taken, together with the query (which was the same for all fourteen orientations), they actually amounted to a different overall query for each group; the judges might have judged these together in such a way that they reformulated the original query to form a different query. Furthermore, it was observed in other experiments by Cuadra and Katter (and by others) that the ease and certainty of judgment is directly correlated with the degree of agreement; since the largest difference was on the problematic use orientations, is it possible that the difficulty of judging rather than use orientations was the overriding factor? In any case, it was shown that the artifacts of particular experimental instructions and conditions significantly could affect results. Furthermore, as an exercise in logic, it was shown in this review how the same results may be interpreted differently, with neither interpretation being necessarily "right."

IV.

In still another experiment in their study Cuadra and Katter (1967) investigated how the amount of academic training in a given subject area (equated with "knowledgeability") affected the interjudge agreement. Nine psychology journal abstracts were judged against each of eight short queries by 230 seniors and first-year graduate students majoring in psychology. The students were grouped into four groups according to academic credits (ranging from three to sixty hours) and their scores on a test on knowledge of authors in psychology. The findings were as follows: the average correlation of agreement within each group for the four levels of experience from lowest to highest experience were: .41, .41, .49, and .44. The groups with the lowest academic training agreed among themselves the least, and those with intermediate training agreed the most, while those with the highest training in their median struck an agreement. It was somewhat surprising to find those with the highest academic training not achieving the highest agreement; however, neither were the differences between the agreements of all groups that large, nor was the level of "knowledgeability" between the groups that different. What is a significant finding is an indication of a degree of correlation between judges: somewhere between .40 and .50. As human agreement correlations go, in judgmental situation, this is not a low figure.

V.

Rees and Schultz (1967) conducted their experiment as mentioned with 184 judges in the following groups arranged according to their educational and practical experience in relation to the research project and documents judged: twenty-nine medical scientists, forty M.D.'s medical experts (of those fourteen researchers and twenty-six nonresearchers), twenty-five M.D. residents, twenty-nine medical students and sixty-one medical librarians. They judged sixteen documents to three research stages of a research project in diabetes, or more precisely in sugar transport in the intestine. The average overall correlation of agreement within each

group was: .66 for medical scientists, .57 for M.D.'s-researchers, .50 for M.D.'s-nonresearchers, .42 for M.D. residents, .44 for medical students, and .47 for medical librarians. The medical scientists had the highest agreement among themselves. Closer examination of data showed that the highest specialization group (scientists) judged relevance most stringently (could be interpreted as judging the smallest number of documents as relevant), and the other groups were more and more lenient (judging larger numbers of documents as relevant) as the specialization decreased. The medical librarians overall rated the documents as being most relevant. But quite importantly it was found that, regardless of the actual ratings of individual documents, all the judgmental groups agreed almost unanimously on the ordering or relative positions of the documents with regard to relevance ratings, with a high degree of consistency, on all document representations and at all the research stages. This is probably the most significant finding of the study. Thus, even if the indicated degree or score of relevance varied from group to group, the relative ordering of documents as to their relevance was equivalent across all groups. These findings are obviously related to the behavior of groups as a whole and not necessarily to each individual in a group.

In comparison to Cuadra/Katter findings as to the agreement due to "knowledgeability," the Rees/Schultz findings may be more representative, because the educational and professional differences between groups were more pronounced and defined.

VI.

Let us turn to another problem: the relation between relevance judgments and testing of information retrieval systems. As a result of empirical or experimental observations on the considerable amount of disagreement and general instability of people's relevance ratings, many critics stressed the potential unreliability of data from tests of retrieval systems. The relevance judgments by people over some set of documents retrieved by or contained in a system are used as a basis on which effectiveness measures for the given system are calculated. It has been stressed that the test data may, to some extent, be used to compare differently implemented functions within a system (if even that), but that comparisons between various systems based on data from unconnected independent tests are fairly meaningless. Thus, a statement ". . . my system operates at seventy-five per cent recall and fifty per cent precision . . ." may indicate a result that is not comparable to other systems tested under different conditions. The major criticism of any and all testing was based on variability of relevance judgment. This was the point of view of the critics of retrieval tests and of the experimenters in relevance judgments—a view which in effect dismissed test results or, at most, pointed out that test results should be viewed with great caution. Needless to say, the evaluators of retrieval systems took a dim view of this criticism. They argued that there is a large speculative inference made, unsupported by experimental evidence, from the results of relevance judgments experiments to the evaluation of results of retrieval systems test experiments. The evaluators were right: It is a large and speculative step; however, the inference cannot be ignored, because it does cast considerable doubt on the reliability of test results.

There was only one experiment conducted which was devoted to the problem: Are the measures indicating the effectiveness of performance of retrieval system unreliable because the relevance judgments are unstable? Lesk and Salton (1968) conducted an experiment to find out if the same ranking order of effectiveness of three different retrieval methods would be preserved when four sets of different relevance judgment treatments were applied as bases for calculations.

In the experiment, each of eight people stated six queries, and then each assessed relevance to his queries of an entire test collection composed of 1,268 abstracts in the field of information and library science. Either the relevance or nonrelevance of each abstract for each query was judged by query authors (these judgments were called the A judgments). Next, an independent set of relevance judgments was obtained for each query by asking each person in the test group to judge for relevance six additional queries originated by six different people, not including himself (B judgments). Thus, for each of the forty-eight queries, four different relevant sets became available. The A set: the abstracts assessed as relevant by query authors; the B set: assessed by subject experts; the C set: abstracts assessed as relevant by either A or B judges; and, the D set: abstracts assessed as relevant by both A and B judges. The overall average agreement between A and B judges was .31 (calculated as the number of relevant abstracts judged so by both judges over the number of relevant abstracts judged by either judge). By way of comment: The results showed the following interesting aspect that was not investigated directly prior to this experiment, but it was observed indirectly in other experiments and in practice time and again. The relevant set of one judge was to a great extent a subset of the relevant set of the other judge; that is, the intersection between the two judgments in comparison to the smaller set of the two judgments, is generally large. Thus, the two groups of judges have generally a large number of relevant documents in common. When the figures in the Lesk/Salton experiments are recalculated for each pair of judgments the *smaller* set of either of the two judgments was about sixty percent comprised of documents found in the larger set.

Next in the Lesk/Salton experiment the total collection of abstracts was treated by three different automatic text processing methods, and then each was searched by the forty-eight queries. The A, B, C, and D relevance sets were applied to the output of the three processing methods to calculate the performance measures of precision and recall. Here are the findings: Regardless of which relevance set was applied, the relative ranking of the three processing methods remained the same. For instance, if a given indexing procedure was ranked on the basis of relevance set A as performing first, it was so ranked on the basis of all other relevance sets. Furthermore, the actual recall/precision graphs and data differed minimally from processing method to processing method when any of the relevance sets was applied. Thus, in this experiment, the relative instability in relevance judgments did not affect comparative figures on performance of retrieval systems; the average recall and precision data were relatively insensitive to differences in relevance judgments. These results can be explained as follows: (a) one relevance set (e.g., set B) was to a large extent a subset of another relevance set; thus, we are dealing with quite similar sets on the basis of which performance was computed; and (b) when the documents were ranked as to relevance by different judges then it can be seen that the highest ranked documents were identical among the judges. Thus, when the ranked judgments A, B, C, and D were used in the experiment to evaluate the ranked systems output, they had to produce the same results because the top rankings were the same.

The same finding, that the relative ranking of documents as to their relevance is similar among groups of judges even when relevance ratings (i.e., relevance value on a scale) may be quite different, was one of the principal findings of the Rees/Schultz study. Clearly, many additional experiments on different systems under different conditions with differently obtained judgments must be performed before we can make general conclusions under which conditions test data from different experiments are comparable. But the Lesk/Salton experiment is very much a step in the right direction, connecting the results of relevance judgment experiments with results of test experiments. In general, given a well-defined test methodology (as Lesk/Salton's) test results may not be as unreliable as acclaimed by relevance experimenters and test critics.

In conclusion, it seems that, although the relevance disagreements may be large in general, the basic disagreement is not entirely on different relevance sets but on the size of the basically same set. People with educational and/or professional connections and similarities seemed to agree quite well on the same basic documents that are relevant and on their order; they disagree on how many additional documents should be included as relevant. The experiments to date have investigated the amount of disagreement. It is suggested that what should be done as the next step is to investigate the nature of these disagreements and agreements.

Part 6. Synthesis

General Conclusions and Implications From the Experiments

The experiments on relevance were fixed effect experiments; the results are not really applicable beyond the range of effects built into any given experiment. Still one is tempted to draw certain general conclusions based on the similar trends of behavior exhibited by a variable, as seen in several experiments. However, the conclusions made below should be viewed with caution, since a healthy amount of intellectual speculation, based on inconclusive experimental evidence, was built into these inferences. The conclusions presented here are an attempt by this reviewer to weigh and cumulate the results of all experiments, independent of the conclusions derived by the individual experimenters. Given this necessary caution, it is hoped that the following conclusions may serve as a practical guide for decision making in relation to processes, operation, experiments, and theories where relevance and relevance judgment are involved. Basically, the conclusions are an attempt to answer the question: "What have we learned from relevance experimentation on the behavior of relevance-related variables?" The conclusions are organized by the classes of variables as reviewed below.

1. *Documents and Document Representations*
    a. It may be expected, with a considerable degree of certainty, that documents or objects conveying information are of all other variables, the major variable in relevance judgments, in particular, and in relevance as a relation between sources and destination in a communication process, in general.
    b. Although there are a number of factors aligned with documents as a variable, it seems that the most important of the factors that would affect relevance is the subject content of documents as related to the subject content of a query.
    c. Not only content, but also elements of style may be expected to affect relevance judgment.
    d. The more specific the subject content of a document, the more relevance agreement may be expected.
    e. A considerable difference between judgments made from titles and judgments made on full texts of the same articles may be expected; titles should be utilized with considerable scepticism and caution for a judgment of what is in the text.
    f. Some difference, more or less, may be expected between judgments from abstracts and judgments made on full texts; abstracts,

depending on their type, length, detail, etc., may be utilized for judgment of what is in a text with much less caution than titles.

Again, many factors in documents and document representations will affect relevance judgments, but the subject content of documents as related to subject content of queries may be expected to be, in most situations, the major factor, the major aspect, the major variable, with which we have to contend in relevance judgments. This is in support of theories that view relevance as a relation between documents and a query, or more specifically, as a measure of the effective contact between a source and destination in a communication process; this also supports contentions that a system's output itself (the documents) is the major variable involved in relevance judgments. In other words, since documents or any conveyors of information are provided by a source in a communication process, this confirms the involvement of a source not only in relevance judgment, but also in relevance as a property of information, in general.

2. *Queries*
    a. The more the judges (in the sense of user delegates) know about a query, the more agreement among judges on relevance judgments may be expected and the more stringent the judgment becomes.
    b. The more the judges discuss the inference about queries and answers, the more agreement may be expected.
    c. These findings confirm the empirical observations about the necessity for question negotiation and general close cooperation between users and system operators.
    d. In a strange way, these findings may also explain the wide distribution of judgments in experiments that incorporated queries in their design, with relatively little explanations about them; in other words, the significant differences may be primarily due to the type of queries.
    e. There seems to exist a close similarity and correlation between texts of queries and texts of relevant documents which can not be found betwen texts of queries and texts of nonrelevant documents.
    f. Texts of documents may be a most important aspect that triggers relevance judgments in relation to stated queries.
    g. In other words, if one can find a statement in a document resembling a statement in the query, one can be assured of a high probability of the document being considered relevant by a user who stated the query.
    h. The less one knows about a query, the more he tends to be lenient in judgment — everything tends to become relevant; or, in spe-

cific terms, the less a system operator or user delegate, in general, is familiar with the query, its content, eventual use, or the problem in relation to which the query is being asked, the wider the disparity in judgments and the more documents will be considered as relevant.

To reiterate: It may be expected that stated, written queries on one hand and documents considered relevant by a user on the other hand, have considerable textual similarity such as similar terminology, phraseology, semantics, and even syntax; documents into which queries can be mapped have a high probability of being relevant, and conversely, the less a query can be mapped into a document the higher the probability that the document will be considered not relevant. It may be expected that precisely stated *and* understood queries will produce a high degree of relevance agreement between a user and a user delegate. From practice, these observations support the contentions of the importance of question negotiation in the question answering process. Furthermore, these findings confirm the reiterative feedback-type of involvement of a destination with a source in establishing relevance of information in a communication process.

3. *Judgmental Conditions and Situations*

This particular class of variables was investigated in only two experiments (Cuadra/Katter and Rees/Schultz), but not extensively. As mentioned, the results from the two experiments somewhat contradicted each other. For instance, Cuadra and Katter found a difference in the ratings because of differences in definitions of relevance, while Rees and Schultz found that differently defined aspects of relevance were not significantly affecting the ratings. It is concluded here, on the basis of a closer examination of data from both studies, that different definitions of relevance offered to judges produce only slight differences in ratings. Here are the conclusions enumerated:

a. Not surprisingly, changes in experimental conditions may introduce changes in judgments.
b. From the mere fact that one may define relevance to users in different ways, one need not expect different ratings.
c. The more pressure existing in judgmental situations, the higher ratings of relevance (i.e., "more" relevant) may be expected.

The last conclusion supports the observation well-known to retrieval practitioners: . . . "the more desperate a user is for information, the more relevant everything becomes . . . ." On the basis of the findings that slight differences in ratings were found from different definitions of relevance, this intriguing question suggests itself: Is it possible that no definition of "relevance" may be necessary, because the concept is so basic and so well

understood? In their theory, Maron and Kuhns (1960) understood relevance in this way and treated it as a primitive concept.

4. *Mode of Expression*

This variable was also investigated in only two experiments: Cuadra/Katter and Rees/Schultz. The results between the two studies were basically in agreement. Here are the conclusions:

a. Different kinds of scales (rating, ranking, and ratio scales), which are used to record the relevance judgments, may produce slightly different judgments.
b. The more categories a rating scale has (scales of up to some ten categories were tested), the more judges may be certain in their judgment; in any case, they may be more at ease with a scale having more than two and up to some ten categories.
c. It is not clear what type of scales are most reliable for use in recording relevance judgments; it seems that some form of a ratio scale may have some advantage over other types of scales for reliability.
d. On the scales tested judges (at least those with a higher level of subject knowledge) may tend to agree with themselves over a short period of time with a high degree of agreement; in other words, people, or at least subject specialists, are intra-reliable as relevance judges to a very high degree.
e. Regardless of the number of categories in a rating scale, it may be expected that the end points of the scale will be used most heavily, i.e., documents tend to be rated as either very relevant or very nonrelevant.
f. The judgments of different judges on one and the same document do not tend to be normally distributed; the distribution of judgments may be expected to be skewed in one direction and not to be uniform.
g. Most significantly, although the ratings of degree of relevance may be scattered, the relative position of documents as to their relevance, especially among the documents with high relevance, may be expected to be remarkably consistent even among groups of judges with differences in subject education.

The last conclusion partially explains why ratio scales may tend to have a higher reliability — they utilize the seemingly natural ability of people to position documents as to relevance with high agreement and on the other hand avoid the problem of ranking scales which allow documents only a rigid compartmentalization as to position or order. The conclusions are in support of the theories treating relevance as a comparative and dependency relation, or more specifically treating it as a measure depending not only on the query but also on the whole set of documents upon which judgment is performed.

5. *People*

People, as a variable, were present to some extent in all other variables; thus, the conclusions from other classes of variables should be taken into account. Following conclusions are made:

a. It may be expected that a greater subject knowledge on the part of a group of judges will produce a higher agreement on relevance judgment, i.e., people who know the same subject thoroughly will agree more among themselves; subject knowledge seems to be the most important factor affecting the relevance judgment as far as people's characteristics are concerned.

b. It also may be expected that the greater the subject knowledge in a group, the fewer documents will be judged relevant; that is, the judgment will be most stringent; conversely the less the subject knowledge, the more lenient the judgment is.

c. It seems that less subject-oriented groups (e.g., subject information retrieval specialists, subject librarians) tend to assessing relatively high relevance ratings; as suppliers of documents and delegates of users, it may be expected that these groups will judge more documents as relevant (from a set of documents) than the users; that they will be inclined to provide a user with all or most relevant material that a user himself would consider relevant and in addition some or considerably more material that he would not consider relevant; however, it may be expected that the order of highest ranked documents as to relevance will be very close between a person with extensive subject background (i.e., subject specialist) and a supplier of information (i.e., delegate) with a lesser subject background.

d. Within the subject background of delegates it seems that the factor that considerably affects a high relevance agreement is the familiarity with and knowledge of subject terminology.

e. It may be expected that a professional or occupational involvement with the problem that resulted in a query will increase the agreement of relevance judgment among and between groups of both subject specialists and those serving subject specialists with information such as subject retrieval specialists and librarians; professional involvement affects positively, as to agreement, the relevance judgment, even where the intensity of subject knowledge varies.

f. As to the amount of agreement on relevance of a set of documents a suggested norm of what may be expected is: the correlation of agreement on relevance among people with the greatest subject knowledge and most direct professional involvement with the subject of the query will probably be somewhere between .55 and .75; the correlation of agreement on relevance among people serving subject specialists with information will probably be somewhere between .45 and .60.

g. A different intention of use for documents by people may produce different judgments, suggesting that intended use becomes a part of a query; in addition to the subject content of a query the explication of intended use may benefit a closer understanding between a user and a delegate and thus, increase relevance agreement.

h. It may be expected that people generally will agree over a set of documents to a higher degree as to what is *not* relevant than to what is relevant; judging relevance is not the complement of judging nonrelevance.

i. Tests of retrieval system performance, given of course that they are well designed and controlled, may produce reliable comparative results within test experiments, regardless of relative instability of relevance judgments (instability within the range elaborated under *e.*)

j. In any case, relevance judgment is not at all a subjective event, in the sense of being even closely associated with random distributions.

Thus, people's subject knowledge seems the most important factor within people affecting the relevance judgment. The less we know the more everything becomes relevant, and the more we know the more stringent we become in our judgment. The theories that dealt with relevance on the basis of conditional probabilities are certainly finding support in their approach from experimental observations. In general, these findings may be projected as follows: At a destination, the content of a destination's file, store or memory in relation to the content of the query will have the greatest effect on establishing relevance of information sent by a source in response to the query.

From the Reflections on the Experiments to the Future

There is no doubt that we in this field have learned a great deal about relevance from relevance-related experimentation. At the minimum we have learned that we cannot and should not make positive and definite statements about a phenomenon as complex as relevance from anecdotal evidence. However, neither can we make quite positive statements from experimental results, as was mentioned in the introduction to general conclusions. In reviewing the relevance experimental efforts in the *Annual Review of Information Science and Technology*, King (1968) expressed this feeling in a classic remark:

"The reports (i.e., relevance experiments by Cuadra/Katter, Rees/Schultz, and others) also reveal the hazards of using relevance assessments blindly. The prescriptions are given for avoiding such pitfalls, however, and one must conclude that, since relevance as a concept cannot be avoided, it must be used. However, it is comforting to know that one can now properly feel nervous in using it."

It is a sad reflection on relevance experimentation that there were such serious shortcomings, which seemed to have first, introduced confusion along with clarification and second, they effected a seeming impasse of activities on relevance at present, as mentioned at the beginning of this paper. Therefore, it seems that relevance experimentation is still in its infancy, suffering from an assortment of infantile diseases and that much remains to be done. Through the analysis of the sources of these shortcomings, we may arrive at some explanations for the reasons of the impasse and at guidelines and recommendations for the future. All the shortcomings enumerated below are interrelated and their order of presentation is not meant to imply any order of importance. The shortcomings may be grouped into three groups: conceptual (under sections I and II), methodological (sections III, IV, and V), and environmental (section VI).

I.

First, a subtle but significant change occured in the conception of relevance. This change seems to be a source of considerable confusion and delimitation of efforts. Relevance as a phenomenon was equated with relevance judgment. A complex reiterative or feedback-type relation involving a communication process between a source and a destination, and including a source and its stores of knowledge and a destination and its stores of knowledge was treated at times solely as a discriminatory preferential response at the destination. Considerable confusion in the minds, in the discussions, in the experiments, and in the interpretations of results was inevitable, because different contexts were utilized. A repetition of what is meant by each may be helpful to underline this important point. Relevance, as a relation between a source of information and a destination to which information is transmitted by a communication process, is a measure of effective contact between the source and the destination, thus, it involves both ends of a process and both stores, files, and memories. Relevance judgment is only one of a variety of available indicators of the effectiveness of contact at the destination. For example: In education while knowledge is usually being communicated, no relevance judgment is performed at the destination (the student), but the effectiveness is examined or indicated in other ways. In effect, it may be said that the source and the destination are involved in a selection type of judgment while both are utilizing its stores, files, or memories of knowledge, and both are affecting each other in that process. It may be self-evident but still important to note that a source cannot send anything that it doesn't have, meaning in general that queries for which there is no counterpart knowledge in a source cannot be fully or at all answered by a communication process. In answering such queries, other processes, such as synthesis, creativity, experimental observations, etc. are more than involved in addition to communication as defined here. Equivalently, a destination can hardly assess relevance of information in relation to queries for which there is no counterpart knowledge of some kind and to some degree in the destination. In assessing answers to such queries a destination may have to involve other processes such as learning, observation, etc. in addition to communication as defined here.

Furthermore and unfortunately, relevance judgment was often viewed as stimuli introduced discriminatory response, which may not necessarily imply any communication process. By way of comment: A communication process may or may not include a judgment, but if it does, the judgment is a part of the process; conversely, a judgment may or may not be a part of a communication process and, thus, a given judgment certainly could be considered without a communication process — a relevance judgment cannot. Analogously, we may observe that, if blondes have more fun judging relevance, which may be a perfectly sound, interesting, and valid observation on a given judgmental process and situation, unfortunately, it has no relevance on relevance in a communication process and situation.

The interpretation of experimental results reflected the casual interchange of these two distinct aspects. It is suggested here that the considerations of relevance judgments in isolation and without involvement in explicit communication process might shed some but generally little light on relevance as a phenomenon in a communication process. The failure to explicitly distinguish between the two may be among the primary causes of our (hopefully) temporary stagnation in work on relevance.

II.

Let us now discuss what is termed the second shortcoming. The experimental work on relevance was done without any serious considerations and support of theories, either sketchy or fully formulated theories. There are a number of communication theories in general and relevance theories in particular that could have been used as an experimental base, at least in part and on a trial and error basis. Speculatively, examples are: information theory, general semantic theory, general system theory, cybernetic theories, epidemic communication theory, the measure theory of relevance, the logical (conceptual relatedness) theory of relevance, the probabilistic and other statistical distribution theories of relevance, some behavioral information processing theories, etc. The theoretical and experimental work on relevance were conducted, as mentioned, in isolation of each other.

On the other hand, experiments may be done without an explicit connection with a theory, but the results should eventually be used for formulating theories and models; however, neither this was done in connection with relevance experimentation. The history of science provides a lesson: Experimentation without connection to or from theories eventually becomes circular, stagnant, insignificant and sterile, introvert and always ending with soul-splitting orientation toward methodological problems. Relevance experimentation has yet a way to go to reach that stage, but not far. It is suggested here that the serious lack of cumulation of experimental findings on relevance may be, to a great extent, attributed to the lack of a relation of experiments to theoretical structures.

III.

This brings us to the third shortcoming, which relates to the general one-sided orientation and approach that the relevance experiments initially took. Briefly, there seems to be an orientation toward psycho- and socio-metrics, and psychology and behavioral sciences in general, as an only and exclusive approach to the proper study of relevance. As an illustration, in another review of relevance studies Paisley (1968), in the *Annual Review of Information Science and Technology*, formulated this conviction:

". . . the discussion of situation-specific preferential discriminatory response helps to move relevance research into the mainstream of psychometrics, where it belongs."

Needless to say that these approaches have a great deal to offer, and they should be used to a much greater extent than they were, but they should not be used to the exclusion of all other approaches. There are other behavioral approaches available, and there are also approaches available from other fields, such as linguistics (e.g., Gifford/Baumanis, 1969), logic (e.g., O'Connor, 1969), systems analysis (e.g., Lesk/Salton, 1968), mathematics (e.g., Goffman/Warren, 1969), a variety of statistical distribution approaches (e.g., Bradford, 1948), etc. These approaches have not been exploited fully, but, concluding from the results of the few studies where they were, they might offer as much as, if not more than, the psychometric approaches.

It might be worthwhile here to examine some general shortcomings of psychometrics, in order to better understand relevance experimentation problems. In the first place, psychometrics is almost totally oriented toward the study of reactions and not actions. The study of the actions in a communication process may have been equally as important in the understanding of relevance as a phenomenon as the study of reactions in

a relevance judgment. Secondly, it happens that psychometrics carries along with it at present, an overly orientation toward methodology as a problem area — that is, answers to problems are often sought in techniques not substance. Kaplan (1964) in his book, *The Conduct of Inquiry,* commenting on the future of behavioral science in general (of which psychometrics is a part), states that:

". . . . Many behavioral scientists, I am afraid, look to methodology as a source of salvation . . . Methodology is not turned to only as and when specific methodological difficulties arise in the course of particular inquiries; it is made all encompassing, a fact in which the tormented inquirer can hope to be reborn to a new life. There are indeed techniques to be mastered and their resources and limitations are to be thoroughly explored . . . but there are behavioral scientists who, in their desperate search for scientific status, give the impression that they don't care what they do if only they do it right; substance gives way to form . . . Their work might become methodologically sounder if only they did not try so hard to be so scientific . . . The label "behavioral science" also counts on insistence on the use of certain techniques, involving either brass instruments or advanced mathematics, preferably both . . . All these connotations belong to scientism, not to science . . . ."

These extremely harsh words are quoted here explicitly to point out some of the blind alleys into which an indiscriminate use of psychometrics might lead the research on relevance.

IV.

The fourth shortcoming identified here stems from the emphasis on the techniques of analysis of the experimental results which, it seems, impaired rather than enhanced the experimentation as a whole. Nobody can deny the importance of sound analysis techniques; however, there is a difference between a sound and sophisticated analysis technique and a significant, sound, and sophisticated experiment or sound and valid conclusions; the first does not necessarily imply the others in that order.

The case in point are the two largest relevance studies: Cuadra/Katter and Rees/Schultz. There is no doubt that these rank among the top experimental studies done in information science to date, and nothing can detract from that. But precisely because they had so many good points, their shortcomings must also be seriously examined.

The Cuadra/Katter study paid a considerable amount of attention to analysis techniques, so much so that it seriously neglected the control of variables in some of the fifteen experiments. For instance: certain experiments used as subjects "library school students and librarians," without distinction between the two groups, while another experiment in the same study did formulate as a hypothesis and later found in results that "knowledgeability," equated with the amount of professional training significantly affects the relevance judgment — shouldn't it be then taken that students of library science and practicing librarians are actually two separate groups each by itself possibly introducing differences in results? The same occurred in another experiment, where "seniors and library school students" comprised the population. The criteria for selection of a population in this instance are not consistent with their own hypotheses and findings. It is the impression of this reviewer that such deficiencies in design were the result of reliance on and emphasis of analysis techniques to such an extent that, at times, it seems that a consideration of given techniques dictated the selection of an experiment and not vice versa. Furthermore, it seems to this reviewer that the sophistication of these techniques made the experimenters overconfident in the arriving at some of the interpretations and conclusions, which were unnecessarily broad and definite at times.

On the other hand, the Rees/Schultz study, to some extent, made vague conclusions, because it seems that the avalanches of data from its own analyses impaired interpretation; (I was involved in that study and, thus, I am criticizing myself). The results from a series of extremely complex analyses of variances simply overwhelmed the whole study. Such a sentiment was expressed by King (1968):

"... Obviously, the next thing to do is to spell out in detail the significance of findings from the thorough CWRU (Case Western Reserve University) study by carefully interpreting the results ..."

While in the first (Cuadra/Katter) study too many conclusions and interpretations were made; in the second study (Rees/Schultz) there were too few — both as the result of sophisticated analysis techniques. The general lesson to be learned here for reference is this: neither let us run with a solution (e.g., analysis technique) to find a problem to which it can be applied, nor, on the other hand, let us impose upon a problem too complex solutions (too complex analysis methods). Rather, let us balance the two, problem and solutions, in a precise order.

V.

The fifth shortcoming relates to the over-complication of the experiments. It seems, retrospectively, that in many studies too many variables were attacked at the same time. This led to unwieldly experiments and too few positive results and too shallow knowledge. To paraphrase, when everything under the sun is varied at the same time, little is learned about anything. True, it may be hard to really isolate a small number of variables at a time, but it is suggested here that a simplification of experiments, dealing only with one or two variables and

aspects in any one study, but dealing with them comprehensively, may lead to a better understanding.

VI.

The sixth and last shortcoming doesn't have anything to do directly with relevance studies, but with the environment of the field in which the studies are done. The field of information science, within which relevance work is by and large conducted, lacks a long and firm tradition in experimentation or theory building or cumulation of knowledge or connecting of theories and experimentation. Such tradition is just emerging. Thus, all the problems of the field of information science as a whole are, to some extent, reflected in the work on relevance. In other words, the shortcomings and problems of relevance work are related to and based on the shortcomings of the field as a whole, to some extent. As the field as a whole makes strides in solving some of its general problems, no doubt the work on relevance will be upgraded. The seeming impasse of the activity on relevance may have been to some degree affected by the general environment provided to relevance activity by information science. As all other, and especially new fields, information science goes through periods of intensive interest and concentration on individual areas of investigation, while other areas of the field are somewhat neglected. Sometimes and especially in new fields, rapid changes in concentrations on individual or even isolated areas take regular appearances of fads. It seems that work on relevance might have been one of such fads which passed — thus, in part, the impasse.

There is still another environment-related problem: Relevance work is primarily directed toward information retrieval and librarianship. There is no evidence that any serious communication occurred between some practical areas of information retrieval or librarianship and any work on relevance, even though some work on relevance may have significant implication for some practical aspects. For instance, findings from experiments on document representations may be used in design decisions on what to disseminate to users; findings on the degree and nature of agreement between subject specialist and subject librarians may be used for selection of people in reference and in defining procedures for a reference process; findings on queries may be used in defining the question negotiation procedures, etc. It may be worthwhile to seriously investigate why there isn't any contact between experimental and theoretical work, on the one hand, and the practical world on the other, but realizing that in such investigation anecdotal evidence is not sufficient. Does the work on relevance have no relevance to practice, or is it that practice cannot recognize the relevance of the work on relevance to its own problems, or could it be that the workers on relevance in their conclusions and interpretations just cannot make themselves relevant to the practical world? However, a note of caution should be sounded: immediate practicality of a finding in science is *not* a measure of its value or validity. Thus, relevance activity should not be judged on the criterion: what good is it to practice right away?

Finally, in discussing environment, it is worthwhile to mention the changing and uncertain nature of financial support for the work or relevance. Government funding agencies, the prime supporters of such work in the past, added and subtracted, changed and varied, prolonged and curtailed, encouraged and discouraged, the support over the last decade to such an extent that sustained orderly efforts in the area of relevance, based on government support have not been possible. The funding agencies in the past or present have had no consistent, clear, long-range policy in relation to the work on relevance. Such erratic support does not add to a success, but we shouldn't be too critical: neither does consistent support guarantee a success. As a matter of fact, it is possible that the field of information science as a whole needs to make a more consistent effort about relevance on its own before the funders can make any policy.

In summary, the experimentation and general work on relevance had among others, these serious shortcomings which, it is suggested, impaired for the moment further progress:

. . . the concept of relevance and the concept of relevance judgment were confused with each other;

. . . theoretical and experimental work was unconnected: there was no cumulation of knowledge; works were done in isolation of each other;

. . . a one-sided orientation to psychometrics as an only approach to experimentation was taken; the discussion of psychometric problems overwhelmed the area of relevance;

. . . in experiments an undue emphasis was given to the techniques of analysis of results at the expense of the considerations involving the quality of experiments as a whole;

. . . quite often too many variables were varied all at the same time; controls in experiments were questionable; and the general environment of information science as a field within which relevance activity was conducted proved not to be encouraging; relevance assumed trappings of a fad; furthermore, there was little or no communication between the world of practice and any relevance activity; the funding for relevance work was erratic.

Part 7. Relevance-Related Distributions

The theories (reviewed in Part 2) concentrated in specifying relationships underlying relevance and the conditions under which these relationships hold, while the hypotheses and experiments (Parts 4 and 5) were basically concerned with variables affecting relevance

judgments. From these reviews it became evident that relevance ought to be approached from the point-of-view of the source and of the destination and their respective files, stores or memories, and from the point-of-view of the relationships between them as realized in the communication process. Of all variables documents (or in general any conveyors of information) were found to be most significant. The results suggest that in specifying or assessing relevance, both the sources and destinations engage in a process of selection and of ordering documents.

Any selection processes and especially any ordering processes have associated with them a distribution. Such a distribution may be random or it may follow a pattern. One of the major conclusions from the experimentation was that relevance is not associated with a random distribution under circumstances encountered in the reality of communication processes in general, or retrieval and library situations in particular. However, at this time we cannot say what kind of distribution may be associated with relevance for the simple reason that it was never investigated.

Consequently, it is of significance and of great practical importance to study the nature of distributions which may be associated with relevance at the source and at the destination. The aim of this Part is to suggest those distributions which may describe the patterns in which relevance may manifest itself. If we can eventually through empirical and experimental observations identify these distributions correctly, then their properties may be utilized for a more formal and orderly as well as a more effective and efficient design of operations in information systems.

The distribution patterns of a great many communication-related phenomena and manifestations were investigated. As a result there exist a large body of literature reporting empirical and experimental observations on such distributions; a number of empirical laws on the relation between the observed variables were derived from the distribution patterns; following the statement of laws, many theoretical generalizations of and correlations between various distributions were further derived. Some of these communication-related phenomena and manifestations for which distribution patterns were investigated are by their nature closely related to relevance, which is also a communication-related phenomenon. Although an implicit recognition of this relation was always present, the resulting distributions were rarely explicitly recognized as related to relevance.

The notion of expressing relevance through distributions stems both from the above synthesis of theories and experiments and from observations on the distributions of communication-related manifestations, such as:

. . . the frequency of utilization of different periodicals from a library collection (Urquhart, 1959);

. . . distribution as to productivity of authors as science (Lotka, 1926) and the generalizations to the growth of science (Price, 1963);

. . . citation practices and networks in science (Price, 1965);

. . . distribution of frequency of appearance of words in texts and subsequent generalizations to distributions of things ranked in order of size (Zipf, 1949);

. . . most importantly, the distribution of the scatter of articles on a subject over journals (Bradford, 1948);

. . . relation between numbers of authors and distribution of journals in a subject area (Goffman and Warren, 1969).

One empirical finding relating to the distributions associated with these communication manifestations is remarkable and most significant: the same mathematical model is applicable to the distribution of most (if not all) of them. This general statistical distribution model is a probability density function associated with a law that in information science is becoming to be known as the Bradford-Zipf law. Most recently Fairthorne (1969) provided a most comprehensive historical review of and correlation between the laws and distributions of interest to information science, thus only the salient findings on the above enumerated frequencies and distributions will be reviewed below in order to enable a suggestion of their relation with relevance.

1. Utilization of a Source

In the practice of librarianship and information retrieval these are well-known empiricisms: A small part of a collection of documents satisfies most of the requests put to that collection; in a large collection a large proportion of the collection is rarely used, some of it never. Substantiating this experience are the data from a number of studies on utilization of library and information retrieval collections. A description of one of the more significant studies conducted follows.

Urquhart (1959) studied the distribution over different periodicals of the 53,000 external loan requests filled by the Science Museum Library in London during 1956. The library had 9,120 different current periodicals; of those 4,821 were never requested that year and 2,190 were requested only once, 791 were requested twice, 403 three times, 283 four times, etc. On the other hand, the most popular periodical was requested 382 times and 60 periodicals were requested more than 100 times each. In percentages, half of the requests were satisfied by the top forty periodicals and eighty percent of the requests were satisfied by less than ten percent of the available periodicals.

The results of Urquhart's study clearly indicate that utilization of a collection (i.e., source) is heavily weighted toward a small section of that collection. Other studies, such as by Badger and Goffman (1964) on frequency of retrieval of documents from a large information retrieval file, which is a different type of source, substantiate this finding. There is a direct relation between "periodicals sent out on request," "retrieved documents" by a source and relevance in general: first, the source sent out periodicals or retrieved documents in response to a request from a destination desiring relevant answers, and second, whatever the destinations eventually selected as relevant answers was selected from what the source sent.

It may be suggested that answers, and thus relevance in general and over a large number of queries as far as a source is concerned, largely depends on or is derived from a small portion or subset of the file that the source contains. Furthermore, it seems clear that a source's file, even in relation to a large number of queries and destinations, is not utilized in a random fashion at all but the frequency of use *does* follow definite patterns. It is interesting to note that here, from a different set of data, we again arrived at the same important conclusion as from previously reviewed experiments: Relevance is not associated with a random distribution.

2. The Productivity of Authors

Since relevance depends in part on documents (or conveyors of information in general) and since documents are written (produced) by authors, it may be worthwhile to examine some relations between authors and a literature, i.e., a set of documents in a given area.

Lotka (1926) formulated from his observations on the frequency of contributions of individual authors in a decennial index of Chemical Abstracts and a historical bibliography of physics till 1900 a simple empirical law which states that the number of people producing n papers is proportional to $1/n^2$. For instance, in sciences, for every 100 authors who produce only a single paper during a longer period of time, there may be expected, the law says, that there are twenty-five authors with two papers, eleven with three papers, six with four papers, etc. With some correction of the law for authors with highest productivity or highest scores, it was found on a variety of data that Lotka's law is remarkably true.

These observed regularities prompted Price (1963) to study and correlate the patterns of distribution and growth of science, its literature, authors and manpower, and the utilization of literature. Among others, Price elaborated on the exponential growth of the scientific literature and speculated on the effects which may happen when this exponential growth starts leveling off, as all logistic growths must. He ascribed the growth of literature to the growth of the number of scientists, and not to any increased productivity of individuals. By the way, the average productivity of authors in science was found to be remarkably consistent over time in general.

Next, Price elaborated on Lotka's law, corrected it for highly prolific authors and substantiated it with other data. The point is this: A large proportion of a total literature is actually produced by a small proportion of the total number of authors; thus, literature (documents) is neither distributed as to its producers in a random fashion nor a normal distribution. One third of the literature is associated with less than one tenth of authors; or more specifically, on the high score, about five to ten per cent of authors produce over fifty per cent of all literature and on the low score some seventy-five per cent of authors produce only twenty-five per cent of all literature. Price pointed out that the distribution that follows Lotka's law is similar to the distribution obtained from Pareto's famous law on income distribution; (i.e., if we plot a number of people as to the size of income, there are a lot of people with low income and we proceed monotonically to a small number of millionaires). Fairthorne (1969) and many others pointed the equivalence between Pareto's and Bradford-Zipf's distributions.

In elaborating on Urquhart's data, Price noted that the distribution of utilization of journals follows exactly the same Pareto-type curve as the distribution of authors. Thus, the production as well as utilization of literature follow basically the same type of distribution patterns. Eventually, relevance may to a large extent not only be derived from a small portion of a source's file but possibly also from a small number of authors in the literature.

3. *Citation Patterns*

Citation of a document in another document is a type of indication of relevance in the same sense as a judgment is. Thus, a pattern of citations is a type of relevance distribution. The question is: What patterns do citation networks take? Are they random or are they weighted heavily toward a small proportion of documents? Price (1965) studied the networks of scientific papers as formed by the special relationship that papers have through citations. He found pretty much the same picture and distribution as found for the utilization of a collection and productivity of authors. The citations found in new papers are of two types: overall some fifty per cent of all citations are less than ten per cent of old papers and the other fifty per cent are some fifty per cent of old papers. Some forty per cent of old papers are not being cited by each year's new crop of papers. Half of the citations, to quote Price:

". . . tie these new papers to a quite small group of earlier ones, and generate a rather tight pattern of multiple relationships. Thus, each group of new papers is "knitted" to a small, select part of the existing scientific literature but connected rather weakly and randomly to a much greater part."

This small part of earlier literature Price called the "research front." He also established the "dying" or half-lives of literature through citations. These findings suggest these notions as to relevance: A small part of literature (at least in science) is highly relevant; fur-thermore, some part "ages" over time so that it becomes nonrelevant — thus, relevance is clearly a time dependent phenomenon.

4. *Zipf's Law*

Zipf (1949) formulated a law based on the study of word counts of large text samples. If all the unique words in a text are arranged (ranked) in order of decreasing frequency of occurrence, Zipf found that for a given word with frequency f and ranked r, the product of frequency times rank provides a constant C which is approximately the same for all words, i.e.:

$$f \cdot r = C \qquad (1)$$

It was found that in a more general case the resulting cumulative distribution of a variety of items ranked in order of size by some natural selection can be approximated by a function of the form

$$f(i) = \frac{c}{i^k} \qquad (2)$$

where $f(i)$ is the number of items that occur i times and C and k are constants. In other words, it was found that there is a general distribution form which accounts for a great many distributions of things ranked in order of size resulting from a given type of selection. In the case of Zipf's law as stated under (1) k = 1.

Simon (1955) elaborated on a class of empirically derived skew distribution functions which approximate form (2) and called them Yule distribution functions after the British statistician, G. U. Yule, who in 1924 constructed a probability model with distribution of approximate form (2). Simon pointed out that the Yule distribution actually describes many diverse and unconnected phenomena (such as distribution of words in texts by their frequency of occurrence (Zipf), distribution of scientists by number of papers published (Lotka), distribution of cities by population (Zipf), distribution of incomes by size (Pareto), distribution of biological genera by number of species (Yule), and other distributions), but that underlying all these phenomena is a general stochastic model and process that leads to that stationary distribution. This is in the same sense by which, for instance, the normal distribution describes a variety of phenomena, but it does not imply that the underlying causes and mechanisms are equivalent. In other words, a study of distribution patterns of phenomena can be done without assuming a proximity of causes. It is of importance to state and investigate the particular stochastic model and process underlying these phenomena because it affords a method of description and prediction.

Even of more importance is to investigate the basic mechanisms that permeate and govern the various phenomena that manifest themselves in Zipf's distribution patterns with the appropriate understanding that a distribution may be only a clue to and never an explanation of the underlying causes and mechanisms. The more we know about the nature of mechanisms the more we can tell about the nature of the phenomenon. On the most generic level the mechanism that governs the mentioned phenomena, and others to be described in the next section, seems to be one of efficiency of selection from a finite number of choices, i.e., it is some kind of a criterion of efficiency of selection that often arises naturally and socially.

On a more specific level in relation to human behavior Zipf thought of this mechanism as one of economy of human behavior and consequently he formulated his widely praised but also attacked Principle of Least Effort. To quote Zipf as to the implications:

". . . if Least Effort is indeed fundamental in all human action, we may expect to find it in operation in any human action we might choose to study. In short any human action will be a manifestation of the Principle of Least Effort in operation, if this Principle is true . . . ."

On a more specific level the mechanisms governing each phenomenon may differ and they will have to be investigated separately. However, and most importantly regardless of the actual Zipf law or some other interpretation of the mechanisms, the "distribution-approach" as a tool affords us a way of looking at a variety of hard to investigate phenomena of which relevance is one.

In relation to relevance the Zipf law, even if not describing it, is certainly suggesting an approach to investigation of relevance distributions, of subsequent stochastic models and processes, and possibly even of the governing mechanisms. That such an approach may be warranted follows from the experimental observations on the definite distribution patterns of relevance-related communication manifestations as well as from theories (substantiated by some experimental observations) that viewed and described relevance in terms of conditional probabilities, which in turn are the basis for stochastic processes. Zipf's law was treated here, at some length for two reasons: first, it has an extensive amount of theoretical, empirical, and critical work associated with it and second, as it will be shown, the Bradford distribution which is most closely associated with relevance is in part equivalent to generalized Zipf's distribution.

5. *Bradford's law*

All the reviewed findings on distributions are best expressed and are most significantly connected with relevance through the Bradford law on the scattering of literature and the associated Bradford distribution. This law is a fundamental discovery which originated from empirical observations by Bradford (1948) on the dispersion in scientific journals of papers in two subject areas: applied geophysics and lubrications. Since it was found in numerous studies following Bradford's formulation that the law holds in a variety of other subject areas, as well as for other parameters and not only journals it is accepted today that the Bradford law describes the dispersion patterns of sciences-related literature as well as its uses and users in general. It is possible that it also pertains to the humanistic literature.

Bradford's original question was: To what extent do different journals contribute articles devoted to a given subject? Even this original question which led to the formulation of the Bradford law can be directly and unambiguously interpreted in terms of the concept of relevance. Namely, the notion of "devoted to a subject" is directly related to the notion of "relevant to a subject"; it is trivial to mention that the journals that contain articles devoted to a subject cannot help but also contain articles eventually relevant to a query on the subject.

Bradford (1948) formulated the law as follows:

". . . if scientific journals are arranged in order of decreasing productivity of articles on a given subject, they may be divided into a nucleus of periodicals more particularly devoted to the subject and several groups or zones containing the same number of articles as the nucleus, where the number of periodicals in the nucleus and succeeding zones will be as $n: n^2: n^3. . . .$"

In other words, if the first nuclear zone contains a given A number of articles produced by a given J_1 number of journals, the second zone will contain approximately the same A number of articles produced by J_2 number of journals, the third zone will have approximately the same A number of articles as the first and second zone produced by J_3 number of journals, etc. The Bradford law states that a subdivision of journals into zones can be such that:

$$J_2 = J_1 b \text{ or } \frac{J_2}{J_1} = b; \text{ and}$$

$$J_3 = J_2 b \text{ or } \frac{J_3}{J_2} = b \text{ and}$$

again

$$\frac{J_3}{J_1} = b^2;$$

or in general the number of journals in the ith zone will be:

$$J_1 = J_1 b^{i-1}$$

where $i = 1, 2, 3 . . .$ and the constant b is the Bradford multiplier for a given number of divisions (greater than 1) into zones. Thus, the ratio of the number of journals in successive zones is:

$$J_1 : J_2 : J_3 : . . . = 1: b: b^2. . . .$$

Bradford suggested that the distribution following his law be plotted as the cumulated sum of articles (R(n)) on the ordinate (y-axis) versus the logarithm of the cumulated sum of the journals (log n) on the abscissae as shown in Figure 3: this remained the usual way of representing the distribution. Bradford also discussed the properties of the distribution noting that the resulting graph has two distinct parts: it starts as a curve of an exponential nature and then commences as a straight line of a linear nature. Eventually the linear part of the distribution was recognized as the Zipfian component and the exponential part as the Bradford restriction on the distribution.

Leimkuhler (1967) was first to propose the Bradford distribution in the form of a mathematical equation of a continuous function:

$$F(x) = \frac{\ln(1 + \beta x)}{\ln(1 + \beta)} \quad (0 \leqq x \leqq 1)$$

where $F(x)$ is the cumulative fraction of articles, x is the corresponding fraction of the most productive journals and β is a constant related to the given subject collection and associated to the Bradford multiplier b as: $\beta = b-1$.

Brookes (1968, 1969 and 1969a) noted that the distribution can be expressed in two parts, one for the Bradford restriction and one for the Zipfian component (Figure 3):

$$R(n) = \alpha n\beta \qquad (1 \leqq n \leqq c) \qquad (3a)$$
$$= k \log n/s \qquad (c \leqq n \leqq N) \qquad (3b)$$

where $R(n)$ is the cumulated sum of items (e.g., articles) contributed by 1, 2, 3 . . . n number of sources (e.g., journals); log n is the logarithm of cumulated journals; α is the number of articles published in the most productive journal, i.e., point A on the ordinate; β is a constant related to the collection, determining the curvature of AC; k is the constant indicating the slope of the linearity CB; and c and s are as indicated in Figure 3. When N, the rank of the last journal is large enough then k = N, and then the slope of linearity indicates the total number of journals in the collection producing $R(N)$ number of articles, i.e., expression (3b) can be rewritten as:

$$R(N) = N \log N/s \quad (c \leqq n \leqq N).$$

The Bradford law, although formulated in 1948, was mostly a curiosity until the late sixties when its remarkable stability, practical applicability, potential, and connection to other human communication laws were recognized through theoretical generalizations and experimental observations on a wide variety of data and situations considerably beyond the scatter of journals. Moreover, this empirical law was arrived at and it is being verified by the methods usual in sciences; thus, it does have the usual scientific acceptance and it should be

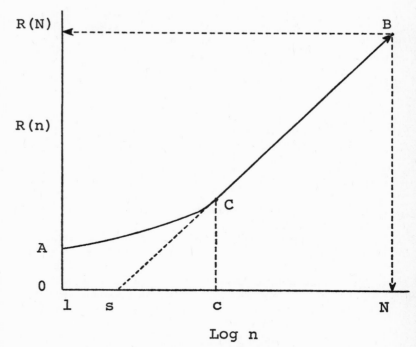

Fig. 3. A Typical Bradford Distribution Showing the Bradford Restriction (AC) and the Zipf Linearity (CB).

understood within the appropriate scope and limitations of other empirically derived laws.

The works in connection with Bradford's law and distribution were summarized and generalized in a number of excellent reviews of recent origin, cited below; thus, no real historical elaboration is needed here, but a short historical summary follows.

Vickery (1948) first undertook a theoretical generalization of Bradford's law over any n number of zones, showed a method for arriving at b, the Bradford multiplier, and corrected the method of fitting the Bradford law to a theoretical curve. Kendall (1960) while applying the law to the bibliography of operations research and of statistical methodology was first to draw a parallel and note the similarity between Bradford's and Zipf's distributions.

Leimkuhler (1967) summarized most, if not all, different Bradford distribution data available to that time and derived a formal equation for the Bradford distribution as a probability density function as stated above.

Brookes (1968, 1969 and 1969a) reviewed further data, and restated the Bradford distribution function in a form (see above) that enabled a clear connection with the Zipf distribution. Brookes (1968) noted that:

". . . Zipf's law has been found to pervade many similar human phenomena which involve a wide choice from a finite number of possibilities. It is not at all surprising and it is certainly very convenient, that Zipf's law should also embrace the scatter of papers relevant to a given topic among the scientific journals (i.e., the Bradford law). . . .''

Brookes (1969) also provided numerous examples on the practical application of the law. In a powerful discussion he noted the direct usefulness of the law to bibliographic services:

". . . (the Bradford law) . . . seems to offer the only means discernible at present of reducing the present quantitative untidiness of scientific documentation, information systems and library services to a more orderly state of affairs capable of being rationally and economically planned and organized. . . .''

Brookes in effect tied the Bradford law most closely to relevance.

Fairthorne (1969) in a paper that has all the earmarks of a classic review was concerned with the mathematical and statistical tools, their characteristics and limitations, applicable to 'bibliometrics' — "the quantitative treatment of the properties of recorded discourse and behavior appertaining to it." He enumerated about a dozen of empirical laws on a wide variety of phenomena and correlated some twenty derivations of these laws, tying the Bradford law to its appropriate class or family of hyperbolic distributions. Most importantly he warned of the fallacies of equating the distributions with the mechanisms underlying the given phenomenon. He also noted the power of the "distribution approach" in studying a communication behavior and that the behavior could be studied without invoking any hypothesis about the proximate causes of such behavior.

A considerable amount of theoretical and experimental work in connection with Lotka's, Zipf's, and Bradford's law was done in Russia. It seems that this activity was spurred in large part by the translation of Price's (1963) book *Little Science, Big Science* into Russian in 1966. For instance, Kozachkov and Khursin (1968) examined the trends of growth of scientific publications according to a generalized model of what is termed in Russia the Lotka/Bradford/Zipf distribution. They established and tested with extensive data a dependency relation between the growth of literature and the number of scientists and denied an existence of a universal law of exponential growth of publications applicable to all subject areas. In another work, Kozachkov (1969) went the furthest so far of anyone in his attempts to connect relevance with other communication manifestations. He related the notion of relevance to a number of problems in informatics (the term for information science in Russia) and scientology (science of science), stating that relevance is proved to be intricately connected with the process of scientific cognition. He connected relevance with a number of known distributions (Lotka, Zipf, Bradford) and in these terms discussed the growth, scatter, losses, and obsolescence of relevant information.

Two other interesting studies are more than worth mentioning because they enlarge the horizon of our views on the Bradford law. Zunde and Dexter (1969), as a result of experiments on indexing consistency, formulated a model of completeness of information representation that in essence follows the Bradford distribution. Namely, the model was formulated after they found that a plot of exhaustivity or completeness of indexing (or information representation) versus the number in a group of decision makers or indexers whose individual choices of indexes are combined, provides a distribution equivalent to Bradford distribution. Thus, the choices of index terms for a document by people from a set of finite choices are distributed in a Bradford manner. The second example relates Bradford to a library. Goffman and Morris (1970) demonstrated that the Bradford law holds for the journal use in a large medical library and it even held for the distribution of library users in relation to frequency of use. Furthermore, for a given subject it holds under a subject heading of *Index Medicus* over a period of three years. Consequently, they suggested on the basis of the data of all the three parameters studied a method for establishing a minimal nucleus of periodicals in a given subject for a library. Their work is an example of the practical potential of the law.

Let us conclude the discourse on the Bradford law (which as it was demonstrated may have a close connection with the pattern of a distribution of relevant information) with a short discussion on the possible mechanisms governing the phenomena demonstrating themselves through the law. Not much theoretical or experimental work was done on unearthing these mechanisms. This is an area badly in need of investigation, because many explanations are clearly lacking. The Bradford law is an empirical finding not well understood in a theoretical sense. On a generic level Brookes (1969) explained the underlying mechanism as follows:

". . . The Bradford/Zipf distribution can be expected to arise when selection is made of items characterized by some common element, which are all equally open to selection for an equal period and subject to the 'success-breeds-success' mechanism (i.e., those items, once successfully selected, have a higher probability of being selected again and so forth), but when a selection of a most popular group is also, but to a weaker extent, subject to restriction. It is thus, a general law of concentration over an unrestricted range of items on which is superimposed a weaker law of dispersion over a restricted range of the most frequently selected items."

Fairthorne (1969) provided numerous general and specific explanations of the mechanisms:

". . . (Bradford/Zipf distribution) is characteristic of any phenomena that are self similar in that their parts differ from the whole only in scale.

. . . Principles of this kind exist in many activities,

but arise out of the nature of the activity rather than as manifestations of a universal principle. . . . The basis for such methods (used in these distribution studies) are the combinatorial properties of compounds built up by repetitoin and combination from a fixed repertory of elements."

In conclusion he states:

"This survey has shown the hyperbolic distributions to be the inevitable result of combinatorial necessity and a tendency to short-term rational behavior whenever a group of people have to use a repertory of given elements to form compounds, and when one aspect of the 'cost' or inconvenience of these elements is dominant. Usually the elements and their use arise from the way people choose to observe, arrange, or talk about things, not from the nature of the things themselves. Therefore designers and administrators can cheat these laws by changing the elements, their costs, and the rules for using them. The laws themselves give the limits of improvement and a yardstick for quality control. Disobedience of the laws is more significant than obedience, because it indicates that conditions have changed."

6. *Structure of Subject Literatures*

As defined, a set of documents on a subject comprises a subject literature. This can be interpreted even in a more abstract sense than physical documents and literature. A unification of all the previous notions on utilization, origination, growth, obsolescence, citation, and scatter of literature (and quite a few other notions) provides a description of the structure of a literature. Since relevance is related to and dependent upon literature, the structure of literature may tell us a great deal about relevance. Until very recently, there were no works that studied the structure of a literature in a unified manner as mentioned above. As an example of how powerful and interesting such studies may be we are summarizing here the study by Goffman and Warren (1969). They studied and compared two total subject literatures from their inception: on mast cell, (1877 up to 1964) and on schistosomiasis, (1852 up to 1962) — that is, they studied the literatures for a span of approximately a century. Their first finding was that although there were three times as many schistosomiasis authors as mast cell authors, three times as many journals containing schistosomiasis articles as mast cell articles, and three times as many journals containing one schistosomiasis article as containing one mast cell article, the ratio of journals to authors for each literature was a constant. In other words, the number of authors and not the number of papers determined the scatter of a literature among its set of journals, i.e.,

$$\frac{J}{a} = W \qquad (4)$$

where J is the number of journals, a is the number of authors, and W is a constant found to be approximately .27.

Next they studied the Bradford distribution of the literature, but with an entirely new notion: namely, trying to find the conditions under which a *minimal* nucleus can be specified, which represents the most significant set of journals for a given literature because it is the smallest core of periodicals devoted to that subject. A minimal nucleus is obtained when there is a maximal (m) number of subdivision in the sense of Bradford and thus b, the Bradford multiplier, is minimal (b_m). The smallest number of articles, A/m, which can effect a division of the J journals in the sense of Bradford must be greater than Z/2, where Z is the number of journals with one article. Subsequently, they showed that:

$$\frac{A}{m} \approx J_m \approx b_m \frac{Z}{2} \approx g \frac{Z}{2} \qquad (5)$$

and thus

$$b_m \approx g$$

where A is the total number of articles, m is the maximal number of zones, J_m is the number of journals in the mth (last) zone and

$$g = A/a$$

i.e., the average number of papers per author. Most interestingly the minimal Bradford multiplier b_m is roughly equal to the average number of papers g. It was also shown that the average number of papers per author was invariant over time, i.e., average rate of production of literature per authors is constant with respect to time. In addition, the study showed that the Bradford law held for the bibliography of individual authors. In conclusion, it seems that the expressions (4) and (5) constitute an additional empirical law (the Goffman/Warren law) which should be taken into account in a study of the structure of a literature and thus, in the study of relevance.

7. *Summary of the General Implications for Relevance*

A variety of communication-related manifestations were reviewed above, and a consistency in patterns of distribution was stressed. A specific connection to relevance of each of the manifestations was made and as a result an existence of a class of relevance-related distributions was inferred. The widely documented observations that an equivalent distribution and model is applicable to the process associated with: (a) utilization of a collection (source); (b) productivity of authors — originators of science literature; (c) citation patterns; (d) vocabulary distribution; (e) scattering of information over its sources; and, (f) completeness of information representation, implies a general law of distribution in processes in human communication which involve knowledge. Therefore, it is reasonable to assume or hypothesize that the same basic distribution laws that apply to other communication manifestations related to relevance will also apply to relevance.

8. *A Hypothesis on Relevance Distribution*

Since a distribution of relevant answers at a source (as selected and considered relevant by the source from its file) and in conjunction with a distribution of relevant answers at a destination (as selected and considered relevant by the destination from the set of answers supplied by the source) in a communication process was not yet investigated, it may be appropriate to conclude this part, as well as the whole review, with a hypothesis to that effect. In brief, the hypothesis states that both distributions with respect to the relevance of answers at the source and the destination over a large number of queries will be of a Bradfordian nature.

As a background to the hypothesis the following is assumed. Relevance is considered a measure of an effective contact between a source and destination in a communication process where information is transmitted; effective contact means that the information transmitted resulted in accumulation of knowledge at the destination (Goffman and Newill, 1967). There are obviously many instruments by which an effective contact may be attempted, one of them being information retrieval. The hypothesis is not concerned with any one particular instrument but with the distribution occurring at the source and at the destination, however, it is particularly applicable to information retrieval systems.

It is assumed further that a source is instigated by a query to select from its store (file) a set of answers to be sent to the destination. The answers are sent by the source because the source considers them relevant and this is *relevance at the source*. The source consists of a set of conveyors of information, i.e., documents. It is assumed that the source's store contains subject literature or literatures; thus, we know that the documents in the store may very likely be distributed in the sense of Bradford. It is also assumed that the queries are on the subjects of the source's store. The destination selects a subset from the set of answers sent by the source which it considers relevant, and this is *relevance at the destination*. A distinction is made between relevance at the source and relevance at the destination because the two sets are usually not identical, although they are not independent at all. We are implying that there are two selections and two relevancies: a selection of relevant documents by the source and a subsequent selection of relevant documents at and by the destination. The decisions as to relevance may be either dichotomous (relevant — not relevant) or some ordering with ability to assign thresholds.

First, the part of the hypothesis concerning the source:

Over a large number of queries, posed by all of the destinations (users), those documents selected as relevant by the source, and thus, provided as answers to destinations of all queries, are distributed in the sense of Bradford.

Second, the part of the hypothesis concerning the destinations: The documents selected as relevant to a large number of queries by all destinations (users) from those answers supplied by a source, are distributed in the sense of Bradford.

However, the two distributions (source's and destination's) are not equivalent in size. The source's distribution will contain more documents than the destination's; thus, the size or number of zones, size of minimal nuclei or the Bradford multipliers will differ. Since it was observed that the ordering of highest rated documents is consistent in general, it is hypothesized that the documents in the nucleus at the destinations will be to a large extent a subset of the documents in the nucleus at the source, and that real differences between the two assignments of relevance will occur on documents in the lowest placed zones. In other words, a high agreement between a source and the destinations will be on the more (not necessarily most) frequently retrieved documents.

In practical terms, the hypothesis implies that, regardless of queries, some documents in a file of a library or a retrieval system will be requested or retrieved time and again, and these documents will comprise a very small proportion of the total collection, i.e., a small number of documents will be answers to a large number of queries. Most documents in the collection will rarely be used or retrieved, a good proportion never. As to the users, the hypothesis implies that of the documents provided or sent by a library or retrieval system, a relatively small number of documents will reoccur time and again as being relevant to a large number of users and a large number of documents will be selected as relevant by users very few times. In other words, a small number of individual documents satisfies a large number of users.

This hypothesis is certainly testable under a variety of experimental conditions. If it is observed on a number of occasions that it is correct, we may achieve three important things: We may further our knowledge on relevance and open an entirely new area of relevance investigations, i.e., the area of relevance distribution; we may directly and not only by inference connect relevance to other communication processes; and we may have some extremely important practical implications on the design, organization, and operation of our information systems. The observations from an experiment by Saracevic (1970) substantiated this hypothesis.

Epilogue

To reaffirm the thought with which the review started: Our present concern over relevance stems mostly from the "amount" of existing nonrelevance which endangers communication. We are investigating relevance in order to suppress nonrelevance. We know that we cannot eliminate nonrelevance but we hope to make it bearable. The mounting problems of our society and the shortness of time we have to solve them demand effective information synthesis, transmition, and organization for decision making that affects us all. Since the investigations on relevance may directly aid in the fulfillment of such demands, this activity may have important social usefulness. With the fantastic developments in information technology, we know how to communicate more efficiently. Unfortunately more and more of what our information systems contain is less and less worth communicating. Thus, regardless of technology, it is becoming more difficult to communicate anything that is of worth. The modern saying summarizes it best: Communications have improved tremendously, so much more so than what we have to say to each other.

References

BADGER, G., JR., and W. GOFFMAN, "An Experiment with File Ordering for Information Retrieval." *Proceedings of the American Documentation Institute*, Washington, D.C., Vol. 3 (1964), pp. 379–81.

BARHYDT, G. C., "The Effectiveness of Non-user Relevance Assessments." *Journal of Documentation*, Vol. 23, No. 2 (June, 1967), pp. 146–49.
The table for this article appeared in *Journal of Documentation*, Vol. 23, No. 3 (October, 1967), p. 251.

BRADFORD, S. C., *Documentation*. London: Crosby, 1948.

BROOKES, B. C., "The Derivation and Application of the Bradford-Zipf Distribution." *Journal of Documentation*, Vol. 24, No. 4 (December, 1968), pp. 247–65.

BROOKES, B. C., "Bradford's Law and the Bibliography of Science." *Nature*, Vol. 224, No. 5223 (December 6, 1969), pp. 953–56.

BROOKES, B. C., "The Complete Bradford-Zipf 'Bibliography'" *Journal of Documentation*, Vol. 25, No. 1 (March 1969), pp. 58–60.

CUADRA, C. A., *On the Utility of the Relevance Concept*. Technical report SP–1595. Systems Development Corp., Santa Monica, Calif. 1964.

CUADRA, C. A., and R. V. KATTER, *Experimental Studies of Relevance Judgments*. TM–3520/001, 002, 003/ 00. 3 vols., Systems Development Corp., Santa Monica, Calif., 1967.

CUADRA, C. A., and R. V. KATTER, "Opening the Black Box of 'Relevance'." *Journal of Documentation*, Vol. 23, No. 4 (December 1967), pp. 291–303.

DOYLE, L. B., "Is Relevance an Adequate Criterion for Retrieval System Evaluation?" *Proceedings of the American Documentation Institute*, Part 2, Washington, D.C., (1963), pp. 199–200.

DYM, E. D., "Relevance Predictability: I. Investigation Background and Procedures." In *Electronic Handling of Information: Testing and Evaluation*, A. Kent, O. E. Taulbee, J. Belzer, and G. D. Goldstein, eds. Washington, D.C.: Thompson Book Co. (1967), pp. 175–85.

FAIRTHORNE, R. A., "Empirical Hyperbolic Distributions (Bradford-Zipf-Mandelbrot) for Bibliometric Description and Prediction." *Journal of Documentation*, Vol. 25, No. 4 (December 1969), pp. 319–43.

GIFFORD, C., and G. J. BAUMANIS, "On Understanding User Choices: Textual Correlates of Relevance Judgments." *American Documentation*, Vol. 20, No.1 (January 1969), pp. 21–26.

GOFFMAN, W., "On Relevance as a Measure." *Information Storage and Retrieval*, Vol. 2, No. 3 (December 1964), pp. 201–03.

GOFFMAN, W., and V. A. NEWILL, "Methodology for Test and Evaluation of Information Retrieval Systems." *Information Storage and Retrieval*, Vol. 3, No. 1 (August 1966), pp. 19–25.

GOFFMAN, W., and V. A. NEWILL, "Communication and Epidemic Processes." *Proceedings of the Royal Society, A.*, Vol. 298, No. 1454 (May 2, 1967), pp. 316–34.

GOFFMAN, W., and K. S. WARREN, "Dispersion of Papers Among Journals Based on Mathematical Analysis of Two Diverse Medical Literatures." *Nature*, Vol. 221, No. 5187 (March 29, 1969), pp. 1205–07.

GOFFMAN, W., and T. G. MORRIS, "Bradford's Law Applied to the Maintenance of Library Collections." Cleveland, Ohio: Case Western Reserve University (1970). In print.

HILLMAN, D. J., "The Notion of Relevance (I)." *American Documentation*, Vol. 15, No. 1 (January 1964), pp. 26–34.

KAPLAN, A., *The Conduct of Inquiry*. San Francisco: Chandler (1964).

KATTER, R. V., "The Influence of Scale Form on Relevance Judgment." *Information Storage and Retrieval*, Vol. 4, No. 1 (March 1968), pp. 1–11.

KENDALL, M. G., "The Bibliography of Operational Research." *Operational Research Quarterly*, Vol. 11, No. 1/2 (March-June 1960), pp. 31–36.

KENT, A., M. BERRY, F. U. LEUHRS, and J. W. PERRY, "Machine Literature Searching VIII. Operational Criteria for Designing Information Retrieval Systems." *American Documentation*, Vol. 6, No. 2 (April 1955), pp. 93–101.

KING, D. W., "Design and Evaluation of Information Systems." In *Annual Review of Information Science and Technology*, Vol. 3, C. Cuadra, ed., Chicago: Encyclopaedia Britannica (1968), pp. 61–103.

KOZACHKOV, L. S., and L. A. KHURSIN, "Model of Scientific Publication Growth Based on the Lotka-Bradford-Zipf Law." (In Russian) *Nauchno Technikheskaya Informatsiya*, Series 2, No. 7 (1968), pp. 3–10.

KOZACHKOV, L. S., "Relevance in Informatics and Scientology." (In Russian) *Nauchno-Tekhnicheskaya Informatsiya*, Series 2, No. 8 (1969), pp. 3–11.

KUHNS, J. L., and C. A. MONTGOMERY, "A Comparative Study of Fragment Versus Document Retrieval." *Proceedings of the American Documentation Institute*, Vol. 1, Washington, D.C. (1964), pp. 369–77.

LANCASTER, F. W., Letter to the Editor. *American Documentation*, Vol. 19, No. 2 (April 1968), pp. 206.

LEIMKUHLER, F. F., "The Bradford Distribution." *Journal of Documentation*, Vol. 23, No. 3 (September 1967), pp. 197–207.

LESK, M. E., and G. SALTON, "Relevance Assessments and Retrieval System Evaluation." *Information Storage and Retrieval*, Vol. 4, No. 3 (August 1968), pp. 343–59.

LOTKA, A. J., "The Frequency Distribution of Scientific Productivity." *Journal of the Washington Academy of Sciences*, Vol. 16, No. 12 (June 19, 1926), pp. 317–23.

MARON, M. E., and J. L. KUHNS, "On Relevance, Probabilistic Indexing, and Information Retrieval." *Journal of the Association for Computing Machinery*, Vol. 7, No. 3 (July 1960), pp. 216–44.

MOOERS, C. S., "Coding, Information Retrieval, and the Rapid Selector." *American Documentation*, Vol. 1, No. 4 (October 1950), pp. 225–29.

NATIONAL ACADEMY OF SCIENCES, *Proceedings of the International Conference on Science Information*, 2 Vols., NAS, Washington, D.C., 1959.
See: (a) Vickery, B.C., pp. 855–86;
     (b) Vickery, B.C., pp. 1275–90;
     (c) Summary of the discussion of the Area 4 (pp. 803–11) and Area 6 (pp. 1395–1409).

NATIONAL SCIENCE FOUNDATION, *Summary of Study Conference on Evaluation of Document Searching Systems and Procedures*. NSF, Washington, D.C. (1964).

O'CONNOR, J., "Relevance Disagreements and Unclear Request Forms." *American Documentation*, Vol. 18, No. 3 (July 1967), pp. 165–77.

O'CONNOR, J., "Some Questions Concerning 'Information Need.'" *American Documentation*, Vol. 19, No. 2 (April 1968), pp. 200–03.

O'CONNOR, J., "Some Independent Agreements and Resolved Disagreements About Answer-Providing Documents." *American Documentation*, Vol. 20, No. 4 (October 1969), pp. 311–19.

PAISLEY, W. J., "Information Needs and Uses." In *Annual Review of Information Science and Technology*, Vol. 3, C. Cuadra, ed., Chicago: Encyclopaedia Britannica (1968), pp. 1–30.

PERRY, J. W., "Superimposed Punching of Numerical Codes on Handsorted Punched Cards." *American Documentation*, Vol. 2, No. 4 (October 1951), pp. 205–12.

POLLOCK, S. M., "Measures for the Comparison of Information Retrieval Systems." *American Documentation*, Vol. 19, No. 4 (October 1968), pp. 387–97.

PRICE, D. J. de S., *Little Science, Big Science*. New York: Columbia University Press, 1963.

PRICE, D. J. de S., "Networks of Scientific Papers." *Science*, Vol. 149, No. 3683 (July 30, 1965), pp. 510–15.

RATH, G. J., A. Resnick, and T. R. Savage, "Comparisons of Four Types of Lexical Indicators." *American Documentation*, Vol. 12, No. 2 (April 1961), pp. 126–30.

REES, A. M., "Semantic Factors, Role Indicators Et Alia, Eight Years of Information Retrieval at Western Reserve University." *Aslib Proceedings*, Vol. 15, No. 12 (December 1963), pp. 350–63.

REES, A. M., and T. SARACEVIC, "Conceptual Analysis of Questions in Information Retrieval Systems." *Proceedings of the American Documentation Institute, Part 2*. Washington, D.C. (1963), pp. 175–77.

REES, A. M., and T. SARACEVIC, "The Measurability of Relevance." *Proceedings of the American Documentation Institute*, Vol. 3, Washington, D.C. (1966), pp. 255–334.

REES, A. M., D. G. SCHULTZ, et al, *A Field Experimental Approach to the Study of Relevance Assessments in Relation to Document Searching*. 2 Vols. Cleveland, Ohio: Center for Documentation and Communication Research, School of Library Science, Case Western Reserve University (October 1967).

RESNICK, A., "Relative Effectiveness of Document Titles and Abstracts for Determining Relevance of Documents." *Science*, Vol. 134, No. 3484 (October 6, 1961), pp. 1004–06.

RESNICK, A., and T. R. SAVAGE, "The Consistency of Human Judgments of Relevance." *American Documentation*, Vol. 15, No. 2 (April 1964), pp. 93–5.

SARACEVIC, T. et al, *An Inquiry into Testing of Information Retrieval Systems*. 3 Parts. Cleveland, Ohio: Center for Documentation and Communication Research, School of Library Science, Case Western Reserve University (1968).

SARACEVIC, T., "Comparative Effects of Titles, Abstracts, and Full Texts on Relevance Judgements." *Proceedings of the American Society for Information Science*, Vol. 6, Washington, D.C. (1969), pp. 293–99.

SARACEVIC, T., *On the Concept of Relevance in Information Science*. Ph.D. Thesis. Cleveland, Ohio: School of Library Science, Case Western Reserve University (1970).

SHIREY, D. L., and M. KURFEERST, "Relevance Predictability. II: Data Reduction." In: *Electronic handling of Information Testing and Evaluation*, A. Kent, O. E. Taulbee, J. Belzer, and G. D. Goldstein, eds. Washington, D.C.: Thompson Book Co. (1967), pp. 187–98.

Simon, H. A., "On a Class of Skew Distribution Functions." *Biometrika*, Vol. 42, Nos. 3 & 4 (December 1955), pp. 425–40.

Swanson, D. R., "Searching Natural Language Text by Computer." *Science*, Vol. 132, No. 3636 (October 21, 1960), pp. 1099–1104.

Swets, J. A., "Information Retrieval Systems." *Science*, Vol. 141, No. 3577 (July 19, 1963), pp. 245–50.

Tague, J., "Matching of Question and Answer Terminology in an Educational Research File." *American Documentation*, Vol. 16, No. 1 (January 1965), pp. 26–32.

Taube, M., and Associates, "Storage and Retrieval of Information by Means of the Association of Ideas." *American Documentation*, Vol. 6, No. 1 (January 1955), pp. 1–17.

Urquhart, D. J., "Use of Scientific Periodicals." In: *Proceedings of the International Conference on Scientific Information*, National Academy of Sciences, National Research Council, Washington, D.C. (1959), pp. 277–90.

Vickery, B. C., "Bradford's Law of Scattering." *Journal of Documentation*, Vol. 4, No. 3 (December 1948), pp. 198–203.

Zipf, G. K., *Human Behavior and the Principle of Least Effort*. Cambridge: Addison-Wesley (1949).

Zunde, P., and M. E. Dexter, "Indexing Consistency and Quality" *American Documentation*, Vol. 20, No. 3 (July 1969), pp. 259–67.

Part Two
Information
Systems

A system — a network of interacting elements — is a primary object of current study in many new and some classical sciences. Increasingly, it is of great concern to modern, complex societies and to mankind in general. Natural systems, which primarily carry out physical and biological processes, are dazzling, but the complexities of social systems, which primarily carry out social processes, are overwhelming. When we realize that an element of a system may be another system, this dichotomy of systems into natural and social appears more artificial than real, especially since social systems do not exist without containing some elements of natural systems. Perhaps the only distinction we can make is that, while the laws and processes of nature underlie natural systems, the ethical and social values and behavioral processes of man are the foundations of social systems. Furthermore, man supplements, fortifies, and extends the physical and biological processes of natural systems by building artificial, man-made systems. While all social systems are man-made not all man-made systems can be interpreted as being social systems, since many of them only carry out physical and biological and not necessarily social processes.

Information systems are viewed here as those carrying out man's communication processes. As such, they are social systems which, in most but not all instances, involve natural and/or physical man-made systems as elements. A number of information systems, probably the most significant and complex ones, are devoted to the communication of knowledge, of what man has found, experienced, deduced or induced. At the foundation of these systems lies the so-far unchallenged ethical belief that knowledge is good, beneficial, and even necessary for the continuous pursuit of a better society and a better man. Examples of such knowledge-communicating information systems are libraries, scientific societies, journals, and more recently, information retrieval systems, all kinds of data processing systems, all kinds of signal-transmission systems, command-control systems, etc.

Many of these systems are used for entirely different purposes — some to enhance further creation of knowledge; some to assist decision-making of an ethical, economical, political nature; some to preserve "all" knowledge indefinitely; some to control the exponential growth of literature; some to permit transmission of all kinds of physical signals representing or potentially representing information, etc. The growth in number, complexity, and importance of modern information systems is in direct proportion to the increase in the complexity of modern societies and in the inabilty to provide necessary information by previously existing means (systems). Old systems are being modified and many new ones are being proposed, built, modified, abandoned, and/or invented.

Most of the effort in information science has been devoted to problems related to information retrieval systems, to computers as technology for information systems, and to problems of representing information. Admittedly, information retrieval systems, computer technology, and information representation are highly significant, but they are not the only tools for use in or the only functions of information systems.

The selections in this Part understandably reflect these biases of the field as a whole. A general point of confusion, which continues to plague the field, is worth mentioning. As the selected works indicate time and again, our greatest deficiency in approaching and studying information systems has been our inability to divorce, when necessary, consideration of the system as a whole from the consideration of the processes being carried out and of the technology involved.

All information systems, regardless of purpose or kind, have some structural and functional elements in common. The works related to the structure of information systems are presented in Chapter 4. The functions common to all information systems are represented by selections in respective chapters on Acquisition, Information Representation, Organization of Information Stores, Question Handling and Search Procedures, and Dissemination. Many articles appearing under given functions have elements of generalizability, and suggest solutions to a number of real, practical problems encountered in design, development, and operation of a variety of information systems.

This brings us to a concluding point. Translations into practice and making generalizations about information systems are extremely hard to do; by necessity, they are left to each person to attempt individually.

Chapter Four
Structure of Information Retrieval Systems

The works selected for this Chapter may be viewed as relating to the construction of models (i.e., analogies) of particular types of information systems, namely information retrieval systems, or more broadly, libraries. With some attempt at translation, these models could be viewed as representing the structure, or some part thereof, of most information systems.

Each of the three selections illustrates a different approach to the construction of models and their representations. It is of interest to observe and compare the approaches, because they point to the possible avenues that could be taken.

Hillman (Article 15) studied the representation of retrieval processes from a formal, mathematical, and logical point of view, and settled a long controversy about the appropriateness of Boolean algebra versus propositional calculus for representation of these processes. Baker and Nance (Article 16) take a systems approach in specifying an information retrieval system or library model, including behavior of the system in the context of its environment. They are not so much concerned with representing the processes but with showing the interaction of different functions with environmental factors. Kochen (Article 17) is essentially concerned with a technological model, showing the order of processes and interaction among elements in a computer-based retrieval system. He is also concerned with the economic factors, technical feasibility, data-based accumulations, etc., as they relate to the application of technology.

In this class of selections would belong a considerable number of articles, presenting algorithms for the solution of given problems or, as applicable, for representation of certain processes; articles dealing with the structure of all kinds of information systems; and the as yet nonexisting articles showing equivalence relationships, where applicable between all kinds of information systems.

15 Two Models for Retrieval System Design

DONALD J. HILLMAN
American Documentation
Vol. 15, No. 3, July, 1964

It is a common fallacy, underwritten at this date by the investment of several million dollars in a variety of retrieval hardware, that the algebra of George Boole (1847) is the appropriate formalism for retrieval system design. This view is as widely and uncritically accepted as it is wrong.

— Calvin Mooers (1)

The purpose of this paper is to examine this fallacy and to seek clarification of the basic issues involved in the dispute it has generated. Clearly, some statement is needed which not only will account for the impropriety of a Boolean algebra as a model for retrieval system design but will also explain its allegedly undeserved popularity. Both Mooers (2) and Fairthorne (3) have addressed themselves to this task in a number of publications, and I have made grateful and copious use of their views in presenting my own estimation of the situation (4). Nevertheless, not all has been said that needs to be said, for there remains a residue of unanswered queries whose stubborn survival continues to give trouble.

Grateful acknowledgment is made to the National Science Foundation for generous support under Grant No. G24070 of the research upon which this article is based.
I wish to thank the referee of this paper for several suggestions as to its improvement.

It is upon these obstinate survivors that I wish to focus attention, since their presence serves only to obstruct our decision whether to accept or reject a Boolean algebra as an appropriate model for retrieval system design. They manage, moreover, to hinder this important decision by introducing into the argument wholly irrelevant considerations, whose only effect is to divert attention from the real issues. I shall attempt to describe these diversionary tactics, to point out their irrelevance and thus hope to arrive at a clearer understanding of the grounds upon which our choice of a model for retrieval system design *must* be based.

Consider first the role assigned to a Boolean algebra in the method of coordinate indexing, as originally planned and developed by Mortimer Taube and his associates (5). The choice of this model is apparently dictated by such considerations as the following:

If any given scientific field can be analyzed into simple terms or ideas so that all or most of the concepts of the field can be expressed in these terms or in truth functions of them (i.e., logical combinations) then mechanical aids can make important contributions to organizing and searching for information in such a field. . . . In order to see more clearly why this is true, we can turn now to a more formal presentation of the nature of coordinate indexing for machines. . . .

In a field, Q, with terms a, b, c . . . etc., coordinate indexing allows only the relations

a

not a

a and b

a or b.

(In terms of machine searching, if we search for 'a or b' we will get everything that is 'a and not b,' everything that is both 'a and b.' The search will reject only those things which are 'not a and not b'.)—(6)

The subsequent development of the method was essentially concerned with the introduction of various types of constraints, such as roles, links and precoordinations. In its original form, however, the method claimed to use a Boolean algebra "to emphasize the possibility of constructing an indexing system which would dispense with syntactical relationships of any kind among terms and which would restrict itself to the class operations allowed in a Boolean Algebra" (7).

It will be noticed that the method here described deals with *class* operations, which immediately raises an initial query. Why, it might be asked, is it claimed that the method is based on a Boolean algebra rather than on some algebra of classes or sets? There is, of course, an obvious answer to this question: every algebra of sets is a Boolean algebra. This familiar theorem, which apparently provides so conclusive an answer to our query, seems to guarantee the acceptability of the method of coordinate indexing, at least on grounds of clarity. I shall argue, however, that this apparent clarity is deceptive, that, straightforward as the claims made for the method may seem, there are certain problems of interpretation to be resolved and a number of serious confusions to be eliminated before we can begin to appraise the utility of coordinate indexing.

A *sine qua non* of this enterprise is to establish precise meanings for the concepts that figure so prominently in discussions of the method in question. Many difficulties have resulted from the failure to do exactly this, as I shall shortly try to show. One such difficulty stems from neglect of the difference between algebras and other types of systems. In general, an *algebra* may be regarded as a system constituted by a set of arbitrary elements and the operations by which they may be combined. A *calculus*, on the other hand, is usually thought of as an organized method for performing inferences by manipulating symbols in accordance with formal rules. Stated thus, the distinction is not, of course, very precise, although it is comparatively easy to attain the required degree of precision. For example, we frequently identify a calculus with a *logistic system* — i.e., a system which provides effective criteria for recognizing well-formed formulas, proofs, proofs as a consequence of a set of well-formed formulas, and the validity of such proofs. Some authors prefer to state the distinction in other ways. Thus Curry (8) uses the term *algebra* to denote systems with free variables

but no bound variables, and the term *calculus* to designate systems with bound variables.

It is not my intention to enumerate the different ways in which distinctions like these may be made, but to point out the necessity for adopting one form of each relevant distinction and to keep this clearly in mind when discussing the theoretical foundations of retrieval systems. Otherwise confusions result which hamper all efforts to build workable systems on a solid basis of theory.

Let us therefore state immediately what is denoted by the term "a Boolean algebra." This is most appropriately accomplished in the form of an explicit definition.

Definition 1: A *Boolean algebra B* is a set of elements, a, b, c . . . satisfying the following conditions:

(a) B has two binary operations, $\cap$ and $\cup$, such that

(i) $a \cap a = a$ and $a \cup a = a$

(ii) $a \cap b = b \cap a$ and $a \cup b = b \cup a$

(iii) $a \cap (b \cap c) = (a \cap b) \cap c$ and $a \cup (b \cup c) = (a \cup b) \cup c$

(iv) $a \cap (b \cup c) = (a \cap b) \cup (a \cap c)$ and $a \cup (b \cap c) = (a \cup b) \cap (a \cup c)$

(b) B has a binary relation, $\leq$, such that

(i) for all a, $a \leq a$

(ii) if $a \leq b$ and $b \leq a$, then $a = b$

(iii) if $a \leq b$ and $b \leq c$, then $a \leq c$

(iv) the statements '$a \leq b$,' '$a \cap b = a$' and '$a \cup b = b$' are mutually equivalent.

(c) B contains two elements O and I such that

(i) $0 \leq a \leq I$, for all a

(ii) $0 \cap a = 0$ and $I \cap a = a$

(iii) $0 \cup a = a$ and $I \cup a = I$

(d) B has a unary operation of complementation,$'$, such that

(i) $a \cap a' = 0$ and $a \cup a' = I$

(ii) $(a \cap b)' = a' \cup b'$ and $(a \cup b)' = a' \cap b'$

(iii) $(a')' = a$.

This definition is by no means the most elegant that can be constructed. Nevertheless, it is a serviceable formulation in that it makes perfectly explicit how the class of all subclasses of a given class *forms* a Boolean algebra, as may be swiftly verified. It is, however, important to bear in mind that a Boolean algebra, in the sense defined, is an *abstract algebraic system*, whose elements are not necessarily classes. An excellent way of emphasizing this point is to refine the notion of a Boolean algebra in the following way:

Definition 2. A *partially ordered system* is any set of elements a,b,c . . . with a binary relation $\leq$, such that:

(i) $a \leq a$, for all a

(ii) if $a \leq b$ and $b \leq a$, then $a = b$

(iii) if $a \leq b$ and $b \leq c$, then $a \leq c$.

Definition 3. A *lattice* is a partially ordered system in which every two elements a and b have a greatest lower bound, denoted by $a \cap b$, and a least upper bound, denoted by $a \cup b$.

Definition 4: A *distributive* lattice is a lattice satisfying the following conditions:
    (i) $a \cap (b \cup c) = (a \cap b) \cup (a \cap c)$
    (ii) $a \cup (b \cap c) = (a \cup b) \cap (a \cup c)$

Definition 5: A *Boolean algebra* is a distributive lattice containing elements 0 and I, with $0 \leq a \leq I$, for all a, and in which each a has a complement a', such that $a \cap a' = 0$ and $a \cup a' = I$.

It is not for pedantic reasons that I refer to this alternative, though familiar, characterization of a Boolean algebra, but for the very good purpose of accentuating the fact, not always explicitly recognized by the exponents of Coordinate Indexing, that a Boolean algebra may have as elements entities other than classes. If this is borne in mind, then it does no harm to talk of "the class operations allowed in a Boolean Algebra," for this is a useful way to identify such operations. Moreover, it has been shown by M. H. Stone(9) that *every* abstract Boolean algebra is isomorphic to an algebra of sets or classes. However, this theorem is not to be interpreted as demonstrating that every Boolean algebra deals *exclusively* with sets or classes. It is, in fact, well known that propositions form a Boolean algebra. In particular, the algebra of propositions under the connectives for negation, conjunction and inclusive disjunction is a Boolean algebra. This latter theorem brings me to the point where I must now join issue with Taube in his discussions of the theoretical foundations of Coordinate Indexing.

It is apparent that Taube has chosen the concept of a Boolean algebra as the basis of his method, on the grounds that such an algebra can represent the class operations involved in organizing and searching for required information. That this is an *appropriate* formalism for retrieval system design has been energetically disputed by Mooers and Fairthorne. Before examining this dispute, it seems to me essential that Taube's position be clarified in a number of important respects. Such clarification is especially necessary in view of the fact that Taube rarely makes explicit the nature of his assumptions, and on several occasions conflates the notion of an algebra with that of a calculus, which leads him to commit at least one serious error, as I shall now attempt to show.

We have seen that a Boolean algebra may be considered as a purely abstract system given by a domain of arbitrary elements together with certain operations defined on the domain and satisfying certain conditions. On the other hand, a Boolean algebra can also be regarded as a formal calculus given by some specific set of postulates. Examples of such postulate sets are abundant (10) each determining not a single Boolean algebra but a *class* of algebras. This is because no postulate set is categorical in terms of its primitives. For ease of reference, however, let us refer to the following axiomatization of a Boolean algebra.

The primitive concepts of our postulate set consist of a nonvoid class K of undefined objects α, β, γ . . . a binary operation $\cap$ and a unary operation $'$. The axioms are then:

A1. If $\alpha, \beta \epsilon K$, then $\alpha' \epsilon K$ and $\alpha \cap \beta \epsilon K$.
A2. If $\alpha, \beta \epsilon K$, then $\alpha \cap \beta = \beta \cap \alpha$.
A3. If $\alpha, \beta, \gamma \epsilon K$, then $(\alpha \cap \beta) \cap \gamma = \alpha \cap (\beta \cap \gamma)$
A4. If $\alpha, \beta, \gamma \epsilon K$, and $\alpha \cap \beta' = \gamma \cap \gamma'$, then $\alpha \cap \beta = \alpha$
A5. If $\alpha, \beta, \gamma \epsilon K$, and $\alpha \cap \beta = \alpha$, then $\alpha \cap \beta' = \gamma \cap \gamma'$
A6. If $\alpha, \beta \epsilon K$, and $\alpha = \beta$, then $\alpha' = \beta'$
A7. If $\alpha, \beta, \gamma \epsilon K$, and $\alpha = \beta$, then $\alpha \cap \gamma = \beta \cap \gamma$ and $\gamma \cap \alpha = \gamma \cap \beta$.

Definitions, as conventions of notational abbreviation, are introduced thus:

D1. $a_1 \cap a_2 \cap a_3 \cap \ldots \cap a_n =_{df} (\ldots ((a_1 \cap a_2) \cap a_3) \cap \ldots)$ $\cap a_n$ i.e., parentheses are associated to the left.
D2. $\alpha \leq \beta =_{df} \alpha \cap \beta = \alpha$
D3. $0 =_{df} a \cap a'$
D4. $1 =_{df} 0'$
D5. $\alpha \cup \beta =_{df} (\alpha' \cap \beta')'$

As rules of transformation, we need only substitution and detachment. From the axioms, with the help of definitions and rules, we may now prove theorems in the customary way.

Having now explained what different things *could* be meant by the phrase "a Boolean algebra," let us go on to determine what Taube has in mind when he uses the phrase. It is here, I think, that we begin to unearth some basic confusions. Moreover, it is precisely here that the promulgation of irrelevant arguments has drawn our attention away from the key issues involved in the use of a Boolean algebra and has led to unnecessary delay in judging it to be an inappropriate formalism for retrieval system design. In order, therefore, to clear away certain obstacles in the path of this decision, I shall now attempt to dispose of an argument which introduces wholly irrelevant considerations into the discussion of the utility of a Boolean algebra for retrieval theory.

First, let us think of a Boolean algebra as a formal postulational system, as previously illustrated. It is well known that formal systems may be interpreted in a number of different ways. Although the concept of an interpretation is understood in different ways, I propose to say that we have an *interpretation* of a formal system in a given subject matter if to every elementary statement of the formal system there corresponds a statement of the subject matter, called an *interpretant*. If the interpretant of every elementary theorem is true, then the interpretation will be called *valid;* if every elementary statement whose interpretant is true is a theorem, then the interpretation will be called adequate. Thus, an interpretation will be thought of as a correspondence between statements, each of the two corresponding members being a statement with its own criterion of truth (11).

Now one of the best known interpretations, in the sense defined, of a Boolean algebra regarded as a formal postulational system, is the so-called *calculus of classes*. If the binary operations denoted by $\cap$ and $\cup$ in the formal system are thought of as designating class intersection and class union, respectively, the unary operation ′ is thought of as designating complementation, and the relation ≤ is regarded as designating class inclusion, then the calculus of classes is both a valid and adequate interpretation of the axiomatic system of Boolean algebra previously described, whose elements are then regarded as class-variables. An equally well-known interpretation of the same formal system is supplied by the two-valued *calculus of propositions*, which formalizes the use of the so-called truth-functional connectives. In this calculus, we employ propositional variables p, q, r . . . of which we assume a potentially infinite list to be available, and truth-functional compounds of these. The latter are molecular formulae arrived at by combining propositional variables with the aid of the truth-functional connectives. Certain obvious rules of formation specify the well-formed truth-functional compounds, and a knowledge of these will be assumed. There are two truth-values, 1 and 0, such that each truth-functional compound takes just one of these values for a given assignment of truth-values to its variables. That the truth-value of any compound is wholly determined by the truth-values of its variables constitutes the *extensionality* property of the propositional calculus. Such truth-values are calculated with the aid of *truth-tables;* viz., matrices exhibiting all possible combinations of truth-values for the variables of a given compound and the value of the compound for each combination. The basic truth-tables for certain important connectives may be written as follows:

p	~p	.	1	0	v	1	0	≡	1	0	⊃	1	0
1	0	1	1	0	1	1	1	1	1	0	1	1	0
0	1	0	0	0	0	1	0	0	0	1	0	1	1

With the aid of these tables, we may now verify the following:

1. (p.q) ≡ (q.p)
2. p.(q.r) ≡ (p.q).r
3. If (p.q) ≡ p, then (p.~q) ≡ (r.~r)
4. If (p.~q) ≡ (r.~r), then (p.q) ≡ p
5. If p ≡ q, then ~p ≡ ~q
6. If p ≡ q, then (p.r) ≡ (q.r) and (r.p) ≡ (r.q)

These rules show that the laws of our Boolean algebra hold for the calculus of propositions with "~", "·" and "≡" substituted for "′", "∩" and "=", respectively. The set {1,0} forms, in fact, a two-element Boolean algebra with respect to the operations "~" and "·".

If we now wish to set up the calculus of propositions as a deductive system, it is necessary to supply axioms. This may be done in many ways, one of which runs as follows (12).

Let K be a non-null class whose members are p, q, r . . ., let "p·q" be the result of a binary operation defined on K, "~p" the result of a unary operation defined on K, and "↔" an equivalence relation defined between the members of K. Then we have:

A1. If p,q∊K, then ~p and p.q are uniquely determined members of K

A2. If p,q∊K, then (p.q)↔(q.p)
A3. If p,q,r∊K, then (p.q).r↔p.(q.r)
A4. If p,q,r∊K and (p.q)↔p, then (p.~q)↔(r.~r)
A5. If p,q,r∊K and (p.~q)↔(r.~r), then (p.q)↔p
A6. If p,q∊K and p↔q, then ~p↔~q
A7. If p,q,r∊K and p↔q, then (p.r)↔(q.r) and (r.p)↔(r.q)
A8. If p∊K, then p↔p
A9. If p,q∊K and p↔q, then q↔p
A10. If p,q,r∊K, p↔q and q↔r, then p↔r.

These axioms show that (K, ~, ·, ↔) is a Boolean algebra with respect to the equivalence relation "↔". This means that the calculus of classes and the calculus of propositions are both interpretations of the same formal system of Boolean algebra. The relation "↔" which replaces the equality sign does not, of course, belong to the object language of the propositional calculus, but to its metalanguage. In a like sense the relation "=" belongs to the metalanguage of a Boolean algebra.

The axiomatization described above is designed to show the exact relationship between the propositional calculus and a Boolean algebra. It is not necessary for us to derive any theorems at this stage, since we have established what we set out to prove. However, before leaving this topic, we should mention that there exists an alternative formulation of the propositional calculus which is exactly equivalent to the concept of a Boolean algebra with respect to an equivalence relation. This is the notion of a Boolean propositional logic, which may be described as a quadruple (K, T, ⊃, ~) satisfying the following (13). Let K and T be undefined classes, "~" a unary operator and "⊃" a binary operator. Then

B1. If p∊T, then p∊K.
B2. If p,q∊K, then p⊃q∊K and is uniquely determined.
B3. If p∊K, then ~p∊K and is uniquely determined.
B4. If p,q,r∊K, then [p⊃(q⊃r)]⊃[(p⊃q)⊃(p⊃r)]∊T.
B5. If p,q∊K, then p⊃(q⊃p)∊T.
B6. If p,q∊K, then (~p⊃~q)⊃(q⊃p)∊T.
B7. If p,p⊃q∊T, then q∊T.

Here, K is to be interpreted as the class of propositions, and T the class of true propositions. If we define T and ⊃ as follows:

Definition 1. p∊T = ₐf p∊K · p↔~(p·~p)
Definition 2. p⊃q = ₐf ~(p·~q)

then the system (K, ~, ·, ↔) is equivalent to the system (K,T,⊃,~).

We have now shown that the propositional calculus is a Boolean algebra with respect to the equivalence relation "↔", and have introduced the concept of a Boolean propositional logic. We have deliberately avoided the development of the propositional calculus as a *logistic system*, concentrating instead on the connection between a Boolean algebra and one of its interpretations, the propositional calculus.

Needless to say, there are many different, though equivalent, formulations of the calculus of propositions. Each separate formulation, that is to say, differs in axiomatic structure but not in the set of all tautologies which are derivable as theorems. Each system of propositional calculus here referred to has all and only tautologies as theorems, and is thus said to be deductively complete (and consistent). The question may now be raised whether *this* interpretation of a Boolean algebra is as appropriate for retrieval system design as the class interpretation, always provided that the latter does constitute an appropriate model. Mortimer Taube, in a number of publications, has provided one answer to this question by arguing that these two interpretations of a Boolean algebra are *not* equivalent, and that, whereas the calculus of classes can function as an appropriate model for retrieval system design, the calculus of propositions *cannot*. It is this argument that I should like to examine, since it seems to incorporate certain irrelevancies whose joint effect is to divert attention from the real issues affecting the use of Boolean algebras and to postpone a needed decision.

Let me start by stating where I agree with Taube in his overall position. In describing the logician's increasing interest in the propositional calculus, Taube says:

> Just about the time this propositional interpretation of symbolic logic was at an apotheosis, there grew up a recognition that digital machines, being two-valued, could be described or modeled in the propositional calculus. And since the propositional calculus and quantification were tending to usurp the whole of logic, the digital computers came to be considered universal information handling machines or universal automata. So general has this view become that any discussion of mechanizing the storage and retrieval of information is apt to assume that the proper and only devices are those which have been designed for computation, the rapid solution of mathematical problems. — (14)

Now, insofar as Taube claims that digital computers do not, *per se*, provide us with all that is necessary for the construction of efficient retrieval devices, I would tend to agree with him. My agreement is based on the fact that much investigation remains to be carried out into the theory of retrieval systems before too heavy a commitment is made to existing high-speed computational devices. However, I disagree with Taube over the *grounds* for his separation of retrieval devices from computers. The basis for this separation is Taube's claim that the logic of retrieval automata is the calculus of classes but *not* the calculus of propositions, which he regards as the logical apparatus for the analysis of computers.

> The calculus of propositions is not identical with the calculus of classes nor even completely analogous with it. A more basic difference which seems directly related to the difference between computers and storage and retrieval devices is found in the fact that, if two propositions are true, the proposition which expresses their conjunction is true; but if a class x has members and the class y has members nothing follows concerning the membership of the product $x \cap y$. — (15)

I do not here propose to examine the claim that the calculus of classes represents the logic (i.e., model) of retrieval automata. Instead, I shall argue that Taube's contention that the class and propositional calculi are not analogous cannot be upheld, and that the elaboration

of this contention serves only to prolong the unnecessary controversy regarding the place of Boolean algebras in the theory of retrieval system design. A consequence of my argument will be that the calculus of classes is *not* preferable as a model to the calculus of propositions, since *neither* calculus can function in this role. I shall hope to show that they are analogous to each other, so that they stand or fall together. The question is *not* whether one interpretation of a Boolean algebra is more suitable than another, but whether a Boolean algebra is *itself* an appropriate formal system for retrieval theory, no matter how it is interpreted. Once this has been made clear, our decision whether to accept or reject Boolean algebras can be made without being hampered by the wholly irrelevant considerations alluded to above and more amply described in what follows.

As the first step toward establishing a precise analogy between the calculus of classes and the calculus of propositions, we may cite the well-known result that to every theorem X of the pure calculus of propositions — i.e. the calculus whose primitive propositional symbols are an infinite list of variables denoting members of any class of propositions closed under the operations of negation, conjunction, and inclusive disjunction — there corresponds a theorem $Y = 1$ of the calculus of classes, where Y is obtained from X by replacing negation, conjunction, and inclusive disjunction respectively by complementation, logical product, and logical sum, and by replacing propositional variables by class variables. In addition to this, every theorem of the pure propositional calculus having the form of an equivalence, $X \equiv Y$, has a corresponding theorem in the calculus of classes which is obtained by replacing the main occurrence of "$\equiv$" by "$=$", and by replacing negation, conjunction, inclusive disjunction, and propositional variables as before.

It is not, of course, surprising that the two calculi should exhibit so close a relationship. Each is, after all, a different interpretation of the same formal system, a fact to which Taube gives explicit recognition (16). Indeed, there are formulations of propositional calculus which can be *shown* to be Boolean algebras or even Boolean *rings* (17). Nevertheless, Taube claims to have found theorems of propositional calculus which do *not* correspond to theorems of the calculus of classes (18). Specifically, he considers the following theorem of propositional calculus:

(A) $\sim(p \equiv q) \equiv (p \equiv \sim q)$

and claims that its analogue

(B) $x \not\equiv y \equiv x = \bar{y}$

in the calculus of classes is *false*. Let us examine this argument in further detail.

Since we know that every theorem of the pure calculus of propositions having the form of an equivalence has a corresponding theorem in the calculus of classes, our task is to determine what *really* is the analogue of (A) in the calculus of classes. Because (A) is a tautology, its theoremhood is guaranteed for the calculus of propositions. Hence (A) has a corresponding theorem in the calculus of classes. Our rules for finding this theorem call first for an elimination of all *secondary* occurrences of the material biconditional "$\equiv$"in (A). This is easily accomplished with the help of the definition "$p \equiv q =_{df} (p \cdot q) v (\sim p \cdot \sim q)$." (A) then becomes:

(A') $\sim [(p \cdot q) v (\sim p \cdot \sim q)] \equiv [(p \cdot \sim q) v (\sim p \cdot q)]$

(A'), being logically equivalent to (A), may be thought of as the same theorem in a different guise. We now replace the *principal* (and only) occurrence of "$\equiv$" in (A') by "$=$", elsewhere replacing "$\sim$", "$\cdot$" and "v" by "$'$", "$\cap$" and "$\cup$", respectively. We then obtain, as the analogue of (A'):

(B') $[(A \cap B) \cup (A' \cap B')]' = [(A \cap B') \cup (A' \cap B)]$,

where "A" and "B" are class variables replacing the propositional variables "p" and "q" of (A'). It remains now to show that (B') is a true statement of the calculus of classes. This is a comparatively simple matter. Thus,

$[(A \cap B) \cup (A' \cap B')]' = (A \cap B)' \cap (A' \cap B')'$
$= (A' \cup B') \cap (A \cup B) = [(A' \cup B') \cap A] \cup [(A' \cup B') \cap B]$
$= [(A \cap B') \cup (A \cap A')] \cup [(B' \cap B) \cup (A' \cap B)]$
$= (A \cap B') \cup (A' \cap B)$. *Q.E.D.*

An alternative method for reaching essentially the same conclusion is to eliminate *all* occurrences of "$\equiv$" from (A) in favor of the primitive connectives "v", "$\cdot$" and "$\sim$". This is most easily accomplished by rewriting (A) in *disjunctive normal form* as follows:

(A'') $(p \cdot q) v (p \cdot \sim q) v (\sim p \cdot q) v (\sim p \cdot \sim q)$

The analogue of (A'') in the calculus of classes then becomes:

(B'') $(A \cap B) \cup (A \cap B') \cup (A' \cap B) \cup (A' \cap B')$,

which is immediately reducible to $A \cup A' = 1$.

Either demonstration shows that (A) *does* have an analogue in the calculus of classes, viz., (B') or (B''), which is, moreover, as good a theorem of the calculus of classes as is (A) in the calculus of propositions. This result now entails that (B), as originally cited by Taube, is *not* the correct analogue of (A) in the calculus of classes, so that the argument that the calculus of propositions is not analogous to the calculus of classes is already beginning to crumble. If this is the case, then clearly an erroneous assumption has been made at some stage of Taube's argument, and it will be instructive to locate this and to trace it to its source.

The argument, as Taube presents it, is made to depend on a purported disanalogy of certain theorems of propositional calculus with their alleged counterparts in the calculus of classes. Three such examples are selected in support of the argument, one of which we have already discussed and found to be inconclusive. The other two run as follows (19):

(C) $[p \supset (q \lor r)] \equiv [(p \supset q) \lor (p \supset r)]$ is a theorem of propositional calculus, whereas its counterpart $[x \subset (y \cup z)] \equiv [(x \subset y) \lor (x \subset z)]$ is false in the calculus of classes

(D) $[(p \cdot q) \supset r)] \equiv [(p \supset r) \lor (q \supset r)]$ is a theorem of propositional calculus, whereas its counterpart $[(x \cap y) \subset z] \equiv [(x \subset z) \lor (y \subset z)]$ is false in the calculus of classes.

The first thing to notice with respect to these two examples is that neither of the alleged class statements can occur as a formula of the calculus of classes. Specifically, the symbols "$\equiv$" and "$\lor$" do not belong to the primitive vocabulary of the calculus of classes, nor are they ever introduced by definition. If they *are* introduced as additional primitives, then the calculus of classes augmented by propositional connectives is simply no longer analogous to the calculus of propositions. How, then, do we construct the correct analogues of the propositional formulas in question? Referring once again to the result concerning correspondences between theorems of the calculus of propositions and theorems of the calculus of classes, it is easy to show that the correct analogues are "$[A' \cup (B \cup C)] = [(A' \cup B) \cup (A' \cup C)]$" and "$[A \cap B)' \cup C] = [(A' \cup C) \cup (B' \cup C)]$," respectively. Obviously, these two equations represent true statements of the calculus of classes. Equally obviously, the alleged analogues cited by Taube are not false statements of the calculus of classes, because they do not belong to the calculus of classes in the first place. Where, then, do they belong?

The examples (A), (B), (C), and (D), claims Taube, are used by Quine in his *Mathematical Logic* and constitute "a simple demonstration that the calculus of propositions is not identical with the calculus of classes nor even completely analogous with it" (20). A scrutiny of *Mathematical Logic*, however, reveals that Quine is in fact claiming something quite different from Taube's interpretation. Quine's *actual* argument runs as follows:

(a) The propositional forms $[\sim(\varphi \equiv \psi) \equiv . \varphi \equiv \sim \psi]$, $[\varphi \supset . \psi \lor \chi : \equiv : \varphi \supset \psi . \lor . \varphi \supset \chi]$ and $[\varphi . \psi . \supset \chi : \equiv :$
$\varphi \supset \chi . \lor . \psi \supset \chi]$
are tautologous forms in the theory of statement composition. — (21)
(b) The respective analogues of these forms, *viz.*, "$(y)(x) x \neq y . \equiv . x = \bar{y}$," "$(z)(y)(x) x \subset y \cup z . \equiv . x \subset y . \lor . x \subset z$" and "$(z)(y)(x) x \cap y \subset z . \equiv . x \subset z . \lor . y \subset z$" are false in the extended theory of classes. — (22)

It is quite obvious that Quine does *not* say that the formulas of (b) belong to the calculus of classes, but to the much more comprehensive *extended* theory of classes. This theory is part of the method set out in *Mathematical Logic* for obtaining a system adequate for mathematics, a method, moreover, which ranks on a par with Zermelo Set Theory and the functional calculus. Thus, Quine's extended theory of classes is *not* the ordinary calculus of classes, so that Taube was mistaken in thinking that the disanalogies cited by Quine are disanalogies between the propositional calculus and the calculus of classes. There are no disanalogies between these two systems; such disanalogies as do exist are between the propositional calculus and a theory which takes particular account of the relation "ε" between classes, which the *calculus* of classes most certainly does not.

The key to the error seems to be the mistaken belief that the symbols "∨" and "≡" belong to the calculus of classes. These symbols, *do*, of course, have their rightful place in *Mathematical Logic*, where they are correctly used. There are, however, ways of misusing these symbols, and I think that this is what has happened in Taube's illustrations. We might diagnose the trouble as stemming from a confusion of object and syntax languages as follows. Apparently, Taube has taken a theorem in the calculus of propositions, such as "$[p \supset (q \vee r)] \equiv [(p \supset q) \vee (p \supset r)]$," translated this into its counterpart "P implies Q or R if and only if P implies Q or P implies R" of a syntax language for the calculus of propositions, has then translated the latter into its alleged analogue "X is included in the union of Y and Z if and only if X is either wholly included in Y or wholly included in Z" of a class syntax language, and has finally paraphrased this into its counterpart "$[x \subset (y \cup z)] \equiv [(x \subset y) \vee (x \subset z)]$" of a theory of classes augmented by truth-functional connectives. This, of course, is an illegitimate maneuver. First of all, it is not the case that the last formula even *belongs* to the calculus of classes. Nor is there any reason to believe that truth or meaning is preserved throughout this process.

There is one further argument of Taube's requiring examination before we proceed to a summary. He has criticized the calculus of propositions for conflating the notions of *element and member,* which he thinks are "fundamentally distinct for the logic of classes" (23). If by "the logic of classes" Taube means "the calculus of classes," then an excellent (although cavalier) way of meeting this criticism is to say that these notions are *not* distinct for the calculus of classes, because they never occur there. Quine, who discusses these notions in his *Mathematical Logic*, says that "ε" expresses the notion of membership, but that the universe of discourse must be divided into things that can be members and things that cannot. Only the former are called *elements.* The rule of class existence provides for the existence of the class of all elements satisfying any condition φ: If β is not α nor free in φ, then $[(\exists \beta)(\alpha)(\alpha \varepsilon \beta \cdot \equiv \cdot \alpha \varepsilon V \cdot \varphi]$ (24). This rule corresponds to the *Aussonderungsaxiom* of Zermelo. The rule of *elementhood* in *Mathematical Logic* is then designed to provide for the existence of just those classes that exist in Quine's *New Foundations For Mathematical Logic* (25). What these classes are does not, of course, concern us here.

Presumably, however, Taube does not mean to use the terms "element" and "member" in their standard (i.e., logical) interpretation. Instead, he proffers the following explanation, which I quote at some length.

(a) Let us think of a "value" or an "element" as any constant to which the variables in an algebra (once it is interpreted) might be equated. — (26)
(b) Both the algebra of propositions and the algebra of classes conform to every law of the Boolean algebra. *In addition,* the algebra of propositions satisfies Shannon's Postulate 4, quoted above, i.e.,
$$p \equiv T \text{ or } p \equiv F$$

Note: We write "$p \equiv T$" rather than "$p = T$" for two reasons: it uses the customary symbol of the usual algebra of propositions, and it emphasizes the fact that we are dealing with a truth functional, rather than, say, a modal, algebra of propositions.

But this *additional* postulate has usually no counterpart in the algebra of classes. This is where the question of members comes in. Let us see what the situation is.

Let us assume — a thing not usually assumed in the algebra of classes, but still consistent with that algebra — that this number of individuals is finite. (This assumption is appropriate to the construction of storage and retrieval machines, since the universal class can be thought of as the class of all stored items, any subset of which is to be retrieved.) Let us designate this number by "n." In terms of it, a postulate analogous to Shannon's Postulate 4, above, may be formulated. Indeed Shannon's Postulate 4 follows immediately from the assumption that $n = 1$. (Here "1" is the cardinal number, not the Boolean constant.) LAW OF VALUES: If there are n members of V, then there are 2^n distinct values available for the variables "X," "Y," "Z," etc.

It may be seen how Shannon's Postulate 4 follows from the above laws of values. Where $n = 1$, there are two distinct values for the variables in question. Since the Boolean algebra postulates two constants, 0 and 1, these two values must be identified with those two constants.

But what is this one member of the "universal class," "T" in the algebra of propositions? (Von Neumann suggests that we may take "T" or "1" as short for "$p \vee \sim p$" and "F" or "O" as short for "$p \cdot \sim p$" where p is some (unspecified) sentential constant. Thus "T" and "F" are propositions, or elements, or values, in the algebra of propositions.) We may call it truth, or the actual state of affairs. From one point of view, there is only one actual state of affairs, namely, the universe as it is, hence there is only one member of the universal class "T". Different propositions either describe this universe, and are equivalent to T, or fail to do so and are equivalent to F. The calculus of propositions does not discriminate propositions with respect to their meaning, or the aspect of truth of the universe that they report; but only with respect to their truth or falsity.

It is here that the algebra of propositions, so to speak, confuses element or value, with member. For we can take truth to be either the one and only member of 1, or to be that element 1 itself. This is because the universal class is a unit class. — (27)

Let us, for the moment, assume with Taube that the calculus of classes is constructible from a finite number *k* of individuals. Then for each value of *k* there exists a Boolean algebra of *order* 2^k. It is, moreover, possible to show that algebras of unequal orders differ from each other. Thus, for the algebra of order 2^0 we may formulate certain laws that hold for no other algebra — e.g., $\vdash a = 0$, for all a, $\vdash a = b$, for all a and b, $\vdash a \cup b = a$, for all a and b, etc. (The symbol "$\vdash$" is read "it is provable that.") Similarly, for the algebra of order 2^1 (Binary Boolean algebra), we have "$\vdash$ if $a \subset (b \cup c)$, then $a \subset b$

or a ⊂ c," "⊢ a ∩ b = 0 or ⊢ a ∩ b′ = 0," "⊢ a = 0 or
⊢ a = 1," whereas none of these laws holds for any algebra
of order 2^k, for k > 1. Thus, there *are* differences between
algebras of unequal orders. Whether these differences
suffice to establish the nonequivalence of the calculus of
classes and the calculus of propositions remains to be
seen. For if B is a Boolean algebra in which K has m
elements (1 < m < ∞), where K is a class of undefined
elements, then there is some atomistic Boolean algebra A
to which B is isomorphic. If n is the number of atoms
in K, then $m = 2^n$. It is now apparent that Taube uses the
terms "member" and "element" to mean "atom" and
"element," respectively. This seems to be the only possible interpretation we can give to Taube's distinction,
but I fail to see what it accomplishes. For there exists a
calculus of classes isomorphic to a two-element Boolean
algebra. Moreover, the truth-values Truth and Falsity
form a two-element Boolean algebra with respect to the
operations ∩ and ′, and may therefore be identified with
the elements 1 and 0. Viewed from this perspective, is
it then true to say that the calculus of propositions confuses atoms with elements? Is it the case that the propositional calculus confuses propositions with their truth-
values? Saying that this is so is tantamount to claiming
that there are only two distinct propositions, there being
only two truth-values in the logic in question. This,
however, is quite wrong, since no special assumption as
to the number of elements in K is forced on us. Even if
we consider propositions to be identical if they are equivalent to each other, this means only that the class of true
propositions is a maximal sum ideal.

Since it seems that Taube's final criticism rests upon
a misapprehension of the relationship between propositions and their truth-values, it becomes necessary to
clarify the nature of this relationship. Let us, therefore,
define a function v on the algebra of propositions which
has as its only values 1 and 0, and for which the following
statements hold.

(A) $v(p′) = v(p)′$ and $v(p ∩ q) = v(p) ∩ v(q)$.

Such a function is a *homomorphism* of the algebra of
propositions onto the two-element Boolean algebra of
truth-values. Let T be the class of propositions p, such
that $v(p) = 1$. Then T is a maximal sum ideal. Conversely,
if T is a maximal sum ideal, and we define v as (a) $v(p)$
= 1, if p ε T and (b) $v(p) = 0$, if p ∉ T, then we may
easily show that v is a homomorphism of the algebra of
propositions onto the two-element Boolean algebra of
truth-values. Then the truth-value 1 may be identified
with the class of all true propositions.

If we now consider the relationship between propositions and truth-values in the light of the above explanation, then it becomes clear that the calculus of propositions most certainly does *not* confuse elements with
members or atoms. The existence of the homomorphism
not only establishes the precise nature of the connection,
but eliminates the logical possibility of confusion.

On the basis of the foregoing, therefore, it seems to me
that Taube's complaint concerning the inability of propositional calculus to distinguish between membership and
elementhood is just irrelevant. We can no more claim a
preferential status for the calculus of classes on these
grounds than we could on previously considered ones.
Thus our conclusion must be that the calculus of classes
and the calculus of propositions have exactly the same
status as models for retrieval system design. It is, therefore, misleading and irrelevant to attempt to evaluate
their efficacies relative to each other, for the basic question concerns the status of a Boolean algebra *as such*
as a legitimate model for system design. It seems to me
that Taube has confused this question with that concerning the utility of a *wholly different* formal system — viz.,
Quine's *Mathematical Logic* — and has also failed to
distinguish propositions from their truth-values. Now it
may well be the case that a system, say, of axiomatic
set theory or functional calculus is better adapted to the
theory of retrieval system design, but this has nothing
to do with the choice between propositional calculus and
the calculus of classes. It certainly *does* have an effect,
however, on the decision whether to accept a Boolean
algebra itself, and this brings us much closer to the heart
of the matter. Now that we have cleared away the irrelevancies engendered by the *artificial* controversy concerning the choice between the calculus of classes and the
calculus of propositions, we can turn our attention to the
genuine problems awaiting solution.

One of the matters affecting the decision to reject
Boolean algebras in favor of some other formal system
is the problem of complementation. Both Mooers and
Fairthorne have correctly stressed the serious difficulties
of interpretation posed by this operation, and have
proposed alternative models for retrieval system design.
It is not my intention to consider their theories in the
present paper. My major purpose has been to clear the
ground for a more mature appreciation of them, and to
establish the conditions for future theoretical investigations. Having rid ourselves of the lingering and quite
irrelevant problems discussed above, we can proceed in
a number of promising directions. We can, for example,
investigate the properties of those systems in which
complementation is not definable. One such system is
the system P^p of positive propositional calculus (28). It
is to be noted that this system is *not* an interpretation
of a Boolean algebra, in that no operation of complementation is definable within it. Thus here no controversy
can erupt of the type described earlier. Another profitable
venture is to consider lattice theory (Mooers) or Brou-
werian logics (Fairthorne). Many valuable results have
already been gleaned in these areas. In more recent times,
Mooers (29) has constructed a model involving the topological notions of open and closed sets, limit points, continuity and transformations. One highly significant consequence of this is his theorem (30) to the effect that a
retrieval prescription which is based on *NOT* and which
is not expressible as an open-operator polynomial cannot
be linked to a continuous transformation from the infor-

mation space of events {e} to the prescribing space of events {p}. This theorem alone is sufficient to establish the inability of a Boolean algebra to function as an appropriate model for "the experimental information-gathering process" (31).

It is in these directions that our investigations should proceed, unhampered by all those irrelevant problems that dissipate our useful energies. If I have helped to remove some of the veils concealing these directions, I shall consider my purpose in writing this paper to have been accomplished.

References

1. Mooers, Calvin, comments in R. A. Fairthorne. 1961. *Towards Information Retrieval.* Butterworths, pp. xxi–xxii.
2. See, for example, A Mathematical Theory of Language Symbols in Retrieval, 1958, *International Conf. on Scientific Information,* Washington, D.C., **2**: 1327–1364; and Some Mathematical Fundamentals of the Use of Symbols in Information Retrieval, 1959, *Proc. International Conf. on Information Processing,* UNESCO, Paris (15–20 June).
3. *Towards Information Retrieval, passim.*
4. *Study of Theories and Models of Information Storage and Retrieval.* 1962. Supported by The National Science Foundation under Grant No. G24070. Report No. 1, Problems, Systems and Methods (Aug. 3); Report No. 2, The Boolean Algebra Model (Aug. 3); Report No. 3, A Positive Model for Systems of Special Classification (Aug. 29).
5. See Studies in Coordinate Indexing, Washington, D.C., *Documentation Incorporated,* **I–V,** 1953–59.
6. Jaster, J. J., Murray, B. R., and Taube, M. 1962. The State of the Art of Coordinate Indexing, *Documentation Incorporated* (Feb.) 18–19.
7. *Ibid.,* p. 20.
8. Curry, Haskell B. 1963. *Foundations of Mathematical Logic.* New York: McGraw-Hill Book Co., p. 126.
9. The Theory of Representation for Boolean Algebras. 1936. *Trans. Amer. Math. Soc.,* **xi**: 37–111.
10. See, for example, E. V. Huntington. 1904. Sets of Independent Postulates for the Algebra of Logic. *Trans. Amer. Math. Soc.,* **5**: 288–309; New Sets of Independent Postulates for the Algebra of Logic. 1933. *Ibid.,* **35**: 274–304; and H. M. Sheffer. 1913. A Set of Five Independent Postulates for Boolean Algebras, with Application to Logical Constants. *Ibid.,* **14**: 481–488.
11. For a full discussion of truth-criteria, see A. Tarski. 1956. The Concept of Truth in Formalized Languages. *Logic, Semantics, Metamathematics* (Oxford): 152–278.
12. See P. Rosenbloom. *The Elements of Mathematical Logic,* pp. 29–30.
13. *Ibid.,* p. 31.
14. Taube, M. 1958. Future Research in Theory. *Information Storage and Retrieval* (ed. Mortimer Taube and Harold Wooster, Columbia), p. 94.
15. *Ibid.,* p. 95.
16. See M. Taube. 1959. The Distinction between the Logic of Computers and the Logic of Storage and Retrieval Devices. *Studies in Coordinate Indexing,* **V**: 19–20.
17. See, for example, Alonzo Church. 1956. *Introduction to Mathematical Logic,* **1** (Princeton), pp. 103–104.
18. Taube, M. Future Research in Theory. 1958. *Information Storage and Retrieval,* (ed. M. Taube and H. Wooster, Columbia), p. 94.
19. *Ibid.,* p. 95.
20. *Idem.*
21. Quine, W. V. 1955. *Mathematical Logic* (Rev. ed., Harvard), pp. 57, 61.
22. *Ibid.,* pp. 183, 188.
23. Taube, M. 1959. The Distinction Between the Logic of Computers and the Logic of Storage and Retrieval Devices. *Studies in Coordinate Indexing,* **V**: 20.
24. Quine, W. V., *op. cit.,* p. 162.
25. Quine, W. V. 1953. New Foundations for Mathematical Logic. *From a Logical Point of View* (Harvard), pp. 80–101.
26. Taube, M., *op. cit.,* p. 20.
27. *Ibid.,* pp. 21–23.
28. See my *Study of Theories of Models of Information Storage and Retrieval,* Report No. 3, pp. 16–20.
29. See, Some Mathematical Fundamentals of the Use of Symbols in Information Retrieval. 1959. *Proc. International Conf. on Information Processing,* UNESCO, Paris (15–20 June), pp. 315–321.
30. *Ibid.,* p. 319.
31. *Ibid.,* p. 316.

16 The Use of Simulation in Studying Information Storage and Retrieval Systems

NORMAN R. BAKER
RICHARD E. NANCE
American Documentation
Vol. 19, No. 4, October, 1968

Much of the work that has been accomplished in studying information storage and retrieval systems (ISRS) has dealt with subsystem problems, e.g. the composition of the descriptor file, the imposed relations between indexing terms, or the descriptor file organization. In general, the focus has been to improve the system performance in terms of maximizing the relevance ratio, minimizing the noise factor, or minimizing system response time. The application of simulation to ISRS has tended to follow this same direction. In other words, most of the research has dealt with optimizing or simulating the operations of ISRS from the point of view of system effectiveness.

In this paper, the ISRS will be viewed relative to system utility, i.e. how useful the system is to the users of the system. The first two sections constitute a brief state-of-the-art of the use of simulation in studying ISRS. The first section briefly summarizes three typical applications. The second section identifies criteria which have been proposed for use in evaluating or designing ISRS

and provides support for the observation that previous studies have restricted their attention to system effectiveness. An overall model that includes the ISRS and its users and funders is developed in the third section. This model provides the framework within which system utility can be evaluated simultaneously with system effectiveness. The overall model is operationalized in section four with a university departmental library as the ISRS component. The results that such an analysis can produce are also discussed.

1 Typical Applications of Simulation to ISRS

Bourne and Ford[1] discussed the usage of a simulation model at Stanford Research Institute in 1964. The system modeled in this study was described in terms of (1) time and cost data for equipment, personnel, materials, and procedures; (2) the statement of interdependencies existing among materials, equipment, and the search requests; and (3) the constants describing the file size and the cost discounting operation. The model was representative of a machine-based information system, and the purpose of the simulation was to provide direct

Paper presented at the *Thirty-Second National Meeting of The Operations Research Society of America*, Chicago, Illinois, November 1–3, 1967. This research was sponsored by The National Science Foundation's Office of Science Information Services, Grant GN–519.

Present affiliation: Southern Methodist University, Dallas, Texas.

economic evaluations of alternative system configurations under different operating conditions.

A second simulation model of an ISRS was reported in 1966 by Charles R. Blount and his associates at HRB-Singer(2). This report described the construction of a general model of machine-based information retrieval systems. The retrieval system was described by the specifications within the model of:

a. Operations requiring processing time.
b. Linkages existing between different processing components in the system.
c. Service units available within the system.
d. Availability of the service units in terms of their reliability and schedule.
e. Processing load exerted on the system by volume and type of user queries.

Similar to the work of Bourne and Ford, the model allowed the researcher to define a system configuration and, by way of the simulation, to determine a measure of the system's performance. The work reported by Blount et al. considered the measure of performance to be the system response time, i.e. the interval between the initial statement of the query and receipt of the system's response to the query. Possible later extensions of the model were to include constraints on costs, response time, equipment, and/or operation in order to ascertain, by simulation, the alternative system structures that satisfied the stated constraints.

A third simulation effort that involved a specific and explicit ISRS was related by Haas(3) in 1964. An attempt was made to model the Columbia University libraries in terms of patron sets, facilities, and available information objects. Also included in the model were provisions for probabilistic representations of the path flow of patrons through the library and the success of patrons in satisfying their needs by interaction with library resources. The purpose of the simulation was to provide estimates of demands on library resources that would be used as input to a linear program. The linear program then would provide a product-mix description of the library resources that would maximize "patron satisfaction." Unfortunately, this project was not completed.

Previous simulation models of ISRS have concentrated on the tangible characteristics of the problem of information retrieval and usage. In doing so, the models consider the user only as providing an input to the system from which he expects to receive an output. The evaluation of the output is expressed in statistics that ignore the user's judgment of the usefulness of the retrieved information. Likewise, the provision of funds for retrieval system operation is treated only in the sense that a certain system design will incur a specified expected cost when subjected to a given set of input queries. Moreover, the dynamic interactions between the retrieval system, the users, and the funders are overlooked. It is the time-varying patterns of behavior of the retrieval system, the users, and the funders that may provide the most extensive information regarding retrieval system performance.

2 The ISRS as Part of a Larger System

The significance of environmental considerations in ISRS design and evaluation has been noted by other authors. Vickery(4, p. 163) has defined what he believes to be the proper view for the designer of retrieval systems:

In designing a retrieval system for a certain situation, it is clear that we must take into account the environment—the needs of the users, the costs and benefits of each step in the whole documentary operation. It is this complete environment which determines what are the functions of the system.

This statement seems equally applicable to the evaluation of retrieval systems as well as to their design.

Vickery's statement takes on added meaning in the light of the simulation studies discussed previously. Evaluation of system performance in terms only of response time or retrieval costs ignores the accompanying costs to the user of filtering through a mass of retrieved documents to find a few that are pertinent to his problem, or the cost of inconvenience incurred by the user in his attempt to interact with the retrieval system. Further complications arise in the situations where the user bears no burden for the retrieval system costs. Ernst(5, p. 243) alluded to this same problem when he noted that:

A tremendous amount of qualitative and semi-quantitative data suggests that these user costs provide the primary reason why mechanized information retrieval systems have had only limited success; yet this factor is almost completely omitted from consideration in existing system evaluation.

This is not meant to suggest that the simulation models and methods previously discussed are not useful. The point emphasized here is that one must clearly distinguish the problem toward which the simulation procedure is directed. This delineation of simulation purposes is cited by Chapman(6) in his treatment of the issues involved in simulating information systems. Chapman's provocative article categorizes simulation approaches with regard to three basic questions involved (1) the proposed problem, (2) the answer wanted, and (3) how to get the desired answer. Previous simulation studies have attacked the problem of retrieval system design or evaluation in terms of what Ernst(5) has referred to as system "effectiveness"—the ability of a system (or a component thereof) to perform the function for which it was designed. Ernst(5, p. 239) offered an alternative evaluation in terms of system "utility," which he defined in the following manner:

A far broader form of evaluation concerns what might be termed the "utility" of a system. In this case it is necessary to be concerned with how a system will suit a broad spectrum of needs, including consideration of the magnitude of each need, the value of fulfilling it, and a variety of factors related to the financial costs, timeliness, and inconvenience to the users of the system.

This concept of "utility" is adopted in later discussions.

The recently reported study of the information-seeking behavior of X-ray crystallographers by Rubenstein et al (7) further substantiated the importance of "user costs." In this study the users were given, at no charge, access to information services that they had stated in advance would be useful. In the control group of nine subjects only 19% of the available information services were used; while in the experimental group of six subjects none of the services were accessed. Apparently, even though the information services provided to the users were viewed, a priori, as beneficial, the costs to the user from learning how to use these services, or the costs expected to result from using the services, were prohibitive.

The effect of the previous argument is to suggest the inclusion of the user in an active sense in the analysis of the retrieval system—a suggestion that has been stated explicitly by Parker(8, p. 27). This is precisely what has been done. In order to handle the situation in which the user has no direct concern for retrieval system costs, the system definition includes as components (1) the information storage and retrieval system, (2) the users of the retrieval system, and (3) the funders of the retrieval system. Two significant features of the system model are that the retrieval system may, or may not, be machine-based and that the actions of each system component are influenced by the actions of the other system components.

3 A General Model of the ISRS/User/Funder Complex

The discussions of previous sections indicate that in order to describe, design, or evaluate an information retrieval system, it is not sufficient to consider the ISRS as a separate entity. The behavior and "utility" of an ISRS is constrained and influenced by actions of the funders and the users. The information storage and retrieval system is constrained to satisfy at least minimally both the funders and the users. In order to avoid confusion by the use of the term "system" in differing contexts, the convention is adopted to refer to the larger ISRS/user/funder structure as a "complex."

Funder-ISRS Action and Interaction

The funders are defined to be those persons who provide the resources that enable the ISRS to operate. Because of their direct control over resources, the funders have an opportunity to exert control over the ISRS. The funders typically reserve the right to evaluate the performance of the ISRS and future allocations, both amounts and kinds of resources, are often partially influenced by the outcome of the funder evaluation.

Two different control constraints can be imposed by the funders—resource constraints and operational constraints. The most obvious resource constraint is the over-all resource constraint $B=\{B_i; i=1, 2, \ldots, m\}$ which constrains the ISRS to utilize no more than B_i of resource i. A more binding resource constraint is the activity resource constraint $\overline{D}=\{\overline{D}_{ij}; i=1, 2, \ldots, m; j=1, 2, \ldots, n\}$ which contrains the ISRS to spend no more than $\overline{D}_{ij}$ of resource i for information retrieval system activity j. Examples of activities might include: (1) output of information, (2) indexing procedures, and (3) checking for errors in the users' formulation of the query. In addition to a maximum activity constraint, the funders can also impose a minimum activity constraint $D=\{D_{ij}\}$ which restricts the ISRS to use no less than D_{ij} of resource i for activity j. It is clear that $0 \leqq D_{ij} \leqq \overline{D}_{ij} \leqq B_i$. Further, $\delta=\overline{D}_{ij}-D_{ij}$ is a measure of the amount of control by the funders relative to activity j. The two extreme cases are "complete freedom" when $D_{ij}=0$ and $\overline{D}_{ij}=B_i$ and "complete control" when $D_{ij}=\overline{D}_{ij}$. Clearly any number of alternatives exist between these two extremes and overall possible activities.

Operational constraints are not so direct as resource constraints and often become attempts to influence rather than constraints per se. The concern is with funder statements to the ISRS that take the form of defining acceptable operating characteristics. For example, statements such as (1) "provide a complete collection of documents relevant to thermo-physical properties," (2) "utilize a descriptor language incorporating no more than six characters per word," and (3) "require no more than 5,000 words in the descriptor file" can be made by the funders and function as operational constraints imposed on the system. Although not as direct as the resource constraints, the operational constraints also act to influence the behavior and "utility" of the ISRS.

The previous comments have assumed that there is one dominant funder or that there are several funders who act as one funder. If there are several funders who operate somewhat independently, for example in the situation where each user purchases service from the ISRS, then opportunities for funder control are minimized. However, it is still possible for the funders to attempt to influence the behavior of the ISRS by putting conditions on the continued availability of their resources. For example, the users could purchase services from another source that better satisfies their needs.

User-ISRS Action and Interaction

The reward-cost theory of behavior(9, 10, 11) provides a base for hypothesizing user behavior. Each user is faced with a complex decision problem. For any given need for information, the user must identify one or more sources that could be approached in search of need satisfaction. The set of possible sources could include such items as: contact someone who could provide the information; search a private collection of books, journals, and papers; let the need go unsatisfied (for some reasonable length of time), etc. Regardless, once alternative sources have been identified, some expectations or measures of attractiveness, relative to specific needs and sources, are established. Simon's principle of "satisficing" (*12*) suggests that sources are identified and expectations or measures are established only until a sufficient number of satisfactory sources has been generated. Thus, the user is unlikely to identify all possible sources and may, or may not, establish expectations or measures for all the sources that are identified.

Reward-cost theory also provides a possible explanation of how expectations and measures are determined. The units of exchange to the user from the user-ISRS interaction are rewards and costs. Rewards are defined in terms of need satisfaction, i.e. the user is rewarded from interaction with the ISRS (or any other source) to the extent that his need or needs are satisfied. Costs are defined as factors that inhibit or deter opportunities for rewards. When there are several alternative sources, a cost arises whenever a source is selected and the need is not satisfied. Thus, the reward-cost expectations are a function of factors such as likelihood of need satisfaction, time, energy, and money necessary to determine if the selected source will result in need satisfaction, and the convenience of using the system. For example, see the Rubenstein et al. study of X-ray crystallographers(*7*).

Once expectations have become well defined, reward-cost theory suggests that the user is required to give less attention to reward-cost evaluations and searching for alternative sources. Only when the environment begins producing outcomes that are not commensurate with expectations will a user return to a consideration of the reward-cost consequences of his behavior. At this point the process repeats itself, and, very likely, the user will reorder this assessment according to current expectations. Two interesting implications can be drawn. First, the signal for reassessment is under the control of the information sources being utilized, i.e. reassessment is initiated when outcomes are not in line with expectations. If an ISRS is not being utilized, then any changes it may implement will not signal reassessment unless the ISRS employs special means of informing the user. Second, even if reassessment is signaled and takes place, those sources that have low current expectations may never be reassessed if a satisfactory information source is found prior to their being reassessed.

An Overall Flow Model

Figure 1 is a flow model that is intended to summarize the discussions of this section and to serve as a general model of the complex comprised of the ISRS and the users and funders of the ISRS. To complete the model it is necessary to observe that the users may attempt to communicate dissatisfaction. This communication can be made directly with the ISRS and/or indirectly by way of the funders. Note that the special case where the users and funders are identical presents no conceptual difficulty in the model.

One last point is worth mentioning. Feedback from either the users or the funders can be interpreted in two ways. The first is to interpret the feedback as attempts to influence and/or control the future behavior of the ISRS. On the other hand, feedback can be viewed as an opportunity for the ISRS to learn more regarding user and funder expectations. Either interpretation suggests the possibility of modified behavior on the part of the ISRS. It may be in the best interests of the ISRS to stress the learning aspects of feedback in order to lessen the possibilities of external control and/or influence.

4 An Operational Application of the General Model

In the discussion of the general model of the ISRS/user/funder complex and from the model of Fig. 1, one can distinguish two characteristics: the importance of feedback in determining the behavior of the components, and the significance of time in the reflection of behavior. An attempt to operationalize the model will in most cases introduce two further characteristics: the inability to portray decisions or policies controlling behavior with simple functional forms (e.g. linear or continuous functions), and the immense size of the complex that is under analysis. These four characteristics—importance of feedback, significance of time, presence of ill-structured functions, and the immense size of the problem—suggested the applicability of the simulation technique, industrial dynamics(*13*), in the study of a departmental library at Purdue University.

Model of the Complex

A library is an information storage and retrieval system, but an information storage and retrieval system is *not* a library. The truth of this statement becomes apparent when one observes the interaction of users with a departmental library. The need for study space, although somewhat independent of the information function, is a prime need of the student user. Following the concept of system "utility" defined by Ernst(*5*), all major needs that bring a user to the departmental library should be considered.

An overview of the model of the library/user/funder complex is shown in Fig. 2. The focal point of interest in the study is the library, which has been divided into five sections or sectors. The funding and user portions of the complex are modeled in one sector for each. By considering a departmental library, the analysis has excluded virtually all the processing work associated with library operations. The model focuses on those activities undertaken by the library that precipitate interaction with the users and/or funders. These activities include: (1) ordering of materials, (2) book loan, (3) periodical loan, (4) provision of service personnel, and (5) provision of space for storage of collection or for study.

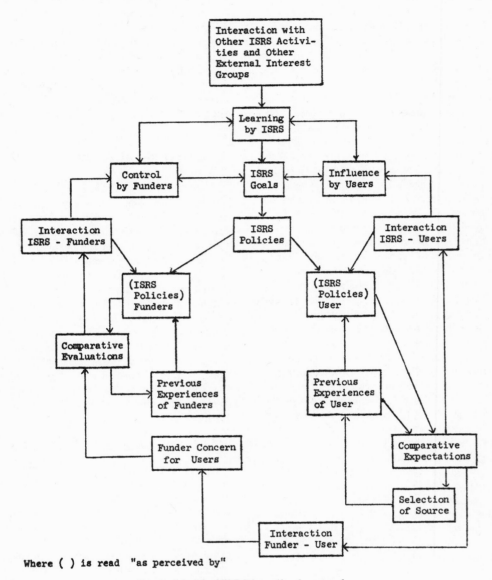

Where ( ) is read "as perceived by"

Fig. 1. Model of ISRS/user/funder complex.

In Fig. 2, broken lines indicate the flow of information and solid lines indicate material flows. Note that the sector of users needs emits only information. The user interacts with the library in an attempt to satisfy one or more needs through usage of library resources, and in the process the user may communicate his satisfaction or dissatisfaction with library services. The reaction of the library may be to provide the services sought by the user or to communicate the unavailability of the resource(s) in demand. Thus the double arrows on some of the information flow lines in Fig. 2 indicate that these communication channels are duplex.

The interaction of the users with the funders is in the form of communication of needs and the ability or inability of the library to satisfy these needs based on the users' past experiences. This, in turn, may precipitate statements of plans, explanations, and commitments by the funders.

Funders interact explicitly with the library in providing operating funds and information concerning the avail-

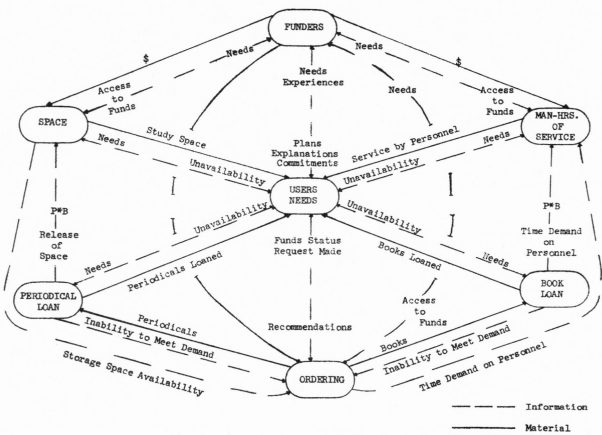

FIG. 2. Model of library/user/funder complex.

ability of funds. The specification of operating constraints is implicit in the modeling of library policy structure and the provisions for policy alterations. Funder evaluation of library operation is not incorporated in the model because it has not appeared as a factor in funder-library interaction. Communication from the library to the funders generally consists of the expression of requests for additional funds to be used for space, personnel, and/or collection increases.

It is beyond the scope of this paper to present the individual sector models in full detail. Future publications will deal with detailed presentation of models, data collection procedures, and analysis of results. However, it is possible to present a brief description of the model and to identify the factors that, a priori, are expected to have significant effect on the overall behavior of the library/user/funder complex. Table 1 contains a list of the sectors, a description of the model of each sector, and an identification of the variables expected to have significant influence on the behavior of the complex.

Objective and Expected Results of the Simulation

In this particular study of university departmental libraries, the objective is to gain insights into the relative

effects of varying library control practices. Library control procedures for collection inventories, loan policies, access to stacks, and space usage exhibit marked variations when identified for the departmental libraries at Purdue University. The simulation analysis is expected to provide a better understanding of the effect of library control procedures on: (1) the behavior of varying sets of library users and (2) the feedback effect on the funders of the library and on the library itself.

Other possible uses of this specific application of the general model are:

1. To investigate the effects of shifts in user demand on staff requirements, budget expenditures, and space utilization.
2. To obtain a view of the library/user/funder complex when subjected to projected information needs under varying budget allocations and over an extended period of time.
3. To reflect the effect of increased communication between the users and funders and to portray the result of increased funder sensitivity to user demands and requirements.

A pilot study dealing with the modeling of one departmental library has been completed. The results of the preliminary simulation runs are most promising and

TABLE 1. Description of models of individual sectors

Sector	Described by	Emphasized
Users' needs	User's contact with library; development of user pressure on funders and library for increased services.	Factors contributing to users' need satisfaction.
Ordering of material	Flow of users' recommendations into orders by library and subsequent arrivals of collection additions.	Sources of recommendations, factors affecting the proportion of users' recommendations which are ordered.
Book loan	Flow of books from library to user and delays in return of books; library policy for loan and return of books and reaction to loss of books.	Factors affecting users' return of books either late or on time, library policy reaction to delay.
Periodical loan	Flow of periodical issues into collection as generated by subscriptions, binding delay in conversion of periodicals into bound form, library policy for loan and return of periodicals and reaction to loss of periodicals.	Factors affecting the users' return of periodicals either late or on time, library policy reaction to delay.
Man-hours of service sector	Usage of service time in accomplishing the demand on personnel arising in other sectors.	Factors requiring expenditure of time by library staff, decisions as to increase or decrease in staff size.
Space	Flow of storage space available into used space for storage, usage of study space by users, transfer of space from study to storage category.	Policy statement for transfer of study space to storage space.
Funding	Flow of allocated money into encumbered then expended accounts for books and for periodicals, flow of money from outside sources into library budget.	Policy for requesting money from outside sources, effect of budget size, transfer of money from book to periodical account.

support expectations that the objective of the study will be realized. The preliminary results also support the belief that the other possible uses of the simulation are feasible. The study is now at the stage where final sector models are being drawn and computer programs are being written. Further reports and publications are expected in the fall of 1968.

5 Concluding Comments

The objectives of writing this paper were to:

1. Summarize existing simulation studies of ISRS.
2. Identify that existing studies have not considered the behavior of ISRS within its overall environment and to support this claim by appropriate citations to the literature.
3. Present a point of view and an associated model that can be utilized in relating the ISRS to its users and funders.
4. Briefly describe how the overall model is being used in a simulation study of departmental university libraries.

The claim at this point in our research is that one description of the ISRS/user/funder complex has been developed and that this description was found to form a foundation upon which it was possible to model university departmental libraries. A more general discussion of the overall model can be found in a recent paper by Baker (14). The manner in which one proceeds from the overall model to an operational model is unique to each study and is dependent upon the specific ISRS, or any other such

activity, under study and the particular objectives of the study.

A better understanding of information storage and retrieval systems is especially crucial at this point in our history. Simulation appears to be a relevant approach for studying such systems and especially pertinent to the study of an ISRS in interaction with its users and funders. It can be anticipated that further specific applications of the general descriptive model will be directed toward other problems in information storage and retrieval and that other researchers in this area will suggest additional descriptive models that can be utilized to provide better understanding of ISRS.

References

1. BOURNE, C. P., and D. F. FORD, Cost Analysis and Simulation Procedures for the Evaluation of Large Information Systems, *American Documentation*, 15:142–149 (April 1964).
2. BLOUNT, C. R., R. T. DUQUET, and P. T. LUCKIE, A General Model for Simulating Information Storage and Retrieval Systems, HRB-Singer, Inc., Science Park, State College, Pennsylvania, April 1966.
3. HAAS, W. J., A Description of a Project to Study the Research Library as an Economic System—Columbia University Libraries, Minutes of the Sixty-third Meeting, The Association of Research Libraries, January 26, 1964.
4. VICKERY, B. C., *On Retrieval System Theory*, 2nd ed., Butterworth and Company, London, 1965.

5. ERNST, M. L., Evaluation of Performance of Large Information Retrieval Systems, in *Information System Sciences*, Spartan Books, Inc., Washington, D.C., 1964, pp. 239–249.

6. CHAPMAN, R. L., The Case for Information System Simulation, in *Information System Sciences*, Spartan Books, Inc., Washington, D.C., 1964, pp. 477–484.

7. RUBENSTEIN, A. H., G. J. RATH, R. W. TRUESWELL, and D. J. WERNER, Some Preliminary Experiments and a Model of Information-Seeking Style of Researchers, Northwestern University, Evanston, Illinois, October 1966.

8. PARKER, E. B., The User's Place in an Information System, *American Documentation*, 17:26–27 (January 1966).

9. BLAU, P. M., *The Dynamics of Bureaucracy*, Revised edition, University of Chicago Press, Chicago, 1963.

10. HOMANS, G. C., *Soial Behavior: Its Elementary Forms*, Harcourt, Brace, and World, New York, 1961.

11. THIBAUT, J. W., and H. H. KELLY, *The Social Psychology of Groups*, John Wiley & Sons, Inc., New York, 1959.

12. MARCH, J. G., and H. A. SIMON, *Organizations*, John Wiley & Sons, Inc., New York, 1958, pp. 140–141.

13. FORRESTER, JAY W., *Industrial Dynamics*, published jointly by The M.I.T. Press and John Wiley & Sons, Inc., New York, 1961.

14. BAKER, N. R., Quantitative Models of Servicer/User/Funder Behavior in Service Organizations, presented at XIV International Meeting of TIMS, Mexico City, August 1967.

17 Systems Technology for Information Retrieval

MANFRED KOCHEN
From "The Growth of Knowledge"
Edited by Manfred Kochen.
John Wiley & Sons, Inc., N.Y., 1967

1. Introduction

This article attempts to sketch an overall picture of the kind of a worthwhile, computer-based IR system that could be realized at this time. The judgment of what is worthwhile is evidently personal. It reflects the conviction that priorities should be assigned as follows: (1) tutorial information service based on synthesis and evaluation; (2) aids to bibliographic control; (3) current awareness; and (4) retrospective searching. All four services are important and should be provided by a good IR system.

Service 1 aims primarily to help a practitioner keep up his understanding of topics that he needs to apply in everyday judgments and actions. Its typical user is a practicing doctor, ten years out of professional school, who wishes to *understand* the latest advances in toxicology rather than just be *informed* of the antidote for a particular poison or the engineer who wishes to understand the formulas and data that he uses rather than looking them up and routinely applying them.

Service 2 is intended mainly to help the librarian who is responsible for managing a document collection and maintaining it in a useful form. He is the intermediary between the IR system (library) and the user. He regards aids to bibliographic control — for example, cataloging, indexing, circulation control — as a way of amplifying *his* performance in the face of mounting arrearages.

Services 3 and 4 aim chiefly to help the information specialist. He is a professional searcher in an information center who extracts from library materials answers to questions posed by researchers at the frontiers of their specialties. His answers are fragments of knowledge — information — rather than a teachable, unified presentation. The professional searcher, like the librarian, is an intermediary between the IR system and the ultimate user. He regards aids to current awareness (for example, dissemination schemes and newsletters) and aids to retrospective search (for example, computer search of an index to produce a bibliography or computer search of text to extract a paragraph) as a way of amplifying *his* ability to meet his obligation.

It is, of course, possible to consider completely automating the roles of both the librarian and the searcher. However, this has not been shown to be either feasible or advantageous, and will not be considered here. Both roles may, of course, be filled by the ultimate user himself. A researcher may, for example, spend one quarter of his time doing his own literature searching and maintaining current awareness entirely on his own; he may even be his own librarian and rely almost entirely on his private collection of books, journals, reprints, and so on. He may not even be able to make effective use of a search specialist. It is highly questionable whether such a user could use an automated version of the search specialist more effectively, as those who argue for direct user — IR system interaction would have to show.

2. Projection of an IR System: Tutorial Information Service Based on Evaluation and Synthesis

Figures 1 to 4 show, without detail, how services 1 to 4 can be provided. Consider Fig. 1a — a system for building up the files to be used in the tutorial information service. Suppose that the system contains a central processing unit like that of an IBM 7090 or 360, and a large auxiliary memory like an IBM Datacell. The process begins by loading the memory with references to documents. Suppose, for the sake of exposition, that these are documents that have been indexed and abstracted by the dozen or so people at the Highway Research Information Service (2). About 5000 of these references — title, author, index terms with roles and links, and abstracts — have been stored on magnetic tape during 1965, with continuation at this rate. Before each such record from the tape is loaded into the Datacell, it is compared with all the records for all documents loaded so far to determine if it "belongs together" with one or more of these. If it does, an appropriate link (two pointers) is set up.

Deciding whether two or more documents "belong together" is a complicated problem. Criteria for "belonging together" include the presence of inconsistencies, of gaps, of needless redundancy, and above all, the likelihood that the several documents *together* add up to more than the same documents *separately*. Suppose that we could think of a document as a sentence generated by a special grammar. The grammar is such that *any* sentence it produces can refer to or be referenced by another such sentence, is attributable to an author (speaker), and does not deviate from conventionalized rules of well-formedness (rules of formation), logical and material truth, and relevance. Then, two sentences "belong together" if they are contradictory, logically coupled (for example, by equivalence or implication), or if they coimply a nontrivial third sentence.

Suppose that somehow a tentative grouping of documents that "belong together" is built up. Before references and groupings are stored in the Datacell, they are evaluated. At least one evaluator is assigned to prepare an evaluation report for each document. He is chosen on the basis of interest, availability, competence, and objectivity. He is to record his personal evaluation of some aspect of the document for a particular purpose. He is to do this by responding to a kind of modernized checklist or preformatted message, possibly by using a keyboard and a text-displaying cathode-ray tube. The preformatted messages used in recording evaluations are to represent the information that various people need in order to decide how deeply to delve into a document, if at all. Eventually, the evaluation report can be prepared much sooner, perhaps as a by-product of refereeing.

Using the evaluation reports, an editorial board decides if and when a tentative grouping of documents that "belong together" is worth acting on. If so, the board commissions a selected expert to produce a "work of synthesis." This can be a new scholarly research paper that resolves an inconsistency indicated by the group of documents, or it can be an original research paper that fills a gap, or it can be just a flag to authors and editors indicating that this is a crowded field in which there is already much redundancy. It might also be a survey/review paper, book, or tabulation.

For each new work created through this novel IR system, three types of secondary records are also generated. The first type is a bibliographic record. It includes data resulting from descriptive cataloging. The second type is a biographic record. It is essentially a dossier on the author. The third is a topical record. It contains units of an indexing/query language relevant for coupling to the contents of a document.

Like the form in which the evaluation report is stored, the three types of record as well as the work of synthesis itself are represented in novel forms. Digital information technology has greatly extended the options and media for storing, transmitting, displaying, processing, and creating representations of documented records. It is somewhat analogous to the way in which motion picture technology has enriched the media for man's expressive powers beyond still photography. How can these new opportunities be well-utilized?

Consider the form of the biographic record, for example. It is to be treated as consisting of elementary, undecomposable segments. Each such segment represents an item of information — the value of a variable — that is deemed significant for users of that kind of record. Record identification number is one segment; author's last name is another; so is city of birth, and so on. Many of these segments within one record must be interlinked, as author's last name is to author's first name. This can be done in a variety of ways: by a generalization of the idea of pointers; by the use of n-place relations; or by the use of what is known as "links" in information retrieval. There are also links from a minimal segment in one record to a minimal segment in another record, in the same file; links from a minimal segment in one

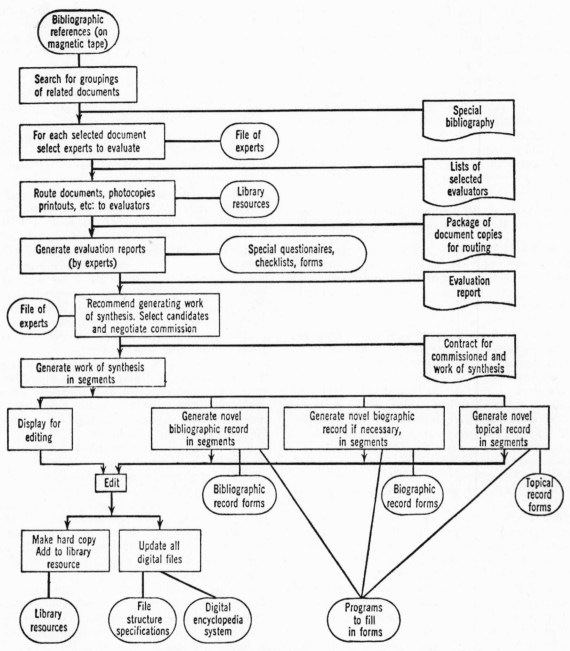

Fig. 1a. Construction and maintenance of subsystem 1: evaluation and synthesis.

record to segments in other files; links of a segment that is an aggregate of minimal segments to other such macro-segments.

The reason for storing documents in this segmented from is to make it possible to search the files with one or more segments specified and to retrieve one or more segments related to what is given in a known way. For example, suppose that "John E. Green," "Miami," and "1965" are given as search specifications (author, city

of birth, and date of birth) and the pseudonym used by that author in 1943 is wanted. The three input segments may be adequate to specify a unique record identification number, and linked to that will also be the desired datum.

Whereas Fig. 1a sketches an arrangement that helps to maintain the system for the tutorial information service, Fig. 1b shows the procedure for providing the service. All the above-mentioned records, evaluation reports, and works of synthesis constitute a "digital

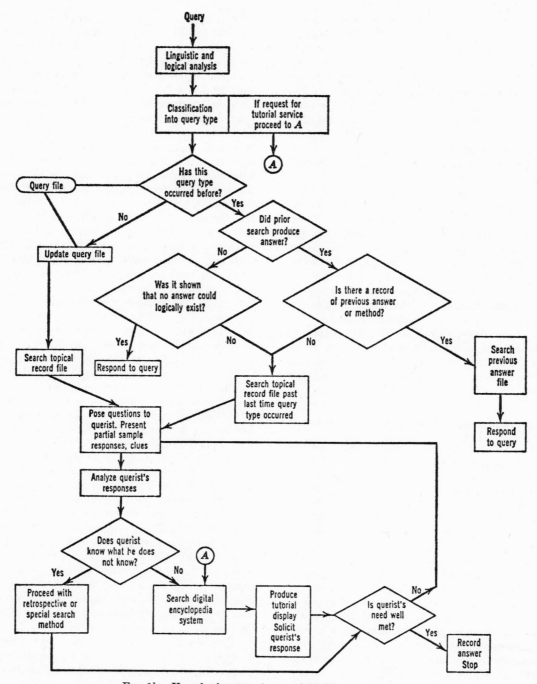

FIG. 1b.   Use of subsystem 1: tutorial information service.

encyclopedia system." Suppose, for example that a querist who is using it wants to know "the maximum temperature on the lunar surface." Linguistic analysis of the query could transform it into "find x such that x is the maximum temperature on the surface of the moon." Logical analysis could further classify the query as incomplete, because it did not specify whether the maximum was to be taken over all points on the lunar surface, over all time, or both. Further logical-semantic analysis, using the topical record file (that is, some substantive understanding of physics), would quickly reveal that "temperature on the surface" is either meaningless or incomplete. It must be the temperature of a thing — of a rock or a spacesuit, for example. If the querist did not know or realize this, he might appreciate being tutorially informed or at least reminded.

If, indeed, several hundred temperature measurements have been reported, the querist might be well served, first, with an overview of the different purposes of the measurements, the different techniques used, and the general nature and classification of the results. He might then be able to reformulate a query based on this increased understanding. That query might be in form suitable for "conventional" retrospective searching. The increase in understanding gained up to the point of reformulating the original query might, however, be far more valuable than any specific fragment of information, even the final answer.

There are evident advantages to a system that helps to digest, to limit, and to master the bulk of retrieved information. Many people would welcome being kept up-to-date by competent and trusted sources. But the process of synthesis, with its selection, re-elaboration, discarding, and re-evaluation of knowledge, could also be a source of anxiety about authoritarian control of the worst kind. These are not groundless fears, for there are real dangers of malfunction due to accident, mismanagement, seizure of control by irresponsible leaders, deliberate abuse or misuse, and so on. It is of critical importance to investigate the stability of the system under such disturbances, and to design sufficient safeguards and protective devices to keep undesirable deviations under control.

3. Bibliographic Control and Current Awareness

Figure 2 sketches a procedure for creating a variety of files pertaining to the items collected by a library, so as to enable the library to control circulation, acquisitioning, inventory, access, and so on. The key problem is, of course, cataloging for better access. Access and aids to current awareness are important to the researcher at the frontier of his specialty in need of a well-defined fragment of knowledge. "Keeping up," the theme of the preceding section, is important to the average person who needs better understanding, to the practitioner, and to the specialist who must borrow from other specialties. The queries posed by such a person often reflect partial ignorance about what it is that he needs to know and what it is that he might yet learn. Sometimes he does not know precisely what questions to ask until he is halfway toward answers. Sometimes answers precede the questions. Frequently he is unaware of just what he does not know that, if he realized it was known, he would find of great interest. Often people who have queries of this kind are too inhibited, pessimistic (actually realistic in terms of services that they have been conditioned to expect), or insecure about how to proceed to even try to pose them.

Most of the research effort in information retrieval has been expended on various ingenious schemes for automatic indexing, that is, subject cataloging. Some schemes are simple — they use a word or a phrase to

index a textual document if the phrase occurs both in the text and in a subject authority list. Other schemes use a phrase to index a document if it is repeated in that document sufficiently often. A variant of this is to require a high enough frequency with which a potential index phrase co-occurs with selected other terms in sentences of the document. Still another scheme requires an index term both to satisfy a frequency criterion and also to be the subject of a sentence in an abstract of the document. Some schemes look for those phrases in a text for which the variance among documents in the same class is significantly less than the variance between documents of different classes. A variant of this scheme is to look for phrases for which the in-document repetition frequency contrasts sharply with the frequency of occurrence of that term in the general language.

There are many more such schemes (5). Many have been analyzed and some have been implemented on a small scale and found to produce more or less impressive results in comparison with conventional ways of indexing. There is no convincing evidence, however, that fully automatic, high-quality indexing on a scale large enough to be practical is feasible and advantageous. Useful aids to bibliographic control are more likely to emerge as by-products of the processes of document generation.

The time when new materials are added to a library — whether they have been cataloged previously, are being recataloged, or are cataloged for the first time — seems the most appropriate one for checking to see if the new items can meet any standing requests for documents on a topic. This means checking a description of the topic against descriptions of the newly arriving items, and notifying the originators of the standing request when there is a match. This method is used in selective dissemination procedures. Proper indexing is only one of the problems in making such schemes successful. Maintaining a current and good description of the standing requests is another. Comparing such descriptions without the rigidity of letter-by-letter matching is yet another. The idea that holds the greatest promise toward improvement of this service is to use all available clues about the originator of the standing request as well as about the authors, including responses to past notices of documents that are classified by type of author.

Computer aids for several of the boxes shown in Fig. 2, which represent processes, have been successfully implemented. Providing aids to current awareness, such as those sketched in Fig. 3, presents problems similar to those discussed above.

4. Retrospective Searching

Although they are assigned the lowest priority here, aids to this type of service have received the greatest emphasis. One of the simplest schemes for retrospective searching — based on coordinate indexing — is also useful to illustrate the kind of "systems arithmetic" that it is

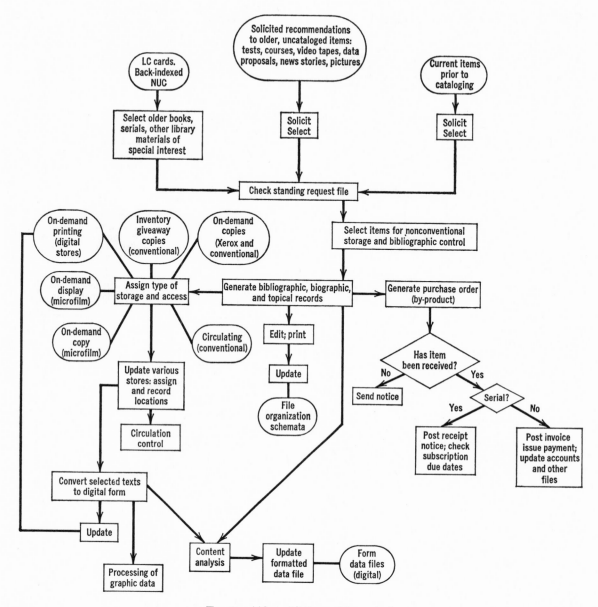

Fig. 2. Aids to bibliographic control.

possible and valuable to do before deciding on any system. The systems analysis illustrated here shows how cost and universal availability of conveniently usable, sophisticated, yet little used private terminals can limit — perhaps fundamentally — the competitive advantages over systems that use modern technology over systems that do not.

Retrospective search requests can be usefully classified into 5 types: (*a*) Known-item search, (*b*) 24-hour–2 week search, (*c*) ½-hour–24-hour search, (*d*) search for data to be delivered in 5 minutes or more, (*e*) search for data to be delivered within 5 minutes (see Fig. 4).

Strictly speaking, only (*b*) and (*c*) are called retrospective searching, in that a list of references to past documents is the desired response to such requests. A broader interpretation of the request would, however, include delivery of the documents — or at least more documents than are available in a traditional citation — in the desired response. If "search" is interpreted to include location of a needed document, then (*a*) is clearly retrospective searching too.

Requests (*d*) and (*e*) have either documented data or a statement asking that the original request be revised or clarified as the desired response. The latter, however,

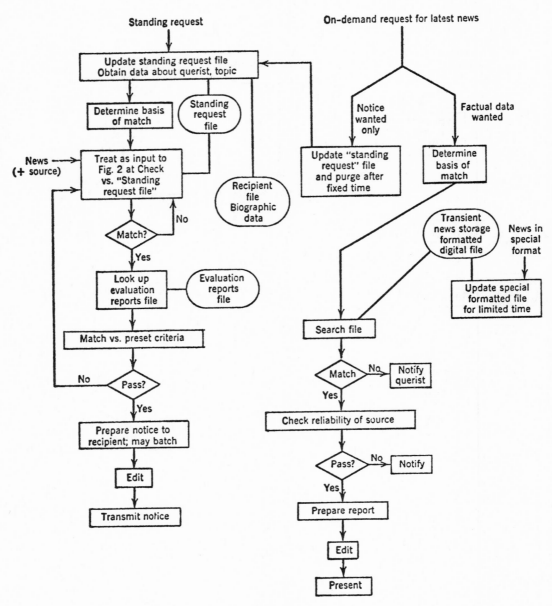

Fig. 3. Current awareness.

is part of the desired response for (a), (b), and (c) as well. In no case should the response to (d) and (e) consist of undocumented data.

Typical queries illustrating (a) through (e), respectively, are:

(a) Do you have the book by Price with the diagram showing growth of literature? Response: Do you mean *Science Since Babylon* by de Solla Price?

(b) Produce a bibliography on the effect of radiation on the production of cancer in mice. Response: 20-100-item list of titles and authors; followed by delivery of a selected dozen or so.

(c) Is there a publication on the IBM photo-optical system I can refer to in the paper to be finished tomorrow? Response: News-story.

(d) What is the maximum temperature on the surface of the moon? Response: Do you want the mean free path between collisions of molecules or the temperature of a particular object there?

(e) What is the antidote for cobalt poisoning, needed to rescue a recent victim? Response: Information adequate to effect rescue.

Retrospective literature searches are conducted by the Engineering Societies Library at $7/hour and by the Science and Technology Division of the Library of Congress at $8/hour, to name only two such services. At the

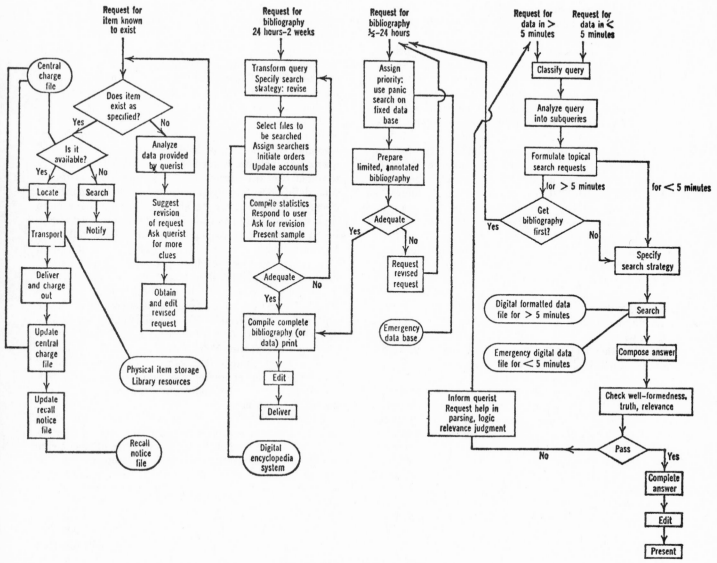

FIG. 4. Retrospective search.

ESL, for example, an annotated bibliography can be supplied in about two weeks at a cost of approximately $50 on the average. The full resources of this library, including a good subject catalog, but no machines, are used. If Cleverdon's results (1) were to generalize to the ESL service, the recall ratio would be between 0.7 and 0.9 and the relevance ratio about 0.2.

Can any of the numerous proposed computer-based retrospective search systems do significantly better in at least one aspect, such as quality, convenience, or cost? Convenience is often equated with the very short response times characteristic of on-demand service. Consider a "time-shared" system that is aimed at providing on-demand man-machine conversational service at stations remote from the central store and control. Suppose

that it had to store the equivalent of the catalog plus indexes for a library, such as those used by ESL in its search service. Assume that the system has three parts: a central processor and multiplexor (CPU), a central store for the index, and N_T remote terminals.

Let U be the total number of users (subscribers) of this system, and suppose that each one poses, on the average, u queries/month. Thus Uu queries/month must be serviced. If the N terminals are equally distributed among the U users, so that S users, with $S = U/N$, share a terminal, queues at a terminal may form or its use may have to be scheduled. One way to minimize queueing is to assign to a user one primary terminal and a secondary terminal which is to be used if the primary one is busy, and so on. If the user's place of work is distant from these terminals, he should be able to sample its status by telephone. Still, he may wish to schedule his use.

Ideally, of course, each user should have his private terminal. At present this may be economical for touch-tone dataphones. One way to use these in on-demand retrospective searching is for the querist to key in numerical codes for subject headings that he looks up in a subject authority list. He uses this like a telephone book. Suppose that he seeks articles on the effect of alcohol on reaction time. He keys in, say, number 0021 for the predicate "effect of ——— on ———," followed by 0000, for "space," followed by 0123 for "alcohol," then 0000 for "space," then 6730 for "reaction time." Before he has had time to key in more items, he hears a pre-recorded message on the telephone: "You want documents on the effect of alcohol on reaction time? Press Y if yes, N if no."[1] He presses Y. The recording continues: "Press H if in humans, D if in dogs, C if in cats, R if in rats." He presses H and listens. "Press T if you are interested in the effects of alcohol on humans in tracking tasks, R if in picture recall, W if in heeding a warning signal, D if in signal detection, N if you don't care in what task."

At the other end there is a computer with an audio-response unit, such as the IBM 7770 & 7772 ($1200/month for 32 words), and other sophisticated devices for accessing complete prerecorded messages. It also has a magnetic disk on which an index is stored. Suppose, for the sake of this calculation, that the index is stored as a table. The table has as many entries as there are subject headings in the authority list, say T. The number that the querist looked up in his directory is the (dialable) address of a table entry. The entry consists of all the document identification numbers that have been posted under the subject heading corresponding to this entry. Let D denote the total number of documents in the library which are thus indexed. Each document identification number must consist of at least $\log_2 D$ bits, and more for error detection/correction purposes.

Although each user may have his private touch-tone dataphone [$1/month more than ordinary telephones, plus $25 for a (Modulator) subset, plus $9/month for local telephone line charges, or more for long distance, plus $3/month for a special card dialer], a diversity of more expensive terminals will be needed. Some of these are (very expensive) high-speed printers; others are ordinary typewriter terminals such as the IBM 1050, 2741, or teletypewriters.

Consider a general expression for the cost, C, of providing such aids to retrospective search. It is the sum of four major terms. The first is the cost of using the terminals and being on-line. The second is the cost of using high-speed large storage for the coded index (for

1. Suppose that the letters are coded from 1010 for A to 1035 for Z.

example, magnetic disks). The third is the cost of using lesser-speed very large storage of information that can be displayed to the user in English rather than in code (for example, Datacells, microfilm, etc.). The fourth is the cost of using the central processing unit (CPU plus core memory). These give a lower limit on the cost per query, as compared with the $50 or so charged by the Engineering Societies Library.

1. The first term is the product of N_T, the number of terminals, and c_T, the cost, say in dollars/month, per terminal. If S users agree to share a query terminal, U/S query terminals are needed. The cost of renting a query terminal can vary from the $38/month for the touch-tone dataphones already mentioned, to $150/month for a simple teletypewriter, to about $500/month for more sophisticated teletypewriters or display units with keyboard input, scope display, and some local buffering. Low-cost remote-control I/O terminals with keyboard and display vary in purchase price from about $4000/unit (for example, Sanders Model 720 or Bunker Ramo Teleregister Model 203 on the basis of 8 units) to $6000. To this cost must be added the cost of a control unit which varies from $3500 (for controlling 8 units) to $20,000 (for controlling 12 units). These devices vary in viewing area (from $5'' \times 7''$ to $6\frac{1}{2}'' \times 8\frac{1}{2}''$), in the number of characters that can be displayed (from 32 to 1196), in the character repertoire (from 50 to 64), and especially in the ability to produce vertical/horizontal line drawings.

Updating the files with incoming documents is at least as much of a problem as servicing requests for retrospective search. Let D' be the number of documents per month received by the library. Suppose that the terminals, like those used to service queries but at the more sophisticated end of the spectrum, are used to enter data about these new acquisitions. Suppose, further, that entering these data ties up the terminal for about $\frac{1}{2}$ hour/document. Assuming 22×8 work-hours/month, about 350 documents/month can be entered on one terminal, and $D'/350$ terminals, used solely for this purpose, would be needed. Thus

$$N_T = U/S + D'/350.$$

To estimate c_T, assume a cost of $250/month for the terminal alone, averaged over the various terminal types. To this should be added the service charge for being on-line, which varies from $5 to $30 per terminal hour, typically about $500/month for 25 hours of on-line use during the month. Experience with the existing time-sharing systems indicates that a querist would rarely get off the terminal before half an hour elapsed. Again, one terminal used full-time could accommodate about 350 queries, or uses, per month. If each of U querists posed u queries per month, and these were to arrive in a strict time order, then only $350/u$ querists could be serviced by one fully used terminal. Furthermore, with $S = 350/u$, one of the S querists may find a queue of as many as

$S-1$ other queries ahead of him, or, say, $(S-1)/2$ on the average. Thus he could expect to wait $(S-1)/2 \times \frac{1}{2}$ hours before his query gets attention. Once it does, he has the capability for on-line interaction with the system during the half hour while his query is being serviced on the terminal. However, queues for getting on a terminal are hardly tolerable.

To complete the estimation of c_T, the cost of a full-time skilled operator for the terminal as an intermediary between the querist and system should be assumed. Long-distance telephone charges (about \$25/hour, less for WATS) will be ignored here, as will be the services of subject experts to supervise updating and general overhead, which may be as high as 150 per cent of the total cost. A sum of \$350/month is estimated to cover all these costs.

Thus $c_T = \$1100/$month,[2] if each terminal is used only 25 hours/month, that is, with 25/175 or $\frac{1}{7}$ utilization. Telephone congestion theory suggests that it may be possible to accommodate about $\frac{1}{5}$ of all U users on terminals simultaneously (to avoid queueing even at peak loads). This would make $S = 5$. The number of queries per user per month, u, is probably quite small and variable. Realistic values for u might be around 1 query/user/month. This would suggest using only 2.5 hours/terminal/month, something that is not now offered commercially. A 25 hour/month terminal would have to be shared by $S = 50$ rather than five people, with a possible two-week wait for one of the 50 to get on with his monthly query.

The existing or forthcoming commercial time-sharing services will hardly be able to accommodate more than about 200 simultaneous users without unwelcome delays in response time. That is, U could be about $5 \times 200 = 1000$. Quite possibly, if each terminal were to be used only 2.5 hours/month, shared by five rare users, then U may be increased. The cost of the terminal (\$250/month) may then be the dominant figure in c_T. It is likely, however, that the use of terminals for retrospective searching will be less than a few per cent of the total varied uses of the terminal and the time-sharing system. If, say, five people with retrospective search requests share a terminal that is used 25 hours/month with users of other services, they may have to wait on a queue. If they insist on on-demand service and have only one query/month each, they will want a 2.5 hours/month terminal, at, say, \$800/month.

2. The second term in the expression for C is the product of K, the number of characters or bytes which have to be in high-speed storage, and c_K, the cost of high-speed storage (\$/character or byte). It will be necessary to store the coded index in this way. This is a table with T entries, where T is the number of subject headings in the subject-authority list. Each entry contains as argument a code for the subject heading. This

2. $\$1100 = (250 + 500 + 350)$.

must be at least $\log_2 T$ bits long, including code identification and check bits. Each entry contains a list of on the average t coded document identification numbers indexed under that term. It is well known that $t = Dd/T$, where d is the average number of index terms per document. The latter varies from 1.6 subject headings per book cataloged by the Library of Congress to as much as 100 in special cases. A typical value for d may be 10. Each document identification number must be at least $\log_2 D$ bits long, plus code identification and check bits.

Taking $D = 2^{20}$ (about a million documents), $T = 2^{15}$ (about 32,000 subject headings) and allowing six bits for code identification and enough additional bits for single-error correction plus double-error detection, about $t \times 32 + 27$ bits per entry should be allowed. That is about $320 \times 32 + 27$ or about 1285 bytes/entry.[3] Altogether, about $10 \times 2^{22} \doteq 40 \times 10^6$ bytes of storage would be required for this index. The cost of this, estimated at \$8000/month for 250 million bytes or characters of disk storage, or 32/million characters/month, is about \$1300/month. Adding to this the cost of an audio-response unit would make it about \$2500/month.

These costs would, of course, decrease if shared with other types of uses, but at a resulting loss of convenience measured by increased waiting times at various queues.

3. The third term in the expression for C is for the use of Datacells or their equivalent. A Datacell costs \$2800/month. Each stores 418 million bytes with about $\frac{1}{2}$-second random access time. Up to eight Datacells can be controlled by one unit costing \$700/month. How many Datacells are needed?

Suppose that, as before, $D = 2^{20}$, and that $D' = 2^{13}$ documents/month. That is, the library grows at 96,000 documents/year, about 9.6 per cent. Assume that a technology such as that of Datacells has an obsolescence period of five years, so that a five-year expansion should be planned for. Thus data about $2^{20} + 5 \times 96000 = 1.5$ million documents must be stored. The data to be stored about each document must spell out what is coded in the index table in order to facilitate communication with the user. Assume for each document about 200 characters' worth of data about the author, about 800 characters' for descriptive cataloging (title, collation, etc.), and about 500 characters' for subject cataloging. A Library of Congress Catalog card has, on the average, 440 characters, so that the 1500 characters assumed here can display nearly three times as much information as can be placed on such cards. Thus about $1.5 \times 10^6 \times 1500 = 2250$ million characters (or bytes) need to be stored. This would require 6 Datacells at a cost of \$17,500/month.

4. During the half hour on a terminal that is needed to enter or service a query, at most a few, say T_q, minutes on the Central Processor are needed. To see this, consider servicing a query. A typical query may require the look-

3. $t = \dfrac{2^{20} \times 10}{2^{15}} = 320$, 1 byte = 8 bits.

ing up of ten coded subject headings in high-speed storage. For each, a list of about 320 document identification numbers are read out (taking a fraction of a second). These 320 lists are searched for numbers common to all of them. This will require about $(320)^2$ comparisons (6) if each list is unordered, less if it is ordered. Each comparison takes no more than, say, 100 microseconds, as a liberal upper limit. Thus no more than ten seconds are needed to do the searching. Updating the index requires sorting and merging. If done weekly, this may take at most an hour of CPU time or, say, $T_U = 4$ hours/month. Typical costs[4] of CPU time are $c_p = \$180$/hour or $3/minute. Thus no more than $4 \times 180 = \$720$/month is required for updating. Allowing $T_q = 1$ minute of CPU time/query adds $\$(Uu/60) \times 3$/month to this fourth term.

5. The total cost is:

$$C = [N_T c_T] + [K c_K] + \left[\frac{(D + 5 \cdot 12D')}{400 \times 10^6} \right.$$

$$\left. \times I \times 2800 + 700 \right]$$

$$+ \left[\left(Uu \frac{T_q}{60} + T_u \right) c_p \right]$$

$$= \left[800 \left(\frac{U}{S} + \frac{D'}{350} \right) \right] + 2500$$

$$+ 17,500 + \left(\frac{Uu}{60} + 4 \right) \cdot 180.$$

If $S = 5$ and $u = 1$, and U is of the order of 1000, it is clear that the first term dominates. The second and fourth terms combined measure the cost of the central configuration, including CPU and high-speed memory. It is negligible in comparison with the other two terms.

If $u = 1$, then U is the number of queries per month to be processed. The cost per query is then, approximately $C/U = 800(1/S + 8000/350 \cdot U) + 20,000/U + 180(1/60 + 4/U)$, with $D' = 8000$.

With $S = 5$ and $U = 1000$, the cost per query is approximately $183. Compare this with the $50 or so per query by conventional methods. Of course, conventional methods do not permit online querying, nor searches of the sophistication possible here, and they do deliver bibliographies within two weeks. If a request for retrospective searching could be met within two weeks, and if the average wait is $\frac{1}{2}((S-1)/2)$ hours for access to a terminal used 25 hours/month, then two-week ($12\frac{1}{2}$

4. At a University Computing Center. It is noteworthy that CPU costs are decreasing even as CPU speeds are increasing. Cost of human labor is increasing.

hour) access can be obtained with $S = 49$, at a cost per query $800(\frac{1}{49} + \frac{1}{44}) + 23 = \$53$/query.

To reduce the cost per query is to reduce the terminal cost, c_T, or to increase S, the number of users sharing a terminal.

Increasing S means possible delays in getting on the terminal. In a sophisticated service there would, presumably, be a variety of modes and priorities of terminal use, with users who pay more per query having to wait less than others to get on the terminal.

Decreasing c_p means giving up some of the display features of the terminal and foregoing the services of a trained operator. The minimal cost of such a terminal is probably that of a dataphone with audio responses as described earlier, with $38/month for equipment rental plus, say, $62/month for being on-line with such an instrument no more than 2.5 hours/month and shared by five users. When there are, say, 10,000 such users, the cost per query could go down to $100/5 + 23 = \$43$.

5. Technological Advances

Some examples of recent technological developments were introduced when we discussed feasibility and advantages—technical and economic—of a possible retrospective search system. These devices and their use in a system were described in a very sketchy manner, with numerous approximations. It is also important to realize that they are only a small sample of the equipment that is commercially available now and that is becoming available at a very rapid rate.

Processing units are already very fast, in the nanosecond range. In one nanosecond light travels about a foot, so that in a processing unit which is a foot long the travel time for a signal may be as much as the switching time. Nonetheless, trends towards integrated circuit technology and microminiaturization make it reasonable to anticipate CPU's at drastically lowered costs, perhaps one for every few terminals.

Current sort-merge programs for files of up to 25,000 variable length records exist for an IBM 7090 and require 30 minutes maximum. Faster programs that use blocking techniques are being developed. The estimate of an hour/week for updating an index on the newer machines, such as the IBM system 360, is surely a conservative upper limit.

Of the three parts of a system—the central processor, the large, slower auxiliary stores, and the terminals—the latter are most likely to be congested if utilized at a high rate. The CPU is most likely to be idle while there are queues to obtain access to the large shared stores. This suggests utilizing the fast CPU for processing tasks other than those of routine updating and servicing of queries. Preparation of concordances as aids to indexing is a possibility. For an average text of 3000 words, it now takes about five minutes of IBM 7090 time to prepare a concordance. A Permuted Title Index for 2000 to 3000 documents can be made in about 30 minutes. Syntactic analysis of sentences in documents to be indexed for file updating is another possibility.

In addition to large digital stores, such as the IBM Datacell and RCA's RACE, a number of devices are under development, for example, a trillion-bit file being developed by IBM for the Atomic Energy Commission in Livermore. Such very large memories would be applicable for storage of full text, graphic data, and special formatted files. The contents of the National Union Catalog, for example, would require storage of this capacity. So would the "Digital encyclopedia system" file shown at the bottom of Fig. 1a. The "Emergency digital data file" in Fig. 4 would require faster access time to probably not as large a data base, and disks (magnetic or photoscopic) may suffice. Core storage would probably be reserved for the housekeeping functions of the central processor. There would be no direct transmission into core except from auxiliary disk-type memories. The latter might be used mainly to let a limited amount of (expensive, fast) core memory act as if it were much larger by swapping program segments back and forth between core and disks (with return from core to disk via drum, for example). Disks would also be used to store a coded version of the index.

Beyond digital storage techniques, there are impressive developments in microform transport, copying, and recording technologies. The IBM 1350 photo-image system, for example, transports a 70×35 millimeter film chip through pneumatic tubes at 25 feet per second to a station where a chip image is created by contact with the microfilm in an aperture card. It can service about 1000 random requests for chips in one hour. Such stores are close to that end of a spectrum of information stores exemplified by Xerox copies and books/journals in conventionally printed form. Technologies for long-distance transmission of Xerox copies and slow-scan television are also advancing impressively, but the kind of systems illustrated arithmetically in Section 4 may show that such techniques are not yet competitive with airmail transport of tapes or hard copies.

Whereas conventional voice-grade telephone lines permit transmission of about 2000 bits/second, at standard rates, experiments in transmission of digital data over a transatlantic cable have shown that 8000 bits/second can be reliably transmitted ($20,000/month for a leased line). If time-division communication systems replace current methods during the next decade, costs can be expected to decrease further. Important trade-off studies involving the use of high-capacity (and high-cost) channels for transmitting rarely requested, centrally stored data, as compared to duplicating (for example, on microfilm) much of the central store at each regional center, are required. The possibility of implementing a network of such regional centers—each one of them servicing, through concentrators, local computing centers—is one of the most important developments in systems technology. There are already a wealth of options among communication channels. The amount of traffic in digitally encoded messages is already nearly equal to the amount of voice traffic over telephone lines and is growing at a much faster rate. With Voice PCM (Pulse Code Modulation) the distinction between transmission of analog or digital signals may become very subtle. Table I gives a general view of what is commercially available in the communications industry.

Terminals have already been mentioned. Input of text via punched cards requires the labor of keypunching and verification, about 1 cent/word. Storage on magnetic tapes is economical for archival purposes; a reel of tape costs about $32 and can readily store 30,000 references (titles, authors, and other descriptive data and subject headings). A charge of about $5 is made for having

TABLE I

Analog	Bandwidth	Digital	Kilobits per second
		TWX	100
Voice	4 KC	TELEX	100
		Dataphone	2.4
Telpak A	48 KC	Telpak A	18–20
Telpak B	100 KC	Telpak B	36–40
Telpak C	240 KC	Telpak C	100
Telpak D	1 MC	Telpak D	500
Half-Video	2 MC	T-1 carrier	1500 short-haul
Video	4 MC	T-2	6000
"Exotic"	up to 20 MC	T-4	220 000

an operator mount a reel of tape, however. It takes several minutes to search a reel of tape. Automatic character-reading devices exist now only for limited fonts. The IBM optical reader ($3,000/month), for example, reads 480 characters of a single font from about 400 documents/minute. Another commercially used reader, by Rainbow, can also read a single standard font at comparable speed, high reliability, and at a cost of $84,000; this firm is also delivering custom-made multifont readers, at considerably higher cost, to special customers Voice-recognition devices are still very far from practical availability. On the display side, there are impressive advances in photocomposing technology. Current devices produce only 12 pages/hour and use about one minute of computer time per page. Devices that produce a multifont transparent master of high quality, including graphics, at 600 characters/second, and are driven by magnetic tape, are under development. So are sophisticated terminals permitting on-line editing. Facilities for producing copies of such masters at two to ten cents/page are now commercially available.

The quantity and quality of current accomplishments in information systems technology match the pace at which it is advancing. An attempt at completely cataloging the state of the art would thus be obsolete before it is complete. The state of the art and growth in software is now nearly the same as that in hardware. Indeed, some software systems are beginning to look for hardware implementations of significant functions.

Modes of use—for example, standard operating procedures—and system design techniques are still in a primitive stage of development. Application areas have yet to be logically structured, and this article is a contribution toward structuring the area of information retrieval in its relation to systems technology.

A minimal system for retrospective search, such as that sketched in Fig. 4 and discussed in Section 4, is barely realizable at this time even with the impressive current state of information systems technology. The Central charge file, for example, should allow a person who knows of the existence of a certain paper but does not recall the exact title or even all details of the author's name to (a) ascertain the existence of this item in the library and (b) to determine its availability, within seconds or minutes at most. As many as half of all items cataloged in a library may be unavailable at one time, for one reason or another. To determine whether the library holds an ill-specified but existing item, the entire catalog would have to be available and would have to be searched with intelligence. Storing the catalog of a million-item library so as to allow user-machine conversation could be accomplished with a Datacell, as already indicated, but the response times will be in seconds. Delivering the wanted item can also be accomplished with recently announced technology, for example, the IBM photo image retrieval system.

Tying all the different technologies together into a total system requires special interfaces and considerable system-design and development work that is very costly and time-consuming. To implement a reasonably sophisticated retrospective search system in, say, three years would require a major, concerted effort—almost at the pace of a crash program. It is hard to imagine that retrospective searching could seem sufficiently worthwhile to generate this kind of urgency. Users may continue to complain about current inadequacies in retrospective search, but it is questionable whether they will enthusiastically invest in or buy an improved retrospective search service, if only that is offered. Even if improved current awareness services are also added, it is doubtful whether this will make much difference.

It is assumed here that a genuine latent need exists for an improved tutorial information service, such as that shown in Figs. 1a and b. The assumption that such service is worthwhile and could generate the sense of urgency needed to mobilize the needed resources for the realization of a system in a reasonable time period is based on the dramatic increase of interest on the part of universities (for example, EDUCOM) and new business enterprises generated by recent developments in closer man-machine coupling (for example, computer-based instruction and on-line debugging).

What would it take to demonstrate, by construction and operation of a significant prototype, that such a system is technically and socioeconomically feasible? An analysis such as was undertaken in Section 4 for a retrospective search system, is much more difficult in this case because there are as yet no good procedures for grouping documents that "belong together," and no good designs for a data structure such as that underlying the "Digital encyclopedia system" which allows storage and retrieval of record segments.

I. Technical feasibility

   A. Standard operating procedures and forms for management and users of a tutorial information service

      1. What information does a user need to decide how deeply to delve into a document, if at all? Answers to this are prerequisite to the design of a questionnaire or checklist for the evaluation report. The applicability of current techniques in survey design supports belief that useful answers can be obtained.

      2. What types of instruction does a user need as a function of how much he already understands? The impetus to research on such questions due to computer-based instruction is quite likely to produce partial answers. Such answers are critical for rational design of data structures to represent the works of synthesis, so as to allow a user to get as much or as little detail as he needs, and to decide when and where to plunge into deeper detail if a short synopsis of a topic is given. Similar questions also relate to design of data structures for representing bibliographic, biographic, and topical records.

      3. By what criteria can the extent to which a querist's need is met be determined?

      4. In a man-machine conversational mode, which functions in the processes of linguistic/logical query analysis, query classification, query reformulation, recognition of query recurrence, judgments of relevance, etc., should be assigned to hardware, which to software, which to clerical-type people with standard operating procedures, which to other types of people?

      5. What languages should be available for different kinds of users in which to formulate the questions, instructions, and responses to the system?

      6. What procedures are there for guaranteeing the integrity of messages that are generated, stored, transmitted, processed, or displayed in the system? For preventing, detecting, or correcting errors? For safeguarding against accidental or deliberate invasion of privacy or confidentiality of sensitive data or mismanagement of the system?

B. Data Bases
1. There are already a large number of significant collections of indexed documents on magnetic tape. MEDLARS has now over 15 reels of tapes with about 30,000 references (subject heading, title) per tape. NASA has a similarly large number. EURATOM has close to 100,000 references in *Nuclear Science Abstracts* on tape, and the collection amassed by Chemical Abstract Services is equally impressive. How can all these tapes, in their different formats and their great number and diversity, be used together, if a total, integrated search service were to be developed?
2. Vast quantities of text (and graphics) are printed by means of linotype machines or transmitted in digital codes over communciation channels, making it feasible to process such data by digital computers. The full text of the *New York Times*, for example, exists on (uncorrected) perforated paper tape. It is possible, although not simple, to read such tapes into disks or cores and perform content analyses on the text by computer.

C. Software
1. What are efficiently automated procedures for managing the on-line generation of evaluation reports, bibliographic, biographic, and topical records by many users "simultaneously"? Experience in the development of timesharing systems should be applicable to this problem.
2. What are effective algorithms and programs for grouping related documents? What information should be supplied about each document to make possible decisions about whether two documents "belong together"?
3. What are good strategies and programs for loading data into a data structure (updating files) and searching data structures in response to various queries?
4. What are efficient procedures for parsing sentences in the one or several languages used in a conversational mode? For translating certain command sentences into actual operations? For transforming interrogative sentences into answer-searching routines?

D. Hardware
1. What interfaces must be provided to permit a variety of on-line terminals of differing sophistication to be tied into the same system?
2. On what basis should priorities be assigned to the development of the numerous competing technologies for very large memories? It is more a question of providing guidance for the idea- and technology-rich hardware development arts than searching for new technologies or developments that would meet the needs

which are now not being met. This guidance will not come from a better understanding of needs to be met but, rather, from what can be put on the market that is sufficiently attractive in flexibility, convenience of use, reliability, and cost.
3. How can hardware be used to support software developments?

II. Socioeconomic feasibility
A. Generating and satisfying demand
1. How valuable is convenience in using a computer? Programmers with access to an on-line terminal for debugging can do in a few days to one week what it took them two to four weeks to complete by using the conventional facilities of a computing center (one to eight hours turn-around time). Students with ten hours of preprogrammed tutorial instruction in elementary statistics could pass the same examination with higher grades than students who studied the same topic in an one-semester college course. Problems that would otherwise not be programmed, topics otherwise not studied, questions otherwise not asked, would be undertaken if it were sufficiently "convenient" to do so. People who would otherwise not avail themselves of information systems technology would do so if it is sufficiently "convenient."
2. How much less is a ten-second response worth than an one-second response, assuming the same response? How does this relation vary with the types of queries to which the responses are relevant?
3. How does the accuracy and precision of a response relate to its value. A response to "What is the elevation of Boulder, Colorado?" asserting "Between 2,000 and 8,000 ft. above sea level" is accurate but imprecise; the response, "Between 6153 and 6159 ft. above sea level" is more precise but inaccurate. Which is more valuable?
4. What is the distribution of users over services of different value (that is, quality)? Relatively few users will pay a high price for very high-quality service and probably very few will pay anything for *very* low-quality service. How does quality of service rendered relate to convenience (that is, response time, simplicity of conversational language, adequate features for display and generation of information input, etc.), to precision, accuracy, and complexity of the question?
5. What is the frequency of use—in, say, queries per user per month—as a function of query type and the distribution of response quality over query types?

B. Costs and Supply

1. How does the cost of supplying a terminal vary with the quantity purchased and the quality? What are the prime determinants of quality for different-purpose terminals? How much less costly is an input-only device than a device with input as well as printer or display capability? How much more costly is a device permitting hard-copy production in addition to display?

2. How does the cost of a large memory vary with the total storage capacity, the mean and variance of the time to produce a response, and the serial read-rate?

3. How do these costs vary with time, not assuming revolutionary technological advances?

4. What are the costs of software support as a function of system size, quality of service, and time schedule of implementation? How are these costs changing with time?

5. What is a reasonable projection for availability of hardware and software as a function of time between order placement and delivery?

C. Organizational

1. How can the best minds capable of literature synthesis in a field of knowledge be motivated to contribute new works of synthesis in novel forms? What will compete with the prestige of leading professional publications, the royalties of a good publishing enterprise, the existing system of editors, referees, reviewers, promotion, and distribution?

2. How can top creative minds in a field of knowledge be motivated to submit objective, thoughtful, critical, and informative evaluation reports? How can this system improve on the existing procedures for evaluating literature both before and after publication?

3. What is the best way of managing an enterprise involving so many intimate man-machine partnerships? How should the management tasks be divided between machines and men?

4. What determines the inherent stability of a tutorial information system? Under what conditions will the system be able to control perturbations due to injection of *some* deviant inputs, some misuse or abuse? What can be done to allay inherent fears about authoritarian control, bias toward special interests, and stifling of full creativity and freedom of expression?

6. Conclusions

The preceding list of questions is a formidable one. Some of the questions are best answered by constructing a system with "quick-and-dirty" solutions to problems for which there is as yet no sound basis, and using the system to compile the needed empirical data upon which to build a rationale.

It can, of course, be argued that considerably more theoretical research is needed before any attempt at construction should be made. It might, for example, be required that an information-retrieval system must: mechanically recognize whether input strings are well-formed, whether they are questions or declarations; formally produce output strings in response to input strings which are not only well-formed but logically true and relevant. Then theoretical problems pertaining to structural ambiguity of sentences, for example, to the use of first-order predicate calculus (which is undecidable), would be considered fundamental. It is, of course, unrealistic to impose such requirements on an IR system which, if successfully implemented and managed, could still be an exciting enterprise and have significant social impact. Therefore, such theoretical questions were not included among those to be answered in showing the technical and socioeconomic feasibility of a tutorial information service.

It is true that there are deep theoretical problems underlying these questions. It is far from clear, however, that existing theoretical work can shed much light on them. The creation of a new theory suitable for the fundamental problems that are relevant to *real* rather than hypothesized systems will probably have to be preceded by a phase of empirical data gathering. We are, perhaps, in a stage comparable to that of the early life sciences, when naturalistic observations and classification of empirical data were a far more reputable activity than speculative theorizing, even if it was mathematically sophisticated and profound.

For these reasons, a well-managed and boldly conceived enterprise for a tutorial information system appears to be the most recommendable next major step. This does not, of course, reduce the current critical need for more and better high-level investigations into the mathematical and conceptual underpinnings of more rationally designed information-retrieval systems. Such research into basic problems is inevitably a slow process, and its progress and progress on IR systems technology can occur independently. The success of the proposed tutorial information system for a specific subject area depends almost entirely on entrepreneurial-managerial genius in mobilizing the high-quality resources that could now be brought to bear on such a project.

References

1. CLEVERDON, C. W., "Report on the Testing and Analysis of an Investigation into the Comparative Efficiency of Indexing Systems," ASLIB Report, Coll. Aeronautics, Cranfield, Bucks Co., U.K., October 1962.

2. IRICK, PAUL, "Highway Research Information Serv-

ice," *Traffic Engineering and Control,* October 1965, pp. 385–388; see also IRICK, P. E., and W. N. CAREY, JR. The New Highway Research Information Service, *Highway Res. News,* No. 18, March 1965, pp. 5–15.

3. KOCHEN, M., *Some Problems in Information Science,* New York: Scarecrow Press, 1965.

4. KOCHEN, M., *Information Retrieval System Theory,* in preparation.

5. NATIONAL SCIENCE FOUNDATION, *Current Research and Development in Scientific Documentation,* No. 14, 1965.

6. WONG, E., "Time Estimation in Boolean Index Searching," *High-Speed Document Perusal,* final report on contract AF49(638)-1062 by M. Kochen to AFOSR, 5/1/62, pp. 69–81.

Chapter Five
Acquisition

Acquisition implies some kind of a selection process by which the content of the system (or more precisely the system's file) will eventually be determined. The question that has to be asked is: "How and on what basis is the selection process to proceed?" Inquiry into this whole area of acquisition in relation to information science is remarkably negligible, although its importance is obvious — acquisition determines what content will ultimately be supplied to a user. In practice, selection is more or less based on some intuitive notion of what the system ought to have; or on subjective judgments about the quality of materials to be included; or on some comprehension of "everything" and "all" in a field, area, discipline or mission. It is usually implied that selection is based on future uses, but the relation between selection and utilization is almost never explicated.

The selections presented here are merely representative of the research methodologies and approaches that are possible in arriving at a more formal and explicit base on which selection processes can be carried out, rather than of the research work being done, of which there is practically none.

It should be mentioned that within the literature there are practically no articles which deal with acquisition for any information systems other than for libraries, from either a theoretical or experimental point of view. Clearly, this is an open area for research.

Buckland and Woodburn (Article 18) address themselves to the question of how many copies of each item a university library should provide. They suggest a method for estimating the total demand and in the process used, some new measures of service, as well as an original methodology of investigation.

Morris and Goffman (Article 19) use Bradford's law of dispersion of literature, which is showing more and more potential usefulness and applicability, in a study of the utilization of periodical collections. On the basis of the data accumulated, the authors seek to link dissemination with acquisition.

Other articles found in the literature that could pertain to this chapter were numerous but not research-oriented. These included articles that present and debate the operational aspects of acquisition, as well as articles that discuss the criteria of quality in a selection policy.

18 An Analytical Study of Library Book Duplication and Availability

M. K. BUCKLAND
I. WOODBURN
Information Storage & Retrieval
Vol. 5, No. 2, July, 1969

1. Introduction

A major difficulty in libraries is deciding how many copies of a given book should be made available for students. Even when the librarian knows which titles are likely to be in demand, there remains the problem of estimating how many copies of each will be needed. If too few are provided, then library users will be unable to find the documents which they need, and the library is failing in one of its fundamental tasks; if too many copies are provided, then money has been wasted and the library's budget is being inefficiently used, in that the cost of buying, processing and storing the redundant copies could have been more profitably used for other purposes. This problem is especially acute where a number of students are taking the same or similar courses.

It would, therefore, seem convenient if an examination of the various factors concerned could provide guidance in this matter. In particular we have been interested in establishing, for any given item, the relationship between:

    i. The number of requests,
    ii. The loan period,

    iii. The number of copies, and
    iv. A standard of service.

It is, in fact, convenient to combine the first two of these factors: if the number of requests occurring during any given span of time is divided by the number of loan periods in the same span of time, then we have an "average request rate per loan period." The effect on the average request rate of an increase or decrease in the number of requests will be clear. So too is the effect of a change in the loan period: to lengthen the loan period is to reduce the number of loan periods in any given span of time, and so the average request rate per loan period is increased; conversely the shortening of the loan period decreases the average request rate per loan period. This report uses the concept of an average request rate throughout, but it should not be forgotten that the effect of a change in the length of the loan period can readily be assessed by calculating a new request rate.

Although the work to be described may well be applicable in many other libraries, it must be stressed that we have not undertaken it merely as a theoretical exercise. This paper describes an attempt to see whether, and how far, an analytical approach could be used to guide day-to-day decisions about duplication in an actual reserve collection within the University of Lancaster Library. This collection is known as the Short Loan Collection: all material known, or expected, to be in heavy demand is removed from the open shelves to this collection which is located, on closed access, behind the service desk. This means that a reader wanting an item from the collection has to ask for it and, if it is available, a member of the library staff will issue it.

With a view to increasing the number of readers who can use each copy, and thus reducing duplication, the loan period is short — normally about four hours. There are twenty-two such loan periods in a week: each weekday has four (morning, afternoon, evening and overnight), and Saturday has two (morning, and from noon until Monday morning). At whatever time an item is borrowed, it *must* be returned or re-borrowed by the end of the same loan period; this rule is strictly enforced by a scale of heavy fines.

In general the teaching staff are relied upon to give prior notice of books which are likely to be heavily used, and of the appropriate number of copies of each, since it is they who direct the student's reading.

2. The Poisson Distribution

Although it may well be possible, by keeping careful records, to establish the average number of requests per loan period for a given title, it does not follow that precisely this number of requests will be made in each individual loan period. In fact, the actual number of requests appears to fluctuate somewhat haphazardly from one individual loan period to another.

Statisticians have often found, when examining this sort of situation, that in the long term there is a predictable regularity in the extent of such fluctuations, which can be described by the Poisson distribution.

$$P(s) = \frac{e^{-r}r^s}{s!}$$

This states the probability $P(s)$ of s requests being made in a single loan period, where r is the average request rate and e is a constant (approximately 2.71828).

For example, if the average request rate were one request per loan period, then we should not expect that there would be precisely one request in each. Instead we should expect that although there often was one request in a loan period, there would sometimes be none, two, or three, and on rare occasions four or more. The Poisson distribution indicates that if the average request rate is one per loan period, then in 100 loan periods, one could *expect* no requests to occur in about thirty-seven of them, one request to occur in about thirty-seven of them, two requests in about nineteen of them, three

requests in about six and four requests to occur only about once.

This formula has been used in many different fields; the outstanding example of its use in librarianship is the planning of the National Lending Library [1]. It has also figured in other studies, notably those by Morse at the M.I.T. Science Library [2].

3. Establishing a Relationship Between Duplication, Availability and the Pattern of Requests

The objective of this analysis is to derive a relationship between:

1. Request pattern,
2. Number of copies,
3. Immediate availability.

In investigating the request pattern, we assume initially that there is an ascertainable average request rate for a given title, and that the Poisson distribution can adequately describe the variations in the observed numbers of requests in individual loan periods.

The concept of immediate availability is based on the simple fact that when a item is requested it is either available there and then, or else it is not. The immediate availability rate is the proportion of requests which are immediately satisfied, and can conveniently be stated as a percentage:

Percentage availability =

$$\frac{100 \times \text{No. of requests immediately satisfied}}{\text{total No. of requests}}$$

This concept is admittedly a somewhat crude measure of the standard of service; for example, it does not take fully into account the fact that requests which are not immediately satisfied can almost invariably be satisfied on some later occasion if the user has sufficient time and persistence. However, such delays are *prima facie* undesirable, and in the circumstances immediate availability seemed to us to be a reasonable measure of the standard of service. Accordingly throughout this report the terms "available" and "satisfied" are used to mean *immediately* available and *immediately* satisfied.

In order to establish the availability rate we need to know both the number of satisfied requests and the total number of requests. If the number of requests for a title in one loan period is equal to, or less than, the number of copies available, then all requests will be satisfied. If the number of requests exceeds the number of copies, and if, as we assume, a copy cannot be borrowed more than once within a single loan period, then the number of satisfied requests cannot exceed the number of copies. We define n as the number of copies of a given title and s as the number of requests for it in any single loan period so that when $0 \leq s \leq n$ then s requests are satisfied and when $s > n$ then n requests are satisfied. Since

$P(s)$ expresses the relative frequency of s requests being made in a loan period

$$\text{Percentage availability} = \frac{100 \left[\sum_{s=0}^{n} sP(s) + \sum_{s=n+1}^{\infty} nP(s) \right]}{\sum_{s=0}^{\infty} sP(s)}$$

We now have a relationship involving:

    i. The number of requests,
    ii. The loan period,
    iii. The number of copies, and
    iv. Percentage availability.

From this we can calculate the dependence of the availability rate on such factors as

    a. the length of the loan period, and
    b. the number of copies in stock.

In the case of the Short Loan Collection a reduction in the length of loan period has been considered undesirable, and our attention has, therefore, been focused on predicting the correct number of copies. This information, which is now being used, is reproduced as Table I.

We would stress that this approach is best suited to comparatively simple situations such as the Short Loan

Collection being investigated. In a typical open access library, items are used in at least two ways: they are consulted inside the library for short periods and they are borrowed for comparatively long and widely varying periods. Consequently, the librarian is likely to be especially interested in possible variations in loan policies, and in the interplay of two or more kinds of use. (For example, how far can he afford to allow the borrowing of material which is traditionally confined to the library?) Furthermore, in such a situation, the librarian is — understandably — concerned with the effects of various and sometimes expensive arrangements for reservations and recalls, and with the delays involved in meeting requests which have not been satisfied immediately. For this more complex situation a different approach would seem to be called for.

4. Is the Use of the Poisson Distribution Justifiable?

The results in Table I were based on the hypothesis that the pattern of requests predicted by the Poisson distribution would be similar to the actual pattern of requests in the collection concerned.

The ideal situation for testing this hypothesis would be where it was feasible to record *all* requests (not only satisfied requests) without the user's knowledge, and where the user could not tell in advance whether or not an item was available. The Short Loan Collection within

TABLE I

PERCENTAGE AVAILABILITY IN RELATION TO THE REQUEST RATE AND THE NUMBER OF COPIES PROVIDED. IN THIS TABLE THE REQUEST RATE IS GIVEN ON A PER DAY BASIS (FOUR LOAN PERIODS PER DAY) INSTEAD OF PER LOAN PERIOD. THE NUMBERS HAVE BEEN ROUNDED

Requests per day	Copies provided									Copies required for		
	1	2	3	4	5	6	7	8	9	80%	90%	95%
0.4	95	100								1	1	1
0.5	94	100								1	1	2
0.6	93	100								1	1	2
0.7	92	100								1	1	2
0.8	91	99	100							1	1	2
0.9	90	99	100							1	1	2
1	88	99	100							1	2	2
2	79	97	100							2	2	2
3	70	93	99	100						2	2	3
4	63	90	98	100						2	2	3
5	57	86	96	99	100					2	3	3
6	52	81	94	98	100					2	3	4
7	47	77	92	97	99	100				3	3	4
8	43	73	89	96	99	100				3	4	4
9	40	69	86	95	98	99	100			3	4	4
10	37	65	83	93	98	99	100			3	4	5
12	32	58	78	89	96	98	99	100		4	5	5
14	28	52	72	85	93	97	99	100		4	5	6
16	25	47	66	80	90	95	98	99	100	4	5	6
18	22	43	61	76	86	93	97	98	99	5	6	7
20	20	39	57	71	82	90	95	98	99	5	6	7

the University of Lancaster Library corresponds closely to this ideal situation; consequently for a period of two weeks during May 1967 all requests were examined. Satisfied requests were already being recorded on the date labels in each item: the date stamped recorded the day of issue, and its position on the date-label the loan period within that day. Arrangements were made for the library staff to note briefly on a piece of paper the details of each request which was not immediately satisfied. Users are unlikely to have known in advance whether or not an item would be available, since it is not normally possible for them to see if there is still a copy of a desired item on the shelves; however, we cannot rule out the possibility that one user may occasionally have learned from another that all copies were already on loan. To the best of our knowledge none of the users was aware that data concerning their requests was being collected.

During these two weeks 2010 requests were recorded, and the immediate availability rate for the collection as a whole was established as 90 per cent. We then decided to compare this figure with the readers' subjective assessment of the level of availability. A brief questionnaire was distributed bearing a numbered scale from 0 (also marked "Never") to 10 (also marked "Always"). A consensus of opinion emerged indicating a subjectively perceived 70 per cent availability compared with the recorded 90 per cent — a salutary reminder that opinion is a poor substitute for fact.

A small random sample of twenty-five titles was taken from the collected data and the distribution of request frequency examined. Some patterns emerged more than once. For example, more than one title had been used once in one loan period and not at all in the remaining forty-three loan periods. Thirteen different patterns of use emerged: in each case the total number of requests occurring during the fortnight was divided by the number of loan periods during the survey (forty-four) in order to produce an average request rate per loan period for each title. The Poisson distribution was then used to predict a pattern of requests for each average request rate. Table II shows the comparison between observed and predicted distributions. The level of agreement is encouraging; for five of the thirteen patterns, representing seventeen of the twenty-five titles, the degree of matching could not have happened by chance more than five times in one hundred. The remaining patterns are not statistically significant, but nevertheless add to the overall impression of an adequate match between theory and practice. In view of this similarity, we feel that the use of the Poisson distribution for this purpose is justified.

5. Planning for Future Demand

We have demonstrated how a simple table could be produced to show the minimum number of copies required for different levels of availability and for various average request rates. If it is known in advance what the average request rate will be, then it is a very simple matter to discover how many copies will be needed to maintain any desired level of availability. Unfortunately,

TABLE II

COMPARISON OF OBSERVED AND PREDICTED REQUESTS PATTERNS

R	O	P	O	P	O	P	O	P	O	P
0	15	14.12	23	24.37	26	28.57	29	29.90	35	33.50
1	13	16.05	16	14.40	17	12.34	13	11.55	7	9.14
2	11	9.12	5	4.25	1	2.66	2	2.23	1	1.25
3	5	3.45	0	0.84	0	0.38	0	0.29	1	0.11
4	0	0.98	0	0.12	0	0.04	0	0.03	0	0.008
5	0	0.22	0	0.01	—	—	—	—	—	—
6	0	0.04	—	—	—	—	—	—	—	—
7	0	0.007	—	—	—	—	—	—	—	—
	Chi-sq.: 2.967		Chi-sq: 1.362		Chi-sq: 3.457		Chi-sq: 0.548		Chi-sq: 7.566	
	DF: 7		DF: 5		DF: 4		DF: 4		DF: 4	
0	31	32.74	33	32.74	34	35.05	40	40.18	37	35.86
1	13	9.67	9	9.67	10	7.97	4	3.65	5	7.34
2	0	1.43	2	1.43	0	0.90	0	0.17	2	0.75
3	0	0.14	0	0.14	0	0.07	0	0.005	0	0.05
4	0	0.01	0	0.01	—	—	—	—	—	—
	Chi-sq: 2.816		Chi-sq: 0.428		Chi-sq: 1.524		Chi-sq: 0.205		Chi-sq: 2.913	
	DF: 4		DF: 4		DF: 3		DF: 3		DF: 3	
0	43	43.01	42	42.04	42	41.10				
1	1	0.98	2	1.91	1	2.80				
2	0	0.01	0	0.04	1	0.10				
	Chi-sq: 0.012		Chi-sq: 0.048		Chi-sq: 9.742					
	DF: 2		DF: 2		DF: 2					

R = No. of requests
O = Observed frequency
P = Frequency predicted by the Poisson distribution

it may not be easy to predict the average request rate for any given title.

The information which could normally be made available to the librarian is the number of students who have been advised to read an item and the span of time during which they are all expected to read it (e.g. the date by which an essay should be completed). If b students request an item once only during a period of time containing p loan periods, then the request rate can be written

$$r = \frac{b}{p}$$

It would be rash, however, to assume that each item will in fact be requested once and once only by each student. Some may not request it at all because they have access to another copy elsewhere, or because they simply do not bother. Others may make more than one request because one borrowing was insufficient or because the book was not available when first requested. These conflicting tendencies might cancel each other out but it may be better to assume that

$$r = x . \frac{b}{p}$$

where x is a quantity, a parameter, which corresponds to this variation in user behaviour. Further investigation might reveal that the value of x tended to remain constant for a particular group of students, or for a particular course, or even for a particular title — but such an investigation would be laborious. In any case the people most closely concerned — the Service Desk staff and the teaching staff — should be able to estimate from their experience the number of requests for each item.

The main difficulty in the use of this approach for planning for future demand lies in predicting the average request rate. It is necessary, therefore, to explore the consequences of inaccurate prediction.

For example, if the average request rate is expected to be between 0.5 and 1.5 requests per loan period, then we can examine the likely consequences of different decisions about the number of copies to be provided. (See Table III.)

TABLE III

Average request rate	Availability resulting from the provision of			
	1	2	3	4 copies
	(%)	(%)	(%)	(%)
0.5	78.7	96.7	99.6	99.96
1.5	51.8	81.3	94.0	98.4

Similarly, if the request rate could only be established as lying between two and four per loan period, then at least we should have the information in Table IV.

TABLE IV

Average request rate	Availability resulting from the provision of			
	3	4	5	6 copies
	(%)	(%)	(%)	(%)
2	89.1	96.2	98.9	99.7
4	66.3	80.5	89.7	95.1

6. Adjusting Existing Provision

The librarian may well wonder whether there are sufficient copies of a given item and, if not, how many additional copies there ought to be.

The number of satisfied requests for a given title is normally easy to discover from date labels or issue records, but he also needs to know the number of unsatisfied requests before he can establish the availability rate. If he considers that this is too low, then he has to decide how many additional copies are required. This can easily be done by reference to a table such as Table I, provided that he knows the average request rate (defined as the total number of requests during a given span of time). Again he needs to measure, or at least estimate, the number of unsatisfied requests.

At the collection actually studied, it happened to be easy to record unsatisfied requests once it had been decided to do so. Nevertheless, the situation might well arise, at Lancaster or elsewhere, in which data on unsatisfied requests was needed retrospectively for a period during which it had not been collected; in different circumstances it may not be practicable to record the number of unsatisfied requests at all. In such cases it is necessary to rely on an estimate.

7. Estimating the Request Rate from the Number of Satisfied Requests Alone

Assuming that data on satisfied requests is available, the problem of estimating the total number of requests in any period of time (and hence the request rate) is in the following form: let us imagine the case where there are three copies of a book and that we have tabulated the data on satisfied requests. If no requests were made during a loan period then there can have been no satisfied requests, and we know from our data how often this has happened. Similarly, when one or two requests were made, and there are three copies, then all requests will have been satisfied and, again, we know the frequency of this occurrence. So far we may be confident that the total number of requests and the number of satisfied requests were the same; but the trouble begins with the remaining loan periods in which three satisfied requests have been recorded. We only know that *at least* three requests were made; we do not know on how many of these occasions there were four or more. Yet this is the crucial information: three requests could be satisfied, but if there were more, then at least one request must have gone unsatisfied. What we really need to know is the number of occasions upon which four, five, six, etc., requests were made.

However, if we are justified in assuming that, for any given item, the fluctuations in the number of requests in individual loan periods correspond to the type of fluctuations predicted by the Poisson distribution, it is possible to estimate from the incomplete data which we have, what the average request rate is most likely to have been. Furthermore it is also possible to gain an impression of the amount of confidence we are entitled to place in the answer.

Since the available data includes only satisfied requests, it can be tabulated as in Table V where n is the number of copies, i.e. we can only observe the number of occasions f_n when n or *more* requests were made.

TABLE V

No. of requests per loan period	Observed frequency
0	f_0
1	f_1
2	f_2
.	.
.	.
.	.
$n-1$	f_{n-1}
$\geqslant n$	f_n

If we assume that in any given loan period the actual number of requests will follow a Poisson distribution, then the likelihood of observing the tabulated data is given by

$$L = \prod_{s=0}^{n-1} \left(\frac{e^{-r}r^s}{s!} \right)^{f_s} \cdot \left[1 - \sum_{s=0}^{n-1} \frac{e^{-r}r^s}{s!} \right]^{f_n}$$

$$\therefore \log L = \sum_{s=0}^{n-1} f_s \log \left(\frac{e^{-r}r^s}{s!} \right) + f_n \log \left(1 - \sum_{s=0}^{n-1} \frac{e^{-r}r^s}{s!} \right)$$

If we take a series of possible values of r, the request rate, then the corresponding values of L will indicate which value of r (the average request rate) is most likely, and will also give some indication of the extent to which this value is more likely than other possible values. An example is given in Table VI, where the likelihood function, L, shows a peak, albeit a rather flat one, corresponding to a request rate of 0.39. We therefore conclude that 0.39 is the request rate most likely to result in the data observed. However, since this method was not necessary at Lancaster, its reliability has not been examined.

It would also seem reasonable to attempt to apply this approach to the special case of gross underprovision (when all copies are borrowed every loan period): What

TABLE VI

Data	
No. of requests per loan period	Observed frequency
0	29
1	13
$\geqslant 2$	2
Result	
r	Log L
0.35	−34.39303
0.37	−34.31419
→0.39	−34.28505←
0.41	−34.30062
0.43	−34.35666

is the lowest request rate which would produce this effect? Consequently, what is the lowest number of additional copies required?

In this special case (see example in Table VII) the likelihood function has no peak but rises to the limit of 1 and, therefore, log L to 0, as the postulated request rate rises. However, by adopting some reasonable threshold, one can at least estimate the lowest request rate likely to have produced this effect. From the data given in Table VII it would seem reasonable to conclude that, in this hypothetical example, the request rate is likely to have been at least six requests per loan period and that the number of copies provided should be increased accordingly.

7. Further Applications

The entire analysis has been concerned with individual items, and the problem has been regarded as one of ensuring that there is sufficient duplication for each item to reach a specified level of availability. A librarian might wish to tackle rather different problems, and the approach outlined in this report could still be useful. For example, if he cannot afford to bring all titles in his stock up to a specified level of availability, then his

TABLE VII

Data	
No. of requests per loan period	Observed frequency
0	0
1	0
$\geqslant 2$	44
Result	
r	Log L
2	−22.91898
4	−4.22604
6	−0.77016
8	−0.13304
10	−0.02198

problem becomes one of selecting the titles of which extra copies will bring the greatest benefit to readers. Since the individual items are normally considered separately, the consequences of buying additional copies of any two or more items can be compared, so that the final selection results in a greater increase in satisfied requests than any other possible selection.

Although the analysis has been concerned with individual titles, it is important to remember that no distinction is made between items having the same average request rate. Consequently, the items in a given collection can be grouped according to their request rates. By considering each group separately and then aggregating the results, it would be possible to answer such questions as: What would be the effect on the collection as a whole of a change in the length of loan period?

8. Conclusions

We originally began to examine the Short Loan Collection at the University of Lancaster Library with two aims: Firstly, how well was it working? Secondly, how far could a quantitative approach be helpful in taking routine decisions about the number of copies to be provided?

When we realized that the unsatisfied requests could conveniently be recorded, the availability rate was determined and discovered to be somewhat higher than we or the readers had subjectively expected. The next stage was to develop a mathematical relationship for individual items, between

    i. The number of requests,
    ii. The loan periods,
    iii. The number of copies, and
    iv. The degree of immediate availability, which had been chosen as the standard of service.

The number of requests and the number of loan periods were related to produce an average request rate. The assumption was made, and subsequently tested, that the Poisson distribution could justifiably be used to relate the average request rate to the number of copies and the degree of availability likely to be achieved. Consequently a table has been produced which can be used in a predictive manner insofar as the request rate itself can be predicted. It can also be used in a corrective manner, but, of course, any corrective action would have to be taken promptly else the circumstances might change.

In order to assist the librarian a method of estimating the average request rate from incomplete data was devised. No attempt has been made to indicate what level of availability the librarian ought to endeavour to achieve; nor has a serious attempt yet been made to isolate and relate the factors determining the demand for library services; these factors might very well include the level of availability achieved. The analytical approach described in this paper appears to be adequate for the circumstances investigated, but it might not be suitable in more complex situations.

The main conclusions are clear. A mathematical relationship between the factors concerned can indeed be established. It should be stressed that there is nothing specific to libraries in this relationship. It, and the availability tables, would apply in any kind of service situation where items are borrowed, or used temporarily, if the same assumptions can be made. The results displayed in Table I illustrate the most important aspect of duplication: that the marginal benefit of adding an additional copy falls off steadily as the level of availability rises. Conversely, as the level of availability rises, so the cost of achieving an extra 5 per cent availability also rises. Doubling the number of copies will not double the availability achieved.

References

1. D. J. URQUHART and R. M. BUNN. *J. Docum.*, 1959, **15,** 21.
2. P. M. MORSE. *Library Effectiveness; A Systems Approach*. M.I.T. Press, Cambridge, Mass. (1968).

19 Bradford's Law Applied to the Maintenance of Library Collections

WILLIAM GOFFMAN
THOMAS G. MORRIS

In a recent article[1], B. C. Brookes pointed out that Bradford's law of dispersion "seems to offer the only means discernible at present of reducing the present quantitative untidiness of scientific documentation, information systems and library services to a more orderly state of affairs capable of being rationally and economically planned and organized." Much of this untidiness and disorderliness is the result of an inability to determine the minimum size or lower limits of a useful collection of information sources. In this communication we report on an application of Bradford's law to the maintenance of a dynamic library collection through the establishment of such lower limits; the upper limits being a function of budget reach their own level by natural processes. We shall limit our discussion to the acquisition of periodicals in a medical library although the method should be equally applicable to most scientific libraries.

Bradford's law of dispersion[2] states that if the journals containing articles on a given subject are arranged in descending order of the number of articles they carried on the subject, then successive zones of periodicals containing the same number of articles on the subject forms the simple geometric series $1:n:n^2: \ldots \ldots$.

Bradford called the first such zone the nucleus of periodicals particularly devoted to the given subject. Clearly, the nucleus is arbitrarily defined since it depends upon the number of articles chosen to effect the partitioning of the periodicals into zones. Hence, Bradford's law, although an interesting phenomenon was of little practical use. It has been shown, however, that there exists a minimal nucleus in the sense of Bradford[3]. That is, a core of journals can be separated from the top of an ordered list of periodicals dealing with a given subject which represents the most significant information sources for that field. This minimal nucleus, moreover, does not necessarily consist of only the most productive periodical but may contain any number of journals depending upon the extent of dispersion of the subject's literature among the many periodicals. Thus, it is possible to set lower bounds on the number of journals which must be contained in a collection devoted to a given subject.

1. Formulation of an Acquisitions Policy

Brookes has also pointed out[1] that Bradford's law "can be expected to arise when selection is made of items, characterized by some common element, which are all equally open to selection for an equal period and subject to the 'success-breeds-success' mechanism". Hence, Bradford's law should apply to the use of periodicals in a library as well as to the dispersion of articles among journals. These are both acquisitions processes, namely processes of acquiring items relevant to some need by means of selection.

Table I shows the distribution of journal use in the Allen Memorial Medical Library, Cleveland, Ohio during its peak month of March, 1968.

TABLE I

JOURNAL CIRCULATION FOR MARCH 1968

No. of Journals	Circulation Per Journal
1	18
1	12
2	11
1	10
3	9
7	8
4	7
12	6
15	5
28	4
36	3
75	2
186	1

Use is here defined as circulation. Clearly, Bradford's law holds for this distribution. Table II shows the minimal nucleus and its successive zones of periodicals.

TABLE II

MINIMAL NUCLEUS OF JOURNALS CIRCULATING IN MARCH 1968

Zone	Times Circulated	No. of Journals	Bradford Contant (n)
1	113	11	—
2	108	16	1.5
3	107	21	1.3
4	110	28	1.3
5	110	38	1.4
6	110	55	1.4
7	109	93	1.7
8	109	109	1.2
	876	371	Average 1.4

The minimal nucleus of journals circulated during March, 1968 consisted of eleven titles that were borrowed 113 times, followed by sixteen periodicals circulating 108 times, twenty-one journals 107 times and so on. Consequently, successive zones of periodicals circulating about the same number of times formed the approximate

geometric series $1:(1.4):(1.4)^2: \ldots :(1.4)^7$. It is interesting to note that half the circulation for March was accounted for by only 76 journals.

Assuming that journal circulation in this library obeys Bradford's law, as seems to be the case, the following acquisitions policy can be formulated. In establishing such a policy it is important to base the selection of journals on expected future demand. Hence,

1. First establish the minimal nucleus and its successive zones of periodical circulation at various successive time intervals. The length of these intervals will vary from library to library with the density of use. Some libraries may compute the nucleus each month, others every three months and so forth. This is necessary since the nucleus may vary with time.

2. On the basis of these observations, establish an "epidemic curve", i.e., the rate of change of circulation, for each periodical circulating in the library.

3. Predict the expected circulation on the basis of these "epidemic curves", at some appropriate future date, say a year in advance.

4. The expected minimal nucleus should belong to the minimal collection in the library's inventory at that point in time.

As a safety factor is may be a good policy for the library not to delete a given journal from its collection until its predicted decline in circulation is verified by fact.

If the budget allows, it may be in the library's interest to include those periodicals which are of greatest interest to its best customers, provided they already do not appear in the minimal nucleus of circulating journals. Table III shows the distribution of users of journals in the Allen Library for the peak month of March, 1968 and Table IV shows the minimal nucleus and its successive zones of users during this time period.

Use is again defined as circulation. The user distribution for March, 1968 obeys Bradford's law whence the

TABLE III

DISTRIBUTION OF USERS FOR MARCH 1968

No. of Users	Circulation Per User
2	12
2	10
2	9
9	8
3	7
6	6
18	5
29	4
44	3
68	2
211	1

TABLE IV

MINIMAL NUCLEUS OF USERS FOR MARCH 1968

Zone	Circulation	No. of Users	Bradford Constant (n)
1	118	13	—
2	108	18	1.4
3	107	24	1.3
4	109	31	1.3
5	109	40	1.3
6	108	54	1.4
7	108	105	1.9
8	109	109	1.1
	876	394	Average 1.4

minimal nucleus of users consisted of thirteen individuals who borrowed journals 118 times, followed by eighteen individuals using periodicals 108 times, twenty-four individuals with 107 and so on. Thus, successive zones of users borrowing about the same number of journals formed the geometric series $1:(1.4):(1.4)^2: \ldots :(1.4)^7$. We note that about half of the circulation is accounted for by only 86 users. We can thus:

1. Establish the minimal nucleus of users of the library.
2. Determine the areas of interest of the members of this nucleus, in terms of Index Medicus subject headings. For medical researchers this can be done by selecting the headings from Index Medicus under which their most recent publications have been indexed. For clinicians, residents and interns this may be done by interest profiles.
3. Establish the minimal nucleus for each subject heading represented by user nucleus. This is done by applying Bradford's law to the distribution of articles among journals under each of the subject headings.
4. The totality of such minimal nuclei should then be added to the library's collection.

That the distribution of articles among journals as indexed in the Index Medicus satisfies Bradford's law is shown in Tables V and VI which give the distribution of articles and minimal nucleus of journals for the subject heading Transplantation-Immunology in Index Medicus for the years 1965–1968.

The minimal nucleus for transplantation-immunology, not surprisingly, consists of the single periodical TRANSPLANTATION, the second zone contains the journals NATURE and SURG FORUM, the third ANN NY ACAD SCI, PROC SOC EXP BIOL MED and J IMMUNOLOGY and so on.

Because it has been shown that Bradford's law applies to a portion of a literature as well as its totality[3], any part of the transplantation-immunology literature could

TABLE V

DISTRIBUTION OF ARTICLES UNDER HEADING
TRANSPLANTATION-IMMUNOLOGY

Journals	Articles Per Journal
1	124
1	71
1	66
1	54
1	40
1	28
1	25
1	24
1	22
1	19
1	17
3	15
1	13
2	12
1	10
6	9
4	8
6	7
1	6
9	5
19	4
20	3
34	2
155	1

TABLE VI

MINIMAL NUCLEUS FOR TRANSPLANTATION-IMMUNOLOGY
1965–1968

Zone	Articles	Journals	Bradford Constant (n)
1	124	1	—
2	137	2	2.0
3	122	3	1.5
4	122	6	2.0
5	122	11	1.8
6	129	20	1.8
7	126	35	1.8
8	118	74	2.1
9	120	120	1.8
	1120	272	Average 1.8

have been chosen for this experiment. In practice it would be best to take the most recent publications in establishing the minimal nucleus for a given field.

In summary, it has been shown that the distributions of both circulating periodicals and their users in a medical library appear to obey Bradford's law. Hence, a smallest core of periodicals which must belong to the library's collection can be defined. This core should consist of the minimal nucleus of circulating journals plus the minimal nuclei of periodicals devoted to the subjects of most interest to the library's nucleus of users. As the budget allows, successive zones of periodicals corresponding to circulation and user interest can be added. As a result, the library collection can be maintained in an orderly and viable state thus providing its patrons with the most potentially useable materials for the funds at its disposal.

References

1. BROOKES, B. C., *Nature,* 224, 953 (1969).
2. BRADFORD, S. C., *Documentation* (Crosby Lockwood, London, 1948).
3. GOFFMAN, W. and WARREN, K. S., *Nature,* 221, 1205 (1969).

Chapter Six
Representation
of
Information

Of all problem areas in information science, the area associated with representation of information has produced the largest number of investigations; even at a glance, the size of this section of the book supports this fact. It is not surprising, since the area itself encompasses many levels, many fragmented, isolated aspects or sub-areas — all of which can be approached from many viewpoints. The amount of attention given this one area, however, was disproportionate to the number and magnitude of other problem areas in the field of information science as a whole. Not that the general area of representation of information is an insignificant one. On the contrary, it is highly important, because it incorporates or affects most, if not all, other areas of concern. But neither is it the only problem area nor the only one to be approached in isolation.

The prominence given to representation of information in information science can be directly attributed to assumptions made in the practice of information systems over the ages. The basic assumption can be paraphrased as follows: given a "good" scheme for representing information, the problem of providing the information to users is practically solved, and everything else will follow the scheme well — the fact is that it often does. Thus, in libraries, the concern is with classification, subject headings, and cataloging; in information retrieval systems, with indexing languages and indexing; in computer-based systems, with programming languages and coding; and in signal transmission systems, with coding.

Not unlike many other fields which tended to be identified through works in one major area of effort, for a while information science was almost synonymous with works on information representation or, even more limited, with the works on indexing. Only in the last few years has attention been focused on other areas, mostly because of the valiant efforts of a relatively small number of investigators.

The seven sections of this chapter may suggest that the works are not really connected or closely related. However, in one way or another, all of the selections deal with the general problem of representing information, regardless of their approach, subject, or emphasis. In the first section, "Structure of Languages," works are presented that take an overall view of languages. Gross (Article 20) discussed the syntactic structure of natural languages in terms of models possibly applicable to purposes of information science. This work, closely related to several other modern linguistic efforts (such as those stemming from Chomsky), indicates the role which linguistic studies can have in the general framework of information science.

Furthermore, linguistics is related to information science through semantic studies (such as Articles 22 and 23) and statistical studies on the behavior of words (e.g., Article 21). Booth (Article 21) reviewed the various empirical laws on the statistical occurrences of words in texts and arrived at a law of his own. Studies such as this one could serve as a base for applied and practical studies on indexing and other processes by which information is represented.

Doyle (Article 22) investigated and proposed methods by which semantic relations between words in texts may be discerned. While the semantic studies in Chapter One deal more with the basic properties of meaning, Doyle addressed himself to the semantic interrelation between words in the text as processed within a retrieval system. In the last article of this section, Feldman and Rovner (Article 23) presented the structure of a computer programming language suitable for associative processing.

Other works which would fall within the first section would include similar articles on syntactic and word structure of languages and numerous works from the area of computer science on programming languages, pattern recognition, artificial intelligence, structure of algorithms suitable for computer processing, etc.

The next two sections (B and C) are closely related. They deal with indexing as a major area of investigation in information science. Section B deals with problems of the organization of terminology. In studying the vocabularies of indexing languages, Moss (Article 24) took a philosophical approach; Gotlieb and Kumer (Article 25) introduced the notion of and the techniques for an indexing vocabulary based on semantic (rather than pure statistical) association; and Zunde and Slamecka (Article 26) formalized the function of optimum distribution of index terms by postings. In the same section would belong works dealing with the study of thesauri, subject headings, and other sets of terminological structures employed for tagging information.

Section C deals with studies, each of which aims to obtain some reasonable set of index terms for documents by automatic means, employing and exploiting the association of words in texts. Jones and Curtice (Article 27) reviewed the properties of existing association measures and provided a framework for comparison. Maron and Kuhns (Article 28), in an article which already has become a classic, took an overall view of the information retrieval problem and proposed probabilistic (associative) measures for indexing. Lesk (Article 29) studied and tested experimentally the application of various association parameters and procedures within the confines of a highly developed laboratory. In many ways O'Connor (Article 30), in his experimental study, comparing automatic and manual assignment of index terms illuminated the basic problems of automatic indexing.

Articles in Section D deal with the exploitation of citations as a special property by which scientific papers are linked. As such, these works are closely related to articles in Chapter 2, describing the behavior of literature. Margolis (Article 31) critically examined the dynamic processes of citation from the point of view of citation indexing. Martyn (Article 32) compared the retrieval process from citation and subject indexing. The works on bibliographic coupling clearly would belong to this section.

Section E is devoted to abstracting, one of the most popular means for representing information, but one that is not investigated a great deal. Borko and Chatman (Article 33), arrived at a set of criteria which can serve as qualitative measures for comparing or evaluating abstracts. Edmunson (Article 34) presented methods and measures suitable for automatic extracting from texts of sentences which could serve as an abstract.

The section on classification and coding is meagerly represented. The origins of work in the area of classification can be traced to Greek philosophers. Over the centuries, the organization of information collections and stores has been firmly based on some principle of classification. The research on classification was and continues largely to be implanted in philosophy. It is of interest to note that, although the modern information systems explicitly abandoned classification, they still implicitly deal in classification — witness the internal structure of modern thesauri, for instance. The articles selected in this section represent some approaches to and viewpoints of classification and coding as they pertain to information science. Wahlin (Article 35) reviews succinctly and critically a number of classification schemes from the point of view of their application in information systems. Borko and Bernick (Article 36) present experimental work on automatic classification. Buck (Article 37) offers an encoding scheme which exhibits quite original features.

When the literature of information science is reviewed, it becomes obvious that the area of classification eludes serious investigations, and the area of encoding is geared mainly to the practical aspects of computer-manipulated codes. Intuitively, it would seem that both areas warrant more attention, but classification, in particular, seems in need of new and fresh approaches. By application of mathematics highly interesting theories of classification are being developed in Russia, (see their journal Scientific and Technical Information).

The last section (G) in the present chapter is devoted to another important, but neglected, area of study, that of bibliographic description and representation. This area has been and still is almost entirely within the realm of library science. Efforts to automate bibliographic representations in large collections have uncovered a staggering array of conceptual rather than merely technical problems, which the prescriptive approach used in the past can no longer adequately handle. It is suggested here that the problems associated with the structure of bibliographic representations are worthy of both applied and basic studies. Vickery (Article 38) enumerates a series of problems encountered in the automation of bibliographic records, suggesting the areas that require resolution. Lubetzky and Hayes (Article 39) describe the important role of bibliographic representation in information systems.

The selections in this chapter can be related to many efforts, both within and outside the field of information science: in the fields of linguistics, computer science, signaling, library science, information retrieval, and even philosophy. It seems that, in the area of information representation, numerous works in information science are strongly influenced by other disciplines and by practical information systems, too. But it also seems that the real theoretical and experimental work has hardly begun.

A. Structure
of
Languages

20 On the Equivalence of Models of Language Used in the Fields of Mechanical Translation and Information Retrieval

MAURICE GROSS
Information Storage & Retrieval
Vol. 2, No. 1, April, 1964

The majority of MT and IR projects have been primarily concerned with the construction of grammars and computer programs aiming to produce syntactic analyses for the sentences of a given natural language.

In certain cases, the grammar and the recognition routine are completely amalgamated into a single program and the grammatical information is no longer available for a program that would synthesize sentences. The interest of synthesizing sentences has been shown, synthesis by the output of a transfer grammar, Yngve [5], or synthesis at random, Yngve [6]. This sort of grammar cannot pretend to hold for models of languages, unless one admits that human beings use alternatively two disjoint devices; one for reading, the other for writing; and probably two others, one for hearing, the other for speaking. One would have to construct four types of corresponding devices for each language in order to translate and to retrieve information automatically.

Rather frequent are the cases where the grammar is neutral between the programs of analysis and synthesis; these grammars following Chomsky [7] [8], we will call generative grammars.

We shall now make more precise the concepts of grammar and language, and examine the requirements a grammar has to meet [9].

We consider the finite set $V = [a_i| \ 0 \leqslant i \leqslant D]$ V is called vocabulary, the a_i's are words, a_o is the null word. On V the operation of concatenation defines the set $C(V)$ of strings on V, any finite sequence of words $T = a_{i1} \ a_{i2} \ \ldots \ a_{ik}$ with $0 \leqslant i_1, \ i_2 \ \ldots \ i_k \leqslant D$ is a string on V, $C(V)$ is a free monoid whose generators are the a_i's.

(1) A subset L of $C(V)$ is called a language on $V : L \subset C(V)$.

(2) A string S, such that $S \in L$, is a sentence of the language L.

(3) A finite set of finite rules which characterize all and only the sentences of L, is called a grammar of L. (Productions of a combinatorial system: Davis [32].)

(4) Two grammars are equivalent if they characterize the same language L.

This abstract and most general model is justified empirically as follows:

The words (or morphemes) of a natural language L form a finite set, i.e. the vocabulary or lexicon V of the language L.

Certain strings on V are clearly understood by speakers of L as sentences of L, others are clearly recognized as nonsentences, so L is a proper subset of $C(V)$.

Many facts show that natural languages have to be

considered as infinite. The linguistic operation of conjunction can be repeated indefinitely, the same thing for the embedding of relative clauses as in the sentence: {*the rat* [*the cat* (*the dog chased*) *killed*] *ate the malt*}. Many other devices of nesting and embedding exist in all natural languages and there is no linguistic motivation which would allow a limit on the number of possible recursions.

We wish to construct a grammar for a natural language L, that considered abstractly enumerates (generates) the sentences of the language L, and associated with a recognition routine it recognizes effectively the sentences of L.

The device so far described is a normative device which simply tells whether or not a string on V is a sentence of L; equivalently, it is the characteristic function of L. This minimum requirement of separating sentences from non sentences is a main step in our construction. The construction of this normative grammar requires the use of the total grammatical information inherent in L, and under these conditions it should be natural to use this same information in order to give as a by-product a description of the organization of a sentence S_1 in L. This can be done simply be keeping track of the grammar rules that have been involved in the analysis of S_1. This particular ordered set of rules is called the derivation of S_1. This by-product is of primary importance; it is a model for the understanding of L by its speakers (Chomsky [9], Tesnière [10]); parallelly any MT or IR realization requires the machine to have a deep understanding of the texts to be processed. Furthermore a normative device would not tell whether a sentence is ambiguous or not; the only way to describe the different interpretations assigned to an ambiguous sentence is to give them different descriptions.

The basic requirements for a formalized description of natural languages, almost trivial in the sense that they make practically no restrictions on the forms of grammars and languages, do not seem to have been widely recognized in the fields of MT and IR, nevertheless they are always unconsciously accepted.

Chomsky [11, 8, 12] has studied a large variety of linguistic and formal constraints that one can reasonably put on the structure of grammars. The grammars so constrained range from finite-state grammars to the device described above, which can be viewed as arbitrary Turing Machine.

These grammars in general meet a supplementary requirement; each derivation of a sentence has to provide a particular type of structural description which takes the form of simple trees or, equivalently of parenthesized expressions; both subtrees and parentheses are labelled, i.e. carry grammatical information. Certain types of grammar have been proved inadequate because of their inability to provide a structural description for the sentences they characterize (type 1 grammars in Chomsky [8]).

Many authors in the field of MT and IR start from the postulates:

(1) A grammar is to be put, together with a recognition routine, into the memory of an electronic digital computer.
(2) The result of the analysis of a sentence is to be given in the form of a structural description.

In order to minimize computing time and memory space, further constraints were devised aiming to obtain efficient recognition routines. In general these constraints were put on the structural description and much more attention has been paid to giving a rigorous definition of the structural description than to the definition of a grammar rule. Discussions of this topic can be found in Hays [2], Lecerf [3] and Plath [13]. The nature of grammatical rules is never emphasized and often the structure of the rules is not even mentioned. Nevertheless the logical priority order of the operations is the following:

— the recognition routine traces a derivation of a sentence S according to the grammar.

— the derivation of S provides a structural description of S. The structural descriptions generally have a simple form, that of a tree terminating in the linear sequence of the words of S. These trees (or associated parenthesized expressions) are unlabelled in [2], [3] and [13]. Yngve uses a complex tree with labelled nodes corresponding to well-defined rules of grammar. Other structures than trees could be used [10] in order to increase the amount of information displayed in the structural description. The question of how much information is necessary in the structural description of a given sentence in order to process it automatically (translation or storage and matching of information), has never been studied. Many authors look for a minimization of this information, which is quite unreasonable given the present status of the art; our guess is that the total amount of information available in any formalized system for a sentence S will never be sufficient for a completely mechanized processing of S and that these minimal structural descriptions will have to be considerably enriched. In Section 6 we will show that for many sentences one tree is not sufficient to describe relations between words.

Among the simple models which have been or are still used, we will quote:

Immediate constituent analysis models as developed in [7], [14], [15] and [16] where two substrings B and C of a sentence S can form a larger unit A of S only if they are contiguous ($A = BC$).

Categorical grammars developed by Bar-Hillel where categories of substrings are defined by means of the basic categories (Noun, Sentence) and of the immediate left or right environment.

Predictive Analysis models ([17], [18], [19]) where

the grammars are built such that the recognition routine can use a pushdown storage, which is a convenient programming tool.

Dependency and projective grammars developed respectively by Hays [20] and Lecerf [3], which lead to the simple analysis programs their authors have described.

1. Chomsky's Context-Free Languages*

The grammars of the most general type we have described in the previous section can be viewed as arbitrary Turing Machines or equivalently [32] as combinatorial systems (Semi-Thue Systems) where the sentences are derived from an axiom S by the means of a finite set of rewriting rules (productions): $\varphi \rightarrow \psi$.

The sentences are defined on the terminal vocabulary V_T as in Section 1. The strings φ, ψ are defined on a vocabulary $V = V_N U V_T$, where V_N is the non-terminal vocabulary which includes an initial symbol S meaning sentence.

The arrow between φ and ψ is to be interpreted as 'is rewritten'.

A context-free grammar is a finite set of rewriting rules $\varphi_i \rightarrow \psi_i$ *where* φ_i and ψ_i are strings on V such that:

φ_i is a single element of V_N
at least one φ_i is S
ψ_i is a finite string on V.

The language generated by a context-free grammar is called a context-free language.

Example
Grammar: $\begin{cases} S \rightarrow aSb \\ S \rightarrow c \end{cases}$

This grammar can generate (recognize) all and only the sentences of the type

$$\underbrace{a \ldots \ldots a}_{n \ times} \; c \; \underbrace{b \ldots \ldots b}_{n \ times}$$

noted $a^n \, c \, b^n$, for any n.

The sentence $aaa \, c \, bbb$ is obtained by the following steps:

$\begin{array}{lll} S & \Rightarrow & aSb \\ aSb & \Rightarrow & aaSbb \\ aaSbb & \Rightarrow & aaaSbbb \\ aaaSbbb & \Rightarrow & aaa \; c \; bbb \end{array}$ these four lines represent the derivation of the sentence.

The associated structural description is the following:

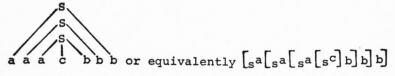 or equivalently $\left[_S a \left[_S a \left[_S a \left[_S c \right] b \right] b \right] b \right]$

*In the section we shall follow closely Chomsky [12] where a complete survey of these languages and their bibliography can be found.

The context-free grammars can be associated with restricted Turing Machines such as restricted infinite automata or equivalently, pushdown storage automata.

We give an informal description of the pushdown storage automaton (PDS automaton). For a more precise description see Chomsky [12].

The PDS automaton is composed of a control unit which has a finite set of possible internal configurations or states $\{S_j\}$ including an initial state S_o. The control unit is equipped with a reading head which scans the symbols a_i of a finite string written on successive squares of an input tape which is potentially infinite and can move, let us say, only from right to left.

$\{a_i | 1 \leqslant i \leqslant p\}$ is the set of symbols; $V_I = eU\{a_i\}$ is the input vocabulary which includes a null element e; the input strings are defined on V_I.

The control unit is equipped with a second head which allows it to read and write on a storage tape which can move in either direction and is also potentially infinite. It writes on successive squares of the storage tape strings on a vocabulary: $eU\{A_k | 1 \leqslant k \leqslant q\}$ which can include V_I. The storage tape vocabulary is $V_o = eU\{A_k\}U\sigma$, where e is the null element, and σ a special symbol which is never printed out.

The squares on which the strings are written are occupied simultaneously by both a_i (or A_k or σ) and e; either infinite side of the string can be thought of as filled with the blank symbol $\#$.

A situation Σ of the PDS automaton is a triplet $\Sigma = (a_i, S_j, A_k)$; if the PDS is in the situation Σ it is also in the situations where the elements a_i or A_k or both are replaced by e. There is an initial situation (a_i, S_o, σ) where the input head is positioned on the leftmost square of the input string, and the storage head on the symbol σ.

A computation starts in an initial situation and is directed by a finite number of instructions I, $\Sigma \rightarrow (S_r, x)$; when the automaton returns to the initial situation the first time, $x = \sigma$.

From the situation Σ, where the automaton is in state S_j, the automaton switches into the state S_r and moves its input tape one square left if the first element of Σ is an a_i, otherwise (for e) the tape is not moved.

If x is a string on $\{A_k\}$, it is printed on successive squares to the right of the square scanned on the storage tape, and the latter is moved $\lambda \, (x)$ (length of x) squares to the left.

If $x = \sigma$ the storage tape is moved one square right, nothing is printed and the square A_k previously scanned is replaced by the blank symbol $\#$.

If $x = e$ the storage tape undergoes no modification. After an instruction I has been carried out, the automaton is in the new situation Σ' whose first element is the symbol of the input string now being scanned, the second element is S_r, the third element can be either the same A_k if $x = e$ or A_m, if $x = A_m$, or if $x = \sigma$, the rightmost symbol of A_k written on the storage tape. If in this new situation Σ' a new instruction I' can be applied (i.e. there is an I' whose left member is Σ'), the computation goes on, otherwise it is 'blocked'.

An input string is accepted by a PDS automaton if starting in an initial situation, it computes until on its first return to S_o it is in the situation $(\#, S_o, \#)$ the storage tape is blank, and the first blank is the one at the right of the input string (the latter has been completely scanned).

A set of strings on V_I accepted by a PDS automaton will be called a pushdown language.

We can define context-free grammars and pushdown automata on the same universal alphabet V_U; we then have the following theorem by Chomsky [12] and Schützenberger [33].

Theorem 1

The pushdown languages are exactly the context-free languages.

2. Equivalences of Languages

(1) The equivalence of context-free languages and immediate constituent languages has been proven by Chomsky [8]. He proved that for any context-free grammar there exists a grammar whose rules are all of the form $A \to BC$ or $A \to a$ where the capital letters (members of the nonterminal vocabulary) represent structures and the a's morphemes.

Sakaï's model is exactly the immediate constituent model. His grammar has rules of the form $BC = A$, his recognition routine builds, for a given sentence, all binary trees compatible with the grammar.

(2) The equivalence of Bar-Hillel's categorical grammars and context-free grammars is proved in [22].

(3) Theorem 1 proves the equivalence of the predictive analysis and the context-free analysis. The recognition routine described in Kuno and Oettinger can be schematized by PDS automaton of Section 2 in the following way: $\{a_i\}$ is identified with the set of syntactic word classes $\{s_j\}$ given by a dictionary; $\{A_k\}$ is identified with the set of predictions $P = \{P_i\}$. The symbol S, meaning sentence and π meaning period (end of sentence) are P_i's. The set I of instructions contains:

$$I_1 : (e, S_o, \sigma) \rightarrow (S_1, e)$$
$$I_2 : (e, S_1, e) \rightarrow (S_2, S)$$
$$I_3 : (s_j, S_2, P_k) \rightarrow (S_{PK}, \sigma)$$
$$I_4 : (e, S_{PK}, e) \rightarrow (S_2, x)$$
$$I_F : (s_j, S_2, \sigma) \rightarrow (S_o, \sigma)$$

The set of the states is $\{S_0, S_1, S_2, [S_{PK}|P_k \in P]\}$.
The device computes as follows:

I_1 and I_2 are initialization instructions; I_2 places on the storage tape the prediction S (sentence).

To I_3, I_4 corresponds the use of the grammar rules; P_k is the rightmost prediction on the storage tape; s_j is the syntactic class of the scanned word on the input tape. If s_j and P_k are compatible then by an I_3 the automaton switches into the state S_{PK} and erases P_k;

then by an I_4 it switches back into the state S_2 and prints a string x of predictions which is a function of P_k and s_j (x may be null).

I_F ends the computation, it comes after an I_3 where s_j was compatible with the 'bottom' prediction π (period); π was erased, then I_F applied and leaves the automaton in the situation $(\#, S_o, \#)$, where the storage tape is blank and the string accepted.

In a situation (e, S_{PK}, e) following a situation (s_j, S_2, P_k) there may be different possible strings x corresponding to a single pair (s_j, P_k); the automaton, which is non-deterministic in this case, will choose one at random; if its choices are right all along the computation, the input string will be accepted, if not the computation will block. These conventions do not affect the class of languages accepted by the automaton. Intuitively, an acceptable string may be rejected several times because of a wrong guess, but there exists a series of right guesses that will make the automaton accept this string.

The actual device gives as an output a syntactic role r_n for each s_j, where r_n provides a structural description; this does not affect the class of languages accepted by the PDS automaton.

The automaton described above is precisely one which was previously used for predictive analysis, where only one (so-called 'most probable') solution (acceptance) was looked for [23]. The new scheme [17] gives all possible solutions for an input sentence. It can be considered as a monitoring program which provides inputs for the PDS automaton described above and enumerates all possible computations the automaton has to do for every input string. If a sentence contains homographs then the corresponding input strings are enumerated and fed successively into the automaton; the latter instead of making a guess when in a non-deterministic situation, tries all of them; they are kept track of by the monitoring program; when a computation blocks, the storage tape (subpool) is discarded and a new computation is proposed to the automaton.

3. Dependency Languages

We will turn to the dependency grammars as defined in Hays [20]. The linguistic conception originated by Tesnière differs from that of Immediate Constituent Analysis; here the morphemes are connected in terms of the intuitive notions of governor and dependent:

Example

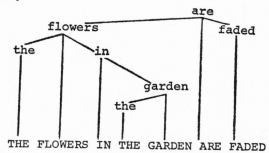

The two basic principles which determine the shape of the dependency model are quoted as follows: ([20] pp. 3, 4).

(1) Isolation of word order rules from agreement rules.

(2) Two occurrences (words) can be connected only if every intervening occurrence depends, directly or indirectly, on one or the other of them.

(1) Corresponds to the fact that recognition routine and grammar are separated.

(2) Defines both grammar and language. The grammar consists of a set of binary relations between a governor and a dependent. Two occurrences can be connected only if a certain contiguity holds: IN and GARDEN are connected only if the (direct) dependency GARDEN-THE holds; FLOWERS and ARE can be connected only if the indirect dependency IN-THE and the direct one FLOWERS-IN, hold.

Theorem

The dependency languages are exactly the context-free languages.

This theorem has been proven by Gaifman and independently by the author. Gaifman [34] has obtained a stronger result showing that the set of the dependency trees is a proper subset of the set of the context-free trees.

We give below the part of our proof which yields the following result; the dependency languages are context-free languages.

We now construct a PDS automaton of the type of Section 2 which accepts the dependency languages. Like the previous machine, it will not give a structural description of the analysed string but the restriction that the device be normative has no effect on the class of accepted strings.

Let $V = \{a_i\}\ i \neq 0$ be the vocabulary of the language. We will take as the input vocabulary of the automaton $V_I = V U e$.

Let $V_o = e U \{A_k\} U \sigma$, $k \neq 0$ be the output vocabulary where the A_k's are syntactic classes.

The set $\{I\}$ of instructions contains

$$I_1 : (e, s_o, \sigma) \rightarrow (S_D, e)$$
$$I_2 : (a_i, S_D, e) \rightarrow (S_D, A_i)$$
$$I_3 : (e, S_j, A_j) \rightarrow (S_j, \sigma)$$
$$I_4 : (e, S_j, A_k) \rightarrow (S_j, \sigma)$$
$$I_5 : (e, S_j, A_k) \rightarrow (S_k, \sigma)$$
$$I_6 : (e, S_j, e) \rightarrow (S_D, A_j)$$
$$I_7 : (e, S_s, \sigma) \rightarrow (S_o, \sigma)$$

The main operation of the computation is to connect a dependent to its governor; when this is done the dependent is erased from the storage.

I_1 initializes the computation.

I_2 is a dictionary look-up instruction; A_i a syntactic class of a_i is printed on the storage tape.

I_3 guesses that there is a connection to be made with the A_i immediately to the left of the scanned A_j, A_j is

erased but remembered since the automaton switches into a corresponding state S_j.

I_4 and I_5 compare the syntactic classes A_j and A_k: the automaton switches into either the state S_j or S_k corresponding to the fact that either A_j or A_k is governor. For a given pair (A_j, A_k) there is generally either an I_4 or an I_5 according as A_j or A_k is governor (in case the agreement is unambiguous). If they cannot be connected at all, the machine stops and the string is not accepted. If the next accessible A_r on the storage tape is to be connected with A_j or A_k then an instruction: $(e, S_j, A_r) \rightarrow (S, \sigma)$ or $(e, S_k, A_r) \rightarrow (S, \sigma)$ can be applied (either of these instructions can be an I_4 or an I_5). If the next accessible A_r is not to be connected with A_j or A_k then instructions I_6 and I_2 are applied. Before the automaton uses an instruction I_5 where it forgets A_j it has to make the guess that no dependent on A_j will come next from the input tape.

I_6; the automaton transfers A_j from its internal memory to the storage tape, it switches into state S_D where it will use an instruction I_2.

I_7 is a type of final instruction; from the state S_s where the automaton remembers the topmost governor A_s, it switches into the state S_o after the direct dependents of A_s have been connected (i.e. erased); the situation following I_7 will be $(\#, S_o, \#)$.

This non-deterministic automaton is equivalent to a recognition routine that would look for one 'most probable' solution. As in the case of the predictive analysis discussed above a monitoring program that would enumerate all possible computations would provide all possible solutions.*

Remarks

The instructions I_3 and I_4 (or I_5 for a governor A_j (or A_k)) remember this governor in the form S_j (or S_k). If this governor were modified by the agreement then it could be rewritten S_m with $m \neq j$ (or $m \neq k$). This would not change the structure of the automaton, nor would it modify the class of accepted languages.

It might be convenient for the diagramming of a sentence to think of null occurrences having a syntactic class; then their position could be restricted (between consecutive $A_j A_k$, for example) and in this case too a modification of the automaton shows that the class of accepted languages is the same.

In the case of I_5 we have the following indeterminacy about the guess the automaton has to make; if the guess is wrong, namely the next coming A_r can be connected to A_k; two cases are possible: (1) A_r can be connected to A_j the governor of A_k, then the computation may still follow a path which will lead to an acceptance (in

---

* The author has written in COMIT a recognition routine of this type. The automation above is a schematization of a part of the program which gave, after one scan from left to right, all the solutions compatible with the grammar.

this case the sentence was ambiguous), (2) A_r cannot be connected to A_j. The string will not be accepted since the content of the storage tape will never become blank.

The cases of conjunction, double conjunction and subordinate conjunctions in the 'secondary structure' require the automaton to have states where it remembers two syntactic types. For example, in the string acb a conjunction c depends on governor b on its right, and the item a equivalent to b and preceding c is marked dependent on c. We will have the following instructions:

$$(C_0) \quad (a, S_D, e) \;\rightarrow\; (S_D, A_a)$$

$$(C_1) \quad (c, S_D, e) \;\rightarrow\; (S_c, e)$$

$$(C_2) \quad (e, S_c, A_a) \;\rightarrow\; (S_c^a, \sigma)$$

$$(C_3) \quad (b, S_c^a, e) \;\rightarrow\; (C_c^a, A_b)$$

$$(C_4) \quad (e, S_c^a, A_b) \;\rightarrow\; (S_D, e)$$

(C_1) remembers the conjunction c read after A_a
(C_2) erases A_a from the storage but remembers it
(C_3) reads and looks up b
(C_4) connects A_a, c, A_b and forgets the dependents A_a and c.

Relationship Grammars

Four classes of grammars, all based on the concept of dependency, are defined by Fitialov.

The author remarks that the languages described by these grammars are all phrase-structure languages in the sense of Chomsky [8]. According to Chomsky [8], [12] phrase-structure grammars include at least context-free and context-sensitive grammars. In his paper Fitialov mentions the use of contexts, and it is not clear which type of phrase-structure grammars are Fitialov's grammars.

The construction of a PDS automaton very similar to the one above, which is perfectly straightforward, shows that Fitialov's languages are context-free. They are probably powerful enough to describe the whole class of context-free languages, which remains to be proved.

Projective Languages

Lecerf [24] works on the principle that the dependency representation of a sentence S_1 and the immediate constituent analysis of the same sentence S_1 are both of interest since they show two different aspects of linguistics [3].

This mathematical theory deals with infinite lexicons and doubly structured strings are defined. We will impose the restriction of finiteness on the lexicon.

The recursive definition of the G-structures is the following:

Let $M = \{m_i\}$, a lexicon where the m_i's are words:
A syntagma is represented by $[S_k]$; the m_i's are S_k's;

S is the set of all possible syntagma
$S = \{[S_k]\}$.
There is an operator represented by $([S_k])$ corresponding to each syntagma which can be applied to the right or the left of any syntagma in order to construct a new one.
Right operation $[S_j] . ([S_k])$ is noted

$$[[S_j] . ([S_k])] \in S.$$

Left operation $([S_k]) . [S_j]$ is noted

$$[([S_k]) . [S_j]] \in S.$$

Example

$$[([([the]) . [man]]) . [[hit] . ([([the]) . [ball]])]]$$

Lecerf proved that the operation of erasing the parentheses provides the tree of the immediate constituent analysis where the dots are the nonterminal nodes. On the other hand, the operation which consists of erasing the brackets and dots provides the tree of the dependency analysis.

We will point out some properties of this model. The language defined by right or left adjunction of an operator to a syntagma is obtained when we erase the structure markers (parentheses, brackets, dots). These adjunctions then reduce to the simple operation of concatenation. The language defined is the set of all possible combinations of words. It is the monoid $C(M)$.

Clearly what is missing is a set of rules which would tell which syntagma and which operators can be combined, but this problem is not raised.

If, following the author, we admit that his model characterizes both the dependency languages and the immediate constituent languages, we have two good reasons to think of the 'G-structures' as being context-free, but no evidence at all. In this case the 'G-structures' would be redundant since Gaifman gave an algorithm which converts every dependency grammar into a particular context-free grammar.

Yngve's Model

The grammar described in Yngve [6] consists of the following types of rules defined as a vocabulary $V = V_N U V_T$
(1) $A \rightarrow a$
(2) $A \rightarrow BC$
(3) $A \rightarrow B \ldots C$ where any single element of V can occur between B and C in rule (3).

The restriction of the depth hypothesis makes the language a finite state language [6]. Without depth, rules of type (1) and (2) show that the language is at least context-free.

Matthews [25] studied a special class of grammars;

grammars containing rules of types (1), (2), (3) are shown to be a subclass of Mathews' 'one-way discontinuous grammars', which in turn are shown to generate context-free languages.

The structural description provided by these rules are not simple trees and cannot be compared to the other structures so far described.

4. Applications of the General Theory of C.F. Grammar

The context-free grammars, have found applications in the field of programming languages. We extend here remarks already made by Chomsky [9] and Ginsburg and Rose [26] to the case of natural languages. The two theorems mentioned below derive from the results obtained by Bar-Hillel *et al.* [27].

Ambiguity

An empirical requirement for a grammar is that of giving n structural descriptions for an n-ways ambiguous sentence. A grammar of English will have to give, for example, two analyses of the sort given below, for the sentence: (A) They are flying planes

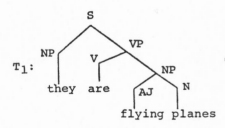
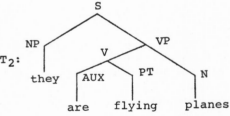

When constructing a *c-f* grammar for natural languages the number of rules soon becomes very large and one is no longer able to master the interrelations of the rules: rules corresponding to the analysis of new types of sentences are added without seeing exactly what are the repercussions on the analysis of the former ones. We use here an example mentioned in [17]. The grammar used at the Harvard Computation Laboratory contains the grammatical data necessary to analyse the sentence (A) in two different manners. Independently it contains the data necessary to analyse the sentence (B) in the manner shown below:

(B) The facts are smoking kills

T_3:

the facts are smoking kills

The dictionary shows that TO PLANE is also a verb and KILL also a noun.

The result of the analysis of sentences (A) and (B) is three solutions for each of them (the three trees described above: T_1, T_2, T_3).

Any native speaker of English will say that (A) is twice ambiguous and (B) is not ambiguous at all; the wrong remaining analyses are obtained because of the grammar in which rules have to be made more precise.

Obviously T_3 has to be suppressed for (A) and T_1 and T_2 for (B). This situation arises very frequently and one may raise the more general question of systematically detecting ambiguities in order to suppress the undesirable ones. A result of the general theory of c.f. grammars is the following.

Theorem. The general problem* of determining whether or not a c.f. grammar is ambiguous is recursively unsolvable [21].

The meaning of the result is the following: there is no general procedure which, given a c.f. grammar, would tell, after a systematic inspection of the rules, whether the grammar is ambiguous or not. Therefore the stronger question of asking what rules produce ambiguous sentences is recursively unsolvable as well. We can expect that the problem of checking an actual grammar by other means than analysing samples and verifying the structural descriptions one by one is extremely difficult.

Translation

A scheme widely adopted in the field of MT [5] consists of having two independent grammars G_1, G_2 for two languages L_1, L_2 and a transfer grammar T going from L_1 to L_2 (or from L_2 to L_1). A result of the theory of c.f. grammars is the following:

Theorem. Given two c.f. languages L_1 and L_2, the problem of deciding whether or not there exists a mapping T such that $T(L_1) = L_2$ is recursively unsolvable [26].

Of course a translation from L_1 to L_2 need not be an exact mapping between L_1 and L_2, but there may be a large sublanguage of L_2 which is not in the range of any particular grammar T constructed empirically from L_1 and L_2; conversely some sublanguage of L_1 may not be translatable into L_2; in any case, one should expect that

* Except in a very simple case of no linguistic interest.

the problem of constructing a practically adequate T for L_1 and L_2 is extremely difficult.

These results derived from the general theory show the interest of this theory. The results so far obtained mostly concern the languages themselves; very little is known about the structural descriptions. Studies in this field could provide decisions when a choice comes between different formal systems: for example, this theory could decide which one of the systems described above is more economical according to the number of syntactic classes, or to the number of operations necessary to analyse a sentence. Such questions, if they may be answered, require further and difficult theoretical studies on these systems.

5. Adequacy of Context-Free Models

Many natural languages present to a certain extent, the features of context-free languages. An example of strings which are not context-free has been given by Bar-Hillel and Solomonoff:

N_1, N_2, ... AND N_k ARE RESPECTIVELY A_1, A_2 ... A_k where a relation holds between each noun N_i and the corresponding adjective A_i. These strings cannot be generated for any k by a context-free grammar.

More obvious is the inadequacy of the context-free structural descriptions. Chomsky [7, 11, 12] pointed out that no c.f. grammar can generate the correct structure for a sequence of adjectives modifying a noun.

c.f. structures:

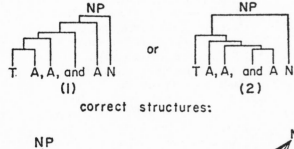

(1)   (2)

correct structures:

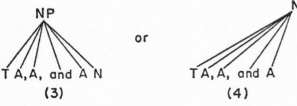

(3)   (4)

In the cases (1) and (2) above the Noun Phrase has been given too much structure by a c.f. grammar. Very frequent too are the cases where no structure can be given at all by a c.f. grammar: the ambiguous phrase:

THE FEAR OF THE ENEMY

cannot be given two different structures showing the two possible interpretations, the same remark applies to phrases of the type:

VISITING RELATIVES.

Another case of lack of information in the structural description given by a context-free grammar is the following:

(i) THE EXPERIMENT IS BOUND TO FAIL

BOUND and TO FAIL have to be connected but nothing can tell that EXPERIMENT is subject of TO FAIL.

Once a context-free structure is given to (i) it is not very simple to give a different one to the sentence:

(ii) THE EXPERIMENT IS IMPOSSIBLE TO REALIZE

where EXPERIMENT is object of TO REALIZE.

In any case, if two different structures are given to (i) and (ii), nothing will tell any more that these two sentences are very similar.

All these examples are beyond the power of context-free grammars. Adequate treatments are possible when using transformational grammars (Chomsky) but these grammars, more difficult to construct and to use, have been disregarded in the field of MT on the grounds that they could not be used in a computer, which is false. The programming language COMIT uses precisely the formalism of transformations. Matthews is working on a recognition routine which is using a generative transformational grammar [28], [29].

The interest of a word for word translation being very limited [30] a scheme of translation sentence for sentence motivated the construction of grammars.

Every sentence requires to be given a structural description, and a transfer grammar maps input trees into output trees. Considered from a formal point of view, a transfer grammar is precisely a transformational grammar.

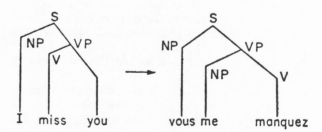

The construction of a transfer grammar between two context-free grammars raises serious problems.

Let us consider the following example of translation from English to French taken from Klima [31].

(a) HE DWELLED ON ITS ADVANTAGES

an almost word for word translation gives the French equivalent:

(a′) IL A INSISTE SUR SES AVANTAGES

but let us consider the passive form (p) of the sentence (a):

(p) ITS ADVANTAGES WERE DWELLED ON BY HIM

in French (a′) has no passive form and (b) has for

translation the sentence (a′). What is required for the translation of (p) is either a transformation of a French passive non-sentence (p′) (obtained almost word for word):

(p′) *SES AVANTAGES ONT ETE INSISTE SUR
　　　PAR LUI

into the sentence (a′) or a transformation of (p) into (a), made before the translation. The two solutions are equivalent from the point of view of the operations to be carried out but the second seems more natural.

In the latter case, since the passive sentences are described by the means of the active sentences and a transformation, no context-free description of the passive sentences is longer required in the source grammar. Many other cases of the type above show that the use of a transformational source grammar will simplify the transfer grammar, moreover Chomsky has shown that transformational grammars simplify considerably the description of languages. These are two good reasons for MT searchers to become interested in models which are less limited than context-free models.

References

1. Y. Bar-Hillel: *Language* (1953), **29**, 47–48.
2. D. G. Hays: *Grouping and Dependency Theory*. The Rand Corporation (1960).
3. Y. Lecerf: Programme des Conflits, Modèle des Conflits Euratom, Rapport Grisa No. 4 (1960).
4. A. Sestier, and L. Dupuis: La Place de la Syntaxe dans la Traduction Automatique des Langues, Ingénieurs et Techniciens, Paris (1962).
5. V. H. Yngve: *Mechanical Translation*, 1959, **4**, No. 3, 59.
6. V. H. Yngve: First International Conference on Machine Translation, Teddington, England (1961).
7. N. Chomsky: *Syntactic Structures*. Moutons', Gravenhage (1957).
8. N. Chomsky: *Information and Control* (1959), **2**, 137–167.
9. N. Chomsky: On the Notion 'Rule of Grammar'. Symposia in Applied Mathematics, Vol. XII, American Mathematical Society, Providence, R.I. (1961).
10. L. Tesnieres: *Syntaxe Structurale*. Klincsieck, Paris (1960).
11. N. Chomsky: *IRE Trans. Infor. Theory, IT* 2, 113–114 (1956).
12. N. Chomsky: *Handbook of Mathematical Psychology*. (Ed. by D. Luce, E. Bush, E. Galanter) (1962).
13. W. Plath: First International Conference on Machine Translation, Teddington, England (1961).
14. Z. S. Harris: *Methods in Structural Linguistics*. University of Chicago Press (1951).
15. Z. S. Harris: *Language* (1957), **33**, 283–340.
16. R. Wells: *Language*, 1947, **23**, 81–117.
17. S. Kuno and A. Oettinger: Multiple syntactic analyser — Harvard Computation Laboratory (to appear in the proceedings of the I.F.I.P. conference, Munich, 1962).
18. A. Oettinger: *Automatic Syntactic Analysis and the Pushdown Store*. Proceedings of Symposia in Applied Mathematics, Vol. XII, American Mathematical Society, Providence, R.I. (1961).
19. I. Rhodes: A new approach to the mechanical translation of Russian. National Bureau of Standards, Report, No. 6295 (1959).
20. D. G. Hays: *Basic Principles and Technical Variations in Sentence Structure Determination*, The Rand Corporation (1960).
21. M. P. Schutzenberger: On a family of formal power series (to be published).
22. Y. Bar-Hillel, C. Gaifman and E. Shamir: *Bull. Res. Council Israel* (1960), **9**, F, No. 1.
23. M. Sherry: First International Conference on Machine Translation, Teddington, England (1961).
24. Y. Lecerf: Une représentation Algébrique de la Structure des Phrases dans diverses Langues Naturelles. Notes aux comptes-rendus de l'Académie des Sciences Paris, 1961, **252**, No. 2, 232.
25. G. H. Matthews: One-way discontinuous grammars (to be published).
26. S. Ginsburg and F. R. Rose: Some recursively unsolvable problems in algol-like languages. System Development Corporation — S.P. 690 (1962).
27. Y. Bar-Hillel, M. Perles and E. Shamir: Zeitschrift für Phonetik, Sprachwissenschaft und Kommunikationsforschung — Band 14, Heft 2 (1961).
28. G. H. Matthews and S. Rogovin: *German Sentence Recognition, Mechanical Translation*, Vol. 5, No. 3, M.I.T. Cambridge, Mass. (1958).
29. G. H. Matthews: First International Conference on Mechanical Translation, Teddington, England (1961).
30. E. S. Klima: First International Conference on Machine Translation, Teddington, England (1961).
31. E. S. Klima: Correspondence at the grammatical level. Q.P.R. No. 64, R.L.E., M.I.T. Cambridge, Mass. (1962).
32. M. Davis: *Computability and Unsolvability*. McGraw-Hill, New York (1958).
33. M. P. Schützenberger: *Some Remarks on Chomsky's Context-free Languages*. Q.P.R. No. 63, R.L.E., M.I.T., Cambridge, Mass. (1961).
34. H. Gaifman: *Dependency Systems and Phrase Structure Systems*. Rand Corporation — P. 2315 (1961).
35. Ya. Fitialov: *On Models of Syntax for Machine Translation*. J.P.R.S. 13197 — 28 March 1962.

21 A "Law" of Occurrences for Words of Low Frequency

ANDREW D. BOOTH
Information and Control
Vol. 10, No. 4, April, 1967

Although Zipf's law is well-known to linguists and to students of language statistics, there is another "law" enunciated by Zipf (1938) which holds for words of low frequency of occurrence and which is not well known. The interest of several linguistic friends suggested to the author that the following note might be of general interest, particularly because it shows that Zipf's second law is only partially true and can be replaced by a more general statement which has a greater range of validity.

1. Zipf's First Law

This law, first stated by Estoup (1916) and popularized by Zipf (1949), can be stated, briefly, as follows: The number of occurrences of each different word in a text is counted and the words are then arranged in a table in which the first word is the most frequent, the second word the second most frequent, and so on. The order of any word in the list is called its *rank* (r) and the number of occurrences of that word its *frequency* (f). Zipf's first law then states that:

$$rf = c,$$

where c is a constant for any particular text.

Table I, derived from a word frequency analysis of a paper by Stiles (1961), illustrates the sort of variation involved. It will seem that the "law" is by no means exactly obeyed but, considering its simplicity, that it is in fair agreement with the data. When more extensive data, such as those of Dewey (1923), are used better agreement results, and this extends to the four or five thousand different words of a 100,000-word sample.

TABLE I

A TYPICAL RANK-FREQUENCY TABLE

Word	Rank (r)	Frequency (f)	rf
The	1	245	245
Of	2	136	272
Terms	3	98	294
To	4	81	324
A	5	65	325
And	6	61	366
In	7	55	385
We	8	52	416
Request	9	49	441
Documents	10	40	400
Which	20	26	520

TABLE II

Word Counts for Four Texts

Text:	W.R.U.1	W.R.U.2	W.R.U.3	Eldridge
Total No. words (T):	4325	4409	8734	43,989
No. different words (D):	1001	1211	1698	6,002
Words occurring once (I_1)	541	710	887	2,976
Words occurring twice (I_2)	152	227	273	1,079
Words occurring 3 times (I_3)	94	91	151	516
Words occurring 4 times (I_4)	56	41	90	294
Words occurring 5 times (I_5)	36	32	62	212

However, these things are well known, and it is the purpose of this note to illustrate and explain the second, and more general, "law" which holds for words of very *low* frequency of occurrence and not for those of high frequency.

2. Low-Frequency Word Occurrences

When the complete word frequency count is made for a text, it is found that words of high rank, that is of low frequency, occur in such a way that many words have the same frequency. Thus, Table II gives the analysis of three texts processed at the Center for Documentation and Communication Research, Western Reserve University, and of the sampling of newspaper English published by Eldridge (1911). We now calculate the ratios I_1/D, i.e., the ratio of the number of words occurring once to the number of different words for each of the texts; these are shown in Table III.

TABLE III

Ratios of Single Occurrences to Vocabulary

Text	Different words, D	Words occurring once, I_1	I_1/D
W.R.U.1	1001	541	.54
W.R.U.2	1211	710	.58
W.R.U.3	1698	887	.52
Eldridge	6002	2976	.50

The next problem is to investigate the remarkable constancy of the ratio of single occurrences to the number of different words in the text, i.e., to the vocabulary. Assume that, in a sufficiently large corpus, the ranks of words do actually differ so that ranking is possible, and let the probability of occurrence of a word of rank r be $p(r)$. The composition of a text whose length is T is thus:

$T\,p(1)$ occurrences of the word of rank 1
$T\,p(2)$ occurrences of the word of rank 2
$\cdots\cdots\cdots\cdots\cdots\cdots\cdots\cdots$
$T\,p(r)$ occurrences of the word of rank r, etc.

To find the number of words which actually occur once we could proceed as suggested by Zipf (1938), who asserted that a word will occur once if

$$1.5 > T\,p(r) \geqq .5. \tag{1}$$

Zipf's law (first) suggests that

$$p(r) = k/r, \tag{2}$$

where k is constant for the text so that

$$1.5 > kT/r \geqq .5$$

or

$$r_{max} = \frac{kT}{.5}, \qquad r_{min} = \frac{kT}{1.5},$$

where the number of occurrences I_1, or $(r_{max} - r_{min})$, is

$$I_1 = kT(2 - \tfrac{2}{3}) = \tfrac{4}{3}\,kT. \tag{3}$$

To find the number of different words, D, which occur under these assumptions, we have

$$T p(D) \geqq .5 \tag{4}$$

since D is simply the highest rank of any word.

Equations (2) and (4) lead immediately to

$$D = 2kT, \tag{5}$$

so that $I_1/D = \tfrac{2}{3}$.

It is easy to show, following the same argument, that the condition for a word to occur n times is simply:

$$(n + \tfrac{1}{2}) > T p(r) \geqq (n - \tfrac{1}{2}),$$

from which it follows that:

$$I_n = kT/(n^2 - \tfrac{1}{4}). \tag{6}$$

This is the form in which Zipf stated his "second law," and it leads immediately to:

$$I_n/I_1 = 3/(4n^2 - 1). \tag{7}$$

It is clear that, although this method of approach predicts the constancy of the ratio I_1/D for different text lengths, it produces a small discrepancy in actual value of this ratio: .67 predicted as compared with the values of .54, .58, .52, and .50 for our texts.

The values of I_n/I_1 also leave something to be desired, as shown by Table IV, where the values of this ratio, predicted by (7) and calculated from the Eldridge text are shown.

3. A More General "Law"

It is trivial to extend the arguments of the previous section to "laws" of word frequency other than Zipf's. We shall take the more general case:

$$p(r) = \frac{k}{r^\alpha} \quad (a > 0). \tag{8}$$

We shall also assume, in place of (1), that the condition for a single occurrence is

$$2 > Tp(r) \geqq 1,$$

or, in general, for n occurrences:

$$(n+1) > Tp(r) \geqq n. \tag{9}$$

By using (8) and (9), and following our previous argument, we thus obtain:

$$I_n = (kT)^{1/\alpha} \left[\frac{1}{n^{1/\alpha}} \quad \frac{1}{(n+1)^{1/\alpha}} \right]. \tag{10}$$

Again, the number of different words, D, in the text is given by

$$Tp(D) \geqq 1$$

where

$$D = (kT)^{1/\alpha} \tag{11}$$

This leads to

$$I_1/D = \left(1 - \frac{1}{2^{1/\alpha}} \right), \tag{12}$$

which shows that even when Zipf's law is replaced by the more general form (8), the ratio I_1/D is still independent of the text length.

The proximity of the calculated values of I_1/D to .5 suggests that Zipf's first law is, at least, a good first approximation to the true state of affairs, and, with $a = 1$, we obtain from (12) $I_1/D = .5$, and from (10)

TABLE IV
PREDICTED AND CALCULATED VALUES OF I_n/I_1

Source	I_1/I_1	I_2/I_1	I_3/I_1	I_4/I_1	I_5/I_1
Predicted by Eq. (7)	1	.20	.086	.048	.030
Calculated from Eldridge	1	.36	.17	.10	.07

TABLE V
PREDICTED AND CALCULATED VALUES OF I_n/I_1

Source	I_1/I_1	I_2/I_1	I_3/I_1	I_4/I_1	I_5/I_1
Predicted by (13)	1	.33	.17	.10	.071
W.R.U.1	1	.28	.17	.10	.07
W.R.U.2	1	.32	.13	.06	.05
W.R.U.3	1	.31	.17	.10	.07
Eldridge	1	.36	.17	.10	.07

TABLE VI
MORE EXTENSIVE DATA FOR I_n/I_1

Source	I_6/I_1	I_7/I_1	I_8/I_1	I_9/I_1	I_{10}/I_1
Calculated from Eq. (13)	.048	.036	.028	.022	.018
Eldridge	.051	.035	.028	.029	.015

$$I_n/I_1 = 2/n(n+1). \tag{13}$$

The values of I_n/I_1 for the fours texts of Table II, and the predicted values, calculated from (13) are shown in Table V. It is clear that the agreement is remarkable. The smallness of the data sample makes it unprofitable to calculate values of I_n/I_1 for $n > 5$ in the case of the three W.R.U. samples, but the series can be continued to $n = 10$ for the Eldridge material and leads to results shown in Table VI, which are still in good agreement.

4. Mandelbrot's Law

Mandelbrot has shown (1957), under quite general conditions, that word frequency should follow a law of the type:

$$p(r) = (B-1)V^{B-1}(r+V)^{-B}, \tag{14}$$

where B and V are constants. Inserting this in Eq. (9) we obtain:

$$(n+1) > T(B-1)V^{B-1}(r+V)^{-B} \geqq n,$$

whence

$$r_{max} = \left[\frac{T(B-1)V^{B-1}}{n} \right]^{1/B} - V$$

$$r_{min} = \left[\frac{T(B-1)V^{B-1}}{n+1} \right]^{1/B} - V,$$

so that

$$I_n = (r_{\max} - r_{\min}) =$$
$$[T(B-1) \, V^{B-1}]^{1/B} \left[\frac{1}{n^{1/B}} - \frac{1}{(n+1)^{1/B}} \right], \quad (15)$$

which is identical to (10) if we put $a = B$ and $k = (B-1)V^{B-1}$.

It follows that the statistical evidence, presented in Tables V and VI, affords no indication which would enable us to discriminate between Zipf's law, the more general form given by Eq. (8), and Mandelbrot's revision.

5. Conclusion

The revised form of Zipf's second law seems in excellent accord with the observed facts. There is no reason to suppose, however, that the rather arbitrary assumption used to deduce I_1 would be equally valid in languages other than English. Nevertheless, the important feature of the demonstration is that the general form of the law of occurrence for low frequency words is independent of the detailed validity of Zipf's law for the distribution as a whole.

Equation (11) gives a means of estimating the Zipf constant, k, for a given author, and this in turn provides a measure of his richness of vocabulary. The implications of the Mandelbrot relationship (14) for vocabulary size estimation have been previously discussed by Mandelbrot himself (1960).

References

DEWEY, G. (1923). "Relative Frequency of English Speech Sounds." Harvard Univ. Press.

ELDRIDGE, R. C. (1911). "Six Thousand Common English Words." Clement Press, Buffalo.

ESTOUP, J. B. (1916). "Gammes stenographiques," 4th edition, Gauthier-Villars, Paris.

MANDELBROT, B. (1957). "Théorie mathématique de la loi d'Estoup-Zipf." Institut de Statistique de l'Université, Paris.

MANDELBROT, B. (1960). *Am. Math. Soc. Symp. Appl. Math*, pp. 180–219.

STILES, H. E. (1961). *Assoc. Computing Machinery* **8**, 271–279.

ZIPF, G. K. (1935). "The Psycho-Biology of Language," p. 40. Houghton-Mifflin, Boston.

ZIPF, G. K. (1938). *Psychol. Record* **2**, 347–367.

ZIPF, G. K. (1949). "Human Behaviour and the Principle of Least Effort." Addison-Wesley, Cambridge, Mass.

22 Semantic Road Maps for Literature Searchers

LAUREN B. DOYLE
*Journal of the Association
for Computing Machinery
Vol. 8, No. 4, October, 1961*

1. Wanted: New Ways to Use Computers

The retrieval of documented information is one of today's most widespread technical problems, affecting almost every large professional group, corporation, and government bureau. Because document retrieval is in part an information processing problem, much hope for a solution has been vested in computers. But large, fast, reliable ones have been around now for five years, and people have steadily realized that the overall task of information retrieval is not one of those rote jobs for which digital computers are made to order. Cataloging and searching are intellectual tasks, and have been thought of as rote not because they are menial and straightforward, but because they are unpalatable and unwanted. Many people do like to use their minds, yes — but not for plowing through and discarding irrelevant material.

Successful use of computers in a problem area depends as much on our understanding of the problem as it does on the capabilities of the computers. It so happens that in most successful computer applications to date, problems have been fairly well understood. Therefore,

mathematicians, programmers, and equipment designers have been the chief head-scratchers in engineering and business applications.

Many people have assumed that this would also be the case in information retrieval. Accordingly, the rush to put computers to work in this area has led primarily to their use as *searching* instruments, and much activity has centered around the design and operation of searching machinery.[1] Boundary conditions have been assumed, such as an ideal searcher who knows what he wants and who knows how to express it in terms understood by the machine, and such as ideal correspondence of descriptors to the documents they describe; then attention has been focused on optimizing the processes between these boundaries. The resulting theories and systems in most cases seem highly adapted to the needs of machine but not adapted to the needs of humans.

We are, after all, dealing with the elemental situation of an author talking to a reader — even if by means of a buffer storage which will grow more and more

---

1. However, it is noted that there has been a recent steep increase in interest in automatic indexing.

mechanical. The basic problem is to increase the mental contact between the reader and the information store, so that the reader can proceed unerringly and swiftly to identify and receive the message he is looking for.

Existing machine searching systems have, however, physically and psychologically enlarged the gap between the reader and the information store. For example, a literature searcher is given the intellectual burden of formulating a search request. When people get over the glamour of using a computer to search a library, there will surely be feelings of frustration and suspicions that the job of deciding what is and is not relevant has been taken out of their hands.[2] Putting ourselves in the shoes of a searcher, we ask: "What have we neglected to consider, that computers might do?" One possible answer, in view of the Gestalt powers of humans, is: "Give the searcher something to look at."

A supermarket is about the same size as a library and, as is well-known, does not have a card catalog. A shopper simply scans the shelf labels, proceeds to the right shelf, and homes in on what he wants — usually in less than a minute. But this is not feasible in a library; its variety of "edibles" is much greater and, more important, the labels do not adequately characterize the products. If only a searcher could "see" the characteristics of books, as if they were toys, or tools, or other functionally shaped articles of merchandise, there would not be so much of a problem.

This gives us the rudiments of a more human-oriented approach to computer usage: suppose we try to make books and documents *visible* to the searcher and organize them well enough so that, as in the supermarket, the shopper can quickly home in on the item of his choice. In this context, the role of the computer changes. It becomes a tool of analysis of books and articles; it no longer searches — it arranges and labels things so that humans can search them. The things to be searched, of course, are not the books themselves, but only proxies which adequately mirror the nature of the books.

The major theme of this article is that natural characterization and organization of information can come from analysis of frequencies and distributions of words in libraries. Others have made use of frequencies of words in text, though for more limited goals. Luhn [2] has by-passed syntactical analysis by taking advantage of the information content of the most frequently used topical words in articles. His auto-abstracts and auto-encodements are suggestive of the proxies we seek to generate. Edmundson [3, a or b] *et al.* take a further step in a desirable direction by bringing in information from *outside* the article being analyzed: words and terms are given greater value as topical clues, as the contrast increases between frequency of use within the article

2. Calvin Mooers gives considerable attention to these problems in his 1959 Western Joint Computer Conference talk, "The Next Twenty Years in Information Retrieval" [1].

and rarity of general usage. In these efforts information theory is at last truly beginning to impinge on information retrieval. Syntactical words have been recognized as having low information content, frequent topical words within articles as having much information, and generally infrequent topical words as having even more information. There may be even greater reservoirs of information which have not yet been discovered.

The massive frequency analyses that we will discuss may seem to demand equipment which is not yet in a state of easy availability, such as photoelectric character readers and billion-bit memories. It is worth emphasizing, however, that the present rate of solution of the intellectual problems of machine-aided literature searching is sufficiently slow that these advanced devices will be in common use long before literature searchers will truly benefit from their presence. This being the case, there is much reason for retrieval research workers to pretend that the machines of 1965 are with us today.

2. Classification Versus Coordination

This article hopes to paint a new picture of library classification, in terms of what we know or can find out about word frequencies. As a backdrop for this, some discussion is required of current attitudes regarding the problem of library classification.

At present, there appear to be two major schools of thought on the organization of categories into classification systems. We can think of them as "radicals" and "reactionaries," without, however, intending to connote anything unpleasant. The "radicals" believe that the traditional classification systems of libraries are inadequate, especially for use in mechanized retrieval, and that new principles of organization are required, such as those of coordination indexing. Taube [4] says: ". . . classification fails . . . in the arbitrary disassociations which are imposed on related ideas by the requirements of the system . . ." and ". . . classification systems are not truly effective instruments for displaying to the browser or searcher *all* of the ideas in any system which are associated with any given idea with which the system is entered . . ."

Taube, of course, uses the term "classification system" to pertain to hierarchical arrangements of categories, such as the Dewey system or the Library of Congress system, and does not apply this term to the "radical" systems, of which his own Uniterm indexing system is one. Later in this section it will be shown that not only are the radical systems rightly viewed as classification systems but that they actually contain hierarchical substructures, and that it is important to appreciate this point in order to sketch out newer, even more radical ways of dealing with categories.

The "reactionary" school of thought takes the position that, even though the traditional classification systems might not be entirely adequate, it is necessary to have a systematic arrangement of categories (which usually works out to be overtly hierarchical). This school feels that the "radicals," having diagnosed the ills of Dewey *et al.*, are actually "anarchists" in shifting to coordination indexing and other formulations which disavow any sort of category grouping. Foskett [5] says: " . . . Vickery [6] has shown how several workers who ostensibly reject any form of classification, preferring mechanical sorting or other nonsystematic coding, have actually begun to introduce, however reluctantly, some of the groupings that have long been commonplace features of classification schemes. . ." Thus, the implication of the reactionaries is that one cannot really get rid of classification structure; it will tend to creep into retrieval system operation because it is semantically necessary.

The reader may feel that there is something unduly extreme about the labels "radical" and "reactionary." However, it turns out that traditional classification structure and the structure generated by coordination indexing *are* extremes, at either end of an important continuum (though neither structure, as we shall see, is altogether extreme). The continuum is that of statistical dependence-independence.

To explain this we introduce the idea of "precision." Precision, n/T, is the most typical number, n, of items of information that a retrieval system will deliver in response to a typical search request, out of a total of T items. (In statistical terms n/T would be the mode.) A retrieval system which usually selects about 100 documents out of 1000 would not be very precise, though it would still be useful, in that it would cut down by 90 per cent the number of documents a searcher would have to inspect. If a system usually delivers two or three documents out of a million, it is highly precise.

Now, on the continuum of statistical dependence-independence, coordination indexing is at the independent or "zero redundancy" extreme. This can be explained in terms of precision. If one has a dictionary of 1000 labels to use in tagging documents, he has available 499,500 possible two-term logical-product coordination search statements. If one also has a million documents to label and is restricted, let's say, to two and only two label assignments to each document, he has an average of two documents retrievable in response to each possible search statement. If one assigns the two labels to each document in a random manner so that one has "statistical independence of label assignment," then two will be not only the average number of documents retrieved but also the most typical number.

Two out of a million is a rather high degree of precision. There are some conceivable methods of label assignment which will give greater precision than random assignment — for example, assigning labels in such a manner that the mode is one rather than two. However, most departures from "equal likelihood" of assignment of the documents to the 499,500 categories corresponding

to the search statements will lead to *much less* precision — this includes, we suspect, the departures which occur in real-life retrieval systems. A look at the statistically dependent end of the continuum may bring this out.

The assertion has been made above that traditional classification systems are almost as extreme in the direction of statistical dependence as coordination systems are in the direction of independence. That is, there exists a state of extreme statistical association among the attributes of items in some reservoirs of data, such that hierarchical structures are the most appropriate schemes for retrieval purposes.

We can make perverse use of the coordination principle to demonstrate this degree of extremity. Figures 1 and 2 are fanciful maps of intersections made possible by two-term coordination. In each case, tallies could be placed in squares as a result of searching at random through books and magazines; whenever a two-word combination is encountered, a tally is placed in the corresponding square. (In real systems each tally would be replaced by a reference.) Figure 1 demonstrates the ultimate extreme in statistical dependence. The label "Napoleon" invariably retrieves tallies only when coordinated with "Bonaparte," and similarly each other label correlates maximally with one other label. Figure 2 shows a somewhat lesser degree of dependence, because some labels, such as "Thomas" and "John," have fruitful coordinations with *several* other labels.

It becomes evident that masses of data which consistently lead to the kind of coordination behavior shown in Figure 2 permit and encourage the formation of hierarchies. Under the category "Thomas" are subcategories such as "Jefferson" and "Huxley." When one begins to encounter large numbers of cases where there are Jeffersons which are not Thomases, or Shakespeares which are not Williams, then one finds hierarchical classification cumbersome, though still useful.

Of course, in this example there is admittedly no significance in the fact that Beecham, Huxley, and Jefferson have the same first name, and therefore no point in dealing with the hierarchical structure — it is sufficient to deal only with the subcategories in this case. However, and this is the important point about hierarchical schemes, whenever the labels for information items *consistently* configure themselves as in Figure 2, there is undoubtedly some significance to the categories as well as to the subcategories. In such a case, the subcategorized items are empirically established as a species of the categorized items, and thus hierarchies become capable of providing semantic guidance to searchers.

Now let us enlarge the number of labels and tallies in the Figure 2 example in order to compare it quantitatively with the results of the random label assignment described earlier. Suppose we assume 1000 labels, 250 of which are first names, and 750 of which are last names. Let us also assume that we have contrived, as in the

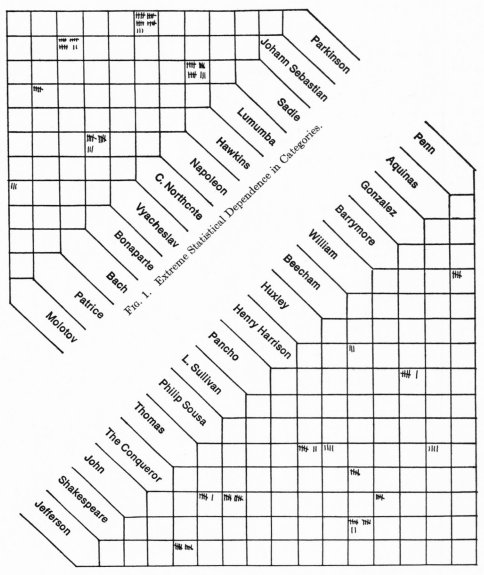

FIG. 1. Extreme Statistical Dependence in Categories.

FIG. 2. A Degree of Dependence Leading to Hierarchy Formation.

Figure 2 example, to choose names such that each first name "belongs" to several other last names, in that several well-known people have the same first name.

We will go through the text of books and magazines until a million occurrences of names corresponding to combinations of the 1000 labels have been picked out. As in the random assignment example, there are 499,500 *possible* categories (500,500 if such names as "Humbert Humbert" are taken into account). However, because of the extreme statistical dependence which has been imposed, we now find that only 750 of the 499,500 categories will contain tallies (this assumes that the names have been chosen cleverly enough that such cross-connections as

"Pancho Shakespeare" or "Ludwig van Bonaparte" are never encountered in text). The categories with the tallies should have an average of 1333 each, and the mode should be in the neighborhood of 1333. This contrasts with a mode of 2 in the random assignment example. By traveling from the statistically independent extreme to the statistically dependent extreme, we have decreased precision by a factor of about 650.

What can one do to make the retrieval precision of data with statistically dependent attributes as good as that for data with independent attributes? One way is to increase the number of ordinates. For example, in looking for the name "Thomas Jefferson," we could also look for some third attribute (such as "Monticello" or "Louisiana Purchase") to allow us to make three-term instead of two-term coordinations.

There are an infinite number of possible third attributes for each of the 750 frequently occurring names, but let's assume that only k of them actually apply to each name, on the average. If we stick to the extreme degree of statistical dependence we initially chose (e.g. "Monticello" would never be associated in text with any other name except "Jefferson"), precision will probably be improved by a factor of k. If k is not large, precision will still be poor and a fourth ordinate may have to be brought in — or a fifth, or sixth — before retrieval precision becomes as good as 2 out of a million.

If this is done, note what is generated: a five or six-level hierarchy! Also note that of the trillions of *possible* five- or six-term coordinations in such a case, only a mere million will result in the retrieval of information.

As a result of considering reservoirs of items whose attributes are distributed with both extreme independence and extreme dependence, we have developed an appreciation for the effect which the statistical nature of language could have on precision in retrieval of text items; we have deliberately chosen these extremes in order to highlight the effect. We have seen that coordination indexing is maximally efficient when the possession of one attribute by an item has zero correlation with the possession of any other attribute: that is, under such conditions one can achieve maximum precision[3] with a given number of ordinates. When attributes become more strongly associated, precision must be degraded, so that more ordinates must be added to each search request statement to maintain precision.

It has been shown that degrees of precision of the order of two out of a million can be obtained with as few as 1000 labels and two ordinates. Under actual document retrieval conditions, we now hypothesize, it would probably take five or six coordinated terms to get this kind of precision, on the average, and furthermore that the result of any one such high-powered coordinating foray would be grossly unpredictable. We may come to see (Section IV) that use of semantic ordinates in searching not only gives poor precision, but also poor *accuracy*, and that the inaccuracy has much to do, though indirectly, with statistical dependence.

Earlier in this section it was suggested that coordination systems are best viewed as classification systems, and actually contain hierarchical substructures. We are now in a good position to appreciate this.

As an illustrative example, a common practice is the combination of two or more uniterms to form a multiword term [7, 10]. For instance, it may be found that searchers using the ordinates "magnetic" and "tape" are

retrieving almost as many documents as those using the ordinate "tape" alone. So the documentalist, to prevent waste motion by the searcher and by the machine, forms the ordinate "magnetic tape," and may actually throw out the "tape" ordinate.

Continued consolidations of this sort may result in some rather complicated labels, such as "magnetic tape recording head adjustment." At such a point, as one scans the index of terms used in the coordination system, one sees structures which begin to take on the appearance of hierarchies. For example:

> magnetic
> magnetic cores
> magnetic drum
> magnetic drum recording head
> magnetic tape
> magnetic tape drive
> magnetic tape parity
> magnetic tape recording head

This would be merely an accidental effect of alphabetical ordering of the multiword terms, but it is not surprising to find coordinate indexers departing from alphabetical lists of terms in order to give searchers more adequate semantic guidance to available labels. As Mrs. Richmond points out [10], this idea has been infiltrating cataloging and indexing practice for many years.

There is a further, less superficial, kinship between coordination and classification systems. A coordination system is a "do it yourself" system of forming subcategories, and though subordination is disclaimed by the advocates of such systems, it is nevertheless inherent; the subcategory "cigarette production," formed by coordinating the categories "cigarette" and "production," is subordinate in every sense to each of those categories. The same effect could be accomplishd in a traditional classification system by having a category "cigarettes" with a subcategory "production" in one hierarchical location, and a category "production" with a subcategory "cigarettes" in another location. Awareness of the difficulty of doing this in a traditional system should not affect our perception of the inherent similarity.[4]

One realization which comes to us as a result of looking at it this way is: when librarians hand control of subcategory formation over to the customer, they relinquish two other kinds of control — over the names of the subcategories and control over the quantities of materials in them. Because of this the librarian assigning uniterms to a document can have no clear idea of how these assignments are going to affect its relationship to other topically close documents. In short, the librarian is

---

3. Strictly speaking, as was shown earlier, *near*-maximum precision.

4. The argument for coordination, then, is not that it lacks subordination of subcategories, but that a given subcategory can be subordinated to numerous and varied categories, thus giving indexing access from a variety of viewpoints, whereas in a regular hierarchy only one approach route is usually given.

no longer in contact with the microstructure of the library. This must lead to uncontrollable precision and also to poor accuracy (Section IV).

These disadvantages do not matter much in a small library, and, as Jonker [8] points out, such disadvantages are heavily outweighed by the reduction of the cost of indexing brought by Uniterm and other keyword methods. The saving is so great that cost of overall operation of a library is usually reduced, at some inconvenience to searchers. However, since this article aims to anticipate technology several years in the future, it is less concerned with cost and more concerned with the welfare of the searcher.

It is also less concerned with small libraries than with large ones. The disadvantages of hierarchies are wellknown, because these are the schemes which are presently used in large libraries. According to Saul Herner [11], the newer and more unconventional schemes have not yet been used in libraries of great size. When they are so used, it is a good bet that the difficulties to which we have alluded will begin to be conspicuous.

This section has delved into the properties of classification systems at some length, in order to highlight conditions which ought to be avoided in formulation of new methods. Both classification and coordination are seen to have their advantages and disadvantages. Among the advantages, we need the flexibility of coordination systems and the semantic utility of hierarchies. We would also like good precision and some degree of control over the smallest subcategories, which hierarchies afford.

It is conceivable that the computer can help us to generate a vastly more flexible representation of library structure. The "supermarket" model of Section I sounds suspiciously like the traditional one-dimensional layout of the Dewey System. Computers, however, should enable us to integrate the "see also's" and the unusual conjunctions of topics with master semantic organization in a thoroughly natural way.

The most extensively discussed idea of this section is that the distribution statistics of library labels ought to be considered when one chooses a structural scheme for a retrieval system. In the following section, some smallscale empirical data will be presented which, we hope, will shed some light on at least the qualitative aspects of label distribution.

3. Topical Intersections

The statistically dependent placement of words in text (and hence of labels on documents) is a natural consequence of the way people think and communicate. The preceding section has pictured hypothetical examples to show that word association can have detrimental effects on retrieval system performance. There is, however, no reason why phenomena whose causes are traceable to the nature of human thought should adversely affect the retrieval of information. Such phenomena can indeed be put to work to aid retrieval: the same cognitive processes which lead to the highly correlated placement of words in text can also lead to the recognition of such pairs by literature searchers. And so we are going to take a close look at highly correlated word pairs — to see if we can get any ideas about how to use them.

Table I shows ten "topical intersections" formed by word distributions in 600 abstracts of SDC[5] internal documents. A topical intersection is a library subset in which every document contains *both* of two designated topical words or terms.

Since abstracts are brief summaries of articles, it is assumed that whenever a content word appears even once in the abstract, it is a topical clue to the contents of the article. Five hundred such topical words were selected for study, though at the time of selection no particular experiments were in mind. A computer program was written to process the keypunched text of the 600 abstracts and to print out data on all topical intersections, i.e. on all possible pairings of the 500 words with each other. The data were: a_1, the number of abstracts in which one word of a pair appears; a_2, the number of abstracts in which the other word of the pair appears; and a_3, the number of abstracts in which both words appear.

If one assumes that the probability of occurrence of one word in an abstract is totally independent of the probability of occurrence of the other word, one can compute the expected size of the intersection as $a_1 a_2 / A$, the expected number of abstracts in the intersection, where A is the total number of abstracts, in this case 600.

The topical intersections having the greatest interest to us are those for which the actual (observed) number of abstracts in the intersection, a_3, is much greater than the expected number, $a_1 a_2 / A$. This is so because of our assumption that statistical dependence is a natural phenomenon in language, and therefore we choose for study those cases which show the widest departures from apparent statistically independent behavior. In case some reader prefers the contrary and less reasonable assumption) i.e. that words are distributed in text as though assigned randomly to the text) and objects to our procedure as leading to explanations of statistical flukes rather than of genuine correlations, the author took the trouble to compute standard deviations of actual values from expected values for the 15 topical intersections formed by the six most frequent topical words in the 600 abstract corpus. The median number of standard deviations per intersection was found to be 2.2, and three of the intersections were more than 4.5 sigmas deviant.

In Table I the *ratio* of the actual number, a_3, to the expected number, $a_1 a_2 / A$, was taken as a crude measure

5. System Development Corporation.

TABLE I

Column	1		2	3	4	5	6	7*	8*	9	10
	Intersections (Subscripts show number of abstracts containing the word; a_1 and a_2 designate these subscripts and not the word itself)		Expected Size of Intersection	Actual Size	Ratio (Actual/Expected)	Number of Abstracts in Which					
						Words Occur Adjacently	Words Are Not Adjacent And Are Part of Multiword Term or Syntactically Linked	Related by Antecedence		Related Otherwise:	
	a_1	a_2								Different	Slight or None
	Feedback $_{51}$	Characteristics $_{61}$	5	35	7	1	25 (words connected by "and")	0	0	2	0
	Production $_{92}$	Schedule(s,d) $_{73}$	11	36	3.3	8	6 (words connected by "for")	4	1	6	3
	Requirement(s) $_{66}$	Sector(s) $_{52}$	5.7	18	3.2	0	9 (words connected by "for" and multi)	0	2	0	1
	Manual $_{72}$	Input(s) $_{63}$	7.5	21	2.8	5	3 (multi)	2	0	7	1
	Problem(s) $_{210}$	Package(s) $_{58}$	20	53	2.65	37	1 (multi)	8	2	0	1
	Program(s,-ed,-ing) $_{137}$	Model(s) $_{50}$	11.5	29	2.5	2	11 (several multi terms)	5	4	6	0
	Training $_{92}$	Aids	7.7	19	2.5	13	1 (words connected by "for")	2	1	2	0
	Flight(s) $_{98}$	Analysis $_{62}$	10	23	2.3	0	15 (multi)	0	0	0	2
	SAGE $_{02}$	System(s) $_{97}$	17	39	2.3	19	3 (several multi)	2	0	4	5
	Meeting(s) $_{79}$	SDC $_{62}$	8	16	2.0	0	4 (words connected by "at")	0	0	9	1
Totals						85	78	23	10	36	13

Total cases where words are related as in column 5 or 6 196

Total cases where words are related otherwise 49

* Column 7 includes cases where both words are in the same sentence; column 8, cases where words are in different sentences.

of correlation for a given word pair. Undoubtedly, much better measures[6] can be derived on theoretical grounds, but it is not yet time to worry about this.

Out of the 500 selected topical words there are 35 which appear in 50 or more of the 600 abstracts. Attention was confined to these in order to yield intersections large enough to be considered good samples. The ten intersections having the largest ratios of actual/expected size (number of abstracts) were chosen, with the qualification that no word be selected twice. Thus, in having 20 different words in the 10 intersections, we have enough semantic variety for the purpose of this discussion.

Column 1 lists the component words of the intersections, and the subscripts indicate the values a_1 and a_2. Columns 2, 3, and 4, respectively, give values for a_3, $a_1 a_2 / A$, and the ratios thereof. Columns 5 through 10 show the number of abstracts in which the component words have the relationship indicated in the column heading. Proximity of the component words in text was used as a criterion for deciding in which column a given abstract should be represented, e.g. if the two words were adjacent to each other in the text, other cases of occurrence of either of these words were ignored. This policy did not exclude many cases because most of the time the words appeared only once in an abstract. Columns 5 through 10 do not add up to the numbers in column 3 because only 550 of the 600 abstracts could be conveniently surveyed for this tabulation.

In columns 5 and 6, it was noted that meanings were "stabilized." For example, though the word "program" was often used in two senses in these abstracts, i.e. "computer program" and "training program," it referred only to computer programs in columns 5 and 6, where it was syntactically tied to the word "model." Other words for which this was true were "manual," "problem," "production," and "analysis." Meanings in columns 5 and 6 were specific and consistent. Indeed, the size of the numbers in these columns shows that the unexpectedly large sizes of the intersections are due mainly to these adjacent or near-adjacent occurrences. We draw the following tentative conclusions:

(a) Some of the strongest word correlations in text are correlations in adjacent or near-adjacent placement.

(b) A likely cognitive explanation for this is the tendency of the mind to handle word pairs (and often larger groups of adjacent words) as if they were one word; naturally the meanings of the component words will be dependent because they are subordinate parts of a larger semantic unit.

Cases without close syntactic connection between component words were assigned to columns 7-10, partly on

6. Among other things, the ratios tend to increase with library size (because the expected number will become smaller as A increases with respect to typical, i.e. modal, a_1 and a_2 values) and cannot be used for comparing cases from one library to another unless a_1, a_2, and A are all comparable in magnitude.

the basis of whether semantic relationships agreed with those in columns 5 and 6. Columns 7 and 8 contain instances where the component words were used in the same senses as in columns 5 and 6, but where the "adjective" component was omitted because an antecedent made things clear. As an example, the phrase "program revision and checkout of the new model" could have been written "program revision and checkout of the new *program* model," which of course would not have been necessary. Columns 9 and 10 contain cases where different relationships existed between the component words, either because one of the words did not pertain to the other component, on an antecedent basis or otherwise, or because one of the components had an entirely different meaning.

If the strongest correlations encountered are those of *adjacent* placement of words in text, some light is shed on the remarks in Section II about coordination indexing. Adjacent word correlations, we would expect, would be the first ones to disturb the operation of a coordination system, their effects setting in even in small collections. Fortunately, these effects are also easiest to handle — by the simple expedient of forming a term out of the two components.

In the 600-abstract "library" of Table I, even adjacent correlations would not lead to intersections large enough to constitute a bother. The intersections of Table I are atypically large in this collection because the component words occurred in at least 50 abstracts. As practiced information searchers know, these are the kinds of words to avoid using, if possible; they are "poor precision" words. In the 600-abstract library, typically consulted two-word intersections would contain about three abstracts each. However, if a library retains a specialized nature, intersections will grow in proportion to library size (probably somewhat less than direct proportion). At the 5000-document level, formation of two- and three-word terms would seem to be desirable, leading to greater precision per search ordinate and less work by the searcher.

What happens if the specialized library grows to 50,000 documents? Are there residual correlations which cannot be dealt with by term formation? Inspection of some of the nonadjacent correlations in the 600 abstracts seem to indicate that there are (see also [9]). The 600-abstract corpus is not large enough to permit this to be established without statistical analysis too exhaustive to be worthwhile. It seems quite safe to assume that even words which do not occur adjacently in text can have correlations for occurrence in the same textual unit (sentence, paragraph, article, abstract) which are much too high to behave as if they had been randomly sprinkled into the text. Statistical analysis has its place; it can reveal the existence of a signal in a packet of noise, but when a given symbol is agreed upon by convention to be a signal, it seems slightly redundant to prove that it is indeed a signal by statistical means. Accordingly, when one finds an apparent high correlation for the presence of the word "rocket" in the same articles with the word "satellite," it seems unreasonable to insist on proof that this could not have happened by chance. Statistics, however, *can* help us to predict the effects of these correlations on retrieval precision in large libraries, but for this we need larger (and more varied) samples.

What is the nature of the assumed residual correlations? If all high adjacent correlations can be removed by consolidation of adjacent words to form terms, then the residual correlations are between words which are not adjacent in text. We can call them nonadjacent or *proximal* correlations. The topical intersection in Table I which shows proximal correlation to the greatest degree is "meeting-SDC." The cases in column 6 (representing the most recurrent close-knit phrase involving "meeting" and "SDC") refer to meetings *at* SDC. This is as close as we come to adjacent correlation for this pair of words. Columns 9 and 10 have cases involving a hodge-podge of relationships between "meeting" and "SDC" usually either SDC personnel attending a meeting, or a meeting between SDC and other group(s) without specifying a location.

The largest topical intersection which could be found in the output data for the 600 abstracts which was practically of pure proximal correlation origin was that for "SAGE" and words with the root "operat—" (operate, -ing, -ion, -ional, -or, etc.). Only two abstracts containing adjacent occurrences (SAGE operations, as it happened) were found. In other cases, references were to parts of the system, e.g. becoming operational at such-and-such date, operating procedures for this or that facility; or obliquely to the system as a whole, as in use of operations research in analysis of SAGE.

The ratio of actual/expected was about 1.5. The sample size, about 25 abstracts in the intersection, was large enough to give confidence. The word "operate" is frequently used in describing what takes place on a macroscale in the SAGE System: the functioning of direction centers, air squadrons, radar sites, etc. Documents discussing small-scale features of the system, or discussing the internal workings of SAGE contractors, relatively infrequently use the words "SAGE" or "operate."

In each of the cases of proximal correlation discussed we can think of authors having in their heads a "discussion referent," which involves labelled mental models of the things being discussed. The probabilities of output of words known by an author, as a document is written, must be affected accordingly. We have now perceived two types of word correlation and can speculate that two different cognitive processes seem to be responsible for each type of correlation, one (adjacent correlation) involving the habitual use of word groups as semantic units, and the other (proximal correlation) having to do with the pattern of reference to various aspects of that which is being discussed (e.g. when one talks about "juries," there is a high probability that one will also

refer to "lawyers"). We can call the statistical effects, respectively, "language redundancy" and "reality redundancy."

While we are talking about various kinds of redundancy in word distribution in libraries we might mention a third kind: in addition to language redundancy and reality redundancy there is "documentation redundancy." This kind of redundancy is more theoretically unesthetic than it is practically odious. It occurs as a result of the series documents, the progress reports, newsletters, etc., which repeatedly and periodically refer to the same spectrum of topics; and documents dealing with routine matters. An example of this in Table I is the intersection "feedback-characteristics," which is generated by a subgroup of documents, all of which are worded similarly and hence have nearly identical abstracts. Documents of this type are best dealt with by tying whole groups of them up in bundles, and there is no need for us to be further concerned with them here.

Additional kinds of redundancy are likely to exist, such as redundancy of personal style and word choice. Evidences of further kinds of redundancy have so far not been perceived by this author, though undoubtedly they will rear their heads when is becomes possible to analyze larger samples.

Ordinarily, in studying various phenomena of reality redundancy, one would have to factor out the overshadowing effects of language redundancy because, as we saw in Table I, proximal correlations tend to be weaker than adjacent correlations. In some studies, however, the reverse is true — effects of language redundancy are overshadowed by those of reality redundancy. This is so, for example, when one's analysis is in terms of numbers of different words (word types) rather than numbers of occurrences (tokens).[7]

One can put such a happy circumstance to use in automatic determination of subject words. Word types in a given corpus of literature which are most thoroughly involved with special topics should appear in a limited subject spectrum, and the corresponding tokens should correlate strongly with certain other words in placement within the same documents. Such topically-involved words can be revealed by inventorying the *number of other word types* coexisting with the word in N documents containing a total of P tokens. If the word is a good subject word, inventory should show many token duplications in the N documents and therefore fewer word types. If the word is a poor subject word, many different fields will be involved in the samples and therefore many word types. If N and P can be held reasonably constant, the number of word types should be an interesting measure of the value of a word as a subject word.

In the pool of 600 abstracts used in deriving the data

7. A word type is a distinct sequence of alphanumeric characters bounded by spaces or punctuation; a word token is an occurrence of a word type in text.

of Table I, we do not have a complete inventory of the word types, but only of the 500 selected words. These words, however, should suffice for an initial test of the measure, and we can count the number of word types for any given word by counting the number of topical intersections in which the word is involved. This is done in Figure 3 for more than 100 of the most frequent of the 500 selected words. N and P could not be held constant, but the measure can be obtained by dividing the solid curve (number of topical intersections) by the value of some function of the dashed curve (number of abstracts in which a word appears) at the ordinate which represents a given word. Words are arranged from left to right in order of frequency. Note that not all of the points on the solid curve are labelled, but only the extreme values, to give readers an idea of which subject words turned out to be the "best" (i.e. troughs on the curve) and which "worst" (peaks).

Figure 3 admittedly does not answer the question, "Is this a good test for subject words?" It is not clear why one should think of "characteristic" and "request" as being better subject words than "equipment" and "input." However, an answer of sorts is possible because six months before it was possible to count topical intersections, the author subjectively partitioned words into five categories, in accordance with what their value as subject words seemed to be. We are therefore able to compare these value judgments with the results of the topical intersection count:

mainly a matter of personal curiosity satisfaction, and not a carefully planned and reasoned experiment. However, two realizations led to a change of heart:

a. The hypothesis that the best subject words should be those with the strongest proximal correlations is much to the point, because these are the very words that people will try to use in literature searching, with obvious implications for retrieval precision. In other words, if the hypothesis is true, we are assured that the residual correlations left over after elimination of adjacent correlations (by term consolidation) will operate in the same way as the adjacent ones did, i.e. the word combinations which correlate most strongly will be the ones most often used in search request statements.

b. It is possible that the "judgment of the computer" as to what constitutes a good subject word is actually better than that of a human. The cases where the results of the "topical intersection test" of Figure 3 differed from the judgment of the author may not have been so much due to the insufficiency of the test as to the faulty human judgment involved. A word like "meeting," though capable of being used in many senses, may actually be used predominantly in a single sense in a given corpus, and may therefore be a useful, accurate ordinate for retrieval. How could human judgment possibly single out such a case?

Now it is true that "a good subject word" is not merely a selective word but one which also has meaning to human searchers which is related to what it selects.

| | Number of Words Having | | |
Category	Above Average Measure*	Below Average Measure	Ratio of Above/Below
1. Unambiguous and specific	1	7	0.14
2. Specific, but possibly ambiguous	4	7	0.57
3. Specific, ambiguous in general, but probably not ambiguous in this corpus	9	14	0.64
4. Unspecific, possibly ambiguous	10	12	0.83
5. Very unspecific and very probably ambiguous	28	14	2.0

* The noncorrespondence in overall form between the two Figure 3 curves indicates that direct proportionality does not apply. At the same time, it is not known what the functional relationship should be. Therefore, the author "distorted" the values taken from the dashed curve, (mostly those from the upper end where a "saturation effect" appears to set in) in order to bring its gross form into line with that of the solid curve, and "aboves" and "belows" were picked on this basis.

Only one out of eight of the words judged best by the author were above average in number of topical intersections (and therefore poor). Words judged worst had more topical intersections than average in two out of three cases.

The author was at first reluctant to include Figure 3 and a discussion thereof in this article, not only because it did not seem to have a direct bearing on the trend of the discussion, but also because the experiment was

Therefore exploiting the "judgment of the computer" depends on our being able to inform searchers what the predominant sense of the word actually is. Section V describes one way in which this might be done indirectly.

This section has analyzed some topical intersections and has come up with the conclusion that there are at least three more or less independent kinds of redundancy in text: language redundancy, documentation redundancy, and reality redundancy. We think we know what

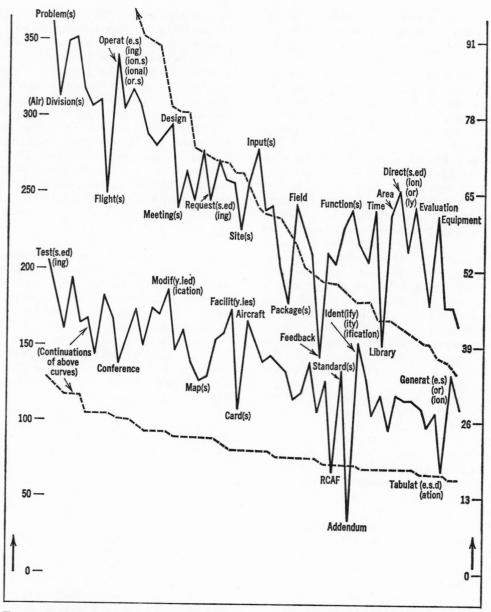

FIG. 3.   Solid Curve Index: Number of other word types coexisting with the words plotted. Dashed Curve Index: Number of abstracts containing the word.

NOTE: Points on solid curve occur in order of frequency of abstracts containing the word. These frequencies are shown by the dashed curve for all but the ten most widely distributed words. In general, the lower the point on the solid curve (with respect to its neighboring points) the better it is as a subject indicator. Thus, words such as "addendum" and "tabulation" are revealed to be highly particular subject indicators, at least for this library. (See discussion.)

to do about the first two kinds in formulating a retrieval system. For language redundancy, we combine the offending words into terms. For documentation redundancy, we combine the offending documents into bundles. What can we do with reality redundancy? This will be the topic of the following section.

4. Associations and Their Consequences

Information theory has brought us increased appreciation of the importance of the unexpected; the relationship between unexpectedness and information content was appreciated in some quarters even before the rise of information theory: for example, the newspaper world with its maxim, "Man bites dog — that's news!" In this section, attention will be drawn to the importance of the *expected*.

Literature searchers find and value both the unexpected and the expected. When something unexpected is found, one thereby obtains information; when the expected is found, one obtains confirmation. However, when one formulates a search, the unexpected is hardly ever involved. Search requests are practically always constructed out of familiar combinations of terms. If a searcher tries to be "cute" and choose an unusual combination of terms, the result of his search will hardly ever be satisfactory. Either there will be no documents satisfying his request, or else the ones that do will have either an incidental or inappropriate relationship between the terms of his request. This is one of the reasons (though not the major reason) why searchers using coordination systems tend to use meaningful, familiar combinations.

When the "unexpected" reveals itself in the text of a document, what form does it take? Does it involve new combinations of words? Usually no. A physical scientist, for example, who reports a new phenomenon does so in terms of the usual words that people in his field would use. Another scientist, to inform himself about this revelation, could dig up this report only by following standard search paths.

This is why hierarchies have been, and still are, important. They provide familiar conceptual grooves by which people can steer themselves to areas of interest. Sometimes, however, the "unexpected" does occur on a search request level. It is quite true that the recent expansion of knowledge, especially in interdisciplinary directions, has given rise to unexpected new pathways of access to information. Provision for these pathways has proved exceedingly troublesome for maintainers of classification systems.

Actually, the new pathways are only initially unexpected. If the pathways persist, they soon will be in the "expected" category in the minds of literature searchers. Those who have devised methods such as co-ordination indexing, where everything is potentially related to everything else, have possibly overemphasized the importance of unexpected relationships. Though there have been and will continue to be a vast number of new and unexpected conjunctions of ideas, it will nevertheless be true that *at any given moment* the number of unexpected relationships will be quite small in comparison to the number of familiar ones. For a layman conducting a search, the number of unexpected conjunctions may be appreciable; but not large enough to preclude tipoff signals to the searcher as a normal part of system operation.

For these reasons, it is probably psychologically sound to give a literature searcher some kind of a structure, whether hierarchical or otherwise, rather than to give him an infinitely flexible and therefore totally disorganized array of terms. Such a structure might have to be revised every so often in order to keep up with the changing topical spectrum; in the past this has not been feasible, but we hope computers can change the picture. The librarian's need for flexibility of organization and the searcher's need for semantic guidance are difficult to reconcile only in contemporary practice, and not in principle.

We are ready to discuss the setting up of a master framework, a kind of "semantic road map" that people can use as a guide to the literature. The framework will presumably be derived partially or wholly by computer analysis of text on a library-sized scale. We do not know exactly what will be involved in such use of a computer, but this need not prohibit discussion of basic principles and above all should not inhibit empirical efforts to find out what the principles are.

We would like the framework to express whatever we can find out about the "reality redundancy" in documentation since, as has been pointed out earlier, the very cognitive processes which cause this redundancy will also enable literature searchers to read correct meaning into the redundant combinations.

Two kinds of structures can be envisioned at this point, hierarchical and associative. The difference between the two is simply that associative structures involve no indications of subordination between categories. Hybrid arrangements are conceivable: one can have either hierarchies with associated cross-linkages, or association maps with arrows pointing toward subcategories. Whatever structure is decided upon should square with the degree of associativeness found in documentation. As we saw in Section II, hierarchies are at one extreme of the continuum of statistical dependence-independence; thus we probably need more pathways than are provided by a pure hierarchy, but many fewer than are provided by a coordination system.

The respective disadvantages of either pure-hierarchical or purely associative structures seem to require a compromise. Any kind of association map has the difficulty that one does not know where he is going on it; in a hierarchy one goes from the general to the specific and vice versa. This, in theory, makes it easy to go from any one subcategory to any other subcategory, by mentally going up the hierarchy to whether level of generality is required and then down again. Thus, the somewhat "artificial" ordering of topics in a hierarchy makes it possible for a searcher to have a fairly good mental picture of library structure. This, in many ways, tends to offset a lack of cross-connections in hierarchies because a searcher, knowing that a topic like "hypnotism" can come under other categories besides psychology, knows how to get to those other categories.

Some such macro-organization may turn out to be essential. Any association map derived from a library corpus will be very difficult to represent two-dimensionally: it will be quite large and probably each topical word or term will be associatively linked to 10 or 12 others. Nothing short of a push-button-controlled display console may be required to bring desired "two-dimensional components" of the map into view. Printouts of the map components are conceivable, but much page flipping would be required in a search. Neither button pushing nor page flipping can be done intelligently unless the searcher has some notion of the overall organization — which he wouldn't have if a standard organization were not somehow imposed. In other words, if we are going to generate an association map by computer analysis of libraries, we cannot permit the associative chips to fall where they may.

Having argued that the master framework should be an association map whose gross organization is decided by humans, and whose details are determined by computer analysis, we now consider that there are two kinds of association maps, psychological and empirical. A psychological association map would result if some eager human decided to organize in detail all knowledge. Such a psychological association map would also result if all literature searchers were asked to draw a small map of the associations which lead to their search request statements (in using a system such as coordination indexing) and all these small maps integrated to form a big one.

This map, as we have speculated, should have some similarity to an empirical map, determined by computer analysis of text. But also, each person would find an empirical map different from his expectations (i.e. his psychological map); and to the extent that it is different it *conveys information*. When we talk about differences between psychological and empirical associations, we are getting very close to making a statement about what "infor...ation" really means to the human mentality. If knowledge is the state of the association network in a human mind, then information is that which alters this state (in a nonrandom way). If a literature searcher finds an unexpected connection between "fish" and "transuranium chemistry," and after investigation realizes that someone has studied the up-take of plutonium by fish in the neighborhood of Eniwetok Atoll, information has indeed been conveyed.

However, as indicated earlier in this section, we do not expect most information transfer to be triggered in this way. A more reasonable expectation is that the vast bulk of information will come as a result of people reading a document after having retrieved it by means of a highly expectable combination of words (whether by search request or by recognition of an index entry). This is appropriate; we only want the association map to lead to the document, not to convey information. However, we continue to be interested in the "fish" example, because it is a kind of information, a very significant kind of information: it is information about *what is in the library*. There is a vast reservoir of such information in text, but it can not be fully tapped unless Edmundson's "special field frequency" idea [3] is extended to

document subsets of many sizes, down to and including subsets containing two documents.

If we visualize an association map as looking something like the cardiovascular system (without implying anything about actual form but only with the idea of speaking in terms of the arteries, arterioles, and capillaries of the system), we can make statements about the difference in derivation and function of these various components. Arteries can be thought of as associational relationships involving thousands of documents, such as that between "computer" and "programming." Arterioles, pathways of much smaller scale, lead to specific aspects of a subject, such as "programming" and "chess," which may involve dozens to hundreds of documents. Capillaries, the smallest pathways, can involve from a few dozen documents down to, at the least, one document (not zero, since we are dealing with an empirical map).

Most of the expected associations will naturally be concentrated in the arteries and arterioles. Because changes in the artery region are not rapid, there will be minimum need for flexibility and maximum opportunity for human design. Such design would have as its goal good overall routing of searchers to arterioles. Presumably, searchers can find an arteriole by looking in an index of terms, but there are undoubtedly many times when productive starting points for a search are not in mind. At these times a map of the gross structure will guide the searcher's imagination.

The arteriole-sized elements (and smaller), which will be the ones that will be strongly (in some cases devastatingly) affected by year-to-year changes in the literature, have to be flexibly organized, and it is at this level that we expect the computer to do most of the work. The arterioles, of course, lead one to the capillaries and the best principles (i.e. heuristics) for this remain to be worked out. In some areas, document word frequencies[8] will provide a basis for organization; in other areas meaningful organization will not be possible, and simple serial searching and recognition by humans of automatically generated proxies for documents will have to be relied upon. Some arteriole-sized elements will be "unexpected," but, as reasoned earlier, they will not be unexpected for long in the minds of searchers.

The capillaries are the smallest elements, and should have the most interesting function. Ideally, we hope these linkages will answer the searcher's question: "What does this document talk about that no other document talks about?" An unusual link such as fish-transuranium just about answers the question. Unfortunately, in most cases, individual documents will only reinforce already well-populated linkages; and in many other cases unique

8. If one deals with, say, the dozen most frequent content words in a document, an enormous amount of information (i.e. in the sense of "number of bits") is at hand, more than adequate to position any document proxy in the proper place (or places) on a map.

linkages will be formed, but will be due to unusual choices of words by authors.

Generally speaking, our hope that capillaries will allow us to make clean-cut discriminations between topically close documents will not work out, and some work must be done by the searcher. The main task at this level, therefore, is to give the searcher enough information about each undiscriminated document to permit him to narrow his focus by recognition.

Before ending this section on associations, it is necessary to tie up an important loose end. Several times earlier it was stated that in a coordination system one cannot cope with lack of precision by bringing additional ordinates into play; bringing in a fourth ordinate, or even a third ordinate, is overwhelmingly likely to lead to inaccuracy, that is, the rejection of relevant documents.

The cause of such a universal state of affairs resides in the fact that both librarians and authors generate words and terms from their own "psychological association maps." If librarians assigning descriptors to documents religiously stick to words used by an author, then the pattern of descriptor assignment is determined by the associations of authors. If librarians improvise, adding descriptors judged relevant, then the associations of librarians determine descriptor patterns. In either case, a decision has to be made about "where to stop" in assigning labels.

If labels were not associated, such a decision would be easy. But, unfortunately, labels imply each other, in an associative sense. "Eye" implies "glasses" and "production" implies "factory." With one search ordinate, the implications (and hence the empirical associations in text) are not very strong. "Eye" can imply "hurricane," "needle," "retina," and many other terms which are grossly unrelated to each other and therefore might give valid discrimination in searching. Suppose, however, one has three search ordinates, such as "camera," "satellite," and "weather." Now certain other labels become very strongly implied, such as "Tiros," "stabilization," "telemetering," etc. "Stabilization," for example, refers to the elementary fact that one needs to point a camera in order to take a picture. The searcher who discovers that his three search ordinates have yielded a hundred references, and who tries to use "stabilization" (the aspect which interests him) as a means of narrowing down, assumes that the motivation (of the librarian) to apply that label must have been proportional to the extent to which stabilization was discussed.

If every author writing a document could be caused to either fully discuss something or *not* discuss it, such an assumption would be justified. In reality, chances are that nearly half of the 100 authors in this case make some reference to the stabilization problem, and very few of them have stabilization as a principal topic. Thus the probability that a librarian will apply the label "stabilization" to a document is likely to be governed, we hypothesize, more strongly by the philosophy of label

application of that librarian on that particular day than by its appropriateness (which after all can be judged only in awareness of the contents of the other 99 documents; such an awareness is difficult enough in a hierarchical system, but it is doubly difficult in a system where librarians are out of touch with subcategories).

Thus, a single word is too intrinsically crude as a discriminating device. The reason it is not crude as a second ordinate and often not crude as a third ordinate is that it takes two and sometimes three ordinates to get one "in the right ball-park" on the association map implicit in the pattern of label assignment. Once the position on this map has been determined, there is more lost than gained by the blind use of further ordinates.

5. Searching the Literature

As many people have realized, there is a certain amount of futility in trying to boil down the contents of a document to some residue which will tell what it is about, either by human or automatic means. Yet, at the same time, such boiling down cannot be avoided if intelligent and nonlaborious selection by human searchers is to be accomplished. We have to give the searcher enough information about each document so that he won't be making rejections "in the dark" (as with coordination indexing), but not so much information as to prohibit convenient scanning of numerous proxies of documents (as in auto-abstracting). The decision as to what is "just the right amount of information" depends on the need for discrimination of a document from topically close documents, and this decision is perhaps best made by a computer, which is the only agency capable of having "full consciousness" of the contents of a library.

The idea that proxies for documents should be derived in relation to the host library and particularly in relation to topically close documents has probably occurred to many others, but immediately discarded in further thinking because it is technologically impossible to implement. On the other hand, it is a theme of this article that retrieval research should anticipate future technology. If retrieval thinkers five years ago had looked toward 1960, chances are that we would be making much wiser use of present equipment than we are. But then, the trends of computer development were not so obvious then as they are today, and so there is much less excuse for us than for past workers.

Now it is time to take a look at "what it might be like" to search the literature in 1965. The sample system about to be presented is completely arbitrary, except insofar as it follows the principles outlined herein. The final form and use of association maps can be determined only by extensive research and experimentation.

Shown in Figure 4 are a "capillary" region of an association map (upper left) and some proxies of documents from which the associations in this capillary were derived (middle and lower right). These maps are true empirical

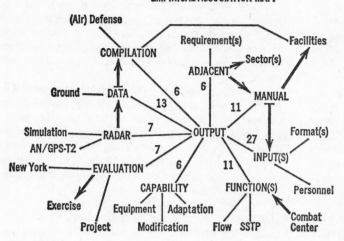

EMPIRICAL ASSOCIATION MAP.

2nd order association

REJECTS

(Negative or uncertain positive correlation with OUTPUT)

Inputs—Intelligence
Inputs—Room
Function—Supervisor
Function—Position
Capability—Frame
Capability—Missile
Evaluation—Criterion
Evaluation—KCADS
Evaluation—Boston
Evaluation—Room
Evaluation—Lincoln (Lab)
Data—Technical

FIVE DOCUMENT PROXIES

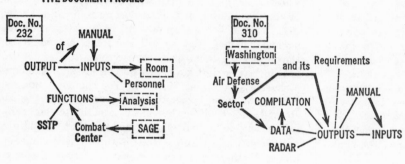

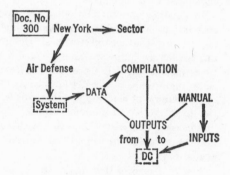

PSYCHOLOGICAL ASSOCIATION MAP.

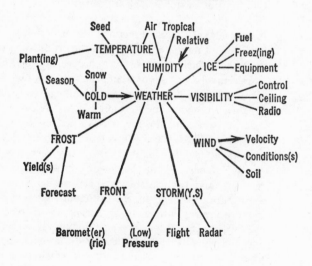

Fig. 4

maps, derived by easily programmable heuristics from the same data (600 abstracts) that went to make up Table I. In the lower left-hand corner is a "psychological" association map made in advance of the empirical map for purposes of comparison of form. The map was made by the author, more or less as a doodle, imagining the associations that might be found in a corpus of articles which talk about the weather (e.g. on agriculture, meteorology, navigation, military operations, etc.). Unfortunately, the thought did not occur (until too late) to use the same semantic starting point and reservoir of material as was used in the empirical map.

The empirical map was generated by finding the eight words correlating most strongly with "output" in occurrence in the same abstracts, and then finding in turn three other words correlating with each of the eight words and also positively correlating with "output." The rejects among these secondary associations (listed at the upper right of Figure 4) had either negative or uncertain positive correlations with "output," even though they had high correlations with those words directly associated with "output."

In general, the correlations were proximal. Adjacent correlations are indicated by double-lined arrows pointing toward the second word of the pair. Three-word terms such as "adjacent manual facilities" can be sometimes picked out. A line crossing the base of the arrow at right angles indicates that the word at the base is always the beginning of a term; in other words, there cannot be the term "adjacent manual inputs," for example. The numbers on the paths connecting with "output" show the number of abstracts containing both words of the connected pair.

The five proxies are made up mainly of words from the empirical map shown. The notation is similar, with the added feature that sometimes it is possible to introduce syntactic connectives (again by means of easily programmable heuristics);[9] in such a case, single-lined arrows are used to show which is the word following the connective. The proxies were derived by applying simple word selection priority rules to the corresponding abstracts; in a real system the proxies would probably be formed out of the most frequent topical words in the corresponding documents.

Assume that a literature searcher is seated at a TV-like display console, which he can operate by means of buttons and typewriter keys. Assume, also, that somehow (we are not equipped to discuss how) he is steered through the "arteries" and "arterioles" of a enormous

9. An example of such a heuristic is a routine which computes the number of letters separating two words in text; if the numbers of letters is not greater than, say, 15, and if there are no intervening punctuation marks, the corresponding words can be extracted as "connectives." The heuristics actually employed would probably have to be more complicated than this.

empirical map and that it becomes evident to him that "output" is a word which will lead to documents of interest. (Note: the word "output," being common, would have to exist at many points on the map; but the searcher has been led to his particular occurrence of "output" by a process superficially resembling coordination.)

The controls of his console enable him to bring the Figure 4 map onto the screen. He is now able to see primary and secondary associations to the word "output," and the chances are that some of these will "ring a bell." Note that, instead of depending on his imagination to think up a search request, he is depending on his *recognition* of semantic relationships. We have put him in close touch with the contents of the library, qualitatively and quantitatively.

When he singles out a particular intersection for further investigation, he is informed how many documents are in the intersection; in other words, he knows whether he has arrived at a capillary or is still in an arteriole, by the size of this number, and he then knows whether to try for a map with smaller intersections or to start requesting individual document proxies. In this case, assume he singles out the intersection "output-manual," hoping that he will get some information on the output of manual air defense sectors.

Using typewriter keys, he indicates his interest in this intersection by typing "manual." The computer program can, at this point, generate the proxies and put them in storage slots ready to be called onto the screen, either collectively or individually, by the searcher. Of the five proxies shown in Figure 4, the top three refer to "manual inputs" rather than "manual sectors," and the word "outputs" refers to still other things. The proxy at the lower right uses "manual" in a completely irrelevant sense, and also contains several words not associated with the "output" capillary in any way. The proxy labelled "304" is the only one that has a chance of being relevant. It does not say "manual sectors," but it does say "manual facilities," a more general term — this is an example of a document which might be passed over in a coordination search involving use of the ordinate "manual sector." Here is a case illustrating the advantage of recognition over search request formulation.

As it turns out, document 304 appears to talk about outputs of SAGE DC's (Direction Centers) and not that of manual facilities. However, by the very mention of "manual facilities" the document has a chance of being relevant, and the searcher has the option of calling in more information about the document. At this point, it is quite appropriate to make use of abstracts (auto or otherwise). In a literature search like this, the author may individually inspect 100 or more proxies, in various topical intersections of more or less equal promise, and may pick out a dozen or so proxies of potential interest, reading the corresponding 12 abstracts.

One might think, "But surely it's easier to read 88 abstracts than to look at 88 of those things in Figure 4." Such a contention would ignore several factors:

(1) The proxies can be evaluated at a glance when one gets used to the notation and knows what to look for; the eye lights immediately on the words "manual" and "output," which are always in the same spatial location with respect to each other. What we are after at this stage of the retrieval process is speedy and confident rejection of irrelevant documents. Rejections, in most cases, should take less time than reading the corresponding abstracts (which, remember, all would contain the words "manual" and "output").

(2) Proxies can be designed to conspicuously indicate the things about a document which make it different from its closest topical relatives; note that for each proxy in Figure 4, a dotted line is drawn around all words not appearing in the capillary display. In systems where more information about a document is available in storage than is shown in the proxy, searchers can request as much additional information as is required to make distinctions between related documents.

(3) The proxies are subject to flexible control in both generation and grouping. Such flexibility lends itself to evolutionary processes.

Methods of this kind not only help clarify the picture in a specific search, but can serve as the basis of highly systematic and rapid browsing. In such a way we, indeed, fulfill the goal described in Section I, of "increasing the mental contact between the reader and the information store." We give the searcher the advantageous illusion of proceeding along ordinates of meaning in his browsing, rather than along the usually irrelevant ordinates of page length and shelf location.

References

1. MOOERS, C. N. The next twenty years in information retrieval. *Amer. Documentation* **11** (1960), 229–236.
2. LUHN, H. P. Auto-encoding of documents for information retrieval systems. In *Modern Trends in Documentation*, Proceedings of a symposium held at the University of Southern California, April, 1958, Pergamon Press Ltd., New York, pp. 45–58.
3a. EDMUNDSON, H. P., OSWALD, V. A., JR., and WYLLYS, R. E. Automatic indexing and abstracting of the contents of documents. Planning Research Corp. Document PRC R-126, ASTIA AD No. 231606, Los Angeles, 1959.
3b. EDMUNDSON, H. P. and WYLLYS, R. E. Automatic abstracting and indexing — survey and recommendations. *Comm. ACM* **4** (May, 1961).
4. TAUBE, MORTIMER. Machines and classification in the organization of information. Documentation, Inc., Technical Report No. 2, ASTIA AD No. 22426, Washington, D.C., 1953.
5. FOSKETT, D. J. The construction of a faceted classification for a special subject. Preprints of papers for the International Conference on Scientific Information, Area 5, Washington, D.C., Nov., 1958, 53–74.
6. VICKERY, B. C. Developments in subject indexing, *J. Documentation* **2** (1955), 1–12.
7. BARTON, A. R., SCHATZ, V. L., and CAPLAN, L. N. Information retrieval on a high-speed computer. Proc. Western Joint Comp. Conf., San Francisco, Mar., 1959, 77–80.
8. JONKER, FREDERICK. The descriptive continuum: a generalized theory of indexing. Preprints of papers for the International Conference on Scientific Information, Area 6, Washington, D.C., pp. 21–41.
9. DOYLE, L. B. Programmed interpretation of text as a basis for information retrieval systems. Proc. Western Joint Comp. Conf., San Francisco, Mar., 1959, 60–63.
10. RICHMOND, PHYLLIS A. Hierarchical definition. *Amer. Documentation* **11** (Apr. 1960), 91–96.
11. HERNER, SAUL. Retrieval questions most susceptible to mechanization. Third Institute on Information Storage and Retrieval, Washington, D.C., February, 1961 (in press).

23 An Algol-Based Associative Language

JEROME A. FELDMAN
PAUL D. ROVNER
*Communications of the Association
for Computing Machinery
Vol. 12, No. 5, August, 1969*

1. The LEAP Language

1.1 Introduction

Associative processing, the accessing of data through a partial specification of its content, has long been a subject of interest in computer science. Although it is no longer considered a panacea, associative processing has proved to be of great value in artificial intelligence, operating systems, and computer aided design, as well as being a major aspect of information retrieval. Various proposals for building large hardware associative memories have not materialized [15], and essentially all the applications to date have depended on software schemes of some sort. In this paper we present a programming language for software associative processing systems and describe a particular scheme which seems to have several nice properties.

There are two basic problems in designing any programming system: ease of use and efficiency of execution. In this section we discuss a programming language which users have found convenient for associative processing; in Section 2 we describe an implementation of the lan-

guage which is quite efficient over a range of problems.

The language LEAP is a version of ALGOL [27] extended to include associations, sets, and a number of auxiliary constructs. The problem of describing a programming language in a journal-size article is quite difficult, especially if the system contains new ideas. The problem is exacerbated in this case by the fact that LEAP is really a family of languages, each adding a different set of features to the ALGOL base. Besides the constructs described here, there are forms of LEAP with matrix operations, property sets, and on-line graphics [34, 35]. Even the associative language has two compilers: one which does dynamic-type checking at execution time and another (described here) which does not. This notion of fluid language specification is contrary to the current emphasis on standardized languages and will be considered further.

The fluidity of the LEAP design is largely due to its implementation by means of the translator-writing system VITAL [11, 25]. Our variation of ALGOL (described in [25, 44]) was purposely designed with the possibility of being extended, and various application groups have tailored it to their needs. With such a system and a good linkage editor, there seems to be no advantage to standardization. We view the design of better universal languages to be like the design of better crutches — not of direct interest to those possessing complete facilities.

This attitude toward programming has also influenced the style of this paper. Rather than attempt to spell out every nuance of the language, we have concentrated on the major features. Although LEAP is even less context-free than other programming languages, we have expressed the form of constructs in Backus-Naur form. The sections on semantics and pragmatics, as well as the examples, serve to delimit the syntactically correct constructs which are meaningful. For expository purposes we have used a slightly different syntax in this paper than is actually implemented. A reference manual [44] and a complete formal description of LEAP in the notation of VITAL (cf [25]) are available from the authors. The formal description does not include the data-structure implementation, which was done separately and is described in Section 2 of this paper. A translator-writing system capable of automating data-structure design would be a significant contribution to the field [12].

Both the LEAP language and the data structure underlying it incorporate constructs whose meaning is not immediately obvious. As an aid to understanding we will establish some notational conventions for this paper. We incorporate in the text, with appropriate typography, three kinds of constructs from the LEAP syntax: reserved words (e.g. *set*), nonterminal symbols (e.g. ⟨set expression⟩) and identifiers (e.g. *fifth*). There are several terms which we will define and then use only in the sense defined; these will appear in italics when defined and will otherwise appear in the text with no special typography. These technical terms to be defined are: item, set, itemvar, local, association, form, component, bound, and datum.

Some of the technical terms coincide with constructs in the language and data structure. For example, there is a LEAP construct, ⟨set expression⟩, whose value is a set. One kind of ⟨set expression⟩ is an ⟨identifier⟩ declared with the declarator *set*. The definition of the technical terms is best motivated by considering the properties of the mythical associative memory.

The essential fact about an associative memory is that it does not rely on explicit addresses. A reference to information contained in a memory cell is specified by a partial description of its contents. All cells in the memory which meet the specification are referred to by the statement. A conventional coordinate-addressed memory can be thought of as a special case in the following way. Each cell of the associative memory will be a pair consisting of a conventional cell and its address:

associative cell | address | conventional cell |

To access a cell in this special associative memory, one specifies the contents of one particular part (the address field) of a cell. In the general associative memory a cell can be accessed by specifying the contents of any part of the cell.

The following example may help point out the importance of this seemingly minor difference. Suppose one were to store the contents of a telephone directory in a computer memory. There are several ways in which the data could be organized so that the telephone number of a given person could be found fairly quickly. However, the problem of going from a telephone number to its owner is rather difficult. One could, of course, enter a second directory ordered by numbers rather than names, but this entails representing the same information twice in the memory. There are several other possibilities; all of these lead to compromises between inefficiency in time and inefficiency in storage. In an associative memory either question could be answered in one memory access and without any redundant information being stored in the memory.

This example is so clear and striking that it should be suspect. First of all, it is often the case that one person has several telephone numbers or that several people are listed for the same number. This is the so-called multiple-hit situation and is at the root of most of the problems encountered in using associative memories. Many other difficulties arise in the design of hardware associative memories [15] and there is a sense in which they are inherently impractical (cf Section 2.1). However, the idea of referring to information by a partial specification of its contents is intriguing and has found its way into a number of programming systems (cf Section 2.1). Let us consider the behavior of an associative memory each of whose cells contains an ordered 3-tuple:

3-element associative cell | a | o | v |

written (a, o, v) or in accordance with LEAP syntactic "sugar" as $a \cdot o \equiv v$. The symbols a, o, and v can be thought of as mnemonics for attribute, object, and value; we will not concern ourselves here with the rationale for choosing three fields.

The elements of the 3-tuple are drawn from a universe of items which are represented inside a machine by their internal names and are otherwise uninterpreted. A 3-tuple of items is an association. The items constituting an association are its components. Typical associations might be:

$$father \cdot john\ doe \equiv don\ doe$$
$$end \cdot line \equiv point$$

If a universe of associations were stored in an associative memory, any partial specification should lead to retrieval. Letting x, z represent unspecified positions in an association, Table I enumerates the partial specifications (forms) possible in a 3-element associative memory. The representation and manipulation of associations

TABLE I

Form Name	Form	Example	Interpretation
F0	$a \cdot o \equiv v$	$son \cdot john\ doe \equiv don\ doe$	The association itself, if in memory
F1	$a \cdot o \equiv x$	$son \cdot john\ doe \equiv x$	Sons of john doe
F2	$a \cdot x \equiv v$	$son \cdot x \equiv don\ doe$	Father of don doe
F3	$x \cdot o \equiv v$	$x \cdot john\ doe \equiv don\ doe$	Relation of john doe to don doe
F4	$a \cdot x \equiv z$	$son \cdot x \equiv z$	All father, son pairs
F5	$x \cdot z \equiv v$	$x \cdot z \equiv don\ doe$	All associations with don doe as third component
F6	$x \cdot o \equiv z$	$x \cdot john\ doe \equiv z$	All associations with john doe as second component

and forms were the major motivations for the development of LEAP and the data structure described in Section 2.2 Table I also contains examples of the application of the seven forms along with an intuitive interpretation of their meanings. With this background we can define all the remaining technical terms except "bound," which is covered in Section 1.4.

The data space manipulated by LEAP includes a universe of *items* and a universe of *associations*.

The universe of items is divided into three subclasses differing in the way an item enters the universe of items:

(1) a *declared* item results from each declaration of an ⟨identifier⟩ to be of type **item**. The declaration is processed once at translation time; items are not declared dynamically;

(2) a *created* item results from the execution of a **new** expression;

(3) an *association* item results from the execution of a ⟨bracketed triple⟩, $[a \cdot o \equiv v]$. This item permanently denotes the association (a, o, v).

An item of type (1) or (2) may have an associated *datum* of ⟨algebraic type⟩ which can be used or altered like an ALGOL variable. An item of type (2) or (3) can be deleted from the universe of items by a **delete** statement; no item is automatically deleted at block exit.

An *itemvar* is a variable whose value is an item (it is a reference [41, 42] to an item). A *local* is an itemvar which obeys special building rules and is used only in a restricted set of contexts (cf Section 1.4; the earliest use of locals was in the string processing languages [4]). A *set* is a finite unordered collection of items containing at most one occurrence of an item.

An *association* is an ordered triple (a, o, v) of items which corresponds to the informal concept of association described above. The items a, o, v are called the *components* of the association. The totality of associations created during the execution of a program (and not subsequently removed by **erase** statements) is called the *universe of associations*. Whenever an association is created from its component items (by execution of a ⟨bracketed triple⟩, or of a **make** statement), the universe of associations is searched for an association with the same components, and a new association is constructed only if this search fails. Thus the universe never contains more than one association with the same components. Once an association has been created, its component items cannot be changed.

Many of the ideas in the associative language LEAP have occurred before. If we consider an association to be a triple we see that the earliest list processing systems

attribute of *object* is *value*

[23, 28] included some associative processing in their attribute or property lists. By considering an associative structure as a colored, directed graph we can relate our work to string and tree manipulation languages. Both these developments have been recently surveyed in [4]. Another field in which associative structures have played a central role is information retrieval [7]. Sets have appeared in simulation languages [40], among others.

The LEAP system is a continuation of our earlier work [10, 34, 35] on associative processing. The new problems attacked were the development of a convenient language for handling complex collections of associations and the extension of the hash-coding structure techniques to a paging system. We were also interested in the implications of LEAP as a nonprocedural language; the sequencing of associative retrieval statements is decided by the translator, and the complexity of this process (cf [16]) portends a difficult future for nonprocedural systems. The LEAP system has been running on the Lincoln Laboratory TX-2 since early 1967 and has been used in a number of applications, some of which are discussed in Section 3.

1.2 Data Types of LEAP

The augmenting of ALGOL with associative processing required the addition of four new ⟨type⟩ declarators corresponding to the notions: item, itemvar, local, set. A ⟨declaration⟩ is formed from ⟨type⟩ declarators as in ALGOL 60.

1.2.1 Syntax

⟨simple type⟩ ::= **real** | **integer** | **boolean**
⟨algebraic type⟩ ::= ⟨simple type⟩ | ⟨simple type⟩ **array**
⟨leap type⟩ ::= **item** | **itemvar** | **local**
⟨type⟩ ::= ⟨algebraic type⟩ | ⟨leap type⟩ | set | ⟨algebraic type⟩ ⟨leap type⟩
Examples of declarations:

set	*sons*
real item	*pi*
local	*x*
boolean	*married*

1.2.2 Semantics

An ⟨identifier⟩ declared to be of ⟨algebraic type⟩ behaves exactly like an ALGOL 60 variable. An ⟨identifier⟩ declared with **item (itemvar, local)** denotes an item (itemvar, local). An item whose declaration is qualified by an ⟨algebraic type⟩ has an associated datum of that type. All items are treated as if they were declared in the outermost block. If an itemvar (local) has its declaration qualified by an ⟨algebraic type⟩, then the item which is the value of the itemvar (local) is assumed to have a datum of that type for algebraic operations. An ⟨identifier⟩ declared with *set* denotes a variable which takes on sets as values.

1.2.3 Pragmatics

The division of variables into ⟨algebraic type⟩, ⟨leap type⟩, and a combination of the two is for efficiency reasons. Variables of ⟨algebraic type⟩ require less space and yield more efficient code. A variable of strictly ⟨leap type⟩ requires less storage than one with ⟨algebraic type⟩ as well. Sets are implemented by a linked list ordered by the internal names of items; this allows the system to carry out binary set operations in an amount of time proportional to the sum of the sizes of the sets rather than the product of their sizes, as would be the case for unordered lists.

An itemvar (local) is implemented as a register which can contain a pointer to an item. An item with an associated datum specifies a cell (or array of cells) containing the datum. Thus, for example, the following program would write out the value "4."

```
begin integer itemvar x;   integer item a;
    datum(a) ← 3;
    x ← a;
    datum(a) ← 4;
    write(datum(x))
end
```

The treatment of all declared items as if they were declared in the outermost block is one of the unfortunate compromises that is forced upon any attempt to combine lists or associations with ALGOL block structure. The creation and deletion of lists and associations is a dynamic process which does not follow a stack discipline and requires some non-ALGOL storage allocation scheme. LEAP uses explicit delete commands for created items; deletion could be extended to declared items, but we find this distasteful.

1.3 Expressions

The additional expressions required for LEAP are divided into those which yield algebraic values and those whose values are leap types. The use of τ in a production is a shorthand notation for two productions, one with τ replaced by "retrieval" and one with τ replaced by "construction."

1.3.1 Syntax

⟨additional arithmetic primary⟩ ::= **datum** (⟨item primary⟩) | **count** (⟨retrieval set expression⟩)

⟨additional boolean primary⟩ ::= ⟨retrieval item expression⟩
in ⟨retrieval set expression⟩ | ⟨retrieval set expression⟩ ⊂ ⟨retrieval set expression⟩ | ⟨retrieval set expression⟩ = ⟨retrieval set expression⟩ | **istriple** (⟨item primary⟩) | **datum**(⟨item primary⟩)

⟨algebraic expression⟩ ::= ⟨arithmetic expression⟩ | ⟨boolean expression⟩

⟨item primary⟩ ::= ⟨item identifier⟩ | ⟨itemvar identifier⟩ | ⟨local identifier⟩

⟨retrieval item expression⟩ ::= ⟨item primary⟩ | ⟨selector⟩ ⟨item primary⟩

⟨construction item expression⟩ ::= ⟨item primary⟩ | **new** | **new**(⟨algebraic expression⟩) | ⟨bracketed triple⟩

⟨bracketed triple⟩ ::= [⟨item primary⟩·⟨item primary⟩ ≡ ⟨item primary⟩]

⟨τ set primary⟩ ::= ∅ | ⟨set identifier⟩ | {⟨τ item expression list⟩} | (⟨τ set expression⟩) | (⟨τ derived set⟩)

⟨τ item expression list⟩ ::= ⟨τ item expression⟩ | ⟨τ item expression list⟩, ⟨τ item expression⟩

⟨τ set factor⟩ ::= ⟨τ set primary⟩ | ⟨τ set factor⟩ — ⟨τ set primary⟩

⟨τ set term⟩ ::= ⟨τ set factor⟩ | ⟨τ set term⟩ ∩ ⟨τ set factor⟩

⟨τ set expression⟩ ::= ⟨τ set term⟩ | ⟨τ set expression⟩ ∪ ⟨τ set term⟩

⟨retrieval associative expression⟩ ::= ⟨retrieval item expression⟩ | ⟨retrieval set primary⟩ | **any**

⟨construction associative expression⟩ ::= ⟨construction item expression⟩ | ⟨construction set primary⟩

⟨τ derived set⟩ ::= ⟨τ associative expression⟩ ⟨associative operator⟩ ⟨τ associative expression⟩

⟨τ triple⟩ ::= ⟨τ derive dset⟩ ≡ ⟨τ associative expression⟩

⟨associative operator⟩ ::= ·| ' |*

⟨selector⟩ ::= **first** | **second** | **third**

Examples

count (*sons*) — **datum** (*bill*) + 3
{*bill, tom*} ⊂ *sons* ∪ (*father'don*)
number[·*part·hand* ≡ *finger*] ≡ **new** (5)

1.3.2 Semantics

The distinction between ⟨construction item expression⟩ and ⟨retrieval item expression⟩ is primarily semantic and gives rise to the further (construction, retrieval) distinctions. In LEAP, an expression is sometimes used to create new items or associations (construction type) or to retrieve information about existing items or associations (retrieval type).

Any ⟨item primary⟩ yields an item as its value. If the item has an associated algebraic datum then **datum** will yield its value; otherwise, **datum** is undefined. The unary operator **count** returns an integer equal to the number of elements in the set specified by its argument. The notions of membership, set containment, and set equality have their usual meaning.

The predicate **istriple** returns **true** if the item specified by its argument is an association item. A ⟨selector⟩ applied to such an item will yield the corresponding component; otherwise, it is undefined. A ⟨construction item expression⟩ may be the operator **new**, which causes a new item to be created and assigned an internal name. If *new* is given a parameter of ⟨algebraic type⟩, the created item has an associated datum of that type.

The execution of a ⟨bracketed triple⟩ causes a new association to be created and placed in the universe of associations (unless it is already present) and then produces an association item which denotes this association.

Any set construct can be of either retrieval or construction type, depending on its context. The symbol ∅ denotes the empty set, a list of item expressions denotes the set containing the values of the item expressions, and the set operations −, ∩, ∪ have their conventional meanings. A ⟨τ derived set⟩ is defined in terms of the universe of associations. If the two operands are both ⟨τ item expressions⟩s with values P and Q then

P·Q is the set of items X such that P·Q ≡ X is in the
    universe of associations,

P ′ Q is the set of items X such that P·X ≡ Q is in the
    universe of associations,

P ∗ Q is (P · Q) ∪ (P ′ Q).

If the ⟨τ associative expression⟩ S has a set $\bar{S}$ as its value, the value of P·S is the union of P·Q for all Q in $\bar{S}$; P′S, P∗S, S·Q, S′Q, and S∗Q are defined analogously.

The ⟨τ triple⟩ is a generalization of the 3-tuple $a \cdot o \equiv v$ which is the Leap representation of an association. The meanings of a ⟨construction triple⟩ and of a ⟨retrieval triple⟩ are quite different and are discussed in connection with the corresponding operators in Section 1.4.

1.3.3 Pragmatics

The use of *datum* can be avoided by adding another depressing convention to the translator; our decision to include *datum* was meant to impose a discipline we believe to be important for effective use of Leap.

Sets are discussed briefly in Section 1.2.3. We were led to include the various set operations after noticing that associations are naturally set-valued and thus all the set manipulation routines would be needed in the system in any event. The Leap syntactic construct ⟨τ triple⟩ is used to represent both the association and the form of Section 1.1.

1.4 Statements

There are relatively few new statement types in Leap because the control structure of Algol was largely adequate for our purposes.

1.4.1 Syntax

⟨additional statement⟩ ::= ⟨set statement⟩ |
    ⟨associative statement⟩ ⟨loop statement⟩
⟨set statement⟩ ::= ⟨set identifier⟩ ←
    ⟨construction set expression⟩ |
    put ⟨construction item expression⟩ **in** ⟨set identifier⟩ |
    remove ⟨retrieval item expression⟩ **from** ⟨set identifier⟩
⟨associative statement⟩ ::= **delete** ⟨retrieval item
    expression⟩ | ⟨itemvar identifier⟩ ←
    ⟨construction item expression⟩ |
    datum (⟨item primary⟩) ← ⟨algebraic expression⟩ |
    make ⟨construction triple⟩ | **erase** ⟨retrieval triple⟩
⟨loop statement⟩ ::= **foreach** ⟨associative context⟩ **do**
    ⟨statement⟩
⟨associative context⟩ ::= ⟨element⟩ | ⟨associative context⟩
    and ⟨element⟩
⟨element⟩ := ⟨retrieval triple⟩ | ⟨boolean expression⟩

Examples

put *tom* **in** *sons*
sons ← *sons* ∪ {*tom*}
make *father·tom* ≡ *bill*
foreach x **in** *sons* **do datum**(x) ← **datum**(x) + 2
foreach *father·x* ≡ *bill* **do put** x **in** *sons*

1.4.2 Semantics

The assignment statements to an ⟨itemvar identifier⟩ and to the datum of an ⟨item primary⟩ are discussed in Section 1.2.3. The set-assignment statement assigns the value of the ⟨construction set expression⟩ to the ⟨set identifier⟩. The **put** (**remove**) operation is simply a more efficient way of doing union (subtraction) of a single element. An item which was created (e.g. by a **new** expression) can be destroyed by **delete**. The internal name associated with this item will be reassigned, and it is the user's responsibility that there are no uses of a deleted item.

The **make** statement causes the association represented by a ⟨construction triple⟩ to be placed in the universe of associations if it is not already there. This may entail the creation of new items and associations, as the following example will show.

Example

make *number·*[*part·hand* ≡ *finger*] ≡ **new** (5)

In the processing of this statement, the system
1. forms an association *part·hand* ≡ *finger*,
2. creates an item from the association formed in 1,
3. creates a new integer item with its associated datum
    initialized to 5,
4. forms the association from *number* and the items of
    2 and 3.

The *erase* statement causes an association to be removed from the universe of associations; it will never lead to the creation of a new entity.

erase *number* · [*part* · *hand* ≡ *finger*] ≡ **any**

This will cause the removal of the association formed in step 4 above. Neither the association *part* · *hand* ≡ *finger* nor any item will be removed.

If a ⟨construction set expression⟩ occurs in the ⟨construction triple⟩ which is the operand of **make**, all associations formed by using each element of the set in turn will be placed in the universe of associations. If a ⟨retrieval set expression⟩ (or **any**) occurs in the ⟨retrieval triple⟩ which is the operand of **erase**, all associations formed by using each element of the set (or of the universe of items) in turn will be deleted from the universe of associations.

Example. If *sons* is a ⟨set identifier⟩ and *x* is a ⟨local⟩, then the statement

make *father* · *sons* ≡ *john*

is equivalent to

foreach *x* **in** *sons* **do make** *father* · *x* ≡ *john*

The ⟨loop statement⟩ is the raison d'etre for the entire system and is considered in some detail. The simple case in which the ⟨associative context⟩ is just ⟨local⟩ *in* ⟨set expression⟩ (one instance of ⟨boolean expression⟩) is discussed first. The ⟨set expression⟩ is evaluated once and the ⟨statement⟩ is executed once for each member of the resulting set. The local is the loop variable and is assigned (bound to) the successive elements of the set; it is treated as an itemvar within the ⟨statement⟩. The local is said to be bound within the body of the loop.

Example

foreach *x* **in** *sons* **do datum**(*x*) ← **datum**(*x*) + 2   (1)

This is a loop over a ⟨set expression⟩ which is simply a set *sons*. If *x* has been declared *integer local*, then the effect of this statement will be to increase by 2 the datum associated with each item in *sons*.

The ⟨loop statement⟩ over a general ⟨associative context⟩ is much more complicated. An ⟨associative context⟩ determines a set of simultaneous associative equations which the system must solve to determine the values of the loop variables. A loop variable is a local appearing in the ⟨associative context⟩ which has not been bound in an enclosing loop. First, let us consider the case where there is only one loop variable occurring in a single ⟨retrieval triple⟩.

foreach *father* · *x* ≡ *bill* **do put** *x* **in** *sons*   (2)

We assume that *father* and *bill* are items, *x* is an unbound local, and *sons* is a set; the ⟨algebraic type⟩ of any

of these variables is irrelevant. The system first computes the set of items {$o_1, \ldots, o_k$} which appear in an association:

father · o_i ≡ *bill*

Now the body of the loop is executed *k* times, once with each o_i as the value of *x* (considered to be an itemvar within the body). If *sons* was initially empty it will be precisely the set {$o_1, \ldots, o_k$} at the end of the execution of 2. If $k = o$, the body of the loop is not executed.

In this simple case the ⟨loop statement⟩ could be replaced by

sons ← *sons* ∪ (*father*'*bill*).

Next we examine a more complex ⟨associative context⟩ still involving only a single loop variable.

Example

foreach *father* · *x* ≡ *bill* **and** *sex* · *x* ≡ *male* **do put** *x* **in** *sons*

This statement is much the same as (2) except that the set of values for *x* is made up of these items satisfying both associations. The set {$o_1, \ldots, o_k$} is computed as above and then each o_i is retained if and only if the association *sex* · o_i ≡ *male* is in the universe. This keeps *bill's* daughters out of the set *sons*. Notice that the order in which the two associations are processed can be expected to have a marked effect on performance; i.e. there are probably many more males than children of *bill*. This situation is discussed further in Section 3.

In general, there will be several loop variables each of which occurs several times in the ⟨associative context⟩. The ⟨associative context⟩ can be thought of as specifying a set of simultaneous relational equations which may have one or more solutions. A solution is an assignment of one item to each loop variable such that the ⟨associative context⟩ is *satisfied* (cf next paragraph). The assignments (if any) which are solutions are computed in advance and the body of the loop executed once for each assignment.

An ⟨associative context⟩ is *satisfied* by some assignment if all of its ⟨element⟩s are satisfied under that assignment. A ⟨boolean expression⟩ is satisfied if it has the value *true*. A ⟨retrieval triple⟩ containing no ⟨set expression⟩ is satisfied by an assignment if the association it specifies is in the universe of associations. A ⟨retrieval triple⟩ containing a ⟨set expression⟩ (or **any**) is satisfied if there are, in the universe of associations, any of the associations formed by substituting elements of the set (or arbitrary items) in the position occupied by the ⟨set expression⟩.

A ⟨retrieval triple⟩ in an ⟨associative context⟩ must have either one or two occurrences of unbound locals. The ⟨associative context⟩ is a powerful construct and must be used with some care, but the simple cases are fairly intuitive.

Example

foreach *father* · (*father* · *x*) ≡ *z* **do make** *grandad* · *x* ≡ *z* (3a)
foreach *father* · *x* ≡ *y* **and** *father* · *y* ≡ *z* **do make**
  grandad · *x* ≡ *z*.

The statements (3a) and (3b) above are entirely equivalent (the current compiler actually will transform (3a) into (3b) supplying a dummy local). Assuming *x*, *y*, *z* are unbound locals, the statement (3b) requires solving for three loop variables. It is clearly inadequate to solve for each loop variable independently; the system must form an assignment of items which satisfies the associative context. For example, if the associations of the universe were

$$father \cdot tom \quad \equiv bill$$
$$father \cdot pete \quad \equiv tom$$
$$father \cdot bill \quad \equiv don$$
$$father \cdot george \equiv clyde$$

the statement (3b) would yield assignments

$$(x, y, z) = (tom, bill, don)$$
$$(x, y, z) = (pete, tom, bill)$$

and after the execution of (3b) the universe would also contain the associations

$$grandad \cdot tom \equiv don$$
$$grandad \cdot pete \equiv bill$$

1.4.3 Pragmatics

The implementation of sets is discussed briefly in Section 1.2.3. The implementation of **make** and **erase** depends heavily on the structure and is discussed in Section 2.2. The ⟨loop statement⟩ over ⟨local⟩ **in** ⟨set expression⟩ is implemented separately for efficiency. The ⟨associative context⟩ loop is by far the most complex construct in LEAP. The formation of assignments entails building many partial assignments which later must be discarded. This is in itself a significant data structure problem and has been implemented with a hash-coded triple scheme associating an assignment number, a local, and an item. This, combined with the order of processing considerations mentioned in connection with (3) above, makes the compilation of the ⟨association context⟩ loop statement decidedly nontrivial. This problem is discussed briefly in Section 2 and at great length in Hilbing's dissertation [16].

1.5 Procedures

The treatment of procedures in LEAP is in no way novel so we content ourselves with an informal statement of the differences. There are no function procedures in LEAP of ⟨leap type⟩. The ALGOL-like language underlying

LEAP [25] classifies parameters as either **value**, as in ALGOL 60, or **reference** (address). Parameters in LEAP may be specified with **set, item, itemvar** as well as the ALGOL 60 specifiers. A formal parameter specified by **set** or **itemvar** (and not by **value**) can be used to return a value.

Example

procedure *pip* (**integer value** *m* ; **real intemvar** *u2*) ;
  begin integar local *x* ; **foreach** *height* · *u2* ≡ *x* **and** *m* > *x*
  do datum(*u2*) ← 0, **end**

1.6 Sample Programs

begin comment This program will find the polygon in some figure which has the largest perimeter and will write its name, number of sides, and its perimeter. We assume that there are items representing figures, objects (components of figures), and lines, and that there are associations in the universe of the form *part* · figure ≡ object, *type* · object ≡ *polygon*, and *side* · object ≡ line. We also assume the number of sides of a polygon is stored as its datum and the length of a line is stored as its datum, the data base is assumed to be built in an outer block ;
item *part, side, type, polygon* ;
real *sum, max* ;
ical *x* ;
real local *y* ;
integer itemvar *largest* ;
itemvar *figure* ;
read(*figure*) ;
max ← 0 ;
foreach *part* · *figure* ≡ *x* **and** *type* · *x* ≡ *polygon* **do**
  begin *sum* ← 0 ;
    foreach *side* · *x* ≡ *y* **do**
      sum ← *sum* + **datum**(*y*) ;
    if *sum* ≥ *max* **then**
      begin *largest* ← *x* ; *max* ← *sum* **end**
  end ;
write(*largest*, **datum**(*largest*),*max*)
end

begin comment This program will determine if *mary* is related to *joe* by virtue of the fact that *mary's* paternal aunt is married to *joe's* paternal uncle and, if so, will record that fact ;
item *father, mary, joe, sex, married, male, related, reason* ;
local *x, y* ;
set *uncles* ;
boolean *switch* ;
uncles ← ∅ ; *switch* ← **false** ;
foreach *father* · *x* ≡ (*father* · (*father* · *joe*)) **and**
  sex · *x* ≡ *male* **do put** *x* **in** *uncles* ;
foreach *father* · *x* ≡ (*father* · (*father* · *mary*)) **and**
  married * *x* ≡ *y* **and** *y* **in** *uncles* **do**
  begin
  make *related* · *mary* ≡ *joe*
    make *reason* · [*related* · *mary* ≡ *joe*]
    ≡ [*married* · *x* ≡ *y*] ;

```
        switch ← true;
      end;
    write (switch)
end
```

2. The LEAP Data Structure

2.1 Introduction and Brief Literature Review

The most important construct in LEAP is the ⟨associative context⟩, which implicitly specifies a collection of items. In this section we present a rather elaborate two-level storage scheme which was designed to facilitate the processing of ⟨associative context⟩s. The problem of retrieving the objects from memory which are associated with a given object has been a central concern in list-processing systems since their inception.

The early list-processing languages (e.g. LISP [23], IPL [28]) achieved a form of associative memory through the use of property (description) lists. This enabled one to specify the name of a property (attribute) and an object from which the system would retrieve the value or list of values. This facility freed the user from remembering which ordinal number he had mentally associated with a property. The property list was implemented as a list of (property, value) pairs linked to the object. When a retrieval was to be made, the system would search the property list of the specified object for the specified property and would return the associated value. Although this feature of list-processing systems is heavily used, there are serious problems with it from both a usage and an implementation standpoint. All the more recent attempts to realize associative processing on conventional computers may be viewed as attempts to solve problems in one or both of these areas.

The problem with property lists from a user's point of view is that they are one-way. If one has stored *"son (john) = don"* there is no direct way to find the x such that *"son(x) = don."* This problem became particularly bothersome in computer graphics and led to the development of languages such as L[6] [19], CORAL [31, 39], AED [33], APL [8], and ASP [20], which have recently been surveyed [14]. These languages automatically provided two-way links and, for reasons described in the next paragraph, replaced the property list with a block (record) of continuous storage.

The abandonment of the property list was a victory for economy over flexibility. The property list requires two cells per association and requires searching at each retrieval. The idea of using a continuous block of storage for the property list should be attributed to Ross [32]. The idea is simple: by assigning a relative address to each attribute (e.g. *son* ~ 3) one can achieve rapid retrieval and still use only one cell per association. The usual implementation is to place the address of the top of the block (internal name of the object) in an index register and assemble a load or store instruction having that index field and with the attribute number in the address field. This scheme is efficient and has been used in a great variety of systems but it too has drawbacks.

The first difficulty is that the size of the continuous blocks must be specified in advance. If a new attribute is applied to an object, at least a partial recompilation is required. A further problem occurs on deciding which small integer to associate with each attribute name; there are three basic approaches to this problem in the literature. (1) Require that each pointer variable be declared to point to only a fixed kind of block. This enables a compiler to compute, at translation time, the relative position in that kind of block which corresponds to a given attribute [41, 42]. This is efficient in its use of time and storage but is not sufficiently flexible for the kinds of applications considered here. For example, the APL system [8] was developed because of the inadequacy of PL/I structures for computer graphics. (2) Require the user to explicitly give the relative locations of attributes in every structure statement [39] (and to some extent [8, 20]). This is efficient and flexible enough but has proved too difficult to program. (3) Assign a unique relative address to each attribute name [19]. This requires the user to schedule the way attributes appear in various kinds of blocks and generally leads to wasted storage.

These three approaches all deal with a dilemma which arises from the fact that every attribute does not apply to each object. If an attribute is assigned the same relative position in the blocks used to represent different kinds of objects, some locations will always be wasted. If the relative position varies among blocks, then the system will have to determine which kind of block is being treated before applying an attribute. In addition, all these schemes share the problem that the entire block of storage for an object must be allocated on the first use of that object.

The data structure schemes discussed above were designed for problems for which the associative structure is rather simple and is contained in main memory. More recently, there have been attempts to extend these systems to a paging environment [3, 6, 9]. The only previous work on systems capable of handling all seven associative forms (cf Table I) and large data bases has been in query languages and information retrieval [7]. The thrust of these efforts has been rather different; they have generally emphasized data bases too large for drums or disks and have allowed for much slower response rates.

There has been, in addition, a great deal of work on hardware associative memories. The engineering problems have proved much more difficult than imagined and there are some a priori arguments against the construction of such a device. Suppose the associative retrieval problem is specified as follows. Given a set of N words of length M, where $\log N < M < N$, find the exact match, if any, of some word. The expected value of the number of retrieval operations is *two* for the hash-coded memory and *one* for the parallel search device. If we assume, realistically, that the memory is not always full, the hash-coding scheme is even more competitive. Furthermore the hash-coding scheme requires matching only on addresses (log N digits, as opposed to M digits). One expects $M \gg \log N$ so that the hash-coding scheme requires considerably less hardware. The cases $M > N$ (the number of words is less than their length) and $M < \log N$ (there are more digits in an address than in a word) are generally agreed to be different problems. The situation is more complex and the complete argument is beyond the scope of this paper. The point is that an associative machine will have to do more in parallel than exact matching to justify its existence. Designers of such devices have realized this and current associative memory designs might better be called array computers. There is, however, no existing design capable of implementing the ⟨associative context⟩ loop in parallel, and we expect hash-coding techniques to remain competitive for this problem.

2.2 The Answer

The hash-coded associative memory scheme presented here is an attempt to solve the associative processing problem for a large range of applications. Hash-coding (scrambling) is a well-known technique for processing symbol tables, etc. [24, 26], and there was early speculation [29] that hash-coding could lead to efficient associative processing. The scheme described here is an extension of our earlier work [11, 35], which is designed to work efficiently in a particular time-sharing system [13].

The motivation for our work on associative data structures is a desire to efficiently realize the features of a hardware associative memory in a conventional computer. This requires that associations be represented in such a way that any one of the seven forms of Table I provides efficient access to all associations matching the partial specification represented by that form. We also require that an association can be formed from any three items in the universe of items. It should also be possible to allow an association to include, as a component, the internal name corresponding to another association. We would like the system to be efficient in time and storage; the time-sharing system used [13] had some marked effects on this aspect of the design.

The problem then is to represent a universe of associations (3-tuples of items) so as to best realize the design criteria. A dictionary phase converts all item identifiers to internal names, which are just integers in a certain range. Each of the forms of Table I gives rise to a primitive associative retrieval request upon the universe of associations. These primitive requests are used in implementing the ⟨associative context⟩ loop and the ⟨associative expression⟩ ⟨associative operator⟩ ⟨associative expression⟩ constructs of LEAP. The discussion of the implementation of the seven primitive requests

specified by Table I occupies most of the remainder of this section. For this discussion we denote an association by (A, O, V) and think of it as a 3-tuple of integers. The primitive requests may be multi-valued and may assign values to more than one local. For example, if the universe was

$$(son, don, john)$$
$$(son, don, joe)$$

the following answers would result from primitive requests.

Primitive Request	Answer
son·john doe ≡	*(son, don, john)*
(son, john, joe)	**null**
(son, don, x)	$x = \{john, joe\}$
(x, don, joe)	$x = son$
(x, don, z)	$(x, z) = \{(son, john), (son, joe)\}$
(x, don, don)	**null**

The basic ideas underlying the implementation are simple. Let us consider an instance of the request arising from form F1:

$$(son, don, x)$$

If the internal name of son is 17,453, and don is 21,411 and x is unspecified, the following would result. The two higher-order digits of son specify that page 17 is to be searched. The location on page 17 where the search is to start is the hash of the remaining digits 453 with 21,411, which might be $4530 + 2140 = 6670$. At location 6670 on page 17 there will be a cell of the general form:

O	4	conflict list
A-use		value list

In this case O = 21,411, and the 4 indicates that the cell is the head of a list of values (cf Table II). Notice that the hash function $\oplus$ has the property that $A' \oplus O = A \oplus O$ implies $A = A'$ so that one need not explicitly store the A value in a cell. The values (internal names of john, joe) are stored in a list starting in the bottom right of the cell. The conflict list is used when more than one (A, O) pair hash to the same location. In this case the stored O is enough to resolve the ambiguity. The A-use field is a link in a list of all uses of the attribute (in this case son = 17,453) in any association. This list contains precisely those associations specified by the F4 form (son, x, z). The system insures that both the values list and the a-use list are kept on one (variable size) page.

The first (A) component of the triple dominated the organization of page 17 in a number of ways. It was the high order digits of the A component that determined

TABLE II

CELL TYPES AND THE PURPOSE OF EACH

Cell Type	Purpose of a Cell of That Type
0	A two-register free block
1	Represents an association in a collection of associations
2	A one-register free block
3	Represents a collection of associations in a "conflict" situation
4	Represents a collection of associations
5	Represents an association which has been bracketed
6	Represents an association
7	Represents an association in a "conflict" situation

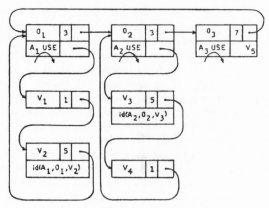

FIG. 1. A segment of the structure on an A-type page (cf. Table II).

the page on which the F1 form was answered. All the answers to the F4 form, which has only the A component specified, were stored on this page. For these reasons the page is referred to as an A-page and would actually be denoted A17.

The system is completely symmetric and has O-pages and V-pages which are analogous to the A-page. The O-page is used to answer the requests specified by form F3 and F6. The V-page is used to answer requests specified by forms F2 and F5. The associative retrieval request F0, which has all components bound, can be answered from any of the three kinds of pages.

Since several different cases arise in storing associations, the structure can get quite complicated. Figure 1 depicts a segment of the storage of an A-type page under the following conditions. The three pairs (A_1, O_1), (A_2, O_2), and (A_3, O_3) all hash-code to the same address; i.e. there is a three-way conflict. The associations represented are:

$$(A_1, O_1, V_1) \quad (A_1, O_1, V_2) \quad (A_2, O_2, V_3)$$
$$(A_2, O_2, V_4) \quad (A_3, O_3, V_5)$$

The associations (A_1, O_1, V_2) and (A_2, O_2, V_3) have been bracketed (cf Section 1.3). The system generates a new internal name (e.g. id (A_1, O_1, V_2)) for each bracketed triple; this internal name is stored in the bottom of the type 5 cell and is treated in the same manner as the internal identifier of any other item, except that its value is an association. The predicate *istriple* and the ⟨selector⟩s enable one to identify and dismember an item which represents a bracketed triple. The interpretation of the various cell types is given in Table II. The situation depicted in Figure 1 is a worst case and will occur infrequently.

The requirement that all answers to a primitive associative retrieval request lie on one memory page leads to variable size pages. There is the further complication that each page must contain five kinds of cells: use-list headers, one-word and two-word associative cells, and one-word and two-word free storage cells. These require-

ments have led to a rather complicated storage arrangement, which is discussed elsewhere [10, 34, 35]. In addition to the retrieval primitives, there are primitives corresponding to the *make* and *erase* commands of LEAP. The system has been in operation for some time and has proved to be sufficiently fast and compact for real-time work in a time-sharing environment.

As the reader has undoubtedly discovered, the price for this generality and efficiency is storage space. Each association is represented on an A-type, an O-type, and a V-type page; this requires approximately twice (not thrice) the storage of our earlier scheme [10] because some of the information is implicit in the address at which the association is stored. The major justification for this storage redundancy is that it is only wasteful of secondary storage; the main memory requirements are actually smaller than those of any other known scheme for answering all the primitive associative requests of Table I.

There are some additional considerations which make the redundant storage scheme less costly. Representing the information in three different ways makes it possible to choose different page distribution strategies for each type. The system does not normally update the three affected pages when a *make* or *erase* is executed; it merely records the fact that the page must be updated the next time it is brought into main memory to be accessed. An obvious addition would be an update command which caused the system to do the updating when time was available.

3. Conclusions

The associative programming language LEAP and the hash-coded associative memory system have been in active use since early 1967. Although there have been many modifications of the system, the basic design has remained intact and appears to be sound. LEAP has become the basic applications programming language for TX-2, although many problems do not require an associative version. The associative features have found application primarily in computer graphics.

We briefly describe some typical applications; more detailed information can be requested through the authors. One application is an interactive program for the design of integrated circuits and the layout of their masks. Another involves an interactive system for pole-zero calculations in circuit design. There is also a program for displaying constrained [38] figures, a significant nonprocedural problem. There are also two large interactive programming systems which have been written in LEAP. The first is a system for synthesizing animated cartoons from a set of continuous wave-forms specifying the motion of parts of the picture [2]. The second is the recently completed implementation [36] of the two-dimensional programming language Ambit/G [5]. In addition, a graphical debugging package for associative structures has been written.

The predominance of uses in interactive graphics systems is a result of the interest of the user community. While LEAP is unabashedly a special purpose language, we anticipate applications in many areas of question-answering [22, 30] and artificial intelligence. There are continuations of some of the LEAP ideas in [1, 18, 21] which may extend the application areas. A major extension of LEAP to include time-sharing programs on a common associative structure is under development at Stanford University.

Our experiences with the LEAP language and data structure suggest several possible extensions of each. The complete data structure scheme described in Section 2 has not yet been used to nearly its capacity and may be unnecessarily complicated for small graphics applications. More particularly, it would be very useful to develop a scheme which did not require a page access to ascertain that an association was not in the store.

In general, the order in which an ⟨associative context⟩ is processed can have a profound effect on the performance of the system. For example, consider two equivalent specifications of the brothers of bill.

$$father' \ (father \cdot bill) \equiv x \ \textbf{and} \ sex \cdot x \equiv male \qquad (4)$$

$$sex \cdot x \equiv male \ \textbf{and} \ father' \ (father \cdot bill) \equiv x \qquad (5)$$

The second version will require time (and space for assignments) proportional to the number of males in the universe. A study of methods for optimal rearrangement of associative statements has been completed [16], and the methods developed there could be incorporated into the compiler.

In the associative language, as in most high level languages, the full form of certain constructs (e.g. ⟨loop statement⟩) becomes tedious; the system could benefit from a simple macro processor [12]. The language also suffers from the lack of item and set functions, although procedures which have the same effect are available. At a more basic level, we would like the ability to manipulate entire assignment structures defined by associative contexts (cf 1.4.2). Finally, a truly complete associative system would include a facility for implicitly solving for associations which are not explicitly represented in the structure; this requires a theorem-proving program as part of the access mechanism. A step along this path has been taken in the TRAMP effort [1], but much is yet to be done.

The study of software associative processing is expanding rapidly and there are a large number of associative languages under development. Most of these are less ambitious than LEAP (but see [43]), but the proposals for graphical (two-dimensional) languages [5, 37] deserve some mention. An associative structure is quite naturally looked upon as a colored, directed graph, and it seems that associative processing is a natural area for graphical languages. After an early attempt to extend [10] to a graphical associative language using [39], we decided that this was not feasible with current technology. Ironically, the only currently available graphical language was implemented in LEAP [36] as a term project. It is too early to predict the usefulness of this system and, in any event, the problems of associative processing will be with us for some time to come.

References

1. ASH, W., AND SIBLEY, E. TRAMP, an interpretive associative processor with deductive capabilities. Proc. ACM 23rd Nat. Conf., Brandon Systems Press, Princeton, N.J., 1968, pp. 143–156.
2. BAECKER, R. M. A study of the on-line computer aided generation of animated displays. Ph.D. diss., M.I.T, Cambridge, Mass., 1969.
3. BOBROW, D. G., AND MURPHY, D. L. Structure of a LISP system using two-level storage. Comm. ACM 10, 3 (Mar. 1967), 155–159.
4. —— (Ed.) Symbol Manipulation Languages and Techniques. North-Holland Publ., Amsterdam, 1968.
5. CHRISTENSEN, C. An example of the manipulation of graphs using the AMBIT/G programming language. Proc. Symp. Interactive Systems in Experimental Appl. Math., Washington, D.C., 1967.
6. COHEN, J. A use of fast and slow memories in list-processing languages. Comm. ACM 10, 2 (Feb. 1967), 82–86.
7. CUADRA, C. A. Annual Review of Information Science and Technology. Wiley, New York, 1966.
8. DODD, G. G. APL, a language for associative data handling in PL/I. Proc. AFIPS 1966 Fall Joint Comput. Conf., Vol. 29, Spartan Books, New York.
9. EVANS, D., AND VAN DAM, A. Data structure programming system. Proc. 1968 IFIP Cong., North-Holland Publ., Amsterdam.
10. FELDMAN, J. A. Aspects of associative processing.

Tech. Note 1965-13, MIT Lincoln Laboratory, Lexington, Mass., Apr. 1965.

11. ——. A formal semantics for computer languages and its application in a compiler-compiler. *Comm. ACM* **9,** 1 (Jan. 1966), 3–9.

12. ——, AND GRIES, D. Translator writing systems. *Comm. ACM* **11,** 2 (Feb. 1968), 77–113.

13. FORGIE, J. W. ET AL. A time and memory sharing executive program. Proc. AFIPS 1965 Fall Joint Comput. Conf., Vol. 27, Pt. 2, Thompson Book Co., Washington, D.C.

14. GRAY, J. C. Compounded data structures for computer aided design; a survey. Proc. ACM 22nd Nat. Conf., P-67, 1967, pp. 355–365.

15. HANLAN, A. E. Content addressable and associative memory systems. *IEEE Trans. EC-15,* 4 (Aug. 1966), 509–521.

16. HILBING, F. J. The analysis of strategies for paging a large associative data structure. Ph.D. diss., Industrial Engineering, Stanford U., Stanford, Calif., Mar. 1969.

17. ITURRIAGA, R., STANDISH, T. A., KRUTAR, P. A., AND EARLEY, J. C. Techniques and advantages of using the formal compiler writing system FSL to implement a formula ALGOL compiler. Proc. AFIPS 1966 Spring Joint Comput. Conf., Vol. 28, Spartan Books, New York, pp. 241–252.

18. KAY, A. FLEX, a flexible extendable language. Tech. Rep. 4–7, U. of Utah, Salt Lake City, Utah, June 1968.

19. KNOWLTON, K. C. A programmer's description of L⁶. *Comm. ACM* **9,** 8 (Aug. 1966), 616–625.

20. LANG, C. A., AND GRAY, J. ASP—A ring implemented associative structures package. Proc. ACM 23rd Nat. Conf., Brandon Systems Press, Princeton, N.J., 1968.

21. LAURANCE, N. A compiler language for data structures. Proc. ACM 23rd Nat. Conf., Brandon Systems Press, Princeton, N.J., 1968, pp. 387–394.

22. LEVIEN, R., AND MARON, M. A computer system for inference execution and data retrieval. RM-5085-PR, The Rand Corp., Santa Monica, Calif., Sept. 1966.

23. MCCARTHY, J., ET AL. Lisp 1.5 Programmer's Manual. MIT Press, Cambridge, Mass., 1962.

24. MAURER, W. D. An improved hash code for scatter storage. *Comm. ACM* **11,** 1 (Jan. 1968), 35–38.

25. MONDSHEIN, L. F. VITAL compiler-compiler system reference manual. Tech. Note 1967-12, MIT Lincoln Laboratory, Lexington, Mass., Feb. 1967.

26. MORRIS, R. Scatter storage techniques. *Comm. ACM* **11,** 1 (Jan. 1968), 39–44.

27. NAUR, P., ET AL. Revised report on the algorithmic language ALGOL 60. *Comm. ACM* **6,** 1 (Jan. 1963), 1–17.

28. NEWELL, A. (Ed.) *Information Processing Language —V Manual.* Prentice-Hall, Englewood Cliffs, N.J., 1961.

29. ——. A note on the use of scrambled addressing for associative memories. Unpublished paper, Dec. 1962.

30. RAPHAEL, B. Sir, a computer program for semantic information retrieval. Proc. 1964 Fall Joint Comput. Conf., Vol. 26, Pt. 2, Spartan Books, New York.

31. ROBERTS, L. G. Machine perception of three-dimensional solids. Tech. Rep. No. 315, MIT Lincoln Laboratory, Lexington, Mass., May 1963.

32. ROSS, D. T. A generalized technique for symbol manipulation and numerical computation. *Comm. ACM* **4,** 3 (Mar. 1961), 147–150.

33. ——. The AED approach to generalized computer aided design. Proc. ACM 22nd Nat. Conf., P-67, 1967, pp. 1367–1385.

34. ROVNER, P. D., AND FELDMAN, J. A. An associative processing system for conventional digital computers. Tech. Note 1967-19, MIT Lincoln Laboratory, Lexington, Mass., Apr. 1967.

35. ——, AND ——. The LEAP language and data structure. MIT Lincoln Laboratory, Lexington, Mass., Jan. 1968. In abbreviated form, Proc. 1968 IFIP Cong., Brandon Systems Press, Princeton, N.J.

36. ——. An AMBIT/G programming language implementation. MIT Lincoln Laboratory, Lexington, Mass., June 1968.

37. SAVITT, D., LOVE, H. H., AND TROOP, R. E. ASP; a new concept in language and machine organization. Proc. AFIPS 1967 Spring Joint Comput. Conf., Vol. 30, Thompson Book Co., Washington, D.C., pp. 87–102.

38. SUTHERLAND, I. E. Sketchpad: A man-machine communication system. Proc. AFIPS 1963 Spring Joint Comput. Conf., Vol. 23, Spartan Books, New York, pp. 329–346.

39. SUTHERLAND, W. R. On-line graphical specification of procedures. Tech. Rep. No. 405, MIT Lincoln Laboratory, Lexington, Mass., May 1966.

40. TEICHROEW, D., AND LUBIN, J. F. Computer simulation—Discussion of the technique and comparison of languages. *Comm. ACM* **9,** 10 (Oct. 1966), 723–741.

41. VAN WIJNGAARDEN, A. (Ed.) Draft report on ALGOL 68. Mathematisch Centrum, MR 93, Amsterdam, The Netherlands, 1968.

42. WIRTH, N., AND HOARE, C. A. R. A contribution to the development of ALGOL. *Comm. ACM* **9,** 6 (June 1966), 413–431.

43. CHILDS, D. L. Description of a set-theoretic data structure. Proc. 1968 Fall Joint Conput. Conf., Vol. 33, Thompson Book Co., Washington, D.C., pp. 557–564.

44. ROVNER, P. D. The LEAP users manual. MIT Lincoln Laboratory, Lexington, Mass., Dec. 1968.

B. Indexing
Vocabularies

24 Minimum Vocabularies in Information Indexing

R. MOSS
Journal of Documentation
Vol. 23, No. 3, September, 1967

Vocabularies are collections of words, generally though not always selected for some particular purpose. The most common examples are the lists of foreign word equivalents in language text books. Words may be spoken or written. In library work we have been concerned mainly with the written word. The written word is an attempt to overcome limitations of space or passage of time in making contact between individuals. It is an expression of faith that what is written will be of use to others or at any rate bring reward to authors.

In information work, a greater element of the spoken word is being introduced, since this is a much faster, though less permanent, method of communication. In both library and information work, however, there is a tendency to forget that much of what is known never gets into print because of lack of time in setting it down, because publication is not always certain, because people hesitate to commit themselves, and because, perhaps most fortunately, of sheer human inertia.

The use of language, whether spoken or written, is to convey or communicate 'thoughts', 'ideas', and 'knowledge', none of which can be satisfactorily defined. There is in language not only a factual element, but also an 'emotion' or 'feeling'. In scientific work we are not or ought not to be concerned with these last although the much sought-after or elusive 'style' in technical and indeed all writing has some affinity with emotion or 'art'. Thus, the science with which information workers deal is never entirely scientific.

1. Signs

The basic forms of human communication — giving and receiving information — are speech and signs. Written words are marks or signs. 'Words are a particular case of signs[1].' Because we are so familiar with them, we do not think of them as signs but this is what they are. (They also require some form of supporting surface or storage). Particular signs — letters of the alphabet — correspond to particular sounds except in English where we are still arguing about it. Very different marks or signs can convey the same ideas as a glance at European (Roman), Arabic, and Japanese alphabets will show.

Speech is variable. Signs point. Written language is a

combination of the two. Signs give written language a somewhat greater precision than the spoken word. They bring some element of constancy to what was previously largely, though not entirely, variable — the grammar of the language also gives some constancy even to the spoken word.

The written or printed word is not the only form of script for speech, though it remained so for a long time. In the last century shorthand came into vogue for dictation in business and offices but in the present century technical advance in the shape of the tape recorder has already pushed shorthand into the background.

'Throughout almost all our life we are treating things as signs. All experience, using the word in the widest possible sense, is either enjoyed or interpreted (i.e. treated as a sign) or both, and very little of it escapes some degree of interpretation.[2]'

To all such signs* Ogden and Richards gave the name symbols.

Symbols are intended to communicate knowledge, to show meaning, but there is always a considerable element of uncertainty and personal interpretation about this.[3] The element of interpretation is markedly present at the original recording stage when the writer is committing his researches to paper, and relying on his personal judgment to express sense-experience and scientific-experience in verbal form. But it is also present at the reading stage when what has been written must be interpreted through the sense-experience of the reader.

So far as symbols are concerned, uncertainty is most marked in the case of word-symbols. For more precise records, mankind has had to invent symbols restricting the element of interpretation and thus allowing greater precision. The earliest form of shorthand symbols for certain words and situations was, and is, Number. The digits, 0 to 9, indicated succession or sequence. This sequence is the basis of all filing methods.

With the increasing pace of scientific discovery and with the necessity of obtaining greater precision, scientists have had to devise new forms of specialist shorthands and symbols. Among the best-known are perhaps the chemical symbols representing the elements. Mathematical instructions can now be given in symbols ranging far beyond the original ones of add, subtract, and equals.

* According to Ogden and Richards,[35] the first scholar to introduce a consistent theory of signs was William of Occam, still probably the most effective operator in the widespread pastime of scholastic knifing.

'Occam is best known for a maxim which is not to be found in his works, but has acquired the name "Occam's razor". This maxim says: "Entities are not to be multiplied without necessity". Although he did not say this, he said something which has much the same effect, namely: "It is vain to do with more what can be done with fewer." That is to say, if everything in some science can be interpreted without assuming this or that hypothetical entity, there is no ground for assuming it. I have myself found this a most useful principle in logical analysis'[36].

Circuit diagrams in electronics are given in the form of well-established symbols for components. Recently, organic chemical symbols have entered the three-dimensional field with the atomic models which can be constructed from standard elements. Note, however, that by itself a symbol is not enough; for effective communication to be established, it also has to have an identifiable — and pronounceable — name. Natural language is still necessary. Although science, with the help of these appropriate specialist symbols, may diminish uncertainty it does not abolish it nor is it entirely able to dispense with everyday language. There will, therefore, always be some information problem.

Criticism sometimes made by scientists to the effect that Librarians (and in this context this includes Information Scientists) think only in terms of words and not of science are not altogether valid, since at the 'sandwich' or middleman stage between the author and the inquirer occupied by the Library, the only symbols at present common to all specializations are those of natural or everyday language. If anything, the criticism against librarians is that they have thought not enough in terms of words and too much in terms of shelf-class numbers. However, this does not invalidate the general criticism that information workers should pay much more attention to the words, terminologies, and contexts used for specialist sciences and technologies than they, at present, do.

2. Restrictions of Indexing Language as Compared with Everyday Language

Information in print is conveyed by documents of varying form and size containing anything from a few to several hundred thousand words and symbols. 'Meaning' in this situation comes not only from the words and symbols used but also from context, the grammar of the language, from the author's art in piecing his material together, and from the degree of understanding which the reader brings to it. 'A word acquires meaning by an external relation'.[4]

The librarian has no such aids. Within the capacity of a small indexing card or its equivalent he must get a sufficient collection of words to give some indication of the subject of a document and also leave room for a filing number. Historically, library methods of cataloguing and classifying have been generally restricted to locating documents, mostly books on shelves. Orthodox library classifications met their first serious obstacle with the journal series, and there, if shelf-classification was required, had to be content with classification of series rather than articles. However, the intensification of scientific research has meant that the library user needs, more often than not, not only to get straight to particular articles but also to particular facts; part of the confusion in information retrieval lies in the uncertainty as to whether we are trying to locate documents or some part of their contents.

More often than not, it is the latter which is required in the information approach. This means that the user or someone acting for him has to scan the document rapidly or to examine the contents list or index, assuming it has one or the other. This, in turn, assumes that he has been able to pick the right document or documents, a situation increasingly improbable even in orthodox library work. 'Analytical' cataloguing was the first attempt to try to incorporate some of the contents and details of books directly into the library catalogue. In fact, the library approach, which is virtually only a 'browsing' facility, though still required in some instances may have to be discarded altogether in information work to meet the greater demand there for direct routing to specialized facts, opinions, and symbols.

Taking information recording to the next stage, the two approaches correspond to the 'route signs' provided for the majority of specialist documents, i.e. contents list and index. (These in turn correspond to the 'term on item' and 'item on term' approaches of classification and co-ordinate indexing.) The contents list is a collection of words, generally consisting of the actual chapter headings and corresponding page numbers, small enough to be scanned ('browsed') fairly rapidly just as are the titles of books on a shelf. The index is the reverse of this; in a way it is the embodiment of the information requirement in miniature; it is intended for reference to particular words, points of fact or symbols representing them and for their subsequent identification at a particular place by page numbers In a contents list, the sequence of page references is that of normal succession. In an index, the sequence is random. Order in an index is determined by the internationally accepted order of the alphabet, A–Z, which imitates that of simple numerical succession. All forms of organization are based on succession and, here, I submit that all our recorded knowledge so far is entirely dependent, for reference or retrieval, on alphabetical order. This is the hidden major premise of all information retrieval. Without words there is no alphabetical order. Without alphabetical order there is no retrieval. The specialist symbols now being used in various schemes do not yet have any agreed order for reference and there seems little realization that, for retrieval, they will need it. Yet anyone who has had even brief experience with, for example, UDC, will know the ambiguities which can result from symbols which have no stated order. If there is one thing certain among all the conflicts and uncertainties of library classification, it is that no classification has yet managed to do without an index and there is no indication that any classification beyond the smallest ever will. Librarians may have been able to memorize parts of their artificial language with their numerical (class number) order but they have never been able to familiarize themselves with them adequately enough to dispense with the alphabetical index altogether.

Recognition of this simple but neglected fact also enables us to end the confusion caused by the old argument as to whether we are classifying, indexing, and/or retrieving documents, subjects, or facts. We are, in fact, always indexing words, and it makes no difference whether the words symbolize documents or subjects within them. In theory, there is no reason why every word in every document should not be indexed in one gigantic index. In practice, the quantity of this renders it virtually impossible for the foreseeable future even in the computer age. In an information store, therefore, we index neither document nor subject. Only words can be indexed. It is always words symbolizing a document or subject, in particular those from titles or their equivalent in the form of subject headings (which are virtually the words the indexer thinks the title ought to be) which are indexed. Though other symbols may eventually be capable of being arranged in a sequence, for a long time to come the only symbols which all the different specialists and non-specialists have in common and in which there is any sort of agreement for indexing, storage, and reference are the words of everyday speech and their printed equivalents, for even among specialists, the habit of labelling or denoting the most complex symbols by some form of word caption is too deeply ingrained to be easily superseded.

In the library/information situation, the function of words as symbols is to provide 'that peculiar character of being directed towards one thing rather than another which we here call reference'.[5]

Reference is, in fact, all that we seek in that stage of information with which the library is historically associated and which is now more fashionably called 'retrieval.' In attempting to locate information in answer to some question or in anticipation of some need, the librarian is not concerned with explanation, with meaning, or purpose. He is concerned there only with identification, with directing to 'this' rather than 'that'. The situation faced in information is virtually always that of question and answer. The librarian is, however, not required to solve the problem, he is required only to show where a solution lies or may lie. For this limited purpose, as for the wider activities dealt with in everyday communication, 'Language if it is to be used must be a *ready* instrument. The handiness and ease of a phrase is always more important in deciding whether it will be extensively used than its accuracy',[6] a characteristic which will inevitably tell against any form of library classification involving complex notation.

For Ogden and Richards, all of what is usually called meaning resolved itself into this element of reference, into the interpretation of sign situations or symbols. 'A symbol, usually a set of words in the form of a proposition or sentence, is true when it correctly records an adequate reference. It correctly records an adequate reference when it will cause a similar reference to occur in a suitable interpreter.'[7] Much of the confusion generated by the word 'Retrieval'[8] might have been avoided had we been content with this good old library and scholarly word, 'reference', a word which in the library context has, too often, sorrowfully degenerated into a restriction on lending designed to suit the ease and convenience of librarians rather than that of their customers.

Taking the most pessimistic view of the information retrieval situation, every symbol, every noun, name, verb, and quite a few adjectives can provide a potential point of reference or source of questions. On this reckoning, the only thing that is ever going to solve our own information retrieval problem is a concordance of the library's stock plus relevant items from the published abstract and indexing journals; and not only this, but also a means of keeping it up-to-date day by day or minute by minute. Obviously this is asking the impossible at the present stage of development and for a long time to come. We have to be content with a situation, therefore, whereby only a small proportion of the available reference can be indexed, and exactly what the proportion or selection will be, will vary from library to library. Indexing and information retrieval will remain for a long time to come as much an art as a science.

Assuming that we manage to index a fair proportion of our stock and its associated auxiliary abstracting items, every success in retrieval will depend on this preliminary indexing, or equivalent information storage. It cannot be stressed too often that no retrieval system or method can produce an answer which has not previously been stored there. This is the fundamental, limiting factor in all information storage or retrieval. It is so obvious that it is almost universally ignored and people have gone on searching for or at any rate talking about 'systems' and machines as the solution of the information problem, ignoring or forgetting that a library system is not a manufacturing process which converts input materials to a new form of output product but merely a store in which the only available output is what has previously been put there.

If we regard an indexing symbol (i.e. word or headings plus storage number) as the record of speech or sound — which it is — information has always to negotiate its own particular 'sound barrier'. Expensive machinery may eventually enable us to cross this and get back more easily but it will still be there. So far as information goes, the easiest way of beating the sound barrier is, as yet, not by elaborate machinery, but by reducing the number of occasions on which we have to cross it, that is, by reducing the indexing vocabulary. Only when library information has been reduced to a much simpler pattern than we have at present, can machines be effectively utilized.

3. Information—Variables: Information Retrieval —Constants

The use of the word information, like the use of most abstract nouns ending in '-ation', has caused unnecessary confusion, not all of it accidental. Information can refer to:

Presentation and publication
Communication
Intellectual content and meaning
Storage as in a library
Reference to the store (retrieval), location transfer
A status war between librarians and information scientists
Publicity and propaganda

With the first and last of these we are not now concerned. With the penultimate, nothing that we can say will have any effect.

Communication implies some form of contact between people. Conversation is the most rapid though not necessarily the most effective and rarely the most permanent way of ensuring that what is communicated will be retained. Where, for reasons of time, space, or cost, people cannot communicate directly some form of record has to be made and referred to later.

Intellectual content includes knowledge, meaning, understanding, and ability to interpret symbols, as, for example, the results of a scientific experiment or the interpretation of a legal text. Also the ability to formulate, express, and communicate further information.

Storage is the record of all these things.

Reference can be reference to the store or to the intellectual content. In the library situation reference is made via indexing symbols. In the case of the individual seeker this reference can be assisted by his skill and by his knowledge of sources of probable locations. The more complex the subjects the more difficult reference becomes and the more nearly it then approximates to intellectual content. Though the two overlap there are wide areas between which it is possible and, if any progress is ever to be made, necessary to draw an arbitrary division both for retrieval applications and for the 'labelling' (indexing) stage which must precede it. Such division corresponds to the approximations or substitutions which are the basis of most logical or mathematical progress.

'Every application of logic or mathematics consists in the substitution of constants for variables: it is therefore essential, if logic or mathematics is to be applied, to know what sort of constants can be substituted for what sort of variables.'[9]

Figure 1 shows the symbolic division between information and information retrieval.

The left side contains the area of variables, of uncertainty, a much larger area than that of our own particular field of storage and retrieval; the right, the area of constants, of an arbitrarily imposed certainty. The aim is so to standardize procedures, so to substitute the constants of indexing terms for the variables of everyday language, that, eventually there will be very little remaining on the left. Thus, as a first step, all discussion about the interpretation and meaning of words and sym-

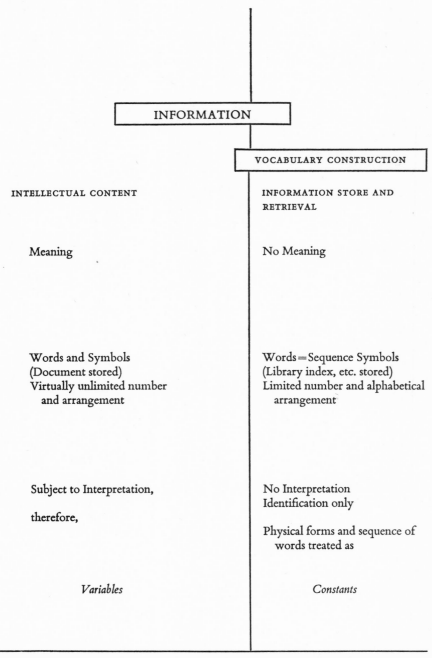

FIG. 1. Symbolic representation of information and retrieval situation.

bols should be restricted to intellectual content. On the other side, input and retrieval, it is essential for words to be treated solely as marks or signs, to be taken at their face value, allowing no time or effort to be wasted at the input or labelling stage on involved arguments as to 'what this really means' and to one-upmanship explanation that it really means something else. All arguments of this nature must be restricted to the vocabulary construction stage, which used to precede indexing, but now generally runs concurrently with it, particulary in a developing science or when indexing is commenced before the vocabulary is completed. Because of the vagaries and lack of precision of words, and because of the apparently ever-increasing complexity of scientific terminologies, for this arbitrary division to be effective, the first element of control has to be the written word, as yet the only constant in information retrieval.

In meaning, it is not a constant for some greater or

lesser element of interpretation comes into words both at the recording stage and at the reading stage. For purposes of location, however, it must be treated as such. Thus, for indexing purposes, the first constant is the readily recognizable pattern to which, presumably, we have long been accustomed by the time we get to the stage of library information. The second is the alphabetical order by which every index is arranged.

Further progress then depends on the choice of words, on their reduction to more easily manageable proportions, and on whether or not the choice of some words rather than others will improve the degree of constancy. These are questions within the province of a minimum vocabulary.

4. Minimum Vocabularies

'I call a vocabulary a "minimum" one if it contains no word which is capable of a verbal definition in terms of other words of the vocabulary. Two minimum vocabularies dealing with the same subject matter may not be equal; there may be different methods of definition, some of which may lead to a shorter residuum of undefined terms than others do. The question of minimum vocabularies is sometimes very important. Peano reduced the vocabulary of arithmetic to three words. It was an achievement in classical physics when all the units were defined in terms of the units of mass, length, and time . . .[10]

'There are as a rule a number of ways in which the words used in a science can be defined in terms of a few among them. These few may have ostensive definitions, or may have nominal definitions in terms of words not belonging to the science in question, or . . . they may be left without either ostensive or nominal definition, and regarded merely as a set of terms having the properties which the science ascribes to its fundamental terms. Such a set of initial words I call a "minimum vocabulary" for the science in question, provided that a) every word used in the science has a nominal definition in terms of these words, and b) no one of these initial words has a nominal definition in terms of the other initial words.'[11]

'Nominal definition' or 'verbal definition' corresponds to speech (language). It consists of defining words in terms of other words. It is the standard, and so far the only, method of dictionary definition.* In the context of

library and information work, it corresponds to the synonyms or the ubiquitous 'see' references of the dictionary catalogue.

'Ostensive definition', may be defined as 'any process by which a person is taught to understand a word otherwise than by the use of other words.'[12]

The most frequent method is by pointing and repeating the appropriate words. Broadly speaking, ostensive definition corresponds to the sign-situation symbols in Ogden and Richards. So far as is known, the infant learns by a process of 'ostensive' — 'in use' — definition. Similarly one can learn much more of a foreign language rather more rapidly and rather more comfortably this way than by the older word-exchange methods of teaching which so many of us had to suffer.

'Ostensive definition, in its earliest form, requires certain conditions. There must be a feature of the environment which is noticeable, distinctive, emotionally interesting, and (as a rule) frequently recurring. . .† In general, though not universally, repetition is necessary for an ostensive definition, for ostensive definition consists of the creation of a habit, and habits, as a rule, are learned gradually.'[13]

It follows from these definitions of 'nominal' and 'ostensive' that the basis of minimum vocabulary is a set of undefined terms.

'Everything said in a science can be said by means of the words in a minimum vocabulary. For whenever a word occurs which has a nominal definition, we can substitute the defining phrase; if this contains words with a nominal definition, we can again substitute the defining phrase, and so on, until none of the remaining words have nominal definitions. In fact, definable terms are superfluous, and only undefined terms are indispensable. But the question which terms are to be undefined is in part arbitrary. Take, for example, the calculus of proposition, which is the simplest and most complete example of a formal system. We can take "or" and "not" as undefined, or "and" and "not"; instead of two such undefined

---

* The same distinction occurs again in the approach of other British philosophers of the empirical school. "In a dictionary we look mainly for what may be called *explicit* definitions; in philosophy, for definitions *in use*. . . We define a symbol explicitly when we put forward another symbol, or symbolic expression which is synonymous with it. The provision of these criteria enables us to see that the vast majority of the definitions which are given in ordinary discourse are *explicit* definitions. In particular, it is worth remarking that the process of defining *per genus et differentiam* to which Aristotelian logicians devote so much attention always yields definitions which are explicit in the

foregoing sense.' (Ayer, A. J. *Language, truth and logic.* Gollancz, 2nd ed., 1956, p. 59–60.)

† What happens when a situation does occur frequently enough?

'We do not often have occasion to speak, as of an indivisible whole, of the group of phenomena involved or connected in the transit of a negro over a rail-fence with a melon under his arm while the moon is just passing behind a cloud. But if this collocation of phenomena were of frequent occurrence, and if we did have occasion to speak of it often, and if its happenings were likely to affect the money market, we should have some name, as "wousin", to denote it by. People would in time be disputing whether the existence of a wousin involved necessarily a rail-fence, and whether the term could be applied when a white man was similarly related to a stone wall.' (A. Ingraham, Swain School Lectures, 1903, p. 121–82, on Nine uses of language. Quoted in Ogden and Richards, *op. cit.*, p. 131.)

When enough suffering infants have learned wousin, someone will put it in a thesaurus.

terms, we can take one, which may be "not this or not that" or "not this and not that." Thus in general we cannot say that such-and-such a word *must* belong to the minimum vocabulary of such-and-such a science, but at most that there are one or more minimum vocabularies to which it belongs.'[14]

Undefined terms were used above when making an arbitrary division between the treatment of words in information (meaning) where definition was involved and in information retrieval (reference) where, at the indexing stage, no definition was allowed. In the stage now reached, the basis of *all* definition is a core of undefined terms. Definition of all the other terms, i.e., 'nominal definition', is stated in terms only of those undefined terms. If this approach is not only adequate but necessary for the purpose of explanation and understanding of science it is that much the more likely to be adequate for the markedly simpler task of indexing and identifying the written records of such sciences. It confirms that the separation of definition and meaning from the indexing stage is the prerequisite of standardized indexing.

It should be noted, however, that the question of exactly which words are to be incorporated in a minimum vocabulary is, Russell says, in part arbitrary. Equally, for an indexing vocabulary, the initial selection of words is empirical and can, so far, only be made by trial and error in a particular situation. It would be a mistake to believe that there is one and only one correct minimum either for the whole of science or for any particular science. But at any one time there is generally an adequate body of agreed fact in most applied sciences and from this it is possible to provide a starting point, either of a few, a few dozen, or even a few hundred words. The minimum aimed at is not one which is static and fixed for all time but one which will change, alter shape, and often grow as new discoveries in a science have to be accommodated until these newer discoveries enable the terms and structure of the list to be reduced again.

For the comparatively limited purposes of information indexing within special subject areas an initial selection of words may be adequate and it may not be necessary to reduce the vocabulary any further. However, in the more complex sciences and especially where a haphazard collection of trivial and technical terms is in use — as, for example, in many parts of organic chemistry — or where a vocabulary threatens to become unwieldy it may require some further reduction. Often this can be done by straightforward reduction of numbers, by synonymous equating of some terms with others. But it is also possible to reduce the size by imposing a further pattern of logical organization.

'All nominal definitions, if pushed back far enough, must lead ultimately to terms having only ostensive definitions, and in the case of an empirical science the empirical terms must depend upon terms of which the ostensive definitions are given in perception. The astronomer's sun, for instance, is very different from what

we see, but it must have a definition derived from the ostensive definition of the word "sun" which we learnt in childhood. Thus an empirical interpretation of a set of axioms, when complete, must always involve the use of terms which have an ostensive definition derived from sensible experience. It will not, of course, contain *only* such terms, for there will always be logical terms'.[15]

('Logical terms' consist of words such as 'or', 'not', 'some', 'all', etc.[16] In an indexing vocabulary, these, if used are included as part of the structure of mathematical or administrative relationships. It is important to note that such relationships have to be built into the vocabulary at the construction stage. They cannot be included at the indexing or retrieval stage if previous provision has not been made for them.)

Taking astronomy as an example, Russell shows that a minimum vocabulary for what may be called the geography of astronomy could be deduced which would contain only two proper names, 'the sun' and (say) 'Sirius'. However, while this would, theoretically, be adequate for astronomy in the abstract, enabling all other astronomical locations to be derived from them, that part of astronomy which is considered as a record of observations depends not on an abstraction, 'the sun', but on being able to observe it, to point to it, to record it.

'Astronomy is not *merely* a collection of words and sentences; it is a collection of words and sentences chosen, from others that were linguistically just as good, because they described a world connected with sensible experience . . . and the sentences in which sensible experience breaks in are such as "that is the sun".'[17]

Similarly, in dealing with physical phenomena such as copper conducting electricity, the name copper can now be defined as element 29. If necessary, elements can then be defined in terms of atomic or nuclear particles. These in turn can be redefined as mass and electric charge and mass is an equivalent of energy. At this level of abstraction, physics is part of pure mathematics and is discussed by means of quantum theory. But Planck's constant 'h' is given as about 6.55×10^{-27} erg secs. 'No one would have thought of introducing just this quantity if there had not been experimental reasons for doing so.'[18] Again, energy, for example, though also an abstraction, depends for definition ultimately on experiments such as those of Joule. Its constancy has been established by the determination of the mechanical equivalent of heat. The physical definition of heat, rapid agitation of particles ultimately rests on the human sensation of feeling heat.

'. . . any minimum vocabulary for physics must be such as to enable us to mention the experiences upon which our physical beliefs are based. We shall need such words as "hot", "red", "hard", not only to describe what physics asserts to be the condition of bodies that give us these sensations, but also to describe the sensations themselves. . . It is obvious that "red" has a meaning independent of physics, and that this meaning is relevant in collecting data for the physical theory of colours, just as the pre-scientific meaning of "hot" is relevant in establishing the physical theory of heat.

'The main conclusion of the above discussion of minimum vocabularies is that every empirical science, however abstract, must contain in any minimum vocabulary words descriptive of our experiences. Even the most mathematical terms, such as "energy", must, when the chain of definition is completed until we reach terms of which there is only an ostensive definition, be found to depend for their meaning upon terms directly descriptive of experiences, or even, in what may be called the "geographical" sciences, giving names to particular experiences.'[19]

Thus, ultimately, a minimum vocabulary rests not merely on terms which are basic to the particular science but on those terms employed to describe or to denote sense experience. It is these which, in the last resort, are the undefined terms. If there are any such things as 'keywords', then these are they.

However, 'experience' is private to each one of us and no universal degree of precision can be attached to any words signifying what is experienced. Thus, even for a familiar description such as 'red' no exact standard can be laid down.

'Any definition of "red" which professes to be precise is prententious and fraudulent.'

Only approximations can be made. When deciding whether anything was red or not, there will be some colours which all agreed were 'red'; there will be others which all agreed were not, 'while in the middle there will be a region where we have no preponderant inclination either towards *yes* or towards *no*. All empirical concepts have this character — not only obviously vague concepts such as "loud" or "hot", but also those that we are most anxious to make precise, such as "centimetre" and "second".'[20]

The manner in which, and partly also the extent to which, undefined terms can be substituted for defined is determined by structure. Structure can refer, first, to the scientific composition of the thing under consideration.

'To exhibit the structure of an object is to mention its parts and the way in which they are interrelated.'[21]

In this first sense, structure depends upon the degree of knowledge at the time, as in the physical and chemical examples quoted earlier.

In the second sense, structure refers to the grammar and form of the language.

'Logic is concerned with sentences that are true in virtue of their structure.'[22]

Exactly parallel forms of structure are found in vocabularies for information storage and retrieval. There, however, description is effectively restricted to lists of words, not to statements and sentences, and the logical structure is, therefore, that much more limited. At present, there are, in fact, two quite different forms of structure in use in information retrieval: the 'generic/specific' relation of biological[23] and library shelf-classification and, secondly, the Boolean 'and/or/not' logic[24] of co-ordinate indexing vocabularies and thesauri. Part of the problem at the present time is that these two forms have so far proved irreconcilable.

There is, moreover, some evidence that indexing vocabulary structure can be affected by the efficiency or otherwise of any visual or electronic aids chosen to supplement it. An example is in co-ordinate indexing where, because of the ability to superimpose more than two cards in 'Peek-a-boo', much simpler vocabulary structures can be effective than is the case with 'Uniterm-type cards', where 'roles' and 'links' have been introduced partly because of the virtual restriction to two cards during the retrieval stage. With the development of more advanced aids, and especially computers, this situation is likely to intensify. Thus, the size and structure of our indexing vocabulary will depend not only on the current state of scientific or other special-subject knowledge and on the form of indexing relationships adopted but also on the efficiency of the particular filing or electronic aids employed.

The variables are still formidable but if the historical pattern of scientific and intellectual development prevails also in retrieval vocabularies there is some hope of ultimate order.

'. . . a science is apt to acquire a smaller minimum vocabulary as it becomes more systematic. The ancients knew many geographical facts before they knew how to assign latitudes and longitudes, but to express these facts, they needed a larger number of undefined words than we need.'[25]

Likewise, it is probable that the confused terminology of library and information retrieval at the present time reflects the inadquate state of the art. As further progress is made in standardizing the operations involved a good many of the fetish words now employed will be relegated to the museums of linguistic and bibliographical curiosity.

5. Basic English

In practice, there has already been one example of a minimum vocabulary, and this not merely for a particular science or speciality but for the entire structure of a natural, everyday language. This is Basic English,[26] the simplified version of the English language developed by Ogden as a result of the earlier studies on meaning and symbols. In Basic English, the vocabulary is reduced to a list of some 850 words in which it is possible to say everything which needs to be said.

During the war, Basic English gained the support of Sir Winston Churchill — and of President Roosevelt — as a means of rapid teaching of English throughout the world in the post-war era.[27] Unfortunately, this lead was not followed and one more opportunity of obtaining easier communication and understanding was lost. The original Basic English list may now need to be modified for scientific work but it could still provide a starting point for a minimum vocabulary in a general library. Perhaps the recent appearance of a scientific dictionary in Basic English may lead to renewed interest in this approach.[28]

6. Conclusion

Most indexing and information theory has been directed towards 'systems', complex methods, artificial languages, and theoretical ideals, towards if anything a maximum vocabulary. But the exceedingly complex classification and retrieval theories which have appeared on both sides of the Atlantic could only be justified if — and not always then — there was any certainty that the things being indexed were ever going to be asked for. There is, however, so far no evidence that anything other than a small proportion of what is written ever gets adequate use again.[29] We are aiming to supply maximum retrieval in order to meet a minimum demand.

In practice, however, the special library world is already largely committed to minimizing retrieval vocabularies, if only because specialization — and economics — restrict the subject areas dealt with there. In many such areas, it is adequate to have the minimum vocabulary of undefined terms based on commonly used terms within that area, though here it should be mentioned that the success of 'Peek-a-boo' for small-scale accurate indexing and retrieval shows that one of the most pressing problems to be solved is the relative merit of single word and word-pair vocabularies. The names of a great many of the scientific and technical developments of the last century have been accommodated within a pre-existing vocabulary by pairing of words.[30] Since, taken to its ultimate conclusion, this means that theoretically a vocabulary can be squared, it may well be that the only way of controlling this new form of information 'explosion', to use the current regrettably fashionable term, is to reduce a vocabulary still further.

'A minimum vocabulary for what we experience is a minimum vocabulary for all our knowledge. That this must be the case is obvious from a consideration of the process of ostensive definition.'[31]

Basing a vocabulary on terms of everyday sense-experience should give a better opportunity of avoiding much of the interminable argument which has gone in information retrieval over 'meaning'.

At the vocabulary construction stage, meaning is certainly involved though to a lesser extent than in the wider natural language, from which the vocabulary terms have to be drawn. In retrieval, we have to accept that we lose the whole grammatical structure of the language, its order, and parts of speech; we are left only with a collection of nouns and names, to make sense of which we must rely on a 'law of averages' in the filing method to secure effective separation in retrieval.

If structural refinements are necessary to improve retrieval accuracy, it seems we should examine the possibility of correlating the structural relationships with the habitual and accepted grammatical structures, rather than by continuing to invent entities such as 'roles', 'facets', and 'analets', which are open to misinterpretation and wide differences of opinion. Thus existing relationships in indexing vocabularies correspond roughly to conjunctions; the next step could be the provision of a relationship corresponding to prepositions. Perhaps the most effective measure would be the drastic reduction of the indexing terms corresponding to verbs — in fact, this is often unconsciously achieved in many specialist vocabularies. Richards considered that the reduction in the number of verbs to eighteen was the key to the discovery of Basic English.[32]

Similarly, there is reason to believe that if a vocabulary can be made or kept small enough all relationships can be eliminated.

'There is doubtless some limit below which a vocabulary can be totally free and without complications such as roles, links, and thesauri. Where the limit lies and how areas outside that limit can best be handled has not been determined.'[33]

It is fairly inevitable that the crossover point between a vocabulary without relationships and one which will come at the point where the vocabulary becomes too large to memorize or scan completely within a minute or two. Equally, a vocabulary with a high proportion of elementary or everyday terms is more easily memorized and used than one which has not. There can be more than one form of minimum vocabulary and there can be more than one minimum vocabulary for a particular subject. The success of small-scale examples in 'Peek-a-boo' indexing encourages us to seek ways of employing the same principles in larger capacity library storage.

References

1. RUSSELL, B. *Human knowledge: its scope and limits*, Allen and Unwin, 1948, p. 199.
2. OGDEN, C. K. and RICHARDS, I. A. *The meaning of meaning*, Kegan Paul, p. 136, 1923.
3. Ibid., p. 306, *et seq.*
4. RUSSELL, B. *op. cit.*, p. 268.
5. OGDEN, C. K. and RICHARDS, I. A. *op cit.*, p. 149.
6. Ibid., p. 16.
7. Ibid., p. 200.
8. BATTEN, W. E. *Aslib Proceedings*, vol. 19, no. 6, 1964, p. 340. '. . . some of them might find their mission a lot easier to approach if their creed had been called in the first place "information extraction" rather than "information retrieval". It was much too late to try and change the terminology, but there was little doubt that the process was one of extraction rather than retrieval and that the part which they were trying to mechanize and cheapen was the step of setting aside that part of the collec-

tion which need not be read at all. Personally he doubted whether it would ever be feasible to dispense entirely with true intellectual effort in the final output stage.'

9. RUSSELL, B. *op. cit.*, p. 89.
10. Ibid., p. 94.
11. Ibid., p. 259.
12. Ibid., p. 78.
13. Ibid., pp. 79–80.
14. Ibid., p. 259.
15. Ibid., p. 258.
16. Ibid., p. 275.
17. Ibid., p. 262.
18. Ibid., pp. 265–6.
19. Ibid., p. 264.
20. Ibid., p. 277.
21. Ibid., p. 267.
22. Ibid., p. 269.
23. Ibid., p. 83. '. . . In biology before Darwin, "species" was a prominent concept . . . There was an elaborate hierarchy of genera, families, orders, etc. This kind of classification, which was and is convenient in biology, was extended by the scholastics to other regions, and impeded logic by creating the notion that some ways of classifying are more correct than others.'
24. Van Nostrand's Scientific Encyclopaedia, 3rd ed., 1958, p. 399.
25. RUSSELL, B. *op. cit.*, p. 260.
26. OGDEN, C. K. *Basic English: a general introduction with rules and grammar*, 7th ed., Kegan Paul, 1938.
27. CHURCHILL, SIR WINSTON. *The Second World War*, vol. 5, 1952, p. 587.
28. GRAHAM, E. C. ed. *The science dictionary in Basic English*, Evans Brothers, 1965.
29. Survey of information needs of physicists and chemists. *Journal of Documentation*, vol. 21, no. 2, 1965, p. 83.
30. MOSS, R. Post co-ordinate indexing *in* 'Information Storage and Retrieval Systems', Proceedings of a Seminar, November 18–19, 1965, Institute for Industrial Research and Standards, Dublin, p. 28.
31. RUSSELL, B. *op. cit.*, p. 283.
32. RICHARDS, I. A. *Basic English and its uses*, pp. 28–9. 'The reduction of the verbs to 18 was the key to the discovery of Basic . . . these "operators", in combination with other Basic words, translate adequately more than 4,000 verbs.'
33. JASTER, J. J., MURRAY, B. R., and TAUBE, M. *The state of the art of co-ordinate indexing*. Prel. ed. Washington, Documentation Inc., Feb. 1962, 259p. (AD275 393), pp. 197–200.
34. OGDEN, C. K. and RICHARDS, I. A. *op. cit.*, p. 102.
35. RUSSELL, B. *History of western philosophy*, Allen and Unwin, 1946, p. 494.

25 Semantic Clustering of Index Terms

C. C. GOTLIEB
S. KUMAR
*Journal of the Association
for Computing Machinery
Vol. 15, No. 4, October, 1968*

1. Introduction

The problem of establishing a quantitative association between index terms has been attempted by various research workers. Usually the terms have been drawn from a natural language vocabulary consisting of words occurring with high frequency in a document collection. Association measures have been defined [6, 14, 16, 17] as some function of the frequency of co-occurrence of these words in the documents. These association measures are essentially statistical; two words such as *data* and *processing* may have a strong association with respect to the given context, but may have very little or no semantic association with one another. In other words, the association measure is heavily dependent on the document collection, which is not a stable context and can change rapidly.

Thus the main problem in attempting to establish a semantic association for natural language words is the strong dependence of their semantics on contexts. Spärck-Jones [15] has suggested that two words may be considered semantically equivalent or synonyms if in a given context (an expression or a sentence) the words can be interchanged without changing the meaning. Such a grouping of interchangeable words is then used as a basis for a semantic classification. Lewis et al. [7] make the hypothesis that two synonyms occur very infrequently in the same sentence, but have similar contexts when they occur separately. They then use this hypothesis for statistically discriminating words into synonyms and antonyms.

In this paper an attempt is made at defining an association measure between index terms which are drawn from the vocabulary of a structured indexing system [5, 8, 18], and which may consist of single words, collections of words, or syntactic phrases. The association measure, which is based on a priori (preassigned) semantic relationships between terms, rather than their co-occurrence in a document corpus, is then used for grouping index terms into clusters or concepts. The resulting collection of concepts gives a new association dictionary. Such an association dictionary can be useful in a document retrieval process for supplementing the original request terms with associated terms. Two possible approaches in generating such a dictionary are described: (i) a fixed dictionary based on fixed values of certain system parameters, and (ii) a user-controlled dynamic dictionary in which the parameters are allowed to change. In Section 7, some experimental results are given.

2. Structure of Index Term Representations

A structured indexing system usually consists of a vocabulary of index terms, V, and a semantic association mapping, Γ, giving the relation in which a term appears with respect to other terms of the system. Two types of semantic associations between terms may be distinguished, (a) semantic inclusion, Γ_n, and (b) semantic relatedness, Γ_r. The mapping Γ_n is antisymmetric and transitive and hence (V, Γ_n) defines a partially ordered structure on index terms. The relatedness mapping Γ_r is irreflexive and symmetric.

A classification of index terms according to the inclusion relationship [2] is almost never possible, particularly when the index terms deal with diversified elements such as physical entities, names, scientific disciplines, and abstract notions. Instead a relatedness mapping Γ_r is used to express more general semantic associations, other than inclusion. In some indexing systems [8], a single cross-reference mapping Γ is given so that $y \in \Gamma x$ implies that y may be either included in x or related to x. In other indexing systems [5, 18], the inclusion and related references are segmented, and for each term x, $\Gamma_n x$ specifies the set of terms included in x, and $\Gamma_r x$ specifies the set of terms related to x. Given Γ_n and Γ_r we can define a single Γ such that $\Gamma x = \Gamma_n x \cup \Gamma_r x$.

We use the single mapping Γ. In the Library of Congress' *Subject Headings* [8], which forms the data corpus for the experimental work (see Section 8), Γ corresponds to the "see also" references of a term. Further, we can define Γ^{-1} by $\Gamma_y^{-1} = \{x \mid y \in \Gamma x\}$, and Γ^{-1} corresponds to the "xx" references of a term.

3. Definition of an Association Measure Between Index Terms

Let $\phi(x) = \{x \cup \Gamma x \cup \Gamma^{-1} x\}$. This set gives all the immediate semantic relatives of a term x, i.e. all terms related to x by a single reference. Of the various formulas available [12], the following simple formula is chosen to define an association measure, $a(x, y)$, between a pair of terms:

$$a(x, y) = \left| \frac{\phi(x) \cap \phi(y)}{\phi(x) \cup \phi(y)} \right|,$$

where $\mid \phi \mid$ = number of elements in set ϕ.

The distance between two terms x and y can be defined from this as $d(x, y) = 1. - a(x, y)$. The distance function satisfies the conditions of a pseudometric [12], i.e.

(i) $d(x, x) = 0.$,   *reflexive;*

(ii) $d(x, y) = d(y, x)$,   *symmetric;*

(iii) $d(x, y) + d(y, z) \geqq d(x, z)$,   *triangle inequality.*

Note that $d(x, y) = 0. \nLeftrightarrow x = y$; also $d(x, y)$ and $a(x, y)$ lie in the range 0.0 to 1.0.

Thus, given a vocabulary of index terms, V, we have an "association matrix" between index terms, the elements of which are real numbers in the range 0.0 to 1.0.

If we replace the nonzero elements of the association matrix with ones, we get the adjacency matrix of a graph. This graph has an edge between any pair of terms which has a nonzero association. Since many term-pairs will have very small non-zero associations, this graph will have many edges. The graph will be more manageable if we associate an edge between terms only when they have an association measure greater than a suitably chosen threshold, T.

A T-graph of index terms can thus be defined as follows: For a term $x \in V$, let $\sigma(T)x$ consist of all terms whose association with x is greater than or equal to a threshold T, chosen in the range 0.0 to 1.0. The T-graph $[V, \sigma(T)]$ or $[V, M(T)]$ (where $M(T)$ is the set of edges of the graph) will be symmetric and reflexive and its number of edges will be a function of the chosen threshold T. The effect of threshold and the question of deciding an appropriate value are discussed in Section 5.

4. Graph-Theoretic Methods of Grouping Index Terms Into Concepts

Various methods of grouping objects into clusters have been suggested [3, 9, 10, 11, 13]. In this section two graph-theoretic methods of grouping index terms into clusters (which are then regarded as concepts) are contrasted: (a) using connected components of the T-graph, and (b) using maximal complete subgraphs (m.c.s.'s) or cliques of the T-graph.

4.1 Concepts Defined from Connected Components

A connected component of a graph is defined as a subgraph in which every pair of vertices is connected by a chain of edges [1]. Also, the different connected components constitute a partition of nodes of the graph. If we have a T-graph $[V, M(T_1)]$, with threshold T_1, then by increasing the threshold to a larger value T_2, we get a T-graph $[V, M(T_2)]$, where $M(T_2) \subset M(T_1)$. If $[V, M(T_1)]$ has $C_1, C_2, \ldots, C_{n1}$ as the node partitions into connected components, then the graph $[V, M(T_2)]$, corresponding to the larger threshold T_2, will have node partitions $P_1, P_2, \ldots, P_{n2}$ with each partition P_j contained in some partition C_i.

Each connected component of a T-graph may be regarded as a distinct concept such that $C^1 = \{x \mid y \in C^1, a(x, y) \geqq T\}$. It follows that every index term in a concept will have an association greater than or equal to the threshold T with *some* other member of the concept, and every member will have an association less than T with all index terms not in the concept. The major shortcoming of this definition is that in the resulting concept, some pairs of terms may not be strongly related to each other. In the extreme case a long chain of terms might be found in a single concept, and although neighboring pairs will be related, relatedness is not transitive, and it will often happen that a pair of distant terms along the chain will have very little semantic association.

4.2 Concepts Defined from Maximal Complete Subgraphs or Cliques

Therefore, the following definition of a concept appears more reasonable: In a concept every pair of members has an association greater than or equal to the chosen threshold T, and there does not exist a nonmember having an association greater than or equal to T to *all* members of the concept. Formally, $C^2 = \{x \mid y \in C^2 \Rightarrow a(x, y) \geq T\}$. For reasons which are made clear below, we call this a "sharp concept."

Sharp concepts correspond to maximal complete subgraphs of the T-graph. (In a maximal complete subgraph, or m.c.s., there is an edge between every pair of vertices and any vertex not belonging to the m.c.s. cannot be connected by an edge to all vertices of the m.c.s.) It is possible to enumerate all the maximal complete subgraphs from our T-graph, and these correspond to all sharp concepts. The family of m.c.s.'s of a graph does not partition either the nodes or the edges of the graph. A node may belong to more than one m.c.s. and the m.c.s.'s can overlap. For our purposes of grouping index terms into concepts, it is necessary to recognize that a term can belong to more than one concept. This is an inevitable property of the fuzziness in natural language.

In a random graph the number of m.c.s.'s can become quite large, and it is possible that the total number of such overlapping maximal complete subgraphs can exceed the total number of nodes itself. We would like to have a manageable number of concepts. Also, on intuitive grounds, it is desirable that any term should not belong to more than a few concepts. There must, therefore, be some means of controlling the number of concepts. In Section 6, a systematic method of merging overlapping sharp concepts into larger diffuse concepts is discussed.

5. Choice of Threshold

A graph G, for which an edge is defined for every pair of terms with a nonzero association, is clearly unsatisfactory, since many term-pairs may have small nonzero measures between them. The T-graph, $[V, \sigma(T)]$, which associates an edge with pairs of terms only if their association measure exceeds a threshold value T, in effect

deletes some edges from the above graph G. The effect of changing T_1 to a larger value T_2 is to remove additional edges for which the association is greater than or equal to T_1 but less than T_2. In the limiting case of $T = 1.0$ we get a graph with approximately $|V|$ edges, i.e. isolated terms with loops on each term.

The functional dependence of $\sigma(T)$ or $M(T)$ on T will not be continuous; at discrete intervals along T, $\sigma(T)$ and $M(T)$ will increase in steps. For a given node x, $\sigma(T)x$ is the set of terms related to x using threshold T, and as T changes from 1.0 to 0.0 the family defines a "local topological structure" for the term x.

For a given vocabulary of index terms, the functional dependence of $M(T)$ or better $\theta(T) = (2 \mid M(T) \mid - \mid V \mid)/\mid V \mid$, where $\theta(T)/\mid V \mid$ is the density of the T-graph, may be used as a basis for selecting a suitable threshold value T. $\theta(T)$ gives the average number of edges per node or the average degree of the T-graph, and it increases as T decreases. For small T we get a large number of edges per node and hence very general concepts, i.e. concepts with many terms. On the other hand, for large T we get a large number of narrow concepts. The value $\theta(T)$ can therefore be used as a guide to determine the extent of generality of concepts. Also, T must be so chosen that the graph model is fairly stable in the region of the chosen T, i.e. small perturbations in the value of T should not affect the graph considerably. As a rough guide, the value $\mid \Delta\theta(T) \mid/\mid \Delta T \mid$ may be used to give the sensitivity of the generality of concepts to the parameter T. For concepts to be stable, the parametric sensitivity should be kept as low as possible. This can be decided from the plot of $\theta(T)$ against T, so that in the neighborhood of the chosen T, the function is as flat as possible. We therefore have two criteria to help choose a suitable threshold, and hence a T-graph of index terms. For an example, see Section 7.

6. Systematic Merging of Overlapping Sharp Concepts Into Larger Diffuse Concepts

The concepts should be groups of index terms such that terms belonging to a group are strongly connected to each other with respect to some relatedness criterion, and the groups themselves are weakly connected to each other, i.e. they are as disjoint as possible. If we start building up the clusters from maximal complete subgraphs we can be assured that pairs of terms belonging to a sharp concept will have associations greater than or equal to the threshold T. The second criterion, i.e. the concepts should be as weakly connected as possible, can be realized by defining concepts in such a way that the distance between them, defined below, will be larger than a specified value.

Since concepts are subsets of the total vocabulary of index terms, and therefore sets in themselves, the distance between two concepts C_i and C_j may be defined as

$$d(C_i, C_j) = 1. - \frac{|C_i \cap C_j|}{|C_i \cup C_j|}.$$

We can now define a new graph, with concepts as its nodes, and for which two nodes are connected with an edge, if and only if the distance between the corresponding concepts is less than a minimum distance threshold δ. Concepts which belong to a maximal complete subgraph of this new graph can be combined to form a new "diffuse concept," thus giving a new family of concepts.

6.1. Merging of Clusters in a Fixed Dictionary

As an illustration of the procedure, consider the arbitrary T-graph of Figure 1. The sharp concepts corresponding to the maximal complete subgraphs are:

$$C_1 = \{1, 2, 3, 4\}, \qquad C_4 = \{2, 5, 6\},$$

$$C_2 = \{2, 3, 4, 5,\}, \qquad C_5 = \{1, 3, 7, 8, 9\},$$

$$C_3 = \{1, 2, 6\}, \qquad C_6 = \{5, 10\}.$$

The distance matrix for the new concepts is

$$D = \begin{array}{c} R_1 \\ R_2 \\ R_3 \\ R_4 \end{array} \begin{bmatrix} 0.0 & 0.5 & 0.75 & 0.833 \\ 0.5 & 0.0 & 0.875 & 0.8 \\ 0.75 & 0.875 & 0.0 & 1.0 \\ 0.833 & 0.8 & 1.0 & 0.0 \end{bmatrix}.$$

Some of the distances between the new concepts are the still less than the chosen threshold δ. Therefore, if we wish to assure that the final concepts have distances greater than δ, then we must treat the new concepts as the nodes of a new graph for which edges exist if the distance between the corresponding concepts is less than δ, and the process must be repeated until the final concepts have distances greater than δ and are therefore weakly connected with respect to a chosen minimum distance threshold δ.

In the last example, the new graph would be as given in Figure 3. The new concepts would be

$$S_1 = R_1 \cup R_2 = C_1 \cup C_2 \cup C_3 \cup C_4 = \{1, 2, 3, 4, 5, 6\},$$

$$S_2 = R_3 \qquad = C_5 = \{1, 3, 7, 8, 9\},$$

$$S_3 = R_4 \qquad = C_6 = \{5, 10\}.$$

Graph

Adjacency matrix

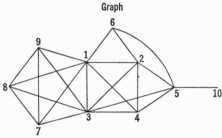

$$\begin{bmatrix} 1 & 1 & 1 & 1 & 0 & 1 & 1 & 1 & 1 & 0 \\ 1 & 1 & 1 & 1 & 1 & 1 & 0 & 0 & 0 & 0 \\ 1 & 1 & 1 & 1 & 1 & 0 & 1 & 1 & 1 & 0 \\ 1 & 1 & 1 & 1 & 1 & 0 & 0 & 0 & 0 & 0 \\ 0 & 1 & 1 & 1 & 1 & 1 & 0 & 0 & 0 & 1 \\ 1 & 1 & 0 & 0 & 1 & 1 & 0 & 0 & 0 & 0 \\ 1 & 0 & 1 & 0 & 0 & 0 & 1 & 1 & 1 & 0 \\ 1 & 0 & 1 & 0 & 0 & 0 & 1 & 1 & 1 & 0 \\ 1 & 0 & 1 & 0 & 0 & 0 & 1 & 1 & 1 & 0 \\ 0 & 0 & 0 & 0 & 1 & 0 & 0 & 0 & 0 & 1 \end{bmatrix}$$

FIG. 1. Example of T-graph.

The distance matrix between the sharp concepts is

$$\begin{array}{c} C_1 \\ C_2 \\ C_3 \\ C_4 \\ C_5 \\ C_6 \end{array} \begin{bmatrix} 0.0 & 0.4 & 0.6 & 0.833 & 0.714 & 1.0 \\ 0.4 & 0.0 & 0.833 & 0.600 & 0.857 & 0.8 \\ 0.6 & 0.833 & 0.0 & 0.5 & 0.857 & 1.0 \\ 0.833 & 0.600 & 0.5 & 0.0 & 1.0 & 0.75 \\ 0.714 & 0.857 & 0.857 & 1.0 & 0.0 & 1.0 \\ 1.0 & 0.8 & 1.0 & 0.75 & 1.0 & 0.0 \end{bmatrix}.$$

For $\delta = 0.50$ (an arbitrary value between 0.0 and 1.0), we get the graph shown in Figure 2. The diffuse concepts, corresponding to maximal complete subgraphs of this graph, would be:

$$R_1 = C_1 \cup C_2 = \{1, 2, 3, 4, 5\},$$

$$R_2 = C_3 \cup C_4 = \{1, 2, 5, 6\},$$

$$R_3 = C_5 \qquad = \{1, 3, 7, 8, 9\},$$

$$R_4 = C_6 \qquad = \{5, 10\}.$$

In the new distance matrix below ($\delta = 0.5$), all distances are greater than δ and hence S_1, S_2, S_3 are the final diffuse concepts:

$$D = \begin{array}{c} S_1 \\ S_2 \\ S_3 \end{array} \begin{bmatrix} 0.0 & 0.778 & 0.857 \\ 0.778 & 0.0 & 1.0 \\ 0.857 & 1.0 & 0.0 \end{bmatrix}.$$

Note that for $\delta = 0.0$, using the above procedure, we get original sharp concepts obtained from the T-graph as our final concepts also, whereas for $\delta = 1.0$, we get a final concept for each connected component of the T-graph.

The finest grouping of terms into concepts for any threshold T corresponds to using $\delta = 0.0$. However, if the number of such concepts tends to be larger than is desirable, then we can use some value of δ greater than 0.0 to combine sharp concepts systematically into diffuse concepts, thus reducing the total number. (In the example illustrated above, six sharp concepts have been

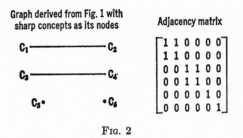

Graph derived from Fig. 1 with sharp concepts as its nodes

Adjacency matrix

$$\begin{bmatrix} 1 & 1 & 0 & 0 & 0 & 0 \\ 1 & 1 & 0 & 0 & 0 & 0 \\ 0 & 0 & 1 & 1 & 0 & 0 \\ 0 & 0 & 1 & 1 & 0 & 0 \\ 0 & 0 & 0 & 0 & 1 & 0 \\ 0 & 0 & 0 & 0 & 0 & 1 \end{bmatrix}$$

FIG. 2

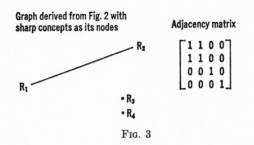

Graph derived from Fig. 2 with sharp concepts as its nodes

Adjacency matrix

$$\begin{bmatrix} 1 & 1 & 0 & 0 \\ 1 & 1 & 0 & 0 \\ 0 & 0 & 1 & 0 \\ 0 & 0 & 0 & 1 \end{bmatrix}$$

FIG. 3

systematically merged to give three final diffuse concepts, using $\delta = 0.5$.)

A block organization of the procedure for merging concepts in a fixed dictionary is given in Figure 4.

6.2. *Merging of Clusters in a Dynamic Dictionary*

In the generation of a fixed family of clusters, it is desirable that clusters should be as disjoint as possible and that the largely overlapping intermediate clusters which are formed at interim stages should not be of much significance. In a dynamic dictionary we allow clusters to grow gradually during the various stages of the merging. Also, clusters can be generated locally around a user request term.

We define a threshold δ_1 as the smallest nonzero distance from a cluster containing the request term to any other cluster. In the example of Figure 1, if the request term is term 4, then (see the distance matrix between sharp concepts in Subsection 6.1) $\delta_1 = d(C_1, C_2) = 0.4$. Using this value, the adjacency matrix of the graph of sharp concepts becomes that shown in Figure 5.

We now define new clusters corresponding to only those maximal complete subgraphs of this graph, where at least one of the nodes corresponds to a cluster containing request term 4; other clusters are held unchanged. In our example C_1 and C_2 contain request term 4. We thus get

$$D_1 = C_1 \cup C_2 = \{1, 2, 3, 4, 5\},$$
$$D_2 = C_3 \qquad = \{1, 2, 6\},$$
$$D_3 = C_4 \qquad = \{2, 5, 6\},$$
$$D_4 = C_5 \qquad = \{1, 3, 7, 8, 9\},$$
$$D_5 = C_6 \qquad = \{5, 10\}.$$

The new distance matrix is

$$\begin{matrix} D_1 \\ D_2 \\ D_3 \\ D_4 \\ D_5 \end{matrix} \begin{bmatrix} 0.0 & 0.67 & 0.67 & 0.75 & 0.833 \\ & 0.0 & 0.5 & 0.857 & 1.0 \\ & & 0.0 & 1.0 & 0.75 \\ & symmetric & & 0.0 & 1.0 \\ & & & & 0.0 \end{bmatrix}$$

Now we can choose a new threshold, $\delta_2 = d(D_1, D_2) = d(D_1, D_3) = 0.67$. The new graph is shown in Figure 6. The new clusters are:

$$E_1 = D_1 \cup D_2 \cup D_3 = \{1, 2, 3, 4, 5, 6\},$$
$$E_2 = D_4 \qquad\qquad = \{1, 3, 7, 8, 9\},$$
$$E_3 = D_5 \qquad\qquad = \{5, 10\},$$

and the distance matrix is

$$\begin{matrix} E_1 \\ E_2 \\ E_3 \end{matrix} \begin{bmatrix} 0.0 & 0.778 & 0.857 \\ & 0.0 & 1.0 \\ symmetric & & 0.0 \end{bmatrix}$$

In the next step, δ_3 can be chosen equal to $d(E_1, E_2) = 0.778$, giving

$$F_1 = E_1 \cup E_2 = \{1, 2, 3, 4, 5, 6, 7, 8, 9\},$$
$$F_2 = E_3 \qquad = \{5, 10\}.$$

Finally δ_3 is chosen equal to $d(F_1, F_2) = 0.9$, and we then get a single cluster, $G = F_1 \cup F_2 = \{1, 2, 3, 4, 5, 6, 7, 8, 9, 10\}$.

It is to be noted that in this merging process δ is chosen automatically by the algorithm. For a given request term we are thus able to access more and more terms in discrete steps.

In a clustering procedure such as this we need some criterion to terminate growth. For a request term x, if C_x^i are the clusters to which the term x belongs, then $| \cup_i C_x^i |$ gives the total number of terms which have been accessed at that stage. When clusters consist of only m.c.s.'s, $| \cup_i C_x^i | = | \sigma(T)x |$. The ratio $| \sigma(T)x |/| \cup_i C_x^i |$ will decrease monotonically, or will at least be nonincreasing, during the subsequent stages of clustering. We can terminate the process when this ratio becomes less than some specified value, say γ.

For the example just considered, the ratio $| \sigma(T)4 |/| \cup_i C_x^i |$ at the various stages of the merging is as shown in Table I.

For γ equal to, say, 0.6 the process can be terminated at stage 4.

A block organization of the procedure for merging clusters in a dynamic dictionary is given in Figure 7.

7. Experimental Results

7.1 *Data Corpus*

In the selection of a possible data corpus on which to carry out experimental work, the following were con-

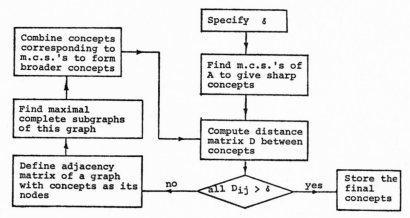

Fig. 4. Block diagram for concept merging procedure with fixed dictionary A: Adjacency matrix of the T-graph.

TABLE I

The Ratio $|\sigma(T)4|/|\cup_i C_i{}^i|$ at the Various Stages of Merging

m.c.s.	Cluster	$|\sigma(T)4|/|\cup_i C_i{}^i|$
Stage 1	$\{1, 2, 3, 4\}$	1.0
Stage 2	$\{1, 2, 3, 4, 5\}$	1.0
Stage 3	$\{1, 2, 3, 4, 5, 6\}$	0.833
Stage 4	$\{1, 2, 3, 4, 5, 6, 7, 8, 9\}$	0.555
Stage 5	$\{1, 2, 3, 4, 5, 6, 7, 8, 9, 10\}$	0.5

sidered: (a) Engineers Joint Council, *Thesaurus of Engineering Terms*, 1st ed. [5]; (b) US Department of Health, Education and Welfare, *MEDLARS Medical Subject Headings* [18]; and (c) Library of Congress, *Subject Headings*, 6th ed. [8].

The first two indexing systems deal with only a restricted field. The last system covers the whole field of knowledge and has been used more extensively than any other single system. It has grown over a period of time through the contribution of many specialists, and as mentioned in its Introduction, "The list is the product of evolutionary changes, . . . semantic changes and varying theories of subject headings practice over the years." One of the main motivations in choosing it as our data corpus was that very little attempt has been made in the past to use it in a mechanized retrieval process, in spite of its being the most widely used system in the North American continent and perhaps the world.

In this list there are about 43,000 terms for each of which there may be "see also" references, which mean either "inclusion" or "relatedness." In preparing the corpus in a form suitable for computer use, each index term was associated with an identifying integer, and eventually a magnetic tape file was constructed in which each record consisted of a term, its identifying number, and all terms referred by it. It was then necessary to match each of approximately 60,000 referred terms with a main term. This required extensive searching, and to do this by sequential processing a second magnetic tape file was prepared, in which a record consisted of a term, its identifying number, one referred term only, and a blank field for its identifying number. This file was then sorted, first on the main terms and then on the referred terms, using IBSYS SORT package to produce a sorted "descendants file" and a sorted "ancestors file," respectively. Using these sorted files, it was possible to perform a local binary search (within a block only) for all referred terms in a reasonable time (about 10 minutes on a 7094 II), and thus assign identifying numbers to all referred terms. Two other tape files were prepared using separate programs. These consisted of semantic connections arising out of subdivided headings, e.g. ART; ART — HISTORY; etc., and inverted headings, e.g. ART; ART, ABSTRACT; etc. Using the four files a final file was prepared, consisting of identifying numbers only, each record consisting of a main term and all terms referred from, or to, this term, i.e. the relatives of the

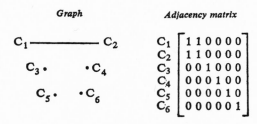

Fig. 5. Graph and matrix for $\delta_1 = 0.4$.

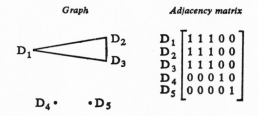

Fig. 6. Derived graph and matrix for $\delta_2 = 0.67$.

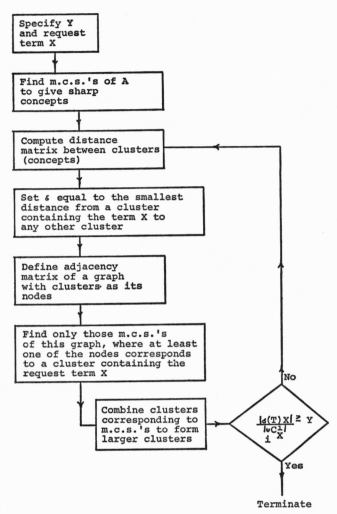

```
┌─────────────────┐
│ Specify Y       │
│ and request     │
│ term X          │
└─────────────────┘
        │
        ▼
┌─────────────────┐
│ Find m.c.s.'s of A │
│ to give sharp   │
│ concepts        │
└─────────────────┘
        │
        ▼
┌─────────────────┐
│ Compute distance │
│ matrix between clusters │
│ (concepts)      │
└─────────────────┘
        │
        ▼
┌─────────────────┐
│ Set δ equal to the smallest │
│ distance from a cluster │
│ containing the term X to │
│ any other cluster │
└─────────────────┘
        │
        ▼
┌─────────────────┐
│ Define adjacency │
│ matrix of a graph │
│ with clusters as its │
│ nodes           │
└─────────────────┘
        │
        ▼
┌─────────────────┐
│ Find only those m.c.s.'s │
│ of this graph, where at least │
│ one of the nodes corresponds │
│ to a cluster containing the │
│ request term X  │
└─────────────────┘
        │
        ▼
┌─────────────────┐
│ Combine clusters │
│ corresponding to │
│ m.c.s.'s to form │
│ larger clusters │
└─────────────────┘
```

FIG. 7. Block diagram for concept merging procedure with dynamic dictionary A: Adjacency matrix of a connected component of the T-graph containing the request term x.

term. Isolated terms (those which had no terms referred from or to it) were eliminated as they did not influence the connective structure of the indexing system. There were 34,832 main terms in this final working file. It was found that there were 2,155 terms with no ancestors (descendants only) and 20,608 terms with no descendants (ancestors only).

7.2 Evaluation of Association Measure

For a number of selected terms the association measure

$$a(x, y) = \left| \frac{\phi(x) \cap \phi(y)}{\phi(x) \cup \phi(y)} \right|,$$

with all other index terms, was computed. Sample values of computed association measures are given in Tables

II–IV. The entries are listed in order of decreasing association measures.

The following observations may be made about these measures:

(i) The maximum association measure for any term with any *other* term is quite small. This is not unexpected. True or even near-synonyms are not usually available in an indexing system since a limited vocabulary of terms has to be defined to cover a wide field of knowledge.

(ii) No great significance can be attached to small quantitative differences. For example, the association measure between *electrons* and *cosmic rays* is 0.174, whereas that between *electrons* and *x-rays* is 0.116, although both *cosmic rays* and *x-rays* would seem to have almost the same association with *electrons*.

(iii) In spite of (ii) the relative ordering of terms according to the measure does not violate our general notions of semantic closeness, and are usually reasonable.

(iv) One of the significant points about the measure is that it can reveal close association between terms which may not happen to refer to one another in the indexing system. For example, it was found that the term *physics* has the second highest association measure with the term *matter — properties*, although *matter — properties* is not one of the fifty terms referred from, or referring to, *physics*.

7.3 Determining a Suitable Threshold

In Section 5 it was shown how a threshold T can be defined which essentially determines the density of edges of the graph. Because of the size of the data corpus, it was not possible to compute the average number of edges per node, $\theta(T)$, for all values of T from 1.0 to 0.0. This would have required too much computer time. Hence, samples of 50, 100, and 200 terms were taken for the purpose. The sample plots exhibited reasonable similarity, and could therefore be considered as representative of the total. A sample plot for 200 terms is given in Figure 8. Note that the plot procedes upward by a series of steps.

For any term x there are many terms y in the indexing system such that $|\phi(x) \cap \phi(y)| = 1$. These give rise to large jumps in the number of edges at threshold values, such as $\frac{1}{3}$, $\frac{1}{4}$, . . . , $\frac{1}{10}$, etc. Similarly, for any term x there are appreciably many terms y in the indexing system such that $|\phi(x) \cap \phi(y)| = 2$. These give rise to smaller jumps at threshold values such as $\frac{2}{3}$, $\frac{2}{4}$, $\frac{2}{5}$, $\frac{2}{7}$, $\frac{2}{9}$, . . . , etc., and add to the jumps at $\frac{2}{6}$, $\frac{2}{8}$, $\frac{2}{10}$, etc. The jumps at $\frac{3}{5}$, $\frac{3}{7}$, etc. were found to be negligibly small.

The threshold should be chosen in one of the stable regions $1.0 \leqslant T^{-1} < 3.0$, $3.0 \leqslant T^{-1} < 4.0$, $4.0 \leqslant T^{-1} < 5.0$, . . . , $9.0 \leqslant T^{-1} < 10.0$, etc. where the sensitivity $|\Delta\theta(T)|/|\Delta T|$ is very small. The average

TABLE II

Terms Related to "Machine Accounting"
Number of relatives $= |\phi(x)| = 7$

Term (y)	Number relatives of y $|\phi(y)|$	$\|\phi(x)\cup\phi(y)\|$	$\|\phi(x)\cap\phi(y)\|$	Association measure $a(x, \cdot y) =$ $\dfrac{\|\phi(x)\cap\phi(y)\|}{\|\phi(x)\cup\phi(y)\|}$	Distance $d(x,y) =$ $1.-a(x,y)$
Machine accounting	7	7	7	1.0	0.0
Accounting machines	7	8	6	0.750000	0.250000
Tabulating machines	7	9	5	0.555556	0.444444
Bookkeeping machines	3	7	3	0.428571	0.571429
Calculating machines	13	15	5	0.333333	0.666667
Punched card systems	16	18	5	0.277778	0.722222
Card system in business	8	13	2	0.153846	0.846154
Electronic calculating machines	10	15	2	0.133333	0.866667
Accounting—problems, exercises, etc.	2	8	1	0.125000	0.875000
Accounting—study and teaching	2	8	1	0.125000	0.875000
Comptometers	2	8	1	0.125000	0.875000
Income accounting	2	8	1	0.125000	0.875000
Productivity accounting	2	8	1	0.125000	0.875000
Accounting examinations	3	9	1	0.111111	0.888889
Accounting—examinations, questions, etc.	3	9	1	0.111111	0.888889
Accounting and price fluctuations	3	9	1	0.111111	0.888889
Average of accounts	3	9	1	0.111111	0.888889
Fiscal year	3	9	1	0.111111	0.888889
Municipal finance—accounting	3	9	1	0.111111	0.888889
Statistics—charts, tables, etc.	3	9	1	0.111111	0.888889
Surplus (accounting)	3	9	1	0.111111	0.888889
Accounting—law	5	11	1	0.090909	0.909091

TABLE III

Number of relatives $= |\phi(x)| = 21$

Electrons	21	21	21	1.0	0.0
Protons	9	22	8	0.363636	0.636364
Neutrons	13	26	8	0.307692	0.692308
Nuclear physics	32	43	10	0.232558	0.767442
Positrons	6	22	5	0.227273	0.772727
Collisions (nuclear physics)	8	24	5	0.208333	0.791667
Atoms	15	30	6	0.200000	0.800000
Matter—constitution	9	25	5	0.200000	0.800000
Cosmic rays	6	23	4	0.173913	0.826087
Particle accelerators	6	23	4	0.173913	0.826087
Cathode ray tubes	8	25	4	0.160000	0.840000
Electric discharges through gases	10	27	4	0.148148	0.851852
Ions	10	27	4	0.148148	0.851852
Nuclear shell theory	4	22	3	0.136364	0.863636
Auger effect	5	23	3	0.130435	0.869565
Mesons	5	23	3	0.130435	0.869565
Transmutation (chemistry)	5	23	3	0.130435	0.869565
Magneto-optics	7	25	3	0.120000	0.880000
X-rays	27	43	5	0.116279	0.883721
Electromagnetic theory	8	26	3	0.115385	0.884615
Radioactivity	42	57	6	0.105263	0.894737
Matter	11	29	3	0.103448	0.896552

TABLE IV

TERMS RELATED TO "ELECTRONIC CALCULATING MACHINES"

Number of relatives = $|\phi(x)| = 10$

Term (y)	Number relatives of y $|\phi(y)|$	$\|\phi(x) \cup \phi(y)\|$	$\|\phi(x) \cap \phi(y)\|$	Association measure $a(x,y) = \dfrac{\|\phi(x) \cap \phi(y)\|}{\|\phi(x) \cup \phi(y)\|}$	Distance $1.-a(x,y)$ $d(x,y) =$
Electronic calculating machines	10	10	10	1.0	0.0
Electronic office machines	4	11	3	0.272727	0.727273
Cybernetics	7	14	3	0.214286	0.785714
Calculating machines	13	19	4	0.210526	0.789474
Electronic calculating machines—design and construction	2	10	2	0.200000	0.800000
Magnetic memory (calculating machines)	2	10	2	0.200000	0.800000
Translating machines	3	11	2	0.181818	0.818182
Electric network analyzers	4	12	2	0.166667	0.833333
Accounting machines	7	15	2	0.133333	0.866667
Machine accounting	7	15	2	0.133333	0.866667
Tabulating machines	7	15	2	0.133333	0.866667
Punched card systems	16	23	3	0.130435	0.869565
Information theory	10	18	2	0.111111	0.888889
Electronic apparatus and appliances	22	29	3	0.103448	0.896552
Comptometers	2	11	1	0.090909	0.909091
Electronic apparatus and appliances—maintenance and repair	2	11	1	0.090909	0.909091
Electronic apparatus and appliances—patents	2	11	1	0.090909	0.909091
Electronic apparatus and appliances—testing	2	11	1	0.090909	0.909091

number of edges per node in these regions is roughly as shown in Table V.

It can be seen that for T^{-1} less than 4.0, the resulting T-graph would have very few edges. On the other hand, T^{-1} equal to or greater than 7.0 would result in a large number of edges per node and hence very broad concepts, i.e. concepts with too many terms. Thus the choice of a suitable threshold narrows down to one of the

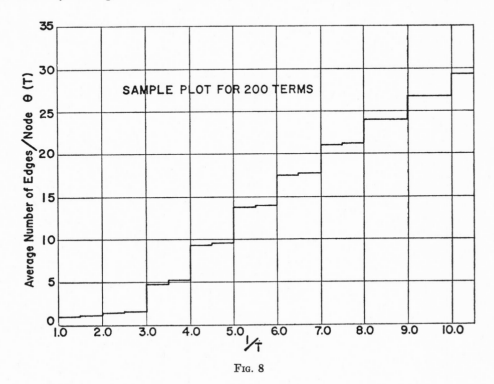

FIG. 8

TABLE V

Average Number of Edges per Node

Range of T	$\Theta(T)$
$1.0 \leqslant T^{-1} < 3.0$	Less than 2
$3.0 \leqslant T^{-1} < 4.0$	5.0
$4.0 \leqslant T^{-1} < 5.0$	9.5
$5.0 \leqslant T^{-1} < 6.0$	14.0
$6.0 \leqslant T^{-1} < 7.0$	18.00
$7.0 \leqslant T^{-1} < 8.0$	21.00
$8.0 \leqslant T^{-1} < 9.0$	24.00
$9.0 \leqslant T^{-1} < 10.0$	27.00

regions $4.0 \leqslant T^{-1} < 5.0$, $5.0 \leqslant T^{-1} < 6.0$, $6.0 \leqslant T^{-1} < 7.0$, etc. (Within a region, change of threshold was found to have little effect on the T-graph and the concepts.) A value of $1/T = 5.0$ ($T = 0.2$) was used to determine sharp and diffuse concepts in the following subsections.

7.4 Sharp Concepts

As a T-graph with over 34,000 nodes is too large for a manipulation, a procedure was developed which built the connected subgraph of the T-graph for a given T, and for any starting node. The subroutine for finding m.c.s.'s has an argument called XLOCK such that the routine finds all complete subgraphs of the highest order less than or equal to XLOCK. Initially, XLOCK is set to an arbitrary high value, so that m.c.s.'s of the highest order present are found. XLOCK is then assigned a value 1 less than the order of the last-found complete subgraph, so that the next lower order complete subgraphs can be found. Complete subgraphs which are subsets of an m.c.s. are ignored. After all the m.c.s.'s for the connected subgraph are found, the nodes and edges belonging to the connected subgraph are removed, and the adjacency matrix of another connected subgraph is built by a similar operation.

As an example, starting with the term *electronic calculating machines* and using $T = 0.2$, the sharp concept classes corresponding to the m.c.s.'s are as given in Table VI.

7.5 Merging of Concepts in a Fixed Dictionary

It can be seen that terms belonging to sharp concepts exhibit strong semantic associations, although they cannot in general be regarded as true or near-synonyms. As mentioned in Subsection 7.2, one should not expect near-synonyms in the indexing system. In general, terms belonging to sharp concepts have the same level of specificity, although some sharp-concept classes also include generic and specific terms. For example, in sharp concept 8, *mathematical instruments* is generic to *slide rule* and *planimeter*.

The distance matrix between the sharp concepts,

$$d(C_i, C_j) = 1. - \frac{|C_i \cap C_j|}{|C_i \cup C_j|},$$

is given in Table VII.

It may be noted that all distances are equal to or greater than 0.5 except for any concept with itself. For a minimum distance threshold, δ, less than 0.5 the diffuse concepts obtained by using the procedure of Section 6 would be the same as the sharp concepts of Table VI. Some diffuse concepts for $\delta \leqslant 0.5$ are shown in Table VIII. For $\delta = 0.5$, sharp concepts 1 and 2 combine to give the diffuse concept 1.2. Also, sharp concepts 4 and 5 combine to give the diffuse concept 4.5. All other sharp concepts remain unchanged.

For $\delta = 0.6$, sharp concept 3 further combines with the diffuse concept 4.5 to give a more diffuse concept, 4.5.3. The diffuse concept 1.2 and all other sharp concepts remain unchanged.

Increasing δ further to 0.7 results in combining sharp concepts 10, 11, 13, 14, 16, and 17 to give the still broader diffuse concept 10.11.13.14.16.17. Sharp concepts 6, 7, 8, 9, and 12 and diffuse concepts 1.2 and 3.4.5 remain unchanged.

For $\delta = 0.8$, all sharp concepts combine to give three diffuse concepts, the broadest being diffuse concept 3.4.5.7.9.12.13.14.16.17.10.

For $\delta \geqslant 0.833$, all sharp concepts of Table VI combine to give one diffuse concept class.

Thus by increasing δ, sharp concepts combine to give increasingly broad and diffuse concept classes. It may be noted, however, that a term belonging to a diffuse concept does not necessarily have association measures greater than or equal to T to all terms in the concept. Examples are *bookkeeping machines* and *calculating machines* in 1.2, *electronic office machines* and *electric network analyzers* in 4.5.3, *automatic timers* and *logarithms* in 10.11.13.14.16.17, *oral communication* and *automatic control* in 3.4.5.7.9.10.12.13.14.16.17, etc.

7.6 Choice of δ in a Fixed Dictionary

When diffuse concepts are used for index term association transformation, it is likely that a term would be replaced by many terms which have association measures less than T. Retrieval precision, P, has been defined [4] as:

P = [number of relevant documents retrieved]/ [total number of documents retrieved].

Let us define the normalized degree of a term i in its diffuse concept as:

D_i = [number of terms in diffuse concept to which term has association measures greater

TABLE VI

Sharp Concepts for $T = 0.20$
Starting term: "electronic calculating machines"

1 Calculating machines
   Accounting machines
   Machine accounting
   Tabulating machines
   Punched card systems
2 Accounting machines
   Machine accounting
   Tabulating machines
   Bookkeeping machines
3 Electronic calculating machines
   Electronic calculating machines—design and
      construction
   Electronic office machines
   Magnetic memory (calculating machines)
4 Electronic calculating machines—design and
      construction
   Magnetic memory (calculating machines)
   Translating machines
5 Electronic calculating machines—design and
      construction
   Magnetic memory (calculating machines)
   Electric network analysers
6 Automatic Control
   Automation
   Servomechanisms

7 Cybernetics
   Communication
   Information theory
8 Slide rule
   Mathematical instruments
   Planimeter
9 Oral communication
   Communication—juvenile literature
   Communication
10 Automatic control
   Automatic timers
11 Slide rule
   Logarithms
12 Translating machines
   Machine translating
13 Electronic calculating machines
   Cybernetics
14 Cybernetics
   Automatic control
15 Tabulating machines
   Statistics—charts, tables, etc.
16 Electronic calculating machines
   Calculating machines
17 Calculating machines
   Slide rule

than or equal to T]/[total number of terms in diffuse concept].

It is reasonable to expect that the loss of precision resulting from the use of a diffuse concept instead of a sharp concept will increase as D_i decreases. For sharp concepts $D_i = 1$ for every term. For diffuse concepts we should try and keep D_i large. The measure, D_i, for any term can be computed from the adjacency matrix of the diffuse concept, in which an element is 1 if corresponding terms have an association greater than or equal to threshold T. As an example, the adjacency matrix of the diffuse concept 4.5.3 ($\delta = 0.6$) is given in Table IX. The normalized degrees for various terms in this diffuse concept are given in Table X.

It can be seen that measures for different terms, be-

TABLE VII

Distance Matrix Between Sharp Concepts

1	2	3	4	5	6	7	8	9	10	11	12	13	14	15	16	17
0.0	0.5	1.0	1.0	1.0	1.0	1.0	1.0	1.0	1.0	1.0	1.0	1.0	1.0	0.833	0.833	0.833
	0.0	1.0	1.0	1.0	1.0	1.0	1.0	1.0	1.0	1.0	1.0	1.0	1.0	0.80	1.0	1.0
		0.0	0.6	0.6	1.0	1.0	1.0	1.0	1.0	1.0	1.0	0.80	1.0	1.0	1.0	1.0
			0.0	0.5	1.0	1.0	1.0	1.0	1.0	1.0	0.75	1.0	1.0	1.0	1.0	1.0
				0.0	1.0	1.0	1.0	1.0	1.0	1.0	1.0	1.0	1.0	1.0	1.0	1.0
					0.0	1.0	1.0	1.0	0.75	1.0	1.0	1.0	0.75	1.0	1.0	1.0
						0.0	1.0	0.8	1.0	1.0	1.0	1.0	0.75	1.0	1.0	1.0
							0.0	1.0	1.0	0.75	1.0	1.0	1.0	1.0	1.0	0.75
								0.0	1.0	1.0	1.0	1.0	1.0	1.0	1.0	1.0
									0.0	1.0	1.0	1.0	0.67	1.0	1.0	0.67
										0.0	1.0	1.0	1.0	1.0	1.0	0.67
											0.0	1.0	1.0	1.0	1.0	1.0
												0.0	0.67	1.0	0.67	1.0
													0.0	1.0	1.0	1.0
														0.0	1.0	1.0
															0.0	0.67
																0.0

Symmetric

TABLE VIII

SOME DIFFUSE CONCEPTS FOR $\delta \leqq 0.5$

Minimum distance threshold, δ	Diffuse concept	Terms
0.5	1.2	Calculating machines Accounting machines Machine accounting Tabulating machines Punched card systems Bookkeeping machines
0.5	4.5	Electric network analyzers Translating machines Electronic calculating machines—design and construction Magnetic memory (calculating machines)
0.6	4.5.3	Electric network analyzers Translating machines Electronic calculating machines—design and construction Magnetic memory (calculating machines) Electronic calculating machines Electronic office machines
0.7	10.11.13.14.16.17	Automatic control Automatic timers Cybernetics Electronic calculating machines Calculating machines Slide rule Logarithms
0.8	3.4.5.7.9.10.12.13.14. 16.17	Electronic calculating machines Electronic calculaing machines—design and construction Electronic office machines Magnetic memory (calculating machines) Translating machines Electric network analyzers Cybernetics Machine translating Calculating machines Slide rule Automatic control Communication Information theory Automation Servomechanisms Automatic timers Oral communication Communication—juvenile literature
>0.833	All sharp concepts of Table VI combine to give one diffuse concept class	See Table VI.

longing to the same diffuse concept, can vary considerably. An average normalized degree, $\bar{D}$, may be defined where $\bar{D} = (1/n) \sum_i D_i$, $n =$ no. terms in the diffuse concept. For example, $\bar{D}$ for 4.5.3 is 0.778 (or 28/36). $\bar{D}$ corresponds to the density (Section 5) of the subgraph for the diffuse concept, i.e. it equals $(2.0 \mid m(\delta) \mid - \mid v \mid)/\mid v \mid^2$, where $\mid m(\delta) \mid$ is the number of edges in the subgraph and $\mid v \mid$ is the number of nodes in the subgraph. For a maximal complete subgraph its value is 1. As a concept becomes more diffuse, its subgraph becomes less dense, and its average normalized degree becomes smaller. If we take the average for all concepts resulting from some choice of δ, and plot its functional dependence on δ, this will give a criterion for choosing δ.

TABLE IX

ADJACENCY MATRIX OF DIFFUSE CONCEPT 4.5.3 ($\delta = 0.6$)

Diffuse concept 4.5.3	Adjacency matrix
Electric network analyzers	1 0 1 1 0 0
Translating machines	0 1 1 1 0 0
Electronic calculating machines—design and construction	1 1 1 1 1 1
Magnetic memory (calculating machines)	1 1 1 1 1 1
Electronic calculating machines	0 0 1 1 1 1
Electronic office machines	0 0 1 1 1 1

TABLE X

NORMALIZED DEGREES FOR TERMS OF DIFFUSE CONCEPT 4.5.3

Term	No. terms having association measure greater than or equal to T	No. terms having association measure less than T	Total no. terms in diffuse concept	Normalized degree, D_i
Electric network analyzers	3	3	6	0.5
Translating machines	3	3	6	0.5
Electronic calculating machines— design and construction	6	0	6	1.0
Magnetic memory (calculating machines)	6	0	6	1.0
Electronic calculating machines	4	2	6	0.667
Electronic office machines	4	2	6	0.667

TABLE XI

MINIMUM NORMALIZED DEGREES FOR DIFFUSE CONCEPTS OF SECTION 7.5

Minimum distance threshold δ	Diffuse concept	Min. no. terms having association measure greater than or equal to T with any term	Total no. terms in diffuse concept	Minimum normalized degree $\min_i D_i$
0.5	1.2	4	6	0.667
0.5	4.5	3	4	0.75
0.6	4.5.3	3	6	0.50
0.7	10.11.13.14.16.17	2	7	0.286
0.8	3.4.5.7.9.10.12.13.14.16.17	3	15	0.167

(Recall that we used the functional dependence of $(2.0 \mid M(T) \mid - \mid V \mid)/ \mid V \mid$ on T as a basis for selection of T.) This would involve the determination of all sharp and diffuse concepts of the T-graph for all possible values of δ, and is therefore not practicable.

As an alternative, it is possible to define $\min_i D_i$ as the *minimum normalized degree* of a diffuse concept. The $\min_i D_i$ for various diffuse concepts of Section 7.5 is given in Table XI.

As the effect of increasing δ is to combine sharp concepts into broader and more diffuse concepts, the mini-

mum normalized degrees for some diffuse concepts can become very small. Therefore, while an increase in δ reduces the number of final concepts, it also increases the possibility of very low precision. δ can be decided by computing the minimum normalized degrees for diffuse concepts belonging to a connected component of the T-graph, and then choosing a value such that the minimum normalized degree for any diffuse concept does not become less than some nominal value, say γ. This value of δ corresponds to the *maximum* value of the minimum distance threshold consistent with the requirement that

TABLE XII

Illustration of Merging Process of Subsection 6.2
Term requested: "accounting machines"

m.c.s.		Cluster	$\mid \sigma(T)x \mid / \mid \cup_1 C_x^1 \mid$	Remarks
Stage 1	1	Calculating machines *Accounting machines* Machine accounting Tabulating machines Punched card systems	1.0	
	2	*Accounting machines* Machine accounting Tabulating machines Bookkeeping machines	1.0	
Stage 2	1.2	Calculating machines *Accounting machines* Machine accounting Tabulating machines Punched card systems Bookkeeping machines	1.0	From Table VII we find that $\delta = 0.5$ is the smallest value of δ which will cause the two clusters containing *accounting machines* to merge.
Stage 3	1.2.16	Calculating machines *Accounting machines* Machine accounting Tabulating machines Punched card systems Bookkeeping machines Electronic calculating machines	0.857	From the new d_{ij} matrix we find that $\delta = 0.857$.
	1.2.15	Calculating machines *Accounting machines* Machine accounting Tabulating machines Punched card systems Bookkeeping machines Statistics—charts, tables, etc.	0.857	
Stage 4	1.2.16.15	Calculating machines *Accounting machines* Machine accounting Tabulating machines Punched card systems Bookkeeping machines Electronic calculating machines Statistics—charts, tables, etc.	0.75	We now find $\delta = 0.25$.
Stage 5	1.2.16.15.13	Calculating machines *Accounting machines* Machine accounting Tabulating machines Punched card systems Bookkeeping machines Electronic calculating machines Statistics—charts, tables, etc. Cybernetics	0.67	Now $\delta = 0.89$.
Stage 6	1.2.16.15.13.14	Calculating machines *Accounting machines* Machine accounting Tabulating machines Punched card systems Bookkeeping machines Electronic calculating machines Statistics—charts, tables, etc. Cybernetics Automatic control	0.6	Next $\delta = 0.9$.

the minimum normalized degree of every concept in the family is greater than or equal to γ. For any specified value γ, the program can automatically determine the value of γ. In the example considered, if γ were 0.4, then δ equal to 0.6 would define a desired family of concepts.

7.7 Merging of Clusters in a Dynamic Dictionary

In Table XII we illustrate the merging process of Subsection 6.2 by considering the example of Table VI and requesting the term *accounting machines*. This process could be continued to produce larger and larger clusters. It may be noted that at any stage we get a comparatively small number of clusters containing the request term.

8. Concluding Remarks

Further examination for terms drawn from the fields of humanities and social sciences indicate that the methods described in this paper do have the strong ability to group conceptually related terms. It is possible, using the procedures, even to reorganize an indexing system which has developed in bits and pieces through years of manual effort. The reorganization procedure is highly automatic.

Although many new retrieval aids are currently being investigated, few of them can be applied to current indexes or to very general indexes such as the Library of Congress' *Subject Headings* list. The actual effectiveness of the particular dynamic dictionary proposed in this paper would have to be assessed in an implementation which would involve a large group of people, and require careful planning. It is, however, believed that such an implementation is feasible, and there is enough promise in the results to justify a pilot project for constructing and using a dynamic dictionary.

References

1. BERGE, C. *The Theory of Graphs and Its Applications*. Wiley, New York, 1962.
2. BIRKHOFF, G. *Lattice Theory* (rev. ed.). Amer. Math. Soc. Colloq. Publications, Amer. Math. Soc., Providence, R.I., 1948.
3. BONNER, R. E. On some clustering techniques. *IBM J. Res. Devel.* **8**, 1 (Jan. 1964), 22–32.
4. CLEVERDON, C. W. Report on the testing and analysis of an investigation into the comparative efficiency of indexing systems. ASLIB-Cranfield Research Rep., Oct. 1962. Cranfield, Bedford, England.
5. ENGINEERS JOINT COUNCIL. *Thesaurus of Engineering Terms* (1st ed.). New York, May 1964.
6. GIULIANO, V. E., AND JONES, P. E. Linear associative information retrieval. In Howerton, P. W., and Weeks, D. C. (Eds.), *Vistas in Information Handling, Vol. 1*, Spartan Books, Washington, D. C., 1963, Ch. 2, pp. 30–46.
7. LEWIS, P. A. W., BAXENDALE, P. B., AND BENNETT, J. L. Statistical discrimination of the synonymy/antonymy relationship between words. *J. ACM* **14**, 1 (Jan. 1967), 20–44.
8. LIBRARY OF CONGRESS. *Subject Headings* (6th ed.). Washington, D. C., 1957.
9. MARON, M. E., AND KUHNS, J. L. On relevance, probabilistic indexing and information retrieval. *J. ACM* **7**, 3 (July 1960), 216–244.
10. MEETHAM, A. R. Graph separability and word grouping. Proc. 21st National Conference ACM, July 1966 (ACM Pub. P-66). Thompson Book Co., Washington, D. C., pp. 513–514.
11. NEEDHAM, R. M. Applications of the theory of clumps. *Mech. Transl. Comput. Linguist.* **8** (June and Oct. 1965), 113–127.
12. RIAL, J. F. A pseudo-metric for document retrieval systems. Rep. W-4595, The Mitre Corp., Bedford, Mass.
13. ROCCHIO, J. J. Document retrieval systems — optimization and evaluation. Harvard U. doctoral th., Rep. No. ISR-10 to the National Science Foundation, Harvard Computation Lab., March 1966.
14. SALTON, G. Associative document retrieval techniques using bibliographic information. *J. ACM* **10**, 4 (Oct. 1963), 440–457.
15. SPÄRCK-JONES, K. Experiments in semantic classification. *Mech. Transl. Comput. Linguist.* **8** (June and Oct. 1965), 92–112.
16. STEVENS, M. E. (Ed.). Proc. Symposium in Statistical Association Methods for Mechanized Documentation. US Government Printing Office, NBS Misc. Pub. 269, Dec. 1965.
17. STILES, H. E. The association factor in information retrieval. *J. ACM* **8**, 2 (April 1961), 271–279.
18. US DEPARTMENT OF HEALTH, EDUCATION AND WELFARE. *MEDLARS Medical Subject Headings* (3rd ed.). Washington, D. C., Jan. 1964.

26 Distribution of Indexing Terms for Maximum Efficiency of Information Transmission

PRANAS ZUNDE
VLADIMIR SLAMECKA
American Documentation
Vol. 18, No. 2, April, 1967

Organization of indexing data in a manner that permits retrieval of the greatest amount of information is a premise fundamental to an efficient performance of all information storage and retrieval systems. In this context an index may be considered a channel linking the information store and the user or searcher. The problem may be viewed as that of organizing information store— that is, the indexing "terms" (subject descriptors) and their "postings" (document identification numbers, for instance)—so as to make a maximum use of channel capacity, permitting the transmission of information from the store to the user with maximum efficiency.

For a given system, indexing terms can be grouped by the number of postings they carry, to form a frequency spectrum characteristic of that system at a particular time. This paper reports the development of a distribution function of term groups by number of postings which allows information transmission with maximum efficiency, and it proposes a measure of evaluation of a system's efficiency in this respect.

The solutions are developed subject to three assumptions. First, no distinction is made between useful and useless information; only the amount of information, not its subjective value, is considered. Second, the possible effects of indexing language and of the function and form of index terms are not taken into consideration, as they are likely to vary from one vocabulary to another. Third, the channel is assumed to be a noiseless one; that is, if term T_1 is addressed, the probability of retrieving it with all its postings is equal to 1.

The efficiency of a statistical information transmission model is defined as

$$\eta = \frac{I(T,Y)}{C} \qquad (1)$$

where $I(T,Y)$ is the transinformation and C is the channel capacity. The channel capacity is in turn defined as

$$C = [I(T,Y)]_{\max} = [H(T) - H(T/Y)]_{\max} \qquad (2)$$

In this equation, $H(T)$ is the source entropy, which in our case is the entropy derived from the relative frequencies of indexing terms by the number of postings, and $H(T/Y)$ is the conditional entropy or average uncertainty given that a particular symbol has been received as to the symbol which was transmitted.

Since the channel was assumed noiseless, the conditional entropy

$$H(T/Y) = 0$$

and the transinformation

$$I(T,Y) = H(T)$$

Thus

$$C = [H(T)]_{\max} \qquad (3)$$

In information theory, the entropy or measure of uncertainty of a complete finite scheme is given by

$$H(T) = - \sum_{t=1}^{n} p(t) \log p(t) \qquad (4)$$

where $p(t)$ is the probability of the occurrence of the event T (in our case, the probability of term group T_i having t postings).

From Eq. (1) we see that the efficiency of an index system is highest when transinformation is equal to the channel capacity. Since in our case the channel capacity is equal to maximum source entropy, the problem is to find such a frequency distribution of term groups by number of postings which produces maximum source entropy. The solution is subject to two constraints:

$$\sum_{t=1}^{n} p(t) = 1 \qquad (5)$$

and

$$\sum_{t=1}^{n} t p(t) = \bar{t} = \text{const} \qquad (6)$$

The first constraint states that the sum of the relative frequencies is equal to one (viz., we have a complete finite scheme). The second constraint states that there is a fixed amount of postings in a given system, expressed as the average number of postings per term.

Using the method of calculus of variation and Lagrange undetermined multipliers, we can write:

$$\delta H(T) = - \Sigma [\ln p(t) + 1] \delta p(t) = 0 \qquad (7)$$

$$\alpha \Sigma \delta p(t) = 0 \qquad (8)$$

$$\beta \Sigma t \delta p(t) = 0 \qquad (9)$$

Adding Equations (7), (8), and (9), we get

$$\Sigma [\ln p(t) + \alpha + \beta t] \delta p(t) = 0 \qquad (10)$$

hence

$$\ln p(t) + \alpha + \beta t = 0 \qquad (11)$$

or

$$p(t) = e^{-\alpha} e^{-\beta t} \qquad (12)$$

To find the Lagrange constants α and β, we turn to the constraints equations. Substituting Eq. (12) into Eq. (5), we obtain

$$\sum_{t=1}^{n} e^{-\alpha} e^{-\beta t} = 1 \qquad (13)$$

hence

$$e^{-\alpha} = \frac{1}{\sum_{t=1}^{n} e^{-\beta t}} \qquad (14)$$

Substituting the expression for $e^{-\alpha}$ into Equation (12), we obtain

$$p(t) = \frac{e^{-\beta t}}{\sum_{t=1}^{n} e^{-\beta t}} \qquad (15)$$

Substituting the expression in Eq. (15) for $p(t)$ into the second constraint Equation (6), we find

$$\frac{\sum_{t=1}^{n} t e^{-\beta t}}{\sum_{t=1}^{n} e^{-\beta t}} = \bar{t} \qquad (16)$$

The summation limits are the lowest and the highest number of postings under any one term in our vocabulary

(i.e., 1 and n). This range of postings is, obviously, bounded; we can, however, extend the upper summation limit to infinity by simply considering the remainder in our series as the sum of terms corresponding to the frequency of terms with "$k+1$ and more" postings, provided k is large enough.[1] Both series in the numerator and denominator are convergent series for $\beta > 0$. Under this assumption, the sum of the series in the denominator is easily established. Thus

$$\sum_{t=1}^{\infty} e^{-\beta t} = \frac{e^{-\beta}}{1 - e^{-\beta}} \qquad (17)$$

The limit of the series in the numerator can be found as follows:

$$\sum_{t=1}^{\infty} t e^{-\beta t} = \frac{\partial}{\partial \beta} \left[- \sum_{t=1}^{\infty} e^{-\beta t} \right] = \frac{\partial}{\partial \beta} \left[- \frac{e^{-\beta}}{1 - e^{-\beta}} \right] = \frac{e^{-\beta}}{(1 - e^{-\beta})^2} \qquad (18)$$

Hence

$$\bar{t} = \frac{\dfrac{e^{-\beta}}{(1 - e^{-\beta})^2}}{\dfrac{e^{-\beta}}{1 - e^{-\beta}}} = \frac{1}{1 - e^{-\beta}} \qquad (19)$$

and

$$\beta = - \ln \left(1 - \frac{1}{\bar{t}} \right) \qquad (20)$$

By substituting the values of β into the equation, we obtain the frequency distribution function that maximizes the source entropy:

$$p(t) = \frac{\left(1 - \dfrac{1}{\bar{t}} \right)^t}{\sum_{t=1}^{\infty} \left(1 - \dfrac{1}{\bar{t}} \right)^t} \qquad (21)$$

The limit of the convergent series in the denominator is easily obtained as

$$\sum_{t=1}^{\infty} \left(1 - \frac{1}{\bar{t}} \right)^t = \bar{t} - 1 \qquad (22)$$

and finally we write

$$p(t) = \frac{\left(1 - \dfrac{1}{\bar{t}} \right)^t}{\bar{t} - 1} \qquad (23)$$

Example. For an information storage and retrieval system with 1,000 documents, each of which is indexed by 22 terms on the average, with a vocabulary of 2,000 terms and the average number of posting per term $\bar{t} = 11$, the optimum frequency distribution of term groups to produce the maximum average amount of information per term would have approximately 182 terms with one posting, 165 terms with two postings, 146 terms with three postings, and so on. The percentage

[1] The effect of the approximation error should be evaluated in each particular instance. For small k and β ($\beta \ll 1$), it might be significant.

of terms which should have 100 or more postings can be calculated as follows:

$$\sum_{t=100}^{\infty} p(t) = \sum_{t=100}^{\infty} p(t) - \sum_{t=1}^{\infty} p(t)$$

$$= \sum_{t=1}^{\infty} \frac{\left(1 - \frac{1}{\bar{t}}\right)^t}{\bar{t} - 1} - \sum_{t=1}^{\infty} \frac{\left(1 - \frac{1}{\bar{t}}\right)^t}{\bar{t} - 1}$$

$$= 1 - \frac{1}{\bar{t} - 1}\left[\frac{1 - \frac{1}{\bar{t}}}{\frac{1}{\bar{t}}} - \frac{\left(1 - \frac{1}{\bar{t}}\right)\left(1 - \frac{1}{\bar{t}}\right)^{100}}{\frac{1}{\bar{t}}}\right]$$

$$= (t - 1)\left(1 - \frac{1}{\bar{t}}\right)^{100} = 0.00072$$

Thus, in this example of a system, 0.072% of terms (between one and two terms) should have 100 or more postings. The percentage of terms with high numbers of postings clearly depends on the average number of postings per term: the greater this average, the higher the percentage of heavily posted terms.

An immediate use of the concept of term group distribution is in the evaluation of existing information systems. Figure 1 compares the actual and optimal term group distribution curves of two information systems, that of the Defense Documentation Center (in 1960) and a private experimental one (*1*). Although the actual distribution curves of both systems (solid lines in the graph) differ from their optima (broken lines)—implying a less-than-efficient use of channel capacity—the

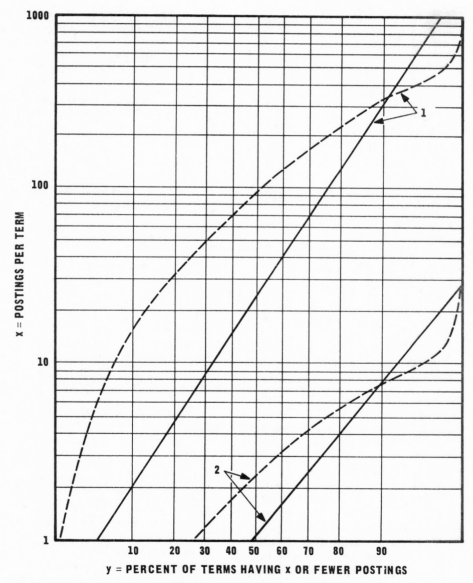

FIG. 1. Actual vs. optimum term-group cumulative distribution in two information systems; 1 = Defense Documentation Center System (1960); 2 = private experimental system (1960)

comparison of the efficiency coefficient will show that the deviation is considerably more serious in the experimental index.

To calculate the efficiency coefficient of a given system, we calculate the transinformation $I(T,Y)$ from the given frequency distribution of term groups. Next, the channel capacity for the system can be derived as follows.

It has been shown (2) that, for a discrete random variable with

$$\Sigma p(t_i) = 1 \quad \text{and the mean} \quad \Sigma t_i p(t_i) = \bar{t}$$

$$H(I) = -\sum_{i=1}^{n} p(t_i) \ln p(t_i) \leqq \ln M(\beta) + \beta \bar{t} \quad (24)$$

with equality if and only if $p(t_i)$ is the maximizing function of the entropy equation. Then

$$M(\beta) = \sum_{i=1}^{n} e^{-\beta t_i} \quad (25)$$

where β is given by

$$\beta = -\ln\left(1 - \frac{1}{\bar{t}}\right) \quad (26)$$

Furthermore, we have already shown that

$$\sum_{i=1}^{n \to \infty} e^{-\beta t_i} = \frac{e^{-\beta}}{1 - e^{-\beta}} \quad (27)$$

Substituting the expression for β into the Equation (27), we get

$$M(\beta) = \sum_{i=1}^{\infty} e^{-\beta t_i} = \frac{\exp\left[+\ln\left(1 - \frac{1}{\bar{t}}\right)\right]}{1 - \exp\left[\ln\left(1 - \frac{1}{\bar{t}}\right)\right]} = \bar{t} - 1 \quad (28)$$

Thus, we can rewrite Equation (24) as follows:

$$[H(T)]_{\max} = \ln M(\beta) + \beta \bar{t} = \ln (\bar{t} - 1) - \bar{t} \ln\left(1 - \frac{1}{\bar{t}}\right)$$

$$= \bar{t} \ln \bar{t} - (\bar{t} - 1) \ln (\bar{t} - 1) \quad (29)$$

which is the expression for channel capacity.

According to the last equation, the channel capacities of the experimental system with $\bar{t} = 3.9$ and of the DDC system with $\bar{t} = 148$ would be 2.22 nits and 6 nits, respectively. By interpolating the graph reproduced in Houston and Wall's article (1) (since complete data were not available to us), we obtained approximately 1.66 nits actual source entropy (= transinformation in the given core) for the experimental system and 5.4 nits for the DDC system. Hence, the efficiency coefficients are approximately 0.75 (75%) and 0.9 (90%), respectively.

In their article Houston and Wall, having investigated a number of indexes for frequency distribution of postings under the terms, came to the conclusion that the distribution is lognormal for all indexes. Furthermore, they derived an empirical probability distribution function, which is supposed to give the frequency spectrum of all actual indexes, if the sample they investigated was representative enough. The proposed function is:

$$p(x) = \frac{0.17}{x} \exp\left[-\frac{(A \log x - B)^2}{2}\right] \quad (30)$$

where

$x =$ number of terms with x postings ($x = 1,2,3, \ldots$)
$A = 2.0 - 0.14 \log_{10} P$
$B = 0.67 \log_{10} P - 2.4$
$P =$ total number of postings

It can be shown that the average source entropy for this type of distribution can be approximated by

$$H(X) = -\sum_{i=1}^{n} p(x_i) \ln p(x_i)$$

$$\cong \left[-\frac{0.17 \ln 0.17 \sqrt{\pi}}{\sqrt{2} A \log e} + \frac{0.17 \sqrt{\pi} \ln 10 (0.67 \log P - 2.4)}{\sqrt{2} \log e (2.0 - 0.14 \log P)^2}\right.$$

$$\left.+ \frac{0.17 \sqrt{\pi}}{2 \log e (2.0 - 0.14 \log P)}\right] \left\{\operatorname{erf} \frac{(0.67 \log P - 2.4)}{\sqrt{2}}\right.$$

$$+ \operatorname{erf}\left[\frac{1}{\sqrt{2}} (2.0 \log x_n - 0.14 \log P \log x_n\right.$$

$$\left.- 0.67 \log P + 2.4\right]\right\} - \frac{0.17 \ln 10}{\log e (2.0 - 0.14 \log P)^2}$$

$$\exp\{-\tfrac{1}{2}(4.0 - 0.56 \log P + 0.0196 \log^2 P) \log^2 x_n$$

$$- \tfrac{1}{2}[-2(2.0 - 0.14 \log P)(0.67 \log P - 2.4) \log x_n$$

$$+ (0.67 \log P - 2.4)^2] - \tfrac{1}{2}(0.67 \log P - 2.4)^2\}$$

$$+ \frac{0.17}{2 \log e (2.0 - 0.14 \log P)}\left\{-[(2.0 - 0.14 \log P) \log x_n\right.$$

$$- (0.67 \log P - 2.4)]$$

$$\exp\left[-\frac{[2.0 - 0.14 \log P) \log x_n - (0.67 \log P - 2.4)]^2}{2}\right]$$

$$\left.- (0.67 \log P - 2.4) \exp\left[-\frac{(0.67 \log P - 2.4)^2}{2}\right]\right\} \quad (31)$$

It has been observed that the maximum number of postings per term is approximately $t_{\max} = 0.03P$. Substituting this value in Equation (31), we get

$$H(X) = \left[\frac{-0.2793 + 0.5867 \log P}{(2.0 - 0.14 \log P)^2}\right]$$

$$\times \left[\operatorname{erf}\left(\frac{0.67 \log P - 2.4}{\sqrt{2}}\right)\right.$$

$$\left.+ \operatorname{erf}\left(\frac{1.543 \log P - 0.14 \log^2 P - 0.646}{\sqrt{2}}\right)\right]$$

$$- \left[\frac{0.9014}{(2.0 - 0.14 \log P)^2}\right][\exp(-0.0098 \log^4 P$$

$$+ 0.2162 \log^3 P - 1.2852 \log^2 P + 1.0268 \log P - 0.2076)$$

$$- \exp(0.2245 \log^2 P + 1.61 \log P - 2.88)]$$

$$+ \frac{0.1957}{2.0 - 0.14 \log P}[0.14 \log^2 P - 2.8832 \log P + 5.446]$$

$$\times \exp(-0.0048 \log^4 P + 0.4036 \log^3 P - 4.9188 \log^2 P$$

$$+ 15.7019 \log P - 14.8294) - (0.67 \log P - 2.4)$$

$$\exp(-0.2245 \log^2 P + 1.61 \log P - 2.88) \quad (32)$$

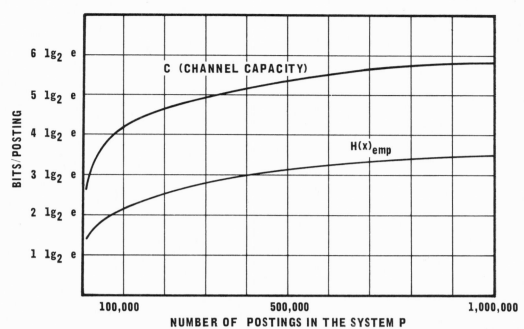

FIG. 2. Actual source entropies $H(X)_{emp}$ and channel capacities C of systems with indexing terms distributed according to Eq. (30)

Houston and Wall also propose in their paper an empirical formula relating the total number of terms in the index with the total number of postings:

$$T = 3,300 \log (P + 10,000) - 12,600$$

where T is the total number of terms and P—total number of postings. The formula is valid for the range of P from 10,000 to 1,000,000. Then

$$\bar{p} = \frac{P}{T} = \frac{P}{3,300 \log (P + 10,000) - 12,600} \quad (33)$$

Substituting this expression into Equation (29), we obtain the channel capacity as a function of P. On the other hand, from Equation (32) we can calculate the actual source entropy for indexes for various values of P, if the frequency distribution of their postings conforms with Houston and Wall's formula. The corresponding efficiency coefficient will be the ratio of these values.

In Fig. 2, channel capacities and source entropies of indexes that obey the empirical distribution formula of Houston and Wall are plotted as functions of the total number of postings P.

A fuller discussion of the uses of this technique in the design of information systems and in the control and optimization of the indexing and storage apparatus of existing systems is in preparation.

References

1. HOUSTON, N., and E. WALL, The Distribution of Term Usage in Manipulative Indexes, *Am. Doc.*, 15:109 (1964).
2. KULLBACK, S., *Information Theory and Statistics*, Wiley, New York, 1959, p. 34.

C. Probabilistic and Statistical Indexing

27 A Framework for Comparing Term Association Measures

PAUL E. JONES
ROBERT M. CURTICE
American Documentation
Vol. 18, No. 3, July, 1967

1 Introduction

Many statistical formulas, almost all of them based on the single theoretical foundation offered by the 2×2 contingency table, have been introduced as candidates for measuring the degree, Aab, of association between two index terms a and b. Generally speaking, no firm relationship between the choice of association measure and its effect upon evaluated performance has been established. In part this has occurred because no opportunity for large scale in-use "tuning" of the measures to the specific needs of an operational retrieval system has been pursued to an experimental conclusion. The study of these measures has tended to stay in a research context, and few practice-oriented appraisals have been made. Nevertheless, a few comparative side-by-side appraisals of the effect of using different formulas have been conducted in pilot experiments.[1] While clear-cut preference for one formula over another (because it is a better discriminator of terms judged to be related) has not emerged from the experimental tests so far reported, the insight and experience that has been gained in laboratory tests has been valuable.

Not surprisingly, each formula has been found to have some attributes and some deficiencies. Apparently, each formula does provide, in practice, a set of associated terms among which there are many "reasonable" ones. What is annoying is that no clear-cut criterion for choice among the alternates has emerged. As a result, few candidate measures have been permanently dismissed from consideration, and a rather large set of formulas remains available.

The argument behind a typical association measure, when developed along statistical or theoretical lines, offers little or no basis for distinguishing among them. The reasoning suggests comparing the number of observed co-occurrences with the calculated number of expected co-occurrences. Given two formulas, it will generally be found that substantially this *same* supporting rationale is proffered for both; there are many ways of measuring statistical surprise or the unexpectedness of an observation,[2] and a large number of the available formulas can responsibly claim to do so. Figure 1 exhibits some of the more familiar measures and records their theoretical interpretation or rationale.

The fact that a large number of formulas has apparently survived the efforts of critical researchers to select among them is a curious problem which faces the serious student of associative retrieval. There definitely are differences in how various formulas behave. But choosing which is "best," even under stated conditions, is a problem which has only rarely been approached. In this paper we develop some of the tools we found helpful for comparing ranked term listings (profiles) produced by the use of term association measures, in practice.

The research reported in this paper was sponsored in part by NASA under Contract No. NASW–1051, and in part by the Air Force Systems Command, Electronic Systems Division, Decision Sciences Laboratory, under Contract No. AF 19(628)–3311 with Arthur D. Little, Inc. The paper is identified as ESD–TR–67–231. Reproduction in whole or in part is permitted for any purpose of the U. S. Government.

[1] See, for example, Kuhns (*1*) and Dennis (*2*).

[2] Goodman and Kruskal (*3, 4*) develop and elaborate this point.

If $\underline{a}$ and $\underline{b}$ are index terms, tallies of numbers of documents indexed (or not indexed) by the combinations of $\underline{a}$ and $\underline{b}$ are revealed in the 2 x 2 contingency table:

	$\underline{a}$	not $\underline{a}$	Total
b	fab	fb − fab	fb
not b	fa − fab	N − fa − fb + fab	N − fb
Total	fa	N − fa	N

where fa and fb are the frequencies of terms a and b respectively, fab is the number of co-occurrences of a and b , and N is the collection size.

Various measures based on this table are:

(I) $\quad \text{Aab} = \dfrac{\text{fab}}{\text{fb}}$ The conditional probability given that term b is assigned to a document, that term a is also assigned.

(II) $\quad \text{Aab} = \text{fab} - \dfrac{\text{fafb}}{\text{N}}$ The difference between the observed number of co-occurrences and the expected number based on chance.

(III) $\quad \text{Aab} = \text{Log}_{10} \dfrac{\left(\left| \text{fabN} - \text{fafb} \right| - \dfrac{\text{N}}{2} \right)^2 \text{N}}{\text{fafb } (\text{N} - \text{fa})(\text{N} - \text{fb})}$ The chi square formula using marginal values of the 2 x 2 table and Yates correction for small samples

(IV) $\quad \text{Aab} = \dfrac{\text{fab}}{\text{fa} + \text{fb} - \text{fab}}$ The number of co-occurrences normalized by the number of documents indexed by only one of the terms.

(V) $\quad \text{Aab} = \dfrac{\left(\text{fab} - \dfrac{\text{fafb}}{\text{N}} \right)}{\sqrt{\dfrac{\text{fafb}}{\text{N}}}}$ The number of standard deviations the observed co-occurrence falls to the right of the expected number of co-occurrences.

FIG. 1. The derivation of association measures based on the 2×2 contingency table

2 Equivalent Association Measures

In practice, the use of one of the available statistical association measures serves two purposes. The first is to *select*, for a given header term, a list of associated terms, a process typically accomplished by specifying a threshold for the measure above which terms count as "associated." The second application is to provide a quantitative measure of the degree of association between the associated terms and the header. A convenient way to portray the result of applying the association measure to the data is to rank the co-occurring terms in a printed list, displaying the terms in decreasing order of the association measure being used. The order in which the terms are presented on such a "profile"

exhibits whether one term is more[3] associated with the header term than another term is.

In attempting to choose among association formulas, we postulated that our first concern was to find a measure which yields an acceptable *ranking* of associated terms. The magnitudes of the numerical values for the degree of association are initially of no interest. What matters is whether the most closely associated term under formula A is one of the most closely associated terms under formula B. If so, the formulas are similar; if not, dissimilar. Generalizing these ideas, two formulas which yield the same (or substantially the same) ranking

---

[3] This is true except where there are ties produced by the association measure in use.

of terms in the profile are equivalent from this point of view.

The notion of equivalent rankings is important principally because this is the practical way to tell the formulas apart. One prepares profiles using several formulas and examines them to see which one places the most suitable terms at or near the head of the list. Attention to the numerical values assigned is secondary. Since we are trying to relate the behavior of the formulas to the kinds of things a person comparing such profiles side-by-side would look for, the ordering is the property to examine first.

3 Generating a Spectrum of Association Measures

The objective of comparing the ranking behavior of various formulas is well served by finding a useful way to place them all into the same mathematical form. One way to do this is to develop a general expression that generates all the formulas of interest and that reduces to any specific one by a choice of parameters in the general expression. But a glance at the expressions for Aab in Fig. 1 shows that a general expression that would include, for instance, formula III as a special case would be too complicated to manage. Fortunately, by directing attention to the approximate *ranking* produced by a formula, it is possible to use a simple, readily understandable model for generating a useful spectrum of alternatives. We shall treat the process of forming an association list as a stylized method of *retrieving* certain documents.

Let term a with frequency fa be the header term for which we wish to develop a profile. Let some other term b, with frequency fb, co-occur with a fab times, as shown by the matrix in Fig. 2. Let us now think of a as defining (as it clearly does) a set of documents:

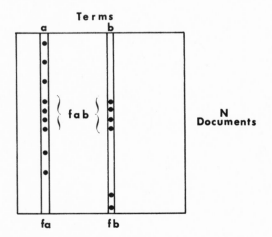

Terms

N Documents

fa   fb

FIG. 2. Document-term matrix showing that term a (frequency fa) co-occurs with term b (frequency fb) exactly fab times

those documents indexed by a. Let us think of the other terms b in the vocabulary (candidates for being "associated" with a) as single-term requests, and define the objective of each of these searches to be the retrieval of those documents indexed by a. In short, the a-indexed documents (and only those) are "relevant." The b indexed documents are "retrieved."

With this conceptual attitude, the familiar Recall and Precision measures can be defined for each term b (with respect to the given term a). They measure—with the usual disclaimers—the goodness of b as a substitute for a.

The Recall of term b is the proportion of documents indexed by term a which are also indexed by term b:

$$\text{Recall}_b = \frac{fab}{fa} \qquad (1)$$

The precision of term b is the proportion of documents posted to b which are also indexed by term a:

$$\text{Precision}_b = \frac{fab}{fb} \qquad (2)$$

We now have two measures of b's capability to be used in lieu of a. But we want only one since the degree to which b is associated with a is a single number. Therefore we wish to combine Recall and Precision into a single measure. The product suggests itself since a term b with both high Recall and Precision should have a high association value. But since we have no idea whether to consider Recall more important than Precision or vice versa, we multiply them together with adjustable exponents. Thus a spectrum of directly interpretable measures of the association of term b with term a is provided by

$$Aab = \left(\frac{fab}{fb}\right)^{(1-n)} \left(\frac{fab}{fa}\right)^{n} \qquad (3)$$

where n is such that $0 \le n \le 1$. Varying n generates a variety of association measures, each representing a different interpretation of the relative importance of Recall and Precision in this viewpoint towards association measures.

Since we ascribe little merit to the actual numerical value Aab given by a measure, putting emphasis rather on the resulting profile term ranking, we allow ourselves to alter a given measure—including this one—so long as the ranking remains invariant under the alteration. Two alterations of this kind which yield equivalent rankings are important:

a) Any positive power of a formula which yields non-negative association measures produces the same ranking of terms as the original formula.

Proof: $Axy > Axz > 0$ and $k > 0$ implies $Axy^k > Axz^k > 0$

b) Also, we will usually be allowed to strike the factor fa from the measure, since it is the same constant for all the terms in a's profile and therefore does not affect the ranking.

Applying these rules to Equation 3 yields the equivalent formulation

$$A_{ab} = (fab)^{(a-n)}\left(\frac{fab}{fb}\right)^n = \frac{fab}{fb^n} \qquad (4)$$

The model presented above thus yields a spectrum of measures of the type $A_{ab}=fab/fb^n$. Each such measure is "rank-equivalent to" (produces the same ranking as) a formula derived from a specified weighting of Recall and Precision in this framework.

4 Graphical Interpretation of the Rankings Produced

The next task is to find, for the more complex statistical formulas, which choice of n produces substantially the same ranking of terms. This will allow us, if we choose, to interpret those other formulas in a common framework. Let us therefore examine more closely the way the choice of n affects the ranking and develop some of the apparatus for relating n to more complex measures.

Figure 3 shows a graph of the (fb, fab) space which is of interest because of the form of Equation 4. Each term which co-occurs with the header term can be placed as a point on this graph according to its frequency (fb) and the number of times it co-occurs with the header term (fab). (Note that all terms must be located on or below 45° line, since $fb \geq fab$.)

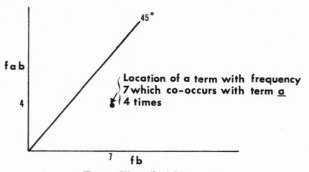

Fig. 3. The (fb, fab) space

Figure 4 indicates what the distributions of fab and fb might be [4] for the terms which co-occur with a given header term. An association measure is represented dynamically as a curve of stated shape which moves in this space, and the ranking of terms on a profile according to that measure is the order in which this curve passes points which represent co-occurring terms.

[4] It would be possible empirically to derive the distribution of (fb, fab) by sampling a large portion of the data. While we have the raw data, we have not determined the detailed distribution. However, it is known by observation that the points strongly tend to be distributed in the manner shown in Fig. 4, with a very high density of points in the lower left-hand corner, trailing off horizontally and upwards. For the present purposes this crude description of the distribution is probably sufficient, though more accurate data would be helpful in future work.

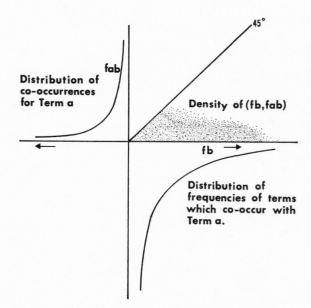

Fig. 4. Distribution of points in the (fb, fab) space

Viewing the measures in this way allows us to perceive which areas of the space are passed first and therefore which terms are likely to be highly ranked.

In Fig. 5 we have shown the curves and movements for various values of n in Equation 4.

When $n=1$, we have a straight line rotating clockwise about the origin. This is the representation of the measure

$$A_{ab} = \frac{fab}{fb}$$

which is pure Precision in terms of our model. Note that the maximum value attainable arises when $fab=fb$, i.e., term b co-occurs with term a each time it occurs. Thus, a term with the values $fb=1$, $fab=1$, or equivalent must be ranked number 1. No distinction is made between such a term and one with values $fb=10$, $fab=10$, although there seems to be more evidence in support of saying the terms are associated in this latter case.

The graphical representation of the case for $n=\frac{1}{2}$ is

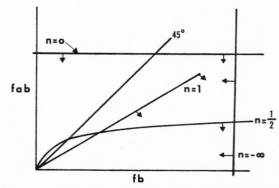

Fig. 5. Graphical representation of various association measures suggested by the model

a curve as shown in Fig. 5 again rotating clockwise about the origin. The measure for $n=\frac{1}{2}$ is

$$Aab = \frac{fab}{fb^{\frac{1}{2}}}$$

In contrast to the case for $n=1$, this formula ranks a term with values $fb=10$, $fab=10$ higher than a term with values $fb=1$, $fab=1$. This phenomenon is quite apparent in the dynamic graph since different areas are covered first by the movement of the corresponding curves. The bend in the curve for $n=\frac{1}{2}$ causes it to be well above the point $fb=1$, $fab=1$ when it crosses the point $fb=10$, $fab=10$. In general, measures of the type fab divided by some root of fb tend to bend more sharply as n approaches 0.

The limiting case when n does reach 0 is given by a horizontal line which moves straight downward with decreasing fab. This measure ranks the terms in order of co-occurrence count. (This is pure Recall.)

Not all possible ranking rules fall within the scope of the model, of course. For example, the extreme case represented by a vertical line that moves from right to left is not strictly within the scope of the model, since n would have to be $-\infty$. It is of interest as an extreme, however, and for this reason is shown in Fig. 4. It corresponds to the measure

$$Aab = fb$$

The dynamic graphical behavior of the formulas produced by the model supplies a means for visualizing the effects which various choices of n will have on the ranking of terms. Other more complex statistical formulas can also be treated within this same framework.

We shall show in the next section that the graphical behavior of these other formulas often resembles the graphical behavior of those generated by the simple model with a suitable choice of n.

5 Relationship with Other Measures

In general, the shape of a curve corresponding to some association formula outside our fab/fb^n framework can be obtained by setting the measure equal to a constant, provided the formula is a function of (fab, fb). The constant represents a particular threshold value; the movement of the curve corresponds to alteration of the threshold. As the threshold is reduced, the curve moves downward and a ranking results.

The measure given by

$$Aab = fab - \frac{fafb}{N} \tag{5}$$

where N = collection size, has been suggested by Maron and Kuhns (5). When set to a constant (to represent a particular threshold K), and solved for fab, Equation 5 becomes

$$fab = K + \frac{fafb}{N} \tag{6}$$

The graphical representation of fab as a function of fb is thus a straight line with small [5] slope fa/N, emerging from the vertical axis at point $fab=K$.

As the threshold is reduced, this nearly horizontal line moves vertically downward. The ranking it produces can be expected to be very similar to a ranking by fab alone, except that the slope of the line is fa/N rather than zero. Note that we cannot strike fa or N from the formula without disturbing the ranking since they are not pure additive or multiplicative constants.

A similar graphical interpretation is given for

$$Aab = \frac{fab}{fa + fb - fab} \tag{7}$$

a measure suggested by Doyle (6).

When set to K and solved for fab we get

$$fab = \frac{K}{K+1}fb + \frac{K}{K+1}fa \tag{8}$$

Again a linear relationship exists between fb and fab as in the previous case. However, the slope of the line approaches zero as the line moves from the top of the graph (where the slope is 1) to the bottom. (This one requires more effort than the rest to see clearly in the dynamic graph.)

In the formula suggested by Dennis (2) and given by

$$Aab = \frac{fab - \dfrac{fafb}{N}}{\sqrt{\dfrac{fafb}{N}}} \tag{9}$$

we may eliminate fa and N as constants. Setting Aab to K and solving for fab yields

$$fab = K\sqrt{fb} + \frac{fa}{N}fb \tag{10}$$

this is seen to be representable as the sum of the square root curve (i.e., $n=\frac{1}{2}$ and a straight line with slope fa/N. Since we would expect fa/N to be small, Equation 9 should yield a ranking similar to the case when $n=\frac{1}{2}$.

A measure investigated by Stiles (7) and given by

$$Aab = \log_{10} \frac{\left(|fabN - fafb| - \dfrac{N}{2}\right)^2 N}{fafb(N-fa)(N-fb)} \tag{11}$$

is approximately equivalent to the ranking produced by the measure

$$\frac{(fab - \frac{1}{2})^2 N}{fafb} \tag{12}$$

when $fa \times fb$ is less than N. (See Fossum (8).) Striking out N and fa we can see that this measure will approximate the case when $n=\frac{1}{2}$. The representation of this measure then will be a curve very similar to

$$fab = K\sqrt{fb} \tag{13}$$

The formulas treated above (except for Doyle's) are thus convertible, without extraordinary difficulty into a form where a value of n in fab/fb^n can be assigned as a crude descriptive parameter. We do this because of

---

[5] Only a handful of terms a (in the NASA vocabulary, 10 out of 18,000) have fa/N in excess of .03.

a desire to compare the formulas within the simpler framework provided by the Recall and Precision model discussed earlier. The relations will be clearer after studying the illustrative examples in the next section.

6 Illustrative Example

The relationships among the various formulas discussed in the preceding section are illustrated in the example presented in Fig. 6. For reasons of space and clarity, the length of the association lists is radically curtailed. The data are drawn from the NASA collection statistics, a collection we noted earlier which contains about 100,000 documents and 18,000 index terms.

Figure 6 illustrates the 15 top associates for the header term "Rocket Motor Case" as ranked by each of 9 measures. The set of co-occurring terms was first restricted to include only those terms b such that 2% or more of their occurrences were co-occurrences with "Rocket Motor Case," i.e., $fab/fb \geqq .02$. This restriction cut the set of candidates to about $\frac{1}{3}$ of the set of all terms that co-occurred with the header term, and was necessary because of computer program limitations. This selection governs all the lists compared in Fig. 6.

Five of the rankings shown are produced by arranging the term b according to five choices of n in Equation 4. The remaining 4 rankings were produced by measures in Fig. 1.

Figure 7 shows the position of the curve representing each of the measures as it selects its 15th term. That is, in the positions indicated, each of the measures has chosen 15 terms associated with "Rocket Motor Case." The thresholds corresponding to these positions vary, and for a particular measure the threshold is merely the value of that measure for the term ranked 15. Thus, by setting the measure equal to the threshold represented by the 15th ranked term, the equation of the curve at that point results.

The various term lists shown in Fig. 6 are arranged systematically according to the average slopes of the corresponding curve in Fig. 7, beginning with the vertical line (fb) and rotating counter clockwise until we reach the 45° line. This arrangement corresponds to increasing n from $-\infty$ to $+1$ for those measures derived from the model; the other measures are interspersed.

Inspection of the lists in Fig. 6 will quickly indicate that they all contain a good proportion of terms which most evaluators would judge to be associated with the header term, "Rocket Motor Case." This is not particularly surprising in a vocabulary of 18,000 terms. There are probably 150 good associates for each middle frequency term in a vocabulary of this size. Even if it were practical to print the top (say) 200 terms here, side-by-side appraisal of the comparative rankings would

require more effort than the reader would expect (or want to devote). Fortunately, however, we can characterize each list by describing the types of terms which tend to appear at the top of the list. These characteristics are features of the measure which generated the particular list. Given a specific application for which the list is to be used, we could then hope to assess in advance which measures would be expected best to meet the application's requirements. Essentially, all that is needed is some statement about which characteristics of highly associated terms are desirable for the given application.

The list for $N = -\infty$ i.e., ranking by fb alone, is surprisingly good, even when we recall the 2% selection restriction mentioned above. That is, merely selecting the high frequency terms which co-occur with the header more than 2% of the time—then ranking them by decreasing frequency—yields a list of words that is far from ridiculous. This indicates, in fact, that the term co-occurrence phenomenon is a stronger effect than one might be predisposed to suspect. Naturally, this list contains terms which tend to be very general, broad, highly used vocabulary terms (by construction). It has the noteworthy attribute that there are hardly any terms appearing on this list which one needs special knowledge to understand. (The vertical line representing this measure was at $fb = 637$ when the 15th term was chosen.)

The terms on the list for $n = 0$, i.e., ranking by fab, are quite similar to those on the list for $n = -\infty$. Note, however, that the constituent terms "case" and "motor" have moved into prominence on this list. (The horizontal line which represents this measure had the Equation $fab = 31$ when the 15th term was chosen.)

The ranking of the top 15 terms for the measure $fab - fafb/N$ is precisely that of the previous measure, fab. Thus the factor $fafb/N$ was not great enough to influence the ranking up to this point. Note the line at this point has already turned clockwise to a very small slope, the equation of the line being

$$fab = 28 + .00243fb$$

The list given by the measure suggested by Stiles (7) differs significantly from the previous lists. Technical terms, like "Hydro test," "deep draw," and "closure" begin to be included. This list and the next two are extremely similar, with only minor permutations of terms. (The curve for this measure was obtained by plotting actual points since the equation is quite complex.) However, Fig. 7 exhibits the obvious similarity of this and the next two measures, showing that the approximation in Equation 12 is indeed valid for this header term. The equations of the curves for the measures given by

$$\frac{fab - \dfrac{fafb}{N}}{\sqrt{\dfrac{fafb}{N}}} \quad \text{and} \quad \sqrt{\dfrac{fab}{fb}}$$

$$fb \ (n = -\infty)$$

Rocket
Propellant
Solid
Steel
Rocket Engine
Fabrications
Titanium
Motor
Glass
Grain
Insulation
Welding
Fracture
Bonding
Cryogenics

$$fab \ (n = 0)$$

Case
Motor
Rocket
Rocket Engine
Solid
Propellant
Steel
Fabrication
Winding
Filament
Solid Prop. Rocket Eng.
Filament Winding
Titanium
Fiber
Glass

$$fab - \frac{fafb}{N}$$

Case
Motor
Rocket
Rocket Engine
Solid
Propellant
Steel
Fabrication
Winding
Filament
Solid Prop. Rocket Eng.
Filament Winding
Titanium
Fiber
Glass

STILES

Case
Motor
Winding
Rocket
Filament Winding
Stretch Forming
Deep Draw
Hydrotest
Filament
Rocket Engine
Closure
Fiberglass
Stretch
Steel
Fabrication

$$\frac{fab - \dfrac{fafb}{N}}{\sqrt{\dfrac{fafb}{N}}}$$

Case
Motor
Winding
Filament Winding
Deep Draw
Rocket
Stretch Forming
Hydrotest
Filament
Rocket Engine
Closure
Fiberglass
Stretch
Spiral Wrap
Steel

$$\frac{fab}{fb^{1/2}} \ (n = 1/2)$$

Case
Motor
Winding
Rocket
Filament Winding
Deep Draw
Stretch Forming
Hydrotest
Filament
Rocket Engine
Closure
Fiberglass
Stretch
Spiral Wrap
Steel

$$\frac{fab}{fa + fb - fab}$$

Case
Motor
Winding
Filament Winding
Filament
Closure
Fiberglass
Glass Fiber
Stretch Forming
Stretch
Solid Prop. Rocket Eng.
Rocket Engine
Reinforced Plastic
High Strength
Fabrication

$$\frac{fab}{fb^{2/3}} \ (n = 2/3)$$

Case
Deep Draw
Motor
Spiral Wrap
Stretch Forming
Hydrotest
Seepage
Winding
Filament Winding
Altair Missile
Stretch Project
Closure
TU 290 Motor
Turks Head Mill
Polaris A2A Missile

$$\frac{fab}{fb} \ (n = 1)$$

Altair Missile
Polaris A2A Missile
Seepage
Spiral Wrap
Stretch Project
TU 290 Motor
Turks Head Mill
Deep Draw
Environmental Temp.
Fuzz
Helical Winding
Stretch Forming
Hydrotest
Vasco Jet
Wing IV Motor

FIG. 6. The top 15 associates of the term "Rocket Motor Case" as ranked by each of nine association measures

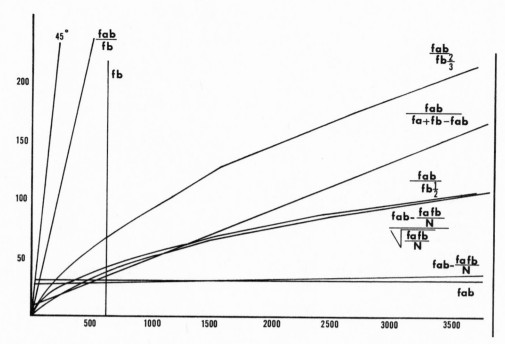

FIG. 7. Graphical representation of various association measures as they select term no. 15

are $fab = 1.58 \sqrt{fb + .00243fb}$ and $fab = 1.73 \sqrt{fb,}$ respectively.

The ranking by $fab/fa + fb - fab$ contains many of the previously seen terms, plus some specific additions such as "high strength" and "reinforced plastic." The curve representing this measure is given at this point by

$$fab = .041fb + 10$$

Next, the list for $n = \frac{2}{3}$, i.e., $fab/fb^{\frac{2}{3}}$, shows the addition of some very specific, highly technical terms such as "seepage," "Polaris A2A missile" and "Turks head mill." The equation of the curve when it has chosen the 15th term is

$$fab = .9fb^{\frac{2}{3}}$$

Finally, the list given by fab/fb when $n = 1$ is presented. Almost all 15 terms on the list are low frequency, highly specific terms. The equation of the line is

$$fab = .46fb$$

at this point.

The discussion above, in conjunction with an inspection of the curves representing various measures, shows that the lists corresponding to various n tend to become more specific and technical in nature as n goes from $-\infty$ to $+1$.

7 Conclusion

The ranking of associated terms produced by using a particular association formula is capable of being evaluated subjectively (though crudely) for its value in a particular application. A gross parametrization of the range of possibilities to consider is presented, and the parameter n is suggested as a summary statistic. It appears to covary with the kinds of subjective characteristics of the lists that bear upon choosing a formula for a particular application. In particular as n moves toward 1 the lists become increasingly specific and specialized.

It is important to repeat that we ascribe no great theoretical importance to the parametrization in terms of n. We regard it as a convenient way to encapsulate a host of crude but interesting empirical observations. We recognize that there are workers who care about, and situations that call for, very detailed attention to the exact value of the association coefficient. We regard the present development principally as a way to narrow the field to isolate the principal behavioral features of a formula with useful properties. The exact choice, once this rough one has been made, of the particular formula best suited to the application is a matter that those closest to the situation are best qualified to study.

Given the framework developed here, we now turn in conclusion to summarizing our own experience, observations, and impressions as they relate to the spectrum of profiles.

1. As a rule one can find people and applications for which each of the lists generated (e.g., in Fig. 6) is evaluated as "best." The choice depends *both* on characteristics of the person using the list and on the nature of the intended application.

2. *People*—even technical specialists tend to reject the lists where n approaches 1 because of the prominence

given to extraordinarily technical, specific, and mysterious terms. People tend to find unfamiliar terms like "Turks Head Mill" disconcerting. However, for fully automatic associative retrieval (when a request is expanded into a profile, and that profile—without being inspected—is used as the weighted search prescription) the formulas with n near 1 appear to give the best performance.

3. For the purpose of preparing a Thesaurus listing for use by subject matter specialists either during query formulation or during an interactive retrieval process, the formulas in the vicinity of $n = \frac{1}{2}$ appear to be most satisfactory. As a rule, the more special knowledge of the field which one can count on the user possessing, the more we can move toward formulas with higher values of n. The range $\frac{1}{3} \leqq n \leqq \frac{2}{3}$ seems most interesting for applications of this type.

4. We have had only limited experience with the effort to use an association profile in preparing a printed Thesaurus for general use. Preliminary indications are that measures in the low range of n $(0 \leqq n \leqq \frac{1}{3})$ tend to be preferred.

To make a very broad summary statement, there is a tendency for n to vary more or less in accordance with "how far along in the retrieval process one is." By this we mean that a requestor, entering the retrieval situation for the first time, who is not too sure of what he is looking for or how to express it, is likely to have a preference for lists with low values of n. As he moves along through the search or gains experience with the collection, the vocabulary, the field, etc., higher values of n become appropriate. (Concurrent with these developments, of course, are considerations of whether the requestor is expanding or narrowing his search at the time he is inspecting a particular association list. Higher values of n tend to be most appropriate for narrowing.) Finally, as the requestor nears the point where he is ready to look at documents, a fairly high value of n seems to be most appropriate.

Adjusting the parameter during the course of an interactive search with the requestor on-line may be of value if this apparent trend is substantiated and if the practicalities of the system permit.

But for the present we suggest this view mainly as a bridge by which the experience, intuition, and judgment of those closely involved in a particular retrieval application can be related to the choice of an association measure.

References

1. KUHNS, J. L., The Continuum of Coefficients of Association, *Statistical Association Methods for Mechanized Documentation,* National Bureau of Standards Miscellaneous Publication 269, Washington, D. C., 1965.

2. DENNIS, S. F., The Construction of a Thesaurus Automatically from a Sample of Text, *Statistical Association Methods for Mechanized Documentation,* National Bureau of Standards Miscellaneous Publication 269, Washington, D. C., 1965.

3. GOODMAN, L., and W. KRUSKAL, Measures of Association for Cross-Classifications, *Journal of American Statistical Association,* 49:732–764 (1954).

4. GOODMAN, L., and W. KRUSKAL, Measures of Association for Cross-Classifications. II: Further Discussion and References, *Journal of American Statistical Association,* 54:123–163 (1959).

5. MARON, M. E., and J. L. KUHNS, On Relevance, Probabilistic Indexing and Information Retrieval, *Journal of the Association of Computing Machinery,* 7:216–244 (1960).

6. DOYLE, L. B., Indexing and Abstracting by Association, *American Documentation,* 13:378–390 (1962).

7. STILES, H. E., The Association Factor in Information Retrieval, *Journal of the Association of Computing Machinery,* 8:271–279 (1961).

8. FOSSUM, E. G., et al., *Organization and Standardization of Information Retrieval Language and Systems,* UNIVAC, Blue Bell, Pa., 1966.

28 On Relevance, Probabilistic Indexing and Information Retrieval

M. E. MARON
J. L. KUHNS
*Journal of the Association
for Computing Machinery
Vol. 7, No. 3, July, 1960*

1. Introduction

One of the really remarkable characteristics of human beings is their ability to communicate with and operate on information formulated in ordinary language. We somehow are able to determine the meanings of words and sentences so as to make judgments about sameness of meaning, redundancy, inconsistency, relevance, etc., in spite of the fact that ordinary language is extremely complex and fraught with vagueness and ambiguity. Since there are no strict rules which prescribe how words are to be put together to convey various kinds and shades of meanings, it is difficult indeed to think of using machines to perform the following kinds of operations on ordinary language: automatic analysis to detect and remove redundant information, automatic abstracting of relevant information, automatic verification of information (i.e., given some items of data, deciding whether or not they are inconsistent with any other data already in storage), automatic deduction (i.e., logical derivation), automatic correlation of data so as to establish trends and deviations from trends, and so on. Yet, if the capabilities of digital computers are to be exploited to the fullest ex-

tent, we would hope that someday they can be programmed to operate on ordinary language on the basis of its meaning (content). It appears that as a first step in the direction of the automatic processing of ordinary language, as typified by the above examples, the problems of information identification and retrieval must be met and dealt with successfully. We therefore turn our attention to the problems of mechanizing a library.

There are a number of obvious difficulties associated with the so-called "library problem" (i.e., the problem of information search and retrieval). The one usually cited relates to the fact that documentary data are being generated at an alarming rate (the growth rate is exponential — doubling every 12 years for some libraries), and consequently considerations of volume alone make the problem appear frightening. However, the heart of the problem does not concern size, but rather it concerns meaning. That is to say, there have been a number of "hardware" solutions to the problem of library size (e.g., use of microfilm, microcards, minicards, magnacards, etc.), but the major difficulties associated with the library problem remain, namely, the identification of content, the problem of determining which of two items of data is "closer" in meaning to a third item, the problem of determining whether or not (or to what degree) some document is *relevant* to a given request, etc.

The jumping-off point for our approach to automatic information retrieval is the recognition that the core of the problem is that of adequately identifying the information content of documentary data. In the discussion that follows we introduce arithmetic (as opposed to logic alone) into the problem of indexing and thereby pave the way for the use of mathematical operations so as to compute a number, called the relevance number, which is a measure of the probable relevance of a document for a requestor. Thus, the fundamental notion which acts as a wedge to drive an opening into the basic problem of information retrieval is that of the relevance number, which provides a means of ranking documents according to their probable relevance. However, the solution to the problem of information retrieval involves more than ranking by relevance — it involves the proper selection of those documents which are to be ranked. In order to get at this "selection" problem, it is necessary to establish various measures of closeness of meaning, and an approach to this semantical problem is via statistics. We define various measures of closeness between documents and between requests for information so that given an arbitrary request a machine can automatically elaborate upon a search in order to retrieve relevant documents which would not otherwise have been selected.

We divide the paper into three parts: (a) discussion of the conventional approach to the library problem, (b) an exposition of the solution given by Probabilistic Indexing, (c) a discussion of some preliminary experiments to test these new techniques and procedures.

2. Conventional Approach to an Automatic Retrieval System

2.1 The Role of Indexes

Because, at least for the immediate future, no machine can actually read a document and decide whether or not its subject matter relates to some given request subject, it is necessary to use some intermediate identifying tags, namely, an indexing system. An index to a document acts as a tag by means of which the information content of the document in question may be identified. The index may be a single term or a set of terms which together tag or identify the content of each document. The terms which constitute the allowable vocabulary for indexing documents in a library form the common language which bridges the gap between the information in the documents and the information requirements of the library users.

In principle, an indexer reads an incoming document, selects one or several of the index terms from the "library vocabulary," and then coordinates the selected terms with the given document (or its accession number). Thus, the assignment of terms to each document is a go or no-go

affair — for each term either it applies to the document in question or it does not. Furthermore, the processes of indexing information and that of formulating a request for information are symmetrical in the sense that, just as the subject content of a document is identified by coordinating to it a set of index terms, so also the subject content of a request must be identified by coordinating to it a set of index terms. Thus, the user who has a particular information need identifies this need in terms of a library request consisting of one or several index terms or logical combinations thereof.

2.2 The Mechanization

Given a set of tags (index terms) which identify the content of each document and a set of tags which describe a request for information, the problem of automatic searching resolves itself to that of searching for and matching tags or combinations thereof. Once a set of index terms has been assigned to each document in the library, this information can be encoded in digital form, put on a suitable machine medium, and searched automatically. In the past, literature searching has been done automatically on punched cards using the IBM sorter, on magnetic tape using an electronic computer such as the IBM 709, on photographic film as a continuous strip such as in the case of the Rapid Selector, or in discrete records on photographic film as, for example, in the Minicard system. In each case a machine searches and retrieves (either copies of the document, abstracts, or a list of accession numbers) by matching document index terms with the terms and logic of the given request.

2.3. The Notion of Semantic Noise

The correspondence between the information content of a document and its set of indexes is not exact because it is extremely difficult to specify precisely the subject content of a document by means of one or several index words. If we consider the set of all index terms on the one hand and the class of subjects that they denote on the other hand, then we see that there is no strict one-to-one correspondence between the two. It turns out that given any term there are many possible subjects that it could denote (to a greater or lesser extent), and, conversely, any particular subject of knowledge (whether broad or narrow) usually can be denoted by a number of different terms. This situation may be characterized by saying that there is "semantic noise" in the index terms. Just as the correspondence between the information content of a document and its set of indexes is not exact, so also the correspondence between a user's request, as formulated in terms of one or many index words, and his real need (intention) is not exact. Thus there is semantic noise in both the document indexes and in the requests for information.

One of the reasons that the index terms are noisy is

due to the fact that the meanings of these terms are a function of their setting. That is to say, the meaning of a term in isolation is often quite different when it appears in an environment (sentence, paragraph, etc.) of other words. The grammatical type, position and frequency of other words help to clarify and specify the meanings of a given term. Furthermore, individual word meanings vary from person to person because, to a large degree, the meanings of the words are a matter of individual experience. This is all to say that when words are isolated and used as tags to index documents it is difficult to pin down their meanings, and consequently it is difficult to use them as such to accurately index documents or to accurately specify a request.

2.4 Conventional Stopgags

Many workers in the field of library science have attempted to reduce the semantic noise in indexing by developing specialized indexing systems for different kinds of libraries. An indexing system tailored to a particular library would be less noisy than would be the case otherwise. (In a sense, to tailor an index system to a specific library is to apply the principle of an ideoglossary, as it is used in machine language translation, to remove semantic ambiguity.) In spite of careful work in the developing of a "best" set of tags for a particular library, the problem of semantic noise and its consequences remain, albeit, to a lesser extent.

Another attempt to remove the semantic noise in request formulations has to do with the use of logical combinations of index terms. That is to say, if two or more index terms are joined conjunctively, it helps to narrow or more nearly specify a subject. On the other hand, the same set of terms connected disjunctively broadens the scope of a request.[1] Thus, using logical combinations of index terms, one would hope to either avoid the retrieval of irrelevant material or avoid missing relevant material. However, although a request using a set of index terms joined conjunctively does decrease the probability of obtaining irrelevant material, it also increases the probability of missing relevant material. The converse holds for a request consisting of a disjunction of index terms. This difficulty in the conventional approach is inherent in its go or no-go nature.

The fact that conventional searching consists in matching noisy tags implies that the result of a search provides documents which are irrelevant to the real needs of the requestor, and, even worse, some of the really relevant documents are not retrieved. Thus, in spite of specialized indexing systems and in spite of the use of logical combinations of index terms, the major problem is still that of properly identifying the subject content of both documents and requests. The problem of accurately representing the information content of a document by means of some kind of tags in such a way that a machine can operate on these tags in order to search for documents with the same meaning, related meanings, relevant meanings, etc., is still unsolved.

In the following section we shall present the basic notions of the technique of Probabilistic Indexing and show that this approach to the library problem improves retrieval effectiveness both by reducing the probability of obtaining irrelevant documents and by increasing the probability of selecting relevant documents. Furthermore, the technique of Probabilistic Indexing provides as the result of a search an ordered list of those documents which satisfy the request, ranked according to relevance.

3. Derivation of the Relevance Number

3.1 Initial Remarks

To say that index tags are noisy is to say that there is an uncertainty about the relationship between the terms and the subjects denoted by the terms. That is to say, given a document indexed with its assigned term (or terms), there is only a probability that if a user is interested in the subject (or subjects) designated by the tag he will find that the document in question is relevant. Conventional indexing consists in having an indexer decide on a yes-no basis whether or not a given term applies for a particular document. Either a tag is applicable or it is not — there is no middle ground. However, since there is an uncertainty associated with the tags, it is much more reasonable and realistic to make this judgment on a probabilistic basis, i.e., to assert that a given tag may hold with a certain degree or weight. Given the ability to weight index terms, one can characterize more precisely the information content of a document. The indexer may wish to assign a low weight such as 0.1 or 0.2 to a term, rather than to say that the term does not hold for the document. Conversely, the indexer may wish to assign a weight of 0.8 or 0.9 to a term, rather than to say that it definitely holds for a document. Thus, given weighted indexing, it is possible to more accurately characterize the information content of a document. The notion of weighting the index terms that are assigned to documents and using these weights to compute relevance numbers is basic to the technique which we call *Probabilistic Indexing*.

3.2 Notions of Relevance and Amount of Information

One of our basic aims is to rank documents according to their relevance, given a library request for information. The problem then is to take relevance, which is a primi-

1. We use the words "conjunction" and "disjunction" to denote the logical connectives "and" and "or " This usage is continued when classes, instead of propositions, are under discussion (as in the case for a possible interpretation of the index terms mentioned above), although in this case "intersection" and "union" are more appropriate.

tive notion, and explicate it — in the sense of making the concept precise — hopefully, to give a quantitative explication. If we cannot have a quantitative measure for relevance, at least we would like a comparative measure so that ranking of documents by relevance will be possible. In some sense the problem of explicating the notion of relevance (which is the basic concept in a theory of information retrieval) is similar to that of explicating the notion of amount of information (which is the basic concept of communication theory). In Shannon's work on information theory we find that one notion of amount of information has been explicated in terms of probabilities so that one can establish a quantitative measure of the amount of information in a message.[2] We approach the notion of relevance also in a probabilistic sense.

3.3 First Step

By "$P(A,B)$" we mean the probability of an event of class B occurring with reference to an event of class A. We shall be interested in the following classes of events:

(a) D_i:
   obtaining the ith document and finding it relevant.

(b) I_j:
   requesting information on the field of interest (subject, area of knowledge) designated by the jth index term I_j.

(c) A:
   requesting information from the library.

Thus

$P(A.I_j,D_i)$ = the probability that if a library user requests information on I_j, he will be satisfied with document D_i.

As the first step in the explication of relevance we assert: If $P(A.I_j,D_1) > P(A.I_j,D_2)$, then D_1 is more relevant than D_2.

3.4 Next Step

In the elementary calculus of probability, one can immediately derive by the inverse inference schema (closely associated with Bayes' Theorem):

$$P(A.I_j,D_i) = \frac{P(A,D_i) \cdot P(A.D_i,I_j).}{P(A,I_j)} \qquad (1)$$

2. C. E. Shannon and W. Weaver, *The Mathematical Theory of Communication*, The University of Illinois Press, Urbana, Illinois (1949).

For any given request I_j, $P(A,I_j)$ is a constant, and consequently we may rewrite (1) as follows:

$$P(A.I_j,D_i) \sim P(A,D_i) \cdot P(A.D_i,I_j) \qquad (2)$$

where $P(A,D_i)$ is the a priori probability of document D_i, and $P(A.D_i,I_j)$ is the probability that if a user wants information of the kind contained in document D_i he will formulate a request by using I_j. Thus, if we can obtain the values called for in the right-hand side of (2), then we can compute a quantity proportional to the value $P(A.I_j,D_i)$. We call this quantity the *relevance number* of the ith document with respect to the given request.

Immediately the problem of estimating these values confronts us. Consider first the estimate of $P(A.D_i,I_j)$. In principle, one could obtain an estimate of this probability via a statistical sampling process, but such a procedure would of course be extremely impractical, and it turns out that it is unnecessary. When an individual indexes a document (i.e., when he decides which terms to use to tag a document) he intuitively estimates this probability — in the conventional case automatically converting the probabilities to either 0 or 1. We now assert that the weight of a tag for a document, i.e., the degree with which the tag holds for a document, when properly scaled, can be interpreted as an estimate of $P(A.D_i,I_j)$. Thus we have from (1) and (2)

$$P(A.I_j,D_i) = a_j.P(A,D_i).\omega_{1j}, \qquad (3)$$

where "ω_{ij}" denotes *the degree to which the j-th index term applies to the i-th document*, $P(A,D_i)$ is the a priori probability of document D_i, and a_j is the scaling factor times the reciprocal of $P(A,I_j)$. If we interpret the a priori probability so that it corresponds to statistics on document usage, i.e., so that $P(A,D_i)$ is the quotient of the number of uses of document D_i by the total number of document uses, then it is easy to show on the basis of (1) and (3) that ω_{ij} and $P(A.D_i,I_j)$ are related by

$$\omega_{ij} = \beta_j.P(A.D_i,I_j), \qquad (4)$$

where

$$\beta_j = \frac{\sum_i P(A, D_i) \cdot \omega_{ij}}{P(A, I_j)}. \qquad (5)$$

In other words, in (4), β_j plays the role of an error factor in the estimation of $P(A.D_i,I_j)$ by the value ω_{ij}; (5) tells us how to estimate, in turn, the value of this error factor by using all the weights for a given tag as well as the statistical data $P(A,I_j)$. An improved estimate, therefore, is given by redefining the weight of a tag as follows:

$$w_{ij} = \omega_{ij}/\beta_j = \text{improved estimate of } P(A.D_i,I_j). \quad (6)$$

We call this value "the modified weight." The reader is referred to the Appendix for the details on the extension of the weight of a single index term to the weight of any Boolean functon of index terms.

To summarize, library statistics provide us with $P(A, D_i)$, the weights coordinated with the index terms, when properly scaled, give us estimates of $P(A.D_i,I_j)$, and consequently we can compute the value of the relevance number $P(A.I_j,D_i)$ by means of which documents can be ranked according to their probable relevance to the requestor.

3.5 Question Concerning Estimation

At this point one might raise the following question. If the indexer is required to estimate $P(A.D_i,I_j)$, why not have him estimate $P(A.I_j,D_i)$ directly, since this is the goal of the computations? Actually this is not quite correct since the general goal of the computations is the determination of $P(A.R,D_i)$, where R is any Boolean function of the index terms. Clearly the indexer cannot make a single estimate of $P(A.R,D_i)$ since the value depends on the particular request R and hence there would have to be as many estimates of $P(A.R,D_i)$ as there would be R's. In order to avoid this situation, it would be necessary to transform $P(A.R,D_i)$ so that R goes from the reference class to the attribute class. Once we do this the problem is to compute $P(A.D_i,R)$ given all of the values of $P(A.D_i,I_j)$ as j varies over the range of tags that are contained in R. Thus, it turns out that $P(A.R, D_i)$ cannot be estimated directly — we must obtain it from $P(A.D_i,R)$, which in turn must be computed from $P(A.D_i,I_j)$.[3] That is to say, we need the value of $P(A.D_i, I_j)$ anyway, and any other estimates are superfluous.[4]

4. Automatic Elaboration of the Selection Process

4.1 Initial Remarks

The technique of Probabilistic Indexing, as we have seen, allows a computing machine, given a request for information, to derive a relevance number for each document. This relevance number is a measure of the

3. See Appendix.
4. Even if every request were of the elementary form $P(A.I_j, D_i)$, it would be better to estimate $P(A.D_i,I_j)$ and compute $P(A.I_j,D_i)$ rather than to estimate the latter directly. This second argument in favor of the estimation of $P(A.D_i,I_j)$ over $P(A.I_j,D_i)$ appears when we consider the consistency of the comparative values. The indexer looks at each document, then runs through the various possible index terms which apply. In general $P(A.D_i,I_j)$ will vary over a much larger range than $P(A.I_j,D_i)$ as j varies, and therefore it is easier psychologically for the indexer to rank correctly the values over the larger range.

document's relevance. The result of a search is an ordered list of those documents which satisfy the request, ranked according to their relevance numbers. We would prefer to have a technique which not only decides which of a given class of documents is most probably relevant, next most probably relevant, etc., but which also decides whether the class itself of retrieved documents is adequate (at least in the sense of determining whether or not it excludes some documents which are relevant to the user's *information needs* but are not computed as probably relevant due to inadequacies in the user's description of his information need). That is to say, if we consider the request as a *clue* which the user gives to the library to indicate the nature of his information needs, then we should raise the following question: Given a clue, how may it be used by the library system to generate a best *class* of documents (to be ranked subsequently by their relevance numbers)? Thus given the clue, how can we elaborate upon it automatically in order to produce a best class of retrieved documents? Let us turn our attention to this problem.

4.2 Search Strategies and the Notion of Closeness

A library request (a clue) is a Boolean function whose variables are index terms, each of which, in turn, selects a class of documents via a logical match. That is to say, all of those documents whose index terms are logically compatible with the logic and the tags of a request R constitute the class of retrieved documents C. Our goal is to extend the class C in the most probable "direction," and this can be done in two ways. One method involves the transforming of R into R', where R' in turn will select a class of documents C' which is larger than C and contains more relevant documents. A second method does not modify R but rather uses the class C to define a new class C''. A set or rules which prescribe how to go from a given request R to a class of retrieved documents is called a strategy. A strategy, in turn, involves the use of several different techniques for measuring the "closeness" between index terms and between documents. Before proceeding, let us introduce some further notations to make more precise what we have been saying.

We understand by "basic selection process" the rule which uses the request to select the class of documents whose tags are logically compatible with the logic and tags of the request, and we denote this basic selection process by the functional notation "f." Thus f is the transfer function from inputs (requests) to output (class of retrieved documents) and we write

$$f(R) = C \quad (7)$$

where, again, R is the request and C is the class of retrieved documents. The problem is to enlarge C so as to increase the probability that it will contain relevant documents and to decrease the probability that it will contain irrelevant documents. We approach this problem in the following way: Suppose R' is a request similar in meaning to R; then we can take as a possible modification of f, say f',

$$f'(R) = f(R) \vee f(R') = C \vee C' \qquad (8)$$

(where "$\vee$" designates class union). This modification can be made precise if we are able to invent a closeness measure on the request space to measure similarity in meaning. Since we are not sure what "meaning" is and much less able to assign a numerical quantity to it, this is rather difficult; but we shall show later that statistics can provide such measures. For the present, suppose we actually do have such a measure; then we can generate a modified selection function f' by defining $f'(R)$ to be the union of all classes $f(R')$ where the "closeness" between R and R' exceeds some specified number, say ϵ. Symbolically, this is written

$$f'(R) = \bigcup_{[Q(R,\,R')\,>\,\epsilon]} f(R'). \qquad (9)$$

Analogously, if we have a "distance" function in the document space[5] which gives "distance" as a numerical measure of dissimilarity of information content, then a completely different modification f'' of f arises via

$$f''(R) = C'' \qquad (10)$$

where C'' consists of all documents whose distance from $C = f(R)$ is less than ϵ.

Thus, we see that a machine strategy can elaborate upon the basic selection process in order to improve the search in one of two different ways. The first is to establish a measure for "closeness" in request space so as to formulate R', given R. The other way is to use the class of documents C, obtained by the initial request R, to define a new class C''. Both of these methods are discussed below.

4.3 Notion of Index Space

Geometrically speaking, one may think of the set of n index terms which constitute the library catalog "vocabulary" as points in an n-dimensional space. The points in this space are not located at random, but rather, they have definite relationships with respect to one another, depending on the meanings of the terms. For example, the term "logic" would be much closer to "mathematics" than to "music." One always finds, when looking up index terms in the catalog of a conventional library, other

5. We use "distance" in document space, "closeness" in request space. The reason is that our measures in request space have the nature of "coefficients of association" rather than the properties of mathematical distance functions.

terms listed under "see" and "see also." This cross-indexing ("see/see also") aspect of a library indicates some of the relationships that index terms have for one another; i.e., it indicates some of the relationships between points in index space.

The numerical evaluation of relationships between index terms can be made explicit by formulating probabilistic weighting factors between them. Once numerical weighting factors are coordinated with the distances, the cross-indexing aspect of a library can be mechanized so that, given a request involving one (or many) index terms, a machine could compute other terms for which searches should be made. That is to say, a request places one at a point, or several points, in index space, and, once the "closeness" measures between points are arithmetized, a machine could determine which other points to go to in order to improve the request. Thus, the elaboration of a request on the basis of a probabilistic "association of ideas" could be executed automatically.

4.4 Automatic Groping in Index Space

There are at least two different kinds of relationships that can exist between the points in index space, viz., semantical relationships and statistical relationships. The most elementary semantical relationship is that of synonymity, but in addition to synonymity there are other semantical relationships such as "partially implied by" and "partially implies." Such relationships between terms are based strictly on the meanings of the terms in question — hence the word "semantical." Another class of relationships is statistical, i.e., those based on the relative frequency of occurrence of terms used as indexes. The distinction between semantical and statistical relationships may be clarified as follows: Whereas the semantical relationships are based solely on the meanings of the terms and hence independent of the "facts" described by those words, the statistical relationships between terms are based solely on the relative frequency with which they appear and hence *are* based on the nature of the facts described by the documents. Thus, although there is nothing about the meaning of the term "logic" which implies "switching theory," the nature of the facts (viz., that truth-functional logic is widely used for the analysis and synthesis of switching circuits) "causes" a statistical relationship. (Another example might concern the terms "information theory" and "Shannon" — assuming, of course, that proper names are used as index terms.)

Once the various "connections" between the points of index space have been established, rules must be formulated which describe how one should move in the maze of connected points. We call such rules "heuristics." They are general guides for groping in the "maze" in the attempt to create an optimal output list of documents for any arbitrary request. The heuristics would enable a machine to decide, for a given set of request terms, which index terms to "see" and "see also," and how deep this search should be and when to stop, etc. Generally speaking, the heuristics would decide which index terms to look at next, on the basis of the semantical and statistical connections between terms, and the heuristics would decide when to stop looking, on the basis of the number of documents that would be retrieved and the relevance numbers of those documents. (Remember that each point in index space defines a class of documents, viz., all of those documents which have been assigned the index terms in question with a nonzero weight.) Given this understanding of heuristics, we see that an overall search strategy is made up of components, some of which are heuristics; i.e., the sequence of devices, rules, heuristics, etc., which lead from inputs (requests) to outputs (classes of retrieved documents) is the strategy.

4.5 Three Measures of Closeness in Index Space

In order to clarify the notion of developing heuristics which would determine how a computer should "grope" in index space, consider the following example. Assume that we compute the frequency, $N(I_j)$, with which each term is used to tag a document, and also that we compute the frequency, $N(I_j.I_k)$, with which pairs of terms are assigned to documents. We can then compute the conditional probability $P(I_j,I_k)$ that if a term I_j is assigned to a document then I_k also will be assigned:

$$P(I_j, I_k) = \frac{N(I_j.I_k)}{N(I_j)} \qquad (11)$$

We do this for all pairs I_j, I_k.

Assume now that I_j' is the index term which has the highest conditional probability given I_j; i.e., I_j' is the index term for which $P(I_j, I_k)$ is a maximum. Then given a request, $R = I_j$, for all documents tagged with I_j, we form a new request, $R' = I_j \vee I_j'$, which searches for all documents tagged with either I_j or I_j'. Thus, the rule is now to consider R' instead of R.

This procedure tells us which tags are closest (in one sense) to given ones, but we still have no *measure* of the "closeness" (hereafter written without quotes) and such a measure is needed as a part of the associated computation rule. That is to say, we elaborate upon R and obtain R' by searching for documents indexed under tags closely related to those in the original request, but clearly the relevance numbers that we derive for these additional documents should be weighted down somewhat in order to indicate that they were obtained only from tags which are close to those in the original request. We measure the closeness as follows: Let $p_j = P(I_j, I_j')$ and normalize p_j over the set of tags used in the request so that

$$\bar{p}_j = \frac{p_j}{\sum p_j} .$$

Now, instead of using $w_i(I_j')$ (the weight assigned to I_j' for the ith document) in the search computation, we replace it by $\bar{p}_j.w_i(I_j')$. The extended search that we have just described is an elementary form of only one of a class of possible heuristics based on the statistical relationships between tags.

A second elementary heuristic which looks even more promising is called the "inverse conditional" search, and it involves measuring closeness of tags to I_j in terms of the conditional probability from I_k to I_j (instead of conversely as described above). That is to say, we compute the $P(I_k,I_j)$ which is maximum as I_k varies, and this provides the tag which most strongly implies the given tag I_j. Thus instead of asking for that tag which is most strongly implied (satistically) by an arbitrary tag in the request, we ask for the tag which most strongly *implies* (statistically) the given tag. Using this method to determine the closeness of tags we establish a measure for the closeness by normalizing the probability as before. That is, define

$$p_j = P('I_j, I_j),$$

$$\bar{p}_j = \frac{p_j}{\sum p_j}$$

and, again, the corresponding computation rule is now $\bar{p}_j.w_i('I_j)$, where $'I_j$ is the I_k which makes $P(I_k,I_j)$ a maximum for a given I_j.

Having discussed two possible measures of closeness, viz., the conditional probability $P(I_j,I_k)$ and the inverse condition probability $P(I_k,I_j)$, we now consider a third statistical measure which appears to be the most promising of the three. This is one of several possible *coefficients of association* between predicates.[6]

The particular coefficient we have chosen arises in the following way. Consider the tags I_j and I_k, and partition the library by four classifications, viz., documents indexed under both I_j and I_k, those indexed under I_j but not I_k, those indexed under I_k but not I_j, and those not indexed under either. Letting $"\bar{I}_j"$ denote the complement of the class I_j, etc., these four classes are given by $I_j.I_k$, $I_j.\bar{I}_k$, $\bar{I}_j.I_k$, $\bar{I}_j.\bar{I}_k$, respectively. The classification and the number of documents is shown most conveniently in a table:

	I_k	$\bar{I}_k$	
I_j	$x = N(I_j,I_k)$	$u = N(I_j,\bar{I}_k)$	$N(I_j)$
$\bar{I}_j$	$v = N(\bar{I}_j,I_k)$	$y = N(\bar{I}_j,\bar{I}_k)$	$N(\bar{I}_j)$
	$N(I_k)$	$N(\bar{I}_k)$	n

We have adjoined to the table the row and column sums and n (the total number of documents).

6. G. U. Yule, On measuring association between attributes, *J. Royal Stat. Soc.,* 75 (1912), 579–642.

Now, using the notation of formula (11), we say that I_j is *statistically independent* of I_k if

$$P(I_j, I_k) = P(I_k). \qquad (15)$$

This can be shown to be equivalent to

$$P(I_j, I_k) = P(I_j) \cdot P(I_k); \qquad (16)$$

so that rewriting in terms of frequencies we have an additional equivalence:

$$N(I_j . I_k) = N(I_j) \cdot N(I_k)/n. \qquad (17)$$

For any pair I_j, I_k, (17) suggests that we look at the excess of $N(I_j . I_k)$ over its independence value; i.e., the quantity

$$\delta(I_j, I_k) = N(I_j . I_k) - N(I_j) \cdot N(I_k)/n. \qquad (18)$$

It can be shown that this function δ has the property

$$\delta(I_j, I_k) = \delta(\bar{I}_j, \bar{I}_k) = -\delta(\bar{I}_j, I_k) = -\delta(I_j, \bar{I}_k), \qquad (19)$$

and thus δ is associated with the difference over independence values in all four classifications. Yule[7] lists some basic properties that a coefficient of association between I_j and I_k should have. We call this coefficient "$Q(I_j, I_k)$". (1) $Q(I_j, I_k)$ should be zero when $\delta(I_j, I_k) = 0$ and, moreover, $Q(I_j, I_k)$ should vary as $\delta(I_j, I_k)$ for fixed n and fixed row and column totals; (2) the maximum of $Q(I_j, I_k)$ should occur when I_j is contained in I_k ($u = 0$), or I_k is contained in I_j ($v = 0$), or I_j and I_k give the same class ($u = v = 0$); (3) the minimum of $Q(I_j, I_k)$ should occur when I_k is contained in $\bar{I}_j$ ($x = 0$), or $\bar{I}_j$ is contained in I_k ($y = 0$), or I_j is the complement of I_k ($x = y = 0$); (4) it should have a simple range of values, say from -1, to 1. A coefficient[8] that has all of these properties is:

$$Q(I_j, I_k) = (xy - uv)/(xy + uv), \qquad (20)$$

where the intimate connection with δ is indicated by the fact that the numerator of Q is, in fact, $n\delta$.

The generation of a heuristic now proceeds by the rules for the previous measures. Given $R = I_j$, we select the term I_k (different from I_j) with the maximum coefficient $Q(I_j, I_k)$. This value will be between 0 and 1, or no term will be selected. Then R is extended to

$$R' = I_j \vee I_k,$$

and in the search computation we multiply the weight $w_i(I_k)$ by $Q(I_j, I_k)$.

We now have the possibility of generating more elaborate heuristics. The heuristics just described can be called "one-deep." Applying the procedure again, we arrive at "two-deep" heuristics. At this second level, however, several possibilities arise. Having gone from I_j to $I_j \vee I_k$, we can now find the term most closely associated to I_k, say I_l, thus obtaining (two-deep chain search):

$$R'' = I_j \vee I_k \vee I_l.$$

Alternately, we can choose the term of second highest association with I_j, say I_m, thus obtaining (two-deep hub search)

$$R'' = I_j \vee I_k \vee I_m.$$

We also have the possibility of changing the measure of closeness for the second search, thus building as complex a search strategy as we wish.

4.6 *Heuristics in the Document Space*

Having shown how to generate heuristics by elaborating on the original requests, let us now look at the problem of implementing formula (10). We call such heuristics "extension heuristics"; i.e., we extend an initially retrieved class of documents by considerations concerning this class itself — holding that this class gives clues as to the meaning of the original request. Now we would prefer not only to extend this class by measures of distance between documents but also introduce such measures into a "generalized" relevance number computation. That is to say, we would like to combine heuristics in such a way that documents with associated ranking numbers are retrieved, not just classes of documents. We would also like to use the values $w_i(R)$ in the computation.

First, we note that the Pythagorean distance between two rows of the probabilistic matrix gives a measure of dissimilarity of information content (as well as dissimilarity of distribution of information) between documents corresponding to these rows. Call this distance, $\Delta(D_i, D_j)$. We can use this distance function to compute the distance of any document from the class C of documents retrieved by the basic selection process. This is all the theory required to implement formula (10).[9]

Next is the problem of defining the generalized relevance number. There are infinitely many possibilities here, and which is the "best" is still an open problem.

---

7. Loc. Cit.

8. The coefficient recommended by Yule, *loc. cit.*, is not Q, but $Z = (\sqrt{xy} - \sqrt{uv})/(\sqrt{xy} + \sqrt{uv})$. The range of variation of both Q and Z is the same and since both lead to equivalent heuristics we have chosen Q for its computational simplicity. For refined work we might adopt Z.

9. Another measure of dissimilarity is to take, not the Pythagorean distance, but the sum of the absolute values of the differences between rows; i.e., $\sum_k |w_{ik} - w_{jk}|$; in fact, several other measures of dissimilarity appear worthy of study. Our discussion is perfectly general, and the reader may take $\Delta(D_i, D_j)$ as any such measure.

However, an extremely natural one arises as follows: We consider the values $w_i(R)$ as measures of closeness between R and the documents. To combine these values with $\Delta(D_i,D_j)$, we convert closeness to "distance" by some device such as considering the negative of the logarithm of $w_i(R)$. We define

$$d(R,D_i) = -\log w_i(R). \quad (21)$$

D_i will be retrieved by R if and only if $d(R,D_i)$ is finite; thus this characterizes the class of retrieved documents. Now take that document D_i in the class of retrieved documents such that $\Delta(D_i,D_j)$ is a minimum.[10] Then we take

$$g(R,D_j) = \sqrt{\Delta^2(D_i,D_j) + \log^2 w_i(R)} \quad (22)$$

as the measure of "distance" between R and D_j.[11] Note that if D_j is a retrieved document, then $\Delta(D_iD_j)$ is zero and

$$g(R,D_j) = -\log w_j(R).$$

Furthermore, if D_j has not been retrieved (initially),

$$g(R,D_j) > -\log w_i(R),$$

where i is the accession number of the document nearest to D_j. Thus the ranking by the g-function will always put an adjoined document below its associated document in the class C. We may now finish the computation by subtracting the logarithm of the a priori probability of a document from its g-value (analogous to multiplying $w_i(R)$ by $P(A,D_i)$ to obtain the relevance number). The final heuristic is then obtained by choosing a suitable cutoff point in the list of adjoined documents — taking only those with generalized relevance numbers less than some specified value.

4.7 *Extension of the Request Language*

It is obvious that the richer the request language the more precise is the user's description of his information need. However, as the language becomes descriptively richer, the processing of retrieval prescriptions becomes more complex because of the difficulties discussed in section 1. A rather simple extension of our request language does, however, present itself. This richer language also has the virtue of adaptability to the automatic procedure we envisage. That is, we permit the requestor to assign numerical weights to index terms according to how important a role he wishes them to play in the processing

10. If D_i is not unique, choose the one in the minimal set with the largest $w_i(R)$.

11. It may be preferable to "weight" each of the components $\Delta(D_i,D_j)$, $\log w_i(R)$ in (22). Suitable values of these weights are to be determined by experimentation.

of his request. These request weights can be used to scale down the index term weights and/or to serve as control numbers in search strategies.

4.8 *Search Strategies*

We have presented some of the heuristics that appear to have the best possibility of being useful components of a search strategy. We also have formulated some principles for a general approach to the problem of automatic elaboration of the selection process. Let us now illustrate these ideas by constructing an over-all search strategy.

First we list the variables involved:
1. Input
   a. The request R
   b. The request weights
2. The Probabilistic Matrix $[w_{ij}]$
   a. Dissimilarity measures between documents (e.g., Δ-values)
   b. Significance measures for index terms (An index term applied to every document in the library will have no significance, while an index term applied to only one document will be highly significant. Thus significance measures are related to the "extension number" for each term, i.e., to the number of documents tagged with the term — the smaller this number, the greater the significance of the index term.)
   c. "Closeness" measures between index terms (e.g., Q-values, etc.)
3. The a priori Probability Distribution
4. Output (by means of the basic selection process, i.e., the logical match plus the inverse inference schema (1) with all of its ramifications and refinements)
   a. The class of retrieved documents, C
   b. n, the number of documents in C
   c. Relevance numbers
5. Control Numbers
   a. n_0, the maximum number of documents that we wish to retrieve
   b. Relevance number control; e.g., we may ignore documents with relevance number less than a specified value.
   c. Generalized relevance number control. Similar to the above, but this applies to the computation described in section 4.6.
   d. Request weight control; i.e., we elaborate on index terms in the request if their request weight is higher than some specified value.
   e. Significance number of index term control; i.e., we give index terms of certain significance (defined in terms of their extensions) special attention.
6. Operations
   a. Basic selection process; denote this by "f."
   b. Elaboration of the request by using "closeness"

in the request space. Denote this by "*H*." Thus the operation *H* will transform the request *R* into a new request *R'*. More precisely *H* is the heuristic: elaborating the index terms in *R* with request weights greater than the request weight control number and/or index term significance greater than a specified value.

c. Adjoining new documents to the class of retrieved documents by using "distance" in the document space. Denote this by "*h*." Thus the operation *h* will transform the class *C* of retrieved documents into a new class, say *D*. More precisely, *h* is the heuristic: trim *C* to documents having relevance number greater than the control number and then annex to *C* all of the documents with generalized relevance number in a certain range.

d. Merge: any merging operation between two classes; e.g., forming their intersection, their union, trimming by using relevance number and then forming union, etc.

Next we combine these to obtain the strategy shown in Figure 1. This strategy is to be regarded as a particularly simple example, its goal to obtain a specified number of documents (say n_0) having the best chance of satisfying the request. Thus, the decision to elaborate, centers on answering the question: Is the number of documents selected greater than or equal to n_0? In Figure 1 we refer to the heuristic *H* as simply "elaborate the request." The actual transfer function *H* involves using control numbers to limit the elaboration. Furthermore, these control numbers can be varied from one ap-

plication of *H* to the next. Similarly we refer to the heuristic *H* as simply "extend the class," but we point out that this too involves control numbers. Finally, a word about the classes *C, C', D,* etc. These are actually lists of documents ranked by relevance numbers. Thus the instruction "trim *C* to n_0" means "cut off the list to the n_0 documents with highest relevance numbers." The output of the system will be an ordered list of document accession numbers.

5. Experimental Results

5.1 An Initial Remark

The previous discussion (sections 3 and 4) indicates that there are two basic hypotheses that we wish to verify. The first hypothesis asserts that the relevance number which we compute for each document, given a request, is, *in fact*, a measure of the probable relevance of the document. The second hypothesis asserts that the automatic elaboration of a search does, *in fact*, produce relevant documents which are not retrieved by the original request. In order to empirically verify the above hypotheses and to gain further insights into these problems, we conducted some preliminary experiments, the results of which we now summarize.

5.2 Experimental Setup

A collection of 110 articles from *Science News Letter*[12] formed the experimental library. Our choice of articles

12. Published by Science Service, Inc., 1719 N Street, N.W., Washington, D. C.

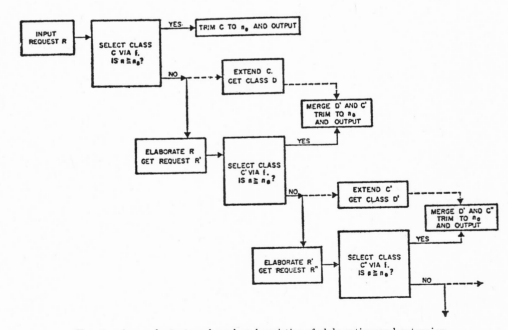

Fig. 1. A search strategy based on heuristics of elaboration and extension.

from *Science News Letter* was dictated to a large extent by the fact that these articles are relatively brief, pithy, clearly written, interesting, and easy to index by non-experts. This made not only the indexing but the subsequent evaluation of retrieved documents a reasonably uncomplicated task.

Since the methods of Probabilistic Indexing are applicable to any indexing system, we were not limited in our choice of a set of tags to be used. The only constraint was that the number of tags in the index list be comparable with the size of the library. Instead of "truncating" an existing index system and using its tags to index the documents, we adopt the following procedure: Each document was read and the key content-bearing words were selected and listed. There were a total of 577 different keywords (as they are called) in the list. These words were sorted into categories on the basis of their meanings. It turned out that the keywords could be sorted into 47 fairly well-defined categories. In many cases a particular keyword could belong to more than one category; consequently, there were 919 occurrences of the keywords in the 47 categories. The names of the 47 categories became the tags that constituted an index term list. These 47 index terms were then assigned to the documents by working backwards as follows: For each category we determined which keywords it contained and each document which contained the keyword in question was coordinated to the corresponding category. That is to say, given the categories, the keywords in each category, and the documents associated with each of the keywords, we then were able to determine which documents should be coordinated with each category, and thus the documents were indexed by assigning to each the names of the corresponding categories. Next, Probabilistic Indexing requires that we indicate the degree with which each tag holds for the document by assigning weights to the index terms. In order to assign the corresponding weight, each document was reread and then the indexer decided for each of the tags coordinated to each document the degree with which it held. We had decided previously that an adequate set of values for the weights was eighths, i.e., the values $1/8, \ldots , 8/8$.

5.3 Experimental Evaluation of the Measure of Relevance

The problem which we now consider is: How well does our relevance number perform in ranking documents according to relevance? First, we must be careful to distinguish a user's information need N from his request formulation R. In a real library system N will never be known, only its description R in a rather artificial language, viz., a Boolean function whose variables are index terms. The library indexing system only relates documents to this request language, but we want to relate documents to information need. A bridge between request language and information need is through statistical data relating library users with the utility they derive from documents. Such statistical data are given by the a priori probability distribution. This is shown by the theoretical development which states that the probability of a document satisfying the request, i.e., the probability of a document giving the desired information item N, is proportional to the product of the a priori probability $(P(A,D_i))$ and the value $(w_i(R))$ of the extended weight function[13] for the request describing that need. In a sense then, this quantity is a measure of the degree of relevance of a document for the information need of the requestor. We say "in a sense" because of its unavoidable probabilistic nature. It is a *probabilistic estimate* of the relevance of a document for the information need of the requestor. With this qualification in mind we call this quantity "relevance to information need" or "probable relevance." We have:

$$(\text{relevance to information need}) \sim P(A,D_i) \cdot w_i(R) \quad (23)$$

We conjecture that our computational procedure for computing the values of the extended weight function is a measure of "relevance to request formulation." We will present the supporting data in subsequent sections, but in anticipation of this we state the result. The inverse inference theorem plus experimental data implies.

$$(\text{relevance to information need}) \sim P(A,D_i) \quad (24)$$
$$(\text{relevance to request formulation})$$

5.3.1 The Result Predicted by the Inverse Inference Theorem

The content of the inverse inference theorem (formula (23)) can be illustrated by the following hypothetical experiment: Consider a document in the experimental library. It consists of many information items. Select one of these. Let a library user describe this item in the library request language. Let the library system now operate on the request, producing a collection of documents. (If the library indexing system is adequate and the formulation of the request is accurate, the original document from which the information item was derived should appear in this retrieved collection.) We now ask the library user to prepare a list:

L_1: the retrieved documents ranked according to relevance to the information item

We ask another person to prepare a second list:

L_2: the retrieved documents ranked according to relevance to the request formulation

To facilitate the processing of this comparative data, we ask that the documents be classified into five categories:

13. See Appendix.

I. Very Relevant; II Relevant; III Somewhat Relevant; IV. Only Slightly Relevant; V. Irrelevant.

Suppose now we simulate an a priori probability distribution and repeat the above experiment many times, each time selecting a document (from which to obtain an information item) by using the simulated distribution. For each request we obtain lists L_1 and L_2 and third list L_3:

L_3: the retrieved documents ranked according to the magnitude $P(A,D_i) \cdot w_i(R)$

The inverse inference theorem now tells us what we may expect to find, namely, that the list L_3 will agree with list L_1 *in the long run*. More precisely, for each instance of a particular request R there are many information items (or needs) that would be formulated by R, one for each requestor who uses R. If for each list L_1 that originated with these requestors we computed the mean relevance evaluation for each document in L_1 by using the category numbers I, II, III, IV, V, then the resulting ranking should agree with list L_3.

5.3.2 The Experimental Design

The result predicted above is difficult to test empirically because it would require such a large sample, but an experiment designed on a much smaller scale can give us some valuable information. Since it is designed primarily to test both the basic selection process and the search strategy by elaborating the request as well as the computational schema for $w_i(R)$, a flat a priori probability distribution is assumed, i.e., all $P(A,D_i)$ are taken to be equal. The significance of this for the probable relevance concept is clear by looking at formula (23).

$$\text{(relevance to information need)} \sim w_i(R). \quad (25)$$

The interpretation of this by the phrase "in the long run" still holds, however. That is, we would not expect a single list of type L_1 to compare with its corresponding list of type L_3 (this last being the ranking of documents by the values $w_i(R)$ in the case of equal $P(A,D_i)$). This can be seen by noting that as the information need becomes more specific the evaluations in a list of type L_1 would tend to split into the two classifications of Very Relevant or Irrelevant, but the ranking by the values of $w_i(R)$ always varies gradually. On the other hand, a list of type L_2 might conceivably be expected to agree with the list L_3 in a single case. This is the content of the experimental result stated in subsection 5.3.1.

5.3.3 Hypothesis to be Tested

We can formulate our goal as that of attempting to confirm that the value $w_i(R)$ that we compute for each document selected by a given request is, in fact, a measure of relevance with respect to the request formulation. If our basic notion is correct, it implies the following hypothesis which we call H_1.

H_1: if a document is relevant to a request, then a high number $w_i(R)$ will be derived for it.

How to verify, confirm, test this hypothesis empirically? We did the following: A number of documents from our experimental library were selected at random and for each document a question was formulated which could be answered by reading the corresponding document. Several persons who acted as test subjects were briefed as to the nature of the library, the indexing system, etc., given a set of questions and asked to formulate a library request for information on the basis of which, hopefully, relevant documents would be retrieved (so as to answer the question). Given the library requests that these test subjects formulated, we proceeded to search and select the accession numbers of those documents satisfying the logic of the request. For each request a list of documents (i.e., a list of the corresponding accession numbers) was generated, and the documents in the lists were ranked according to the number $w_i(R)$ that was computed for each. We then examined each list to determine whether or not the so-called "answer" document was on the list, and if it was we recorded its relative position on the list. We made the (natural) assumption that the answer document (i.e., the document on the basis of which the question was formulated) would be relevant to the request. We then determined the number of times that the correct answer document retrieved was associated with a high number $w_i(R)$. The results can be summarized as follows: 40 library requests were made, and in 27 cases the answer document was retrieved. The number of documents on the output lists ranged from a minimum of one (in four cases) to a maximum of 41. In the majority of the 23 cases which contained more than a single document, the answer document appeared towards the top of the list.

The results showed that if the answer document was on a list, then it was computed to have a high number $w_i(R)$ in most of the cases. This evidence thus supports the hypothesis H_1, which asserts that if a document is relevant a high value $w_i(R)$ will be computed for it. However, it was not always the case that the answer document was computed to have the highest number; i.e., there were documents other than the answer document for which a high number was derived. Thus, the question arises: "If a document has a high number $w_i(R)$, is it relevant to the request?" This represents the converse of the original hypothesis H_1. We shall form this as an hypothesis and call it H_2.

H_2: if a document has a high number $w_i(R)$, then it is relevant to the corresponding request.

If we can confirm H_2 as well as H_1 we will have, in fact, confirmed an hypothesis H^* which is stronger than each.

H^*: the methods of Probabilistic Indexing will derive a high number $w_i(R)$ for an arbitrary document *if* and *only if* the document in question is relevant to the request.

In order to determine if there were relevant documents other than the answer document on a list, we had to have evaluation data from the users themselves. We obtained a sample of this information from the test subjects in the following way: Four test subjects were given the actual documents corresponding to the retrieval lists, and they were asked to read each document and decide whether they considered it to be Very Relevant, Relevant, Somewhat Relevant, Only Slightly Relevant or Irrelevant. Thus for each document retrieved they would judge to which of these five categories it belonged, and we in turn compared their judgments with the numbers $w_i(R)$ which we had computed for each document. A fifth person prepared control lists, i.e., evaluations for the same requests.

In order to facilitate the comparison we standardized the values $w_i(R)$; i.e., we multiplied each value by the reciprocal of the highest value to force the numbers on each list to vary from 1 to 0, — 0 being the value assigned to unretrieved documents. We also divided the numbers into three categories: *high* (value equal to or greater than 0.75), *medium* (value between 0.75 and 0.25), and *low* (value equal to or less than 0.25). The results show quite definitely that if a document had a high number $w_i(R)$ that document was judged by the evaluator as Very Relevant or Relevant, in most cases. Conversely, if the number $w_i(R)$ was low, the evaluators rated the corresponding document as either Only Slightly Relevant or Irrelevant in most cases.

Thus the data support the following: "If a document is relevant to a request, then there is a strong probability that the document will have a high number $w_i(R)$ computed for it." Furthermore, the data support the converse; viz., "If a document is computed to have a high number $w_i(R)$, there is a strong probability that it is relevant to the request." Thus the data support both H_1 and H_2, and taken jointly we see that the data do support and confirm the stronger hypothesis H^*; viz., a high number $w_i(R)$ will be derived if and only if the document in question is relevant to the request. The details of the analysis show how the values $w_i(R)$ associated with these documents were distributed among the five categories. Computing the average value and the variance in each of the five categories, we obtained the following results.

Document Rating	Mean	Variance
I. Very Relevant	0.81	0.043
II. Relevant	0.72	0.053
III. Somewhat Relevant	0.54	0.043
IV. Only Slightly Relevant	0.40	0.110
V. Irrelevant	0.18	0.013

Thus we see that the values of the numbers that we computed decrease, on the average, as we go from category I (Very Relevant) to category V (Irrelevant).

Although this result tends to confirm our hypotheses H_1, H_2, and H^*, we prefer to look deeper into the situation. Let us call categories I or II simply "Relevant" and category V, as before, "Irrelevant." Note that Relevant and Irrelevant are not negations of each other since we have the intermediate categories III and IV consisting of documents neither totally Relevant nor Irrelevant. Now the hypotheses H_1, H_2, H^* say two things:

1. Relevant is equivalent to High.
2. Irrelevant is equivalent to Low.

Also these hypotheses imply two weaker statements:

3. Relevant implies not-Low.
4. Irrelevant implies not-High.

The statistical confirmation of these statements can be accomplished by using the theory of the coefficient of association between predicates as outlined in section 2.6. That is to say, each of the statements above calls for a study of a matrix of the kind defined on p. 301, i.e., a sorting of the total class of retrieved documents according to the properties:

1. Relevant and High
2. Irrelevant and Low
3. Relevant and Low
4. Irrelevant and High

We would expect to find the Q-values in (1) and (2) to be near $+1$ (maximum positive association), and the Q-values in (3) and)4) near -1 (maximum negative association). These values are in fact:

$$Q(\text{Relevant, High}) = +0.70$$
$$Q(\text{Irrelevant, Low}) = +0.90$$
$$Q(\text{Relevant, Low}) = -0.92$$
$$Q(\text{Irrelevant, High}) = -1.00$$

Since these values are fairly sensitive, we introduce a control on the study by assuming that these predicates are statistically independent, then computing the probabilities of the Q-values having been as close or closer to the anticipated values by chance. For the four distributions we calculate these control probabilities to be 0.041, 0.006, 0.010, 0.059, respectively.[14]

5.4 *Elaboration of the Selection Process*

5.4.1 *Initial Remarks*

The relevance number, as we have seen, provides a means of ranking documents according to their probable relevance. However, the solution to the problem of retrieval effectiveness involves more than ranking by relevance — it involves the proper selection of those documents which are to be ranked. Before we describe the results of the experiments that were conducted to

14. Precisely, if Relevant and High are independent, then the probability of their Q-value having the property $0.70 \leqq Q \leqq 1.00$ is 0.041 (similarly for the other classifications).

test our methods for improving the selection process, let us take one more look at the relevance number as a filter to eliminate low relevance documents. In particular, let us consider the usefulness of the relevance number on unelaborated requests.

In our experiments, 40 different library requests were made and a total of 379 documents were retrieved (using the basic process of selecting those documents whose tags are logically compatible with the logic and tags of the request). Let us compare the results of probabilistic searching and so-called "binary" or conventional searching. We can do this by assuming that all the tags which are assigned to documents with a nonzero weight are, in fact, assigned to the corresponding documents in the conventional system. Thus when the basic selection process is the same (viz., the unelaborated logical matching process), the same documents will be retrieved in both cases; however, in the conventional system the retrieved documents are not ranked by any criteria of relevance. For each of the retrieval lists if n documents have been retrieved and the answer document is present, then using the conventional search technique the requestor must read, on the average, $(n + 1)/2$ documents. If the answer document is not present, then all of the retrieved documents must be read (in order to determine that no relevant information was retrieved). These considerations (inadequate though they be, since they presuppose that only an answer document produces a satisfactory search result) give us a criterion with which to compare the probabilistic and binary searches. This criterion is the total number of documents that would have to be read for all 40 searches in order to find the answer documents. The results are as follows:

Type of Search	Total Number of Documents Retrieved	Total Number of Documents that would have to be Read
Binary	379	235
Probabilistic[15]	379	181

Thus we see that a conventional system would require the user to read approximately 30 percent more retrieved documents to obtain the same number of answer documents. These two different searches, each using the basic selection process, produced 27 answer documents out of a possible 40. Note that the binary search as defined above is more extensive than might be expected in the sense that we have used all the tags with nonzero weights as binary tags. In an actual conventional system those tags with a low weight would probably not be coordinated with documents. That is to say, the use of weighted tags encourages more tags to

15. A flat a priori probability distribution was used.

be applied to a given document than would be the case if weights were not allowed. In a previous study where documents were indexed independently by two different indexers, one using probabilistic indexing, the other using binary indexing (i.e., either a tag holds for a document or it does not), it was found than 70 percent more answer documents were retrieved in the probabilistic search and only 32 percent more documents had to be read.

The above comparison presupposes that the user is looking for some specific information (viz., the answer document) and that he knows when he has found it. It might be realistic to make no such assumption; therefore, let us consider the following comparison. Given a request for information, a probabilistic search is made, but beforehand we tell the user to read only those documents which have a computed relevance number greater than 0.5. That is to say, "before the facts" we give the requestors a guide to use in reading the 40 lists presented to them. It turns out that of the 379 documents in the 40 lists there are only 225 which have a relevance number greater than 0.5. Furthermore, it turns out that if the users had adopted the strategy of reading only those retrieved documents which had relevance numbers greater than 0.5, then they would have found 25 of the 27 answer documents.[16] Now compare this with the case of conventional retrieval where the users would have to read all of the 379 retrieved documents (since there is no way to distinguish between any two documents in the same list). In this latter case the users, of course, would find all 27 answer documents, but again at the "cost" of reading all 379 documents. Thus we see that a conventional system would require that users read 68.5 percent more documents than for the probabilistic system and they would gain only 7.4 percent in increased number of answer documents.

These considerations indicate that the relevance number can be used to filter out irrelevant material. That is to say, if we use the relevance number associated with documents to separate the relevant from the irrelevant, we are providing the user with a valuable tool.

5.4.2 Automatic Elaboration

We have described two methods for automatically elaborating upon the selection process which is involved in information searching. One method establishes a measure of distance in document space and the other method involves measures of closeness in request space. We shall not consider the former since as yet no experimental tests have been completed. For closeness in request space we have described three different statistical

16. In one of the two remaining cases the relevance number of the answer document was just under 0.5, and in the other case the answer document had a rather low number but it was third in a list of only three.

measures, viz., forward conditional probabilities, inverse conditional probabilities, and coefficients of association. We now raise the questions: "How good are the proposed statistical measures of closeness in elaborating upon a request?" and "Which of the three measures that have been discussed is the best?" Again, in the case of the automatically elaborated request we generate the new request R' given the initial request R by formulating the following type of disjunction for each tag in R:

$$\text{if } R = I_j, \quad \text{then} \quad R' = I_j \vee (a)I_j'$$

where a is the measure of closeness between I_j and I_j', and I_j' is the term that gives maximum a with respect to I_j. We would like to be able to establish the following:

(1) That the elaborated request catches relevant documents which are not selected by the original (unelaborated) request.

(2) That, although the elaborated request catches more documents, the relevance number can be used as a guide for eliminating the ones with low probable relevance.

5.4.3 Some Testing (Evaluation) Problems

Since we are really interested in the overall retrieval effectiveness of the selection process, we would like to know how many of the relevant documents in the entire library have been caught by the elaborated requests. In order to determine this it would be necessary for us to present the requestor the entire library so that he, in turn, could judge which relevant documents, if any, were not retrieved. That is to say, in order that a user properly judge whether or not he did, in fact, receive all relevant documents as the result of a search, he would have to be familiar with the entire contents of the library. Because of this difficulty, we see that such an evaluation would be impractical to conduct. We must, therefore, lower our sights and look for a substitute type of evaluation. The substitute that we have adopted consists in, again, using the answer documents as a measure of retrieval effectiveness. That is to say, since we *know* that the answer documents are relevant, we can automatically elaborate upon those original requests which did not catch the answer document in order to see whether the elaborated request succeeds in retrieving it. Such a test would allow us to establish some measure of the retrieval effectiveness of the automatic elaboration procedures. We can compare the total number of documents for the elaborated requests with what would be the case for the unelaborated request. This we have done and the results are discussed in the following section.

5.4.4 Results and Their Evaluation

Of the 40 requests that were made, the answer document was retrieved in 27 cases and it was not retrieved in 13 cases. We conducted three different types of elaborated requests for each of the 40 cases. The results are as follows:

1. Using the method of request elaboration via forward conditional probabilities between index tags, we retrieved the correct answer document in 32 cases out of the 40.

2. Elaborating the requests via the inverse conditional probability heuristic, we retrieved the correct document in 33 of the 40 cases.

3. Using the coefficient of association to obtain the elaborated request, we obtained success in 33 cases of the 40.

Thus we see that the automatic elaboration of a request does, in fact, catch relevant documents that were not retrieved by the original request.

We now raise the question: "Because of the small size of the library and the large percent of the total library that is selected by the elaborated request, are the above results statistically significant?" That is to say, what is the probability of doing as well or better just by selecting at random, for each of the 13 requests for which the answer document was not originally retrieved, a sample of size equal to that given by the elaborated requests. We have made the corresponding calculations and it turns out that probability of doing as well or better by chance is less than 0.034 for both the forward and inverse conditional probability elaborations and less than 0.001 for the coefficient of association search. Thus the above results are indeed statistically significant.

Could the number of answer documents have been improved? That is, could 40 out of 40 answer documents have been retrieved? We looked at the seven cases for which the answer document was not retrieved when elaborating via the coefficient of association, and in three cases the indexing was at fault. That is to say, in three of the seven cases the answer document was poorly indexed (a fact of life that must be faced by all libraries). In one case the request formulation was very poor and no reasonable elaboration would help. In one case the answer document was caught by a different heuristic (viz., the forward conditional), and in the remaining two cases, again, the requests suffered by being poorly formulated.

Now consider the fact that, although the automatic elaboration of a request does catch relevant documents that would not otherwise have been selected, it also increases the total number of retrieved documents. (We point out at this time that of the three heuristics which we considered, the one which elaborated via the coefficient of association gave the greatest ratio of answer documents to total documents retrieved.) In order to have the advantages of an elaborated request (namely, the relevant documents that it obtains) and in order to avoid the disadvantages (namely, the larger number of total documents), we now introduce the relevance number to truncate the output lists. That is to say, we use the relevance numbers to separate out the highly relevant from the less relevant documents by adopting the following rule: Only those documents which are selected by the elaborated request and which have a standardized relevance number greater than 0.5 are to be retrieved. Our experiments with the coefficient of association heuristic show that of a total of 661 documents that were selected by the elaborated requests only 446 (or 67.5 per cent) have a standardized relevance number greater[17] than 0.5. Furthermore, if we adopt this rule, then 32 out of the 33 (or 97 per cent of the) answer documents which are selected by the automatic elaboration would still be retrieved; i.e., 32 of the 33 answer documents had relevance numbers greater than 0.5.

We conclude by observing that to a very large degree the procedures for automatically elaborating upon a request are empirical; i.e., their development and refinement must rest on further empirical testing and experimentation. Hopefully the results of further tests will shed light on and provide new insights into the difficult and intriguing problems of information identification, search, and retrieval.

Appendix

Extension of the Weight Function

Before looking at the computational procedure for deriving the relevance number given any arbitrary request R, we must explain the meaning of the language of the request. We allow two logical operations between index terms, viz., "and" and "or." We abbreviate "I_1 or I_2" by "$I_1 \vee I_2$," "I_1 and I_2" by "$I_1.I_2$"; the first is called a disjunctive request, the second, a conjunctive request. The different interpretations of the logical combinations $I_1.I_2$, $I_1 \vee I_2$, as used in request formulations are shown in Table I. Note how the "$\vee$" in side a retrieval prescription becomes an "and" in the retrieval instructions. We can say that a disjunctive request is actually several requests, but the searches are to be conducted simultaneously.

17. For the computations we used a flat a priori probability distribution.

By extending the notation for a request to include logical combination of tags, we can consider every request R (i.e., every Boolean function of index terms) as an event class. For example, $R = I_j$, $R = I_j. I_k$, $R = I_j \vee I_k$, etc. We have shown that if it is possible to compute $P(A.D_i,R)$ then we can rank documents according to probable relevance by taking the relevance number to be

$$P(A,D_i) \cdot P(A.D_i,R);$$

for, by the inverse probability calculation

$$P(A.R,D_i) = \left(\frac{1}{P(A,R)}\right) \cdot P(A,D_i) \cdot P(A.D_i,R), \quad (1)$$

so that $P(A.R,D_i)$ is proportional to $P(A,D_i) \cdot P(A.D_i,R)$. Now we note that $P(A.D_i,R)$ is an *extension* of the modified weight function in the sense that:
If $R = I_j$, then

$$w_{ij} = w_i(R) = P(A.D_i,R). \quad (2)$$

Thus the problem is to extend the function $w_i(I_j)$, whose values are given only for $I_1, \ldots, I_n$, to any Boolean function of these terms. We denote this extension by $w_i(R)$ and we require this extension to satisfy the rules of probability since we intend for it to be an estimate of $P(A.D_i,R)$. In particular, we require:

$$0 \leq w_i(R) \leq 1, \quad (3)$$
$$w_i(I_1.I_2) \leq w_i(I_1), \quad (4)$$
$$w_i(I_1 \vee I_2) + w_i(I_1.I_2) = w_i(I_1) + w_i(I_2). \quad (5)$$

We note the important fact that (5) allows us to compute the weight of a disjunction if the weight of a conjunction is known. Successive applications of (5), combined with logical transformations, allow the weight of any request to be written as sums and differences of weights of single terms or conjunctions. Thus the problem of the extension of the weight function is reduced to the extension to conjunctions. For these weights we also have certain restrictive conditions. If we let $p = w_i(I_1)$ and $q = w_i(I_2)$, then it can be shown that $w_1(I_1.I_2)$ must be less than or equal to the minimum of

TABLE I

Interpretation of Logical Connectives

Request:	$I_1.I_2$	$I_1 \vee I_2$
Logical meaning	User requests information on the "subject" designated by $I_1.I_2$	User requests information on the "subject" designated by $I_1 \vee I_2$
Retrieval instruction meaning	Search for documents indexed under I_1 and I_2	Search for documents indexed under I_1 *and* search for documents indexed under I_2
Class meaning	User obtains documents indexed under both I_1 and I_2	User obtains documents indexed under I_1 or I_2 or both

the two numbers p and q and must be greater than or equal to $p + q - 1$ if this is positive, otherwise it must be greater than or equal to 0. We write this condition as

$$\max[0, p+q-1] \leqq w_i(I_1.I_2) \leqq \min[p,q]. \quad (6)$$

We have decided to take as the initial w-value of a conjunction its independence value, i.e.,

$$w_i(I_1.I_2) = w_{i1} \cdot w_{i2}. \quad (7)$$

The relevance number for a conjunction $I_1.I_2$ is then given by

$$P(A,D_i) \cdot w_{i1} \cdot w_{i2},$$

and the relevance number for a disjunction $I_1 \vee I_2$ becomes by (5)

$$P(A,D_i) \cdot [w_{i1} + w_{i2} - w_{i1} \cdot w_{i2}].$$

Several remarks need to be made about use of the independence value. Note that we do not say that the tags are independent — in fact they are not — but the word "estimate" is useful to avoid making a false assumption. First, we estimate $w_i(I_1.I_2)$ by $w_{i1} \cdot w_{i2}$. Second, we use the independence value relative to the class D_i, that is, we take

$$P(A.D_i.I_1.I_2) = P(A.D_i.I_2), \quad (8)$$

but not

$$P(A.I_1.I_2) = P(A.I_2). \quad (9)$$

We believe the former estimate is more accurate than the latter. In section 4.5 we discussed a coefficient of association between index terms. This coefficient Q lies in the interval $[-1, 1]$ with $Q = 0$ being the point of independence. The joint occurrence of two events will have a probability in excess of its independence value only if the corresponding value of Q is positive. We have two intervals to schematize this situation (p and q are the probabilities of the separate events and Q their coefficient of association):

```
┌─────────────────────┐
0        Q →         1
```

Interval of Positive Association

```
┌─────────────────────┐
```
$p \cdot q \uparrow$ Probability $\rightarrow$ $\uparrow \min[p,q]$
Corresponding Interval of Probability Value

An investigation of the statistical correlation between tags via the computation of Q and then a subsequent study of which pairs of tags were used in requesting shows that Q had positive values for almost all of these pairs. This indicated that computations were called for with estimates of $w_i(I_1.I_2)$ taken at the upper end of the scale, i.e., where

$$w_i(I_1.I_2) = \min[w_{i1}, w_{i2}]. \quad (10)$$

The results were not as successful as when using the independence value. A possible explanation lies in noting that independence is a three-term relation as formulas (8) and (9) show. It could well be that the probability value for tags I_1 and I_2 relative to the reference class A lies closer to the maximum value ($\min[p, q]$), while the probability value for I_1 and I_2 relative to $A.D_i$ lies closer to its independence value. In our computations we have assumed this to be the case.

29 Word-Word Associations in Document Retrieval Systems

M. E. LESK
American Documentation
Vol. 20, No. 1, January, 1969

1 Introduction

Word normalization procedures in document retrieval systems traditionally use manually constructed thesauri and term lists. Recently automatic methods dependent on statistical co-occurrence of words have been proposed for the determination of word meanings and the selection of synonymous words, and it has been asserted that the use of such word-occurrence statistics can substitute for thesauri in retrieval systems (1, 2).

Word association procedures can be investigated through the SMART automatic document retrieval system, which is capable of simulating a wide variety of proposed computerized text analysis systems in an experimental retrieval environment (3, 4). Completely automatic processing of text and questions followed by the evaluation of the test results by a variety of performance measures is easily performed. Existing test collections and dictionaries are used to analyze and evaluate the performance of association procedures for document retrieval.

This research was supported in part by the National Science Foundation under grant GN-495.

2 Method

In the SMART retrieval programs, documents are translated into "concept vectors" consisting of a list of concepts with attached weights. Each concept represents a piece of information found in the text by the analysis routines, and the weight reflects the number of times it was found and the importance attached to it. The concepts may represent words, groups of synonymous words, phrases, or anything else reflecting the content of documents. In a word matching system, for example, each English stem is a concept, and the number of occurrences of a stem is its weight. The concept vector then represents a frequency list of the words in the text or query. Retrieval tests are performed by matching queries against documents to find the documents with the most similar concept vectors.

To simulate a word-word association process, the concept vectors of the requests and documents are augmented by concepts found to be related to the original concepts. The association procedures construct a list of strongly associated word pairs. All the words paired with each word in the concept vector of a document are added to that concept vector. The expanded concept vector is used for retrieval in exactly the same fashion as the original concept vector, and the results compared.

Related word pairs are determined by the following algorithm. For each word in the document collection, a list of the documents in which it has occurred and its frequency is compiled. For each pair of words, the corresponding lists are compared and a measure of similarity between the two concepts evaluated. The normal measure of similarity is the "cosine" correlation, defined by

$$r_{ij} = \Sigma_k \, w_{ik} w_{jk} / \sqrt{\Sigma_k \, w^2_{ik} \cdot \Sigma_k \, w^2_{jk}}$$

where w_{ik} is the weight of word i in document k, and r_{ij} is the correlation between concept i and concept j. Alternatively, the "overlap correlation" may be used; it is defined as

$$r_{ij} = \Sigma_k \min(w_{ik}, w_{jk}) / \min(\Sigma_k \, w_{ik}, \Sigma_k \, w_{jk})$$

Experiments with both correlation coefficients, however, produce only very small differences in performance in association retrieval runs, and the cosine correlation alone is used in all further tests in this paper. An example of the correlation procedure is shown in Table 1. All pairs of words whose correlation exceeds a previously set cutoff are used as associated pairs in the expansion procedure.

Many options are available in this procedure. The cutoff may be adjusted arbitrarily; the procedure may be iterated, with word similarities measured by the correlation of the lists of related words determined by the previous iteration; the weights with which the new words are added to the concept vector may be changed; and words occurring outside specified frequency ranges may be omitted from the procedure.

Experiments were performed on three document collections, all used for many SMART experiments. The Cranfield collection, 200 abstracts in aeronautics collected by the Aslib-Cranfield project in England, is used for most of the investigation. Evaluation is based on a set of 42 actual research questions, with relevance judgments by the researcher himself. The other collections are the IRE collection, consisting of about 780 abstracts in computer science, and the ADI collection of 82 short papers in documentation. These collections have prepared questions with relevance judgments by the authors.

The major procedures used for evaluation in the SMART system have been described earlier (3, 4). They are the recall-precision curve and four measures: rank recall, log precision, normalized recall, and normalized precision. The measures vary from 0.0 to 1.0, with 0.0 representing the worst possible performance and 1.0 representing perfect performance. These measures all reflect both recall and precision, requiring perfect recall and perfect precision to produce a value of 1.0; but the rank recall and normalized recall measures both reflect recall more than precision, while the log and normalized precision reflect precision more strongly. The "quasi-Cleverdon" recall-precision curves shown here are recall-precision curves averaged over the set of 42 requests.

TABLE 1. Example of concept-concept association procedure

a. Document—Term assignment

			Document		
	1	2	3	4	5
Terms	cat	cat	cat	dog	dog
	dog	lion	bear	lion	bear
	fish	mouse	tiger	wolf	mole
	mouse	bird			

b. Term—Document assignment

					Term					
	cat	dog	fish	mouse	lion	bird	bear	tiger	wolf	mole
Occurs in	1,2,3	1,4,5	1	1,2	2,4	2	3,5	3	4	5

c. Computations of association

	Cosine	Overlap
$r_{cat, \, dog}$	$(1 + 0 +)/\sqrt{(1 + 1 + 1)(1 + 1 + 1)}$ $= 1/3 = 0.33$	$1/3 = 0.33$
$r_{cat, \, mouse}$	$(1 + 1)/\sqrt{3.2}$ $= 2/\sqrt{6} = 0.82$	$1/2 = 0.50$

For a cutoff of 0.45, "cat" would be found related to "mouse" but not to "dog." The vector of document 3, after expansion, would then include "cat, bear, tiger, mouse."

3 Results

Table 2 shows the distribution of associated word pairs as a function of word frequency, using the cosine correlation at a cutoff of 0.6. The largest number of correlations is between words of very low frequency (1 or 2). With the correlation measure used it is very easy for low frequency words to appear highly correlated, since any pair of words, each with frequency 1, which happen to occur in the same document are given a correlation of 1.0. With a collection size of 200 and with 1179 words occurring only once, there will be over 7000 correlations above cutoff of words of frequency 1 purely from random associations. If words of frequency 2 are also considered, the total number of random correlations above 0.6 would be about 12,000. The observed 18,000 associations are not significant data, therefore, but largely chance. Since these correlations could represent a major part of expanded document vectors, they might seriously perturb the run. To eliminate these chance correlations, all correlations involving a word occurring fewer than three times are removed from our retrieval runs. The expected number of chance correlations above cutoff, among words of three occurrences, is only 1 or 2.

TABLE 2. Word-word associations tabulated by word frequency

Frequency of one word of the pair	Number of words of that frequency	Number of pairs	Average number of pairs per word	Approx. weight in text expansion	Percent weight in expansion
1	1179	18894	16.0	18900	17
2	382	6924	18.1	13800	12
3	199	1855	9.3	5600	5
4	126	1003	8.0	4000	4
5	103	957	9.3	4800	4
6	83	588	7.1	3500	3
7	61	554	9.1	3800	3
8	55	416	7.6	3300	3
9	41	254	6.2	2300	2
10	34	229	6.7	2300	2
11–14	87	819	9.4	9800	9
15–19	54	293	5.4	5300	5
20–29	86	481	5.6	12000	11
30–39	43	87	2.0	3000	3
40–49	25	101	4.0	4500	4
50–59	18	105	5.8	5800	5
60–69	13	32	2.5	2100	2
70–79	8	3	0.4	200	0
80–89	7	34	4.9	2900	3
90–99	6	2	0.3	200	0
100–124	6	5	0.8	600	1
125–149	5	39	7.8	5400	5
150–174	1	0	0.0	0	0
175–199	2	1	0.5	200	0
200+	4	4	1.0	1000	1
All	2628	28680	10.91	111500	100

Complete elimination of chance associations requires the removal not only of very rare words but also of very frequent words. The expected random correlation between two words, each occurring in 100 documents, (half the collection) is about 0.5, close to cutoff. Associations between more frequent words are therefore also deleted from retrieval runs.

The remaining associations represent nonrandom word co-occurrences. This does not necessarily imply that the words are related semantically. Co-occurrences also result from quirks of an author's style or from peculiarities of word usage with document collections. Since it has been suggested that word associations can be used instead of thesauri, it is important to know whether word-word pairs produced by an association process reflect semantic meanings accurately.

To investigate semantic properties, a list of word-word associations from a collection in aerodynamics (the Cranfield collection mentioned earlier) was prepared and analyzed for significance. The cutoff was 0.6 (cosine method). Word pairs were judged as significant or nonsignificant; significant pairs were those which seemed to be composed of semantically related words. The words are judged to be semantically related if they would normally be used together in discussions of the same topic, considering the most common technical definitions of the words. For example, "per" and "cent" is considered a significant pair; so is "atmosphere" and "satellite." On the other hand, "machine" and "evaluating" is judged nonsignificant; so is "km" and "200," or "leading" and "edge." There is a great deal of subjectivity in such decisions, but all were made by the author and are believed reasonably consistent.

All the word pairs are classified by frequency of components and by correlation. The resulting table is then examined to see if any combination of parameters yields a particularly high ratio of significant to nonsignificant associations. Overall only 16.2% of all associations are judged significant. Figure 1 and Table 3 show the variation of significance with correlation level. There is a small increase in the fraction of pairs judged significant

TABLE 3. Effect of correlation level on significance

Cutoff	Significance %	Number of pairs
.6–.7	15.6	185
.7–.8	16.0	75
.8–.9	17.3	52
.9–1.0	20.0	20
All	16.2	332

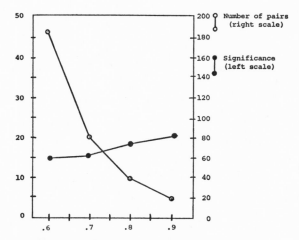

FIG. 1. Variation of significance with cutoff

at higher correlations, but the number of correlations above cutoff decreases so rapidly as the cutoff is increased that this is not a practical way of improving the quality of information produced by the association scheme. Even at a cutoff of 0.9 (which means that if two words occurred five times each, all five would have to be co-occurrences; or if each occurred ten times, nine would have to be co-occurrences) only 20% of the correlations were judged significant. High cutoffs should not be used in the word-word association process if the aim is to recover a sizable number of significant pairs.

Classification by word frequency also yields no particularly superior choice of options. Table 4 shows the variation of significance with the frequencies of the words in the associated pair. High frequency words, as might be expected, show somewhat more reliable relationships; but the amount of statistical scatter in this corner of the table (since the number of high-frequency words is so small) makes the numbers doubtful. In any event, even the best numbers (e.g., correlations of words above 20 occurrences, based on eight pairs) are relatively poor; only 37% are significant relations. There is, in short,

TABLE 4. Dependence of word-pair significance on word frequency as shown by percentage of significant correlations

Frequency of words	Frequency of words							
	3	4	5–6	7–8	9–10	11–19	20+	All*
3	19	10	11	13	16	14	15	14
4		0	9	0	40	18	20	12
5–6			12	33	16	22	19	21
7–8				0	0	20	0	5
9–10					0	43	25	25
11–19						50	29	33
20+							37	37

* The "all" column shows the percentage of significant correlations among all pairs which have the frequency of their lower frequency word indicated by the row frequency, not the percentage among all pairs with a word of the indicated frequency either as maximum or minimum frequency component.

no choice of frequency or correlation cutoff which will yield reliably significant pairs. Examination of more complete tables showing both frequency and correlation dependence of significance also discloses no particularly good combination. It is believed, then, that for a collection of this size (40,000 words) the statistical association process cannot be used to yield reliable indications of generalized word meanings.

Confirmation of this comes by comparison of word association pairs with dictionaries, phrase lists, and hierarchies. The IRE collection, for which a thesaurus of 700 concepts and about 3000 stems, a phrase list of 400 entries, and a complete hierarchy exist, is used for this test. A word-word association run was performed and the pairs checked against all these dictionaries. The association process identifies only 1 pair which is considered synonymous by the thesaurus; no pairs are considered phrases in the phrase dictionary; and only 2 pairs even represent words which are directly related through the hierarchy.

An investigation of larger collections also proved fruitless. A collection of 110,000 words (the ADI collection) yields 19.7% significant associations, ranging from about 10% in the lower frequency ranges to 50% in the higher frequency ranges. Because of the longer documents in this collection, though, these results are not properly comparable with those from collections of abstracts, and further work on such longer collections is needed to determine whether reliable word relationships can be obtained from longer collections.

Since few of the word associations represent obvious semantic relationships, it may well be asked what they do arise from. Usually, they represent relations of "local" semantic meanings peculiar to this collection of documents. That is, the meaning of a word in one particular document collection may differ widely from the normal meaning of the word. When the meanings of the words within the collection are considered, it is found that about 73.1% of the pairs are significant. For example, consider the associated pair "scheme" and "machine." This was rated nonsignificant, since the words in their normal technical meanings are not related. However, the 10 occurrences of the word "machine" in the collection all imply "digital computing machine"; although the collection discusses compressors, engines, etc., none of these is referred to as "machines." The "local meaning" of "machine" is therefore "computer." Similarly, the major local meaning of "scheme" turns out to be "algorithm" (to be used in a digital computer program). Clearly "algorithm" and "computer" is a significant pair.

To determine the fraction of significant pairs with local interpretations, the list of pairs was rechecked, with each word looked up in a concordance of the text to determine its true local meaning. The results are shown as a function of frequency in Table 5 and as a function of cutoff in Table 6. Nearly three-quarters of the pairs are now meaningful. The remaining pairs which are not

TABLE 5. Significant associations using local pairs as shown by percentage of significant correlations

Frequency of words	Frequency of words							
	3	4	5–6	7–8	9–10	11–19	20+	All
3	61	55	59	73	83	77	77	68
4		67	65	80	80	82	70	72
5–6			100	80	79	78	78	81
7–8				67	100	100	64	78
9–10					50	100	100	94
11–19						50	67	63
20+							88	88

composed of related words are generally stylistic quirks. For example, the word "addition" is used only as part of the phrase "in addition," which appears in only a few abstracts. The word "addition" is thus associated with the other words in these abstracts even though it has no significant meaning in this collection.

Nonsignificant pairs are also derived simply from accidental preferences by one particular author for certain words. If one abstract contains many instances of one word, a few instances of another word in the same abstract may appear to be a major amount of overlap.

The majority of associations, though, are locally significant pairs. About three-fourths of the associations fall into this category, and only 20% are significant in the absolute sense. (Additional explanations of local meanings are given in Table 7a, and a sample list of word pairs with significance judgments is shown in Table 7b.) As a result of this peculiarity of the association process, it is not directly useful for determining word pairs that should be connected in a thesarus; but it can point out word relations not normally apparent and thus serve as an aid to dictionary constructors.

These experiments were run on collections of 40,000 words. In larger collections the apparent meanings of words may approximate their common meanings more closely. This will be the subject of future investigation, but the presence of apparently meaningless correlations has already been noted in larger collections (5).

The properties of second-order associations were also investigated. These are word pairs which need not co-occur in any documents but rather have common first-order associations. Almost all second-order associations,

TABLE 6. Effect of correlation level on local significance

Cutoff	Percent significant	Number of pairs
.6–.7	71	185
.7–.8	79	75
.8–.9	76	52
.9–1.0	95	20
All	71	332

TABLE 7a. Associated pairs with local meanings

Word₁	Word₂	Local usage₁	Local usage₂
km	density	altitude in earth's atmosphere	density of air in atmosphere
km	200	altitude in earth's atmosphere	height in km of atmospheric phenomena
cold	turbojet	temperature of exhaust from jet engine	turbojet
models	wire	models	material of which models are built
eccentricity	contracts	ellipticity of satellite orbit	contraction of satellite orbit
leading	edge	leading edge of shock tube front	front in shock tube

however, were first-order associated terms. They generally arise from large blocks of words, all of which were used to discuss some subject, and all of which were first-order associations of each other. For example, the words "height," "atmosphere," "density," "km," etc. are used in a set of documents about the measurement of the density of the upper atmosphere. They were all first-order associations, and all became second-order associations. Stylistic quirks were not eliminated by the repetition of the association process; and the total number of pairs was diminished by a factor of from 8 to 10. Second-order associations did not produce useful synonyms; even the one or two complete synonyms in the first-order associations (e.g., "error," as in "error function," and "erfc," its abbreviation) tended to disappear in second-order. The use of second-order associations appears to offer no ad-

TABLE 7b. Examples of word-word associations with significance judgments

Word pair		Significance	
		Overall	Local
absorption	diurnal		
accepted	fractions		
addition	entering	x	
addition	rate	x	
afterbodies	reaction		
background	beam		x
beam	view		x
believed	extremely		
blade-to-blade	rear		
blasius	erfc	x	x
centrifugal	impeller		x
channels	compressibility		x
check	multiple		x
check	reflection		x
complementary	threepoint		

vantages over first-order associations and loses a great amount of material.

It is therefore concluded that the use of associative procedures for the determination of word meaning in a general sense is not advisable with moderate sized collections, since the vast majority of the associations produced reflect specific local meanings of words. No choice of word frequencies or associative procedures appears to offer a way around this difficulty.

4 Retrieval Experiments

Although the association process is not suited for investigations of absolute word meanings, it is nevertheless useful in retrieval systems. Figure 2 shows a comparison between word-word association retrieval runs and straight word stem matching for three collections. It is seen that for two of the collections (the ADI and IRE collections) the improvement offered by associative strategies is only over small ranges and doubtfully significant. For the Cranfield collection the associative strategy shows a definite superiority.

The purpose of the associative method, originally, is to produce word relations missed by the stem matching procedure, and thus take the place of a synonym list or thesaurus. It would be expected that such a procedure would be a recall-oriented device. However, this is not quite what happens. Associative procedures improve performance in two distinctly different ways. First, they do occasionally retrieve a document that is missed in stem matching, by introducing new word relations which provide some request-document overlap. More often, however, *precision* is improved by promoting documents which were already retrieved but at a moderately low level. This is done by increasing the *weight* of significant words which previously matched in the request and document by adding associated words to both vectors. This increases the weight of the significant words (by adding words which co-occur with them) and improves performance. Most of the improvement shown by the association process is produced by the precision effect. Jones and Jackson (6) have also used word associations to improve the precision of searches.

The precision effect might seem to correspond to the role of the list of nonsignificant words in a thesaurus, just as the recall effect corresponds to a synonym list. In practice, however, the nonsignificant words needed for this are often missed in thesaurus construction. For example, the thesaurus constructor may easily fail to recognize the uselessness of "addition," "hand," "order," and "example" if he does not know that they occur only in the combinations "in addition," "on the other hand," "in order to," and "for example." Also, high-frequency words, even if they have retained their semantic sense, are often of no value for retrieval because they occur so often as to provide no discrimination between documents. In a thesaurus made without the aid of a complete concordance, and even with this aid in many cases, such errors are quite likely.

The two effects of the associative process can be seen in Table 8. This table shows the changes in rank position of relevant documents from the word stem matching process to the associative retrieval run, using a frequency

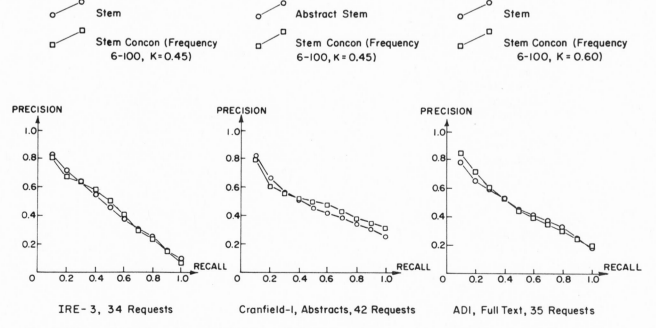

FIG. 2. Comparison of word stem dictionary with addition of statistical word-word association (stem concon)

TABLE 8. Changes in rank positions of relevant documents for two analysis methods

Rank in word stem process	Rank in association retrieval process						
	1–9	10–19	20–29	30–49	50–99	100–200	total
1–9	67	12	0	4	3	1	87
10–19	16	7	4	5	4	0	36
20–29	7	2	2	2	1	3	17
30–49	2	0	1	3	5	2	13
50–99	2	2	1	1	11	5	22
100–200	2	2	1	2	7	9	23
Total	96	25	9	17	31	20	
Net change	+9	−11	−8	+4	+9	−3	

range of 6 to 50 and a cutoff of 0.45. The number of documents which changed from each range of rank positions in the associative run is shown in the main block of the table and the net change in each rank group is shown at the bottom. It is observed that the associative process removes relevant documents from ranks 10–29, but not 30–99. It also removes documents (but many fewer) from the very low rank positions. The documents in ranks 10–29 which are promoted up to ranks 1–9 are generally those which have had their significant terms upweighted by the process indicated above. The majority of documents promoted from ranks 100–200 had no significant matching terms before associations were added. Of 6 relevant documents which move up over 100 rank positions, all were improved by the recall effect. But in the 10–29 groups, which lost a total of 38 relevant documents, 25 going up and 15 down, nearly every case of improvement is due to the precision effect. This represents a significant improvement in the performance of the relevant documents in this range. In fact, the largest change of ranks in the entire table is the promotion of 16 relevant documents from the 10–19 range to the 1–9 range. In the 100–200 range, a total of 14 documents were promoted out of this range, while 11 were dropped down into it. But it should be noted that if we consider the range 20–99, as many documents (10) dropped from these ranges to the 100–200 range as were promoted to them. The net loss of documents from the 100–200 range is due entirely to the four promotions to rank positions 1–20, all caused by the recall effect.

The mechanism of precision improvement, as previously stated, is to reinforce the apparent weight on significant terms by adding their associated terms. This process works because the significant terms generally have more associated pairs than the nonsignificant terms. It may be wondered why this should be so. This feature of the associations derives from the greater concentration of the significant terms in the abstracts. The nonsignificant terms are generally widely spread among the abstracts, so that it is difficult for any term to match their occurrences. The significant terms are clustered in a few abstracts, and another term can match them easily, since only one or two co-occurrences of terms which occur several times in each document they appear in is necessary to produce a correlation above cutoff. That is, if terms occur once in each of 10 documents, they must occur in six common documents to correlate at a 0.6 level; but if they occur three times in each of three documents, they need only co-occur in two documents to correlate at a level of .67. The tendency of significant terms to bunch up is shown in Table 9, which shows the distribution of occurrences of the 10 words occuring 15 times. It is seen that no nonsignificant term occurs in fewer than 12 documents; none occurs more than three times in a document; and their average ratio of number of occurrences per document is only 1.1. The significant terms never occur in more than 10 documents; every one appears at least three times in some document; and they average 1.8 occurrences per document.

An example of the effect of this is shown by query Q116. This query contained 12 words in the word stem matching system, of which the key word was "dissociated." "Dissociated" was outweighed in the search by such high-frequency words as "wind," "high," "pressure," etc. which are too frequent in this collection to be of much use as search terms. However, none of those words had any related pairs, while "dissociated" introduced eight new words. As a result, while "dissociated" represented only 8% of the original query, it and its associations represented 28% of the new query. The additional weight given to this important term (since all its associations were also introduced into any document which contained the word) caused 3 relevant documents in rank positions 21, 23, 27 to be promoted to positions 1, 6, 7. Note that "dissociation" already appeared in these documents before expansion, but it was not emphasized enough.

Recall-effect improvement (introducing new terms missed in the original search) is shown by a question in the ADI collection, QB2, on the "testing of automatic information systems." This failed to match one relevant document which spoke of "evaluating documentation techniques." The association procedure connected "auto-

TABLE 9. Distribution of occurrences of significant and nonsignificant words

Word	Significant?	Number of documents	Occurrences								Occur. per document
			1	2	3	4	5	6	7	8	
airfoil	yes	8	3	3	2						1.9
affect	no	13	11	2							1.2
converge	yes	8	4	2	1	1					1.9
correct	no	14	13	1							1.0
km	yes	7	5	1						1	2.1
magnitude	no	14	13	1							1.0
plan	yes	10	7	2	1						1.5
practical	no	12	10	1	1						1.25
previous	no	14	13	1							1.0
vortex	yes	7	4	1		1	1				2.1

matic" in the query with "experiment" and "reduce"; "reduce" in turn was related to "documentation.") This provided enough overlap to raise the document from 77th place in the rank list of retrieved documents to ninth. It should be noted that the useful relations were locally significant pairs (e.g., "automatic" and "experiment"; but "experiment" and "test" were not associated).

An example from the Cranfield collection is query 226, whose key term was "Navier-Stokes" (equation). Document 08C did not contain this word, but it was introduced by the association procedure from the word "steady." The word "numerical" was introduced into both query and document from "Navier-Stokes" and "steady," respectively. Again, note the locally significant pairs; the thesaurus did not connect "Navier-Stokes" with any of these terms. As a result of these associations, this relevant document was promoted from rank position 143 to rank position 4.

The results of retrieval experiments can be used to determine the best set of parameters for the association process. The conclusions agree well with those deduced from the examination of the pairs in the previous discussion. We noted there, for example, that words that are either very frequent or very rare tend to have nonsignificant associations. The fraction of meaningful correlations can also be increased by raising the cutoff. The effect of this on retrieval is shown in Fig. 3, where recall-precision curves for the stem dictionary directly, without any associations added, and for two different association strategies, are compared. When all words, of whatever frequency, are used in the association process, the resulting curve is usually inferior to the normal word matching run. But when the frequencies of words employed in the association process are restricted to the range 6 to 50, and the cutoff is raised, the resulting recall-precision curve is everywhere superior to the stem curve.

We have also noted that words occurring only three or four times have fewer significant occurrences than words of six or more occurrences. The effect on retrieval of

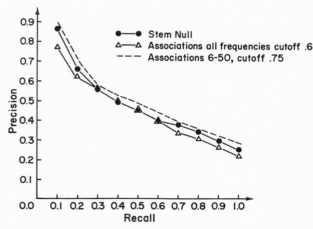

FIG. 3. Recall-precision curves for association runs—Cranfield collection: Limitation of association process

TABLE 10. Rank-recall and log precision for various frequency ranges *

a. Rank recall for different frequency ranges

Minimum frequency	Maximum frequency			
	25	50	100	None
None				.2991
3	.2840	.3051	.3126	.3070
6	.2933	.3162	.3148	.2887
10	.2838	.3123	.2970	.2561

b. Log precision for frequency ranges

Minimum frequency	Maximum frequency			
	25	50	100	None
None				.4642
3	.4684	.4823	.4756	.4647
6	.4711	.4888	.4738	.4453
10	.4488	.4737	.4567	.4179

* All runs with cosine correlation, cutoff 0.6, expansion weight 1.0.

variations in the frequencies of words used in the association process is shown in greater detail in Table 10. For both recall and precision purposes the optimum frequency range appears to be 6–50, although the differences in performance are small. The majority of the improvement obtained by restricting frequency of words processed is obtained by removing the associations involving words of frequency 1 and 2.

The effect of varying the cutoff used in the association process is shown in Table 11. The useful range of cutoffs seems to be 0.45–0.75, for the cosine correlation. As a high cutoff produces the fewest but most reliable associated pairs, it is expected to be preferable for precision uses, whereas a low cutoff produces the largest number of pairs and therefore has an advantage if maximum recall is needed. The table indicates that 0.45 is the best cutoff, although the high cutoff of 0.75 is good for precision.

Table 12 shows the effect of varying the relative weight of the associations (a weighting of 1 makes a word introduced into a document vector by the association process of equal importance to a word in the original document). Weights below 1 are preferable, especially for precision purposes. Figure 4 indicates the changes in performance

TABLE 11. Effect of varying cutoff *

Cutoff	Rank recall	Log precision
.30	.3247	.4770
.45	.3409	.4982
.60	.3162	.4888
.75	.3116	.4932
.90	.2933	.4608

* All runs cosine correlation, frequency range 6–50.

TABLE 12. Effect of varying weight of associations *

Weight	Rank recall	Log precision
.125	.3009	.4668
.25	.3224	.4991
.5	.3239	.4952
1.0	.3162	.4888
2.0	.3007	.4712

* All runs 6–50, cosine correlation, cutoff 0.6.

as the weighting is varied. To sum up, then, for high precision one should have low weights and high cutoffs, while for high recall, higher weights and lower cutoffs are desirable.

We have also noted that additional iteration of the association process is not useful in finding synonyms, nor is it of great value in retrieval. Figure 5 shows curves for 0, 1, and 2 iterations of the association procedure, with frequencies of 6–50 and a cutoff of 0.60. The first iteration curve is seen to be superior.

The performance differences shown by the various options in the association process are small. It is particularly difficult to choose a set of options which maximize either the precision effect or the recall effect over an entire set of requests. Nor does a fine adjustment of cutoff, frequency, or weight have a major effect on retrieval performance. This is just what is expected from the analysis of the associated pairs, since no set of parameters produces an unusual number of significant pairs. In general, the use of associated pairs produces improvement in performance over most of the range compared with word stem matching if words with very low and high frequencies are omitted. Procedures which decrease the number of associated pairs (restricting the frequency range used, raising the cutoff) or lower the weight of the associations are best for precision; procedures which increase the number of associated pairs or their weight are best for recall, but the effect is small.

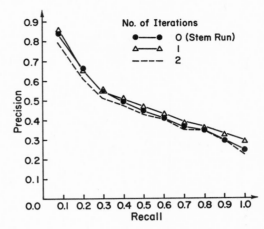

FIG. 5. Recall-precision curves for association runs—Cranfield collection: Effect of iteration

It is often hypothesized that association procedures can simulate the operation of a thesaurus or other classical word normalization procedures. This simulation can be tested on the Cranfield collection, because it has a thesaurus and a form of indexing. The indexing, although very detailed and exhaustive (averaging over 30 terms per document), was not carried through a rigorous term normalization, and the results with it may perhaps be unusual. It is felt, however, that in terms of overall performance the exhaustivity and high quality of the indexing compensates for the lack of normalization, so that results should be roughly comparable.

As expected from the earlier discussions in this section, the association procedure operates in a unique and virtually independent way, simulating neither indexing nor thesaurus. Out of 42 requests the thesaurus improves the performance of 24, the indexing improves the performance of 24, and the association procedure (with a frequency range of 6–100, cutoff of .45, weight of 1.0) improves 25. Yet only 12 requests are improved by all three methods (even on a random basis at least eight would be improved by all three). Table 3 shows two-by-two contingency tables for co-improvement of requests by thesaurus and association, and Table 14 shows two-by-two contingency tables for co-improvement of requests by indexing and association. None of the tables are significant, i.e., there is no covariation of association results and thesaurus results or of association results and indexing results. A set of recall-precision curves for thesaurus and associations is shown in Fig. 6 and for indexing and associations in Fig. 7. The curves cross, and the order of superiority depends on the operating range of the system. In short, the association process (a) does not detect the same word relationships as a thesaurus or an index, (b) does not use them in the same way, and (c) does not have the same effect on retrieval.

The operation of associative retrieval as a precision device can be demonstrated by noting that the mechanism proposed (promotion of relevant material near the top

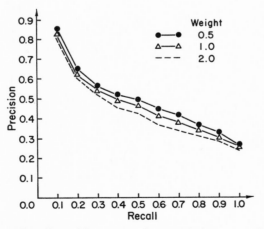

FIG. 4. Recall-precision curves for association runs—Cranfield collection: Variation of weights

TABLE 13. Contingency table for covariation of thesaurus association methods

a. Improvements of association methods over null and thesaurus

	Request improved by association over null	Request not improved by association over null	Total
Request improved by thesaurus over null	15	9	24
Request not improved by thesaurus	10	8	18
Total	25	17	42

b. Large improvements of association methods over null and thesaurus

	Request greatly improved (rank recall up by .1) by association over null	Request not greatly improved by association over null	Total
Request greatly improved (rank recall up by .1) by thesaurus over null	5	3	8
Request not greatly improved by thesaurus over null	9	25	34
Total	14	28	42

TABLE 14. Contingency tables for covariation of indexing and association methods

a. Improvements of association methods over indexing

	Request improved by association over null	Request not improved by association	Total
Request improved by indexing over null	16	8	24
Request not improved by indexing over null	9	9	18
Total	25	17	42

b. Large improvements of association methods over indexing

	Request greatly improved by association	Request not greatly improved by association	Total
Request greatly (rank recall up .1) improved by indexing	4	5	9
Request not greatly improved by indexing	10	23	33
Total	14	28	42

of the rank list) requires a moderately good performance to begin with. When the performance of associative retrieval methods is compared between requests having good performance with the stem dictionary and requests having bad performance in the stem dictionary, it is seen that few requests with bad performance in the stem dictionary are improved by the association process. Table 15 shows that although 20 requests have a rank recall with the stem dictionary above 0.2 and 22 have a rank recall below 0.2, 10 of the 14 requests which improved in the association process had a rank recall above 0.2.

To sum up, 25 requests have a rank recall increase of 0.1 with some method, but only two requests improved this much on all three methods. More requests were

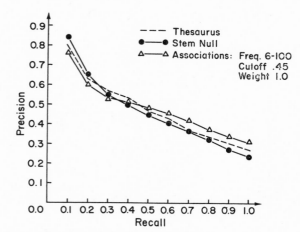

FIG. 6. Recall-precision curves—Cranfield collection: Comparison of association and thesaurus

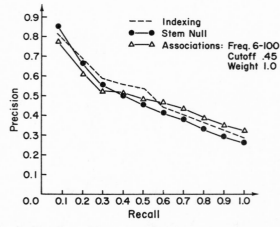

FIG. 7. Recall-precision curves—Cranfield collection: Comparison of association and indexing

TABLE 15. Contingency table for covariation of association improvement and bad performance in stem dictionary

	Large improvement with association (rank recall up .1)	Not large improvement with association	Total
Rank recall in null above .2	10	10	20
Rank recall in null below .2	4	18	22
Total	14	28	42

improved by the associative process alone than were improved both by the thesaurus and by the associative process. It seems fair to conclude that associative retrieval and the use of a thesaurus are essentially independent methods of improving request performance. "Which method is better?" can therefore be asked only in the sense of "considering the average collection and request, which method has the higher probability of better performance?" Figure 8 shows comparative recall-precision curves for thesauri and association methods for three collections using good association strategies. For two of the three collections, the thesaurus is definitely superior, and on the third collection (Cranfield) the difference in performance is nonsignificant. For this Cranfield collection, the thesaurus performs worse than for the other collections; if the thesaurus performance were comparable, it would also be superior to association methods on Cranfield as well as on the other two collections. The reason for the poorer performance of the

Cranfield thesaurus is believed to be that it was originally constructed for a different purpose and is not optimally designed for our system. Even with the performance curves as shown in Fig. 8, however, it is clear that on the average requests should be entrusted to a thesaurus rather than to an association scheme for maximum performance.

5 Conclusions

Experimental results with associative retrieval procedures indicate that

(a) In small collections associations are not useful for determining word meanings or relations, since the majority of the associated pairs depend on purely local meanings of the words and do not reflect their general meaning in technical text;

(b) Associative retrieval is not an effective recall device but rather a precision device in many cases, operating by increasing the weight of significant terms rather than by introducing new significant terms; and

(c) As a method of improving both precision and recall, a properly made thesaurus is generally preferable to associative procedures.

The usefulness of an associative method in operational retrieval experiments will probably be restricted to aiding dictionary constructors by pointing out unusual word relationships in a document collection, and as an alternative option for requests which do not perform well in a thesaurus. The method does not appear to be a reliable substitute for a thesaurus for the typical retrieval operation.

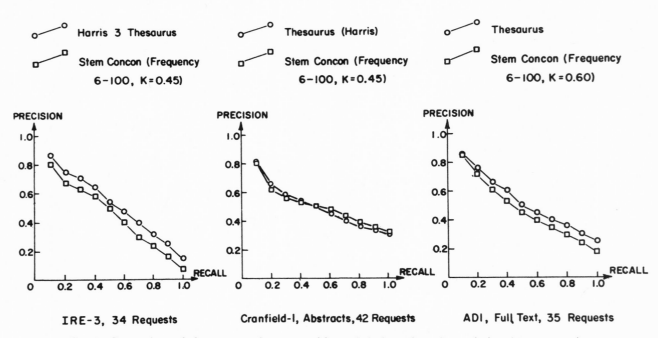

FIG. 8. Comparison of thesaurus performance with statistical word-word association (stem concon)

References

1. GIULIANO, V., and P. JONES, Linear Associative Information Retrieval, *in* P. Howerton (Ed.), *Vistas in Information Handling,* Spartan Books, Washington, D. C., 1963.
2. DOYLE, L. B., Indexing and Abstracting by Association, *American Documentation,* 13 (No. 4):378 (1962).
3. SALTON, G., and M. LESK, The SMART Automatic Document Retrieval System—An Illustration, *Communications of the ACM,* 8 (No. 6):391 (1965).
4. SALTON, G., and M. LESK, Computer Evaluation of Indexing and Text Processing, *Journal of the ACM,* 15 (No. 1):8 (1968).
5. JONES, P. E., V. E. GIULIANO, and R. M. CURTICE, Development of String Indexing Techniques, Report ESD-TR-67-202, AF19(628)-3311, *in Papers on Automatic Language Processing,* Vol. 3, Arthur D. Little, Inc., Cambridge, Mass.
6. JONES, K. S., and D. M. JACKSON, *The Use of the Theory of Clumps for Information Retrieval,* Cambridge Language Research Unit, Cambridge, England, 1967.

30 Automatic Subject Recognition in Scientific Papers: An Empirical Study

JOHN O'CONNOR
*Journal of the Association
for Computing Machinery
Vol. 12, No. 4, October, 1965*

1. Introduction

Many methods have been proposed in recent years for subject identification of scientific papers by computer; for a review see [18]. Some of these methods have been tested empirically [4, 5, 7, 12, 21, 24, 26, 27, 30, 31]. The basis of each test has been comparison of subject specification-document pairs formed by knowledgeable humans and pairs formed by computer. The specifications have been subject terms such as "digital logical circuitry", or "learning and reinforcement"; extended subject characterizations such as "automata theory, computability and effective computability, finite-state sequential machines, Turing machines and other tape automata"; or subject questions such as "how could one calculate the efficiency of a hydrogenous scintillation counter?"

This paper describes the results of an empirical test which differs from those cited in several ways. (1) The literature was in biomedicine, rather than in physics, the

1. There have been previous studies using biomedical titles [3, 13, 15, 17] but not full texts. The inadequacy of titles alone for some purposes is indicated by some of these tests [3, 15, 17].

computer sciences or psychology.[1] (2) About 60 percent of the papers were longer than 1000 words (the average length 2000), rather than letters to the editor [27, 26] or abstracts [4, 5, 7, 12, 21, 24, 30, 31]. (3) Two subject specifications were studied intensively — for one specification, 300 documents humanly paired with it were examined, while for the other specification 55 papers paired with it were studied. (4) Some new automatic recognition rules were formulated and tested, and several recognition rules previously suggested but not applied were also tested.

2. The Sample

A coordinate indexing retrieval system serves the Merck Sharpe and Dohme (hereafter MSD) pharmaceutical research center. The system is described in detail in [16] and [22]. It should be noted here that the indexing is done by subject specialists, spending an average of 10 minutes per paper.

The population sampled for this study was the 10,000 documents indexed at MSD in 1955, omitting reviews (so indexed at MSD) because they present special indexing problems, and foreign language papers. A few abstracts from the April, 1962 *Federation Proceedings* were also used.

Most of the sample documents were fully keypunched, and a computer generated both an alphabetical word frequency list for each document and a cumulative word frequency list for the corpus. Marks had been added to each document by a pre-editor (informed but not a subject specialist) for titles, headings, summaries, figures (verbal material in tables, diagrams, etc.), references and footnotes. The computer was programmed so that in the word frequency lists each word was marked for the document places (title, heading, etc.) in which it occurred.

The subject specifications studied were two MSD indexing terms. Subject specification-document pairs formed by knowledgeable humans were provided by the MSD indexing. Important and doubtful cases of MSD indexing were discussed with Mrs. Claire Schultz, now of the Institute for the Advancement of Medical Communication, who established the MSD system and supervised its operation for a number of years.

3. Toxicity

Toxicity was the first index term studied. In the MSD system it primarily refers to drug toxicity — undesirable side effects of drugs. However a few papers on poisoning by insecticides, industrial processes, snakebite, etc. are also included under the term. At MSD, *toxicity* is a frequently used term, assigned to 15 percent of the collection in 1955. Of course in searching it is always used in combination with other terms.

To develop computer rules for assigning *toxicity*, 110 *toxicity* and 200 non-*toxicity* papers (Group 1) were examined. These rules were then tested (manually) on a further 180 *toxicity* and 100 non-*toxicity* documents (Group 2). The rules were also tested on 23 *toxicology* papers from the April, 1962 *Federation Proceedings*.

Twenty-eight papers indexed *toxicity* at MSD, which were hard cases for various rules, were judged by Mrs. Schultz to be "incorrectly indexed *toxicity*" or "not important to be indexed *toxicity*". There papers were excluded from the sample.

Of the papers not indexed *toxicity* at MSD, 11 were judged to be papers which should have been so indexed and were included in the sample as *toxicity* papers.

The following property characterized 14 other papers not indexed *toxicity*: Nine years after the indexing it was not possible to say why they should or should not have been indexed *toxicity*. These papers were excluded from the study.

Thesaurus Group for Toxicity. Automatic subject identification by means of a thesaurus is now a familiar idea. A thesaurus group for a subject specification is a set of words and phrases with semantic or factual relations to that specification which make them good clues for it in the document collection searched. A thesaurus

group can be compiled from textbooks, index authority lists, dictionaries, etc., discussion with experts, cerebral (human) study of documents or mechanical processing of documents.

A beginning for a *toxicity* thesaurus group was provided by the stem, "toxic . . .", and the following cross-references (reduced to stem form) from the MSD index authority list: poison. . ., side effect, drug allerg. . ., drug reaction, drug sensiti. . . . Choice of stem forms was aided by the cumulative word frequency list; for instance "sensiti. . ." includes "sensitiv. . .", "sensitis. . ." and "sensitiz. . .". Obvious plurals such as "side effects" are understood here.

Reading the *toxicity* papers in Group 1 provided many additions. The resulting thesaurus group was the following:

toxic . . . , poison . . . , lethal dose, LD, side effect,[2] drug allerg . . . , drug reaction, drug sensiti . . . , intoxicat . . . , venom . . . , side action,[2] side reaction,[2] adverse effect, adverse reaction, ill effect, idiosyncra . . . , overdos[2] . . . , overtreat[2] . . . , intoleran . . . , contraindicat . . . , salicylism, goitrogen . . . , nephrotoxic . . . , neurotoxic . . . , hypervitaminosis, untoward, undesirable, deleterious, irritat . . . , irritan . . . , harm . . . , risk . . . , danger . . . , hazard. . . .

The stems, words and phrases of the thesaurus group will be called "keywords".

Toxicity Thesaurus Group Applied to Group 1. Of the 110 *toxicity* papers in Group 1, 80 percent contained at least one *toxicity* keyword. Figure 1 shows the keyword distribution in document places and in different length documents.

"Toxic. . ." and "side effect" each selected about 20 percent of the papers, and "poison. . ." selected 7 percent. "Intoxicat. . ." and "danger" added 5 percent each, three other keywords selected 3 percent each, two selected two percent, and 10 each selected a single paper. A total of 13 other keywords occurred in papers but were not needed to select any. Papers containing several keywords were assigned to the word which occurred most in documents containing just one.

Nonrecurring Toxicity Expressions. A brief example of a *toxicity* paper which contained no keywords is the following abstract:[3]

A Rare Complication Due to Isoniazid Treatment of Tuberculous Meningitis in Childhood.

A six-year-old girl with primary tuberculosis in the right upper lobe and tuberculous meningitis was treated with intramuscular streptomycin and oral

2. There may be a hyphen after "side" or "over."
3. Weisner, E. A rare complication due to isoniazid treatment of tuberculosis meningitis in childhood. *Amer. Rev. Tuberc.* 72 (July 1955), 11.

isoniazid. Following good improvement, she suddenly became very sick on the eighty-first day of treatment with these signs and symptoms: pallor, headaches, vomiting, apathia, drowsiness, vascular collapse, tremor, hyper-reflexia, difficulty of urinating, and drop of lymphocytes in the blood differential count, without temperature elevation. This condition lasted two days and disappeared promptly when the isoniazid was discontinued, while streptomycin was continued and an antihistaminic was added.

It is believed that cerebral edema occurred on an allergic basis caused by isoniazid in a patient predisposed by previous meningitis.

"Complication due to isoniazid" would be a useful addition to the *toxicity* thesaurus if it could be expected to recur in other *toxicity* papers. But such recurrence is very unlikely.

Examples of such nonrecurring expressions from other *toxicity* papers which lack keywords are the following:

> convulsion two hours after the administration
> Teratogenic effects of cholinergic drugs
> hypertension following the administration,
> cortisone may have caused the eruption
> insulin-induced hypoglycemia.[4]

Expressions such as these suggest a computer indexing rule composed of three lists and some order and word distance requirements. The "S-list" contains names of substances and words such as "administration" which indicate probable contact with a substance; the "D-list" contains names of disorders; and the "connective list" contains "due to", "after", "effects of", etc.

Substance, Disorder and Connective Lists. For this study, the S-list was considered to be a drug manual, supplemented by a complete scan of a medical dictionary for S-words such as "inoculation", "injection", etc. and further supplemented by S-words such as "administration" which were in Group 1 *toxicity* expressions but not in the dictionary.[5] The D-list was also assumed to be compiled by medical dictionary scan, supplemented by further D-words such as "aggravating" and "damage"

4. Many other examples of such expressions are found in [20]. Full texts of several papers without *toxicity* keywords are found in [19].

5. The dictionary used was *Dorland's Illustrated Medical Dictionary* [8].

appearing in Group 1 *toxicity* expressions. These assumed lists were used in the study by looking up, whenever appropriate, any apparent S- or D-word to see if it had a dictionary meaning which would cause its selection in a scan. The few obvious drug names not in the dictionary were assumed to be in a 1955 drug handbook.[6]

The connective list consists of connectives appearing more than once in Group 1 *toxicity* expressions and some inflectional variants of them. The complete list follows:

action of (DCS),[7] effect of (DCS), attribut . . . to (DCS), after (DCS, CSD), due to (DCS), during (DCS, CSD), follow . . . (DCS), following (DCS, SCD), followed by (SCD), if (DCS, CSD), when (DCS, SCD), induc . . . (SCD), induc . . . by (DCS), caus . . . (SCD), caus . . . by (DCS), produc . . . (SCD), produc . . by (DCS), result . . . in (SCD), result . . . from (DCS), relat . . . to (DCS, SCD), relat . . . with (DSC, SCD), relation . . . between_____ and _____ (CSD, CDS), connect . . . between_____ and _____ (CSD, CDS).

Toxicity Connection Forms. A *toxicity* connection expression contains an S-word, a D-word and a connective in an order permitted for that connective, and sufficiently near to one another.

Examples of permitted order are: D after S, after S D, D related to S, etc, The notations in the connective list given above indicate permitted orders.

Nearness of S, D and connective words is measured by the number of intervening words in the same sentence. A maximum of three is permitted.

The nonrecurring *toxicity* expressions quoted earlier are all connection expressions.

An expression form containing a connective, and D and S as variables, for example "D after S", with no more than three intervening words will be called a connection form. Thus the computer indexing rule described here consists of a set of connection forms, an S-list and a D-list.

The effect of omitting order requirements was tested on 85 non-*toxicity* papers. Eight of the 85 would be

6. A few non recurrent D-expressions were observed, such as "morphine-like effect" and "increased the number of organisms in the trachea", but they were not in needed clue expressions.

7. The notations after each connective are explained below.

Title	Heading	Abstract	Summary	Figure	Reference	Main Text Word Length			
						0–500	500–1,000	1,000–1,500	Over 1,500
20	17	8	6	1	1	7	9	6	12

A paper which can be entered in more than one column is entered in the furthest left column.

An abstract is a summary published independently, for instance in the "Abstracts" section of a journal. A summary appearing as part of a larger paper is called a "summary".

Fig. 1. Keywords in Group 1 *toxicity* papers.

falsely selected besides those which would be otherwise falsely selected by the final form of the *toxicity*-rules. Thus order requirements seem desirable.

Further Toxicity Connection Forms. Some *toxicity* expressions in Group 1 suggest other connection forms in which only one S- or D-variable occurs. These forms are: postvaccin . . . D, postinject . . . D, complication of S, reaction to S, sensiti . . . to S, hypersensiti . . . to S. In the last four forms, one word may intervene before the S-word.

Another connection form is SD. This is illustrated by "penicillin anaphylaxis", "insulin hypoglycemia", "immunization adenitis". The S-words in expressions of this form must be nouns to avoid such unwanted expressions as "watery diarrhea", "therapeutic failure", "treated myxedema".

The selectivity of all connection forms is improved if the S-words are not treated as such when followed by any one of: defici . . . , deplet . . . , depriv . . . , sensiti . . . test.

Connection Forms Applied to Group 1. All but one of the *toxicity* papers in Group 1 which had no keywords contained at least one connection form.[8] Figure 2 shows the connection form distribution among these papers.

A Toxicity Paper Without Keywords or Connection Forms. One *toxicity* paper in Group 1 contained neither keywords nor connection forms. Its text follows.[9]

Indications for Vitamin B_{12}

Q.—In what conditions is vitamin B_{12} definitely indicated? Advertisers suggest its use in a wide variety of conditions.

A.—It has been suggested that cyanocobalamin (vitamin B_{12}) increases the weight of premature babies and underweight children, that it has some general tonic effect in adults, and that it is of value in the treatment of diabetic neuropathy. The main weight of scientific and clinical evidence does not support these claims and suggests its use should be largely confined to the treatment of Addisonian pernicious anaemia, in which its therapeutic efficacy appears to be identical with that of liver extract, including its ability to prevent and ameliorate the nervous complications of the disorder. Its cost is less

8. There were also connection forms in some papers containing keywords.
9. Indication for vitamin B_{12}. *British Medical J. 1* (May 1955), 1232.

than that of liver extract, the amount needed for injection is smaller, and it does not cause allergic reactions. In consequence it is probable that cyanocobalamin will replace liver extract in the future. It is occasionally effective in other high colour-index anaemias (the megaloblastic anaemias of pregnancy, infancy, malabsorption, and the Tropics), but in these folic acid is usually the drug of choice. Subacute combined degeneration of the cord hardly ever occurs in these latter anaemias, but it is wise for maintenance purposes to supplement folic acid with parenteral therapy with cyanocobalamin or liver extract, since severe peripheral neuritis may occur in patients taking folic acid alone for a long time.

Toxicity Expressions Which Are Neither Keywords nor Connection Expressions. The only *toxicity* expression in this paper is "neuritis may occur in patients taking folic acid", which appears in the last sentence. Other *toxicity* papers in Group 1 also contain *toxicity* expressions which are neither keywords nor connection expressions. Examples are the following:

sulfonamides favored the implantation of these organisms

22 percent of the infants in the high-oxygen group and none in the low-oxygen group developed irreversible RLF

symptoms occurring in patients on reserpine

patients who were given 1.8gm. of streptomycin daily suffered permanent loss of vestibular function

Further Observations on the Metabolic Effect of Quinidine: Evidence Suggesting Impairment of Glucose Utilization

excessive and prolonged menstrual flow in women receiving salicylic acid

salicylates and bishydroxycoumarin may block the utilization of vitamin K.

About five percent of the *toxicity* expressions in Group 1 *toxicity* papers were in this class.

A computer rule which would identify most of them is the following: S and D in the same sentence, in either order, with at most four words between them. However this rule would be too undiscriminating. It selected 32 of the 65 non-*toxicity* papers examined. To anticipate a bit, even when all the rules for reducing overassigning, described below, were used and the papers otherwise

Title	Heading	Abstract	Summary	Figure	Reference	Main Text Word Length			
						0–500	500–1,000	1,000–1,500	Over 1,500
12	1	3	1	0	0	1	2	2	See note*

* Main texts of papers longer than 1500 words were not searched for connection forms.
A paper which can be entered in several columns is entered in the furthest left column.

FIG. 2. Connection forms in Group 1 *toxicity* lacking keywords.

overassigned by those rules were excluded, it still selected 18 of the 65.

The author has not found any other computer rule which would identify these *toxicity* expressions.

Another one percent of the Group 1 *toxicity* expressions were multisentence *toxicity* expressions. For example:

> The patient was given 400,000 units of procaine penicillin in the deltoid muscle with prior aspiration of the syringe plunger. Approximately sixty seconds later the patient complained of tingling all over, vomited twice, stated he "couldn't breathe", and collapsed.

Overassigning Toxicity. Of the 200 non-*toxicity* papers in Group 1, 28 percent contained *toxicity* keywords. Figure 3 shows the keyword distribution among these papers. The value for each column is the sum of the numbers entered in it. Their meaning will be explained shortly.

Another 11 percent of the Group 1 non-*toxicity* papers contained connection forms.[10] Figure 4 shows their distribution. As in Figure 3, the value for a column is the sum of the numbers in it.

Four kinds of overassignment could be distinguished. Some papers were selected accidentally. For example:

> the patient had noticed heat intolerance
> Three Cases of Sclerema with Recovery after Treatment with Cortisone.

Some papers reported only absences of *toxicity* which were not noteworthy. Other papers described slight *toxicity* of unsurprising kinds.

The remaining overassigned papers referred to facts about *toxicity* already familiar to users of the MSD system. For example:

> Effect of Hypothalamic Lesions on Steroid-Induced Atrophy of Adrenal Cortex in the Dog.
>
> This dual action of chlorpromazine may explain, to some extent, the published observations of its usefulness as an antiemetic agent in man in such a wide variety of conditions causing nausea and vomiting. These include drug toxicity, infections, intoxication, neoplasms, radiation sickness, cardiovascular diseases, increased intracranial pressure, ...

These four kinds of false selection will be called "accidental", "absent *toxicity*", "slight *toxicity*", and "familiar *toxicity*". In Figures 3 and 4, the four numbers in each column represent the four kinds of overassigning, in the order just given.

Of the 39 percent Group 1 papers overassigned, 17 percent were accidental, 14 percent were "familiar *toxicity*" and about 4 percent each were "absent *toxicity*" and "slight *toxicity*".

Of the 39 percent overassigned, 15 percent consisted of papers longer than 1500 words even though only keywords were searched for in those papers.

Reducing Overassigning. Rules were developed to reduce false selection in Group 1. Sometimes very strong forms of two rules could not both be selected because some *toxicity* papers would thereby be missed. Alternatives were chosen which appeared to minimize overassigning and to be generally plausible.

The selectivity of eight keywords was increased by requiring an S-word at most two words distant from each of their occurrences. These keywords were: intoleran . . . , deleterious, harm . . . , irritat . . . , irritan . . . , danger . . . , hazard . . . , risk . . . . This rule removed seven papers longer than 1500 words and one abstract from accidental overassigning.

Most of the accidental overassigning by connection forms was caused by ambiguous S- and D-words, for example, administration, hypercalcemia, reaction, sensitivity. Administration may be of a virus in an experiment, hypercalcemia may be "within physiological limits", a reaction may be chemical, and bacteria may have a sensitivity to antibiotics. These ambiguous S- and D-words, or analogous ones, were needed for connection forms. No means of reducing this ambiguity was found.

Six of the "absent *toxicity*" papers could be omitted from selection by requiring that no keyword have "non"

10. There were, of course, also connection forms in some papers containing keywords.

							Main Text Word Length			
	Title	Heading	Abstract	Summary	Figure	Reference	0–500	500–1,000	1,000–1,500	Over 1,500
Accidental	0	0	2	1	0	0	1	2	1	15
Absent Toxicity	0	0	2	1	0	0	0	1	0	5
Slight Toxicity	0	2	1	0	0	0	1	2	0	0
Familiar Toxicity	0	1	2	0	1	2	2	2	1	9

A paper which can be entered in several columns is entered in the furthest left.

FIG. 3. *Toxicity* keywords in Group 1 non-*toxicity* papers.

	Title	Heading	Abstract	Summary	Figure	Reference	Main Text Word Length			
							0–500	500–1,000	1,000–1,500	Over 1,500
Accidental	2	1	1	4	1	0	3	1	0	Not searched
Absent Toxicity	0	0	0	0	0	0	0	0	0	
Slight Toxicity	2	0	0	0	0	0	0	0	0	
Familiar Toxicity	1	2	0	1	0	2	0	1	0	

A paper which can be entered in several columns is entered in the furthest left.

Fig. 4. *Toxicity* connection forms in Group 1 non-*toxicity* papers lacking *toxicity* keywords.

as a prefix or have a negation within four words of it, and no connection expression contain a negation as an intervening word or have one within four words of it. The negations are the following: no, not, none, free . . . . This rule prevented overassigning of an abstract, a summary, a paper shorter than 1000 words and three papers longer than 1500 words.

No means of reducing "slight *toxicity*" overassigning was found. Examples of *toxicity* clues in these papers are are the following:

Side Reactions
mild and transitory side reactions

Untoward Reactions
mephenesin might be contraindicated in patients under the influence of a barbituate. . . . This was not substantiated.
without any serious side effects

Progesterone-Induced Withdrawal Bleeding as a Simple Physiologic Test for Pregnancy

The only side reaction encountered was a transient subfebrile temperature

Only one patient experienced an untoward reaction; he manifested excitation and restlessness following administration of the usual dose, but he responded without undue stimulation of psychomotor areas when the dose was decreased to 50 milligrammes.

Each block of expressions in this list is taken from a a separate paper.

Reducing Overassigning by Emphasis Measure. A *toxicity* fact familiar to MSD users, which appears in a paper indexed at MSD, is also likely to be familiar to the author of the paper. That is, it probably appears as background in his paper. Therefore he may emphasize it less than new results. Thus emphasis measures might reduce "familiar *toxicity*" overassigning.

Syntactic Emphasis Measure. It has been suggested that syntactic centrality in a sentence or clause measures emphasis or "importance" in a message [6, 29]. Several "familiar *toxicity*" examples illustrate this:

The delayed depressor response which begins approximately five hours after the subcutaneous administration of Pitressin to DCA-hypertensive rats can be also elicited . . . (from a summary).

Effect of Hypothalamic Lesions on Steroid-Induced Atrophy of Adrenal Cortex in the Dog.

Effects of antihistaminic drugs on the ventricular arrhythmias induced by aconitine.

. . . it contains a factor termed vitamin U, which is capable of preventing the development of histamine-induced ulcers in guinea pigs . . . (from a brief paper)

A few *toxicity* papers had their most central *toxicity* clue in a somewhat nested position.

Perforation of a Post-gastrectomy Stomal Ulcer during Cortisone Therapy
. . . one patient died of pancytopenia following drug therapy.
. . . the increasing frequency of toxic manifestation . . . have suggested . . . .
. . . his condition was interpreted as a transfusion reaction . . .

The basic idea of [6, 29] can be roughly summarized as follows: How many modifying phrases and words must be added to a core clause (or core word, in a title or heading) before the nested expression is reached, preserving grammaticality during the additions. As is well-known, an obstacle to satisfactory computer use of this measure is syntactic ambiguity (to the computer). For instance in the first "familiar *toxicity*" example above, the structure might be formally interpreted as "the response to DCA-hypertensive rats can be elicited". This difficulty might be met (crudely speaking) by giving preference in ambiguous cases to modifiers which are closer in word distance to the core.

By this measure, the second set of *toxicity* clues above, those from *toxicity* papers, appear to be less deeply nested than the first set. A syntactic indexing rule would then be that a paper have at least one *toxicity* clue no more deeply nested than are the clues in this second set.

Of course this rule would have to be precisely formulated for computer use.

This rule removed five connection-form papers from overassigning. The false clues in these papers occurred in a title, two headings, a summary and a paper shorter than 1000 words. Four overassignments were "familiar *toxicity*", and one of the heading selections was accidental.

Document Place Emphasis Measure. The document place (title, heading, summary, etc.) of an expression indicates emphasis. However 39 of the Group 1 *toxicity* papers contained a keyword or connection form only in the main text as Figures 1 and 2 indicate.

Figure material appears in 30 percent of the *toxicity* papers, almost all longer than 1500 words. Half of these papers have *toxicity* clues (usually keywords or connection forms) in their figures. However each of these latter papers is already selected by keywords or connection forms in other document places so that *toxicity* expressions in figures are not needed as clues. Ignoring them reduced overassigning by two papers.

Reference material occurs in 50 percent of the *toxicity* papers, 30 percent longer than 1500 words. Titles of cited papers appear in 30 percent of the papers. In 25 percent of the *toxicity* papers a keyword or connection form appears in their references. But these papers are already selected by keywords or connection forms in other document places; therefore reference *toxicity* expressions are not needed as clues. Ignoring them reduced overassigning by four "familiar *toxicity*" papers.

Frequency as an Emphasis Measure and for Reducing Accidental Overassigning. In a paper the frequency of clues for a subject specification [11] might indicate the emphasis on that subject in the paper and thus be useful in reducing "familiar fact" overassigning. And frequency of clues might also help to reduce accidental overassigning, if accidents are rare enough.

Absolute frequency could not be used for *toxicity* because five of the *toxicity* papers each contained only one keyword or connection form, though they also contained other *toxicity* expressions.

A requirement of at least one keyword or connection form per W-words of text reduced *toxicity* overassigning in Group 1. The W for summaries was 200, for abstracts 300 and for other texts 1200. This relative frequency rule removed six "familiar *toxicity*" papers, all longer than 1500 words. It also removed seven accidental papers longer than 1500 words, an accidentally selected summary and an accidentally selected abstract (all overassigned by keywords). Two "absent *toxicity*" papers longer than 1500 words were also removed.

Sentence and Paragraph Positions as Emphasis Measures. Several authors [1, 2] have suggested that occurrence in first and last sentences of paragraphs or first and last paragraphs of sections indicates emphasis.

This approach did not help reduce overassigning for summaries and abstracts since they usually have few paragraphs and few sentences per paragraph.

Requiring a *toxicity* expression in a first sentence or a first paragraph, in the main text of a paper containing a summary, removed two "familiar *toxicity*" papers longer than 1500 words, and a "familiar *toxicity*" and an accidental paper each shorter than 1000 words (all overassigned by keywords). This rule also removed redundantly seven longer papers, three accidental, three "familiar" and one "absent", already omitted by the frequency rule.

This rule had to be restricted to papers accompanied by summaries so that three *toxicity* papers would not be missed. One paper,[11] a 1500 word meeting report, contained index-worthy *toxicity* material which was not centrally emphasized in the paper. Another paper[12] (erroneously not indexed *toxicity* at MSD) was a 1200 word meeting report which contained three references to possible toxicity of new drugs and dosages, none in the first paragraph or a first sentence. The remaining paper,[13] 800 words long, contained in its first paragraph and first sentences only *toxicity* expressions which were neither keywords nor connection forms. An example is the following:

> . . . the use of only one of these steroids may alter the functions of an important gland such as the adrenal, thereby disturbing the balance in the pituitary and other glands.

The rule for papers containing summaries may not be ad hoc, however. Of the Group 1 *toxicity* papers 50 percent contained summaries and only one of these (selected by clues in its summary) did not have a *toxicity* expression in a first sentence or first paragraph of the main text.

Remaining Overassigning. Figure 5 shows the resultant overassigning by keywords in Group 1.

Figure 6 shows the resultant overassigning by connection forms in Group 1.

Overassigning by keywords was reduced from 28 percent to 9 percent, and overassigning by connection forms reduced from 11 to 7 percent. Thus total overassigning was lowered from 39 to 16 percent of the non-*toxicity* papers in Group 1.

Of this 16 percent, 7 percent was accidental overassigning (mostly by connection forms) and about 4 percent each were "slight *toxicity*" and "familiar *toxicity*" (mostly by keywords).

"Toxic . . ." caused 3 percent of the keyword overassigning, an accidental, a "slight" and four "familiar" papers. "Side effect" overassigned an "absent", a "slight", and a "familiar" paper.

11. Pash, J. Resuscitation of the newborn. *Australian Med. J. 2* (Oct. 1955), 538–539.
12. Progress in chemotherapy of tuberculosis. *New Engl. J. Med. 252* (Apr. 1955), 600–601.
13. Lamb, J. H. Abuses and uses of the corticosteroids. *Southern Med. J. 48* (July 1955), 782–785.

	Title	Heading	Abstract	Summary	Main Text Word Length			
					0–500	500–1,000	1,000–1,500	Over 1,500
Accidental	0	0	0	0	0	1	1	1
Absent Toxicity	0	0	1	0	0	0	0	0
Slight Toxicity	0	2	1	0	0	0	0	0
Familiar Toxicity	0	1	2	0	2	1	1	1

FIG. 5. Overassigning by *toxicity* keywords in Group 1 non-*toxicity* papers.

Of the 23 percent overassigning removed, 14 percent consisted of papers longer than 1500 words. The frequency rule alone eliminated half these papers.

Resulting Sensitivity of Keywords. Seven of the *toxicity* papers containing keywords did not have them in positions or frequencies enabling the papers to be selected by the rules. However combinations of key words and connection forms selected three of these papers, an abstract and two papers less than 1500 words long. The other four papers, two longer than 1500 words, one shorter than 1500 and one shorter than 500, were selected by connection forms in a heading, the summary, and the main texts respectively.

Thus keywords alone selected 73 percent of the Group 1 papers.

Group 1 Toxicity Rules Applied to Group 2. The rules developed for group 1 selected 92 percent of the 180 *toxicity* papers in Group 2.

Seventy-six percent were selected by keywords. The details are in Figure 7.

Another five papers contained keywords but not in positions or frequencies to satisfy the rules. These papers were selected by connection forms, two in titles and one each in a heading, a summary, and a text shorter than 500 words.

In the 13 percent of the papers containing no keywords selection was made by connection forms. The details are in Figure 8.

Group 2 Toxicity Papers Missed by Group 1 Rules. A total of 14 papers were missed by the rules. The rule changes needed to select them are indicated below.

Adding "iododerma" (eruption caused by iodine) and "hypercortisonism" (morbid effects of an excess of cortisone) to the thesaurus group would select two of these papers. Both these words are in Dorland, and a scan of that medical dictionary for all such specific *toxicity* terms would have added them.

Another paper required "associated with" as a connective. On checking it was found that several occurrences

of "associated with" had been overlooked in Group 1 and should have been included in the connective list.

A paper needed "enlargement" as a disorder term, occurring in the expression "adrenal enlargement caused by estrogen treatment". "Enlargement" appears neither in Dorland nor in Stedman, a more recent medical dictionary.[14]

The best *toxicity* clue in another paper was its title, "Injury to Guinea Pigs that Follows a High Intake of Phosphates." This changed the permitted word distance for connection forms from three to six.

The only *toxicity* passage in one paper was the following:

It is suggested that the eruption may be due to hypersensitivity or allergy, because some cases give a history of recent upper respiratory infection or of the administration of sulphonamides.

It seemed best, though not ideal, to simply take "hypersensiti . . ." as a clue in this instance and add it to the thesaurus group.

Two papers changed the clue frequency requirement for summaries from at least one keyword or connection form per 200 words to at least one per 300. Six other papers[15] lowered the frequency limit for main texts from one in 1200 to one in 2000 words.

Two papers, besides easing the frequency rule, required identification of connection forms in long texts. These papers were 4000 and 5000 words long.

Another paper contained as a needed *toxicity* clue the sentence:

Severe glossitis, atrophy of lingual papillae, and cheilosis developed in two patients with "megaloblas-

14. The dictionary referred to here is *Stedman's Medical Dictionary* [23].
15. One was the paper which needed "hypersensiti . . ." as a keyword.

	Title	Heading	Abstract	Summary	Main Text Word Length			
					0–500	500–1,000	1,000–1,500	Over 1,500
Accidental	2	0	1	4	3	1	0	Not searched
Absent Toxicity	0	0	0	0	0	0	0	
Slight Toxicity	2	0	0	0	0	0	0	
Familiar Toxicity	0	1	0	0	0	0	0	

FIG. 6. Overassigning by *toxicity* connection forms in Group 1 non-*toxicity* papers.

				Main Text Word Length			
Title	Heading	Abstract	Summary	0–500	500–1,000	1,000–1,500	Over 1,500
35	31	10	17	9	12	9	14

FIG. 7. Selection by keywords of Group 2 *toxicity* papers.

tic anemias" during therapy with small daily doses of Vitamin B_{12}. . . .

Here "during therapy" is not deeply nested to a human reader, but to a computer program using the syntactic emphasis rule which was sketched for Group 1, it would be too deeply nested for acceptance. On the other hand, by correct nesting analysis "anemias" would be too deeply nested for acceptance. Therefore advantage could not be taken of the fortunate accident (in terms of the connection form rule) that "anemias" is near "during". Thus selection of this paper required lowering somewhat the degree of syntactic centrality required in sentences. However there seemed no reason to ease the requirement for titles and headings as well.

In the syntactic rule for Group 1 it was not explicitly specified that hyphenated words be treated as units, though that seems natural for measuring nesting. One Group 2 *toxicity* paper, which was counted as selected, required this condition for its title:

Inhibition of cholesterol-induced hypercholesteremia and atherogenesis by fat-free diet in chicks.

Further Overassigning in Group 1. Some of the rule changes described above increased the overassigning in Group 1.

Adding "iododerma" and "hypercortisonism" to the thesaurus overassigned no further papers. It appeared to the author that addition of all such specific *toxicity* terms would cause no further overassigning.

No more overassigning resulted from adding "associated with" to the connection list, and "enlarg . . ." to the D-list.

Changing the connection-form word distance from three to six overassigned three more accidental papers (a summary and papers less than 500 and 1000 words long), an "absent *toxicity*" and a "slight *toxicity*" (both abstracts).

Adding "hypersensiti . . ." to the thesaurus overassigned one accidental paper (in the title).

Changing the frequency for summaries overassigned (by connection form) one further accidental paper.

Changing the frequency for main texts overassigned two accidental and one "absent *toxicity*" papers, all longer than 1500 words. The change would also have added two longer "familiar *toxicity*" papers, but they had no clues in first sentences or first paragraphs.

Overassigning by connection forms was determined in papers longer than 1500 words only for the non-*toxicity* papers of Group 2, since this testing takes a long time. And, for the same reason, there were no tests for occurrences of the connection form SD even in these papers. Beyond papers already overassigned in Group 2, connection forms in longer papers overassigned an additional four accidental and one "familiar *toxicity*" papers. This is not a large enough number for the sample size to make any useful estimates about such overassigning in Group 1.

Changing the syntactic centrality requirement caused no further overassigning.

In summary, the required changes in indexing rules added another five percent to the overassigning in Group 1, mostly accidental papers, selected equally by keywords and connection forms. And connection forms in longer papers would cause an undetermined further overassigning.

Overassigning in Group 2. The *toxicity* rules developed for Group 1 overassigned 18 percent of the 100 non-*toxicity* papers in Group 2.

Keywords accounted for 13 percent of the overassigning. The details are in Figure 9.

The five percent overassigning by connection forms is shown in Figure 10.

Two of the "absent *toxicity*" papers could be removed by adding "without" to the negation list. There was no apparent way of reducing the other overassigning.

Further Overassigning in Group 2. The changes in frequency rules required by Group 2 *toxicity* papers overassigned five more Group 2 non-*toxicity* papers. Three of them were added by keywords, two long "familiar *toxicity*" papers, and an accidental paper shorter than 1500 words. The other two were accidental papers added by connection forms in summaries.

As noted earlier, connection forms in long papers added four accidental and one "familiar *toxicity*" papers to the overassigning.

				Main Text Work Length			
Title	Heading	Abstract	Summary	0–500	500–1,000	1,000–1,500	Over 1,500
9	1	7	4	2	1	0	Not searched

FIG. 8. Selection by connection forms of Group 2 *toxicity* papers lacking keywords.

	Title	Heading	Abstract	Summary	Main Text Word Length			
					0–500	500–1,000	1,000–1,500	Over 1,500
Accidental	0	0	0	1	0	2	0	0
Absent Toxicity	0	0	1	0	1	1	0	2
Slight Toxicity	0	1	0	0	0	0	0	1
Familiar Toxicity	0	1	0	0	0	1	0	1

FIG. 9. Keyword overassigning in Group 2 by Group 1 *toxicity* rules.

Thus the changes in Group 1 rules required to select all Group 2 *toxicity* papers would add another 10 percent to the overassigning in Group 2.

MSD Indexing Errors. Eleven of the 325 papers, or about three percent, which were not indexed *toxicity* at MSD should have been so indexed.[16]

Twenty-eight of 307 papers, or about nine percent, indexed *toxicity* at MSD should preferably not have been so indexed.[16] And 15 percent of all MSD papers were indexed *toxicity*. Thus about 14 percent of all MSD papers were correctly indexed *toxicity*.

Combining the results of the preceding paragraphs, about 80 percent of the MSD papers which should have been indexed *toxicity* were so indexed. Allowing for sampling errors, between 70 and 88 percent of the MSD papers which should have been indexed *toxicity* were so indexed.

The overassigning of *toxicity* by MSD indexers was one or two percent.

Some of the MSD indexing errors were really clerical errors. For example if clerical processing omitted one index term in 200, then as many as three of the 11 missed *toxicity* papers might have represented clerical errors. In general correct *toxicity* identification by MSD indexers *might* have been near 95 percent.

Seven of the 11 *toxicity* papers missed by the MSD indexers (or clerical mistakes) were selected by keywords and the other four by connection forms. In Group 2, two were missed by the Group 1 rules because of frequency and one in Group 1 had no first sentence or first paragraph clue.[17] The others were not difficult cases for the rules.

Comparison of Computer Indexing and MSD Indexing. "Computer indexing" here is understood to mean indexing by the rules derived from Group 1 without further

16. Based on material given above [p. 324].
17. Progress in the Chemotherapy of Tuberculosis. See [p. 330, footnote 12].

changes. The aplication is to Group 2 except where otherwise indicated.

The computer rules selected 92 percent of 180 *toxicity* papers. Allowing for sampling error, these rules would select between 88 and 95 percent of the *toxicity* papers. Thus the computer rules would be roughly comparable to, or perhaps superior to, MSD indexers in identifying *toxicity* papers.

However the computer rules overassigned 18 percent. Allowing for sampling error, they would overassign between 10 and 26 percent. By contrast the MSD indexers overassigned one or two percent.

Several possible trade-offs are worth noting. Keywords alone selected 76 percent of the *toxicity* papers in Group 2 and overassigned 13 percent. Combining these results with those for Group 1, keywords alone selected 75 percent of the *toxicity* papers and overassigned 10 percent.[18]

The following trade-offs were only determined for Group 1. Use of both keywords and connection forms as clues and increase of the required clue frequency in main texts to one per 600 words selected 90 percent of the *toxicity* papers and overassigned 12 percent. Addition of the requirement that word distance for connection forms be zero decreased selection of *toxicity* papers to 80 percent and decreased overassigning to eight percent. Addition of the further requirement that all main texts (not just those with separate summaries) have a *toxicity* clue in a first sentence or first paragraph reduced selection to 79 percent and overassigning to seven percent.

Application of Toxicity Rules to Federation Proceedings Toxicology Abstracts. The Group 1 *toxicity* rules were applied to the 23 *toxicology* abstracts in the April,

18. However it should be noted that thesaurus overassigning in Group 1 would be 13 percent rather than nine percent (and perhaps comparably higher in Group 2) without the use of *S*-words with some keywords ("intoleran . . .," "deleterious," etc.).

	Title	Heading	Abstract	Summary	Main Text Word Length			
					0–500	500–1,000	1,000–1,500	Over 1,500
Accidental	0	0	1	0	2	0	1	Not searched
Absent Toxicity	0	0	0	0	0	0	0	
Slight Toxicity	0	0	1	0	0	0	0	
Familiar Toxicity	0	0	0	0	0	0	0	

FIG. 10. Connection form overassigning in Group 2 by Group 1 *toxicity* rules.

1962 *Federation Proceedings*.[19] Sixteen of the abstracts were selected by keywords, nine in titles. Fourteen of the 16 were selected by "toxic . . ." and one each by "poison . . ." and "lethal dose". Two more abstracts were selected by connection forms in their texts.

The best clue in one of the remaining abstracts was its title:

Boric Acid Accumulation in Brain after Repeated Injections

However "accumulation" might not already be on the D-list since the closest entry in Dorland's medical dictionary is "accumulator" defined as a storage battery.

The best clue in another abstract was the following:

. . . the drug solution was instilled and it was permitted to remain in contact with the tissues until cardiac arrest occurred.

"Contact" is in Dorland, but it is questionable that it would be on the S-list on the basis of the definitions given there. And "until" is not on the connective list. With these additions to the lists the abstract can be selected by connection form.

Another abstract missed required either "weakness", which is not in Dorland, as a D-word or a clue nested to the following extent:

Others have reported a TOCP metabolite, potent as both an anticholinesterase and an agent that produces hen ataxia. . . .

The best clue in another abstract was the following sentence:

Tar C was the least deleterious of the three tars

By the rules, this is not a *toxicity* clue because "deleterious" is separated by three words from the nearest S-word, "tars".

The rule changes required to select the four abstracts just described would cause no further overassigning in Group 1 and Group 2.

The 23rd *toxicology* abstract was completely missed by the rules. Its text follows:

A Versatile Apparatus for Studying the Effects of Gases, Aerosols and Drugs on Ciliary Activity in the Non-immersed Mammalian Trachea. Sam P. Battista,* Joseph DiNunzio,* and C. J. Kensler. Life-Sciences Division, Arthur D. Little, Inc., Cambridge, Massachusetts.

19. *Federation Proceedings, Vol. 21, No. 2.* pp. 449–453. Federation of American Societies for Experimental Biology, Washington, D.C., Mar.–Apr., 1962, Waverly Press, Baltimore, 1962. These abstracts were indexed by their authors.

Most of the major problems encountered during pharmacological studies on non-immersed cilia are ascribed to a failure to adequately maintain proper temperature and/or humidity. Less frequently recognized is the more subtle but none-the-less important need to control the volume and viscosity of the fluid film in which the cilia must operate, the size and density of the particle used to measure ciliary activity and finally the inherent differences in sensitivity of the cilia to the test agents. The apparatus was designed so that the certain parts of the cycle of operation, including the exposure time (as short as 18 seconds), could be operated automatically or by push button. Consistent ciliary activity was obtained when a 12% egg white Tyrode's solution was applied at a constant rate of 0.003 ml/min. to the lower end of the trachea and the upper end elevated 10 degrees. In this way a small volume of fluid of constant composititon and viscosity, together with tracer particles, are carried against the force of gravity by ciliary activity. The apparatus can also be used to study the effects of compounds applied in Tyrode's solution.

It is not clear how this paper could be selected by computer except perhaps at the cost of much overassigning. However Mrs. Schultz suggested that it would probably not be so important to users for this abstract to be indexed *toxicology* as to be indexed under some other headings.

Note on Syntactic Measure of Distance. Words in an expression which are far apart by word distance may nonetheless be syntactically close. For example,

Injury to Guinea Pigs that Follows a High Intake of Phosphates

contains the syntactic sequence: Injury-that-Follows-Intake. Thus syntactic distance might be better than word distance for measuring word relations [9].

Syntactic distance for connection forms was tried. A distance of one intervening word was needed by Group 1 *toxicity* papers. This distance was required by just one *toxicity* clue:

apnea was due to excessive sedation

A distance of one sufficed for the Group 2 *toxicity* papers.

This syntactic distance overassigned 15 accidental and one "slight *toxicity*" papers in Groups 1 and 2. By comparison, a word distance of three for connection forms overassigned 15 accidental papers,[20] while a word distance of six overassigned 18 accidental, one "absent

20. Four other papers, not counted here, were overassigned by "reaction to ——*S*" and other forms described on [p. 494]. No syntactic alternatives to these forms appeared desirable.

toxicity" and one "slight *toxicity*" papers.[20] Most of the syntactic overassignments were also word distance false selections. Examples of those which were not are the following:

Meningitis has been produced experimentally in adult rhesus monkeys by the inoculation [of bacteria]. . . It is postulated that failure to stain the Golgi apparatus in blocks of frozendried tissue might be due to gas in tissue spaces. . . .

Use of syntactic distance in computer indexing rules would raise the problem of structures ambiguous to the computer. Resolving ambiguities by connecting pairs of words which were closer, by word distance, rather than pairs further away *appeared* to work for Group 1 and Group 2. However this rule failed in a *Federation* abstract for the following needed clue:

The ureter, bladder or urethra was then isolated, washed with warm saline, the drug solution was instilled and it was permitted to remain in contact with the tissues until cardiac arrest occurred.

The desired sequence is either "contact-until-arrest" or "solution-until-arrest". The former cannot be obtained because "with the tissues" intervenes. The latter cannot be obtained because the clause "it . . . tissues" intervenes.

Word distance was also used to relate some thesaurus words with accompanying S-words and *toxicity* clues with negation words. In these cases syntactic distance *appeared* to work about as well as word distance.

4. Penicillin

The other MSD term studied was *penicillin*. At MSD this term was assigned to seven percent of the collection in 1955.

To develop computer rules for assigning *penicillin*, 17 *penicillin* and 200 non-*penicillin* papers (Group A) were examined. These rules were then tested with an additional 38 *penicillin* and 90 non-*penicillin* papers (Group B).

Five papers indexed *penicillin* at MSD were judged by Mrs. Schultz to be incorrectly so indexed. These five were then included with the non-*penicillin* papers.

Five papers not indexed *penicillin* were judged to be papers which should have been so indexed. They were included with the *penicillin* papers.

Of two other papers not indexed *penicillin* it was not possible to say, nine years after indexing, why they should have been indexed *penicillin* or why they should not have been. These papers were excluded from the study.

Identification and Overassigning in Group A. Every *penicillin* paper contained the word "penicillin". The distribution is shown in Figure 11.

No other expressions appeared to be plausible *penicillin* clues.

Of the 200 non-*penicillin* papers six percent contained the word "penicillin". The distribution is shown in Figure 12.

Among these papers eight referred to routine clinical uses of penicillin which were not noteworthy. Another clinical paper which was less than 1500 words long, an experimental paper shorter than 500 words, and an experimental paper with "penicillin" in a figure contained other familiar facts about penicillin as part of the background. The remaining paper was a long general discussion of drug toxicity testing which included familiar facts about penicillin in its illustrations.

Reducing Overassigning-Syntactic Emphasis Measure. The overassigning just described suggests that emphasis measures might reduce false selection.

Syntactic emphasis measure did not help much. In one long non-*penicillin* paper the only occurrence of "penicillin" was the following:

None of the patients received any other drugs during the entire period of treatment except one patient who was treated with penicillin for three days because of intercurrent infection.

However the greatest nesting in the other non-*penicillin* papers is illustrated by the following:

In a second similar experiment the mice received extensive chemotherapy with penicillin and aureomycin to determine whether control of secondary infection would prevent destruction of the eye.

In nine *penicillin* papers the most central occurrence of "penicillin" was nested at least as much as in the sentence just quoted. It was more nested in seven of these papers. For instance:

For example, there are many agents available today which possess high antimicrobial activity, but for reasons of *toxicity* (neomycin, polymyxin), low tissue concentrations (nitrofurantoin, carbomycin), or poor penetration into the cerebrospinal fluid (penicillin), their selection for treatment simply on the basis of *in vitro* activity may lead to poor results.
S.C.M. was treated for two days with penicillin without any effect on his pyrexia . . .
In doubtful cases where a bacteriological examination is not feasible a combination of hydrocortisone with penicillin and streptomycin is indicated.

The first of these quoted sentences indicates that a syntactically unemphasized reference to penicillin in a paper might be index-worthy.

In summary, one false selection in Group A could be avoided by syntactic emphasis measure.

Title	Heading	Abstract	Summary	Figure	Reference	Main Text Word Length			
						0–500	500–1,000	1,000–1,500	Over 1,500
1	0	2	2	3	1	1	1	0	6

FIG. 11. "Penicillin" occurrences in Group A *penicillin* papers.

Document Place Emphasis Measure. Eight *penicillin* papers contained "penicillin" only in the main text.

The three *penicillin* papers with "penicillin" in figures also contain the word in main text (with frequencies of 1/1400, 7/3900, 14/2700). This is not true of the two non-*penicillin* papers with figure "penicillin" occurrences. Thus not using clues in figures (also not used by the *toxicity* rules) would remove two papers from overassigning.

One of the *penicillin* papers with "penicillin" in a reference contains one main text occurrence in 1400 words, and the other contains 29 main text occurrences in 4400 words.

Frequency Emphasis Measure. Requiring at least one occurrence of "penicillin" per 200 words of abstract removed the non-*penicillin* abstract (which had one occurrence in almost 500 words). Summaries needed a frequency of one clue per 300 words.

Requiring more than one main text occurrence of "penicillin" would omit five of the eight non-*penicillin* papers overassigned by main text occurrences (three long papers and two less than 1000 words long). However it would also miss five of the ten *penicillin* papers selected by main text occurrences (three long papers, a paper shorter than 1500 words, and a paper shorter than 500 words).

The ineffectiveness of relative frequency in main texts is indicated in Figure 13.

The data of the preceding two paragraphs indicate that relatively unemphasized (at least as measured by frequency) references to penicillin in a paper might be worth indexing. For example a 3200 word *penicillin* paper, "Preparation of the Patient for Intestinal Surgery", contained the following as its only reference to penicillin:

Strains of *Micrococcus pyogenes* resistant to penicillin, streptomycin, aureomycin, oxytetracycline and sometimes to erythromycin are found growing rapidly in the intestine of some patients who have followed this regime of preparation.[21]

21. From Griffin, G. D. J., Judd, E. S., and Dearing, W. H. Preparation of the patient for intestinal surgery. *Postgrad. Med. 18* (July 1955), 18.

And a 2900 word *penicillin* paper, "Hematoma of the Orbit", contained only the following reference to penicillin:

Subsequently the child was given intensive therapy with penicillin, streptomycin, chloramphenicol, and then erythromycin when the organism was found to be most sensitive to this antibiotic.[22]

In general, some unemphasized facts may be familiar material which is not worth indexing, but other unemphasized facts may require indexing.

Sentence and Paragraph Position Emphasis Measure. Of the fourteen *penicillin* papers with main texts 12 (the other two were abstracts) had at least one main text "penicillin" occurrence in a first sentence or first paragraph. One of the exceptions had one "penicillin" occurrence in 1700 words and the other had two occurrences in 2500 words. The former paper had no summary. The latter paper, describing a case of toxoplasmosis, reported the ineffectiveness of several therapeutic agents, including penicillin, which was mentioned twice in 2500 words.[23]

Only three of the nine non-*penicillin* papers with a "penicillin" occurrence in the main text contained "penicillin" in a first sentence or first paragraph. Five of the six excluded papers had summaries.

Thus the requirement of at least one first sentence or first paragraph occurrence of "penicillin" in papers with summaries would reduce main text overassigning from nine papers to four. However it would also miss one *penicillin* paper.

Indexing Rules for Group A. Using only "penicillin" occurrences in title, headings, abstracts, summary, and main text, imposing a relative frequency requirement on abstracts, and a slight restriction on syntactic nesting would select all *penicillin* papers in Group A and decrease the overassigning from six to four percent.

Application of Group A Rules to Group B Penicillin

22. From Roberts, W. Hematoma of the orbit (Report of two cases). *Amer. J. Ophthalmology 40* (Aug. 1955), 218.

23. Beverly, J. K. A., Skipper, E., and Marshall, S. C. Acquired toxoplasmosis (With a report of a case of laboratory infection). *Brit. Med. J. 1* (Mar. 1955), 577–578.

Title	Heading	Abstract	Summary	Figure	Reference	Main Text Word Length			
						0–500	500–1,000	1,000–1,500	Over 1,500
0	0	1	0	2	0	1	1	2	5

FIG. 12. "Penicillin" occurrences in Group A non-*penicillin* papers.

	Main Text Length						
	0–500	500–1,000	1,000–1,500	1,500–2,000	2,000–2,500	2,500–3,000	3,000–3,500
Penicillin papers	3	3	3	1	0	1	1
Non-*penicillin papers*	2	2	2	2	0	1	0

Fig. 13. Relative frequencies of "penicillin" occurrences in main texts.

Papers. The indexing rules developed for Group A selected 97 percent of the Group B *penicillin* papers, missing only one of 38. The distribution of clues is shown in Figure 14.

The missed paper was an abstract with one "penicillin" occurrence in 210 words. Reducing the required frequency for abstracts to one clue per 300 words for this abstract would cause no further overassigning in Group A or, to anticipate, in Group B.

The most deeply nested required clue was the following:

Parenteral administration of 3 to 5 million units of penicillin should be carried out daily.

In only five other Group B *penicillin* papers was the most central clue nested as deeply as in the following sentence:

Alternatively the patient may receive a monthly injection of 1,200,000 units of benzathine penicillin.

This contrasts with Group A where seven out of 17 *penicillin* papers had the most central clue at least this deeply nested.

Three of the papers selected by main text occurrences contained only one "penicillin", two of them shorter than 600 words and the other one 3500 words long. Fourteen main text papers had at least one "penicillin" per 500 words, five more at least one per 1000, and four at least one per 1500. A 2100 and a 5700 word paper each had two "penicillin's" and a 3500 paper contained one.

Four of the 18 papers with summaries had no "penicillin" in a first sentence or first paragraph of main text. Three of these papers had only main text clues; they are the long papers referred to at the end of the preceding paragraph. Four of 12 papers without summaries, all shorter than 500 words, had no first sentence or first paragraph occurrence of "penicillin".

Overassigning by Group A Rules in Group B. The Group A rules overassigned about four percent of the Group B non-*penicillin* papers, falsely selecting four papers out of 90.

All four papers were overassigned by main text occurrences with the following frequencies: 2/1100, 3/1800, 1/2800, 2/9000. None of the four, each with a summary, had "penicillin" in a first sentence or first paragraph.

No other Group B non-*penicillin* paper contained any occurrence of "penicillin".

Comparison of Computer Indexing and MSD Indexing. Five of 285 papers, or about two percent, which were not indexed *penicillin* at MSD should have been.[24]

Five of 60 papers, or about eight percent, indexed *penicillin* at MSD should not have been.[24] And seven percent of all MSD papers were indexed *penicillin*. Thus about six percent of all MSD papers were correctly indexed *penicillin*.

Combining the results of the preceding two paragraphs, about 75 percent of the MSD papers which should have been indexed *penicillin* were so indexed. Allowing for possible clerical mistakes[25] and sampling errors, between 60 and almost 100 percent of the MSD papers which should have been indexed *penicillin* were so indexed.

The overassigning of *pencillin* by MSD indexers was between less than one percent and less than two percent.

The Group A computer indexing rules applied to Group B selected 97 percent of the *penicillin* papers. Allowing for sampling error these rules might select 85 to almost 100 percent of the *penicillin* papers. They also overassigned four percent in the Group B sample, and this might mean anywhere from less than one percent to 10 percent overassigning.

A trade-off in Group A suggests itself. Adding to the Group A rules the requirements of a main text clue frequency of at least one per 1500 words and a main text clue in a first sentence or first paragraph (whether or not the paper has a summary), would cause a selection of 76 percent of the *penicillin* papers and an overassigning of less than two percent. In Group B these rules would select 79 percent and overassign nothing.

5. Discussion

The subject recognition rates in six of the previous studies ranged from 30 to 70 percent with corresponding

24. Based on material given above [p. 335].
25. See [p. 333].

Title	Heading	Abstract	Summary	Main Text Word Length			
				0–500	500–1,000	1,000–1,500	Over 1,500
3	2	2	4	4	4	5	13

Fig. 14. *Penicillin* clues in Group B *penicillin* papers.

overassigning less than seven percent [4, 5, 12, 24, 26, 30].[26, 27] The results in the other four tests were 100 percent recognition and five percent overassigning [21], 94 percent recognition and 40 percent overassigning [7], 80 percent recognition and 10 percent overassigning [7], 80 percent recognition and 13 percent overassigning [27] and 60 percent recognition and 10 percent overassigning [31].

No general conclusions can be drawn from the empirical work so far reported, including the study described here. It is not clear that the varieties of subject specifications, documents, and collections have been adequately sampled. It is also not clear how many of the human judgments used as standards in these studies were idiosyncratic.[28] Further, not all proposed recognition methods have been tried.

However an empirical test can show that some phenomena which were previously only speculative possibilities or not even thought of, do sometimes occur. Some examples provided by the work reported in this paper are summarized below.

All of the recognition methods previously tested have shared the assumption that any subject requires at most a few dozen clue words and phrases to identify it in any paper in which it occurs. However the connection form *toxicity* papers require S- and D-lists containing probably thousands of words each.

All previously proposed recognition methods have assumed that common words such as "if", "when", "after", "produce", "cause", etc. can be ignored except perhaps for their grammatical roles. However the common words in connection forms are used for their meanings.[29]

Connection form rules illustrate that it is possible by appropriate generalization to formulate rules for identifying subjects expressed by nonrecurring expressions. However it is not clear a priori what subjects other than *toxicity* can and should be automatically recognized by such rules.

The *toxicity* paper and *toxicity* expressions which contain neither keywords nor connection forms indicate that

a humanly identifiable subject *might* not be computer identifiable. However the conclusion is not certain. A much larger set of *toxicity* expressions, neither keywords nor connection forms, than this study provided might display recurring forms which would suggest further computer recognition rules. These forms might be represented in the sample only by miscellaneous single instances. As a parallel, if the sample had included only one connection form expression the connection form rules might not have been formulated.

The complete index sets and texts of 35 MSD papers were briefly compared in a search for further "hard cases". It is the author's *impression* that almost all of the index terms could be automatically assigned to these papers by appropriate thesaurus groups. However this leaves open the question of how to construct sufficiently comprehensive thesaurus groups and the question of how much overassigning such thesaurus groups would produce.

Two of the exceptions were *toxicity* connection form papers. The other two exceptions were *oral administration* papers which contained only these expressions:

phenothiazine feeding
medicated mash
administered in the drinking water
food medication

These examples suggest the rule that a sentence contain a "drug word" and a "food-drink word" separated by at most two other words. However this rule was not tested on other papers.

Suppose that important failures of an automatic subject recognition method proposed for a particular application would be infrequent but not sufficiently infrequent. Nonthesaurus MSD *toxicity* papers may illustrate this. Then a sample of documents and subject specifications used for testing that recognition method in that application might appear adequate but lead to incorrect reliance on that recognition method.

It has been suggested that automatic subject recognition can be improved by augmenting papers with words closely associated statistically with the words in the papers [10, 14, 25].[30] A paper to be augmented is usually represented by an unordered list of its words or some part of the list. However it is not clear that such augmentation would add *toxicity* keywords to *toxicity* papers which lack them. An example is the *toxicity* paper, "A Rare Complication Due to Isoniazid . . . ".[31] The word list for this paper contains disorder, treatment, substance, physiological and pediatric words, together with common words. It is the author's impression that such a word list, or any part of it, is not especially likely to belong to a *toxicity* paper in the MSD collection. Nor does it seem that a different categorization of the word list

26. Maron, Borko and Williams do not explicitly report overassigning rates. However in each case approximately one subject category was assigned to each paper, and the number of subject categories is known, so the average overassigning can be estimated from the recognition rate.

27. A useful estimate of overassigning in the Stevens test appears impossible because of the rather inconsistent human indexing which she used as a standard.

28. Some of the studies [4, 5, 7, 26, 27] used judgments agreed on by two or three subject specialists. The work reported here used, in effect, two specialists for "hard cases".

29. "Grammatical" rather than "syntactic" is used in this context to prevent a possible confusion. Some writers use "syntactic" to refer both to grammatical relations among words in a text and relations among referents of the text which are expressed by that text. This broader usage of "syntactic" seems unfortunate since it blurs an important distinction.

30. For a brief summary, see [18, pp. 441–2].

31. Given in full [p. 325].

would increase the probability. If not, then association procedures could not add *toxicity* keywords to this paper. This conclusion also *appears* to be true of the other connection form papers and the Group 1 paper which lacked both keywords and connection forms.[32] These are not conclusive counter-examples but they indicate a possible problem for recognition by statistical association.

Giuliano and Jones [9] have also suggested adding sentence co-occurrence or syntactic information to the word list representing a paper. Sentence co-occurrence would change the word list for "A Rare Complication Due to Isoniazid . . ." into five sublists (counting the title as a sentence). The inadequacy of such a refinement for this paper is suggested by the figures given earlier for co-occurrences of *S*-words and *D*-words.[33] What would happen if syntactic information were added to the five sublists is unclear. The author sees no strong reason to believe the addition would help automatic recognition in this case. It is his impression that similar remarks apply to the other non-keyword *toxicity* papers in the sample.

An automatic recognition rule of a general kind, such as a frequency or sentence-paragraph position requirement, may work for one subject specification in an application and not for another. For example a main text frequency of one clue per 2000 words selected all *toxicity* papers in Groups 1 and 2 but missed 10 percent of the *penicillin* papers in Group A and B. And the first sentence-first paragraph rule which selected all *toxicity* papers missed 15 percent of the *penicillin* papers.

If a recognition rule overassigns x percent of the collection and correctly identifies y percent of the collection, then let x/y be called the *overassignment ratio* of the rule. For example the Group 1 *toxicity* rules have an overassignment ratio, allowing for sampling errors, between 0.5 and 1.5, and the *penicillin* rules would overassign between 0.1 and 1.5. In other studies the average overassignment ratios were between 0.3 and 1.5 except for a 94 percent recognition costing 8.5 [7] and an 80 percent recognition costing 2.0 [7, 27].

The subject specifications in previous studies, except [24], would not usually be used conjunctively in searching, while an MSD search is usually specified by a conjunction of index terms. The possible importance of the difference is indicated by the following example. Suppose MSD indexing was automatically produced, an MSD search was specified by index terms A, B and C, each term was overassigned with ratio 1.0, and assignments and overassignments by the recognition rules were all statistically independent. Then only one eighth of the papers selected by the conjunction of A, B and C would correctly have all three terms, which means an overassignment ratio of 8.0.

On the other hand most MSD searches are intended to select a small fraction of one percent of the collection, while almost every subject specification used in previous recognition studies was satisfied by at least one percent of the collection searched.[34] Automatic recognition rules for subjects occurring in far less than one percent of the collection in the applications previously studied would perhaps have much higher overassignment ratios than the ratios found in those studies.

Overassigning can inflate the storage of a retrieval system, perhaps to an unacceptable degree. For example, suppose automatic recognition rules are used to produce a book-form subject index for wide distribution. A high recognition rate and an overassignment ratio of 1.0 would mean an index twice as large as the recognition rate alone would require and thus might be unacceptable. On the other hand if a subject index automatically produced was to be stored on punched cards, for instance, which had surplus coding space then the increased storage would not be a problem.

It was the author's impression after examining the Group 1 papers overassigned by Group 1 *toxicity* rules that about half the overassigned papers could be confidently rejected by a post-editor examining an average of two clue sentences and headings per paper. About a quarter of the papers overassigned by the Group A *penicillin* rules could be similarly rejected. The average paper not rejected would require the same time to examine as a rejected paper. The post-editing would apparently not be clerical work, but it was not clear how much special knowledge would be required. No attempt was made to determine how much further examination of context would be required to further reduce overassigning.

The preceding paragraph suggests the following possibility. The output of an automatic recognition system for a subject specification should be not only identification of the selected papers but also copies of the clue sentences and headings which led to their selection. Such an output might facilitate rejection of overassigned papers.

The occurrence of *toxicity* keywords in titles of only 20 percent of the *toxicity* papers and of "penicillin" in titles of only 7 percent of the *penicillin* papers illustrates the inadequacy of permuted title indexes for some purposes.

On the other hand *toxicity* keywords occurred in the titles or headings of 37 percent of the *toxicity* papers. This suggests that a permuted title and heading index might sometimes be a significant improvement on a permuted title index. However keywords in headings had an overassignment ratio near one. And "penicillin" occurred in headings of only 4 percent of the *penicillin* papers.

Papers longer than 1000 words, not used in earlier

32. Given in full [p. 327].
33. See [pp. 327 and 328].

34. Two of the **17** subjects in the Salton tests occurred in 0.5 of the collection and two more in 0.8 of the collection [21].

empirical studies, posed no special problem for *toxicity*. For example, 60 percent of the non-*toxicity* papers were longer than 1000 words, but a smaller proportion of the papers overassigned by either Group 1 or Group 2 rules were of that length. And the trade-offs suggested above for *toxicity*[35] would cost about equally many longer and shorter *toxicity* papers while the overassignment reductions were also about equally divided. More affirmatively, for longer papers the main text frequency rule (without trade-off modifications) and first sentence-first paragraph rule reduced overassigning primarily among the longer papers. The frequency result contrasts with Swanson's [28] that frequency did not help. However he tested absolute rather than relative frequency.

Longer papers would perhaps provide a greater problem for *penicillin* than shorter ones. Eighty-five per cent of the *penicillin* overassigning was in longer papers, while only 65 percent of *penicillin* papers were longer. The main text frequency rule and first sentence-first paragraph rule, which worked well for long *toxicity* papers, could only be used for *penicillin* at the cost of some *penicillin* papers. However these rules made possible the trade-offs suggested for *penicillin*. The trade-offs would cost about equal proportions of longer and shorter *penicillin* papers but would remove from overassigning all of the longer non-*penicillin* papers.

The new recognition rules used in this study with some success were connection forms, negations forbidden near clues (for *toxicity*), and S-words required near some keywords. The last rule somewhat resembles Salton's "statistical phrases" [21], but the S-list is very long and a word nearness closer than sentence co-occurrence is used.

The previously untested recognition techniques applied here with some success were a syntactic emphasis measure, a first sentence-first paragraph emphasis measure, and a syntactic distance measure.

Using several hundred *toxicity* papers in the study helped to indicate the forbidden negation and keyword S-word rules. The large sample on which the *toxicity* rules were based (Group 1) also may have helped make possible a recognition rate above 90 percent. The only other studies reporting recognition rates over 80 percent were Salton's [21], still in the early phase in which the corpus searched is that used to build the thesaurus, and Dale's [7] in which this recognition rate cost 40 percent overassigning.

References

1. Automatic Abstracting. Rep. No. C 107-3U1, Comput. Div., Ramo Wooldridge, Canoga Park, Calif., Feb. 1963.
2. BAXENDALE, P. Machine-made index for technical literature—An experiment. *IBM J. Res. Develop.* **2,** 4 (Oct. 1958), 354.

35. See [p. 333].

3. BERNARD, J., AND SHILLING, C. Accuracy of titles in describing content of biological sciences articles. Amer. Institute of Biological Sciences, Washington, D.C., May, 1963.
4. BORKO, H., AND BERNICK, M. Automatic document classification: Part II. *J. ACM* **11,** 2 (Apr. 1964), 138–151.
5. ———. Toward the establishment of a computer based classification system for scientific documentation. Rep. No. TM-1763, System Development Corp., Santa Monica, Calif., Feb., 1964.
6. CLIMENSON, W. D., HARDWICK, N. H., AND JACABSON, S. W. Automatic syntax analysis in machine indexing and abstracting. In *Machine Indexing*, pp. 305–325. American U., "publisher" 1961.
7. DALE, A. G., AND DALE, N. Some clumping experiments for associative document retrieval. *Amer. Doc.* **16,** 1 (Jan. 1965), 5–9.
8. *Dorland's Medical Dictionary.* 23rd., W. B. Saunders, Philadelphia, 1957.
9. GIULIANO, V., AND JONES, P. E. Studies for the design of an English command and control language system, Sec. V. Rep. No. CACL-1, Arthur D. Little, Inc., Cambridge, Mass., June 1962.
10. ———. Linear associative information retrieval. In *Vistas in Information Handling, Vol. 1,* ch. 2. Howerton and Weeks (Eds.), Spartan Books, Washington, D.C. 1963.
11. LUHN, H. P. A statistical approach to mechanized encoding and searching of literary information. *IBM J. Res. Develop.* **1,** 4 (Oct. 1957).
12. MARON, M. E. Automatic indexing: an experimental inquiry. *J. ACM* **8,** 3 (July 1961), 404.
13. MONTGOMERY, C., AND SWANSON, D. R. Machinelike indexing by people. *Amer. Doc.* **13,** 4 (Oct. 1962), 359–366.
14. NEEDAM, R. A method for using computers in information classification. Preprints and Proc. Conf. Internal. Fed. Inform. Proc. Soc., Munich, 1962.
15. NEWILL, V. A., AND GOFFMAN, W. Searching titles by man, machine, and chance. *Proc. Amer. Doc. Instit., 1964,* pp. 421–423, Spartan Books, Washington, D.C., 1964.
16. *Nonconventional Technical Information Systems in Current Use.* No. 2, p. 24. National Science Foundation, Washington, D.C., 1959.
17. O'CONNOR, J. Correlation of indexing headings and title words in three medical indexing systems. *Amer. Doc.* **15,** 2 (Apr. 1964), 96–104.
18. ———. Mechanized indexing methods and their testing. *J. ACM* **11,** 4 (Oct. 1964), 437–449.
19. ———. Mechanized indexing studies of MSD toxicity, part I (Appendix D). AD 436 523. Defense Documentation Center, Cameron Station, Alexandria, Va.
20. ———. Mechanized indexing studies of MSD toxicity,

part II (Appendix B). AD 437 868, Defense Documentation Center, Cameron Station, Alexandria, Va.

21. SALTON, G. ET AL. Information storage and retrieval. Rep. No. ISR-8, Computation Labs, Harvard U., Cambridge, Mass., Dec. 1964.

22. SHULTZ, C. K. Chapter in *Punched Cards*, J. Perry and R. Casey (Eds.), 2nd ed., Reinhold Publish. Corp., New York, 1958.

23. *Stedman's Medical Dictionary*. 20th ed., Williams & Wilkins, Baltimore, 1961.

24. STEVENS, M., AND URBAN, G. H. Training a computer to assign descriptors to documents: Experiments in automatic abstracting. *Proc. Spring Joint Comput. Conf. 1964*, pp. 563–575, Spartan Books, Washington, D.C., 1964.

25. STILES, H. E. The association factor in information retrieval. *J. ACM* **8**, 2 (Apr. 1961), 271.279.

26. SWANSON, D. R. Searching natural language text by computer. *Sci.* **132**, 34 (Oct. 1960), 1099.

27. ——. Interrogating a computer in natural language. Preprints and Proc. Conf. Internat. Fed. Inform. Proc. Soc., Munich, 1962.

28. ——. Research procedures for automatic indexing. In *Machine Indexing*, pp. 281–304, American U., 1962.

29. THORNE, J. P. Automatic language analysis. Indiana U., Bloomington, Ind., Dec. 1962. AD 297 381, Defense Documentation Center, Cameron Station, Alexandria, Va.

30. WILLIAMS, J. H., JR. A discriminant method for automatically classifying documents. *Proc. Fall Joint Comput. Conf. 1963*, pp. 161–166, Spartan Books, Washington, D.C., 1963.

31. ——. Results of classifying documents with multiple discriminant functions. IBM Federal Systems Div., Bethesda, Md., 1964. Delivered at Symposium on Statistical Association Methods for Mechanized Documentation, Washington, D.C., Mar. 1964.

D. Citation Indexing

31 Citation Indexing and Evaluation of Scientific Papers

J. MARGOLIS
Science
Vol. 155, No. 3767, March, 1967

As a result of the recent expansion of scientific literature, more time and effort are being devoted to the selection of what is to be read than to the actual reading. To cope with the demand there has been a corresponding growth of abstracting and indexing services as well as of sophisticated computer-based systems for information storage and retrieval such as the "Medlars" development (1). Against this rapidly shifting background it is almost impossible to say what is the prevalent attitude of users toward scientific publications, but presumably most readers still try first to ascertain the nature of an article's contents by reference to its author, title, or other subject descriptors.

The use of the bibliography as a point of departure is a relatively new approach, which became practicable only with the compilation of citation indexes (2). It is self-evident that the contents of an article determine to what papers the article will refer. Perhaps less obvious is the fact that in some respects the bibliography appended to an article specifies uniquely, if indirectly, its subject (3). The practice of appraising a paper by noting the references it cites is probably quite common. When a busy research worker scans the current periodicals he

may be able to decide at once from the list of references whether an article with an interesting title is worth reading. He may, for example, be inclined to reject a paper that does not mention some important contributions on the subject. More generally, each item on the list provides a clue, and the total "spectrum" of such clues will often identify the theme. For those who can read the code, this identification is an act of instant and effortless recognition — effortless, that is, compared with evaluation of any part of the contents. However, this approach can be useful only to the reader who is already familiar with the literature, and, in any case, it depends on finding the article first, either by chance or by way of the existing subject-oriented information channels.

The appearance of a comprehensive *Science Citation Index* (4) has made it possible for the first time to systematize this procedure for general use. The structure and operation of the *Index* have been described in detail elsewhere (2, 5-7). In essence, it is produced by listing all the items cited in papers (sources) in a multidisciplinary selection of scientific, technical, and medical periodicals (613 journals in 1961 and more than 1500 in 1966). The items are in the form of line entries, arranged alphabetically by the name of the first author, followed by the year, name of the journal, volume, page, and certain other coded information. Under each citation are listed all the citing (source) articles, identified in a similar manner. The *Index* is produced quarterly (with a cumulative issue at the end of each year) and lists only the source papers published in the journals being processed at the time. No such restrictions apply to the cited items. Anything that may appear in the list of references, from "personal communications" to citations of Lewis Carroll or Confucius, is a legitimate entry.

For the purpose of retrieving the most up-to-date information, the search of the current *Index* usually starts with one or more specific items, which, one believes, are bound to be cited by any article that is worth reading. Since publications belonging to the recent "research front" (8) form a tightly interwoven network and an average paper carries approximately 15 references, the user need not be particularly careful, for a generic search, in his selection of entry points. A search based on, say, five respectable citations will, almost inevitably, lead to all the important papers in the source journals but, probably, also to a number of irrelevant papers. The latter must be treated as "noise" (2), which can, however, be reduced by various screening procedures. First of all, the author's name and the source journal may already be a sufficient reason for immediate exclusion. Next, by reference to full titles listed in the *Source Index* that accompanies the *Citation Index*, a large proportion of the irrelevant items can be eliminated. Using a process of "bibliographic coupling" (6), one may narrow the search at will by accepting only those items which cite two or more of the starting references. Lastly, with the aid of the existing subject indexes, one may use any combination of citation and subject descriptors as a basis for an automatic search program (3).

One of the most attractive features of citation indexing is the fact that it is essentially an algorithmic process (9). Once the panel of source publications and the computer system have been specified, the rest does not require specialized scientific knowledge. However, this process cannot eliminate all errors in the original material, so the *Index* contains many inaccuracies, mostly in the volume or page number, and variations in initials, which may sometimes cause the same item to be listed as two or more nonconsecutive entries. By and large, these are only a minor nuisance and do not cause failure in retrieval for the user who starts with a few definite references and hopes to be guided to the most recent papers that have cited these. All the same, this means that the *Index* cannot be used without some intellectual effort, as it could be were it not for these defects.

Errors, variations in spelling, and homographs — that is, multiplicity of authors with identical names and initials — are a more serious drawback in statistical studies. This can be corrected for or tolerated when one is dealing with individual items, but at present there appears to be

no way of reducing a survey of author citations to clerical work, let alone to computer processing.

Another remarkable aspect of a citation index is its self-organizing nature, which stems from the "ancestor"-versus-"descendant" relationship between the cited and citing publications, respectively. Every time an author refers to other papers he becomes an unwitting contributor not only to the size of the system but also to its integration. What is more, the very existence of the *Science Citation Index* will almost certainly have various feedback influences on the writing and citing habits of future authors. This would, in turn, be reflected in the contents of the *Index* and could progressively increase its usefulness. While it is very difficult to anticipate all that can happen to such a self-regulating system, some of the possibilities are examined below.

1. Citation Habits

It is self-evident that the healthy operation of citation indexing depends on citation habits. These must vary enormously from article to article, but statistical regularities discovered in the *Index* point to the existence of certain vague norms of citation behavior (10). Authors of original contributions are probably the best-qualified critics of the literature in their field, but, since reviewing is not their primary aim, their selection of references is apt to be somewhat casual. Granted that really important papers are usually cited and trivial ones usually ignored, there remains a wide area in between which is influenced by familiarity, language, loyalty, and self-interest, all of which contribute either to the general level of semantic noise or to retrieval loss. Extended use of citation indexing may well lead to general improvement of standards, as a result of editorial policy and recognition of moral obligations on the part of the authors. But a more realistic motive, and one that enhances the self-organizing features of the system, could be the author's self-interest in feeding the *Index* with relevant information so that he may reach his readers. He knows that his article may be overlooked if it does not cite pertinent literature. Haphazard citation of respectable publications of a general nature, such as textbooks or monographs, may also be against the author's interest because many readers may be discouraged by the large numbers of entries for such frequently cited works, from using them as a point of departure. Thus, from the writer's point of view it pays to exercise care in the choice of bibliography.

On the debit side, such a user-oriented outlook might promote an unjustifiable increase in the number of references, since this number, of course, determines the number of times the source paper is listed in the *Index*. However, even now many leading journals discourage the inclusion of exhaustive bibliographies, and an extension of this policy may be sufficient to prevent such a practice, especially because it would be in the interest of "evaluation-oriented" writers not to be overgenerous in acknowledging a debt to others.

In his book *Little Science, Big Science* (*11*), de Solla Price remarks that most scientists "have a secret hope that some standard will be found for the objective judgment of their own caliber and reputation. . . ." The value of a scientific paper can be measured by the influence it has on others, and citation indexing provides, as a by-product, a measure of the impact of articles, authors, and journals (*12, 13*). For example, of all cited papers listed in the *Science Citation Index* for 1961, 75 percent were cited once only, 12 percent twice, 6 percent three times, and only about 1 percent six times or more (*8*). It is reasonable to expect that the best contributions would have been among those cited most, while relatively unimportant papers would have attracted few, if any, citations. Among papers cited only a few times, however, many may have failed to be noticed because of the language or journal in which they appeared, or for other reasons which have nothing to do with their quality; indeed, some may even be too far ahead of their time (*6*). Moreover, a high score cannot be taken at face value in every case. A paper may be heavily cited because it provoked criticism or described a minor improvement of an established method, or simply because the author himself cited it frequently in subsequent publications (such citation of one's own work may, of course, be justified). Thus, impact and quality do not always go thogther, and it would be preposterous to suggest that the most cited author would be automatically entitled to a Nobel prize (*14*).

Quite apart from accidental or deliberate irregularities,

a yearly "popular poll" of a mere 0 to 6 "votes," the range of "votes" received by about 99 percent of publications, would suffer from too much random variation to be reliable. This sampling error might be reduced, by fields, in one or the other of two ways: through a wider coverage of sources or through a cumulative citation count over a number of years. The latter procedure, however, introduces another factor — the survival value, which, on its own, may be more telling than the immediate impact.

2. Survival Value

According to results of the present pilot survey of recent papers (Fig. 1), which agree with the earlier data from the *Science Citation Index* for 1961 (*8*), the average citation rate tends to reach a peak during the 3rd year after publication and to fall off by 50 percent every 3 to 5 years thereafter. This, however, is the pattern for the entire population of cited papers and not necessarily for the top 1 to 2 percent, which could conceivably have quite a different survival profile. An examination of 200 articles published in 1958 and cited a total of 1600 times in the two issues of the *Index* (1961 and 1964) showed that papers cited, on the average, 1, 5, 13.4, or 23 times in 1961 were likely to be cited, in 1964, 0.4, 2.5, 9.5, or 16 times, respectively (the coefficient of variation of these estimates being in the region of 30 percent). Only 12 percent of the 200 articles were cited more often in their 7th than in their 4th year. It appears, therefore, that most articles which are heavily cited in any one year continue to be cited a proportionately

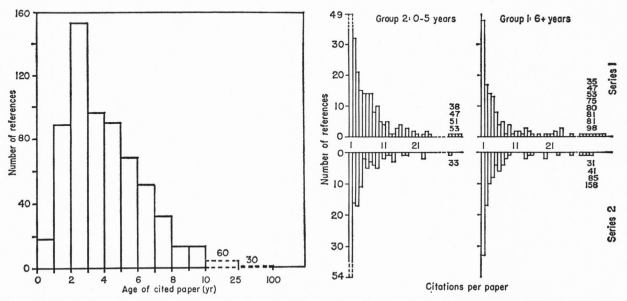

FIG. 1 (left). Age distribution for references cited in a sample of biomedical papers published between 1961 and 1965. FIG. 2 (right). Frequency distribution of citations to papers in series 1 and 2 of Table 1. Papers cited more than 30 times are grouped together, and indicated by individual blocks and figures opposite.

large number of times in subsequent years but that their survival profile is not very different from the average. On the other hand, a small proportion of papers have survival profiles showing unusual longevity. Future studies of this kind may show whether there is anything special in these contributions which could qualify them for some "Journal of Really Important Papers" (8).

3. Indirect Influence

The total influence of a scientific paper extends beyond its direct impact, for its influence may continue, and possibly grow, through successive generations of other publications. When comprehensive citation indexing is a few years older, it will be interesting to follow these relationships quantitatively and determine whether a high impact value tends to run through bibliographic chains. Since only a small percentage of papers are heavily cited, one would imagine that "clones" of such papers would be quite conspicuous against the general background (15). In the present context it is convenient to speak of the references cited in an article as the article's "ancestors" and of the subsequent source papers which cite the article as its "descendants."

On the basis of the two complete issues of the *Index* (for 1961 and 1964) available at the time of writing (4), only a limited survey of the "ancestry" and "progeny" of highly cited papers was possible. First, a random selection, from the *Index* for 1964, of "research articles" (as distinguished from reviews and monographs) published in 1961 which the *Index* showed as having received 10 or more citations in 1964 was retrieved. Each of these "series 1" articles was matched by an article which had appeared in the same journal and volume and which was cited once only in 1964 ("series 2"). Next, all the papers cited by articles in the two series were located in the *Index* for 1961, and a count was made to determine their citation scores in 1961. The neighboring entries in the *Index* which were discovered to be multiple listings of a single item resulting from inaccuracies in volume or page number as given by the citing article were also included in the count. All the same, as noted above, a

survey of this type is subject to error because of inaccurate entries which cannot be easily traced.

When the citation scores were tabulated according to the age of the cited papers in 1961, the papers fell into two groups: (group 1) those published before 1955 and (group 2) the more recent ones (0 to 5 years old). In group 2, the mean citation score for items referred to in the articles of series 1 was twice as high as the mean citation score for items referred to by papers of the control series (series 2) (see Table I and Fig. 2). This might possibly mean that the authors of these more-cited papers were more selective in the choice of references, especially of references to recent papers which had not had time to become widely known through textbooks and reviews. The possible argument that the *Index* could have influenced the reading habits of the authors may be discounted, because, unlike the later *Indexes*, which are completely up to date, the *Index* for 1961 was based on experimental files and was not generally available till 1964.

In the second part of the survey, these relationships were traced forward. A sample of papers published in 1958 and cited 10 or more times (mean number of citations, 11.6) in 1961 was compared with papers cited once only in 1961. The citing (source) articles were followed into the *Index* for 1964. The mean citation score for a descendant paper of the first series was 2.5 citations; that for a descendant paper of the second series was 1.0.

When all the data are combined and three generations of papers separated by 3-year intervals are considered, the relationship between the citation score of a paper and the scores of its ancestors or references (that is, the papers it cites) and its descendants or citations (the papers that cite it) would appear to be roughly as shown in Table II. The tendency for the ancestors to have higher citation scores than the descendants may at first appear surprising, since the *Index* covers only a very select fraction of the citing journals while the population of ancestors is quite unrestricted. However, in this system, selection operates backward, because it is the descendants who choose their ancestors.

It must be recognized that the figures based on a 3-year

TABLE I

Data, from the *Science Citation Index* for 1961, for Papers Cited in Two Series of Papers Published in 1961 Which Were, in Turn, Cited in Subsequent Papers, as Noted in the Index for 1964. For the Meaning of Series 1, Series 2, Group 1, and Group 2, See Text. (For Frequency Distributions, See Fig. 2.)

1	2	3	4	5		6		7	
				No. of papers cited by papers of col. 2		No. of times papers of col. 5 were cited in *Index* for 1961		Means, per paper, for citations of col. 6	
Series No.	No. of papers in series (all published in 1961)	No. of citations, in *Index* for 1964, of papers of col. 2	Average, per paper, for the citations of col. 3	Group 2	Group 1	Group 2	Group 1	Group 2	Group 1
1	17	238	14 (10–24)	214	134	1331	1230	6.2	9.2
2	17	17	1	174	97	522	705	3.0	7.3

TABLE II

CITATION FREQUENCY (IN NUMBER OF CITATIONS DURING THE 3RD YEAR AFTER PUBLICATION) OF THREE GENERATIONS OF PAPERS, 3 YEARS APART. "MIDDLE GENERATION" IS A HYPOTHETICAL TEST SAMPLE, RECONSTRUCTED FROM DATA ON PAPERS PUBLISHED IN 1958 AND IN 1961, FOR COMPUTING THE NUMBER OF CITATIONS TO DESCENDANT (CITING) AND ANCESTOR (CITED) PAPERS (SEE TEXT).

Middle generation	Ancestors	Descendants
12	6	2.5
1	3	1.0

span between generations are not optimal but are dictated by the fact that the *Indexes* for 1961 and 1964 were the only ones that had been published at the time of writing. For instance, a paper written in 1958 and cited 12 times in 1961 is likely to have been cited 15 to 18 times in 1960 and 60 times in the period 1958–64 (see Fig. 1). Second, the arithmetical mean values do not convey the whole picture, because the frequency of citations does not follow a normal distribution but follows a reciprocal cube curve (see Fig. 2), the number of papers cited n times decreasing approximately as $1/n^3$ (8). When this is taken into account, we find that at least 50 percent of "fertile" articles are directly linked with a small "elite" group of equally fertile ancestors and successors.

4. Networks of Publications

Although it is quite reasonable to expect general statistical trends in populations of papers, the place of an individual contribution can be determined only from its unique relationship to the whole body of scientific literature, which resembles a self-organizing growing network, where every paper is linked with its bibliographic ancestors and descendants. The texture of this network is not homogenous but shows a hierarchy of structures and substructures depending on the scale of observation. If we had a plot of these interrelationships for all papers published in the past century, during which time the present form of scientific journals became established, we could expect to see a reasonably faithful map of the history of science outlined by bibliographic connections (15). It would reflect the development, divergence, and confluence of major disciplines, fields, and ideas; classical contributions would be distinguished by thick bundles of connections with the later literature, while the less important elements would be lost in the background. Further, we would note that the network doubles in size every 10 to 20 years, most of the growth taking place along the leading edge of the "research front" (8) characterized by increased tightness of the mesh due to relatively more frequent references to recent papers.

At present we can only study theoretically general properties of such networks or examine in detail limited areas in a specific field or journal (2, 8, 15). More comprehensive investigations of this nature will become possible as further volumes of the *Index* becomes available.

5. Estimation of Indirect Impact

However much we may deplore it, a count (or, more cynically, weight) of publications is commonly used as a measure of scientific productivity. Against this background the introduction of an independent measure, such as may be provided by citation data, can only improve matters. Granted that a short-term citation count is unreliable and that historical evaluation takes too long, there must be an intermediate period when citation networks begin to show sufficient organization to be susceptible of meaningful analysis. One can only make an educated guess as to how long this process will take. A great deal depends on the interval of latency between successive generations of papers. As was noted earlier, papers 2 to 3 years old have the greatest chance of being cited. At this rate, by 1970 we shall have citation data pertaining to at least five well-stocked generations of papers. It is hard to believe that this information will not be used for the evaluation of journals, institutions, and individual workers. One can only hope that it will be used with discretion.

A reasonable objection to a simple citation count is the argument that it may tend to favor applied research papers at the expense of the fundamental contributions on which they are based. It is also likely that publications in a new field, with only a few workers, will be cited less often than those in a crowded field. This bias could be, at least in part, corrected by use of the indirect method of scoring discussed below. By analogy to more familiar systems, this would be like estimating the distribution of a particular genetic character in a population of descendants, or more graphically, like calculating the stress on a given node of a suspended network, assuming that all the nodes are of equal weight and that stresses are evenly distributed along weightless connections. Quantitatively, these models are equivalent and could be dealt with formally by application of the theory of graphs (16), but for the present purpose a more elementary treatment will suffice.

First, let us consider a simple case in which each node has two ancestors and two descendants (Fig. 3): the total contribution, or influence, of a given node would then increase at each level by one unit, because with each duplication only one half would be transmitted downward. An interesting feature of these models is the fact that the above description applies equally well to open-ended, branching structures (Fig. 3A) and to networks proper, where some of the nodes have ancestors related to each other by common descent, thereby completing a loop (Fig. 3B). In the latter case the original influence would be diffused among fewer members, but the total would remain the same as in an open branching system.

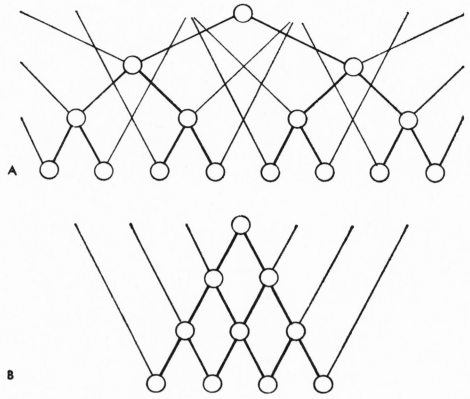

Fɪɢ. 3. A system of nodes connected into an open-ended (A) or looped (B) network. In the two cases the same downward stress is transferred to the apical node.

This greatly simplifies mathematical treatment of complex networks.

If, at any level, there are more descendants than ancestors per node, the influence will be proportionally increased. The general expression for calculating the total contribution (C) of a given node after n generations would, therefore, be

$$C = \sum_{i=1}^{n} \frac{p_1 p_2 p_3 \ldots p_i}{q_1 q_2 q_3 \ldots q_i} \ldots \quad (1)$$

where p_1, p_2, p_3, $\ldots$ are the arithmetical mean numbers of descendants and q_1, q_2, q_3, $\ldots$ are the harmonic means of the numbers of ancestors per node in the 1st, 2nd, 3rd, $\ldots$ nth generation.

When one applies Eq. 1 to bibliographic networks reconstructed with the aid of the *Science Citation Index*, instead of considering the total number of references (q) in a citing paper, it would be proper to consider only the references to journals listed as sources in the *Index* (that is, to exclude references to monographs, private communications, or periodicals not covered by the *Index*). In Table III, the values q are based on these "eligible" items. In the papers surveyed in Table 1, 80 percent of the references, in both groups, were eligible for inclu-

sion, and the data in Table III were calculated on this assumption.

For example, in order to estimate the total indirect impact of a paper A_0 in the period 1958–64, we would first list all the direct citations A_1, B_1, C_1 $\ldots$ of A_0; then the second-generation — A_2, B_2, C_2, $\ldots$ of A_1; next, D_2, E_2, F_2 $\ldots$ of B_1; and so on. Each count is independent of the others, so that C_1, A_2, and D_2 could well refer to a single item, counted three times as a descendant of A_0, A_1, and B_1, respectively. After determining the mean number of citations per paper and the harmonic means of eligible references (q) in each generation, one can calculate the total score, as described. In dealing with large populations, average values obtained from sample counts at each level could be used. In any case, citation data are already stored in a form suitable for automatic processing, so that dealing with large samples does not present insuperable technical difficulties.

Actual trials of this method of scoring cannot be attempted until two or three more volumes of the *Index* become available, but, as an illustration, the following hypothetical example could be reconstructed from partial data based on the *Indexes* for 1961 and 1964. To fill the gaps, citation frequency was assumed to vary with the age of a paper roughly as shown in Fig. 1. Thus, an article published in 1958 with 10 citations listed in the

TABLE III

CALCULATION OF INDIRECT-IMPACT SCORE FOR THE PERIOD 1958–64. THESE SCORES ARE ESTIMATES BASED ON AVERAGE VALUES FOR A SAMPLE OF PAPERS PUBLISHED IN 1958 AND CITED 10 TIMES IN 1961. THE PROBABLE CITATION FIGURES FOR THE YEARS 1958, 1959, 1960, 1962, AND 1963, NOT COVERED BY THE *Index* WERE INFERRED FROM THE DATA OF FIG. 1.

Generation* of descendants (i)	Mean number of citations from i to $i-1$ (p_i)	Mean of reciprocals of references per paper† ($1/q_i$)	Indirect-impact score† for each generation	
			Extent of the network ($p_1 p_2 p_3 \ldots p_i$)	Fractional impact $\frac{p_1 p_2 p_3 \ldots p_4}{q_1 q_2 q_3 \ldots q_i}$
1	55	0.10	55	5.50
2	11	.15	605	9.07
3	2.2	.20	1331	4.00
4	0.7	.20	932	0.56
5	.1	.20	93	.01
6⎫ 7⎭	Negligible			
Totals	†		3016	19.14

* Note that *generation* does not refer to the number of years since publication of the first paper.
† See text.

Index for 1961 would, typically, have collected about 55 citations by the end of 1964. Of the citing articles, each could be expected to have a mean of 11 citations, and so on (Table III). The total score applies to the period of 6 to 7 years (depending on the exact date of publication), so that the mean yearly score would be 430 to 500, expressed as the extent of the network, or approximately 3.0 in terms of fractional transfer of impact. By comparison, an average 1958 paper cited twice in 1961 is likely to have a yearly score of less than 10 and 0.3 on the respective scales, but the individual scores would be subject to a very large variation: the papers whose descendants had high citation rates would have high indirect citation scores. Among them could well be found important fundamental contributions which had a small initial impact but became cornerstones of large fields of knowledge.

Even though the above methods of indirect scoring may lessen the bias against theoretical papers or papers in a small emerging field, the score could serve only as an index for matching comparable papers or groups of papers. Neither scale has any objective meaning as a measure of the actual transfer of information. First, the influence passed on by a scientific paper (unless it be purely a review) consists not only of the paper's "genotype" but includes the author's original contribution. In terms of the genetic model this would be equivalent to recurrent mutations which would progressively dilute the pool of the original genes. If we could objectively define the fraction of a contribution $1/r$ which represents the debt to its predecessors, then the transferable impact could be expressed as p/qr instead of p/q. Second, not every cited reference has an equal share in this debt. To correct for this, a relative numerical value would have to be allotted each reference according to some scheme of

citation relationship indicators (*12, 17*) and converted into a fraction $(1/s)$ of the total bibliographic debt $(1/r)$ of the paper.

When the terms rs are substituted for q in Eq. 1. the general expression for assessing the influence of papers becomes

$$\sum_{i=1}^{n} \frac{p_1 p_2 p_3 \ldots p_i}{r_1 s_1 r_2 s_2 r_3 s_3 \ldots r_i s_i}$$

Until we can determine objectively what part of the paper represents truly original work and what is the relative degree of indebtedness to each cited reference we cannot speak of quantitating the influence of published papers. It may, however, be interesting to assign some arbitrary values to r and s as defined above, in order to test the applications of this approach.

6. Conclusions

Evaluation by means of citation patterns can be successful only insofar as published papers and their bibliographies reflect scientific activity and nothing else. Such an innocent description is becoming less and less tenable. The present scientific explosion gave rise to more than a proportional publication explosion, which not only reflects the scientific explosion but has its own dynamics and vicious circles. Publication of results is probably the main means of accomplishing the almost impossible task of accounting for time and money spent on research. Inevitably, this puts a premium on quantity at the expense of quality, and, as with any other type of inflation, the problem worsens: the more papers are written, the less they count for and the greater is the pressure to publish more. What makes matters worse is the fact that the sheer volume of the "literature" makes it increasingly difficult to separate what is worthwhile from the rest. Critical reviews have become somewhat of a rarity, and editorial judgment is usually relegated to referees, who are contemporaries and, perhaps, competitors of the authors — a situation which has its own undesirable implications (11, 18). It requires little imagination to discover other vicious circles, all arising from distortion of the primary reasons for publishing the results of scientific inquiry.

There are, it is true, signs of adjustment to this crisis, partly due to some easing of the pressure to publish at all costs, and partly due to the readers' changing attitudes toward the flood of publications. An increasing amount of research is now being carried out in the form of collective projects in large institutions where publication is no longer the standard method of accounting for individual work. At the same time there is apparent an increasing tendency for scientific journals to polarize into the relatively few leading ones which carry important information and the many subsidiary journals which serve as vehicles for interim local accounting and, in a way, substitute for detailed intradepartmental reports. This division is a result not of some arbitrary decree but of normal competition between journals, as a result of which, however, the strong usually get stronger and the weak get weaker. Were it not for these changes and also for a striking improvement in abstracting, indexing, and alerting services, most research workers would have found long ago that, even in their own specialized fields, new information is accumulating faster than it can be sorted out. These developments can provide only a temporary reprieve, so long as there remains a strong incentive to publish the greatest possible number of papers. A new scale of values based on citations is by no means infallible or, in many cases, even fair, but at least it provides an alternative to the existing one, which is at the root of the crisis.

It might, of course, be asked whether wide acceptance of such new standards would not lead to deliberate abuses. A little reflection shows that the system is less open to manipulation than might appear. First, the referees are expected to see to it that the submitted papers cite work which is pertinent to the subject. An increased awareness of the usefulness of citation indexing as a tool for retrieval and evaluation will make this aspect of refereeing more important, and what now passes for minor carelessness or discourtesy could easily come to be regarded as serious malpractice. Second, as noted above, careful selection of references is in the author's own interest, because it helps him to reach his readers. There is, therefore, some room for hope that healthy feedback in the system will tend to keep it viable. At the basis of this hope lies the supposition that, in the long run, only good work can ensure recognition.

As Martyn (2) has pointed out, as an information-retrieval method, citation indexing is rather "noisy." The word *noisy* may apply even more to the problem of evaluation. Whereas in information retrieval much of the unwanted information can be filtered out by suitable search strategy (2, 6), this is not so easy to do for the purpose of evaluation, because a simple descendence relationship between papers is still an ideal far removed from actually (7). The situation would be much better if we could at will exclude all citations which do not indicate real indebtedness. A scheme of citation relationship indicators, first mentioned by Garfield (12) and elaborated by Lipetz (17), would be a help, but, even if it were technically feasible, to provide such indicators would greatly add to the production costs of the *Index*.

Another possible way to minimize the effects of "noise" it to increase the size of the samples on which the reckoning is based. Now that research has become a rather popular occupation, it seems that a kind of public vote may have to be accepted as a factor in evaluation. Since this is the case, there is something to be said for extending the "franchise" to minimize accidental effects. An index which attempted to process all scientific publications would be several times the size of the present *Index*, and, what is more, it would not necessarily be an improvement as a tool for information retrieval because most of the significant work is already concentrated in the present *Index*. Whether this attempt will ever be considered worthwhile remains primarily a matter of policy and economics. In the meantime there is an urgent need for more experience with the existing services.

It is not the purpose of this article to advocate evaluation of scientific work by some kind of public opinion poll; its purpose is to recognize a possible trend in this direction. Any judgment by public acclaim is subject to obvious fallacies, but we must not be carried away by the analogy to the Stock Exchange or to electoral practices. The fact that, in this case, the "public" consists of authors whose contributions are generally linked creates quite a new pattern of organization. In this discussion some of the aspects of this pattern have been explored through analogy to idealized genetic or mechanical network models, but the very uniqueness of the system, with its many self-organizing ramifications, makes it a new field which deserves close study, since these developments may have profound effects on the future of scientific communication.

References and Notes

1. "The Medlars story at the National Library of Medicine," *U.S. Dept. Health Educ. Welfare Publ.* (1963).
2. J. MARTYN, "An examination of citation indexes," *Aslib Proc.* **17,** 184 (1965).
3. G. SALTON, *J. Ass. Computing Machinery* **10,** 440 (1963).

4. E. GARFIELD and I. H. SHER, *Science Citation Index* (*1961*) (Institute for Scientific Information, Philadelphia, 1963); *Science Citation Index* (*1964*) (Institute for Scientific Information, Philadelphia, 1965).

5. *Effective Use of the Science Citation Index. A Programmed Text* (Institute for Scientific Information, Philadelphia, 1964).

6. E. GARFIELD, *Science* **144,** 649 (1964).

7. ———. *Rev. Intern. Documentation* **32,** 112 (1965).

8. D. J. DE SOLLA PRICE, *Science* **149,** 510 (1965).

9. E. GARFIELD, paper presented at the American Documentation Institute symposium on statistical associative methods for mechanized documentation, Washington, D.C., 1964.

10. N. KAPLAN, *Amer. Documentation* **16,** 179 (1965).

11. D. J. DE SOLLA PRICE, *Little Science, Big Science* (Columbia Univ. Press, New York, 1963).

12. E. GARFIELD, *Science* **122,** 108 (1955).

13. ——— and I. H. SHER, *Amer. Documentation* **14,** 1965 (1963).

14. E. GARFIELD, *ibid.*, p. 289.

15. ———. I. H. SHER, R. J. TORPIE, *The Use of Citation Data in Writing the History of Science* (Institute for Scientific Information, Philadelphia, 1964).

16. C. BERGE, *The Theory of Graphs and Its Applications* (Methuen, London, 1962).

17. B. LIPETZ, *Amer. Documentation* **16,** 81 (1965).

18. B. GLASS, *Science* **150,** 1254 (1965).

19. I thank DRS. E. GARFIELD and I. H. SHER for valuable criticism and generous help with biblographic material, and PROFESSOR H. O. LANCASTER, DR. P. J. CLARINGBOLD, and DR. S. J. PROKHOVNIK for helpful discussions of the mathematical models.

32 An Examination of Citation Indexes

JOHN MARTYN
Aslib Proceedings
Vol. 17, No. 6, June, 1965

In the past few years two methods of information access using the citations given in published papers have been developed. These methods are citation indexing and bibliographic coupling, and although they are closely related it is important clearly to distinguish between them. In essence, bibliographic coupling is a concept developed by M. M. Kessler of the Massachusetts Institute of Technology, concerned with the relation existing between two documents by virtue of their joint descent from a third — that is, two documents are said to be coupled if they both cite the same document, and the strength of the coupling is determined by the number of citations they have in common.[1] We are here primarily interested in citation indexing and will therefore only discuss Kessler's work as it becomes immediately relevant to this subject. A citation index is 'an ordered list of cited articles each of which is accompanied by a list of citing articles. The citing article is identified by a source citation, the cited article by a reference citation. The index is arranged by reference citations.'[2] It is helpful at this stage to think of the source citations as descendants, and the reference citations as their ancestors.

It will be easier to see what this means if at this point we look at two sample pages, taken from the *Science*

Citation Index for the first quarter of 1964, produced by the Institute for Scientific Information, Inc. The first page (Figure 1) is from the Source Index. We see, for example, that an author named DEAN, A. C. R., has a paper called 'Some basic aspects of cell regulation' in *Nature*, vol. 201, beginning on p. 232, in 1964: HINSHEL, W. C., was a co-author. It has ninety-six references (ninety-six ancestors) and is an issue, part or supplement, no. 4916. The number 49833 is the ISI accession number. Although we are not told so here, one of the references is to a paper by J. E. M. Midgley, in *Biochim Biophys Acta*, vol. 61, p. 513, 1962.

If we now go to the Citation Index (Figure 2) and look at the entries under Midgley, J. E. M., we find that his 1962 paper was cited by, as we know, Dean and Hinshel; it was also cited by three other authors in the first quarter of 1964, so, as Kessler would say, all those four papers are coupled at strength one (and maybe more). What has happened is that the citations given in the 1964 papers by these authors have been sorted alphabetically by cited author, thus bringing these four references to Midgley's paper together. Midgley's paper has four descendants in the period covered by this index.

This is an example of one sort of citation index —

```
JAN 14          DAYAL HM      SAXENA BN    NIGAM SS                        DEBONO AHC
ITCH              I J EX BIOL   2  62 64   N   2R   N1      49991            BR J SURG
                  ERADICATION OF MITES FROM FUNGAL CULTURE                   LUNG TRA
JAN 28            COLLECTION
STING YARN                                                                DEBORGER L
                DAYES L .    SEE DOSSETOR JB  CAN MED A J  90  471            B S CHIM B
S                                                                           1.2-CYCL
EM 239  43      DAYKIN DR      INT BUS MAC
S                 3121800 US          64  P  2R  FEB 18                    DEBRAY C
YC  28  23        CL307/88 PULSE GENERATING CIRCUIT
                                                                          DEBRIE AVL
VI     50389    DAYKIN PN    SEE BLOOR JE     CAN J CHEM    42  121          3119319 US
RANDS IN        DAYSTR INC   SEE BLANCO E     3120650 US                     CL95/89
                DAYSTR INC   SEE FREEMAN RW   3122018 US                     MACHINES
                DAYSTR INC   SEE LENDER RJ    3119962 US
N7323  49339    DAYSTR INC   SEE PRATT WW     3119919 US                  DEBROW PL
IES             DAYT PERF I  SEE BLEICHER RL  3118260 US
                DAYTON PG    SEE FINSTER M    ANESTHESIOL   25  94        DEBRUIN HJ
SYLV EL PRO     DAYTON PG    SEE WEINER M     AM J MED SC  247  75          REV SCI IN
FEB 25          DCRUZ IA     SEE NAMIN EP     AM J CARD     13  124          PRECISIO
                DCRUZ IA     SEE NAMIN EP     AM J CARD     13  124          DIFFUSIO
                DCRUZ IA     SEE WEINBERG M   J THOR SURG   47  40
ON  170 195     DEACON GER                                                DEBRUIN HJ
                  NATURE      201  561 64   E NO R  N4919  50438             3120776 US
                  INTERNATIONAL INDIAN OCEAN EXPEDITION                      CL82/33
JAN 28
IT FOR          DEAKIN ST    SEAL CORP                                     DEBRUIN HJ
                  3120418 US          64  P  8R  FEB 4                       3122037 US
        154 197   CL339/126 ELECTRIC SOCKET CONTACTS                        CL81/9.5
                DEAL LA                                                    DEBRUYN WT
                  3119321 US          64  P  2R  JAN 28                      3121923 US
VI     49908      CL99/277.1 APPARATUS FOR AGING ALCOHOLIC                   CL20/52.
EXOSES TO         SPIRITS
ODIUM IN                                                                   DEC NV
                DEALFARO V   PREDAZZI E   ROSSETTI C                       DECASTRO
                  NUOV CIMENT  31  42 64    25R  N1     50607
      23 T 17     ANALYTICITY IN ANGULAR MOMENTUM IN POTENTIAL            DECATUR PS
                  SCATTERING                                                3116984 US
VI     50319    DEALY JM     GREEN AA    ALB PIP SUP                         CL34/79
                  3119635 US          64  P  6R    JAN 28
                  CL287/108 H-BEAM PILE CONNECTORS                        DECC LIM
VI     50319                                                              DECENCIO D
                DEAN ACB     MASON MK                                     DECHAMPL.J
                  GUT         5  64 64      12R  N1.  51679               DECHAMPL.J
/    43  32       DISTRIBUTION OF PYLORIC MUCOSA IN PARTIAL               DECHAMPL.J
ED  60 320        GASTRECTOMY SPECIMENS                                   DECHAMPL.J
                                                                         DECIUS JC
                DEAN ACR     HINSHELW.C                                   DECKEL FW
                  NATURE      201  232 64    96R  N4916  49833            DECKEL FW
VI    52239       SOME BASIC ASPECTS OF CELL REGULATION                  DECKEL FW
MPOSITION OF                                                             DECKEL H
                DEAN DC      SEE DESANCTI.RW  CIRCULATION  29  14          DECKEL H
                                                                         DECKEL H
CT  '87  49     DEAN DJ      LIEBERMA.J   ALBRECHT RM  ARNSTEIN P         DECKER DG
                             BAER GM      GOODRICH WB
                  PUBL HEALTH  79  101 64     25R  N2    51186            DECKER HL
VI    51248       PSITTACOSIS IN MAN & BIRDS                                3121260 US
SILLECTOMY                                                                  CL20/22
                DEAN FM      JONES PG    MORTON RB    SIDISUNT.P
                  J CHEM SOC   411 64      10R  JAN   51086               DECKER K
JAN 14            ADDUCTS FROM QUINONES & DIAZOALKANES .4.                  B S CHIM B
JCTION            TROPONES FROM ACETYLQUINONES                              SUR LA B
                                                                           CLOSTRID
                DEAN RA
      51  71      CAN J MATH   16  136 64    8R  N1    49515              DECKX R
      26  47      FREE LATTICES GENERATED BY PARTIALLY ORDERED              CLIN CHIM
                  SETS & PRESERVING BOUNDS                                  MODIFIED
                                                                           SUITABLE
MAR  3          DEAN RE      ANDREW JH   READ RC                            METABOLI
IL FLANGE ON      J AM MED A   187  27 64    15R  N1    49430
                  RED CELL FACTOR IN RENAL DAMAGE FROM                    DECORDOV.SF
                  ANGIOGRAPHIC MEDIA - PERFUSION STUDIES OF IN              3120871 US
JR  16  312       SITU CANINE KIDNEY WITH CELLULAR & ACELLULAR             CL166/55
IE  144 299       PERFUSATES
    17  185                                                               DECOSTAN.PF
                DEAN RL      SEE ALBRONDA HF  ARCH G PSYC  10  276           3120672 US
                DEAN WV      SEE TOWELL BH    3123141 US                     CL15/250
BECK JC         DEANE        SEE ZIMMERMA.    J HIST CYTO  12  6
I7   50884                                                                DECRAENE EP
UPON            DEANE EH     WILSON RJ   EASTM KOD C                      DECROLY P
IANSPORT          3117508 US          64  P  4R  JAN 14
                  CL95/89 VISCOUS SOLUTION PROCESSING DEVICE              DECROOCQ D
4493P1 51025                                                               B S CHIM F
E & N-BUTANE    DEANE GE                                                    LA CONST
                  J EXP PSYCH  67  193 64    3R  N2    50762                MELANGES
                  HUMAN HEART RATE RESPONSES DURING
SMITH S           EXPERIMENTALLY INDUCED ANXIETY - FOLLOW UP             DEDEN C
I4914 49368       WITH CONTROLLED RESPIRATION                             DEDERICK MM
ARIANT OF
EGG             DEANE P                                                   DEDEURWA.R
                  J AM STAT A  59  278 64    B  1R  N305  51382             J POL SCI
II   50000        ECONOMIC TRENDS IN SOVIET UNION                          VISCOMET
                                                                           TEMPERAT
                DEANGELI.A   AM OPT COMP
                  3122962 US          64  P  16R  MAR 3                   DEDIC AM
      90  12      CL85/1 RING-LIKE RETAINING DEVICES                        3117689 US
                                                                           CL217/60
                DEANS T
                  NATURE      201  599 64    L NO R  N4919  60438         DEDINSKY JP
                  ISOTOPIC COMPOSITION OF STRONTIUM IN                      3116497 US
                  CARBONATES                                                CL9/6 CO
```

FIG. 1

probably the best known, certainly the most widely publicized. The source material in the *Science Citation Index* is drawn from about seven hundred journals in 1964 (613 in 1961), all items in these journals, with the exception of ephemera such as advertisements and announcements, being processed. 'The emphasis in journal selection has been the multidisciplinary journals. These are, generally, recognised as important in each country, but are only selectively and fragmentarily covered by the discipline oriented indexing services.'[3] The journals broadly cover the whole field of science, with emphasis to some extent on the life sciences. Other citation indexes have been confined to one subject area, such as the *Genetics Citation Index,* also produced by the Institute for Scientific Information, in 1963, and the index to statistics which is being produced by Dr. John W. Tukey.

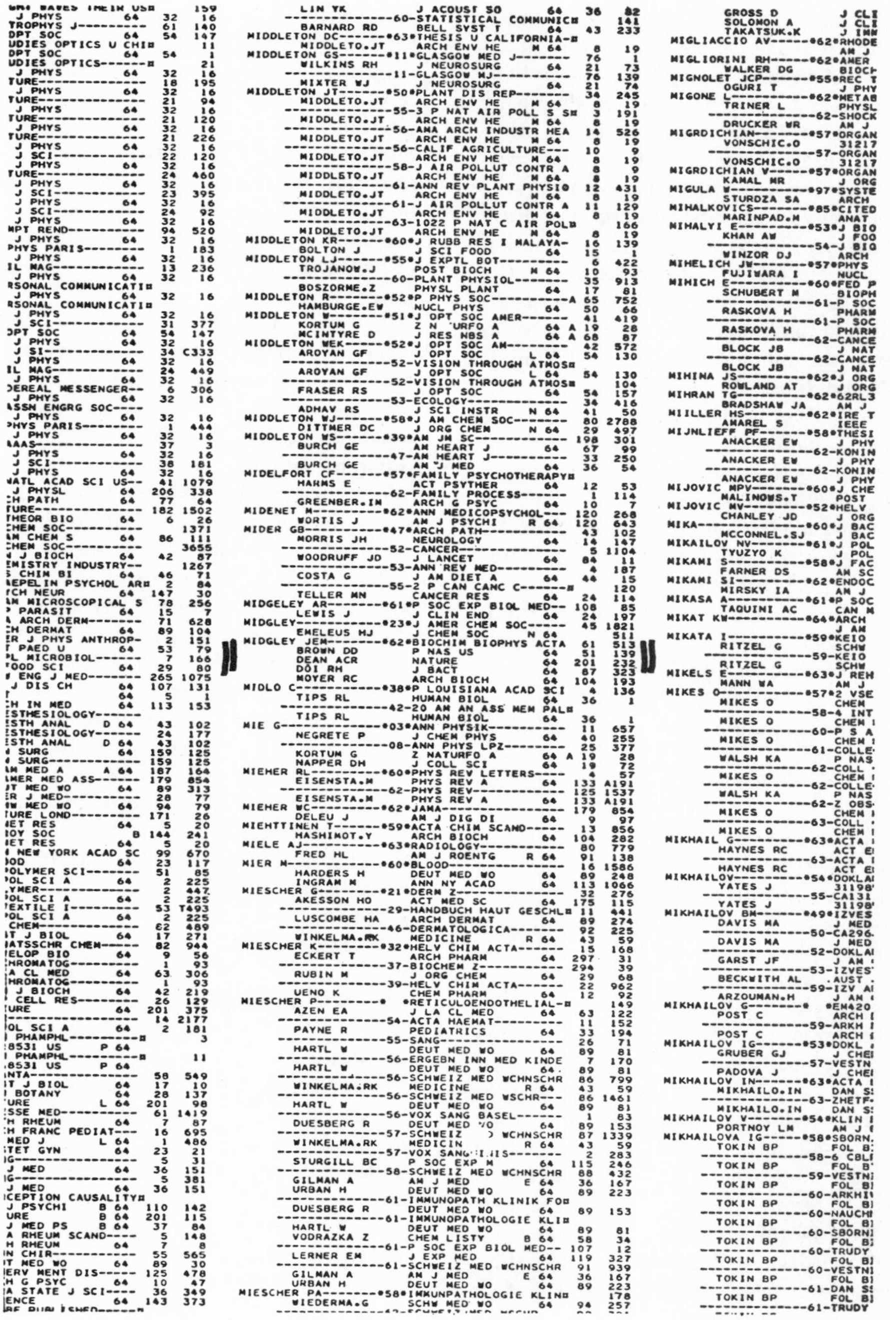

Fig. 2

Some have been produced as indexes to the material appearing in one journal, the outstanding example being the index to volumes 1–31 of the *Annals of Mathematical Statistics*.[4] This has a citation index to papers appearing in the *Annals*, arranged by author, which gives the reference to the paper, a reference to the abstract or abstracts of the paper (eight abstracting journals were searched to provide this), references to papers in the *Annals* citing the original, and references to papers in *other* journals citing the original, these last being produced by searching thirty-seven journals in the statistical field, the proceedings of three Symposia, and three presentation volumes. In addition a subject index in great depth to papers and often to the content of specific pages is given, and, a most interesting feature, a 'forwards' citation index, collecting and listing the citations *to* other journals by

Representation of Information   355

authors of papers appearing in the *Annals*. This index was produced without the aid of a computer. The index to the *Journal of the American Statistical Association*, vols. 35–50, also includes in its author index a note of subsequent citing papers in the journal, but in no other journal, and so is on rather a small scale. It also was hand-prepared. Tukey[5] reports two other citation indexes, one a *Bibliography of non-parametric statistics*, by I. R. Savage, Harvard University Press, containing 'for each item, indications of the other items in the bibliography which were known to refer or, in the compiler's judgment, should have referred to the item in question;' the other is the annual index to Institution of Radio Engineers, *Transactions of the Professional Group on Information Theory*, 1958 to date, which contains, as an 'Index to footnote references', an author-ordered list of footnote citations from that volume to all items. A citation index to the published proceedings of the two United Nations International Conferences on Peaceful Uses of Atomic Energy was compiled by Itek Laboratories for experimental purposes, and the work involved has been reported by Ben-Ami Lipetz.[6] The index is not publicly available. Another index was prepared by Lipetz in a limited part of the field of physics,[7] in connection with an experimental evaluation of the impact of a citation index, and I shall mention this in more detail at a later stage.

Finally the Short Papers contributed to the Theme Sessions of the 26th Annual Meeting of the American Documentation Institute, in December 1963 published in two volumes under the title *Automation and scientific communication*, contains a Citation Index to all the references cited in the papers, arranged by author and giving the full bibliographic details, including titles, of all citations, and additionally a KWIC index to these references. This was prepared on an IBM 1401.

We have seen that citation indexes can be prepared covering a large part of the field of science and technology, or specific areas, or to one journal-series, or indeed to any body of literature. They can be annual, cumulative, or 'once-for-all' jobs, depending on the nature of the subject and the material. They can be arranged by author, by journal or even, if specific to a particular journal, by initial page of the cited item, as Tukey has suggested, although this last arrangement seems rather exotic. They are flexible devices and can be arranged in whatever way most suits the convenience of the user. They can be prepared by hand, but this is a considerable undertaking, and if the scope is to be at all wide, or if speed of production is important, then a computer must be used. To demonstrate this last point, we may note that the 1961 *Science Citation Index* has 102,000 source articles from 613 journals, giving a total of 1,370,000 citations, which when sorted and arranged give references to 890,000 papers by 258,000 authors. The majority of these papers were cited only once in 1961, but many were cited more than once, the most frequently cited

being a paper by O. H. Lowry,* which was cited more than five hundred times.

Machine processing has its own problems, however, the most obvious one at the moment being that of inaccurate citation by authors. J. E. Terry[8] notes that of forty-six citations discovered in the course of a search involving the 1961 *Science Citation Index* for material in physics, eleven contained errors in the page number, volume number or year, and one quoted the wrong journal; in every case the mistake had been made by the citing author.

In using the *Science Citation Index* for retrieving references in the fields of biology and chemistry I have also found errors in citation, although the proportion was very much lower than that found by Terry (which incidentally suggests the possibility that physicists have different citation habits from chemists and biologists). We all know that papers frequently contain incorrect citations, but perhaps had not realized that the incidence of error was so high. This error-rate is, of course, no reflection on the compilers of the *Science Citation Index;* to check every citation in every paper processed is an impossible task, and one which more properly should be carried out by authors, referees, and editors. Another sort of error which frequently occurs is misfiling the authors of citations; as an example, if a paper by SNAPE, F. J., is cited by three authors, the first referring simply to SNAPE, the second to SNAPE, F. and the third to SNAPE, F. J., this results in three separate author entries for the three isotopes of SNAPE, first for SNAPE *per se*, and the second and third for the forms SNAPE, F. and SNAPE, F. J. This sort of error, though, is only a minor irritation.

Citation indexes have had a mixed reception. I will risk a generalization, and I emphasize that it *is* a generalization, based largely on personal contacts, and say that scientists are on the whole in favour of them, while librarians are much more cautious. As an illustration of the scientist's view — perhaps an extreme view — Dr. J. M. Hammersley,[9] reviewing the Index to the *Annals of Mathematical Statistics* in *Nature*, said 'Librarianship in the future will become a task less for the bibliophile and more for the electronic engineer. With the publication of these indexes . . . the writing is already on the library wall'. Examples of the librarian's view are harder to come by, but a representative view is expressed by E. M. Keen,[10] who wondered '. . . whether the citation index would look so attractive if similar effort was being expended on conventional indexes.'

We know that following up references cited in relevant papers is the scientist's most favoured method of obtaining information;[11] it is not therefore very surprising that a device which allows them to move forwards in time as well as backwards is greeted with enthusiasm. I suggest

* Protein measurement with the Folin phenol reagent. *Journal of Biological Chemistry*, vol. 193, 1951, p. 265.

that there is another attraction for the scientist. We know too that using a library card index to gain information is second in unpopularity among scientists only to asking a librarian for assistance.[11] (We do not know why this antipathy exists, we only know at present that it does, and deploring the fact does not change it.) A citation index allows them to attack the literature directly, in a way to which they are accustomed, without benefit of intermediaries, and I believe that this is a factor which possibly influences the scientists' initial acceptance of the Citation Index. To borrow an idea from John Tukey,[12] the librarian is concerned with information retrieval, whereas the scientist is more interested in information *access*; regarded as a retrieval tool, the Citation Index is not as efficient as some more conventional approaches to the literature, but as an *access* tool it functions very well.

Before we discuss specific methods of using it we must be clear on one point. The Source Index is in effect an author index to all items published in the titles covered by the *Science Citation Index* in the particular year for which the Index is issued, but the Citation Index itself is *not* an author index, and should not be used as such. It is an index to specific documents which are cited by those other documents which form the Source Index, and is arranged by first author purely for the convenience of the user. It should not be used for compiling author bibliographies, firstly because it lists first authors only and secondly because a first author's paper will only form an entry *if* it has been cited by one of the items in the Source Index.

We enter the Index with a citation or citations, which can be obtained in various ways. Perhaps we choose one specific paper we know to be highly relevant to our subject of interest and use this as our entry-point, in which case the sort of question we are asking is 'What use has been made of this information? Has this information been modified? Has this idea been followed up?' If we take the most recent relevant paper and use its bibliography as our entry citations we are asking 'What work is there parallel to this?', arguing along the line that the greater the number of citations two papers have in common (the greater the strength of the bibliographic coupling), the greater is the probability that they are about the same subject.

How many citations we use to enter the Index has, of course, a profound influence on the return we get from it. It must be remembered that citation of a particular paper in a given year is a low-probability event[13] — in other words, the average paper is not cited very often. To illustrate this I used 389 references to work published in 1958, 1959, and 1960, on the subject of Biological Control of Insect Pests and Weeds, as citations with which to enter the 1961 *Science Citation Index;* 123 items were cited in 1961, 266 (68 per cent) were not. Another example: using 1,045 references between 1950 and 1963 on the subject of the semi-conductor properties

of Gallium as entry-points to the *Science Citation Index* for the first six months of 1964, 163 items were cited, 882 (84 per cent) were not. Assuming that this citation rate would hold for the last six months of 1964 (assuming, that is, that about 163 more citations can be expected in that period, giving about 326 for the whole year), we get a non-productive rate of 69 per cent, remarkably close to the 68 per cent we obtained in 1961 with the biological literature. We cannot yet say, based only on these two observations, that our chances of getting anywhere in the Citation Index when we enter it with any one citation are about three in ten, but I think we can say that if further work showed the probability to be around 0.3 we would not be terribly surprised.

If you *do* get anywhere, then by the process Dr. Garfield calls 'cycling' your returns increase quite rapidly. For example, Figure 3 is a partial map of what happened when I used a paper by White, H. G. and Logan, R. A. (Gallium phosphide surface-barrier diodes. *Journal of Applied Physics*, vol. 34, p. 1990–7) published in 1963, as an entry-point to the 1964 Citation Index, in search of material on Gallium semi-conductors. White and Logan were cited three times in 1964, by Cowley in the *Journal of Applied Physics*, by Thomas in *Physical Review*, A and by Spitzer in *Physical Review*, A. In the bibliography to Thomas's paper is a reference to Hopfield, *Physical Review Letters* 1963. Hopfield's paper was cited by Gross in the *Doklady Akademiyaemii Nauk SSSR*, and Gross also cited Fuller, *Journal of Applied Physics* 1963. Fuller cited his 1963 paper in another paper in the *Journal of Applied Physics* in 1964. So it can be seen that by taking White and Logan's paper in 1963 as an entry-point, getting to the papers which cite it in 1964, using their bibliographies as entry-points and repeating the process, we can find fifteen 1964 references relevant to our subject. It can also be seen that whatever

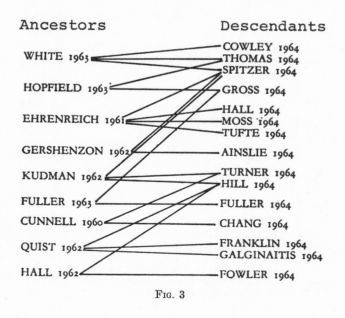

Fig. 3

paper we choose as a starting-point in this network, either source-item or citation, we can retrieve all the others by cycling.

This is, I repeat, a *partial* map. When we note that Ehrenreich's 1961 paper was cited in fact not four times, as shown on our map, but eight times, and that Hall's 1964 paper carried fifty-three citations, Spitzer's thirty-one, Thomas's twenty-six, and so on, it is evident that the full source-citation map is much more complex. This means that a citation network is an inherently 'noisy' system, using 'noise' to describe material retrieved which is not immediately relevant to our search subject. There are, as we shall see, ways of reducing the noise.

To see what sort of return we get from the *Science Citation Index* and how much noise is produced we have carried out some small-scale tests. What we have done is to take a bibliography on a specific subject and divide it into two parts, one part being a number of references which, by virtue of their being published within the time-period covered by an issue of the *Science Citation Index*, are eligible for inclusion as source items, and the other part being earlier items which may serve as entry-points to the Citation Index. We have a bibliography on the semi-conductor properties of Gallium from 1950 to April 1964, including 1,094 references, which divide into 1,045 references in 1963 and earlier, and forty-nine references to 1964.* So there are forty-nine references (all journal references) which are eligible for inclusion in the 1964 Citation Index as Source Items, and 1045 possible entry-points to the Citation Index proper. Of the forty-nine references we might find as source items, we in fact find 22 (45 per cent), the remainder being in journals which are not covered in the first three quarters' volumes of the *Science Citation Index* (although two journals which will add eight references to the coverage will be included in the 1964 Annual issue, and this will make our percentage figure 61 per cent). This coverage figure, incidentally, can be compared with figures obtained using the 1961 *Science Citation Index* to examine a bibliography on Biological Control of Insect Pests; of the forty-three possible source items, twenty (47 per cent) were in journals covered for that issue of the Index. This means that, in these two examples, using the *Science Citation Index* we are going to find only about half of the relevant references published in the year in which we are interested.

This sounds like a condemnation of the Index, but a little thought will correct this impression. A bibliographic approach to coverage of abstracts journals[14] has shown that percentage coverage of twelve topics by the best-performing abstracts journal for each topic ranges from 87 per cent to 34 per cent, the mean percentage coverage by best service being 65 per cent. Further, these abstracts services were specific to one area of science, whereas the *Science Citation Index* is general to the whole field. To be able to cover about half the literature by taking about 2 per cent of the world's journals suggests not only that the journals are in this instance well-chosen, but that the distribution of journals by size looks something like this (Figure 4).

This is substantiated by Professor Derek J. de Solla Price:[15] 'It is probable that 80% of all scientific papers can be had from about 1,000 journals, and that 80% of all chemical papers would come from the biggest specialised journals totalling less than 100 in number, and even that better than 95% of the chemical literature could be had from less than 200 of the most eminent journals'. The study of *Physics Abstracts* by Keenan and Atherton[16] shows that 50 per cent of the items abstracted are drawn from nineteen journals. In 1959 Urquhart[17] reported 50 per cent of the demand on the Science Library to have been met by 350 titles only, which again supports our hypothesis.

Returning to our Gallium semi-conductor bibliography, you will remember that we had 1,045 pre-1964 references, and forty-nine references to 1964, of which twenty-two were listed as source items. We have used all the 1,045 pre-1964 citations as entry points to see how many of the twenty-two relevant 1964 items we can locate, how much 'noise' we get, and whether or not we find anything relevant which was not included in our original 1964 bibliography. Of the 1,045 citations, 163 led us somewhere, as I have already told you; eighty-three of these guide us to twenty out of the twenty-two source items we are seeking. We do not find two of our source items, as neither of them cites any of our 1,045 references. Two pre-1964 citations guide us to four source items each, six to three each, eleven to two each, and sixty-three pre-1964 citations guide us to one source item each; there is, of course, considerable overlap, illustrated by the fact that of Spitzer's thirty-one citations in his 1964 paper, eighteen are to items in our pre-1964 bibliography, which means we find his paper eighteen different times. We can split up the 163 references which led us to source items, relevant or 'noise', as follows: fifty-five lead to relevant source items only, eighty to 'noise' source items (i.e. items not included in our twenty-two 1964 items) only, and twenty-eight lead to both relevant and 'noise' items.

In addition to the twenty source items of the 1964 bibliography we were also led to sixty-seven 'noise' items which appeared between January and April 1964, and we have sorted them into three groups on the basis of title only. Thirty-six are probably not relevant to the subject of Gallium as a semi-conductor, twenty-seven may or may not be relevant, and four — and this is the point — definitely are. (For interest, I mention that first I, a non-chemist, sorted the titles, and subsequently

---

* Section 11 of Gallium: *propriétés principales; bibliographie* by Dr. P. de la Breteque *and* L'Institut de Recherches de la Societé Française pour l'Industrie de l'Aluminium, in collaboration with l'Aluminium Suisse SA (formerly Aluminium–Industrie–Aktien–Gesellschaft). Marseilles, June 1962, and supplements in June 1963 and June 1964.

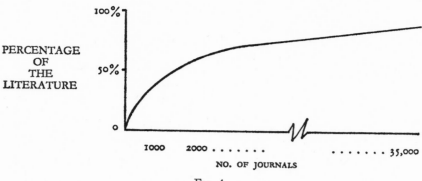

PERCENTAGE OF THE LITERATURE

100%

50%

0

1000   2000 35,000

NO. OF JOURNALS

FIG. 4

a colleague who is a chemist sorted them and we reached identical conclusions, without looking over each other's shoulder.) So we have found at least four new items relevant to our search, and I am awaiting with interest the publication in June of the next supplement of our Gallium bibliography, to see if they are picked up from the literature. If we class everything except that which is known to be relevant as 'noise', then we have altogether twenty-four 'signals' to sixty-three 'noises', a signal-to-noise ratio of 2:5, which we can crudely interpret as meaning that, in this particular case, of every seven references we found using the index two were highly relevant and five were not. All those which were not relevant to the search-subject, Gallium as a semiconductor, were relevant either to Gallium alone or to semi-conductors alone.

This seems to be a high proportion of noise to be receiving and supports the view that citation indexing is inherently noisy. However, at both the source and citation ends of the cycling process we have the ability to use a filter to screen off some of the noise. This filter is provided by the titles of source and citation items. In the first Cranfield Project report,[18] C. W. Cleverdon pointed out that KWIC indexing would have retrieved 97 per cent of the test documents known to have been relevant to the test questions, which, he says, is 'an interesting commentary on the effectiveness of the titles of the reports and papers used in the project'. A. Resnick[19] has confirmed that (to recipients of a selective dissemination of information service) there is no significant difference between the usefulness of titles and of abstracts for the purpose of determining relevance of documents of work interests, and there have been several other experiments reported all indicating that titles are a fairly effective guide to the relevance of documents. So, when using a Citation Index, you enter it with a citation to something you know is relevant; if you are led anywhere you are led to one or more entries in the Source Index, and can find there the full titles of the sources. You inspect these titles and seek copies only of those which look relevant; then when you are examining the bibliographies of the papers so selected, you will choose as fresh entry-points to the Citation Index only such

references as either the title, or the citing part of the source item you have, imply are relevant. You thus block off probably not all, but certainly a number, of the 'red-herring' channels in your citation network, and can steer your search in the most-desired direction. You can also use authors as blocks. That is, you may know that Snape is working along a different line to the one in which you are interested, and so may block not only channels leading to Snape but possibly also those leading to any co-authors of Snape. And of course journal titles can be used as blocks in the same way. Provided that the user of the Citation Index has access to a library and can consult his source items without difficulty, and has such reasonable knowledge of the literature of his field as any reputable scientist has, I do not consider that the 'noise' generated by a Citation Index is an important factor in its use. You are *not* snowed-under by references because not only are your chances of getting anywhere with any one citation limited, but you are interacting with the system at every stage in the process of cycling, and can, in Tukey's terminology, 'thin' at will, thus controlling your search-product to some extent throughout.

By now you must by nursing a growing suspicion that I am secretly in the employ of Dr Garfield. This is, I assure you, not so. My remarks about the ability of the user to modify his search-pattern at will are the result of an opportunity I had of watching scientists using the Citation Index to gather references relevant to current research projects, an experience which I found most instructive and illuminating, not least because the scientists in question were able to make effective use of the index, and even tell us ways of using it, after not more than about ten minutes' discussion and inspection of it.

Naturally there are things one cannot do with the index, because it is essentially only a guide to the existence of information and not a container of information in itself, in the sense that an abstracting service is. It is not, and in the nature of things never can be, a substitute for all the more formal bibliographical tools, but neither is it in the strict sense supplementary to them. It is an additional tool in its own right. This point has been brought out by T. A. Waldhart,[20] who compiled a bibliography on the subject of lasers, using seven conventional abstracting or indexing services and the *Science Citation Index* for 1961. As only the Applied Science and Technology Index and Solid State Abstracts contributed a higher proportion of unique references than SCI, he concluded that while SCI may be claimed in this instance as supplemental to ASTI and SSA, it could be claimed on the same grounds that the other five services individually were supplemental to SCI. It is interesting to note that it took him 380 minutes to produce 124 references from the conventional services and 120 minutes to produce forty from SCI, an average in each case of three minutes per reference. We must also note that of the thirteen unique references produced by SCI all but three were *covered* in one or more of the conventional services, but were not *found* because they were not indexed under the terms by which the indexes were searched.

We must also note that one of the charms of a citation index is that it is produced with no intellectual effort, and can be used without any great intellectual effort. Its production and its use are essentially clerical processes and if, as Tukey and Waldhart suggest, a Permuted Title Index to the source citations were added to allow a subject approach, it would still be a clerical job to produce it. Given the computer programmes (which already exist), the only point at which human intervention is needed is in the input stage. The rest is mechanical.

A little earlier I suggested that librarians might be less inclined readily to accept the *Science Citation Index* than scientists and research workers. If this be true there are a number of possible reasons, two of the more definable being the publicity associated with its appearance and its price. It seems generally agreed that some of the publicity has made rather exaggerated claims for the indispensability of the Index, but in all fairness any commercial venture nowadays must be announced with a certain amount of drum-beating, even though to some ears the beat of a drum is not music. The price is a more serious factor than this. The Index costs $1,250 a year to educational, hospital, and non-profit-making/non-Government supported organizations, and $1,950 a year for other organizations, with pre-publication reductions and a considerable reduction for second copies. This is a great deal of money, particularly when one realizes that for the same money an organization in the second category could buy *Chemical Abstracts, Physics Abstracts, Electrical Engineering Abstracts, Nuclear Science Abstracts, Biological Abstracts, Index Medicus, Engineering Index*, the 'Rubber Bible', and Whitaker's, and still have a sizeable sum left over. However, the *Science Citation Index* is, remember, a commercial venture, and is not now subsidized in any way from Federal or other resources. The price is reasonable in that the production of this Index is a very costly process, and if the Index is to be economically viable the price must

obviously cover the cost. It is unfortunate that not all British special librarians are funded on the same scale as some of their counterparts in the United States.

The question we are frequently asked at Aslib is 'Should I buy a copy of the *Science Citation Index*?' In a sense this is not a meaningful question, because, to be realistic, if a literature-access tool is of any use at all (and we have seen that the *Science Citation Index* is of use) and allows you to approach the literature in a different way to that permitted by your existing tools, you will almost certainly buy it if you have the money. To put this a different way, if you cannot afford the Index, you have no problem, and if you can afford it you will probably buy it — it is, after all, only the cost of a copy-typist. This is, I realize, a gross over-simplification, but I feel very strongly that fully effective literature exploitation is something that cannot be done on a tiny budget, and that if an organization insists on attempting to operate information services on a shoestring then it is short-sighted and unrealistic, and cannot expect perfection in its services. This may seem to be a digression from our subject, but I have allowed myself to digress because I think the price of this service is not of the highest relevance.

Not *every* scientist greets the appearance of a Citation Index with enthusiasm. Dr Ben-Ami Lipetz has made an attempt to evaluate the impact of a citation index in physics on the literature-use habits of physicists.[7] He prepared a citation index in which it was possible 'to look up a known reference in either the *Physical Review* or the *Journal of Applied Physics* to learn whether, and precisely where, it was cited in four of the leading Soviet physics journals which are published in English translation by the American Institute of Physics'. Copies of the index were given to 470 physicists, and the increase in the demand on libraries for the Soviet physics translation journals was studied to assess the impact of the Citation Index. A questionnaire was also used, to which 260 physicists responded; of these 260, twenty-nine said they hadn't looked at the index, 189 had only looked it over, forty-two claimed to have used it. Only a small increase in use of the Soviet literature was noted, and it was concluded that although citation indexing in physics can produce a measurable impact on literature-use, its effect is not very large or dramatic. This is not very surprising, for several factors are operating here, such as resistance to the scientific literature originating outside one's own language-group. Analysis of the comments of the 260 respondents shows 122 (47 percent) generally in favour of citation indexing, seventy-nine (30 percent) neutral, and fifty-nine (23 percent) more or less not in favour of the idea.

We know something of the performance characteristics of the *Science Citation Index*, but we do not yet know much about its use characteristics — I mean, how in practice scientists will use it, what they will expect it to do, and how well they will be satisfied with the results.

Will it be used, like an abstracts journal, about equally for current awareness and for retrospective search? The ultimate test of any system or service is the degree of its acceptance by the user — the most perfect system, on intellectual terms, is of limited value if the user is resistant to it, and a defective system of greater value if it is used to a greater extent. If scientists like and will use the *Science Citation Index*, then it is worth having a copy available in the library even though you are personally convinced that your Classified Card Index is more use; particularly if the scientists do not use the card index. Therefore I feel that the need now is for some user evaluation of the *Science Citation Index;* we need to have it available for a few years, so that we may see the scientists' reaction over the long term.

References

1. KESSLER, M. M. Bibliographic coupling between scientific papers. *American Documentation,* vol. 14, no, 1, January 1963, p. 10–25.
2. GARFIELD, E. "Science Citation Index" — a new dimension in indexing. *Science,* vol. 144, no. 3619, May 1964, p. 649–54.
3. *Science Citation Index.* 1961. Philadelphia, Pa., Institute for Scientific Information, 1963. (Introduction, p. xvii.)
4. GREENWOOD, J. A., OLKIN, I., *and* SAVAGE, I. R. *Annals of Mathematical Statistics.* Indexes to vols. 1–31, 1930–1960. University of Minnesota, 1962.
5. TUKEY, J. W. The citation index and the information problem. Princeton University Statistical Techniques Research Group, Annual Report for 1962.
6. LIPETZ, BEN-AMI. Compilation of an experimental citation index from scientific literature. Lexington, Mass., Itek Laboratories, June 1961.
7. LIPETZ, BEN-AMI. Evaluation of the impact of a citation index in physics. American Institute of Physics, September 1964.
8. TERRY, J. E. *Science Citation Index*: an international interdisciplinary index to the literature of science. *Journal of Documentation,* vol. 21, no. 2, June 1965, p. 139.
9. HAMMERSLEY, J. M. Guides to statistical literature. *Nature,* vol. 202, no. 4930, 25th April 1964, p. 330.
10. KEEN, E. M. Citation indexes. *Aslib Proceedings,* vol. 16, no. 8, August 1964, p. 246–51.
11. MARTYN, J. Report of an investigation on literature searching by research scientists. London, Aslib, 1964.
12. TUKEY, J. W. In discussion.
13. KESSLER, M. M., *and* HEART, F. E. Concerning the probability that a given paper will be cited. Massachusetts Institute of Technology, November 1962.
14. MARTYN, J., *and* SLATER, M. Tests on abstracts journals. *Journal of Documentation,* vol. 20, no. 4, December 1964, p. 212–35.
15. PRICE, D. J. DE S. Is technology historically independent of science? Paper given at a Symposium on the Historical Relations of Science and Technology. Montreal, December 1964.
16. KEENAN, S., *and* ATHERTON, P. The journal literature of physics. New York, American Institute of Physics, 1964.
17. URQUHART, D. J., *and* BUNN, R. M. A national loan policy for scientific serials. *Journal of Documentation,* vol. 15, no. 1, March 1959, p. 21–37.
18. CLEVERDON, C. W. Report on the testing and analysis of an investigation into the comparative efficiency of indexing systems. Cranfield, College of Aeronautics, October 1962.
19. RESNICK, A. Relative effectiveness of document titles and abstracts for determining relevance of documents. *Science,* vol. 134, no. 3484, October 1961, p. 1004–5.
20. WALDHART, T. J. A preliminary analysis of the Science Citation Index. Thesis, University of Wisconsin, 1964.

E. Abstracting

33 Criteria for Acceptable Abstracts: A Survey of Abstracters' Instructions

HAROLD BORKO
SEYMOUR CHATMAN
American Documentation
Vol. 14, No. 2, April, 1963

1. Introduction

As part of a present research investigation into abstracting and related information-reprocessing functions, we have carried out a survey of the instructions published by various journals and services to guide abstracters in the preparation of copy. A letter of inquiry was sent to 315 sources selected from *A Guide to U. S. Indexing and Abstracting Services in Science and Tech-. nology* (1961, Science and Technology Division, Library of Congress, for the National Federation of Science Abstracting and Indexing Service, June). The text of the letter was as follows.

Dear Sir:

The System Development Corporation is supporting a research project in scientific journal abstracting. In the course of this project we hope to develop some criteria for the adequacy of an abstract, and some more or less mechanical procedures for abstracting articles. Your cooperation would be appreciated.

Your organization publishes abstracts and I am therefore writing to inquire whether you have a prepared guide or set of instructions for use by your abstractors. I would appreciate receiving a copy of such a guide or any material which sets standards for abstracts, and if possible a few samples.

Are the abstracts which you publish designed primarily to alert your readers to current papers which they themselves would want to read in full; or are they designed to furnish the reader with broad coverage of new developments in their field, substituting thereby for the reading of the original paper?

Thank you for your cooperation.

Very truly yours,

Responses have been received from 183 sources, 130 of which contained usable information (see alphabetic bibliography at the end of this paper). Results of the survey are presented under the headings of Function, Content, and Form. We have not distinguished between instructions for abstracts written by the author for submission of his own article and abstracts written by professionals for abstracting journals or services. Only instructions expressly presented to guide the abstracter were analyzed; no analysis was made of actual practice as determined, for example, by close examination of the published abstracts themselves. Such an analysis definitely should be done, both to discover the relation between theory and practice and to uncover the more subtle aspects of linguistic and information-retrieval behavior involved in the preparation of abstracts. In the meantime, we must satisfy ourselves with surveying how editors say abstracts should be written.

2. Function

The nature of an abstract reflects the editor's purposes, which in turn reflect the desires of the reader. Therefore, one cannot separate function from use: an editor's constant problem is to estimate what sort of presentation his readers really want.

In response to our question concerning the functions of abstracts, a distinction between two basic types clearly emerged; these may be called by different names and entail some difficulties in definitions, but the distinction seems fairly clear. One kind of abstracting is usually referred to as "informative" ("informational," "direct"); it provides the reader with the basic informational content of the article. The other is the "descriptive" abstract ("indicative," "alerting"), whose function is to "direct," "alert," provide "current awareness," "acquaint . . . with the gist of the article," "bring reader's attention to important articles they may have overlooked" (33), and to "permit the reader to decide whether the article or book reviewed would be of value or interest to him" (66), etc.

Definitions and examples

Definitions of the two approaches are not easy to formulate or to express; one injunction concerning the writing of the informative abstract warns "Do not state what the report is about but what it tells . . ."; another defines an abstract as a "Condensed Version, not a description"; a third states that the descriptive abstract is one which "tells what the article is about," while the informative abstract "transmits information." Metaphor is used: the descriptive abstract is called a "prose table of contents" (3). Perhaps the clearest formulation is the following:

The informative abstract . . . is more nearly a condensation of the information in the report. It contains the principal ideas, methods, and data but omits excess wordage and detailed explanation . . .

The indicative or descriptive abstract consists of generalized statements of the content of the article, is ordinarily shorter than the other type, and is characterized primarily by the absence of qualitative and quantitative data. It is often little more than a listing of the principal subjects presented in narrative form . . . (79).

But even better than definitions are examples; some editors show how the same article can be abstracted in both styles. It is worthwhile to quote two of these and to discuss some implicit principles of composition and style.

For Meteorology:

Informative: Brinell and scratch hardness tests were made on single ice crystals with a modified Olsen Baby Brinell Hardness Tester and a Spencer Microcharacter, respectively. Hardness increased with decrease in temperature; Brinell hardness numbers ranged from about 4 at −5C to 17 at −50C. A similar temperature dependence for scratch hardness was noted. The single ice crystal was harder parallel to the c-axis than in the normal direction.
[Descriptive]
Indicative: The experimental procedures and results of Brinell and scratch hardness tests on single ice crystals are given. The effects of temperature and c-axis orientation on hardness are discussed, and the experimental data are tabulated and graphed (79).

For Chemistry:

Informative: Close-packed molecular and crystal models can be built easily and inexpensively by dipping balls of various materials into latex of 60% concentration. Desired colors can be obtained by dipping the balls into a quick-drying water insoluble paint before the latex is applied. Slight pressure is all that is needed to stick the balls together to form a model. They can be separated by a quick jerk.
Descriptive: A simple method of building close-packed molecular and crystal models is described. It has proved its pedagogic value as well as its many advantages to the research worker. Two diagrams and four photographs are included. The method was evolved in the author's laboratory (3).

Prominent in the descriptive abstract are terms like "are given," "are tabulated," "are graphed," "are listed," "is indicated," etc. These terms, generally set in the passive, can conveniently be referred to as "metatext terms"; they tend to highlight the process of writing the article rather than the research upon which the article is based. The style is that of an outsider: "Procedures . . . are given," "effects . . . are discussed," "a method . . . is described," "diagrams . . . are included."

In the informative abstract, however, the abstract author, by identifying himself grammatically with the abstracter, refers not to the mere processes of writing the article but to the actual experimental or investigative activities of the real author or to the behavior or state of the organisms or things being studied ("scratch hardness tests were made," "hardness increased," "hardness numbers ranged," "a similar temperature dependence . . . was noted [*was*, not *is:* the notation was part of the original author's experimental activity, not of his writing-up of the results]").

Types of abstracts

The Informative Abstract

The function of the informative abstract is generally to obviate the necessity of reading the article at all; the original should be "reviewed in sufficient detail to make it unnecessary for the reader to consult the original article" (112); it should "include every fact the reader will want, rather than simply to alert him" (33); it should be written "so that the reader will not have to refer to the original article" (106); it is "intended for the use of a reader who does not have access to or cannot use, the original" (64). Some editors, however, imply that the informative abstract should not replace the article; the reader "can determine which articles can be referred to in order to secure the information he may need" (64). One distinguishes, rather wistfully, ideal from real functions: "Although ideally, readers should be stimulated to go to the original source to read the full article, we have found that many, if not the majority, of our readers use this department as a means of 'keeping up' on new developments because of what they feel to be our broad coverage" (68).

The Indicative Abstract

Alerting is a quite separate function, and editors warn that their abstracts are not intended to replace the original article; the descriptive abstract is designed "to tell the reader what subjects he will find discussed in the article — to act as a guide to the article, not as a substitute for it" (104), "to alert our readers to current papers which they themselves would want to read in full" (20), "to give the essential information in scientific articles so that the reader may decide for himself whether the abstract gives him enough information or whether he wishes to read the original article in full" (98). "It is not intended that reading the review should be a replacement for reading the original paper. The primary purpose is to give the user . . . a basis for deciding whether or not he needs to read the original paper" (83). The purpose of the descriptive abstract is "not to condense the whole subject matter into a few words for quick reading, but rather to give a clear indication of the object and scope of the paper and the results achieved, so that the reader may determine whether the full text will be of interest to him" (85).

Combined Informative and Indicative Abstracts

Some journals indicate a desire to perform both an indicative and an informative function. One policy is to write descriptive or indicative abstracts for survey, lecture, and other articles which "contain too much information (especially if it is a review); [or where] the information in the article is well known (a discussion); [or if] the article concerns mathematics which is difficult to verbalize" (16). Informative abstracts, on the other hand, are called for in the case of research reports (116), so that the research can be disseminated widely.

One editor comments realistically that:

> While we intend to give the reader broad coverage of new developments in their field to take the place of the original paper, we sometimes succeed, and at other times, we must be content with alerting the reader to current papers which he may wish to read in full (91).

Another puts the same thought as follows:

> . . . the abstract is not meant as a replacement of the original but in many cases it may have to serve as an adequate substitute (79).

Function summary

The results of our survey of policy concerning the function of abstracts may be summarized as follows:

Informative:	23	17.7%
Descriptive:	48	36.9%
Both:	32	24.6%
Other or unclear:	4	3.1%
No information:	23	17.7%
	130	100.0%

These differences do not apparently correspond to any contrast in subject matter or field, as, for example, the difference between pure science and technology.

3. Content

It is interesting to note how extensively editors agree on and can specify the kinds of information they wish abstracts to contain. There are, of course, differences among the requirements of the various disciplines — as will be demonstrated below — but the degree of similarity is impressive. A neat dichotomy manifests itself: "what to include" vs. "what to exclude." It is generally agreed that abstracts should include the four main topics (purpose, methods, results, and conclusion) and, where applicable, specialized information and should exclude all excessive verbiage, as in the case of detailed explanations and in the repetition of known results.

Purpose

The abstracter is instructed to state the purpose of the article. This concept is expressed by a number of terms which more or less mean the same thing: "the reasons for the work that was performed" (116); "what was sought" (116); the "objectives" (9); "nature of the problem" (67); "goals," "object," "the reason for the investigation," "the problem" (85). Another term, "scope" (79, 116, 7, 91, 53, 31), adds the implication of magnitude or size of the undertaking. In two cases the inclusion of purpose is only requested if it is not evident from the title (116, 131). A few formulate purpose as "hypothesis" (100).

Methods

This is a summary term for the "way" (85), the "approach," the "treatment," how the results were sought, rather than what was sought (21, 110, 116). Here again we have a proliferation of similar terms, although slight differences emerge, corresponding to differences in subject matter and approach. The hard sciences and technology ask for a description of apparatus, equipment and material (26, 53, 91, 7, 93) or a categorization into "laboratory" or "field techniques" (53). One of the more explicit social science journals specifies its requirements quite exhaustively.

How does the author do it? What data are used? What is their origin? What method(s) of isolating data are used? Are the data qualitatively and/or quantitatively manipulated? What tests, scales, indexes, or other summarizing techniques are used? What are the major distinctions or breaks? What concepts are developed? What classification scheme is used? How, in other words, is analysis and/or synthesis accomplished? (108)

For reasons of brevity, many journals request that a description be limited to new methods only (53, 26, 7, 91, 104); in one set of directions, abstracters are asked to describe particularly carefully the methods with the "greatest value and originality" but are warned that "in the majority of cases . . . the method is typical and should be described very briefly (usually by name . . .)" (116).

Results

Although a few journals ask simply for "what was learned," or (39) ". . . something missing?", the majority distinguish between results and conclusions (110, 38, 79, 32, 53, 116, 43). This dichotomy, of course, is based on classical experimental procedure, in which the experimenter secures findings and then proceeds to interpret them. Obviously, it is sometimes necessary for the abstracter to make a selection among results.

Frequently . . . there are too many specific results for inclusion. To prepare a truly informative abstract, the abstractor should reflect that which was found to be *new* . . . (21).

There is an emphasis on "principal" events (26, 43, 100), "new or verified" (26, 16, 53, 9, 19), and "of permanent value" (26, 53), "major" (100), ones which are "significant" (79), and "important" (17). One journal requests that "negative results . . . be generalized" (32).

Conclusions

The conclusions — the "interpretations" of the results or "significance" — are "what [the investigation] meant, or how it may be of value or interest to investigators in similar fields . . ." (21). Its purposive character is often stressed by such accompanying "recommendations" (116); "applications" (79, 53); "suggestions," "evaluation," and "new relationships" (108). More explicitly, "Are the hypotheses, ideas, concepts, theories, etc. [i.e., the purpose] accepted or rejected"? (108).

Miscellaneous and specialized information

In addition to these four major categories, directions of one sort or another are often given regarding special or supplementary information which is to be included in the abstract. Examples of these specialized instructions include: Give length of article (67); give status of research as in progress reports (100, 21); give new terms and their definitions (7, 91). Some instructions are so specialized as to be idiosyncratic. These are listed by subject field.

Pharmacology: . . . how many individuals there were in the experimental series; whether human or animal, and the species; what percentage reacted, etc.; and in the case of a new drug, its composition . . . (118).

Chemical Market Analysis: Company, location, plans, dates, capacity, trade name, nature of product, patents, unit consumption factor (33).

Biology: name of organism . . . new genera, new classifications and distribution records, absorption spectra . . . (26).

Sociology: type of question (open-ended, multiple-choice, true-false, etc.), and the manner of administration . . . The *N* used in the study, the basic breaks made, the geographic or social characteristics of respondents or sources . . . scales must be named: Guttman, Thurstone, Likert, etc. (108).

Geology: orient [paper] in place and geologic time . . . locate local stratigraphic names in the general geologic column . . . [name] new minerals, fossils, etc. (53).

Medicine: full details of diagnosis and treatment, technic and procedures . . . (drug dosages, operative techniques) . . . (87).

In addition, special instructions are provided for abstracting books, bibliographies, and patents.

Books: Abstracts of books should reflect their extent, which can usually be determined from the table of contents . . . (89).

Bibliographies: Abstracts of bibliographies should indicate the extent, scope, period covered, arrangement and number of references, and indexes included (89) . . . can best be annotated by citing the scope of the bibliography and giving the time span covered by the entries and their method of arrangement, i.e., whether by topic or alphabetically by author (21).

Patents: . . . what the invention is or to what it relates . . . (a) its construction, if a machine, apparatus, device or article; (b) its identity, if a chemical compound, or its ingredients, if a mixture, including the production thereof if not obvious; or (c) the procedure involved, if a process . . . its manner of operation (how it works) . . . (56).

Statistical Data

The attitudes of the editors toward the quotation of statistics and numbers in the abstract differ. One journal feels that "Numerical results represent the heart of the abstract" (106); others ask that they only be included if relevant ("statistics . . . if necessary to support the author's conclusions, may be used in the final portion of the abstract" (87, 54), "New numerical data . . . if space permits" (9, 19); one requests that "Numerical data . . . be summarized with extreme or mean values being cited wherever possible" (79). On the other hand, at least one journal suggests that numerical data not be included: "If at all possible, please avoid the use of mathematics" (17), and another asks abstracters to "reduce the number of mathematical formulae used to a minimum" (62). A similar difference of attitude occurs with respect to graphs, illustrations, tables, and charts: "graphs and illustrations will all be included" (112), "utilize information and relationships given in graphs and charts" (20), or at least "Important tabulated data, graphs, illustrations, maps, etc., should be cited" (79), "Diagrams, graphs, photographs, tables . . . are to be noted at the end of an abstract when they are pertinent" (16) (but 16 goes on to warn against excessive liberality in annotation). Many journals, however, expressly exclude such materials (67, 120, 26, 53, 31, 17, 9), and one even requests that "citations and references to the tables, illustrations, or other material . . . be avoided" (52).

Reference Citations

Practice similarly varies with respect to the citation of references. Some journals have a regular quantitative measure:

If more than 1 and less than 40 references appear with the article, note 'reference' at the end of the abstract. If 40 or more appear, note 'bibliography' (3).

Others request citation if more than 15 references are made (32), or more than 4 (20); some request that all references be cited either unqualifiedly or at the discretion of the abstracter ("noteworthy bibliography" (67), "occasionally it necessary to cite literature references (89)).

Items to exclude

Abstracters are requested to exclude "detailed descriptions" (53), particularly of "experiments or organisms" (26, 120) or of "methodology" (12); "statements generally should not be amplified by the use of examples" (52), or at least general headings should be provided where details are excessive (20). Other exclusions relate to unsubstantiated remarks or generally known facts: "Speculation by the author or general conclusions which do not follow immediately from the results . . . ought to be omitted" (34); the abstracter should not include any "facts already well established" (50), including "basic . . . information that is well known to the profession" (87, 54), "surveys of the literature" (87, 54, 67), "or references to other men's experiences, except as the author adopts [sic] particular findings to his own work" (87). One journal even suggests that abstracters "try to avoid repeating any information already given . . . in recent abstracts of articles by the same author or on the same subject" (104). An obvious and necessary general exclusion is made explicit in three journals: do not include "additions, corrections, or any information not contained in the original published paper" (26, 53, 120). A few format restrictions are also indicated: "headings should be avoided" (52), and "long lists of names" (26, 53, 120). Finally, the most widespread exclusion pertains to information which is already implicitly included either in the title (79, 116, 26, 52, 50, 17, 120, 20, 19, 9, 21, 89) or the table of contents (52), and a few journals warn against taking from the author's own abstract *verbatim* (94).

Content summary

Regarding the content of an abstract, regardless of whether the abstract is intended to be informative or descriptive, it is generally agreed that an adequate abstract should include — as a minimum — a statement concerning the purpose, methods, results, and conclusions reached by the author of the original article. In addition, depending upon the specialized subject field of the nature of the article being abstracted, the abstracter may be required to include other data. In all instances it is suggested that the abstract be brief and nonrepetitive.

4. Form

Many journals give directions concerning the form in which the abstract is to be written. It is convenient to distinguish between the following aspects of form: Style, Length, and Abstracter Comments.

Style of abstract

"Style" in the present context means writing style, not format instructions (paragraphing, typing, indenting, abbreviations, etc.). An essential conflict arises in attempting to communicate information through abstracts: How can one be concise without being obscure? This tension is the constant theme of editorial comment on abstract style.

> That style is best in an abstract which more *quickly* conveys the necessary information. Clarity is essential; vividness is not . . . Brevity is important but is to be measured by the amount of information conveyed in a given space, not by the number of lines (93).

> The abstractor should develop the practice of critically rereading the completed abstract and should chop ruthlessly at all verbiage before forwarding it to the reviewer. Complete and clear sentences in good, idiomatic English is the desired result (89).

Requests to improve clarity and uniformity necessarily lead to generalized directions; abstracters are asked to write abstracts which are "straightforward" (9), "direct," "terse" (9), "concise" (83), "brief" (93), "objective" (9), "smooth-reading" (20), "complete" (9), "possessed of continuity" (79), "properly emphasized" (9), "specific" (20), etc. The value of such directions is somewhat questionable, since telling a less-than-competent writer to be concise, straightforward, etc., is like telling a shoeless person to pull himself up by his bootstraps; but the editor's predicament is understandable, since its difficult to describe good style in other than general terms. Some journals do manage, however, to give rather specific instructions about abstract style, and it is worthwhile to examine what they say.

Phrase Structure

As a means of packing a great deal of information into a small space, one journal suggests using phrases for clauses and words for phrases (9). Aside from the fact that some clauses are shorter than some phrases and some words longer than some phrases, it may be that phrase transformations of clauses are harder to understand than the original clauses themselves. Two other journals suggest converting subject-predicate constructions into participle or nominalized constructions:

Example:	*Not:*
Showing or indicating	it is shown that
determination of	are found to be determined
using or with	by means of (20)

. . . say, 'Using operational methods . . . ,' instead of 'Through the use of operational methods . . .' (17).
Another journal may be referring to the misuse of this practice when it warns against dangling participles.

> Dangling participles are undesirable. . . . The noun that is modified by a participle should always appear in the same sentence or clause that contains the participle . . . (32).

Sentence Structure

The word "telegraphic" crops up regularly in discussions of abstract style.[1] It usually means a style in which grammatical or function words (articles, for example) are omitted or reduced in number. Sometimes it refers to a more radical stylistic revision in which verbs are eliminated as well, and the abstract tends towards a mere listing of topics. Most of the journals examined dislike telegraphic abstracts: ". . . be terse but not telegraphic (e.g., do not omit a's, an's and the's . . ." (9); ". . . complete, clear sentences in correct English should be used. Avoid abstracts that read like jotted notes or a telegram. Use article (a), (an), and (the): their omission often detracts from clearness and makes reading tiresome" (32) (cf. also 116, 70, 66, 31, 89, and 104). A couple of journals, however, do not require complete sentences (although they dislike dropped articles).

> Shall we insist upon complete sentences? Not always. There is much to be said for phrases that are in essence subtopics and which convey in briefest form what the articles is about. The title 'A new method of training' conveys the same information as the sentence in the test 'A new method of training is described' (93).

But the editor hastens to add:

> . . . a steady diet of 'telegraphic sentences' or 'headlines' becomes very tiresome. Often few words are saved: 'Reliability and validity promising' is probably not read much faster than 'The reliability and validity were promising.' A certain variety of structure contributes to readability. We can only say: strive to save not only the time but the effort of the probable readers (93).

Another editor states that:

> Complete sentences are not necessary but a complete thought must be conveyed. Example: Determination of phase equilibria in terms of alloy composition and temperature. Do not eliminate all definite and indefinite articles, since they are needed to give sense to the abstract (20).

At least one journal allows the deletion of articles but does not specify whether it is always permissible: "Say 'Author concludes . . .' instead of 'The author concludes'" (17).

Verb Form

In striving for consistency and readability of abstracts, attention must be paid to the mood and tense of the verbs. Most abstracters' manuals devote some space to a

1. This term is used by the Western Reserve Documentation Center to represent a much more powerfully reduced kind of abstract, which also serves as an index.

discussion of the verb form, and the instructions are fairly uniform.

Passive vs. active voice. The well-known rhetorical principle that verbs should be placed in the active mood as much as possible to increase vividness does not always find acceptance in abstract-writing: "Abstracts should usually be written in the passive voice of either present or past tense" (116). The reasons for using the passive, even at a loss of rhetorical vividness, are to maintain impersonality, to eliminate constant reference to the author, and to cut down on metatext constructions, i.e., locutions like 'the authors felt that . . .,' or 'it is the author's contention that . . . .'

> Preferred: 'The circuit requirements for tunnel diode converter operation are discussed.' Rather than: 'This paper discusses the circuit requirements for tunnel diode converter operation.' 'The patent cites the circuit . . .' The author states the circuit . . .' (110).

As was pointed out above, the use of the passive voice is the one stylistic feature which is usually typical of the descriptive or altering abstract. In the informative abstract, the passive voice is regularly replaced, explicitly or by example.

An abstract is a condensed version of the original— *not a description of it.*

> WRONG: 'The usual causes of death from oral malignancy are reviewed . . .'
> RIGHT: 'Death usually results from . . .' (67).

Sometimes the choice of mood is determined by the position of the verb. One journal states a clear preference for placing the verb at the end of the sentence.

> . . . the position of the verb is at the end of the sentence. This is preferred (though not demanded) . . . (110).

Most journals take a more flexible point of view.

> We use active verbs wherever possible in order to avoid such weak verb forms as 'is,' 'was,' 'are,' and 'were.' However, we use the passive voice where a direct statement would push the main subject of the abstract to the end of the first sentence; i.e., for subject emphasis we are thus forced to say: 'The relative absorption coefficients of ether, water, and ethylene were measured . . .' (16).
> A sentence should be constructed so that the verb is near the subject. The long series of modifiers that sometimes separate subject and verb can often be changed into adverb modifiers occurring either before the subject or after the verb (32).

Tense. Practice concerning tense varies too.

> The past tense is used in describing experimental work, including the procedure, equipment, conditions,

theoretical bases, and data obtained. The present tense is used in giving conclusions derived from the experimental data.

> Example: The engine *was mounted* on a large test stand, and *was used* to show that aromatic gasolines *are* relatively low in antiknock response to tetraethyllead (16).

Instructions about the use of the perfect tense are as follows:

> Present tense is used throughout the abstract, except for presenting statistics and case references (87).
> The present tense is used when referring to an action going on now or when discussing the report itself. The use of the present perfect is to be avoided. For example, the phrases 'data are given,' not 'data were given,' and 'an experiment was performed,' not 'an experiment has been performed,' should be used (89).
> The past perfect tense is preferred, (e.g. company *has begun,* or *was to begin*) (33).

One source associates the present tense with descriptive abstracts and the past with informative abstracts.

> The . . . present tense is preferred in descriptive abstracts which summarize what is described, presented, discussed, tabulated, etc. Simple past tense is generally preferred for informative abstracts. . . . Specific conclusions should be stated in the past tense. General truths and general conclusions may be stated in the present tense. The use of mixed verb forms or shifting of tenses in abstracts is usually undesirable (116).

There is general advice to maintain consistency in tenses.

> The use of mixed forms in an abstract should be avoided unless justified by a change in viewpoint. For example, the past perfect tense should be used for work done before the present study . . . past tense to describe the procedure . . . present tense to discuss the report itself . . . and future tense to discuss future projects (rarely suitable in abstracts) (32). . . . mixing of [verb] conventions within a single abstract should be avoided (89).

Point of View

Another stylistic matter commented upon is that of "point of view"; the point of view is the rhetorical perspective or stance which the author assumes. One may write in his own behalf, or from someone else's point of view, or "omnisciently" (as in a panoramic novel where the author enters the minds of many characters), or neutrally. There is often a close correlation between one's notion of the function of abstracts and his rhetorical point of view: in informative abstracts, the abstracter is completely identified with the author, while in descriptive abstracts, the abstracter stands apart, behind locutions like "X was attempted" or "The author believes Y." Those journals which urge informative abstracts are the most likely to make observations like the following:

We use direct statements rather than indirect ones wherever possible. The author speaks, not the abstractor (16).

The abstractor . . . should use sparingly such phrases as 'the author believes,' 'it is concluded by Smith for this work,' et cetera (12).

It may be assumed that any statement in the abstract is essentially that of the author, hence such expressions as 'The author concludes' are redundant (93).

Minor Stylistic Recommendations

Directions abound in rhetorical prohibitions of one kind or another, some of which can be found in the usual handbooks and others of which demonstrate hardly more than the personal peeves of editors. One journal proscribes the excessive use of relative clauses (along with superlatives and "grandiose phrases" (79), while another requests "full use" of relative clauses, along with adjective "to save repeating words" (104). It is hard to see, *in vacuo*, quite what the evils or advantages of relative clauses might be. A few journals provide sizeable lists of points to be guarded against; there are both grammatical and lexical, and a few may be quoted.

Such expressions as '10 times longer' or '5 times smaller,' sometimes found in scientific literature, are not exact. The first of these expressions is ambiguous, and the second one is meaningless. The writer of '10 times longer' probably means '10 times as long,' but he could mean '11 times as long' (32).

The expression 'such as' should not be followed by the redundant 'etc.' after a series of examples (32).

The word 'data' is plural and should be so treated consistently. 'Data' should be referred to as 'they' and not as 'it' and should always have plural qualifiers (89).

Avoid split infinitives. For example, say 'to increase greatly' rather than 'to greatly increase' (89).

Medical writing is cluttered with many words that are overused or misused. Here is a list of words and phrases frequently encountered in medical articles, with comment indicating [our] editorial preference:

all of—omit *of*
autopsy—a noun; adjective is *postmortem*
average—use *about* . . . [etc.] (87).

Length of abstract

As one might expect, practice varies widely concerning optimal abstract length, Indeed, even the measuring stick varies: number of words, percentage of the original article, number of lines, number of sentences, and amount of the page covered. The results are most com-

pactly presented in a table (Table I). The numbers in parenthesis refer, as always, to the specific journals listed in the bibliography.

TABLE I
MEASURING STICKS FOR OPTIMAL ABSTRACT LENGTH

Number of words:

50–100 (85)	200 (12, 92, 19)
100–(56, 61)	250 (21) (116)
100–500 (108)	300 (18)
125–150 (34)	400–800 (62)
150 (31)	2000 (66)

Percentage of the original article:

less than 3% (26)
4%–6% of medium length articles, less for longer one (9)

Number of lines:

3–8 (20)
5–20 (106)
28 (16)

Number of sentences:

one or two (118)

Amount of the page (8 x 11 double-spaced covered):

¾ of a page (68)
1½ pages (67)
not more than three pages (113)

Few journals are so brave as to leave abstract length unspecified.

No specific limits on length of abstract have been set for survey reports. The author should keep in mind the value of a concise abstract to a busy reader and should write what is needed for the abstract but no more. Short, compact papers generally require actually shorter but proportionally longer abstracts than large, detailed papers. There are many different arbitrary limits set by scientific and technical journals on the length of abstracts, some in terms of a word limit and some in terms of a ratio or percentage limit (52).

Most journals recognize that abstract length should be flexible to accommodate the different kinds of materials abstracted (9, 317, 83, 62, 93, 98, 104, 116, etc.); frequently, articles from foreign or difficult-to-obtain journals are given longer treatment, while contributions which review the literature are abbreviated.

Comments by the abstracter

While the primary role of the abstracter is to summarize the content of the original article, some journals allow—or even encourage—the abstracter to critically comment on the value or correctness of the information. The degree of freedom in this regard varies from a *carte blanche* to complete prohibition, as a few representative quotations will illustrate.

Many of our reviewers go well beyond an abstract, into a critical evaluation. . . . We have no fixed rules on which items receive critical review and which are in effect abstracts. If the reviewer has comments pro or con, he is free to include them (27).

With regard to critical comments, such items as correctness, relation to other work, novelty, etc., should be discussed. Preface such remarks by 'Reviewer believes . . .' or an equivalent opening. If novelty of the paper is discounted, give references to support contention (17).

Criticism and personal comment are not required and should not be included in the text of the abstract, except when mistakes or misprints are discovered. An abstract is not a public discussion against which the author might have to defend himself. However, whenever you are reluctant to share the slightest responsibility with the author, you can always express this by using such terms as: 'It is claimed, postulated, inferred,' etc. (50, 104).

A special class of abstracter's comments deal with cross-referencing and indexing of abstracts. Attitudes toward the free inclusion of cross-references range from liberal ("Indicate . . . any code number of cross-references you deem applicable" (17); ". . . show correlation with earlier works (if important)" (53), "Compare the reference in question to others of similar or contrasting purpose, especially when there is a conflicting opinion" (66)) to conservative. ("A comparison of the present work with the work of others or with what has been known previously about a topic should be avoided. Reference to the work of others may be included, however, if the present work is a development from other work and it is necessary to show the basis from which the development was made" (52). "Do not fill your abstract with references to earlier work—the ones to include are those which aid in understanding the abstract, and the reader must turn to the original paper for the full bibliography" (104).) Most editors prefer to cross-reference by abstract number (104, 32, 16, 100, 17); one requests authors to "Cross out all references in the text to journals and to previous abstracts. Leave in the names of previous investigators referred to" (106). Abstracts are sometimes tied in with indexing systems, and instructions are given for facilitating the transfer of information (9). "Abstracts should contain or make specific reference to all of the information [in the articles] that is suitable for index entries." Abstracters are requested to "underline . . . important words for subject indexing" (53) taken from the body of the text or from the title (106). The indexing may be done by the abstracter himself (62) or by the editor and his staff (83).

Form summary

The form to be used in the writing of abstracts was discussed under the headings of style, length and ab-stracter's comments. Style refers to the style of writing. All editors agree that abstracts should be concise and clear. The bulk of material in the instruction manual is devoted to specifying how conciseness and clarity are to be achieved. Most editors insist that the abstracts be written in complete sentences. The use of the passive verb form is typical of the descriptive abstract, and active verb forms are more likely to be found in the informative abstract. The tense of the verb is also significant, although opinion differs more widely about the proper tense than about the proper mood. The present tense is preferred. The past tense frequently denotes work done prior to the present study. Here again, however, there is a significant difference between the verb forms used in descriptive and in informative abstracts. The present tense is most often associated with the former, while the past tense occurs more often in the informative abstract. The length of the abstract is quite variable but is most likely to be in the 100–500-word range. Thus we see that, although a great deal of latitude is possible, there is present a core of consistency so that all abstracts have more in common with each other than they have with any other prose form.

5. Conclusions

As a prelude to stating our conclusions, let us first review the aims and purposes for undertaking this study. Our main purpose was to study the literature on the preparation of scientific abstracts and to specify a set of criteria by which the adequacy of an abstract could be judged. We recognized at the onset that, because of the variation in subject matter, user requirements, cost, and other factors, a single universal set of criteria may not be reached, and that two or more restricted sets of criteria might be needed.

Why the interest in criteria for abstracts? It is already possible to prepare an extract of an article by means of a computer program. The early efforts to evaluate these extracts failed partially because there were no criteria by which they could be judged. As our computer technology improves, it should be possible to prepare 'better' extracts and possibly true abstracts. Before such a time comes, we should have ready a means for measuring the adequacy of the abstract—be it man-made or computer-prepared. It was with these thoughts in mind that this study was conceived.

As a general conclusion, it is of interest to note that abstracts have a great deal in common, and, hopefully, these common elements could be specified. Differences in subject matter do not necessarily require different kinds of abstracts. However, there seems to be a real difference—both in content and, especially, in form—between informative and indicative abstracts. Content-wise, the informative abstract contains more detailed quantitative and qualitative data than does the indicative abstract. Style-wise in the informative abstract, the abstracter identifies with, and writes from, the point of view of the experimenter; that is to say, he uses an active verb form in the same tense, after the past tense, as in the original article. In contrast, the descriptive abstract is most often written in the passive mode and in the present tense.

Criteria for an adequate abstract

Distilling the essence from the 130 manuals of instructions, we list as our criteria for an adequate abstract the following.

Content

Purpose: A statement of the goals, objectives, and aims of the research or reasons why the article was written. This statement should be included in both the informative and indicative abstracts.

Method: A statement about the experimental techniques used or the means by which the previously stated purpose was to be achieved. If the techniques are original or unusual, or if the abstract is informative, more detail should be included.

Results: A statement of the findings. The informative abstract tends to be more quantitative than the descriptive abstract.

Conclusions: A statement dealing with the interpretations or significance of the results.

Specialized content: Certain subject-matter fields require that the abstract contain specialized information. Medical journals, for example, require that the abstract contain details of diagnosis and treatment, drug dosages, etc., where applicable. In writing or evaluating abstracts in these fields, the specialized requirements must be considered.

The abstract is to be brief (100–500 words) and non-repetitive.

Form

More variation is possible in the form of the abstract. Therefore, form criteria must be applied judiciously and cautiously. The major criteria are clarity of content and conciseness of expression. Having recognized the existence of great variation in form, we can nevertheless specify general differences between the informative and indicative abstract.

Informative	*Indicative*
1. Active voice	Passive
2. Past tense	Present
3. Discusses the research	Discusses the article which describes the research

Plans for future research

Obviously, it is not sufficient to simply state our notions of acceptable criteria. The criteria themselves must be subjected to critical analysis and evaluation. Our first plans then are to circulate this report, request criticism, and, in the light of suggestions, revise the criteria as necessary. A special group from whom comments will be solicited are the editors of the abstracting journals who cooperated in the initial part of the study. Would they accept these criteria?

Next, we plan to evaluate published abstracts against these criteria. Are the published abstracts adequate as judged by these measures?

Third, we plan to give these criteria to subject-matter specialists, request them to write abstracts in accordance with these rules, and send the results to the journal editors for evaluation.

Last, our long range plans call for the translation of these rules into computer programs for the automatic preparation of extracts and abstracts.

Bibliography

1. *Abstract Bulletin of the Institute of Paper Chemistry.*
2. *Abstract Review.* (National Paint, Varnish, and Lacquer Association).
3. *Abstracts (Continental Can Company, Inc.),* "Guide for Abstractors."
4. *Abstracts of Articles on Geodesy and Related Fields* (Corps of Engineers, Army Map Service).
5. *Abstracts of Bioanalytic Technology* (John Crerar Library for the American Association of Bioanalysts).
6. *Abstracts of Military and Aviation Ophthalmology and Visual Sciences* (Ophthalmological Foundation, Inc.).
7. *Abstracts of Photographic Science and Engineering Literature,* "Directions for Preparation of Abstracts For" (Columbia University in collaboration with the Society of Photographic Scientists and Engineers).
8. *Abstracts of the New World Archaeology* (Society for American Archaeology).
9. *American Institute of Physics Style Manual* [provides directions for: *American Journal of Physics, Journal of Applied Physics, The Journal of Chemical Physics, Journal of Mathematical Physics, Journal of the Acoustical Society of America, Journal of the Optical Society of America, Noise Control, The Physical Review, The Physics of Fluids, Physics Today, The Review of Scientific Instruments, Reviews of Modern Physics*].
10. *American Journal of Enology and Viticulture,* "Guide to Authors" (University of California, College of Agriculture).
11. *The American Journal of Occupational Therapy* (American Occupational Therapy Association).
12. *The American Review of Respiratory Diseases,* "Directions to Abstractors" (published for the Ameri-

can Thoracic Society by the National Tuberculosis Association).

13. *Anesthesia Abstracts* (Burgess Publishing Company).

14. *Ansco Abstracts* [publication ceased with the December 1961 issue].

15. *APCA Abstracts* (Air Pollution Control Association).

16. *API Abstracts of Refining Literature,* "API Technical Abstracts Manual" (American Petroleum Institute).

17. *Applied Mechanics Reviews,* "Review Preparation Guide" (The American Society of Mechanical Engineers).

18. *Archives of Physical Medicine and Rehabilitation,* "Agreement" (American Congress of Physical Medicine and Rehabilitation).

19. *ARS Journal* (American Rocket Society) [see *American Institute of Physics Style Manual*].

20. *ASM Review of Metal Literature,* "Abstractors' Manual . . ." (American Society of Metals).

21. *ASTIA Guidelines for . . . Cataloging and Abstracting* (*Technical Abstracts Bulletin,* Armed Services Technical Information Agency).

22. *The Auk* (The American Ornithologists' Union).

23. *Battelle Technical Review* (Battelle Memorial Institute).

24. *Behavioral Science* (Mental Health Research Institute, University of Michigan).

25. *Bibliography and Index of Geology Exclusive of North America* (Geological Society of America).

26. *Biological Abstracts,* "To Those Who Write for and Use *Biological Abstracts:* A Guide" (University of Pennsylvania).

27. *Bird Banding, A Journal of Ornithological Investigation* (Published for the Northeastern Bird Banding Association).

28. *Bulletin of the American Association of Petroleum Geologists,* XVII (1952), 645, "A Scrutiny of the Abstract," by Kenneth K. Landes.

29. *Bureau of Mines Manuscripts* (U. S. Department of the Interior, Bureau of Mines) [to appear shortly].

30. *Cave Notes* (Cave Research Associates).

31. *Ceramic Abstracts,* "Your Guide to Abstracting" (The American Ceramic Society, Inc.).

32. *Chemical Abstracts,* "Directions for Abstractors and Section Editors of" (American Chemical Society).

33. *Chemical Market Abstracts* (Foster D. Snell, Inc.).

34. *Child Development Abstracts and Bibliography,* "Guide for the Preparation of Abstracts" (Society for Research in Child Development, Purdue University).

35. *Civil Engineering* (American Society of Civil Engineers).

36. *Clinical Clippings* (Francis Roberts Agency).

37. *Combustion* (International Combustion (Export) Limited).

38. *Computer Abstracts on Cards,* "Instructions for Filing and Using" (Cambridge Communications Corporation).

39. *Corrosion Abstracts* (National Association of Corrosion Engineers).

40. *Current Abstracts* (*Pertinent to Solid Propellant Research*) (The Solid Propellant Information Agency, The Johns Hopkins University Applied Physics Laboratory).

41. *Current Literature on Venereal Disease* (Department of Health, Education, and Welfare, Public Health Service).

42. *Dental Abstracts* (American Dental Association) [cf. Journal of the American Dental Association].

43. *Digest of Neurology and Psychiatry* (The Institute of Living).

44. *Diseases of the Colon and Rectum* (J. B. Lippincott Company).

45. *Dissertation Abstracts,* "Suggestions for the Preparation of Manuscripts for Microfilming" (University Microfilms, Inc.).

46. *Distillation Literature Index and Abstracts* (Applied Science Laboratories, Inc.).

47. *dsh Abstracts* (Deafness, Speech, and Hearing Publications, Inc.).

48. *Electronic Industries.*

49. *Electronic Technology* (ILIFFE Publications, Ltd.).

50. *Excerpta Medica* (Excerpta Medica Foundation) [Twenty-four Divisions].

51. *Gastroenterology* (Mount Sinai Hospital, New York, N.Y.).

52. *Geophysical Abstracts,* "Abstract" (United States Department of the Interior, Geological Survey) [Same instructions for *Geochemical Prospecting Abstracts*].

53. *Geoscience Abstracts,* "Specifications for" (American Geological Institute).

54. *Geriatrics* [same instructions as for *Modern Medicine,* 87].

55. *The Glass Industry* (Ogden Publishing Group).

56. Government Patents Board, "Abstract Definition" [now defunct].

57. *GP* (The American Academy of General Practice).

58. *Historical Abstracts* (Eric Boehm).

59. *Hospital Planning Abstracts* (American Hospital Association).

60. *Hospital Topics* (Gordon M. Marshall).

61. *International Abstracts of Biological Sciences,* "Principles of Abstracting Used by" (Pergamon Press).

62. *International Journal of Abstracts Statistical Theory and Method,* "Instructions for New Abstractors . . . " (International Statistical Institute).

63. *Journal of Abdominal Surgery* (The American Society of Abdominal Surgeons).

64. *Journal of Occupational Medicine,* "Instructions for Abstractors" (Industrial Medical Association).

65. *Journal of Soil and Water Conservation* (Soil Conservation Society of America).
66. *Journal of the American Concrete Institute,* "Guide to Preparing Current Reviews" and "Recommended Standards for Bibliographies."
67. *Journal of the American Dental Association,* "Preparation of Abstracts for."
68. *Journal of the American Dietetic Association,* "Instructions for Abstractors."
69. *Journal of the American Leather Chemists Association.*
70. *Journal of the American Medical Association,* "Suggestions to Authors of Manuscripts Submitted to."
71. *Journal of the American Oil Chemists' Society.*
72. *The Journal of the American Optometric Association.*
73. *Journal of the American Physical Therapy Association.*
74. *Journal of the American Podiatry Association.*
75. *Journal of the American Veterinary Medical Association.*
76. *Journal of the International College of Surgeons.*
77. *Lab World* (Sidale Publishing Company).
78. *Leukemia Abstracts* (Research Information Service).
79. Library of Congress Scientific Division [Instructions given in "Preparing for Technical Abstract," by John Sherrod, *American Meteorological Society Bulletin,* October 1957, pp. 496–497, are 'typical' for the following: *Aeronautical and Space Serials — A World List* [scheduled for publication in December 1961]; *Aerospace Medicine and Biology: An Annotated Bibliography; Air Pollution Bibliography; Bibliography on Saliva; Bibliography on Snow, Ice, and Permafrost . . .; Bibliography on the International Geophysical Year* [scheduled for publication in early 1962]; *Chinese Scientific and Technical Serial Publications in the Collections of the Library of Congress* [scheduled for publication in December 1961]; *Cold Weather Agriculture; Report on a General Survey of the Low Temperature and other Problems Affecting Plant Growth and Development; Cold Weather Operation of Diesel Engines; A Bibliography; Effects of Cold on Man; An Annotated Bibliography, 1938–51 Foreign Literature on Industrial Applications of Radioisotopes; A Guide to the World's Indexing and Abstracting Services in Science and Technology* [scheduled for publication in early 1962]; *A Guide to U. S. Indexing and Abstracting Services in Science and Technology; Infrared; A Bibliography; An Interim Bibliography on the International Geophysical Year; Japanese Scientific and Technical Serial Publications in the Collections of the Library of Congress* [scheduled for publication in December 1961]; *Journals in Science and Technology Published in Japan and Mainland China; A Selected List; List of Russian Serials Being Translated into English and other Western Languages; A List of Scientific and Technical Serials Currently Received by the Library of Congress; Mainland China Organizations of Higher Learning in Science and Technology and Their Publications; Marine Borers: A Preliminary Bibliography; The Polar Bibliography; Scatter Propagation; Selected Foreign References, 1955–1960; Scientific and Technical Serial Publications in the Soviet Union, 1945–1960, Revised and Enlarged Edition* [scheduled for publication in early 1962]; *Soviet Science and Technology: A Selected Bibliography on the State of the Art, 1956–1960* [scheduled for publication in December 1961]; *Thermal Properties of Certain Metals.*
80. *List of Publications and Patents* (United States Department of Agriculture Southern Utilization Research and Development Division).
81. *Lithographic Abstracts* (Lithographic Technical Foundation).
82. *Materials Research & Standards* (American Society for Testing and Materials).
83. *Mathematical Reviews,* "Instructions for Reviewers" (American Mathematical Society).
84. *McCutcheon Synthetic Detergent File* (John W. McCutcheon, Inc.).
85. *Mechanical Engineering,* "An ASME Paper" (The American Society of Mechanical Engineers).
86. *Meteorological and Geoastrophysical Abstracts* (American Meteorological Society).
87. *Modern Medicine,* "Style Guide for Science Writers."
88. *Modern Plastics.*
89. *Nuclear Science Abstracts,* "Guide to Abstracting & Indexing for" (United States Atomic Energy Commission).
90. *The Paper Industry* (Fritz Publications, Inc.).
91. *Photographic Science and Engineering* (Society of Photographic Scientists and Engineers) [See *Abstracts of Photographic Science and Engineering Literature,* 7].
92. *Proceedings of the IRE,* "Information for IRE Authors" (The Institute of Radio Engineers).
93. *Psychological Abstracts,* "Policies and Procedures of" (American Psychological Association).
94. *Psychosomatic Medicine* (American Psychosomatic Society, Inc.).
95. *Public Health Engineering Abstracts* (Department of Health, Education, and Welfare, Public Health Service).
96. *Public Works* (Public Works Journal Corp.).
97. *Quality Control and Applied Statistics,* "Instructions for Abstractors" (Interscience Publishers).
98. *Radiology,* "Suggestions to Abstractors for Radiology" (The Radiological Society).
99. *Rehabilitation Literature* (National Society for Crippled Children and Adults).

100. *Research Digest* (Bureau of Community Planning, University of Illinois).

101. *Review of Allergy and Applied Immunology,* "Procedure Re."

102. *Rocket Reviews and Rocket Abstracts* (American Rocket Company).

103. *Rubber Age* (Palmerton Publishing Company, Inc.).

104. *Science Abstracts,* "Notes for Abstractors" (The Institution of Electrical Engineers).

105. *Sci-Tech News,* "Documentation Digest, Guide Sheet for" (Science Technology Division of the Special Libraries Association).

106. *Semiconductor Abstracts,* "Reviewers Instructions" (Battelle Memorial Institute).

107. *The Sight-Saving Review* (National Society for the Prevention of Blindness, Inc.).

108. *Sociological Abstracts,* "Abstracting Instructions."

109. *Solar Energy: The Journal of Solar Energy Science and Engineering* (Association for Applied Solar Energy).

110. *Solid State Abstracts,* "Instructions — Outline — Pre-Index for" (Cambridge Communications Corporation).

111. *Sport Fishery Abstracts* (Bureau of Sport Fisheries and Wildlife, United States Fish and Wildlife Service).

112. *Strain Gage Reading* (Stein Engineering Services, Inc.).

113. *Surgery, Gynecology, & Obstetrics,* "The Preparation of Abstracts" (American College of Surgeons).

114. *Surveying and Mapping* (American Congress on Surveying and Mapping).

115. *Tappi* (Technical Association of the Pulp and Paper Industry).

116. *Technical Translations,* "Rules for Abstracting" (Office of Technical Service, United States Department of Commerce).

117. *Textile Technology Digest* (Institute of Textile Technology).

118. *Therapeutic Notes,* "Suggestions to Abstractors" (Parke, Davis & Company).

119. *Tobacco Abstracts* (North Carolina State College).

120. *Transfusion,* "A Guide for Preparation of Abstracts" (J. B. Lippincott Company).

121. *United States Navy Medical Newsletter* (Department of the Navy, Bureau of Medicine and Surgery).

122. *Upper Respiratory Infections* (The Wm. S. Merrell Company).

123. *Urban Transportation Research and Planning Current Literature* (United States Department of Commerce, Bureau of Public Roads).

124. *United States Government Research Reports* (Office of Technical Services, United States Department of Commerce) [see *Technical Translations,* 116].

125. *Vacuum* (Pergamon Press).

126. *Vitamin Abstracts* (Association of Vitamin Chemists, Inc.).

127. *The Volta Review* (Alexander Graham Bell Association for the Deaf).

128. *Wildlife Review* (United States Department of the Interior, Fish and Wildlife Service).

129. The Williams and Wilkins Company [five journals in the medical field].

130. *World's Poultry Science Journal* (The World's Poultry Science Association).

34 New Methods in Automatic Extracting

H. P. EDMUNDSON
*Journal of the Association
for Computing Machinery
Vol. 16, No. 2, April, 1969*

1. Introduction

Historical Background

Shortly after research in automatic translation began, interest was aroused in the possibility of automatically abstracting documents. Emphasis was placed on the production of indicative abstracts (i.e. abstracts that allow a searcher to screen a body of literature to decide which documents deserve more detailed attention) rather than on the production of informative abstracts (i.e. abstracts that can serve as substitutes for the document).

Also, it was hypothesized that an extract of a document (i.e. a selection of "significant" sentences of a document) can serve as an abstract. This hypothesis concerning the substitutability of extracts for abstracts has been discussed in [1, 2, and 4]. All automatic abstracting methods to date have only extracted documents, i.e. the computer has selected sentences of the document and listed them in text order. Although it has been recognized for some time that this kind of automatic abstract might better be called an "automatic extract," "abstract" is often used as the generic term.

The original method of Luhn assigned weights to each sentence of the document according to statistical criteria, in fact, a simple function of the number of high frequency words occurring in the sentence. Common words such as "the," "and," "at," and "are" were disregarded because of their very high frequency alone, and the remaining words were assigned frequency weights that provided sentence weights for measuring sentence significance. The extracts produced by this strictly statistical method were of sufficient quality to encourage further research [3, 6]. However, a purely statistical method of producing extracts was suspected of being inadequate, and hence other methods were sought [7].

Summary of Present Study

The objective of this study was twofold: first, an extracting system to produce indicative extracts, and second, a research methodology to handle new text and new extracting criteria efficiently. The purpose of the present paper is to make the results of this study more readily available.

The research methodology comprised a study of the abstracting behavior of humans, a general formulation of the abstracting problem and its relation to the problem of evaluation, a mathematical and logical study of the problem of assigning numerical weights to sentences, and a set of extracting experiments employing cyclic improvement.

The extracting system developed uses four basic methods to produce automatic extracts of technical documents approximately 4000 words in length with the IBM 7090–7094 (and has been reprogrammed for the Univac 1103A and CDC 1604). The automatic extracts are believed to be of sufficiently high quality to be used in the screening of large collections of documents. The system has been parameterized to permit modification of both prestored and generated word lists, to readjust weights assigned to text characteristics, to permit selection from 15 combinations of the four basic methods of extracting, and to alter the length of an automatic extract.

Three different evaluation schemes were applied to the resulting automatic extracts. Comparison of the automatic extracts and corresponding "target" extracts of 40 documents, which had not been used in the developmental research, showed that a mean of 44 percent of the sentences were coselected. Also, the mean similarity rating, in terms of a subjective evaluation of content by information type, was 66 percent. These are to be compared with a mean of 25 percent coselected sentences and a mean of 34 percent similarity rating between target extracts and random extracts, respectively. Statistical comparison of the automatic and the corresponding target extracts for the documents used in the developmental phase showed a mean of 57 percent coselected sentences with a standard deviation of 15 percent. A sentence-by-sentence analysis of the corresponding automatic and target extracts of 20 of these documents resulted in a judgment that 84 percent of the computer-selected sentences could be classified as extract-worthy; i.e. they would be worthy of selection in an extract of unrestricted length.

The following sections of this paper treat the research methodology used in the study, the extracting system, and the outlook for further research.

2. Research Methodology

Research Steps

The work reported here relies on the detection and use of sentence "significance." Within sentences selected by humans in forming an extract, there exist certain clues that, independent of subject content, tend to indicate that those sentences are significant. The goal was to replace the subjective notion of "significant" by an operational procedure. A methodology was sought whereby a computer could produce extracts as useful as conventionally created abstracts. The approach was to look for selection criteria among manually selected and rejected sentences.

The research steps, in chronological order, were:

(1) select a corpus of documents;

(2) study the characteristics — both in terms of content and machine-recognizability — of traditional manual abstracts of documents;

(3) specify the desired form and content of the "target" (manual) extracts;

(4) manually produce, for an experimental library of documents, target extracts that meet both the content and machine specifications;

(5) develop a system that assigns numerical weights to machine-recognizable characteristics;

(6) program a computer to produce automatic extracts;

(7) cyclically improve the program by comparing the automatic extracts and their target extracts; and

(8) evaluate the extracting system on a new group of documents not previously used in the experimental development.

The steps of the research methodology are shown in Figure 1.

Selection of the Corpus

For the purpose of determining initial weights and parameters, preliminary statistical data (on common words, sentence length, and sentence position) were obtained from 200 documents in the fields of physical science, life science, information science, and the humanities; hereafter this collection is called the heterogeneous corpus.

For the extracting experiments a different corpus, consisting of 200 documents in chemistry, was used. These documents were contractor reports to various government agencies and ranged in length from 100 to 3900 words, with an average of 2500. The limitation on document length was imposed by the limited computer storage available for the text of a document under the present program. These technical reports, written by chemists, chemical engineers, and physicists, were highly formatted and terse, and contained equations and experimental data.

Since a fair evaluation of experimental results required that the system be tested on documents different from those used in developing it, the chemistry corpus was divided into an experimental library of documents to serve as the data base and for experimentation, and a test library of documents reserved for evaluation of the extracting program after experimentation had been completed.

Target Extracts

Specification of Target Extracts. A set of instructions for human extractors was developed comprising the following specifications for the content and form of the target extracts, and the systematic procedures for composing them.

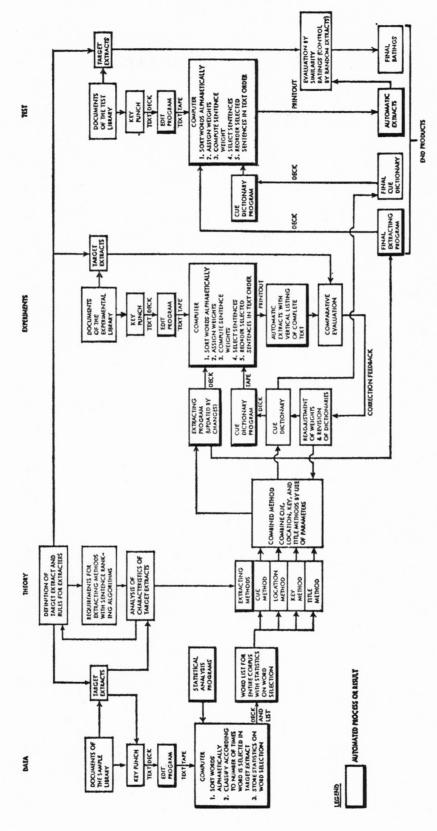

Fig. 1. Research methodology for automatic extracting study.

1. Sentences were selected only if they were eligible in terms of content. A sentence was called *eligible* if it contained information of at least one of the following six types:

Subject Matter. Information indicating the general subject area with which the author is principally concerned (i.e. *what*?).

Purpose. Information indicating whether the author's principal intent is to offer original research findings, to survey or evaluate the work performed by others, to present a speculative or theoretical discussion, or to serve some other main purpose (i.e. *why*?).

Methods. Information indicating the methods used in conducting the research. Depending on the type of research, such statements may refer to experimental procedures, mathematical techniques, or other methods of scientific investigation (i.e. *how*?).

Conclusions or Findings. Information indicating the author's conclusions or the research results.

Generalizations or Implications. Information indicating the significance of the research and its bearing on broader technical problems or theory.

Recommendations or Suggestions. Information indicating recommended courses of action or suggested areas of future work.

2. Sentences were selected to minimize redundancy in the extract. A sequence of sentences was said to be *non-redundant* if their information content was not repeated by reiteration, paraphrasing, or direct implication.

3. Sentences were selected to maximize coherence. A sequence of sentences was said to be *coherent* if all crucial antecedents and referents were present, no semantic discontinuities were present, and the sequence of ideas progressed logically.

4. The number of sentences selected was predetermined by a rule. Even though 25 percent of the sentences of the document was used as the length parameter for this research, this is not proposed as the optimal figure because it depends both on the purpose the extract is to serve and on the length and nature of the document.

An example of a target extract appears in Figure 2.

Preparation of Target Extracts

Analysis Procedure. To systematize the manual preparation of target extracts by humans, an analysis sheet itemizing every sentence was completed for each document. Here the extractor recorded his judgment about the eligibility of the sentence, his findings on its dependency on other sentences (e.g. antecedents), and whether the sentence was selected for the target extract. To facilitate comparisons, columns were also provided to record sentence selections by the various automatic methods and by a random-selection procedure used to evaluate the comparison scores described below.

Composition Problems. Much of the target-extracting effort was devoted to locating duplications of information throughout the document. A typical chemistry document had a summary at the beginning, an orientation section, a methods section, a discussion section, and, frequently, a conclusion that rephrased the initial summary. Hence the same information often appeared in several places in a document. Occasionally, however, nearly the entire document comprised research conclusions. When a hierarchy, either of significance or of generality, could not be established, no abstract could logically be composed by extracting. In this case a description representation was appropriate. However, if the document did contain a description of itself, this description rarely amounted to 25 percent of the sentences; if it did not, then the present extracting rules did not yield a coherent extract. Furthermore, to select 25 percent of the sentences, it was occasionally necessary to select several less condensed sentences instead of an equivalent, but more succinct, one. Although the 25 percent length parameter seemed workable for most documents, in some case it was manifestly not appropriate.

An attempt was made to classify eligible sentences as to qualitative degree of "extract-worthiness" (a concept analogous to that of quantitative weightings). However, in practice it did not prove satisfactory for sentence selection since it was often impossible to determine if a sentence, seen only in the context of an extract, reported a well-known fact, a result of some previous experiment, or a conclusion of the document being extracted. Furthermore, a sentence was often anaphoric, i.e. depended on another one for its meaning (and there may even have been a series of such dependencies), requiring the selection of both even though the other sentence did not qualify in terms of content. Certain words or phrases such as "this," "therefore," and "since" frequently indicated this situation, and studying their occurrence seemed necessary to the refinement of the automatic method. The more an author used such words for reasons of structuring and style, the more difficult it was to extract sentences from context without destroying their function in the document.

In the composition of maximally coherent and meaningful target extracts, it was noticed that requirements of antecedents, deletions of text due to preediting, minimization of redundancy, and restrictions on the length parameter often took precedence over a sentence-by-sentence rating of extract-worthiness. In the evaluation step it was found that target extracts consistently differed from automatic extracts in precisely these aspects.

Automatic Extracts

Guiding Principles for Automation. The following principles were devised to guide the development of automatic extracting methods so as to yield close approximations to target extracts:

1. Detect and use all content and format clues to the relative importance of sentences that were originally provided by the author, editor, and printer.

ABSTRACT BASED ON HUMAN SELECTION

EVALUATION OF THE EFFECT OF DIMETHYLAMINE BORINE AND SEVERAL OTHER ADDITIVES ON COMBUSTION STABILITY CHARACTERISTICS OF VARIOUS HYDROCARBON TYPE FUELS IN PHILLIPS MICROBURNER (AD87730)
R. L. BRACE

1	0	SUMMARY
2	1	AT THE REQUEST OF THE NAVY BUREAU OF AERONAUTICS, PHILLIPS PETROLEUM COMPANY UNDERTOOK THE EVALUATION OF DIMETHYLAMINE BORINE AS AN ADDITIVE FOR IMPROVING THE COMBUSTION CHARACTERISTICS OF AVIATION GAS TURBINE TYPE FUELS.
2	2	BECAUSE OF THE SMALL AMOUNT (100 GRAMS) OF DIMETHYLAMINE BORINE RECEIVED FROM CALLERY CHEMICAL COMPANY. THIS EVALUATION HAS BEEN LIMITED TO THE MEASUREMENT OF ITS EFFECT ON THE FLASH-BACK CHARACTERISTICS OF THREE PURE HYDROCARBONS (TOLUENE, NORMAL HEPTANE AND BENZENE) IN THE PHILLIPS MICROBURNER.
2	3	DIMETHYLAMINE BORINE CONCENTRATIONS OF FROM 0.1 to 1 0 PER CENT BY WEIGHT WERE EVALUATED.
3	1	FOR COMPARATIVE PURPOSES TWO COMMON IGNITION ADDITIVES (AMYL NITRATE AND CUMENE HYDROPEROXIDE) WERE ALSO EVALUATED DURING THIS STUDY. AS WELL AS CONCENTRATIONS UP TO 20 PER CENT BY WEIGHT OF PROPYLENE OXIDE - A RELATIVELY HIGH FLAME VELOCITY FUEL.
3	2	PREVIOUS STUDIES IN PHILLIPS 2 INCH TURBOJET ENGINE TYPE COMBUSTOR HAD INDICATED THAT SUCH MATERIALS COULD SUBSTANTIALLY INCREASE THE MAXIMUM RATE OF HEAT RELEASE ATTAINABLE. ESPECIALLY WITH LOW PERFORMANCE FUELS SUCH AS THE ISO PARAFFIN TYPE HYDROCARBONS - PARTICULARLY WHEN OPERATING UNDER SEVERE CONDITIONS FOR COMBUSTION (I. E., HIGH AIR FLOW VELOCITY OR LOW COMBUSTION PRESSURE).
4	4	WITH RESPECT TO THE DIMETHYLAMINE BORINE. ITS EFFECT AS A FUEL ADDITIVE WAS NOTEWORTHY. 0.1 WEIGHT PER CENT IN TOLUENE BEING EQUIVALENT TO 20 PER CENT BY WEIGHT OF ADDED PROPYLENE OXIDE.
4	5	IN GENERAL, ADDITIVE CONCENTRATIONS OF ONE PER CENT BY WEIGHT IN THE SEVERAL PURE HYDROCARBONS WHICH NORMALLY DIFFERED QUITE WIDELY IN PERFORMANCE, PRODUCED UNIFORMLY SUPERIOR COMBUSTION STABILITY CHARACTERISTICS AS MEASURED USING THE PHILLIPS MICROBURNER.
5	0	I. INTRODUCTION
8	0	II. DESCRIPTION OF PHILLIPS MICROBURNER (MODEL 1A)
10	0	III. DESCRIPTION OF TEST APPARATUS
14	0	IV. DESCRIPTION OF TEST FUELS
15	2	THESE FUELS REPRESENT VARIATIONS IN CHEMICAL STRUCTURE WHICH WILL IN TURN PROVIDE INDICES OF BOTH GOOD AND POOR COMBUSTION STABILITY PERFORMANCE.
17	0	V. TEST PROCEDURE
21	0	VI. RESULTS
24	1	THE REGION OF STABLE OPERATION IS DEFINED AS THE STATE OF FLASH BACK— THE CONDITIONS OF COMBUSTION WHERE THE FLAME WOULD BECOME ANCHORED TO A FLAME HOLDER - AS IN STABLE GAS TURBINE OR RAM JET COMBUSTOR OPERATION - IF THE FLAME HOLDER WERE PROVIDED IN THE BURNER TUBE.
25	0	VII. DISCUSSION
26	2	THE ASSUMPTION IS MADE THAT THE GREATER THE ALLOWABLE BEAT INPUT RATE AT A GIVEN VELOCITY. THE GREATER THE DEGREE OF STABILITY.
31	3	ALL FOUR ADDITIVES INDICATED THEIR ADDITION TO BE SUBJECT TO THE EFFECT OF DEMINISHING RESULTS UPON FURTHER ADDITION - THAT IS, THEIR EFFECT WAS NOT ESSENTIALLY A BLENDING EFFECT.
32	1	MENTION SHOULD BE MADE OF THE FACT THAT DURING THE COMBUSTION OF THE DIMETHYLAMINE BORINE-HYDROCARBON FUEL BLENDS NO NOTICEABLE ODORS OR SMOKE WERE OBSERVED.
33	0	VIII. CONCLUSIONS
36	1	3. THE ADDITION OF ADDITIVE CONCENTRATIONS (UP TO 1 PER CENT) OF AMYL NITRATE. CUMENE HYDROPERIOXIDE, AND DIMETHYLAMINE BORINE ALL RESULTED IN IMPROVED STABILITY PERFORMANCE, THE GREATEST INCREASES WERE SHOWN WHEN BLENDED WITH A FUEL OF POOR PERFORMANCE CHARACTERISTICS - SUCH AS TOLUENE.
36	2	BENEFICIAL EFFECTS WERE APPRECIABLY LESS WHEN BLENDED WITH A FUEL OF GOOD PERFORMANCE CHARACTERISTICS - SUCH AS N-HEPTANE.
37	0	IX. RECOMMENDATIONS
38	1	BASED ON THE EVALUATION OF THE EFFECTS OF ADDITIVES ON THE FLASHBACK LIMITS OF THE ADDITIVE-FUEL BLENDS TESTED IN THE MICROBURNER (MODEL 1A) IT IS RECOMMENDED THAT DIMETHYLAMINE BORINE SHOULD BE FURTHER INVESTIGATED.
38	2	THIS FUTURE WORK SHOULD INCLUDE STUDY OF COMBUSTION STABILITY AND COMBUSTION EFFICIENCY EFFECTS IN THE PHILLIPS 2 INCH COMBUSTOR AND AN INVESTIGATION OF ITS INFLUENCE ON COMBUSTION CLEANLINESS.

*Sic

FIG. 2. Target extract.

2. Employ mechanizable criteria of selection and rejection, i.e. a system of reward weights for desired sentences and penalty weights for undesired sentences.

3. Employ a system of parameters that can be varied to permit different specifications for extracts.

4. Employ a method that is a function of several linguistic factors (syntactic, semantic, statistical, locational, etc.).

Clearly, a computer can operate only on machine-recognizable characteristics of text (e.g. occurrence of certain words, position of a sentence in a paragraph, number of words in a sentence). A text characteristic was said to be *positively relevant* if it tended to be associated with sentences manually selected to comprise an extract, *negatively relevant* if it tended to be associated with unselected sentences, and *irrelevant* if it tended to be associated equally with selected and unselected sentences (see [5]). The task was to find relevant characteristics of the text and program the computer to recognize and weight them.

The Four Basic Methods. The automatic extracting system was based on assigning to text sentences numerical weights that were functions of the weights assigned to certain machine-recognizable characteristics or clues. For computational simplicity the sentence weights were taken as sums of the weights of these characteristics. The four basic methods (called Cue, Key, Title, and Location) to be discussed next used different sets of clues to the probable desirability of selecting a sentence for the automatic extract.

It was necessary to distinguish two types of word lists. A *dictionary* was regarded as a list of words with numerical weights that formed a fixed input to the automatic extracting system and was independent of the words in the particular document being extracted. A *glossary* was regarded as a list of words with numerical weights that formed a variable input to the automatic extracting system and was composed of words selected from the document being extracted.

1. *Cue Method.* In the Cue method the machine-recognizable clues are certain general characteristics of the corpus provided by the bodies of documents. The Cue method is based on the hypothesis that the probable relevance of a sentence is affected by the presence of pragmatic words such as "significant," "impossible," and "hardly." The Cue method uses the prestored Cue dictionary of selected words of the corpus. The Cue dictionary comprises three subdictionaries: Bonus words, that are positively relevant; Stigma words, that are negatively relevant; and Null words, that are irrelevant. The final Cue weight for each sentence is the sum of the Cue weights of its constituent words.

The Cue dictionary was compiled on the basis of statistical data and refined by linguistic criteria. Initial statistical data were obtained from 100 documents of the heterogeneous corpus for which target extracts had been prepared. A concordance program provided the following statistics for each word: frequency (number of occurrences in the corpus), dispersion (number of documents in which the word occurred), and selection ratio (ratio of number of occurrences in extractor-selected sentences to number of occurrences in all sentences of the corpus) (see [4]).

The following classes were then defined and listed by a computer program: Null candidates — dispersion greater than a chosen threshold and selection ratio between two chosen thresholds; Bonus candidates — selection ratio above the upper threshold; Stigma candidates — selection ratio below the lower threshold; and Residue — dispersion less than the threshold and selection ratio between the thresholds.

These categories were modified in three further steps. First, since most of the counterintuitive assignments occurred with low-frequency words, certain words were reclassified on this basis as Residue. Second, the statistics for 20 documents of the chemistry corpus were examined, and those additional words that exceeded a frequency threshold were also assigned, according to their selection ratio, to the Bonus, Stigma, and Null dictionaries. The final Cue dictionary contained 139 Null words, 783 Bonus words, and 73 Stigma words. The Null dictionary was created to list words excluded from the Key and Title glossaries, which are discussed next. Furthermore, it constituted a reservoir of common words that might, upon further research, be transferred to the Bonus or Stigma dictionaries.

Linguistic analysis of the experimental data revealed the following classes of Cue words: Null — ordinals, cardinals, the verb "to be," prepositions, pronouns, adjectives, verbal auxiliaries, articles, and coordinating conjunctions; Bonus — comparatives, superlatives, adverbs of conclusion, value terms, relative interrogatives, causality terms; Stigma — anaphoric expressions, belittling expressions, insignificant-detail expressions, hedging expressions; and Residue — positives, technical terms, and archaic terms.

2. *Key Method.* The principle (but not the algorithm) of the Key method is like the one first proposed by Luhn for creating automatic extracts (see [6]). Its machine-recognizable clues are certain specific characteristics of the body of the given document. It is based on the hypothesis that high-frequency content words are positively relevant.

The Key method compiles a Key glossary for each document, ideally consisting of topic words statistically selected from the body of that document. The words comprising a Key glossary were selected by listing all words not in the Cue dictionary in order of decreasing frequency of occurrence in the document. The frequencies were cumulated, from the highest downward, to a given percent of the total number of word occurrences in the document. Non-Cue words with frequencies above this threshold were designated Key words and were assigned positive weights equal to their frequency of occurrence in the document. The final Key weight of a sentence is the sum of the Key weights of its constituent words.

Initially, Key words were defined as non-Cue words of the highest Cue-weighted sentences, and their Key weights were taken to be their frequency of occurrence in that set. In the final system, Key words were chosen from a given percent of the total number of words in the document, and their Key weights were taken to be their frequency of occurrence over all words in the document. It was felt that the change from a fixed threshold to a fractional threshold was an improvement because of increased coverage and flexibility. Moreover, both statistical and linguistic investigations have supported the shift from the narrower environment of high Cue-weighted sentences to the wider environment of all text words.

3. *Title Method.* In the Title method the machine-recognizable clues are certain specific characteristics of the skeleton of the document, i.e. title, headings, and format. The Title method is based on the hypothesis that an author conceives the title as circumscribing the subject matter of the document. Also, when the author partitions the body of the document into major sections he summarizes it by choosing appropriate headings. The hypothesis that words of the title and headings are positively relevant was statistically accepted at the 99 percent level of significance.

The Title method compiles, for each document, a Title glossary consisting of all non-Null words of the title, subtitle, and headings for that document. Words in the Title glossary are assigned positive weights. The final Title weight for each sentence is the sum of the Title weights of its constituent words.

The weights assigned to the words of a Title glossary were determined on the basis of their effect in the combined weighting scheme of the four methods. Content words of the title were given heavier weights than content words of the headings. However, the initial assignment of weights led to a difficulty in the ranking of all sentences of the document when the Title method was used, since one weight was an exact multiple of the other, and this caused many ties among sentence weights. To minimize the occurrence of ties, title words were assigned a weight relatively prime to that of heading words.

4. *Location Method.* In the Location method the machine-recognizable clues are certain general characteristics of the corpus provided by the skeletons of documents, i.e. headings and format. The Location method is based on the hypotheses that: (1) sentences occurring under certain headings are positively relevant; and (2) topic sentences tend to occur very early or very late in a document and its paragraphs. These location characteristics of sentences were tested for correlation with selection ratios, and statistically derived weights were assigned to reflect the probable relevance of sentences according to the occurrence under certain headings and their position in a document and a paragraph.

The Location method uses the prestored Heading dictionary of selected words of the corpus that appear in headings of documents, e.g. "Introduction," "Purpose," "Conclusions." In addition to assigning positive weights provided by the Heading dictionary, the Location method also assigns positive weights to sentences according to their ordinal position in the text, i.e. in first and last paragraphs, and as first and last sentences of paragraphs. The final Location weight for each sentence is the sum of its Heading weight and its Ordinal weight.

To investigate the importance of headings for a sentence, all words occurring in the headings of 100 documents of the heterogeneous corpus and 20 documents of the chemistry corpus were listed, excluding prepositions, articles, and highly specific words. A set of words was common to both corpora, and a selection ratio was computed for each. Selection ratios were found to confirm the intuitive appraisal of heading-word importance. Weights proportional to the selection ratios were then assigned to each of these heading words, and the remaining heading words were assigned the same weights as their synonyms in that set. Deletions were made on the basis of low frequency and unrelatedness to the desired information types (i.e. subject, purpose, method, conclusion, generalization, recommendation). The resulting Heading dictionary contained 90 words.

To investigate the importance of sentence position — both within a paragraph and in the document as a whole — 300 sentences were randomly picked from the heterogeneous corpus, and selection ratios computed. These data were used as the basis for the assignment of Ordinal weights to the positional characteristics of a sentence according to whether it occurred in the first paragraph, last paragraph, and as first sentence, or last sentence. Intermediate sentences and paragraphs were assigned zero weights. The final weights adopted reflected the gross behavior of the above selection ratios.

Rationale of the Basic Methods. Extracting clues may come from two structural sources: (1) the *body* (text) of the document; and (2) the *skeleton* (title, headings, format) of the document. Also, clues may come from two linguistic sources: (1) *general* characteristics of the corpus and language (e.g. value-judgment words); and (2) *specific* characteristics of the individual documents (e.g. high-frequency words).

The two structural sources and the two linguistic sources of clues yielded four opportunities to create basic methods of automatic extracting which were defined simply by the class of clues upon which they rely. When applied to word clues this classification yielded four distinct word lists. These distinctions and standardizations of terminology permitted the following convenient classification of the four methods and their corresponding word lists (see Figure 3).

		Structural Sources of Clues:	
		Body of Document (Text)	Skeleton of Document (Title, Headings, Format)
Linguistic Sources of Clues:	General Characteristics of Corpus	CUE METHOD: Cue Dictionary (995 words) (Includes Bonus, Stigma, and Null subdictionaries)	LOCATION METHOD: Heading Dictionary (90 words) (Location method also uses ordinal weights)
	Specific Characteristics of Document	KEY METHOD: Key Glossary	TITLE METHOD: Title Glossary

Fig. 3. Rationale of the four basic methods.

Experimental Cycles

Seventeen experiments were performed in the course of the research to verify the significance of the various extracting clues, to refine the Cue and Heading dictionaries, to adjust weights, to reprogram the four basic methods, to improve the output format, and to evaluate the extracting methods (singly and in all possible combinations).

In the final system the relative weights among the four basic methods were parameterized in terms of the linear function

$$a_1 C + a_2 K + a_3 T + a_4 L$$

where a_1, a_2, a_3, and a_4 are the parameters (positive integers) for the Cue, Key, Title, and Location weights, respectively. Moreover the length parameter P was modified so that it can be adjusted to any integral percent of the number of sentences in a document. Thus by means of a single program card, the values of a_1, a_2, a_3, a_4, and P can be specified as desired. Also, the 7090–7094 system was modified to extract documents of 4000 words instead of 3000 words (as initially programmed).

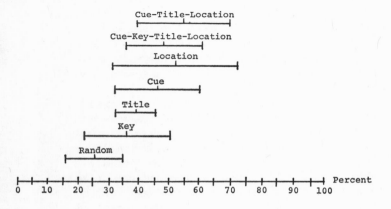

Fig. 4. Mean coselection scores of the methods.

Selection of Preferred Method

The percent of the number of sentences coselected in both the automatic and the target extracts was computed for each of the extracting methods, separately and in combination. The mean percentages for the most interesting methods are shown in Figure 4, with the intervals encompassing the sample mean plus and minus one sample standard deviation. The corresponding percentages for the random extracts (i.e. a random selection of 25 percent of the sentences) and the automatic extracts are given for comparison. The Cue-Title-Location method is seen to have the highest mean coselection score, while the Key method in isolation is the lowest of the automatic methods.

On the basis of these data it was decided to omit the Key method as a component in the preferred extracting system. These data confirm the hypothesis set forth previously (see [4]) that Key words, although important for indexing, may not be as useful for extracting. This decision has important consequences for an extracting system since avoiding frequency-counting the entire text results in considerable simplification and shorter running time for the computer program.

Evaluation of Preferred Method

Studies of Evaluation. Two different studies of evaluation of the preferred method were conducted: (1) subjective similarity ratings by evaluators, with respect to each of the information types, of the automatic extracts versus the corresponding target extracts and random extracts of the same length; and (2) statistical error analysis in terms of the percent of extract-worthy sentences in the automatic extract computed as the sum of coselected sentences, plus sentences cointensional (i.e. conveying the same information) with sentences of the target extract, plus additional sentences judged to be extract-worthy. No attempt was made to evaluate the utility of the target extracts for the screening purposes that they were designed to serve, and no conclusions were drawn about the utility of the automatic extracts from the relative evaluation methods utilized in this study since that was the subject of another study.

Subjective Similarity Ratings. The first evaluation study involved a gross evaluation of the similarity of the automatic extracts to the corresponding target extracts for a group of documents that had not been used in the developmental phase. Automatic extracts generated by the Cue-Title-Location method and target extracts were prepared for a sample of 40 documents from the test library. Individual raters were asked to subjectively score the similarity between two pairs of extracts for each document: target and automatic; target and random. For each pair of extracts the similarity with respect to each of the six information types was considered in turn and reported on a five-point scale: no similarity, moderate similarity, considerable similarity, complete similarity, and not applicable.

Comparison between target and automatic extracts yielded a mean similarity rating of 66 percent (with 44 percent of the sentences coselected); while target and random extracts had a mean similarity rating of 34 percent (with 25 percent of the sentences coselected). For both, the sample standard deviation of the mean was 3 percent.

Statistical Error Analysis. The second evaluation study involved detailed comparison of extracts produced by the Cue-Title-Location method with the corresponding target extracts for 20 documents from the experimental library. Every sentence in a document can be classified uniquely by considering all combinations of the following properties: worthy to be in an extract of unrestricted length, in the target extract, in the automatic extract, and the negations of these properties. Eight classes result, of which two define the most significant types of statistical error, namely, type 1 error — sentence is worthy and in the target extract but contains information not in the automatic extract; and type 2 error — sentence is not worthy and is not in target extract but is in the automatic extract.

The 20 extracts comprised 311 sentences, of which 37 percent were classified as type 1 errors and 16 percent as type 2 errors. Of the computer-extracted sentences, 57 percent were identical with sentences in the target extracts, 10 percent were cointensional with other sentences in the target extracts, and 17 percent were judged to be extract-worthy. The sum for these three sets was 84 percent, a measure of the percent of extract-worthy sentences. The 16 percent type 2 errors accounted for 100 percent of the computer-extracted sentences.

The identification of both meaning-similarity and extract-worthiness in running text was a highly subjective matter. Therefore this analysis represented careful and considered judgment. The sentences selected automatically, but judged not extract-worthy (type 2 errors), contained extraneous detail and represented "noise."

They cluttered the extract and often interfered seriously with its coherence. The sentences resulting in type 1 errors represented information included in the target extract but not in the automatic extract. Their significance can be discovered only by studying the sentences in question.

The second study revealed the reasons for the apparent useful qualities of the automatic extracts. The number of coselected sentences showed only part of the actual correspondence between automatic and target extracts. When the number was expanded to include the automatically selected sentences cointensional with target extract sentences, the total roughly represented the degree to which the automatic process included the information in the target extract. The category of additional worthy sentences included some, but not all, eligible sentences that might be included in an extract of unrestricted length. It served as a reminder that for any document there are many possible abstracts differing in both length and content. This category and the preceding two comprised the total of extract-worthy sentences. Their average of 84 percent, even though uncorrected for redundancy in the automatic extract, appears to represent a promising achievement in the automation of the extracting process.

Extracting System

General Characteristics

The cardinal feature of the extracting system is its flexibility. The system was parameterized, whenever possible, to allow easy modification of both the weights within a single extracting method and the relative weights of the methods in combination. This was accomplished by making it possible to modify both prestored dictionaries and program-generated glossaries, to readjust weights assigned to text characteristics, to permit the use of 15 combinations of the four basic methods of extracting, and to alter the length parameter that determines the length of the automatic extract. The operating system comprises two input programs: (1) Edit Program — creates the text tape used by the extracting program; and (2) Cue Dictionary Program — feeds Cue dictionary into extracting program. It also comprises four basic extracting programs: (1) Cue Routine — weights sentences according to match of text words with Cue dictionary; (2) Key Routine — weights sentences according to frequency of word occurrence; (3) Title Routine — weights sentences according to match of text words with title and heading words; and (4) Location Routine — weights sentences according to location in document and appearance under words of the Heading dictionary.

The IBM 7090 edit program has 1707 instructions and occupies 30K of core. The Cue dictionary program tape has 704 instructions and uses 23K of core. The extracting program has 2427 instructions and uses 32K of core. The flowchart of the extracting system is shown in Figure 5.

Input Procedures

Preediting. The text must have a length of at most 4000 words and is manually preedited according to pre-edit instructions, which cover the problems of formatting, graphics, special symbols, special alphabets, etc. Figure 6 shows a preedited document. The notations used are defined and discussed in [1].

Keypunching. The keypunch instructions are based on the preedit instructions and are subject to the conditions imposed by present input and output hardware. They contain rules and examples of sufficient generality to cover a wide variety of textual situations.

Edit Program. The edit program creates the text tape used by the extracting program. Text written in free format is punched on cards according to the keypunch instructions. The edit program interprets these cards, recognizing title, headings, author, paragraph boundaries, sentence boundaries, number of sentences in document, punctuation, capitalization, etc. The program also recognizes input errors, which are then printed together with a vertical listing of text described below.

Cue Dictionary Program. The Cue dictionary program creates a Cue dictionary tape to be used by the extracting program when it is identifying Cue words and compiling the Key and Title glossaries. The input to the program consists of at most 1000 words and their weights; the words are punched one word per card and must be in alphabetical order. The output consists of a binary tape containing only one record, in which each

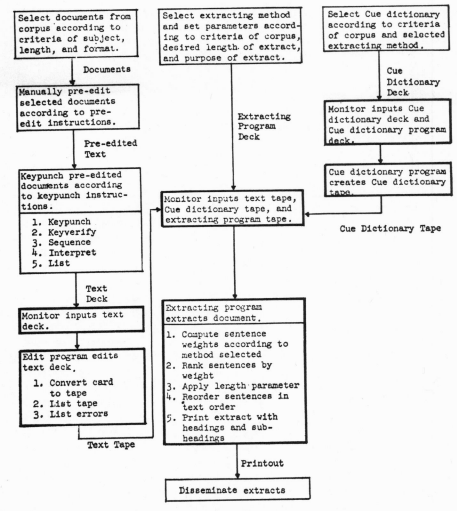

Note: Heavy boxes denote computer operations

FIG. 5. Extracting system.

entry takes four computer words. Certain input errors can be detected, and these, as well as a BCD listing of the Cue dictionary, are printed on an output tape.

Processing Steps

Cue Method:

1. Compare each word of text with Cue dictionary.
2. Tag all Bonus words with weight $b > 0$, all Stigma words with weight $s < 0$, all Null words with weight $n = 0$.
3. Compute Cue weight C of each sentence by summing its Cue word weights b, s, and n.
4. Rank all sentences in decreasing weight order.
5. Select sentences whose rank order is less than length parameter P percent of the number of sentences in the document.
6. Select all headings.
7. Merge selected sentences under their proper headings.
8. Output title, authors, and results of step 7.

Key Method:

1. Compare each word of text with Cue dictionary.
2. Create table of distinct, nonmatching text words (as Key-word candidates).
3. Compute frequency k of each Key-word candidate.
4. Sort table in decreasing frequency order.
5. Create a Key glossary from all Key-word candidates whose total frequency (when summed in decreasing frequency order) exceeds threshold of W percent of the total number of word occurrences in document.
6. Compare each text word with Key glossary, and tag each matching word with weight k equal to its frequency of occurrence in text.
7. Compute Key weight K of each sentence by summing its Key-word weights k.
8. Rank all sentences in decreasing weight order.
9. Select sentences whose rank order is less than length parameter P.
10. Select all headings.
11. Merge selected sentences under their proper headings.
12. Output title, authors, and results of step 11.

Title Method:

1. Compare each word of title and headings with Null dictionary.
2. Create a Title glossary of nonmatching words.
3. Tag all words of Title glossary that come from title with weight t_1. Tag all words that come only from subtitle or heading with weight t_2.
4. Compare each word of text with Title glossary. Tag each matching word with corresponding weight, t_1 or t_2.
5. Compute Title weight T of each sentence by summing its word weights.

6. Rank all sentences in decreasing weight order.
7. Select sentences whose rank order is less than length parameter P.
8. Select all headings.
9. Merge selected sentences under their proper headings.
10. Output title, authors, and results of step 9.

Location Method:

1. Compare each word of headings with Heading dictionary.
2. Tag each matching word with weight h given in Heading dictionary.
3. Compute Heading weight H of each heading by summing its Heading-word weights h.
4. Tag each sentence with Heading weight H of its heading.
5. Tag each sentence of first paragraph with Ordinal weight O_1 and of last paragraph with Ordinal weight O_2. Tag first sentence of every paragraph with Ordinal weight O_3 and last sentence of every paragraph with Ordinal weight O_4.
6. Compute Ordinal weight O of each sentence by summing its Ordinal weights O_1, O_2, O_3, and O_4.
7. Compute Location weight L of each sentence by summing its Heading weight H and Ordinal weight O.
8. Rank all sentences in decreasing weight order.
9. Select all sentences whose rank order is less than length parameter P.
10. Select all headings.
11. Merge selected sentences under their proper headings.
12. Output title, authors, and results of step 11.

Combined Methods. The four basic methods described above yield 15 combined methods that have in common the following sequence of steps:

1. Select desired values for parameters a_1, a_2, a_3, a_4, and P.
2. Compute total weight $a_1C + a_2K + a_3T + a_4L$ of each sentence by summing its weighted single-method weights C, K, T, L.
3. Rank all sentences in decreasing weight order.
4. Select sentences whose rank order is less than length parameter P.
5. Select all headings.
6. Merge selected sentences under their proper headings.
7. Output title, authors, and results of step 6.

Output Procedures

Extracting Output. An extract of a document can be produced by any combination of the four basic methods of calculating sentence weights. The extracting output is an extract containing the following information: document number, methods used to produce the extract, title of the document, author(s) of the document, all headings (identified by zero as a sentence number), and the selected sentences (all tagged with paragraph and sentence number). Figure 7 shows an automatic extract produced by the combined Cue-Title-Location method.

Research Output

1. *Key-word lists.* Two lists of Key words for the document are printed, one in frequency order and the other in alphabetical order.

2. *Sentence-weight lists.* Two lists are printed, giv-

ing each sentence number in the document and its computed weight. One is in sentence order and the other in weight order. The weight is the sum resulting from the method or methods used.

3. *Vertical listing.* A list is printed, one word to a line, of every word (of the document) in text order together with punctuation before (open quotation mark, open parenthesis, initial capitalization, etc.), first punctuation after (comma, hyphen, period, etc.), second punctuation after (hyphen, closed parenthesis, closed

PHILLIPS PETROLEUM COMPANY - ACQUISITION DIVISION - REPORT 425-5M-7832

SPECIAL REPORT

NAVY CONTRACT FOR N-2C-1857, Aerogothiil 7

EVALUATION OF THE EFFECT OF DIMETHYLAMINE BORINE AND SEVERAL OTHER ADDITIVES ON COMBUSTION STABILITY CHARACTERISTICS OF VARIOUS HYDROCARBON TYPE FUELS IN PHILLIPS MICROBURNER △/A P87730/△

By R. L. Brace

SUMMARY

At the request of the Navy Bureau of Aeronautics, Phillips Petroleum Company undertook the evaluation of dimethylamine borine as an additive for improving the combustion characteristics of aviation gas turbine type fuels. Because of the small amount (100 grams) of dimethylamine borine received from Callery Company, this evaluation has been limited to the measurement of its effect on the flash-back characteristics of three pure hydrocarbons (toluene, normal heptane, and benzene) in the Phillips Microburner. Dimethylamine borine concentrations of from 0.1 to 1.0 per cent by weight were evaluated.

For comparative purposes two common ignition additives (amyl nitrate and cumene hydroperoxide) were also evaluated during this study, as well as concentrations of up to 20 per cent by weight of propylene oxide - a relatively high flame velocity fuel. Previous studies in Phillips 2 inch turbojet engine type combustor had indicated that such materials could substantially increase the maximum rate of heat release attainable, especially with low performance fuels such as the iso paraffin type hydrocarbons - particularly when operating under severe conditions for combustion (i. e., high air flow velocity or low combustion pressure).

The assumption has been made in this fuel evaluation that the greater the allowable heat input rate for a given velocity, the greater the degree of combustion stability. On this basis, the data indicate that all of the additive materials tested caused an increase in stability performance; a fuel of relatively low performance such as toluene being benefited to a greater extent than a high performance fuel such as normal heptane. These data are in agreement with previous additive studies by Phillips. With respect to the dimethylamine borine, its effect as a fuel additive was noteworthy; 0.1 weight per cent in toulene being equivalent to 20 per cent by weight of added propylene oxide. In general, additive concentrations of one per cent by weight in several pure hydrocarbons which normally differed quite widely in performance, produced uniformly superior combustion stability characteristics as measured using the Phillips Microburner.

I. INTRODUCTION

At the request of the Navy Bureau of Aeronautics the Jet Fuels Group has evaluated the effects of the addition of small amounts of dimethylamine borine ((CH₃)₂ NH:BH₃) on the combustion stability performance of several hydrocarbon fuels. The dimethylamine borine was supplied to Phillips by the Callery Chemical Company.

Due to the small quantity of this material obtained the evaluation was conducted in the Phillips Microburner (Model 1A) which is a slightly modified version of the original Phillips Microburner (Model 1).

II.△ DESCRIPTION OF THE PHILLIPS MICROBURNER (MODEL 1A)

The design of the original Phillips Microburner (Model 1) was discussed in detail in Reference 1. The only significant change in burner detail was the substitution of a LeRoy Lettering Pen for the LeRoy pen fuel nozzle in the Model 1. The details of the Model 1A are shown in Figure 1.

Fig. 6. Preedited document (cont'd on next page).

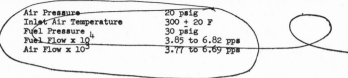

III. DESCRIPTION OF TEST APPARATUS

The fuel system on the Phillips Microburner (Model 1) was designed so as to handle small quantities of highly corrosive substances. In the present evaluation it is not necessary to consider the effect of corrosion, consequently a continuous flow system providing greater flexibility and easier handling was incorporated which requires only slightly more fuel per test than the original. This new system includes a source of nitrogen gas, a surge tank, a pressurized fuel tank, a small capacity Brooks Rotameter, and a flow control valve.

The air heater circuit was modified so as to include a mercury relay and bimetallic thermoswitch thus providing automatic air temperature control.

The details of these modifications and of the test apparatus are shown in schematic in Figure 2.

IV. DESCRIPTION OF TEST FUELS

The chemical and physical properties of the hydrocarbon fuels tested are summarized in Table I. These fuels represent variations in chemical structure which will in turn provide indices of both good and poor combustion stability performance.

The additives evaluated, dimethylamine borine, propylene oxide, amyl nitrate, cumene hydroperoxide, were blended into the hydrocarbon fuel by weight in concentrations ranging from 0.1 to 20 per cent.

V. TEST PROCEDURE

The conditions at which this study was made in the Microburner (model 1A) were:

Air Pressure	20 psig
Inlet Air Temperature	300 ± 20 F
Fuel Pressure	30 psig
Fuel Flow x 10^4	3.85 to 6.82 pps
Air Flow x 10^3	3.77 to 6.69 pps

Once the air temperature was established the air flow was set at the desired rate and the fuel turned on. Ignition of the then fuel-rich mixture was accomplished by applying a lighted, portable propane torch to the top of the burner tube. The fuel flow was then gradually decreased until the flame holding at the burner tube rim flashed back into the tube. At the point of flashback the following were recorded:

Cold Air Temperature
Inlet Air Temperature
Air Rotometer Reading
Fuel Rotometer Reading

After checking the point at least once more the air flow was increased another increment and the process repeated.

Fig. 6 (continued).

quotation mark, etc.), paragraph number, sentence number within the paragraph, word number within the sentence, Cue weight, Key weight, and Title weight. After the last word of each sentence is printed, the Cue, Key, Title, and Location weights for that sentence are printed.

Time and Cost Factors

Automatic extracts were produced by the combined Cue-Title-Location method at a minimum rate of 7800 words per minute on a corpus of 29,500 words. After the first 4000 words the rate increases linearly with the size of the corpus.

The total system cost (edit, extracting, output) was approximately 1.5 cents per word; keypunching costs (including verification) accounted for two-thirds of this. The above times and costs concern the present research only and should not be misinterpreted in connection with the question of the economic feasibility of automatic extracting.

3. Outlook

This research should be regarded as an interim report. Nonetheless, the direction of future investigation and the problems to be investigated next are becoming clearer. It is now beyond question that future automatic abstracting methods must take into account syntactic and semantic characteristics of the language and the text: they cannot rely simply upon gross statistical evidence.

It is believed that the research methodology outlined here has been, and will continue to be, fruitful. Future research should adhere to the principle of parameterization to gain flexibility and permit continuing improvement of abstracting methods. The present set of weights is subject to continuing experimentation to permit maxi-

ABSTRACT BASED ON HUMAN SELECTION

EVALUATION OF THE EFFECT OF DIMETHYLAMINE BORINE AND SEVERAL OTHER ADDITIVES ON COMBUSTION STABILITY CHARACTERISTICS OF VARIOUS HYDROCARBON TYPE FUELS IN PHILLIPS MICROBURNER (AD87730)

R. L. BRACE

PAR	SENT	
1	0	SUMMARY
2	1	AT THE REQUEST OF THE NAVY BUREAU OF AERONAUTICS, PHILLIPS PETROLEUM COMPANY UNDERTOOK THE EVALUATION OF DIMETHYLAMINE BORINE AS AN ADDITIVE FOR IMPROVING THE COMBUSTION CHARACTERISTICS OF AVIATION GAS TURBINE TYPE FUELS.
2	2	BECAUSE OF THE SMALL AMOUNT (100 GRAMS) OF DIMETHYLAMINE BORINE RECEIVED FROM CALLERY CHEMICAL COMPANY, THIS EVALUATION HAS BEEN LIMITED TO THE MEASUREMENT OF ITS EFFECT ON THE FLASH-BACK CHARACTERISTICS OF THREE PURE HYDROCARBONS (TOLUENE, NORMAL HEPTANE AND BENZENE) IN THE PHILLIPS MICROBURNER.
2	3	DIMETHYLAMINE BORINE CONCENTRATIONS OF FROM 0.1 to 1.0 PER CENT BY WEIGHT WERE EVALUATED.
3	1	FOR COMPARATIVE PURPOSES TWO COMMON IGNITION ADDITIVES (AMYL NITRATE AND CUMENE HYDROPEROXIDE) WERE ALSO EVALUATED DURING THIS STUDY, AS WELL AS CONCENTRATIONS UP TO 20 PER CENT BY WEIGHT OF PROPYLENE OXIDE – A RELATIVELY HIGH ELAME VELOCITY FUEL.
3	2	PREVIOUS STUDIES IN PHILLIPS 2 INCH TURBOJET ENGINE TYPE COMBUSTOR HAD INDICATED THAT SUCH MATERIALS COULD SUBSTANTIALLY INCREASE THE MAXIMUM RATE OF HEAT RELEASE ATTAINABLE, ESPECIALLY WITH LOW PERFORMANCE FUELS SUCH AS THE ISO PARAFFIN TYPE TYDROCARBONS – PARTICULARLY WHEN OPERATING UNDER SEVERE CONDITIONS FOR COMBUSTION (I.E., HIGH AIR FLOW VELOCITY OR LOW COMBUSTION PRESSURE).
4	4	WITH RESPECT TO THE DIMETHYLAMINE BORINE, ITS EFFECT AS A FUEL ADDITIVE WAS NOTEWORTHY, 0.1 WEIGHT PER CENT IN TOLUENE BEING EQUIVALENT TO 20 PER CENT BY WEIGHT OF ADDED PROPYLENE OXIDE.
4	5	IN GENERAL, ADDITIVE CONCENTRATIONS OF ONE PER CENT BY WEIGHT IN THE SEVERAL PURE HYDROCARBONS WHICH NORMALLY DIFFERED QUITE WIDELY IN PERFORMANCE, PRODUCED UNIFORMLY SUPERIOR COMBUSTION STABILITY CHARACTERISTICS AS MEASURED USING THE PHILLIPS MICROBURNER.
5	0	I. INTRODUCTION
8	0	II. DESCRIPTION OF PHILLIPS MICROBURNER (MODEL 1A)
10	0	III. DESCRIPTION OF TEST APPARATUS
14	0	IV. DESCRIPTION OF TEST FUELS
15	2	THESE FUELS REPRESENT VARIATIONS IN CHEMICAL STRUCTURE WHICH WILL IN TURN PROVIDE INDICES OF BOTH GOOD AND POOR COMBUSTION STABILITY PERFORMANCE.
17	0	V. TEST PROCEDURE
21	0	VI. RESULTS
24	1	THE REGION OF STABLE OPERATION IS DEFINED AS THE STATE OF FLASH BACK- THE CONDITIONS OF COMBUSTION WHERE THE FLAME WOULD BECOME ANCHORED TO A FLAME HOLDER – AS IN STABLE GAS TURBINE OR RAM JET COMBUSTOR OPERATION – IF THE FLAME HOLDER WERE PROVIDED IN THE BURNER TUBE.
25	0	VII. DISCUSSION
26	2	THE ASSUMPTION IS MADE THAT THE GREATER THE ALLOWABLE BEAT INPUT RATE AT A GIVEN VELOCITY, THE GREATER THE DEGREE OF STABILITY.
31	3	ALL FOUR ADDITIVES INDICATED THEIR ADDITION TO BE SUBJECT TO THE EFFECT OF DIMINISHING RESULTS UPON FURTHER ADDITION – THAT IS, THEIR EFFECT WAS NOT ESSENTIALLY A BLENDING EFFECT.
32	1	MENTION SHOULD BE MADE OF THE FACT THAT DURING THE COMBUSTION OF THE DIMETHYLAMINE BORINE – HYDROCARBON FUEL BLENDS NO NOTICEABLE ODORS OR SMOKE WERE OBSERVED.
33	0	VIII. CONCLUSIONS
36	1	3. THE ADDITION OF ADDITIVE CONCENTRATIONS (UP TO 1 PER CENT) OF AMYL NITRATE, CUMENE HYDROPERIOXIDE, AND DIMETHYLAMINE BORINE ALL RESULTED IN IMPROVED STABILITY PERFORMANCE, THE GREATEST INCREASES WERE SHOWN WHEN BLENDED WITH A FUEL OF POOR PERFORMANCE CHARACTERISTICS – SUCH AS TOLUENE.
36	2	BENEFICIAL EFFECTS WERE APPRECIABLY LESS WHEN BLENDED WITH A FUEL OF GOOD PERFORMANCE CHARACTERISTICS – SUCH AS N-HEPTANE.
37	0	IX. RECOMMENDATIONS –
38	1	BASED ON THE EVALUATION OF THE EFFECTS OF ADDITIVES ON THE FLASHBACK LIMITS OF THE ADDITIVE-FUEL BLENDS TESTED IN THE MICROBURNER (MODEL 1A) IT IS RECOMMENDED THAT DIMETHYLAMINE BORINE SHOULD BE FURTHER INVESTIGATED.
38	2	THIS FUTURE WORK SHOULD INCLUDE STUDY OF COMBUSTION STABILITY AND COMBUSTION EFFICIENCY EFFECTS IN THE PHILLIPS 2 INCH COMBUSTOR AND AN INVESTIGATION OF ITS INFLUENCE ON COMBUSTION CLEANLINESS.

*
Sic

FIG. 7. Automatic extract.

mum specification of desired content of automatic extracts. Even now ways can be conceived to reduce both the number and size of experimental cycles with more powerful statistical and computational techniques.

It is highly desirable that the extracting system be modified to accommodate longer documents (in fact it has been reprogrammed for the UNIVAC 1103A to accommodate documents of approximately 40,000 words). To reduce operating time and costs, ways to make the programs more efficient should be investigated. Reprogramming can help, but the greatest need for improvement is in the method of inputting text. In this connection it is also important to devise ways of automatically capturing chemical and mathematical symbols in machine form. Clearly there are extracting clues that have not yet been exploited — in captions of figures and tables, in footnotes and references, and in larger linguistic structures such as phrases and clauses. Better ways must be sought to identify those specific characteristics of documents that are significant for automatic extracting (such as presence or lack of headings, technical or literary content, etc.) and to correlate these characteristics with some combination of extracting method, set to weights, and length parameter that will give better automatic extracts.

Further investigation of methods of evaluating automatic extracts is needed to increase their speed, simplicity, and discrimination. Future research should involve sharper statistical analysis of the two types of error with the purpose of modifying the program to minimize them. Study should be made to discover machine-recognizable clues to determine the proper length of an extract. The extent to which redundancy appears in automatic extracts and ways of minimizing it should be investigated. Linguistic clues to coherence should be identified and expressed in machine-recognizable form, perhaps in the form of a word-and-phrase dictionary indicating the need for selecting antecedent sentences. In summary, the main differences between manual and automatic extracts can now be described and procedures outlined to minimize them.

Although automatic extracts of the future may differ both in content and appearance from traditionally composed manual abstracts, these differences do not appear as insuperable barriers to their usefulness. In spite of the recognized problems it is now felt that automatic extracts can be defined, programmed, and produced in an operational system to supplement, and perhaps compete with, traditional ones.

References

1. Automatic abstracting. RADC-TDR-63-93, TRW Computer Div., Thompson-Ramo-Wooldridge, Inc., Canoga Park, Calif., Feb. 1963.
2. EDMUNDSON, H. P. Problems in automatic abstracting. *Comm. ACM 7,* **4** (Apr. 1964), 259–263.
3. EDMUNDSON, H. P., and WYLLYS, R. E. Automatic abstracting and indexing — survey and recommendations. *Comm. ACM 4,* **5** (May 1961), 226–234.
4. Final report on the study for automatic abstracting. C107-1U12, Thompson-Ramo-Wooldridge, Inc., Canoga Park, Calif., Sept. 1961.
5. KUHNS, J. L. An application of logical probability to problems in automatic abstracting and information retrieval. Joint Man-Computer Indexing and Abstracting, Sess. 13, First Congress on the Information System Sciences, Nov. 1962.
6. LUHN, H. P. The automatic creation of literature abstracts. *IBM J. Res. Develop. 2,* **2** (1959), 159–165.
7. RATH, G. J., RESNICK, A., and SAVAGE, T. R. Comparisons of four types of lexical indicators of content. *Amer. Docum. 12,* **2** (Apr. 1961), 126–130.

F. Classification and Coding

35 Classification Systems and Their Subjects

EJNAR WÅHLIN
American Documentation
Vol. 17, No. 4, October, 1966

A General Analysis of Different Kinds of Classification Systems Characterized by Different Types of Subject

By way of introduction I may quote a statement from the FID/CR Conference at Elsinore in the autumn of 1964 (1):

> The Conference listed as its aims:
>
> the improvement of existing classifications, including work on methods for construction of thesauri and related tools;
>
> the achievement of better design in new classifications;
>
> the exploration and implementation of compatibility among classification systems and thesauri, including standardized vocabularies;
>
> the convertibility of the records of material indexed in one system into another;
>
> and the study of the interaction between classification systems and computer technology in the process of system analysis and programming.

These recommendations have the great merit that they go deep into the core of the problem and may therefore be considered fruitful. Most of these points are discussed in this report.

The words "classificaton," "classification systems," and "systems" occur in all five paragraphs above. It is important to know exactly what kind of systems are referred to here.[1]

Financial support by The Swedish Council for Building Research and The Swedish Council for Technical Research.

[1] Concerning the nomenclature in the sequel, I shall consider "classifications" and "classification systems" as synonymous. "System" is sometimes used in a wider sense to express contexts which cannot be presented as written schemes, but the word is not used in the sense of "information system."

With regard to the scope of the system we talk of *universal systems,* comprising all fields of knowledge, and *specialized systems,* covering only a limited field. The general and traditional structure of classification systems is the *hierarchical* (tree-structure), but among specialized systems *faceted* systems are a particular type. These differ from the traditional *discipline systems* not only in structure but also in being entirely based on concepts.

Examples of adjectives used to denote the meaning of the word classification in special contexts are mentioned by R. Mölgaard'H (in the proceedings of the Elsinore Conference 1964): "informative, topological, dynamic, synthetic, faceted, hierarchical, factor-analytical, natural, arbitrary, general, special, and topographical."

The most important and fruitful approach seems to me, however, to characterize the systems according to *the subject of the system,* i.e., what the designer of the system wanted to arrange and classify, but very little attention seems to have been paid to this problem. We find in the literature that some experts, in writing about classification systems, have classification of *knowledge concepts,* or *ideas* in mind, others classification of *documents,* while sometimes the subject is *terms, things,* or other phenomena. I shall not maintain that some of them are right, others wrong. In fact, different kinds of classification systems with different types of subjects may be necessary in documentation.

The types of systems I wish to deal with are all "general," in the sense that they are not restricted to a special subject field, and they are all of importance for documentation. They are all types of *systems in existence,* having been devised by different professional groups for different practical requirements.

I shall first discuss *systems of science:* several systems of this kind have been devised and here we have a background to the document systems. I shall not discuss systems of knowledge as I do not think that there exists any reliable system comprising all knowledge for the specific purpose of classifying knowledge, but I shall deal with *systems for documents* based on their knowledge content. I will interpret the heading Mathematics in a document system as "Documents on Mathematics" and the subheadings as "Documents on Algebra," etc. There are other systems (even if not called classification systems) where the heading Mathematics has another significance, e.g., "Teaching of Mathematics" (in a timetable) or "text on mathematics" (in a handbook).

Even if a document system is *based on concepts,* I will avoid presenting it as a system for concepts, because the purpose is not to classify concepts, but to classify documents.

A universal system for concepts (made with the purpose to classify concepts) does not exist and is not easily made because there doesn't exist any definite collection of concepts from which we can pick up concepts and arrange them.

On the other hand concepts are usually expressed by terms and we can talk of *systems of terms* as we really have a definite stock of terms. The terms here are the subjects and should determine the structure of the system.

Also "practical systems" used in industry and commerce for registration purposes will be discussed. A *system for products* should be designed according to the structure of the collection of products uninfluenced by documentation aspects.

The essential point in this presentation is to show how and why these systems have come about, how they have developed, what role they play or should play in documentation, and to indicate principles on which we can create for every type of subject a new system designed to fulfill its function in the best possible way, all systems forming a *system of systems* in which every individual system—as far as possible without disturbing its primary function—has common features with the other systems.

1 The System of the Sciences and the Systems within the Sciences

Science and System

According to Albert Einstein, science is the striving, with the aid of thought, to arrange the observable phenomena of our world into, as far as possible, a coherent

system, an attempt to reconstruct our existence with the help of the formation of *concepts.* The main purpose of documentation is to classify scientific literature and make it accessible. The structure (or system) of science can then not be without significance.

The order between the individual sciences should not be a question of prestige. Only by arranging a science in a certain series is it possible to know what is *before,* what is *within,* and what is *behind,* and thus to get a definition of each science.

The history of the system of the sciences is described by, among others, Bliss (2) and, in Swedish, by Allen Vannerus (3). The latter has made very thorough studies and presents a system that is still of interest. He defines the "systematics of the sciences" as follows:

What must be done is to bring the sciences, this characteristic and highly important element in our spiritual culture, under the form of a *system* in order to obtain an insight not only into their multiplicity but also into their affinities.

In older times the natural starting point for philosophers was the human mind rather than nature. To quote from Francis Bacon (4):

The parts of human learning have reference to the parts of man's understanding, which is the seat of learning: History to his *Memory,* Poetry to his *Imagination,* and Philosophy to his *Reason.* . . . Thus I have made, as it were, a small globe of the intellectual world.

During the 18th century most natural sciences developed rapidly, but the continuity was still obscure. Fossils of plants and animals in rock were sometimes interpreted by scientists as products of "Vis plastica," i.e., a supposed power of nature to reproduce living beings in stone. The history of creation and the chronology of the Bible were for most scientists a reality. Obviously the time was not ripe for a coherent system of science.

In the 19th century—in conjunction with the development of the theory of evolution—a picture became clear of the relations between the sciences which in broad outline still holds today and which implied a radical reversal of the earlier order of sequence between the sciences. This very important reversal seems not to have been observed in books on the history of the system of science. It is moreover paradoxical that during that century, when it first became possible to speak of a general picture of the sciences which could be accepted in the whole western world, the interest in the system of the sciences began to die out both among philosophers and librarians. H. E. Bliss is here an exception, as de Grolier (5) points out:

His principal effort was directed to one point; to draw bibliographic classification nearer to what he termed "the scientific and education consensus"—the scientific and pedagogic order of subjects of study. His work from this standpoint has historical importance.

A documentalist now engaged on the relation between the sciences is the Pole, Z. Dobrowolsky (6), who wants to create a new "encyclopaedic classification."

This would be important, not only for the development of documentation but also for the furtherance of scientific research by furnishing a basis for rational organization of research within all fields of knowledge and on an international level.

It is true that documents nowadays cannot as easily as before be fitted into traditional folds, since scientific progress has meant that different sciences are to an ever increasing extent woven together and make use of one another. But this does not signify that a system is lacking.

Systems Within the Sciences

Apart from the structure of the whole field of science (the system of science), most sciences have developed rather detailed and fixed systems or structures of their own. Linne's "Systema Naturae" is an example, perhaps not quite up to date, but in his time bringing order out of chaos. The systems of the chemical elements, of atoms and electrons, of the stars and the galaxies, of the hereditary factors, etc., are other well known systems, forming a basic layer in the individual sciences and in the whole field of science as well.

Main Sequence in Science

A division of the entire field of science into only three main groups—which can scarcely be questioned—becomes clear from the following:

1. In the beginning there existed only lifeless matter and energy. The processes which went on are described in the sciences of mechanics, physics, chemistry, astronomy, geophysics, etc., with mathematics as basic science. The heavenly bodies and our earth appeared.
2. The origin of life signifies the start of a new epoch in natural history with a new series of phenomena and concepts. Living matter, plants, and animals evolved.
3. When some higher mammals developed into man, still another phase starts. Language arises, nature is exploited, societies and cultural activities come into being, and the stock of concepts was rapidly increased.

We have here a simple tripartite principle:

Matter (i.e., inorganic matter and energy)
Life (i.e., living matter and physical life)
Culture and society (man as an individual and in society)

This principle corresponds with that advanced by the British librarian, James Duff Brown (7), who at the beginning of this century suggested the simple series:

Matter—Life—Mind—Record

Figure 1 shows two philosophical systems from the first half of the 19th century and the library systems of Bliss and Brown constructed a century later which all—by and large—exhibit the sequence mentioned above. In contrast thereto, UDC (and Dewey) exhibit quite another structure representing a picture antiquated already in Dewey's time, and this also applies to many library systems used today.

Nowadays—with our strong trend toward specialization—these questions are considered a little old-fashioned. The field of knowledge is regarded by many documentalists as a coherent mass without distinguishable dividing lines; or the only way to divide it is according to some of the well-known traditional library systems. Only very occasionally is a new voice heard. It was therefore a strange coincidence that, at the time of writing this paper, the author happened to read an article in a Swedish newspaper entitled "Science with or without method." Dr. Boris Tullander (8), Lecturer in Economic Methodology at Uppsala University, writes, though not with a thought for documentation:

> There are at least three areas of our existence which are sharply distinguished. One may call them (1) the sphere of the material—mechanical relations, (2) the sphere of the organic—biological relations, (3) the sphere of the psychological—sociological relations. These relations, or "causa nexi," are geared to one another but they also represent a distinct advance and one immediately recognizes the differences.

Coming down to a lower level the principles for further division are not so self-evident.

A division of the sciences not consistent with that above is advocated by Maurice Korach (Hungary) in an interesting analysis (9) of the nature of the sciences:

Pure sciences	Natural sciences	Technical sciences, technologies
Mathematics	Zoology	Agricultural technologies
Physics	Botany	
Chemistry	Mineralogy and petrography	Industrial technologies
etc.	Astronomy	———
	etc.	

This division seems to aim at the general character of the sciences and not at their knowledge content (e.g., Zoology and Botany between Chemistry and Petrography). Perhaps we have to admit that the system of science can be regarded from different aspects. The documentation aspect, however, seems better justified by the scheme advocated above.

Disciplines or Concepts

To set up a fixed and detailed scheme, with the traditional disciplines as building blocks, has its difficulties even if we are agreed on the principle of their sequence. There have been successive changes in the composition of the sciences. Philosophy originally comprised nearly all science, but later had to relinquish bit by bit. The limits between mechanics, physics, and chemistry are

	COMTE	SPENCER	BLISS	BROWN	UDC

I	Mathematics
	Astronomy
	Physics
	Chemistry
		Logics
		Mathematics
		Mechanics
		Physics
		Chemistry
		Astronomy
		
		Geology
			A. Philosophy
			    General Science
			     Logic, Mathematics, etc.
			B. Physics
			C. Chemistry
			D. Astronomy
			    including Geology,
			    Geography
				Matter	Generalities
					0 Bibliography
					   Libraries, etc.
					
					   Philosophy
					1 Ethics
					   Psychology
					
					   Religion
					2 Theology

II	Physiology	Biology	E. Biology
			F. Botany
			G. Zoology
			H. Man
			     Physical
			     Medicine
				Life	3 Social sciences
					   Law
					
					   Philology
					4 Linguistics
					5 Pure sciences

III	Sociology	Psychology
		Sociology
			I. Psychology
			    Social
			     Education
			K. Sociology
			    Ethnology
			    Human Geography
			    Travel and Description
			L/O. Social-Political
			    History
			P. Religion and Ethics
			Q. Social Welfare,
			    Applied Ethics
			R. Political Science
			S. Law
			T. Economics
			U. Useful Arts, Industries
			    Trades
			V. Fine Arts, Philosophy
			W/Y. Literature and Language
			Z. Bibliography
				Mind
				
				Record[1]
					Applied sciences
					6 (Medicine, Tech-
					   nology)
					
					   Arts
					7 Entertainment
					   Sport
					
					   Literature
					8 Belles lettres
					
					   Geography
					9 History
					   Biography

1) Record = Literary forms, History, Geography and Biography

FIG. 1. Two philosophical systems from the first half of the nineteenth century and two library systems constructed a century later compared with another and with UDC

debatable. Atomic and nuclear physics have broken away from classical physics to form a new fundamental physics related to optics and the theory of electricity. Space science is another example and similar conditions prevail over the entire science register. When we come to the applied sciences, it is difficult to draw a frontier with pure science and no generally accepted subdivision of technology exists. Within sociology the difficulty is still greater, not to speak of psychology.

In the introduction we distinguished between traditional discipline systems and concept systems. By subdividing the total field of science *according to concepts* one obtains a basis for a system free of the traditional boundary lines.

This will not imply a revolution in the sequence, as one can follow in broad outline the sequence presented in Table 1 and thus make use of the already disentangled relations. But now we are more free to follow the principle of introducing new basic concepts in such a way that each new group can make use of earlier concepts and no group need make use of concepts from subsequent groups. One can also, within the pure basic sciences, obtain a close agreement with the system for units of measure, magnitudes, and physical "dimensions" as shown in Table 1.

A more extensive sketch of the sciences and their objects, embracing the introductory groups, is shown in Table 2.

TABLE 1. The Pure Sciences, Their Magnitudes and Basic Units of Measure

Science	Magnitudes [1]	Dimension	Units of measure [2]
Arithmetic	Number	0	—
Algebra and analysis	Mathematical quantities	0	—
Geometry	*Length*	1	m
	Area, etc.	1^2	m^2
Chronology	*Time*	t	s
Kinematics	Velocity	$v = 1/t$	m/s
	Acceleration, etc.	$a = 1/t^2$	m/s^2
Statics	*Force* [3]	F	kp or Newton [4]
	Moment of a force	$F \times 1$	kpm
	Pressure, etc.	$F/1^2$	kp/m^2
Dynamics	*Mass*	m	kg
	Kinetic energy, etc.	$m \times v^2$	$kg\, 1^2/t^2$

[1] Basic magnitudes in italics.
[2] m = meter, s = second, kg = kilogram, kp = kilopond (1 kilopond is the gravity of 1 kg under certain conditions).
[3] In statics force can be considered as a fundamental magnitude; but if, as in the mks system, mass is a fundamental magnitude, force will be derived by Newton's law: force = mass $\times$ acceleration ($F = m \times a$).
[4] 1 Newton is that force that will give the mass of 1 kg an acceleration of 1 m/s^2.

TABLE 2. The Pure (Exact) and the Natural Sciences and Their Respective Concepts

I. The pure and inorganic material sciences

A. Pure nonmaterial sciences (= exact sciences)	*Concepts*
Mathematics	Number and mathematical quantities
Geometry	Space [1]
Chronology	Time [1]
Kinematics	Motion
Statics ⎱ Mechanics	Force
Dynamics ⎰	Mass [2]

B. Pure material sciences

Physics	Matter
Chemistry	and
	Energy

C. Sciences of the universe and the earth (= inorganic natural sciences)

Astronomy	Universe
Geophysics	The earth
Geology	The solid surface of the earth
Hydrology. Oceanography	The water on the face of the earth
Meteorology	The atmosphere
Space science	The space around us

D. Technology

II. The biological sciences (= organic natural sciences)

A. General biology	Life
B. Botany	Plants
C. Zoology	Animals
D. Anthropology. Medicine	Man

III. ——

[1] The concepts space and time are not the same as in Ranganathan's space and time facets; they do not embrace geography and history.
[2] Mass is not to be mixed up with matter or material. Mass is ideal matter, characterized only by weight and inertia.

The more dynamic the development in our stock of knowledge, the more important it is, in the construction of a system of sciences, to build on simple, permanent, fundamental concepts. Concepts such as number, force, mass, energy, heat, atom, molecule, metals, wood, electricity, cell, heredity, sex, organs of sense, etc., stand through all times whatever the developments in society and technology. Changes in the sequence of the fundamental concepts are—after Newton and Darwin—rare. Einstein's theories may have led to a new conception of the most elementary basic concepts, but this is hardly of practical significance for documentation.

For dividing the field of technology this principle is of importance by creating a firmer ground for classifying those parts of technology which constitute applied science. We shall come back to this question in Section 2.

To extend the system of sciences to all areas influenced by the activity of man is exactly the purpose and the aim of science, because science is the knowledge of systematical relations between concepts, even if we cannot construct a hierarchy comprising all details of science.

By document systems is meant systems designed for classification of documents, whether for arrangement on the shelf or for organization of card indexes or printed indexes, each document being classified according to its knowledge content. As earlier intimated we can, when trying to classify a certain piece of knowledge, use different principles for different purposes. Therefore we have a more pragmatic approach if we talk of classifying documents according to their knowledge content than if we talk of classifying knowledge.

Hierarchical Document Systems

In this category we can distinguish between universal and specialized systems. The field of interest is here divided from the above in classes, subclasses, etc., down to a certain level. For each document we try to find one or more places where the document as a whole has its domicile.

Universal Document Systems

This is the category of the well-known library systems as Dewey, UDC, etc. The systems used in the book trade also belong here.

A. *Main Structure*

The main structure of these systems is generally influenced by the division into disciplines as adopted in the universities. The production of scientific literature followed in old days this division in broad outline and could therefore be easily fitted in the pattern.

The similar organization of studies at the occidental universities meant that the building blocks in the schemes of different countries were roughly the same, which facilitated an international diffusion of certain systems.

The traditional sequence, starting with philosophy, religion, and sociology, was accepted by Dewey and was characteristic also of the UDC based on Dewey's scheme. For the applied sciences one special main group was introduced.

As time went on, the document systems acquired an increasingly detailed structure, especially within the practical fields, and the connection with the traditional disciplines was partly dissolved.

The subdivision of the applied sciences and other practical fields was generally based on the differentiation into industries and professions and did not stand in any carefully thought-out correspondence with the system of sciences, but partially duplicated the latter. This was a natural arrangement, for within other fields—mathematics, biology, law, art, etc.—it was to a large extent particular professional categories that corresponded to the document groups, both as authors and readers.

B. *Principles of Subdivision*

We will first investigate the principal structure of UDC—as a representative for this category of systems. The main classes have already been dealt with. On lower levels UDC displays in some parts real generic divisions, e.g., in language, botany, zoology. In other parts we have non-generic but strictly hierarchical divisions, implying that the subclasses are equal and parallel. This is valid, e.g., for anatomy, for physics (the traditional subdisciplines), for many parts of technology, etc.

To a great extent, however, the subclasses correspond *to different aspects* of the class, the aspects having their domicile in other parts of the system. An example:

631.   Agriculture, farming in general. Agronomy
  .1   Farm management
  .2   Farms and farmyards
  .3   Agricultural implements, tools and machinery (e.g., ploughs)
  .4   Soil science (e.g., physical properties)
  .5   Growing, cultivation methods (e.g., ploughing)
  .6   Rural engineering (e.g., drainage)
  .8   Fertilizers. Manuring (e.g., nitrogen fertilizers)
  .9   Other topics

Most subclasses are applications of one special science or technique (economy, building, machinery, geology, etc.). We have now definitely left the "tree of knowledge" and the connection with the systematic of sciences. The system is a tool for collecting—in a collection comprising more than agronomy—all documents written for agronomists. The codes could also have been derived by combining 631 with other UDC-numbers.

C. *Precoordination of Concepts*

It may be reasonable to ask how in a document system we can introduce a limited number of concept combinations from the very great number of possible combinations, and if it is possible to design rules regulating which concept of two should have preferences. Is a universal document system perhaps on the whole an absurdity?

First, we have to consider that a document can often (depending on the size and the character of the collection) be classified only with the help of a single concept.

Second, to a certain extent, precoordinated concept combinations can be introduced and be a valuable feature.

Not all combinations of concepts have any real importance; the number studied and written about in the literature is in fact limited in relation to the number of possible combinations, even if it is large. A specialized documentalist will recognize certain types of combinations which often recur.

If a document deals with the concepts a and b in relation to one another, and both of them are represented in the system, the document can naturally be classified both under a and b. But if ab is an important combination, which has caused a great production of literature, there may be reason to introduce this combination in the scheme.

Let us take an example that is applicable both for a universal collection and for a special collection (e.g., a building trade library), but perhaps *not* for a specialized research institute.

On a purely generic basis the literature on concrete would be classified according to type of concrete. But as the literature is dominated by normal concrete made of Portland cement and ordinary stone material, it is perhaps more appropriate to form a system such as the following:

Concrete
    Manufacture of concrete
    ———

    Properties of concrete
      General
      Mechanical properties
        Strength
        Hardness
    ———

    Physical properties
    ———

    Special types of concrete

Combinations of concepts such as *concrete : strength* thus have their given place in this arrangement. The combination *strength : concrete* should in such case not be used.

In many cases the priority of the concepts *a* and *b* can be questioned but in other cases one sequence is definitely to be preferred. The building library will surely prefer to bring together all documents on concrete instead of bringing together all documents on strength. "Stronger" concepts like special materials, things, etc., will have preference over "weaker" concepts, e.g., properties.

We thus conclude that *concept combinations, if carefully selected, can be valuable features* in a document system, but it seems very hard to make such a selection if the structure of the system is not logically built up.

D. *Postcoordination of Concepts*

Even if the system includes the most important combinations today, new important combinations will come forward and we must have a method for coding them. How does UDC function in the case of unforeseen combinations? Let us first see how UDC is presented by FID. We quote from the General Introduction to the trilingual edition (my italics) (10):

The Universal Decimal Classification (UDC) is a scheme for classifying the whole *field of knowledge*. . . .

a classification in the strictest sense, depending on the analysis of idea content, so that related *concepts* and groups of concepts are brought together.

. . . an integrated pattern of correlated *subjects*. . . .

. . . constructed on the principle of proceeding from the general to the more particular by the (arbitrary) division of the whole of human *knowledge*. . . .

We also read that:

it should not be regarded as a philosophical classification of *knowledge*.

a practical system for numerically coding *information*, so designed that any *item*, once coded and filed correctly, can be readily found from whatever angle it is sought.

. . . the introduction of an auxiliary apparatus of connection and relation signs, lacking in the original Dewey system, has made the UDC really universal, in the sense that it permits almost any desired combination and modification of basic numbers to denote the most complex *subjects*.

It may be true that the system permits coding of practically any combination of concepts by linking two concepts with the colon sign or with the use of the auxiliary tables. But is this coding of such a nature as to provide sufficient guidance for searching? The concepts to be combined for forming complex subjects are to a large extent already combinations of concepts (type *ab* or *abc*). The same concept is for that matter often located in more than one place in the system.

Can one not often express a certain combination of concepts in different notational ways. Perhaps *ab : lm* has the same signification as *al : bm*, etc., but how is one to choose the right entrance, especially if a concept is to be found in more than one place in the system?

This combining of concepts, which cannot in themselves be regarded as simple, fundamental concepts selected on a strictly logical principle, leads to a fairly complicated procedure. Is this not a compromise between two logical principles? The principles are as follows:

1. Classification with the aid of a document system based on both generic and other strictly hierarchical structures and moreover on certain precoordinated structures (*ab* and *lm*) and

2. Indexing with the aid of a number of equivalent terms (*a, b, l, m*).

E. *How to Get a Modern Universal Document System?*

The first condition for a new universal system is that it should be linked up with the scientific pattern which has been generally accepted for more than 100 years (cf. Bliss) and the second, that it should be designed on the basis of fundamental concepts instead of traditional headings.

These questions have been dealt with above with respect to the system of science. A proposal for the main structure of a document system based on these principles has been made by the author (11). Here the possibility is also advanced of different universal document systems for different main fields of activity, each system being universal but designed from a special aspect. (See Section G.) The proposal mentioned is especially intended for technology and called *TUS*, i.e., *Technological Universal (Document) System*. The main groups are (cf. Table 2):

1. Abstract concepts .... I A
2. Force. Energy .... I B
3. Matter. Materials .... I B
4. World .... I C
5. Life. Man II
6. The individual. Humanistic fields III
7. Society III
8. Material culture III
9. History. Geography. Biography III

The principle behind the main groups is explained in Section 1, p. 203. One important factor for a system intended for technology is naturally the principle for the division of technology. This question has here been solved in such a way that all technical subjects, which can be related to fundamental concepts belonging to those parts of the system which are dependent on the system of science, are located in connection with these fundamental concepts; while those parts of technology which are best characterized by their purpose, e.g., Transport, Building, etc., are collected in one main group, called "Material Culture" or "Functional Material Culture." This group will contain subjects of primary interest to man and society (automobiles, buildings, etc.), while that which lies behind (the engine, installations, theory) is considered as secondary and appears in connection with the fundamental concepts. Strictly speaking, two separate bases for classification have been used:

	A	B
(1)	Applied sciences	Nonapplied sciences
(2)	Not of primary interest to man and society	Of primary interest to man and society

These two principles of classification, however, lead to a great extent to the same result. We find the same tendency to division of technology into two parts if we study the titles of the main branches of technological teaching:

A. By science: mechanical, chemical, electrical (etc.) engineering
B. By purpose: housebuilding, shipbuilding, aviation, mining, etc.

TUS has in the first place to be judged from the viewpoints of special fields of activity, which only collect documents for their own needs. Every field has its own main number in the system, under which the specific documents will be collected, but has to spread out other documents over the whole system as far as possible. Different applications of the system for different types of document collections are discussed in the sequel.

These principles for designing a universal system were advanced as early as 1949 at a conference on Building Documentation in Geneva (12). In the last years it has been possible to go a little further on this road and TUS has now been constructed in detail as regards those parts which are of interest to the housebuilding field. It has been adopted for a bibliography comprising 25 years of the Swedish journals *Arkitektur* and *Byggmastaren* (13). By way of experiment the whole of UDC in its trilingual edition has also been rearranged under TUS headings, which permits a considerable concentration of related fields of knowledge which are widely dispersed in UDC.

The principle of attaching applied science to fundamental concepts was advanced already by J. D. Brown. Now, after 60 years, it is fascinating to hear this voice from the grave:

> Its basis [Brown's system] is a recognition of the fact that every science and art springs from some definite source, and need not, therefore, be arbitrarily grouped in alphabetical, chronological or purely artificial divisions, because tradition or custom has apparently sanctioned such usage. The division seen in most classifications in vogue—Fine Arts, Useful Arts and Science, are examples of the arbitrary separation of closely related subjects, which in the past have become conventional, and it may seem heretical even at this late time to propose a more intimate union between exact and applied science.

Brown's system was perhaps imperfect in some ways, but it nevertheless seems remarkable that the statement above did not influence the international development in classification.

F. *Limitations on the Use of a Hierarchical Universal Document System*

The scheme need not enter more deeply into details than a generally applicable differentiation of documents allows. When we come down to a certain level, perhaps the 3- or 4-digit level, we can no longer find principles of classification which can be generally accepted. The best subdivision for one institute or library may not be suited to others. A certain institute may very well arrange a detailed classification for its own use, but in an international standard one should not go too deeply into detail. Even if a subdivision on modern principles into only a few groups could be generally accepted, very much would be gained. Other methods of search can then be employed both within a class and in combination with other classes. Faceted systems, coordinated indexing, or permutated indexing may have their place here.

The question whether one can classify a document in a document system so that it can easily be retrieved is tied up also with the size and the degree of specialization of the collection in which the document is to be stored. In a small collection comprising many fields of knowledge a single concept may suffice to provide a safe anchorage, and a universal document system is thus best suited for such a collection. Perhaps the widest application for universal document systems is in filing of documents in offices and for every man's use.

If the collection grows larger, still with unchanged composition, more documents will come under every class number. This can hardly imply that the possibility of finding relevant documents will decrease. But if we want to use this bigger collection with full effectiveness, it may be reasonable to try to refine the indexing and search methods.

If we now compare with a very specialized collection, it is quite clear that the advantage of the universality of the system becomes smaller in the same degree as the documents are assembled under fewer headings. To characterize every document, we are forced either to get the class numbers in question more detailed in a way that best corresponds to the collection or to use other methods of indexing.

We have here, of course, presumed that the aim of the system is to display the collection in the widest possible way, and not to concentrate documents according to field of activity, as the character of some groups of UDC seems to indicate.

G. Different Applications of a Document System for Different Fields of Activity

By fields of activity is meant fields with a common need for documentation, their own special journals, etc. These fields may be scientific or social, sectors of industry or professions. Every part of the universal scheme corresponds to one or more fields of activity.

We also have a hierarchy—apart from the hierarchy in the document system—that could be exemplified by:

All science	= "universal field"
Technology	= "suprafield"
Building and civil engineering	= "field"
Architecture	= "subfield"

With increasing specialization the special document collections are more important than the universal, and the first aim of a universal system is to be a tool for special collections.

If we try to apply the principles mentioned above and draw up system structures suitable for (1) the universal field, for (2) some suprafields, for (3) some fields, and for (4) some subfields of activity, it is not probable that we shall get the same result in all these cases. This is one reason why the system presented above (TUS) is adapted to a "suprafield" technology.

I do not think that it is suitable to aim at different document systems for the fields and subfields under technology, but it may be justified to have *different applications* of the same system. If we have a document "Electrical Installations in Buildings," the classification allotted when publishing the document will consist of two equivalent notations: *b* for building and *e* for electrical. The "electrical library" may use *b* and the building library *e*

as primary classification. While this is a simple example, the problem as a whole is rather complicated and cannot be thoroughly studied without the background both of a certain document system and of the outline of a division into fields of activities and their documentation activities.

It is conceivable however that documents, as an aid both for filing in different collections and for distribution to the proper categories, might be classified both according to knowledge content and to receiver categories (fields of activity).

Specialized Hierarchical Systems

Among the reasons why there are hundred or thousands of special systems in use in most countries, one is that the UDC numbers are too long and that specialized spheres of interest disappear in the universal collection. This is not a weighty reason, for one often overlooks the simple course of substituting the most heavily loaded numbers by letters and making a selection from the main system in which irrelevant titles are weeded out. A more weighty reason is that the structure of UDC has proved unsuitable for many particular fields. The absence of a main group for materials, for instance, seems to be a serious defect. Only a radical revision would suffice in face of such criticism.

If one could get all those who now use special systems to use a common universal system instead, the circle of users of the universal system would be multiplied many times over. The picture is, however, not complete without paying consideration to the faceted systems.

Faceted Document Systems

The faceted systems drawn up in England are all intended for special fields. They are not, as are hierarchical specialized systems, constructed by dividing the special field of knowledge from above in certain parts. Instead they are constructed from *below* by organizing the most important concepts (represented by certain terms) in a limited number of series (facets) and the documents are characterized by means of one concept from some (or all) of the facets. Thus there is no precoordination of concepts involved. If we consider each facet as one classification system, the concepts represent the "subjects," but for the system taken as a whole the documents represent the subjects. The faceted principle is more related to indexing than to classification in general sense.

What is here of special interest is that members of CRG are striving at the design of a universal document system with faceted structure. Main facets are Things, Activities, and Properties. A series for things arranged according to "integrative level" have been published. For further information it is better to refer to various publications of the members of CRG, especially perhaps to Foskett's *Classification and Indexing in the Social Sciences* (14), where, moreover, a very interesting and exhaustive analysis of the whole classification problem is given. We quote from this book:

> What is certain is that a general classification scheme is needed, that none of the existing schemes are satisfactory, and that we have enough ideas about the structure of a new scheme to make the effort to produce one worthwhile.

If we compare this project with UDC or with the enterprise to design a new hierarchical document system along the lines advocated above or other projects going on, it would be better not to try to formulate an opinion concerning which may be the best way. Research and experiments in more directions and with organized comparisons may be better than any attempt to compel the development into a single track.

3 Other Systems Based on Knowledge Content

Editorial Systems

Every author of a textbook, and every scientific writer, is faced with the same problems as the documentalist, the systemization of knowledge in some way or another; but in the editorial field these problems are not at all objects for organized studies. The editor of a technological compilation, for example, or of a code of standards, is presented with the problem of arranging a number of "facets." These must be chosen so as to bring out the most important concepts as headings; the number of facets must not be so small that they cannot accommodate the desired contents. Nor must it be too large, for then there will be too many entries. The editor will then have great problems in deciding on the choice of location of the knowledge elements and the reader will meet with difficulties in finding the information he requires [2].

Just as important as it is to keep documents in order, so it is to bring order into their contents by editing the documents.

Here, as within documentation, we have the struggle between the alphabetical and the systematic principle. The alphabetical has a great significance in encyclopaedic works, especially the bigger ones of a general nature, and in books of reference, owing to the fact that the general public do not want to choose between different possible entries but go direct to a title-word they have in mind. Just as a document may occur several times in an alphabetical index, so information can be duplicated in an alphabetical work, perhaps linked together by cross ref-

erences. For books intended for learning and education the systematic form is the obvious choice.

Editorial systems have significance on the universal plane as well. Compilations of this kind exist both with the classical disciplines (mathematics, mechanics, physics . . .) as headings, and with concept headings (number, space, time, mass . . .). Table 3 shows the systems in some modern encyclopaedias from different countries which conform closely to Table 2.

Books of this kind should follow the systematics of science, i.e., present knowledge in a natural sequence, implying that elementary phenomena are described before the more complicated and that new fundamental concepts are not introduced until the presentation so demands. Cross references should go backwards (toward the beginning of the book) and the need for them should be minimal.

Educational Systems

The most important phase in the distribution of knowledge is the education organized by society. Systems are necessary for dividing up the sphere of knowledge taught at each school and university into curricular subjects. Obviously these systems must be based on the system of science. It should be possible to give every subject a definition by reference to a universal system.

All educational planning should be based on a systematic analysis of the specified requirements of knowledge for different occupational groups. The relation between education and documentation is mutual and sig-

TABLE 3. Some Modern Encyclopaedic Works with Systematic Structure (by Subject)

Larousse Metodique (Librarie Larousse, Paris 1959)

Aritmetique	Astronomie	Biologie
Algebre	Physique	Botanique
Geometrie	Chimie	Zoologie
Mecanique rationelle	Geologie	etc.

Universitas Litterarum (Walter de Gruyter, Berlin)

Matematik	Mineralogie	Medizin
Physik	Palaentologi	Psykologie
Chemie	Botanik	Volkerkunde
Astronomie	Zoologie	Sociologi
Geologie	Anthropologie	etc.

Kleine Enzyklopadie (Verlag Enzyklopadie, Leipzig 1960)
Natur

Zahl	Kraft (energi)	Leben
Raum	Stoff	Tier
Zeit	Weltall	Pflanze
Mass u. Gewicht	Erde	Mensch

Fakta (Bokforlaget Fakta AB, Stockholm, 1955–1961) and *Facta* (Ediciones Rialp, Madrid; 1962–1966)

Mathematics	Geology	Countries and peoples
Mechanics	Meteorology	Humanistic fields
Physics	Biology, general	Society
Chemistry	Plants, Animals	Technology
Astronomy	Man	Home and environment

---

2. An application of a specialized system with decimal notation has been realized on a large scale in the Swedish building handbook **BYGG**, published in the 1940's in four volumes (in the 1960's increased to 6 volumes), with three numerals before the colon and a maximum of three after (e.g., 242:518 Concrete; strength; compression; testing). This system has also been used for filing of documents and is often preferred to existing library systems. The same notation principles but with a universal system are used in the general encyclopaedia Fakta (Table 3).

nificant, but have the relations between curricular subjects and document systems anywhere been investigated?

Systems for Patents and Legal Texts

Both in a patent specification and in a code of laws, certain relations are established between concepts which have a legal force. The problem of classifying or indexing such texts is, as is well known, closely akin to the general problem of documentation and these questions have been dealt with in the documentation literature. In fact such texts should be ideal experimental subjects owing to their concentrated form and the care with which concepts are selected, clothed in word form and syntactically compiled.

4   Term Systems

General

Vocabularies in different languages have not been created at one time as the result of a general study, but have developed successively among different peoples insofar as they have felt a need for words. Science, technology, and social organizations are constantly producing many new concepts and require an extended and exactly defined vocabulary. The creation of new words is a slow process, and it is therefore not remarkable that the connection between concepts and words is poor. The nomenclature organizations have the difficult mission of guiding the development into the proper paths.

The stock of terms is of great interest in documentation. The knowledge contained in documents can, as is well known, be indexed, either by a number (or several numbers) in a document system ("item-entry") or by a number of concepts or terms characteristic of the document. If we index by terms ("term-entry") it is important to draw up a list of terms (descriptors or key words) which should be given priority both by the indexer and by the searcher. These terms are collected in a special word list, often called a "thesaurus."

Different Ways of Arranging Terms

The commonest and simplest method of arranging terms is *alphabetically*, a convenient but, as we know, an often deceptive method. As complement to all other classifications, however, the alphabetical is indispensable.

Then we have the *grammatical* division according to parts of speech which determine to a certain extent what syntactical role the word can play. The trilogy things, activities (processes), and properties correspond by and large to the three main parts of speech, the substantives, the verbs, and the adjectives, but the context between concepts and parts of speech is, as well known, not always ambiguous. Prepositions and other small words explain—together with a more or less extensive system of case-declensions—the syntactical context between the words.

The logic of natural speech, however, seems to be insufficient in qualified information retrieval, and different sets of "role indicators" have been devised by different documentation schools or experts.

There is also the *etymological* classification, which is based on the origin of words and cuts across the grammatical classification. Words are organisms which are born, develop, change their meaning and spelling, and sometimes die. The etymological classification corresponds to the natural genus-species division in the plant and animal kingdoms. The synonyms are representatives of different etymological individuals, joined in the same concept category. The words "hound" and "dog," for example, come in different etymological places but in the same concept category and so do "hen" and "poultry." Composite words correspond to biological crossings.

We can also classify words *semantically*, on the basis of the concepts the words are to convey.

Concepts can to some extent be expressed by *symbols* or *pictures* without the help of words. Geometrical figures can be easily illustrated; the elements, too, by means of their electron shells; chemical compounds by their molecular diagrams; cells, tissues, plants, and animals can be illustrated, as can technically produced objects. (Maps, diagrams, and tables can also exhibit very complicated relations without words.) Illustrated glossaries are not unknown and have a function to fulfill within documentation.

The language of symbols is an intermediate step between concepts and words. Can one imagine a complete universal system of systematically arranged symbols?

Terms can also be expressed by *definitions*, a new term being defined by means of other already defined terms. This implies a certain systematic arrangement, e.g.:

3. A figure bounded by *three* straight
   lines: triangle
4. A figure bounded by *four* straight
   lines: quadrangle
   4.1   Ditto with right angles: rectangle
   4.11 Ditto with right angles and
         equal sides: square

Here, as a matter of fact, we are approaching the editorial principle of presenting knowledge in text books by building a system of concepts step by step (cf. Section 3).

To a certain extent terms can be easily arranged in groups which are, more or less, generally accepted, such as the elements, chemical compounds, rock species, plants, animals, etc. If we strive at a fixed unambiguous location for every word, we must always keep to the fundamental meanings of the words. Granite, for instance, is a geological term (a species of rock) and not a building material or a product from the quarrying industry, for the definition of the word belongs to the sphere of geology. Rose is a botanical term; dog, a zoological.

Lists of terms arranged with regard to the semantic signification of the words are needed within documentation. A scheme for a complete, systematic list of terms, in which each term is as far as possible located according to its meaning, we shall here call an *unambiguous semantic term-concept system* or, more simply, a *term system*.

The elementary terms in the sciences are generally not created for the sciences, but for more primitive needs of man. Hot and cold are originally not physical terms, they are expressions for certain feelings of man. However, the sciences have need of such elementary terms, and allot them fixed positions and clear definitions. We will get a good guidance for an unambiguous location if we give preference to the more fundamental locations in the series of the sciences and concepts as shown in Table 2.

To a very large extent even terms considered to be "general" can thus be assigned a place according to the sciences. Large, small, increase, decrease will go to Mathematics; long, short, round to Geometry; rapid, slow to Kinematics; force, equilibrium to Statics; hot, cold to Thermodynamics; beam, reflex to Optics; granite and syenite to Geology, etc.

Survey of Existing Term Lists

One might have expected there to exist a systematically arranged glossary of all our technical terms; at all events in some language; in fact there appears to be none, at least none that is up-to-date.

A well-known, systematic glossary of universal character is Roget's *Thesaurus* published in England in 1852—which was enlarged in 1952 (15) and has a wide use as dictionary of synonyms for writers and editors. The original system has been retained, but this is unacceptable for modern science and technology as physical and technical concepts are derived from the human senses, which leads to corresponding gaps in physics and technology. Example:

Matter	Intellect
Organic matter	Communication of ideas
Sensation	Modes of communication
Touch, Heat,	Publication
Taste	. . . journalism,
	. . . radio,
	. . . television

Coordinate indexing has brought a new wave of interest in technical terms, and attempts are being made within all branches of technology to perfect their stocks of words. There have been discussions concerning the use of UDC as a systematic term list; but UDC is not constructed as a term system, and the same terms may occur 5 to 10 times or more, whereas a large number of the elementary words are missing. One would first have to rebuild UDC so that the same term occurs only once, and the principles of such adjustment of the system would then have to be investigated, which to some extent is equivalent to constructing a new system.

It is imaginable, however, that large parts of UDC, e.g., within chemistry and electrotechnics, could be used. And as UDC is published in several languages, the use as far as possible of this system, and possibly other classification systems, should be valuable.

Example from the trilingual edition of UDC:

German 621.375	English	French
Rohrenverstarker	Valve amplifiers	Amplificateurs a lampes
Magnetische Verstarker	Magnetic amplifiers (transductor)	Amplificateurs magnetiques
Kristallverstarker Transistoren	Crystal amplifiers (transistor)	Amplificateurs a cristal Transistors
Dielektrische Verstarker	Dielectric amplifiers	Amplificateurs dielectriques

A glossary of terms common to the whole of technology and intended for coordinative indexing is the Engineering Joint Council (EJC) *Thesaurus* (16). The terms are alphabetically arranged, but with references to "broader terms," "narrower terms," and to otherwise related words ("refer to"), and from words which should not be used as descriptors to the respective descriptors. These arrangements may be interpreted as a system of "micro-hierarchies," but no attempt has been made to bring together all terms into a single systematic totality.

A number of special thesauri have been compiled for different fields, and in them one sometimes finds a systematic classification of the terms of that field. In a thesaurus published by Euratom (17) for nuclear technology, for instance, we find a classification of the vocabulary into 42 groups (key word groups). It may be of interest to see whether two institutions select and arrange the terms within the same field in the same way. Within the field of radiation and electromagnetic waves Euratom arranges the key words in four groups:

72. Optics
73. Magnetism
84. Radiations
85. Elementary particles

If we compare the 17 key words under Radiation in Euratom with the 28 "narrower terms" under Radiation in EJC, we find that *only one* is exactly the same in the two groups, namely Cosmic Radiation, while the following three are similar in their import but differ in spelling and linguistic form.

Cerenkov radiation	—	Cherenkov radiation
Gamma rays	—	Gamma radiation
X-rays	—	X-radiation

Otherwise the selection of terms is entirely different in the two thesauri. The compatibility between them is obviously very poor. As regards special thesauri the following points may also be noted: The barrier between science and technology that is characteristic of UDC does not exist here. The key word groups thereby have a more homogenous character, and the structure is more rational.

Concerning terminology, on the other hand, one notes a diverging tendency since each special branch of technology uses general terms in a specialized sense for the branch. In a thesaurus for roadbuilding, words such as base, bed, carpet, coat, deep, junction, etc., appear in the key word group "Road." This may be acceptable if road documentation is to be considered an isolated activity, but if this activity is to be included in a broader context, one will have to deal with different vocabularies. Closer agreement between terms and headings is found in key word groups such as "Mathematics—Mechanics" and "Optics."

An interesting example of a list of terms is *Medical Subject Headings* (18) of *Index Medicus*, a list of biomedical terms arranged both alphabetically and systematically ("categorized list"). We quote:

> The Categorized List is an attempt to bring related terms together where the indexer and searcher can view a panorama of subject headings and select the most appropriate heading for his needs.

The introductory categories are:

A. Anatomical terms
B. Organisms
C. Diseases
D. Chemicals and Drugs
E. Analytical, Diagnostic, and Therapeutic Technics and Equipment

Example of subcategories:

A1. Parts of the Body
A2. Musculoskeletal system
A3. Digestive system

The terms ("subject headings") have usually been unambiguously locatable within a main category, but thereunder they often occur within several subcategories. Example: "Hand" occurs both under A1 and A2. As cross references are given, this perhaps is of no particular inconvenience, but by adjustment of the category headings it should be possible to achieve unambiguous locations to a greater extent. Generally speaking, one may say that A, B, and C of *Index Medicus* could be incorporated in a universal system of terms.

It is interesting to compare these categories with the headings which are usual in document systems:

Index Medicus (term categories)	*UDC* (subject fields)
A. Anatomical terms	58. Botany
B. Organisms	59. Zoology
C. Diseases	61. Medical Sciences

The pattern in the "realm of knowledge" is not the same as in the "realm of terms." Botany, Zoology, and Medicine have largely the same stock of terms as the groups A, B, and C. But if terms are collected and arranged from the bottom *upwards* as in a thesaurus, one comes automatically upon certain groups which do not always agree with the traditional sciences and are found in document systems for which the classification is made from the top *downwards*.

One can easily find out which classification of a collected stock of biomedical terms results in the largest number of duplicate locations. That, at all events, Zoology and Medicine have a common stock of anatomical terms is natural since, anatomically, man is an animal. Thus the A, B, and C grouping above must in this case be better for the term system. But the following term categories are also conceivable:

Botany	Zoology and Medicine
Anatomical terms	Anatomical terms
Organisms	Organisms
Diseases	Diseases

In a universal term system, of course, the group Chemicals must not come under the heading Biomedicine, but appear earlier in the systematic sequence. One may then perhaps find that Drugs as well can be removed from the medical field.

In the field of materials technology I have made some attempts to systematize the stock of terms (materials, processes, properties), and the result suggests that an unambiguous systematic grouping of these terms is not a hopeless task. It is also quite clear that one arrives at hierarchies of an entirely different kind than in a document system, as will be shown.

In the section on document systems (2.1.1.C) we have given an example of a possible subdivision of a document collection on concrete, corresponding to the composition of the stock of documents. In a term system only words relating exclusively to the concept "concrete" may appear under the heading—words such as standard concrete, lightweight concrete, etc.—while terms for properties and processes appear elsewhere. In the document system the hierarchies are to a certain extent expressions of combinations of concepts which have been regarded as suited to a collection of documents and a document on "Strength of Concrete" has here a fixed location. In the term system one is concerned only with generic hierarchies (each term being defined by superior headings). The same document has to be indexed with help of two terms (as in a faceted system). (Fig. 2.)

A universal, systematically (and alphabetically) arranged thesaurus can be created by successively sifting the vocabularies from different subject fields through the "screen" of a universal system. The dilemma is that a universal term system is lacking. There are two ways of creating such a system: by way of theoretical speculation or, practically, by proceeding from a universal document system. This must, however, be successively adjusted to a systematized arrangement adapted to terms,

1. Hierarchy in a document system

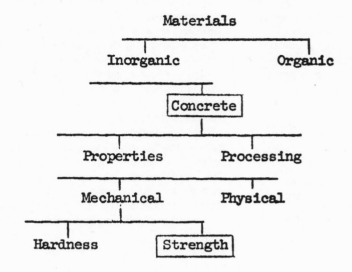

2. Hierarchy in a term system

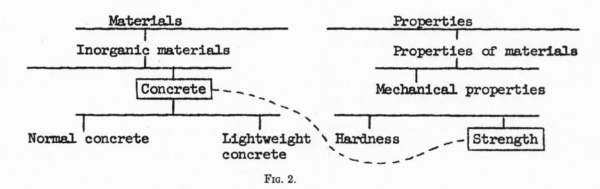

Fig. 2.

as is shown by the comparison between *Index Medicus* and UDC. The more conceptual and the less bound to tradition the system used, the easier it seems to be to transform it to a term system.

Attempts on a smaller scale with assortments of vocabularies from different quarters have been started with the help of TUS as a provisory term system. Every term is given a number according to TUS and then sorted both on the basis of this number and alphabetically. With the aid of punched cards a project of this kind can be very well carried out on a large scale and the value would be greatest if the work could be conducted on a universal basis.

To avoid misunderstandings it should be emphasized that a term system constructed on the principles presented here will be quite different from a concept system for classifying documents. It has been shown that a document system of the normal model is not suited as a term system. But can a term system be used as a document

system or as the framework—in one sense or another—of a document system?

Obviously many traditional subject fields will be broken down (cf. *Index Medicus*). But if we think not of the universal libraries but primarily of the special libraries where often this breakdown has already been made, it may be wise to postpone expressing an opinion until the question has been examined.

Opinions among documentation experts concerning the possibility of creating a universal system of terms can be illustrated by some quotations. Vickery (19) puts the question:

> Is a universal descriptor language possible which embraces all subject fields, and is usable in all retrieval systems? . . . Perhaps the present area of specialization in retrieval will be succeeded by a synthesis, leading to the general use of a common "interlingua."

This question comes back unaltered in the second issue of his book (1964). Evidently nothing has happened in three years that has made it possible for Vickery to give an answer to his question.

Mortimer Taube had some doubts on the possibility and wrote: ". . . no one has actually produced a general categorization or classification of a total vocabulary."

The universal facets of CRG must in this connection be of interest as Foskett presents the theory of integrative levels as a principle for dividing terms into groups. The relation between document systems and term systems here comes in a new light.

5 Practical Systems

By practical systems is here meant systems used in industrial enterprises, in trade, and in other practical connections, aimed at the classification of products, costs, etc., and for filing purposes.

Product Systems

Systems for technically produced things we may call *product systems*. All industrial enterprises need such systems to maintain order in their manufactures and often spend large amounts of money on them. They are used for stockkeeping, for registration of drawings, for filing of documents on products, for costing and industrial planning. Often an entire trade has a common system (e.g., the hardware trade, the furniture trade).

Products can be classified from different points of view. They cannot as natural things (plants, etc.) be classified according to genus-species relations, but the raw material and the industrial production process offer a counterpart to some extent. Material, shape, and purpose are for many products the most important factors; and a concrete drainpipe may thus be classified as *pipe*, as *concrete product,* or as *products for sewage.*

These remarks apply primarily to bulk materials and to semimanufactured products. The classification of *machinery* and *apparatus* offers greater difficulties since, in this case, the principle of function (a particular physical principle, for example), or a category of user, may offer the best classification (e.g., electrical or optical equipment, office supplies, etc.). A universal system would seem to be necessary as a basis or background for compiling a comprehensive system for the latter categories.

The degree of complexity can also be used as a first principle of classification, and under the main groups derived in this way various principles of subdivision can be employed.

Product systems in industry are often used also for classifying documents concerning products; this is sometimes their main aim. Sometimes these systems acquire the character of complete document systems, with space also for sciences, social questions, and the like. In such case they often compete with the system used in the library, which in turn may be elaborated in detail into a product system. UDC tends in this direction but is generally not used as product system; as a rule industrial enterprises draw up their own systems which they consider better suited to their specialties.

The existence within the same firm of two or more schemes with different structure, but comprising partly the same concepts and terms, cannot be an ideal solution. This now seems to be the rule, however, and a big firm or institution sometimes has even three, four, or more schemes which perhaps could be replaced by a single one.

The need for a document system which is also a complete industrial product system—or at all events constitutes a basis for such a system—is fully legitimate. One may then ask whether this is an unreasonable requirement, or can one imagine a universal classification system which can serve satisfactorily both as document system and as a basis for a universal thing-and-product system?

It is naturally not possible to construct a universal product system simply by adding together a number of such industrial systems, as they usually overlap to a great extent. Perhaps a universal product system could be made as a faceted system with facets for material, shape, function, etc.

A standardized facet for materials and another for form may be the best way to start with, if we strive at some uniformity in this field, and these facets could in some way be included in a universal document system. The function facet could also be a connecting link with a universal document system.

Systems for Processes and Labor

Materials and products are the "substantive facet," in industry, processes, and labor the "verb facet," and properties the "adjective facet." Processes include both intellectual work and manual and mechanical work. In this context we shall not be concerned with intellectual work. To get a classification for processes and labor is more difficult than for materials and products.

Some processes can easily be classified according to processed material (in the building trade woodwork, concrete work, etc.), but not all material processes or material treament can be classified thus, as they are applicable to all or some kinds of materials (e.g., welding, drilling). Other processes must be classified on the basis of the finished product (e.g., installation or assembly work) or as "auxiliary processes" which cannot be related to either a particular material or a product. However, it is not impossible to get a generally acceptable division of the processes in industry; such a division is essential and has already been accomplished thousands of times. We have in fact only to consider which solution is the best one, if we want to get a standardized system of this kind.

It would be possible to obtain some correspondence

between systems for processes and systems for materials and products, and it also seems possible to include a category of material treatment processes in a universal document system.

Systems for Properties

It seems to be difficult to construct a universal system for properties of all kinds. For the properties of materials, on the other hand, a system associated with the systematics of science may be fairly easily constructed, as certain special institutes have devoted much effort to studies of all the properties of materials. The study of materials indeed consists to a large extent of determining their properties expressed in units of measure. These units, which are composed of a limited set of basic units (cf. Section 1), are a good guide to the systematics of properties, which is closely related to the classical subdivisions of the natural sciences:

Mechanical properties
Thermal properties
Electrical and magnetic properties
Chemical properties,
etc.

A system for properties of materials is valuable for all industrial enterprises producing materials in their specification of properties. It is also of interest for testing materials and for general consumer information. This is a necessary step also when drawing up a list of terms for technology.

Summary

The purpose of this paper is to point out the fact that we in documentation have use not only of one kind of classification systems but of different types distinguished by *different types of subjects*.

The discussions are often confused as the primary purpose of the classification is not made clear. Some experts talk of classifying knowledge, others of classifying concepts, ideas, terms, etc. We will get a more fruitful and pragmatic approach if we consider the type of subject of the general library classification systems to be *documents,* even if the system is constructed on the basis of fields of knowledge or on concepts.

In documentation we also have a need of a classification system for terms, a *term system,* based on the semantic signification of the terms. The demands on the hierarchical structure is always determined by the subject thus for term systems by the terms themselves. The patterns in the "realm of knowledge" is not the same as in the "realm of terms." To investigate principal differences in these different patterns seems to be an important task.

Further on we have in all industrial enterprises, etc., need for practical systems with different objects, e.g., *systems for products*. These can be used for specifications of products, for cost calculations, etc., and also for filing of documents on the products.

It is important in developing classification systems of different kinds to strictly have the subjects in mind. It may be that we want to use a document system for classifying terms or a term system or a product system for classifying documents or a document system for classifying products, but we have to be aware of the fact that we then are using these systems for a secondary purpose.

References

1. BRUGGHEN, W. VAN DER, Report on the FID in 1964, *Revue Internationale de la Documentation,* 32 (No. 2) : 60, 1965.
2. BLISS, H. E., *The Organization of Knowledge and the System of the Sciences.* New York, 1934.
3. VANNÉRUS, A., *Vetenskapssystematik,* Alb. Bonniers förlag, Stockholm, 1921.
4. BACON, FRANCIS, *Of the Proficience and Advancement of Learning,* 1605.
5. DE GROLIER, E., *A Study of General Categories Applicable to Classification and Coding in Documentation,* Printed in the Netherlands, Unesco, 1962.
6. DOBROWOLSKY, Z. (Warzawa), *Analysis of Classification Systems,* Report to the 2nd FID/CR Meeting in Stockholm, 1963. Stenciled copy.
7. BROWN, J. D., *Subject Classification,* London, 1906.
8. TULLANDER, B., Vetenskap med och utan metod (Science with and without method), *Svenska Dagbladet,* Stockholm, March 1965.
9. KORACH, M., The Science of Industry, Chapter 13, *in* N. Goldsmith and A. McKay, eds., *The Science of the Sciences,* Bungay, Suffolk, 1964.
10. *Universal Decimal Classification,* Trilingual abridged edition, British Standards Institution, London, 1958.
11. WÅHLIN, E., Principles for a universal system of classification based on certain fundamental concepts and an outline of a variant adapted to technology, *Journal of Documentation,* 1963 (4):173–186.
12. WÅHLIN, E., *Basic Principles and Outline of a New Universal System of Classification,* Proceedings from the Conference on Building Documentation, Genève, 1949. Stenciled copy.
13. WÅHLIN, E., *25-year Bibliography for the Journals Byggmästaren and Arkitektur,* Byggmästarens förlag, Stockholm, 1966.

14. FOSKETT, D., *Classification and Indexing in the Social Sciences,* Butterworths, London, 1963.
15. *Roget's International Thesaurus,* Thomas Y. Cromwell Co., London, 1962.
16. *Thesaurus of Engineering Terms,* Engineering Joint Council, New York, May 1964.
17. *Euratom-Thesaurus,* Presses Academiques Européennes, Bryssel, February 1964.
18. *Medical Subject Headings,* National Library of Medicine, 1965.
19. VICKERY, B. C., *On Retrieval System Theory,* Butterworths, London, 1961.

36 Automatic Document Classification

HAROLD BORKO
MYRNA BERNICK
*Journal of the Association
for Computing Machinery
Vol. 10, No. 2, April, 1963*

1. Introduction and Related Research

The problem of automatic document classification is a part of the larger problem of automatic content analysis. Classification means the determination of subject content. For a document to be classified under a given heading, it must be ascertained that its subject matter relates to that area of discourse. In most cases this is a relatively easy decision for a human being to make. The question being rased is whether a computer can be programmed to determine the subject content of a document and the category (categories) into which it should be classified. This question has practical implications. Technical libraries are being inundated by vast quantities of literature. Some automatic or semiautomatic procedures must be developed to handle the initial processing of this material. Unless such help is provided there will be an unreasonable delay in the processing of the document prior to its distribution to the interested user.

Content analysis, be it done by humans or by machines, is a complex task involving the analysis of meaning, a relatively uncharted area. However, the pioneering work of Luhn [5] has shown that a statistical analysis of the words in the documents will provide some clues as to its content. For example, a document that contains the words "boys", "girls", "teacher", "school", "arithmetic", "reading", etc., probably deals with education. Luhn wrote of the process of communicating notions by means of words, and he suggested that, "the more two representations agreed in given elements and their distribution, the higher would be the probability of their representing similar information."

Maron [6] applied a formalized statistical approach to the problem of automatic indexing which involved ". . . (1) the determination of certain probability relationships between individual content-bearing words and subject categories, and (2) the use of these relationships to predict the category to which a document containing the word belongs." Using selected individual words in a document as clues, the computer was able to predict into which one of a number of predetermined subject categories the document most probably belongs. Borko [2] in a previous study demonstrated that the classification categories themselves could be derived by means of factor analysis.

The present research is based upon these earlier studies, and the experiment is designed to demonstrate the relationship of the classification system and the procedures for automatic document classification. It is our thesis that if it were possible to derive a set of categories which would provide a best possible description of a domain of documents the task of classification would be simple, and in fact could be done automatically. To test this hypothesis it is necessary to:

(1) construct an empirically based mathematically derived classification system,
(2) devise a set of procedures by which documents can be automatically classified into these categories, and
(3) determine the accuracy of the classification by comparison to a criteria.

There are a number of assumptions implied by the above statements which should be made explicit. The assumption that it is possible to derive an empirically based classification system has been substantiated [2]. However, it has not yet been proved that a classification system so derived is the best possible classification system for a given set of documents. This experiment will be testing the hypothesis that a classification system derived by factor analysis provides a sound basis for automatic document classification and would result in more accurate classifications than those achieved by Maron in his experiment [6].

2. Methodology

2.1 Selection of the Data

In his study, Maron [6] selected abstracts of computer literature as a suitable collection of documents on which to carry out his research on automatic indexing. These abstracts had been published in the *IRE Transactions on Electronic Computers*, Vol. EC-8 [1]. By selecting for our research the same corpus of documents that Maron used, we are provided with an opportunity to compare classification categories as well as automatic indexing procedures. Consequently, this body of data was chosen for further study.

In keeping with Maron's basic research design, the 405 abstracts of computer literature were divided into two groups. Group 1 consisted of the 260 abstracts which were published in the March and June issues of the 1950 *IRE Transactions on Electronic Computers*. This was designated as the Experimental Group. The classification system was derived by an analysis of the documents in the Experimental Group as were the statistical techniques for automatic indexing. Group 2 contained 145 abstracts; this was the Validation Group. It was put aside until after all the statistical procedures were worked out; these techniques were then applied to the documents in Group 2 in order to test the validity of the procedures.

2.2 Selection of Index Terms

In keeping with the notion that the new experiment should be as close as possible to Maron's original research, so that the results could be meaningfully compared, we decided to use the 90 clue words which Maron had selected. It is important to note that Maron selected these words in such a manner that they would be good predictors of his 32 classification categories. It was known in advance that the classification categories derived through factor analysis would not, in all probability, be the same as the categories which Maron derived on the basis of a logical or intuitive analysis of the documents. In fact, as will be shown, the classification systems were different. Nevertheless, it was decided to use Maron's clue words as index terms because one of the assumptions underlying the factor analysis technique is that the method is relatively independent of the words used provided that the words are representative. This assumption has never been adequately tested, and it is a point to which we will return in the discussion of results of the study.

The 90 index terms are listed in Appendix A.

2.3 Derivation of the Classification Categories

Maron considered the classification system of computer literature used by the IRE to be inadequate in that it was not discriminative enough and had too few categories. Prior to proceeding with his experiment he devised a set of 32 subject categories which he felt were more logically descriptive of the material. Classification categories should be determined by the documents to be classified and by the use and function of the information system. The present research project attempts to derive a classification system which meets the above criterion. The preferred classification system is operationally defined to mean a classification system which would enable one to classify documents (within the confines of that system) with a minimum of effort and a maximum of accuracy. In a similar vein, "minimum of effort" would be defined as a routine procedure which could be performed on a computer, and the standard for "maximum of accuracy" would be either human performance or the counterpart of performance of another semiautomatic system. The application of factor analysis to problems of classification is described in the paper by Borko [2]. Underlying this application are the assumptions that documents can be classified on the basis of words they contain and that documents containing similar sets of words belong to the same category. At the start of the computation, the documents selected for examination, i.e. the 260 abstracts in the Experimental Group, were keypunched. By means of a computer program [7], counts were made of the number of times each of the 90 index terms appeared in each of the documents. These frequency counts were arranged in the form of a data matrix with the index terms on the horizontal axis and the document identifying numbers on the vertical axis. Within each individual cell in the matrix was recorded the number of occurrences of the particular term in the given document. For example, under the word "logic" we have recorded the fact that it appeared two times in document #1, zero times in document #2, etc. Based upon the frequencies in the data matrix, correlation coefficients were computed for each of the 90 index terms correlated with each of the other terms. This resulted in a 90 × 90 correlation matrix. This matrix was then factor analyzed.[1]

The technique of factor analysis is based upon matrix algebra. Its purpose is to reduce the original correlation matrix to a smaller number of factors or eigenvectors. The determination of the number of eigenvectors to extract is based upon some rules of thumb and the judgment of the investigator. In practice, a number of sets, ranging in size from 15 to 32, were extracted, rotated and interpreted. As a result of this analysis, it was determined that the set of 21 orthogonal factors was the most adequate and most meaningful when interpreted as classification categories. The factors were interpreted and named on the basis of the terms with high loadings which appeared on each of the factors. The naming of the factors is a subjective process performed by the experimenter. Some of the titles initially suggested were modified to reflect the experience of subjects who attempted to classify Group 1 documents in these subject categories. Appendix B contains the factor loadings and subject category titles given to factors 7, 11 and 15. Appendix C contains a complete list of the factor names, that is, the interpretations of each of the 21 factors.

2.4 Classification of Abstracts by Humans

Having derived a classification system for computer literature which consists of 21 subject categories, we could now proceed to the next stage of the study and classify all 405 abstracts, Groups 1 and 2, into these categories. The classification of the abstracts is the criterion against which the efficiency of automatic classification will be measured; consequently, the classification must be done as accurately as possible. To insure a high degree of accuracy, the documents were classified by five subjects and the two investigators. While no claim is made that the above procedure resulted in a perfect classification of the abstracts, the final results were sufficiently reliable and accurate so that they could be

1. A discussion of computer aids to factor analysis has been described by Harman [4] and by Fruchter [3]. In this study the calculations were performed on an IBM 7090 using programs available at the System Development Corporation.

used as a criterion by which to evaluate the accuracy of automatic classification.

2.5 Automatic Classification

The initial experiment work was performed exclusively on the documents in the Experimental Group. A classification schedule was established, and procedures for automatic classification were devised, checked and revised. A method was sought which, most importantly, resulted in an accurate classification and, secondly, was to be simple and mechanical so that it could be performed automatically by means of a computer analysis of the data. A predictive function based upon the words in the documents and their factor loadings was developed. Additional trial and error performances evaluated the efficiency of using raw factor scores, normalized factor scores and even some power functions. The final prediction formula was a function of the sum of the products of the normalized factor loadings and the index term.

$$P = f(L_1 \times T_1 + L_2 \times T_2 + \ldots + L_n \times T_n),$$

where $P \equiv$ predicted classification, $L_n \equiv$ normalized factor loading of term n for a given category, and $T_n \equiv$ number of occurrences of the nth term.

After the rules had been tried and found acceptable for the classification of the documents in the Experimental Group, they were applied with no further modification to the Validation Group.

The data available for computer processing include:
(1) the complete abstract of the document
(2) the selected set of 90 index terms (see Appendix A)
(3) the 21 subject categories (see Appendix C)
(4) the factor loadings of each significant term on each of the categories (see Appendix B)
(5) the normalized factor loadings of each significant term on each of the categories (see Appendix B)
The procedural steps for automatically classifying the documents are:
(1) Each document, in machine readable form, is analyzed by the computer. A list of the index terms and their frequencies of occurrence in each document is recorded.
(2) The category, or categories, containing the index term is assigned a value equal to the product of the number of occurrences of the word in the abstract and the normalized factor loading of the word in the category. If more than one index appears in a category, the products are summed.
(3) After each index term has been considered, the category having the highest numerical value is selected as the most probable subject classification for the document in question. (See example in Appendix D.)

All documents in the Experimental Group were classified in accordance with these rules. The documents in the Validation Group were similarly classified.

3. Results

This study was designed to construct an empirically based, mathematically derived classification system for a given body of computer literature and to determine whether the derived subject matter categories would provide an adequate basis for automatic document classification.

3.1 The Classification System

Starting with the set of Maron's 90 index terms (see Appendix A) and applying the mathematical procedures of factor analysis, a classification system for organizing computer literature was derived. All classification systems, whether logically or mathematically derived, must be meaningful. It is the investigators' contention that the empirically derived classification system is a meaningful one. (See Appendix C for a listing of the three classification systems.) It is also contended that use of the mathematically derived classification system facilities automatic document classification by enabling one to apply the procedures outlined in Section 2.5.

3.2 Automatic Document Classification: Experimental Results and Discussions

The results of this portion of the study are discussed in two parts: (1) the classification of the documents in the Experimental Group, and (2) the classification of the documents in the Validation Group. For both groups, the results are compared with those obtained by Maron. It should be pointed out that because we are using fewer categories, 21 as compared with 32, the figures are biased in our favor. To make the results more directly comparable, one could correct for coarse grouping of the data. However, as will be seen, the results are such that they do not warrant this additional sophisticated statistical treatment.

There was one other point of difference between the two studies which may have a bearing upon the results. Whereas both began their experiment with the same set of 90 index terms, the rotation of factors resulted in ten terms which did not have significant loadings on any of the 21 factors. Therefore, only 80 terms were usable for automatically classifying documents in this experiment.

As is indicated by the figures in the table, Maron's technique was superior in classifying the documents in the Experimental Group. The surprising point is not that Maron did so well, but that the factor technique did so poorly when working with the specific body of data on which the classification system and the factor loadings were derived. A possible explanation is that the

3.2.1 Experimental Results: Group 1, Experimental

	Maron	Borko
Total number of documents in Group 1	260	260
Number of documents with no clue words	12	17
Errors preventing automatic classification	1	0
Number of documents available for automatic classification	247	243
Number of documents correctly classified	209	154
Percent correct classification	84.6%	63.4%

factor-analytic method is a generalizing technique designed to deal with common properties and not with the specific variances found in a population sample. In contrast, Marion's technique capitalizes on the specific variance in the sample and, therefore, as we shall see, does far better in the automatic classification of the documents in Group 1 than for Group 2.

3.2.2 Experimental Results: Group 2, Validation[2]

	Maron	Borko
Total number of documents in Group 2	145	145
Number of documents with no clue words	20	16
Number of documents with one or more clue words	125	129
Number of documents correctly classified	—	60
Percent correct classification	—	46.5%
Number of documents with two or more clue words	85	90
Number of documents correctly classified	44	44
Percent correct classification	51.8%	48.9%

For emphasis, we repeat that in neither Maron's study nor the present one were the documents in the Validation Group used to determine any of the automatic classification procedures. All of the prior statistics were accumulated from an analysis of the documents in Group 1. This includes the selection of the index terms, the derivation of the classification schedule, and the methods for automatic classification. Group 2 is a new set of documents upon which the techniques developed in the course of analyzing the documents in Group 1 are to be tested. The automatic classification of the documents in Group 2, therefore, provides a significant test of the prediction schema. This holds true for both studies.

The results are strikingly similar. Both studies correctly classified exactly 44 documents. The percentage figures differ slightly because of a difference in the base number. It would have been of some interest to know if they were the same 44 documents, but Maron's data are not available. Even if the data were available, the information

2. There is a discrepancy in some of the figures used in these two experiments. Unfortunately, Maron no longer has his original work sheets available, and so we were unable to resolve the differences. However, the discrepancies are minor and they do not detract from the results.

would be of little practical value because the classification categories are different.

In interpreting the results, it should be remembered that while the absolute numbers are the same, the overall performance of Maron's system is somewhat superior, for he had the more difficult task of classifying into a larger number of categories. Maron makes the statement that ". . . the more clue words in a document, the better the automatic indexing." In contrast, a prediction technique based upon the factor loadings appears to have little dependence on the number of clue words in the article. That is to say, the number of documents containing one or two clue words were classified with almost the same degree of accuracy as those containing a larger number. This makes sense when one realizes that factor analysis is a generalizing technique designed to minimize the specific variance of the individual words. As a result, a method of automatic document classification based upon factor loadings enables one to classify documents containing a minimum of index terms.

4. Conclusions

In Maron's pioneering paper on automatic indexing, he demonstrated that it was possible to have a properly programmed computer "read" a set of documents, separate out those which could not be automatically classified and then correctly classify approximately 50 percent of the remaining documents according to subject category. The present study, using different methods, arrived at similar conclusions, thus demonstrating once again that automatic document classification is possible.

In addition, the present study tried to improve the accuracy of prediction. It was our contention that had a more optimal set of classification categories been used, together with a prediction formula based upon the derivation of these categories, the percentage of correct predictions would have increased. The experimental results do not bear out this prediction. Why? With a clarity of perception made possible only by hindsight, it can be seen that the experimental design confounded two hypotheses which should have been tested separately. One hypothesis states that factor analysis can be used to derive a set of classification categories which best describes a given set of documents. The second hypothesis states that a prediction formula based upon the derivation of these categories, i.e. factor scores, would result in a high percentage of correct classifications. In the study just reported, both hypotheses were tested at the same time. We derived the classification system, and we automatically classified the documents by our formula. Had the results been more strikingly positive, this more efficient experimental design would have been justified. Since our results show no improvement over Maron's we want to determine whether this is because the mathematically derived categories are not optimum or because the prediction equation based on the factor loadings is not as discriminating as the formula used by Maron. To make this determination two new experiments have been designed.

In the first of these experiments, we assume that the mathematically derived set of classification categories used in the study just reported was, in fact, optimum, but that the method of predicting correct document classification was not as good as Maron's prediction equations. To test this hypothesis, we will start with the derived schedule of 21 classification categories and select a new set of clue words in the manner suggested by Maron; then we will use Maron's prediction equation for automatic classification. If our method of automatic classification was at fault, this new experiment should result in improved automatic prediction.

In the second experiment, we assume that the initially derived set of classification categories for computer literature was not optimum. This assumption is based on the fact that the index terms used were not derived on a frequency basis, such as is normally the case in factor analysis studies. To test this hypothesis, a new classification system will be derived based upon other index terms. The documents of Groups 1 and 2 will be classified into the new categories, and the two different procedures for automatic document classification tested and compared.

It is anticipated that these additional experiments will enable us to further improve our methods for automatic document classification.

5. Concluding Remarks

At this point the reader could reasonably ask why we do not do the suggested experiments before publishing these results. In fact, it would be unreasonable not to raise this question, and so it should be answered. Our prime motive is to provide a note of caution to all researchers interested in the classification problem and in the application of factor analysis. The response to our previous efforts in this area have been gratifying — almost enthusiastic — and we feel that as a result of our more recent experiences more caution, perhaps even skepticism, is necessary. Also, it is our belief that experiments that are not completely successful can still contribute to our knowledge.

This experiment has, by applying the method to a new set of data, verified the usefulness of factor analysis as a technique for deriving classification categories. The experiment has also shown that automatic document classification is possible; indeed, by verifying Maron's results, additional supporting evidence was provided. However, there is a large gap between the demonstration of experimental possibilities and their practical applications. Considerably more work must be done to refine the methods and the accuracy of automatic classification procedures. We will be continuing our efforts in this area of research.

Appendix A. List of Index Terms

1.	abacus	23.	decoder	46.	matrix	69.	scientific
2.	adder	24.	definition	47.	mechanical	70.	section
3.	analog	25.	delays	48.	mechanisms	71.	shift
4.	arithmetic	26.	differential	49.	memory	72.	shuttle
5.	average	27.	diffusion	50.	monte (carlo)	73.	side
6.	barium	28.	division	51.	multiplication	74.	simulation
7.	boolean	29.	element	52.	network	75.	solution
8.	bound	30.	elements	53.	networks	76.	speech
9.	carry	31.	equation	54.	numbers	77.	square
10.	character	32.	equations	55.	office	78.	stage
11.	characters	33.	error	56.	parity	79.	storage
12.	chess	34.	expressions	57.	plane	80.	switching
13.	circuit	35.	fields	58.	printed	81.	synthesis
14.	circuits	36.	file	59.	process	82.	tape
15.	code	37.	films	60.	processing	83.	traffic
16.	coding	38.	function	61.	program	84.	transistor
17.	communica-	39.	functions	62.	programming	85.	transistors
	tions	40.	generator	63.	programs	86.	translation
18.	complexity	41.	information	64.	pseudo-random	87.	transmission
19.	compressions	42.	language	65.	pulse	88.	UNCOL
20.	control	43.	library	66.	randomness	89.	unit
21.	conversion	44.	logic	67.	recording	90.	wire
22.	counter	45.	magnetic	68.	register		

Appendix B. List of Subject Categories

Term No.	Word	Factor Loading	Normalized Factor Loadings
Factor No. 7. Mathematics—Arithmetic Computations			
5	average	.8784	.277
51	multiplication	.8091	.255
59	process	.7058	.222
28	division	.5610	.177
32	equations	.2187	.069
			1.000
Factor No. 11. Cybernetics—Intelligent Mechanisms & Processes			
48	mechanism	.9806	.405
70	section	.9549	.395
59	process	.2688	.111
12	chess	.2150	.089
			1.000
Factor No. 15. Equipment—Magnetic Film Memory Devices			
34	magnetic	.6442	.201
49	memory	.6313	.197
37	films	.5287	.165
79	storage	.4809	.150
67	recording	.3465	.108
29	element	.3307	.203
30	elements	.2412	.076
			1.000

Appendix C. List of Subject Categories: Derived by Factor Analysis

Factor Number   Factor Name

MATHEMATICS:
    7   Arithmetic Computations
    1   Differential and Integral Equations, Systems of Equations
  13   Random Number Generation and Random Samples
    8   Code Compression and Conversion
  18   Boolean Algebra and Matrices

EQUIPMENT:
  10   Parity Checking; Problems of Logical Complexity
  12   Logical Circuitry and Design
    3   Pulse Counters, Arithmetic Units, Components & Circuits
    6   Shift Registers and Decoders
  15   Memory and Storage Devices
    5   Character Readers and Techniques
  14   Digital and Analog Control Systems, Analog Computers, Function Generators
  16   Data Transmission
    4   Switching Networks

APPLICATION:
    2   Industrial Material Movement Simulation Studies
    9   Programming Languages & Auto Codes, Linear Programming
  17   File & Data-Processing Systems; Magnetic and Paper Tape; Input, Output, and Data Conversion
  11   Cybernetics, Intelligent Mechanisms
  19   Speech & System Simulation Studies
  20   Information Processing, Storage & Retrieval
  21   Computers and Programs Applied to Scientific and Engineering Problems; Mechanical Translation

Appendix C'. List of Subject Categories: Maron

1. Logical design and organization of digital computers
2. Digital data transmission systems
3. Information theory
4. Intelligent machines and programs
5. Number theory
6. Cybernetics
7. Pattern recognition techniques
8. Digital computer storage devices
9. Language translation and information retrieval
10. Digital counters and registers
11. Error control techniques
12. Number systems and arithmetic algorithms
13. Arithmetic units
14. Digital logical circuitry
15. Analog circuits and subsystems
16. Digital switching components
17. Physical characteristics of switching and memory materials
18. Automatic control and servomechanisms
19. Input-output devices
20. Analog-to-digital conversion devices
21. Analog system descriptions
22. Business applications of digital computers
23. Scientific and mathematical applications of digital computers
24. Real-time control system applications of digital computers
25. Digital computer programming
26. Applications and theory of analog computers
27. Simulation applications of computers
28. Glossaries, terminology, history and surveys

29. Numerical analysis
30. Boolean algebra
31. Switching theory
32. Combined analog-digital systems and digital-differential analyzers

Appendix C″. List of Subject Categories: IRE

A. Equipment
  1. Theoretical Design
  2. Components and Circuits
  3. Subsystems
  4. Digital Computers
  5. Analog Computers
B. Systems
  1. Theoretical Design
  2. Descriptions
  3. Applications
  4. Testing
C. Automata
  1. Natural
  2. Artificial
D. Programs
  1. Automatic Programming, Digital
     Computers
  2. Applications, Digital Computers
  3. Techniques, Digital Computers
  4. Testing, Digital Computers
  5. Applications, Analog Computers
E. Mathematics—Logic
  1. Theoretical Mathematics
  2. Symbolic Logic
     Boolean Algebra, Number Systems
  3. Numerical Analysis
  4. Theoretical Linguistics
  5. Information Theory
  6. Linear Programming
F. Personnel
G. Bibliographies
H. Biographies
I. Standards
J. Summaries and Reviews

Appendix D

ABSTRACT # 42

Word Number	Word	Frequency
3	analog	1
16	coding	1
21	conversion	2
86	translation	1

Word Number	Frequency	1	Categories 14	8	16	21
3	1	.0773	.1363			
16	1			.2408	.1259	
21	2			.1211		
86	1					.3325
Sum of Products		.0773	.1364	.4830	.1259	.3325

Each entry in the row labeled "Sum of Products" is the sum of the normalized factor loadings of each word contributing to that category times the frequency of appearance of the word in the abstract.

The category with the greatest total is, in this case, category 8 with a total of .4830 (.2408 from word 16 plus 2 times .1211 from word 21). Thus, Abstract No. 42 is classified in category 8.

References

1. Institute Radio Engineers, 1959. Abstracts of current computer literature. *IRE Trans. EC-8*, Nos. 1, 2 and 3.
2. Borko, H. 1962. The construction of an empirically based mathematically derived classification system. Proc. Spring Joint Comput. Conf. **21,** 279–289.
3. Fruchter, B., and Jennings, E., 1962. Factor analysis # 1. In H. Borko (Ed.), *Computer Applications in the Behavioral Sciences,* Prentice-Hall, Englewood Cliffs, N.J.
4. Harman, H. H., 1947. *Modern Factor Analysis.* University of Chicago Press, Chicago Ill.
5. Luhn, H. P. 1957. A statistical approach to mechanized encoding and searching of literary information. *IBM J. Res. Dev. 1,* 309–317.
6. Maron, M. E. 1961. Automatic indexing: an experimental inquiry. *J. ACM 8,* 407–417.
7. Olney, J. C. 1960. FEAT, an inventory program for information retrieval. FN-4018, System Development Corp., Santa Monica, Calif.

37 Studies in Information Storage and Retrieval: On the Use of Godel Indices in Coding

R. CREIGHTON BUCK
American Documentation
Vol. 12, No. 3, July, 1961

1 Introduction

During the past eighteen years, *Mathematical Reviews* has acquired an extensive body of detailed information dealing with the mathematical literature. Most of this is presently available in the form of published abstracts or reviews, with or without value judgments on the contents. As in most fields of research, it is becoming increasingly difficult to make efficient use of such information because of the rapid increase in the general level of activity.

Recently, there has been some discussion of the possible use of mechanical or electronic means to assist the mathematical community in the time-consuming but necessary labor of literature search. This is also closely tied in with the present system of mathematical publication, and the use of referees. At the moment, the proposal to prepare a cumulative subject index of *Mathematical Reviews,* extended backward perhaps to 1930 or 1935 with the material from the *Zentralblatt,* has been shelved; work has been started, however, on a cumulative author index.

In other fields, notably chemistry, the use of mechanical storage and retrieval systems for specific document collections has grown, and seems to be meeting with general success. These have many special features not present in the mathematical area. Moreover, their information needs are seldom as specific or their subject area as broad as those in mathematics. Finally, the number of documents involved in these collections is comparatively small, whereas we have at present approximately 70,000 papers reviewed and must plan for a system to accommodate perhaps 150,000. There are many reasons, then, to believe that it will not be possible to devise a system which will better serve the entire community of mathematicians than the present one; it has been suggested that we formalize the present system and offer subsidy to a small group of mathematical scholars who will themselves serve as the storage and retrieval system, responding to inquiries with

This is work done at the Mathematics Research Center, United States Army, under contract DA-11-022-ORD-2059.

appropriate references in the published literature. Each of these specialists may wish to have assistance from a specialized document file, which in turn may be used in conjunction with a mechanical (or electronic) retrieval system.

Although I myself feel that this is the solution which we might ultimately adopt, it seems desirable to study the entire problem to see where the difficulties lie. The results obtained will be of value in dealing with the smaller, more specialized collections, and may be of interest to documentalists in general.

The present note consists of two parts. In the first, we discuss some of the general aspects of the storage and retrieval problem to serve as orientation and background. In the second part, we discuss the more technical problem of the design of coding systems suitable for machine use.

I wish to acknowledge helpful discussions on this general subject with many individuals; let me single out particularly Preston Hammer of Wisconsin, Jack Herriot of Stanford, Van Quine of Harvard, Clifford Maloney of the Department of the Army, and Dr. Nowlan of I.B.M., San Jose.

2 Taxonomy

The central problem in the design of a storage and retrieval system is the construction of an appropriate coding system for the classification of documents. Among other things, it should reflect to some degree the inherent taxonomy of the subject being classified. As a crude illustration of this, the simplicity of the classification of chemical compounds by structural formula lies behind the success of the systems that have been adopted in the chemical field. Accordingly, one does not expect such a system to succeed except where there is some degree of homogeneity in the subject matter; a general library covering many different fields has too much diversity of structure to permit efficient use of the types of retrieval systems currently being studied.

Mathematics has been suggested as a field which is suitable for the type of classification schemes that have been used elsewhere, and one in which worthwhile experimentation could be carried out. Since the classification scheme is one that must take account of innovations and changes in the terminology and even the direction of mathematical research, it is almost certain that the classification scheme represented by the present subject index of *Mathematical Reviews* is unsuitable. Indeed, one notes that it has already been necessary to abandon certain subject headings, and adopt new ones such as "topological algebraic structure" to meet current needs. Finally, the greatest barrier to the adoption of such a system is the matter of cost and time. With the present body of some 70,000 documents, a large part of the initial cost will go toward the re-examination and classification of each of these papers by a person who is himself highly trained and who is qualified to determine its subject classification accurately. It is therefore of the utmost importance to design a classification and coding system for mathematical papers which, as suggested above, mimics the inherent structure of mathematics, rather than an artificial system of historic divisions and subdivisions.

All classification schemes must, of necessity, have much in common. Let us assume that we are concerned with a certain collection of documents. Since they can be identified by serial number (e.g. acquisition number), we can represent this collection as a finite set of integers

$$S = \{ 1, 2, \ldots, N \}$$

In the case of *Mathematical Reviews*, N is of the order of 10^5; for a smaller specialized collection (e.g. differential equation theory) N might be on the order of 10^3. We also have a somewhat ill-defined and chaotic set Σ, together with a mapping $x \to \bar{x}$ from S into Σ. We interpret $\bar{x}$ as the contents or subject matter of document x. We do not assume that this mapping is one-to-one.

The general retrieval problem can now be stated as follows: *How can we determine all documents* x *such that* $\bar{x}$ *deals with some aspect of a specific subject* ω? The key phrase is "deals with." To give meaning to this, it is evident that one must first introduce into Σ some type of pseudo topology in terms of which we can speak of two subjects α and β in Σ as being "near" or "related."

The most general way to achieve this is to define a sequence of coverings or partitions of Σ

$$\left\{ \sigma_i^{(1)} \right\}_{i=1}^{k_1} , \qquad \left\{ \sigma_i^{(2)} \right\}_{i=1}^{k_2} , \ldots$$

where each covering $\left\{ \sigma_i^{(j)} \right\}_{i=1}^{k_j}$ is a collection of sets having Σ for their union, and such that each set is a subset of one of the sets in the preceding covering. The content of each document x can be described or "located" within Σ by indicating the set in each successive covering that contains $\bar{x}$. This description can be given in a numerical form by listing in a sequence the indices of the appropriate sets. We thus arrive at a sequence valued function f defined on S with

$$f(x) = \langle a_1, a_2, a_3, \ldots \rangle$$

whenever $\bar{x}$ lies in each of the nested sequence of sets

$$\sigma_{a_1}^{(1)} \supset \sigma_{a_2}^{(2)} \supset \sigma_{a_3}^{(3)} \supset \ldots$$

Note that the coordinates a_j obey $1 \leqq a_j \leqq k_j$ and that k_j will increase with j.

With this as the taxonomy on Σ, the retrieval problem takes on this form: from an inquiry, one determines a pair of integers $\langle j, w \rangle$ specifying a depth j (or fineness) of covering, and the index w of one of the sets in this covering, and the query is satisfied by all documents x with $\bar{x}$ in the set $\sigma_w^{(j)}$.

If this system is translated into the language more familiar to documentalists, the taxonomy described above is an abstract subject index, and the classification code f is an abstract decimal system.

Certain special "covering taxonomies" can be generated in a simple way. We start with a collection

$$\{ C_1, C_2, \ldots, C_r \}$$

of subsets of Σ, and form all the sets that can be obtained from these by multiple intersections. The basic sets C_j are chosen to be not disjoint from each other, so that the resulting covering of Σ is as fine as possible. This is the abstract version of a *concept cluster* or "Uniterm" system. The content of a document x is described by listing the indices of the basic sets C_j to which $\bar{x}$ belongs. This leads to a simple sequence valued coding function g, with

$$g(x) = \langle b_1, b_2, \ldots, b_m \rangle \qquad b_j < b_{j+1}$$

whenever

$$\bar{x} \ \varepsilon \ C_{b_1} \frown C_{b_2} \frown \ldots \frown C_{b_m}$$

In this system, a query takes the form of asking for all documents treating a specific concept cluster. In terms of the code g, this means that we want all documents x such that $g(x)$ contains a specific sequence $\langle w_1, w_2, \ldots, w_q \rangle$ as a *subsequence*. In the next section, we shall discuss another method of recording a concept cluster describing the contents of a document, and correspondingly, an alternate procedure for recovering the document in answer to an inquiry; to this we have given the name Gödel indices, and we defer its description until then.

Assume then that a taxonomy on Σ has been selected, along with a particular code in which the classification of a document can be recorded, or the nature of an inquiry stated. There remains the problem of finding all documents $x \ \varepsilon \ S$ which treat a topic ω. The decision to accept or reject a document x is made by a comparison between the coded description of the contents of x, and the coded form of the inquiry. The nature of this comparison is determined, of course, by the nature of the code. Since we are dealing with machines designed to handle numerical data, we may assume that any code used will be a function F defined on S (or more precisely, determined by the selected taxonomy) whose values are sequences of integers:

$$F(x) = <c_1, c_2, c_3, \ldots>$$

We may also assume that there is an upper bound to the index of the last non-zero entry. The coded form of a query will also be a sequence $<w_1, w_2, w_3, \ldots>$, and document x will be rejected unless each entry c_j of $F(x)$ bears a specified relationship to the corresponding entry w_j. This relationship could, for example, be merely one of size; we might ask for $c_j \geqq w_j$ for all j. Since the entries are integers, one could ask for divisibility relations, or other criteria more complicated to apply. It might also be desirable to accept also documents x whose coded descriptions satisfy the acceptance criterion for all but one, or all but k, entries. This can be reduced to the preceding, however, by introducing additional query sequences w, obtained by altering in turn each subset of k entries.

The direct approach would be to scan the entire collection of documents, item by item, for each $x \ \varepsilon \ S$, make the appropriate test, and accept or reject x. With the use of wider tapes, increased transport speeds, and faster reading speed, it may be possible to employ this approach with relatively large document collections. At the moment it would seem quite feasible to store the serial numbers and contents descriptions of about 10^5 documents on a full-length standard magnetic tape at the rate of about three documents per inch, allowing a contents description code of at most 60 decimal characters; this could then be completely scanned for a specific inquiry in less than ten minutes. The high cost of machine time would make it expedient to wait until there was a supply of inquiries, and then to scan the complete tape for all inquiries at the same time.

Alternatively, either as a result of the original classification process, or a number of separate passes of the master tape, one might start with a collection of *partial solutions*. For definiteness, suppose that the acceptance criterion for a document with code $<c_1, c_2, \ldots, c_r>$ and inquiry code $<w_1, w_2, \ldots, w_r>$ is that $c_j \geqq w_j$ for all j. Let us assume that each individual entry may take on only the values 1, 2, 3. The partial solutions will consist of $2r$ subsets of S, namely:

all x with $<c_1, \ldots, c_r> \geqq <2, 1, 1, 1, \ldots, 1>$
all x with $<c_1, \ldots, c_r> \geqq <3, 1, 1, 1, \ldots, 1>$
all x with $<c_1, \ldots, c_r> \geqq <1, 2, 1, 1, \ldots, 1>$
etc.

For convenience in referring to these, denote these sets by W_1', W_1'', W_2', etc. Then a specific inquiry can be answered without searching through the complete document file, but may instead be obtained by forming the appropriate intersections of these sets W_j. For example, if the inquiry code is $<2, 3, 1, 2, 3, 1, 1, 1, \ldots>$, then the sought-for documents are simply those in the set

$$W_1' \frown W_2'' \frown W_4' \frown W_5''$$

The speed with which an intersection of sets can be obtained on a machine depends roughly upon the total number of elements in all the sets. The routine used depends of course upon the manner in which the sets are represented. Assuming first that we have a relatively small number of relatively small subsets of a rather large set, then two simple procedures come to mind. For simplicity, let us suppose that each set is stored as a deck of cards bearing the serial numbers of the members of that set. We then store deck 1 in the machine, and run deck 2 through, comparing each of its members with the members of deck 1 on a less-or-equal basis; since the decks can be initially arranged in order of increasing serial number, we stop the comparison routine whenever we reach a number in deck 1 larger than the one we are trying to match. Those numbers in deck 1 that had no match are dropped, and the remainder compared in the same way with those in deck 3, and so on. At the end, the machine carries only the numbers common to all the sets. The second procedure is even simpler; stack the separate decks together, and arrange the whole pile in order of increasing serial number. Duplicate cards will drop together and the final arrangement will have blocks of r duplicates for each number that belongs to all of the r sets. Various methods can be used to pick out these blocks, and thus obtain the desired set intersection.

Of course, if the entire set S from which the subsets are chosen is itself relatively small, then some variant of direct coincidence scanning can be used to obtain the intersection of the sets. The simple "peek-a-boo" system is one example of this. Here, the individual members of the "universal" set S have each an assigned position on a large stencil. Each of the sets is then represented by such a stencil with holes punched at the appropriate locations, corresponding to the members of that set. The coincidence scanning is effected by superimposing the stencils and noting the holes that are common to all the stencils. This particular form of the system is limited to a set S with about 10^4 members. In another variant, the stencils are replaced by tapes; each member of S again has an assigned location on a tape, and the given subsets are represented by tapes with indicators (holes, pulses, etc.) at the locations belonging to its members. The tapes are then run through separate readers, stepping in unison, with the printer set to respond only when a signal appears at the same location on all the tapes. (In passing, we note that this system is well adapted to the modification in which we desire all elements that belong to at least m of the r sets.)

Returning to the retrieval problem, the adoption of one of these procedures allows one to answer specific inquiries without having to search the entire document file each time. If the resulting system is examined, it will be seen that we have constructed from the original coding system a new concept cluster taxonomy, whose basic sets are the partial solution sets W. Let us illustrate this by showing that the original coding function g for a concept cluster taxonomy with basic sets C_1, ..., C_r can be replaced by a different coding function F whose partial solutions, in the sense described above, are precisely the sets C_i. To achieve this, set

$$F(x) = <c_1, c_2, \ldots c_r>$$

where each entry c_i takes only the values 1 or 2, with $c_i = 2$ if and only if the document contents x lies in the set C_i. Thus a concept cluster whose g code was $<2, 3, 7>$ (indicating that we are concerned with the set $C_2 \frown C_3 \frown C_7$) would now be coded as the sequence $<1, 2, 2, 1, 1, 1, 2, 1, 1, \ldots, 1>$. Note that the criterion for acceptance of a document for an inquiry ω with code $<w_1, w_2, \ldots, w_r>$ is indeed that $c_i \geqq w_i$ for all $i = 1, 2, \ldots, r$. It is immediately evident that the partial solution sets for the code F are simply the original sets C_i.

From this discussion, we see that any numerical coding system having the structure of F will permit the construction of partial solutions, and that these in turn correspond to the creation of a secondary taxonomy of the concept cluster variety. The fundamental machine operations can thus be reduced to the formation of set intersections. Whether or not this is preferable to the more direct process of scanning the entire document file depends upon the size of the collection, and the type of machines which are available.

3   Code Construction

This section will be concerned with the specific problem of devising a numerical code function which will serve both to describe and to compare individual concept clusters. Two possible choices have already been mentioned. In the first, the code of a cluster is simply the list of concept indices present in the cluster and recorded in increasing numerical order. The cluster consisting of concepts C_3, C_5, C_6, and C_9 would be indicated by the sequence $<3, 5, 6, 9>$. To determine whether two concept clusters are related by inclusion, one examines their coded descriptions, and asks if the sequence for one is a subsequence of the sequence in the other. For convenience, we retain the letter g to denote this code. The second procedure, for which we used the letter F, gave rise to a sequence-valued code in which the coordinate entries were only allowed to be 1 or 2, with a "2" indicating that the appropriate concept was present in the cluster. If, for example, we are dealing with a total of 15 distinct basic concepts, then the same cluster mentioned above would have the F code

$$<1, 1, 2, 1, 2, 2, 1, 1, 2, 1, 1, 1, 1, 1, 1>$$

One disadvantage of the F code is thus immediately evident. In most systems of the Uniterm or concept cluster variety, there are apt to be several thousand basic concepts (or terms) which enter into clusters; the F code would therefore have code words consisting of several thousand characters, most of which will be a "1", with a few occurrences of "2" scattered among them. On this ground alone, we must reject the F system; a compressed code, with low redundancy, will enable us to store more document descriptions in a given length or volume.

To give us a basis for comparisons, let us suppose that we have a set of 10^3 basic concepts, and that they will occur in clusters of at most 10 (and frequently in clusters of only 4 or 5). The code g will then have symbols that consist of a sequence of at most 10 integers, each of which has at most three digits, ranging from "1" to "999." Inserting needed blanks, this will produce a code word for an individual concept cluster that consists of at most 40 characters. It is a little harder to estimate the expected word length; assuming, for example, that all concepts are equally likely to enter into a cluster, one finds that the expected number of digits per concept is $321/111 = 2.891$, and a 5-concept cluster will be coded by a word with roughly 19 characters. This estimate is maximal, however, for in practice, one assigns lower indices to the concepts that tend to occur more frequently as part of a cluster, which has the effect of reducing the expected word length. The difference will probably be slight, however; it is reasonable to assume that most code words will be from 20 to 35 characters in length.

How can we bring about a greater efficiency? One suggestion that has been widely discussed is that of code contraction, which produces shortened code words at the expense of possible ambiguity and 'false drop out.' A simple example will show the basic idea. We start by replacing the original concept labels by new ones which are themselves sequences, composed of "0" and "1" entries. Since $_{14}C_4 = 1001$, we can obtain enough of these by using sequences each 14 digits long, comprised of 4 occurrences of "1" and 10 occurrences of "0" Thus, a typical label for one of the 10^3 concepts might be 00101100000100. A cluster of concepts is then labeled by a similar sequence which is obtained by coordinate-wise addition of the sequences that label the individual concepts present in the cluster. For example, one might have a 2-concept cluster, whose code is given by

first concept	= 00101100000100
second concept	= 10100001010000
code	= 10201101010100

By this device, we have constructed a coding system for the concept clusters in which each code word is never more than 14 characters long (assuming that we do not have more than 9 coincidences in the labels for the concepts in a cluster). The contraction must of course have been effected by a many-one mapping;

many different clusters will have the same code word. In the example above, there are $(_6C_3)/2 = 10$ different clusters that receive the label 10201101010100. It is the hope of those who advocate the use of this device that most of these extraneous concept clusters will prove in practice to be empty, corresponding to content descriptions that no document will fit. If this is the case, then the occurrence of a few cases of false drop-out will be not too serious a drawback.

Some improvement in this system results if an effort is made to select labels for the basic concepts which avoid some of the overlaps between corresponding co-ordinates. In this way, there will be fewer clusters that have the same associated code word. Unfortunately, one must go to much longer code words to achieve this. With length 14, for example, we can produce only 11 code words (of the total of 1001) that contain four digits "1", with mutual overlaps of one, namely:

11110000000000	10001000001100
00011110000000	01000100001010
10000011100000	00101000000011
01001000110000	00000100100101
00100101010000	00010001001001
	00000010010110

Since we need 10^3 distinct code words, it would be necessary to go to extremely long words, even if we relax somewhat the stringent overlap condition.

Some years ago, Gödel met and solved a somewhat related coding problem in his general approach to con-sistency problems. His device suggests a similar scheme for coding concept clusters which, to the best of my knowledge, has not been exploited. The result-ing code is a simple numerical one, with a specific integer associated with each cluster; to these integer labels, we give the name *Gödel* indices. As before, suppose that we have a collection of r basic concepts, $C_1, C_2, \ldots, C_r$. Then the Gödel index of a concept cluster $C_{b_1} \frown C_{b_2} \frown \ldots \frown C_{b_m}$ is defined to be

$$N = p_{b_1} p_{b_2} \cdots p_{b_m}$$

where p_n is the n-th prime number. The key to the success of this code lies in the fact that the inclusion relationship between concept clusters can be replaced by the divisor relation between their Gödel indices.

Let us examine how this would be used in a retrieval situation. We may suppose that we have written on a tape the succession of document serial numbers x, each followed by its Gödel index $G(x)$. An inquiry is trans-lated into a particular subject in the taxonomy, and receives its own Gödel index q. We want all docu-ments x such that x treats at least the subject of the inquiry; this means merely that q must divide $G(x)$, with no remainder. We therefore scan the entire tape, and at each entry, test to see if q divides the listed index $G(x)$.

The speed and efficiency of this procedure depends chiefly upon the transport and reading speed of the tape, and the space which will be required for a Gödel index. There is some reason to believe that this system will be a decided improvement over the original sequence-valued code g with which we opened this sec-tion. The reason for this is twofold. First, the product of integers takes less storage room than does the list of factors; using "B" to denote a blank, compare 13B23B67 with 2033. Secondly, the use of the arith-metical operation of division is simpler than the match-ing process which is necessary in the case of the g code, for some machines.

Unfortunately, there is a second factor at work which tends to lengthen the code words. The n-th prime number, p_n, is somewhat larger than $n \log n$, so that the product $\prod\limits_{j=1}^{m} p_{b_j}$ can be expected to exceed $\prod\limits_{j=1}^{m} b_j \prod\limits_{j=1}^{m} \log b_j$; although $\prod\limits_{j=1}^{m} b_j$ takes less space to record than does the list of factors $b_1, \ldots, b_m$ the additional $\prod\limits_{j=1}^{m} \log b_j$ tends to decrease this advantage. For ex-ample, if $<b_1, b_2, b_3, \ldots, b_m> = <10, 15, 20, 80>$, then its g code is 10B15B20B80, using 11 characters, while the Gödel code is simply the number $39580151 = (29)(47)(71)(409)$ using only 8 characters. It is perhaps reasonable to expect a saving of 20 per cent in the space needed for code characters if Gödel indices are used for coding concept clusters.

There is also another advantage in the adoption of this method of coding clusters. One often wishes to indicate that certain concepts in a cluster are the domi-nant interest in the document being classified, whereas certain others, although present, are of minor concern. When this is the case, the Gödel index system will per-mit one to show this easily; one need only attach exponents to the corresponding primes to show the degree of intensity which that concept bears. This per-mits one to scan the document file for those documents that treat certain concepts with a prescribed degree of intensity. Another way in which the same device can be used to advantage is as an indication of specializa-tion. One concept C_1 may be itself rather broad, but may be the first in a chain of more specialized concepts, each a specialization of the preceding. If the first has the Gödel index 2, then the later ones can be coded as 2^2, 2^3, etc.

One unfortunate aspect of the use of Gödel indices is the relative intractability of the primes. They are difficult to generate, analytically, and are rather erratic in their distribution. At the expense of sacrificing the uniqueness of the coding, and with a compensating gain in ease of use and brevity of code length, another pro-cedure might be used. Since it differs from the previ-ous system in certain essential ways, a new name is desirable; I have chosen to adopt the designation "Landau indices" for reasons that are possibly self-evident.

Let us examine the essential structure of the Gödel index system. We see at once that the key lies in the fact that the positive integers under multiplication form a semigroup with a set of generators which are the primes. Factorization into these is unique, and an integer q cannot divide an integer s unless the prime factors of q are also present in the prime factorization of s. The positive integers, under multiplication, have certain sub-semigroups. If N is any integer, then the set $\{N + 1, 2N + 1, 3N + 1, \text{etc.}\}$ is such. We could apply a sieve procedure to select the "primes" in this semigroup—those integers which cannot be expressed as a product of integers in the semigroup. We will get, of course, all the ordinary prime numbers which happen to belong to the semigroup, but we will also get other numbers. For example, with $N = 6$, the semigroup is

7 , 13 , 19 25 31 37 43 49 55 61 67

73 79 85 91 97 103 109 115 121

127 133 139 145 . . .

and among those listed, only the three that are underlined *fail* to be pseudo primes in the system. In this semigroup, however, factorization into pseudo primes is not unique; 3025 can be expressed either as $(25)(121)$ or as $(55)(55)$, both prime decompositions. If we were to use the pseudo primes in such a semigroup to replace the ordinary primes in the Gödel code, we would gain in conciseness (due to the somewhat slower rate of growth of the pseudo primes) but we would again meet the possibility of ambiguity. The code number q of an inquiry may arise as the product of a specific set of pseudo primes, but q may divide the code index s of some document which does not in fact treat the concept cluster of the inquiry; this would happen, for example, if s arises as a product of certain pseudo primes which do not happen to be among those in the specific prime factorization of q.

Since uniqueness must therefore be sacrificed in any case, the restriction to the use of only the pseudo primes in the semigroup is not so vital. One might therefore consider the construction of Gödel type codes for concept clusters using *all* the elements in the semigroup, whether they be "primes" or not. With $N = 1$, when the semigroup becomes the set of consecutive integers

$$\{2, 3, 4, 5, 6, 7, \ldots\},$$

this leads to much ambiguity. There are too many composites, and there is too much false drop-out, in response to an inquiry. However, with $N = 6$, or 30, the composites are rather sparse, and the likelihood of false drop-out from this cause does not seem large. Taking $N = 6$, the system would work as follows: A concept cluster with indices $b_1, b_2, \ldots, b_m$ would receive the code

$$S = (6 b_1 + 1) (6 b_2 + 1) \ldots (6 b_m + 1).$$

As before, if an inquiry has code number q, we would scan the file looking for documents whose code numbers are multiples of q, and be assured that we will obtain all relevant documents, together with a small number of quite unrelated documents arising because of the composite structure in the semigroup of some of the numbers $6b + 1$, and the absence of unique factorization.

It is also possible to make another essential simplification which has the effect of decreasing the length of the code words used; the resulting system will be called the Landau code. Observe first that the function H, defined by $H(t) = 6t + 1$, maps the set $I = \{1, 2, 3, \ldots\}$ onto the set $P = \{7, 13, 19, 25 \ldots\}$. H is one to one, but is not an isomorphism of these two sets as multiplicative semigroups, since $H(ab)$ is not in general equal to $H(a)H(b)$. However, being a one-to-one mapping of I onto P, we can carry back the binary operation in P into I to obtain a new multiplication operation there. Denoting it by "$*$", we define it by

$$a*b = H^{-1}\{H(a)H(b)\}$$

which can be explicitly calculated to be

$$a * b = 6ab + a + b.$$

We are therefore assured that the set I is a semigroup under $*$, and that $H(a*b) = H(a)H(b)$, so that H is now an isomorphism between $<I, *>$ and $<P, \cdot>$. We can therefore use the semigroup $<I, *>$ to replace $<P, \cdot>$, and thus obtain a coding function which results in smaller numbers for the same concept clusters. Specifically, the Landau index of the cluster $C_{b_1} \frown C_{b_2} \frown \ldots \frown C_{b_m}$ is to be the integer

$$s = b_1 * b_2 * \ldots * b_m.$$

(The operation $*$ is associative so that this product can be computed either from left to right or in blocks.)

We illustrate this with several examples. The cluster whose g code is 5B10 (indicating the set $C_5 \frown C_{10}$) will have Landau code $315 = (6)(5)(10) + 5 + 10$. The cluster used earlier, whose g code was 10B15B20B80 and whose Gödel code was 39580151, now has the Landau code 53845625. The clusters 4B31 and 9B14 both have Landau code 779. The gain in the Landau code over the Gödel code occurs when larger numbers b_j are involved, for the size of the Landau code is determined by the size of $6 \prod_1^m b_j$, whereas that of the Gödel code word is on the order of $\prod_1^m b_j \log b_j$. As another example, the cluster with g code 50B100B500, using 10 characters, has a Gödel code of 9 characters, but has a Landau code word 90480650 with 8 characters. This is more or less typical. With $10^3 - 1$ concepts, the longest possible g code word will have 39 characters, and the corresponding Landau code word will have 36 characters.

The retrieval procedure for the Landau code has a different routine for testing whether to accept or reject a document. If an inquiry has Landau code q, and a document has Landau code s, then we do not ask if q divides s; rather, we must ask if there is an integer t with $s = q * t$. This can be reduced to ordinary arithmetic operations, for the requirement is equivalent to asking that $(s - q)/(6q + 1)$ be an integer—that is: *does $H(q)$ divide $s - q$?* With this as the testing routine, we can then scan the document tape, with the write-out being the serial numbers of all acceptable documents x.

It is hoped that it will be possible to carry out some experimentation with these Gödel type systems as a further check upon their feasibility. It is the author's belief that they may have certain definite advantages over the g code, and over other coordinate or superposition codes; some of this stems from the fact that in using these codes, one employs the arithmetical capacity of a computer.

G. Bibliographic
Representation

38 Bibliographic Description, Arrangement, and Retrieval

B. C. VICKERY
Journal of Documentation
Vol. 24, No. 1, March, 1968

Description
Retrieval
Filing
Location

A good deal of work is now going on concerned with the development of bibliographic entries for use in computer systems. Both the Library of Congress and the British National Bibliography are working in this field, as well as some Continental national bibliographies, and individual institutions such as the University of Newcastle are developing their own formats. There is some danger that we will soon be faced with a variety of incompatible machine records, even more difficult to use in an integrated way than the existing variety of catalogue formats.

There is an understandable pressure to standardize as soon as possible, but this may well prove even more dangerous if it is carried out too precipitately. It is not just a question of deciding on the best current practice, and all agreeing to use this in computer systems. A machine record is not simply a different physical means of recording a traditional bibliographic entry, for use in a traditional way. The only reason for creating it, in fact, is that the machine offers us the possibility of using it in ways hitherto untried because of their expense. The record becomes wide open to far more flexible manipulation.

Before deciding on a standard format, we must look closely at all the purposes that bibliographic records can be made to serve, given this flexibility of manipulation, and at the forms that they may take in order to serve these purposes. This paper takes a preliminary look at these problems.

1. The Functions of Bibliographic Records

A bibliographic record consists of a set of elements A, B,C,D, etc., where A may be author, B title, C publisher, and so on. The elements can serve four purposes: a, collectively, the elements in a record describe and identify a bibliographic item (book, serial, article, patent, etc.), b, each element can in principle serve as a retrieval key by which records that share a common characteristic can be selected (e.g., all books written by Enid Blyton), c, the symbolic forms in which each element is recorded (letters, numerals) may facilitate clerical arrangement of records into an ordered sequence (e.g., by using alphanumerical filing rules), d, one or more elements can indicate the locations where the item itself is stored.

The traditional bibliographic record is a catalogue entry. This is sometimes almost a narrative description of a book, and even the most stylized entry retains traces of the narrative form, as can be seen from Fig. 1. The entry itself primarily serves purpose a, bibliographic

A — Advanced data processing in the university library, by Louis A. Schultheiss, Don S. Culbertson ₍and₎ Edward M. Heiliger. New York, Scarecrow Press, 1962. — D / F

J — 388 p. illus. 22 cm. — M

V — "Final report of the University Library Information Systems Project of the University of Illinois at Congress Circle, Chicago." — C

L — Includes bibliography. — B

T — 1. Information storage and retrieval systems. I. Illinois. University. University at Congress Circle, Chicago. Library. II. Title. III. Title: Data processing in the library.

S — Z699.S35   025.078   62–10128 rev ‡ — Q

Library of Congress   ₍r62q²40₎ — R

FIG. 1.

description. To it are added various headings serving purpose *b*, the main heading at the top of the entry, and other headings shown in the tracings near the bottom. (The lettering in this figure will be referred to later.)

To design an optimal bibliographic record it is necessary to consider all its functions. Design principles for catalogue entries have largely been developed for each function in isolation. This situation is illustrated by the exsitence until recently of independent codes: for descriptive cataloguing — purpose *a*; for author/title entry, for subject headings — purpose *b*; and filing rules — purpose *c*.

The possibility of manipulating bibliographic records by data processing equipment requires reconsideration of their structure. Fitting them into machine record format must inevitably modify them. So far, modification has been in the direction of retaining the traditional catalogue format but adding extra retrieval keys (see Fig. 2 for the Library of Congress machine-readable catalogue record.[2] The MARC record will be further amplified in 1968). Other modifications have been proposed to facilitate clerical or computer filing.[2] It has not been demonstrated that these modifications produce a record that optimally serves all the purposes listed earlier. The structure of record used by a specialist agency for reports and articles has departed further from traditional catalogue format (Fig. 3).

To design an optimal bibliographic record it will be necessary to determine: the bibliographic elements that should be included in it, to serve the purposes of description, retrieval, filing, and location; the symbolic structure each element needs if it is to serve these purposes; the most efficient ways of assembling records into a master file.

2. Bibliographic Elements

Below I give a list of elements found in bibliographic records. The letters and numbers are inserted only to aid reference. The list is not exhaustive (other elements are to be found in Fig. 3), but does include many items in current cataloguing codes. Illustrations of the elements are indicated by letters in Figs. 1 and 3.

A *Personal name*–
subfields may be —
1. surname
2. forenames or initials
3. dates
4. epithets
5. relator

'relator' includes author, editor, illustrator, annotator, cartographer, commentator, committee chairman, compiler, composer, continuator, contributor, dedicatee, engraver, indexer, librettist, reviser, sponsor, translator, prefacer, publisher, printer, person as subject, pseudonym.

B *Corporate name*
subfields may be —
1. hierarchical divisions of corporate body
2. relator

'relator' includes author, sponsor, publisher, printer, publisher's agent, affiliation of person, facsimile publisher, corporate name as subject.

C *Place name*
subfields may be —
1. hierarchical specification of place
2. relator

'relator' includes place of publication, printing, presentation (e.g. conference), availability (e.g. on sale), place as subject.

D *Title* — with subfield 2, relator
'relator' includes main title, alternative title, subtitle, binder's title, caption title, cover title, half title, running title, translated title, transliterated title, supplied title, series title, abbreviated title (e.g. coden), masthead title, former and subsequent titles (for serials).

E *Related work* (e.g. index, supplement, special number, commentary, concordance, abridgement, continuation, extract, separate, facsimile, revision, translation, dissertation, adaptation, parody).

TYPE OF ENTRY	FORM OF WORK	BIBLIO	ILLUS	MAPS	SUPPLEMENT NUMBER	CONFERENCE OR MEETING	JUVENILE WORK	RECORD INDICATOR
REL SOC OR INST	MONOGRAPH	YES	YES	NONE	NONE	NO	NO	NEW RECORD

LANGUAGE DATA: CLASS	LANG 1	LANG 2	PUBLICATION DATA: KEY	DATE 1	DATE 2	PLACE	NAME	HEIGHT
SINGLE	ENGL		SINGLE	1963	1964	ERROR	PLOU	22 CM

TYPE OF SECONDARY ENTRY: A   S   SERIES: NO   LENGTH OF RECORD - 921

VARIABLE FIELDS:

MAIN ENTRY	10	BRUDERHOF COMMUNITIES.
TITLE STATEMENT	20	EBERHARD ARNOLD; # [A TESTIMONY OF CHURCH-COMMUNITY FROM HIS LIFE AND WRITINGS ON THE EIGHTIETH ANNIVERSARY OF EBERHARD'S BIRTH]
IMPRINT STATEMENT	30	WOODCREST,N.Y. PLOUGH PUB. HOUSE [1963,C1964]
COLLATION STATEMENT	40	XI1; 43 P. ILLUS., PORT. 22 CM.
NOTES	60	PART OF THE MATERIAL WAS FIRST PUBLISHED IN ENGLAND IN 1953 AS THE AUTUMN ISSUE OF THE PLOUGH.
NOTES	60	CONTENTS.---INTRODUCTION.---SONGS AND POEMS.---EBERHARD ARNOLD'S LIFE AND WORK; BY EMMY ARNOLD.--A PERSONAL WORD BY EBERHARD ARNOLD.--EXCERPTS FROM EBERHARD ARNOLD'S LECTURES AND WRITINGS.--EXCERPTS FROM EBERHARD ARNOLD'S LETTERS.--LETTERS FROM FRIENDS [RECOLLECTIONS OF EBERHARD ARNOLD]--BIBLIOGRAPHY (P.38-40)--ADDENDUM: LETTER FROM HERMAN BUDDENSIEG.
SUBJECT TRACING	70	1.ARNOLD, EBERHARD, 1883-1935.
PERS AUTHOR TRACING	71	1.ARNOLD, EBERHARD, 1883-1935.
L.C. CALL NUMBER	90	BX8129.B68A7
DEWEY CLASS. NUMBER	92	922.8743
L.C. CATALOG CARD NO.	94	64-709
DIAGNOSTIC NOTES		FIXED FIELD PLACE MISSING

FIG. 2.

F   *Date* — with subfield 2, relator 'relator' includes publication date, copyright date, cover date, presentation date (e.g. conference or article), duration date (for serial), coverage date.

G   *Edition statement*

H   *Subset statement* (e.g. volume 2, number 4)

J   *Pagination statement*

K   *Illustrations statement* (e.g. illustrations, maps, portraits, diagrams, plates, tables, facsimiles, plans, charts)

L   *Bibliography statement*

M   *Size*

N   *Frequency* (of serial)

P   *Price*

Q   *Book number* (e.g. publisher number, national bibliography number, report number, patent number)

R   *Knowledge number* (e.g. class number)

S   *Location statement* (e.g. call number, holding library)

T   *Subject statement* (e.g. subject headings, descriptors, contents note, abstract)

U   *Language*

V   *Literary form* (e.g. collected works, selected works, single work = monograph, collective work = symposium or conference proceedings, serial, newspaper, annual, biography, correspondence, dictionary, encyclopaedia, tabular data, committee report, patent, standard specification, code, bibliography, history)

W   *Physical form*

X   *Intellectual form* (e.g. teaching text at various levels, popular, experimental study, theoretical study, state of the art survey).

Most of the elements listed are familiar in cataloguing, but a few features need comment. All personal names are grouped together, and the relation of each to the bibliographic item recorded is indicated by a 'relator'. The same is true for corporate names, place names, titles, and dates. Provision is made for the specific statement of language, literary form, physical form, and intellectual form. If the entry in Fig. 1 were reorganized according to the above list, the following record might result:

Personal	— Schultheiss/Louis Avery/–/–/ author
	— Culbertson/Don S./–/–/ author
	— Heiliger/Edward M./–/–/ author
Corporate	— Illinois/University/Library/Information Systems Project/ affiliation
	— Scarecrow Press/ publisher
Place	— New York/publication
	— Chicago/Congress Circle/ affiliation
Title	— Advanced data processing in the university library/main
Date	— 1962/Publication
Pagination	— 388

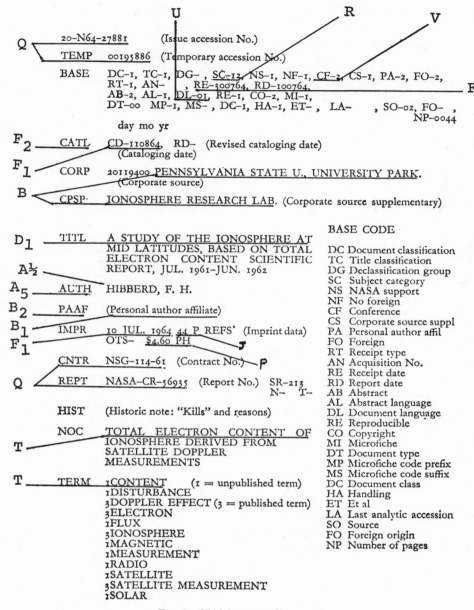

Q 20-N64-27881 (Issue accession No.)
TEMP 00195886 (Temporary accession No.)
BASE DC-1, TC-1, DG- , SC-12, NS-1, NF-1, CF-2, CS-1, PA-2, FO-2,
RT-1, AN- , RE-300764, RD-100764,
AB-2, AL-1, DL-01, RE-1, CO-2, MI-1,
DT-00 MP-1, MS- , DC-1, HA-1, ET- , LA- , SO-02, FO- ,
NP-0044

day mo yr

F₂ CATL CD-110864, RD- (Revised cataloging date)
(Cataloging date)
F₁ CORP 20119400 PENNSYLVANIA STATE U., UNIVERSITY PARK.
(Corporate source)
B CPSP· IONOSPHERE RESEARCH LAB. (Corporate source supplementary)

D₁ TITL A STUDY OF THE IONOSPHERE AT MID LATITUDES, BASED ON TOTAL ELECTRON CONTENT SCIENTIFIC REPORT, JUL. 1961–JUN. 1962
A½
A₅ AUTH HIBBERD, F. H.
B₂ PAAF (Personal author affiliate)
B₁ IMPR 10 JUL. 1964 44 P REFS' (Imprint data)
F₁ OTS- $4.60 PH
CNTR NSG-114-61 (Contract No.)
Q REPT NASA-CR-56935 (Report No.) SR-213
N- T-

HIST (Historic note: "Kills" and reasons)

NOC TOTAL ELECTRON CONTENT OF IONOSPHERE DERIVED FROM SATELLITE DOPPLER MEASUREMENTS
T

T TERM 1CONTENT (1 = unpublished term)
1DISTURBANCE
3DOPPLER EFFECT (3 = published term)
3ELECTRON
1FLUX
3IONOSPHERE
1MAGNETIC
1MEASUREMENT
1RADIO
1SATELLITE
3SATELLITE MEASUREMENT
1SOLAR

BASE CODE

DC Document classification
TC Title classification
DG Declassification group
SC Subject category
NS NASA support
NF No foreign
CF Conference
CS Corporate source suppl
PA Personal author affil
FO Foreign
RT Receipt type
AN Acquisition No.
RE Receipt date
RD Report date
AB Abstract
AL Abstract language
DL Document language
RE Reproducible
CO Copyright
MI Microfiche
DT Document type
MP Microfiche code prefix
MS Microfiche code suffix
DC Document class
HA Handling
ET Et al
LA Last analytic accession
SO Source
FO Foreign origin
NP Number of pages

FIG. 3. NASA master file record.

Bibliography — Bibliography
Size — 22 cm.
Book number — 62–10128 rev (LC)
Knowledge number — 025.078 (Dewey)
Location statement — Z699.S35
Subject statement — Information storage and retrieval systems
Language — English
Literary form — Project report

This is not presented as an optimal record, nor even as preferable to the conventional entry — it is simply a stage in analysing bibliographical descriptions.

3. Record Structure for Retrieval

All elements of a bibliographic record serve the functions of description and identification. Traditionally, only a few elements are used for retrieval. In a sample survey of Library of Congress catalogue cards, Henriette Avram found the number of file entries per work in a dictionary catalogue to be distributed as follows[3]:

Entries	1	2	3	4	5	>5
% of sample	22	22.3	35.8	25.1	10.3	4.3

Most commonly there were three entries per work, rarely more than five. In Fig. 1 there are fourteen bibliographic elements (excluding the numbers at the foot), and five of these are used as entries, so that this is not a typical card.

The current trend in information retrieval is to increase the number of access routes to a bibliographic record, and we must consider which elements are likely to be needed as retrieval keys. Traditional catalogue headings are A1 (personal surname), B1 (corporate name), C (place as subject), D (title for serials and some other works), R (knowledge number), a limited range of T (subject statements), and sometimes V (literary form). The following additional keys may be needed:

A5 (e.g. to retrieve cartographers or printers)
B2 (e.g., to retrieve publishers)
C2 (e.g., to retrieve places of presentation)
E (e.g., to retrieve concordances or translations)
F (to select items by date)
K (to select illustrated items)
L (to select items containing a bibliography)
N (to list serials by frequency)
Q (to list in book number order)
S (to list in location order)
U (to select items by language)
W (e.g., to select microforms)

If a bibliographic element is to be used as a retrieval key its rendering in the record must be standardized. That is to say, it must be possible to locate all occurrences of a particular element within a file. This requires that retrieval keys be symbolized in such a fashion that they can be arranged in a conventional order; that when the same element occurs in more than one record, either it is represented by identical symbols or its occurrences are linked, as by a *see also* reference; and that when two or more elements differ from each other they be distinguished by some individualizing symbol.

These requirements cut across the traditional emphasis on transcribing bibliographic elements exactly as they occur on title pages and elsewhere. Cataloguing codes are largely concerned with providing standard rules for choice and rendering of name and place headings. As shown in Fig. 1, retrieval headings are entered into the bibliographic record twice — once 'as on title page' and once in a standardized form. As long as the proportion of elements in the record that is to serve the retrieval function remains small, this duplication may be permissible. But if a much higher proportion is to serve as retrieval keys, then duplication becomes wasteful. Since standardization, as defined above, is essential for retrieval, the demand for exact transcription may then have to give way.

Once this is granted, the rendering of each element becomes a matter of balancing optimum symbolization for retrieval against the need for title-page language recognizability. For retrieval, lists of bibliographic elements must be scanned and matched, and this work is minimized if the elements are in the form of brief coded symbols. Fig. 3 shows a string of retrieval keys in 'base

code', but other keys (corporate source, author, subject terms) are left in title-page language for ease of recognition.

There would be a good case for leaving an element in title-page language if it served no retrieval or filing function, but there is no element that may not need to be pressed into service in one of these ways. Title-page language is still to be preferred when *a*, it is itself the most suitable symbolization for retrieval and filing — as is the case, say, with dates in arabic numerals, or *b*, the descriptive function of the element is more important than the other functions — as is the case, say, with book titles. For machine filing, Hines and Harris[2] have already suggested replacing title-page Roman numerals by Arabic, and eliding prefixed personal names (e.g., 'von Braun' to be recorded as 'vonBraun'). For cataloguing old books, Cox and Hunt[4] have introduced codes for personal name relations, countries and towns of publication, languages, and illustration processes. The use of codens for serial titles is now well established. Other elements that could be coded are the relators for corporate name, for place name, for title and for date, the related work and illustrations statements, serial frequency, and literary, physical, and intellectual form. Where it is necessary to retain recognizability in the visual records either the codes could be mnemonic abbreviations or a code dictionary giving natural language equivalents could be stored, for substitution on print-out. Suggested treatment of the various bibliographic elements can be summed up as follows:

A1/4 — personal name — standardized
   5 — relator — coded
B1 — corporate name — standardized
   2 — relator — coded
C1 — place name — standardized, perhaps partly coded
   2 — relator — coded
D1 — title — generally as in title page (but not for serials)
   2 — relator — coded
E — related work — perhaps coded
F1 — date — standardized
   2 — relator — coded
G — edition — standardized
H — subset — standardized
J — pagination — standardized
K to S — coded
T — subject — at present, both standardized terms (subject heading, descriptors) and 'free text' terms have their advocates.
U to X — coded

A coded version of the entry in Fig. 1 might read as follows:

A — au — Schultheiss/Louis Avery
A — au — Culbertson/Don S.
A — au — Heiliger/Edward M.

B	— pub	— Scarecrow Press
B	— affil	— Illinois/University/ Library/Information Systems Project
C	— pub	— New York
C	— affil	— Chicago/Congress Circle
D	— main	— Advanced data processing in the university library
F	— pub	
J	— 388	
L	— b	
M	— 22	
Q	— 62–10128	
R	— 025.078	
S	— Z6999.S35	
T	— Information storage and retrieval systems	
U	— E	
V	— 09	

Since virtually all bibliographic elements may serve as retrieval keys, the essential feature of record structure is that there should be access to any element or combination of elements in a record. Ways of achieving this are as varied as the range of record media and retrieval mechanisms available.[5]

4. Problems of Clerical Filing

The filing sequence of a set of bibliographic records can be completely haphazard, but scanning — particularly visual scanning — is aided by the use of ordered files. Arranging in an ordered sequence (filing) can be reduced to a purely clerical operation if we can specify the sequence of elements in a record that are to be used for ordering, and the elements use symbols which can themselves be placed in a standard sequence (e.g., alphabetic order).

In conventional catalogues, only two or three filing sequences are specified — the basically alphabetic order of the dictionary catalogue (or two alphabetic orders in the divided catalogue), and numerical or alpha-numerical orders for book numbers, knowledge numbers, or locations. The filing rules used are not always precisely specified. For knowledge numbers, only Ranganathan's Colon Classification specifies a unique filing order. Some sequences of headings in the dictionary catalogue have to be visualized by the filer — they are not signalled by the record structure. If filing is to be purely clerical, all its rules have to be spelled out and incorporated in the record.

Consider first a particular subfield — say, A5, personal name relator. The prolific Scriblius Polymath (1812–1984) may in various records be an author, editor, annotator, commentator, indexer, reviser, translator, publisher, printer . . . If his works are to be arranged according to relator, what sequence of relators is to be adopted? If other than alphabetical, a sequence code must be devised — say, author 01, editor 02, translator 03, com-

mentator 04, etc, If these codes are used in the record, natural-language recognizability is lost. As mentioned earlier both code and natural word could be recorded — the one for filing and retrieval, the other for a legible description (see Fig, 3, where a legend on the printed record translates the 'base codes' into natural language).

Within a particular element (say, personal name), either a fixed sequence of subfields must be established, resulting in a fixed filing order within the field, or it must be possible to vary the sequence — for example, to list personal names first by date, next by relator, and only then by surname, to get a chronological survey of literary contributions. The next stage of complexity is a filing order based on more than one bibliographic element. For example, in the General Catalogue of the British Museum, having arrived at a particular author, his works are arranged as follows:[6]

> Collected works (filing element V)
> according to language (U)
> Selected works (V)
> according to language (U)
> Correspondence (V)
> Single works (V)
> arranged by title (D)
> each followed by its translations and other related works (E)
> arranged by language (U)

Still more complex is the arrangement in the General Catalogue of entries beginning with the same word, e.g. ROSE (Fig. 4). To file in the preferred order requires a scan of elements A1, A2, B1, C1, and T in all records, and those containing the words ROSE are then filed in the sequence T, C, A2 B, A1 (and this is a somewhat simplified version of the actual filing rules illustrated in Figure 4).

Machine manipulation offers the possibility of considerably more varied filing sequences for special listings. In principle, we may require any combination of elements to be a determinant of sequence — for example, monographs (V), containing illustrations (K), arranged by knowledge class (R), and date (F). The cost of achieving such flexibility may be high, perhaps too high — and we may have to accept more limited facilities. As Nugent points out, a machine program for clerical filing would be neither short nor simple — but neither are the rules it would be based on, nor the bibliographic data on which it would operate.[7]

5. Section I.—Arrangement of Headings in Relation to Each Other

The following list illustrates the system adopted. The word ROSE has been chosen for the purpose of convenience, and most of the examples are imaginary.

Not a proper noun.	ROSE (flower, tool, etc.).	Entries under such a word as ROSE, with its variety of meanings, are arranged alphabetically in one group, irrespective of language, except that in the case of words identical in form but etymologically distinct, e.g., BUT (English) and BUT (French), LOVE (English) and LOVE (Danish), the heading is repeated and entries are grouped separately.
Place.	ROSE (without epithet).	cf. London; Cambridge.
	ROSE, *House of.*	cf. Anjou, *House of.*
	ROSE, John, *Count of.* (Place unascertained, or a character in fiction.)	
	ROSE, *Italy.*	cf. London, *Ontario;* Cambridge, *Mass.*
	ROSE, *Italy, Diocese of.*	
	ROSE, *Italy,* Henry, *Bishop of.*	
	ROSÉ, *Spain.*	The accent does not affect the arrangement.
	ROSÉ, *Spain, Diocese of.*	
	ROSÉ, *Spain,* Carlos, *Bishop of.*	
	ROSE, *U.S.A.*	
	ROSE, *U.S.A., Diocese of.*	
	ROSE, *U.S.A.,* William, *Bishop of.*	
Personal name.	ROSE.	
	ROSE, *Abbot.*	
	ROSE [da Pietro], called *the Grammarian.*	The epithet determines the order.
	ROSE, *pseud.*	
	ROSE, *Saint.*	
	ROSE, *Ship.*	
Compounds, other than compound surnames, arranged, irrespective of meaning, in alphabetical sequence.	ROSE AMELIA, *Queen.*	
	ROSE AND COMPANY.	
	ROSE AND CROWN.	e.g. an inn or the title of a periodical.
	ROSE AND CROWN, *Diocese of.*	cf. Bath and Wells.
	ROSE BROTHERS.	
	ROSE COMMEMORATION FUND.	
	ROSE CULTIVATION MANUALS.	
	ROSE GARDEN.	
	ROSE GARDEN JONES FUND.	
	ROSE GARDENERS CLUB.	
	ROSE GAZETTE.	
	ROSE JONES HOSTEL.	Rose, Christian name: Jones, surname.
	ROSE-JONES INSTITUTE.	Rose-Jones, surname.
	ROSE LIMITED.	
	ROSE-ON-SEA.	
	ROSE RIVER COLONY.	
	ROSE 7689.	
	ROSE UNIVERSITY COLLEGE.	
	ROSE WILHELMINA, *Queen.*	
	ROSE, WILSON AND COMPANY.	
Possessives.	ROSE'S INSTITUTE.	
Body of persons so named.	ROSE, *Clan of.*	
	ROSE, *Family of.*	
	ROSE, *Messrs.*	
Surnames, plus round brackets.	ROSE (J.) *Artist.*	
	ROSE (J. de)	
	ROSE (J. Albert)	
	ROSE (John)	
	ROSE afterwards SMITH (John)	
	ROSE (John) AND SONS.	ROSE (John) calling himself George Rose.
	ROSE (John) *Agent.*	
	ROSE (John) *2nd Earl.*	
	ROSE (John) *Musician.*	ROSE (John) called the Grammarian
	ROSE (Sir John)	
	ROSE (Sir John) AND SONS.	ROSE (John) of London, Ontario
	ROSE (John de)	
	ROSE (John von)	
	ROSE (John Daniel)	
	ROSE (John D'Arcy)	
	ROSE (John de Lancey)	
	ROSEBERY.	
	ROSEBUD.	
	ROSE-JONES (John)	Compound surname read as [one word.
	ROSEMARY.	

Fig. 4.

6. Questions to be Answered

Current work on bibliographic records for machine handling—of which the references at the end of this paper are a sample—appears to be concerned mainly with modifying the record so that it becomes amenable to machine manipulation, but preserving as far as possible the conventional structure and layout of the catalogue. From the viewpoint of bibliographic continuity, this approach is commendable; but there is no guarantee that the result will be optimally efficient, either in terms of economic machine use or in terms of provision for users of the record. All that I have tried to do in this paper is disrupt the conventional record into its elements, as a preliminary to considering how best they may be reassembled.

To determine the structure of an optimal bibliographic record needs much more information than is at present available. Some of the questions to be answered are as follows:

1. Are there further bibliographic elements to be identified?
2. How often is each element used in recording, and in records serving what functions?
3. How, and how often, is each used in retrieval and filing? To what extent would each be used more in these functions if there were access to the record by any element?
4. For each use of an element, how important is its descriptive function, and the need to retain visual recognizability?
5. Can we identify preferred filing sequences, so that the more frequently used can be readily provided, and the rarely required can be sacrificed?

Such general questions as these must be answered before detailed problems of record structure can be tackled. In view of the current activity towards developing standard machine-readable records, it is urgent that answers be obtained.

References

1. AVRAM, H. D., and MARKUSON, B. E. Library automation and Project MARC. In: *The Brasenose conference on the automation of libraries,* London, Mansell, 1967. pp. 97–123.
2. HINES, T. C., and HARRIS, J. L. *Computer filing of index, bibliographic and catalog entries.* Newark, Bro-Dart, 1966.
3. AVRAM, H. D. Fields of information on Library of Congress catalog cards. *Library Quarterly,* vol. 37, no. 2, 1967, pp. 180–192.
4. HUNT, C. J. The computer production of catalogues of old books. In: *Newcastle Seminar on the organization and handling of bibliographic records by computer.* Newcastle-upon-Tyne, Oriel, 1967. pp. 137–149.
5. MEADOW, C. T. *The analysis of information systems.* New York, London, Wiley, 1967.
6. *Guide to the arrangement of headings and entries in the General Catalogue of Printed Books in the British Museum.* (London, The Museum, 1940.)
7. NUGENT, W. R. The mechanization of the filing rules for the dictionary catalogs of the Library of Congress, *Library Resources and Technical Services,* vol. 11, no. 2, 1967, pp. 145–166.
8. CURRAN, A. T., and AVRAM, H. D. *The identification of data elements in bibliographic records.* Final report of the special project on data elements for the Subcommittee on Machine Input Records (SC–2) of the Sectional Committee on Library Work and Documentation (z–39) of the US Standards Institute, May 1967.

39 Bibliographic Dimensions in Information Control

SEYMOUR LUBETZKY
R. M. HAYES
American Documentation
Vol. 20, No. 3, July, 1969

1 Books and Information

The records of man's thought and experience stored in libraries, mostly though not exclusively in the form of books, have traditionally been viewed as presenting two aspects involving two distinct problems: First, how are they, as concrete entities, to be individually identified and entered in a catalog so that they could readily be found when needed; and second, how are they, as sources of information on various subjects, to be characterized and related so that they could be found by those in search of the information desired? The first question naturally led to the use of author and title entries alphabetically arranged, thus creating the original "alphabetical catalog" now commonly referred to as the "author-and-title catalog;" and the second question led to the formulation of "subject headings" and the use of subject entries to form a "subject catalog." This situation early gave rise to the issue of which of the two catalogs was more essential to the library user, and the arguments on both sides reverberated loudly at the hearings held by a Royal Commission in London in 1847–1849 on the alphabetical catalog designed by Panizzi for the library of the British Museum (1). It was apparent that neither catalog was, alone, quite sufficient, that both catalogs were needed to serve their respective purposes, but that the

alphabetical catalog was more urgently needed to serve the elemental function of a library—which is to be able to tell whether or not it has a particular book. As one of the witnesses at the hearings commented: "I think the first object of a catalogue is that persons going to consult it, if they have an accurate knowledge of the title of the book they want, may be able to find it at once in the catalogue. . . . But, for those who know not the exact title of a book, it would be very desirable to have it placed (also) under the subject to which it relates and then to refer by a cross-reference to the title of the book (1, Question 7917)." Twenty-five years later, Charles Ammi Cutter, viewing the two catalogs as parts of "the catalog as a whole," provided rules for their integration into one "dictionary" catalog (2); but the result appeared as little more than a mere alphabetical interfiling of the author and title entries with the subject entries rather than involving any interrelation between them. The standard cataloging rules subsequently issued were expressly limited to the entry of publications by author and title as a distinct problem (e.g., *Catalog Rules: Author and Title Entries*, 1908; *A.L.A. Cataloging Rules for Author and Title Entries*, 1949). It is quite understandable, therefore, that those concerned with the problem of information should have regarded the problem of "descriptive" cataloging as irrelevant to their purposes and should have taken little notice of the important revision of the cataloging rules in the past fifteen years (3) which has culminated in an International Conference on Cataloging Principles (1961) (4) and a new code of *Anglo-American Cataloging Rules* (1967) (5).

This paper is an outgrowth of discussions between the two authors about the relevance of bibliographic cataloging (on a study of which the first is presently engaged under a grant from the U. S. Office of Education) to the problem of information control (with which the second is particularly concerned). The paper was prepared as part of the work under grant OE-1-7-071089-4284.

2 The Book and the Work

But the notion of "cataloging" and "cataloging rules" as concerned merely with the description of the physical book or record—a notion undoubtedly sustained much too long by the ambiguous term "descriptive cataloging" often used to distinguish it from subject cataloging—has undergone a profound change and has come to assume a character which makes it very pertinent and of increasing importance to the problem of information control.

The essence of the modern concept of cataloging, which might more appropriately be called "bibliographic cataloging," has gradually emerged from a growing realization of the fact that the *book* (i.e., the material record) and the *work* (i.e., the intellectual product embodied in it) are not coterminous; that, in cataloging, the *medium* is not to be taken as synonymous with the *message*; that the *book* is actually only one representation of a certain *work* which may be found in a given library or system of libraries in different media (books, manuscripts, films, phonorecords, punched and magnetic tapes, braille), different forms (editions, translations, versions), and even under different titles; that a library user may need a *particular* edition cited, or may do with *any* available edition or translation of the work, or may need to know what editions and translations of the work the library has so that he could select the one or ones which would best suit his needs (earliest, latest, illustrated, well-edited, original, or translation in a language he knows); that, to serve all these purposes, a book must be treated not only as a particular publication, but also as the representation of a particular work by a particular author, so that the catalog will reveal to an inquirer not only whether a particular *book* is in the library but also what editions and translations of a particular *work* the library has and what works it has of a particular author; and finally, that failure to do so will obviously minimize the potential value of the library to its users.

The meaning of the last point is illustrated in the observations of a reviewer (*6*) commenting on a recent bibliography of translations. In that bibliography, the publications appear to be treated only as such, and not as representations of particular *works*, with the result that "the same work appears under several titles, for example, Gogol's *Sinel*, which shows up as 'The Cloak,' 'The Greatcoat,' 'The Mantle,' and 'The Overcoat' . . ." all interfiled alphabetically with other publications representing different works. The reviewer then goes on to consider the consequences: "Let us imagine that the user of this bibliography is looking for translations of Chekhov's short story *Gore*. After having gone through seventeen pages of tightly printed listings, he will have come up with a long list of titles, such as 'Heartache,' 'Misery,' 'Trouble,' 'The Lament,' 'In Trouble,' 'Woe,' 'A Misfortune,' 'A Bad Business,' 'Sorrow,' 'Grief,' etc., each of which might well be a translation of *Gore*. But he will not know which of these titles actually do represent *Gore* . . . nor if he has found all of the translations of *Gore*." An awareness of the distinction between *books* and the *works* embodied in them, or of the problems and principles of bibliographic cataloging, would have caused the bibliographer to avoid such consequences.

3 Author and Work as "Subjects"

The treatment of a publication as the representation of a particular work by a particular author implies three levels of identification—of the publication itself, of the work represented by it, and of the author of the work. This lends the catalog bibliographic dimensions only sporadically provided by the former cataloging rules. But these dimensions are important not only to the effective control of the books and the works in the library, but also to control of the information contained in them. To illustrate, assume a reader is in search of information about the life and work of Sir Isaac Newton. This reader, in a research library, would reasonably expect to find there both some of Newton's own works and some works about him. He would also be aware, or be advised, that some of the editions of Newton's works might include valuable bibliographical, historical, and critical information about him not found elsewhere—that is, that the editions of an author's works are often also valuable sources of information about him. With this in mind, he will undoubtedly want to know both what works of Newton and what works about him the library has. Proceeding now to the author-and-title catalog, he will readily find under *Newton, Sir Isaac* a list of all of the editions of his works which the library has, including those in which the name *Isaac* appears as *Isaak* and *Newton* as *Neuton*, because the importance of identifying an author—or other person or corporate body—by one particular name and by only one form of the name has long been recognized and followed in cataloging. By the same token, he will find in the subject catalog, under the same form of name, a list of all the works which the library has about Newton. But if in the course of his study our reader's attention were directed specifically to Newton's *Principia*, and he wanted to see some of the editions of this particular work and some other works about it which the library has, then he would find obstacles in his way, because the identification of a *work* has not been recognized and has not been followed under the former cataloging rules (except in certain cases specifically provided—as in the so-called "anonymous classics," e.g., "Bible"). Thus, in returning to the author-and-title catalog, he might or might not find under Newton's name an edition entitled *Principia*, and in either case he would not discover what editions or translations of this work the library had unless he had the perspicacity and tenacity to examine all the entries under Newton's name. Only then would he have found *The First Three Sections of Newton's Principia* under *F*, *The Mathematical Principles of Natural Philosophy* under *M*, *Philosophiae naturalis principia mathematica* under *Ph*, *Principia: The Mathematical Principles of Natural Philosophy* under *Pr*, and *The Three First Sections . . . of Newton's Principia* under *T*, interfiled with such unrelated titles as *Arithmetica universalis, Interpolation Tables, Lettres inedites, Opticks, Opuscula mathematica, Tables for Renewing and Purchasing Leases,* and *Universal Arithmetick* (*7*). (Note also the separation of *The First Three Sections of Newton's Principia* and *The Three First Sections . . . of Newton's Principia,* of his *Arithmetica universalis* and *Universal Arithmetick*). Under the circumstances, one would rationally be at a complete loss about how to find, in the subject catalog, any materials about this variously named work of Newton. This is, of course, analogous to the situation described by the above-mentioned reviewer in trying to locate the translations of Checkov's *Gore* (a situation which, ironically, might well be described by this title, including all the connotations of "Trouble" and "Grief"). It is the consequence of failure to recognize the identity of a work which may be embodied in different publications under different titles and to provide appropriately for such identification. Under the new cataloging rules, all the editions and translations of Newton's *Principia* would be represented as such, thusly:

Newton, Sir Isaac
    [Principia] Philosophiae naturalis principia mathematica . . .
    [Principia. *English*] The mathematical principles of natural philosophy . . .
    [Principia. *French*] Principes mathématiques de la philosophie naturelle . . .
    [Principia. 1–3] The first three sections of Newton's Principia . . .
    [Principia. 1–3] The three first sections . . . of Newton's Principia . . .
    etc.

And, accordingly, the materials about this work would logically be found in the subject catalog under the heading *Newton, Sir Isaac. Principia.*

4 Misconceptions of Bibliographic Cataloging

Despite the extensive discussions which accompanied the revision of the former *A. L. A. Cataloging Rules* and the development of the new *Anglo-American Cataloging Rules,* the essential character of the new concept of bibliographic cataloging and its implications for the systematic structure and effectiveness of both the author-and-title catalog and the subject catalog remain deplorably malunderstood. Some of those concerned with the problem of information in the library appear in-credibly oblivious of the fact that information is found in the library not in any abstract form of "information" as such but only as embodied in the works represented by books and other materials, and that these materials must therefore necessarily and properly be considered as an organic part of the problem of information. One such individual (*8*) claims that "The over-emphasis on authorship in our bibliographical apparatus obscures both the fact that libraries are essentially institutions for the preservation of thought processes and the fact that the value of these thought processes is independent from the form in which they appear and from the individuals who create them." Apart from the dubious validity of the assertion that the value of "thought processes"—which presumably means ideas or information—does not depend on the reputation of their authors or editors, this writer simply ignores the fact that libraries actually do not deal in any abstract "thought processes" but in records representing the works of men, and that it is these records that libraries must buy, preserve, catalog, and make available to their users. Nor does this writer indicate how libraries might tangibly handle "thought processes"—a consideration which led another student (*9*) of the problem of information to say that the problem "stems, as we know, from the insubstantiality of information, and is not lessened by our obstinate refusal to admit that all we are able to organize are the documents that house the information." Others appear disposed to belittle "cataloging" as a low-level form of indexing. "The methods used in indexing range from the relatively straight-forward system of providing bibliographic data, well described by conventional library rules, to more sophisticated attempts to establish dictionaries and other hierarchical systems which . . . will lead the person to the desired information (*10*)." But as the foregoing and the following may indicate, the bibliographic and subject systems in use represent not a range of sophistication but a range of purposes to be served, any of which may be "straight-forward" or "sophisticated" depending on the competence and skill of the practitioner. And most continue to confuse the *book* with the *work* and to regard the library catalog as merely a list of *books,* or publications, by author, title, and subject. Thus one may find in a paper (*11*) delivered at a recent Institute on the "book catalog"—that is, the catalog printed in book form—that "A catalog should be designed to answer questions as to what *books* [italics added] are in the library—questions of physical accessibility." Although earlier in that paper the author speaks of "individual works," there is nothing to indicate an awareness of any distinction between the "books" and the "works," or of the implications of such distinction for the functions which the catalog should be designed to serve. Likewise, in the last paper of that Institute (*12*), one is told that "Possibly the simplest and most frequent type of library request is that for a particular *book or work* [italics added] identified by title, author, or other descriptive bibliographic information." The intended synonymity of "book" and "work" is here further confirmed by the inscription under a key of an illustrated computer console, which reads (*12*, p. 114):

Specific Work

For requesting a specific book, journal, or report by means of author, title, publisher, or other descriptive (non-subject) information.

Nowhere in these papers is there any apparent concern about the *work* as distinct from the *book*.

Failure to understand fully the purposes and principles of bibliographic cataloging has also led, more recently, to the notion that use of the computer in the production of the catalog makes the traditional method of cataloging, employing a "main entry," now obsolete (*13, 14*). That is, instead of having the cataloger always decide whether the "main entry" for a given publication is to be under author, title, or other heading—a decision requiring knowledge of the cataloging rules and principles as well as discrimination in their application—a basic entry would simply be made under the title of the publication; and this entry would then automatically be provided by the computer with the indicated author, subject, and other headings to form the desired catalog entries. The idea appears irresistibly attractive and promising the long yearned-for simplification of bibliographic cataloging—and has indeed been urged on other occasions before (*15*) and used in some cases (*16*)—but it ignores the basic function of the "main entry" as the nucleus of the catalog (*17*). For when the main entry is designed to represent a publication as an edition of a particular work by a particular author, the result is that the added entries under the subject and other added headings will similarly be related; but if the basic entry is to be under the title of the publication, the entries under a given subject heading will be indiscriminately arranged alphabetically by the wording of their titles rather than their intrinsic interrelation. This has already been noted by one library where the idea was adopted (*18*) and where, as a result, one will find under the heading *Symphonies*, in the subject catalog, not an arrangement of the symphonies by composer and composition (i.e., author and work)—as any rational approach would appear to warrant—but of titles of publications such as *Four Complete Symphonies* . . . under *F, The Great Symphonies of* . . . under *G, The Nine Symphonies of* . . . under *N,* and then *Symphonia* . . . , *Symphonie* . . . , *Symphonies* . . . , *Symphony no.* . . . , *Symphony in* . . . , *Symphony of* . . . , *Symphony on* . . . , *Synfoni* . . . , and other variations of such titles, regardless of the works and the composers represented by them.

5 Bibliographic Problems in Information Control

The foregoing illustrates the relevance of the problems and principles of bibliographic cataloging to those of information control. There is, however, at least one important method of information control whose problems are entirely the same as those of bibliographic cataloging. This is the method which employs authors and works symbolically as "subject headings" to designate the subject fields or ideas represented by them and to relate the sources in which the authors and the works are cited—as is done in the *Science Citation Index*. Here, as is explained (*10*), "The searcher starts with a reference or an author he has identified . . . then enters the *Citation Index* section and searches for *that particular author's name* [italics added]. When he locates the author's name, he then checks to see which of several possible references fits the particular one that he is interested in. Under the year, journal volume, and page number of this particular reference, he then looks to see who has currently cited *this particular work* [italics added]." But if the *Index* is to be a dependable and effective guide to the sources in which a "particular author" or a "particular work" is cited, then obviously the authors and works listed in it must be adequately and *unambiguously* identified—as they are required to be in bibliographic cataloging. But are they so treated in the *Index*? One might assume from the foregoing quotation emphasizing "that particular author's name" and "this particular work" that this was the intention; but if that was the case, the methodology adopted here was ill calculated to accomplish the desired ends. The identification of an author by the surname and initials cited is inevitably bound to separate references to the same author when he is variantly cited and to confuse references to different authors having the same surname and initials; and identification of a *work* by the source in which it appeared is inevitably bound to separate references to a work which appeared, with or without modifications, in more than one source. The combination of the two factors scarcely promises to make the pursuit of sources related to a "particular author" or a "particular work"— the declared objectives of the *Index*—a successful experience.

To confirm this conclusion, a member of the research staff of the University of California Institute of Library Research, Mrs. Nancy Brault, was asked to verify some names and citations of the *Science Citation Index*. Picking up a copy of the 1966 cumulation, she turned to the name Gibbs as a name which is neither very common (like Smith) nor very uncommon, and from the citations found in columns 7105–7109 she selected the names Gibbs (without initials), Gibbs A, Gibbs A J, Gibbs C J, Gibbs F, Gibbs F A, and Gibbs J W. She then went to some of the sources cited for a more adequate identification of the authors and their works and returned with the following telling results:

1. Two of the works cited under Gibbs (without initials) belong to two different authors. The author of *65–J Chem Phys 43 139* will be found to be Julian H. Gibbs, who is listed also under Gibbs J H as author of *54–J Chem Phys 22 1460, 55–J Phys Chem 59 644, 58–J Chem Phys 28 373*, and others; and the author of *76–T Connecticut Acad 3 343* will be found to be Josiah Willard Gibbs, who is listed also as Gibbs J W where the same item and other items are cited (see below).

2. Gibbs A, the author of *53–Parasitology 43 143*, will be found to be Alfred J. Gibbs, who is listed also under Gibbs A J as author of *59–Parasitology 49 411*; at the same time it will be found that other items listed under each of these two names belong to different authors, active in different fields, and associated with different institutions.

3. Gibbs C J, author of *65–J Water PC 73 1417*, will be found to be Charles V Gibbs, not C J Gibbs. A misprint or error in the citing article *J Water PC 38 685* entailed a misplacement of this author and his confusion with other authors. At the same time, there is nothing under Gibbs C V, where one would look for him.

4. Gibbs F and Gibbs F A will be found to be the same author, Frederic Andrews Gibbs. Some items will be found under one name, some under the other, and some under both of these names; in addition, some items will be found represented, under one or both of these names, under as many as 4 and 6 variant citations (e.g., *50–Atlas Electroencepha, 50–Atals [!] Electroencepha 1, 50–Atlas EEG 1*, and *50–Atlas Electroencepha 1* under Gibbs F A, all referring to the author's *Atlas of Electroencephalography*, 2nd edition, vol. 1, published in 1950; *64–Atlas EEG, 64–Atlas Electroencepha 3*, under Gibbs F, and *Atlas 3, 64–Atlas EEG 3, 64–Atlas Electroencepha 2* [i.e., 3], and *64–Atlas Electroencepha 3*, under Gibbs F A, all six referring to vol. 3 of the above work published in 1964.)

5. Gibbs J W will be found to be Josiah Willard Gibbs who, as already noted, is one of the authors listed also under Gibbs (without initials). The principal interest in this case, however, is the fact that the entries under this name illustrate how reproductions of a "particular work," identified as they are in the *Index* by source of publication, may appear in it as so many different works. J. W. Gibbs' writings, which first appeared in scientific periodicals, were later collected and republished in 1906 and 1961 under the title *The Scientific Papers of J. Willard Gibbs*, and in 1928, 1948, and 1957 under the title *The Collected Works of J. Willard Gibbs*. Any one of the author's papers may therefore be cited as found in any or all of these sources without indication that they represent the same *work*. Thus his paper "On the Equilibrium of Heterogenous

Substances" will be found cited as *Collected Works 1 300, 06–Scientific Papers 1 219, 28–Collected Works 1 219, 48–Collected Works 1 219, 75–Conn Acad Sci T 3 108, 75–T Connecticut Acad 3 108, 76–T Conn Acad 3 108*, and so on. One will also note that here, as in the foregoing paragraph, variations in the citation of the source (*Conn Acad Sci T, T Connecticut Acad, T Conn Acad*) serve further to separate the references and cap the confusion. If these conditions, found in a small sampling of entries under a few ordinary names, in the space of not more than four columns of only one year's cumulation, are any indication of the bibliographic conditions obtaining generally in the *Index*, it is difficult to see how a person interested in the subject field or the ideas represented by a certain author or certain work can effectively use the *Index* to locate the sources related to "that particular author" or "this particular work." Perhaps even more significant would be the effects of these conditions upon studies which by their nature, depend upon the identification of "particular works by particular authors," such as the use of citations to identify families of papers (*19, 20*).

This is not intended and is not to be construed as a criticism of the *Science Citation Index*—a valiant and useful undertaking where economic and other practical considerations dictate a course of action not conducive to ideal results. It is adduced, however, as a prime example of an important method of subject or information control, the problems of which are entirely the same as those of bibliographic cataloging and therefore ones that could benefit from the solutions evolved in bibliographic cataloging.

6 Epitome

The "information" found in the materials of a library is not in the form of nuggets that can be collected, sorted, and labeled in isolation. Rather, it is part of the collective work and thought of men, and of the fabric of the particular works in which it is found. It is pertinent, therefore, that in organizing this information cognizance should be taken of the authors who created it, the particular works of which it is an organic part, and the materials embodying these works. Together, the authors, the works, and the materials may be said to constitute the determinant dimensions of the information found in bibliographical sources.

References

1. Gt. Brit. Commissioners Appointed to Inquire into the Constitution and Government of the British Museum, *Report of the Commissioners . . . with Minutes of Evidence*, London, 1850.

2. CUTTER, C. A., *Rules for a Printed Dictionary Catalog,* Washington, 1876, p. 5.

3. GORMAN, M., A-A 1967: The New Cataloging Rules, *Library Association Record,* 70:27–32 (February 1968).

4. International Conference on Cataloguing Principles, Paris, 1961, *Report,* London, 1963.

5. *Anglo-American Cataloging Rules,* North American Text, American Library Association, Chicago, 1967.

6. TERRAS, V., [Review of] The Literatures of the World in English Translations, *Library Quarterly,* 38:115 (January 1968).

7. *Cf.* U.S. Library of Congress, *A Catalog of Books Represented by Library of Congress Printed Cards issued to July 31, 1942,* 108:448–450. Edwards Brothers, Ann Arbor, Michigan, 1944.

8. KRAFT, M., An Argument for Selectivity in the Acquisition of Materials for Research Libraries, *Library Quarterly,* 37:288 (July 1967).

9. BATTEN, W. E., We Know the Enemy—Do We Know Our Friends?, *Library Journal,* 93:946 (March 1, 1968).

10. MALIN, M. V., The Science Citation Index: A New Concept in Indexing, *Library Trends,* 16:375 (January 1968).

11. WEBER, D. C., The Changing Character of the Catalog in America, *Library Quarterly,* 34:21 (January 1964).

12. SWANSON, D. R., Dialogues with a Catalog, *Ibid.,* p. 115.

13. PARKER, R. H., Book Catalogs, *Library Resources & Technical Services,* 8:344–348 (Fall 1964).

14. SIMONTON, W., The Computerized Catalog: Possible, Feasible, Desirable? *Ibid.,* p. 399–407.

15. AHLSTEDT, V., Unit Cataloging, *Libri,* 1:113–170 (1950).

16. BOGGS, S. W., and LEWIS, D. C., *The Classification and Cataloging of Maps and Atlases,* Special Libraries Association, New York, 1945.

17. LUBETZKY, S., VERONA, V., and JOLLEY, L. The Function of the Main Entry in the Alphabetical Catalogue, in International Conference on Cataloguing Principles, Paris, 1961, *Report,* London, 1963, pp. 139–163.

18. JOHNSON, R. D., A Book Catalog at Stanford, *Journal of Library Automation,* 1:13–50 (March 1968).

19. KESSLER, M. M., An Experimental Study of Bibliographic Coupling between Technical Papers, *IEEE Trans. Information Theory* IT9: 49–51 (1963).

20. GARNER, R., A Computer-Oriented Graph Theoretic Analysis of Citation Index Structures, in *Three Drexel Information Science Research Studies,* 1–46 (especially 14–15).

Chapter Seven
Organization
of
Information
Stores

Storing information records (books, articles, data sheets, etc.) and their representations (catalogs, indexes, etc.) has always vexed information systems. In the past, both the method of storing (filing, shelving, etc.) records and the organization of stores were usually influenced by the medium of the records; but today, quite often we have the reverse situation — the media of the stores affect or even dictate the organization and the medium of the records.

The first step most often taken in the traditional pattern of problem-solving was to define and examine the problem fully, then to find the solution to it. However, within the fields concerned with information, the rapid development of information technology has forced the reversal of the traditional pattern; thus, the solutions have gone begging for problems. Perhaps the best example of this is the employment of the computer and microfilm to a great variety of information handling problems, problems which were neither fully defined nor understood. Nevertheless, many benefits accrued from this reversal; the problems themselves became the focus, were critically examined, and fresh approaches brought considerable illumination. Thus, both the problem-stating and the problem-solving aspects were fortified. As a matter of fact, the rise of information science is due, to a great extent, to the problems encountered in the deployment of information technology.

The number of existing articles and even books that pertain to the organization of information stores (especially computer stores) is staggering. Because the subject is covered very adequately elsewhere, the small selection of articles in this chapter merely exemplifies the variety of research efforts in this area.

Leimkuhler (Article 40) presented a formal file organization and searching structure, which is suitable for the optimization of literature searching, by utilizing the special properties of literature behavior, such as those governed by Bradford's law of dispersion. Thompson, Benningson and Whitman (Article 41) addressed themselves to the efficiency and optimization of searching by utilizing classification properties of literature-related data bases. Booth (Article 42) investigated formally the possible geometrical and architectural arrangements of library stacks. Utilizing the properties of usage of items in the library, he suggested organizing a library in the manner of a push-down store.

The three works selected have one thing in common: each utilized some observed and/or behavioral property of the stored records as the base on which the store should be organized. In itself, this approach suggests the manner in which future work on information stores may proceed.

40 A Literature Search and File Organization Model

FERDINAND F. LEIMKUHLER
American Documentation
Vol. 19, No. 2, April, 1968

1 Introduction

A basic consideration in the design of information systems is the organization of data files for efficient storage and recall operations. A familiar example is a library classification system for storing books on shelves in a manner that enables users to find documents on the same subject in close proximity to one another.

There is a close analogy between the problems of file organization and those of military search and reconnaissance operations, which are concerned with the design of efficient search patterns that allocate available search effort over target areas in an optimal manner (*1*). A fundamental design principle in search theory is that the expected search effort is minimized by always distributing the effort sequentially so as to maximize the probability of target detection with the effort expended thus far (*2*, p. 332).

Consider the task of locating a pertinent piece of information in the literature by a systematic examination of a collection of source documents. If it takes about the same effort to examine each item, then the items should be searched in decreasing order of their probabilities of yielding the information sought. In this way, the probability of success is always maximum for the effort expended, and search effort is minimized. Such a strategy, however, requires sufficient prior information to be able to rank all the items in the file according to their probabilities of yielding the target.

As an alternative to complete ranking of the file items, the file could be organized into several zones of decreasing target likelihood, where all items in any zone are judged to have target-yield probabilities that are less than items in preceding zones and greater than items in succeeding zones. By not having to discriminate between items in the same zone, there is a less stringent prior information requirement. At the same time, there is some loss in search efficiency, since within any zone the file is unordered.

Let a file of n items be arranged in a sequence, $j = 1, 2, \ldots, n$, with target probabilities, p_j, associated with each item. If the file is organized so that $p_i \geqq p_{i+1}$, then the search effort, measured by $\sum_{j=1}^{n} j \, p_j$, is minimized.

With partial ordering, however, each item is judged to be a member of zone k, $k=1, 2, \ldots, m$, having a common zone probability, $p_k > p_{k+1}$, where p_k is equal to the average probability for all items in the zone. If n_k denotes the cumulative number of items in zone 1 through k and p_k denotes the cumulative probability of finding the target in the first n_k items, then the expected search effort is defined for m zones and a file of n items by

$$E_m = \sum_{k=1}^{m} (n_k + n_{k-1} + 1)(P_k - P_{k-1})/2 \quad (1)$$

Eq. (1) reduces to $(n+1)/2$ for $m=1$, and to $\mu = \sum_{j=1}^{n} j \, p_j$ for $m=n$, so that $\mu \leqq E_m \leqq (n+1)/2$. By evaluating E_m in this range, the relative advantage of increasing file discrimination can be determined.

2 Model

Without loss in generality, let a real number, x, in the interval $(0,1)$ define a sequence of file items in the order of search, and $G(x)$ define the probability of finding the target in the interval $(0, x)$ for a particular arrangement of the file. $G(x)$ is monotone nondecreasing, $G(0)=0$ and $G(1)=1$. If $G(x)$ has a continuous finite derivative, $g(x)$, for every x, $g(x)$ is the target density function of the file. For a given collection of file items, let $F(x)$ or F_x be the target distribution function when the items are arranged in *optimal search order* where f_x is a monotone nonincreasing function of x so that $F(x)$ is maximum for all G at each level x.

Associated with target distribution function, F_x, we define a family of search functions $F_x^{(m)}$, $m=1, 2, \ldots$, which are piecewise linear approximations of F_x consisting of m line segments as shown in Fig. 1. The target search function, $F_x^{(m)}$, corresponds to a partial ordering of the file into m zones, each having uniform target detection density within the zone, which is less than that of the preceding zone. Thus, the density function for $F_x^{(m)}$ is a monotone nonincreasing step-function with finite drops at points $x_k^{(m)}$, $k=1, 2, \ldots m$, of amounts equal to $(F_k - F_{k-1})/(x_k - x_{k-1})$, since $F_k^{(m)} = F_k$ at the points x_k. When $m=1$, $F_x^{(1)} = x$, and generally, as m increases, $F_x^{(m)}$ approximates F_x more closely.

The expected search effort with a search function $F_x^{(m)}$ over a partially ordered file is defined as follows:

$$E_m(x_1, x_2, \ldots x_{m-1}) = 1/2 \sum_{k=1}^{m} (x_k + x_{k-1})(F_k - F_{k-1}) \quad (2)$$

$$E_m \leqq E_1 = 1/2$$

$$E_m \geqq \lim_{m \to \infty} E_m = \int_0^1 x \, f(x) \, dx = \mu_x$$

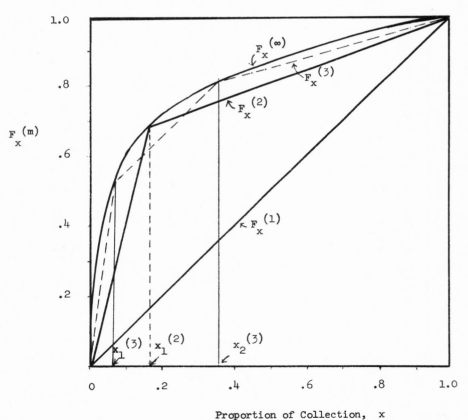

FIG. 1. Search functions, $F_x^{(m)}$, for the target distribution function $F_x = \ln(1 + \beta x)/\ln(1 + \beta)$, $\beta = 269$

Since the zone limits, x_1, x_2, $\ldots$, x_m, can take on arbitrary values in the interval $(0, 1)$, E_m can take on as many values for given F_x and m. Of particular interest are the zone limits which minimize E_m and permit a meaningful comparison of the gain in search efficiency with larger values of m, i.e., greater discrimination between file items.

For a given target distribution function, F_x, over a completely ordered file, a partially ordered search function $F_x{}^{(2)}$ consists of two zones, $(0, x_1)$ and $(x_1, 1)$, respectively, which are searched in that order. The expected search effort is given by

$$E_2(x) = (x_1 + 1 - F_1)/2 \tag{3}$$

where

$$E_2' = (1 - f_1)/2$$
$$E_2'' = (-f_1{}^1)/2 > 0$$

Thus, E_2 is minimum for $x_1{}^*$ such that $f(x_1{}^*) = 1$.

For example, if $F_x = x^{-\frac{1}{2}}$, $f_x = \frac{1}{2}x^{\frac{1}{2}}$, and $\mu_x = 0.33$, then one would expect to examine one third of the completely ordered file before finding the target, while with no ordering, one would expect to examine half the items in the file. The best that can be done with the partial ordering into two zones is to identify and search the most likely 71% of the items first, $x_1{}^* = 0.25$, and, if unsuccessful, examine the remaining items. The expected search effort for this strategy is 0.375, a reduction of 25% from 0.50, out of a possible reduction of 0.33% with complete ordering. If a three-zone search is employed $x_1{}^* = 0.11$, $x_2{}^* = 0.44$, and $x_3 = 1$, and the expected search effort is only 0.35, which is quite close to the best that can be done.

In general, suppose F_x is known and sufficiently well-behaved that a unique set of points, $x_1{}^*$, $x_2{}^*$, $\ldots$, $x_{m-1}{}^*$, exist on the interval $(0, 1)$ and minimize E_m, then the $m-1$ necessary equations for the extremum can be written as

$$f(x_k) = (F_{k+1} - F_{k-1})/(x_{k+1} - x_{k-1}), \quad k = 1, 2, \ldots m-1 \tag{4}$$
$$F_o = 0 = x_o < x_k < x_m = F_m = 1$$

after setting the partial derivatives of $E_m(x_k)$ equal to zero. Eq. (4) can be solved simultaneously to yield the optimal search strategy with m zones.

3 Literature Scatter

The significance of partial ordering in scientific literatures was first advocated by S. C. Bradford as a "law of scattering" (3), which holds that when documents are arranged in decreasing order of productivity the number of documents increases geometrically with the useful references they contain. Various attempts have been made to apply Bradford's law to documents used and cited in different scientific disciplines (10, 11).

By restating Bradford's model in terms of proportions and inverting the relationship, a more useful mathematical function, called the Bradford distribution, can

be obtained (5). Let x denote the fraction of more productive documents in an ordered collection, and

$$F(x) = \ln(1 + \beta x)/\ln(1 + \beta) \tag{5}$$
$$0 \leq x \leq 1, 0 \leq \beta$$

$F(x)$ defines the proportion of total productivity (references) contained in the fraction of documents x (titles). β is a factor related to the subject field and the completeness of the collection. The inverse relationship

$$x = (b^F - 1)/(b - 1) \tag{6}$$
$$b = 1 + \beta$$

is the continuous version of Bradford's law of scattering relating the proportion of documents to the proportion of references they contain.

The mean value and the density of the Bradford distribution are as follows:

$$\mu_x = 1/\ln(1+\beta) - 1/\beta \tag{7}$$
$$f_x = \beta/(1 + \beta x)\ln(1 + \beta) = (1 + \beta\mu_x)/(1 + \beta x) \tag{8}$$

An important property of the Bradford distribution is its applicability to incomplete collections of source documents. If a subset of the total collection contains the most productive portion of that collection and consists of a fraction, α, of the total collection, then the distribution of references within the subset also follows the Bradford distribution but with a modified parameter, β_α, which is linear with α, i.e., $\beta_\alpha = \alpha\beta$ (5).

In a very thorough search of 1,282 abstracting journals for the period 1940–1958, a total of 9,810 useful papers on thermophysical properties were obtained (4); and the distribution of journal productivity was recorded for the 50 most productive journals, which yielded 51% of the references. These data were found to be closely approximated by a Bradford distribution with parameter $\beta = 269$ for the entire set of journals, and $\beta_\alpha = 10.5$ for the more productive subset of 50 journals (5). This β value agrees very closely with measures of scatter that Cole (6) obtained in his study of specialized literatures. Bradford (3) suggested a β value of 125 for scientific journals. Evidence from other literature searches indicate β values in a wide range (100–300), which can be due to either more or less inherent scatter or more or less completeness of the collections searched. A plot of the Bradford distribution fitted to the results of the search for thermophysical properties data is shown in Fig. 2.

4 Literature Search

Let a collection of source documents be arranged in order of decreasing productivity and their reference content follow the Bradford distribution. Furthermore, let the reference content be a measure of the likelihood that a given document contain the target information sought in a particular search. Then the expected search length or search effort, is defined by μ_x in eq. (7). Alternatively, if the documents are arranged into two zones

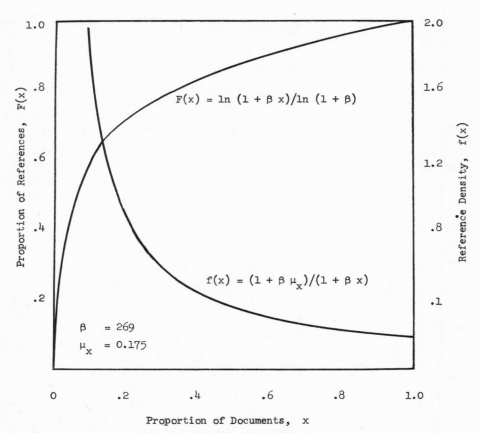

$$F(x) = \ln(1 + \beta x)/\ln(1 + \beta)$$

$$f(x) = (1 + \beta \mu_x)/(1 + \beta x)$$

$$\beta = 269$$
$$\mu_x = 0.175$$

Proportion of Documents, x

FIG. 2. Bradford distribution fitted to results of search for
thermophysical property data

having more productive and less productive documents, and the items in the more productive zone are examined (randomly) first, then the search effort is defined by eq. (3), which is minimized when

$$f(x_1) = 1 = (1 + \beta \mu)/(1 + \beta x_1) \tag{9}$$

which implies that $x_1{}^* = \mu$.

For example, the collection of abstracting journals on thermophysical properties had a β value of 269 and $\mu = 0.175$, i.e., one would expect to search through 17.5% of the collection if the journals were ranked in decreasing order of productivity. This is considerably less than the expected effort of 0.50 with random search. But if the collection is grouped into two zones, consisting of the 17.5% most productive journals in the first search zone and the remainder in zone two, and the zones are searched randomly, then the expected search effort is only 0.24, which is quite close to the best attainable effort of 0.175. The probability of succeeding in zone 1 is 0.69, $F(\mu)$, i.e., better than two thirds of the time the target is found without recourse to the second zone of source documents.

The search efficiency can be improved slightly by going from a two- to three-zone file organization. For a three-zone plan the expected search effort is given from eq. (2) as

$$E_3(x_1, x_2) = (x_2 + 1 - F_2 + x_1 F_2 - x_7 F_1) \tag{10}$$

which is minimized under the conditions $f_1 = F_2/x_2$ and $f_2 = (1 - F_1)/(1 - x_1)$ from eq. (4). Under the assumption of a Bradford distribution these conditions reduce to the form

$$1 + \beta x_1 = \beta x_2/\ln(1 + \beta x_2) \tag{11}$$

$$1 + \beta x_2 = \beta(1 - x_1)/\ln[(1 + \beta)/(1 + \beta x_1)] \tag{12}$$

By eliminating x_1, the equation

$$1 + \beta x_2 = \frac{(\beta + 1) - \beta x_2/\ln(1 + \beta x_2)}{\ln(\beta + 1) - \ln[\beta x_2/\ln(1 + \beta x_2)]} \tag{13}$$

can be easily solved iteratively for x_2, which is then substituted in eq. (11) to find x_1.

For the example, with $\beta = 269$, the optimal limits for a three-zone search plan are: $x_1{}^* = 0.075$, and $x_2{}^* = 0.36$. These yield an expected search effort of $E_3{}^* = 0.20$, which is a reduction of about 0.04 under the two-zone search plan and only 0.025 above the best that can be expected with complete ranking of all items. The probability of the search proceeding beyond zone 1, the 7.5 most productive percent of the collection, is $1 - F_1 = 0.45$, and the probability of proceeding beyond zone 2 is $1 - F_2 = 0.18$.

The relative improvement in search efficiency decreases rapidly with the use of more zones in the organization of the file.

In Fig. 3, values for E_1, E_2^*, $\mu = E_\infty$, and F_μ are plotted for values of $\beta \leqq 500$, where $F\mu$ is the probability of success in the first zone of a two-zone search plan. The relative efficiency of zone searching appears to be quite stable over the entire range of Bradford distributions considered, and in the range 100–500 the values change less than 0.05 for all curves. This range is considered the most meaningful from the data available. Relatively small values of β would apply to search situations with very small scatter or target dispersion, as, for example, within the few most productive journals on a particular topic. In general, as the references are distributed over larger numbers of source documents it is optimal to search a slightly smaller proportion of the total collection first; however, in most situations it appears that the initial search should encompass between 15–20% of the collection, with a probability of success of about 0.67 in that part of the collection.

5 Remarks

This research grew out of a larger study of library storage systems. Faced with an exponential growth in acquisitions, research libraries are fighting a losing battle with the problems of physically processing and shelving books under a theoretically unlimited bibliographic classification system. Other studies (7, 8) have shown that uniform shelving of the entire collection is relatively inefficient with regard to spatial and economic considerations. The present study indicates that uniform shelving may be relatively inefficient with regard to user search and retrieval activities.

The suggestion here is that a "two-bin" system of document storage will better serve the user, whereby he first consults a small, more active file of the more useful items before proceeding to a larger secondary file. Based on the empirical evidence at hand, the smaller file should contain about 20% of the pertinent documents and satisfy about two thirds of the user needs.

The economic advantages of a two-bin system to a research library needs to be more fully explored. The

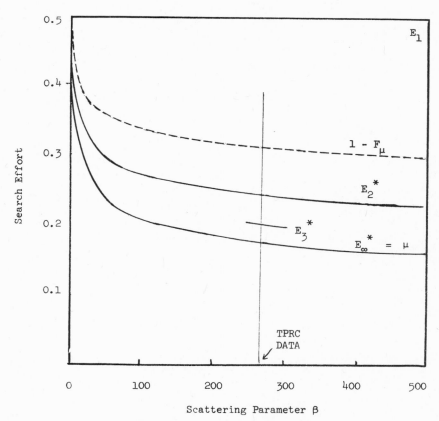

FIG. 3. Optimal expected search effort, E_m^*, for m zones when file content has a Bradford distribution with parameter β

model assumes that the user is seeking a readily recognizable item, which, when found, terminates the search, and it is assumed also that there is some mechanism available for easily dividing the collection into zones of high and low success probabilities for a given target. However, many libraries formally and informally divide their collections today into groupings that are considered to be more or less pertinent to the needs of a given class of users. This may be done for reasons of economy or user service and implemented by means of descriptors, citations, usage, age, language, source of publication, or some combination of such characteristics (9). The model is intended to aid in the formalization and justification of such schemes on a more rigorous basis. It should be useful in exploring problems such as the determination of the optimal size and makeup of depositories and browseries, the allocation of materials among branch libraries, and the design of regional information networks.

References

1. Enslow, P. H., Jr., A Bibliography of Search Theory and Reconnaissance Theory Literature, *Naval Research Logistics Quarterly,* 13(2):177–202 (June 1966).

2. Dobbie, J. M., Search Theory: A Sequential Approach, *Naval Research Logistics Quarterly,* 10(4):223–334 (December 1963).

3. Bradford, S. C., *Documentation,* Public Affairs Press, Washington, D.C., 1950.

4. Cezairliyan, A. O., P. S. Lykoudis, and Y. S. Touloukian, A New Method for the Search of Scientific Literature through Abstracting Journals, *Journal of Chemical Documentation,* 2:86–92 (1962). *See also* Thermophysical Properties Research Center Report 11, Purdue University, 1960.

5. Leimkuhler, F. F., The Bradford Distribution, *Journal of Documentation,* 23(3):197–207 (September 1967).

6. Cole, P. F., A New Look at Reference Scattering, *Journal of Documentation,* 18(2):58–64 (June 1962).

7. Leimkuhler, F. F., and J. G. Cox, Compact Book Storage in Libraries, *Operations Research,* 12(3):419–427 (1964).

8. Lister, W. C., Least Cost Decision Rules for the Selection of Library Materials for Compact Storage, Ph.D. Thesis, Purdue University, 1967. (U.S. Government Clearinghouse Report PB 174441.)

9. Jain, A. K., A Statistical Study of Book Use, Ph.D. Thesis, Purdue University, 1968. (U.S. Clearinghouse Report PB 176 525.)

10. Stevens, R. E., *Characteristics of Subject Literatures,* American College and Research Libraries Monograph Series 7, 1953.

11. Vickery, B. C., Bradford's Law of Scattering, *Journal of Documentation,* 4(3):198–203 (1948).

41 A Proposed Structure for Displayed Information to Minimize Search Time Through a Data Base

DAVID A. THOMPSON
LAWRENCE A. BENNIGSON
DAVID WHITMAN
American Documentation
Vol. 19, No. 1, January, 1968

1 Introduction

In the design of information retrieval techniques, the question arises regarding how a data base should be structured and displayed in order to minimize user search time to retrieve any single item from the data base.

Several authors have suggested various classification schemes (*1, 2, 3*) including the use of explicit decision tree structures to accommodate the decision-retrieval process of the investigator (*4, 5, 6*). However, we have found none who have suggested an optimal structure for such a classification scheme from the standpoint of the user, and we would like to develop such a structure in this paper.

2 Information Structure Types

The most common structure for data bases or information collections will be referred to here as the "table of contents" structure, and represents the format of the Engineering Index, the Library of Congress classification system, Index Medicus, and many others. A second information structure noticed with increasing frequency in the literature is that of a "decision tree." These two schema are illustrated in Fig. 1.

The "table" format is that of an implicit decision tree, wherein the successive levels of decision occur from left to right rather than from top to bottom, and the

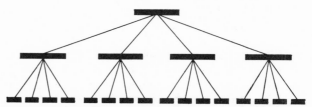

FIG. 1a. The structure of a "table of contents" data base array. It has 2 levels, and 4 alternatives at each decision node in this example.

FIG. 1b. The structure of a "decision tree" data base array. It has 2 levels, and 4 alternatives at each decision node in this example.

hierarchical relationships are indicated by headings and subheadings rather than by the more obvious drawn branches of the tree. The table makes a more efficient use of display area; the tree defines the decision sequence and the importance hierarchy more clearly. Because of their close logical similarity, they will be treated together in this paper, and both referred to as decision trees.

3 Searching the Tree

Consider a large data base to be structured as, and to appear as, a very large physical tree. The tree has a complex proliferation of branches extending from the main trunk with many levels of successively smaller branches from each of the larger branches, and so forth. In searching such a data base, an investigator sees only a small portion of this tree at one time. The question that concerns us is how much of the tree should he see at one time in order to minimize his total tree search time? That is, if we visualize him searching the tree through a window which he scans over the data base structure how large should that window be?

Let us define "window size" in the following terms: the height of the window will refer to the number of decision levels that may be viewed at any one time; the "window width" will refer to the number of alternatives displayed at any decision node. Thus, in Fig. 2a, the window height is one level and the window width is five alternatives; in Fig. 2b, the height is two levels and the width is five alternatives.

Some window height greater than one level is probably desirable. This would permit the searcher to back up a level following a poor decision, or perhaps to look ahead at the consequences of selecting a certain alternative. However, this paper will deal solely with an analysis of window width, or the optimum number of alternatives to display at any one decision node in order to minimize the investigator's search time through a given data base.

4 Analysis of Search Time

In this preliminary development of a search model, we shall establish search time as a monotonic criteria upon which to judge optimality of window width. The objective function for our determination of optimal window width then becomes one of minimizing expected search time. The search process corresponding to this search time is the procedure the investigator goes through in selecting a single satisfactory item in a data base of a fixed size. Beginning at the apex of the decision tree, he examines the alternatives available to him at the first decision node, selects one of them, which in turn leads to a subsequent decision node with its own alternatives, etc. Finally, he has traced through the whole tree to the data base stored on the last level of branches. Figure 1b

Fig. 2a. Portion of a decision tree as viewed through search window. Window "height" is 1 level and window "width" is 5 alternatives. Black node indicates decision presently under consideration.

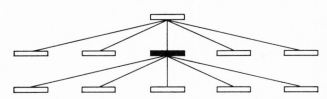

Fig. 2b. Portion of a decision tree as viewed through search window. Window "height" is 2 levels and window "width" is 5 alternatives (assumed the same for all decisions). Black node indicates decision presently under consideration, having been selected in preference to its "sister" alternatives at the decision node above it. In this example, only the alternatives to be selected among at the decision node are displayed.

illustrates such a data base of 16 items with the search assumed to start at the highest level, then moving to one of the decision nodes at the intermediate level, and finally to one of the data items (a two-level search).

The time of the search process consists of two components:

1. *Decision time* required for visually orienting to an alternative branch, focusing on the word or statement describing the alternative, and deciding whether or not the alternative is the direction in which to continue the search; and

2. *Window shift time* required to shift the viewing window to the next level of the tree and visually to orient oneself to the new display. Physically, the window through which one scans the tree may be a portion of a page, an index card, a computer-driven CRT, etc. Consequently, the time to shift the window from one portion of the tree to the next successive portion consists of handling or machine time and/or visual saccade time.

We shall assume that the total tree search time consists of the sum of the individual alternative decision times and the window shift times.

The notation we shall use to describe the tree is as follows:

N = total number of end items in the data base to be differentiated among and stored at the end of the last level of branches. In Fig. 1, $N = 16$.

L = total number of levels in the tree, to be searched one at a time in succession. In Fig. 1, $L = 2$.

n = number of alternative branches under each decision node. In the present analysis, this is assumed to be the same for all nodes, although relaxation of this assumption will be discussed later. In Fig. 1, $n = 4$.

T = expected total tree search time.

T_w = expected total window shift time.

t_w = time to shift the window once to an adjacent level, assumed to be the same for all levels.

T_d = expected total decision time.

t_d = time to read a single alternative and make a single decision about it. It is assumed in this model that reading and deciding occur simultaneously.

n_d = expected number of decisions made at any given level.

$\gamma = t_d/t_w$

We will show that the optimal structure for the visual search of a data base is a function of γ but independent of N.

To determine the number of individual decisions required in searching a tree, it is necessary to discriminate between two principal decision processes:

1. *Relative decision-making* is a judgment process where each alternative under a decision node is examined and the alternative is selected which best satisfies a certain criterion (e.g., the largest, the most similar, the most promising).

2. *Absolute decision-making* is a judgment process where each alternative is examined and accepted or rejected, not in comparison with its "sister" alternatives but rather in terms of some common, absolute standard of comparison. As soon as an alternative is accepted, the searcher immediately shifts to the next level to examine the subalternatives under the just selected alternative and the unexamined sister alternatives are not considered.

Depending on the nature of the information in the tree and the familiarity of the investigator with this information, either of these search techniques may be used. Both will be analyzed here.

If the relative decision-making strategy is used, then $n_d = n$ and the expected total decision time is the time required to make n decisions[1] at each of L levels, or

$$T_d = n L t_d \qquad (1)$$

If the absolute decision-making strategy is used, the expected number of alternatives that will be examined before a satisfactory one is found (and the search at that level ends) may be found as follows. Assuming that each alternative branching from a node is equally likely for selection, the probability of selecting the kth alternative, $p(k)$, is $1/n$ and

$$n_d = \sum_{k=1}^{n} k\, p(k) = \sum_{k=1}^{n} k\, \frac{1}{n} = \frac{n+1}{2}$$

[1] This assumes that each alternative is examined only once, and the results carried in short-term memory during subsequent examinations. If one assumes that pair-wise comparison is made of all alternatives, then $n_d = n(n-1)/2$, and all subsequent calculations involving n_d are increased by an amount $(n-1)/2$.

Because decision time is a linear function of the number of alternatives considered at each level, the expected value of the total decision time is the expected value of the individual decision time multiplied by the total number of decisions in a search, or

$$T_d = \frac{(n+1)\, L\, t_d}{2} \qquad (2)$$

In either of these two cases, the time required to shift the window $L-1$ times over the L levels of the tree is

$$T_w = (L-1)\, t_w \cdot \qquad (3)$$

Consequently, the total expected time to search the complete tree may be determined from Eq. 3 and either Eq. 1 or 2:

$$
\begin{aligned}
T &= T_d + T_w \\
&= n L t_d + (L-1)\, t_w \qquad \text{(relative)} \qquad (4)\\
&= \frac{(n+1)\, L\, t_d}{2} + (L-1)\, t_w \qquad \text{(absolute)} \qquad (5)
\end{aligned}
$$

A total data base of size N may be searched by selecting among n alternatives at each decision point on each of L levels, where $N = n^L$. In log form, $\log N = L \log n$, or

$$L = \frac{\log N}{\log n} \cdot \qquad (6)$$

Equation 6 may be substituted in Eq. 4 and 5 to obtain an expression in terms of n, the variable to be optimized so as to minimize T; N, which is fixed for any given data base; and the average times t_d and t_w:

$$T = \frac{n \log N}{\log n} t_d + \left(\frac{\log N}{\log n} - 1 \right) t_w \qquad \text{(relative)} \qquad (7)$$

$$T = \left(\frac{n+1}{2} \right) \left(\frac{\log N}{\log n} \right) t_d + \left(\frac{\log N}{\log n} - 1 \right) t_w \qquad \text{(absolute)} \qquad (8)$$

Taking the partial difference of T with respect to n for each of these expressions, we determine the value of $n = n^*$ which minimizes T for the search of any given N.

$$0 = \frac{\Delta T}{\Delta n} = \frac{t_d \log (N)}{2} \left[\frac{n^* + 2}{\log (n^* + 1)} - \frac{(n^* + 1)}{\log (n^*)} \right] + t_w \log N$$
$$\left[\frac{1}{\log (n^* + 1)} - \frac{1}{\log (n^*)} \right] \qquad \text{(absolute)} \qquad (10)$$

$$0 = \frac{\Delta T}{\Delta n} = t_d \log (N) \left[\frac{n^* + 1}{\log (n^* + 1)} - \frac{n^*}{\log (n^*)} \right]$$
$$+ t_w \log N \left[\frac{1}{\log (n^* + 1)} - \frac{1}{\log (n^*)} \right] \qquad \text{(relative)} \qquad (11)$$

where Δn is identically equal to 1.

The optimal n^* is a function of the ratio of average decision time and average window shift time but independent of the size of the data base.

5 Selecting Optimal Search Parameters

Equations 7 and 8 have been plotted in Fig. 3 for T as a function of n at various levels of $\gamma = t_d/t_w$. It is noted that T has a distinct minimum which becomes

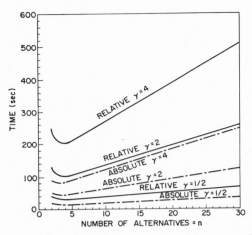

FIG. 3. Expected total time of search versus number of alternatives for both absolute and relative judgment searches and tree values of γ. $N = 1,048,576$

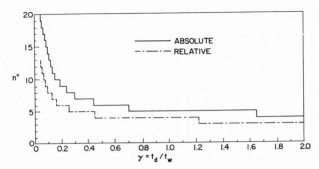

FIG. 4. Optimum number of alternatives (n^*) at each level versus values of $\gamma = t_d/t_w$ for both absolute and relative judgment problems

more sharply peaked as γ increases. In other words, as the time to make decisions becomes longer relative to the time to shift the window, nonoptimal structuring becomes relatively more costly.

In order to obtain a typical value of γ, predetermined time standards of visual operations were consulted (8). The decision time, t_d, is nominally one second for inspection of a simple "chunk" of information; and the value of window shift time, t_w, is approximately $\frac{1}{2}$ second (assuming minimal handling or machine time). Consequently, the ratio $\gamma = t_d/t_w$, should have a value of about two.

Figure 3 illustrates the consequences of a γ equal to 2 for various values of n on the time to search a tree, and the sensitivity of search time to changing γ values. It will be seen that tree search time reaches a minimum typically for $n = 4$. The value of n^* is always between 3 and 5 in the cases investigated (for values of $\gamma \geq \frac{1}{2}$) under both the relative and absolute judgment strategies. The penalty cost in time wasted in searching a nonoptimally structured tree is also indicated. A poorly structured data base display might require two or more times the information retrieval time by the investigator than would an optimally displayed data base.

More generally, Fig. 4 illustrates the optimal values, n^*, for any value of γ. Here it may be seen that n^* is rather small and the decision tree branches, as seen through the search window, are relatively narrow except in the case of very small values of γ. The smaller values of γ would result from ungainly manual handling methods, sluggish machine cycle times, or reduced decision times. As γ increases to more typical values, n^* rapidly approaches the asymptotic values of 3–4.

Relationships such as those presented in Fig. 3 and 4 may be used to measure the relative efficiency of the structure of any given data base and its manual or machine constrained search procedures in terms of the approximate search time required and the search time

requirements under optimal conditions, granting the assumptions that have been made.

6 Discussion of Results

These results seem to be at variance with the apparent assumptions of the structure of most data bases we have observed. The Library of Congress classification system, Index Medicus, the Engineering Index, Psychological Abstracts, Dictionary of Occupational *Titles,* the STAR Index, and several other classification systems commonly in use are very low in height and extremely wide. Typically, the trees observed are only 2 or 3 levels deep and 40 to 50 alternatives wide at a given decision node. The Library of Congress classification system (7) is over 30,000 branches at the first level with as many as 107 entries under one of these branches.

Although a user-oriented data base would be no wider than four to five alternatives at any one decision node, and as deep as necessary, it should be noted that, for values of γ less than one, the tree search time curves (Fig. 4) are reasonably flat in the range of three to eight alternatives per node. Consequently, in this situation some flexibility in designing the tree structure is possible without appreciably affecting the investigator's search time. (Things do not always come precisely in fours or fives.)

7 Discussion of Assumptions

Several assumptions have been made in this paper which will require subsequent analysis to determine the effect of their relaxation. The number of alternatives per decision node, n, has been assumed to be the same for all nodes in the tree. This would be impossible in a practical situation—information does not come organized that way. However, we would assume that if the recommended n^* were considered to be an average n rather than a constant n our recommendations would still apply.

In addition, we have made the somewhat unrealistic assumption that the investigator would go right through the tree from top to bottom making exactly one decision at each level. However, we have found from some preliminary studies that this seldom happens, and that, in the cases of incorrect decisions, it is necessary to back up one level and select a new alternative from among the ones previously rejected or ignored. In fact, as indicated earlier, provision should be made for backup in the design of a retrieval system. Nevertheless, we feel that, unless this phenomenon were to influence the t_d or the t_w times, our recommended n^* values would still apply.

Moreover, we have assumed that all alternatives have an equal likelihood of being inspected, and that the decision time, t_d, is not a function of n. Relaxing these assumptions would not be difficult—it would simply mean new, more complex formulations along the same lines of the ones presented in the paper that would probably not change the results of the basic formulations significantly.

Finally, as a consequence of our "equal likelihood" assumption, we have assumed that the alternatives under consideration at a decision node had no ordering in their array that would assist in searching—such as relative importance, alphabetical, or frequency of use. Obviously, were the alternatives arrayed in such a manner, the time to search them would be less than we have assumed since now some alternatives are more likely to be selected than others and the pattern of the array would assist in ignoring the less likely, but only in the case of an investigator who is familiar enough with the tree to know what key word he is searching for in the language of the tree. The naive investigator, who is learning the tree as he searches it, is not helped by an alphabetical array when he does not know what specific words represent the concept he is researching; nor is he assisted much by importance or frequency-of-use rankings unless he is willing to put his faith in the top word of the list. That is, the more knowledgeable the investigator in terms of knowing the vocabulary of the tree being searched, the greater the value of such an infor-

mation coding procedure to reduce the effective window width.

8 Conclusion

It is clear that much work remains to be done to develop general theories of the display and search of large data bases. However, we now feel that we are able to recommend a general structure shape for librarians and others working in the field of information storage and retrieval who would like some guidelines for information classification, and some suggestions for future analysis. To our knowledge, guidelines on optimal classification tree sizes have not existed previously.

References

1. MILLS, J., *Rutgers Series on Systems for the Intellectual Organization of Information,* Vol. I: *The Universal Decimal Classification,* Rutgers University, New Brunswick, N.J., 1964.
2. TAUBE, M., *Studies in Coordinate Indexing,* Documentation, Inc., 1953.
3. VICKERY, B. C., *Rutgers Series on Systems for the Intellectual Organization of Information,* Vol. V, *Faceted Classification Schemes,* Rutgers University, New Brunswick, N.J., 1966.
4. CENTER for DOCUMENTATION and COMMUNICATION RESEARCH, *Information Retrieval in Action,* Western Reserve University Press, Cleveland, Ohio, 1963.
5. DUGGAR, B. C., et al., *Design and Use of Information Systems for Automated On-The-Job Training,* Vol. 4, *Graphical Symbology and Logic Diagrams for Use as Training Aids,* Technical Document Report No. ESD-TDR-64-234 V4, Dio-Dynamics, Inc. Cambridge, Mass., 1965 (AD 616 551).
6. JONKER, F., *Indexing Theory, Indexing Methods, and Search Devices,* Scarecrow Press, New York, 1964.
7. Library of Congress, *Subject Headings,* 7th ed., Washington, D.C., 1966.
8. BIRNS, S., et al., *Management of Office Costs,* McGraw-Hill, New York, 1962.

42 On the Geometry of Libraries

A. D. BOOTH
Journal of Documentation
Vol. 25, No. 1, March, 1969

The following problem suggested itself whilst the optimum physical layout of a library was being considered. The analysis and conclusion, however, have a wider relevance and, in particular, seem to throw light both on the statistics of natural language and upon the process of data storage in the human brain.

In the library context the problem to be investigated is: which is the layout which minimizes the distance travelled by the user or, more generally the access mechanism, in extracting books.

The solution which comes most obviously to mind is to arrange the books so that those to which reference is most frequently made occupy positions which are closest to the point of entry. We shall now show that this arrangement minimizes access time.

Let f_i be the frequency of use of book $b_i (i = 1 \ldots N)$ and let b_i be shelved so that its access distance is l_i. If the books are assumed ordered so that $f_1 > f_2 \ldots > f_i \ldots > f_N$ then the total access distance to the collection in some interval of time is*

$$D = \sum_{i=1}^{N} l_i f_i$$

* In subsequent formulae the limits of summation will be omitted.

We now show that if $l_1 < l_2 < \ldots < l_i \ldots < l_N$, i.e. the books are arranged so that their access distances are less as their frequency of use increases, then D is a minimum.

This follows because the interchange in shelving position of two books, b_i and b_j say, changes D by the quantity:

$$Q = (l_j f_i + l_i f_j) - (l_i f_i + l_j f_j)$$

i.e.
$$Q = -(l_i - l_j)(f_i - f_j)$$

and, by assumption, $f_i > f_j$ and $l_i < l_j$,

whence $Q \geqslant 0$

equality occuring only when $f_i = f_j$ or $l_i = l_j$.

Any change from the inverse frequency ordering thus generally increases access time except in the case $l_i = l_j$.

1. The Frequency of Use Law

In the preceding analysis no assumption has been made regarding the way in which frequency of book use is distributed amongst members of the collection. This item of information will be needed in the following sections of the paper in order to make quantitative comparisons between different geometrical arrangements.

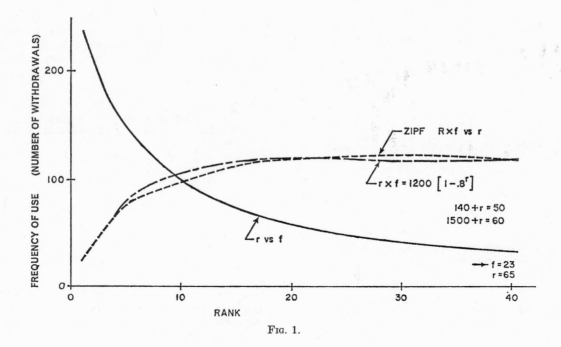

FIG. 1.

It is fortunate that data of the kind required are available. Fleming and Kilgour[1] have provided an analysis of the withdrawal frequency of serials from a large library, their data are shown in graphical form, in Fig. 1 (solid line).

Now a general 'law' of behaviour for frequency-structured collections has been suggested by Zipf.[2] This 'law', initially proposed for word frequency distribution in language, can be simply expressed as:

$$f = K/r$$

Here the items considered are assumed to be arranged in a list so that the most frequently occurring comes first and has frequency f_1 and rank $r = 1$; the second most frequently occurring comes second and has rank 2 and so on.

Zipf's law has been shown to apply to such diverse collections as words in English and Greek, and to U.S. cities in order of population.

To test its applicability to library withdrawals the information of Fleming and Kilgour has been plotted in the form rank vs rank $\times$ frequency. This is shown in the dotted curve of Fig. 1. It is evident that, for $r > 10$, Zipf's law is an excellent approximation to the facts. For $r < 10$ it appears that a better approximation would be

$$r \times f = 1200\{1 - (0.8)^r\},$$

this is shown in the chain dotted curve of Fig. 1.

The deviation from Zipf's law occurs only for small values of r. It seems probable that this is due to the fact that insufficient duplicate copies have been provided to satisfy the large user demand for the most frequently used books, and to verify this, a study is being mounted at the Cleveland Health Sciences Library. For the present, however, it will be assumed that Zipf's law does apply to withdrawals with the reservation that some modification in detail may be needed to our conclusions when new evidence is available.

It is worth noting, however, that such modification is likely to be small since only the first few items are affected.

2. Library Geometry

We shall consider next the implications of the result just obtained to library layout.

The first, and most elementary configuration is one in which the access point (A, Fig. 2) is at one end of a single long shelf upon which the books are arranged in descending order of frequency of use.

If it is assumed that the average book thickness is p and that the distance of A from the start of the shelf is l then the distance travelled by the access operator (human or mechanical) in unit time is:

$$D_{20} = \sum (l + ip)f_i$$
$$= l \sum f_i + p \sum i f_i \qquad (1)$$

This value can clearly be improved if the access point is situated at the mid-point of the collection and, in this case, shown in Figs. 2.1 and 2.2, is simply

$$D_{21} = l \sum f_i + \frac{p}{2} \sum i f_i \qquad (2)$$

Organization of Information Stores   457

FIG. 2.0.   Linear shelf — end access.

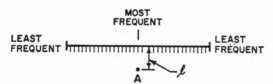

FIG. 2.1.   Linear shelf — central access.

FIG. 2.2.   Linear shelf — two-sided access.

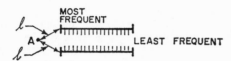

FIG. 2.3.   Linear shelf (corridor) — end access.

It is clear that, for small values of l and large numbers of books, N

$$D_{21} \to \frac{1}{2} D_{20}$$

Naturally the single linear shelf would be unacceptable in human library design although in a mechanized library the linear mechanism needed to search it would be attractively simple.

The next, and obvious, extension of this analysis is to assume that the books are arranged on shelves in the usual manner. If the stack is assumed to be S shelves high, and that shelf length is great compared with S so that vertical access time can be neglected, the analogues of (1) and (2) are:

$$D_{20} = l \sum f_i + \frac{p}{S} \sum i f_i \qquad (3)$$

and

$$D_{21} = l \sum f_i + \frac{p}{2S} \sum i f_i \qquad (4)$$

It is clear that, of the arrangements examined D_{21} (Equation 4) is the most efficient.

In practice a library would be unlikely to take the form shown in Fig. 2.3 unless the only space available was in the form of a long corridor and in this case a slight extension of the preceding analysis shows that the optimum arrangement would be that shown in Fig. 3,

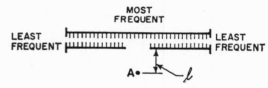

FIG. 3.   Linear corridor — central access.

here,

$$D_3 \doteq \sum f_i + \frac{p}{4S} \sum i f_i \qquad (5)$$

The analysis can be extended to more usual configurations such as those shown in Fig. 4.

Analytical expressions could be given for each of the cases Figs. 4.1 and 4.2. They would, however, be extremely complicated since for optimum performance the books must be arranged in spherical zones whose distance from A increases as the frequency of use decreases. The problems of cataloguing such a collection for access and those of designing a mechanical selection system would be considerable, but the general result which can be stated is that, if D_{42} is the access distance for the configuration, Fig. 4.2, and D_{41} that for configuration, Fig. 4.1, then *very* approximately

$$D_{42} \approx \tfrac{1}{2} D_{41} \approx \frac{1}{T} D_3$$

where T is the number of rows of shelves in Fig. 4.2.

We now answer the question: by how much is the frequency-of-use ordered linear collection more efficient than a normal one where subjects or author names form the basis of arrangement?

The answer will be given for the specific case of the stack arrangement, Fig. 2.3, for which

$$D = l \sum f_i + \frac{p}{2S} \sum i f_i \qquad (6)$$

When no frequency order is imposed the access distance for each transaction is, on average:

$$D_{23}^1 = \sum \left(l + \frac{Np}{2 \times 2S} \right) f_i$$

$$= l \sum f_i + \frac{p}{2S} \sum \frac{N}{2} f_i$$

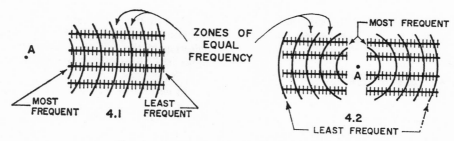

FIG. 4. Optimum use of conventional stacks.

For a large collection, when l is ignored, and it is assumed that Zipf's law is obeyed, $f_i = K/i$ we thus have:

$$D_{23} = \frac{p}{2S} \sum Ki/i = \frac{KNp}{2S}$$

and

$$D_{23}^1 = \frac{p}{2S} \sum \frac{KN}{2i} = \frac{KNp}{4S} \sum \frac{1}{i}$$

$$\approx \frac{KNp}{4S} \log_e N$$

Thus

$$\frac{D_{23}^1}{D_{23}} = \tfrac{1}{2} \log_e N$$

This increases with the size of the collection and shows, for example, that the mean access distance for a collection of 10,000 volumes using frequency ordering is 9.2 times less than that involved when subject or author arrangement is adopted. Yet again, for 100,000 volumes the frequency-of-use ordering wins by a factor of 11.5, and so on.

3. More Complex Geometries

We consider next some more complex stacking arrangements. The first is shown in Fig. 5 and represents, for example, the type of situation encountered in a number of legislative libraries (except for the frequency ordering).

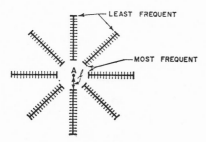

FIG. 5. Radial library.

Here the analysis leads to:

$$D_5 = l \sum f_i + \frac{p}{2R} \sum i f_i \qquad (7)$$

where R is the number of radial stacks.

It is clear that this arrangement wastes space, an attempt to improve it leads to Fig. 6,

FIG. 6. Radial library — optimum packing.

and this naturally suggests Fig. 7.

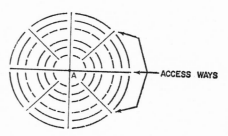

FIG. 7. Concentric circular library.

Analyses of these situations can be produced but are safely left to any reader who has a specific situation in mind.

The second situation which is worth examination is that shown in Fig. 8. Here the collection is disposed upon a circular stack with the access point at its centre. Ac-

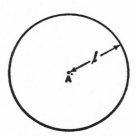

FIG. 8. Circular stack with central access.

cess to any book is now substantially independent of its position or frequency of use. The access distance becomes:

$$D_c = \sum l f_i = l \sum f_i \qquad (8)$$

This would appear to be less than all of the values previously obtained. However this superiority is illusory since, to accommodate the books l must have a minimum value given by:

$$2\pi l = \frac{Np}{S}$$

From which, using (8) we obtain,

$$D_c = \frac{Np}{2\pi S} \sum f_i \qquad (9)$$

To make this strictly comparable with (4) some assumption must be made as to the variation of f_i with i and as before we shall assume Zipf's law to hold so that $f_i = K/i$.

Inserting this relationship into (4) there results:

$$D_{21} = l \sum f_i + \frac{Kp}{2S} \sum 1$$

$$= l \sum f_i + \frac{KNp}{2S} \qquad (10)$$

Now, if $f_i = K/i$,

$$\sum f_i \approx K \log_e N$$

Whence:

$$D_c \approx \frac{KNp}{2\pi S} \log_e N$$

and

$$D_{21} \approx K \left\{ l \log_e N + \frac{Np}{2S} \right\}$$

Now l is a small *constant* so that it is clear that for appreciably large N, $D_c > D_{21}$, and this is simply a reflection of the fact that the larger the collection, the larger the diameter of the circular library used to house it.

It is natural to consider next the case of a spiral shelf arrangement of the type shown in Fig. 9.1. The mathematical problem is that of finding the equation of the spiral for which:

$$D = \sum r_i f_i \qquad (11)$$

is a minimum.

Since p, the mean book thickness, is small compared to the shelf length for, say, 100,000 books, the summation of equation (11) can be replaced by an integral without appreciable loss of accuracy:

$$D = \int_0^{Np} r f ds \qquad (12)$$

where s is now the length of the shelf measured from its origin.

It is shown in Appendix I that

$$D = 0.470\, NpK$$

This is to be compared with the one-sided linear shelf of Fig. 2 for which:

$$D = 1.00\, NpK$$

The spiral shelf thus decreases access distance by 53%, a significant improvement.

Yet again a double spiral of the type shown in Fig. 9.2 might be used. The same analysis applies with the exception the limits of access angles are now (o and π).

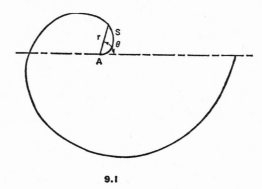

9.1

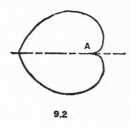

9.2

9.3

FIG. 9. Spiral configurations.

A determination of the resulting value of c and numerical evaluation of D leads to

$$D = 0.351 \, NpK$$

which is to be compared with the

$$D = 0.5 \, NpK$$

which results from the two-sided shelf of Figs. 2.2 or 2.3. The gain in efficiency is, in this case, about 30%.

This type of analysis can be applied to more complex systems such as that of Fig. 9.3 where the limiting angles on spirals are (o and $\pi/2$) but enough has been said to show the general aspects of the method and to illustrate the gains in efficiency which it can produce.

It is interesting to note that, if the spiral single-stack library is allowed to have values of θ greater than 2π a progressive increase in economy is produced. This is because, for large values of n, when the limiting angle is $2n\pi$ so that the stack has n turns,

$$c_n = 2Np/(2n\pi)^2$$

$$D_n \rightarrow 4n\pi c = \frac{2NpK}{n\pi}$$

The value for the linear stack remains NpK.

In human operations, access through stacks, which is implied by this type of library is, of course, impossible. However, for a mechanized library the access device might well operate from beneath the stacks and in this case the above arrangement would be excellent. The choice of n is not, of course, a free one, it is determined by the fact that to extract books from stacks a minimum distance of one book width, w, say, must be allowed. This gives

$$w = c \frac{\pi}{2} = \frac{2Np}{(2n\pi)^2} \cdot \frac{\pi}{2} = \frac{Np}{\pi(2n)^2}$$

or

$$n = \frac{1}{2} \left(\frac{Np}{\pi w} \right)^{\frac{1}{2}}$$

This in turn gives, $D = 4K(Npw/\pi)^{\frac{1}{2}}$
so that the spiral arrangement would, for 10^6 books, reduce the access distance by a factor of order (1,000) over that for the linear, frequency ordered, shelf.

For completeness, the simpler problem, posed by the configuration shown in Fig. 10 is of interest.

Here the access point is in close proximity to the most frequently used books in a circular stack. For the case in which the minimum distance between A and the most frequent book is, say, l, the analysis is intractable. However, when $l = 0$ the situation is as shown in Fig. 11.

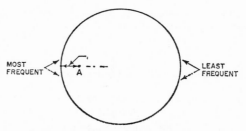

FIG. 10.   Circular stack with non-centric access.

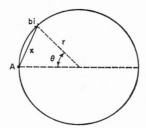

FIG. 11.   Circular stack peripheral access.

The analysis is contained in Appendix II and shows that the access distance D_0 is given by

$$D_0 \approx 0.435 \left(\frac{NpK}{5} \right)$$

It is interesting to compare this value with that obtained from (4) with the same Zipfian assumption and $l = 0$. We get:

$$D_{21} = \frac{p}{2S} \sum K \frac{i}{i}$$

$$= \frac{pNK}{2S} = 0.5 \frac{pNK}{S}$$

This is slightly larger than the $0.435 pNK/S$ given above and shows, as expected, that the shelf configuration of Fig. 11 is more efficient than that of Fig. 2.3 but that the difference (about 13%) is not important.

Thus, whilst aesthetics may make it desirable to consider curved stack configurations such as that of Fig. 11 or the more complex one of Fig. 12, the gains of efficiency

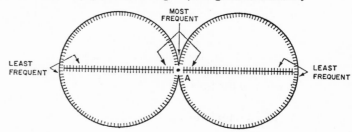

FIG. 12.   Optimum bi-circular stack.

are likely to be small and, although the subject is of interest to the mathematician and to the architect, it may safely be left to them to pursue.

4. The Library as a Push Down Store

The frequency-of-use ordered book collection described above can, of course, be realized by placing the books in the required stacking sequence and replacing them after use. There is, however, another method which will now be described.

Assume that the books are initially in any order on a long shelf. After any book has been withdrawn it is replaced, not in its original position but at the head of the shelf, all other books being pushed down to accommodate it. It is clear that, after a sufficiently long period of operation, on the average each book will occupy a position in the sequence which has the rank of its frequency of use. Naturally, withdrawal of a book will lead to temporary de-arrangement of the sequence but order will be restored when the collection has a reasonable turn-over rate.

The important feature of this result is that a library operated on the push-down principle is self optimizing and will keep itself up-to-date during periods of varying user interest.

An extra benefit of this self-optimizing scheme is that a collection operated in this way is self-purging. We mentioned that deviations from Zipfian behaviour are probably due to inadequate duplication of most frequently used items, in a collection where topical items soon become uninteresting extra copies should be removed when appropriate.

If the self optimizing mode of operation is adopted and the algorithm used is that the copy nearest to the access point is the one retrieved then other duplicates will steadily work their way to the end of the collection where they can be removed with the assurance that no harm will be done. It may be thought that the location of a book in a collection where it has no fixed place would be difficult. This is, however, not so. When a book is withdrawn its catalogue entry is set equal to zero. When it is returned its catalogue number is set equal to the number of this particular transaction in the history of the library. (The first book ever returned to the library is transaction 1, the second 2, and so on.) The location of the book at any time after its return can then be achieved by a relatively simple computer programme.

The computer and self-optimizing library structure should, however, not deter forward looking library designers from using frequency-of-use structured collections and normal fixed-place shelving.

5. The Architecture of Language

The preceding discussion has an implication for language. It has been shown by psychologists that the words

and concepts most frequently used are most readily retrieved by the human brain.

In language the most generally valid law is that of Zipf (*loc. cit.*) which states that, if words are arranged in order so that the most frequently used word is first and has rank 1, the second most frequently used word comes second and his rank 2, and so on; then

$$\text{rank} \times \text{frequency} = \text{constant}.$$

Regarding the human memory as being of the push-down variety, it emerges from the analysis given in the first part of this paper, that the system is such that it minimizes total access time. This in turn suggests, although it does not of course prove, that some mechanism of the type just proposed for library operation is at work in the long-term storage section of the human brain.

This is a direct validation of Zipf's original suggestion that his law implies a principle of least effort.

Appendix I. The Spiral Shelf Solution

The solution to this problem is typical of those to which the calculus of variations can be applied. In this case there is the auxiliary equation which states that the length of the curve is a constant Np and, for a planar library, the second condition that θ_{max}, the angle through which the radius vector, r, moves as its end transverses the stack, S, cannot exceed 2π radians. (This is necessary since the access mechanism is assumed to be unable to jump over, or go under, the stack to locate books.)

Since the integrand in (12) dies not involve derivatives of r or f it is possible to replace the Euler equation of variation calculus by the simpler, but geometrically equivalent, statement that D is minimized by that function r whose rate of change with θ, the polar co-ordinate angle, is least. That is:

$$\frac{d}{d\theta}\left(\frac{dr}{d\theta}\right) = 0$$

This equation can be integrated at once and gives:

$$r = c\theta + d$$

where c and d are constants of integration.

The initial condition $(r = 0, \theta = 0)$ gives $d = 0$ and thus

$$r = c\theta$$

To introduce the fact that the length of the stack is Np and that this occurs when $\theta = 2\pi$ we note that

$$ds^2 = r^2 d\theta^2 + dr^2$$
whence
$$ds^2 = c^2\theta^2 d\theta^2 + c^2 d\theta^2$$

or, integrating:

$$s = \frac{c}{2} \{\theta \sqrt{\theta^2 + 1} + \log_e (\sqrt{\theta^2 + 1} + \theta)\} + e$$

where e is a constant of integration. Since $(s = 0, \theta = 0)$ $e = 0$, c can be determined from:

$$Np = \frac{c}{2} \{2\pi \sqrt{4\pi^2 + 1} + \log_e (\sqrt{4\pi^2 + 1} + 2\pi)\}$$

The integral (12), which gives D, cannot be evaluated unless the form of f is known. If, as before, we assume that the collection obeys a Zipfian use distribution, then $f = K/s$ and the integration of (12) can be performed numerically. It turns out that:

$$D = 0.470 NpK$$

Appendix II. The Circular Stack Solution

The access distance, D_0 is now

$$D_0 = \frac{1}{2s} \sum x_i f_i$$

where $\qquad x = 2r \sin \theta/2$

Now we have the relationships

$$r\theta = ip \qquad\qquad (11.1)$$

with $\qquad \pi r = Np$

Whence $\quad D_0 = \frac{1}{2s} \sum 2r \sin \frac{\theta_i}{2} . f_i \qquad (11.2)$

We next assume that the collection can be represented, as to frequency of use, by Zipf's law, so that:

$$f_i = K/i$$

Equation (11.2) then becomes:

$$D_0 = \frac{K}{S} \sum \frac{r}{i} \sin \frac{\theta_i}{2}$$

or, using (11.1)

$$D_0 = \frac{K}{S} \sum \frac{p}{\theta_i} \sin \frac{\theta_i}{2}$$

Now, approximately, D_0 may be written:

$$D_0 \approx \frac{K}{S} \int_{i=1}^{N} \frac{p}{\theta_i} \sin \frac{\theta_i}{2} \, di$$

or, since $\quad di = \frac{r}{p} \, d\theta$ and $\theta = \frac{ip}{r}$,

$$D_0 \approx \frac{K}{S} \int_{\pi/N}^{\pi} \frac{r}{\theta} \sin \frac{\theta}{2} . d\theta$$

We now put $\quad r = \frac{Np}{\pi}$ (from (11.1)) and $\theta/2 = \phi$ and obtain

$$D_0 \approx \frac{KpN}{\pi S} \int_{0}^{\frac{1}{2}\pi} \frac{\sin \phi}{\phi} \, d\phi$$

whence $\quad D_0 \approx \frac{KpN}{\pi S} Si(\pi/2) = 1.37 \frac{pNK}{\pi S} = 0.435 \frac{pNK}{S}$

References

1. FLEMING, T. P. and KILGOUR, F. G. Moderately and heavily used biomedical journals. *Proc. 2nd Int. Congress on Med. Lib.*, 1963, p. 234–41.
2. ZIPF, G. K. *Human behaviour and the principle of least effort.* Addison-Wesley, Mass., 1949.

Chapter Eight
Question,
Handling,
and
Search
Procedures

In comparison to the input functions of information systems, the output functions received relatively little attention. In information science the problem of representation of information has been treated at great length and indepth, while there have been few efforts devoted to the equivalently important problem of question handling and analysis and of search procedures and strategies. However, a few experiments have revealed that the methodology for handling questions and searching could affect the performance of information systems as much, at least, as the method of representing information, such as indexing. The reason for this relative neglect lies in the aforementioned and widely accepted assumption that, given a "good" method for handling input, the output would not be a real problem. It is suggested here that this is not the case, and that handling of output in information systems continues to be a problem area in dire need of comprehensive research.

The interdependence and interrelation of question handling and search procedures make them so congruent that, at times, it is nearly impossible to distinguish fully between the two. While question handling usually implies a mechanism for entering a request into the system, an analysis of the concepts in the request (e.g., enumeration of near-synonyms and related terms), a translation into the language(s) of the representation used in the system, and an ability to clarify the content of the question with the requestor, the search procedure implies an application of the available logic to the request and the physical manipulation of the file(s). The picture is further complicated by the fact that the question handling is closely related to the function of representation of information, and the search procedures to the organization of the file.

The empirical work in this area has been concerned with devising means and methods which would ensure some optimization of the understanding of the question by the system; with the analysis of the questions; with the interaction with the requestor; with the exploration of complex logic in search statements; and with the physical searching. The experimental work has concentrated on (1) the development of systems which allow direct handling of questions, (2) the testing of the effects of various implementations of question handling, and (3) the effect of search procedures on performance of information systems. The theoretical work has been directed mostly toward devising new logical and mathematical foundations for searching and, specifically, toward building the foundations for iterative searching as the most promising method. The selections in this chapter represent these experimental and theoretical efforts.

Simmons (Article 43) provides a review of efforts to create a "second generation" of computer-based systems which would be able to handle questions stated directly in natural language and to process natural language texts. This goal can be assumed to be the highest ideal of information systems, in general; but it is well-known that we are quite far from achieving it. It should be pointed out that question handling in online systems, operating at present, are closely related to the general works in this area with very similar ideals. However, it is strange that so little theoretical or even experimental work has actually been done on online systems utilization (except on the organization of files); admittedly of high technical competence, the efforts have been distinctly developmental and operational in a technological sense and usually isolated from theory or even from an analysis of needs. Somehow, it seems that the mistakes in the development of the information retrieval systems on the first and second generation computers prevalent during the fifties and early sixties are being repeated in the development of such online systems on the third and fourth generation computers.

In the second article in this chapter, Goffman (Article 44) provides a theoretical framework and an experiment implementing a theory in relation to an indirect search technique for information retrieval. At the base of this method are the relationships between the documents in the file, as opposed to the usual method of matching the relationships between the questions and the documents.

Keen (Article 46) presents results from test experiments in which the effects of various question analyses and search strategies on performance of retrieval systems are investigated.

It seems quite obvious that many more, similar efforts in the general area of output function are needed in order to learn how to exploit what we already have developed in information systems.

43 Natural Language Question-Answering Systems: 1969

ROBERT F. SIMMONS
Communications of the ACM
Vol. 13, No. 1, January, 1970

1. Introduction

Kuhn (1962) has persuasively argued that science progresses by means of its paradigms — its models of the general nature of a research area — and that at the frontiers of research the primary quest is for a good paradigm. The small frontier outpost of language data processing has been characterized by an intensive seeking for a paradigm suitable to guide its researchers as they survey the complex topography of natural language structures. The earliest paradigm — one that led mechanical translators and early information retrievalists into a hopeless cul-de-sac — was that words (i.e. strings of letters) are the units of meaning; that mechanical translation requires simply the discovery and substitution of target language equivalent words; that information retrieval requests and data structures can be adequately represented by some Boolean combination of words.

With each succeeding failure, this paradigm was buttressed with notions of thesaurus classes of words, statistical association probabilities, and superficial syntactic structures. The paradigm still proved inadequate as shown by the conclusions of the recent ALPAC (1967)

report and by a sharp criticism of language processors by Kasher (1966). In the meantime, Chomsky (1965) devised a paradigm for linguistic analysis that includes syntactic, semantic, and phonological components to account for the generation of natural language statements.

He says (p. 141): "The syntactic component consists of a base and a transformational component. The base in turn, consists of a categorical subcomponent and a lexicon. The base generates deep structures. A deep structure enters the semantic component and receives a semantic interpretation; it is mapped by the transformational rules into a surface structure, which is then given a phonetic interpretation by the rules of the phonological component." This theory can be interpreted to imply that the meaning of a sentence can be represented as a semantically interpreted deep structure — i.e. a formal data structure.

From computer science's preoccupation with formal programming languages and compilers, there emerged another paradigm. In this one the elements of a language are formally defined objects in a well-defined syntactic structure. Translation between two such languages is accomplished by a set of transformational rules or functions whose arguments are these structured objects. The set of transforming functions is seen to be the semantics of the system, and the meaning of a program is generally taken to be the effect of its operation.

The adoption and combination of these two new paradigms have resulted in a vigorous new generation of language processing systems characterized by sophisticated linguistic and logical processing of well-defined formal data structures. It is my purpose to examine several of these systems and draw conclusions concerning the state-of-the-art, its principles, its problems, and its prognosis for socially useful applications.

Background

In 1965, the first generation of fifteen experimental question-answering systems was reviewed (Simmons 1965). These included a social-conversation machine, systems that translated from English into limited logical calculi, and programs that attempted to answer questions from English text. The survey concluded that important principles of language processing were being unearthed and that significant progress was being made toward the development of useful question-answering systems. This conclusion was criticized by Giuliano who took the contrary view that there was "... evidence mainly of motion with little real evidence of progress" (Giuliano 1965). Kasher (1966) critically reviewed several example systems to conclude that none met even minimal criteria for successful semantic analysis or logical inference capabilities. Continued efforts in the field indicate that Giuliano's view was unnecessarily pessimistic, and these efforts have gone far toward correcting the inadequacies that Kasher stressed. Most systems developed since that time have included formally described data structures, explicit semantic analysis procedures, and a significant degree of deductive capability.

2. Second Generation Systems

First generation systems were not only handicapped by the lack of adequate linguistic models but in addition were often written in low level languages such as FAP and IPL. Considerable impetus was gained from the appearance of such higher level languages as Comit, Lisp, Slip, Snobol, and Algol, which were commonly available by 1964 and 1965. The additional leverage added by the accessibility of time-shared, interactive consoles greatly eased the task of programming and debugging complicated language processing programs, and as a consequence, numerous language processing systems, many of them variants on the question-answering theme, were constructed. A group of conversation machines typified by Weizenbaum's Eliza and Colby's belief system simulations were experimented with in several settings. A number of excellent approaches to natural lan-

guage-oriented fact retrieval systems and a calculus word-problem-solver were programmed, and efforts continued toward the development of natural text question-answering and paraphrasing systems. For convenience of presentation, the second generation systems will be considered under the headings: conversation machines, fact-retrieval systems, mathematical word-problem-solvers, and natural language text processing.

Conversation Machines

Eliza is a Slip program developed by Weizenbaum (1966) to explore the possibility of programming computers to conduct natural language conversations with humans. Early experiments with Eliza simulated (or caricatured?) the conversational mode of a Rogerian psychotherapist as exemplified in the following brief excerpt from a computer conversation:

Well, my boyfriend made me come here.
YOUR BOYFRIEND MADE YOU COME HERE?
He says I'm depressed much of the time.
I AM SORRY TO HEAR YOU ARE DEPRESSED.
It's true, I am unhappy.
DO YOU THINK COMING HERE WILL HELP YOU NOT TO BE UNHAPPY?
Etc.

The program structure that supports this conversational capability is a set of pattern-operation transformations whose patterns are composed of keywords and whose operations are the substitution of a partially composed English statement in conjunction with some portion of the input sentence. These transformations are provided to Eliza by a prepared script. The script is a high level program[1] whose statements are not necessarily sequential — the flow of control among command statements in the script is guided by the keywords of the input.

If we consider a brief example and its script rule, the central operation of the system can be seen.

Input: you are very helpful

Script: (0 you are 0) = (What makes you think I am 4)

Output: What makes you think I am very helpful? In the input phase, which includes a dictionary lookup, the "you" elicits an associated script rule that matches the text. The pattern (0 you are 0) matches any occurrence of the sequence of words "you are" regardless of what preceded or followed them. At this point Eliza uses the pattern to segment and number the modified input text as follows:

1: (empty); 2: you; 3: are; 4: very helpful

It then rewrites for the number 4 in the right half of the rule, "very helpful," the element labeled 4 by the left

---

1. Similar in structure to parts of the pattern-operation rules of Comit, Meteor, or Snobol.

half, and prints the results: "What makes you think I am very helpful?"

ELIZA has been studied in application to a number of computer-aided instruction problems (Taylor 1968) and to a computer simulation of counseling behavior (Ellis and Tiedeman, 1968) and in each case has shown promising capabilities. The system includes limited features for remembering previously mentioned topics, for tagging keywords in the dictionary, and for operating script rules that refer to the tags.

Colby's simulations of belief systems originally used a set of pattern-operation rules much like those of ELIZA but have since progressed to a more complex organization (Colby and Enea, 1967; Tesler, Enea, and Colby, 1968; Colby and Enea, 1968). In original phases of this research, Colby's program scanned an input statement to discover particular patterns of words. When such a pattern was found, a response associated with the pattern was selected by the program and typed as a conversational reply to the subject's input. The purpose of the conversation was to allow the program to accumulate belief statements held by the subject. Augmentation of this direct word-pattern matching by the addition of pushdown stacks that helped to maintain the continuity of conversations supported Colby's hypothesis that a successful man-machine dialogue system required models of the patient, of itself, and of the world in general. The pushdown stacks in early implementations predicted certain aspects of replies to the computer system's questions; thus a "why" question predicted a "because" type response, and a "yes-no" type question predicted an affirmative or negative reply. Additional information stacks were used to remember pertinent facts known about the subject so that blunders such as the one illustrated in the following dialogue between the person and the program could be avoided.

When my father died my mother was sick for a long time.
TELL ME MORE ABOUT HIM.
My father was a writer. He was kind but rather cynical . . .
IS HE NOW?
He is dead.

The blunder occurred because the system at that time did not store and use the fact that the father was dead.

In the most recent phases of this research a directed graph model of concepts in relation to other concepts has been developed to model the belief systems of the persons being conversed with. Concepts are represented by nodes, and relationships by the labeled connections between nodes. Each node in the graph is associated with a set of attributes that can characterize a belief in terms of its intensity, credibility, etc. The relations that connect concepts are characterized by formal properties that can be used by the model in processes of interpretation and reasoning. Rules of inference are also embedded in this structure in the form of conditional statements with variables. (This type of rule is explained and illustrated in the section on Fact-Retrieval Systems.)

Two 1969 reports (Colby et al.) offer some detail on the system's present methods for evaluating beliefs. The principal inference rule that has been used is of the general form "A implies B", where "implies" is understood to mean a psychological expectation and the A term may involve multiple conditions. An essentially unlimited series of such rules can be applied as follows:

$$A \rightarrow B \quad B \rightarrow C \quad C \rightarrow D \text{ etc.}$$

Such a procedure gives inference power limited only by search time and by the validity of the "implies" relation. Discovering beliefs relevant to a given proposition is accomplished by replacing terms in the proposition by similar, opposite, or complementary terms and applying inference rules to obtain the set of beliefs related to that proposition. Beliefs are evaluated by a technique that computes credibility as a weighted function of consistency and evidential foundation of each belief. The resulting evaluations are used in heuristics that control the depth of search for relevant beliefs. Results with this system show that it is effective for retrieving relevant beliefs — although the cost in computing time is not cited.

Schank and Tesler (1969) describe a semantic system for eventual use in conjunction with Colby's belief model. This system is called a conceptual parser. It is based on a dependency grammar in which each syntactic constituent is tested against a conceptual semantics data base that shows semantic compositions with knowledge of relations that hold in "the real world." The parsing system includes transformations in the form of pattern-operation rules so that it can extricate embedded sentences as in the following example:

John saw Texas flying to California.
Parse:

$$John \overset{P}{\Longleftrightarrow} see \leftarrow Texas$$

$$John \overset{\uparrow P}{\Longleftrightarrow} fly \overset{to}{\Leftarrow} California$$

The symbol "⟺" refers to a subject predicate relation "←" to a direct object, "⇐" to a prepositional dependency, "↑" to a modifier, and the label "P" refers to past tense. The alternate interpretation that "Texas flies to California" is eliminated by the absence of the conjunction of "Texas" and "fly" in the conceptual data base. Schank's system is unusual in basing its semantic analysis on a dependency grammar, but it appears to be as effective as any other system that makes a semantic test following the formation of a syntactic constituent.

The belief system simulations of Colby et al. compose a very active project and one that is significantly advancing capabilities for natural language conversations with computers. There is a balanced use of deductive and inductive forms of inference, and with the eventual incorporation of sophisticated syntactic and semantic analysis procedures this line of research may result in a significant psychological model and an effective language processor.

Abelson and Carroll (1965) have also reported on a computer model of belief systems that is based on a network of logical relations between concepts. It uses an inductive logic to substantiate or reject statements in accordance with its beliefs. This logic is based on the notion of frequency of class instantiation. For example, given the statement:

"Left-wingers mistreat US friends abroad"

the system uses the inductive rule that the sentence will be considered credible if at least half the instances of the concept, "left-wingers," are connected in belief statements with one of the instances of the predicate, "mistreat US friends abroad." Thus, if "administration theorists" is one of two concepts that are considered to be instances of "left-wingers" and is connected to "coddle left-leaning neutrals," which is considered an instance of the first predicate, then the statement is accepted as credible. The system also includes deductive processes and models for rationalizing and denying its input statements.

A most interesting notion of complex meaning — the implicational molecule — is described in a more recent paper (Abelson and Reich 1969). Abelson holds that one of the more important aspects of language usage is pragmatic analysis, i.e. the production of plausible implications from sentences. The implicational molecule is a first approach to pragmatic analysis. Abelson illustrates with three responses to the sentence "I went to three drugstores." "A syntactically based system might respond 'How did you go to three drugstores?' A semantically based program might respond, 'What useful things did you buy in three drugstores?' But a pragmatically based program ought to be clever enough to ask 'How come the first two drugstores didn't have what you wanted?' "

An implicational molecule is a set of sentence classes bound together by psychological implication. Thus a sentence is a propositional element, and implication links bind such elements into a molecule. The set {A does X, X causes Y, A wants Y} is an example of an implicational molecule. Abelson postulates a *completion tendency* as a characteristic of human users of language. So, given some elements of the set, the others may be inferred. Thus, if it is given that A does X and X causes Y, there is some likelihood of inferring that A wants Y; it is even plausible, given only A does X, to infer that X causes some Y that A wants. Implicational molecules are named; the above example is called PURPOSE (Y, A, X) and the program is allowed to infer that A did X

with purpose Y. The idea of implicational molecules is an important addition to a program's capability for conducting connected discourse with humans for filling in unexpressed premises, intentions, purposes, etc.

Abelson's program is stocked with a data base containing beliefs representing "the extreme right wing point of view of a well-known ex-ex-senator." He reports that the use of implicational molecules greatly enhanced the program's capability to simulate actual replies of the senator to input statements. The system, programmed in SNOBOL3 and limited to fixed format sentences for input and output, is a most suggestive model of internal symbolic processes that may intervene between statement and response in a conversational system. For language-processing researchers, both Abelson's and Colby's systems demonstrate methods for using inductive inference in question-answering and conversational machines.

Becker (1969) has presented a detailed analysis of the notion of "analogy" in the context of a general data structure for representing semantic information derivable from English sentences. He suggests that an important aspect of understanding new information is the process of locating previously stored information analogous to it, and making predictions on the basis of this previous experience. Becker outlines a process for inductive inference on the basis of analogies, which is justifiably more complex than methods used by Colby and Abelson. Another approach that may prove useful for inductive inference is McCarthy's (1963) formal system for the Advice Taker that introduces a modal logic for inferring that CAN(a b) and CAN (b c) may imply CANACHULT (a c), i.e. that a can ultimately achieve c.

Fact-Retrieval Systems

Second generation systems include a natural language oriented fact-retrieval system by Elliott (1965) and a generalization of several previous approaches into one system, DEDUCOM, by Slagle (1965). Both of these systems used a formal — but English-like — language as input. Slagle's DEDUCtive COMmunicator was a LISP system that stored LISP expressions of data statements such as:

1. There are 5 fingers on a hand
2. There is one hand on an arm
3. There are 2 arms on a man
   and inference rules in the form of conditional statements that included variables as in the following:
4. If there are m X's on a V and if there are n V's on a Y, then there are mn X's on a Y.

By substituting data statements for the variables in conditional expressions, DEDUCOM answers questions such as the following:

Question: How many fingers on a man?
Answer: 10.

DEDUCOM can be considered as a tour de force in LISP that explores the deductive power of inference rules in

the form of conditionals with variables and transformations — another form of the pattern-operation rule. Such
rules were first introduced to the question-answering
scene by Black (1964), Raphael (1964), and Bobrow
(1964).[2] Although this form of transformation is powerful enough to deduce an answer to a question, given appropriate data statements, its application to a large data
structure is hopelessly expensive without the inclusion
of an appropriate set of tree-pruning heuristics.

Elliott's system, in contrast, operated very rapidly
because of his careful attention to the development of
efficient data structures. Input to this system is in the
form of parenthesized natural English statements such
as the following:

1 (Fact(San Francisco) (is north of) (Mexico City))
The canonical form for an input is:

(Operator(Datum$_1$) (Relation) (Datum$_2$)).

The system builds a directed graph to represent the relations between its data terms. A relation is defined to the
system by a set of properties such as reflexive and symmetric. The pattern of properties associated with a relation is used by the system to call a subroutine that constructs appropriate connections between the data terms.

This system also uses conditional rules with variables,
as in the following form:

(Combine ((B) (is between) ((A) and (C))) IF ((B)
(is less than) (A)) AND ((C) (is less than) (B)))

The use of these conditional transforms gives the system great deductive power, and since it depends mainly
on a strongly ordered data structure, it is able to operate
rapidly in answering most queries.

Neither Slagle nor Elliott chose to confront the problem of syntactic and semantic analysis of English statements and queries but instead explored the implications
of their respective structural models in terms of deductive power and retrieval effectiveness. Both emphasize
the deductive power of conditional transforms with variables, but Elliott introduced the effective idea of characterizing relations by properties which are used in
ordering the data in a directed graph.

Since these 1965 programs, several small scale natural language processors and several very large formal
language data management systems have been developed. These are cited briefly in the section headed Miscellaneous. Of more significance for this review are three
recent fact-retrieval systems, each of which confronts
the semantic problems of English and inclueds a deductive capability for answering questions (as contrasted
with the direct lookup operations of the formal language
systems).

The first of these is a merger of Raphael's earlier line
of thought, first with formal theorem-proving techniques

2. These and other relevant language processing theses
and papers have recently been collected as a book by
Minsky (1969).

(Green and Raphael 1968), then with a natural language
semantic system developed by Coles (1968). Coles' approach to linguistic analysis includes a one-pass predictive syntax recognizer or parser that is automatically
produced from a BNF description of the grammar via
an algorithm developed by Earley (1965). It may be
that such an approach to compiling a parser optimizes
its efficiency with respect to a subset of English, but it
appears to entail the disadvantage of requiring a new
recognizer to be compiled each time the grammar is
changed.

The semantic approach taken by Coles includes the
notion of a model of what is being talked about and an
unambiguous formal language, the predicate calculus,
which can express the facts of the model. His semantic
analyzer must transform constituents of an English
statement about the model into constituents of predicate
calculus statements. Disambiguation is achieved by testing the truth value of the logical statement in terms of
the model. These formidable tasks are accomplished with
the aid of production rules or transformations associated
with each syntactic rule. Coles cites earlier uses of this
technique by Kirsch (1964) and a similar principle used
by Thompson (1964) as the basis for semantic systems.
A recent paper by Kochen (1969)[3] reports the detailed
design of a similar system that uses production rules for
transforming from English into predicate calculus statements and questions about simple diagrams as a stage in
the production of flowcharts of programs for answering
the questions. Because the principle of transforming
natural language constituents into the formal language
of the system is now commonly used in second generation
language processors, it is illustrated here in some detail.

Suppose that the sentence "Each resistor is an element." is to be represented in the predicate calculus as
"$(\forall x)$ [resistor (x) $\Rightarrow$ element (x)]." The following
grammar serves:

$$S \rightarrow NP_1 + PRED \qquad |\rightarrow \text{``}(\forall x) [\alpha(x) \Rightarrow \beta(x)]\text{''}$$
$$NP_1 \rightarrow DET_1 + N \qquad |\rightarrow \text{``}\alpha(x) \leftarrow N(x)\text{''}$$
$$PRED \rightarrow V + NP_2$$
$$NP_2 \rightarrow DET_2 + N \qquad |\rightarrow \text{``}\beta(x) \leftarrow N(x)\text{''}$$
$$DET_1 \rightarrow EACH, EVERY$$
$$DET_2 \rightarrow A, AN$$
$$N \rightarrow RESISTOR, ELEMENT$$
$$V \rightarrow IS$$

The operation of this grammar is similar to that of an
ordinary context-free phrase structure grammar except
that as each rewrite rule is successfully applied, the associated semantic transformation is executed on a separate semantic pushdown list. Thus, with a top-down
approach, the symbol S is selected and rewritten as
$NP_1 + PRED$; NP_1 is then rewritten as $DET_1 + N$;

3. This paper publishes research first reported by Kochen
in 1965.

DET_1 is found in the input sentence to be the initial word, "Each"; PRED is stored on the syntactic pushdown list; N matches the following word "resistor" so the semantic transformation associated with NP_1 now can be applied to the semantic pushdown list giving us

$$a(x) \leftarrow \text{resistor } (x),$$

while the input string is rewritten as

$$NP_1 \text{ is an element.}$$

Returning to the syntactic pushdown list of goals, the term PRED is then rewritten as $V + NP_2$; V is found to match "is" with no semantic transformation required; NP_2 rewrites as $DET_2 + N$, which matches the words "an" and "element" respectively. Now, according to the semantic transformation associated with NP_2, we obtain a semantic pushdown list of

$$\beta(x) \leftarrow \text{element}(x), \quad a(x) \leftarrow \text{resistor}(x)$$

and have an input string of

$$NP_1 \ V \ NP_2.$$

Finally, the semantic transformation in the rule for S gives us

$$(\forall x)[a(x) \Rightarrow \beta(x)], \quad \beta(x) \leftarrow \text{element}(x),$$
$$a(x) \leftarrow \text{resistor}(x)$$

which upon evaluation results in the desired form

$$(\forall x)[\text{resistor}(x) \Rightarrow \text{element}(x)].$$

Coles' variation of this technique is sufficiently strong to translate certain English sentences into a fully quantified predicate calculus — provided that his grammar and transformations are sufficiently detailed to recognize the subtle cues that distinguish various meanings of "each," "every," "the," etc., in their quantificational function and the sometimes even more subtle cues that signify the scope of the quantifier. One strategy that Coles has not fully capitalized upon is to test the semantic well-formedness of each major constituent as it is constructed. This has been found in other studies (below) to be an important pruning heuristic for reducing the number of meaningless constituents that are carried during the analysis.

Green and Raphael's system for answering questions deductively uses the Robinson resolution theorem proving procedure which finds proofs by refutation. The question is taken as a postulated theorem. The resolution procedure then attempts to construct a model that satisfies both the axioms and the *negation* of the theorem; i.e., if the theorem does follow from the axioms, then such a model does not exist, and the resolution procedure

discovers this by deriving a contradiction in its attempt to construct the model. If the theorem is not proved after some given effort is expended, an attempt is made to show that the theorem is false by assuming it true and searching for a contradiction. The process continues until either a proof or a disproof is found, or until some allotted amount of search time is exceeded. With the aid of heuristics to deal with the more closely related axioms first, and to avoid repeating equivalent proofs, the researchers believe that the approach may develop into one of practical usefulness on data bases of reasonable size. The 1969 papers quote a number of difficult example questions that were successfully answered by the system, QA3, using this technique, and show its application to general problem solving and to commanding actions from the SRI robot (Green 1968), Coles 1969).

The resolution method was first experimented with in a natural language application by Darlington (1965), who has since, in two reports (1969), contributed further refinements and additional experiments with the method's effectiveness in a near-English formal language question-answering system. Proponents of this approach to deductive question answering and automated theorem proving generally follow Robinson's (1967) enthusiastic conclusion (in reference to mathematical contexts): "A theorem proving problem can be solved automatically if it can be solved at all . . . by executing a certain purely clerical algorithm. . . ." At the same time, those concerned with question-answering systems have encountered well-known shortcomings in the first order predicate calculus, with reference to representing equality, recursiveness, modality, tense, and the detailed quantificational structure of English. In response to shortcomings of first order logics, Robinson (1968) attempts ". . . to persuade those engaged in mechanical theorem-proving research, and those proposing to start such research, to focus their attention henceforth on mechanizing higher order logic."

In actual fact, researchers are quietly extending the first order predicate calculus by introducing additional operators and quantifiers. (See for example, Green and Raphael's *var* operator and Woods' use of the *iota* quantifier and successor functions.) John McCarthy has contributed a useful formulation of a modal predicate calculus for dealing with the notion of "can" in his Advice Taker, and Pople (1969) has extended these notions somewhat in his goal-oriented language (GOL) for the general problem-solving area.

As a culmination of several years of research on data management systems Kellogg (1968) has developed a system for compiling formal language data management procedures from a subset of natural English statements and questions. Unique to the Kellogg system is a satisfying sense of completeness; first, it is programmed and operating as a complete system; second, it accepts natural language questions and statements and retrieves data or modifies the data base; third, it includes minimally adequate syntactic and semantic analysis approaches that are based on current linguistic theory; finally, it incorporates sufficient logical structure to support deductive procedures based on both mathematical and logical relations. A significant weakness is that, as an experimental system, it is currently limited to operation on data bases that can be contained in core memory; however, the present line of research is aimed at expanding the approach to auxiliary storage.

Kellogg defines a formal language for information management. He requires that such a formal language: (1) be procedural, machine independent and independent of special data requirements or considerations; (2) approach the power of the predicate calculus in its capabilities for composition of functions, nesting of relations, embedding of procedures within procedures and representing quantification over sets; (3) be easy to read and understand. The language he defines in 30 (complex) formation rules is shown by numerous examples to be adequate for expressing complex data retrieval requests and for describing data for storage. His implementation of the quantificational feature is still limited.

The linguistic procedure for translating from an English string into the formal language structure begins with a top-down syntactic analysis based on a context free phrase structure grammar. The lexical structure associated with each English word includes syntactic and semantic word-classes, a list of semantic features, and a list of selection restrictions. As the syntactic parser constructs a constituent, a semantic test is made to discover if the features of the head of the construction satisfy the selection restrictions of the dependent construction. If the test is satisfied, a transformation is effected to compose (i.e. combine) the features and selection restrictions for the resulting constituent. The semantic test and composition functions follow closely the notions outlined by Katz (1967) but are more explicit than the limited descriptions offered by Katz.

Following the semantic composition of a constituent, additional transformations may be signaled to translate it into a portion of the resultant formal language expression. The process, with the exception of the semantic composition functions, can be seen to follow roughly the example previously illustrated by the sentence "Each resistor is an element." Once again we see the application of the powerful pattern-operation rule, this time for disambiguation by use of semantic features and selection restrictions as well as for transformation into a formal language expression that is operable as a program applied to a data base.

The third natural language data base system, designed by Woods (1967, 1968), begins by analyzing the data from an airlines guide into a set of primitive functions and predicates. Predicates include such examples as the following:

CONNECT (X1, X2, X3)	Flight X1 goes from place X2 to place X3.
DEPART (X1, X2)	Flight X1 leaves place X2.
MEALSERV (X1, X2)	Flight X1 has type X2 meal service.
PLACE (X1)	X1 is a place.
FLIGHT (X1)	X1 is a flight.

Examples of primitive functions include the following:

DTIME (X1, X2)	Departure time of flight X1 from place X2
OWNER (X1)	Name of airline that operates flight X1
TZ (X1)	Time zone of place X1

The primitive predicates and functions comprise the elementary operations of a procedural language for managing a data base of airline guide information. Each predicate may be tested as true or false and each function can be operated to return a value. The meanings of the primitives are thus defined by programmed subroutines which may be combined into more complex programs to define additional predicates and functions. The procedural language also includes the data management operators, RECORD, LIST, TEST, PRINT, etc., and a detailed expression of quantification, EACH, EVERY, ALL, SOME, etc., and its scope.

The language processing task is to translate from natural language statements or queries into a quantified formal expression in the procedural language. As input to his semantic system, Woods uses a deep structure syntactic analysis of each sentence in the form of a labeled phrase marker, like that output from the Harvard syntactic analysis system. His semantic system depends on the use of pattern-operation rules whose left halves are Boolean combinations of labeled fragments of phrase markers that include specification of their terminal elements as English words or as semantic class predicates.[4] (By semantic class predicate is meant such predicates as PLACE(Boston) — True: Boston is a kind of place; or AIRPORT(Boston) — True; etc.) The right half of these rules is a function or predicate in the procedural language with its arguments specified as elements from the syntactic subtrees of the left half. These transformations are very powerful in that they incorporate detailed specification of legitimate combinations of syntactic features and semantic class markers (i.e. predicates) as conditions of the formation of (i.e. transformation to) procedural language constituents. They thus include tests for syntactic and semantic well-formedness to allow for selection of sense-meanings or disambiguation of words and phrases.

At all levels of constituent processing, translation from

---

4. Woods shows the correspondence of these structures to semantic markers and selection restrictions of Katz's theory.

English determiners and quantificational terms to quantifiers in the formal language is treated carefully and successfully. It is probably in his detailed description of a method for dealing with quantification that Woods makes his most significant contribution. In other systems large gaps are to be found in the explanation of this process.

Woods' approach shows how "meaning" can be operationally defined as a sequence of subroutines, functions, or operations that a statement calls for a system to perform — so far in the context of a data management task. The extent to which this approach can generalize beyond the data base context remains to be discovered as does its effectiveness in treatment of various subtleties of English usage — that are beyond the immediate goals of Woods' research. One apparent weakness in the approach as so far described lies in Woods' use of syntactically analyzed English as an input to the system. A syntactic parsing that is independent of the semantic operations implies that numerous syntactically valid but semantically impossible interpretations would have to be considered. As he continues his development of the system, Woods expects to adopt a procedure of semantically testing each syntactic constituent as it is formed to dispose of semantically invalid constituents at the earliest possible moment.[5]

Mathematical Word-Problem Processors

Intermediate between data base systems and research on text processing, Charniak's (1969) CARPS is a program that solves calculus word problems. CARPS is a generalization and expansion of techniques introduced by Bobrow (1964) in his STUDENT program for solving algebra word problems. These two systems take a heuristic approach to the analysis of English sentences using pattern-operation rules for both syntactic and semantic operations.

Charniak describes the operation of his system with reference to the following example problem. "Water is flowing into a conical filter at the rate of 15.0 cubic inches per second. If the radius of the base of the filter is 5.0 inches and the altitude is 10.0 inches, find the rate at which the water level is rising when the volume is 100.0 cubic inches."

The first step in analysis is a dictionary lookup during which words may be tagged with syntactic information, common phrases are transformed to a canonical form, and keywords are noted if they have equations associated with them in memory or if they give information about the type of problem (e.g. volume or distance). The next phase is to transform the complicated sentences of the problem into simpler form. This phase is accomplished by pattern-operation rules as shown below with reference

5. Personal communication with Woods.

to the second sentence of the problem. After dictionary lookup this sentence appears as:

(A) (If the radius of the base of the filter (is verb) 5.0 (inches unit) and the altitude (is verb) 10.0 (inches unit), (find Qword (rate Rword) at which the water level (rising verb) when the volume (is verb) 100.0 (IN3 UNIT))

The first relevant pattern is as follows:

(B) IF-ANYTHING-, -QWORD-ANYTHING.

Pattern (B) successfully matches the first clause of sentence (A); its associated operation is to break the sentence into two sentences, the first containing "if the radius . . . and the altitude is 10.0 inches" and the second beginning "Find. . . ." The rule then starts the program over, and again applies rules to each of the sentences. After the input sentences have been simplified, additional pattern-operation rules are applied to transform each sentence into equations or data structures. For example:

(C) ((water NVP) (flowing verb) (at PREP) (rate anything) (15.0 Number) (IN3 UNIT) (Per PER) (Second TIMEUNIT))

is matched by the rule:

(D) ANYTHING-VERB-PREP-ANYTHING-NUMBER-UNIT-PER-TIMEUNIT

Rule (D) classifies the sentence as one in which the noun phrase (NVP), is changing at a constant rate and additional patterns and operations are applied to give the structure

Water
Volume: G0015
Value: (QUOTIENT(TIMES   15.0(TIMES   TIM
(EXPT IN 3)))SEC)

which includes the Lisp equivalent of the formula

$$\frac{TIME \times INCHES^3 \times 15}{SECONDS}$$

The result of these operations is to produce a tree structure of the information contained in the problem as in Figure 1. Final phases of the program establish equations from the structured information and solve them.

Significant in this approach to language processing is the fact that paragraph units of natural (though specialized) text are dealt with. Problems of anaphora and pronominal reference are faced. For example when pronouns are encountered, a function returns the most likely referent. In addition, the accumulation of all information in the problem into a single tree structure provides a form of discourse analysis in which the phrase "the filter" in the second sentence of the problem refers to "the canonical filter" already established in the data structure by the first sentence. Similarly "the altitude," "the water level," and "the volume" all refer back to attributes of the "conical filter."

Although Charniak's (and Bobrow's) systems effectively use pattern-operation rules to syntactically analyze their problems, Charniak concludes that an incremental left-to-right parse would be more efficient. We have previously seen syntactic constituents transformed into predicate calculus statements, LISP functions, and other data structures with use of the pattern-operation rule; in these two programs the operations transform constituents into data structures and mathematical equations.

Natural Language Text Processing

The natural language fact retrieval systems just described define a subset of English and a formally defined data base structure whose content is usually a set of short fact statements. For text-processing applications, a major research task is to analyze a much broader subset of English into a data structure sufficiently general to represent something typical of the wide range of meanings expressed in a corpus of expository text. The natural model for this data structure is the invisible cognitive structure of the human language user. As a consequence, the analytic text-processing research has a pronounced psychological flavor as typified by Quillian's model of semantic memory structure (1967, 1968) and his recent Teachable Language Comprehender (1969), and Simmons' model of verbal understanding (Simmons et al. 1968). It is not surprising that these systems relate strongly to such other psychological models as Colby's and Abelson's simulations of belief structures in their mode of representing conceptual information.

Quillian's original semantic memory encodes dictionary definitions of words as a network of word-nodes connected by syntactic and semantic relations. The definition of an English word such as plant is characterized by a disjunctive set of labeled planes, e.g. plant1, plant2, plant3, etc., to represent the various alternate sense meanings. Within a plane the sense meaning is expressed by a structure such as:

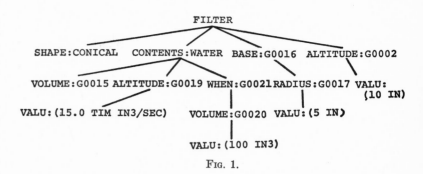

FIG. 1.

Five types of relations are used to connect nodes in the graph. The first is the semantic relation of type or class illustrated by the connection of "plant" and "structure" by a single straight line with an arrow joining a type and token node. The syntactic notion of modification is symbolized by the same arrowed line connecting two tokens, as "structure" and "live." The relations of conjunction and disjunction are symbolized by labeled curved pointers. Finally, a relation signified by an English verb or preposition is shown by twin pointers to the subject and object of such a relational word. The notion of word type is reserved for the head of a sense meaning while a token is the representation of a word type as it is used in defining some other word type.

The result of this structure for each definition is a form of handmade syntactic and semantic analysis, the substructures of which tend to be similar in some respects to deep linguistic structures. Each plane represents the immediate definition of a concept; but a *full concept* is defined as all nodes that can be reached by an exhaustive tracing from the head word type of the plane. If we think of the semantic memory as a horizontal spider web, picking it up by any one node orders all other nodes in a vertical dimension with reference to the node selected. It is this vertical ordering of the web that Quillian defines as a full concept.

A primary operation on the network is to compare and contrast the meaning of any two word-concepts in the memory store and generate an English statement to represent the relationship. Thus, comparing "plant" and "live," the system reports:

1. Plant is a live structure.
2. Plant is structure which get food from air. This food is thing which being has-to take into itself to keep live.

In recent research Quillian (1969) has generalized his semantic network and embedded it in a program called the Teachable Language Comprehender (TLC). When new text is input to TLC, the system relates each assertion of the new text to its semantic memory which represents the facts it already has recorded. Comprehension of new terms is accomplished by a generalization process illustrated in the following example.

Suppose the program is faced with the new phrase, "client's lawyer." The two following facts are already

```
plant1
  ↓
structure
  ↓     and
 live ⤻  ↘vegetable  with3      get
            ↘leaf  ⌐→plant
                  └→from3
                      ↘food  or    or
                    ↳air  water earth
```

stored in its memory: (1) a client is a *person* who employs professionals; (2) a lawyer is a *professional* who represents or advises a person in legal matters. Both of these facts are in the form of a superset class modified and distinguished by subproperties. By the intersection process described earlier, TLC finds that "client" and "lawyer" intersect in the node, "professional" which is a part of the property describing "client" and is the superset class for "lawyer." By letting "lawyer" substitute for the "professional" employed by "client," the system has identified a relationship that exists in the semantic network that may explicate the meaning of the input phrase. A syntactic test of the input is then made to determine if this relationship in memory corresponds to the form of the input; if the test succeeds, the new phrase has been correctly comprehended. In experiments with the above example, TLC demonstrates its understanding of the phrase "lawyer's client" by printing "under discussion is a client who employs a lawyer: this client is represented or advised by this lawyer in a legal matter."

A unique aspect of Quillian's approach is that all syntactic and semantic information is carried in a data base encoded as a network of interrelationships between words and word senses. His notion of a full concept as (essentially) all of a person's knowledge ordered with respect to that concept is a challenging one that adds richness to the idea of semantic analysis. In his view, disambiguation is to be accomplished generally by selecting those word-senses that have the shortest paths between them as the senses that are relevant to the context. This viewpoint is more flexible than Katz's calculus of selection restrictions and semantic markers and is one that can eventually account for the metaphorical usage of words quite as readily as it can for literal usage. However, beyond some limited explorations by Sparck-Jones (1965) there is practically no knowledge of the extent to which semantic distance measures will prove a successful technique for disambiguation.

The long continued line of synthex research has most recently resulted in Protosynthex III (Simmons et al. 1968, Schwarcz et al. (1968) that successfully analyzes a wide range of English sentences and questions, deductively answers many forms of question and generates English sentences either as answers to questions or as paraphrases of an input statement in English. At the base of this system is a model of human conceptual structures expressed as nested (Concept-Relation-Concept) triples. In this model a sentence such as "The angry pitcher struck the umpire who called the game" would be expressed by the following set of triples:

(((Pitcher MOD angry)TMOD the) (strike T past) (umpire SMOD(umpire(call T past) (game TMOD the))))

Each term in a triple is an unambiguous selection in a sense meaning of the word. Each middle term in a triple is a relation — not necessarily well defined. The structure

is a formal language that expresses sentence meanings as a nested set of relational triples — i.e. binary relations.

Transforming from English to this formal language is accomplished by a bottom-up syntactic analysis using the Cocke algorithm.[6] Each constituent found acceptable in terms of the grammar is subjected first to a syntactic transformation, then to a semantic test. The grammar rules combine a phrase structure and a transformational component as in the following example:

ADJ NP — (B Mod A) NP.

Given the possible constituent formed on an adjective and a noun phrase, the rule applies. The transformation is found within the parentheses; in this case it takes from the left half, the Bth element, NP, the literal term Mod, and the Ath element, ADJ, to produce (NP Mod Adj) and the name NP. Sequences such as ABAAC are acceptable elements of the transformation to provide for reference to an element at any level of nesting.

Following the transformation the resulting constituent is tested semantically by looking it up in a list of rules called Semantic Event Forms or SEFs. A SEF is a triple of three semantic class terms. A semantic class is derived for a word, W, by testing it in the frame "W is a kind of _____." Thus pitcher is a kind of gameplayer; gameplayer is a kind of person; angry is a kind of emotion, etc. If the constituent in question were "angry pitcher" the result of the transformation gives "pitcher Mod angry." The SEF rules include (person Mod emotion), and since person and emotion are semantic classes for "pitcher" and "angry," respectively, the semantic test is passed successfully for the person-sense of "pitcher" and fails for the sense "pitcher as a container."

After disambiguation via the SEFs and transformation into the formal language, a question, no matter how complex, is resolved into a nested set of simple questions — i.e. triples. Each of these is looked up in the accumulated data store. If direct lookup is unsuccessful for a triple, attempts are made to deduce the answer using deductive inference rules that are keyed either to properties of the relations in the system or directly keyed to the relational word-concept. Some of these rules are in the form of program functions while others use the familiar pattern-operation form like:

((A sister B) and (B mother C) ⇒ (A aunt C))

Several forms of these rules have been analyzed into classes which can be expressed more succinctly than the above. Using Complex-Product as an operator, the above rule can be expressed:

((sister C/P mother) ⇒ aunt)

with some gain in program efficiency.

The system has been tested on a range of questions

6. Described in Kay (1964).

selected from those provided in Compton's Encyclopedia. The detailed description of the question-answering process by Schwarcz et al. (1968) shows several successful examples and an analysis of certain types of questions that are beyond its scope. The question "Who lost the Battle of Waterloo?" is successfully answered by the statement "Napoleon commanded the French Army which lost the Battle of Waterloo in 1815." The question "Does the monkey get the bananas?" followed by a series of verbal statements describing the situation is also successfully answered with the aid of appropriate inference rules. Answering "how" and "why" questions is not yet possible for the system.

Paraphrase is treated as a special limited form of a question and covered by the same logic. Generation of answers is accomplished by using an inverse of the grammar that accepts formal structure triples and transforms them into English strings that express their meaning.

Weaknesses in this system include inadequate treatment of quantification and a certain awkwardness of structure that results from the complex nesting of data statements. Its syntactic-semantic machinery has been tested on a wide variety of sentences — including some that are very long and complicated — and found to be very powerful. It is presently written in LISP and core-bound. It is also presently very slow. An expanded version that can use disk storage is now being programmed. The syntactic-semantic component of the new system is running — about fifty times faster than the original — and it is believed that the whole revised system will operate rapidly and effectively enough to test it thoroughly on fairly large bodies of text (i.e. 5 to 10 thousand words).

Protosynthex III, although experimental, is another system that offers a sense of completeness — this time as a general purpose language processor. It develops and is based on a psychological model of cognitive structure that is grounded in linguistic and logical theory. It demonstrates that very sophisticated language processing operations are well within the range of today's computing technology — though so far only for small subsets of the language.

Miscellaneous

Several additional systems beyond those reviewed above have been developed (or further developed) in the past few years. Many of them deserve detailed treatment, but to keep this review manageable in size they are mentioned here briefly.

A recent system programmed in SNOBOL3 by Shapiro extends the ideas developed by Elliott. (Shapiro and Woodmansee 1969). It allows more freedom in the definition of relations and, in contrast to Elliott's GRAIS, it remembers new relations after they have been defined. Shapiro's system avoids problems of English syntax and semantics by using a near-English input-output language.

Salton's SMART system has achieved a high level of development as a general purpose document and text retrieval system based primarily on statistical treatment of words in text (Salton 1968). His use of statistical phrase-matching techniques and his approach to developing and using thesauri are noteworthy advances in the information retrieval area. Thompson's now classic DEACON system was carried somewhat further after he left TEMPO but eventually abandoned for lack of research funds. Most recently Thompson has developed the REL system of on-line multi-access consoles, which among other powerful capabilities allows a user to define a subset of English as a query and response language for data management tasks. As of this writing there are no published descriptions of this system.

Tharp and Krulee (1969) describe a still incomplete system to answer English questions from analyzed text. Their approach parses text with a transformational analysis system developed by Petrick (1965). They transform the analyzed text into n-place relational predicates where the verb signifies a relation between the subject and object of the sentence. Conjunctions are relations whose arguments are the conjoined sentences. The resulting predicates are ordered with respect to the adjudged priority of the relational term for accessibility to a retrieval algorithm. Because of limitations of the grammar, the input text is first edited by hand. They propose to incorporate deductive question-answering procedures of the type now common in question-answering systems.

Formal language data base systems are currently receiving much publicity but typically offer little in the way of deductive logic or semantic techniques. One exception in this area is the excellent approach of Levien and Maron (1969). This system expresses information related to a large document collection in the form of relational triples and provides a user language that is a mixture of English and a simple symbolic logic. It includes deductive techniques that provide answers to such complex questions as "What is the organizational affiliation of all authors whose publications are classed as natural language question answering?" Despite attempts at efficient programming for use on a data base of 200,000 statements, retrieval times typically measured in minutes. (Levien's experience casts some doubt on the vaunted efficiency of other data base systems where retrieval times are not so frankly reported.) A group of researchers at Hughes Aircraft (Savitt et al. 1966) designed and developed an approach to a non-Von Neumann type computer based on an associative memory and a pattern-operation type of instruction code. They have most recently simulated the system on an IBM 360 computer. It is probable that a hardware version of this system would prove a great boon to the general area of symbolic processing including applications to information retrieval, data management, language processing, and artificial intelligence research.

On the natural language processing aspect, Rosenbaum

(1968) in addition to providing a detailed transformational grammar for a subset of English has designed (1967) a grammar-based question-answering procedure that capitalizes on the power of transformational rules to show that linguistic deep structures can serve as a data base for a fact file. Schwarcz (1967) outlined a set of principles that serve as a sound basis for question answering. Wilks (1967) shows how pattern-operation rules can be used to produce a rough semantic analysis of the flow of content through a paragraph. Bohnert and Becker (1966) have continued Bohnert's line of research on transforming predicate calculus statements into English forms and have unearthed useful methods for dealing with the difficult problems offered by prepositional phrases, conjunctions, and comparatives. Klein (1968) has published a description of a system that simulates the behavior of a linguist as he develops a grammar and a morphology for a new foreign language. Improved approaches to syntactic analysis have been described by Bobrow and Fraser (1969), by Thorne et al. (1968), and by Martin Kay (1964).

3. Discussion

In this paper the implicit definition of a language processor has been a system that accepts natural language statements and questions as input, uses syntactic and semantic processes to transform them into a formal language, provides deductive and/or inductive procedures for such operations as answering questions, and generates English strings as answers. Most of the systems reviewed in this paper are incomplete with respect to one or more clauses of this definition, but taken as a whole it is apparent that the field has developed techniques for at least minimal management of each of these aspects of language processing. It will prove profitable to examine and summarize the methods now commonly used for syntactic and semantic analysis, the data structures used to represent content, inferential procedures for answering questions, and the approaches used to generate English statements as responses.

Syntactic Analysis

It was surprising to discover that most of the language processing systems depended on a top-down approach to syntactic analysis. In a recent review of parsing algorithms used in formal language compilers, Feldman and Gries (1968) reported that most of the compilers used a basic top-down approach but also used bottom-up techniques as pruning heuristics to prevent the parser from exploring all possible branches of the grammar. It appears that a bottom-up approach is necessarily more economical where a large grammar is involved as must eventually be the case for a natural language processor. The use of the input string to directly select the relevant subset of the grammar eliminates a great deal of explora-

tion of irrelevant rules that all begin with such common elements as S, NP, PRED, etc., each of which must be followed to terminal expressions by the pure top-down system. In the worst but usual case (in natural language work) where all interpretations of a sentence must be found, the top-down approach essentially requires the abortive generation of all strings that are partially well formed with respect to the grammar.

Despite this criticism, syntactic analysis is accomplished effectively with reasonably efficient algorithms by the second generation systems. The grammars typically include a phrase structure component in combination with a transformational capability and, in most cases, can deal successfully with discontinuous constituents. Also, since the lexicon and grammar are clearly separated from the parsing algorithm, the systems generalize to a wide range of natural languages providing the linguistic data is available. With the exception of a few systems such as Kellogg's, the lexical component has received little attention and is used primarily as a means for associating syntactic word-classes to the vocabulary.

It is apparent that the second generation approach to syntactic analysis still generally ignores most of the syntactic subtleties of English including agreement, punctuation, pronoun reference, treatment of comparatives, etc. However, despite the rough and ready nature of the approach, it is quite clear that basic computational procedures are well understood for syntactic analysis, including the transformational component required to obtain various forms of deep linguistic or conceptual structure.

Semantic Analysis

With respect to semantics, the situation is encouraging but not yet well developed. A semantic analysis of an English statement is required at least to select the word-sense or senses appropriate to the context (i.e. disambiguate) and to transform the sentence into one or more expressions in an unambiguous formal language. Katz (1967) also includes the notion of a composition function that will express the meaning of any and every constituent as a combination of the meanings associated with the elements that comprise it. So far, only Kellogg's system uses composition functions in this sense.

The most satisfactory approaches to semantic analysis are seen in systems by Woods, Kellogg, and Simmons — and these leave much to be desired. Each of these systems uses something akin to Katz's semantic markers, but the markers are so far limited to the form of semantic classes and lack the extensive structure Katz now believes to be required in a marker. Kellogg also uses selection restrictions and composition functions that express a meaning of each constituent in terms of a combination of the markers and selection restrictions of the elements that comprise that constituent. Simmons uses semantic event forms which are essentially rules that show allowable combinations of semantic classes, and does not provide any explicit composition function. However, both Kellogg and Simmons use the economical procedure of taking each constituent as soon as it is found acceptable syntactically and testing it for semantic well-formedness. This approach minimizes the number of meaningless syntactic constituents that have to be carried during the parse.[7]

Woods' test for semantic well-formedness occurs after the assumed deep structure analysis. It is accomplished by testing the sequence of semantic classes and English words as being an acceptable left half of a semantic transformation rule. Coles' approach does not explicitly deal with semantic classes, although word-classes that form his grammar rules may in fact be such; and his test of a sequence of class categories as a left element in a transformation rule may thus be a semantic check. For Coles' system, the final check of semantic well-formedness is to test the resulting language translation against a model representing the true state of the relevant universe.

Perhaps the principle of accomplishing semantic analysis via pattern operation rules can be seen most clearly in ELIZA, the simplest of the systems reviewed above. The semantic analysis of a word or a pattern of words for a computer is the selection of either a data structure or a pattern of operations that it signifies. In ELIZA semantic analysis by pattern-operation is frankly simplistic — a pattern of keywords on the left and a formula for constructing a conversational response on the right. For Woods the keywords are structured in syntactic patterns and the operations are keyed by an ordering of subroutines on the right. Despite the complexity engendered by syntactic and semantic word-classes, markers, selection restrictions, etc., the same pattern-operation principle is what supports the semantic capability of the other systems. Disambiguation is accomplished by testing a segment of the English string as an acceptable sequence of semantic units. The semantic content is expressed as a formal language whose elements may be either data structures or procedures.

Quillian's approach to semantic analysis offers an initial exploration of one additional aspect, that of semantic distance between two terms each of which signifies a data structure (concept) in a connected network of such structures. In Quillian's system the semantic content of a constituent would be a combined data structure which included the concepts of each of its elements as well as all concepts on the shortest path between them. This notion offers the advantage of providing a computer definition of meaning that includes some of the associational richness of human uses of the term with respect to language.

It is clear that the pattern-operation rule is today

7. Schank's approach to semantic analysis is essentially similar to Simmons' (though independently derived) except in his use of a dependency grammar to form the syntactic constituents.

serving as the key to semantic analysis. However, no one has yet experimented with more than the barest of literal content — the richness of natural languages in terms of metaphoric and connotational content is completely untouched.

Data Structures for Representing Content

In talking about structures to represent content there is, on the one hand, the linguistic notion of deep structure representation and, on the other, the very common question of convenient computer representation. Chomsky's deep linguistic structures serve the purpose of showing that the complexity of natural language sentences can best be explained as a matter of transformational combination of what are very like simple subject-predicate sentences in base structures. However, because of their linguistic richness, the Chomsky-type base structures are more suited for linguistic research than for computer representation of factual information. Several alternate forms of representation can preserve linguistic detail but offer structures that are more tractable to computation. Bohnert and Kirsch introduced the hypothesis that an appropriate deep structure representation of meaning is the predicate calculus. Several systems follow this notion. Fillmore (1967) has recently offered an attractive linguistic deep structure that resolves into a nesting of attribute value lists that are easily representable as computer structures (see Simmons 1968). Concept networks used by Colby, Abelson, Simmons, and Quillian all depend strongly on the notion of nested attribute value lists to form computer representations for units of meaning. The structure of relational triples to represent meanings as nested sets of binary relations has advantages also.

To the extent that the conceptual content of a natural language statement can be represented both as a convenient data structure and as a defined formal language, operations on some aspects of meaning become both computable and describable. The power and the limitations of such languages can be explored by mathematical and logical methods. Perhaps more important for such cases, the problem of computer "understanding" of natural languages can be seen (as noted by Kellogg and by Thompson 1966) to be a special, vastly complicated case of compiler design.

The systems that have been reviewed above almost invariably depend on associative storage of the syntactic and semantic information they use. To attain associative storage in a sequential computer, such systems as LISP, SNOBOL, or SLIP are usually used. The unfortunate consequence is that all the systems are currently corebound in random access cores that (after including operating and embedding systems) allow 20 to 40 thousand cells of storage. Serious uses of language processing require dictionaries of between 15 and 100 thousand entries, vast quantities of syntactic and semantic information and, eventually, storage of encyclopedias of text. If there is to be any hope for useful language processing systems on sequential computers, there must be a melding of the technology of managing truly large data bases on auxiliary storage with the necessarily associative processing of computational linguistics. Alternate solutions exist, of course, in the provision of 100 million word cores or the development of associative computers — neither alternative appears likely in the immediate future.

A final remark is required on the content of the data structure. Most effort has so far been spent in designing algorithms and computable structures that can conveniently contain the linguistic and factual content required by a language processor. Researchers are keenly aware that lying in wait for them is the gargantuan task of encoding tens of thousands of dictionary items and innumerable syntactic, semantic, and logical inference rules for accomplishing on a large scale those language processing tasks that experiment has shown possible with small subsets of a language. At this moment it is hardly possible to estimate the effort that will be required, but it is safe to assume that researchers will discover an entire new spectrum of problems deriving from the complexity that comes with size.

Inference in Question Answering

After a question and an answering text have been translated into an explicitly structured formal language, the process of question answering can be seen to be essentially one of theorem proving. Several systems embody deductive approaches that use inference rules to ex; and and transform the formal expression of a question until it matches some combination of data structures. In these approaches, the ever-present pattern-operation rule with variables has been a key technique. Recently, the Robinson resolution algorithm used by Green and Raphael has shown itself to be an attractive deductive approach, and methods used by Woods and Kochen suggest the eventual automatic production of programs to accomplish inference. Initial uses of inductive approaches are also to be found, particularly in Colby's, Abelson's, and Becker's work, while McCarthy shows lines along which inductive logics may be formalized. Statistical induction techniques for question answering are used in Salton's SMART and Simmons' Protosynthex I (1964).

The last two systems automatically index large quantities of text and use keyword techniques for retrieving sentences, paragraphs, or articles relevant to a query. The matching of keywords is augmented by statistical controls on word-form and sequence to retrieve text passages whose words (or thesaurus classes) are most highly correlated with semantic elements of the query. It must be noted that these systems work effectively on large, textual data bases with no effort required for providing grammars and sets of inference rules. As document

or text retrieval aids, they already approach the practically useful stage, and develop a statistical correlation approach to inductive inference in question answering.

Since this statistical induction approach coupled with the effective use of automatically produced indexes of the text has proved so effective, it has earned legitimacy as a question-answering technique. Presumably, its eventual place in the scheme is to act as a first stage filter that selects from a large body of data that portion which is obviously relevant to a question. More refined deductive and inductive approaches can then be used on the resulting small — perhaps manageable — selection of relevant material.

Generating Coherent English

Only a few systems have been concerned with generating natural English responses. It is an essential feature of ELIZA, a defined requirement on Protosynthex III, and a continuing concern for Klein's control of style. The process, as might be expected, is the inverse of the analysis of a natural language; but interestingly enough, it is not only a generation in the linguistic sense, it is also a translation — from formal language to English.

The ubiquitous pattern-operation rule is the key to this procedure also. Constituents of a data structure are assigned class names and used as the left half of the transformation. The set of constituents is transformed into other constituents or a segment of a natural language string by the right half of the rule, and the eventual output is the set of well formed English expressions permitted by the grammar (see Simmons et al. 1968). Such a system naturally generates all purely syntactic paraphrases for a given meaning structure. If the meaning structure is based on characteristics (such as semantic markers) whose patterns represent sense meanings of words, the rules for selecting a word to match the pattern will be very like grammar rules, and lexical paraphrase will result by producing all strings whose terminal elements contain the required characteristics. Little more exists, however, than initial experiments with the production of meaningful language statements. Klein's work has shown that the selection and control of stylistic restraints on the choice and placement of words is an area where much research can be profitably centered.

A Unifying Paradigm

Much has emerged from consideration of various language processing systems: the pattern-operation rule; the representation of content as operations or as structures; the use of deep linguistic or conceptual structure versus the use of predicate calculus types of representation; the idea of natural language compilation; the idea of translation from natural language to a formal language representation of meaning. Let us attempt a synthesis.

Four strands of thought can be seen: first, the linguistic

paradigm of deep structures and transformations; second, the computer science approach to compilation, i.e. the transformation using symbol tables and production rules from problem-oriented languages to machine languages of operations and data; third, the psychological notion of cognitive structure composed of concepts and relations; and finally, the basic ideas of logical structure and inference as expressed primarily in the predicate calculus.

These strands of thought are deeply interwoven in the existing systems. For example, Kellogg uses a lexical structure deriving from Chomsky and Katz, with production rules familiar to syntax directed compilers, to transform from an English subset to a formal language resembling the predicate calculus. In each of the question-answering systems the question eventually becomes a formal language theorem whose validity is to be tested with respect to a set of manipulative axioms and accepted data theorems. Psychologically-oriented systems such as those of Abelson, Colby, Quillian, and Simmons are built around simulated or synthesized cognitive structures whose elements are concepts and relations, and which incorporate inference procedures as special cases of concepts. These systems also show concern for inductive as well as deductive inference methods. Coles' and Kochen's approaches are clearly gneralized from the treatment of programming languages, while Woods brilliantly extends LISP ideas and Katzian semantics into a function and predicate-oriented natural language data management system.

I believe these apparently disparate approaches reveal a unifying paradigm in which the four strands are plaited into a single line of thought that can guide further language processing research. The basis of this paradigm is a structure to represent the relevant conceptual content (i.e. aspects of meaning) symbolized by a natural language string. This structure must be a formal language with the power of a higher order logic. Variables and operators in this language can be represented, respectively, as nodes and labeled connections in a directed graph which, with suitable associated information concerning belief values, etc., can be taken as a model of human cognitive structure. Statements in the formal language can be interpreted as procedures that modify the network, accomplish inferences, or do other work; or they can be treated as uninterpreted data structures. Two statements in this language are equivalent if there exist content preserving transformations that can convert one into the other or if, as procedures, they accomplish equivalent results. Establishment of equivalence is a theorem-proving operation where content-preserving transformations are the axioms, and known facts are established theorems; deductive or inductive procedures can thus be used to draw conclusions or to construct predictions.

I believe that such a formal language representation of the content of natural language statements cor-responds in large measure to the semantically interpreted deep structures of Chomsky's linguistic theory, and that his theory, especially as interpreted by Joyce Friedman (1969), describes a suitable approach for generating natural language statements from the formal language representation. Our own experience is that the application of a set of linguistic transformations to constituents of statements in the formal language can produce surface structures in English syntax that generate natural English statements. Thematic control of coherence and connectivity between statements is still largely an unexplored area, but one that is opened to exploration in this framework.

For recognizing natural language strings, the paradigm calls for classes of elements, or combinations of these classes in the surface language string to be tested, first for syntactic well-formedness, then for semantic coherence with respect to context. If these tests are successfully passed by a natural language constituent, it is then transformed into a constituent of the formal language by means of a Chomsky-type transformation, a pattern-operation rule or, most generally, a function. Different natural languages are characterized by differing syntactic and semantic systems. But, since at least approximate translations between statements in natural languages are possible, it is reasonable to assume that the underlying cognitive structures of people who speak each language are structurally similar and can be represented by the same formal language. Translation between two natural languages can thus be seen to result from analysis of one language using its syntax and semantics into the base formal language, followed by a generation using the other languages's semantics and syntax in terms of elements selected from its lexicon.[8]

Question-answering conversational machines, and creative writing devices easily fit within the above paradigm, but each requires differing sorts of logical operations on the underlying formal language. The paradigm will easily generalize to applications that operate between modalities, i.e. picture-to-language, language-to-action, etc., using the formal language as an intermediary.

The nature of a paradigm in science is to yield to better ones, as it is gradually found to be incomplete or inadequate in the face of more finely articulated observations. It can be hoped that this one, emerging from the first decade of research in computational linguistics, will guide us well into the second decade before it becomes obviously obsolete. The second decade can be expected to test it on ever larger subsets of natural language materials in increasingly larger experimental contexts. We can hope that it will be extended to account for anaphoric, thematic, and discourse analysis of the paragraph and of larger units of natural language material.

8. This aspect of the paradigm was foreshadowed long ago by Yngve's (1957) analysis of the automatic translation problem.

4. Conclusions

In reviewing second generation question-answering systems it is apparent to me that significant progress has been made. Syntactic processing is well understood; semantic analysis has been operationally defined for small subsets of English, and certain limited, literal aspects of sentence meaning have been expressed as computable structure. The power of the pattern-operation rule, with or without variables, has been appreciated widely and exploited in application to semantic analysis and the deductive operations required for answering questions.

Significant weaknesses are still prominent. All existing systems are experimental in nature, small, and core-bound. None uses more than a few hundred words of dictionary or a small grammar and semantic system. None can deal with more than a small subset of English strings. Deductive operations, though undeniably powerful, still generally lack adequate heuristic controls to limit the extent of searching an infinite inference tree. Little has been done so far to incorporate inductive inference procedures. Few systems (see Charniak and Wilks) go beyond sentence boundaries in their analyses, and generally acceptable methods for anaphoric analysis and the discovery of pronominal reference have not yet been developed. Such subtleties as the relativity of adjectives and adverbs, thematic sequence, metaphor, etc., have still to be explored.

In conclusion, minimally adequate methods have been developed for dealing with natural languages in small quantity. The next step, managing dictionaries with tens of thousands of entries and correspondingly large grammars and semantic systems will entail a whole new order of complexity and may require the invention of entirely new techniques to accomplish the same goals. I believe the next step requires confrontation of the problem of pure size. The time is almost upon us when we can consider a research program that proposes to exploit and explore existing techniques in application to a question-answering system based on a 20 to 40 million word encyclopedia.[9] Perhaps only with such a program can we expect to discover whether what has been learned so far can be used for an eventual practical question-answering system.

References

1. ABELSON, R. P., and CARROLL, J. D. Computer simulation of individual belief systems. *Amer. Behav. Sci. 9* (May 1965), 24–30.
2. ——, and REICH, C. M. Implicational molecules: a method for extracting meaning from input sentences. Proc. Int. Jt. Conf. Art. Intel., Washington, D.C., 1969, pp. 641–647.
3. ALPAC (Automated Language Processing Advisory Committee). Language and machines — computers in translation and linguistics. Nat. Acad. Sci., Washington, D.C., 1966.
4. BECKER, J. D. The modeling of simple analogic and inductive processes in a semantic memory system. Proc. Int. Jt. Conf. Art. Intel., Washington, D.C., 1969, pp. 655–668.
5. BLACK, F. S. A deductive question-answering system. Ph.D. Th., Harvard U., Cambridge, Mass., June 1964.
6. BOBROW, D. G. A question-answering system for high school algebra word problems. Pro. AFIPS 1964 Fall Joint Comput. Conf., Vol. 26, Pt. 1, Spartan Books, New York, pp. 591–614.
7. ——, and FRASER, B. An augmented state transition network analysis procedure. Proc. Int. Jt. Conf. Art. Intel., Washington, D.C., 1969, pp. 557–567.
8. BOHNERT, H. G., and BECKER, P. O. Automatic English-to-logic translation in a simplified model. AFOSR 66-1727 (AD-637 227), IBM Thomas J. Watson Res. Center, Yorktown Heights, N.Y., Mar. 1966.
9. CHARNIAK, E. Computer solution of calculus word problems. Proc. Int. Jt. Conf. Art. Intel., Washington, D.C., 1969, pp. 303–316.
10. CHOMSKY, N. *Aspects of the Theory of Syntax.* MIT Press, Cambridge, Mass., 1965.
11. COLBY, KENNETH M., and ENEA, HORACE. Heuristic methods for computer understanding of natural language in context-restricted on-line dialogues. *Math. Biosciences 1* (1967), 1–25.
12. —— and ——. "Inductive Inference by Intelligent Machines." *Scientia, 103,* 669–720 (Jan.–Feb. 1968).
13. ——, TESLER, L., and ENEA, H. Experiments with a search algorithm for the data base of a human belief structure. Proc. Int. Jt. Conf. Art. Intel., Washington, D.C., 1969, pp. 649–654.
14. —— and SMITH, DAVID C. Dialogues between humans and an artificial belief system. Proc. Int. Jt. Conf. Art. Intel., Washington, D.C., 1969, pp. 319–324.
15. COLES, L. STEPHEN. Talking with a robot in English. Proc. Int. Jt. Conf. Art. Intel., Washington, D.C., 1969, pp. 587–596.
16. ——. An on-line question-answering system with natural language and pictorial input. Proc. ACM 23rd Nat. Conf. 1968, Brandon Systems Press, Princeton, N.J., pp. 157–167.
17. DARLINGTON, J. L. Machine methods for proving logical arguments expressed in English. *Mech. Transl. Comput. Linguist. 8* (June–Oct. 1965), pp. 41–67.
18. ——. Theorem proving and information retrieval. In *Machine Intelligence 4,* Meitzer and Mitchie

9. Olney's careful preparation of computer usable versions of the entire contents of Merriam-Webster's Collegiate and Pocket dictionaries (Olney, et al. 1968) now completed, sets the stage for such an ambitious undertaking.

(Eds.) Edinburgh U. Press, Edinburgh, 1969, Ch. 11.

19. ———. Theorem provers as question answerers. Unfolioed mss. Proc. Int. Jt. Conf. Art. Intel., Washington, D.C., 1969, abstract p. 317.

20. EARLEY, J. C. Generating a recognizer for a BNF grammar. Comp. Ctr. Rep. Carnegie-Mellon U., Pittsburgh, Pa., June 1965.

21. ELLIOTT, R. W. A model for a fact retrieval system. Ph.D. Th., TNN–42, Computation Center, U. Texas, Austin, Tex., May 1965.

22. ELLIS, ALLAN B., and TIEDEMAN, DAVID V. Can a machine counsel? Proc. CEED-SSRC Conference on Computer-based Instruction, U. of Texas, Austin, Texas, Oct. 1968.

23. FELDMAN, JEROME, and GRIES, DAVID. Translator writing systems. *Comm. ACM, 11,* **2** (Feb. 1968), 77–113.

24. FILLMORE, C. J. The case for Case. In *Universals in Linguistic Theory.* E. Bach and T. Harms (Eds.), Holt, Rinehart and Winston, 1968.

25. FRIEDMAN, J. A computer system for transformational grammar. *Comm. ACM 12,* **6** (June 1969), 341–348.

26. GIULIANO, V. E. Comments. *Comm. ACM 8,* **1** (Jan. 1965), 69–70.

27. GREEN, C. CORDELL, and RAPHAEL, BERTRAM. Research on intelligent question answering systems. Proc. ACM 23rd Nat. Conf., 1968, Brandon Systems Press, Princeton, N.J., pp. 169–181.

28. ———. Application of theorem proving to problem solving. Proc. Int. Jt. Conf. Art. Intel., Washington, D.C., pp. 219–239.

29. HAYS, D. G. *Introduction to Computational Linguistics.* American Elsevier, New York, 1967.

30. KASHER, A. Data retrieval by computer: a critical survey. Hebrew U. of Jerusalem, Jan. 1966. Tech. Rep. No. 22 to Off. of Naval Res., Inf. Syst. Branch.

31. KATZ, J. J. Recent issues in semantic theory. *Foundations of Language 3* (1967), 124–194.

32. KAY, M. A parsing program for computational grammars. RM-4283-PR, Rand Corp., Santa Monica, Calif., 1964.

33. KELLOGG, CHARLES H. A natural language compiler for on-line data management. *AFIPS Conference Proceedings,* Vol. 33, Proc. AFIPS 1968 Fall Joint Comput. Conf. Vol. 33, Thompson Book Co., Washington, D.C., pp. 473–493.

34. KIRSCH, R. A. Computer interpretation of English text and picture patterns. *IEEE Trans. EC* (Aug. 1964).

35. KLEIN, SHELDON, ET AL. The Autoling system. Tech. Rep. #43, Computer Sciences Dept., U. of Wisconsin, Madison, Wisc., Sept. 1968.

36. KOCHEN, MANFRED. Automatic question-answering of English-like questions about simple diagrams. *J. ACM 16,* **1** (Jan. 1969), 26–48.

37. KUHN, THOMAS S. *Structure of Scientific Revolutions.* U. of Chicago Press, Chicago, Ill., 1962.

38. LEVIEN, R. E., and MARON, M. E. Relational data file: a tool for mechanized inference execution and data retrieval. RM-4793-PR, Rand Corp., Santa Monica, Cal., Dec. 1965.

39. ———. Relational data file: experience with a system for propositional data storage and inference execution. RM-5947-PR, Rand Corp., Santa Monica, Calif., 1969.

40. MCCARTHY, J. Situations, actions and causal laws. Stanford Art: Intel. Proj., Memo 2, Stanford U., Stanford, Calif., 1963.

41. MINSKY, M. *Semantic Information Processing.* MIT Press, Cambridge, Mass., 1969.

42. NEWELL, A., and SIMON, H. A. GPS, a program that simulates human thought. In *Computers and Thought,* E. Feigenbaum and J. Feldman (Eds.), McGraw-Hill, New York, 1963.

43. OLNEY, J., REVARD, C., and ZIFF, P. Toward the development of computational aids for obtaining a formal semantic description of English. SP2766/001, Syst. Develop. Corp., Santa Monica, Calif., Oct. 1968.

44. PETRICK, S. A recognition procedure for transformational grammars. Ph.D. Th., Dep. of Modern Languages, MIT, Cambridge, Mass., June 1965.

45. POPLE, H. E., JR. A goal-oriented language for the computer. Ph.D. Th., Systems and Communication Science Dep., Carnegie-Mellon U., Pittsburgh, Pa., 1969.

46. QUILLIAN, M. Ross. Semantic memory. Ph.D. Th., Carnegie-Mellon U., Pittsburgh, Pa., Feb. 1966.

47. ———. Word concepts: a theory and simulation of some basic semantic capabilities. Doc. SP-2199, Syst. Develop. Corp., Santa Monica, Calif., Sept. 15, 1965. (Also in *Behav. Sci. 12,* (Sept. 1967), 410–430.)

48. ———. The teachable language comprehender. Bolt Baranek & Newman, Cambridge, Mass., Jan. 1969, in preparation.

49. ———. The teachable language comprehender. *Comm. ACM 12,* **8** (Aug. 1969), 459–476.

50. RAPHAEL, B. SIR: a computer program for semantic information retrieval. Ph.D. Th., Math. Dep., MIT, Cambridge, Mass., June 1964. In Proc. AFIPS 1964 Fall Joint Comput. Conf. Vol. 26, Pt. 1, Spartan Books, New York, pp. 577–589.

51. ROBINSON, J. A. A review of automatic theorem proving. Proc. of Symposia in Applied Math., Vol. 19, AMS, Providence, R.I., 1967, pp. 1–18.

52. ———. The present state of mechanical theorem proving. Fourth System Symposium, Cleveland, O., Nov. 19–20, 1968, in preparation.

53. ROSENBAUM, PETER. A grammar base question answering procedure. *Comm. ACM 10,* **10** (Oct. 1967), 630–635.

54. ——. English grammar II. Res. paper RC 2070, IBM Thomas J. Watson Res. Cent., Yorktown Heights, N.Y., Apr. 1968.

55. SALTON, GERARD. *Automatic Information Organization and Retrieval.* McGraw-Hill, New York, 1968.

56. SAVITT, D. A., LOVE, H. H., and TROOP, R. E. Association-storing processor study. Tech. Rep. RADC-TR-66-174, Rome Air Develop. Center, Rome, N.Y., June 1966.

57. SCHANK, ROGER C. Outline of a conceptual semantics for generation of coherent discourse. TRACOR-68-462-U, Tracor Inc., Austin, Tex., Mar. 1968.

58. ——, and TESLER, L. G. A conceptual parser for natural language. Proc. Int. Jt. Conf. Art. Intel., Washington, D.C., 1969, pp. 569–578.

59. SCHWARCZ, R. M. Steps toward a model of linguistic performance: a preliminary sketch. RM-5214-PR, The Rand Corp., Santa Monica, Calif., Jan. 1967.

60. ——, BURGER, J. F., and SIMMONS, R. F. A deductive logic for answering English questions. Syst. Develop. Corp., Dec. 1968, in preparation.

61. ——. Towards a computational formalization of natural language semantics. *Proc. Int. Conf. on Comp. Ling.,* held in Sweden, Sept. 1969, in preparation.

62. SHAPIRO, S. C., and WOODMANSEE, G. H. A net structure based relational question answerer: description and examples. Proc. Int. Jt. Conf. Art. Intel., Washington, D.C., 1969, pp. 325–345.

63. SIMMONS, ROBERT F., KLEIN, S., and McCONLOGUE, K. Indexing and dependency logic for answering English questions. *Amer. Doc. 15,* **3** (1964), 196–204.

64. ——. Answering English questions by computer: a survey. *Comm. ACM 8,* **1** (Jan. 1965), 53–70.

65. ——. Linguistic analysis of constructed responses in CAI. TNN-68, Comput. Center, U. Texas, Austin, Tex., Oct. 1968.

66. ——, BURGER, J. F., and SCHWARCZ, R. M. A computational model of verbal understanding. Proc. AFIPS 1968 Fall Joint Comput. Conf., Vol. 33, Thompson Book Co., Washington, D.C., pp. 441–456.

67. SLAGLE, J. R. Experiments with a deductive question-answering program. *Comm. ACM 8,* **12** (Dec. 1965), 792–798.

68. SPARCK-JONES, K. Experiments in semantic classification. *Mech. Transl. Comput. Linguist. 8,* **3 & 4** (1965), 97–112.

69. TAYLOR, EDWIN F. (Ed.) ELIZA: a skimmable report on the ELIZA conversational tutoring system. Educational Res. Center, MIT, Cambridge, Mass., Mar. 1968.

70. TESLER, LAWRENCE, ENEA, H., and COLBY, K. M. A directed graph representation for computer simulation of belief systems. *Math. Biosciences 21,* **2** (Feb. 1968).

71. THARP, A. L., and KRULEE, G. K. Using relational operators to structure long-term memory. Proc. Int. Jt. Conf. Art. Intel., Washington, D.C., 1969, pp. 579–586.

72. THOMPSON, F. B., et al. DEACON breadboard summary. RM64TMP-9, TEMPO, General Electric, Santa Barbara, Calif., Mar. 1964.

73. ——. English for the computer. Proc. AFIPS 1966 Fall Joint Comput. Conf., Vol. 29, Spartan Books, New York, pp. 349–356.

74. THORNE, J. P., BRATLEY, P., and DEWAR, H. The syntactic analysis of English by machine. In *Machine Intelligence 3,* D. Michie (Ed.), American Elsevier, New York, 1968.

75. WEIZENBAUM, J. ELIZA — a computer program for the study of natural language communications between man and machine. *Comm. ACM 9,* **1** (Jan. 1966), 36–45.

76. WILKS, YORICK. Computable semantic derivations. SP 3017, Syst. Develop. Corp., Santa Monica, Calif., Jan. 1968.

77. WOODS, WILLIAM A. Semantic interpretation of English questions on a structured data base. Mathematical linguistics and automatic translation, Rep. NSF-17, 1967, Comput. Lab., Harvard U., Cambridge, Mass., Aug. 1966.

78. ——. Procedural semantics for a question-answering machine. Proc. AFIPS 1968 Fall Joint Comput. Conf., Vol. 33, Thompson Book Co., Washington, D.C., pp. 457–471.

79. YNGVE, V. H. A framework for syntactic translation. *Mech. Transl. Comput. Linguist. 4* (Dec. 1957), pp. 444–466.

44 An Indirect Method of Information Retrieval

WILLIAM GOFFMAN
Information Storage & Retrieval
Vol. 4, No. 4, December, 1968

1. Introduction

The function of an information retrieval system is to provide its users with useful information on request. The most common type of information retrieval system is one whose information source consists of a file of documents. Thus, given a collection of documents and a query, the system has to assign to the query an answer, i.e., a set of documents belonging to the collection which are expected to convey the desired information. Naturally, this answer cannot be chosen arbitrarily but should reflect a relationship between the query and the resulting set of documents. Usually, one says that the documents in the answer are relevant to the query. Hence, the information retrieval process can in general be characterized in terms of two sets S and X and a relation R between their members. The set S stands for queries, the set X a file of documents and the relation R, called relevance, is the property which assigns to every $s \in S$ a certain subset $A(s)$ of X, called an answer to s. That is, $A(s)$ consists of all $x \in X$ for which xRs.

The notion of treating the information retrieval process strictly as a matching procedure between the query and the documents in the file is the basis of most operating information retrieval systems. By this method, the query s is matched directly against each member x of the set X in order to determine the membership of the answer set $A(s)$. Two important defects in this procedure, which we shall call the direct method, have been pointed out in Refs. [1, 2]. One defect in the direct method affects the efficiency of the system in that the entire set of documents X must always be probed in order to determine the subset $A(s)$. The second and more important flaw is related to the fact that the usefulness, hence the relevance, of the information conveyed by a document relative to a query must depend upon what is already known at the time that this information is conveyed. Thus, if a document x has been assessed as relevant to a query s, the relevance of the other documents in the file X may be affected since the value of the information conveyed by these documents may either increase or decrease as a result of the information conveyed by the document x. Hence, the relevance of a document is not absolute but may depend upon what information is conveyed by other documents in the file which is being interrogated, i.e., upon the information acquired during the course of the retrieval process. Consequently, the relationship between a query and a document is not sufficient to establish relevance. On the other hand, the underlying assumption of the direct method is that the relationship between the query and the document is both necessary and sufficient to establish relevance. That is, it is assumed that all documents in a file are independent, from which it follows that there exists, for every query s, one and only one set of documents in the file which constitutes the answer to s; an assumption which does not seem to be consistent with reality.

The purpose of this paper is to demonstrate, by means of an experiment, a search technique for information retrieval based upon a mathematical model in which the defects in the direct method are taken into account. We shall be mainly concerned with the general strategy for finding an answer to a query and not with the related problems of how to represent information contained in documents and queries or what constitutes relevance. The paper is divided into two sections. The first gives a brief exposition of the essential aspects of the theory, a detailed development of which has been given by the author in Ref. [3]. This is followed by the experimental method and results.

2. The Mathematical Model

Consider a query s and a set of documents X. Let $P_s(x)$ denote the probability that document $x \in X$ is relevant to the query s. Assume that with every s there is associated a critical probability $\xi_0(s)$. If $P_s(x) > \xi_0(s)$ then x is said to be relevant to s. Thus, a relevant document will be characterized by having attached to it a probability greater than the critical probability. One can think of the probabilities as indicating a measure of relevance of the documents to which they are attached. The critical probability is then the dividing line between the barely relevant and the not quite relevant. Hence, $\xi_0(s)$ acts as a partitioning point of the set X since xRs only for those members of X with probability greater than the critical probability.

Since two given members of X may not be independent of each other, i.e., the value of the information conveyed by one may be either inhibited or enhanced by the information conveyed by the other, a dependency relation between the members of X must be introduced.

Definition 1: Let p_{ij} be the conditional probability that $x_j \in X$ is relevant to s given that $x_i \in X$ is relevant to s: $p_{ii} = 1$.

Definition 2: Let r_{ij} be the conditional probability that $x_j \in X$ is relevant to s given that $x_i \in X$ is not relevant to s: $r_{ii} = 0$.

Thus, r_{ij} represents the initial probability that x_j is relevant to s and p_{ij} does not depend on s but on x_i.

THEOREM 1: *If the elements of a sequence $Y = (y_j)$, $y_i \in X$, are relevant to s then $p_{j-1,j} > \xi_0(s)$ for every $y_j \in Y$.*

Proof: Consider the following arbitrary sequence Y of elements in X

$$Y = (y_0, y_1, \ldots, y_j, \ldots, y_n).$$

The probability $P_s(y_j)$ that y_j, $j = 0, 1, \ldots, n$, is relevant to s can be defined by recursion as follows:

$P_s(y_0) = r_{i,0}; i = 1, 2, \ldots, n.$
$P_s(y_j) = p_{j-1,j} P_s(y_{j-1}) + r_{j-1,j}[1 - P_s(y_{j-1}) = r_{j-1,j} + \lambda_{j-1,j} P_s(y_{j-1}); j = 1, \ldots, n$
where $\lambda_{j-1,j} = p_{j-1,j} - r_{j-1,j}$. If $P_s(y_0) > \xi_0(s)$, then $r_{i,0} > \xi_0(s)$. If $P_s(y_j) > \xi_0(s)$, then

$$\lambda_{j-1,j} > \left(\frac{\xi_0(s) - r_{j-1,j}}{P_s(y_{j-1})} \right); j = 1, 2, \ldots, n.$$

Suppose $p_{j-1,j} \leq \xi_0(s)$, then $(\xi_0(s) - r_{j-1,j}) P_s(y_{j-1}) > \xi_0(s) - r_{j-1,j}$ or $P_s(y_{j-1}) > 1$, which is absurd.

Thus, a sequence of documents in X will be relevant to a query s, i.e., will belong to an answer $A(s)$, only if, for every document in the sequence with an immediate predecessor, the conditional probability of its relevance, given the relevance of its immediate predecessor, exceeds the critical probability.*

Definition 3: Given x_i, x_j in X, if $p_{ij} > \xi_0(s)$ then x_i is said to converse with x_j. This relation shall be denoted by $x_i C x_j$.

Definition 4: A sequence of elements x_i to x_j such that $x_i C x_{i+1} C \ldots C x_{j-1} C x_j$ is called a communication chain from x_i to x_j; x_i is said to communicate with x_j and is denoted by $x_i \bar{C} x_j$. If $x_i \bar{C} x_j$ and $x_j \bar{C} x_i$ then x_i and x_j are said to be in intercommunication denoted by $x_i I x_j$.

Clearly, for a set of documents to be relevant to a query, it is necessary that there exist a communication chain of its members. Hence, communication is a necessary condition for relevance in the information retrieval process. Thus, an answer $A(s)$ to a query is a closed communication chain of documents, i.e., a communication chain for which there is no $x \in X$ with which the last element in the chain communicates and no $x \in X$ which communicates with the first element. Moreover, an answer need not be unique since there may exist a multiplicity of not necessarily disjoint closed communication chains relative to a given query. Hence, the mapping R of $s \in S$ into the power set of X is generally not one to one but more realistically one to many.

* A model of the direct method results by assuming $p_{ij} = r_{ij}$ for every x_i, x_j in X, i.e., by assuming independence. $A(s)$ is then all $x_j \in X$ for which $r_{ij} > \xi_0(s)$.

THEOREM 2: *Intercommunication is an equivalence relation.*

Proof: (1) $x_i I x_i$ since a document is in intercommunication with itself.

    (2) If $x_i I x_j$, then $x_j I x_i$ for the intercommunication chain from x_i to x_j implies that there is one from x_j to x_i.

    (3) If $x_i I x_j$ and $x_j I x_k$, then $x_i I x_k$ for if there is intercommunication between x_i and x_j and intercommunication between x_j and x_k, there must be intercommunication between x_i and x_k namely the sum of the two.

It follows from Theorem 2 that the set X can be partitioned into communication classes

$$X = \sum_{i=1}^{n} I_i$$

such that, if an element $x \in X$ belongs to a given class I_i then all members of X which are in intercommunication with x also belong to I_i. Consequently, an answer, i.e., a closed communication chain, can be represented as a sequence of partial answers whereby each partial answer belongs to a given intercommunication class. The critical probability which depends on the requirements imposed upon the system by the user, determines the extent of the partition of X. That is, increasing the critical probability leads to a finer covering of X and decreasing it leads to a cruder one.

The notion of relevance which plays a prominent role in information retrieval is also a basic concept in the calculus of entailment. It is interesting to note a connection between the notions of relevance as applied in these two different subject areas.

In logic, a necessary condition for the validity of an inference from a proposition A to a proposition B is that A be relevant to B. Thus, relevance is essential to a valid logical argument. In a recent paper, ANDERSON and BELNAP [4] consider the following system of axioms as capturing the notion of relevance in the calculus of entailment.

(1) $A \rightarrow A$
                                  (identity)

(2) $A \rightarrow B \rightarrow \cdot B \rightarrow C \rightarrow \cdot A \rightarrow C$
                                (transitivity)

(3) $(A \rightarrow \cdot B \rightarrow C) \rightarrow \cdot B \rightarrow \cdot A \rightarrow C$
                                (permutation)

(4) $(A \rightarrow \cdot B \rightarrow C) \rightarrow \cdot A \rightarrow B \rightarrow \cdot A \rightarrow C$
                            (self-distribution)

THEOREM 3: *The relation of communication satisfies axioms 1–4.*

Proof: (1) $x_i \bar{C} x_i$, i.e., a document communicates with itself.

    (2) If $x_i \bar{C} x_j$ and $x_j \bar{C} x_k$, then $x_i \bar{C} x_k$, i.e., if there is a communication chain from document x_i to document x_j and a communication chain from document x_j to document x_k, there is a communication chain from document x_i to document x_k.

    (3) If $x_i \bar{C} (x_j \bar{C} x_k)$ then from x_j it follows that $x_i \bar{C} x_k$, i.e., if a document x_i communicates with a chain of documents x_j to x_k, then from x_j it follows that x_i communicates with x_k.

    (4) If $x_i \bar{C} (x_j \bar{C} x_k)$ then from $x_i \bar{C} x_j$ it follows that $x_i \bar{C} x_k$, i.e., if a document x_i communicates with a chain of documents x_j to x_k, then it follows from the chain x_i to x_j that x_i communicates with x_k.

Thus, the conditions for relevance in information retrieval satisfy the axioms which capture the notion of relevance in the calculus of entailment. Therefore, when we talk about relevance in information retrieval or the calculus of entailment, we are essentially talking about the same thing.

On the basis of Theorems 1, 2 and 3, a file of documents X can be formally probed for an answer $A(s)$ to a query s in the following manner. Given a set of documents X and a query s together with its associated critical probability $\xi_0(s)$:

(1) Construct the matrix M of conditional probabilities p_{ij} for every x_i, x_j in X.

(2) Convert the matrix M to a communication matrix M' by reducing to zero all entries in M which are less than or equal to $\xi_0(s)$.

(3) From M', establish the partition of X into disjoint intercommunication classes I_i as determined by $\xi_0(s)$.

(4) Select at random a representative member of each class. Denote this set by G_1.

(5) Search the set G_1 for documents x_j for which $r_{ij} > \xi_0(s)$. One of three possibilities will result.

    (i) There are no such documents in G_1.
    (ii) There is one such member in G_1.
    (iii) There are two or more such members.

We shall first consider case (ii).

(6) Let x_j denote the member of G_1 for which $r_{ij} > \xi_0(s)$. Enter the intercommunication class to which x_j belongs. Denote this class by I_j. Find that member of I_j which has the highest initial probability of relevance to s. Denote this document by x_0. (This step can be eliminated by taking x_j as x_0.)

(7) Enter the communication matrix M' and con-

struct a communication chain from x_0 as follows: Let x_1 be that member which has the highest conditional probability of relevance, given that x_0 is relevant. This is greater than the critical probability since only such values appear in M'. If the highest conditional probability is shared by two or more documents, then pick the one with the highest initial probability. If there are still more than one pick any one. Let x_2 be that member with the highest conditional probability of relevance, given that x_1 is relevant. If the document with the highest conditional probability is already in the chain, in this case x_0, then pick the member with the next highest one. Continue with this procedure until there are no elements with positive conditional probabilities remaining in the row of M' corresponding to the last element in the chain x_z.

(8) By axiom (3) of the axiomatic system describing the notion of relevance, it follows that if there is a communication chain from some $x \in X$ to x_0 then from x_0, we can infer that the chain extends to x_z. Let x^1 be that member not already in the chain for which the conditional probability of x_0 being relevant, given that x^1 is relevant, is maximum. If there is more than one such element, follow the procedure specified above. As before, continue this procedure until there are no elements with positive conditional probabilities in the column of M' corresponding to x^a, the first element in the chain. The resulting closed communication chain represents an answer $A(s)$ to the query s.

In case (iii), i.e., if two or more members of G_1 have initial probabilities of relevance greater than the critical probability, choose the one with the highest initial probability and proceed as in case (ii). In the event that two or more members share the highest probability, pick any one.

We shall now consider case (i), that is the case where no members of G_1 have initial probability greater than the critical probability. This, of course, does not imply that there are no members of X which are relevant to s. Hence, from the remaining members, select a scond set of representative members of the I_i. Denote this set by G_2. Search G_2 for relevant members. Again, there are three possibilities. In the event that either case (ii) or case (iii) results, proceed in the manner described above. Suppose, however, that there are no relvant members in G_2. Then select a G_3 from the remaining members and so on if necessary. Consider this situation analogous to the classical urn problem of determining the expected number of probes before obtaining a white ball from an urn containing n balls of which k are white. The expectancy E is expressed by the well-known formula

$$E = \frac{n - k}{k + 1}$$

Since we are interested in the case where $k = 1$, probe $(n - 1)/2$ sets G of representative members of X, where n is the number of elements in the largest class I_i, before stopping. Thus, the necessity of searching the entire file is avoided.

The procedure described above has the advantages of (1) requiring no human intervention so that it can easily be carried out by a machine, (2) the possibility of reducing the number of documents which are probed before arriving at an answer to a query and (3) making use of information acquired while the search is in progress, i.e., it is required to find only one relevant document on the basis of the query which will lead to another relevant one and so on, until an answer is generated. If a relevant document is known prior to the search, e.g., one provided by the inquirer, then steps 3–6 of the procedure can be eliminated.

3. The Experiment

An experiment for demonstrating the search procedure developed in section 2, which we shall call the indirect method, must clearly contain the following four constituents: (1) one or more queries, (2) a file of documents, (3) a means of representing the information content of the queries and documents and (4) a means of establishing relevance. The following scheme was adopted in conducting the experiment presented in this section.

Consider an arbitrary scientific paper s. We can say that s represents a certain research question, namely the one with which the author was concerned while carrying out the work reported in that paper. Associated with each scientific paper s is a set of references which the author has cited to support his work in one way or another. Hence, we can infer that the author considered these papers to be relevant, in some sense, to the scientific inquiry repesented by the paper s. Therefore, we shall take the paper s to represent a query and its set of references to represent an answer to the query, i.e., a set of relevant documents. This arrangement seems adequate for this experiment since we are not so much interested in reproducing a real situation as in simulating the information retrieval process for comparative purposes. Moreover, the advantages of using this scheme seem to outweigh the well-known disadvantage due to the sometime arbitrary manner by which certain authors assign references to their articles. These advantages are: (1) the scheme can be quickly and cheaply implemented and (2) the references to an article, regardless of the manner in which they were selected, still represent a well defined set of documents which are relevant to the paper which cited them. Thus, the tedious, time consuming and costly alternative of establishing so called user groups can be avoided. Besides, the relevance assessments of such groups under experimental conditions is perhaps even less reliable than are author citations.

Since our primary concern in this experiment is with the general strategy for finding an answer to a query from a file of documents, we are not too interested in how the information in the query and file is represented as long as it is represented consistently. Consequently, it was decided to utilize a completely automatic scheme for this purpose. The method adopted is one due to BOOTH [5] and consists of having a computing machine (1) make a word frequency analysis of the whole of each input document; (2) sort the words into a list in descending frequency of occurrence; and (3) apply a test to determine unusual frequency. Dean Booth has suggested comparing the frequency of the words with a standard frequency list. Then any word which occurs more than say five times as frequently as in normal usage is regarded as significant. The factor in frequency may be varied according to the amount of detail which is required in the output. This method, though very simple, has the virtue of requiring no human inspection of the documents and is well suited to computer operation, hence it suits our purposes well.

For the experiment, two articles were arbitrarily selected from the journal *Diabetes*, Vol. 12, 1963, to represent queries. These articles are entitled:

(1) *Hypoglycemic Effect of L-leucine During Periods of Endogenous Hyperinsulinism* by G. REAVEN, C. WINKELMAN and C. LUCAS.
(2) *Sensitivity of Beta Cells to Alloxan after Inhibition by Insulin or Stimulation by Glucose* by M. KANEKO and J. LOGOTHETOPOULOS.

Article (1) contains nine citations while article (2) contains sixteen. Of the sixteen references cited by (2), one refers to unpublished experiments, three are in the German language and one refers to a symposium, the proceedings of which were unavailable. Thus, the relevant set for (2) was reduced to eleven documents. Consequently, the file for the experiment consisted of twenty documents, i.e., the union of the two sets of references, nine of which are relevant to query s_1 represented by article (1) and eleven relevant to query s_2 represented by article (2). (The two articles have no citations in common.)

A word frequency analysis of the whole of articles (1) and (2) was made. In each case the words were sorted into lists in descending frequency of occurrence. Since a standardized frequency list for the vocabulary of diabetes research does not exist for comparison, the following convention was adopted for determining the significant words of the articles. Those words in each document whose frequency exceeds 1% of the total number of words in the document were selected as significant. The resulting lists were then subjected to further modification by

the deletion of articles, prepositions, conjunctions, etc., which was carried out automatically. This procedure, although somewhat arbitrary, seemed to produce good descriptions of the contents of each document, but more importantly it provides a consistent, if not accurate, representation of the information content of a set of documents to which it is applied. The word frequency analysis on articles (1) and (2) produced the two lists of significant words shown in Table I.

TABLE I
SIGNIFICANT WORDS IN ARTICLES (1) AND (2)

s_1	s_2
blood	alloxan
concentration	blood
dogs	beta cells
during	diabetes
experiments	effects
effect	glucose
glucose	groups
hyperglycemia	infusion
hepatic	injections
infusion	insulin
insulin	levels
L-leucine	rate
output	rats
periods	severity
	zinc

Each document in the file, i.e., the twenty referenced articles, was analysed in a similar fashion and a list of significant words obtained for each. We denote the members of the file by $x_1, x_2, \ldots, x_{20}$, where x_1 through x_9 stand for the documents relevant to s_1 and x_{10} through x_{20} those relevant to s_2. We shall first apply the direct method to this data.

We match the list of significant words representing each of the queries s_1 and s_2 against the word lists representing each of the documents in the file, and compute estimates of the initial probabilities r_{ij} of relevance of each document x_j in the file to each query by means of the expression:

$$r_{ij} = \frac{m(x_j \wedge s_k)}{m(s_k)} ; \qquad i,j = 1, 2, \ldots, 20.$$
$$k = 1, 2.$$

where $m(x_j \wedge s_k)$ is the number of words common to the lists representing document x_j and query s_k and $m(s_k)$ is the number of words in the list representing s_k. Only an exact match is considered to be a word in common. The computation yields the values shown in Table II.

The next step is to define the critical probabilities $\xi_0(s_1)$ and $\xi_0(s_2)$ in order to establish relevance. The critical probability must be high enough to reject the spurious material yet low enough to capture the desired information. Since we have no way of knowing the amount

TABLE II

Initial Probabilities of Relevance

	s_1	s_2
x_1	0.07	0.06
x_2	0.29	0.19
x_3	0.21	0.19
x_4	0.64	0.26
x_5	0.36	0.26
x_6	0.36	0.19
x_7	0.36	0.26
x_8	0.29	0.26
x_9	0.29	0.26
x_{10}	0.14	0.19
x_{11}	0.07	0.26
x_{12}	0.21	0.26
x_{13}	0.00	0.26
x_{14}	0.21	0.19
x_{15}	0.21	0.50
x_{16}	0.21	0.50
x_{17}	0.14	0.19
x_{18}	0.14	0.25
x_{19}	0.07	0.25
x_{20}	0.14	0.19

of detail required by the authors of s_1 and s_2, we could pick arbitrary values. However, we do know that s_1 was not cited by s_2 nor s_2 by s_1 even though they deal with the same general subject area and appear in the same journal. Thus, we define

$$\xi_0(s_1) = \frac{m(s_1 \wedge s_2)}{m(s_1)}; \qquad \xi_0(s_2) = \frac{m(s_1 \wedge s_2)}{m(s_2)}$$

That is, the critical probability for $s_1(s_2)$ is taken as the smallest value for which $s_2(s_1)$ will not be relevant to $s_1(s_2)$. The computed values are,

$$\xi_0(s_1) = 0.29; \qquad \xi_0(s_2) = 0.26$$

Hence, by the direct method the answers to s_1 and s_2 are,

$$A(s_1) = \{x_4, x_5, x_6, x_7\}$$
$$A(s_2) = \{x_{15}, x_{16}\}$$

i.e., all members of the file with probability r greater than the critical probability for each query. We shall now compare these results to the outputs obtained when applying the indirect method to the same data.

Given documents x_i and x_j in the file, we define estimates of the conditional probabilities p_{ij} as follows:

$$p_{ij} = \frac{m(x_i \wedge x_j)}{m(x_i)}; \qquad i, j = 1, 2, \ldots, 20.$$

where $m(x_i \wedge x_j)$ is the number of significant words shared by the documents x_i and x_j and $m(x_i)$ is the number of significant words representing x_i. In this manner

we construct the matrix M of conditional probabilities p_{ij} for every x_i and x_j as shown in Table III. By replacing all entries in M which are less than or equal to 0.29, i.e., $\xi_0(s_1)$, we obtain the communication matrix $M'(s_1)$ for query s_1, which is given in Table IV.

From $M'(s_1)$ we establish a partition of the file into the following intercommunication classes I_i; $i = 1, 2, \ldots, 10$.

$$I_1 = \{x_1\}$$
$$I_2 = \{x_2, x_3, x_4, x_5, x_6, x_7, x_8\}$$
$$I_3 = \{x_9\}$$
$$I_4 = \{x_{10}, x_{18}, x_{19}\}$$
$$I_5 = \{x_{11}\}$$
$$I_6 = \{x_{12}\}$$
$$I_7 = \{x_{13}\}$$
$$I_8 = \{x_{14}\}$$
$$I_9 = \{x_{15}\}$$
$$I_{10} = \{x_{16}, x_{17}, x_{20}\}$$

If we select representative sets G and search, we will find a relevant document in the intercommunication class I_2 since all documents with initial probability greater than 0.29 belong to the class. The highest probability is attached to x_4. Entering $M'(s_1)$ with x_4 results in the closed communication chain

$$A(s_1) = x_3 \, Cx_4 \, Cx_7 \, Cx_8 \, Cx_5 \, Cx_6 \, Cx_2$$

which consists of the entire class I_2 and contains seven of the nine references to s_1 opposed to only four by the direct method. In each case no spurious material was retrieved which would indicate a good choice of critical probability. If we eliminate the step of starting with the document having the highest probability and instead begin with the known relevant document, the indirect method would yield the following possible outputs.

From x_5, the chain $x_1 \, Cx_6 \, Cx_5 \, Cx_8 \, Cx_7 \, Cx_4 \, Cx_2$
From x_6, the chain $x_1 \, Cx_6 \, Cx_5 \, Cx_8 \, Cx_7 \, Cx_4 \, Cx_2$ or
$x_1 \, Cx_6 \, Cx_7 \, Cx_4 \, Cx_2$
From x_7, the chain $x_1 \, Cx_6 \, Cx_7 \, Cx_4 \, Cx_2$

Although the outputs differ, in each case the result is better than the one obtained by the direct method.

Let us now consider the query s_2. By replacing all entries in the matrix M which are less than or equal to 0.26, i.e., $\xi_0(s_2)$, we obtain the communication matrix $M'(s_2)$ for the query s_2, shown in Table V. From $M'(s_2)$ we establish a partition of the file into intercommunication classes corresponding to the query s_2. These classes are

$$I_1 = \{x_1\}$$
$$I_2 = \{x_2, x_3, x_4, x_5, x_6, x_7, x_8, x_9, x_{14}\}$$
$$I_3 = \{x_{10}, x_{15}, x_{16}, x_{17}, x_{18}, x_{19}, x_{20}\}$$
$$I_4 = \{x_{11}\}$$
$$I_5 = \{x_{12}, x_{13}\}$$

TABLE III
The Matrix M of Conditional Probabilities

(1)	0·50	0·25	0·25	0·50	0·50	0·25	0·50	0·25	0·25	0·25	0·00	0·00	0·25	0·25	0·25	0·00	0·25	0·25	0·00
0·10	(1)	0·16	0·32	0·10	0·21	0·16	0·21	0·10	0·16	0·05	0·10	0·05	0·21	0·10	0·26	0·21	0·16	0·16	0·16
0·11	0·33	(1)	0·55	0·33	0·33	0·55	0·33	0·22	0·11	0·11	0·11	0·00	0·44	0·11	0·33	0·11	0·22	0·22	0·11
0·07	0·40	0·33	(1)	0·33	0·27	0·40	0·27	0·27	0·13	0·13	0·20	0·00	0·20	0·20	0·33	0·13	0·13	0·13	0·07
0·12	0·12	0·19	0·31	(1)	0·31	0·25	0·50	0·19	0·12	0·06	0·12	0·00	0·12	0·25	0·19	0·06	0·06	0·06	0·06
0·25	0·50	0·35	0·50	0·62	(1)	0·62	0·62	0·35	0·25	0·00	0·12	0·00	0·35	0·25	0·35	0·25	0·25	0·25	0·25
0·07	0·13	0·33	0·40	0·33	0·33	(1)	0·40	0·20	0·13	0·13	0·13	0·00	0·27	0·13	0·33	0·20	0·27	0·13	0·13
0·13	0·27	0·20	0·27	0·53	0·33	0·40	(1)	0·13	0·13	0·00	0·13	0·00	0·13	0·13	0·13	0·07	0·20	0·13	0·13
0·07	0·14	0·14	0·28	0·21	0·21	0·21	0·14	(1)	0·21	0·21	0·14	0·00	0·14	0·21	0·36	0·07	0·21	0·21	0·07
0·09	0·27	0·09	0·18	0·18	0·18	0·18	0·18	0·27	(1)	0·36	0·18	0·09	0·27	0·45	0·45	0·36	0·54	0·45	0·27
0·00	0·11	0·06	0·11	0·11	0·00	0·11	0·00	0·11	0·22	(1)	0·11	0·11	0·17	0·17	0·11	0·17	0·22	0·22	0·00
0·00	0·13	0·07	0·20	0·13	0·07	0·13	0·13	0·13	0·13	0·13	(1)	0·27	0·13	0·33	0·13	0·07	0·20	0·07	0·00
0·00	0·08	0·00	0·00	0·00	0·00	0·00	0·00	0·00	0·08	0·08	0·15	(1)	0·23	0·23	0·15	0·00	0·31	0·08	0·00
0·08	0·33	0·25	0·25	0·17	0·25	0·33	0·17	0·17	0·25	0·25	0·17	0·25	(1)	0·08	0·33	0·17	0·42	0·17	0·17
0·05	0·10	0·05	0·14	0·18	0·10	0·10	0·10	0·14	0·23	0·14	0·23	0·14	0·05	(1)	0·32	0·18	0·23	0·27	0·05
0·04	0·19	0·12	0·19	0·12	0·12	0·19	0·08	0·19	0·19	0·08	0·08	0·08	0·15	0·27	(1)	0·35	0·19	0·15	0·15
0·00	0·17	0·04	0·08	0·04	0·08	0·12	0·04	0·04	0·17	0·12	0·04	0·00	0·08	0·17	0·37	(1)	0·12	0·12	0·30
0·05	0·16	0·10	0·10	0·05	0·10	0·21	0·16	0·16	0·32	0·21	0·16	0·21	0·26	0·32	0·26	0·16	(1)	0·32	0·26
0·07	0·20	0·13	0·13	0·07	0·13	0·13	0·13	0·20	0·33	0·27	0·07	0·07	0·13	0·40	0·27	0·20	0·40	(1)	0·20
0·00	0·30	0·10	0·10	0·10	0·20	0·20	0·20	0·10	0·30	0·00	0·00	0·00	0·20	0·10	0·40	0·70	0·50	0·60	(1)

We see the effect of lowering the critical probability, namely the resulting cruder partition of the file into five instead of ten classes as was the case for the higher critical probability of 0.29. As in the search for the answer to s_1, all members with initial probability greater than 0.26 belong to the same class, in this case I_3. Proceeding as before, we arrive at identical closed communication chains starting from either of the documents with initial probability greater than 0.26, i.e., x_{15} or x_{16}. Thus,

$$A(s_2) = x_{13} \ Cx_{12} \ Cx_{15} \ Cx_{16} \ Cx_{17} \ Cx_{20} \ Cx_{19} \ Cx_{18} \ Cx_{10} \ Cx_{11}$$

Hence, the indirect method produced ten of the eleven references to s_2 as opposed to only two by the direct method with no spurious material retrieved by either method.

We could have proceeded with the search for an answer to s_2 in a slightly different manner. Since $\xi_0(s_1) > \xi_0(s_2)$ it follows that every intercommunication class in the partition of the file effected by $\xi_0(s_1)$ is a subset of an intercommunication class in the partition of the file effected by $\xi_0(s_2)$. Hence, every communication chain relative to $\xi_0(s_1)$ is a sub-chain of a communication chain relative to $\xi_0(s_2)$. Consequently, we could have searched

TABLE IV
The Communication Matrix $M'(s_1)$

	x_1	x_2	x_3	x_4	x_5	x_6	x_7	x_8	x_9	x_{10}	x_{11}	x_{12}	x_{13}	x_{14}	x_{15}	x_{16}	x_{17}	x_{18}	x_{19}	x_{20}
x_1	(1)	0·50	0·00	0·00	0·50	0·50	0·00	0·50	0·00	0·00	0·00	0·00	0·00	0·00	0·00	0·00	0·00	0·00	0·00	0·00
x_2	0·00	(1)	0·00	0·32	0·00	0·00	0·00	0·00	0·00	0·00	0·00	0·00	0·00	0·00	0·00	0·00	0·00	0·00	0·00	0·00
x_3	0·00	0·33	(1)	0·55	0·33	0·33	0·55	0·33	0·00	0·00	0·00	0·00	0·00	0·44	0·00	0·33	0·00	0·00	0·00	0·00
x_4	0·00	0·40	0·33	(1)	0·33	0·27	0·40	0·27	0·27	0·00	0·00	0·00	0·00	0·00	0·00	0·33	0·00	0·00	0·00	0·00
x_5	0·00	0·00	0·00	0·31	(1)	0·31	0·00	0·50	0·00	0·00	0·00	0·00	0·00	0·00	0·00	0·00	0·00	0·00	0·00	0·00
x_6	0·00	0·50	0·35	0·50	0·62	(1)	0·62	0·62	0·35	0·00	0·00	0·00	0·00	0·35	0·00	0·35	0·00	0·00	0·00	0·00
x_7	0·00	0·00	0·33	0·40	0·33	0·33	(1)	0·40	0·00	0·00	0·00	0·00	0·00	0·27	0·00	0·33	0·00	0·27	0·00	0·00
x_8	0·00	0·27	0·00	0·27	0·53	0·33	0·40	(1)	0·00	0·00	0·00	0·00	0·00	0·00	0·00	0·00	0·00	0·00	0·00	0·00
x_9	0·00	0·00	0·00	0·28	0·00	0·00	0·00	0·00	(1)	0·00	0·00	0·00	0·00	0·00	0·00	0·36	0·00	0·00	0·00	0·00
x_{10}	0·00	0·27	0·00	0·00	0·00	0·00	0·00	0·00	0·27	(1)	0·36	0·00	0·00	0·27	0·45	0·45	0·36	0·54	0·45	0·27
x_{11}	0·00	0·00	0·00	0·00	0·00	0·00	0·00	0·00	0·00	0·00	(1)	0·00	0·00	0·00	0·00	0·00	0·00	0·00	0·00	0·00
x_{12}	0·00	0·00	0·00	0·00	0·00	0·00	0·00	0·00	0·00	0·00	0·00	(1)	0·27	0·00	0·33	0·00	0·00	0·00	0·00	0·00
x_{13}	0·00	0·00	0·00	0·00	0·00	0·00	0·00	0·00	0·00	0·00	0·00	0·00	(1)	0·00	0·00	0·00	0·00	0·31	0·00	0·00
x_{14}	0·00	0·33	0·00	0·00	0·00	0·00	0·33	0·00	0·00	0·00	0·00	0·00	0·00	(1)	0·00	0·33	0·00	0·42	0·00	0·00
x_{15}	0·00	0·00	0·00	0·00	0·00	0·00	0·00	0·00	0·00	0·00	0·00	0·00	0·00	0·00	(1)	0·32	0·00	0·00	0·27	0·00
x_{16}	0·00	0·00	0·00	0·00	0·00	0·00	0·00	0·00	0·00	0·00	0·00	0·00	0·00	0·00	0·27	(1)	0·35	0·00	0·00	0·00
x_{17}	0·00	0·00	0·00	0·00	0·00	0·00	0·00	0·00	0·00	0·00	0·00	0·00	0·00	0·00	0·00	0·37	(1)	0·00	0·00	0·30
x_{18}	0·00	0·00	0·00	0·00	0·00	0·00	0·00	0·00	0·00	0·32	0·00	0·00	0·00	0·00	0·32	0·00	0·00	(1)	0·32	0·00
x_{19}	0·00	0·00	0·00	0·00	0·00	0·00	0·00	0·00	0·00	0·33	0·27	0·00	0·00	0·00	0·40	0·27	0·00	0·40	(1)	0·00
x_{20}	0·00	0·30	0·00	0·00	0·00	0·00	0·00	0·00	0·00	0·30	0·00	0·00	0·00	0·00	0·00	0·40	0·70	0·50	0·60	(1)

TABLE V

THE COMMUNICATION MATRIX $M'(s_2)$

	x_1	x_2	x_3	x_4	x_5	x_6	x_7	x_8	x_9	x_{10}	x_{11}	x_{12}	x_{13}	x_{14}	x_{15}	x_{16}	x_{17}	x_{18}	x_{19}	x_{20}
x_1	(1)	0·50	0·00	0·00	0·50	0·50	0·00	0·50	0·00	0·00	0·00	0·00	0·00	0·00	0·00	0·00	0·00	0·00	0·00	0·00
x_2	0·00	(1)	0·00	0·32	0·00	0·00	0·00	0·00	0·00	0·00	0·00	0·00	0·00	0·00	0·00	0·00	0·00	0·00	0·00	0·00
x_3	0·00	0·33	(1)	0·55	0·33	0·33	0·55	0·33	0·00	0·00	0·00	0·00	0·00	0·44	0·00	0·33	0·00	0·00	0·00	0·00
x_4	0·00	0·40	0·33	(1)	0·33	0·00	0·40	0·00	0·00	0·00	0·00	0·00	0·00	0·00	0·00	0·00	0·00	0·00	0·00	0·00
x_5	0·00	0·00	0·00	0·31	(1)	0·31	0·00	0·50	0·00	0·00	0·00	0·00	0·00	0·00	0·00	0·00	0·00	0·00	0·00	0·00
x_6	0·00	0·50	0·35	0·50	0·62	(1)	0·62	0·62	0·35	0·00	0·00	0·00	0·00	0·00	0·35	0·00	0·35	0·00	0·00	0·00
x_7	0·00	0·00	0·33	0·40	0·33	0·33	(1)	0·40	0·00	0·00	0·00	0·00	0·00	0·00	0·00	0·33	0·00	0·00	0·00	0·00
x_8	0·00	0·00	0·00	0·00	0·53	0·33	0·40	(1)	0·00	0·00	0·00	0·00	0·00	0·00	0·00	0·00	0·00	0·00	0·00	0·00
x_9	0·00	0·00	0·00	0·00	0·00	0·00	0·00	0·00	(1)	0·00	0·00	0·00	0·00	0·00	0·00	0·36	0·00	0·00	0·00	0·00
x_{10}	0·00	0·00	0·00	0·00	0·00	0·00	0·00	0·00	0·00	(1)	0·36	0·00	0·00	0·00	0·45	0·45	0·36	0·54	0·45	0·00
x_{11}	0·00	0·00	0·00	0·00	0·00	0·00	0·00	0·00	0·00	0·00	(1)	0·00	0·00	0·00	0·00	0·00	0·00	0·00	0·00	0·00
x_{12}	0·00	0·00	0·00	0·00	0·00	0·00	0·00	0·00	0·00	0·00	0·00	(1)	0·00	0·00	0·00	0·33	0·00	0·00	0·00	0·00
x_{13}	0·00	0·00	0·00	0·00	0·00	0·00	0·00	0·00	0·00	0·00	0·00	0·31	(1)	0·00	0·00	0·00	0·00	0·31	0·00	0·00
x_{14}	0·00	0·33	0·00	0·00	0·00	0·00	0·00	0·33	0·00	0·00	0·00	0·00	0·00	(1)	0·00	0·33	0·00	0·42	0·00	0·00
x_{15}	0·00	0·00	0·00	0·00	0·00	0·00	0·00	0·00	0·00	0·00	0·00	0·00	0·00	0·00	(1)	0·32	0·00	0·00	0·00	0·00
x_{16}	0·00	0·00	0·00	0·00	0·00	0·00	0·00	0·00	0·00	0·00	0·00	0·00	0·00	0·00	0·00	(1)	0·35	0·00	0·00	0·00
x_{17}	0·00	0·00	0·00	0·00	0·00	0·00	0·00	0·00	0·00	0·00	0·00	0·00	0·00	0·00	0·00	0·37	(1)	0·00	0·00	0·30
x_{18}	0·00	0·00	0·00	0·00	0·00	0·00	0·00	0·00	0·00	0·32	0·00	0·00	0·00	0·00	0·00	0·32	0·00	(1)	0·32	0·00
x_{19}	0·00	0·00	0·00	0·00	0·00	0·00	0·00	0·00	0·00	0·33	0·00	0·00	0·00	0·00	0·00	0·40	0·00	0·40	(1)	0·00
x_{20}	0·00	0·30	0·00	0·00	0·00	0·00	0·00	0·00	0·00	0·30	0·00	0·00	0·00	0·00	0·00	0·40	0·70	0·50	0·60	(1)

$M'(s_1)$ for an answer to s_2 with the knowledge that the resulting chain must belong to an answer to s_2. In this case the identical chains result from searching either $M'(s_1)$ or $M'(s_2)$. If this were not the case, we could have reduced the critical probability and obtained the missing documents. Thus, given a large set of queries with a wide range of variation in their critical probabilities, we could adopt the general strategy of constructing the communication matrix M' on the basis of the least upper bound of the critical probabilities. By first searching for an answer in M', we obtain a partial answer for each query from the same communication matrix which could then be extended, if required, by lowering the critical probability. In general, if the critical probability for a given query is unknown one could start the search by assigning an arbitrary high value to the query and then gradually reduce it until the required output is obtained.

References

1. W. GOFFMAN, A searching procedure for information retrieval. *Inf. Stor. & Retr.*, 1964, **2,** 73–78.
2. W. GOFFMAN, On relevance as a measure. *Inf. Stor. & Retr.*, 1964, **2,** 201.
3. W. GOFFMAN, and V. A. NEWILL, Communication and epidemic processes. *Proc. Roy. Soc. A*, 1967, **298,** 316–334.
4. A. R. ANDERSON and N. D. BELNAP, The pure calculus of entailment. *J. Symbol. Logic*, **27,** 19–51.
5. A. D. BOOTH, Characterizing documents — A trial of an automatic method. *Computers and Automation,* 1965, pp. 32–33.

45 Variable Length Tree Structures Having Minimum Average Search Time

Yale N. Patt

*Communications of the Association
for Computing Machinery
Vol. 12, No. 2, February, 1969*

1. Introduction

There are many applications in data processing which require that a file be both searched and updated frequently. It has been suggested [1] that the most efficient organization for such a file is a doubly-chained tree structure.

A *tree structure* is a directed graph which contains no closed loops and has at most one branch entering each node. A *root* is a node which has no branches entering it. A *terminal node* is a node which has no branches leaving it. The *filial set* of a node is the set of all nodes reachable from the given node by branches of unit length. In Figure 1 nodes A and I are roots; nodes $C, D, F, G, H, J, M, N, P, Q, R, S, T$, and U are terminal nodes; nodes D, E, and F comprise the filial set of node B.

Double-chaining is one technique for representing a tree structure in a digital computer. Each node is represented by a computer word consisting of three fields. The first field contains the key which is queried during a search. The second field contains the address of another node in the same filial set (to be queried next if the previous query elicits a negative response). The third field

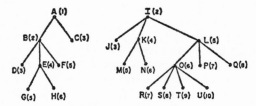

Fig. 1. A doubly chained tree structure.

contains the address of a node in the filial set of the given node (to be queried next if the previous query elicits a positive response). For example, if node E in Figure 1 is being queried, the second field contains the address of node F and the third field contains the address of node G. The term "doubly-chained" then refers to the facts that: (1) all nodes in a filial set are chained together (by means of the second field) and (2) each node is chained to its own filial set (by means of the third field). Items of information in the file are stored as terminal nodes in the doubly-chained tree structure.

The tree is searched as follows: Let k_i represent the ith component of the query item. First the roots are compared in turn (from left to right in the tree representation) with k_1 until a positive response (a match) occurs. Then the computer branches to the filial set of the node for which the match occurred, and proceeds in the same fashion, comparing the nodes in this set with k_2. Each time a positive response is obtained for k_i, the computer branches to the filial set of the node for which the positive response was obtained, and comparisons are made with k_{i+1}. The search continues in this way until a terminal node is reached.

The time required to reach a terminal node is clearly proportional to the number of nodes queried in the search from the left-most root to the terminal node. In this paper, this time is called the *search length* for that node. If $P_r(j)$ is the position within its filial set of the node on the rth level in the path to terminal node j, and $h(j)$ is the level of the tree on which node j appears, then the search length of node j is

$$t(j) = \sum_{r=1}^{h(j)} P_r(j).$$

In Figure 1, the number in parentheses next to each node represents the search length of that node. If there are N terminal nodes, the average search length $\bar{t}(N)$ of the doubly-chained tree structure can be expressed

$$\bar{t}(N) = \frac{1}{N} \sum_{j \in N} t(j) = \frac{1}{N} \sum_{j \in N} \sum_{r=1}^{h(j)} P_r(j).$$

Sussenguth [1] studied the problem of minimizing $\bar{t}(N)$ with the restriction that all terminal nodes lie on the same level of the tree. This paper develops procedures for constructing doubly-chained tree structures for which $\bar{t}(N)$ is minimized and Sussenguth's restriction is removed. In Section 2 a special case is introduced. Tree structures having the property that the filial set of every node in the tree is specified a priori are studied. Sections 3 and 4 treat the more general case, that is, where only the number of terminal nodes is specified, and therefore complete choice of the structure of the tree is available.

2. Tree Structures with Completely Specified Filial Sets

A special case of the variable length, doubly-chained tree structure is one which has the property that the filial set of every node in the tree is specified a priori. One example of a file system which has this structure is a collection of words. The query item would be a particular word and the information desired at the end of the search could be, among other things, its meaning, the number of times it is used in a given report, or its translation into a particular foreign language. The roots would be the 26 possible first letters. The filial set of the first letter "W" would be $(A, E, H, I, O,$ and $R)$, the set of possible second letters of words beginning with the letter "W".

Note that although the filial set of "W" is fixed, the order in which the members of the filial set are searched is not at all predetermined.

Given a file system organized as a doubly-chained tree structure where the filial set of each node is completely specified, it is desired to minimize the average search length. It is clear from the preceding discussion that the only freedom of choice available is the order in which the nodes of each filial set are searched.

THEOREM 1. *The average search length of this type of tree structure is minimized if the nodes of every filial set are ordered according to the number of terminal nodes reachable from each.*

PROOF. Let $A_0 = (a_1, a_2, \ldots a_n)$ be the filial set of node a_0, where a_i is the ith node, ordered from left to right, $1 \leq i \leq n$. Let $K(a_i)$ represent the number of terminal nodes reachable from a_i.

Consider any node a_0 and its filial set

$$A_0 = (a_1, a_2, \ldots, a_n).$$

Let a_{ij} represent a terminal node reachable from a_i; $1 \leq i \leq n, 1 \leq j \leq K(a_i)$. Define

$$T(A_0) = \sum_{i=1}^{n} \sum_{j=1}^{K(a_i)} [t(a_{ij}) - t(a_0)]$$

where $t(a_{ij})$ and $t(a_0)$ are the search lengths of a_{ij} and a_0 respectively.

The defining equation for $T(A_0)$ can be rewritten as

$$T(A_0) = \sum_{i=1}^{n} \sum_{j=1}^{K(a_i)} [t(a_{ij}) - [t(a_0) + i] + i].$$

From the description of the search procedure it is clear that $t(a_0) + i = t(a_i)$. Substituting this into the above equation and separating the two terms under the double summation, we obtain

$$T(A_0) = \sum_{i=1}^{n} \sum_{j=1}^{K(a_i)} [t(a_{ij}) - t(a_i)] + \sum_{i=1}^{n} \sum_{j=1}^{K(a_i)} i.$$

But $\sum_{j=1}^{K(a_i)} [t(a_{ij}) - t(a_i)]$ satisfies the defining equation for $T(A_i)$. Therefore,

$$T(A_0) = \sum_{i=1}^{n} T(A_i) + \sum_{i=1}^{n} iK(a_i).$$

Consider the doubly-chained tree structure. Let A_0 be the roots of the tree. Since $t(a_i) = i$, $t(a_0)$ must equal zero. Then $(1/K(a_0))T(A_0)$ equals the average search length of the tree structure. We can write $T(A_0)$ in terms of its filial set:

$$T(A_0) = T(A_1) + T(A_2) + \cdots + T(A_n) + \sum_{i=1}^{n} iK(a_i).$$

Similarly for any A we can write $T(A)$ in terms of its filial set. Therefore, we can systematically obtain the following set of equations:

$$T(A_0) = T(A_1) + T(A_2) + \cdots + T(A_n) + \sum_{i=1}^{n} iK(a_i).$$

$$T(A_1) = T(A_{11}) + T(A_{12}) + \cdots + T(A_{1m}) + \sum_{i=1}^{m} iK(a_{1i})$$

$$\vdots$$

$$T(A_n) = T(A_{n1}) + T(A_{n2}) + \cdots + T(A_{nq})$$
$$+ \sum_{i=1}^{q} iK(a_{ni})$$

$$\vdots$$

Since the tree is finite the above set of equations is finite. Combining the above equations, we obtain

$$T(A_0) = \sum_{i=1}^{n} iK(a_i) + \sum_{i=1}^{m} iK(a_{1i})$$
$$+ \cdots + \sum_{i=1}^{q} iK(a_{ni}) + \cdots$$

where each filial set A contributes one term to the right side of the composite equation. The average search length, therefore, is minimized if for every filial set A,

$$\sum_{i=1}^{n} iK(a_i)$$ is minimized.

But it can be shown [2] that the summation $\sum iK(a_i)$ is minimum if $K(a_i) > K(a_j)$ implies that $i < j$; that is, if the nodes are ordered according to the number of terminal nodes reachable from each.   Q.E.D.

3. General Case

In this section a procedure is developed for constructing variable length doubly-chained tree structures having minimum average search length if only the number of terminal nodes is specified. It is proved that a tree structure obtained by this procedure does in fact have minimum average search length.

This procedure will be defined inductively. For a tree consisting of N terminal nodes, it is shown how to add an $(N + 1)$st terminal node. Two cases must be considered: if $2^m \leq N < (3/2)2^m$ and if $(3/2)2^m \leq N < 2^{m+1}$.

Case I. $2^m \leq N < (3/2)2^m$. The tree consists of 2^{m-1} terminal nodes of search length m, 2^{m-1} terminal nodes of search length $m + 1$, and $N - 2^m$ terminal nodes of search length $m + 2$. The tree consisting of $N + 1$ nodes is obtained by adding a node to any filial set such that the search length of the added node is $m + 2$. Figure 2

Fig. 2.   Addition of an 11th node to a 10-node tree.

shows one of the ways in which an 11th node can be added to a 10-node tree. Since there are 2^{m-1} nodes of search length $m + 1$, it is always possible to add a node in this way.

Case II. $(3/2)2^m \leq N < 2^{m+1}$. The tree consists of $2^{m+1} - N$ terminal nodes of search length m, $N - 2^m$ terminal nodes of search length $m + 1$, and $N - 2^m$ terminal nodes of search length $m + 2$. The tree consisting of $N + 1$ nodes is obtained by adding two branches to a terminal node of search length m. This reduces by 1 the number of terminal nodes of search length m, and increases by 1 each the number of terminal nodes of search length $m + 1$ and $m + 2$. Figure 3 shows one of the ways in which a 14th node can be added to a 13-node tree.

Fig. 3.   Addition of a 14th node to a 13-node tree.

It should be pointed out that to construct a minimal tree of arbitrarily large N, it is not necessary to start the above procedure at $N = 1$. Clearly there exists a unique m such that either $2^m \leq N < (3/2)2^m$ or $(3/2)2^m \leq N < 2^{m+1}$. If the former, then the procedure may begin at $N = 2^m$. The tree is uniquely defined, having 2^{m-1} terminal nodes of search length m and 2^{m-1} terminal nodes of search length $m + 1$. If the latter, then the procedure may begin at $N = (3/2)2^m$. Again the tree is uniquely defined, this time having 2^{m-1} terminal nodes of search length m, 2^{m-1} terminal nodes of search length $m + 1$, and 2^{m-1} terminal nodes of search length $m + 2$.

The average search length of an optimal tree can be determined readily by summing the search length of each node and dividing by N. If $2^m \leq N \leq (3/2)2^m$,

$$\bar{l}(N) = \frac{1}{N} [2^{m-1}(m) + 2^{m-1}(m + 1) +$$
$$(N - 2^m)(m + 2)]$$
$$= m + 2 - \frac{3 \times 2^{m-1}}{N}.$$

Note that for $N = 2^m$, $\bar{l}(N) = m + \frac{1}{2}$; for $N = (3/2)2^m$, $\bar{l}(N) = m + 1$. If $(3/2)2^m \leq N \leq 2^{m+1}$,

$$\bar{t}(N) = \frac{1}{N}[(2^{m+1} - N)(m) + (N - 2^m)(m + 1)$$
$$+ (N - 2^m)(m + 2)]$$

$$= m + 3 - \frac{3 \times 2^m}{N}.$$

Note that for $N = (3/2)2^m$, $\bar{t}(N) = m + 1$; for $N = 2^{m+1}$, $\bar{t}(N) = m + 3/2$.

The results reported in [1] show that if all terminal nodes lie on the same level of the doubly-chained tree, the minimum average search time which can be obtained is $1.24 \log_2 N$, which is about 24 percent larger than our value.

Let us now prove that the above procedure does in fact yield tree structures having minimum average search length. First a few observations about the search length of the nodes in a doubly-chained tree structure are in order. (1) From each node, it is clear that we can search next at most one of two other nodes. There is then one node which has a search length of one, two nodes with a search length 2, 2^2 nodes with a search length 3, ..., 2^n nodes with a search length of $n + 1$. (2) If $t(k)$ is the search length of node k, there is one node reachable from node k which has a search length $t(k) + 1$, 2 nodes reachable from node k with search length $t(k) + 2$, ..., 2^r nodes reachable from node k with search length $t(k) + r + 1$. (3) By definition a node cannot be both a terminal node and an intermediate node. Therefore, if a node k is used as a terminal node, this eliminates from possible use 2^r of the $2^{t(k)+r}$ nodes of search length $t(k) + r + 1$.

THEOREM 2. *The minimum average search length for a tree consisting of N terminal nodes, $2^m \leqq N \leqq (3/2)2^m$, is $m + 2 - 3 \times 2^{m-1}/N$.*

PROOF. Recall the search lengths of the N nodes in the alleged minimum tree structure of Section 2. There are 2^{m-1} terminal nodes of search length m and 2^{m-1} terminal nodes of search length $m + 1$. If a tree structure is to have a smaller average search length, one of the following three conditions must exist: (a) more than 2^{m-1} terminal nodes of search length m, (b) in addition to the 2^{m-1} terminal nodes of search length m, more than 2^{m-1} terminal nodes of search length $m + 1$, or (c) at least one terminal node of search length less than m. Let us consider the three possibilities.

Consider (a). It has been shown that the total number of possible terminal nodes of search length m is 2^{m-1}. Therefore, condition (a) can never exist.

Consider (b). It has been shown that each node of search length m eliminates one node of search length $m + 1$ as a possible terminal node. Since there are 2^m possible terminal nodes of search length $m + 1$, and 2^{m-1} of them cannot be used because of the 2^{m-1} terminal nodes of search length m, it follows that at most there can be 2^{m-1} terminal nodes of search length $m + 1$. Therefore, condition (b) can never exist.

Consider (c). If there exists a terminal node of search

length $m - s$, where s is a positive integer, then 2^{s-1} nodes of search length m and 2^s nodes of search length $m + 1$ are eliminated from possible use as terminal nodes. Since the number of terminal nodes is fixed, we must account for these eliminated nodes by adding $2^{s-1} + 2^s$ nodes of at least search length $m + 2$. The decrease of s/N in average search length achieved by the terminal node of search length $m - s$ is more than offset by the increase of $(1/N)[2(2^{s-1}) + 2^s]$. Therefore, condition (c) leads to a larger average search length. Q.E.D.

THEOREM 3. *The minimum average search length for a tree consisting of N terminal nodes, $(3/2)2^m \leqq N \leqq 2^{m+1}$, is $m + 3 - 3 \times 2^m/N$.*

PROOF. The proof of this theorem will follow that of theorem 2. Recall the search lengths of the N nodes in the alleged minimum tree structure of Section 2. There are $2^{m+1} - N$ terminal nodes of search length m, $N - 2^m$ terminal nodes of search length $m + 1$, and $N - 2^m$ terminal nodes of search length $m + 2$. If a tree structure is to have a smaller average search length, one of the following three conditions must exist: (a) In addition to the $2^{m+1} - N$ terminal nodes of search length m, more than $N - 2^m$ terminal nodes of search length $m + 1$; (b) More than $2^{m+1} - N$ terminal nodes of search length m; or (c) At least one terminal node of search length less than m.

Let us consider the three possibilities.

Consider (a). Each of the $(2^{m+1} - N)$ terminal nodes of search length m eliminates from consideration one node of search length $m + 1$. There are in all 2^m nodes of search length $m + 1$. But $(2^{m+1} - N) + (N - 2^m) = 2^m$. Therefore, condition (a) can never exist.

Consider (b). Suppose there exist $2^{m+1} - N + s$ terminal nodes of search length m. This eliminates from consideration $2^{m+1} - N + s$ nodes of search length $m + 1$ and $2[2^{m+1} - N + s]$ nodes of search length $m + 2$. This leaves $N - 2^m - s$ allowable nodes of search length $m + 1$ and $2(N - 2^m - s)$ allowable nodes of search length $m + 2$. If all but w of the allowable nodes of search length $m + 1$ are used, only $N - 2^m - s + w$ nodes of search length $m + 2$ can still be used. If all but v of these are used, this still leaves $s + v$ nodes which must have search lengths of at least $m + 3$. Then at best, the average search length of such a tree is

$$\bar{t}(N) = \frac{1}{N}[(2^{m+1} - N + s)(m)$$
$$+ (N - 2^m - s - w)(m + 1)$$
$$+ (N - 2^m - s + w - v)(m + 2)$$
$$+ (s + v)(m + 3)]$$

$$= m + 3 - \frac{3 \times 2^m}{N} + \frac{w + v}{N}.$$

Therefore, condition (b) can never lead to an average search length which is less than the stated minimum.

Consider (c). If there exists a terminal node of search

length $m - s$, then that makes unavailable for use 2^{s-1} nodes of search length m, 2^s nodes of search length $m + 1$, 2^{s+1} nodes of search length $m + 2$.

If all but u of the remaining $2^{m-1} - 2^{s-1}$ nodes of search length m are used, this renders unavailable an additional $2^{m-1} - 2^{s-1} - u$ nodes of search length $m + 1$, and $2(2^{m-1} - 2^{s-1} - u)$ nodes of search length $m + 2$.

If all but v of the remaining $(2^{m-1} - 2^{s-1} + u)$ nodes of search length $m + 1$ are used, this renders unavailable an additional $2^{m-1} - 2^{s-1} + u - v$ nodes of search length $m + 2$.

If all but w of the remaining $(2^{m-1} - 2^{s-1} + u + v)$ nodes of search length $m + 2$ are used, the remaining terminal nodes must be at least nodes of search length $m + 3$. The average search length for this tree structure then is

$$\bar{t}(N) = \frac{1}{N}[(1)(m-s) + (2^{m-1} - 2^{s-1} - u)(m)$$
$$+ (2^{m-1} - 2^{s-1} + u - v)(m+1)$$
$$+ (2^{m-1} - 2^{s-1} + u + v - w)(m+2)$$
$$+ (N - 3 \times 2^{m-1} + 3 \times 2^{s-1} - u + w - 1)$$
$$\cdot (m+3)]$$
$$= m + 3 + \frac{(3 \times 2^m)}{N} + \frac{3(2^s - 1) - s + v + w}{N} .$$

Since s is a positive integer and v and w are non-negative integers, the third term to the right of the equal sign must be greater than zero. Therefore, condition (c) always leads to a larger average search length.   Q.E.D.

Perhaps it is worth examining again the equation for average search length under condition (c) of Theorem 2 above. If there are in fact no terminal nodes of search length less than m (i.e., $s = 0$) and if in addition all available nodes of search lengths $m + 1$ and $m + 2$ are used (i.e., v and $w = 0$), the third term to the right of the equal sign becomes zero and the resulting calculated average search time agrees with our minimum.

4. Storage Capacity Requirements

Since each node in the tree structure is stored as a word in the digital computer, it is worth determining the storage requirements for the minimal search length tree.

Let $f(N)$ be the number of nodes in a tree having N terminal nodes. Recall the method of adding nodes to the tree. It is clear that

$$f(N) = \begin{cases} f(2^m) + (N - 2^m), & 2^m < N \leq (3/2)2^m \\ f[(3/2)2^m] + (2)(N - (3/2)2^m), & \\ & (3/2)2^m < N \leq 2^{m+1}. \end{cases}$$

Combining the above, and noting that $f(2) = 2$, we obtain

$$f(2^m) = 3(2^{m-1}) - 1$$

Therefore, the storage capacity requirements for $2^m < N \leq (3/2)2^m$ is

$$f(N) = f(2^m) + (N - 2^m)$$
$$= 3(2^{m-1}) - 1 + N - 2^m$$
$$= N + 2^{m-1} - 1.$$

The storage capacity requirements for $(3/2)2^m < N \leq 2^{m+1}$ is

$$f(N) = f(2^m) + 2^{m-1} + 2(N - (3/2)2^m)$$
$$= 2(N - 2^{m-1}) - 1.$$

Sussenguth [1] has suggested that one measure of the efficiency of the doubly-chained tree structure is the product of average search length and storage capacity. For $N = 2^m$, our cost according to this criterion is

$$C(N) = [3(2^{m-1}) - 1][m + \tfrac{1}{2}].$$

For large N, this value approaches $(3/2)N \log_2 N$. Sussenguth's cost varies with his choice of filial set size. His minimum cost for a tree having N terminal nodes is

$$C(N) = 3.88(N - 1) \log_{5.3} N.$$

For large N, this value approaches $1.64N \log_2 N$. Therefore, the procedure developed in this paper yields an 8.5 percent improvement in the total cost function defined by Sussenguth.

5. Concluding Remark

By noting the number of nodes reachable from a given node and the search lengths of these reachable nodes, it has been relatively straightforward to construct minimal doubly-chained tree structures for any number of terminal nodes. It is suggested that this method should prove useful in constructing optimal trees under other conditions of optimality; for example, where the number of key elements allowed is bounded, or where the number of different values any key element can have is bounded.

References

1. SUSSENGUTH, E. H., JR. Use of tree structures for processing files. Comm. ACM 6, 5 (May 1963), pp. 272–279.
2. HARDY, G. H., LITTLEWOOD, J. E., AND POLYA, G. Inequalities. Cambridge U. Press, Cambridge, England, 1934, pp 261–262.

46 Search Strategy Evaluation in Manual and Automated Systems

MICHAEL KEEN
Aslib Proceedings
Vol. 20, No. 1, January, 1968

1. Introduction

Document retrieval systems are designed and implemented for the purpose of satisfying the information needs of a group of users, and the final stage of the technical processes required is the search of the stored file of documents or document surrogates. Studies of many aspects of retrieval systems have been made, but work has concentrated on the indexing or input stage, and little attention has been paid to the search or output stage.

The search stage is that part of the operation of a system that is carried out after a document store has been set up together with the necessary physical and semantic rules of access to it, and includes all actions taken from the receipt of a search request to the point where the search for, and examination of, documents is terminated. The search strategy itself is the intellectual part of this process, and requires a series of decisions concerning request and system terminology, decisions that normally vary from request to request and that are subjective in nature, depending for success on the skill of the searcher and effectiveness of the system. An evaluation of the decisions made in searching a particular set of search requests in a given system may, if the evaluation test is designed with care, be used to advance knowledge about searching generally if the test is of an experimental nature, or, if the test is of an operating system, its performance may be capable of improvement. Criteria for evaluation and some new user oriented techniques of performance measurement are discussed in section 2.

The introduction of mechanized methods for document storage and retrieval has not so far radically affected the intellectual aspects of searching. The promise of automation to come should encourage an examination and evaluation in detail of search strategies used in manual systems, and in section 4 a preliminary and brief treatment is given. Automation is discussed and defined in section 3, and, using the experience being gained from one experimental system which is investigating the design of automatic systems, some ideas on the way in which automatic systems will be searched are given in section 5.

2. Evaluation

The evaluation of the search stage may be carried out from the viewpoints of both users and system managers, and several criteria have been suggested.[1] A satisfactory retrieval performance seems to be of paramount importance, since a user whose need is not met by the search is unlikely to be impressed by a short response time or the ease of physically consulting an index. User criteria such as time and effort, and also the management criterion of cost are inseparably linked to particular systems in particular environments, but aspects of systems that involve retrieval performance may more easily be made the subject of evaluation tests, and results taken mainly from experimental simulation tests are presented in this paper.

Since evaluation tests of this type require, in relation to the search requests, a set of relevance decisions, results presented are from tests which use quite small document collections but have exhaustive relevance decisions: that is, every document in the collections used has been examined for relevance to every search request. Details of the different possible techniques for making relevance decisions are not given here, since descriptions of methods used in the three sources involved appear elsewhere.[1, 2, 3]

Retrieval performance effectiveness from a user viewpoint is best reflected by the twin measures of recall (amount of relevant material examined) and precision (amount of examined material relevant), and results of searches may be presented as a graph as seen in Figure 1. A curve, rather than a single point is obtained in these examples by successively searching on up to five search terms in the index, and calculating the recall and precision ratios that are obtained after each term has been searched, to give the five symbols on each curve on the graph. The curves presented are all based on thirty-five search requests, with the recall and precision ratios achieved by each request combined to give an average consisting of the arithmetic mean of the performance ratios of each request.

Several evaluation tests have purported to use what has become the accepted precision ratio,[4, 5] but on examination it is seen that although the searchers examined all documents posted under the search terms used, they then made a selection of the documents they considered probably relevant to the request and based the calculation of precision (and presumably recall) on this selection only. Although this searching technique is clearly an accepted and valuable one the result is highly dependent on the searcher's ability to recognize what is relevant, and introduces a variable that is unwanted for most aspects of an evaluation test. Precision measured this way will be considerably different from the system precision normally calculated, and it is suggested that it be referred to. as a 'Selected Precision Ratio'. The system recall and precision results given in Figure 1 have also been searched this way by a searcher presented only with a written statement of the requests but using the same search terms as were used for the system performance results, and the high selected precision results giving

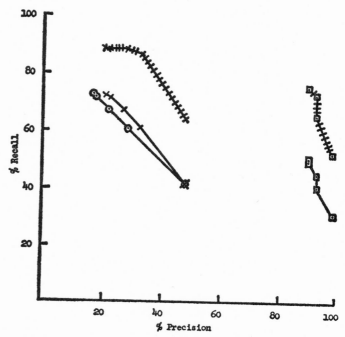

Graph of various kinds of recall and precision ratios from searches in a KWIC index to the full abstracts of a collection in documentation (used by SMART), based on averages over 35 requests.

Fig. 1.

ratios above 90 per cent can also be seen in Figure 1, together with a drop in recall.

Another type of precision ratio of lesser importance, but which may be useful for comparing certain types of indexes is an 'Index Entry Precision Ratio'. For this the total number of documents examined (the denominator of precision) is replaced by the total number of distinct index entries examined, so that in indexes where entries for a given document are made in more than one place these may be accounted for, since it has been the practice in calculating system precision never to count the same document more than once. Search results of this type are again presented in Figure 1 since it is a KWIC index that is being searched, and the necessarily unchanged recall but lower index entry precision may be seen.

A final matter concerns recall, which in experimental tests conducted so far has been calculated on the basis of the total number of relevant documents in the file. However, for users requiring high precision and only say two or three relevant documents, satisfaction is reached before 100 per cent recall is reached if there are many relevant items in the file. Recall can therefore be calculated relative to the user's needs based on the number of relevant documents the user would like to see, to be described as 'Relative Recall'. Assuming that all thirty-five requesters had a high precision need, the position of the relative recall and either system precision or selected precision curves may be seen in Figure 1.

Results presented in this paper use the system recall and precision measures, since data for the use of relative recall is not available. A ratio known as the fallout ratio (amount of non-relevant examined in relation to total non-relevant in file) has certain advantages over precision for experimental work, but its use would not significantly alter the comparisons made here, and precision is a superior measure from the vital user oriented viewpoint. A post-search analysis of individual search results is a necessary part of evaluation work, and a variation of methods in use is described as a 'Hindsight' performance result. This is an extension to a failure analysis in which errors or poor decisions are replaced by the optimum possible decisions, in order to calculate the performance that would be possible if one part of the system were perfect.

3. Manual, Mechanized and Automated Systems

In the context of the search stage, manual systems are those in which intellectual decisions relating to all aspects of a search have to be made at the time of search of a request, and the examination of the index entries is also done by hand. Some systems employ mechanized means to construct the physical index and add new documents (KWIC indexes and some post-co-ordinate indexes, for example), but these are still manually searched. Introduction of mechanization to searching is almost entirely restricted to the physical scanning of the index, so that complex search formulations requiring considerable skill are needed, and the lack of provision for altering the search strategy during the physical search that is commonly experienced with computers makes successful searches difficult to achieve. Promises of future automation are frequently made in vague terms, and the place for, and extent of, human intellect and skill that will still be required is rarely considered.

To automate is more than to mechanize. The concept of automation in engineering adds to the brute force of mechanization the sensitive treatment of control devices, which use sensing and measuring instruments to permit changes to be made during a mechanized operation so that the result may be optimized to meet the circumstances. Feedback may either be applied by the system itself, based on intellectual decisions about foreseen events that have been programmed into the system, or, when abnormal situations occur, the attention of a human operator may be invoked to make the necessary decisions and changes.

In documentation, mechanization is rightly being used in some circumstances to carry out clerical tasks of a repetitive nature, and application to the drudgery of searching pre-formulated requests in a large system such as Medlars is a good example. But any claim to automation requires more than this, and only when the following three elements are met is automation being achieved:

1. Some intellectual tasks are avoided altogether.
2. Some intellectual tasks that are in manual systems performed many times are performed once only and applied by the system as needed.
3. The intellectual tasks that are indispensable are directly provided for by the use of systems that allow direct user-system communication, give a rapid response time, and permit sophisticated user feedback.

An example of the first element would be the replacement of the human indexing task by some form of automatic indexing, which at its simplest uses the natural language of the documents (or document abstracts) as input to the system. Although automatic indexing as a process is devoid of intellect, except for the rules that are programmed into the system, it is not correct to regard the result as containing no intellect at all since it is really the intellect used by the authors who wrote the documents that is being used as a substitute for indexing effort. A second example would be the use of statistical association techniques to reveal relations between words, to be used in place of hand-made classifications and thesauri, but present techniques nearly always give inferior results to the hand-made versions.

The second and third elements suggested as essential to automation are particularly applicable to search strategies, so a list is given of six types of decision which are required in manual search strategies:

1. Translation of user's request into terminology of system.
2. Choice of related vocabulary terms by which to extend the search to cover all possible useful topics.
3. Statement of all search terms in their required logical combinations, necessary only for post-co-ordinate systems.
4. Choice of an order in which the search terms or search statements will be tried.
5. Decision as to point at which search is terminated.
6. Use of feedback to make adjustments to some of the preceding decisions as a result of examining some documents.

Decisions of types 1, 2 and 3 are very critical in mechanized search systems because the entire search formulation must usually be made in advance of the search, and the formulation made directly determines decision 5, usually called the cut-off point. If too few or too many documents are retrieved user satisfaction will suffer, because time and cost often preclude re-searching a request in a large file. Topic 6 is important because the person-to-person interaction between requester and searcher possible in many manual systems permits quite sophisticated feedback during the search and contributes to success. Some requesters prefer not to delegate searching to system operators at all, and wish to browse or examine a few items in order to formulate their need more clearly; and even when information centres serve remotely located users the human searcher is an important intermediary. If these are the topics that are candidates for automation then no known operating system is yet fully automated, but sufficient knowledge is being gained by experimental work to give some results and discussion in section 5.

4. An Analysis of Strategies for Manual Systems

The analysis is based on the six types of decision listed in the preceding section, and after a description of the matters involved in each decision some comments on evaluation with examples are given.

Request translation is the task of taking the search request and representing it by the terms in the vocabulary of the system. If an adequate lead-in vocabulary is provided this can be a clerical task, except that several important decisions may be made at this point. For example, it may be decided that some parts of a search request need never be incorporated in the actual search, or that some notion in the request may always be searched more generically than the requester's statement. These are best described as decisions about the 'exhaustivity' and 'specificity' of the complete search, as defined in reference 3. Also, it may be decided that one of the request notions is quite vital to the whole request, so that this important notion should be included in every individual programme of the complete search formulation, even when extensions to related notions are made, and individual programmes reduce exhaustivity and specificity.

Quality of request translation may be evaluated by post-search analysis, and in one particular test cases of undesirable reduction in exhaustivity and specificity of the complete search were the cause of 65 per cent of the failures due to searching.[3] Such failures limit the precision ratio that can be achieved, and also affect recall to a lesser extent.

Choice of search terms is rarely confined to those suggested by the request words directly translated, and other related vocabulary terms are often included in the search. The decisions as to which related ideas to follow up is determined by the requester's requirements, since a high recall need may require the use of many related terms, but a high precision need is served by use of only those terms which are most closely related, such as real synonyms. Formal provision of useful relations between vocabulary terms is frequently provided by means of classification schemes or thesauri. Such formal aids may

be less necessary than is realised when experienced searchers are used, as one result shows.[6, page 91]

Evaluation of the choice of terms in search programmes is often the subject of a post-search analysis.[3, 6] It is also possible to calculate 'hindsight' performance results to show exactly how much loss in performance is caused by a less than optimum choice of search terms, and an example of this is given in Table I. The manual KWIC index searches previously used in Figure 1 are made on a collection in the subject of documentation, and the KWIC index is made from the full document abstracts rather than just titles, so the data in Table I show how both better recall and precision are attainable in theory.

TABLE I

Evaluation of search term choices made in the KWIC index searches, giving "hindsight" performance results averaged over 35 requests.

	Number of Search Terms	Documents Retrieved	Relevant Documents Retrieved	Recall	Precision
1 Terms selected in search	3.3	20.7	3.1	71.8%	22.3%
2 Terms Matching only with non relevant deleted from 1	2.2	15.7	3.1	71.8%	30.1%
3 Terms matching relevant not retrieved added to 1	4.2	22.1	4.1	89.5%	26.1%
4 Terms in 2 deleted and in 3 added to 1	3.1	17.2	4.1	89.5%	39.1%

Pre-co-ordinate systems require only search term choice and order decisions, but for post-co-ordinate systems there is the additional need to formulate the logical relations in which the individual terms are to be searched, using such relations as AND, OR and NOT. Reduction in exhaustivity and specificity may easily be accomplished by demanding fewer of the search terms in logical product co-ordination, and the question arises as to whether this method of extending the search (to improve recall) gives better performance results than the addition of more related terms. In the context of the aerodynamics collection and the experimental procedures used in the second Cranfield Project, the conclusion is that reduction in search term co-ordination gives superior results to the addition of related terms from the synonym list.[8] Figure 2 shows that, on average, a search demanding three terms in co-ordination achieves 25 per cent recall, so that if the recall is too low either the addition of related synonyms or the reduction in co-ordination to two terms increases recall to around 50 per cent, but the latter method achieves a better precision ratio.

The search term order decision relates to the order in which the choices of search terms and combinations of

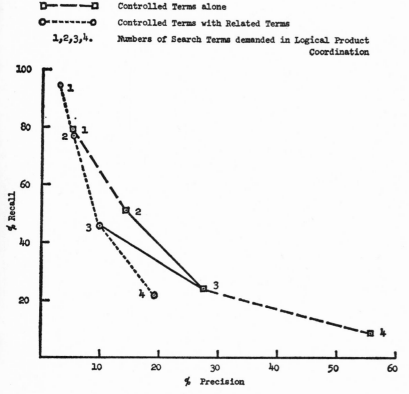

Data from Second Cranfield Project showing effect of changes in search term coordination and use of related terms, from Figures 4.820T and 4.824T[8], using an aerodynamics collection of 350 documents and averages over 77 requests.

Fig. 2.

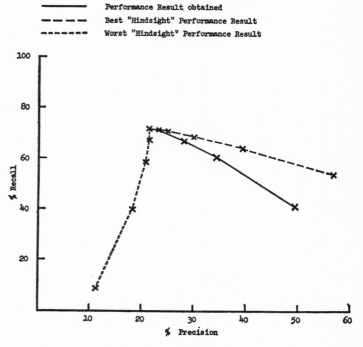

Evaluation of search term order decisions made in the KWIC index searches.

Fig. 3.

search logic will be tried, and naturally the principle used is the order of expected decreasing relevance. The matter of order does not arise in mechanized search systems, where the whole search formulation is usually processed at one time, but in manual systems a good choice of order will result in a quicker and more acceptable search result at higher precision. For example, the manual search of the KWIC index has been analysed for search term order, and Figure 3 gives two additional curves that represent the best and worst possible orders, together with the curve for the actual result.

The search cut-off is the point at which a search is terminated, and in manual systems this may be done as soon as the requester is satisfied with recall, or may be delayed either until the requester is unwilling to examine more documents or until no suitable further choice of search terms can be made. In a non-interactive mechanized search system it is usual to spend a lot of effort on search term choice and logic in an effort to make a correct cut-off, and supplementary information such as term posting frequencies is often used in an attempt to estimate the number of documents that will be retrieved using a given search formulation. Post-search evaluation

of cut-offs may be done as illustrated in Table II. Results from reference 3 are analyzed in terms of the total numbers of documents retrieved, assuming for the sake of this example that where the cut-off equalled the total number of relevant documents in the file ('Timely' Cut-off) this is the perfect result, although the system does not necessarily give 100 per cent recall and precision in such cases. 'Too Late' cut-offs, where more documents are retrieved than there are relevant, can never give perfect precision, and 'Too Early' cut-offs, where fewer documents are retrieved than there are relevant, can never give perfect recall, so the actual results of the 114 requests in a test of two systems are given in Table II.

Feedback in manual systems has undisputed value, but a test in which feedback is monitored for evaluation purposes is not known to have been made.

5. Towards Search Strategies for Automated Systems

The experimental automatic system used to illustrate this section is known as the SMART system, described in.[9, 10, 11] Documents are stored in the system initially in natural language, and a variety of word dictionaries are provided, some manually and some automatically constructed, with other optional types of weighting scheme and search matching functions. Present work is centred on tests that simulate the user-system interaction that will be possible when remote consoles and time sharing

TABLE II

Post-search evaluation of cut-off decisions showing the numbers of search requests that fall into the six possible categories of cut-off type and performance, derived from data in one particular operational test[3].

Performance Achieved	Cut-off Type			
	Too Early	Timely	Too Late	Totals
100% Recall and 100% Precision		7 (23)		7 (23)
100% Recall and <100% Precision			57 (39)	57 (39)
<100% Recall and 100% Precision	8 (17)			8 (17)
<100% Recall and <100% Precision	10 (9)	2 (6)	30 (20)	42 (35)
Totals	18 (26)	9 (29)	87 (59)	114 (114)

n = Searches in W.R.U. Mechanised Search System

(n) = Searches in Facet Index

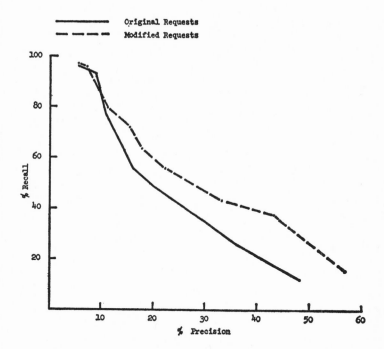

Comparison of original requests searched as received with modified requests having important words tripled in weight, using the SMART automatic system, the collection of abstracts in documentation, a thesaurus dictionary and based on averages over 35 requests.

Fig. 4.

computer equipment become available to permit full scale operational testing.[12,13] No single mode of interaction can yet be advocated, since the ideal amount of human control for automated systems is not yet fully known, and provision of different levels of 'strong' and 'weak' user-system interaction would permit requesters to decide for themselves. Some of the possible search strategies, choices and decisions involved are described, using the six manual steps as a framework.

No human request translation is necessary in SMART since search requests are put to the system in natural language as received. A growing operational system would require any new words encountered to be added to the stored vocabulary dictionaries but no special hand processing of request notions is essential. However, it has been found that long request statements give a better performance than short ones,[7] so that for users willing to interact strongly a few simple rules would improve performance. Even if requesters simply marked the important words in their request the system could automatically assign higher weight to these words, and would give performance improvements such as that seen in Figure 4, where modified requests are seen to perform better than requests searched without identification of the important words. With an automatic system there is no possibility of being less exhaustive or specific than the request statement in some part of the search, so that failures of the type noted earlier are avoided. Relevant to many of the search steps being discussed is the use by SMART of weighting schemes, based mainly on word frequency, which are found to improve retrieval performance compared to nearly all cases where no weighting is used. High frequency words which are of no value for retrieval purposes such as articles and prepositions

are removed automatically by means of a deletion list.

Search term choice is achieved in SMART by means of several pre-constructed and computer stored vocabulary dictionaries. These dictionaries each provide groupings of natural language words on the basis of some well known principle, such as suffix removal to reduce to stems, synonym and near synonym recognition by either a manually constructed thesaurus or a machine computed list of statistical associations based on frequency counts, use of phrases rather than single words, use of hierarchical relations and the use of syntactical rules. Search formulation is therefore not carried out manually at the time of search at all, since al that is required is the choice of one or more of the dictionaries to use. This choice may be determined by use of only those dictionaries that are proved to be the best on average in tests, and Figure 5 shows that in a documentation collection the full synonym dictionary (thesaurus) performs better than those which use types of suffix removal only. This results conflicts with the aerodynamics result in Figure 2 for reasons that are partially known. Another possible strategy would be to provide several dictionaries so that a user dissatisfied with the result on one could try the others, perhaps also using a technique that combines the search results from several dictionaries into one output list. A further possible strategy would be to devise some means of automatically making a pre-search dictionary

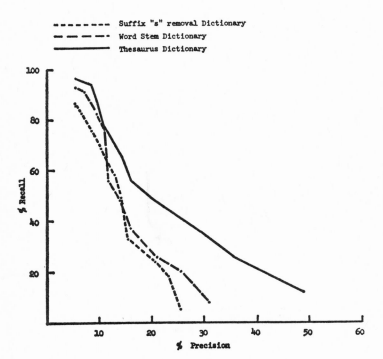

Comparison of merit of three different dictionaries on SMART, using the the collection of abstracts on documentation, and based on averages over 35 requests.

Fig. 5.

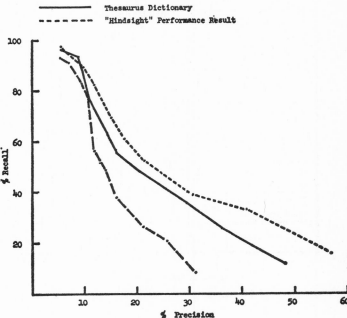

Comparison of two dictionaries with the performance of correct (by hindsight) dictionary choices for the individual requests, using SMART collection of abstracts in documentation, based on averages over 35 requests.

Fig. 6.

choice if it was found, for example, that long requests work better with a dictionary based on word stems, and short requests require a thesaurus. Although some correlations of this kind have been discovered,[7] they are not sufficient to make an accurate enough dictionary choice, but if some method were developed using some factors not so far considered then Figure 6 shows that correct advance choices of the word stem and thesaurus dictionaries would give a better result than either of the dictionaries used exclusively. This is because in this case ten of the requests work better with the word stem dictionary, and twenty-five are better with the thesaurus.

It is not claimed that the use of pre-constructed dictionary groupings gives as good a result as can be achieved by search term choices made at the time of search for an individual request, but evidence is growing to show that procedures used may well give a performance that is satisfactory for many users with resulting advantages in search time, cost and effort. However, any users willing to interact strongly with the system should still be able to use displays of relevant dictionary categories and be able to make individual choices of search terms with as much freedom as is enjoyed in manual systems.

No series of logical statements of search terms have to be manually formulated in SMART. A quite new approach is used that automatically allows progressive

relaxation of the logic to an apparently ridiculously low level. Even documents containing any one of the search terms are matched with the request by the system, even though this means that often 30 per cent to 50 per cent of the documents in the collection are so matched. But all matched documents are not necessarily retrieved because they are all arranged in an order of decreasing match, so that the searcher may examine only the highly matched documents at the top of the list, or he is free without further searching to look at more documents further down the ranked list. The matching algorithms that achieve this ranking employ factors in addition to simply the number of search terms that match in a document, and factors such as the length of the document and the values assigned to each term by the weighting scheme are used. Some loss in precision performance probably occurs because not all the spurious matches (i.e. noise) are successfully relegated to low rank positions on the output list, but the inclusion of the special factors mentioned makes up, in part, for this deficiency, and the avoidance of manually formulated logic is a gain.

Any decisions of the order in which the terms are to be searched is not required, since in common with mechanized systems the complete search is carried out in one operation. The decisions relating to order of use of optional dictionaries have been considered.

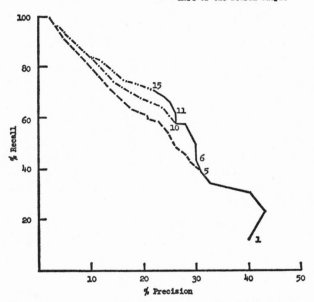

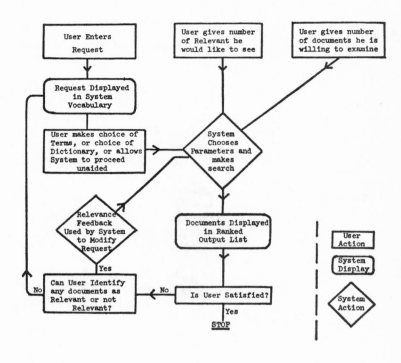

Results of searches using relevance feedback on SMART from[13], using the collection of abstracts in aerodynamics, based on averages over 42 requests.

FIG. 7.

Flowchart of User-system interaction in an automated system

FIG. 8.

The provision of a ranked search output list permits the cut-off decision to be quite independent of search term choice or logic, and allows the searcher to examine as few or as many documents as he chooses. Thus any searches in the manual or mechanized system that exhibited cases of 'early' or 'late' cut-off in Table II could be avoided in a ranking system if the searcher was able to recognise the need to look at a greater or smaller number of documents.

User controlled search strategies for automated systems will probably include a technique of great promise developed for SMART known as 'relevance feedback'. This is achieved by first making an initial search of the request in which the searcher examines just a few of the top ranked documents only, and then makes speedy relevance judgements by indicating which documents probably are, and which probably are not, relevant to his need. This relevance information is then returned to the system so that the original search request may be automatically modified to make it more similar to the documents judged useful, and less similar to documents judged valueless. The modified request is then searched, and this procedure may be iterated many times. Figure 7 uses some of the very first results of this, and it can be seen that this procedure steadily improves performance since an 8 per cent higher precision is gained in two iterations

for users who want 70 per cent recall, compared with the use of a full search without feedback.

A conceptual flowchart of user-system interaction possibilities is given in Figure 8. Users can have the option of aiding terminology choice actively or using stored dictionaries. They should enter the approximate number of relevant desired and indicate the number of non-relevant they will tolerate so that the system can choose the best matching algorithm and weighting scheme; then, on examination of some output users can re-cycle the process by supplying relevance feedback information or making search terminology changes; and certain simple additional parameters will allow a simultaneous bibliographic search, so that using the documents that the user has said are relevant, the system will also search for other documents by the same authors, and documents having strong citation similarity. Experiments with SMART are continuing to simulate all the separate parts of such a system, and future work will move towards a combined system of this type in an operational environment.

References

1. CLEVERDON, C., MILLS, J., and KEEN, M. Factors determining the performance of indexing systems,

vol. **1**: design. Aslib Cranfield Research Project, Cranfield, 1966.

2. Keen, M. Test environment. Report ISR-13, Section I, Department of Computer Science, Cornell University, Ithaca, N.Y., 1967.

3. Aitchison, J., and Cleverdon, C. A report on a test of the Index of Metallurgical Literature of Western Reserve University. Aslib Cranfield Research Project, Cranfield, October 1963.

4. Altmann, B. A multiple testing of the natural language storage and retrieval ABC method: preliminary analysis of test results. *American Documentation,* **18** (1), January 1967.

5. Jahoda, G., Oliva, J. J., and Dean, A. J. Recall with keyword from the title indexes: effect of question-relevant document title concept correspondence. Library School, Florida State University, December, 1966.

6. Cleverdon, C. Report on the testing and analysis of an investigation into the comparative efficiency of indexing systems. Aslib Cranfield Research Project, Cranfield, October 1962.

7. Keen, M. An analysis of the documentation requests. Report ISR-13, Section X, Department of Computer Science, Cornell University, Ithaca, N.Y., 1967.

8. Cleverdon, C., and Keen, M. Factors determining the performance of indexing systems, vol. 2: Test Results. Aslib Cranfield Research Project, Cranfield, 1966.

9. Salton, G., and Lesk, M. E. The SMART automatic document retrieval system — an illustration. *Commun. ACM,* **8,** June 1965.

10. Salton, G. The evaluation of automatic retrieval procedures — selected test results using the SMART system. *American Documentation,* **16,** July 1965.

11. Lesk, M. E., and Salton, G. Design criteria for automatic information systems. Report ISR-11, Section V, Department of Computer Science, Cornell University, Ithaca, N.Y., June 1966.

12. See papers in Report ISR-12, Department of Computer Science, Cornell University, Ithaca, N.Y., June 1967.

13. Keen, M. User controlled search strategies. Proceedings of the Fourth Annual National Colloquium on Information Retrieval, Philadelphia, held May 1967.

Chapter Nine
Dissemination

There is an interesting parallel between the functions of acquisition and dissemination in information systems: both have a selection process as a base, and both have received little attention. However, most often the works related to other functions, especially to question handling and search procedures, are so closely related to dissemination that dissemination is always implied.

It is suggested here that the study of dissemination may be approached from viewpoints other than from the immediate system procedures involved in dissemination, namely dissemination may be approached by a study of the distributions related to the dispersion, utilization, and scatter of recorded knowledge. Fairthorne labeled this approach "bibliometrics": a field which denotes "a quantitative treatment of the properties of recorded discourse and behavior appertaining to it."

The work by Leimkuhler (Article 47) is an example of such an approach. In the forties, Bradford formulated an intriguing law, based on his observations of the scatter of articles on a subject among journals. Leimkuhler derived a general mathematical distribution function implied by the Bradford law, using a formula which makes it possible to use standard statistical methods for summarizing data and testing hypotheses.

Brookes (Article 48) restated the Bradford distribution function n a smplfied form, explored the mechanisms underlying the Bradford law, elaborated on the properties, and most importantly, demonstrated the practical applicability of the law. Fairthorne (Article 49) in a review that has all the earmarks of a classic, summarized and equated some dozen empirical distribution laws and pointed out their usefulness for bibliometric description and prediction. The point is that these "dis-tribution approaches" may lead us to theoretical formalization and description of many structural and functional aspects of communication. However limited these formalizations may be, they are more than those previously available.

It seems logical to make a connection between the distribution laws and approaches and their direct theoretical and experimental application in other selections in the book. These were used in the following studies: Price (Article 7) in a study of network characteristics of science papers; by Goffman and Warren (9) in explicating a structure of two literatures; by Goffman and Morris (19) in deriving methods for acquisition; by Booth (21) in studying recurrences of words; by Zunde and Slamecka (26) in developing a method for optimum distribution of index terms; by Leimkuhler (40) in suggesting a file organization model; by Booth (42) in suggesting a library shelf organization; by Zunde and Dexter (53) in studying indexing consistency; and obviously by studies using statistical association measures for indexing, abstracting, classifying, and retrieving.

It is suggested here that the exploration of various empirical distribution laws related to communication and the exploitation and application of characteristics found in theory, experimentation, and practice may be a most important and significant activity in information science for the time to come. It is possible that only success in that type of investigation may be able to fully solidify information science as a distinct science in its own right. This is because, if we are successful, we may suggest better practical information systems to be built on the basis of some formally observed properties of communication.

47 The Bradford Distribution

FERDINAND F. LEIMKUHLER
Journal of Documentation
Vol. 23, No. 3, September, 1967

The distribution of references in a collection of pertinent source documents can be described and predicted by the relation

$$F(x) = \frac{ln\ (1 + \beta x)}{ln\ (1 + \beta)}$$

where the parameter β is related to the subject field and the completeness of the collection. The model is used to predict the reference yield of abstracting journals in a search for thermophysical property data. It is used also to explain differences among various literature studies of the past in terms of differences in subject and comprehensiveness of search. The model is derived from S. C. Bradford's 'law of scattering' and is called the Bradford Distribution.

1. Introduction

The current revolution in computer-aided, micro-analytic techniques of information retrieval was largely justified by earlier studies of the literature used in scientific research. These studies showed that researcher interest was widely scattered among formal titles and classifica-tions and much more extensive than the coverage provided by existing bibliographic services. The most important measure of scatter used in empirical studies is 'title dispersion' which is defined as the degree to which the useful literature of a given subject area is scattered through a number of different books and journals. Stevens[3] made a comparative analysis of title dispersion data from eight studies as shown in Table I. By inspection of this data, he concluded that the dispersion is smaller in pure science, greater in technology, and greatest in the humanities.

Of particular interest is the work of S. C. Bradford.[1] He studied the title dispersion of useful papers in two areas: applied geophysics and lubrication, by arranging the source titles in order of productivity and then dividing them into three approximately equal groups as shown in Table II. Bradford concluded that the ratios of the titles in successive zones followed a common pattern, and proposed the following 'law of scattering':

If scientific journals are arranged in order of decreasing productivity of articles on a given subject, they may be divided into a nucleus of periodicals more devoted to the subject, and several groups or

TABLE I

TITLE DISPERSION IN EIGHT STUDIES SUMMARIZED BY STEVENS[3]

Subject field	Number of references	No. of journals* with % of references			
		25%	50%	75%	100%
Chemistry	3,633	2	7	24	247
Chemistry	1,085	1	5	19	131
Biochemistry	17,198	3	12	56	851
Physics	1,279	1	3	17	134
Electrical engineering	17,991	3	9	39	—
Radio engineering	1,506	2	8	20	—
Chemical engineering	21,728	3	23	—	—
U.S. history	452	14	54	149	259

* Journals are counted in order of decreasing productivity.

TABLE II

TITLE DISPERSION OF USEFUL PAPERS REPORTED BY BRADFORD[1]

Grouping by yield	Applied geophysics		Lubrication	
	Journals	References	Journals	References
1	9	429	8	110
2	59	499	29	133
3	258	404	127	152

zones containing the same number of articles as the nucleus, where the numbers of periodicals in the nucleus and succeeding zones will be as 1 :n :n² . . . (p. 154).

If this law is applied to the data in Tables I and II, the ratios for zones 2 and 1 and 3 to 2 vary from about 2 to 7. Bradford suggests 5 as a representative number for his data, although the actual ratios are less.

In comparing cumulative periodicals with the cumulative references they yield, Bradford proposed a linear logarithmic approximation. This proposal led to some confusion which B. C. Vickery[4] undertook to clarify by developing a correct method of fitting a theoretical curve to the observed data. Vickery shows that Bradford's law is independent of the number of zones chosen although this affects the value of the ratio multiplier.

A more revealing analysis of title dispersion can be made by first deriving the mathematical formula for the distribution of references in an ordered collection of titles, which is implicit in Bradford's law. This formula, or model, makes it possible to use standard statistical methods for summarizing empirical data and making tests of hypotheses.

2. Restatement of Bradford's Law

Consider a collection of source documents arranged in decreasing order of productivity and divided into m groups of relative sizes $d_1, d_2, \ldots, d_m$, i.e., d_i is the proportion of documents in group i. If the groups are chosen so that each group yields the same number of useful references, then according to Bradford,

$$d_i = b_m d_{i-1} = b_m^{i-1} d_1 \quad i = 1, 2, \ldots, \quad m = 2, 3, \ldots \quad (1)$$
$$0 < d_i < 1 < b_m$$

where b_m is the Bradford multiplier for m divisions. Since the sum of the proportions d_i sum to one,

$$1 = \sum_{i=1}^{m} d_i = \frac{d_1(b_m^m - 1)}{(b_m - 1)}$$

$$d_1 = \frac{(b_m - 1)}{(b_m^m - 1)}$$

$$d_i = b_m^{i-1} d_1 = \frac{b_m^{i-1}(b_m - 1)}{(b_m^m - 1)} \quad (2)$$

The cumulative proportion of documents, $D_{j,m}$, in the first j of m groups and containing the fraction j/m of all references is defined by

$$D_{j,m} = \sum_{i=1}^{j} d_i = \frac{(b_m^j - 1)}{(b_m^m - 1)} \quad j = 1, 2, \ldots, m \quad (3)$$

Now, for all even values of m, $D_{\frac{1}{2}m,m}$ is the more productive portion of the collection containing half of the references, where

$$D_{\frac{1}{2}m,m} = \frac{(b_m^{\frac{1}{2}m} - 1)}{(b_m^{\frac{1}{2}m} - 1)} = \frac{(b_m^{\frac{1}{2}m} - 1)}{(b_m^{\frac{1}{2}m} - 1)(b_m^{\frac{1}{2}m} + 1)}$$

$$= \frac{1}{b_m^{\frac{1}{2}m} + 1)} \quad m = 2, 4, 6 \ldots$$

and since

$$D_{\frac{1}{2}m,m} = D_{1,2}$$

$$b_m^{\frac{1}{2}m} + 1 = b_2 + 1$$

$$b_m = b_2^{2/m} \qquad m = 2, 4, 6, \ldots \quad (4)$$

Next, let m be an odd number and apply equations (3) and (4) to

$$D_{2,2m} = \frac{(b_{2m}^2 - 1)}{(b_{2m}^{2m} - 1)} = \frac{(b_2^{2/m} - 1)}{[(b_2^{2/m})^m - 1]}$$

which contains the fraction $2/2m$ or $1/m$ of all the references. Therefore,

$$D_{2,2m} = D_{1,m} = \frac{(b_m - 1)}{[(b_m)^m - 1]}$$

and

$$b_m = b_2^{2/m} \qquad m = 1, 3, 5, \ldots \quad (5)$$

By defining the parameter b, equation (3) can now be written in a more general form:

$$b = b_2^2$$

$$b_m = b_2^{2/m} = b^{1/m} \qquad m = 1, 2, 3, \ldots$$

$$D_{j,m} = \frac{(b^{j/m} - 1)}{(b - 1)} \qquad j = 1, 2, \ldots, m. \quad (6)$$

Equation (6) states that the smallest proportion of source documents needed to yield the proportion j/m of all useful references is a simple power function of j/m and a parameter b. This is essentially the point argued by Vickery.

Equation (6) can be used to explain, in part, the differences observed in the data of Tables I and II. Bradford, in Table II, divided his collections into three groups, $m = 3$, and obtained a multiplier estimate of 5, $b_3 = 5$, $b = b_3^3 = 125$. The Stevens data of Table I employs a four-way division and should yield a different multiplier value. If Bradford's estimate is correct for the Stevens data, its multiplier value should be $b_4 = \frac{1}{4}b = (125)^{\frac{1}{4}} = 3.34$, which is rather close, especially for the chemistry studies. In general, with more divisions the multiplier is reduced at a decreasing rate.

3. The Bradford Distribution

In the previous section, an expression was developed for defining the smallest fraction of a finite collection of documents containing a given fraction of the number of useful references in the collection. By generalizing this relationship to all real values of the variables and then inverting the relationship, we can obtain an expression for the distribution of productivity in a collection of source documents. We will call this the Bradford distribution.

Let x denote the fraction of documents in a collection which are most productive, $0 \leqslant x \leqslant 1$; and $F(x)$ denote the proportion of total productivity contained in the fraction x, where

$$x_F = \frac{(b^F - 1)}{(b - 1)}, \qquad 0 \leqslant x \leqslant 1, b > 1$$

$$F(x) = \frac{ln\,(1 + bx - x)}{\log b}$$

$$\beta = b - 1$$

$$F(x) = \frac{ln\,(1 + \beta x)}{ln\,(1 + \beta)} \quad (7)$$

$F(x)$, in terms of the single parameter, β or b, is the Bradford cumulative distribution function, (c.d.f.); and the corresponding probability density function (p.d.f.), using natural logarithms is given by

$$f(x) = dF(x) = \frac{\beta}{(1 + \beta x)\,ln\,(1 + \beta)} \quad (8)$$

The mean value, E_x or μ_x, for the Bradford distribution is given by

$$\mu_x = \int_0^1 x f(x)\,dx = \frac{1}{ln\,(1 + \beta)} - \frac{1}{\beta} \quad (9)$$

It is possible to write the expression for $f(x)$ in terms of μ_x, since

$$1 + \beta\mu_x = \frac{\beta}{ln\,(1 + \beta)}$$

$$f(x) = \frac{(1 + \beta\mu_x)}{(1 + \beta x)} \quad (10)$$

The latter form of $f(x)$ more clearly shows the bilinear form of the Bradford p.d.f.

A particularly important analytic property of the Bradford distribution is its relation to population or collection size. Heretofore, we have considered the distribution of productivity or information content over an ordered collection of documents of given size. What about those documents which contain pertinent information but have not been included in the given collection? It is reasonable to expect that any particular collection is always a subset of some larger total population. If we make the assumption, however, that the collection at hand is the *most productive* portion of the total population, then the Bradford distribution can be easily adapted to describing the subset only.

Let the information content in a large collection be distributed according to equations (7) and (8). If we divide this collection at some point, $x = a$, and consider only the most productive fraction from 0 to a, then the *conditional* distribution of content over this smaller collection is defined by

$$g(y\,;a)dy = \frac{f(y)dy}{F(a)}, \qquad 0 \leqslant y \leqslant a \leqslant 1$$

$$= \frac{\beta dy}{(1 + \beta y)\, ln\,(1 + \beta a)} \qquad (11)$$

By introducing a change of variables from y to z, where z is a fraction of the subset a, i.e., $z = y/a$, then the conditional distribution of content in the most productive fraction, a, of a larger collection is given by

$$g(z;a)dz = \frac{\beta a dz}{(1 + \beta a z)\, ln\,(1 + \beta a)} \qquad (12)$$

$$\beta_a = \beta a$$

$$g(z;a)dz = \frac{\beta_a dz}{(1 + \beta_a z)\, ln\,(1 + \beta_a)}$$

$$G(z;a) = \frac{ln\,(1 + \beta_a z)}{ln\,(1 + \beta_a)}, 0 \leqslant z \leqslant 1$$

with mean value

$$\frac{1}{ln\,(1 + \beta_a)} - \frac{1}{\beta_a} \qquad (13)$$

Thus both the distribution of content in the larger collection and in the smaller collection follow the Bradford model with a parameter proportional to the size of the subset.

We are now in a position to offer a much fuller explanation for the differences observed by Stevens and Bradford in their title dispersion data. Earlier, we saw that the ratio factor for the zones depended on the proportion of references in each zone. Now we see that it also depends on the proportion of all possible source documents which are included in the collections studied. These two effects would have to be accounted for first, before one could attribute any remaining differences to qualitative aspects of the particular research field, as was done by Stevens in his conclusions.

4. An Application of the Bradford Distribution

In a more recent study of the scientific literature, Cezairliyan, Lykoudis, and Touloukian[2] reported the results of a comprehensive search of scientific journals for useful papers on thermophysical properties. A total of 9,810 papers were obtained from 1,282 journals for the period 1940–58. The journals were then ranked according to their productivity and data on the fifty most productive journals were reported. This subset of fifty accounts for only 3.9% of the 1,282 journals but 51.31% of 9,810 references.

The Bradford distribution can be readily fitted to the observed productivity of the first fifty journals by estimating the β parameter for the most productive fraction, a, of a larger population. An estimate, β_a, is easily derived by the 'method of moments' from the sample mean, $\overline{z}$, where

$$\overline{z} = \sum_{i=1}^{n} \frac{if_i}{n} = \frac{1}{ln\,(1 + \beta_a)} - \frac{1}{\beta_a} \qquad (14)$$

Here, f_i is the proportion of all references from the n documents ($n = 50$) found in the i-th most productive journal.

For the first fifty journals in the thermophysical properties study, z was calculated as 0.315, and β_a was computed from equation (14) as 10.5 by interpolation from a table of natural logarithms. Since for the data at hand $a = 50/1282 = 0.039$, the estimate of β for the entire collection of source documents is simply β_a/a or 269.24, from equation (12). The fitted curves are plotted in Fig. 1.

On the assumption that the Bradford distribution applies, equation (12) can be used to compute the theoretical scatter of 5,033 references among fifty journals when the β_a value is 10.5. This is done in Table III and compared with actual observations for five successive groups of ten journals each. The resulting chi-square measure for 'goodness of fit' indicates relatively close agreement between the observed and theoretical distributions. A more detailed analysis shows the greatest single difference is associated with the most productive journal which yielded considerably more references, 529, than predicted by the Bradford distribution, 393.

TABLE III

THERMOPHYSICAL PROPERTY REFERENCES OBSERVED IN THE FIFTY MOST PRODUCTIVE JOURNALS AS COMPARED WITH ESTIMATES USING THE BRADFORD DISTRIBUTION WITH $\beta_{.039} = 10.5$

Rank of journals	References		$\frac{(O-E)^2}{E}$
	Obs.	Est.	
1–10	2,377	2,328	1.03
11–20	1,072	1,066	0.04
21–30	662	698	2.86
31–40	525	521	0.03
41–50	397	420	1.26
	5,033	5,033	5.22
Chi-Square with 3 d.f. at 0.05 = 7.82.			

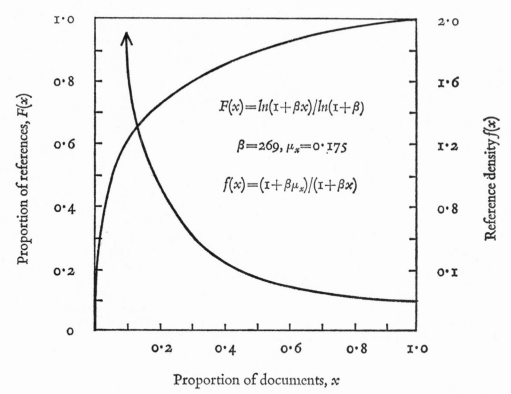

$$F(x) = \ln(1 + \beta x)/\ln(1 + \beta)$$

$$\beta = 269, \mu_x = 0.175$$

$$f(x) = (1 + \beta\mu_x)/(1 + \beta x)$$

Fɪɢ. 1. Bradford distribution fitted to results of search for thermophysical property data.

5. Scattering and the Bradford Distribution

Bradford's 'law of scattering' is the inverse function for the Bradford distribution, i.e. while the latter predicts the number of references for a given portion of the journals, the former speaks of the number of journals required to obtain a given portion of the references. From equation (12),

$$G(z) = \frac{\ln (1 + \beta_a z)}{\ln (1 + \beta_a)}$$

$$z(G) = \frac{(b_a^G - 1)}{(b_a - 1)} \quad b_a = 1 + \beta_a \qquad (15)$$

This is the continuous version of equation (6). For the fifty most productive thermophysical property sources, $\beta_a = 10.5$ and $b_a = 11.5$, and the first 25% of the references, $G = 0.25$, should be contained in the fraction, $z = 0.08$ of the fifty journals, i.e., 4 journals (50 × 0.08) are expected to contain about 1,258 references (5033 × 0.25). Similarly, we can anticipate an additional 1,258 references from the next 7.5 journals, the subsequent 13.5 journals, and the last 25 journals. A comparison of these estimates and the actual observations is made in Table IV.

As already noted, knowledge of the β_a value for the more productive subset, a, of a population implies the β value for the larger population which is inversely proportional to a. For the thermophysical property data, the first fifty journals are only 3.9% of the 1,282 sources identified. Hence, the β value for this larger collection is β_a/a or approximately 269. What about the β value for *all* sources on this subject? It would depend on how thoroughly the 1,282 known sources exhaust the literature. If they constituted a fraction γ of this larger literature, then it has a β value of $269/\gamma$.

It is of interest to note that a β of 269 implies the following b values:

$$b = 270$$

$$b_3 = 270^{\frac{1}{3}} = 6.5$$

$$b_4 = 270^{\frac{1}{4}} = 4.1$$

The above are quite comparable to the zone ratios observed in Tables I and II. Before attributing any differences to the subject fields, as Stevens did, it is necessary to account for differences in coverage of source documents. An observed multiplier, b_m, is an estimate of the 'true' parameter $(a\beta + 1)^{1/m}$. In comparing two studies, with observed multipliers b'_m and b''_m, the ratio $(b'_m/b''_m)^m$ is roughly equal to $(a'\beta' + 1)/(a''\beta'' + 1)$, or just $(a'\beta'/a''\beta'')$ when a and β are large. For example, Bradford suggested a b_3 value of 5 as compared with 6.5 above. Since the ratio $(6.5/5)^3$ is approximately 2.2, we can conclude

TABLE IV

ESTIMATED SCATTER OF THERMOPHYSICAL PROPERTY REFERENCES
ACCORDING TO BRADFORD'S LAW, AND THE OBSERVED SCATTER

Zone	Estimated scatter			Observed scatter		
	Journals	References	Accumulative References	Journals	References	Accumulative references
1	4.0	1,258	1,258	3	1,186	1,186
2	7.5	1,258	2,516	8	1,332	2,518
3	13.5	1,258	3,774	14	1,271	3,789
4	25.0	1,258	5,033	25	1,244	5,033

that either a), Bradford's literature has half as much title dispersion as the thermophysical property literature; or b), Bradford's coverage was only half as complete, or c), some combination of a) and b) exists. In the comparison at hand, one should recognize also the possibility that the literature of 1960 may show a different title dispersion that the literature of 1930, even in the same subject area. With the aid of the Bradford distribution as an analytic model, it is possible to evaluate such characteristics of subject literatures in a more rigorous fashion by using standard statistical methods. In addition, computers can be employed in the analysis of large amounts of empirical data.

6. Linear Approximation

While the Bradford distribution is a precise mathematical statement of Bradford's law, several empirical studies have made use of an approximation formula proposed by Bradford and obtainable from equation (7), as follows:

$$F(x) = ln(1 + \beta x) / ln(1 + \beta)$$

$$= \frac{ln\beta}{ln(1 + \beta)} + \frac{ln\,x}{ln(1 + \beta)} + \frac{ln(1 + 1/\beta\,x)}{ln(1 + \beta)}$$

$$\simeq 1 + (1/ln\,b)ln\,x = 1 + B\,ln\,x \qquad (16)$$

when β and βx are relatively large. Cole[5] has plotted the cumulative fraction of total references against the logarithm of the cumulative fraction of total titles to obtain an approximately linear relation. He showed that the slope, called the reference-scattering coefficient, is a concise and useful measure of literature usage.

In particular, for petroleum literature, Cole obtained the relationship

$$F(x) \simeq 1 + 0.43 \log x \qquad (17)$$

where $F(x)$ corresponds to his symbol R/RT, and x to T/TT. Cole used logarithms with base 10. When equation (17) is converted to natural logarithms and related to equation (16), there is the implication that for Cole's data

$$F(x) \simeq 1 + 0.185\,ln\,x$$
$$\beta = b - 1 \simeq 256$$

This result is remarkably close to the estimate of 269 found above for the thermophysical property literature. The cube root of 257, approximately 6.3, is the ratio factor b_3 for a collection when it is divided into three equally productive zones. This can be compared directly with Bradford's estimate of 5 and with the ratios in Table II.

Kendall[6] has suggested an alternative explanation of the linear approximation formula, in which he considers the number of titles with a reference count greater than some given value. For the Bradford distribution this relation would correspond to the inverse of equation 18, i.e.,

$$x(f) = (1/f\,ln\,b) - (1/\beta)$$
$$= Bf^{-1} - \beta^{-1}$$
$$\simeq B\,f^{-1}, \beta \text{ large,}$$

which is a form of Zipf's[7] law and an approximate Yule distribution, as explained by Kendall. Thus Bradford's law and Zipf's law are essentially just two different ways of looking at the same thing.

References

1. BRADFORD, S. C. *Documentation*. London, Crosby Lockwood, 1948.
2. CEZAIRLIYAN, A.O., LYKOUDIS, P. S. *and* TOULOUKIAN, Y. S. A new method for the search of scientific literature through abstracting journals, *Journal of Chemical Documentation*, vol. 2, no. 86, p. 86–92, 1962. See also Thermophysical Properties Research Center Report 11, Purdue University, 1960.
3. STEVENS, R. E. Characteristics of subject literatures, American College and Research Libraries Mono. Series, vol. 7, 1953.
4. VICKERY, B. C. Bradford's Law of Scattering, *Journal of Documentation*, vol. 4, no. 3, p. 198–203, 1948.
5. COLE, P. F., A new look at reference scattering, *J. Doc.* vol. 18, no. 2, June 1962, 58–64.
6. KENDALL, M. G., The bibliography of operations research, *Operational Research Quarterly*, vol. 11, 1960, 31–6.
7. ZIPF, G. K., *Human behaviour and the principle of least effort*, Addison-Wesley, 1949.

48 Bradford's Law and the Bibliography of Science

B. C. BROOKES
Nature
Vol. 224, December 6, 1969

In 1948 Bradford[1] formulated an empirical law of scientific periodical literature in the following terms:

"If scientific journals are arranged in order of decreasing productivity of articles on a given subject, they may be divided into a nucleus of periodicals more particularly devoted to the subject and several groups or zones containing the same numbers of articles as the nucleus, when the numbers of periodicals in the nucleus and succeeding zones will be as $1 : n : n^2 : \ldots$"

Bradford also drew a graph to illustrate the law (Fig. 1). Along the x axis he ranked the periodicals $1, 2, 3, \ldots n \ldots$ in decreasing order of productivity of papers relevant to the given subject on a logarithmic scale; along the y axis he marked cumulative totals of papers, $R(n)$. When $R(n)$ is plotted against $\log n$, the resulting graph begins with a rising curve AC which at some critical point C runs into a straight line CB. Bradford's formulation of this law is quite clear, but he did not express it in the form of a mathematical equation. As a result of this omission it has taken twenty years for the significance of this law to be recognized.

During these twenty years the law has been regarded only as a statistical curiosity. Its validity has been tested from time to time with varying degrees of apparent success, chiefly because the law has not always been interpreted as Bradford formulated it. There has also been a search for the underlying formula, particularly for series with terms such as $(n + a_n)^a$ which might yield sums of the form required, and more elaborate formulations have been published from time to time. It has only recently been noticed[2] that the law has to be expressed in two parts:

$$R(n) = a\,n^\beta \ (1 \leqslant n \leqslant c) \tag{1a}$$
$$= k \log n/s\,(c \leqslant n \leqslant N) \tag{1b}$$

These two equations refer separately to the rising curve and to the linearity, and satisfy Bradford's verbal formulation and his graph precisely.

The constants are not all independent. The value of a is the number of relevant papers published in the most productive periodical; it clearly increases with the time-span of the bibliography. It is found that $\beta < 1$ always: its value is constant only if the bibliography is restricted to some relatively short time-span, say two to five years. For bibliographies with longer time-spans such as those

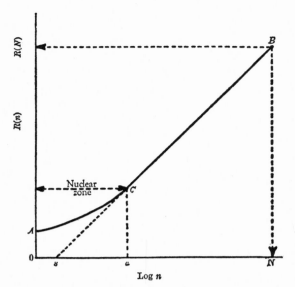

Fig. 1. Bradford's diagram of the "law of scatter" showing the initial curve *AC*, the "nuclear zone" and the linearity *CB*.

recently analysed by Goffman and Warren[3] on mast cells and schistosomiasis, which both ranged over a century, it is found that β takes a series of successively decreasing values — of $0 \cdot 85$, $0 \cdot 73$ and $0 \cdot 40$ for mast cells and of $0 \cdot 91$ and $0 \cdot 86$ for schistosomiasis.

The constant k is the slope of the linearity. All bibliographies are finite and the final increment, from the least productive periodical, cannot be less than 1. If N is the rank of this last periodical, then

$$r(N) = R(N) - R(N-1) = -k \log (1 - 1/N) \approx k/N = 1$$

when N is large enough, as in this case it is. And so $k = N$, that is the slope of the linearity indicates the total number of periodicals in the bibliography. So equation (1*b*) can now be rewritten

$$R(N) = N \log N/s, \ (c \leqslant n \leqslant N) \qquad (1c)$$

Thus the slope of the linearity enables an estimate to be made of the total number of papers to be expected in the complete bibliography. This estimate has been found to be surprisingly exact and the fact is of practical importance — as I shall show later.

It is found that $s \leqslant 1$ and that $s = 1$ for only narrow scientific subjects: as the subject widens, so does s. In fact, s could become an objective measure of subject breadth, for it can be shown that if r wholly independent bibliographies of equal size, each with $s = 1$, are added together to become a composite bibliography then the composite value of s is r.

The value of c, which is related to s, has not yet been found to be less than 3, and that when $s = 1$. So the value of c increases also as the breadth of the subject

increases. As the curve is found to run smoothly into the linearity, certain analytical conditions have to be satisfied: they are that

$$1/\beta = \log_e c/s = R(c)/N$$

For strict conformity with Bradford's law, certain conditions have to be imposed on the bibliography. They are (1) the subject of the bibliography must be well defined; (2) the bibliography must be complete, that is, all relevant papers and periodicals must be listed; (3) the bibliography must be of limited time-span so that all contributing periodicals have the same opportunity of contributing papers.

Nevertheless, it is found that the form of the graph is surprisingly stable even when these conditions are not fully satisfied. The more one analyses sets of bibliographic data in this way, the more one is surprised by the stability of the Bradford law and of the characteristic form of the bibliograph.

1. Mechanism Underlying the Law

The underlying mechanism of this empirical law is not fully understood. The generation of a Bradford distribution is a stochastic process which is at present being explored by computer simulation techniques. There seem to be two mechanisms which compete in part. The linearity arises if successive choices are made initially from a small number of possible items, but only if each item selected becomes a "success" which strengthens the probability of that same item being selected again. As the total number of selections grows, so does the number of items from which selection is made. Gradually a few of the items emerge as the most "popular" choices but, as they do, a restrictive factor comes into play, though it bears only on a limited number of the most popular selections. These most popular selections remain, however, the most popular selections but with their freedom of growth restricted in part. Without such restriction the resulting graphs are always wholly linear (on semi-log paper) and of the form

$$R(n) = k \log n/s$$

where $s \leqslant \frac{1}{2}$, that is, they are Zipf distributions. To obtain the required Bradford-Zipf combination it is therefore necessary to impose on the c most popular choices a restriction of the required intensity and proportional to some as yet unknown function of $(c - n)$ which, for $n < c$, will fade away to zero as n approaches and finally reaches c.

In bibliographical terms the Bradford law implies that when the first papers on a new subject are written they are submitted to a small selection of appropriate periodicals and are accepted. The periodicals initially selected attract more and more papers as the subject develops but, at the same time, other periodicals begin to publish their first papers on the subject. If the subject continues to grow, however, there eventually emerges a Bradford "nucleus" of periodicals which are the most productive of papers on the subject. As this occurs, the pressure of the thrusting new subject on the space of these periodicals increases until restrictions are imposed by limitations of space and by editorial decisions to maintain a balance of scientific interest among all the papers published. Assuming that the initial growth of literature in any new subject follows an exponential law in time, conformity with the Zipf law would require a uniform increase with time of the numbers of papers published on the new subject by each contributing periodical, but this kind of growth does not continue; one relief is the establishment of new specialist periodicals. The initial rising curve of the Bradford nucleus to the Zipf linearity is the indication of the kind of restrictive pressure which leads to a Bradford deficiency from the Zipf expectation of $(a + N \log s)$ papers from the nucleus of periodicals.

If this hypothesis, which combines the free play for all of the "success-breeding-success" mechanism together with restraints on the most popular few is valid, then it should apply to other phenomena subject to similar conditions. Conversely, if these conditions are not fully satisfied, then Bradford–Zipf distributions should not be obtained. So let me specify again the requirements for exact conformity with the law in more general terms.

The Bradford–Zipf distribution can be expected to arise when selection is made of items, characterized by some common element, which are all equally open to selection for an equal period and subject to the "success-breeds-success" mechanism, but when the selection of a most popular group is also, but to a weaker extent, subject to restriction. It is thus a general law of concentration over an unrestricted range of items on which is superimposed a weaker law of dispersion over a restricted range of the most frequently selected items.

The Bradford law remains empirical until it is better understood. But if it can be demonstrated to be widely applicable, reliable and useful in practical operations there is no need to wait until the underlying theory is completely established. In the chaotic field of scientific documentation there is plenty of work for it to do in helping to design information systems, in rationalizing library services and in making more economic and fruitful use of the 29,000 scientific periodicals estimated to be in current production.

2. Bibliographic Applications of Bradford's Law

The collection of a complete bibliography by human search is still an exhausting task even with the bibliographic aids now available. There is unfortunately no indication to the searcher when his task has been completed. All that he knows is that as he approaches the end of his task, his search becomes increasingly un-

rewarding until finally he stops. The advent of computerized bibliographic search systems such as MEDLARS has therefore brought a flood of new bibliographic data. The advantage of the computer is that it completes any search it makes on the literature within the system and maintains a constant standard of "relevance" throughout.

Fig. 2 shows the actual and estimated "complete"

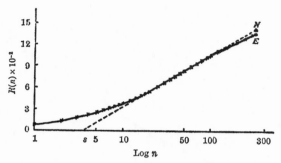

FIG. 2. Bibliograph of MEDLARS print-out on muscle fibres: $N = 313$, $E = 313$; $R(N) = 1{,}402$, $R(E) \equiv 1{,}346$; $s = 3 \cdot 6$, $c = 18$.

bibliograph of a MEDLARS print-out on muscle fibres. It is typical of good bibliography, though even this shows, towards the end, a slight fall-off from the Bradford idea in $R(N)$, though N is correctly estimated. The bibliograph of a good but "selected" (and therefore incomplete) bibliography on computer science is shown in Fig. 3 to indicate its larger deviation from the Bradford ideal.

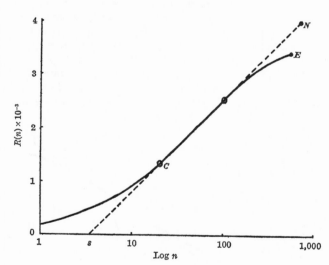

FIG. 3. Bibliograph of a good but "selective" (and therefore incomplete) bibliography on computer science: $N = 750$, $E = 522$; $R(N) = 4{,}050$, $R(E) = 3{,}436$; $s = 3 \cdot 4$, $= 18$.

All such bibliographs of periodical literature so far examined have either corroborated Bradford's law or else the discrepancies have been plausibly accounted for.

The number of abstract serials and other aids to

bibliographic searching now exceeds 1,000 and so they too should be candidates for Bradford analyses. Statistical data on the use of bibliographic aids are, however, scarce. The only published data known to me are those of Wood and Bower[4] of the National Lending Library which refer to abstracting serials used in the social sciences. The bibliograph (Fig. 4) conforms closely with the law — a

Bradford restriction. But this is not surprising because there is no restriction on the number of citations that may be made. Data on citations given by papers in *Physics of Fluids* to papers in other periodicals, also given by East and Weyman[5], seem to conform with the Bradford–Zipf law (Fig. 6), but the estimated end-point is 248 while the actual end-point is 372 citations. The

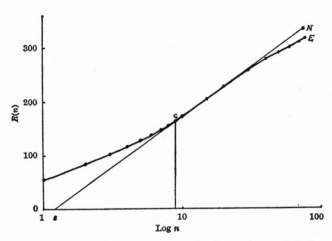

Fig. 4. Bibliograph of the use of abstracting serials in the social sciences (Wood and Bower): $N = 75$, $E = 77$; $s = 1\cdot21$, $c = 9$.

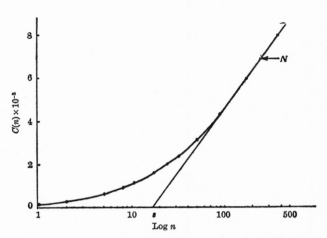

Fig. 6. Bibliograph of citations in *Physics of Fluids* (East and Weyman): the end-point does not conform; $N = 248$, $E = 372$.

fact of practical importance though it would be reassuring to have corroborating evidence from other sources.

Data on citations are readily available but their bibliographs conform only in part to the Bradford-Zipf distribution. Some citation data yield Zipf distributions only. For example, data on citations in *Plasma Physics* — published by East and Weyman[5] — yield two successive Zipf distributions with $s_1 = 1/2\cdot08$ and $s_2 = 1\cdot00$ respectively (Fig. 5). In this case, therefore, there is no

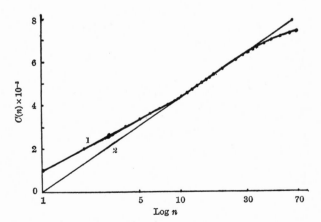

Fig. 5. Bibliograph of citation data in *Plasma Physics* (East and Weyman): two Zipf distributions, $s = 1/2\cdot08$, $s = 1\cdot00$.

explanation is that citations are not bibliographically homogeneous: citations to other papers by papers in *Physics of Fluids* are not all to other papers which would be classified as "physics of fluids": they may refer to mathematics, electronics, and so on. So citations do not conform with the Bradford–Zipf conformity of the distribution of the citing papers.

If the publishers of books of a bibliographically well defined subject, for example mathematics, are ranked 1, 2, 3, . . . n . . ., and $R(n)$ is the cumulative sum of books published within a given period, then $R(n)$ conforms with the Bradford law. The required conditions are fully met.

The issues of books by a library seem to satisfy the Bradford conditions but, until a computerized issue system can do the count automatically, such data cannot be checked without an inordinate amount of clerical work.

3. Practical Applications of the Law

In the management of special libraries the bibliograph offers a check on the completeness of any allegedly complete bibliography — a check that has hitherto been missing. For any specified subject it is necessary to analyse the productivity of only at most the $c + 5$ most productive periodicals in order to estimate the complete bibliography. Thus much time and effort can be saved in trying to estimate the magnitude of the bibliographical area and the cost to the library of attempting to cover the whole or any specified fraction of the complete bibliography. Thus, if f is the specified fraction, this fraction of the complete bibliography is covered most economically if the Bradford ranked series is cut at n where

$$N \log n/s = f N \log N/s, \quad (c \leqslant n \leqslant N)$$

that is where $n/s = (N/s)^f$.

Thus, for $N = 2,000$, $s = 5 \cdot 0$, $N/s = 400$. And so to cover half the output of papers from the 2,000 contributing periodicals it is necessary to take only the $s(N/s)^{\frac{1}{2}}$ or 100 most productive of the 2,000 periodicals. The same technique can be applied to bibliographic aids. It should be noted that the technique is valid only if $n \geqslant c$, but a special library would normally take at least the "nuclear" periodicals in its subject.

If the total expenditure on periodical provision is limited to the fraction f of the sum needed to cover the subject completely, the buying of periodicals may be supplemented by the buying of photocopies of the relatively few relevant papers published in the peripheral periodicals. For $n \geqslant c$, the number of papers expected in the periodical of rank n is N/n; the cost of such papers is therefore approximately An/N each, where A is the average cost of annual periodical subscriptions. As soon as $An/N > P$, the average cost of photocopies, it pays to switch from periodicals to photocopies. We then have

$$An + PN (\log N/s - \log n/s) = f A N$$

an equation for n which can best be solved graphically by reference to the bibliograph.

It is known that scientific periodicals "age", that is interest in and references to back issues decline broadly in conformity with the negative exponential law

$$R(t) = R(0) \, e^{-t/a}$$

where $R(t)$ is the sum of the references to issues of age t or more, and where a is a constant characteristic of each scientific subject. It is therefore possible to organize the periodicals in a special library so that ageing issues are discarded as they reach any prescribed minimum level of utility. If it is worth while just retaining (for a few seconds only) new issues of the nth of the N periodicals, the fraction of the total utility thus discarded is $n/(N \log N/s)$ so that equal increments of utility would be discarded from the remaining collection if the process were continued with the discarding, one by one, of the periodicals ranked $n - 1$, $n - 2$, ... down to $n - c$.

The law could also be applied to the planning of special library systems; the model considered here consists of a national, a regional and a local library. The local special library is assumed to be interested in a scientific subject whose complete periodical bibliography consists of N periodicals with the characteristic constant s. Of these N periodicals, the national library takes all, the regional library takes n_1 and the local library takes n_2, where $c \leqslant n_2 \leqslant n_1 \leqslant N$. Most of the periodicals taken by the regional and national libraries will be in the outer Bradford zones of the subject and therefore contain papers of interest to other special libraries as well.

If it is assumed that the use made of periodicals is proportional to the numbers of relevant papers they contain, then $R(n)$ is proportional to usage. Thus a scientist interested in the subject and seeking specific papers will find $f_2 = R(n_2)/R(N)$ of the papers he needs in his local library, $f_1 = \{R(n_1) - R(n_2)\}/R(N)$ of his residual needs in the regional library, and the remaining fraction, $\{R(N) - R(n_1)\}/R(N)$, in the national library. Substituting $R(n) = N \log n/s$ we obtain

$$n_2/s = (N/s)^{f_2} \text{ and } n_1/s = (N/s)^{f_1 + f_2}$$

It has been shown[6] that f_1 and f_2 can be related to the "viability ratios" of the libraries. If the local library does not attain, for any given potential user, a certain minimum viability, he will by-pass it in favour of the library next in the hierarchy. This factor depends on the user's estimates of the "costs" to him of using the various libraries and varies from one potential user to another. These viability ratios are likely to be lognormal variates. A library operating at the median value of the ratio is attracting half its potential users, and analysis shows that the viability ratio of a local library in relation to a regional library varies inversely as the "distance", measured in terms of user cost, of the local from the regional library. Thus the local libraries more remote from the regional library can operate viably with a smaller stock than those that are nearer.

For all such problems of viability and rationalization of library systems the Bradford–Zipf distribution is of great value. Subject bibliographies can be resolved or composed without difficulty, for example, but its principal advantage is that it has an optimization principle automatically built into it. The Bradford cut-off is the optimum cut-off for all purposes.

4. Theoretical Problems

The Bradford–Zipf distribution is empirically found to be very stable. But it would be reassuring to have a theoretical explanation of its stability. Ordered distributions such as Bradford and Zipf have so far attracted little theoretical attention.

Though the Bradford–Zipf distribution, which is first organized by arranging all the contributing "sources" in order of productivity, is not a conventional statistical distribution, such a distribution can be derived from it by inverting the distribution to express the numbers of periodicals, $p(r)$, expected to produce r papers. The probability density function of this distribution is

$$p(r) = \frac{1}{1 - \gamma^r} - \frac{1}{1 - \gamma^{r+1}}, r = 1, 2, 3 \ldots N/c$$

where $\gamma = e^{-1/N}$ so that $\gamma < 1$. This expression reduces to $p(r) = N/r(r+1)$ when r/N is small enough, but it has to be modified to allow for the Bradford restriction when $r > N/c$.

The behaviour of the Bradford–Zipf distribution for $n < c$ also requires theoretical analysis. It is not clear why the exponent β, if not constant throughout, seems to take a series of distinct discrete values.

In conclusion, when remaining doubts about the applicability of the Bradford–Zipf to bibliographic work, and the reliability of the estimates derived from its application, have been more thoroughly tested, it seems to offer the only means discernible at present of reducing the present quantitative untidiness of scientific documenta-tion, information systems and library services to a more orderly state of affairs capable of being rationally and economically planned and organized.

References

1. BRADFORD, S. C., *Documentation* (Crosby Lockwood, London, 1948).
2. BROOKES, B. C., *J. Doc.*, **25,** 58 (1969).
3. GOFFMAN, W., and WARREN, K. S., *Nature*, **221,** 1205 (1969).
4. WOOD, D. N., and BOWER, C. A., *J. Doc.*, **25,** 108 (1969).
5. EAST, H., and WEYMAN, A., *Aslib Proc.*, **21,** 160 (1969).
6. BROOKES, B. C., *J. Lib.* (in the press).

49 Empirical Hyperbolic Distributions (Bradford-Zipf-Mandelbrot) for Bibliometric Description and Prediction

ROBERT A. FAIRTHORNE
Journal of Documentation
Vol. 25, No. 4, December, 1969

Since 1960, and especially during the past three years, many papers have appeared about particular manifestations and applications of a certain class of empirical laws to a field that may be labelled conveniently 'Bibliometrics'. This term, resuscitated by Alan Pritchard (see page 348), denotes, in my paraphrase, quantitative treatment of the properties of recorded discourse and behaviour appertaining to it.

In this field the law cited is usually that named after Bradford[4,5] or Zipf [59,60] according to whether the interest is in vocabulary or periodical literature or physical access, in the rate of diminishing returns, or in the cumulative yield from a given input. The behaviour is hyperbolic; that is, the product of fixed powers of the variables is constant. This type of behaviour has been observed for a century or so in fields ranging from meteorology to economics, and has given rise to many particular explanations appropriate to the particular fields. Thus it has received many names according to its exponents, in both senses of the word.

A recent note by Buckland and Hindle[10] and subsequent correspondence[20,52,11,8] have outlined the application of the Zipf-Bradford (rectangular hyperbolic, or harmonic) relation to aspects of library management and aligned it with some cognate studies in other fields.

This paper, and its bibliography, supplement Buckland and Hindle. It aims to help present and future workers to build on what has been done already. To this end I, as have others, interpret earlier work as particular applications of a certain type of statistical distribution. Inevitably this attempt at unification is largely a précis of Benoit Mandelbrot's researches.[2,42,43,44,45,46,47]

This approach, besides thwarting wasted effort, has the advantage that it makes available statistical tools that are neutral towards rival explanations of this type of behaviour. Actually, as Fairthorne[17] pointed out in 1958, it is non-conformity, rather than conformity with it, that needs explanation. It is difficult to defeat in situations where the objects or actions of interest are built from a finite repertoire of elements — alphabet, vocabulary, authors, journals, arm and leg movements, species, phonemes — whose co-occurrences are at most weakly correlated and whose quantitative properties are additive. More generally, as pointed out by Mandelbrot[46,47] it is characteristic of any phenomena that are self-similar in that their parts differ from the whole only in scale.

So far as possible I outline mathematical matters plainly and briefly enough to lie within the tolerance of a generally educated reader, while giving enough clues and references for the mathematically skilled to follow up.

The bibliography necessarily and properly overlaps that of Buckland and Hindle, and should be taken as supplementing theirs. With few exceptions I have read all the works that I cite.

1. Empirical Laws

The same social phenomena may have many different causes, acting severally or in concert. Together with the uniqueness of social events, which makes them unrepeatable in detail, this strongly hampers the isolation of social causes. Day to day struggles with these uncomfortable facts make economists, engineers, administrators, librarians, and other servants of social demands, very wary of general principles claimed to be the mainspring of widely ranging phenomena. The wariness varies directly with the generality of the principle. Even in physics some general principles such as the conservation of energy, Hamilton's principle, and Lagrangean equations apply to so many possibilities as to be useless unless these are strictly isolated and controlled within a laboratory or conceptual model. Permissible general principles are those of logic and mathematics, provided that these can be shown to correspond with reality not only before deduction, calculation, and symbol manipulation, but also after.

On the other hand, though causal insensitivity hampers explanation, it correspondingly helps prediction. Provided that the unknown causes are not augmented or replaced by different ones, the general pattern of events is likely to be repeated. Given enough carefully collected and presented data, both the pattern and its persistence can be estimated usefully in numerical terms. This can be very useful, pending explanation. For instance, gravitation is far from being explained, though there is precise and comprehensive enough knowledge of gravitational behaviour to construct stationary satellites and, in due course, live in them. But for wider tracts of useful activity even rougher knowledge will suffice. Often all that is needed is reasonable assurance that water will flow into the sink and not on to the ceiling.

In social situations even this kind of assurance is weakened by the awkward fact that the situations are created by people. All measurements are necessarily retrospective, so social prophecies based upon them are liable to be either self-defeating or self-fulfilling just because they have been made. Indeed, 'quality control' consists of making and then defeating prophecies of future unfavourable behaviour. I use the word 'prediction' in this sense of detecting changes soon enough to correct or allow for them. I do not use it in the sense of successful prophecy, guaranteed in advance of its success.

The indispensable basis of this kind of prediction is careful and extensive observation. This demands not only skill, patience, and endurance, but also inspiration about what may prove relevant. One cannot observe everything. Then the data must be described rationally and conveniently. Description also needs inspiration, because the manner of description is, consciously or unconsciously, a partial explanation.

Not so long ago the presentation of empirical data had an ambiguous status. Many of its devotees compensated for lack of insight and experimental skills with exotically graduated graph paper, 'curve fitting' with typographically elegant expressions inappropriate to the subject matter, arbitrary parameters equinumerous with the data and, as even now, the darker activities euphemistically named 'adjustment of experimental data'. Widespread use and understanding of statistical disciplines has done much to remove the black magic from empirical description. One can discuss and compare similar patterns of behaviour in widely removed fields without assuming that they have the same proximate cause. For instance, the pattern of events known as the Poisson distribution is exhibited both by the number of soldiers kicked to death by horses within a given period, and also by the number of loans in certain libraries within a given period. This does not prove that library borrowers have the motives of homicidal horses. Nor of course, does it disprove it. The deductions are no more than that at any given time most books were not being borrowed and most soldiers were not being kicked to death, that neither the borrowers nor the horses were working in concert between themselves, and that individual drives to borrow or kill were manifested so often on the average. Because rare events, occurring independently of each other at constant average rates, are common in many otherwise unrelated activities, the Poisson distribution can be used in them for prediction, in the sense defined above.

From this antiseptic viewpoint I will discuss a certain class of empirical descriptive 'laws' that long have been known to fit certain phenomena of psychology, meteorology, linguistics, signalling errors, economics and, presumably, any other phenomena with the necessary formal properties. Amongst these are certain types of bibliographic behaviour, as was noted some time ago without much effect. In the past two or three years this has been rediscovered and applied with fair vigour. This resurgence of interest comes because of the growing demands on library and cognate services. Far more people are now working at, and paying for, library and documentary work than earlier. Moreover, workers are now quite as numerate at they are literate, sometimes more so. Only a few years ago writing on such topics in the mathematical frame of mind resembled shouting into a hollow tree. Also we can now delegate heavy computation to automatic machines. Above all, this increased interest has been made possible by those who have collected and presented essential data about who and how many and in what way and when and where and by what name. One can get by without being a skilled mathematician or without having access to a computer or even without an audience. One cannot get anywhere without reliable observers.

Empirical description can take many forms. Hitherto the one most often used in our field is a relation between quantity and yield. For instance Bradford's law relates the number of periodicals, arranged in order of decreasing productivity, to the number of technical articles of specified type contained between them. Direct descriptions of such relations may not be available, or may be too cumbersome, but sometimes we can still describe how they are generated in terms of difference, differential, or integral equations. These cannot always be resolved, even numerically, but detailed solutions are rarely needed. For instance, the equations governing vibrating systems and their more complicated descendants, control systems, are usually far too complex for other than particular numerical solutions at best. But usually what matters is not the exact shape of the vibrations, but under what conditions they will grow, die away, or remain stable. Powerful ways for studying the stability of interconnected systems have been developed during this century.

Goffman and Newill[25,26,27,29,30] have applied these to their 'epidemic' model of the spread of scientific ideas, as manifested by publication. Communication of ideas by recorded discourse is assumed to be governed by processes formally equivalent to communication of disease by microorganisms and of signals by machines. Information Retrieval then corresponds to processes that enhance the spread of infection by favouring the contacts of infectives with susceptibles. Goffman and Newill use control system theory to study the growth, decay, and stability of such processes. Analysis of Selye's bibliography of mast cell research, 1877–1963, and Warren and Newill's of schistosomiasis, 1852–1962 gives grounds for wider application of this model of the growth and dispersion of recorded discourse.

2. Some Examples of Hyperbolic Distributions

At present the Goffman-Newill theory seems to be the only bibliographical model that involves time explicitly, treating the situation as a process. The others give synoptic views of consolidated data. Almost all of them, whatever their starting-point, end with some kind of hyperbolic distribution in which the product of fixed powers of the variables is constant. In its simplest discrete manifestation an input increasing geometrically produces a yield increasing arithmetically. This is the empirical relation between stimulus and response observed by Weber (1846) and between periodicals scanned and articles retrieved observed by Bradford[4] (1934). Different manifestations of the hyperbolic distribution for both discrete and continuous variables are found in many fields and named variously after Fechner, Zipf, Pareto, Bradford, Willis, Berger-Mandelbrot, and others. But these are names associated with particular explanations for particular manifestations of this type of behaviour, not names for the type of behaviour itself.

These manifestations can be regarded as samples from one or other of a family of statistical distributions first studied in detail by Paul Lévy[39] (1925). This has properties as appropriate to some types of behaviour as the Normal Gaussian distribution has to others. I give some examples, in chronological order. All these bear on the bibliometric application.

Coin-Tossing

From the beginning of the eighteenth century there have been extensive studies of problems arising from the situation where two men, traditionally named Peter and Paul, toss pennies. Peter pays Paul one penny if the result is 'heads', Paul pays Peter one penny if the result is 'tails'. One problem is to find the probability that, on the $2n + 1$ throw, one of the players has for the first time to draw upon his capital. That is, that up to this time his losses have never exceeded his gains. For an unbiased penny this probability is

$$p(n) = C(2n, n)/2^{2n}(n + 1) \qquad (1)$$

where $C(2n, n)$ is the number of selections of n items from a collection of $2n$ distinct items.

For large enough n this expression tends to

$$p(n) = (2\sqrt{\pi})/n^{-3/2} \qquad (2)$$

From this point it can be shown that the probability of the interval between successive points of financial equilibrium exceeding $2n$ throws varies inversely with the square root of n. That is, it is a hyperbolic distribution.

This result and discussion of the problem will be found in many textbooks. Feller's[22] treatment is thorough whilst, as usual, Whitworth's[56] classic deals with it elegantly in terms of elementary algebra, under the heading of 'Questions of priority'.

Little more than changes of nomenclature suffice to apply this result to taxonomic trees, random walks, intermittent errors in signalling and, as the first exact equation suggests, to the relation between ideally chosen and assigned descriptors and the size of the collection labelled with them.

Weber-Fechner Psycho-Physical Laws

In 1846 Weber found experimentally that the just noticeable increase of a stimulus is proportional to the initial magnitude of the stimulus. This implies that the stimulus must increase in geometrical progression to produce an arithmetical increase in the response.

Fechner (1860) developed this as support for his philosophical views on the mind-body relation. He assumed that the Weber rule would hold for subdivisions finer than the just noticeable. In the limit this leads to

$$R = k \log (S/s) \tag{3}$$

where R is the number of just noticeable increments of response or sensation above its value at the threshold, S is the magnitude of the stimulus, s its threshold value.

Modestly, but confusingly, Fechner called this the Weber Law. Formally it is the same as the Bradford distribution.

Pareto Distribution

The economist Pareto[48] showed in 1897 that the distribution of wealth in various communities could be represented quite well by taking the proportion of $P(u)$ of incomes equal to or exceeding a given value u as inversely proportional to some power of u, the exponent being greater than zero and not exceeding unity: to wit

$$\begin{align} P(u) &= ku^{-\theta} \quad (1 \leqslant u, 0 < \theta \leqslant 1) \\ &= 1 \quad\quad\ (0 \leqslant u < 1) \end{align} \tag{4}$$

Because it is a more general distribution, and applies to a very wide range of phenomena outside economics, including the coin-tossing problem of equilibrium, it is often called the 'Paretian distribution'.

Willis Taxonomic Distribution

Willis[57] observed in 1922 that for some biological families the number of genera $g(s)$ having exactly s species could be given by the relation,

$$g(s) = k\, s^{-(1+\theta)} \ (0 < \theta \leqslant 1) \tag{5}$$

Alternatively, taking s as a continuous variable, the number of genera $G(s)$ having at least s species is

$$G(s) = K\, s^{-\theta} \tag{6}$$

k, and K being appropriate constants.

Usually θ is around one-half, as in the coin-tossing problem. This is no coincidence. Taxonomic trees can be regarded as generated by successive dichotomies, just as the trees proper to random walks and to coin tossing are generated by successive dichotomies, right-left, or gain-loss, and also as the trees appropriate to sentences are generated by segmentation into words by spaces.

Yule[58] (1924) modelled the Willis distribution by assuming species and genera to multiply at random, but at constant rates whose ratio is θ.

Benoit Mandelbrot[44] treated this distribution from many points of view in 1955.

Fundamentally he took it as a sample drawn from a population conforming to a more general distribution that has many properties desirable in taxonomy and linguistics, amongst others. It is stable, in the sense that parts of it are distributed in the same way. Thus splitting or lumping together of genera or species result in populations that follow the same law, and the relation between families and genera is the same as between genera and species. Later Mandelbrot was to develop this property of stability or self-similarity and apply it to many phenomena, including variations in market prices[46] and intermittent error bursts in communication systems. [2,47] *Mutatis mutandis*, his studies are strongly relevant to bibliometrics.

Lotka's Distribution of Literary Productivity

In a study of literary output by scientists Lotka[40] (1926) found that the number of authors who had published n papers in a given field was roughly $1/n^2$ the number of authors who had published one paper only.

This relation implies that, if it holds good for all authors in a given field, their number would be finite and less than $\pi^2/6$, approximately $1 \cdot 65$, of the number of single-article authors, even if the total were infinite. This is unlikely. The relation underestimates the number of more prolific authors but applies fairly well for the less prolific.

Bradford's Law of Literary Yield

In 1934 Bradford[4,5] published a study of the dispersion of articles on specific topics. He found that if periodicals were ranked into three groups, each yielding the same number of articles on a specified topic, the numbers of periodicals in each group increased geometrically. That is, for successive yields of n articles, one had to search successively a, ab, and ab^2 periodicals if the latter were ranked in order of decreasing yield. Proper choice of origin and scales can reduce this to the Weber-Fechner relation, (3) above.

The relation can be expressed in many ways, and in continuous as well as discrete variables. For instance, in continuous variables,

$$F(x) = k \log (1 + cx) \tag{7}$$

where $F(x)$ is the total yield from the more productive fraction x of the periodicals, and k, c, are constants.

$$f(x) = A/(1 + cx) \tag{8}$$

where $f(x)$ is the yield from a periodical of rank x. That is, x is the proportion of periodicals that have yields not less than $f(x)$. A, c are constants.

$$P(u) = (C/u) - D \tag{9}$$

where $P(u)$ is the proportion of periodicals having a yield not less than u. That is, the expression gives the rank in terms of yield per periodical.

All these are obviously equivalent. The constants are functions of the median, which is the smallest fraction of the periodicals that can produce half the total number of required articles.

Equivalent expressions can be formed for discrete variables, but these are more of a typographical strain than are the continuous expressions. The constants for discrete expressions involve the median and the number of periodicals each having the smallest yield, usually one article per periodical, or the number of periodicals each having the largest yield.

Kendall[35] published this form of the Bradford distribution, and related it to Zipf, in 1960. Though this was known before it does not seem to have achieved publication. The Bradford distribution is treated in more detail below. It is outlined here to relate it to the others in this section.

Zipf and Least Effort

Zipf[59,60] (1935, 1949) greatly developed and extended the scope of an empirical relation, noted by Estoup[14] in 1916, between the rank of a word in order of frequency, and the frequency of its appearance in a long enough text. A 'word' is here any string of letters bounded by spaces and used in the text. It therefore comprises more than dictionary entries. The rank of a word, r, is the number of words, including itself, that have at least the same frequency, $f(r)$, of occurrence.

Zipf's relation is

$$f(r) = k/r \quad (k \text{ approximately } 1/10) \quad (10)$$

He explained this, and other manifestations in many fields, as the consequence of a general principle of Least Effort. In particular applications the practical value of this principle depends on how well one can enumerate actions and their consequences, and estimate the effort they demand. Fortunately in some important and well defined situations relations of this kind can be predicted without calling in the aid of Least Effort, except in the very weak form of excluding any significant amount of obviously irrational behaviour. Therefore occurrence of the Zipf type of relation can be made use of without denying or endorsing the principle.

Benoit Mandelbrot[42,43] (1953, 1954), using considerations based on information theory, obtained a more general and better fitting form. He took the 'effort' or 'cost' of words as the delay resulting from their transmission as a sequence of letter patterns or phonemes, separated by spaces or pauses. Assuming that the aim of language is to allow transmission of the largest variety of signals (i.e. 'information' in the specialized sense of that word in information theory) as is possible with the least delay, he used the techniques for matching codes to message usage. Thus he obtained the relation between word frequency $f(r)$ and rank of word, r as;

$$f(r) = k (f + c)^{-\theta} \quad (11)$$

The constant c improves the fit for common words, which have low r, or if the relation (11) is interpreted as a Bradford distribution, for the most productive periodicals. The exponent improves fit for large r; that is, for the rarer words or less productive periodicals. For most natural languages θ is rather larger than unity, and for languages with constrained vocabularies and rules of use it is less than unity. A perfectly applied indexing language would tend to have a horizontal curve, with θ zero, because every term would be used on the average equally often.

Parker-Rhodes and Joyce[49] (1956) obtained the derivative of the Zipf relation. This gives the number of words $n(u)$ in a given vocabulary that occur in a long enough text with relative frequency u. Their relation is the same as Lotka's, above, for the number of authors of given productivity; to wit

$$n(u) = ku^{-2} \quad (12)$$

They derived this by assuming, amongst other things, that words in the vocabulary are stored and scanned in order of decreasing frequency, that that duration of scansion is proportional to the number of words scanned, and that the language concerned evolved so as to give maximum variety ('information') for a given duration of scansion. They then used maximum likelihood methods to obtain (12).

This entails maximizing the sum of products $u \log u$ taken over the entire vocabulary. Mandelbrot's derivation also requires maximization of this sum of products, although his hypotheses make no assumptions about the manner of storing and scanning. In fact the sum of products $u \log u$ over all elements of choice in a system must arise whenever one tries to estimate the optimal use of a repertory of entities to build up compounds, provided that the 'cost' of a compound is the sum of the costs of its components. This sum is often called the 'entropy', 'negentropy', or '(selective) information', but is not necessarily associated with quantities that deserve these names.

In a series of papers, 1953 through 1958, Fairthorne [15,16,17,18] expounded and applied this Least Cost principle to various problems in documentation and retrieval from coding, through the power required by different alphabets, to the marshalling of books on shelves.

In 1969 Booth,[3] independently developing the last application in detail, inverted the Parker-Rhodes and Joyce argument. Discussing the layout of books in libraries he derived the optimal least-frequent most-distant arrangements by assuming a Zipf distribution of book usage, instead of deriving the Zipf relation from an assumed storage and access procedure. His use of Zipf in this application was, of course, supported by empirical evidence on library borrowing. Booth then suggests the possibility of some equivalent mechanism for average minimum access time in human cognitive processes, very similar to that assumed by Parker-Rhodes and Joyce to derive the Zipf relation.

Buckland and Hindle[10,11] (1969) review applications of Zipf to many aspects of library management. This paper and its bibliography supplements theirs, but does not supplant it.

Distribution of Initial Digits

For a long time people dealing with numerical tabulations have noticed that if the numbers are expressed without zeros on the left, the initial digits occur with roughly logarithmic frequencies. About one third of the initial digits will be '1's, rather under one half will be either '1's or '2's, and so on. It is not difficult to show that for large enough tables, without arbitrary constraints, the relative frequency $P(d)$ of numbers commencing with any of the digits '1' through 'd' is

$$P(d) = log_{10}\,(d+1) \qquad (13)$$

Obviously this will not hold in a tabulation displaying, say, the populations of towns having at least 4,000 inhabitants. Apart from such drastically truncated samples the relation holds very widely. Goudsmit and Furry[31] (1944) and Furry and Hurwitz[23] (1945) showed analytically why it is so stable.

The general form is

$$P(d) = log\,(d+1)/log\,R \qquad (14)$$

where R is the radix of the representation.

If d is taken as a continuous variable, this expression gives the rate of yield of entries per initial digit as

$$p(d) = 1/(d+1)\,.\,ln\,R \qquad (15)$$

The symbol 'd' is not only the name of a numeral, it also represents its rank in order of decreasing frequency. So the distribution of initial digits follows the simple Bradford and Zipf laws.

Although the expression of numbers by 'significant digits' alone necessarily suppresses the absolute magnitude of the number so represented, many people who should know better have taken (14) as a law of distribution of magnitudes in the physical universe; e.g. Benford[1] (1938). It has been remarked[17] that, if so, the law must be awkward to enforce, because the distribution alters if the observer chooses to write down the magnitude in, say, duodecimal instead of decimal nota-

tion. If he wrote it down in binary notation, all entries would commence with a '1'.

It is not a property of the external world, but of how we talk about it. So also is the Zipf-Mandelbrot relation a property of how we are compelled to talk within a framework of words and spaces, not a property of what is talked about. The Bradford relation is probably a property of how editors talk about subjects in terms of authors within a framework of distinct periodicals. Certainly it is not a property of whatever authors write about.

These 'laws' are laws in the legal or arbitrary sense, not laws of nature. As with any social arrangement we can change them if we have the inclination to do so, and the power to persuade others to conform. This option is not available with the laws of nature. Things fall to earth, not away from it, whatever the consensus of opinion.

Some linguists, e.g. Herdan[33] who disapprove of Mandelbrot's explanation of the Zipf relation, also of Zipf's, treat this legal and social aspect of the relation as a weakness. In the context of linguistics, this is a curious objection. Language itself is the supreme social artifact.

How we talk about things, or go about things, is to some extent a matter of convention. There are many ways of doing them without violating natural laws. But there is a hard core of combinatorial necessity. For instance, however we choose our guests at a cocktail party or other such gathering of six people, at least three of them will either be previously known to each other or previously mutual strangers. However we choose our means, these means are necessarily finite and discrete and, like the guests (who are finite and mathematically discrete), must conform to combinatorial laws.

The following example shows how this can lead to a hyperbolic distribution directly without any behavioral hypothesis.

The Length of Rugged Coastlines.
Equi-Populated Regions

The British physicist L. F. Richardson (1881–1953) devoted the last twenty years of his life studying empirically possible proximate causes of war. Amongst these are population densities and boundaries in common. In a posthumous paper[50] (1961) intended as an appendix to his final work[51], itself published posthumously, he studied empirically, experimentally, and mathematically various ways of measuring these factors.

He divided the world into sixty regions of equal population. This is the two-dimensional version of Bradford's approach to literary productivity but, unlike the division of a sequence into quantiles, can be done in many ways. Richardson's regions were determined by the requirements of being simply connected (i.e. not ring-shaped or similarly awkward) and as broad as they were long, so far as this was consistent with common boundaries and leaving existing political boundaries intact.

He found the relation between population (1910 statistics) p, in millions, of a region in terms of its rank r to be

$$p = 1/(0 \cdot 127\, r + 0 \cdot 06)^3 \qquad (16)$$

excluding the population of China. Lack of statistics about this country much hampered his work.

Richardson compares this with the laws of Pareto and Zipf. The latter, he comments, 'offers theoretical, but rather vague, explanation.'

To arrive at this geographical subdivision he had to solve massive mathematical and empirical problems. Amongst these was the estimation of the length of a boundary. Usually one measures the length of an irregular outline by approximating to it with a polygon; for instance, by stepping along it with a pair of dividers of constant opening. Sometimes this leads, conceptually or practically, to a unique limit; whatever the opening of the dividers, the measurement tends to the same limit as the opening is decreased. Curves that considerately conform to such treatment are said to be rectifiable. Not all mathematical curves are rectifiable and, in the physical world, most curves are not. Fortunately one is rarely interested in lengths along the arc, usually we are concerned only with the distance between points that lie on the curve.

Richardson found empirically that the relation between the length $L(u)$ of an outline or curve, and the length u of the side of an approximating polygon or divider opening was (omitting terms that vanish with u)

$$L(u) = ku^{-\theta} \qquad (17)$$

For a rectifiable curve θ is zero, and the length is determinate. For most coast lines it is a small positive number. The west coast of Britain, which is very irregular, has an exponent of $0 \cdot 25$.

Mandelbrot[47] (1967) shows that if θ be written $D - 1$, then D corresponds to a dimension, even though it may be fractional. One of the characteristics of dimension is that a parallelepiped of dimension D can be dissected into N parallelepipeds similar to it in the ratio $N^{1/D}$. For example, you can dissect a rectangle into N similar rectangles whose sides have the ratio $N^{\frac{1}{2}}$ to the side of the original rectangle.

The relation between the ratio of similarity r, the dimension D, and N, the number of similar parts is

$$D = {}^{\circ} - log\, N / log\, r \qquad (18)$$

Mandelbrot suggests that fractional dimensionality is in some way a measure of self-similarity between the parts of a system and the whole. Such self-similarity leads to hyperbolic distributions.

3. Characteristics of Hyperbolic Distributions

These examples come from many disjunct activities and they could be extended indefinitely. For instance, the distribution of prime numbers is approximately a Bradford distribution, because all numbers are unique products of primes. Whatever their origin, all involve hyperbolic distributions which, in terms of a continuous random variable u, are of the form (4); to wit

$$\begin{aligned} P(u) &= ku^{-\theta} \quad (1 \le u < \infty, 0 < \theta \le 1) \quad \text{(4 bis)} \\ &= 1 \qquad (0 \le u < 1) \end{aligned}$$

where $P(u)$ is the probability of the variable exceeding the value u.

The many rather bewildering variations from this form come from expressing it in terms of rank or in terms of probability density, the latter increasing θ by unity. Also, if one expresses the relations in terms of discrete variables, as one should, they look very different. In this survey I have shifted from discrete to continuous variables without giving the rather massive formal justification required, but this does not mean that one can change from discrete to continuous variables without risk of losing essential features.

Essentially the hyperbolic distributions arise from properties of discrete collections, or the attempts to quantize non-discrete phenomena. So for investigation into causes or for theoretical mathematical development, one must treat the problem to begin with in its exact discrete form. For application of the results, the continuous form is much more convenient as a rule, and can be adjusted to fit a given range with reasonable accuracy.

Another source of variation is presentation of these relations in terms of logarithms, so that they become — if one is lucky enough to know the correct origin and scale — straight lines when plotted on logarithmically scaled paper. If the exponent is exactly unity, its cumulative expression, e.g. (3) and (7), plots as a straight line on semi-logarithmic paper. So it will if the exponent is not exactly unity, deviating noticeably from a straight line only for large enough values. Some of the various 'drops' reported (e.g. Groos[32] [1967]) in Bradford plots may be in part due to the exponent not being exactly unity.

The limits of validity of the relation are part of the relation. If they are varied in each application, they must be regarded as additional parameters. Some years ago I remarked, as have others, that a straight line law connecting any empirical data always can be achieved with the aid of suitably scaled logarithmic paper and a robust conscience. Even more can be achieved if you give yourself the option of declaring the limits of the straight line portion only after you have plotted the data.

In many applications the scale and limits are determined, not by the phenomena themselves, but by the sensitivity, resolution, and range of the methods of observation or presentation. For instance, in the Pareto distribution of incomes, no income can be less than the least monetary unit. The same situation arose when selling the Bottle Imp. Because the hyperbolic distribution is self-similar, so a segment of it can be scaled into the form (4), whatever the instruments of observation and mode of reporting. In this it is unique (Mandelbrot[46] [1965]). The uniform, equiprobable, distribution is the special case when the exponent is zero. This is obviously self-similar.

Self-similarity characterizes the Bradford distribution, because if we subdivide any of the original zones into sub zones, they will follow the same law, though with a different parameter. Again, any part of a taxonomic tree is on the average similar to any other part, differing mostly in scale and degree of refinement. Trees of the same kind can represent also the building of words from letters, number-words from numerals; phrases from words and spaces, levels of physical access or administrative access into libraries, encyclopaedias, or computer stores; all numbers from prime numbers; random walks and coin-tossing; and so on indefinitely. It is not surprising that the hyperbolic distribution is so widespread in documentary and managerial contexts, where activities are of similar pattern at different levels by design and by necessity.

These hyperbolic distributions belong to a class studied in detail by Paul Lévy[39] (1925). The most useful ones have the property that the sum of two such distributions is itself a similar distribution. That is, it is stable in the statistical sense. A better known stable distribution is the Normal or Gaussian distribution, which is also the only stable distribution to have finite moments. The hyperbolic distributions have infinite moments, as is easily confirmed. Finite samples from them have finite moments, of course, but these are rather sensitive to sample size.

Distributions with infinite moments are quite respectable. For instance the Cauchy distribution, which is generated by the intercept of a randomly rotating line with a fixed straight line, is a straightforward example. But such distributions do not yield gracefully to the usual powerful methods based on the moments of a distribution. Instead of these one must use the median, quantiles, and their higher equivalents. Indeed, these arise naturally in phenomena giving rise to hyperbolic distributions. Bradford, for instance, divided the range of periodicals into three zones of equal yields.

Looking at them from another point of view, it may be helpful to point out that the Normal Gaussian distribution can be generated from binomial distributions with integer exponents, the hyperbolic from binomial distributions with fractional exponents. For example, the exact expressions for financial equilibrium in coin tossing, (1) above, are the coefficients in the expansion of a binomial square root. This observation gives a clue for modelling discrete processes of indefinite length.

A modern and more accessible treatment of Lévy distributions is given by Gnedenko and Kolomogoroff[24] (1954). Mandelbrot[45] and Fama[21] (1963), applying them to the variation of speculative prices, discuss in some depth the stability of these distributions which, quite reasonably in this context, are what Mandelbrot calls 'Stable Paretian Laws'.

Up to this point I have surveyed the hyperbolic laws as a whole, with bibliometric applications as particular cases. This unifies the formal aspects of this type of behaviour, and collects tools for dealing with it, without invoking any hypothesis about the proximate causes of such behaviour.

I will now outline the rather isolated and amnesic progress of such studies within the field of bibliometrics.

4. The Bradford Distribution

Bradford[4] published in 1934 a paper showing the dispersion amongst scientific periodicals of articles about applied geophysics and about lubrication. The paper was reprinted with minor alterations in 1948.[5] In both of these largely unrelated topics he grouped the source periodicals into three zones, in order of decreasing yield, each zone yielding the same number of required articles. Bradford found the number of periodicals in each zone to increase geometrically. He used this finding to estimate the number of periodicals that contained articles on a specified subject and concluded that, unless many pertinent articles were to be lost, periodical literature must be abstracted by source and not by subject.

Though in public and, rather ambiguously, in private Bradford tended to belittle this finding, he did make use of it. His private conversations gave me the impression that he was sure it was important, but equally sure that he had not enough evidence or explanation to sustain it in public debate.

Vickery[53] (1948) cleaned up and extended the mathematical side of Bradford's communication. In particular he showed that if the relation held generally, it must hold for any subdivision into groups of equal yield, not just for high, medium, and low yielding quantiles.

A dozen years passed before the Bradford distribution again became the main topic of a published paper. In 1960 Kendall[35] showed that it applied to the bibliography of operational research, and studied it from a statistician's point of view. He showed that it was structurally similar to the Zipf relation, and took the important step of regarding any particular manifestation of the relation as a sample of a more general statistical distribution.

There seems little doubt of Kendall's priority of publishing an explicit statistical study of the Bradford distribution and its equivalence to Zipf's.

Though Kendall was the first to publish, the Bradford-

Zipf equivalence was fairly widespread amongst those few already working in the field. This is indicated by Fairthorne[18] (1958) referring to the importance of 'deviations from some Bradford-Zipf-Mandelbrot relation' in the distributions of words and of notions over items indexed by them. Up to 1960 the interest and paid time of the few mathematically inclined workers in documentation was directed mainly on index languages and their coding to deal with unpublished reports and to patent specifications. They were not unacquainted with conventional periodicals and, in those early days, some had even read books with hard covers, but immediate problems lay with unpublished items and their retrieval.

Cole[12] (1962), making use of the papers of Bradford, Vickery, and Kendall, plotted the proportion of total yield $F(x)$ against the logarithm, $ln(x)$, of the most productive fraction of sources that yielded it. He drew his data from the fields of engineering, biology, chemistry, and physics. For all these subjects he got a fairly straight line. For petroleum literature he proposed an empirical formula which can be written, as Leimkuhler was to point out, as

$$F(x) = 1 + 0 \cdot 185 \, ln \, x \tag{19}$$

Leimkuhler[37] (1967) examined existing studies and examples of Bradford's distribution and derived various formulations for discrete and for continuous variables. As Vickery had found, a fundamental parameter is the ratio b_m between the numbers of source periodicals in successive zones, when the periodicals are grouped into m zones of equal yield, with the periodicals in decreasing order of yield. The relation between these ratios for different numbers of zones, m, n, is:

$$b_n^n = b_m^m = b_2^2 \tag{20}$$

This perhaps may be seen more readily if one considers subdivision into mn zones. The ratio b_{mn} should be the same whether you first divide into m zones, and then subdivide each into n or divide into n zones, and then subdivide each into m. The relation (20) between the ratios is the only one that permits this.

Any particular collection is a sample of the actual population of productive periodicals. Assuming that this sample is the most productive part of the actual population, Leimkuhler studied the effect of collection size on Bradford parameters.

Brookes[7, 8] (1968, 1969) reviews the literature from Bradford onwards, and formulates the distribution directly from the consideration that, by hypothesis, the number of pertinent articles yielded by the nth ranking periodical exceeds that of the $(n + 1)$th by $bln \, [n/(n - 1)]$, where b is the ratio between successive equi-yielding zones of periodicals. For the most refined subdivision, this difference of yield must be one article.

The distribution is thus determined by b^2, which is found immediately from the median value, and by the number of periodicals with minimum yield, usually one article per periodical. The last determines the greatest number of zones into which a particular collection can be subdivided.

Brookes aims to derive simple techniques for using the Bradford distribution as a working tool of operational research or quality control.

Leith[38] (1969) showed that his personal collections of references in radiation- and cell-biology follow Bradford distributions. He draws the same conclusion for personal reading that Bradford did for special libraries. That is, by reading only the 'core' periodicals of your specialty you will miss about 40% of articles relevant to it. Qualitatively this review supports his view.

Goffman and Warren[28] (1969) used their studies of mast cell and of schistosomiasis literature, discussed above, also to investigate the Bradford distribution. They found that in both subjects the ratio of periodicals to authors was almost the same, around $0 \cdot 27$, and the average output of authors over five year periods did not vary over the entire eighty years covered by the bibliographies. Moreover, these ratios of articles per author — $1 \cdot 1$ for mast cell literature and $1 \cdot 5$ for schistosomiasis — were roughly equal to the minimal Bradford ratio b corresponding to the most refined subdivision of the periodicals.

These findings of Goffman and Warren hint, to me, that the Bradford distribution of periodical articles arises from an author-editor balance, rather than subject-periodical. Short of publishing one massive periodical containing all articles by all authors, there are two policies for partitioning their output. One is to publish periodicals such that each makes use of as many authors as possible, subject to the constraints of practical publishing; e.g. *Nature, Science, Reader's Digest*. The other policy, also subject to economic constraints, is to publish the output of a group of authors that is changed no more than the attrition of authors demands. To these editorial policies correspond author policies. Both policies are largely unconcerted, and the situation tends to be stable. Because authors commonly write within a special field these days, the situation can be interpreted in terms of subject matter, but it is plausible that the editor-author interaction is basic.

This is speculation, but there is no doubt that after many years the observations of Bradford have at last helped to forge a tool useful in management of and research into bibliographic matters. Many will be glad that his name is used to label this tool.

5. Vocabularies, Coding, Access

Zipf[59, 60] had proposed a general Least Effort principle that was not, perhaps, stated with a precision commensurate with its claimed far reaching consequences. Nevertheless, principles of this kind exist in many activities, but arise out of the nature of the activity rather than as manifestations of a universal principle. For instance, in communication engineering messages must be coded as patterns of physical events so as to allow the greatest variety of patterns to choose from. At the same time they must use as little power, cause as little delay, and be masked as little as possible by extraneous physical events, generically called 'noise'. In 1958 many previous applications of these considerations were united in Shannon's 'Information Theory', a name later changed by him to 'Communication Theory' in the interests of semantic hygiene.

An essential tool in this theory is a measure of average variety or complication of signals. This takes the form of a sum of products, $- p \, log \, p$, summed over the values of p for each element of the repertory of signal patterns. p is the relative frequency or 'probability' of use of the signal pattern, and is therefore less than unity. Hence the minus sign, which is put in to make the sum positive.

This measure is called, in this context, the '(selective) information', a name that ever since has been a lure for loose thinkers.

It has the same form as the measure of thermodynamic entropy and, in certain very circumscribed situations, can be identified with it. For our purposes it is a measure of the average variety, complication, or freedom of choice, allowed by a given repertory of patterns used with stated frequencies. Why and for what they are used does not come into it. This quantity is used a great deal in combinatorial and statistical theory, and crops up over and over again in applications, from Bradford's distribution to problems in sorting and marshalling and access to files. Information Theory has therefore supplied a useful label for an existing concept. Whether it has supplied more than a label is subject to dispute that does not concern us here.

Shannon's theory appeared in the summer and fall of 1948, too late for discussion at the Royal Society Conference on Scientific Information held earlier that year. Nevertheless some people, including some at Aslib, recognized at once its relevance to various documentary problems, especially to coding for what Mooers was to call (the next year) Information Retrieval.

The most thorough study of information theoretic methods appropriate to this problem was not directly aimed at it, but at the more general problem of the coding of messages into words and spaces in natural languages. From 1952 onwards Benoit Mandelbrot attacked this problem. In a symposium paper[42] (1953) he gives, in English and mathematics, a comprehensive and very condensed account of motivation and development. Many ideas of this paper deserve and still await exploitation. Brillouin[6] summarizes the method used in his chapter on coding problems. A less technical summary, in French, was published by Mandelbrot[43] in 1954. Here he is concerned mainly with the application of his techniques to natural languages, but the relevance to indexing and similar languages is obvious. More obvious, in fact, than their relevance to linguistics in general. About this there is some debate because Mandelbrot bases his stand on the views of de Saussure, which are not accepted unanimously by linguists. Fortunately this debate does not affect the validity or invalidity of his methods when applied to other activities.

Concurrently, from 1952 through 1958, a sequence of papers by Fairthorne[15,16,17,18] reprinted later in 1961[19], attempted to explain, mainly in non-technical English the scope and limitations of information theoretic methods in documentation, and stated results concerning vocabularies and their coding, sorting and marshalling, access to files, keyboards, and bookshelves, amongst others.

The basis of such methods are the combinatorial properties of compounds built up by repetition and combination from a fixed repertory of elements. This may be an alphabet of letters and spaces; a set of numerals; a vocabulary of words or phrases with spaces or pauses; fixed teams of authors; periodical title lists; pigeon holes; prime numbers; phonemes; standardized actions in clerical or manipulative activities; and so on. With each of the elements is associated a positive number, its 'cost', which may be its financial cost, its mass, length, distance, or duration, or any other measure of significant inconvenience, from duration of a word to rotation of a typewheel or length of a bookshelf. If the total cost of any compound be the sum of the costs of its elements, and the restrictions on permissible combinations not too arbitrary, the costs of all compounds can be represented analytically or computed. Otherwise, and always as a check, one relies on observation. Zipf, for instance, investigated the cost as being the length of words (number of letters) occurring naturally in various environments. Mandelbrot took his cost as being the duration of words and spaces.

Consider an alphabet of n letters, each of the same length or duration, or requiring the same effort or money to print or write. Suppose, at first, that all combinations of letters are permitted, and that we will ignore the space as a character. That is, words will be considered as isolated occurrences. (In fact spaces and hierarchies of spaces are a most important type of character in segmented sequences.) Clearly there are n one-letter words, n^2 two-letter words . . . n^r r-letter words, and so on. Their costs are $1, 2, . . ., r, . . .$ units respectively. Thus we have the familiar geometrico-arithmetical correspondence between the number of words with their costs that we have observed so often between sources and their yields.

If here we assume that the less costly words are used more often, in isolation, than more costly words and that equally costly words are used equally often, we arrive immediately at the Zipf-Bradford hyperbolic distribution with exponent unity, sometimes called the 'harmonic' distribution.

In most applications by no means all compounds are permitted, there must be special elements with the properties of spaces, and the elements will have different costs. Nevertheless, if one considers the costs averaged in various plausible ways, the result is qualitatively the same. Instead of n being a whole number, and instead of the hyperbolic exponent being unity, both may be fractional.

To determine the values is a technical task. Traditionally information theorists take an unnecessary detour through difference equations. Actually the direct attack is by way of generating functions and their resolution into partial fractions. Fairthorne[18] (1958) developed a very general type, in the form of analytical continued fractions, for a unified treatment of storage and retrieval languages.

The important property of 'vocabularies' generated in this way is that they are insensitive to quite extreme restrictions on rules of use, as noted above when discussing the Initial Digit distribution. Therefore any assumption about fairly rational use of the repertory leads to hyperbolic distributions, whatever the precise linking of cost to frequency of use. Deviations will occur only when the calculated costs cease to be the dominant costs, or inconveniences, because of changed circumstances. These are most likely to affect first the very cheap or very expensive compounds.

Mandelbrot's major contribution has been to bring together and organize a set of phenomena and of appropriate mathematical tools hitherto scattered around. For instance, in his discussion[44] of the language of taxonomy he uses the techniques and concepts of statistical thermodynamics, but based on the Lévy hyperbolic, instead of the Normal Gaussian, distribution. Since then he has continued to develop, sharpen, and apply these tools.

Nevertheless in 1969 one read in a documentation journal the suggestion that the Bradford-Zipf relation was perhaps the symptom of some law or 'information flow', the last two words undefined. The unwillingness, or inability, of information retrieval specialists to retrieve information about information retrieval is notorious. It is also extremely expensive.

As mentioned above, Parker-Rhodes and Joyce arrived at the Zipf distribution of exponent unity by using information theoretic or statistical methods (the distinction is here mainly terminological) but rather differently from Mandelbrot, who obtained a more general result. Many others at that time I know to have been working on similar problems on similar lines. Few if any achieved publication other than as internal memoranda.

Up to the late 1950s the most pressing problems concerned indexing vocabularies and their coding into forms congenial to various devices. All these ingredients were regarded as commercial commodities. Thus, though the growth of indexing vocabularies with the size of the collection came in for much attention, especially after 1950, studies of it were mainly *ad hoc* and confined to one's own system. Nevertheless the approximately straight line relation on log–log paper, and the imuportance of its slope, were fairly well-known. Those with the appropriate background recognized the equivalence of Zipf and Bradford laws. But data were scanty, pressures then as now were on development rather than on research, and there was no audience for publication.

Although it is impossible to give individual credit for unpublished and inaccessible contributions I can, and should, credit the Documentation Committee of the Advisory Group on Aeronautical Research and Development of NATO for their encouraging pioneer work and discussion about mathematization and mechanization of documentary tasks in the early 1950s. As well as encouraging research, it had the more difficult task of discouraging mystique and misunderstanding about both mathematics and machines. Thus it laid a fairly sound foundation for the machines when they were ready for documentary tasks. Unfortunately that was late enough for the foundations to have been forgotten.

Wall[54, 34] (1957, 1964) reports that in 1956 T. E. Boyle of DuPont Engineering Department suggested, in private correspondence, use of Zipf's findings to predict the number of 'keywords' or the like in what are now called 'co-ordinate indexes'. In 1959 Costello and Wall[13] gave an empirical formula relating the number t of indexing terms, of the undisciplined Uniterm kind, and the number of documents n indexed by them.

$$t = 4170 \, log_{10} \, (n + 730) - 11620 \qquad (21)$$

Wall favours a log-normal distribution, rather than a hyperbolic, of the use of indexing terms; that is, the logarithm of the documents per term is dispersed about its mean value according to the normal Gaussian distribution. He seems to have chosen this distribution because the results plotted as a straight line on available 'probability' paper. So they would have on ordinary logarithmic paper. Numerically and graphically there is little difference, because segments of the tail of a Gaussian distribution are not readily distinguishable from segments of a hyperbolic distribution. Unfortunately there is not, so far as I know, any small-sample test of goodness of fit for logarithmic plots.

Houston and Wall[34] (1964) fitted the log-normal distribution to nine indexing vocabularies. Wall[55] elaborated on this work in another paper published the same year. In this he displayed generalized hyperbolic as well as log-normal distributions for various relations in index term use. Also he gave procedures for predicting term use as a function of index size. These are entirely empirical and extremely elaborate, using many arbitrary parameters. The last did not, as an unkind critic commented, outnumber the data, but there was enough to make some theoretical justification and practical interpretation most desirable. However Wall did cite and use extensive data from the more monstrous indexes, vocabularies, and subject heading lists of the time. It is worth noting that he in some cases obtained a Zipf-Bradford relation between the rank of a term and its frequency of assignment.

Zunde and Slamecka[62] (1967) use an information theoretic approach, but seem unacquainted with the work of Mandelbrot and others. Their criterion of index efficiency was matching of input and output 'entropy'; i.e. of variety or complication. This certainly is a measure of the efficiency of signalling. Also it is a measure of the convenience of natural language, in the sense of permissible variety. Natural language has no 'efficiency' in the engineering sense. The least-cost principle applies only to short-term inconvenience, dealt with more or less instinctively.

Index languages, like other deliberately constructed languages, do have efficiencies with respect to the end for which they were constructed. As is well-known, efficiency here by no means implies convenience. If an indexing language were perfectly efficient, every term would be used equally often and every item would be assigned the same number of index terms. Plotted as a cumulative distribution, the perfect indexing system would give a horizontal line along the rank axis, a vertical line, and a line parallel to the axis. Normally index term distributions approximate to this as a S-shaped curve, which become straighter and closer to the simple Bradford line as the index language becomes more convenient (i.e. closer to natural language) and less efficient in the sense of terms needed to index an item.

Zunde and Slamecka do obtain these S-shaped curves, but take goodness of fit with simple Zipf as the criterion of virtue. The more general Mandelbrot relation, had they known of it, would certainly have fitted the plotted curves for overall slope and for common and rare terms. They also accept a log-normal distribution of term usage, and use it to calculate source 'entropy' for collections of various sizes. Probably they get much the same numerical results as they would from any plausible arbitrary distribution, but the log-normal hypothesis certainly does not simplify their calculations.

Zunde and Dexter[61] (1969), investigating the joint use of indexing terms by groups of indexers, arrive at a hyperbolic distribution between a function of the number of distinct terms used by a number of indexers, and the number of indexers. They cite Lotka, Zipf, and Bradford, but not Mandelbrot and the others who have published on information theoretic methods in this field. Internal evidence suggests that they are going to repeat this earlier work unwittingly.

In this they will not be alone. A paper of Krautwurst,[36] citing Zipf and Zunde and Slamecka (1967) purports to apply information theory to analysis of an indexing vocabulary. Apart from listing some of the elementary expressions of information theory, this paper does no more than to put new labels on old curves. One hopes that the resurgence of interest in the information theo-

retic approach does not also mean that it will become fashionable.

6. Conclusions

This survey has shown the hyperbolic distributions to be the inevitable result of combinatorial necessity and a tendency to short-term rational behaviour whenever a group of people have to use a repertory of given elements to form compounds, and when one aspect of the 'cost' or inconvenience of these elements is dominant.

Usually the elements and their use arise from the way people choose to observe, arrange, or talk about things, not from the nature of the things themselves. Therefore designers and administrators can cheat these laws by changing the elements, their costs, and the rules for using them. The laws themselves give the limits of improvement and a yardstick for quality control. Disobedience of the laws is more significant than obedience, because it indicates that conditions have changed.

This survey itself supports Bradford's conclusion from his law; that to know about your speciality you must go outside it. You must be neither too local nor too contemporary. The past is a profitable prelude.

References

1. BENFORD, F. *Proceedings of the American Philosophical Society,* vol. 78, 1938, p. 551.
2. BERGER, J. M. and MANDELBROT, BENOIT. A new model of error clustering on telephone circuits, *IBM Journal of Research and Development,* vol. 7, 1963, p. 224–36.
3. BOOTH, A. D. On the geometry of libraries. *Journal of Documentation,* vol. 25, no. 1, 1969, p. 28–42.
4. BRADFORD, S. C. Sources of information on specific subjects. *Engineering,* 1934, Jan. 26.
5. BRADFORD, S. C. *Documentation,* Crosby Lockwood, 1948.
6. BRILLOUIN, L. *Science and information theory.* Academic Press, 1956.
7. BROOKES, B. C. The derivation and application of the Bradford-Zipf distribution. *Journal of Documentation,* vol. 24, no. 4, 1968, p. 247–65.
8. BROOKES, B. C. The complete Bradford-Zipf 'bibliograph'. *Journal of Documentation,* vol. 25, no. 1, 1969, p. 58–60.
9. BROOKES, B. C. Library Zipf (letter). *Journal of Documentation,* vol. 25, no. 2, 1969, p. 155.
10. BUCKLAND, M. K. and HINDLE, A. Library Zipf. *Journal of Documentation,* vol. 25, no. 1, 1969, p. 54–7.
11. BUCKLAND, M. K. and HINDLE, A. Library Zipf (letter). *Journal of Documentation,* vol. 25, no. 2, 1969, p. 154.
12. COLE, P. F. A new look at reference scattering. *Jour-*

nal of Documentation, vol. 18, no. 2, 1962, p. 58–64.

13. COSTELLO, J. C. and WALL, E. Recent improvements in techniques for storing and retrieving information. In Studies in co-ordinate indexing, vol. 5. Documentation Inc., 1959.

14. ESTOUP, J. B. Gammes stenographiques. 4th edition. 1916.

15. FAIRTHORNE, R. A. Automata and information. Journal of Documentation, vol. 8, no. 3, 1952, p. 164–72.

16. FAIRTHORNE, R. A. Information theory and clerical systems. Journal of Documentation, vol. 9, no. 2, 1953, p. 101–16.

17. FAIRTHORNE, R. A. Some clerical operations and languages. In Proceedings of the Third London symposium on information theory, 1955. Butterworth, 1956.

18. FAIRTHORNE, R. A. Algebraic representation of storage and retrieval languages. In: Proceedings of the International Conference on scientific information, Washington, D.C. 1958. Area 6. National Academy of Sciences, 1959.

19. FAIRTHORNE, R. A. Towards information retrieval. Butterworth, 1961 (reprinted, Archon Books, 1968).

20. FAIRTHORNE, R. A. Library Zipf (letter) Journal of Documentation, vol. 25, no. 2, 1969, p. 152.

21. FAMA, E. F. Mandelbrot and the stable Paretian hypothesis. Journal of Business, vol. 36, 1963, p. 420–9.

22. FELLER, W. An introduction to the theory of probability and its applications. vol. 1, second edition. Wiley, 1957.

23. FURRY, W. H. and HURWITZ, H. Distribution of numbers and distribution of significant digits. Nature, vol. 155, 1945, pp. 52–3.

24. GNEDENKO, B. V. and KOLMOGOROFF, A. N. (trans. K. L. Chung). Limit distributions of sums of independent variables. Addison-Wesley, 1954.

25. GOFFMAN, W. An epidemic process in an open population. Nature, vol. 205, 1965, p. 831–2.

26. GOFFMAN, W. Stability of epidemic processes. Nature, vol. 210, 1966, p. 786–7.

27. GOFFMAN, W. A mathematical approach to the spread of scientific ideas. Nature, vol. 212, 1966, p. 449–542.

28. GOFFMAN, W. and WARREN, K. S. Dispersion of papers among journals, based on a mathematical analysis of two diverse medical literatures. Nature, vol. 221, 1969, p. 1205–7.

29. GOFFMAN, W. and NEWILL, V. A. Generalization of epidemic theory; an application to the transmission of ideas. Nature, vol. 204, 1964, p. 225–8.

30. GOFFMAN, W. and NEWILL, V. A. Communication and epidemic processes. Proceedings of the Royal Society, Series A, vol. 298, 1967, p. 316–34.

31. GOUDSMIT, S. A. and FURRY, W. H. Significant figures of numbers in statistical tables. Nature, vol. 154, 1944, p. 800–1.

32. GROOS, O. V. Bradford's law and Keenan-Atherton data. American Documentation, vol. 18, 1967, p. 48.

33. HERDAN, G. The advanced theory of language as choice and chance. Springer, 1966.

34. HOUSTON, N. and WALL, E. The distribution of term usage in manipulative indexes. American Documentation, vol. 15, 1964, p. 105–14.

35. KENDALL, M. G. The bibliography of operational research. Operational Research Quarterly, vol. 2, 1960, p. 31–6.

36. KRAUTWURST, J. Die Beurteilung eines Thesaurus mit informationstheoretischen Hilfsmitteln. Nachrichtung für Dokumentation, vol. 20, 1969, p. 68–72.

37. LEIMKUHLER, F. F. The Bradford distribution. Journal of Documentation, vol. 23, no. 3, 1967, p. 197–207.

38. LEITH, J. D., JR. Biomedical literature: an analysis of journal articles collected by a radiation- and cell-biologist. American Documentation, vol. 20, 1969, p. 143–8.

39. LÉVY, P. Calcul des probabilités. part 2, chap. 6. Gauthier-Villars, 1925.

40. LOTKA, A. J. The frequency distribution of scientific productivity. Journal of the Washington Academy of Sciences, vol. 16, 1926, p. 317–23.

41. LYNN, K. C. A quantitative comparison of conventional information compression techniques in dental literature. American Documentation, vol. 20, 1969, p. 149–51.

42. MANDELBROT, BENOIT. An information theory of the statistical structure of language. Proceedings of the symposium on applications of communication theory, London, Sept. 1952. Butterworth, 1953, p. 486–500.

43. MANDELBROT, BENOIT. Structure formelle des textes et communication. Word, vol. 10, 1954, p. 1–27.

44. MANDELBROT, BENOIT. On the language of taxonomy: an outline of a 'thermostatistical' theory of systems of categories with Willis (natural) structure. Information Theory; papers read at a symposium on information theory, London, Sept. 1955. Butterworth, 1956, p. 135–45.

45. MANDELBROT, BENOIT. The variation of certain speculative prices. Journal of Business, vol. 36, 1963, p. 394–419.

46. MANDELBROT, BENOIT. Self-similar error clusters in communication systems and the concept of conditional stationarity. IEEE Transactions on Communication Technology, vol. 13, 1965, p. 71–90.

47. MANDELBROT, BENOIT. How long is the coast of Britain? Statistical self-similarity and fractional dimension. Science, vol. 156, 1967, p. 636–8.

48. PARETO, V. Cours d'économie politique. Vol. 2. Section 3. Lausanne, 1897.

49. PARKER-RHODES, A. F. and JOYCE, T. A theory of word-frequency distribution. *Nature,* vol. 178, 1956, p. 1308.

50. RICHARDSON, L. E. The problem of contiguity. *In:* General systems: yearbook of the Society for General Systems Research, vol. 6, 1961, p. 139–88.

51. RICHARDSON, L. F. *Statistics of deadly quarrels* (ed. by Quincy Wright and C. C. Lienau), Boxwood Press, Pittsburgh, 1960.

52. SMITH, D. A. Library Zipf (letter). *Journal of Documentation,* vol. 25, no. 2, 1969, p. 153–4.

53. VICKERY, B. C. Bradford's law of scattering. *Journal of Documentation,* vol. 4, 1948, p. 198–203.

54. WALL, E. Use of concept co-ordination in the DuPont Engineering Department. *In:* Conference on multiple-access searching for information retrieval. Proceedings, 1957. AD-147491, U.S. Defense Documentation Center.

55. WALL, E. Further implications of the distribution of index term usage. *In:* Parameters of information science; proceedings of the American Documentation Institute annual meeting, 1964, vol. 1, p. 457–66. American Documentation Institute, 1964.

56. WHITWORTH, W. A. *Choice and chance.* Chap. 5, 5th edition, 1901 (reprinted, Stechert, 1942).

57. WILLIS, J. C. *Age and area; a study in geographical distribution and origin of species.* Cambridge University Press, 1922.

58. YULE, G. UDNY. A mathematical theory of evolution based on the conclusions of Dr. J. C. Willis. *Philosophical Transactions of the Royal Society,* Series B, vol. 213, 1924.

59. ZIPF, G. K. *Psycho-biology of language.* Houghton-Mifflin, 1935.

60. ZIPF, G. K. *Human behaviour and the principle of least effort.* Addison Wesley, 1949.

61. ZUNDE, P. and DEXTER, M. E. Indexing consistency and quality. *American Documentation,* vol. 20, 1969, p. 259–67.

62. ZUNDE, P. and SLAMECKA, V. Distribution of indexing terms for maximum efficiency of information transmission. *American Documentation,* vol. 18, 1967, p. 104–8.

Part Three
Evaluation
of
Information
Systems

In Part I, we discussed the basic notions of information and of communication processes, and in Part II we investigated the structure and function of systems that are instigated to carry out some of the communication processes — especially those related to knowledge. In Part III, we turn to the studies concerned with evaluation of the workings and performance of information systems in general and information retrieval systems in particular.

The significance of evaluation studies may be interpreted from a number of viewpoints. The theoretician and experimentor uncovered variables, often hidden and disguised, that operate within information systems — variables which warranted special research attention. To the designers, developers, and operators of information systems, evaluation studies were somewhat disappointing, because they did not provide direct, clear-cut answers to the operational problems. These studies, however, did provide enough helpful clues which, in some rare instances, were translated into practical solutions. Finally, evaluation studies established the evaluation effort in itself as an area worthy of basic and applied research.

The evaluation studies also verified the suspected complexity of information systems. They demonstrated that there are no easy answers; revealed that the claims and counterclaims about information systems performance were founded on optimism rather than on fact; and indicated that experimental observations may take precedence over limited practical observations in a debate. What is clearly lacking in the field is a translation function between the evaluation studies and the reality of practical considerations, that is, a connection between theory and experimentation on the one hand, and practice on the other. It is entirely possible that these studies were so inadequate that there was nothing to translate; but it is also possible that there was a general lack of ability on the part of the practitioners (designers, developers, and operators) to translate the results in practical terms. If the latter situation is the case, it presents a grave indictment against the kind of education provided for information systems practitioners. In this context, it is suggested here that a fully and formally educated professional practitioner in information systems should be quite familiar with approaches, methodologies, results, and critical analyses of studies of the type presented in this book. Indubitably, a basic or applied researcher must be thoroughly familiar with such studies. The reverse is

also true: because of the nature of information science, a researcher has to be familiar with practical problems, otherwise his research is conducted in a vacuum.

Again, the organization of this part in itself suggests the structure of the problem area. Chapter 10 deals with studies on the work-related behavior of people in information systems. Chapter 11, divided into two subareas, presents work related to testing the effectiveness of information systems. First, works are presented that deal with performance measures, which are applicable to information systems; and, second, articles are presented that summarize results from some major studies conducted in the field. Finally, Chapter 12 deals with the problem of efficiency and growth of information systems. The significance of economic studies can be exemplified by the truism that, after all is said and done, it is the economics of information systems that makes or breaks them.

The work presented in this part is a direct outgrowth of the work presented in the previous part. Furthermore, the work on the communication processes of information users (Chapters 2 and 3) is closely related to the study of work-related behavior of people in information systems, because they are also information users, even if they are working within the system. It is also worthwhile to suggest that the studies on the basic notions of information (Chapter 1) and the structure of information systems (Chapter 4) may have, but so far have not had, an important relationship to work on performance measures. It must be realized that what constitutes the basis of phenomena and structures involved in information systems is also fundamental to a more formal understanding of objectives. The objectives, in turn, underlie the selection of criteria for performance measures which should reflect the objectives of a system.

Finally, attention is called to the diverse backgrounds of those engaged in evaluation work. We can find logicians and mathematicians interested in the fundamental aspects of measures; systems, industrial and electrical engineers; computer scientists; librarians; information retrieval professionals; physicists; biomedical personnel; psychologists; statisticians; economists, etc. As previously mentioned, many people from many disciplines were engaged in similar problem areas of information science. This merely points to further evidence of the field's multidisciplinary spread, on the one hand, and a unity of problem orientation, on the other.

Chapter Ten
Human Factors
in Information
Systems

That people greatly affect systems of which they are a part and vice versa is clearly not a hypothesis but a tautological statement. But the questions of how and to what extent these effects take place are serious questions that many sciences have asked and investigated. With the rising complexity of our society and of our systems, these questions are growing in importance and significance. New areas have been opened up — human engineering, man-machine interaction, organizational behavior, human factors in systems analysis and operations research, etc. Of special significance to information science are investigations in the general area of the effects of humans on systems and effects of systems on humans. These studies gain in significance from the realization that with the advent of complex machinery an unfortunate side effect occurred which by now is having great social repercussions. Namely, in complex system designs and operations, people were considered too often a nuisance and seen stubbornly to defy orderly manipulations. Furthermore, people have been treated as an adjunct to the systems rather than vice versa. We tried too often in our information systems to become what Boguslaw, in his book New Utopians, *calls "social engineers" . . . "We neglected the human aspects of our systems. In the term man-Machine interface the only capital M is in Machine. We started paying for this neglect and we may even pay a lot more."*

These few sociological observations were brought in here in order to identify a big gap in information science studies. The studies on human factors within systems deal almost exclusively with the human consistency of performing some task, such as indexing. These studies indicate just a meager beginning of what should be done and of what should be a matter of great concern not only to theoreticians and experimentors, but also to educators, designers, developers and operators.

Montgomery and Swanson (Article 50) ask a provocative question about the nature of the indexing process by humans. In the conclusions on the basis of the experiment conducted, they point out that there are some aspects of indexing that are machine-like rather than intellectual.

Tinker (Articles 51 and 52) in his study on indexing and indexers took an approach that can be termed classic — first, he broadly described a theory of meaning in a language and a communication process; second, he designed and carried out a number of experiments examining the effects of various indexing constraints on indexing consistency; and third, on the basis of experiments he designed a new, more efficient indexing scheme.

Zunde and Dexter (Article 53) reviewed the measures and results of previous indexing studies. Next, they devised a new and, to a degree, a qualitative measure of indexers' performance. They then applied this measure in a series of experiments. The significance of their approach is twofold: first, they took the necessary and missing step in linking the consistency with quality, and second, they derived an empirical algorithm which described certain regularities of indexes and indexing.

These selections indicate not only what was done in the area of human factors but even more so they indicate how little was done and how much more has to be done.

50 Machinelike Indexing by People

CHRISTINE MONTGOMERY
DON R. SWANSON
American Documentation
Vol. 13, No. 4, October, 1962

1 Introduction

The key to bringing about substantial and significant improvements in the effectiveness of libraries through automation lies in a deeper understanding of the intellectual processes associated with classification, indexing, and retrieval. Classification and indexing are necessarily the proper points of beginning since, once these operations have been completed, subsequent encoding and machine searching are largely matters of economics; the die is already cast with respect to the effectiveness of the library as an instrument for information retrieval. Indexing, or classification, as an intellectual process is profound in principle and extraordinarily difficult of formalization. In this paper, we suggest that indexing in practice may be of a quite different nature.

A brief study of an existing system for indexing medical literature was carried out through detailed examination of its end product—a monthly index of medical journals. The study was not concerned with how the medical literature could have been or should have been indexed, but only with how it *was* indexed. This approach thus does not involve evaluation in the sense of measuring retrieval effectiveness, but rather is based on the question "To what extent can the human indexing operations that take place in an existing system be simulated by machines?" The issue of whether the indexing is adequate or inadequate for retrieval purposes is thus bypassed. It was concluded that most of the articles studied could have been indexed by machine on the basis of machine "inspection" of article titles alone.

Two closely related studies were also carried out, one on automatic compilation of special bibliographies and the other on the usefulness of titles as a basis for estimating relevance of articles to requests.

2 Study of the *Index Medicus* Entries

The indexing entries studied were selected from the September 1960 issue of *Index Medicus*, a publication of the National Library of Medicine. This indexing system is based upon an alphabetic subject heading list whose 5,000 terms vary widely from the specific to the general. The subject portion of the *Index Medicus* consists of title citations cross-filed under each assigned subject heading and subheading. Throughout this paper we shall take "indexing" to mean that process which leads to the *Index Medicus*; it is perhaps better described as "assignment of articles to pre-established subject categories."

Figure 1 shows a sample set of entries in which we have underlined those words of article titles which are identical to—or near synonyms of—the subject heading (usually one word) under which the title appears. These titles (tagged with a check mark) could thus have been assigned to the proper subject headings by a machine procedure. Titles about which the investigators were doubtful are indicated by question marks; those which did not seem to exhibit a word-plus-synonym match are marked with an X.

One might ask whether or not the checked articles were cross-filed under other subject headings where the relationship between subject title and article title might be less direct. This question is answerable only with considerable difficulty, since the *Index Medicus* itself does not list under any given title the various headings under which that title is cross-filed. One would either have to hypothesize probable subject headings and then confirm the hypothesis by inspection, or consult the indexers at the National Library of Medicine.

An alternative approach is much simpler, however. Let us restate our objective by asking either the question

Paris 36:1144–52/SP, 18 Apr 60 (Fr)

surgery

KIEFER JH, McDONALD JH: The surgical management of nonhypertensive adrenal disease. Illinois Med J 117:207–10, Apr 60

ADVERTISING

PETERMAN RA: The special demands of medical advertising. Mississippi V Med J 82:142–5, May 60

PANKOW LJ: The professional cards. S Dakota J Med Pharm 13:245–6, May 60

ROYO VILLANOVA R: [Professional advertisement by the physician] An Acad Nac Med (Madr) 77:157–94, 1960 (Sp)

AEDES

BOORMAN JP: Observations on the feeding habits of the mosquito Aedes (Stegomyia) aegypti (Linnaeus): the loss of fluid after a blood-meal and the amount of blood taken during feeding. Ann Trop Med Parasit 54:8–14, Apr 60

FOX I: [Resistance of Aedes aegypti to certain chlorinated hydrocarbon and organophosphorus insecticides in Puerto Rico] Bol Ofic Sanit Panamer 48:375–82, May 60 (Sp)

HUDSON A, BOWMAN L, ORR CW: Effects of absence of saliva on blood feeding by mosquitoes. Science 131:1730–1, 10 June 60

metabolism

MICKS DW, FERGUSON MJ, SINGH KR: Effect of DDT on free amino acids of susceptible and DDT-resistant Aedes aegypti larvae. Science 131:1615, 27 May 60

AEROBACTER AEROGENES

infection

ZINSSER HH, LATTIMER JK, SENECA H: Aerogenosis; a plea for clinical bacteriology. J Urol 83:755–8, May 60

metabolism

DEAN AC, HINSHELWOOD C: Variations in the nucleic acid content of Bact. lactis aerogenes during the growth cycle. Proc Roy Soc [Biol] 151:348–63, 2 Feb 60

AEROSOLS

therapy

WEGNER W: [On progresin-aerosol therapy of degenerative peripheral circulatory disorders] Deutsch Med J 11:237–41, 5 May 60 (Ger)

Aerotitis see OTITIS MEDIA

AESCULUS

chemistry

PATT P, WINKLER W: [The active therapeutic principle of horse chestnut (Aesculus hippocastanum). Part 2. On the chemistry of the active substance] Arzneimittelforsch 10:273–5, Apr 60 (Ger)

pharmacology

LORENZ D, MAREK ML: [The active therapeutic principle of horse chestnut (Aesculus hippocastanum). Part 1. Classification of the active substance] Arzneimittelforsch 10:263–72, Apr 60 (Ger)

VOGEL G, UEBEL H: [The active therapeutic principle of horse chestnut (Aesculus hippocastanum). Part 3. On the question of the point of application and the mechanism of action] Arzneimittelforsch 10:275–80, Apr 60 (Ger)

therapy

HUTZEL H: [Clinical experiences in surgery with a horse chestnut extract] Ther Gegenw 99:134–5, Mar 60 (Ger)

toxicology

UEBEL H, PATT P: [The active therapeutic principle of horse chestnut (Aesculus hippocastanum). Part 4. On the toxicology of the active principle] Arzneimittelforsch 10:280–4, Apr 60 (Ger)

Affect see EMOTIONS

AFIBRINOGENEMIA

in pregnancy

REZENDE J de, ROCCO R: [Afibrinogenemia after cesarean section] Rev Ginec Obstet (Rio) 105:433–8, Oct 59 (Por)

pathology

FERRARO C: [Considerations on a severe case of postpartum afibrinogenemia complicated by irreversible renal damage] Quad Clin Ostet Ginec 15:46–64, Jan 60 (It)

AGAMMAGLOBULINEMIA

LINDENMAYER H: [Antibody deficiency syndrome (A- and hypogammaglobulinemia)] Med Mschr 14:185–7, Mar 60 (Ger)

NÜNBERG M, SCOPPOLA L: [Agammaglobulinemia, Syndrome of lack of antibodies] Policlinico [Prat] 67:481–95, 4 Apr 60 (It)

case reports

PISCIOTTA AV, JERMAIN LF, HINZ JE: Chronic lymphocytic leukemia, hypogammaglobulinemia and autoimmune hemolytic anemia—an experiment of nature. Blood 15:748–57, May 60

etiology

HUDSON RP, WILSON SJ: Hypogammaglobulinemia and chronic lymphatic leukemia. Cancer 13:200–4, Jan–Feb 60

in infancy & childhood

GOOD RA, ZAK SJ, CONDIE RM, BRIDGES RA: Clinical investigation of patients with agammaglobulinemia and hypogammaglobulinemia. Pediat Clin N Amer 7:397–433, May 60

Agaricus see MUSHROOMS

Aged see GERIATRICS

AGGLUTINATION

see also HEMAGGLUTINATION

BUERKI F: [An orienting study of animal sera for antibodies against Leptospira by mixed antigens in the complement fixation reaction. Part II. Results in comparison to the agglutination - lysis reaction] Z Immunitaetsforsch 119:333–43, Apr 60 (Ger)

JASINSKA S: [The effect of bacteriophages on agglutination] Arch Immun Ter Dosw 7:625–51, 1959 (Pol)

AGGRESSION

GUSTAFSON JE, WINOKUR G: The effect of sexual satiation and female hormone upon aggressivity in an inbred mouse strain. J Neuropsychiat 1:182–4, Apr 60

AGING

see also GERIATRICS
see also GROWTH

ASTRAND I: Aerobic work capacity in men and women with special reference to age. Acta Physiol Scand 49/Suppl 169:1–92, 1960

BARROWS CH Jr, FALZONE JA Jr, SHOCK NW: Age differences in the succinoxidase activity of homogenates and mitochondria from the livers and kidneys of rats. J Geront 15:130–3, Apr 60

BOHATIRCHUK FP: Micromorphological data on aging bone atrophy as seen in microradiographs and colored specimens. J Geront 15:142–8, Apr 60

BROZEK J: Age differences in residual lung volume and vital capacity of normal individuals. J Geront 15:155–60, Apr 60

BILASH I, ZUBEK JP: The effects of age on factorially "pure" mental abilities. J Geront 15:175–82, Apr 60

BRENT FD: Some aspects of placement systems in industry. Canad Med Ass J 82:1022–30, 14 May 60

CLARK JW: The aging dimension; a factorial analysis of individual differences with age on psychological and physiological measurements. J Geront 15:183–7, Apr 60

GRUNT JA, KNISELY WH: Strain differences and the development of fatty liver in the aged rat. J Geront 15:134–5, Apr 60

HABERMANN V, HABERMANNOVA S: Age difference in nicotinamide mononucleotide synthesis by human erythrocytes. Nature (Lond) 186:389–90, 30 Apr 60

KIRK JE: The glyoxalase I activity of arterial tissue in individuals of various ages. J Geront 15:139–41, Apr 60

KIRK JE: The leucine aminopeptidase activity of arterial tissue in individuals of various ages. J Geront 15:136–8, Apr 60

LOEPER J: [Sulfur and senescence] Presse Med 68:718–20, 16 Apr 60 (Fr)

McFARLAND RA, DOMEY RG, WARREN AB, WARD DC: Dark adaptation as a function of age. I. A statistical analysis. J Geront 15:149–54, Apr 60

PECHTEL C, MASSERMAN JH, AARONS L: Differential responses in young vs. old animals to training, conflict, drugs and brain lesions. Amer J Psychiat 116:1018–20, May 60

QUARTO DI PALO FM, BERTOLINI AM, GASTALDI L: [The metabolism of creatinic bodies in senescent animals] G Geront 8:85–9, Feb 60 (It)

ROWE O: Life for the added years. N Carolina Med J 21:199–201, May 60

SCHRANZ D: Age determination from the internal structure of the humerus. Amer J Phys Anthrop 17:273–7, Dec 59

SZILARD L: Dependence of the sex ratio at birth on the age of the father. Nature (Lond) 186:649–50, 21 May 60

metabolism

HRACHOVEC JP, ROCKSTEIN M: Age changes in lipid metabolism and their medical implications. Gerontologia (Basel) 3:305–26, 1959

physiology

BYKOV VD: [On the problem of the rate of formation of conditioned reflexes as an indication of the development of higher nervous activity in ontogenesis] Zh Vyss Nerv Deiat

Figure 1. Sample Entries of Index Medicus

TABLE 1. RESULTS OF TITLE STUDY (First Sample)

Heading	No. of entries containing synonyms of subject heading.	No. of entries which investigators were unable to resolve.	No. of entries containing no synonyms of subject heading.	Total No. of entries under subj. heading.
Adrenal Cortex	27	11		38
Adrenal Cortex Hormones	54	3	6	63
Air Pollution	28	2	3	33
Allergy	86	5	1	92
Amino Acid Mixtures	51	1	2	54
Antineoplastic Agents	42	1	19	62
Antibiotics	59	8	2	69
Antitubercular Agents	26	5	2	33
Arteriosclerosis	36	1	2	39
Arthritis, Rheumatoid	27	11	1	39
Asthma	31	1	2	34
Biographies	85			85
Bladder	39	1	6	46
Blood Coagulation	33	4	1	38
Blood Proteins	49	10		59
Bone and Bones	52		2	54
Bone Marrow	28		2	30
Brain	115	6	6	127
Calcium	38	1		39
Carcinoma	35	2		37
Central Nervous System	35	1	3	39
Cholesterol	33	1	1	35
Coronary Diseases	36		3	39
Corticotropin	34		5	39
Cortisone	39		5	44
Diabetes Mellitus	66		4	70
Electrocardiography	43	2	4	49
Electroence phalography	71	7	4	82
Enzymes	48		4	52
Epilepsy	25	1	7	33
Erythrocytes	43	3	2	48
Esophagus	37	2	4	43
Estrogens	34	1	3	38
Eye (Opthalomology)	47		1	48
Gastrectomy	38		4	42
Griseofulvin	62		1	63
Gynecology	26		4	30
Heart	49	2	2	53
Heart Defects, Congenital	22	5	4	31
Heart Surgery	27	3	3	33
Leukemia	54	4	1	59
Hospitals	32		12	44
Hospital Administration	25		12	37
Hypertension	72		5	77
Hypothermia	37		2	39
Industrial Medicine	16		19	35
Infant, Newborn	72		6	78
Intestines	44	1	5	50
Iodine	44	1		45
Kidney	94	2	6	102
Kidney Diseases	45	1	6	52
Learning	32		3	35
Lipids	32		3	35
Liver	90		13	103
Liver Diseases	43	2	8	53
Lung	36		7	43
Lung Diseases	35		6	41
Lung Neoplasms	50	1	6	57
Mental Disorders	58		15	73
Military Medicine	36			36
Muscle Relaxants	27	1	4	32
Muscles	46		6	52
Myocardial Infarct	40	1	3	44
Neoplasms	116	2	24	142
Obituaries	42		30	72
Pancreas	35		5	40
Pediatrics	36		3	39
Peptic Ulcer	33	5	5	43
Pituitary Gland	26		7	33
Plants	23	5	2	30
Poliomyelitis	57	1	2	60
Prednisolone	27	3	7	37
Pregnancy	88		26	114
Proteins	65	2	2	69
Psychopharmacology	22	3	9	34
Radiation Effects	33		6	39
Radiation Injury	18		16	34
Radiation Protection	19		17	36
Respiration	57		8	65
Schizophrenia	36		3	39
Skin	77	1	12	90
Skin Transplantation	34			34
Spleen	29		3	32
Staph Infections	29		5	34
Stomach	41		5	46
Stomach Neoplasms	25	3	6	34
Surgery, Operative	44			44
Tranquilizing Agents	34	3	10	47
Tuberculosis	63		4	67
Tuberculosis, Pulmonary	60	3	22	85
Vascular Diseases, Peripheral	39		2	41
Virus Diseases	30	3	8	41
Viruses	39		6	45
	4,093	149	528	4,770

"What proportion of entries in the *Index Medicus* (an entry being defined as the recording of a title under a particular subject heading) could have been created automatically?" or the almost equivalent question "Which subject headings within the *Index Medicus* are amenable to automatic assignment of titles?" Our study proceeded then simply on the basis of examining entries in the *Index Medicus*. The first sample of subject headings selected was essentially random but biased by the requirement that no subject headings with fewer than 30 title citations were included. Subheadings were not considered.

Each title was inspected to determine whether it contained words identical to or essentially synonymous with the corresponding subject heading; medical dictionaries and drug indexes were used to assist in the recognition of synonyms. In the case of multiple-word subject headings, judgments of synonymity were made as follows. If the particular subject heading contained a word which did not occur in any other subject heading, only that word (or its synonym) was required to be present in the titles listed under the given subject heading. For example, some synonym of "tranquilizing" was judged sufficient for the identification of entries to be indexed as *Tranquilizing Agents*; when the particular subject heading did not contain a uniquely occurring word, presence of both elements in the title was required for a match between heading and entry, as in the case of *Stomach Neoplasms*. Matches were found in 4,093 of the 4,770 entries studied, 149 were doubtful, and the remaining 528 did not contain matching words.

The list of subject headings studied is given in Table 1, together with the total number of entries appearing under each one and decisions as to whether particular entries could be indexed automatically. To determine whether the "30-entry" selection criterion might have, for any reason, introduced a bias into the results, a second sample of an equal number of subject headings was taken alphabetically (excluding those previously studied). Of the total of 451 entries examined, 392 contained words matching elements in the subject headings, 12 were unresolved, and 47 were judged difficult or impossible to index by an automatic process. The similarity of the two sets of results indicates that neither sample was significantly biased. The subject headings used for the second sample are listed in Table 2.

It must be presumed, of course, that if a machine were carrying out this matching process, it would have to be provided with a thesaurus or dictionary containing groups of words which are either synonymous or which function as synonyms for purposes of information retrieval. Table 3 illustrates a few examples of such groups of words, collected under subject headings taken from the *Index Medicus*. Here the subject headings can be looked upon as designators for thesaurus groups.

The size of the synonym groups shown is clearly a function of the inclusiveness of the individual subject heading rather than of the number of titles listed under it. For example, the general category *Antibiotics* required two synonyms and 17 names of particular antibiotics

TABLE 2. RESULTS OF TITLE STUDY (Second Sample)

Heading	No. of entries containing synonyms of subject heading.	No. of entries containing no synonyms of subject heading.	No. of entries which investigators were unable to resolve.	Total No. of entries under subj. heading.
Abdomen	26	2		28
Abdominal Wall	1	2		3
Abnormalities	9	2		11
Abortion	13	2		15
Abortion, Criminal	1	1		2
Abortion, Missed	2			2
Abortion, Therapeutic	2	1		3
Abruptio Placentae	2			2
Abscess	2			2
Acceleration	2			2
Accidents	7	2		9
Accidents, Industrial	4	2		6
Accidents, Traffic	10	2		12
Acclimatization	4			4
Accommodation, Ocular	3			3
Accounting	5			5
Acculturation	1	1		2
Acetaldehyde	1			1
Acetamalid	1			1
Acetates	10		1	11
Acetazolamide	6			6
Acetobacter	1			1
Acetone	1			1
Acetylcholine	13			13
Acetylsalicylic Acid	4	3		7
Achromobacter	1			1
Acid-base Equilibrium	2	1		3
Acidosis			1	1
Acids	4			4
Acne	3			3
Acoustic Nerve	3			3
Acridines			1	1
Acromegaly	1			1
Acrylic Resins	2			2
Actinobacillus	1			1
Actinomyces	2			2
Actinomycosis	1			1
Acupuncture	6			6
Acute Renal Failure	6	1	1	8
Adamantinoma	1			1
Adaptation, Biological	1			1
Adaptation, Ocular	3			3
Adaptation, Physiological	2	3		5
Adaptation, Psychological	1	1		2
Addison's Disease	7			7
Adenine	2			2
Adenocarcinoma	7	2	2	11
Adenocarcinoma, Papillary		1		1
Adenofibroma	2			2
Adenoids	1			1
Adenoma	3			3
Adenoma, Chromophobe		1		1
Adenosine Phosphates	4	1		5
Adenovirus	5			5
Adenovirus Infections	5		1	6
Adenylpyrophosphatase	1	1		2
Adhesions	5			5
Adipose Tissue	10			10
Adnexa Uteri	2			2
Adnexitis	2			2
Adolescence	3	1		4
Adonis	1			1
Adoption	3			3
Adrenal Cortical Rest Tumor	1			1
Adrenal Glands	21	2		23
Adrenal Medulla	3			3
Adrenalectomy	11	1		12
Adrenogenital Syndrome	3			3
Advertising	2	1		3
Aedes	3	1		4
Aerobacter Aerogenes	2			2
Aerosols	1			1
Aesculus	5			5
Afibrinogenemia	2			2
Agammaglobulinemia	5			5
Agglutination	2			2
Aggression	1			1
Aging	25	2		27
Agranulocytosis	4			4
Agriculture	3			3
Air	2	1		3
Air Conditioning	1			1
Aircraft	1			1
Alanine	1	1		2
Albumins	3			3
Albuminuria	1			1
Alcohol, Ethyl	7	4		11
Alcohol, Methyl	2			2
Alcoholic Intoxication	2		1	3
Alcoholism	12			12
Alcohols	2	1	1	4
Aldehydes	4			4
Aldolase	9		2	11
Aldosterone	7		1	8
Alfalfa	1			1
Algae	9			9
	392	47	12	451

TABLE 3. FUNCTIONAL SYNONYMS UNDER SUBJECT HEADINGS

Allergy
allergy(s)
allergic
allergen(s)
allergenic
allergology
hyperallergy
sensitization
sensitized
autosensitization
desensitization
hypersensitivity
autoimmune
reaction
reagin
anaphylaxis
anaphylactic
anaphylactoid

Antibiotics
antibiotic(s)
antimicrobial
 primycin
 oligomycin
 rifomycin
 sigmamycin
 trichomycin
 spiramycin
 colimycin
 mitomycin
 neomycin
 paromomycin
 kanamycin
 kanamytrex
 tetracycline(s)
 carcinophylline
 colicine H
 mycerin
 polymixin

Cholesterol
cholesterol
cholesterolemia
hypercholesterolemia
cholesterin
cholesterinemia
hypercholesterinemia

Geriatrics
geriatric(s)
older
old age
old women
elderly
senile
senescent
senior citizens

Intestines
intestine(s)
intestinal
gastrointestinal
enteric
enteromesenteric
enteropathy

Choline
choline
iodocholine
thiocholine
isovalerylcholine

Calcium
calcium
Ca
calcic
hypocalcemia
hypercalcemia
nephrocalcinosis
hypercalciuria

Acetates
acetate(s)
acetic
pentaacetate
tertioamino-acetates
thioacetamide
p-chlorophenoxyacetic

Adipose Tissue
adipose tissue
body fat
fat body
subcutaneous fat
steatonecrosis

Adrenal Cortex
adrenal cortex
suprarenal cortex
adrenocortical
hypocorticism
hypercortisonism
hypermineralocorticoidism
corticostimulating
adrenocorticotropic
corticotrop(h)ic
adrenal
adrenal hyperplasia

Adrenal Cortex Hormones
adrenal cortex hormone(s)
adrenal cortical hormone(s)
adrenal steroid
adrenocortical steroids
adrenal cortical steroid(s)
hormonal steroid
steroid hormones
corticosteroid(s)
cortico-like steroids
corticoid
corticosterone
corticotherapy
cortisone-like
cortisone
17-oxosteroids
17-hydroxycorticosteroids
11-desoxycortisol
glycocorticoids
glucocorticoids
adrenalin

Adrenal Glands
adrenal glands
the adrenal(s)
adrenal disease
adrenal hyperplasia
adrenal hypoplasia
adrenal insufficiency
hypophysial-adrenal
pituitary-adrenal

Corticotropin
corticotropin
adrenocorticotropic hormone
ACTH
adreno-cortical hormones

(taken here as functional synonyms) for the automatic indexing of 59 of a total of 69 titles, while the name of one specific antibiotic substance, griseofulvin, appeared in 62 of the 63 titles listed under the heading *Griseofulvin*.

We conclude that if a computer were provided with the title of each of these articles, the *Index Medicus* subject heading list, and a synonym list or thesaurus group of each subject heading, it could then be programmed to determine which subject headings should be assigned to each article. About 86% of such assignments would be the same as assignments made by human indexing.

The investigation did not show how much more extensively the machine might cross-file a title than would human indexers. That is, if the machine were to test each word of a given title to determine whether that word matched some subject heading, it is presumed that more cross-filing would result. It seems likely that such cross-filing, since it is more exhaustive and more reliable, would represent a significant improvement over human indexing, but the point should be further looked into.

Interesting preliminary evidence thus has been uncovered that present indexing of the medical literature as published in *Index Medicus* is, or could be, (a) based largely on examination of titles, and (b) based on a word-plus-synonym match of titles to subject headings. Clearly these two procedures are mechanizable. It should furthermore be noted that, not only are they mechanizable, but *economically* so, since keypunching and processing of titles alone would be quite inexpensive.

It is of considerable interest to analyze the 14% of the cases that failed to conform to these specifications. About half could not be resolved without more extensive research, and were marked as doubtful by the investigators. The remaining titles fell into two groups:

(1) Those which were inherently ambiguous—for example, "Meeting the Challenge to Society" listed under *Geriatrics*;

(2) Those which were ambiguous within the framework of the *Index Medicus* system of subject headings.

The latter group deserves further comment. The *Index Medicus* subject headings vary in generality from such narrow topics as names of rare myopathies to broad categories of organs and systems. Furthermore, many specific subject headings can be subsumed under more general ones, thus leading to several essentially equivalent and equally appropriate subject headings for some articles. This ambiguity of overlap among the various headings is a problem which is only partially resolved by the cross-reference structure, as the use of cross-references by an individual indexer appears somewhat arbitrary.

Consider, for example, a segment of the complex of subject headings associated with the adrenal system: *Adrenal Cortex, Adrenal Cortex Hormones, Adrenal Glands, Corticotropin, Cortisone, Epinephrine*. Obviously, these categories overlap to a considerable extent, as the adrenal cortex is the outer layer of the adrenal gland, the adrenal cortex hormones, which include cortisone and epinephrine, are those secreted by the adrenal cortex, and

corticotropin is a hormone which specifically stimulates the adrenal cortex. Therefore, articles on cortisone could conceivably be listed under *Adrenal Cortex Hormones* as well as under the more specific heading *Cortisone*, and so forth. In this study, article titles containing a word identical to a specific heading but listed under the general heading were labeled as not indexable by an automatic procedure. In addition to the problem of articles cited under general subject headings where specific ones seemed more applicable, there was the reverse situation of articles which were listed under a subject heading more specific than the title seemed to warrant. Thus, for purposes of automatic indexing by title, such articles were ambiguous with respect to their assignment to one or several potential subject headings. Presumably, reference to the full text is necessary in those cases.

3 Automatic Compilation of Special Bibliographies

The apparently strong reliance placed on titles by indexers suggests the possibility that those who compile special bibliographies in the medical literature may rely upon titles in much the same way. Accordingly, a study similar to the above was made of 302 bibliographies which had been compiled in the UCLA biomedical library in response to requests for information on a variety of topics, ranging from arthrogryposis to Zen Buddhism. A sample of 83 of these was selected for detailed study.

In order to test the effectiveness of *Index Medicus* as a research tool, the 83 requests were first matched against the *Index Medicus* subject headings to determine whether comparable bibliographies could have been compiled from a search of listings under those titles in the *Index Medicus*. This study revealed that only 16 of the 83 requests were identical to subject headings in the *Index Medicus*, while 59 were phrased in more specific terms than the corresponding subject headings. The remaining 8 involved only terms neither listed among the *Index Medicus* subject headings nor defined by the cross-reference structure. These eight seemed to require for their resolution a more sophisticated knowledge of medical terminology than the investigators possessed. Examples of these "non-indexable" terms included "amyoplasia congenita," which might conceivably have been listed under *Muscles* or *Muscular Atrophy*, and "cannibalism," for which *Diet Fads* seemed to be the most vivid (if anthropologically questionable) description. The foregoing results demonstrate the difficulties encountered in translating a bibliographic request into an intermediate language (such as the *Index Medicus* system of subject headings) in order to search the literature.

Again using the existing UCLA bibliographies, an alternative search procedure was then tested which involved direct matching of the words (expanded by lists of synonyms) used by the requester to corresponding words of article titles in the bibliography compiled in response to the particular request. Thus no indexing system was involved. The requests were first examined to determine impressionistically the number of concepts represented in each. The bibliographic citations listed for each request were then matched against the words of the request to establish the number of citations per request containing one or more of the concepts (or synonymous concepts) specified by the requester. A list of the requests included in the study is given in Table 4, together with information on the total number of bibliographic citations per request and the number of such citations containing words identical to or synonymous with those appearing in the request itself. The latter figures are expressed in terms of the number of concepts contained in the request, as indicated by the italicized words; e.g., the request for information on "blood changes in allergic children" listed in Table 3 was interpreted as containing three basic concepts—blood, allergy, and children.

For the eight requests containing three concepts, 37% of the references cited also contained the three concepts either directly or through synonymous words, 45% contained representations of two of the concepts expressed in the request, and the remaining 17% contained one concept. For the fifty titles containing two concepts, 64% of the citations contained some representation of both concepts, 30% reflected only one of the concepts expressed in the request, and 5% did not contain either of the two original concepts in any form. The citations listed for the 25 request titles containing only one concept exhibited a 92% correlation of concepts with the request. Of the total of 3,145 bibliographic citations evaluated, only 5.3% did not contain any terms which corresponded to concepts expressed in the request.

These statistics seem to indicate that the particular special bibliographies which were studied could have been compiled on the basis of title alone. (No effort was made to determine how the bibliographies were actually compiled; only the end result was available for the study.) A direct matching of citations to request titles thus seems to be a simpler and more effective approach to automatic bibliography compilation than does use of an intermediate system of subject headings.

4 Judgment of Relevance Based on Titles

The role which titles apparently play in both the indexing and retrieval of medical literature suggests that the following question is of critical importance: "To what extent can the relevance of a journal article to a given information requirement be judged on the basis of title alone?"

The importance of this question can be brought out most clearly if we consider some portion of an article which, though informative and significant, is not adequately described by the title of the article. If the indexer failed to read diligently beyond the title, the article would not be assigned subject headings relevant to the portion in question. Then, even if it were adequately indexed, it does not necessarily follow that the requester would conclude, from seeing the title alone, that the article was of sufficient probable interest to justify re-

trieving in its entirety. Most bibliographic citation lists that are generated either from using the *Index Medicus* or in response to a request for a specialized bibliography contain so many cited titles that the researcher probably does not have time to examine the full text of more than a small proportion of those cited.

The foregoing question is exceedingly difficult to answer, but a related project at Thompson Ramo Wooldridge Inc., RW Division, on the text searching of physics literature, provided valuable background material (1). This project on text searching included the development of a set of estimates of the relevance of each of one hundred physics articles to each of fifty questions, based on direct examination of the full text of the collection by experts in the subject matter. A similar estimate has been made in which only titles were made available for relevance estimates instead of the entire articles. Comparison of title relevance judgment with judgment based on full text examination indicates that titles are only about one-third effective (i.e., two-thirds of the relevant articles would be judged irrelevant) as a basis for estimating the relevance of the article to a given question. The estimate of one-third does not include "source documents" (Swanson, 1960) for which relevance estimates were over 90% accurate. (A "source document" is one which directly inspired the question and whose language might therefore have influenced the wording of the question.) Combining these two figures yields the conclusion that titles are about 50% effective in relevance judgment.

The study was carried out by examining the titles of each of one hundred articles in an experimental collection of physics documents with respect to each of fifty questions. Two persons, each knowledgeable in the subject matter but not familiar with the contents of the experimental library itself, made independent relevance estimates. These independent estimates were highly consistent with one another. The results may be summarized as follows. For the fifty questions tested, the average number of documents known to be relevant was four, of which the average number judged relevant through title inspection was two. The average number of irrelevant documents judged relevant on the basis of titles was also two. (One of the four relevant documents was always a "source document," as was in nearly all cases one of the two judged relevant on the basis of title.)

This title relevance study also included an analysis of why relevant information was judged irrelevant and why irrelevant information was judged relevant. The following salient features of the results are worth noting. In most cases of relevant information missed, the title did not adequately describe that portion of the article relevant to the question. The reason for such failure cannot be attributed to an inadequate title but simply to the fact that a title cannot possibly encompass the description of all aspects of the article from all points of view, and thus is necessarily limited as an information retrieval tool.

It was observed that 80% of the successful retrievals could also have been performed by a machine through a

TABLE 4. MATCH OF TERMS IN REQUEST TO THOSE IN CITED TITLES

Request (Concepts are indicated by italics.)	Number of Titles Containing Concepts Synonymous with Those Underlined in Request				
	3 Syn. Concepts	2 Syn. Concepts	1 Syn. Concept	No Syn. Concepts	Total Titles Listed in Bibliography
Alcoholism			78		78
Blood changes in *allergic children*	6	7	8		21
Effect of *smog* on *allergy*		1	12		13
Renal handling of *amino acids*		109			109
Effect of *polymixin* on *renal* function		4	21	3	28
Amyoplasia congenita			5		5
Amyotonia congenita			9	3	12
Amygdaloid nuclei			34	2	36
Effect of *morphine* and other *analgesics* on the *nervous system*		83	17		100
Pernicious anemia with *combined system disease*		70	36	13	119
Anesthesia for *neurosurgery*		44	1		45
Psychological aspects of *anesthesiology*		20	3		23
Congenital abdominal aortic aneurysm		21	4		25
Angioneurotic edema			36	5	41
Anorexia nervosa			134	3	137
Psychiatric aspects of *anorexia nervosa*		13	14	3	30
Anoxia			5	4	9
Hypersensitive reactions to *antibiotics*		10	54	5	69
Alterations of physiologic responses of *arteries* with *aging*		34	8		42
Arthrogryposis			26	1	27
Incidence of *asthma* after *removal* of *nasal polyps*		13			13
Atmosphere within *space capsule*		5	8	6	19
Possible *emotional roots* of *low back pain*		17	8	1	26
Fluid and electrolyte *absorption* through *bladder*		17	5	1	23
Current and new trends in the *treatment of bladder tumors*		14	1	1	16
Transurethral resection of bladder tumors		9	1		10
Blood groups in monkeys		6	2		8
Brain abscess with and without congenital heart disease, primarily in *infants*		6	21	1	28
Brain tumors in infants and children		75	1	1	77
Cancer prevention		83	7	1	91
Cannibalism			34	3	37
Carcinoid tumors of the small intestine		17	71	6	94
Cardiac changes with *aging*		17	6		23
Cardiac trauma		24	4		28
Psychoanalysis in *cardiovascular diseases*		20	4		24
Castration, castration complex, and castration anxiety			17	5	22
Carcinoma of the cervix during *pregnancy*	51	15	2		68
Conization in early diagnosis of *carcinoma of the cervix*	11	26	3		40
Incompetent cervix			28	4	32
Fetal salvage in *abruptio placentae* by *caesarian section*		3	58	8	69
Chondroitin sulfates			25	11	36
Psychiatric problems of *college students*		25	6		31
Lymphosarcoma of the *conjunctiva*		4	2		6
Corbiloculare			7		7
Corneal endothelium		73	16		89
Cortisone therapy of acute infections		7			7
Crying			51	5	56
Interpretive dance in *psychiatric treatment*		9	2	4	11
Delinquency as a *symptom*		3	16	4	23
Delirium			80	6	86
Delirium tremens			38	9	47
Depression in adolescents		10	10		20
Trauma and *diabetes*		11	2		13
Diabetes mellitus		26	37	11	74
Alloxan diabetes		20	2		22
Diets for *middle age disease of kidney, heart and liver*		3	18		21
Psychogenic causes of diarrhea		7	3		10
Psychogenic aspects of diarrhea		9	3		12
Effects of *alcohol and drugs* on *driving*		35	4		39
Monostatic fibrous dysplasia			14		14
Ego psychology		76	25		101
Ehlers-Danlos syndrome			35	3	38
Electrocardiogram near *death*		6			6
Electrocardiogram in the aged		16		1	17
Electrohysterography		16	9	3	28
Endocardial fibroelastosis			34	2	36
Enterocele			12	3	15
Rectocele			15		15
Enuresis			168	7	175
Breaking point of the *epiphyses*			19	1	20
Epiglottis			15		15
ABO incompatibility causing *erythroblastosis* in the *newborn*	14	23	6		43
Estrogenic hormones in the *blood*		27	21		48
Metabolism of ethyl alcohol		54	6		60
Toxicology of ethylene dichloride		11		2	13
Toxicology of methylene dichloride		10		2	12
Toxicity of ethylene oxide		10	9	1	20
Steroid treatment of endocrine exopthalmos		6	10	1	17
Experimental method in *science*		1	19	3	23
Design of experiments		6	1	12	19
Fetal electrocardiography in *animals*	11	5	3		19
Fetal electrocardiography		41	24	1	66
Filariasis			7	3	10
	93	1321	1560	171	3145

process of matching words in the retrieval questions to words in the title, taking proper account of synonyms. It was of interest, therefore, to analyze further those instances of successful retrieval in which no such word match was present. It was found in all of these cases that the requester's knowledge of physics permitted associations to be made which could not reasonably be incorporated in a thesaurus or synonym dictionary. For example, an article on total reflection of neutrons was successfully retrieved as being relevant to coherent scattering. This association is not related to the similarity of meaning between total reflection and coherent, but rather to those "facts of nature" which make total reflection under certain conditions a specific consequence of coherent scattering.

In about one-half of the instances of irrelevant associations, the article title contained one or two words in common with the search question, which made that article a reasonable candidate for being considered as possibly relevant to the question. In other cases, the subject matter, independently of word content, appeared closely enough related to the request to justify a conjecture of relevance.

This study suggests that indexing should be based on more than titles and that a bibliographic citation system should present to the requester something more than titles. Whether this additional presented information should take the form of an abstract, a portion of the text of the article, or a list of key words must be determined within the framework of a specific system.

5 Intellectual Aspects of Information Retrieval

In this study, the end product of a particular indexing system was examined and its characteristics described; conclusions are accordingly limited to that system. It may be suggested, though, that a more general investigation of indexing as an intellectual exercise might best proceed by first separating from it its obviously machine-like aspects, and then studying what remains. In the remaining portions, several questions are of crucial interest. Are human indexers both self-consistent and consistent with one another? If so, are they making choices consistent with effective retrieval of the indexed information? If the answer to both questions is "yes," then clearly the intellectual aspects of indexing are of much interest for further analysis. If the answer turns out to be "no," we might reasonably conclude that the only reliable and effective kind of human indexing is that which is already machine-like in nature. In that event, any major advance in the art of indexing must come about through a study of what people ought to be doing, rather than what they are doing.

Acknowledgments

A portion of this work was carried out under sponsorship of the Council on Library Resources, Washington, D.C.

The authors express appreciation to Dr. S. L. Kameny for assisting with the title relevance study.

Bibliography

1. Machine Indexing: Progress and Problems. 1961. Third Institute on Information Storage and Retrieval, The American University, Washington, D.C. See especially papers by H. Edmund Stiles (p. 192), M. E. Maron (p. 236), John O'Connor (p. 266), and Don R. Swanson (p. 281).
2. Swanson, D. R. 1960. Searching natural language text by computer. *Science*, **132:** 1099.

51 Imprecision in Meaning Measured by Inconsistency of Indexing

JOHN F. TINKER
American Documentation
Vol. 17, No. 2, April, 1966

1 Introduction

Personal indexes are satisfactory and comprehensible to those who prepared them (1), but usually cannot be easily used by others; that is, informal indexing from a personal viewpoint is an effective reminder to oneself, but not an effective means of communication. If this difficulty of communication were overcome, personal indexes collected from many individual experts would become a valuable tool, since they would capture much of the expertise of the individuals.

The work described here was undertaken to determine some of the problems involved in combining personal indexes of individuals who cannot work together closely enough to reach a common viewpoint to index consistently. Indeed, traditional methods of language control and arbitrary rules of precedence, imposed to improve indexing consistency, are antagonistic to creativity, which is a more important demand on these individuals.

The approach I have adopted is a simplification of an actual search for documents. In an actual search, the

Presented at the 31st Meeting of the International Federation for Documentation, Washington, D. C., October 1–16, 1965.

individual may remember a document faintly, or not at all, and may have in mind concepts only peripherally related to his lack of knowledge. In this work, we want to determine how the individual would search for a document in his personal index collection of abstracts, given a vivid memory of the document. We can make this determination if we assume that he will search under those index terms he applies to the abstract in indexing it. When we combine and compare the indexing done by many individuals, we gain some idea of the difficulty of transforming a set of reminders into a means of communication.

In taking this approach — that a personal index is the most valuable reflection of a creative scientist — we must relax the control of language and abandon judgment of correctness. Having welcomed the scientist as an indexer, we cannot stifle his expression nor veto his assignments. Our combined index must reflect actual usage of index terms, not hypothetical classification unrelated to the needs and thoughts of users. Our ultimate task is not to criticize or formalize the indexing done by the experts, but to assemble it into a tool of communication.

The indexing step has a large effect on the facility of the communication. The way in which the indexing information is displayed and the weight applied to each index term in retrieving documents will obviously influence the facility of communication, and consequently the utility of the index. However, even if these two factors were optimum, the utility of the index is still affected by the precision of the meaning of the indexing terms. Clearly a system with perfect display and optimum weighting factors is useless to someone who does not understand the meaning of the words that it uses.

Most information theorists seem to assume that meaning is perfectly precise; that is, they assume that concepts are lucidly embodied in documents, and that these concepts can be perceived and labeled with precision. To validate this assumption, they define or appoint a subject expert — someone whose duty it is to provide the standard indexing information. Invoking the subject expert is logically equivalent to the assumption that concepts in documents can be precisely labeled, at least by someone.

The concept of subject expert is unsatisfactory, both in practice and in theory. In practice, the available experts wish to restrict the area of their expertise to so narrow a speciality as to be nearly useless. Furthermore, no two subject experts agree, and neither is altogether comprehensible to the questioner. The indexer usually resorts to using himself as the subject expert, and to doing his best to explain his point of view to the questioner. Sometimes the point of view of the indexer is so foreign to the questioner that the latter will not attempt to use the index.[1]

As a practical expedient, the subject expert is not a useful addition to an information system. As a theoretical expedient, an average or abstraction of subject experts is not helpful either. We can do no better than assert that a subject expert is one who fulfills the assumption given above. Enough is known about the process of perception to make it most unlikely that a real person can fulfill that assumption.

In this paper, we adopt the point of view that a subject expert is neither necessary nor desirable, either as a part of an information system or as a standard of reference. We try to answer two questions: How precisely do ordinary people skilled in the subject perceive and label the concepts embodied in documents? Is this degree of precision such as to pose a difficult problem so severe as to make optimum weighting factors for index terms a minor improvement? In subsequent papers, I plan to investigate the improvement of communication between questioner and answerer as it is influenced by the content and layout of the index itself, always bearing in mind the precision with which the meaning of the indexing terms is understood by the questioners.

Hillman (2, 3) has shown that four factors enter into the definition of relevance: the question, the answer, a degree, and a corpus. The term "relevance" is ordinarily applied to define the relationship between two things, for instance, a question and answer. Many think that relevance either exists or does not exist. However, in many instances we must also admit to degrees of relevance. Out of the many possible answers to a question it is possible to say that some have a great deal of relevance, some less relevance, and others have little or no relevance. Hillman, in his paper, writes in terms of "concepts," suggesting that their interpretation depends on the field of knowledge (corpus) to which they are being applied. Hence, the field must be specified as a part of our definition of the relevance existing between two things. I should like to suggest that this expanded definition of relevance should also be applied to our consideration of words and their meanings. This is an intuitively agreeable course of action, since we are all aware of how a given word may have a number of meanings and of how the specific meaning applied to the word depends on the field of knowledge in which it is being used. I propose that meaning can be defined as the relevance of a word to the concept that it labels.[2] Therefore, if we are to specify the meaning of a word, we must also specify the four parameters suggested by Hillman's work: the word, the abstraction for which it is to stand, the degree of relevance that we wish to exist between the word and the abstraction, and the field of knowledge in which this word will be used.

How then can these ideas aid us to better understand the task of indexing? By assigning a descriptor[3] to a document, the indexer asserts that the descriptor has a high degree of relevance to the contents of the document; that is, he asserts that the meaning of the descriptor is strongly associated with a concept embodied in the document, and that it is appropriate for the subject area of the document. Let us assume that the indexers assign the descriptors in the order of the degree of relevance to the concepts, or that they assign all of the descriptors that they believe have a high degree of relevance. Then the consistency with which a given degree of relevance is associated with a given descriptor-concept pair will reflect the precision of the association strengths. Hence, consistency of indexing serves as a measure of the precision of meaning.[4]

Through measuring the consistency with which a term is applied to a concept, we are able to assess whether or not its meaning is understood with precision. By having a number of abstracts indexed by a number of people, it is possible to discover the consistency with which a given indexing term was used and, hence, how well the meaning of the term was understood.

---

[1] This is the situation of many organic chemists in regard to alphabetical indexes of chemical names.

[2] Harold Wooster suggests that meaning be defined as the degree of synonymy connecting a word and the concept it labels. However, I think it is clearer to use synonymy to name a relation between like things, e.g., one word has a degree of synonymy with another; and to use relevance to name a relation between unlike things, e.g., a word has a degree of relevance to a concept.

[3] In this paper, *descriptor* is used as a synonym for *index term* in accordance with popular usage, but at odds with its *formal definition*.

[4] For another approach to the measurement of the precision of meaning, see references 4 and 5.

2 Part I. Indexing Consistency with Free Choice of Descriptors

In Part I of the experiment, 15 indexers were asked to choose descriptors for 50 abstracts which had been chosen at random from a single abstract journal. The indexers were to select any words or phrases that they considered appropriate. They were not supplied with instructions for making the choice, a word list, or the definition. This resulted in a list of descriptors that contained 1,050 different words and phrases that had been applied to the 50 abstracts. Plural and singular forms of the same word were counted as a single descriptor. The diversity of the responses made it impossible to use these data to arrive at any estimate of the precision with which the descriptors were used. However, several interesting conclusions could be drawn from these data. An average of 3.6 descriptors was assigned by each indexer to each abstract. However, let us remember that the depth of indexing is not the same as the number of index terms applied. Depth of indexing is measured by that proportion of concepts embodied in the document to which index terms are applied. If a document is about two concepts only, the deepest indexing can apply only two terms to it. Conversely, if a UDC number six digits long is applied to a document that embodies a dozen concepts, only one index term is applied — not the six terms implicit in the six digits — and the indexing is shallow. To determine the absolute depth of indexing for the documents used here, an absolute judgment of the number of concepts embodied in each document would be needed. Since we have avoided absolute judgment, we cannot make this calculation. To estimate this number of concepts by taking the consensus of the indexers, we needed the opinion of each indexer regarding the generic relations among the terms he applied — the degree to which each term implies or includes every other term. These opinions, rather difficult to form, were not determined. Consequently, we cannot estimate the depth of indexing and can only guess that it probably is not very deep.

Of the 1,050 descriptors chosen, only 48% of these were actual words or phrases that appeared in the abstract or the title. The indexers apparently found the language used by the author in the abstract inadequate for describing the work performed. As might be expected, a greater number of descriptors were applied to longer abstracts.

CHANCE OF RETRIEVAL

The descriptors assigned by the indexers to the subjects covered in an abstract can be considered to be the search program they would first formulate if they were attempting to find information on those subjects. The probability that the search devised by an average indexer would contain at least one descriptor in common with those chosen for a given abstract by all other indexers participating is given in Equation 1, where C_j is the chance of

Equation 1

$$C_j \, (\%) = \frac{\sum\limits_{i=1}^{i=m} (X_{ij})^2 \quad 2 \leq x \leq n}{\left[\sum\limits_{i=1}^{i=m} X_{ij} \right]^2 \quad 1 \leq x \leq n} \times 100$$

EQUATION 1. Chance of Retrieval for Abstract j, C_j.

retrieval for abstract j, expressed in per cent, X_{ij} is the number of times the descriptor i was applied to the abstract j; n is the number of indexers; and m is the number of descriptors. This new measure of the chance for retrieval is necessary because existing measures of efficiency include a term which requires a judgment of the pertinence of the descriptor choice. No such judgment was made in dealing with these data.

If each indexer applies different descriptors to an abstract, the chance of retrieval is zero; if each indexer applies the same descriptors, the chance of retrieval is 100%. Nearly 62% of the descriptors were used only once; consequently, the chance of retrieval was low, varying from 1.5% to 12%, averaging 6.5%. This I consider to be a good estimate of the success of any initial search if it is made by a searcher familiar with, but not knowledgeable in, the special field of the search and if the searcher is not given indexing aids or the advice of subject experts. The chance of retrieval showed no correlation with the number of words in the title and in the text of the abstract. Of the approximately 1,050 descriptors used, 1%, or 10 words, accounted for 30% of the descriptor-abstract pairs and 2.2% of the descriptors accounted for half of the pairs.

This suggests that a much smaller number of descriptors would be almost as effective for describing these abstracts as the 1,050 actually used. The value of the chance of retrieval for each abstract was plotted versus the number of descriptors chosen for the abstract. The least-squares straight line showed a negative correlation, significant at 99% level. I conclude that, under the condition of free choice of descriptors, the greater the number of descriptors applied, the more difficult is the retrieval.

Some control of the indexing language is obviously the next step in our attempt to eliminate all the variables and measure only the precision of the meaning of the words — the precision with which indexers and questioners knowledgeable in the subject can perceive and label concepts embodied in documents. One possible mode of control would be to restrict the indexing language to that appearing in the documents. There are several objections to this procedure. First, it is not drastic enough. When one attempts to eliminate an undesired variable from a measurement, the best initial strategy is to give the undesired variable two extreme values. In this case, wishing to measure the precision of meaning independently of choice of language, we first give great freedom, then highly restrict choice of language. Free to use the language of the documents, the indexers can still use nearly half of the descriptors. As we shall see, a cut to 10% is not too drastic.

A second objection to the procedure of restricting the language of description to that of the documents arises from the particular document set used. Although many of the abstracts were written by the original authors, many were not. The language in the latter is not that of the author. Thus, we cannot restrict the indexer to the language used by the author. Furthermore, what we wish to estimate is the precision with which the indexer understands the meaning of the words, not the facility with which he picks out the author's words. In forcing the indexer to use any language but his own, we introduce an additional uncontrolled variable into our measurement. Finally, the author's language is not an optimum choice to reach conditions of maximum precision in meaning, because there is no reason to believe that authors use words more precisely than indexers do.

It seems best to begin with the list of freely chosen descriptors, for these represent the natural expression of the group of indexers, if not of each individual indexer. In restricting the list, we can make no "intelligent" choice, for to do so is to reintroduce the subject expert, whose influence we wish to avoid. The list should, then, be drastically reduced in size in an arbitrary way. The list was cut to one-tenth, using a random selection so arranged that terms used by many indexers are more likely to be retained. Chosen in this way, the final list resembles more closely the list used by each individual indexer than would be the case if the list were culled at random without consideration of the frequency of use of the terms.

To examine the effect of reducing the number of descriptors on the chances of retrieval, a small set of descriptors was chosen from the total list of 1,050. Descriptors were chosen for this set by first giving a weight to each descriptor — a weight representing, not its probable utility in retrieval, but the frequency with which it was applied by the indexers. Numbers from 1 to 2,180 were assigned to each descriptor each time it was applied, so that a given descriptor that was applied to 30 abstracts might receive the numbers 1–30 or 70–99, whereas a descriptor that was applied only once would be given only a single number. Numbers were then taken from a random number table (6) and matched against the numbers assigned to the descriptors until a set of 100 descriptors was chosen. This set of descriptors was then compared with our original descriptor-abstract data to find how many times each descriptor in the set of 100 had been applied to the 50 abstracts by the original 15 indexers. We then substituted this new frequency data in Equation 1 to find how restricting the number of descriptors had

affected the chance of retrieval of each abstract. This chance of retrieval is the probability that the first search program would succeed if only the descriptors in the selected list of 100 were used. This chance varied from 0 to 100%, averaging 36%. When the selected vocabulary was used to calculate the chance of retrieval, the correlation with the number of descriptors applied rose to a small positive value, indicating no correlation. That is, the disadvantage of assigning many descriptors to a document, without control of choice, was overcome by restricting the choice of descriptors used in searching (Table 1).

3 Part II. Indexing Consistency with Restricted Choice of Descriptors

In Part II of the experiment, the same 50 abstracts, rearranged in a random fashion, were sent to 9 indexers, all of whom were among the original 15 indexers. These indexers were now supplied with the randomly chosen list of 100 descriptors and requested to apply these to the abstracts. For several of the abstracts, no adequate descriptors appeared in the list; consequently, the subjects were asked whether or not they considered the descriptors they had chosen for each abstract to constitute an adequate description. This opinion showed no correlation with the average number of descriptors chosen, and none with the chance of retrieval.

Restricting the choice of descriptors results in a marked increase in the consistency (7, 8, 9) with which they are applied. In Part I, no descriptor was applied to any abstract by all of the indexers, whereas in Part II, 19 of the descriptors were applied by all of the indexers. However, of these 19 only 6 were applied with perfect consistency; that is, they were either applied 9 times or not at all. The other 13 descriptors were applied consistently to certain abstracts by all indexers but inconsistently to other abstracts. Of the 100 descriptors, 15 describe con-

TABLE 1. Relation of the number of descriptors used for retrieval to retrieval chance and to the correlation of retrieval chance with the number of descriptors assigned to an abstract.

Number of Descriptors Used		Chance of Retrieval, %			Correlation	
		Min.	Max.	Aver.	Z Value	Significant
Part I	1000	1.5	12	6.5	−0.51	Yes
	100	0	100	36	+0.04	No
Part II	100	9.8	56	22	−0.73	Yes
	50	0	67	33	−0.52	Yes
	25	0	100	48	−0.35	Yes
	12	0	100	45	−0.13	No
	6	0	100	23	+0.27	No
Part III	45	8.4	15	12	+0.03	No
	22	14	18	16	+0.17	No
	11	19	91	37	+0.27	No
	6	37	44	41	−0.19	No

cepts that were unknown only a few years ago. Five of these new words, or 33% of them, were among the 19 most precise descriptors, while only 16% of the older words were used precisely. It would be interesting to know if new concepts are understood more precisely than older ones as suggested by these data.

Twelve of the 100 descriptors on the list were used in 34% of the descriptor-abstract pairs. Of these often-used descriptors, only 1 (or 75%) was new. The other 11 descriptors, or 13% of the total, were older words. This suggests that descriptors for older concepts tend to be used more frequently.

The chance of retrieval was calculated for each abstract by means of Equation 1. It varied from 9.8% to 56%, averaging 22%, a substantial improvement over Part I. The correlation of the chance of retrieval with the number of descriptors assigned to the abstract was again strong and negative. Smaller sets of descriptors were chosen from the list of 100 by using the weighting method described in Part I. Sets of 50, 25, 12, and 6 descriptors were chosen. Each set was then used to calculate the chance of retrieval for each abstract with the results shown in Table 1, and graphically in Fig. 1. Again, restricting the number of descriptors excludes the possibility of retrieving some of the abstracts, i.e., the chance of retrieval is 0, but it increases the average chance of retrieval for the sets of 50 and 25 descriptors (dashed curve). However, with the sets of 12 and 6 descriptors, more and more abstracts are irretrievable and the average chance of retrieval diminishes. The correlation between chance of retrieval for a particular abstract and the number of descriptors applied to the abstract is strongly negative for the largest three sets of descriptors (100, 50, 25) and insignificant for the smallest two sets.

4 Part III. Indexing Consistency with Many Indexers

For the third part of the experiment 21 abstracts were selected. Each abstract was one about which there had

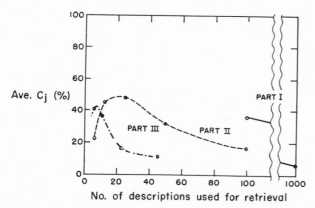

FIG. 1. Relation of the number of descriptors used in retrieval with the average chance of retrieval.

been substantial disagreement among the indexers as to whether descriptors assigned from the list of 100 adequately described the abstract or not. From these 21, the abstracts were chosen that required the use of "new" descriptors; i.e., terms that have been added to the technical vocabulary during the last few years. This eliminated all but 8, and from these 5 were selected at random. The descriptor set made up for these abstracts consisted of all the descriptors that had been assigned to these abstracts by indexers in Part II. This required 28 descriptors. Seventeen additional descriptors were then chosen from the Part II set at random by using the weighting procedure already described to compile a list of 45 descriptors. The abstracts and descriptors were sent to several hundred indexers with backgrounds similar to those of the indexers used in the first two parts of this experiment. Each indexer was asked to assign descriptors from the list of 45 to each of the 5 abstracts and to indicate whether or not they considered the descriptors chosen adequately described the abstracts.

Three hundred and twenty-three indexers responded. There were several differences between the results of Part II and those of Part III and the conclusions that could be drawn from them. The chance of retrieval in Part III was lower than that in Part II; the larger number of indexers had a greater difference of opinion, lowering the chance of retrieval. The correlation of chance of retrieval with the number of descriptors assigned per abstract is insignificant — probably a consequence of the drastic reduction in the number of abstracts. The 12 descriptors most often used accounted for 59.5% of the total number, or nearly twice the fraction of Part II. Of these, 6 were new and 4 showed good precision. The difference in usage of new words and the tendency to use new words less precisely than old words fail to appear in Part III, probably because the particular abstracts were chosen to include frequent use of new words.

No descriptor was used in Part III with perfect precision. The best four descriptors (lead monoxide, modulation transfer function, phase modulation, nuclear reactors) were used by 96%, 93%, 88%, and 85% of the indexers, respectively, for one of the 5 abstracts, and none of the indexers applied any of these terms to more than a single abstract.

The typical graph shown in Fig. 2 shows how "lead monoxide" was handled in each of the three parts of this experiment. As we have already noted, the descriptor was applied in Part III to one of the 5 abstracts by 96% of the indexers and was not applied to any of the other 4 abstracts by any of the 323 indexers. This is shown by the graph labeled "Part III" in Fig. 2. In Part II in which 9 indexers were asked to index 50 abstracts using a list of 100 terms, "lead monoxide" was applied to one abstract by 67% of the indexers and to a second by 78%. None of the indexers applied this term to any of the other 48 abstracts. In Part I in which 15 indexers were asked to index the same 50 abstracts, but without the aid of a descriptor list, the term was applied by 53% of the

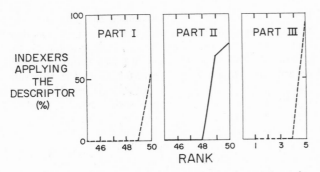

FIG. 2. Graphs illustrating the precision of meaning of "lead monoxide."

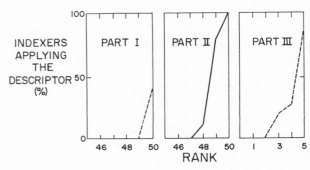

FIG. 4. Graphs illustrating the precision of meaning of "electrophotographic plates."

indexers to a single abstract and it was not applied to any other abstract by any of the indexers.

At this point, it is interesting to observe the behavior of the indexers with respect to some of the other terms. Fig. 3 shows how the term "data processing" was applied. Note the perfect precision in the graph of Part II with which this descriptor was applied. However, in Part I the term was applied by far fewer indexers when they were required to supply the term rather than to assign the term from a list. In Part III, for some reason, the term was applied somewhat less frequently to the one abstract (i.e., less frequently than in Part II), but more frequently to two of the other abstracts. Since the population of indexers is so small in Part II, the results in Part III probably express more accurately the precision with which this term is applied or understood.

An objection might be raised that, although the meaning of a word may be perfectly understood by an indexer, he might fail to apply the word because he considers it useless for retrieval of the particular abstract. This objection is specious: the distinction is too fine to influence the results of this experiment. That is, for the purposes of this experiment, the following statement was taken as a tautology: The word that stands for a concept is useful in retrieving an abstract treating that concept. The terms "lead monoxide" and "data processing" can be used to illustrate this point of view. If a given term is applied to a specific abstract by a large number of indexers, it is fair to say that those who do not apply the term do not

fully understand its meaning. Hence, we can say that the consistency with which a term is applied by a large number of indexers is a good measure of how well that term is actually understood.

Next, an attempt was made to discover whether or not a group of indexers who used one term with precision used other terms with equal precision. To do this, the term "electrophotographic plates" was selected because it had been used throughout the experiment with average precision. Fig. 4 shows how this term was applied to a single abstract by 88% of the indexers. We now reject the 12% of the indexer population that failed to apply the term to abstract 5, and an additional 34% minority who applied it to two other abstracts. By examining how the remaining 54% (174 indexers) applied other terms, we can gain some understanding of whether or not a population that is consistent in its use of a given term is also consistent in its use of other terms. Fig. 5 shows how the term "conductivity" was handled in the three phases of the experiment. The right-hand graph shows how the selected group of 174 indexers applied "conductivity" to the 5 abstracts used in Part III. We note that the selected group, who had been consistent in the application of the term "electrophotographic plates," is not consistent in its application of the term "conductivity." If this same procedure is applied to other pairs of terms, we always find this behavior, i.e., that a given term is applied consistently by a group of indexers is no guarantee that the group will apply some other term with equal consistency.

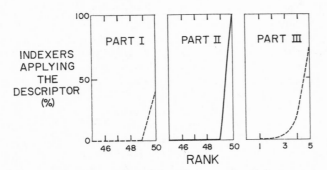

FIG. 3. Graphs illustrating the precision of meaning of "data processing."

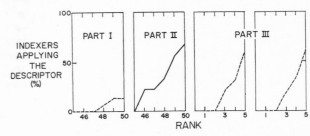

FIG. 5. Graphs illustrating the precision of meaning of "conductivity." The graph on the extreme right shows the results in Part III, with all assignments deleted for indexers who disagree on "electrophotographic plates."

Evaluation of Information Systems

Summary

In Part I of the experiment, 15 indexers chose descriptors for 50 abstracts with no restrictions on the choice of descriptors or on the language with which they were expressed. Many descriptors were chosen, although only a moderate depth of indexing (3.6 descriptors per abstract) resulted. Only about half of the descriptors matched words or phrases of the abstracts. A new measure of retrieval efficiency was needed because no judgment of correctness of the indexing was made. The chance that at least one descriptor applied by one indexer would match the descriptors applied by all the other indexers, the chance of retrieval, was calculated. For the 50 abstracts the average chance of retrieval is 6.5%. The average chance of retrieval rose to 36% (nearly six times as high) when calculated using data from a selected list of 100 terms. In Part I, even though the field of knowledge (corpus) and the concepts embodied in the abstracts were controlled, the consistency of indexing was low. The variety of expressions used for an identical or closely related concept frustrated the attempt to relate precision of meaning to indexing consistency.

In Part II, 9 of the same indexers applied descriptors to the same 50 abstracts, using only the 100 selected terms. The consistency of application increased markedly, and 6 of the terms were used with perfect precision. The chance of retrieval averaged 22%. When an even smaller selected list of descriptors (25) was used, the chance of retrieval rose to a maximum of 48%.

Most descriptors were used imprecisely. Since meaning is defined in terms of the relevance of a word to the concept it labels, descriptors will be imprecisely applied if any one of four factors (the field of knowledge, the concepts, the words, or the degree of relevance) is not controlled. All indexers must have a common understanding of the concepts used in a given corpus of knowledge and the words to be associated with these concepts. They must also have a common understanding of the degree of association (relevance) that exists between a word and the concept for which it stands. Analyses of the results show that three of these factors (field of knowledge, the concepts, and the words) were adequately controlled under the conditions of this experiment. However, because only 9 indexers were used, the degree of relevance cannot be measured with a high degree of confidence. Hence, a larger group of indexers was used in Part III in order to demonstrate more fully the connection between precision of meaning and consistency of indexing.

In Part III of the experiment, 323 indexers applied 45 selected descriptors to 5 abstracts. The consistency of application decreased and the chance of retrieval averaged 16%. Using fewer descriptors from this list raised the chance of retrieval. Graphs, in which the fraction of indexers applying a given descriptor to the abstract was plotted versus the abstracts and ranked so that the highest ranking abstract had the greatest fraction of indexers applying the particular descriptor, illustrate the precision with which the descriptor is used. None of the descriptors in Part III was used with perfect precision. Furthermore, it was shown that precision in the use of one term did not imply that the same indexer would use other terms with precision.

In the experiment, the field of knowledge was constant and well defined, the terms were kept constant, and the concepts embodied in the abstracts were kept constant. Nonetheless, perfect consistency was not obtained. Obviously, a fourth variable is present. I conclude that meaning can be defined as the relevance of a word to the concept it labels, and that the degree of relevance, as it is understood by the various indexers, is the most important variable accounting for these results.

It is clear that the meaning of words is not understood precisely, even when the words labeling scientific concepts are used by competent scientists in their own field of knowledge.[5] Any aid (thesaurus) or procedure(multiple indexing, personal contact) that helps to increase the precision of meaning among a particular group can be expected to increase the effectiveness with which they exchange information. To make an excellent index means must be found that will allow good communication by means of words which are inherently imprecise.

References

1. MARTYN, J. 1964. Literature Searching by Research Scientists. Aslib Res. Dept. 3 pp.
2. HILLMAN, D. J. On Concept — Formation and Relevance. *Proc. Am. Doc. Inst. Meeting, October 5–8. 1964.* Vol. **1**: 23–29.
3. HILLMAN, D. J. 1964. The Notion of Relevance. *Am. Doc.,* **15** (1) : 26–34.
4. OSGOOD, C. E., SUCI, G. J., and TANNENBAUM, P. H. 1957. *The Measurement of Meaning.* Univ. of Ill. Press, Urbana, Ill.
5. FORSTER, K. I., TRIANDIS, H. C., and OSGOOD, C. E. 1964. *An Analysis of the Method of Triads in Research on the Measurement of Meaning.* Tech. Report No. 17, June. AD 603 944. Dept. of Psychology, Univ. of Ill., Urbana, Ill.
6. RAND CORPORATION. 1955. *A Million Random Digits with 100,000 Normal Deviates.* Free Press, Glencoe, Ill.
7. JACOBY, J., and SLAMECKA, V. 1962. *Indexer Consistency Under Minimal Conditions.* November. AD 288 087.
8. SLAMECKA, V. *Final Report, Indexing Aids.* 1963. January. AD 294 859.
9. BORKO, H. 1961. *A Research Plan for Evaluating the Effectiveness of Various Indexing Systems.* July. AD 278 624.
10. CHAPANIS, A. 1965. Color Names for Color Space. *Am. Scientist,* September, pp. 327–346.

[5] A similar suggestion has been made by Alphonse Chapanis in reference 10.

52 Imprecision in Indexing (Part II)

JOHN F. TINKER
American Documentation
Vol. 19, No. 3, July 1968

1 Introduction

In Part I (*1*) we discussed the inherent imprecision of language and the problems of indexing related to this fact. The point, in that paper, was not to find how to bring indexers into agreement on the meaning of a word, but rather to discover how much disagreement in meaning exists among technical workers whose primary job is not indexing. The results suggested that a drastic reduction in the number of allowed indexing terms would increase the precision with which the terms would be used.

However, a limited and inflexible set of indexing terms has serious disadvantages. New concepts cannot be described when the labels are not available and none can be added. Even if adding of labels is allowed, the addition process tends to be slow and difficult. Furthermore, a small set of indexing terms is limited in the richness of description it is capable of. Clearly, limiting the choice of indexing terms to a small set is unsatisfactory.

Instead of the absolute constraint of the indexers' "You must use these terms," we might impose the lesser constraint, "You must begin with these terms." This paper is an investigation of this idea; the indexer was required to choose broad terms for a short list, then freely assigned modifiers to the terms, so that the combination of terms and modifiers described the document and distinguished it from the others in the file.

Each of the resulting sets of terms and modifiers was subjected to a display program which produced a format that resembles the entries in a conventional book index, in which a limited number of principal terms are arranged alphabetically. To each principal term was added a series of phrases that makes its meaning more specific and descriptive. Therefore, computer programs were required that would produce a display, or listing, that showed at each index point all of the sets of terms and modifiers that had been applied to a document, regardless of the length or number of the words.

This report describes the display needed to make such index information useful in manual searching, a computer system to produce the display, application of this indexing system to chemical structure, and finally application to general literature.

2 Design of Listing Programs

The design parameters for the listing program are these:

1. The structure of a chemical will be represented by a series of descriptors, which, in this case, will be words

We wish to thank Mr. F. W. White, of these Laboratories, for his collaboration in the design of the system; D. Barton and H. Bewicke, for writing the computer programs; and T. H. Higgins, for further programing assistance.

or phrases based on traditional chemical nomenclature, and a series of modifiers will be attached to each descriptor.

2. All descriptors and modifiers must appear in a dictionary that controls the acceptance of descriptors and modifiers and governs the order of entries in the final listing.

3. A descriptor or modifier may be of any length and may be composed of any number of words. The order in which the descriptors are displayed in the listing must be completely controllable; i.e., the order of the index is completely subject to the discretion of the person managing the index.

4. The maximum number of descriptors per chemical, or of modifiers per descriptor, must be flexible.

The third parameter is required because of the traditional division of opinion regarding the order of classes. Is it best to display the index in some classificatory arrangement, or is a purely alphabetical arrangement better? Would a mixture of logical grouping and alphabetization give the most lucid display? Clearly, a different order may be required for a different job; the best specification for the program, therefore, is that the order of entries in the index be given by the manager, instead of being fixed. To achieve this flexibility, a dictionary containing each valid term, whether it is a class name, a descriptor, or a modifier, will be created. The order of the final index listing will then be controlled by the order in the dictionary.

3 Chemical Structure

Figure 1 illustrates how the dictionary is used to classify chemicals. Valid descriptors or modifiers are followed by a period; notes or explanatory phrases are shown in parentheses.

The manager who arranged the dictionary (Fig. 1) has chosen to subdivide a class, *heterocyclic compounds*, into *nitrogen heterocycles* and *oxygen heterocycles*. These two labels of smaller classes will be modifiers of the principal class. The next important aspect of this class, he has decided, is the name of the heterocycle. The order in which the names appear need not be alphabetical; the arrangement may be any one that the manager thinks is desirable. For instance, the 6-membered-2-nitrogen ring *pyrimidine* might be first, then the 5-membered-2-nitrogen ring *imidazole*. Two oxygen heterocycles follow. Other descriptors, signifying groups of interest, follow. The last descriptor in Fig. 1 is a single blank (explained on the display by the parenthetical expression). The blank is needed to satisfy a program check that every compound have at least three descriptors; if three are not actually needed to describe the structure, the blank is used. This stratagem was included to avoid accidental omission of descriptors and to allow the program to perform this simple editorial check automatically.

Each word used as a descriptor or a modifier must appear in the dictionary, because the order of a word relative to other words is governed by its position in the dictionary. A word, if omitted from the dictionary, is rejected. Errors from misspellings and inconsistent choice of terms can be controlled by this means. For present purposes, all the words are put into the dictionary after editorial review.

The terms may include blanks but not periods or the special symbol, the commercial *at* sign. The latter, for instance, in the words *antifoggant sensitized@emulsions* is a program format signal. When this term is printed in the index lists, in which a line holds only 25 characters of a term, all the characters after the symbol will be printed on the next line, flush to the right of the print line, so as not to be mistaken for another term.

The first assumption made by the designers of the listing system was that computer collation would not put chemical terms in a suitable order. Even this small

DESCRIPTORS	MODIFIERS
Heterocyclic Compounds.	Nitrogen Heterocycles.
	Oxygen Heterocycles.
Pyrimidine.	Dihydro.
Imidazole.	Tetrahydro.
Pyran.	Perhydro.
Pyrillium.	
2-Oxo.	1,3-Dimethyl.
	1,3-Diethyl.
	1,3-Bis(2-hydroxyethyl).
2-Thiono	1,3-Bis(dimethylaminopropyl).
.(Single Blank)	5-Hydroxy.

FIG. 1. Sample dictionary of chemical descriptors and modifiers

sample shows that character-for-character sorting will not achieve a sensible order for a dictionary of chemical terms. Two difficulties are apparent: the terms are of varying length, indefinitely long (the program accepts terms up to 130 characters in length); and the special characters, which cannot be left out of the terms, influence the sorting order in a way difficult to understand. It is difficult to devise an alogrithm that allows the sorting process to ignore characters that should be ignored in traditional alphabetization of chemicals.[1] For instance, 1,3-*dimethyl* is alphabetized under *M*, *dimethylaminopropyl* under *D*, and *1,3-bis(dimethylaminopropyl)* under *B*. Using a flexible listing order that can be specified for the index solves the ordering problem in this system; editorial work is, of course, a consequence. The advantage of flexibility in the face of a difficult problem was considered sufficient justification for this effort.

The second basic assumption, that descriptors and modifiers can reflect chemical structure effectively, is supported by Fig. 2. The first column of the figure contains the identification number of the chemical. The subsequent columns contain descriptor modifier groups.

Notice the lucidity of the description. For the simple compounds of Fig. 2, the description is nearly identical with the name. More complicated chemicals can be described in this manner much more clearly than by naming them. The descriptor-modifier description is nearly as good as the structure and easier to hold and manipulate in binary form. The general structure representing all four compounds (among others) is shown in Fig. 3; it is relatively enigmatic.

The order of the compounds in Fig. 2 is controlled by the order of words in the display, Fig. 1. The first descriptor (principal descriptor, or class name) is identical for all four compounds, as is its modifier. The next descriptor, which is the next arrangement criterion, is *pyrimidine* for the first three. Compound 604 is last, because *imidazole* comes after *pyrimidine* in Fig. 1.

The listing program has been used successfully to prepare an index to several groups of compounds. Physical properties and test data can be added to the right of the

[1] See, for example, the introduction to the subject index to Vol. 56 of *Chemical Abstracts* (1962).

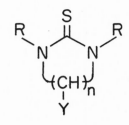

Where R is alkyl, hydroxyalkyl, or
tert - aminoalkyl
Y is hydrogen or hydroxyl;
n is 2 or 3

FIG. 3. Markush structure for a chemical class

descriptors and modifiers. A form of the listing can be produced in which the order is controlled by the value of a data field.

We have used two modifications of the listing program: single- and multiple-entry listings have been produced. The single-entry type lists a compound only once. For example, the listing in Fig. 2 represents the only entry for the four compounds. The first compound in Fig. 2 illustrates how the description of the compound, in the single-entry version, begins at a general level (*heterocyclic compounds*), proceeds stepwise to a specific level (*nitrogen heterocycles, pyrimidine, perhydro*), then shifts to another facet, functional groups (*2-thiono, 5-hydroxyl, 1,3-dimethyl*). The multiple-entry type lists a single compound several times. Figure 4 is one version of the multiple-entry list for four compounds of Fig. 2. The control of the order by the dictionary of Fig. 1 is apparent.

4 Problems of Inconsistency

Neither of these versions can overcome the bad effects of inconsistency in indexing. The single-entry version is a classical classification system with mutually exclusive

836	HETEROCYCLIC COMPOUNDS NITROGEN HETEROCYCLES	PYRIMIDINE PERHYDRO	2-THIONO 5-HYDROXY 1,3-DIMETHYL
639	HETEROCYCLIC COMPOUNDS NITROGEN HETEROCYCLES	PYRIMIDINE PERHYDRO	2-THIONO 5-HYDROXY 1,3-BIS(2-HYDROXYETHYL)
453	HETEROCYCLIC COMPOUNDS NITROGEN HETEROCYCLES	PYRIMIDINE PERHYDRO	2-THIONO 5-HYDROXY 1,3-BIS(DIMETHYLAMINOPROPYL)
604	HETEROCYCLIC COMPOUNDS NITROGEN HETEROCYCLES	IMIDAZOLE PERHYDRO	2-THIONO 1,3-BIS(2-HYDROXYETHYL)

FIG. 2. Sample descriptor-modifier index of chemicals, single entry

836	HETEROCYCLIC COMPOUNDS NITROGEN HETEROCYCLES	PYRIMIDINE PERHYDRO	2-THIONO 5-HYDROXY 1,3-DIMETHYL
639	HETEROCYCLIC COMPOUNDS NITROGEN HETEROCYCLES	PYRIMIDINE PERHYDRO	2-THIONO 5-HYDROXY 1,3-BIS(2-HYDROXYETHYL)
453	HETEROCYCLIC COMPOUNDS NITROGEN HETEROCYCLES	PYRIMIDINE PERHYDRO	2-THIONO 5-HYDROXY 1,3-BIS(DIMETHYLAMINOPROPYL)
604	HETEROCYCLIC COMPOUNDS NITROGEN HETEROCYCLES	IMIDAZOLE PERHYDRO	2-THIONO 1,3-BIS(2-HYDROXYETHYL)
836	PYRIMIDINE PERHYDRO	2-THIONO 5-HYDROXY 1,3-DIMETHYL	HETEROCYCLIC COMPOUNDS NITROGEN HETEROCYCLES
639	PYRIMIDINE PERHYDRO	2-THIONO 5-HYDROXY 1,3-BIS(2-HYDROXYETHYL)	HETEROCYCLIC COMPOUNDS NITROGEN HETEROCYCLES
453	PYRIMIDINE PERHYDRO	2-THIONO 5-HYDROXY 1,3-BIS(DIMETHYLAMINO- PROPYL)	HETEROCYCLIC COMPOUNDS NITROGEN HETEROCYCLES
604	IMIDAZOLE PERHYDRO	2-THIONO 1,3-BIS(2-HYDROXYETHYL)	HETEROCYCLIC COMPOUNDS NITROGEN HETEROCYCLES
836	2-THIONO 5-HYDROXY 1,3-DIMETHYL	HETEROCYCLIC COMPOUNDS NITROGEN HETEROCYCLES	PYRIMIDINE PERHYDRO
639	2-THIONO 5-HYDROXY 1,3-BIS(2-HYDROXYETHYL)	HETEROCYCLIC COMPOUNDS NITROGEN HETEROCYCLES	PYRIMIDINE PERHYDRO
453	2-THIONO 5-HYDROXY 1,3-BIS(DIMETHYLAMINOPROPYL)	HETEROCYCLIC COMPOUNDS NITROGEN HETEROCYCLES	PYRIMIDINE PERHYDRO
604	2-THIONO 1,3-BIS(2-HYDROXYETHYL)	HETEROCYCLIC COMPOUNDS NITROGEN HETEROCYCLES	IMIDAZOLE PERHYDRO

FIG. 4. Sample descriptor-modifier index of chemicals, multiple entry

classes. Although the list can be arranged alphabetically or logically by changing the order of descriptors and modifiers in the dictionary, the subdivision of chemicals by the terms is a classification and entails all the disadvantages inherent in classifying. Hence, any failure to apply an appropriate descriptor, or the use of an inappropriate descriptor, will change the position of the entry in the index. Thus inconsistency in indexing results in dispersion in the index. That is, an item can be found in some area (not a point) with some probability (not a certainty).

The location in the listing of a compound depends on the descriptors and modifiers used to represent the structure and on their order. To increase consistency in the choice and order of terms for a compound, both program checks and indexing conventions are needed. The program checks ensure that the terms are properly spelled, eliminating scatter due to misspelling. Another check makes certain that the order of descriptors within every compound is consistent. Descriptors for a compound must be cited in the order in which they appear in the dictionary. If compound 836 of Fig. 2 were indexed *Heterocyclic compounds, nitrogen heterocycles; 2-Thiono, 5-hydroxy, 1,3-dimethyl; Pyrimidine, perhydro*, the program would

reject it because *2-Thiono* comes after *Pyrimidine* in the dictionary (Fig. 1).

The program checks ensure the correct order of descriptors for a compound but not the order of modifiers for a descriptor. This decision was made because it is sometimes useful to illustrate the order of connections in a substituent group by a series of modifiers instead of a single complicated modifier. The modifier *6-(2-(2-bromopyridyl)ethyl)* can be replaced by the simpler set of three modifiers, *6-ethyl, 2-pyridyl, 2-bromo*. The order now reflects the structure, and the three modifiers cannot be rearranged to follow the dictionary order. Therefore, rules have been established to guide the indexers and searchers in choosing the modifiers and ordering them correctly. In this system, as in more conventional systems, these rules are the principal control of inconsistency.

The multiple-entry version, in which a compound appears in several places in the list, gives more convenient access from various points of view. In the multiple-entry version, one can easily find all compounds to which any descriptor is applied, for instance *2-thiono*, as Fig. 2 shows. The influence of inconsistency has not been lessened by multiplying the paths of approach. However, a searcher may find the multiple-entry list more effective for two reasons. A particular query may have answers that are less scattered from one point of view than from the others. Then, he may have a better understanding of the decision rules that the indexer has applied along one path of approach than he does along others. These advantages must be balanced against the increased cost and size of a multiple-entry listing.

Applied to a restricted class of chemicals, with carefully formulated rules for applying descriptors and modifiers, this indexing system is successful in illustrating the structure of a compound and in collecting similar structures. We were encouraged by this success to attempt to apply the system, with less rigid rules, to different types of subject areas, including journal literature. The index to a sample of literature of photographic science was much less useful than the index to a class of chemicals, and we consider it a poor choice for a general finding key. The data that led to this opinion are of interest and point up the difference in retrieval characteristics that result from replacing a single contributor and rigid but restrictive editorial rules with many contributors and flexible rules.

In one experiment a random selection of 13 abstracts of articles in the field of photographic science was sent to 19 indexers. As in Part I(1), these people were knowledgeable in the field and were potential searchers; but they were not trained indexers. Their indexing of an abstract can be taken to represent the initial formulation of a search strategy designed to locate the abstract. The indexers were given an authority list of only 34 terms, which together form a classification of photographic science. They were asked to choose descriptors from this list and freely add modifiers. The 13 indexers used a total of 425 modifiers. They applied to each abstract an average of 7 terms (2.4 descriptors and 4.6 modifiers).

The first step of the experiment was to process this indexing information through the computer, correcting mistakes and arranging the dictionary for best effect.

Part of the dictionary, which contains both descriptors and modifiers, is shown in Fig. 5. As before, a period is used to denote the end of a term, and the *at* sign indicates the position within a word to shift to the next line, i.e., it is a format symbol. The arrangement of the dictionary is alphabetical, with some exceptions. For in-

```
                    DICTIONARY OF DATE   AUG  7 1967        PAGE   1

  WORD-#   PD USE   WORD                                          NOTES


  00001    NO         •
  00002    NO       ACCURACY OF.
  00003    NO       AC FLASH SYSTEM.
  00004    NO       ADDITIVE.
  00005    NO       ADDITIVES.
  00006    NO       ADDITIVE STABILIZER.
  00007    NO       ALKALI.
  00008    NO       ALPHA PARTICLES.
  00009    NO       ALPHA PARTICLE SENSITIZERS.
  00010    NO       ANALYSIS OF FACTORS&AFFECTING PRECISION.
  00011    NO       ANILINO.
  00012    NO       ANILINOHYDROQUINONES.
  00013    NO       ANTIBRONZING.
  00014    NO       ANTI BRONZING AGENT.
  00015    NO       ANTIBRONZING AGENT.
  00016             ANTIBRONZING AGENTS.
  00017    NO       ANTIBRONZING STABILIZERS.
  00018    NO       ANTIFOGGANT.
  00019             ANTIFOGGANTS.
  00020    NO       ANTIFOGGANT ADDITIVES.
  00021    NO       ANTIFOGGANT AGENTS.
  00022    NO       ANTIFOGGANT SENSITIZED&EMULSIONS.
  00023    NO       ANTIFOGGANT SENSITIZERS.
```

FIG. 5. Part of dictionary of descriptor-modifier index listing program

```
114-02   EMULSION TECHNOLOGY
         ANTIBRONZING AGENTS

102-18   EMULSION TECHNOLOGY     PROCESSING              THEORY
         ANTIFOGGANTS            ANTIFOGGANTS              PHOTOGRAPHIC FOG

102-14   EMULSION TECHNOLOGY     PROCESSING              TRIALKYLIMIDAZOLIUM
         ANTIFOGGANTS            ANTIFOGGANTS                           HALIDES
                                                         ANTIFOGGANTS

102-10   EMULSION TECHNOLOGY     PROCESSING
         ANTIFOGGANTS            ANTIFOGGANTS

102-09   EMULSION TECHNOLOGY     PROCESSING
         ANTIFOGGANTS            DEVELOPER ANTIFOGGANTS
         IMIDAZOLIUM SALTS

102-05   EMULSION TECHNOLOGY     PROCESSING
         ANTIFOGGANT ADDITIVES   ANTIFOGGANT ADDITIVES

110-18   EMULSION TECHNOLOGY     PROCESSING              SENSITOMETRY            THEORY
         ANTIFOGGANT SENSITIZERS PHOTOGRAPHIC FOG        ANTIFOGGANT SENSITIZED   PHOTOGRAPHIC FOG
                                                                    EMULSIONS

31-06    EMULSION TECHNOLOGY     INTERMEDIATE DYE
         DYE SYNTHESIS                          SYNTHESIS

102-20   EMULSION TECHNOLOGY     PROCESSING
         EMULSION ADDITIVES      DEVELOPER ADDITIVES
```

FIG. 6. Sample descriptor-modifier index of abstracts, blank last

stance, word 19 of Fig. 5, *antifoggants,* is not in its traditional alphabetic position.

A preliminary version of the listing is shown in Fig. 6. The order is controlled in this part, by the first modifier, since the principal descriptor is the same. Consequently, the four entries with *antifoggants* as the modifier, precede the entry with *antifoggant additives* as the modifier. Notice also the layout of the long words *trialkylimidazolium halides* (the third descriptor of the third entry) and *antifoggant sensitized emulsions* (the third descriptor of the second from last entry). From these, it can be seen that print format for long words is quite successful. The

format for entries with many descriptors (not illustrated) is also successful; in these cases the fifth descriptor-modifier group appears beneath the second one, the sixth beneath the third, and so on.

Notice the relative positions of the second, third, and fourth entries. All four of the first terms match. The position of 102–10 is determined by its fifth word, a single blank. It comes last, because the dictionary used for this preliminary list is not that of Fig. 5, but one otherwise identical with the blank as the last word. In Fig. 7 is shown a later listing, one made after adding more entries and shifting the blank to the beginning of the dic-

```
114-02   EMULSION TECHNOLOGY
         ANTIBRONZING AGENTS

114-09   EMULSION TECHNOLOGY       ORGANIC CHEMISTRY
         ANTIBRONZING STABILIZERS  MERCAPTANS
                                   HETEROCYCLIC
102-01   EMULSION TECHNOLOGY       IMIDAZOLIUM
         ANTIFOGGANTS              HALIDE
                                   TRIALKYL

102-10   EMULSION TECHNOLOGY       PROCESSING
         ANTIFOGGANTS              ANTIFOGGANTS

102-18   EMULSION TECHNOLOGY       PROCESSING              THEORY
         ANTIFOGGANTS              ANTIFOGGANTS             PHOTOGRAPHIC FOG

102-14   EMULSION TECHNOLOGY       PROCESSING              TRIALKYLIMIDAZOLIUM
         ANTIFOGGANTS              ANTIFOGGANTS                          HALIDES
                                                           ANTIFOGGANTS

114-18   EMULSION TECHNOLOGY       PROCESSING              THEORY
         ANTIFOGGANTS              ANTIFOGGANTS             STABILIZATION
         ANTIBRONZING AGENTS       ANTIBRONZING AGENTS      ANTIBRONZING
         STABILIZERS               STABILIZERS              EMULSION ADDITIVES

102-09   EMULSION TECHNOLOGY       PROCESSING
         ANTIFOGGANTS              DEVELOPER ANTIFOGGANTS
         IMIDAZOLIUM SALTS

102-05   EMULSION TECHNOLOGY       PROCESSING
         ANTIFOGGANT ADDITIVES     ANTIFOGGANT ADDITIVES

110-18   EMULSION TECHNOLOGY       PROCESSING              SENSITOMETRY            THEORY
         ANTIFOGGANT SENSITIZERS   PHOTOGRAPHIC FOG        ANTIFOGGANT SENSITIZED   PHOTOGRAPHIC FOG
                                                                      EMULSIONS
```

FIG. 7. Sample descriptor-modifier index of abstracts, blank first

tionary. The first entry is the same as in Fig. 6; the next two are new entries. Then follows 102–10, which now precedes the two entries with which it shares the first four terms, since the new dictionary has the single blank first. Similar shifting of any term in the dictionary will result in similar readjustment of the order in the listing. This gives the manager great control over the listing sequence, but it puts great responsibility on him to avoid putting duplicate and synonymous words into the dictionary and to produce an order understandable by the searchers who will use the listings.

The entries can be descriptive, and they usually avoid the overly concise representation of other indexing displays. For instance, compare the dual-dictionary display, Fig. 8, with the equivalent listing, Fig. 6. Only the left-hand part of two dual-dictionary frames are shown in Fig. 8.[2] The listing (Fig. 6) gives more information about the item, allowing a searcher to be more selective when choosing answers. The dual dictionary is, of course, more compact.

What is the effectiveness of manual searching of this new display? There are two steps in searching: access and selection. The first consists in locating an entry in the listing and using an initial strategy applied to a few of the terms, the ones most important in controlling the

order in the listing. The second step is accepting or rejecting that item by a more complicated strategy applied to the complete entry. The second step can be readily carried out with this new listing, even for a large file, as Figs. 6 and 7 suggest, since there are an average of seven terms per entry for selecting. Terse entries (the first of Fig. 7) are less useful for this purpose.

For best recall and precision, one would use a simple locating strategy. The locating strategy obviously controls the recall, since anything not located is not retrieved. The selecting strategy controls precision and does not affect recall.

When the locating strategy consists in matching a single descriptor, the maximum recall is the chance of retrieval (1). Averaged over all the 34 required descriptors and the 19 abstractors, the chance of retrieval is 69%. Table 1 shows the data for each abstract as well as the final average.

If the descriptors and modifiers are treated as independent index terms, as they were in producing the dual dictionary shown in Fig. 8, the distinction between a descriptor and a modifier is no longer apparent to the searcher. He then will probably adopt, as locating strategy, a match on any word. Under these circumstances, the chance of retrieval drops to 14%. The constraint on the indexers to choose descriptors has resulted in a fivefold improvement in chance of retrieval, by de-

2. This figure is reproduced from a microfilm produced on a microfilm printer from tapes prepared on a computer. Programing by D. Barton and T. Grout is gratefully acknowledged.

ANTIFOGGANTS

| 102-10 | | | | 102-14 | |

EMULSION TECHNOLOGY

| 102-10
102-20 | | 114-02 | | 102-14 | 102-05 |

FIG. 8. Sample dual-dictionary index of abstracts

TABLE 1. Indexing statistics

Abstract number	Descriptors & modifiers per abstract	Descriptors per abstract	Retrieval chance, %	
			With descriptors only	With descriptors and modifiers
5	7.6	2.5	62	7
16	14.0	2.7	78	17
22	6.2	2.7	62	8
31	4.2	1.6	42	7
42	7.4	2.8	82	18
96	6.6	2.7	66	13
102	5.1	2.0	61	16
110	5.1	1.8	64	10
114	5.6	2.0	59	10
138	7.5	2.6	68	16
157	7.5	3.1	92	25
173	5.5	2.1	84	19
178	8.9	2.8	73	16
Average	7.0	2.4	69	14

creasing the variability of expression for a concept that the indexer chooses to notice.

A more fundamental property, one that also contributes to inconsistency, is imprecision of meaning. If all the indexers have the same understanding of the meaning of a term, they will unanimously apply it, or fail to apply it, to each abstract. The extent to which they deviate from this unanimity is shown on a graph showing the fraction of indexers applying the descriptor as the ordinate. The abscissa of the graph is the rank of an abstract, so that the curve rises to the right. We can define perfect understanding and perfect precision of meaning as yielding a rectangular curve—one with points only at 0 and 100% (1).

Such a graph for a term on the required list of 34 descriptors is shown in Fig. 9. The term is *emulsion tech-*

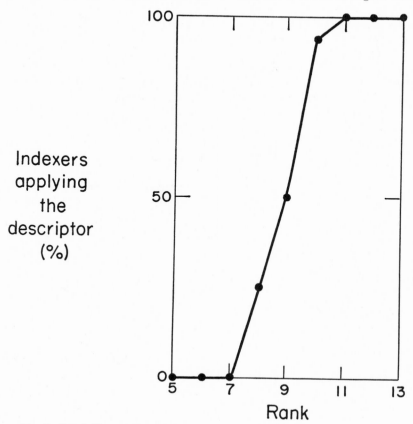

FIG. 9. Graph illustrating the precision of meaning of "Emulsion Technology"

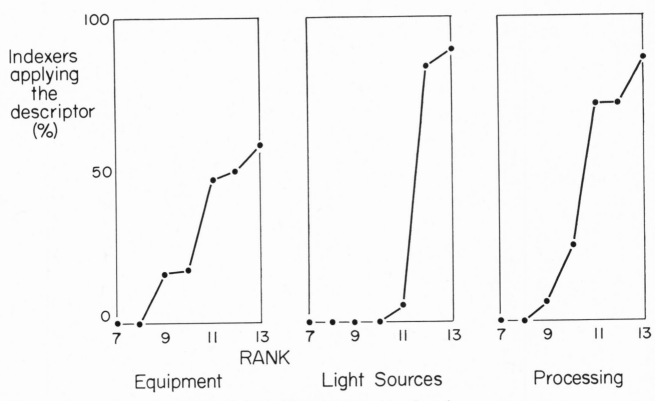

Fig. 10. Graphs illustrating the precision of meaning

nology, the term also shown on Figs. 6 and 7. It is a term that would be expected to have high precision among these indexers, since it describes a subject area in which they are competent. The graph shows that the term is not used with perfect precision, since it is not a rectangular curve. Furthermore, the imprecision is about the same as is observed when terms are chosen freely *(1).* Three other graphs are shown in Fig. 10; all four graphs show about the same imprecision as terms freely chosen. The use of an authority list, in the way we have explained, does not increase the inherent imprecision of words.

We have made no attempt, either in this experiment or in earlier ones *(1),* to discover what precision of meaning

the indexers or searchers could be brought to, but rather that precision of meaning—as expressed by document indexing and document retrieving actions—was already present in the population of ordinary research workers. This information is the first step in our attempts to utilize for indexing the expert's experience and knowledge, and to supply the expert with indexes instead of answers.

Reference

1. TINKER, J. F., Imprecision in Meaning Measured by Inconsistency of Indexing, *American Documentation,* 17 (No. 2):96–102 (1966).

53 Indexing Consistency and Quality

PRANAS ZUNDE
MARGARET E. DEXTER
American Documentation
Vol. 20, No. 3, July, 1969

1 Indexing Consistency

It is well known that any two indexers, indexing one and the same document individually, will select sets of indexing terms which are most unlikely to be identical. In other words, if one compares indexing terms assigned by any two indexers to the same document, one discovers that, as a rule, the indexers differ considerably in their judgment as to which terms reflect the contents of the document most adequately. It is clear that this difference in the judgment of indexers introduces a great deal of uncertainty in any information retrieval system based on human indexing. Although an information system normally would not contain identical documents indexed by different indexers, the implication is that documents which are similar may and often would be indexed so differently that their similarity would not be properly reflected in the sets of indexing terms assigned to these documents. Various tools have been developed to reduce this discrepancy in the judgment of the indexers on such matters as term assignments, but the discussion of these tools is not the purpose of this article.

Since indexing consistency manifests itself in the similarity (or dissimilarity) of indexing terms assigned to a given document by different indexers, and since the selection of indexing terms by an indexer reflects his judgment regarding the information contained in the document and its representation, indexing consistency is

This research was partially supported by the NSE Grant GN-655.

essentially a measure of the similarity of reaction of different human beings processing the same information. Thus, more precisely, we shall define indexing consistency in a group of indexers as the degree of agreement in the representation of the essential information content of the document by certain sets of indexing terms selected individually and independently by each of the indexers in the group.

Previous Consistency Studies

In a survey of indexing consistency studies, Hooper (*1*) cited consistency values ranging from 10% to 80%, depending on the conditions under which the indexing was performed and the measure of consistency used. Jacoby (*2*) reported a mean consistency of 10% when chemical patents were indexed by three experienced and three inexperienced indexers and no indexing aids were used. Consistency values of 35% to 45% were obtained by Slamecka and Jacoby (*3*) for experienced indexers using certain indexing aids, such as controlled vocabulary.

In a third report, Jacoby and Slamecka (*4*) arrived at a consistency of 16.3% for experienced indexers and 12.6% for inexperienced indexers. No indexing aids other than indexing rules were used.

Painter (*5*) reported consistency values of 40%, 42%, 48% and 70% with varying indexing systems and types of documents. Rodgers (*6*) came up with an average consistency of 24% for combinations of two indexers in a group. Korotkin and Oliver (*7*) reported consistencies ranging from 36% to 59% in an experiment in which five psychologists and five nonpsychologists indexed abstracts.

Consistencies up to 80% were reached when indexers were required to use classification schedules and thesauri and had very limited freedom or no freedom at all to use terms not contained in the above indexing aids (5, 7, 8, 9, 10).

Schultz, Schultz and Orr (11) measured the goodness of author indexing by using a set of indexers as a criterion group to establish a weight for each term. The weight for a term for a given document was defined as the square of the number of criterion group indexers selecting the term for the specific document. The goodness of the author's index set was taken to be the sum of the weights of the terms selected. This measure was then normalized by dividing the score for each document by the maximum score possible for the document, the sum of the weights of all terms selected by the criterion group for the document. They found that the mean score for the authors was 76%.

Consistency Measure Used in Previous Studies

The consistency measure used in most previous studies was the ratio of the number of terms selected by all indexers in the group to the total number of different terms selected for the document. For a group of two indexers the consistency measure on a given document is thus defined as

$$c_{ij} = \frac{n(T_1 \cap T_2)}{n(T_1 \cup T_2)} \qquad (1)$$

where T_1 and T_2 denote the sets of terms selected by the first and second indexers respectively, and $n(T)$ denotes the number of elements in set T.

This measure can be extended to $k > 2$ indexers by taking

$$c_{1, 2, \ldots, k} = \frac{n(T_1 \cap T_2 \cap \ldots \cap T_k)}{n(T_1 \cup T_2 \cup \ldots \cup T_k)} \qquad (2)$$

The main disadvantage of such a consistency measure is the underlying assumption that all the indexing terms selected are equally significant and relevant for the representation of the information content of the document. In other words, measures (1) and (2) completely disregard the difference between agreement on significant terms and agreement on insignificant terms. The result, as will be shown in this paper, is that the above measures tend to produce consistently lower consistency measures than one would intuitively be willing to accept. For example, consider three indexers indexing one and the same document on jet propulsion and assume, for simplicity, that each of them assigned three indexing terms to the document as shown in Table 1.

Assume further that the terms JET and PROPULSION refer to the main topic of the document, whereas FLOW and LEVEL refer to topics of marginal importance. From Equation (1), the consistency of any two of these three

TABLE 1. An example of an assignment of terms to one document by three indexers

Indexing term	Indexer		
	1	2	3
JET	x	x	x
PROPULSION	x	x	
FLOW	x		x
LEVEL		x	x

indexers is 0.50 (or 50%). But in effect the indexing consistency of 1 and 2 should be considered much higher than either that of 1 and 3 or of 2 and 3 since the common part of sets I_1 and I_2 contain both of the significant words JET and PROPULSION. Therefore the measures (1) or (2) would be fair measures of consistency only in the absence of any information whatsoever on the relative importance of the indexing terms, but they obviously do not adequately reflect the agreement of indexers' judgment if such information is available.

2 Proposed Consistency Measure

The consistency measure which is proposed here and which is expected to eliminate, at least partially, the shortcomings of the consistency measures of the type expressed by equations (1) and (2) is based on the postulate that there exists no *well defined set* of "relevant," "most indicative," "most pertinent," "most informative," etc., indexing terms for a document, because there exist no objective criteria which would enable us to construct such sets. Indexing performance of human indexers demonstrates this clearly, because if such criteria were available, we could apply them to obtain 100% indexing consistency.

An alternative to a well defined set is a "fuzzy set" which has been proposed by Zadeh (12). Whereas well defined sets have precisely stated criteria of membership, a fuzzy set is a collection of objects which meet the criteria of membership to a varying degree which is assumed as given. More precisely, a fuzzy set A in a set X of objects x is characterized by a membership function $f_A(x)$ which associates with each point in X a real number in the interval [0,1], with the value of $f_A(x)$ at x representing the "grade of membership" of x in A. The nearer the value of $f_A(x)$ to unity, the higher the grade of membership of x in A. If the function $f_A(x)$ can assume only the values 0 and 1, it reduces to the familiar characteristic function of the set A. For further discussion of the fuzzy sets and operations on them, see Appendix.

Consider now the set of all English words and phrases, which are potential indexing terms for any kind of document. We shall say that this set of words and phrases is a fuzzy set with respect to the membership criteria of "being representative of or pertinent to" a given document D, the degree of membership of each term reflecting the degree of agreement as to its significance with respect to the information it conveys about the document indexed. We shall call this set the global (indexing) set U for the document D.

We shall further define the set T_j of indexing terms t assigned by an indexer I_j to the document D to be the subset of the fuzzy set U such that for each $t \, \varepsilon \, T_j$, $f_{T_j}(t) = f_U(t)$. In other words, the set T_j is a fuzzy set obtained by associating with each indexing term t selected by the indexer I_j the membership value which that term t has in the set U. For example, the set $T_1 = \{t_1, t_2, t_3, t_4\} = \{$blood, circulation, heart, disease$\}$ with the membership function $f(t_1) = 0.8$, $f(t_2) = 0.85$, $f(t_3) = 0.95$, $f(t_4) = 0.7$ might represent the set of indexing terms assigned by an indexer I_1 to some document D.

Now let $\{I_1, I_2, \ldots, I_m\}$ be a group of indexers and $\{T_1, T_2, \ldots, T_m\}$ a (well defined) collection of fuzzy sets of indexing terms t assigned by each of these indexers to one and the same document D. We shall define the measure of consistency of the group of indexers I_1, I_2, $\ldots, I_m$ by the expression

$$c^*_{1, 2, \ldots, m} = \frac{\sum_t f_{T_1 \cap T_2 \cap \ldots \cap T_m}(t)}{\sum_t f_{T_1 \cup T_2 \cup \ldots \cup T_m}(t)} = \frac{\sum_t f_{\underset{m}{\cap} T_i}(t)}{\sum_t f_{\underset{m}{\cup} T_i}(t)} \quad (3)$$

where $\sum_t f_{T_1 \cap T_2 \cap \ldots \cap T_m}(t) = \sum_t f_{\underset{m}{\cap} T_i}(t)$ denotes the sum of the membership values of the intersection set of the fuzzy sets T_j, $j = 1, 2, \ldots, m$, and $\sum_t f_{T_1 \cup T_2 \cup \ldots \cup T_m}(t) = \sum_t f_{\underset{m}{\cup} T_i}(t)$ denotes the sum of the membership values of the union set of the fuzzy sets T_j, $j = 1, 2, \ldots, m$.

3 Quality and Exhaustivity Measures

Furthermore we shall define the measure of quality of an index to some document D to be the expression

$$\eta_j = \frac{\sum_t f_{T_j}(t)}{\sum_t f_u(t)} \quad (4)$$

where $\sum_t f_u(t)$ denotes the sum of the membership values of all the elements t of the global set U, and $\sum_t f_{T_j}(t)$ denotes the sum of the membership values of all the elements t of the fuzzy set of indexing terms T_j, assigned by the indexer I_j to the document D.

It should be noted that the measure of quality given by expression (3) can be viewed as the measure of goodness of performance of indexer I_j in indexing document D, where by performance is understood the capabilities of the indexer to select indexing terms which would give maximum information about the document indexed.

Finally we shall define the measure of exhaustivity by the expression

$$\gamma_{1, 2, \ldots, m} = \frac{\sum_t f^*_{\underset{m}{\cup} T_i}(t) \ln f_{\underset{m}{\cup} T_i}(t)}{\sum_t f^*_u(t) \ln f^*_u(t)} \quad (5)$$

where

$$f^*_{\underset{m}{\cup} T_i}(t) = \frac{f_{\underset{m}{\cup} T_i}(t)}{\sum_t f_{\underset{m}{\cup} T_i}(t)} \quad (6)$$

and

$$f_v^*(t) = \frac{f_v(t)}{\sum_t f_v(t)} \quad (7)$$

Essentially this measure indicates that portion of the overall information of the document D which is reflected in the joint output of a group of indexers $\{I_1, I_2, \ldots, I_m\}$. Since $\gamma_{1,2,\ldots,m} \geq \gamma_{1,2,\ldots,s}$ whenever $m > s$, i.e., γ increases or remains unchanged when the number of indexers in the group increases, the change in γ can be considered as the indicator of the proportion of additional information about the document gained due to the contribution of $m - s$ additional indexers.

A problem of practical importance is how to obtain the global set U with its membership function for a document D. Leaving the question open of whether or not it is possible to determine such a set a priori, we shall describe an experimental approach to the construction of such a global set and development of the measures defined by equations (3), (4), and (5), which enabled us to demonstrate the major issues of this investigation. The method used for the construction of the global set —and it is not claimed that this is the only method to arrive at such a set—will be outlined following the description of the experiments performed and data used.

Experimental Data

The data used in this investigation came from two sources. One source of data was a study performed by Schultz, Schultz and Orr (11) in which 285 biomedical documents were indexed by the author, by twelve biomedical scientists who were engaged in research in the area, and by eight professional indexers. For the purposes of this study, data from 29 of these documents was used. Two groups of eight indexers each were selected, the eight professional indexers forming one group and the first eight of the twelve scientists forming the other.

The documents indexed in this study were brief summaries of oral reports on current biomedical research which were presented at the 1962 meeting of the Federation of American Societies for Experimental Biology. These documents consisted of every tenth document in the 1962 meeting issue of the *Federation Proceedings* (Vol. 21, No. 2, March-April 1962.) The 12 scientists who indexed the documents were given a form which listed 373 subject categories from which they could select as many terms as they wished. The form also provided space for writing-in additional terms. The scientists were instructed to choose as many terms as they felt were required to characterize the document. They were also told to index personally, to use the form only when it was natural and helpful, and to let their responses reflect their viewpoints and terminology.

The eight professional indexers indexed the same documents using the same form. They were also encouraged to assign to each document as many terms as they considered necessary.

The other source of data was an experiment performed at Georgia Tech in May of 1968. In this experiment nine graduate students in the School of Information Science each indexed 16 documents. Eight of these documents were selected from the 285 biomedical documents described above. The other eight were selected from *Efficient Reading*, by James E. Brown (13), a collection of articles designed for use in a rapid reading course. Data from eight of the nine graduate students was used for this study. No classification schedules or any other indexing aids were made available to these students. No restrictions were imposed as to the number of terms they were to assign to the documents.

Thus in the first instance we had slightly controlled indexing, in the second, completely free indexing.

A sample document of the biomedical category is shown in Figure 1. Indexing terms which have been assigned to this document by student indexers are given in Table 2.

Derivation of Fuzzy Sets

For each document D, the global fuzzy set U was obtained by the following procedure. Every term assigned by any one of the indexers I_j, $j=1, 2, \ldots, m$, to the document D is an element of the fuzzy set U. The membership function of the global set U is obtained by assigning to each element, i.e., each term in the set, a

PATHWAYS OF INTRACELLULAR
HYDROGEN TRANSPORT.

Bertram Sacktor, Arthur R. Dick and *Eva H. Wormeer*
CRDL, Army Chemical Center, Maryland.

The mechanisms for oxidizing extramitochondrial DPNH in mammalian tissues were studied. Activity measurements were made of the pathways in different tissues, including: heart, skeletal muscle, diaphragm, brain, lung, liver, kidney, spleen and testes, for oxidizing exogenous DPNH by mitochondria and by cytoplasmic or soluble lactic, a glycerophosphate and malic dehydrogenases. Analyses of the oxidized and reduced metabolites in the different tissues were correlated with the potential of the different pathways.

Fig. 1. A sample document from the biomedical collection used in indexing experiment.

Table 2. Terms assigned by student indexers to sample document shown in Figure 1

Indexing term	Student indexer							
	1	2	3	4	5	6	7	8
t_1 analyses					x			
t_2 biochemistry		x				x		
t_3 cellular	x							
t_4 DPNH	x	x					x	x
t_5 extramitochondrial		x	x					
t_6 hydrogen				x	x	x		x
t_7 intracellular					x	x		
t_8 mammalian		x	x		x			
t_9 metabolic	x	x		x	x			x
t_{10} mitochondria		x						
t_{11} oxidase	x	x	x		x		x	x
t_{12} pathways		x				x		
t_{13} tissue		x		x	x			
t_{14} transport		x			x		x	x

membership value equal to the ratio of the number of indexers who assigned that term to the document D to the total number of indexers who indexed that document, i.e., the total number of indexers in the experimental group.

The conceptual justification for this procedure is that the selection of a term by an indexer is an indication that that term is representative—at least in his judgment and to some degree—of the information contained in the document and that it reflects some of that information. Hence every term selected by an indexer in the group should be assigned a membership value greater than zero. The rest of the terms in the vocabulary, i.e., the terms which none of the indexers used, are assumed to have the membership value equal to zero. As to the terms which have been selected, the degree of concensus of indexers in selecting a term is considered to be a proper indicator of their significance in representing the information contained in the document. In other words, the more indexers select a given indexing term, the more representative it should be considered with respect to the contents of the document. A term, which is selected by all indexers in the group, is assigned member-value 1. Thus, the membership values of the elements (terms) of the global fuzzy set U can assume values in the interval [0, 1]; but terms with membership values equal to zero are not shown, since they have no effect on further calculations.

It should be noted that the fuzzy set U thus arrived at and the fuzzy sets T_j of indexing terms selected by each indexer in the experimental group are "fuzzy" with respect to their pertinence or significance in representing information contained in a document, but they are not "fuzzy" with respect to the criterion of being symbols for certain words, i.e., with respect to the partitioning of the vocabulary into a set of terms which have been chosen as indexing terms and a set of terms which have not been chosen as indexing terms. This is true for any fuzzy set: the concept of "fuzziness" pertains to the criteria of membership in a given set, and the same set could be a fuzzy set with respect to one criterion and a well defined set with respect to another.

As an example, the fuzzy global set U and three of the sets T_j for the document D in Figure 1, calculated from the data in Table 2, are given here:

$$U = \left\{ \begin{matrix} t_1, & t_2, & t_3, & t_4, & t_5, & t_6, & t_7, & t_8, & t_9, & t_{10}, & t_{11}, & t_{12}, & t_{13}, & t_{14} \\ \frac{1}{8} & \frac{2}{8} & \frac{1}{8} & \frac{4}{8} & \frac{2}{8} & \frac{4}{8} & \frac{2}{8} & \frac{3}{8} & \frac{5}{8} & \frac{1}{8} & \frac{6}{8} & \frac{2}{8} & \frac{3}{8} & \frac{4}{8} \end{matrix} \right\}$$

$$T_1 = \left\{ \begin{matrix} t_1, & t_2, & t_3, & t_4, & t_5, & t_6, & t_7, & t_8, & t_9, & t_{10}, & t_{11}, & t_{12}, & t_{13}, & t_{14} \\ 0 & 0 & \frac{1}{8} & \frac{4}{8} & 0 & 0 & 0 & 0 & \frac{5}{8} & 0 & \frac{6}{8} & 0 & 0 & 0 \end{matrix} \right\}$$

$$T_2 = \left\{ \begin{matrix} t_1, & t_2, & t_3, & t_4, & t_5, & t_6, & t_7, & t_8, & t_9, & t_{10}, & t_{11}, & t_{12}, & t_{13}, & t_{14} \\ 0 & \frac{2}{8} & & \frac{4}{8} & \frac{2}{8} & 0 & 0 & \frac{3}{8} & \frac{5}{8} & \frac{1}{8} & \frac{6}{8} & \frac{2}{8} & \frac{3}{8} & 0 \end{matrix} \right\}$$

$$T_3 = \left\{ \begin{matrix} t_1, & t_2, & t_3, & t_4, & t_5, & t_6, & t_7, & t_8, & t_9, & t_{10}, & t_{11}, & t_{12}, & t_{13}, & t_{14} \\ 0 & 0 & 0 & 0 & \frac{2}{8} & 0 & 0 & \frac{3}{8} & 0 & 0 & \frac{6}{8} & 0 & 0 & 0 \end{matrix} \right\}$$

4 Results of Consistency Tests

Under all experimental conditions the proposed measure of consistency, which reflects the agreement of a group of indexers on the significance of the selected terms, produced on the average higher consistency values than the measure given by equation (2), which does not reflect any judgment of significance of the terms.

The consistency of one pair of professional indexers was calculated for the 29 biomedical documents. The resulting mean and variance for both the "unweighted" measure c_{ij} and the proposed "weighted" measure c^*_{ij} are given in Table 3.

Consistency was then calculated for all pairs of indexers for a specific document. The average consistency according to the measure c_{ij} was 0.35, and the average according to the proposed measure c^*_{ij} was 0.59. When random samples of pairs of indexes over all documents were calculated, the two consistency values were found to be 0.27 and 0.44 respectively.

When both the "unweighted" and the proposed "weighted" values were calculated for all pairs of professional indexers, it was found that the measure c_{ij} was higher in $2\frac{1}{2}\%$ of the cases, both measures were zero in $7\frac{1}{2}\%$ of the cases, and the measure c^*_{ij} was higher for the remaning 90% of the pairs of indexers.

The calculations were then extended to measure the

TABLE 3. Mean and variance of consistency of one pair of indexers over a sample of 29 documents for consistency measures c_{ij} and c^*_{ij}

	$c_{1,2} = \dfrac{n(T_1 \cap T_2)}{n(T_1 \cup T_2)}$	$c^*_{1,2} = \dfrac{\sum\limits_t f_{T_1 \cap T_2}}{\sum f_{T_1 \cup T_2}}$
Mean	.24	.41
Variance	.01	.02

consistency of three indexers, then of four indexers, and up to the consistency of the entire group of eight indexers using equations (2) and (3), respectively.

Random combinations of three indexers, four indexers, and up to eight indexers were selected from one document. Again, the proposed measure c^*_{ij} tended to yield higher values of consistency than did the measure c_{ij}. The results are shown in Figure 2. Then the same calculations were made for combinations of indexers selected randomly from all documents. The results were quite similar to those for one document as may be seen in Figure 3.

5 Quality Measurements

The indexing quality was calculated, using equation (4), for each indexer on each document for the professional indexers, the scientists, and the students. The "best" and "worst" indexer in each of the three groups was determined, using the average quality for the indexer.

The calculated quality measure for eight professional indexers and eight scientists, based on a sample of 29 documents and for eight student indexers based on a sample of 16 documents is shown in Tables 4, 5, and 6. The documents were ranked for each group according to the difference in quality of the best indexer and the worst indexer, and the results plotted as shown in Figures 4, 5, and 6. It should be noted that the indexer with the best average quality score scored higher in performance quality for most documents individually than the indexer with lowest average quality score. As a matter of fact, there were only two instances where the "poor" indexer of the group performed better than the best in the group by scoring higher [1] on an individual document. This is a strong indication that the proposed optimality measure is an adequate tool in evaluating the overall indexer's performance.

The mean and variance of the quality score and the

---

[1] Two statistical tests were employed, a sign test and the Wilcoxon matched-pairs signed-rank test. Under both tests, the difference in quality between the best and the worst indexer is significant at the .001 level for all three groups of indexers.

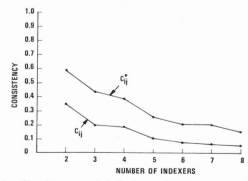

FIG. 2. Consistency of indexing: Values averaged over combinations of indexers for one document

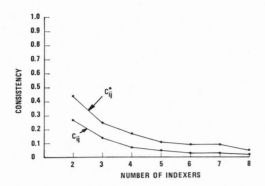

FIG. 3. Consistency of indexing: Values averaged over combinations of indexers and the sample set of documents

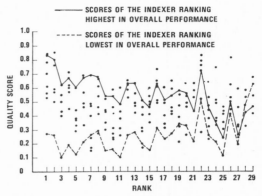

FIG. 4. Quality scores of the first indexer group (professionals) by document

average number of terms were calculated for all indexers. This data is shown in Table 7. It is interesting to note that the quality measure increases with the number of terms when the number of terms is small. But this increase levels off at a given point, and additional terms add little to the quality measure. This seems to suggest an "optimal" number of terms which is, on the average, slightly higher than the average number of terms selected by one indexer.

6 Measurement of Indexing Exhaustivity

The question to be discussed next is how much an index can be improved by "group" indexing, i.e., by having one and the same document indexed by several indexers and then combining the results into a single index for that document. In other words, the problem under investigation was how much more information is contained in the joint product of two indexers as compared to the product of one indexer, or in the joint product of three indexers as compared to that of two, etc.

One approach to answering this question is to consider the number of new terms contributed by another indexer. Calculations were made as to the average number of terms selected by one indexer, two indexers, and so on, out of the total set of terms selected by all eight indexers, by considering all combinations of indexers two at a time, three at a time, etc. These values were then expressed in percentages of the total number of terms resulting from all eight indexers. This data is shown in Table 8.

TABLE 4. Quality scores by indexers (professional) and documents

Document number	Rank	Indexer							
		1	2	3	4	5	6	7	8
6	1	.78	.70	.53	.27	.83	.61	.84	.56
8	2	.59	.85	.50	.26	.80	.50	.57	.76
15	3	.43	.40	.55	.10	.62	.43	.40	.50
7	4	.57	.62	.60	.19	.67	.67	.45	.71
9	5	.38	.33	.44	.12	.60	.37	.29	.44
19	6	.69	.56	.33	.21	.67	.46	.49	.46
2	7	.49	.40	.17	.26	.69	.47	.14	.24
5	8	.61	.27	.41	.29	.68	.46	.66	.54
18	9	.44	.43	.43	.15	.54	.30	.35	.52
4	10	.59	.27	.23	.16	.54	.31	.46	.24
12	11	.38	.31	.60	.10	.48	.31	.26	.43
25	12	.53	.62	.65	.26	.62	.59	.53	.53
30	13	.63	.42	.47	.28	.63	.56	.42	.49
13	14	.31	.29	.40	.20	.51	.31	.17	.46
28	15	.41	.35	.54	.15	.46	.48	.60	.50
1	16	.51	.73	.61	.31	.63	.73	.49	.65
11	17	.34	.51	.60	.23	.51	.31	.49	.40
23	18	.43	.41	.65	.27	.54	.46	.46	.59
14	19	.47	.21	.32	.34	.58	.39	.34	.55
10	20	.46	.54	.26	.33	.56	.49	.33	.49
24	21	.53	.42	.63	.21	.42	.53	.53	.58
21	22	.83	.79	.76	.52	.72	.72	.28	.52
26	23	.23	.32	.47	.26	.44	.38	.53	.47
17	24	.38	.38	.64	.21	.36	.49	.33	.51
29	25	.30	.35	.43	.11	.24	.44	.46	.41
22	26	.62	.44	.81	.41	.50	.53	.47	.47
20	27	.59	.32	.43	.19	.24	.27	.32	.46
16	28	.53	.58	.42	.47	.42	.53	.53	.58
27	29	.67	.54	.64	.62	.46	.41	.54	.62
Average		.52	.44	.50	.26	.53	.47	.44	.51

TABLE 5. Quality scores by indexers (scientists) and documents

Document number	Rank	Indexer							
		1	2	3	4	5	6	7	8
13	1	.53	.13	.60	.60	.53	.67	.53	.47
22	2	.45	.35	.70	.70	.35	.85	.60	.40
5	3	.57	.21	.18	.43	.39	.64	.35	.21
25	4	.84	.42	.42	.89	.53	.84	.63	.42
24	5	.68	.37	.53	.26	.53	.79	.42	.37
12	6	.35	.12	.41	.59	.29	.53	.71	.35
26	7	.38	.38	.25	.56	.50	.75	.44	.38
20	8	.67	.33	.44	.39	.56	.67	.61	.33
10	9	.42	.26	.26	.47	.26	.58	.16	.47
28	10	.64	.28	.40	.52	.48	.60	.56	.32
23	11	.53	.16	.32	.84	.37	.47	.37	.26
1	12	.63	.25	.29	.50	.63	.54	.08	.33
15	13	.52	.24	.24	.48	.24	.53	.57	.29
27	14	.50	.21	.33	.33	.58	.50	.50	.21
16	15	.61	.44	.44	.94	.50	.72	.56	.44
18	16	.24	.05	.38	.57	.24	.33	.38	.43
2	17	.46	.04	.19	.38	.31	.31	.35	.19
6	18	.48	.29	.43	.38	.48	.53	.24	.38
4	19	.41	.14	.23	.45	.41	.36	.14	.14
14	20	.73	.47	.47	.60	.20	.68	.47	.47
19	21	.64	.50	.50	.57	.57	.71	.14	.50
11	22	.38	.19	.19	.31	.25	.36	.13	.19
9	23	.28	.28	.33	.50	.11	.44	.11	.39
21	24	.67	.28	.44	.72	.22	.44	.39	.28
7	25	.65	.30	.30	.50	.55	.45	.15	.30
29	26	.80	.30	.35	.20	.50	.45	.40	.30
17	27	.64	.50	.50	.79	.57	.64	.14	.50
8	28	.31	.25	.25	.38		.31	.44	.56
30	29	.58	.37	.68	.63	.68	.37	.63	.21
Average		.52	.28	.38	.53	.42	.55	.39	.36

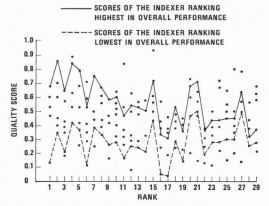

FIG. 5. Quality scores of the second indexer group (scientists) by document

Although the number of terms were quite different, the percentages obtained were practically identical for the scientists and professional indexers, and not greatly different for the students. In all cases, approximately half the terms obtained by eight indexers were obtained by two indexers, and 80% of the terms were obtained by five.

The calculations were repeated using the proposed measure of exhaustivity, equation (4), which reflects the varying degrees of significance of information contents of assigned terms. Average exhaustivity ratios were calculated for groups of 1, 2, 3, . . . , to 8 indexers and the results are shown in Table 8 in columns 3, 5, and 7. The plot of these exhaustivity ratios on a logarithmic scale is shown in Figure 7.

The interesting result of this experiment is that the exhaustivity ratios thus obtained, when plotted on a logarithmic scale with respect to the number of indexers, lie on a straight line for each group of indexers considered. This suggests a general model of indexing exhaustivity

$$\gamma = \gamma_1 + m \log n \text{ and } N \ll T \qquad (8)$$

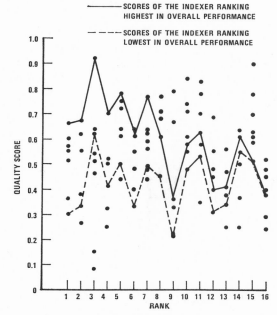

FIG. 6. Quality scores of the third indexer group (students) by document

where γ is the exhaustivity measure, γ_1 is the "average exhaustivity" of one indexer (intercept of the line with the n-axis), n is the number of indexers, $m = \tan \phi$ is the tangent of the angle at which the line intersects the n axis, N is the total number of indexers in the group and T is the total number of different indexing terms used by the group.

To test this model, another calculation was performed independently for a group of 20 indexers. The results are shown in the plot of Figure 8 and can be seen to agree well with the previous findings. However, as N approaches T, the dependence of the exhaustivity coefficient γ on the number of indexers n might be expected to deviate more and more from the expression equation 8 because—and this is intuitively clear—the distribution

TABLE 6. Quality scores by indexers (students) and documents

Document number	Rank	Indexer 1	2	3	4	5	6	7	8
14	1	.51	.66	.57	.60	.36	.60	.30	.55
9	2	.38	.67	.26	.38	.62	.38	.33	.55
10	3	.08	.92	.64	.15	.54	.51	.62	.46
12	4	.32	.70	.52	.32	.25	.52	.41	.50
7	5	.72	.78	.44	.72	.61	.75	.50	.64
15	6	.55	.61	.40	.55	.48	.64	.33	.55
16	7	.59	.77	.64	.48	.56	.62	.49	.44
6	8	.68	.61	.71	.77	.61	.77	.45	.71
2	9	.22	.36	.33	.67	.33	.79	.21	.33
4	10	.74	.58	.48	.84	.55	.71	.48	.61
11	11	.35	.63	.58	.70	.63	.78	.53	.83
1	12	.55	.40	.48	.55	.45	.69	.31	.48
8	13	.41	.41	.25	.56	.56	.47	.34	.38
13	14	.61	.61	.25	.50	.64	.37	.55	.61
3	15	.61	.51	.90	.70	.63	.59	.51	.78
5	16	.40	.38	.24	.45	.52	.48	.38	.38
Average		.48	.60	.48	.56	.52	.60	.43	.55

TABLE 7. Average number of indexing terms assigned, mean quality scores and variances for professional indexers, scientists, and student indexers

Rank	Professional indexers Number of terms	Quality u	δ^2	Scientists Number of terms	Quality u	δ^2	Students Number of terms	Quality u	δ^2
1	7.6	.53	.02	3.21	.55	.02	6.3	.60	.02
2	6.7	.52	.03	3.72	.53	.03	6.4	.60	.02
3	5.4	.51	.01	3.38	.52	.02	5.0	.56	.03
4	6.9	.50	.03	2.54	.42	.02	4.4	.55	.02
5	5.9	.47	.03	2.24	.39	.03	3.2	.43	.01
6	4.4	.44	.04	1.76	.38	.02	4.9	.48	.03
7	5.0	.44	.03	1.48	.36	.02	4.5	.48	.03
8	2.5	.26	.01	1.0	.28	.01	3.2	.43	.01
Average	5.6			2.4			5.0		

TABLE 8. Percentages of the total number of terms and exhaustivity levels as a function of the number of indexers in the group

Number of indexers	Professional indexers		Scientists		Students	
	Percent-age of terms	$100 \cdot \gamma$	Percent-age of terms	$100 \cdot \gamma$	Percent-age of terms	$100 \cdot \gamma$
1	29%	39%	28%	36%	33%	45%
2	46	57	46	55	52	63
3	59	70	60	69	64	74
4	70	79	71	78	72	82
5	79	86	80	86	81	88
6	87	91	88	92	88	93
7	94	96	94	96	94	97
8	100	100	100	100	100	100

law underlying this process would not hold unless $N \ll T$.

Since

$$\gamma(n+1) = \gamma_1 + m \log (n+1)$$

therefore the difference or the rank increment of γ

$$\Delta\gamma_n = (n+1) - \gamma(n) = m \log (n+1) - m \log n$$

can be approximately equated to

$$\Delta\gamma_n = m \log \left(1 + \frac{1}{n}\right) \cong \frac{m}{\log 10} \cdot \frac{1}{n} = m\frac{1}{n}$$

or

$$\Delta\gamma_n \cdot n = m = \text{const.}$$

Thus equation (8) or its equivalent form equation (9) are familiar expressions obtained in other contexts: they can be interpreted—with appropriate changes of the names of variables—either as Bradford's law of information scattering (14), as the law of scientific productivity

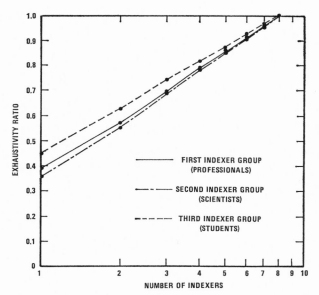

FIG. 7. Plot of the exhaustivity ratios γ versus the number of indexers in the group (on a log scale) for a group of 8 indexers

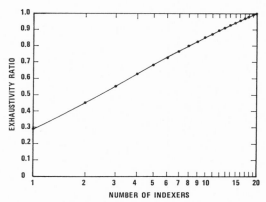

FIG. 8. Plot of exhaustivity ratios γ versus the number of indexers in the group (on a log scale) for a group of 20 indexers

developed by Lotka (15), or as Zipf's law of vocabulary distribution (16). In Bradford's law, the expression of the form of equation (8) relates the cumulative total number of articles to the number of journals in which they were published. Lotka obtained an equivalent functional relationship (although in more general form) between the number of scientists and the number of scientific contributions they make. In the case of Zipf, an expression of the type of equation (9) was obtained relating the word length with the number of word occurrences. We have shown that the same model applies also to express the relation between the level of exhaustivity of information representation or indexing and the number of decision makers (or indexers) whose individual judgments are combined to reproduce the information contents of the object which is jointly observed (specifically, to produce a cumulative index). In other words, this could be considered as the law expressing the dependence of the "completeness" of knowledge on the size of the community which might be expected to contribute to this knowledge.

The fact that the same model is applicable to the process of information scattering (Bradford's Law), growth of scientific productivity (Lotka's Law), vocabulary distribution (Zipf's Law), and, as we have now shown, to the completeness or exhaustivity of information representation as reflected in group indexing, implies that the same basic law of distribution of information flow should underlie all these processes. This topic will be discussed in greater detail in a different paper.

7 Conclusions

Measures of indexing consistency should reflect not only the formal agreement of indexers on a number of terms, but also the significance of terms on which the indexers agree or disagree. This can be achieved if the sets of indexing terms are considered not well-defined sets but fuzzy sets with respect to the significance judgment. A procedure for designing such sets has been proposed and it has been shown that the proposed approach can be extended to define the quality and exhaustivity of indexing. The experimental results on indexing exhaustivity based on this approach warrant the conclusion that the increase of information as a result of group indexing obeys the same law as that of the scattering of information (Bradford), of scientific productivity (Lotka), and vocabulary distribution (Zipf).

8 Appendix

The purpose of this appendix is to expand the concept of fuzzy sets discussed in the text. The definitions are from Zadeh (*12*).

Let A, B and C be fuzzy sets in a set X of objects x with membership functions $f_A(x)$, $f_B(x)$ and $f_C(x)$ respectively. Then the following definitions are made:

Equality: The fuzzy sets A and B are said to be equal, written $A = B$, if $f_A(x) = f_B(x)$ for all x in X.

Subsets: The fuzzy set A is said to be a subset of the fuzzy set B if $f_A(x) \leq f_B(x)$ for all x in X.

Union: The union of two fuzzy sets A and B, written $A \cup B$, is a fuzzy set C where $f_C(x) = \text{Max } [f_A(x), f_B(x)]$, $x \in A$ which may be abbreviated $f_C = f_A \vee f_B$. The union of n fuzzy sets T_1, T_2, . . . T_n is the fuzzy set C where $f_C = f_{T_1} \vee f_{T_2} \vee . . . \vee f_{T_n} = \underset{i}{\vee} f_{T_i}$

Intersection: The intersection of two fuzzy sets A and B, written $A \cap B$, is a fuzzy set C where $f_C(x) = \text{Min } [f_A(x), f_B(x)]$, $x \in A$ which may be abbreviated $f_C = f_A \wedge f_B$. The intersection of n fuzzy sets T_1, T_2, . . . , T_n is the fuzzy set C where $f_C = f_{T_1} \wedge f_{T_2} \wedge . . . \wedge f_{T_n} = \underset{i}{\wedge} f_{T_i}$.

It can be shown that fuzzy sets have the following properties:

$A \cup B = B \cup A$

$A \cap B = B \cap A$

$(A \cup B) \cup C = A \cup (B \cup C)$

$(A \cap B) \cap C = A \cap (B \cap C)$

$A \cap (B \cup C) = (A \cap B) \cup (A \cap C)$

$A \cup (B \cap C) = (A \cup B) \cap (A \cup C)$

$A \cup A = A$

$A \cap A = A$

References

1. HOOPER, R. S., *Indexer Consistency Tests—Origin Measurements, Results and Utilization*, IBM Washington Systems Center, Bethesda, Maryland, Presented at the 1965 Congress International Federation for Documentation 10–15 October, 1965.
2. JACOBY, J., *Methodology for Indexer Reliability Texts*, RADC–IN–62–1, Documentation, Inc., Bethesda, Maryland, March 1962.
3. SLAMECKA, V., AND J. JACOBY, *Effect of Indexing Aids on the Reliability of Indexers*, RADC–TDR–63–116, Documentation, Inc., Bethesda, Maryland, June 1963.
4. JACOBY, J., AND V. SLAMECKA, *Indexer Consistency under Minimal Conditions*, RADC–TDR–62–426, Documentation, Inc., Bethesda, Maryland, November 1962.
5. PAINTER, A. F., *An Analysis of Duplication and Consistency of Subject Indexing Involved in Report Handling at the Office of Technical Services*, U.S. Department of Commerce, Office of Technical Services, Washington, D.C., March 1963.
6. RODGERS, D. J., *A Study of Intra-Indexer Consistency*, General Electric Company, Washington, D.C., September 1961.
7. KOROTKIN, A. L., and L. H. OLIVER, *The Effect of Subject Matter Familiarity and the Use of an Indexing Aid upon Inter-Indexer Consistency*, General Electric Company, Bethesda, Maryland, February 1964.
8. HOOPER, R. S., A Facet Analysis System, Automation and Scientific Communication, *Short Papers, Annual Meeting of the American Documentation Institute*, 2:253 (October 1963).
9. STEVENS, M. E., *Automatic Indexing: A State-of-the-Art Report*, Monograph 91, National Bureau of Standards, Washington, D.C., March 1965, p. 160.
10. BRYANT, E. C., D. W. KING, AND P. J. TERRAGNO, *Some Technical Notes on Coding Errors*, Westat Research Analysts, Denver, Colorado, 1963.
11. SCHULTZ, CLAIRE K., WALLACE L. SCHULTZ, AND RICHARD H. ORR, Comparative Indexing: Terms Supplied by Biomedical Authors and by Document Titles, *American Documentation*, 16(No. 4):299–312 (1965).
12. ZADEH, L. A., Fuzzy Sets, *Information and Control* 8:338–352 (1965).
13. BROWN, JAMES E., *Efficient Reading*, D. C. Heath and Company, Boston, 1962.
14. BRADFORD, S. C., *Documentation*, Public Affairs Press, Washington D.C., 1950, pp. 148–154.
15. LOTKA, ALFRED J., The Frequency Distribution of Scientific Productivity, *Journal of the Washington Academy of Sciences, 16* (No. 12):317–323 (1926).
16. ZIPF, G. K., *Human Behavior and the Principle of Least Effort*, Addison-Wesley Press, Inc., Cambridge, Mass., 1949, pp. 24–25.

Chapter Eleven
Testing

Although "testing and evaluation" are often mentioned in juxtaposition as one, they are two quite distinct and different activities. Pointing out the differences between them may appropriately introduce this chapter. This lack of distinction has been and still is a point of unnecessary confusion, preventing understanding and communication. Testing is concerned with whether the system (or some of its elements) does what it is supposed to do, and evaluation asks whether what it is supposed to do is the right or "best" way of doing it. In other words, testing is concerned with the working of a system (or its elements) as stated in the design, and evaluation is concerned with the statements on which the design of the system is based. In a sense, system evaluation and testing are related to each other as are theory and experimentation in the scientific method.

In many areas, the activity of testing traditionally has been recognized as a highly important one. The primary and practical purposes of testing are:

a) to learn about the workings of systems (or elements thereof) in order to derive bases upon which predictions about their future performance may be made and their past performance may be explained; and

b) to enable orderly change(s) in design, development, and operation of systems (or elements thereof) on the basis of information gathered on their performance.

Although testing activity in information science was voluminous, it was limited to only a few performance areas. Besides the extensive testing of the technological or hardware aspects of information systems (which is really outside the realm of information science), testing in information science was limited to the software aspects of computer technology (e.g., program debugging) and to a limited number of functions of information retrieval systems. In fact, the selections in this book are representative of the literature in the latter area.

The testing activity in information retrieval produced a considerable number of works of theoretical, experimental, and critical natures, which are reflected by the division of this chapter in two sections. Section A contains formal and theoretical works dealing with establishment of performance measures; it also contains one article of a critical nature. Section B contains a selection of articles presenting test experiments and results.

In the first selection of Section A, Swets (Article 54) presents an extensive and critical review of measures proposed to that date and also proposes measures of his own, which are based on conditional probabilities as utilized in statistical decision theory. The significance of Swets' work is that it broadens the treatment of measures as simple ratios with the application of probability theory, as measures are treated in most sciences; he discusses the properties of measures and separates measures from measurement. Brookes (Article 55) proceeds from Swets, critically analyzing Swets' measures, applying them to some experimental data, and proposing improve-

ments by especially taking into account the predictability of performance with a minimum of measurements. Pollock (Article 56) points out the weaknesses of many traditional measures, at least in two respects — first, the ability only to treat probabilities with values of 0 and 1 and, second, the inability to derive a combining, overall, utility function from the measures. On the basis of his criticism, Pollock derives a number of conditions that retrieval measures need to satisfy, and develops a measure — "normalized sliding ratio measure" — with interesting properties that might allow generalization over a wide variety of conditions, as well as other measures. Fairthorne (Article 57) in a most penetrating way asks a number of (so far) unanswered questions about testing of retrieval systems. His critical comments are of value not only to theorists but also to experimentors and operators.

Section B contains articles on test experiments, presenting test results. These articles are significant from a number of points of view. First, they include several, differing variables, which indicate to a designer, developer, or operator the available modes of variation; second, they demonstrate by the fact of experimentation the approaches to and problems of methodology; and, third, regardless of the general and justifiable scepticism about validity and/or reliability of results, they show the general and comparative trends in performance that can be expected from implementation of given sets of variables within a retrieval system.

Cleverdon (Article 58) presents results mostly on the effects of different definitions and implementations of indexing languages. Salton and Lesk (Article 59) present results from the tests of various automatic indexing methods, results which may indeed suggest a base for decision-making in practice. Lancaster (Article 60) presents a performance study of a system, contrasting with the previous selections which were studies of experimental systems. Saracevic (Article 61) presents selected results from an inquiry into testing of numerous variables which affect the performance of a retrieval system, with particular focus on the problems of test methodology and the effect of human factors. Finally, Adams and Lockley (Article 62) present a study of the acceptances and reactions of scientists to a new retrieval system. In the process they present a highly interesting, different, and original methodology for a performance study.

In conclusion, there seems to be a glaring deficiency among test studies: they each stand in isolation, defying comparison and cumulation. It is extremely difficult to add to what we learn about the performance of individual variables from study to study. We glean some general aspects of the behavior of retrieval systems and we even are able to make gross predictions as to how some configurations of variables will perform. But we have not been able to coordinate and cumulate specific knowledge from testing. This remains a high priority problem for future efforts.

A. Measures of Performance

54 Information Retrieval Systems

JOHN A. SWETS
Science
Vol. 141, No. 3577, July, 1963

In the past 5 years, the period of intensive study of information-retrieval systems, ten different measures for evaluating the performance of such systems have been suggested. In this article I review these measures and propose another.

The various measures have much in common. Eight of them evaluate only the effectiveness (accuracy, sensitivity, discrimination) of a retrieval system and are derived completely, in one way or another, from the 2-by-2 contingency table of pertinence and retrieval represented in Fig. 1. The other three measures assess efficiency as well as effectiveness, by including such performance factors as time, convenience, operating cost, and product form.

In some of the measures, in each of the categories just mentioned, the variables considered are combined into a single number. In other measures, of each kind, the separation of two or more variables is maintained, and the numerical value of each is listed. Still other measures consist of a graph showing the relationship between two variables related to effectiveness.

The measure proposed here is one supplied by statistical-decision theory. It compresses the four frequencies of the contingency table into a single number, and it has the advantage that this single number is sufficient to generate a curve showing all of the different balances among the four frequencies that characterize a given level of accuracy. That is to say, this measure, given the validity of the model underlying it, provides an index of effectiveness that is invariant over changes in the breadth of the search query or in the total number of items retrieved. If desired, a second number can be extracted from the fourfold table to characterize the specific balance among the frequencies that results from any specific form of query. This measurement technique has the drawback, at present, that the model on which it is based has not been validated in the information-retrieval setting. The ground for optimism on this score is the fact that the model has been validated in analogous problems of signal detection studied in electrical engineering and psychology.

Before proceeding to the review and proposal, it should be stated that this article deals only with measures of merit — that is, with the dependent variables of an experiment conducted to evaluate one or more retrieval systems. It is not concerned with methodological issues (such as the number of items in the information store, the means of determining relevance, the number and qualifications of judges, and the form and number of queries) in the design of such experiments.

1. Review

In this review I present the measures to some extent in the terms of their originators and to some extent in common terms which will make it easier to compare and contrast them with the measure proposed here. A common vocabulary is achieved by coordinating the variables expressed in the various terms of different writers with the quantities of the contingency table as they are represented in Fig. 1. These translated quantities always appear in

	P	$\overline{P}$	
R	a_{V_1}	b_{K_1}	$a + b$
$\overline{R}$	c_{K_2}	d_{V_2}	$c + d$
	$a + c$	$b + d$	$a + b + c + d$

FIG. 1. The 2-by-2 contingency table of pertinence and retrieval. P and $\overline{P}$ denote, respectively, pertinent and nonpertinent items; R and $\overline{R}$ denote, respectively, retrieved and unretrieved items; $a, b, c,$ and d represent the simple or weighted frequencies of occurrence of the four conjunctions; V_1 is the value of retrieving a pertinent item; V_2 is the value of not retrieving a nonpertinent item; K_1 is the cost of retrieving a nonpertinent item; and K_2 is the cost of failing to retrieve a pertinent item.

brackets. Thus, [a] represents the number of pertinent items retrieved. A quantity such as [a/a+c] represents the proportion of pertinent items retrieved and may be taken as an approximation to the conditional probability that a pertinent item will be retrieved — a probability denoted $[Pr_P(R)]$. It is convenient at times to refer to these quantities in words, so I define them as follows:

$a/a + c = Pr_P(R) =$ conditional probability of a "hit."

$b/b + d = Pr_{\overline{P}}(R) =$ conditional probability of a "false drop."

$c/a + c = Pr_P(\overline{R}) =$ conditional probability of a "miss."

$d/b + d = Pr_{\overline{P}}(\overline{R}) =$ conditional probability of a "correct rejection."

The first measure to be considered is one proposed by Bourne, Peterson, Lefkowitz, and Ford (1), a measure best described as "omnibus." These writers recommend determining a measure of agreement between an aspect of system performance and a related user requirement for each of approximately 10 to 12 requirements.

The measures of agreement are then multiplied by weighting coefficients which represent the relative importance of the requirements, and the products are summed to achieve a single figure of merit.

Bourne and his associates report the results of what they regard as a preliminary investigation, and it is true that the measure has not yet been described in sufficient detail for application. The requirements to be included in the measure have deliberately not been fixed; it is suggested that they will represent such factors as amount of pertinent material missed [c], amount of nonpertinent material provided [b], delay, ease of communication, complexity of search logic accommodated, form in which items are delivered, and degree of assurance that items on a given subject do not exist. Bourne and his associates point out that there are not enough quantitative data available to apply the measure now, but they do present data which demonstrate that users tend to disagree on the relative importance of different user requirements. They do not justify the combining of many different kinds of variables on a single metric.

Bornstein (2), in discussing details of experimental design, proposes consideration of the following four variables: (i) the number of pertinent [a], partially pertinent, peripherally pertinent, and nonpertinent [b] responses to each question; (ii) the time spent by the user in examining materials in each of the four categories of pertinence; (iii) the proportion of acceptable substitutes for "hard copy" which are supplied in each of the four categories; and (iv) the actual coincidence and uniqueness of responses on the four-point scale of pertinence.

Bornstein suggests that analyses of variance be carried out for variables i, ii, and iii for each point on the pertinence scale, the main effects attributed to the different retrieval systems being compared. He suggests that within-cell variance terms and certain interaction effects will also convey valuable information. This procedure yields only relative measures of effectiveness and efficiency, but Bornstein argues that using a known store of information, which is necessary if absolute measures are to be obtained, requires excessive effort and biases the comparison of different retrieval systems.

Wyllys (3) derives a single figure of merit for the efficiency of a search tool as employed at a given stage in the sequential search process. He proposes to obtain the product of four variables: (i) the "restriction ratio" (which is the number of items retrieved at stage k divided by the number of items retrieved at stage $k - 1$, or the reduction in the number of potentially pertinent items that is effected by the search tool); (ii) the cost of using the tool; (iii) the number of pertinent documents eliminated from further consideration [c]; and (iv) a loss function $[K_2]$.

Wyllys states that the cost variable should be defined in accordance with the local situation to weight correctly such factors as time, money, inconvenience, and indexing costs, and that the loss function should incorporate the degree of pertinence of the pertinent documents eliminated.

Verhoeff, Goffman, and Belzer (4) propose a measure which may be translated as

$$M = [a(V_1) - b(K_1) - c(K_2) + d(V_2)],$$

in which $[K_1]$ and $[K_2]$ are non-negative constants, and for which pertinence is defined by each system user.

These writers would maximize the measure for a given retrieval system, over users with different opinions about pertinence, by defining a critical probability

$$\left[Pr = \frac{K_1 + V_2}{V_1 + K_1 + K_2 + V_2} \right]$$

for each item relative to each query, and by retrieving those items having a probability of pertinence greater than the critical probability. This procedure is germane to system design and use rather than to system evaluation, but I mention it because it bears some resemblance to concepts discussed later in this article.

Swanson (5) has proposed a measure $M = R - pI$, where R is the sum of relevance weights of retrieved items divided by the sum of relevance weights (for a given query) of all items in the store; I is the effective amount of irrelevant material, and is defined as $N - LR$ where N is the total number of items retrieved $[a + b]$ and L is the total number of pertinent items in the store $[a + c]$; and p is a penalty $[K_1]$ which takes on arbitrary values.

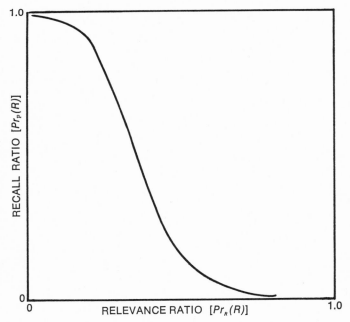

FIG. 2. The plot suggested by Cleverdon (9) to show the trading relationship between the proportion of pertinent items which are retrieved and the proportion of retrieved items which are pertinent.

Borko (6) presented a modification of Swanson's measure in which the irrelevancy score I is redefined. In Borko's measure, I is the number of nonpertinent items retrieved $[b]$ divided by the number of items retrieved $[a + b]$, or $[Pr_R(\bar{P})]$. Borko also prefers to do without the arbitrary penalty on nonpertinent retrievals so that the measure is bounded by $+1$ and -1.

Mooers (7) proposes three ratios: (i) the ratio of the number of crucially pertinent items retrieved to the number of crucially pertinent items in the store; (ii) the ratio of the number of pertinent or crucially pertinent items retrieved to the number of pertinent or crucially pertinent items in the store; and (iii) the ratio of the number of nonpertinent items retrieved to the number of nonpertinent items in the store.

In more general terms, Mooers proposes consideration of three conditional probabilities — of an important hit, of a hit, and of a false drop. He states that, for an excellent system, the first probability should be high and the last should be simultaneously low. He further states that a system is good if the first is near 1.0, and very good if the last is less than .01. The second variable is said to be of less importance than the other two; it should always closely approach 1.0.

Perry and Kent (8) consider several quantities found in the contingency table but focus on two: (i) the conditional hit probability, $[a/a + c]$ or $[Pr_P(R)]$, and (ii) the inverse hit probability $[a/a + b]$ or $[Pr_R(P)]$.

Cleverdon (9) considers the same two variables, which in his terms are the "recall ratio" and the "relevance ratio," respectively. He emphasizes the trading relationship (that is: as the inverse hit probability or relevance ratio increases, the hit probability or recall ratio can be expected to decrease) and suggests that it will be illuminating to plot the recall ratio against the relevance ratio. He expects that a curve will be generated, with an as yet unknown shape, as the restrictiveness of the search query is varied. He has speculated that the curve will look something like the one in Fig. 2. Thus, highly restrictive queries would lead to a relatively high relevance ratio and to a relatively low recall ratio; a less restrictive query would enhance the recall ratio at the expense of the relevance ratio.

Swanson's second proposal (10) is much like the last few discussed. From an experiment on automatic text searching he has plotted the percentage of pertinent items retrieved [or the conditional hit probability, $Pr_P(R)$] against the number of nonpertinent items retrieved $[b]$. His data follow the curve of Fig. 3. The data points forming this curve were generated by a procedure analogous to varying the requirements for proximity, in text, of key words, and by specifying either an "and" or an "or" relationship among a variable number of key words.

The proposal made in the next section, discussed later in detail, is that $Pr_P(R)$ be plotted against $b/b + d$ — that is, against $Pr_{\bar{P}}(R)$ — rather than against b, as Swanson has done, or against $Pr_R(P)$, as Cleverdon has done. One reason is that the quantities $Pr_P(R)$ and $Pr_{\bar{P}}(R)$ contain all the information in the fourfold table of pertinence and retrieval, because the other two, $Pr_P(\bar{R})$ and $Pr_{\bar{P}}(\bar{R})$, are simply their complements. The major point, however, is that, for these axes, statistical-decision theory provides a family of theoretical curves, which are similar in appearance to Swanson's empirical curve, along with two parameters. One of the parameters, the one of major interest, reflects accuracy; it is an index of the distance of a curve from the positive diagonal, the latter corresponding to chance performance. The other parameter reflects the breadth of the query; it indexes a point on a curve by the slope of the curve at that point.

Thus, if it can be generally established that varying the breadth of the query in retrieval systems will generate a curve of the type provided by the theory (and this seems likely), then it is possible to combine the hit and false-drop probabilities, $Pr_P(R)$ and $Pr_{\bar{P}}(R)$, into a single number which is an absolute measure of retrieval-system accuracy, independent of the particular balance between the two probabilities that is struck by any particular form of query, and also to combine the two probabilities in another way into another single number to represent any particular balance between them.

2. Proposal

The relevance of statistical-decision theory to the problem of information retrieval has been observed before. Maron and Kuhns (11) have suggested "an interpretation of the whole library problem as one where the request is considered as a clue on the basis of which the library system makes a concatenated statistical inference in order to provide an ordered list of those documents which most probably satisfy the information needs of the user." Wordsworth and Booth (12) have applied game theory to the problem of deciding when to stop a search. Here I simply call attention to the possibility that statistical-decision theory will provide a measure of retrieval effectiveness that is preferable to the measures proposed to date.

Decision theory is addressed to the problem of assigning a sample, bearing evidence, to one or the other of two probability distributions — one of two (mutually exclusive and exhaustive) statistical hypotheses is to be accepted. An analogous problem is posed in classical problems of signal detection. The measure taken of the input to a detector, in a particular time interval, must be assigned to one of two events — the detection system reports either that noise (random interference) alone existed or that a specified signal existed in addition to the noise. Similarly, a retrieval system takes a measure of a given item in the store, relative to a particular query, in order to assign the item to one of two categories—the retrieval system rejects the item as not being pertinent or retrieves it.

Decision theory describes the optimal process for

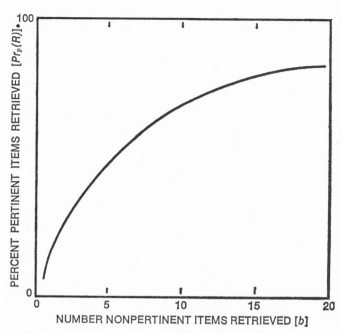

FIG. 3. Curve representing an idealization of data reported by Swanson (10).

making the type of decision with which it deals (13). This process description has been translated directly into a functional specification of the ideal signal-detection device (14) and it has been found to represent quite accurately the behavior of human observers in a variety of detection and recognition tasks (15, 16).

The primary concern here is not with a process, or with system design, but rather with the measurement techniques that accompany the process description. The process model is presented here, though very briefly, because it provides a rationale for the measurement techniques. The model is described in the language of the retrieval problem to display one possible coordination between the elements of the model and the physical realities of retrieval. It is suggested, however, that the measurement techniques may be used to advantage whether or not this particular coordination seems entirely apt.

The model. Let us assume that when a search query is submitted to a retrieval system the system assigns an index value (call it z) to each item in the store (an item can be a document, a sentence, or a fact) to reflect the degree of pertinence of the item to the query. (Maron and Kuhns have described a particular procedure to accomplish this assignment, but let us regard such a procedure, in general, as a feature of all retrieval systems.) Now it may be that for a given need, or for the need as translated into a search query, the items in a given store do in fact vary considerably in pertinence, from a very low value (or no pertinence) to a very high value (or full satisfaction of the need). On the other hand, all of the items may in fact (according to expert opinion or the user's opinion) be either clearly non-pertinent or clearly pertinent to the need. In either case the retrieval system, being imperfect, will view the items as varying over a range of pertinence; indeed, because of the error which will exist in any retrieval system, the value of z assigned to a non-pertinent item will frequently be higher than the value of z assigned to a pertinent item.

Thus, we assume that the retrieval system assigns a fallible index of pertinence, z, and that there exists, apart from the retrieval system, a knowledge of which items are "in truth" pertinent and nonpertinent. We may speculate that the situation is similar to that depicted in Fig. 4. The abscissa represents the degree of pertinence as indexed by z. The ordinate shows the probability of assignment of each value of z. The lefthand function, $f_{\bar{P}}(z)$, represents the distribution of values of z assigned to non-pertinent items, and the righthand function, $f_P(z)$, represents the distribution of values of z assigned to pertinent items. It should be noted that an umpire can determine the condition P or $\bar{P}$ (that is, he can classify all items as being pertinent or nonpertinent) either because, in his opinion, they all fall clearly into one of these two categories or by virtue of selecting arbitrarily a cutoff along a continuum of pertinence.

Figure 4, as described so far, is intended only to portray the assumptions that the values of z assigned to $\bar{P}$ items vary about a mean, that the values of z assigned to P items vary about a higher mean, and that the two distributions overlap. The two distributions are shown as normal and of equal variance. These assumptions, if justified empirically, facilitate the calculation of a measure of effectiveness, but they are not necessary.

It is clear from the representation of the problem in Fig. 4 that if the retrieval system is to accept (retrieve) or reject each item on the basis of the index value z associated with it, a criterion of acceptance must be established by, or for, the system. A cutoff value of z, denoted z_c, must be established such that all items with $z > z_c$ are retrieved and all items with $z < z_c$ are rejected. It may also be seen in Fig. 4 that a trading relationship exists between the conditional probability of a hit, $Pr_P(R)$ [represented by the area under $f_P(z)$, to the right of z_c], and the conditional probability of a false drop, $Pr_{\bar{P}}(R)$ [the area under $f_{\bar{P}}(z)$ to the right of z_c]. If, for example, the acceptance criterion is made more lenient — that is, if z_c is removed to the left — $Pr_{\bar{P}}(R)$ is increased at the expense of increasing $Pr_{\bar{P}}(R)$.

Just where, along the z axis, the cutoff is best set is determined by the values and costs appropriate to a particular retrieval need. If the user is willing to examine a good deal of nonpertinent material in order to reduce the chance of missing a pertinent item, the cutoff should be low. Alternatively, if time or money is an important factor and a miss is not very serious, the cutoff should be high. Similarly, certain a priori probabilities may affect the level of the desired cutoff. If the user has good reason to believe the store contains the item he wants, he may choose to make a relatively thorough

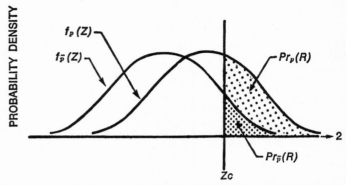

FIG. 4. A representation of the probability distributions, on the index of pertinence z, related to nonpertinent and pertinent items, and of the retrieval criterion z_c.

search; if he is doubtful that the store contains the item he requires, he may prefer a token search, of only the items most likely to be responsive to his query. In practice, the level of the cutoff may be set, though imprecisely to be sure, by the choice of a form of query. The choice of and "and" or "or" relationship among a number of key terms, and the selection of the number of key terms, are ways of determining the breadth of the query and thus the level of the z-axis cutoff.

In the next section I derive a measure of the basic effectiveness of a retrieval system that is independent of the level of the acceptance criterion. If the general representation of the problem in Fig. 4 is valid, then the measure presented is the only one that serves the purpose. Measures of the proportion of hits, or the proportion of hits and correct rejections, or the proportion of hits minus the proportion of false drops, or other measures of this kind, are not adequate, and simply observing various values of two variables, such as the proportion of hits and the proportion of false drops, is an unnecessarily weak procedure.

Of course, the assumption that a real retrieval system has a constant effectiveness, independent of the various forms of queries it will handle, is open to question. It seems plausible, however, that the sharpness of the retrieval system's query language, and its depth of indexing, and also the heterogeneity of items in the store, will determine a level of effectiveness that is relatively invariant over changes in the form of the query. In any event, the assumption is subject to empirical test, and its importance is sufficient to justify the effort of testing. Again, it may be that retrieval systems vary considerably in their ability to handle different forms of query — that is, to adopt different acceptance criteria — some present systems being relatively inflexible. Differences in this respect come under the heading of efficiency, as opposed to effectiveness, and can be taken into account separately. This kind of flexibility will probably be a standard feature of future retrieval systems.

Derivation of the measure. The proposal made here amounts to a recommendation that retrieval-system performance be analyzed by means of the *operating characteristic* as used in statistics. One form of the operating characteristic is the curve traced on a plot of $Pr_P(R)$ versus $Pr_{\bar{P}}(R)$ as the z-axis cutoff varies. One such operating-characteristic curve, calculated on the basis of the assumptions that the underlying probability distributions (of Fig. 4) are normal and of equal variance, is shown in Fig. 5. The complemenary probabilities, of a correct rejection and of a miss, $Pr_{\bar{P}}(\bar{R})$ and $Pr_P(\bar{R})$, are also included in Fig. 5 to emphasize the fact that a complete description of the retrieval system's performance can be obtained from an operating-characteristic curve.

It is evidence that a family of theoretical operating-characteristic curves can be drawn on the coordinates of Fig. 5, bounded by the positive diagonal and the upper left-hand corner, that correspond to different distances between the means of the two probability distributions, $f_{\bar{P}}(z)$ and $f_P(z)$. Since the distance between the means of these two distributions reflects the ability of the retrieval system to segregate nonpertinent and pertinent items, the parameter of this family of curves will serve as a measure of effectiveness.

If the curves are normal, they can be characterized by a single parameter — namely, the distance between the means of the two probability distributions divided by the standard deviation of the distribution of nonpertinent items,

$$\frac{{}^M f_P(z) - {}^M f_{\bar{P}}(z)}{{}^a f_{\bar{P}}(z)}$$

It does no harm to adopt the convention that this standard deviation is unity, and then the parameter is just the difference between the means. This measure, which in this context I shall call E, is simply the normal deviate. It is easily obtained from a table of areas under the normal curve. Figure 6 shows a family of operating-characteristic curves and the associated values of E.

It is possible to relax the assumption of equal variance of the two distributions which was made in drawing the curves of Fig. 6. By way of illustration, Fig. 7 shows a family of theoretical curves calculated on the basis of the assumption that the variance of $f_P(z)$ increases with its mean — in particular, that the ratio of the increment in the mean to the increment in standard deviation is equal to 4.0.

I next describe a convenient way of calculating E in practice, and show how an additional parameter may be obtained, if necessary, to represent the ratio of variances. For the present, it is important to note that the assumption of normality will probably be adequate, and that curves based on quite extreme variance ratios differ very little. It will, in fact, be difficult to obtain enough data to reject the normality assumption or to distinguish among similar assumptions about variance. With the variance ratio as a free parameter, a normal operating-characteristic curve can be drawn to fit closely any steadily rising function. That a steadily rising curve will be obtained in practice is a reasonable expectation; Swanson's data (Fig. 3) certainly fit such a curve.

Having seen how a given level of sensitivity or effectiveness can be measured by a single number E, independent of a particular acceptance criterion, let us observe in passing that the slope of the curve at any point will serve as an index of the particular acceptance criterion, and of the breadth of the search query, which

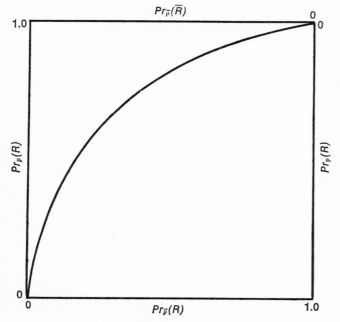

FIG. 5. A typical operating-characteristic curve.

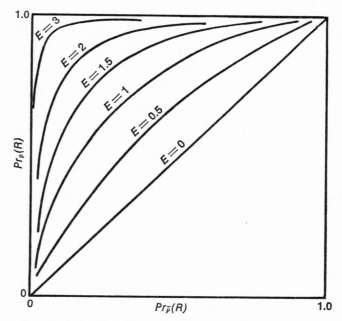

FIG. 6. A family of operating-characteristic curves, based on normal distributions of equal variance, with values of the parameter E.

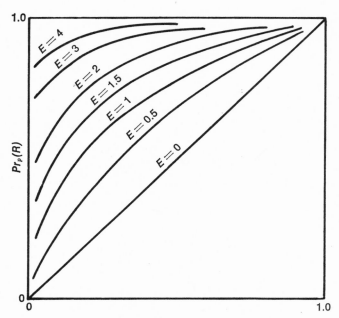

FIG. 7. A family of operating-characteristic curves based on an assumption of increasing variance.

yielded that point. Strictly speaking, it is assumed in statistical theory that the z axis of Fig. 4 is a scale-of-likelihood ratio, $f_P(z)/f_{\bar{P}}(z)$, and then the value of the slope of the operating-characteristic curve at any point is exactly the value of likelihood ratio at which the acceptance criterion must be set to produce that point. Moreover, if the a priori probabilities $[Pr(P)$ and $Pr(\bar{P})]$ and the values and costs are known, then the optimal setting of the acceptance criterion is at the value of likelihood ratio equal to

$$\frac{Pr(\bar{P})}{Pr(P)} \cdot \frac{(V_2 + K_1)}{(V_1 + K_2)}$$

However that may be, the formal assumptions and the full quantitative power of statistical theory have not been emphasized here; although they may ultimately be found to be of value in the retrieval application, the use of the suggested measures does not depend on this finding. The slope may simply be taken as the measure of the acceptance criterion, empirically, without concern for its precise theoretical basis. It is clear that the difference in the slopes at two points of a steadily rising function is a straightforward measure of the effective change in the breadth of a search query.

In brief, the operation of a retrieval system yields entries in the cells of a fourfold contingency table and thus yields estimates of four conditional probabilities, two of which are independent. For any given query or form of query, these two probabilities can be plotted as a point in the unit square of Fig. 6.

The parameter of the theoretical curve on which the point falls is a measure of retrieval system effectiveness; the slope of the curve at that point is a measure of query breadth. It is expected that the various fourfold tables which result from systematically varying the breadth of the queries addressed to a given retrieval system will generate a steadily rising function similar to the ones shown in Fig. 6.

Specifics of measurement techniques. The most convenient way of converting the conditional probabilities of a hit and of a false drop into a value of E is to plot them on normal coordinates — that is, on probability scales transformed so that the normal deviates are linearly spaced (for example, Codex Graph Sheet No. 41,453). On these scales, as illustrated in Fig. 8, the normal operating-characteristic curve becomes a straight line. The points indicated as A and B illustrate that the difference between the normal-deviate values, one taken from the abscissa and one from the ordinate, is equal to E.

The lines shown in Fig. 8, having unit slope, are based on probability distributions, $f_{\bar{P}}(z)$ and $f_P(z)$, of equal variance. In general, the reciprocal of the slope (with respect to the normal-deviate scales) is equal to the ratio of the standard deviation of $f_{\bar{P}}(z)$. Thus, the curves of Fig. 7, if plotted on these scales, would show slopes of less than unity and a decrease in slope with increases in E.

It should be noted that the procedure just given for calculating the value of E — that is, taking the difference between the two normal-deviate values — is not adequate when the operating-characteristic curve has a slope other than unity, for then a single curve will produce different values of E, depending on which point along the curve is chosen. A satisfactory convention often followed in this case is to determine the value of E from the point where the curve crosses the negative diagonal.

Validating requirements. The validity of the decision-theory model and measurement techniques for a given retrieval system can be tested by determining the operating-characteristic curve experimentally. Four or five data points, spread over a range of $Pr_{\bar{P}}(R)$ from approximately 0.10 to 0.90, will establish whether or not the curve rises steadily, and, if it does, these four or five points will establish its slope. Each data point must, of course, be based on a large enough sample to provide a fairly reliable point estimate of a probability. This is admittedly a large number of data, more than many investigators would at present consider economically feasible to obtain. There is, unfortunately, no substitute for adequate numbers of data if retrieval systems are to be evaluated on an empirical basis. Perhaps a small offsetting consideration is the fact that results can be pooled for queries of the same breadth, or of the same logical form.

It is possible to conduct further, and stronger, tests of validity. For retrieval systems that calculate something like the index of pertinence, z, additional information can be obtained by determining directly the probability distributions that underlie the operating characteristic.

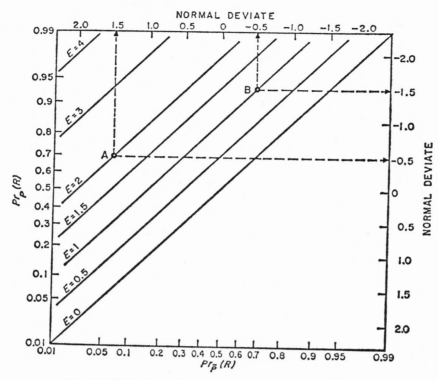

Fig. 8. Normal operating-characteristic curves plotted on double-probability graph paper.

Other tests exist which may be applied appropriately to retrieval systems that do not provide an index comparable to z. An extensive testing program, originally designed for the study of signal detection in psychology, could be directly translated and applied to retrieval systems. A description of this program may be found elsewhere (16). For most purposes, however, a determination of the operating-characteristic curve should be adequate.

If the empirical operating-characteristic curve obtained from a given retrieval system is reasonably well fitted by a linear function on normal-deviate coordinates, the measure E is appropriate to represent the effectiveness of that system. It is to be expected, on rational grounds, that the model will be found to apply generally to a variety of retrieval systems. If this proves to be the case, there will be many current applications of the measure E. This outcome would greatly facilitate performance-cost analysis of available retrieval systems.

References and Notes

1. C. P. Bourne, G. D. Peterson, B. Lefkowitz, D. Ford, *Stanford Res. Inst. Proj. Rept. No. 3741* (1961).
2. H. Bornstein, *Am. Doc.* **12,** 254 (1961).
3. R. E. Wyllys, *Trans. Congr. Inform. System Sci., Hot Springs, Va., 1st* (1962).
4. J. Verhoeff, W. Goffman, J. Belzer, *Commun. Assoc. Computing Machinery* **4,** 557 (1961)
5. D. R. Swanson, *Science* **132,** 1099 (1960).
6. H. Borko, *System Development Corp., Santa Monica, Calif., Field Note No. 5649/000/01* (1961).
7. C. N. Mooers, *Zator Company, Cambridge, Mass., Tech. Note No. RADC-TN-59-160* (1959).
8. J. W. Perry and A. Kent, Eds., *Tools for Machine Literature Searching* (Interscience, New York, 1958), pp. 3–18.
9. C. W. Cleverdon, *Association of Special Libraries and Information Bureaux, Cranfield, England, Interim Rept.* (1962).
10. D. R. Swanson, paper presented at the Congress of the International Federation of Information Processing Societies, Munich (1962).
11. M. E. Maron and J. L. Kuhns, *J. Assoc. Computing Machinery* **7,** 216 (1960).
12. H. M. Wordsworth and R. E. Booth, *Western Reserve Univ. Tech. Note No. 8, AFOSR-TN-59-418* (1959).
13. A. Wald, *Statistical Decision Functions* (Wiley, New York, 1950).
14. W. W. Peterson, T. G. Birdsall, W. C. Fox, *IRE (Inst. Radio Engrs.) Trans. Information Theory* **4,** 171 (1954); D. Van Meter *and* D. Middleton, *ibid.,* p. 119.
15. W. P. Tanner, Jr., and J. A. Swets, *Psychol. Rev.* **61,** 401 (1954); J. A. Swets, *Psychometrika* **26,** 49 (1961).
16. J. A. Swets, *Science* **134,** 168 (1961).

55 The Measures of Information Retrieval Effectiveness Proposed by Swets

B. C. BROOKES
Journal of Documentation
Vol. 24, No. 1, March, 1968

1. Introduction

As Bourne[1] has emphasized in a recent review, direct comparison and critical discussion of the performances of different IR systems are hampered by the adoption of different measures of effectiveness by different workers. It would therefore be helpful to the development of IR systems if a measure of general applicability and acceptability could be contrived. The measure sought should also be interpretable in terms of the different sets of variables used in different systems so that the effects of minor modifications of a variable can easily be related to the overall effectiveness of the system.

Swets[2,3] has proposed a new measure of IR effectiveness which has more advantages than he has already claimed for it and which is a promising candidate for the present vacancy. However, some difficulties of interpreting the measure need to be resolved before it is likely to become generally acceptable.

At the present time the performance of IR systems can be reliably assessed only by meticulously detailed testing of a sizeable collection of documents over all practicable ranges of all the key variables taken one by one. The pioneers of IR measurements had to regard this laborious-

ness as an inescapable part of their exploratory work. Cleverdon,[4] for example, estimates that about 300,000 searches of, for the most part, 1400 documents were made during the Cranfield experiments, though this was an exceptionally comprehensive study. This heavy work of measurement inhibits attempts to measure the total effects of minor modifications to any variable and therefore impedes the progressive refinement of IR systems in operation. The statistical decision theory measures proposed by Swets offer considerable reduction of effort in measuring effectiveness.

The well-known graphs of recall and precision introduced by Cleverdon[5] and the normalized measures introduced by Salton[6] all require measurements to be taken over the whole ranges of the variables (such as level of co-ordination). Swets has demonstrated, however, that the technique he has proposed yields, in general, a straight line instead of a curve of varying curvature and unknown mathematical form. If this linear form can be relied on, then only two experimental points are needed, in principle at least, to obtain his measures instead of the five, six, seven, or more required to plot an unknown curve.

Cleverdon and Salton have rightly emphasized the

need to make many tests to ensure that reliable averages and smooth curves are finally obtained. But the smooth curves by means of which final results are necessarily publicly presented tend to hide from public view the random uncertainities of individual researches which can be illustrated only by very detailed results. Smooth curves suggest that the variables so related are the results of forces as deterministic as those of mechanics, but the results of individual searches reveal that the selection of documents relevant to a given inquiry is a random hit-or-miss process which indexing merely biases towards successful retrieval. By proposing a measure derived from probability theory, Swets emphasizes the fundamentally probabilistic nature of IR. He also sketches, though very tentatively, some plausible probabilistic models of IR systems. If any one of these can be shown adequately to simulate real IR systems, then a new path to theoretical development has been opened.

On these two counts alone, i.e. reduction of measuring effort and the propects of theoretical advance, Swets' proposal is worthy of serious consideration.

2. The Swets Model of an IR System

Consider two distinguishable populations, of m objects A and n objects B, which have a measurable characteristic z distributed with means μ_1 and μ_2 and variances σ_1^2 and σ_2^2 for the populations A and B respectively. Let $f(z/A)$ and $f(z/B)$ be the probability density functions.

Then assigining some arbitrary cut-off value, c, to z, we can ask: What is the ratio of the numbers of objects A to the number of objects B for which $z \geqslant c$? The proportion of the m objects A for which $z \geqslant c$ is equal to the area which lies under the curve A to the right of the ordinate at C, as shown in Fig. 1. Similarly, the proportion of the n objects B for which $z \geqslant c$ is equal to the area which lies under the curve B to the right of the same ordinate. Expressing these proportions in terms of probability theory:

$$P(z \geqslant c/A) = \int_c^\infty f(z/A)\,d_z$$

and

$$P(z \geqslant c/B) = \int_c^\infty f(z/B)\,d_z.$$

We can therefore expect the mixed population for which $z \geqslant c$ to contain

$$m \int_c^\infty f(z/A)\,d_z \quad \text{objects A}$$

and

$$n \int_c^\infty f(z/B)\,d_z \quad \text{objects B}$$

The percentages of the m objects A and n objects B in this mixed population for which $z \geqslant c$ can be obtained by multiplying the two numbers given above by $100/(m+n)$.

If the value of c is varied, these corresponding percentages and their ratio will vary. If the percentages corresponding to A and B for the given value of c are plotted against each other, a curve which characterizes the particular mixed population is obtained. This curve is called the *operating characteristic* or *OC curve* of the system.

If the A and B curves of Fig. 1 overlap then, as the cut-off point c moves from left to right, the corresponding

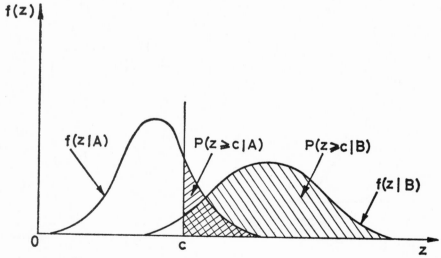

FIG. 1. The statistical model: the 'problem of two means'.

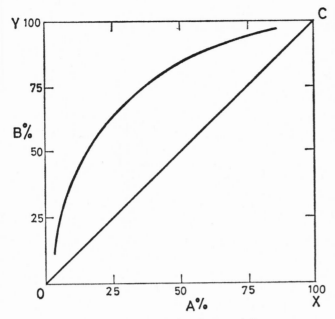

FIG. 2. The operating characteristic.

OC curve of Fig. 2 will be generated. It will start at C (where A = B = 100%), move to the left rapidly at first as the ordinate at c moves through the main part of curve A and will eventually reach O (where A = B = 0%) as c moves beyond the tail of curve B. It will form an arc lying above the diagonal OC. If the A and B curves overlap completely, the OC curve coincides with the diagonal, implying that the proportions of A and B are constant throughout. If the A and B curves do not overlap, the proportion of A falls from 100% to 0% while that of B remains constant at 100%, and the OC curve coincides with the two lines CY and YO.

In the Swets model the component populations A and B are identified with the documents, respectively nonrelevant and relevant to a given inquiry, which together constitute the collection under test. The figures required are those of the *recall ratio*, $P(z/B)$, which Swets prefers to regard as $P(R/r)$, i.e. the probability of retrieving a document given that it is relevant, and of the *fall-out ratio* $P(z/A)$ which Swets regards as $P(R/r)$, i.e. the probability of retrieving a document given that it is *not* relevant. Corresponding values of the recall ratio (Y) and the fall-out ratio (X) are then plotted, on paper with with normal probability scales on both axes, to produce the OC curves.

In his paper Swets presents eighty-two OC curves derived from the published experimental results of Salton and Lesk, Cleverdon, Mills and Keen, and Giuliano and Jones. Within the limits of experimental error, *all are straight lines*.

This result offers the strong presumption that the probability density functions of recall and of fall-out with respect to some mediating variable are both gaussian or very nearly so. (See Appendix). Swets seems to be reluctant to draw this inference but it is easily checked. The detailed results of the Cranfield tests are readily available and one has only to plot the Cranfield figures

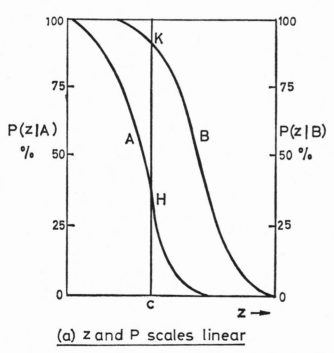

(a) z and P scales linear

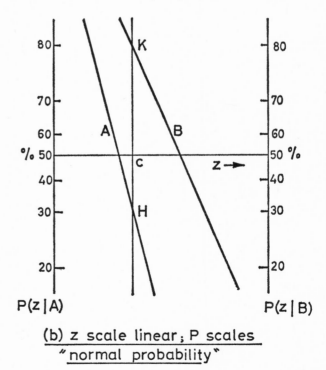

(b) z scale linear; P scales "normal probability"

FIG. 3. Plots of $P(z/A)$ and $P(z/B)$ against z.

of the recall ratio, and similarly the corresponding fall-out ratio, as in Fig. 3(b) on normal probability paper. As expected, the plots produce a series of points which lie on straight lines, or very nearly so (Fig. 5), showing that the distributions of recall and fall-out are approximately gaussian.

However, this inference requires the variable z to be continuous. But in the Cranfield tests the mediating variable was the 'level of co-ordination', a discrete variable which takes only the integral values 0, 1, 2. . . Can the continuous variable of the gaussian distributions be identified with the discrete 'level of co-ordination'? Swets does not mention this difficulty. However, for the present analysis, it suffices to imagine that underlying the discrete variable 'level of co-ordination' there is a continuous variable, z, which conveniently assumes the value $1 \cdot 00$. . ., $2 \cdot 00$. . ., $3 \cdot 00$. . ., and so on, as the level of co-ordination takes the values 1, 2, 3,. . . This point can await clarification if the implications of the Swets measure require it.

The fact that the plots of recall and fall-out drawn on probability paper are straight lines, or nearly so, together with the assumption that z can be regarded as a continuous variable to provide a measure, implies that the Cranfield systems can be represented by statistical models such as shown in Fig. 6. The values of the parameters determined from the graph of Fig. 5 (from figures for Index Language 1.1a (fig. 6.501T) chosen because it had as many as ten co-ordination levels) are:

$$\mu_1 = 1.17, \quad \mu_2 = 5.32, \quad \mu_2 - \mu_1 = 4.15,$$
$$\sigma_1 = 2.13, \quad \sigma_2 = 2.00, \quad \sigma_1/\sigma_2 = 1.065.$$

The equation of the OC curve, obtained by substituting the values in (3), is then

$$Y = 1 \cdot 065 \, X + 2.075$$

but, as this technique requires the drawing of two straight lines through two sets of plotted points, the risk of error is reduced by plotting the OC curves directly as Swets describes.

The main reason for deriving the parameter values is that figures can be attached to components of the model. An improvement of the system would produce an OC curve more remote from O. Such a shift requires at least one of the following improvements in terms of the existing model:

a. A reduction of σ_2, i.e. improvement of the recall techniques.

b. A reduction of σ_1, i.e. an improvement which reduces fall-out.

c. An increase of $(\mu_2 - \mu_1)$, normalized with respect to σ_1 and σ_2, i.e. an improvement in discriminating between relevant and non-relevant documents.

The technique suggested offers a means of measuring in isolation the effects of any modification of recall, fall-

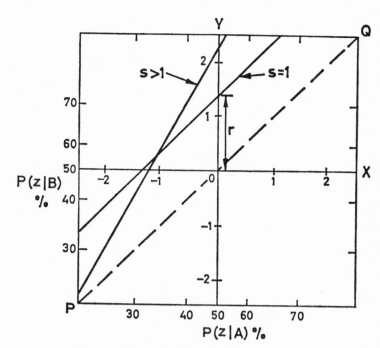

Fig. 4. OC curves: biaxial probability scales.

out, or discrimination, and then of calculating the effect on the system as a whole.

In a large collection of documents the required estimates of m and n, the numbers of non-relevant and relevant documents respectively in the total collection, or in any large experimentally segregated part of it, can be obtained by random sampling. As the techniques of sampling 'attributes' and the associated sampling errors are well-known, there is no reason why the Swets measures are not as applicable to large operational systems, such as MEDLARS, as well as to experimental systems such as the Cranfield collection.

3. The Swets Measure of IR Effectiveness

If in Fig. 7 the OC line AB is parallel to the diagonal PQ and cuts the XY diagonal at I, Swets defines his measure of effectiveness as

$$E = \sqrt{2OI}$$

where OI is the intercept on OR. Incidentally, $\sqrt{2OI}$ is equal to the intercept on the Y-axis. Swets calibrates OR so that the value of E, which is $\sqrt{2OI}$, can be read off directly. For his sample of Cranfield results, Swets found values of E ranging from 1.33 to 1.86 — a reasonable range of discriminable values.

4. Critique of the Swets Measures

If the OC line is *not* parallel to PQ, and Swets finds values of the slope, s, ranging from almost as low as

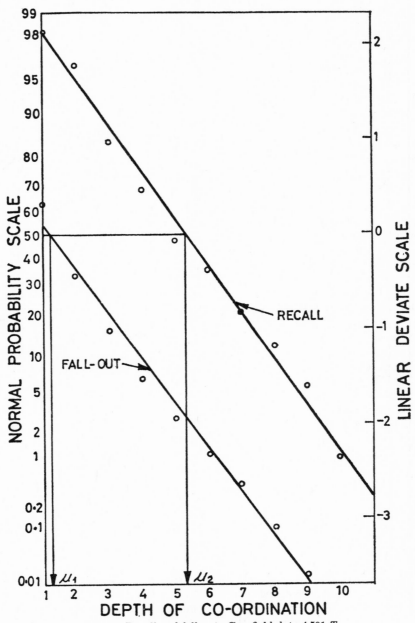

Fɪɢ. 5. Recall and fall-out: Cranfield data 4.501 *T*.

0.5 to almost as high as 2.0, then it is necessary to report both *E*, defined again as $\sqrt{2OI}$, and *s*, the slope. So, in effect, we always need two measures, *E* and *s*, because we need to know that *OC* is parallel to the diagnoal, i.e. that $s = 1 \cdot 00$, if the value of *s* is not reported.

Consider two IR systems S_1 and S_2 for which the Swets measures are E_1, s_1 and E_2, s_2 respectively. Then, if $s_1 = s_2 = s$, i.e. if the *OC* lines are parallel to each other, there is no doubt that, given $E_1 > E_2$, system S_1 is more effective than system S_2. But Swets does not explain how one can compare systems which have different values of *s* only, or different values of both *E* and *s*.

In addition to the difficulties of interpreting different sets of *E* and *s* values, the measures proposed by Swets have some elements of arbitrariness about them which are likely to inhibit wide acceptance of the measures in the precise form in which he defined them. They are:

a. The factor $\sqrt{2}$ by which the key intercept *OI* is multiplied. Why is it needed?
b. The choice of *OR* as the intercepted line providing the measure for lines of all slopes; this choice may flatter the performance of systems whose *OC* lines diverge widely from $1 \cdot 00$. It is noticeable that the highest

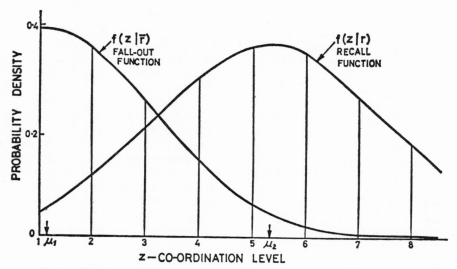

FIG. 6. Statistical model of IR system. Cranfield data 4.501 T.

values of E reported by Swets are associated also with high values of s, but it is necessary either that E and s should be independent or that their functional relationship be understood.

c. The use of $\frac{1}{2}(\sigma_1 + \sigma_2)$ as the normalizing factor for $(\mu_1 - \mu_2)$, which is implicit in the choice of OY as the intercepted line. The arithmetic mean of standard deviations is not, in general, a conventional or meaningful statistical measure. The dependence of E on such a factor will impede development, for example, of the statistical tests needed to discriminate between sampling fluctuations and significant differences in test values of E.

Swets may have good reasons for introducing these seemingly arbitrary elements into his measures but he has not so far explained their relevance to IR and their advantages are not apparent. The defects are, however, remediable.

5. Proposed Modifications

As a subordinate measure of effectiveness, s is needed only if E is not independent of the slope. By calculating the intercept of the line (3) with the line $Y = -X$, it can be shown that, as defined by Swets,

$$E = \frac{\mu_2 - \mu_1}{\frac{1}{2}(\sigma_1 + \sigma_2)}$$

It is suggested that E should be replaced by S, where

$$S = \frac{\mu_2 - \mu_1}{(\sigma_1^2 + \sigma_2^2)^{\frac{1}{2}}}.$$

Here the normalizing factor is the standard deviation of the sum (or difference) of two independent variables

with variances of σ_1^2 and σ_2^2. From a statistical point of view, this normalizing factor is more acceptable than the arithmetic mean of σ_1 and σ_2 because its use simplifies the analysis of sampling variations and the testing of significant differences of the measure of effectiveness since the sampling distribution of S is known.[7]

Geometrically interpreted, S is the length of the perpendicular from O to the OC line which (apart from Swets's factor $\sqrt{2}$) makes S equivalent to E when $s = 1$ but which is increasingly less than E as the value of s diverges from unity (Fig. 7). Thus S corrects the bias in favour of systems with 'sloped performance' which E seems to give when the result and fall-out distributions

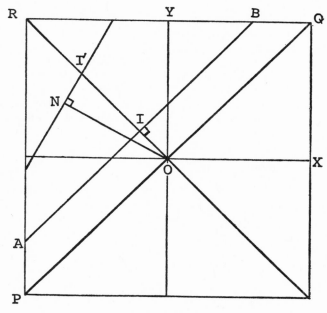

FIG. 7. For AB, $\quad E = \sqrt{2}OI$, $\quad S = OI$.
For $A'B'$, $\quad E = \sqrt{2}OI$, $\quad S = ON$.

are both guassian. Moreover, S is of wider generality than E because it can be determined uniquely from its formula even if the Swets OC curve is not linear.

The index s could be regarded, not as a subordinate measure of effectiveness of the system as a whole, but as a useful description of the system's mode of performance. If $s = 1$, the recall technique and fall-out control are equally effective. If $s < 1$, then $\sigma_2 > \sigma_1$ and so recall is less effective than fall-out control. If $s > 1$, recall is the more effective. Improvement of either recall or fall-out control would of course also improve the effectiveness of the system as a whole and would be reflected in an increase in the value of E.

The main advantage of E and s is that, unlike other measures of IR effectiveness so far proposed, they link IR measurements to a ready-made and well-developed statistical theory and therefore offer the hope of lifting IR development to a new and more objective plane. But the acceptability of E and s is jeopardized by their elements of arbitrariness and by the difficulties of interpreting them in terms of IR system variables.

To sum up, the proposed measure S is defined as

$$S = \frac{\mu_2 - \mu_1}{(\sigma_1^2 + \sigma_2^2)^{\frac{1}{2}}}$$

where μ_1, μ_2, and σ_1^2, σ_2^2 are the means and variances respectively of the frequency distributions of recall and fall-out with respect to the mediating variable (such as depth of co-ordination).

For the Cranfield data quoted earlier in this paper,

$$S = \frac{4 \cdot 15}{(2 \cdot 00^2 + 2 \cdot 13^2)^{\frac{1}{2}}} = \frac{4 \cdot 15}{2 \cdot 92} = 1 \cdot 42$$

but values of S of $3 \cdot 0$ to $3 \cdot 5$ are the distant objective.

The main advantage of S over E is that S is a 'statistic' whose properties are known so that IR systems measured by it can be more meaningfully compared.

One of the next phases of IR investigation must concern the relationship between increased effectiveness, by means of 'feed-back' or other techniques, and 'cost'. For such investigations some measure of effectiveness as general and as statistically convenient as S will be necessary.

Appendix

The particular case for which the probability density functions $f(z/A)$ and $f(z/B)$ are gaussian (or 'normal') is of theoretical and practical interest in statistics. We can then write:

$$f(z/A) = \frac{1}{\sigma_1 \sqrt{2\pi}} e^{-(z-\mu_1)^2/2\sigma_1^2}$$

and

$$f(z/B) = \frac{1}{\sigma_2 \sqrt{2\pi}} e^{-(z-\mu_2)^2/2\sigma_2^2}$$

Definite integrals of these functions are tabulated as the 'normal probability function' and are readily accessible. Other aids to calculation involving these functions are also available. For example, if plots of the percentages of A and B corresponding to given values of c are drawn, using the usual linear scale for the percentages, then typical 'ogive' curves are produced, as in Fig. 3(a). But if the same points are plotted on 'normal probability paper', which has a specially distorted scale for the percentages, then the ogive curves derived from gaussian distributions become straight lines, as in Fig. 3(b).

In a similar way, when corresponding A and B percentages are both plotted on normal probability scales, as in Fig. 4, the OC curve becomes a *straight line*.

The equations A and B of Fig. 3(b), with respect to the linear deviate scales and origin O, are

$$X = -\frac{1}{\sigma_1}(z - \mu_1) \tag{1}$$

and

$$Y = -\frac{1}{\sigma_2}(z - \mu_2) \tag{2}$$

From the graphs of Fig. 3(b) the values of μ_1 and μ_2 for any set of empirical results can be read directly in terms of z and, if the graphs are straight lines, the values of σ_1 and σ_2 are the inverses of the slopes. If the graphs are *not* straight lines, the probability density functions $f(z/A)$ and $f(z/B)$ are not gaussian but their forms can be constructed directly from the graphs of Fig. 3 and their parameters can thus be determined.

The OC curve drawn against normal probability scales can also be derived from (1) and (2) without the use of the special graph paper which has normal probability scales along *both* axes. For a given value of c, the ordinate at $z = c$ cuts the graph of A and B, in Fig. 3, at H and K respectively. If the special paper (Chartwell C5570) is available, the OC curve is drawn by plotting corresponding values of X and Y; if it is not available, the curve can equally well be drawn on ordinary linear graph paper by plotting corresponding values of X_1 and Y_1 on equal linear scales, as shown in Fig. 4.

From (1) and (2) we have (linear scales)

$$X = -\frac{1}{\sigma_1}(c - \mu_1)$$

and

$$Y = -\frac{1}{\sigma_2}(c - \mu_2)$$

Elimination of c yields the equation of the OC curve:

$$\sigma_2 Y = \sigma_1 X + (\mu_2 - \mu_1) \tag{3}$$

which is the equation of a straight line with slope σ_1/σ_2. For the particular case which $\sigma_2 = \sigma_1 = \sigma$ (say) then, putting $\mu_2 - \mu_1 = r\sigma$, (3) reduces to

$$Y = X + r \tag{4}$$

which is a straight line parallel to the diagonal PQ and whose intercept on the Y-axis is r.

If therefore a mixed population has two component populations with unknown means μ_1 and μ_2 and variances σ_1^2 and σ_2^2 with respect to some mediating variable z, then the OC curve can be constructed as described above. If the resulting OC curve is a straight line, it follows that:

a. The variate z is 'similarly' distributed in both populations. Note that if, in equations (1) and (2) $f(z)$ is substituted for z, the same equation (3) is obtained when $f(z)$ is eliminated. This implies that if the OC line (drawn on bi-axial probability paper) is a straight line, it does not necessarily follow that the z-distributions of result and fall-out are gaussian.

b. The slope of the line, σ_1/σ_2, is the ratio of the two standard deviations.

c. The distance of the line from O (Fig. 4) is a measure of the separability of the two component populations.

This is the statistical technique which Swets has applied directly to the results of experiments on IR systems.

References

1. BOURNE, C. P. Evaluation of indexing systems. In: *Annual review of information science and technology*, vol. **1**, ed. Cuadra, C. A., 1966, p. 171–90.
2. SWETS, J. A. Information retrieval systems, *Science*, vol. **141**, July 1963, p. 245–50.
3. SWETS, J. A. *Effectiveness of information retrieval methods*. Bedford, Mass., Air Force Cambridge Research Laboratories, **15**, June 1967 (Report AFCRL-67-0412).
4. CLEVERDON, C. W., The Cranfield tests on index language devices, *Aslib Proc.*, vol. **19**, no. 6, June 1967, p. 173–94.
5. CLEVERDON, C. W., MILLS, J., and KEEN, M. *Factors determining the performance of indexing systems (Aslib–Cranfield Research Project)*. Vol. **2**. *Test results*. Cranfield, College of Aeronautics, 1966.
6. SALTON, G. The evaluation of automatic retrieval procedures—selected test results using the SMART system. *American Documentation*, vol. **16**, July 1965, p. 209–22.
7. For example, KENDALL, M. G., and STUART, A. *The advanced theory of statistics*, vol. **2**, 1961. The problem of two means, p. 139–50.

56 Measures for the Comparison of Information Retrieval Systems

STEPHEN M. POLLOCK
American Documentation
Vol. 19, No. 4, October, 1968

1 Introduction

A definite need exists for the comparison and evaluation of certain characteristics of various information retrieval systems. This paper is concerned only with the ability of such systems to satisfy queries; the effort and time used by these systems or their relative costs are not considered.

It is important to note that information retrieval systems can respond to queries in a variety of ways. The problem at hand is to consider all possible responses and to evaluate and compare them, both with respect to competing systems and in terms of some absolute measure.

Some past procedures that have been used are reviewed and discussed along with some of the difficulties that arise when these procedures are followed. This paper also introduces some possible new procedures and the inherent difficulties and problems with them.

2 Definitions

The following definitions are to be used in the context of this paper only. Although some of the terms are almost self-definitive, or have been discussed at length elsewhere, it is important to list them here so that confusion and ambiguity will be at a minimum.

1. *Documents*. Documents are elemental entities con-

Presented at the 31st National Meeting of ORSA, New York.

taining information. Thus in terms of this definition, a document might be a report, an abstract, perhaps even a file card containing key words or index phrases. We do not differentiate between "data" and "documents."

2. *Library*. The library is the collection of all documents potentially available to the information-seeker (referred to as the "file" or "collection" in some literature).

3. *Query*. A query is a general statement describing the information that is sought. It is a verbalized expression of an underlying need for information. In general, it is a string of words and may be in the form of a direct question or a statement, such as "tell me about. . . . " We assume that the query is the most complete initial basis available for determining the requestor's information need.

4. *Degree of .Satisfaction of Query*. This extremely subjective term will pertain here to a set of values placed upon all documents in the library that summarizes their respective *relevance* [1] *to a particular query*. Such a set of values may be assigned by a particular retrieval system, or by a "panel of judges," and in general is dependent upon the assigning agency and upon the specific query. The units of value are purposely left undetermined, although it will often be convenient (without loss. of generality) to measure values on a 0 to 1 scale, with 1

---

[1] The term "relevance" here is taken to be synonymous with "pertinence." For a discussion of these terms see for example reference *1*, and for a critical appraisal, reference *2*.

being the perfect degree of satisfaction and 0 being the perfect degree of dissatisfaction.

5. *Master Values.* These are hypothesized perfect, "true" or "God-given" values, inherent to each document-query pair, and are not related to any particular information retrieval scheme. The existence of such values is clearly a philosophical question. We shall assume them discernible by the originator of the query, or a suitably selected "typical requestor" jury. All that follows requires the existence of such a set of values.

6. *System.* A system is a general means of searching through the library with the aim of discovering documents that, to some degree, satisfy a particular query. Typically, a system is directed to identify documents that are relevant to a particular query. Examples of systems are human use of a card index file, computer use of a card index file, coordinate retrieval, etc.

7. *List.* A list is the name we shall give to the output obtained when a system is given a query and "sent" to the library. It is a listing of some or all of the documents in the library, together with appended information concerning the system's estimates of the satisfaction value of each of the listed documents. The list may be, for example, one of the forms:

(a) Documents A, B, C, F, G are responsive to the query; the rest are not.
(b) Documents A, B, C are very responsive; documents F, G, H are of interest; the rest are not.
(c) In order of decreasing satisfaction value, relative to the query the documents are A, C, F, B, H, G, K, L . . . etc.
(d) The value of each document, with respect to the query, is:

Document value	A .9	C .8	F .4	B .3	H .2	G .05	K .05	L .03

(e) Combination of the above.

8. *Master List.* The master list is a listing of all documents in the library, along with their master values, (see paragraph 5 preceding). For a particular query, it is often convenient to think of the documents in the master list as being ordered in decreasing master value.

3 Previous Statistics and Measures

In the past, summary statistics have been devised to compare and evaluate Information Retrieval Systems by analysis of the lists produced by competing systems. Many such analyses have compared lists between two competing systems, as well as the list of a specific system with a master list. There are questions concerning the applicability and characteristics of some of these statistics, however, which will be considered after a brief summary of their definitions and behavior.

Precision and Recall Ratios

Perhaps the most widely used statistics, these measures, are defined as follows (*3*).

Recall Ratio. This term is defined only when the values assigned to the documents by a system are either 0 or 1, and, in addition, the master values are also either 0 or 1. In this case, the recall ratio is defined to be the number of documents assigned 1 that have master value 1, divided by the total number of documents in the library that have master value 1; in other words, the fraction of "relevant" documents that are retrieved.

Precision Ratio. This ratio is also defined only when values can be either 0 or 1. In this case, the precision ratio is the fraction of documents that have been assigned value 1 that have master value 1.

These are absolute measures in that the master list must be available to determine the true (or master) values of each document (i.e., which documents have value 0, which have value 1). Any given list of documents in the library will have associated with it a precision and a recall ratio. The higher these ratios, the better the system that produced the list. Unfortunately, as one ratio goes up, there is a tendency for the other to go down (a conclusive experimental result is presented in reference *4*). For example, a retrieval system that assigns the value 1 to all documents in the library will doing so assign value 1 to all documents that have master value 1, and so the recall ratio will be unity. The precision ratio, however, will then fall to just that fraction of documents in the library that have master value 1.

A probabilistic interpretation may be applied to these ratios, which is helpful when we try to modify them somewhat. If a class of queries is posited over which the recall and precision ratios are well behaved statistically, we may define for any given document-query pair the relations

$$r = \text{recall ratio} \quad = \text{prob. } \{R/S\}$$
$$p = \text{precision ratio} = \text{prob. } \{S/R\}$$

where the events $\{R\}$ and $\{S\}$ are defined

$\{R\} = $ document is assigned value 1 by the system (is "retrieved")

$\{S\} = $ document has master value 1 ("satisfies the query")

If N is the number of documents in the library and R^* is the number of documents in the library with master value 1, then the following conditional probability statement holds:

$$p = \text{prob. } \{S/R\}$$
$$= \frac{\text{prob. } \{R/S\} \text{ prob. } \{S\}}{\text{prob. } \{R/S\} \text{ prob. } \{S\} + \text{prob. } \{R/\bar{S}\} \text{ prob. } \{\bar{S}\}}$$
$$p = \frac{r \dfrac{R^*}{N}}{r \dfrac{R^*}{N} + f\left(1 - \dfrac{R^*}{N}\right)} = \frac{1}{1 + \dfrac{f}{r}\left(\dfrac{N - R^*}{R^*}\right)} \quad (1)$$

where $f = $ prob. $\{R/\bar{S}\} = $ false relevance assignment probability (i.e., probability of assigning value 1 when the master value is 0)

With the relation given in equation (1) we see that for a particular query-library pair if we are given any two of the parameters p, r, and f, the third is uniquely determined. Thus any two of these three measures suffice to characterize a system. Some workers (5) prefer to call r the "sensitivity" and $1-f$ the "specificity," after the medical usage of the terms. These measures are also related to the conventional error probabilities of hypothesis testing:

$$\text{"Type 1" error} = a = \text{prob. } \{\bar{R}/S\} = 1-r$$
$$\text{"Type 2" error} = \beta = \text{prob. } \{\bar{S}/R\} = 1-p$$

Rank-Order Statistics

These statistics have their origin in classical problems involving the comparison of various rankings. The statistics can be used in both an absolute way and a relative way. That is, two lists may be compared against each other, or individual lists may be compared against master lists.

Most commonly used rank-order statistics are specific cases of a general rank-correlation coefficient. This coefficient is defined as follows (6).

Consider the two lists of numbers:

$$\text{List A: } x_1, x_2, x_3, \ldots x_N$$
$$\text{List B: } y_1, y_2, y_3, \ldots y_N$$

These are the lists we wish to compare. The following methodology allows us to express, for each list, how much it "matters" to find x_i in position i and x_j in position j.

We define for the A list the score a_{ij} for each pair of numbers (x_i, x_j), $i, j = 1, 2, \ldots N$. A similar score b_{ij} is defined for the B list. The only limitation on these scores is the skew symmetry requirement $a_{ij} = -a_{ji}$, $b_{ij} = -b_{ji}$ (so that $a_{ii} = b_{ii} = 0$).

A general rank-correlation coefficient Γ is then defined to be

$$\Gamma = \frac{\Sigma a_{ij} b_{ij}}{[\Sigma a_{ij}^2 \Sigma b_{ij}^2]^{1/2}} \qquad (2)$$

where Σ indicates a double summation over all $i, j = 1, 2, 3, \ldots N$. Note that when $a_{ij} = x_i - x_j$; $b_{ij} = y_i - y_j$, then Γ becomes the ordinary product-moment correlation coefficient. Also note that unlike the precision and recall measures, a single number results from the use of this technique.

a. *Kendall's τ Statistic.* The simplest and most widely used form of this coefficient is Kendall's τ statistic. Γ is equal to τ when a_{ij} and b_{ij} are defined

$$a_{ij} = \begin{cases} +1 & m_i < m_j \\ 0 & m_i = m_j \\ -1 & m_i > m_j \end{cases}$$

$$b_{ij} = \begin{cases} +1 & n_i < n_j \\ 0 & n_i = n_j \\ -1 & n_i > n_j \end{cases}$$

where m_i and n_i are, respectively the *rank* of the ith element of the A and B lists. This τ statistic exhibits the properties

(1) $\tau = 1$ when the two lists are identical.
(2) $\tau = -1$ when one list is exactly the inverse of the other.
(3) The average value of τ is zero when both lists are random arrangements of the elements x_i and y_i.

It may also be shown that this statistic is a linear function of the number of pairwise interchanges of neighboring elements (x_i, x_{i+1}) required to change the A list into the B list (or vice versa).

b. *Spearman's ρ Statistic.* This coefficient is obtained by assigning

$$a_{ij} = m_i - m_j$$
$$b_{ij} = n_i - n_j$$

the differences in *rank* of the ith and jth elements of the lists. Spearman's ρ may also be shown to have the properties listed above for the τ statistic. In addition, it gives more weight than the τ statistic to the differences in the rank of elements of the list, as they get further apart.

The M-V Statistics

A modification of Kendall's τ has been developed by Venezian and Mazuy (7) called here the M-V statistic. This statistic is related to Kendall's τ and is defined by letting

$$a_{ij} = \begin{cases} +1 & m'_i < m'_j \\ 0 & m'_i = m'_j \\ -1 & m'_i > m'_j \end{cases}$$

where m'_i is a *modified* ranking of the A list. This modified ranking is such that only the first M elements of the list are ranked according to the original ranking, and the remaining $N-M$ elements are grouped together into an $(N-M)$–fold tie with rank $M+1$. Thus

$$m'_i = \min(m_i, M+1)$$

The same holds for b_{ij} and the B list.

This statistic—call it $\tau(M)$—has introduced a free variable M: the length of the list (from the beginning) that will be used in evaluating a rank-order coefficient. The advantage of having such a free variable in the measure of the effectiveness of systems will be discussed in a later section. At this point it suffices to note that the $\tau(M)$ of a particular pair of lists might vary considerably with M.

Salton's Normalized Measures

G. Salton recently proposed a normalization of the "standard" precision and recall ratios (8). These normalized measures account for the fact that the ratios depend importantly upon the length of (dichotic 0–1 type) list presented to the requestor (or presented for evaluation!).

Letting r_i and p_i be the standard recall and precision ratios evaluated for the *first* i *documents of a list,* Salton defines the normalized measures

$$R_{\text{norm}} = \frac{1}{N} \sum_{i=1}^{N} r_i$$

$$P_{\text{norm}} = \frac{1}{N} \sum_{i=1}^{N} p_i$$

These measures are thus averages of the precision and recall ratios over all possible retrieved sequences of the library.

4 The Disadvantages of Previous Statistics and Measures

Precision and Recall Ratios

These ratios have as their primary disadvantage the fact that assigned and master values must be either 0 or 1. That is, a document must be considered to be either relevant to the query or not. No spectrum of relevance in between is allowed. As a consequence, given many documents that are in fact found to be relevant, there is no way of ordering these according to degree of satisfaction.

Another difficulty with precision and recall ratios is the fact that each retrieval system is rated by a *pair* of numbers. Unless a relation exists to convert such a pair into a single number, there is always the problem of having two systems that are incomparable, in the sense that one might have a high recall ratio and a low precision ratio, the other just the opposite, and thus the two systems cannot be realistically compared to one another. This difficulty can be overcome in theory by creating a "utility function" which depends upon both of the ratios. Although the choice of such a utility function is often somewhat arbitrary, it is apparent that any measure of effectiveness by which systems will be evaluated must implicitly have *some* such relation between the relative costs (or advantages) of recall capability and precision capability.

Indeed, such utility functions have been suggested both on a theoretical (9) and an empirical basis (5). The validity of such functions, however, has yet to be fully confirmed. Most seem to be of a simple (but arbitrary) linear form, such as $U = U(r,f) = r - f$ (reference 5), or $U = U(r,p) = r + p - 1$ (reference 10).

Kendall's τ

The major disadvantage with this statistic is the fact that the *entire list* is used as a basis for comparison. In other words, an interchange of elements with master rank 3 and 7, for example, in the system list, will be just as important as interchange of ranks 103 and 107. Users of the system would tend to regard the first interchange as more serious than the second. Clearly, a realistic measure of the list produced by a system should have some means of weighting appropriately the more "important" parts of the list.

The M-V Statistic

The M-V statistic was created to do such a weighting. This statistic counts only the first M elements of the list, puts the rest in a tie for the $(M+1)$st place, and performs the Kendall τ arithmetic. It has two disadvantages, however. First of all, once M has been selected, the process essentially weights the first M members of the list equally—there is no mechanism for making use of the fact that the master list values might well be other than 0 or 1. Secondly, the calculations involve rather meticulous and difficult analysis.

Salton's Normalized Ratios

These ratios require master values of either 0 or 1. They do effectively weight the initial portion of the list, by producing higher measures for the systems that "right off the bat" provide good recall and precision. However, the entire list is always used; in addition, we are again left with two noncomparable measures, and a utility function combining them is necessary. Salton uses as an "overall" measure the expression $1 - 5R_{\text{norm}} + P_{\text{norm}}$, which can be seen to be somewhat arbitrary.

Summary

Perhaps the most glaring fault with the statistics mentioned here (with the exception of Salton's) is that they treat the lists produced by retrieval systems in a fairly abstract, nonoperational way. That is, there seems to be really no direct relation between the lists and the *use* to which the lists must be directed. Salton's measure seems to be the first historical attempt to avoid this criticism but is itself weakened by the arbitrary weights assigned.

5 Toward a Rational Measure of Effectiveness

This section discusses the desirable characteristics of a realistic measure and makes some suggestions towards obtaining a reasonable measure of effectiveness. As exhibited by the M-V modification of Kendall's τ statistic, there is a desirability to modify available statistics to produce something which can be considered to be a more "useful" or more "applicable" measure of the retrieval capabilities of a particular system (as represented by the list it produces). On the other hand, Salton's measures demonstrate the need to compare lists of different or varying lengths.

Perhaps the most straightforward way of looking at this problem is to ask about the end purpose of these lists: what will be done with them? Only by answering this question can the importance of ordering within the lists, number of elements in the list, etc. be determined, and how important it is to avoid various interchanges of elements. The M-V statistic starts to come to grips with this. Parameter M, which indicates the length of the list to be used, may be varied from unity out to N, the entire number of documents in the library. However, the uniform weighing of the portion of the list that *is* counted implies some fairly strong assumptions as to the use to which the list will be put.

Let us examine some ways that the list might be used.

1. The Officer

Consider a requestor who wishes to find only one document of relevance and is willing to read only two or three documents to find it. Let us call him the "officer." To evaluate a system's response with respect to his rather extreme criterion, the chosen measure should give a high score to a retrieval system that places only one, two, or three documents before the officer and insures that these documents have high probability of relevance. The officer is uninterested in exhaustive search and is indifferent to the system's failure to present *all* relevant documents. He does not care about the probability of relevance of the fiftieth document retrieved. He is interested just in finding one and refuses to read beyond three. The system's performance is judged by the first three documents presented, and the system is penalized for "top-of-the-list" failures even though it might have a perfectly good list of relevant documents to follow.

2. The Analyst

It is possible for a requestor to be interested in compiling, say, a 100-document bibliography (responsive to some query), which is to be studied and analyzed at leisure. Let us call him the "analyst." The analyst might be content with a list of perhaps 400 documents from which he can select 100 particularly pertinent documents; he is probably not seriously concerned about the order in which these 400 are presented to him. He does not mind at all if the first three are not relevant if a high proportion of the rest are. On the other hand, the analyst is not impressed by a system that does well for only the first two or three documents and then begins to produce irrelevant material.

3. The Browser

Another possible user of the retrieval system's output —the "browser"—might be interested in a sequential examination and exploration. When the browser is given a list of relevant documents, he goes through them—in order of computed value if a ranking is given, or just randomly if an unranked set is given. The browser proceeds to look through the documents and will stop when he feels that he has obtained enough information or has satisfied himself as to the amount of information that he wants. From the browser's viewpoint, good retrieval performance means that at each stage in the sequential process, probability of relevance of the next item is maximal.

The many possible uses of a list of retrieved documents suggest that a desirable measure of retrieval effectiveness should be responsive to these variable needs. In particular, there should be a "depth of search parameter" available, to be varied such that if the parameter is at one end of the scale, top-of-the-list performance for only one or two documents is emphasized; if the parameter is at the other end of the scale, the whole collection becomes important, perhaps with ranking of the collection relatively unimportant. With the parameter in the middle of the scale, it should be a mixture of the two. The M-V statistic comes close to doing this, and other schemes might also be appropriate for the same objective. The following section will discuss some of these schemes and presents principles upon which a realistic measure of effectiveness should be based.

6 Some P.B.I.'s [2] Concerning Meaningful Measures of Systems

Importance of the Master List

Whatever measure is devised, it is reasonable that it should relate, in *some* way, to the master list. This master list might have values of simply 0 or 1—the document either relevant or not relevant to the query, with no shades of meaning between. Or it might be ordered in terms of satisfaction values, as described earlier. Although the existence and determination of such a master list is beyond the scope of this paper,[3] it is a necessary prerequisite for the computation of an absolute measure that may be applied to any given list produced by a retrieval system. Inasmuch as absolute measures of two different systems may be compared, such measures are also relative. However, it seems at this point that a statistic which merely compares two lists and decides whether or not they are "similar" (in some sense) seems worse than useless. The degree of similarity might be in just that portion of the list which is unrelated to the real *use* of the list of documents.

A Browser's Statistic

A "Browser's" measure seems possible to suit his characteristics described in item 3 of the previous section. We could construe the value of a document to be related to the probability that the particular document will *completely* satisfy the query, thus ending the need for further documents. If this is the case, then one might use, as a measure of effectiveness, the expected number of documents that it takes for a requestor to be satisfied, given a

---

[2] "Partly Baked Ideas"; see reference *11*.
[3] For a discussion of the problems relating to this, see appendix A of reference *12*.

particular *ranked* list. This number may be calculated (in theory) as follows:

Let us call the master value of the ith document (according to a specific query) $V(i)$, and, as assumed above

$$V(i) = \text{probability } \{i^{th} \text{ document satisfies the query}\}.$$

In addition, we make the assumption (probably a risky one) that these probabilities are independent of the examination of previous documents. Thus the probability $f(n)$ that satisfaction occurs with the nth document of the ranked list $(x_1, x_2, x_3, \ldots x_n)$ becomes

$$f(1) = V(x_1)$$

$$f(n) = V(x_n) \prod_{i=1}^{n-1} (1 - V(x_i)) \quad n = 2, 3, 4, \ldots, N$$

where it is assumed that the documents in the list are examined in the order presented, and N is the number of documents in the library. (If the ranking is imperfect, in that it contains K sets of ties, containing $k_r (r = 1, 2, \ldots K)$ documents each, then the probability that satisfaction occurs with the nth document is

$$f(n) = \frac{1}{P} \sum_{p=1}^{P} f_p(n)$$

where

$$P = \prod_{r=1}^{K} (k_r!) = \begin{array}{l} \text{the number of lists that can be} \\ \text{produced by all permutations of} \\ \text{documents within rankings;} \end{array}$$

$$f_p(n) = V(x_n{}^p) \prod_{i=1}^{n-1} [1 - V(x_i{}^p)]$$

and

$$x_i{}^p = \begin{array}{l} \text{document in position } i \text{ of the} \\ p^{th} \text{ permutation of the list,} \\ p = 1, 2, \ldots P) \end{array}$$

Once $f(n)$ is obtained for a given list, a number n may be defined [4] as:

$$n = \sum_{n=1}^{N} n f(n)$$

It is possible to normalize this number by calculating n for the master list. For the master list, we note that the rank of x_i is i, which leads to the normalized measure

$$v = \frac{\displaystyle\sum_{n=1}^{N} n f(n)}{\displaystyle\sum_{n=1}^{N} n (V)n \prod_{i=1}^{n-1} (1 - V(i))}$$

Unfortunately, at first glance this measure does not seem to have any practical conceptual, statistical or algebraic attractiveness.

A Weighted Rank-Correlation Statistic

The M-V statistic is essentially a technique to weigh only certain portions of the list. The portion up to some rank is weighted unity; the portion past this rank is weighted zero. There seems to be a more mathematically tractable device: weighting the whole list in decreasing

---

[4] When $f(n)$ is a nondefective probability mass function (i.e., $\sum_{n=1}^{N} f(n) = 1$), the number n is simply the expected number of documents needed to obtain satisfaction.

importance from the head of the list to the end. The first function of such sort that comes to mind is a simple exponential weighting. It might be possible to adapt Kendall's τ statistic subject to such a weighting. (In fact, the ideal weighting should perhaps be the actual master values of the documents themselves.) This concept of weighting is developed here only in a very general way.

Let us still preserve the formalism leading to the definition of the general correlation coefficient of equation (2). However, instead of having the scores $a_{ij}(b_{ij})$ dependent upon just pairwise comparison *within* the A list (B list), let us define the B list to be the master list, so that

$$n_i = \text{rank of } i^{th} \text{ document in master list} = i$$

$$b_{ij} = \begin{cases} +1 & i < j \\ -1 & i > j \end{cases}$$

$$\sum_{i=1}^{N} \sum_{j=1}^{N} b_{ij}{}^2 = N(N-1)$$

Now let us define a weighting function $W(i)$, such that $W(i)$ is a measure of the importance of having the document with master rank i being assigned rank i by the system (the A list). Then we may define

$$a_{ij} = \begin{cases} +W(i) & m_i < m_j \\ 0 & m_i = m_j \\ -W(j) & m_i > m_j \end{cases}$$

where again

$$m_i = \text{rank of the } i^{th} \text{ document in the A list (system list)}$$

For example, an exponentially weighted list would have

$$W(i) = a^{i-1}$$

where a is some number between 0 and 1. The resulting coefficient would be a function of a. Call this coefficient τ_a.

Note that if $a = 1$, τ_a becomes simply Kendall's τ. When $a = 0$, then τ_a becomes $+1$ when $p_1 = 1$, and 0 when $p_1 \neq 1$ (so that only the first document in the list is counted). A "master weighted" list might have $W(i) = V(i)$.

The algebraic properties of such weighted statistics have yet to be determined.

Cost Matrix Measures

Another way of looking at the value of a system list is by a decision theoretic formulation. Consider a matrix $\{U_{ij}\}$. This matrix represents the utility of having a document, whose master ranking as i, assigned the rank j by the system. If it is possible to associate utilities (or costs) to each such assignment independent of other assignments, then the value (in terms of overall utility) of a given list of assignments may be obtained from such a matrix.

This may be accomplished by constructing an "occupation matrix" 0_{ij}, where

$$0_{ij} = \begin{cases} 1 & \begin{array}{l} \text{when document with master rank } i \text{ is assigned} \\ \text{rank } j \end{array} \\ 0 & \text{otherwise} \end{cases}$$

Using this matrix, one obtains for the utility of the entire list:

$$U = \sum_j \sum_i 0_{ij} u_{ij}$$

This utility matrix may be used to extend the concepts (or our preconceptions) concerning what a retrieval system really does. In particular, one might look at a retrieval system in the following way.

Given a particular query, there is a certain probability that this query will be ranked j given that its true, or master, ranking is i. Thus, a stochastic matrix, P, may be created, where $\{P_{ij}\}$ is simply this probability. The utility matrix was devised to evaluate any particular given list, given an occupancy matrix 0_{ij} consisted of only a single 1 in any column or row. It is possible to conceive of some similar operation of the P matrix on the utility matrix, such that for any given system represented by a P matrix, an overall average effectiveness of the system might be obtained. Before developing such an operation, we should consider some desirable properties that this operation should possess:

The measure obtained should be normalized so that

(a) It is $+1$ when the P matrix is the identity matrix.
(b) It is -1 when the P matrix is the anti-diagonal matrix:

$$P_{ij} = \begin{cases} 1 & i = N - j + 1 \\ 0 & \text{otherwise} \end{cases}$$

(c) It is 0 when $P_{ij} = 1/N$ for all i, j (i.e., when all lists are "randomly" created).

Expected Search Time Measures

When the user is less interested in retrieved content, but is instead concerned with the time (or effort) involved to obtain some specified level, an appropriate measure might relate to the expected time (or effort) needed. Such indicators are developed in references (*13*) and (*14*), and in appendix 5A of (*4*).

A Partial Relevance Measure

Finally, it seems possible to adapt the standard concept of recall and precision ratios to the situation where relevance may be measured in terms other than "0 or 1." This is discussed at length in the next sections.

7 The Normalized "Sliding" Ratio Measure

We now discuss a measure which can be used to compare and evaluate the retrieval quality of a large variety of information retrieval systems, vis-a-vis any specific query. This measure compares pairs of systems and requires the existence of a master list. The measure has a relation to the classical recall and precision ratios and may be looked upon as a generalization of them. It is also related to the "normalized recall" and "normalized precision" measures devised by Salton. The similarity in terminology is coincidental, but apparently the need for a "normalization" of some kind has been instrumental in the coincidence.

8 Assumptions and Ground Rules

1. The library consists of a total of N documents, any of which may be retrieved by the candidate systems.

2. The output of a system is in general a list "L" of documents, $L = \{1_1, 1_2, 1_3 \ldots 1_N\}$ where 1_i is the identifying number (serial number, etc.) of the ith document in the list.

3. This list is further broken down into K groups called *ranks*, $(K \leq N)$ such that the first k_1 documents are in the first rank, the next k_2 documents are in the second rank, and so on, until the last k_K documents are in the Kth rank. Since all documents must be in some rank, r,

$$\sum_{r=1}^{K} k_r = N.$$

4. A fully ranked list is defined to have only one document in each rank, so that all the k_i are equal to unity and the number of ranks K is equal to N.

The opposite case is the pathological one where $K = 1$, so that $k_K = k_1 = N$, and all documents are contained in the first rank.

Many nonautomated retrieval systems will have $K = 2$ ranks (i.e., "relevant" and "nonrelevant"), with k_1 selected documents included in the first rank, and the remaining $N - k_1 (= k_2)$ documents in the second rank. Most automated systems, however, will produce full-ranked lists.

5. If some documents are not contained in the list, they are assumed to be members of an additional last rank.

6. In order to obtain an absolute measure, a master list L^* is assumed to exist, with the properties of general lists described above, having K^* ranks, with k^*_i documents in rank i $(i = 1, 2, \ldots K^*)$. *In addition*, the master list associates a value v_r with a document in the rth rank of the master list.

9 Definition of the "Sliding" Ratio Measure

A formal definition of the measure follows: the discussion will justify its form and discuss its properties.

For any list L and a master list L^*, define

$x_{ij} \equiv$ the number of documents in rank i in L that are in rank j in L^*,

and

$$g_t \equiv \sum_{r=1}^{t} k_r \qquad g_0 = 0 \qquad (t = 1, 2, \ldots K).$$

Then when n is in the region

$$g_t \leq n \leq g_{t+1} \qquad (t = 0, 1, \ldots K)$$

a function $f(n)$ may be defined

$$f(n) \equiv \frac{n - g_t}{k_{t+1}} \sum_{j=1}^{K^*} v_j x_{t+1,j} + \sum_{i=1}^{t} \sum_{j=1}^{K^*} v_j x_{ij} \qquad (3)$$

When $L = L^*$ in the above definitions, then we may similarly define

$$x^*_{ij} = k^*_i \delta_{ij} \qquad [\delta_{ij} = \text{Kroneker delta}]$$

$$g^*_t = \sum_{r=1}^{t} k^*_r \quad g^*_o = 0 \quad (t = 1, 2 \ldots K^* - 1)$$

and so for $g^*_t \leq n \leq g^*_{t+1}$

$$f^*(n) = \frac{n - g^*_t}{k^*_{t+1}} \sum_{j=1}^{K^*} v_j x^*_{t+1,j} + \sum_{i=1}^{t} \sum_{j=1}^{K^*} v_j x^*_{ij}$$

$$= (n - g^*_t) v_{t+1} + \sum_{i=1}^{t} v_i k^*_i \qquad (4)$$

The "Sliding" Ratio Measure is now defined to be

$$\mu(n) \equiv \frac{f(n)}{f^*(n)} \qquad (5)$$

10 Clarification and Discussion of the Measure

Value of a Set of Documents

We assume that there is some sort of "query satisfaction" value, which may be assigned to each document in the library. In addition, we assume that there are K^* levels, or ranks, of this value, so that any document must have one of the values v_r, $r = 1, 2 \ldots K^*$. By ordering all the documents in the library according to these values, the master list is constructed.

One way of interpreting these values is to consider them as measures of the amount of query-related content contained in each document. When interpreted in this way, it is evident that the master value of one document is independent of the values of the other documents in the library. In fact, this is a highly desirable property to assign to the value scale, since the existence of other documents should not affect the "retrievability" of the one in question.

With this interpretation of the value of each document, we see that if we are presented with a specific set of documents, the value of this set can be construed as the sum of the values of the documents contained.

This value provides a rationale for the use of the $\mu(n)$ measure just defined.

Truncation of a List at n Documents

Now let us imagine that the requestor uses (because of constraints on L, or by operational requirements) *only the first* n *documents of a L-list* produced by a system. When the list is fully ranked (as defined in item 4 in the preceding section), there is no question as to what is meant by the "first n" documents: simply those n documents in the first n ranks (each rank has one document). On the

other hand, if the list has many documents "tied" at various ranks, then the concept of truncating the list after the "first n" documents needs enlargement.

When we say the requestor uses only the first n documents of the list, we imply that if, at any point, the first n documents have not yet been obtained, and two or more documents remain, having the same highest rank remaining, then one document is selected from among these, at random.

For example, if there are $N = 5$ documents in the library, the L list is (3, 5, 1, 2, 4) and $k_1 = 1$, $k_2 = 1$, $k_3 = 3$, the list may be written:

Document # 3 5 1 2 4
Rank   1 2 3 3 3

Then if $n = 4$, each of the following sets of documents has equal probability of being the "first 4" of the list presented to the requestor:

(3, 5, 1, 2)   (3, 5, 2, 4)
(3, 5, 1, 4)   (3, 5, 4, 1)
(3, 5, 2, 1)   (3, 5, 4, 2)

If $n = 2$, then the first n documents can be only (3, 5).

Rationale Behind the Ratio $\mu(n)$

Now to explain the $\mu(n)$ measure, we simply imagine that, in fact, the requestor limits himself to selecting only n documents from the L list. If the L list has *any* ordering, this implies that these first n should be selected according to this ordering, with tied documents treated as discussed previously.

The value of the set of n *selected documents, however, depends only upon the master list* L^*. Inasmuch we have assumed that the total value of the n documents selected is equal to the sum of their individual values, we are led to the form of equation (3). The double summation term in the right-hand side of this equation is seen to be the sum of the values of the documents in the first t ranks of the L list. The first (single) summation term represents the average value (weighted over all appropriate combinations) of documents from the $(t+1)$st rank needed to bring the total number of selected documents to n.

It is possible to simply use the $f(n)$ of equation (3) as our measure.[5] However, the value of this function depends very strongly (naturally) upon the master list and associated master values. In order to account for this, we normalize this function by defining the function $f^*(n)$ of equation (4); $f^*(n)$ is simply the total first-n-document value achieved by using the L^* list as the L list; in other words, $f^*(n)$ is the *best* you can do when *required* to select n documents.

The measure $\mu(n)$, then, is a normalized one relative

[5] In fact, if we used $1/N \sum_{n=1}^{N} f(n)$, we would have exactly Salton's "normalized recall" (8) *if in addition* we constrained K^* to be 2 (so that only two relevance values, 0 and 1, are allowed).

to the master list ("the best you can do") and equals unity when $L=L^*$, and is always less than unity when the L list differs from the L^* list.

11 Numerical Examples

1. Fully Ordered Master List and System List (N = 5)

(a) Master List

L^*:	3	5	1	2	4
Rank:	1	2	3	4	5
Value:	10	8	5	2	0

$(K^*=5; \ k^*_1=k^*_2=k^*_3$
$=k^*_4=k^*_5=1)$

(b) System List

L:	3	4	5	1	2
Rank:	1	2	3	4	5

$(K=5; \ k_1=k_2=k_3=k_4$
$=k_5=1)$

(c) g-calculation: $g_0=0; \quad g_1=1; \quad \text{etc.} \ \ldots \ g_i=i$
$\qquad i=1, 2, \ldots 5$
$\qquad g^*_0=0; \ g^*_1=1; \quad \text{etc.} \ \ldots \ g^*_i=i$
$\qquad i=1, 2, \ldots 5$

(d) x_{ij} Matrix

Rank in L^*
1 2 3 4 5

	1	2	3	4	5
1	1	0	0	0	0
2	0	0	0	0	1
Rank in L 3	0	1	0	0	0
4	0	0	1	0	0
5	0	0	0	1	0

(e) $f^*(n)$ calculation
Since $g^*_t=t$, and $k^*_i=1$, $(i=1, 2, \ldots 5)$, equation (4) reduces to

$$f^*(n)=\sum_{i=1}^{n} v_i$$

n	1	2	3	4	5
$f^*(n)$	10	18	23	25	25

(f) $f(n)$ calculation
Since $g_t=t$, and $k_i=1$, equation (3) reduces to

$$f(n)=\sum_{i=1}^{n} \sum_{j=1}^{5} v_j x_{ij}$$

n	1	2	3	4	5
$f(n)$	10	10	18	23	25

(g) $\mu(n)$ calculation: $\mu(n)=\dfrac{f(n)}{f^*(n)}$

n	1	2	3	4	5
$\mu(n)$	1	.55	.78	.92	1

(h) Comments: Note that if only one document is allowed (or desired), then the retrieval system is scored unity (ideal)—the best possible system (the L^* list) would present the same document. Similarly, if the *whole* library of five documents were demanded, the system again scores unity (as would

even the L^* system) because no discrimination was desired. The *behavior* of $\mu(n)$, as n goes from 1 to N, thus indicates the ability of the system. The value of $\mu(n)$ at a particular n is not of interest *by itself*, unless we are ready to concede the constraint of *requiring* n documents to be selected.

(i) Comparison with another system

System list	L'	2	1	5	4	3
	Rank	1	2	3	4	5

By similar calculations as those above

n	1	2	3	4	5
$f(n)$	2	7	15	15	25
$\mu(n)$	.2	.39	.65	.6	1

and so we see that L' list is as poor as or inferior to the L list for *all* values of n.

2. Master List and System Involving Ties (N = 5)

(a) Master List

L^*:	3	5	1	2	4
Rank:	1	1	2	2	3
Values:	9	9	3	3	0

$(K^*=3; \ k^*_1=k^*_2=2,$
$k^*_3=1)$

(b) System List

L:	3	4	5	1	2
Rank:	1	1	1	2	2

$(K=2; \ k_1=3, k_2$
$=2)$

(c) g-calculation $\quad g_0=0; \quad g_1=3; \quad g_2=5$
$\qquad\qquad\quad g^*_0=0; \ g^*_1=2; \ g^*_2=4; \ g^*_3=5$

(d) x_{ij} Matrix

Rank in L^*
1 2 3

	1	2	3
Rank in L 1	2	0	1
2	0	2	0

(e) $f^*(n)$ calculation
$0\leq n<2 \quad f^*(n)=nv_1$
$2\leq n\leq4 \quad f^*(n)=(n-2)v_2+2v_1$
$\qquad\qquad\quad f^*(5)=v_5+2v_1+2v_2$

n	1	2	3	4	5
$f^*(n)$	9	18	21	24	24

(f) $f(n)$ calculation

$0\leq n\leq3 \quad f(n)=\dfrac{n}{3}\sum_{j=1}^{3} v_j x_{1j}$

$$=\frac{n}{3}[v_1 x_{11}+v_2 x_{12}+v_3 x_{13}]$$

$$=\frac{n}{3}[9(2)+3(0)+0(1)]=6n$$

$3\leq n\leq5 \quad f(n)=\dfrac{n-3}{2}\sum_{j=1}^{3} v_j x_{2j}+18$

$$=\frac{n-3}{2}[9(0)+3(2)+0(0)]+18$$
$$=3n+9$$

Evaluation of Information Systems

n	1	2	3	4	5
$f(n)$	6	12	18	21	24

(g) $\mu(n)$ calculation: $\mu(n) = \dfrac{f(n)}{f^*(n)}$

n	1	2	3	4	5
$\mu(n)$	.67	.67	.86	.88	1

(h) Comments: If only one document were called for, then the L list has a ⅓ chance of selecting document #4, which is not first ranked in the L^* list, so that the measure of the system, at $n=1$, is ⅔.

12 The Special Case When $K^*=2$: The Normalized Sliding Precision and Recall Ratios

When documents can have only two degrees of relevance to a query (either "total" or "none"), the master list consists of only two ranks, $K^*=2$ (although it is possible for a system to be "unaware" of this restrictive dichotomy, and thus assign a complete ranking anyway). Then it is possible to readjust the value scale (because values are additive) so that $v_1=1$, $v_2=0$:

Relevant documents (rank 1) are worth one unit, irrelevant documents (rank 2) are worth nothing. Using these restrictions, equation (3) becomes for $g_t \leq n \leq g_{t+1}$

$$f(n) = \frac{n-g_t}{k_{t+1}} x_{t+1,1} + \sum_{i=1}^{t} x_{i1} \qquad (6)$$

and equation (4) becomes

$$\begin{array}{ll} 0 < n \leq R^* & f^*(n) = n \\ R^* \leq n \leq N & f^*(n) = R^* \end{array} \qquad (7)$$

where $R^* = g^*_1 = k^*_1 =$ the number of documents in rank 1 and L^*, i.e., the number of relevant documents.

An examination of equations (6) and (7) (keeping in mind that x_{i1} stands for the number of documents ranked i by the L list that are ranked 1 by the master, i.e., are relevant; and that i can equal only 1 or 2) shows that $f(n)$ is simply the (average) cumulative number of relevant documents in the first n documents. Inasmuch as we have defined R^* to be the number of relevant documents, we see that we may use these terms to write the classical recall and precision ratios (r, p) for a given number n of documents required to be retrieved:

$$r(n) = \frac{f(n)}{R^*}$$

$$p(n) = \frac{f(n)}{n}$$

Under this constraint of requiring n documents to be retrieved, the best retrieval list possible, the master list L^*, will have the classical ratios.

$$r^*(n) = \frac{f^*(n)}{R^*}$$

$$p^*(n) = \frac{f^*(n)}{n}$$

The measure $\mu(n)$ may thus also be looked upon as a normalized "sliding" (with n) precision and/or recall ratio, because

$$\mu(n) = \frac{f(n)}{f^*(n)} = \frac{\dfrac{f(n)}{R^*}}{\dfrac{f^*(n)}{R^*}} = \frac{r(n)}{r^*(n)}$$

$$= \frac{\dfrac{f(n)}{n}}{\dfrac{f^*(n)}{n}} = \frac{p(n)}{p^*(n)}$$

13 Conclusion

Information retrieval systems are certainly here to stay. The variety available and under development tend to support the suspicion that they are indeed useful, or will be when the "bugs are ironed out." When the potential requestor faces up to the fact that he must answer the question, "Which is the most useful (to me) system?" he is bound to turn to the literature on the evaluation of such systems (cf. reference 15). When he does, however, he is apt to be taken back by the obvious fact that the question cannot be answered without a thorough knowledge of the depth and type of the retrieval required. As Fredrick Pohl (16) so nicely put it:

. . . essentially the problem of useful information retrieval is the problem of setting criteria for usefulness. Once the criteria can be unambiguously established, the rest is a matter of detail.

The normalized sliding ratio appears to be one measure upon which a meaningful usefulness criterion can be based.

• Acknowledgment

The author wishes to thank Paul Jones, Vincent Giuliano, and Emilio Venezian for their cooperation and helpful ideas. Much of the work reported here was accomplished while the author was with Arthur D. Little, Inc., Cambridge, Massachusetts.

References

1. Perreault, J. M., Documentary Relevance and Structural Hierarchy, *Information Storage and Retrieval* 3:13–18 (August 1966).

2. Taube, M., A Note on the Pseudo-Mathematics of Relevance, *American Documentation*, 16:69–72 (April 1965).

3. Cleverdon, C. W., and J. Mills, The Testing of Index Language Devices, *Aslib Proceedings*, 15:106–130 (1963).

4. Cleverdon, C., and M. Kean, Factors Determining the Performance of Indexing Systems, vol. 2, Test Results, ASLIB Cranfield Research Project, Cranfield, 1968.

5. GOFFMAN, W., and V. A. NEWILL, A Methodology for Test and Evaluation of Information Retrieval Systems, *Information Storage and Retrieval*, 3:19–25 (August 1967).

6. KENDALL, M. G., *Rank Correlation Methods*, Hafner Publishing Co., New York, 1962.

7. MAZUY, K. K., A Modification of Kendall's Rank Correlation Measure, presented at one Annual Meeting of the Institute of Mathematical Statistics, Amherst, Mass. (August 1964).

8. SALTON, G., The Evaluation of Automatic Retrieval Procedures—Selected Test Results Using the SMART System, *American Documentation*, 16:209–222 (July 1965).

9. GOOD, I. J., The Decision Theory Approach to the Evaluation of Information Retrieval Systems, *Information Storage and Retrieval*, 3 (April 1967).

10. SINNETT, J. D. (LCOL USAF), *An Evaluation of Links and Rolls Used In Information Retrieval* (Thesis),

AFIT School of Engineering, Wright-Patterson AFB, Ohio, 1964.

11. GOOD, I. J., *The Scientist Speaks*, Basic Books, Inc., New York, 1962.

12. GIULIANO, V. E., and P. E. JONES, Study and Test of a Methodology for Laboratory Evaluation of Message Retrieval Systems, Interim Report, Decision Sciences Laboratory, ESD, AFSC, USAF (prepared by Arthur D. Little, Inc.), August 1966.

13. COOPER, W. S., A Single Measure of Retrieval Effectiveness Based on the Weak Ordering Action of Retrieval Systems, *American Documentation*, 19:30–42 (January 1968).

14. CONGER, C. R., The Simulation and Evaluation of Information Retrieval Systems, H. R. B. Singer, Inc., Report #352–R–17, April 1965.

15. HENDERSON, M. M. (Comp.), *Tentative Bibliography on Evaluation of Information Systems*, National Bureau of Standards, Washington, June 1965.

16. POHL, F., Information Science—Fiction or Fact?, *American Documentation*, 16:69–72 (April 1965).

57 Some Basic Comments on Retrieval Testing

ROBERT A. FAIRTHORNE
Journal of Documentation
Vol. 21, No. 4, December, 1965

To test is not to evaluate. Tests reveal to what extent a retrieval system performs in some specific way; what value is or should be put upon such performance is another matter altogether. Clearly one should test only such performance as is necessary to the aim of the system, because one cannot test everything. Thus we must first decide what is the aim of the system, then test to find how well it achieves this aim. These matters can be examined and discussed usefully without going into profound matters such as man's place in the universe, the nature of unrecorded knowledge, the library's place in next year's budget, or whether some individual user's knowledge is changed to his individual satisfaction.

Even to define the aim is difficult, because we deal with essentially social systems. We can lay down necessary, but not sufficient conditions of performance. What, for instance, are the conditions sufficient to inform somebody about something? Even if known they would take us well out of the field of 'Information Sciences' into psychology and beyond it into the personal psychical structure and history of each individual user of the system. Sufficient conditions are out of the question; we must concentrate on necessary ones. As our knowledge grows, so will the conditions known to be necessary. We certainly know that before anyone can be informed, he must be told. Before users can be informed by documents they must be told or notified about them. This is not sufficient, but it is certainly necessary.

1. Documentary Activities in Documentary Terms

To separate aim and achievement from the values of the aims and achievements, we must consider them in terms of documentation, not of the external applications or intentions. For example, the same documentary techniques can be used to look up such expressions as those denoting the square root of thirteen, the melting point of tungsten, the destination and intended time of departure of an aircraft, or the last line of a limerick. These may be demanded for many reasons or non-reasons. They can be looked up or retrieved by the same automatic techniques, but not because they refer to 'facts'. They may not refer to anything at all, let alone to verifiable and verified events outside the library. Automatic retrieval is here possible because what can be generated or written by machine can be retrieved, or indexed, by machine. The idiotic label 'fact retrieval' denotes combined machine generation and retrieval of strings of symbols. Whether the interpretations, if any, of such strings have any bearing on facts in the external world is completely irrelevant to documentation as such. The techniques are the same.

In general, completely automatic techniques of indexing and retrieval cannot be used with texts that cannot be written automatically. But whatever technique is used, it depends only on the ways in which the texts are written, and how and how often documentary services are called for. Whether the reader is informed, misled, or shocked by what is delivered to him, and whatever his motives may have been and may now have become are irrelevant to begin with.

What matter are what sort of documentary entities are asked for; how are they asked for; how well does the system supply what is asked for, when asked for in these terms.

It is not reasonable to demand of a documentary system 'Give me what I need'. The most a documentary system can claim is that the better the user understands his subject matter (including how *other people* talk about it), the better the service he will receive. It cannot substitute for author or reader completely.

In short, documentary systems cannot be expected to *use* the documents in the collection; they can only *mention* them.

Supplying a set of documents is of course a vigorous way of mentioning it.

Necessarily one must find out at least, what sets of documents are supposed to be mentioned, and what terms? How well are they mentioned (referred to, supplied, or notified) when requested in these terms?

2. Varieties of Retrieval

All retrieval systems demand that the items be marked (or can be recognized from existing test marks) according to the way in which they may interest defined types of user.

Furthermore, the interests of users, as described by them, must be connected with the interests satisfied by the items, as described by the indexers (or by the makers of recognition rules).

This entails constraints on what is described, and how it is described, by user and indexer both.

For instance, if the indexer is constrained to use descriptive cataloguing, he can describe only points of bibliographic interest in terms of the cataloguing rules. The user also has to use the language of descriptive cataloguing, and is necessarily constrained to describe only those bibliographic properties he happens to know about.

The advantage of this system is that the user certainly gets what he asks for (correctly) and no more; while the indexer has to consider only a definite number of sharply defined interests.

At the other extreme, the user has no pre-knowledge of the bibliographical characteristics, including the existence, of the type of item that interests him. To compensate for this ignorance, he is constrained to express his interests in some special language, and the indexer to predict in a special language how items may interest this kind of user. The advantage (to the user) of such a system is that the burden of knowing who has written which about what, when, and where has been transferred to the retrieval system. The indexer has also to know what sorts of subject matter are likely to interest what sorts of people, and how these people are likely to express these interests.

For local, contemporary, and specialized use, the inevitable ignorances of indexers and the inevitable ambiguities of request and indexing description can be kept down. However, some ignorance is inevitable; the indexer cannot predict all the ways an item may legitimately interest a user, while the user cannot know his interests beforehand so precisely that he can state exactly what he wants and what he does not want.

Over and above this are the inevitable ambiguities of the indexing and request languages themselves. Certain types or combinations of interests will be too specific or too general for description in any agreed language, or will not be describable at all.

To take an extreme case, no indexing or request language—with one exception—can describe *any* subset of items in the collection. The exception is the language of descriptive cataloguing; one just makes a list of the items. (With ingenuity one can devise apparently different languages to do this. All, however, effectively reduce to a set of proper names, one for each item in the collection.)

On the other hand most 'retrieval languages', as commonly understood, cannot retrieve sizeable and acceptable subsets of items. That is, one cannot frame a rational specification that will apply to an appreciable fraction of the collection. Some classificatory languages, particularly hierarchical classifications, do allow this, at a price.

To be effective, retrieval languages must not only allow description of an appropriate range of interests, but also must be matched to the number and size and other combinatorial properties (e.g., overlap) of the sets of items corresponding to these interests.

The original 'co-ordinate indexing' by means of overlapping 'descriptors' (which were not necessarily dictionary words, but broad notions) was introduced by Calvin Mooers around 1948. This allowed one, amongst other things, to specify items or requirements without implying any pre-existing specific or generic relations between them. That is, no index tag or specification could be formed by 'and', 'or' (in the Boolean sense) operations on other tags or specifications. The only relation permitted between indicia was that of similarity, in the sense of the number of descriptors held in common and, what was the same in this system, the number of descriptors absent from both. The last condition is necessary, if this 'similarity' is to mean anything. Most current 'co-ordinate' systems do not satisfy it. Clearly this was a most useful way of dealing with topics in which no clear structure of discourse had yet emerged, and where requested items were either rare or non-existent.

In research situations, zero subsets are important. They are interests, or 'topics', about which reports may plausibly exist but in fact do not, at the moment. The kind of response of the system to such 'plausible requests' must not be ignored. For often the main reason for using the system is to find whether something exists, rather than to find what and where it is if it does. However, whether 'plausible requests' and zero subsets are amongst the aims of a system or not, we must include the sizes and number of subsets it purports to retrieve as part of its aim.

No retrieval language or method will fit all situations; specific and generic items, few and many interests. Its performance must be judged within its aims. Tests of how it behaves outside its declared aims—e.g., seeing how a true 'co-oordinate' retrieval system copes with requests for broadly specified interests—can contribute much to our knowledge, but should be regarded as a test to destruction.

We see that, even in their own terms, the aims of retrieval systems can vary quite widely, though most today are concerned with retrieval of relatively unrelated rare (or non-existent) items specified and indexed in terms of specialized interests.

Whatever their aims, their performance entails certain necessary, though not sufficient, characteristics. To begin with, these characteristics concern what the user can ask for, how he can ask for it, and how much he gets of what he asks for (as assessed by other people, not by him), irrespective of the wisdom of his request.

B. Results

58 The Cranfield Tests on Index Language Devices

CYRIL CLEVERDON
Aslib Proceedings
Vol. 19, No. 6, June, 1967

The first Aslib-Cranfield project attempted to investigate the operational performance of four different indexing systems, namely the Universal Decimal Classification, a facet classification, an alphabetical subject catalogue and the Uniterm system of co-ordinate indexing.[1,2] In terms of performance, it was found that all systems operated at very much the same level of efficiency.

In the course of the first project, an evaluation was made of a test collection of some 1,100 documents in the index of metallurgical literature of Western Reserve University, and comparison was made with a faceted index, covering the same set of documents, that was compiled at Cranfield.[3] The results from these tests were to establish the measures that can be used in evaluating the operational performance of information retrieval systems. The two measures, namely *recall ratio* and *precision ratio*, were not only important in themselves, but provided a clue to the composition of index languages, for detailed analysis of the results of the two tests showed that each indexing system was made up of a basic vocabulary together with a number of devices. These devices fall into two main categories; there are *recall devices*, which are intended to increase the probability of retrieving more revelant documents. Examples of such recall devices are the grouping of synonyms, the confounding of word forms, or the formation of classes of related terms. On the other hand *precision devices* are intended to ensure that non-relevant documents are not retrieved, and examples of such precision devices are co-ordination (whether pre-co-ordination or post-co-ordination), links and roles.

The analysis of the test results in Cranfield I showed that all indexing systems were an amalgam of recall and precision devices, and that these interacted with each other in such a complex manner that it was impossible to measure their effect on the overall performance of any indexing system. The Universal Decimal Classification, for instance, is a very complex system, and includes every possible device. It incorporates recall devices, such as the control of synonyms, by means of the alphabetical index:

e.g. Air Cushion Vehicles	629.137
Ground-effect machines	629.137
Hovercraft	629.137

World forms are also brought together by the alphabetical index:

e.g. Weld   621.791
Welded   621.791
Welding   621.791

Generic relations are shown in the schedules:

e.g. 662   Beverages
622.3   Wines

Pre-co-ordination of terms frequently occurs in the schedules:

e.g. 533.6.071   Wind tunnels
533.6.071.4   Wind tunnel instruments

Alternatively, co-ordination can be obtained by the use of the colon sign or brackets:

e.g. 338:633.1   Cereal production
942(42)   English history

Links are also shown by the colon sign:

e.g. 669.71 : 621.791   Welding of aluminum

Roles are indicated by the context of the schedules:
e.g. *Input*   Wood (fuel)   662.63
Output   Wood (forestry)   634.08

The second Cranfield project was therefore designed to investigate such index language devices in isolation and in all practical combinations, and attempt to measure the effect which each device had on performance. For this purpose a test collection was established consisting of 1,400 research papers, mainly in the field of aerodynamics. Each document was 'indexed' in three different ways (Fig. 1); first, the most important concepts were selected and were recorded in the natural language of the document. The single words in each of the concepts were then listed, and finally the concepts were combined in different ways to form the main themes of the documents. At the time of indexing, each concept was given a 'weighting' (1, 2 or 3) to indicate its relative importance. The concepts in the main theme of the document would be weighted '1', the less important concepts '2' and the minor concepts '3'.

For the testing, 221 questions were used, these being questions which had been provided by the authors of a number of research papers. The first task was to determine the relevance of every document in the collection to each of the questions. The relevance decisions, which were finally decided by the originators of the questions, were in a scale of from 1 to 4, which had the following requirements.

B1590

Base Document A137

AUTHOR STONE, A.
TITLE   Effect of stage characteristics and matching on axial flow compressor performance

REFERENCE *Trans. American Soc. of Mechanical Engineers,* c–, 1958, p. 1273

Indexer J.M.   Date 17-6-63

THEMES (partitioning)		CONCEPTS (Interfixing)		CONCEPTS (Interfixing)		TERMS & WEIGHTS		TERMS & WEIGHTS	
A	cd effect of a use of ef	a	Stage characteristics	t	Range of operations	Stage	1	Blade	3
B	——— b	b	Stage matching	u	Stage flow co-efficient	Characteristic	1	Range	2
C	cdh	c	Axial flow compressor	v	Mass flow	Matching	1	Operations	2
D	cdi effect of j with k	d	Stage performance	w	Choking flow co-efficient	Axial	1	Mass	2
E	cdl effect of g	e	Test data	x	Surge line	Flow	1	Choking	2
F	cmp effect of n	f	Analysis	y	Change in slope	Compressor	1	Line	2
G	———vo	g	Mach number	z	Knee double valued performance curve	Performance	1	Slope	3
H	cmdq	h	Velocity distribution			Test	1	Knee	3
I	cmdr	i	Temperature co-efficient	aa	Unstalling hysteresis	Data	1	Double	3
J	cmdt effect of sg	j	Flow co-efficient	bb	Inlet guide vane stagger	Analysis	1	Curve	3
K	cmu effect of g	k	Constant flow angle	cc	Uprating stage one	Mach	2	Unstalling	3
L	———v	l	Cascade losses	dd	Uprating stage two	Velocity	2	Hysterisis	3
M	cbv effect of w	m	Idealized compressor	ee	Blade stagger	Distribution	2	Inlet	3
N	cbx effect of o	n	Total pressure ratio	ff	Stage loading	Temperature	3	Guide	3
O	cbxy effect of o	o	Percentage of design speed	gg	Annular area	Co-efficient	3	Vane	3
P	cbz effect of aa	p	Performance			Constant	3	Stagger	3
Q	cu effect of bb	q	Stalling point			Angle	3	Uprating	3
R	———cc	r	Compression surges			Cascade	3	One	3
S	———dd	s	Pitch line blade speed			Loss	3	Loading	3
T	cx effect of ee					Idealized	2	Annulus	3
U	———ff					Total	3	Area	3
V	———gg					Ratio	3	Number	2
W	———vq					Percentage	2	Line	3
						Design	2	Valued	3
						Speed	2	Two	3
						Stalling	2	Pressure	2
						Point	2		
						Surge	2		
						Pitch	3		

FIG. 1. Indexing sheet for document 1590.

	RELEVANT	NON-RELEVANT	
RETRIEVED	a	b	a + b
NOT RETRIEVED	c	d	c + d
	a + c	b + d	a + b + c + d = N (Total Collection)

FIG. 2. 2 × 2 contingency table.

1. References which are a complete answer to the question.
2. References of a high degree of relevance, the lack of which either would have made the research impracticable or would have resulted in a considerable amount of extra work.
3. References which were useful, either as general background to the work or as suggesting methods of tackling certain aspects of the work.
4. References of minimum interest, for example, those that have been included from an historical viewpoint.

In a normal search, the document collection is divided into two groups, consisting of the documents that are retrieved and the documents that are left in the system. Each of these groups can be subdivided into those documents that are relevant and those documents that are not relevant. This is usually presented as in Fig. 2.

For the purpose of evaluating an information retrieval system, performance is presented by plotting the recall ratio $\left(\dfrac{100a}{a + c}\right)$ against either the precision ratio $\left(\dfrac{100a}{a + b}\right)$ or the fallout ratio $\left(\dfrac{100b}{b + d}\right)$. The fallout ratio is particularly useful when comparing performances of document collections of different sizes, but the precision ratio is more satisfactory for most of the results obtained in the Cranfield work.

Three main types of index language were investigated. For the first, single terms only were used; examples of these are given in the final columns of Fig. 1 and all such terms are in the natural language of the documents. It was these natural language terms which were used for the basic index language of this type; for the second Single Term index language, synonyms were grouped; for the third, word forms were confounded. Further Single Term index languages had groups of terms based on different hierarchical classes (Fig. 3).

The second main type of index language used the concepts as given in Fig. 1, with some slight simplifications; again the basic Simple Concept index language used these terms as they occurred in the documents, and fourteen other index languages were formed on the basis of various groupings of these terms (Fig. 4). The third main type consisted of six different index languages which were based on various groupings of a set of controlled terms (Fig. 5).

In addition, there were four further index languages where the index terms represented all the key words in the titles or in the abstracts. In each case these were tested in the natural language and with word forms confounded.

The searches were carried out in such a way that

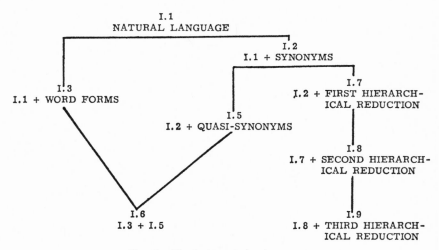

FIG. 3. Single term index languages.

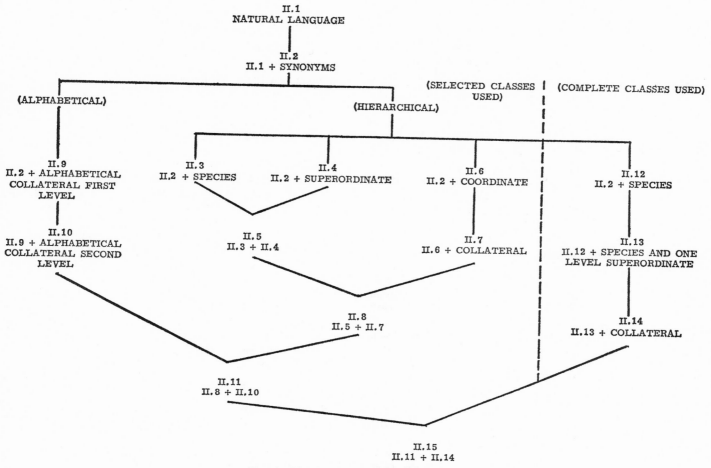

Fig. 4. Simple concept index languages.

there was absolute consistency, except for a single variable, such as the index language or the search rule or the relevance decision. Consider, for instance, the question 'Small deflection theory of simple supported cylinders'. This is the question exactly as stated by its originator, and it contains six key terms. With the basic single term index language, the first search was made for a match in all six terms, and this retrieved three documents. For a match of any five terms, ten documents were

retrieved; for a match of any four terms fourteen documents were retrieved; forty-three documents were retrieved at a match of three terms, 177 documents at a match of two terms and 722 documents when any single term was accepted on its own.

For comparison we consider the results obtained with Index Language I.6; in this case the change is that the single terms are grouped into classes formed by synonyms, word forms and quasi-synonyms. It is now found that at

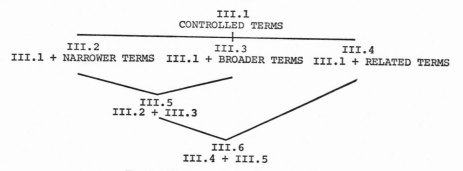

Fig. 5. Controlled term index languages.

a match of all six terms, four documents have been retrieved; at a match of five terms, fourteen documents were retrieved; for a match of four terms, thirty-eight documents were retrieved; 125 documents were retrieved at a match of three terms, this being nearly three times as many as were retrieved at this level with Index Language I.1. However, in this particular case, whereas only two of the six relevant documents were retrieved at a match of three with Index Language I.1., five relevant documents are retrieved with Index Language I.6.

When the results of a number of searches are aggregated, test results are obtained which can be presented in the manner shown in Figs. 6 and 7. The single variable in these two sets of results is the index language; Fig. 6 shows the results for Index Language I.1, which used single terms in the natural language. Figure 7 presents the results for Index Language I.6 where the single terms are grouped into classes formed by synonyms, word forms and quasi-synonyms.

The tables show the number of relevant and non-relevant documents retrieved at various coordination levels and from these figures are calculated the recall ratio, the precision ratio and the fall-out ratio.

These two sets of results can be presented on a recall-precision plot as in Fig. 8; from this it can be seen that at any given recall ratio up to 95 per cent, Index Language I.1 has a higher precision ratio than Index Language I.6.

In addition to the results of the type already shown, many further tests were made to determine the effect of different variables. Figure 9, for instance, shows the effect of introducing certain rules concerning the search strategy, and Figure 10 is a plot showing the effect of the four different levels of relevance. In this latter case a plot showing recall and fall-out ratios is presented. This is done because the effect of changing the relevance levels is to alter the number of relevant documents and thereby change the generality number. Due to this change in generality number, a recall/precision plot would have shown the best performance with documents relevance 1-4 and the worst performance with documents relevance I. While it is practical to make the necessary adjustments in precision ratio, the fallout ratio automatically compensates for the change in the generality number and correctly shows that the best performance is obtained with relevance 1 documents.

The plots and the test results illustrate the inverse relationship, first postulated in the earlier Cranfield work,[2] which exists between recall and precision. Whereas the maximum possible recall ratio of 100 per cent can be

Index Language   I.1.a. (S.T.   Natural language.   Coordination)

Exhaustivity of Indexing 3	Number of Documents in Collection 1,400
Search Rule A	Number of Questions 221 (Subset 3)
Document Relevance 1-4	Number of Relevant Documents 1,590
	Generality Number 5.1

Coord-ination Level	Documents Retrieved Rel.	Documents Retrieved Non-rel.	Recall Ratio a/a+c	Precision Ratio a/a+b	Fallout Ratio b/b+d	x	y	z
1	1,510	159,122	95.0%	0.9%	51.696%	221	221	221
2	1,283	58,122	80.7%	2.2%	18.883%	221	221	221
3	946	21,933	59.5%	4.1%	7.125%	215	220	220
4	606	7,359	38.1%	7.6%	2.390%	187	212	212
5	314	2,380	19.7%	11.6%	0.773%	131	197	197
6	154	699	9.7%	18.0%	0.227%	86	164	164
7	74	216	4.7%	25.5%	0.070%	50	140	140
8	22	43	1.4%	33.8%	0.014%	18	105	105
9	8	5	0.5%	61.5%	0.002%	8	78	78
10	1	0	0.1%	100.0%	0.000%	1	52	52
11	0	0				0	32	32
12	0	0				0	15	15
13	0	0				0	8	8
14	0	0				0	4	4
15	0	0				0	3	3

Fig. 6. Results of searches using index language I.1.

Index Language   I.6.a (S.T.   Synonyms, Quasi-synonyms, Word forms.   Coordination)

Exhaustivity of Indexing   3   Number of Documents in Collection   1,400
Search Rule   A   Number of Questions   221 (Subset 3)
Document Relevance   1 - 4   Number of Relevant Documents   1,590
Generality Number   5.1

Coord-ination Level•	Documents Retrieved		Recall Ratio a/a+c	Precision Ratio a/a+b	Fallout Ratio b/b+d	x	y	z
	Rel.	Non-rel.						
1	1,557	(-)	97.9%	(-)	(-)	221	0	221
2	1,430	116,374*	89.9%	1.2%*	37.783%*	221	44*	221
3	1,165	45,101*	73.3%	2.5%*	14.643%*	218	109*	220
4	848	18,373*	53.3%	4.4%*	5.965%*	206	142*	212
5	503	8,895*	31.6%	5.4%*	2.888%*	169	177*	197
6	295	3,874*	18.6%	7.1%*	1,257%*	119	161*	164
7	161	1,136	10.1%	12.4%	0.369%	83	140	140
8	72	344	4.5%	17.3%	0.112%	54	105	105
9	24	82	1.5%	22.6%	0.027%	25	78	78
10	6	18	0.4%	25.0%	0.006%	12	52	52
11	0	1	0.0%	0.0%	0.0003%	1	32	32
12	0	0				0	15	15
13	0	0				0	8	8
14	0	0				0	4	4
15	0	0				0	3	3

Fig. 7.   Results of searches using index language I.6.

obtained by, if necessary, looking at every document in the collection, the inevitable effect of bringing about any improvement in the precision ratio is a drop in the recall ratio. In reverse, if one wishes to increase the number of relevant documents which are being retrieved, this can only be done by increasing to a greater extent the number of non-relevant documents also retrieved. This is always the case when operating within any given system, although it does not, of course, apply for comparisons between different systems.

It is estimated that some 300,000 test results were obtained in the project, and while the results appeared consistently to show the same trends, it was difficult to present them in a manner which gave a direct comparison between the different systems. Many proposals have been made for a single performance measure, and a large number of these were considered in detail in the project report.[4] All these measures had a similar weakness in that they could only represent a single recall/precision point. This meant that a 'score' of, say, 85 might imply a recall ratio of 80 per cent and a precision of 5 per cent, or a recall ratio of 20 per cent and a precision ratio of 65 per cent or any other of a whole series of single points. The emphasis in the Cranfield work has been on the overall

performance of a system which is obtained by changing a single variable, such as the co-ordination level; this produces a series of points giving a performance curve as already shown in Figure 8, and it was this overall performance curve which we wished to compare. The answer lay in a form of the normalized recall ratio as first used by Professor Salton.

The investigations undertaken by Salton with the SMART system[5] were basically similar to those which were being done at Cranfield. In both cases the intention was to compare the effect of using different devices or options, but there were, of course, important differences, apart from the fact that Salton used a large computer while Cranfield used simple but laborious clerical techniques for carrying out the test searches. The significant difference lay in the fact that the SMART programmes had the facility of being able to present an output in a ranked order of probable relevance (Fig. 11). It was this which enabled Salton to calculate the normalized recall ratio, which is based on the sum of recall ratios calculated after the recall of each single document, and thereby enable direct comparison between systems.

At Cranfield, such direct comparison was difficult, because the measures were calculated at co-ordination level

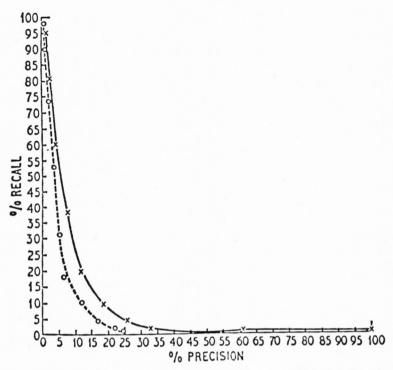

FIG. 8. Recall/precision plot for index languages I.1 and I.6 as given in Figures 6 and 7.

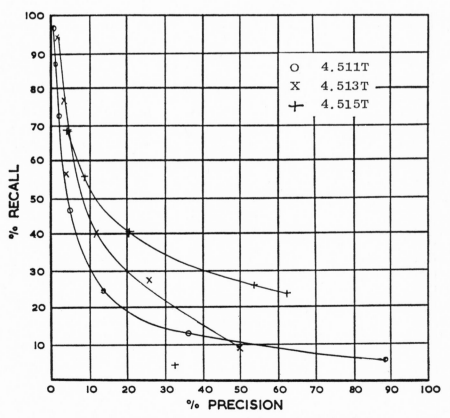

FIG. 9. Effect on performance of changes in search rules.

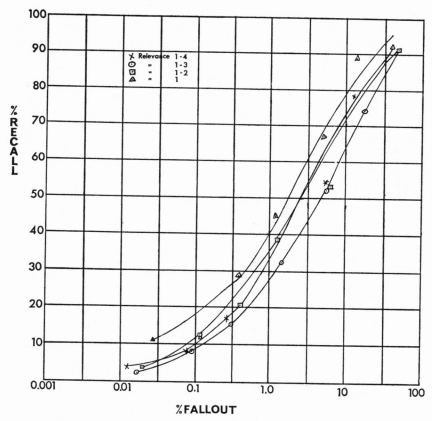

FIG. 10. Effect on performance of variations in document relevance (recall/fallout plot).

ABSTR NEW QS TOP 15 RELEVANT			INDEX NEW QS TOP 15 RELEVANT			CRAN CONCON INDEX F NULL TOP 15 RELEVANT		
1	792	7 712	1	792	3 712	1	597	6 708
2	797	19 711	2	683	69 708	2	792	25 712
3	799	97 713	3	712	80 711	3	717	46 711
4	324	101 708	4	797	139 713	4	799	102 709
5	683	149 709	5	988	153 709	5	748	136 713
6	992		6	572		6	708	
7	712		7	437		7	316	
8	707		8	799		8	451	
9	416		9	682		9	11A	
10	321		10	675		10	11I	
11	655		11	670		11	683	
12	33H		12	316		12	10A	
13	874		13	681		13	670	
14	316		14	701		14	916	
15	919		15	707		15	08D	
RNK REC	= 0.0402		RNK REC	= 0.0338		RNK REC	= 0.0476	
LOG PRE	= 0.2509		LOG PRE	= 0.2433		LOG PRE	= 0.2605	
NOR REC	= 0.6328		NOR REC	= 0.5600		NOR REC	= 0.6923	
NOR PRE	= 0.3390		NOR PRE	= 0.3115		NOR PRE	= 0.3717	
OVERALL	= 0.2911		OVERALL	= 0.2771		OVERALL	= 0.3081	
NOR OVR	= 3390		NOR OVR	= 0.3115		NOR OVR	= 0.3717	

FIG. 11. Examples of ranked output obtained with SMART for question 147.

cut-offs, the effect of which was that (as in the example given earlier) at a given co-ordination level, system A might retrieve fourteen documents while system B would retrieve thirty-eight documents. This variation in the number of documents retrieved effectively stopped any direct comparison, whereas the ranked output presented by SMART made it possible to ascertain the performance after, say, five documents had been retrieved, after ten documents or any other number.

Therefore, the first task was to obtain a simulated rank output for the Cranfield searches. The method adopted was based on the retrieval of relevant and nonrelevant documents at each co-ordination level. If we consider the results for Q.100 when searched in a collection of two hundred documents, the position is as follows:

Documents retrieved

Co-ordination level	Relevant	Non-Relevant
1	1	2
2	3	50
3	3	71
4	4	167

By using such figures, a rank order number could be assigned to each relevant document by means of the equation

$$c_{R_n} = X_c + (n - Y_c) \left(\frac{x_c + 1}{y_c + 1} \right)$$

where c_{R_n} is the rank order number of the nth relevant document to be retrieved

    c   is the co-ordination level at which the *nth relevant document* is retrieved

    x_c is the additional number of *documents* retrieved at coordination level c. (i.e. those not retrieved at a higher co-ordination level)

    y_c is the additional number of *relevant documents* retrieved at co-ordination level c. (i.e. those not retrieved at a higher co-ordination level)

    X_c is the total number of documents retrieved before searching at co-ordination level c. (i.e. at higher coordination levels)

    Y_c is the total number of *relevant documents* retrieved before searching at co-ordination level c. (i.e. higher co-ordination levels)

c_{R_n} is taken to the nearest whole number but if its value falls exactly between two whole numbers, it is taken to the lower whole number for odd numbered questions and to the higher whole number for even numbered questions.

With Question 100, no documents are retrieved at a co-ordination level higher than four, so for this question, the various values are as follows:

Question 100

At level c = 4, then $x_4 = 3$, $y_4 = 1$, $X_4 = 0$, $Y_4 = 0$
At level c = 3, then $x_3 = 50$, $y_3 = 2$, $X_3 = 3$, $Y_3 = 1$
At level c = 2, then $x_2 = 21$, $y_2 = 0$, $X_2 = 53$, $Y_2 = 3$
At level c = 1, then $x_1 = 97$, $y_1 = 1$, $X_1 = 74$, $Y_1 = 3$
∴ For Relevant Document 1, retrieved at level 4:

$$4_{R_1} = 0 + (1 - 0) \left(\frac{3 + 1}{1 + 1} \right) = 0 + 2 = 2$$

For Relevant Document 2, retrieved at level 3:

$$3_{R_2} = 3 + (2 - 1) \left(\frac{50 + 1}{2 + 1} \right) = 3 + 17 = 20$$

For Relevant Document 3, retrieved at level 3:

$$3_{R_3} = 3 + (3 - 1) \left(\frac{50 + 1}{2 + 1} \right) = 3 + 34 = 37$$

For Relevant Document 4, retrieved at level 1:

$$1_{R_4} = 74 + (4 - 3) \left(\frac{97 + 1}{1 + 1} \right) + 74 = 49 = 126$$

The normalized recall ratio was obtained by taking the sum of the recall ratios of seventeen standardized cut-off groups, and dividing by seventeen. Figure 12 shows a typical score sheet based on simulated ranking for forty-two questions with a single language while Fig. 13 presents the results for eight single term index languages.

As Salton had used the Cranfield test collection with the SMART system, it was possible to check the proposed method, and this showed that the Cranfield normalized recall ratios produced a performance ranking which closely matched that obtained with the original SMART measure. This being the case, the results of the tests on thirty-three index languages were recalculated to give the normalized recall ratios.

It must be emphasized that, for reasons which are considered at length in Chapter 5 reference 4, the use of a document output cut-off method means that recall ratios and precision ratios are interdependent. For a single system, the inverse relationship of recall and precision will always hold; however, if in a second system there is, as compared to the first, an increase in the recall ratio, then there must always be a corresponding increase in the precision ratio. Because of this, it is immaterial whether one obtains the normalized recall ratio or the normalized precision ratio.

Figure 14 shows the thirty-three index languages tested at Cranfield in a ranked order based on the normalized recall ratios. The relationship of the index languages to each other is shown in detail in figures 3, 4, and 5. Generally speaking, the Single Term index languages are

Q	REL	1	2	3	4	5	6-7	8-10	11-15	16-20	21-30	31-50	51-75	76-100	101-125	126-150	151-175	176-200
79	3	x									x					x		
100	4		x							x	x					x		
116	6							x		x	x	x	x		x	x		
118	5	x					x	x			xx							
119	6			x		x	x				x	xx						
121	3	x	x	x														
122	5	x				x		x			x	x						
123	4	x		x		x												
126	2	x	x														x	
130	4	x						x	x		x							
132	4				x							x			x		x	
136	6		x	x		x	x	xx										
137	6		x			x		xx	xx									
141	1	x																
145	12	x	x	x	x			x	x	x		xxx	x	x				
146	9		x	x	x	x			x		x	x	x			x		
147	5							x			x	x	x			x		
148	4	x	x		x		x									x	x	
167	4	x				x		x										
170	2		x											x				
181	2			x							x			x				
182	4			x										x	x			x
189	2										x	x			x	x		
190	7	x	x	x			x		x			x			x			
223	2	x	x									x			x			
224	5							x			x	x	x	x				
225	6							x	x		x	x			x	x		
226	7	x	x	x		x						xx	x					
227	2	x		x														
230	7	x	x					x		x	x	xx						
250	8	x	x	x		x	x	x	xx									
261	4	x	x	x	x													
264	2	x	x															
266	5							x	x	x	x			x				
268	5	x	x	x	x		x											
269	4	x	x		x		x											
272	4	x	x		x					x								
273	7	x	x	x	x		x		x		x							
274	5				x		x			x			x			x		
317	2					x		x										
323	5					x			x	x	x	x						
360	8		x		x	x	x	x	xx									
Totals		23	21	13	13	12	11	16	14	10	18	17	8	7	5	6	3	1
Recall		12	22	29	35	41	47	56	62	67	76	85	89	92	95	98	99	100
Precision		55	51	45	42	39	32	26	20	16	12	8	6	4	4	3	3	2

FIG. 12. Document output cut-off score sheet for index language I.1.

found at the head of the list, the Simple Concept index languages at the bottom and the Controlled Term index languages are in the middle position.

There are a number of points of special interest in this table. The only difference between index language I.1 (rank order 3) and II.1 (rank order 33) is that the latter interfixes the single terms of the former, e.g. the single terms 'axial', 'flow', 'compressor' are combined to form the simple concept term 'axial flow compressor' (Fig. 1). However, the effect of this is to change the ranking from 3 to 33.

The only improvement on the Single Term natural language (I.1) is by the control of synonyms or the confounding of word endings. Any further extension of the classes of terms results in a drop in performance. The reverse, however, is true of the group of Simple Concept index languages, where the performance with the natural language terms is so poor that grouping of terms brings about a significant improvement. Intermediary is a third group of index languages, based upon a controlled term vocabulary. Here the broadening of the basic terms by forming groups with related terms brings about a small loss in performance.

Numerous additional tests were made (and are reported in reference 4) to investigate various factors, such as the level of relevance of the documents, the effect of varying the search procedure, or the effect of various precision devices such as interfixing or partitioning. None of these appear in any way to affect the general results as presented in Fig. 14.

When considering the somewhat unexpected results of this project, one must, of course, bear in mind the environment in which the tests were made, but there appears to be nothing in the test design which could have so consistently influenced the results. Certainly it would be absurd to say that in all situations the most effective form of index language is one that combines simple post-co-ordination with natural language single terms which are uncontrolled except for the grouping of synonyms and terms having the same root. Yet that is what happened in this particular environment, and one can only say that it would be an unusual coincidence if a

DOCUMENT OUTPUT CUT-OFF	I-1		I-2		I-3		I-5		I-6		I-7		I-8		I-9	
	R	P	R	P	R	P	R	P	R	P	R	P	R	P	R	P
1	12	55	12	57	12	57	13	60	11	52	10	48	9	43	8	36
2	22	51	23	54	23	54	19	45	21	49	21	49	19	44	16	37
3	29	45	30	47	30	48	28	44	29	46	29	46	28	44	22	34
4	35	42	36	42	37	43	32	38	35	42	33	39	32	38	27	32
5	41	39	41	39	43	40	36	34	40	38	40	38	38	36	33	31
6-7	47	32	48	32	48	32	45	30	47	32	46	31	46	31	40	27
8-10	56	26	55	26	56	26	53	25	55	26	53	25	55	26	47	22
11-15	62	20	63	20	64	20	59	19	62	19	63	20	62	20	58	18
16-20	67	16	67	16	70	17	65	15	66	16	67	16	68	16	63	15
21-30	76	12	76	12	76	12	73	12	73	12	76	12	76	12	72	11
31-50	85	8	85	8	86	8	82	8	83	8	86	8	85	8	82	8
51-75	89	6	89	6	89	6	88	6	89	6	91	6	91	6	89	6
76-100	92	4	92	4	93	4	91	4	92	4	93	4	93	4	93	4
101-125	95	4	95	4	95	4	94	4	95	4	95	4	96	4	95	4
126-150	98	3	98	3	98	3	96	3	97	3	97	3	98	3	97	3
151-175	99	3	99	3	99	3	98	3	99	3	99	3	99	3	98	3
176-200	100	2	100	2	100	2	100	2	100	2	100	2	100	2	100	2
NORMALISED RECALL	65.00		65.23		65.82		63.05		64.47		64.05		64.41		61.17	

SINGLE TERM LANGUAGES

I-1	Natural language	I-6	Synonyms, word endings, and quasi-synonyms
I-2	Synonyms	I-7	Hierarchical reduction first stage
I-3	Word endings	I-8	Hierarchical reduction second stage
I-5	Synonyms and quasi-synonyms	I-9	Hierarchical reduction third stage

FIG. 13.   Recall and precision ratios and normalised recall for single term index languages.
(R = Recall Ratio,   P = Precision Ratio)

situation had been selected which was unique in the whole field of science and technology.

It is necessary to try to explain what has been happening in these tests so as to bring about the results as given. It must be emphasized that with the exception of Languages IV.1, IV.2, IV.3, and IV.4, in all the systems shown in Fig. 14 everything has been held constant except the index language. This is to say that we are dealing with the same documents which have all been indexed in the same way; a set of questions which have been searched in exactly the same way for each index language; a set of relevance decisions which are always the same. The only variation is the relationship of the index terms to the natural language terms of the documents.

This can be considered as a matter of specificity of the index terms. In Index Language I.1 the specificity is exactly the same as that of the single terms of the natural language. Synonyms and word endings provide, overall, a slight reduction in specificity, and also give a small improvement in performance. However, beyond this stage, the further reductions in specificity, provided by the formation of classes based on quasi-synonyms or hierarchical grouping, results in a loss in performance.

In Index Language II.1 the specificity is exactly the same as the concepts of the natural language, and these represent a higher level of specificity that the single terms. 'Constant wall temperature' is a far more specific

index term than the separate single terms 'Constant', 'Wall' and 'Temperature', and, as previously noted, the result of this higher level of specificity brings about a large fall in performance. Because the Simple Concept index terms are over-specific, it is found that the broadening of the classes by any means brings about an improvement in performance. However, this improvement does not result in any Simple Concept index language reaching the level of performance of that obtained by the single terms.

The Controlled Term index languages, with ranks of 10, 11, 14, 16, 17 and 18, occupy an intermediary position. One can suggest that two conflicting factors are present. Some of the index terms were compound terms (e.g. 'Pressure welding' or 'Hydraulic equipment') and were therefore more specific than the single terms. On the other hand, a number of natural language terms were grouped to form a single term, and thereby maintain Rule T-1 of the E.J.C. Thesaurus of Engineering Terms, which warns against being too specific. It is difficult to say which of these factors was responsible for the loss in performance as compared to single terms; the only clue is that any broadening of the classes from the basic terms give a slight loss in performance, and it would therefore seem that, overall, the terms were not sufficiently specific.

This matter of specificity is related to the number of index terms (but *not* code terms) in the index language

ORDER	NORMALISED. RECALL		INDEXING·LANGUAGE
1	65.82	I-3	Single terms. Word forms
2	65.23	I-2	Single terms. Synonyms
3	65.00	I-1	Single terms. Natural Language
4	64.47	I-6	Single terms. Synonyms, word forms, quasi-synonyms
5	64.41	I-8	Single terms Hierarchy second stage
6	64.05	I-7	Single terms. Hierarchy first stage
7=	63.05	I-5	Single terms. Synonyms. Quasi-synonyms
7=	63.05	II-11	Simple concepts. Hierarchical and alphabetical selection
9	62.88	II-10	Simple concepts. Alphabetical second stage selection
10=	61.76	III-1	Controlled terms. Basic terms
10=	61.76	III-2	Controlled terms. Narrower terms
12	61.17	I-9	Single terms. Hierarchy third stage
13	60.94	IV-3	Abstracts. Natural language
14	60.82	IV-4	Abstracts. Word forms
15	60.11	III-3	Controlled terms. Broader terms
16	59.76	IV-2	Titles. Word forms
17	59.70	III-4	Controlled terms. Related terms
18	59.58	III-5	Controlled terms. Narrower and broader terms
19	59.17	III-6	Controlled terms. Narrower, broader and related terms
20	58.94	IV-1	Titles. Natural language
21	57.41	II-15	Simple concepts. Complete combination
22	57.11	II-9	Simple concepts. Alphabetical first stage selection
23	55.88	II-13	Simple concepts. Complete species and superordinate
24	55.76	II-8	Simple concepts. Hierarchical selection
25	55.41	II-12	Simple concepts. Complete species
26	55.05	II-5	Simple concepts. Selected species and superordinate
27	53.88	II-7	Simple concepts. Selected coordinate and collateral
28	53.52	II-3	Simple concepts. Selected species
29	52.47	II-14	Simple concepts. Complete collateral
30	52.05	II-4	Simple concepts. Superordinate
31	51.82	II-6	Simple concepts. Selected coordinate
32	47.41	II-2	Simple concepts. Synonyms
33	44.64	II-1	Simple concepts. Natural language

FIG. 14. Order of effectiveness based on normalised recall for 33 Cranfield index languages.

and if we plot the normalized recall ratio against the number of terms in the index language the result is shown in Fig. 15. This indicates that in the environment of his test, an index language having 2,541 terms was the most efficient.

The second factor which appears to have an important effect on performance is the level of exhaustivity of indexing. Index Languages I.1, IV.1 and IV.3 represent three levels of exhaustivity of indexing; figures are also available for Index Language I.1 when the exhaustivity is reduced by omitting terms weighted 3 and then omitting terms weighted 2 and 3. Figure 16 shows the average number of terms of these five levels of exhaustivity and the normalized recall ratios, and the plot of Figure 17 shows that the performance is optimised at a level of 33 terms; below this figure the results indicate that insufficient terms are being used, but the sixty terms of the abstracts would appear to be at too high a level of exhaustivity, since there is a large drop in performance.

Index Language	Number of Terms	Normalized Recall Ratio
I.9	306	61.17%
I.7	1,217	64.05%
I.3	2,541	65.82%
I.2	2,988	65.23%
I.1	3,094	65.00%
II.13	6,000*	55.88%
II.4	8,000*	52.05%
II.1	10,000*	44.64%
	* Estimated	

FIG. 15. Normalized recall ratios for index languages with varying numbers of index terms.

A clue as to how the exhaustivity of indexing and the specificity of the index language work together is provided by the comparison of Index Languages IV.1 with IV.2, and IV.3 and IV.4. With Index Language IV.1 where only the terms in the titles were used, the exhaus-

Index Language		Average No. of Terms	Normalized Recall Ratio
Titles		7	59.76%
Level 1	Single Term Natural Language	14	62.88%
Level 2	Single Term Natural Language	22	63.57%
Level 3	Single Term Natural Language	33	65.00%
Abstracts		Approx. 60	60.94%

FIG. 16. Normalized recall ratios for five levels of exhaustivity of indexing.

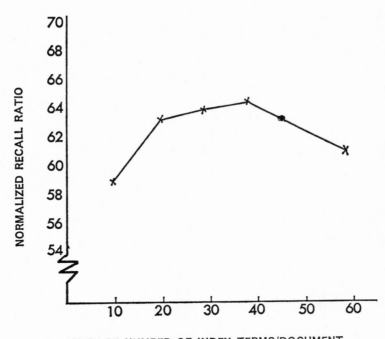

FIG. 17. Plot of normalized recall ratios for five levels of exhaustivity of indexing.

tivity is too low. By moving to Index Language IV.2, where word forms have been confounded, the lower specificity results in an improvement of the normalized recall ratio from 58.94 per cent to 59.76 per cent. With Index Language IV.3, it has been shown that the use of all the terms in the abstracts is at too high a level of exhaustivity of indexing; when in Index Language IV.4 word forms are confounded, the lower specificity now results in a loss in performance from 60.94 per cent to 60.82 per cent.

As with Cranfield I, the outcome of this test is to raise more new questions than questions it answers. It would be absurd for any organization to abandon conventional indexing and controlled index languages, whether thesauri or classification, on the basis of these test results. It would, to the author, seem equally absurd to aver that any system is operating at maximum efficiency unless a careful evaluation of the operational and economic characteristics of the system has been made. For this purpose, this test has shown that the use of single terms in the natural language, with true synonyms and word endings confounded, is a perfectly reasonable — and relatively simple — index language to use for comparison purposes. In practically all circumstances it would seem that such

an index language is more economical than any other; it will be interesting to see whethere in some cases it also turns out to be more efficient.

References

1. CLEVERDON, C. W. Report on the first stage of an investigation into the comparative efficiency of indexing systems. Cranfield, 1960.
2. CLEVERDON, C. W. Report on the testing and analysis of an investigation into the comparative efficiency of indexing systems. Cranfield, 1962.
3. AITCHISON, J., AND CLEVERDON, C. W. Report of a test on the Index of Metallurgical Literature of Western Reserve University. Cranfield, 1963.
4. CLEVERDON, C. W., MILLS, J., AND KEEN, M. Factors determining the performance of indexing systems (Aslib-Cranfield Research Project). 2 vols. Cranfield, 1966.
5. SALTON, G. The evaluation of computer-based information retrieval systems. In Proceedings of the 1965 Congress of the International Federation for Documentation, pp. 125–33. Washington: Spartan Books, and London: Macmillan, 1965.

59 Computer Evaluation of Indexing and Test Processing

G. SALTON
M. E. LESK

*Journal of the Association
for Computing Machinery
Vol. 15, No. 1, January, 1968*

1. Introduction

Throughout the technical world, a growing interest is evident in the design and implementation of mechanized information systems. Over the last few years, the general feeling that something should be done to help organize and store some of the available information resources has given way to the widespread impression that modern computing equipment may in fact be capable of alleviating and solving to some extent the so-called information problem. Specifically, it is believed that the required capacity exists to store many data or document collections of interest, that procedures are available for analyzing and organizing the information in storage, and that real time software and hardware can be used to ensure that the stored information is retrieved in response to requests from a given user population in a convenient form, and at little cost in time and effort [1–3].

Before investing the necessary resources required for the implementation of sophisticated information services, it becomes necessary to generate the detailed system specifications and to determine which of many possible alternative design features should in fact be implemented. This, in turn, must be made to depend on experimentation in a controlled environment to test and evaluate the effectiveness of various possible search and analysis procedures. The SMART document retrieval system, which has been operating on an IBM 7094 for over three years, has been used extensively to test a large variety of automatic retrieval procedures, including fully automatic information analysis methods, automatic procedures for dictionary construction, and iterative search techniques based on user interaction with the system [4–7].

The present study summarizes the result obtained with the SMART system over a two year period starting in 1964, and presents evaluation output based on the processing of three document collections in three different subject fields. Conclusions are drawn concerning the most likely analysis methods to be implemented in an operational environment. The emphasis throughout is on text analysis procedures, since they form an important part of a document handling system. Several operational problems, including the actual network implementation of a retrieval system, are not covered; cost and timing estimates are also excluded, because these are tied directly to the specific environment within which a given system actually operates.

The basic features of the SMART system are first described, and the design of the main experiments is outlined, including the statistical procedures used to test the significance of the evaluation output obtained. The principal evaluation results are then presented, and tentative conclusions are reached concerning the effectiveness of automatic text analysis procedures as part of future information systems. The results derived from the present experiments are also briefly compared with the output obtained with several other testing systems.

2. The SMART System

A. Basic Organization

The SMART system is a fully automatic document retrieval system operating on the IBM 7094. The system does not rely on manually assigned keywords or index terms for the identification of documents and search requests, nor does it use primarily the frequency of occurrence of certain words or phrases included in the document texts. Instead, the system goes beyond simple word-matching procedures by using a variety of intellectual aids in the form of synonym dictionaries, hierarchical arrangements of subject identifiers, phrase generating methods, and the like, in order to obtain the content identifications useful for the retrieval process.

The following facilities incorporated into the SMART system for purposes of document analysis are of principal interest:

(a) a system for separating English words into stems and affixes, which can be used to reduce incoming texts into *word stem* form;

(b) a synonym dictionary, or thesaurus, used to replace significant word stems by *concept numbers*, each concept representing a class of related word stems;

(c) a *hierarchical arrangement* of the concepts included in the thesaurus which makes it possible, given any concept number, to find its "parent" in the hierarchy, its "sons," its "brothers," and any of a set of possible cross-references;

(d) *statistical association* methods, used to compute similarity coefficients between words, word stems, or concepts, based on co-occurrence patterns between these entities in the sentences of a document, or in the documents of a collection; associated items can then serve as content identifiers in addition to the original ones;

(e) *syntactic analysis* methods, which are used to generate phrases consisting of several words or concepts; each phrase serves as an indicator of document content, provided certain prespecified syntactic relations obtain between the phrase components;

(f) *statistical phrase recognition* methods, which operate like the preceding syntactic procedures by using a preconstructed phrase dictionary, except that no test is made to ensure that the syntactic relationships between phrase components are satisfied;

(g) *request-document matching* procedures, which make it possible to use a variety or different correlation methods to compare analyzed documents with analyzed requests, including concept weight adjustments and variations in the length of the document texts being analyzed.

Stored documents and search requests are processed by the system *without any prior manual analysis* using one of several hundred automatic content analysis methods, and those documents which most nearly match a given search request are identified. Specifically, a correlation coefficient is computed to indicate the degree of similarity between each document and each search request, and documents are then ranked in decreasing order of the correlation coefficient [4–6]. A cutoff can then be picked, and documents above the chosen cutoff can be withdrawn from the file and turned over to the user as answers to the search request.

The search process may be controlled by the user in that a request can be processed first in a standard mode. After analysis of the output produced, feedback information can then be returned to the system where it is used to reprocess the request under altered conditions. The new output can again be examined, and the search can be iterated until the right kind and amount of information are obtained [7, 8].

The SMART system organization makes it possible to evaluate the effectiveness of the various processing methods by comparing the output obtained from a variety of different runs. This is achieved by processing the *same* search requests against the *same* document collections several times, while making selected changes in the analysis procedures between runs. By comparing the performance of the search requests under different processing conditions, it is then possible to determine the relative effectiveness of the various analysis methods. The evaluation procedures actually used are described in the next subsection.

B. Evaluation Process

The evaluation of an information search and retrieval system can be carried out in many different ways, depending on the type of system considered — whether it is an operational, experimental with user populations, or laboratory type system; on the viewpoint taken — that of the user, the manager, or the operator; and on other factors, such as the special aims of the evaluation study. A large number of different variables may affect the results of any evaluation process, including the kind of user population, the type and coverage of the document collection, the indexing tools used, the analysis and search methods incorporated into the system, the input-output equipment used, the operating efficiency as well as costs and time lag needed to produce answers, and many others.

In the present context, the viewpoint taken is the user's, and the overriding criterion of system effectiveness is taken to be the ability of the system to satisfy the user's information need. Management criteria such as cost are not taken into account, even though in the final analysis the problem is of primary importance, since the most effective system will not avail if the operations are too costly to be performed. However, costs are difficult to measure in an experimental situation where unusual fluctuations may occur because of many extraneous factors. Furthermore, the immediate need is for a measurement of the effectiveness of the intellectual tools used to analyze and search the stored information, since these are responsible in large part for the retrieval results. Costs can later be taken into account, for example, by providing several classes of service at varying cost.

The evaluation measures actually used are based on the standard *recall* and *precision* measures, where the recall is defined as the proportion of relevant matter retrieved, while precision is the proportion of retrieved material actually relevant. In an operational situation, where information needs may vary from user to user, some customers may require high recall, that is the retrieval of most everything that is likely to be of interest, while others may prefer high precision, that is, the rejection of everything likely to be useless. Everything else being equal, a perfect system is one which exhibits both a high recall and a high precision.

If a cut is made through the document collection to distinguish retrieved items from nonretrieved on the one hand, and if procedures are available for separating relevant items from nonrelevant ones on the other, the standard recall R and standard precision P may be defined as follows:

$$R = \frac{\text{number of items retrieved and relevant}}{\text{total relevant in collection}}$$

and

$$P = \frac{\text{number of items retrieved and relevant}}{\text{total retrieved in collection}}$$

The computation of these measures is straightforward only if exhaustive relevance judgments are available for each document with respect to each search request, and if the cutoff value distinguishing retrieved from nonretrieved material can be unambiguously determined [8–10].

In the evaluation work carried out with the SMART system, exhaustive relevance judgments are used since the document collections processed are all relatively small. Moreover, the choice of a unique cutoff is avoided by computing the precision for various recall values, and exhibiting a plot showing recall against precision. An example of such a graph is shown in Figure 1 and Tables Ia and Ib for query Q145, processed against a collection

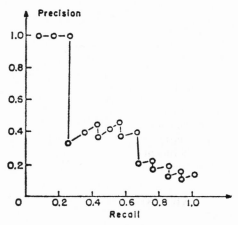

FIG. 1. Performance characteristics for query Q145 (Cranfield-1, word-stem run): Recall-precision plot.

of 200 documents in aerodynamics. A total of twelve documents in the collection were judged relevant to the request, the relevance judgments being performed by a subject expert independently of the retrieval system. The ranks of the relevant documents produced by the search system after ordering of the documents in decreasing correlation order are shown in Table Ia. For the retrieval process illustrated in Figure 1 and Tables Ia and Ib, these ranks range from 1 for the relevant document with the highest request-document correlation to 78 for the relevant item with the lowest correlation. By choosing successive cutoff values after the retrieval of 1, 2, 3, . . . , n documents, and computing recall and precision values at each point, a recall-precision table can be constructed, as shown in Table Ib. The recall-precision graph obtained from this table is represented in Figure 1.

Recall-precision graphs, such as that of Figure 1, have been criticized because a number of parameters are obscured when plotting recall against precision — for

TABLE Ia.

PERFORMANCE CHARACTERISTICS FOR QUERY Q145 (CRANFIELD-1, WORD-STEM RUN): LIST OF RELEVANT DOCUMENTS

Relevant documents		
Rank	Number	Correlation
1	80	.5084
2	102	.4418
3	81	.4212
10	82	.2843
11	193	.2731
14	83	.2631
15	87	.2594
20	88	.2315
40	86	.1856
50	109	.1631
69	84	.1305
78	85	.1193

Recall-precision after retrieval of X documents		
X	Recall	Precision
1	0.0833	1.0000
2	0.1667	1.0000
3	0.2500	1.0000
9	0.2500	0.3333
10	0.3333	0.4000
11	0.4167	0.4545
13	0.4167	0.3846
14	0.5000	0.4286
15	0.5833	0.4667
19	0.5833	0.3684
20	0.6667	0.4000
39	0.6667	0.2051
40	0.7500	0.2250
49	0.7500	0.1837
50	0.8333	0.2000
68	0.8333	0.1470
69	0.9167	0.1594
77	0.9167	0.1428
78	1.0000	0.1538

example, the size of the retrieved document set and the collection size [11]. Such plots are, however, effective to summarize the performance of retrieval methods averaged over many search requests, and they can be used advantageously to select analysis methods which fit certain specific operating ranges. Thus, if it is desired to pick a procedure which favors the retrieval of *all* relevant material, then one must concentrate on the high-recall region; similarly, if *only* relevant material is wanted, the high-precision region is of importance. In general, it is possible to obtain high recall only at a substantial cost in precision, and vice versa [8–10].

In addition to the standard recall and standard precision measures, whose values depend on the size of the retrieved document set, it is also possible to use indicators which are independent of the retrieved set. In particular, since the SMART system produces ranked document output in decreasing order of correlation between documents and search requests, evaluation measures can be generated which are based on the ranks of the set of relevant documents, as determined by the automatic retrieval process, compared with the ranks of the relevant documents for an ideal system where all relevant items are retrieved before any nonrelevant ones.

Two particularly attractive measures with this property are the normalized recall and normalized precision, which are defined as follows [7, 8]:

$$R_{\text{norm}} = 1 - \frac{\sum\limits_{i=1}^{n} r_i - \sum\limits_{i=1}^{n} i}{n(N-n)},$$

$$P_{\text{norm}} = 1 - \frac{\sum\limits_{i=1}^{n} \log r_i - \sum\limits_{i=1}^{n} \log i}{\log \dfrac{N!}{(N-n)!\, n!}}$$

where n is the size of the relevant document set, N is the size of the total document collection, and r_i is the rank of the ith relevant document when the documents are arranged in decreasing order of their correlation with the search request.

These measures range from 1 for a perfect system in which all relevant items are placed at the top of the retrieved list, to 0 for the worst case where all nonrelevant items are retrieved before any relevant one. Furthermore, under certain circumstances the normalized measures can be shown to be closely related to the standard measures as follows [12]:

$$R_{\text{norm}} \approx \frac{1}{N} \sum_{i=1}^{n} R(i)$$

when the number of relevant documents n is small compared to the collection size N, and

$$P_{\text{norm}} \approx \frac{1}{N} \sum_{i=1}^{n} P(i)$$

for large N and n not too small. $R(i)$ and $P(i)$ correspond, respectively, to the standard recall and precision values after the retrieval of i documents.

Two further overall measures of retrieval effectiveness, analogous to the normalized measures, but somewhat simpler to compute, are the "rank recall" and "log precision" measures, defined as

$$\text{rank recall} = \sum_{i=1}^{n} i \Big/ \sum_{i=1}^{n} r_i,$$

$$\text{log precision} = \sum_{i=1}^{n} \ln i \Big/ \sum_{i=1}^{n} \ln r_i,$$

where n is again equal to the number of relevant documents, and r_i is the rank (in decreasing correlation order) of the ith relevant document. Like the normalized measures, rank recall and log precision are functions of the rank of the relevant documents, but contrary to the earlier situation, these measures do not take into account the collection size N.

Under normal circumstances the results of a system evaluation must reflect overall system performance, rather than the performance for individual requests only. In these circumstances, it is convenient to process many search requests and to use an average performance value as a measure of retrieval effectiveness [12]. For the overall evaluation measures (normalized recall and precision, and rank recall and log precision), the averaging process presents no problem, since only a single set of values is obtained in each case for each request. The averaging method is more complex for the standard recall-precision graph, since a continuous set of values is involved, and the number of relevant documents differs from request to request. In the SMART system, the averaging process for the recall-precision graph corresponding to many search requests is performed as follows:

(a) ten specified standard recall values are picked ranging from 0.1 to 1.0;
(b) for each recall level, the number of documents which must be retrieved in order to obtain the specified level is determined;
(c) using the cutoff value thus calculated for the number of retrieved documents, the precision value is generated corresponding to the specified recall;
(d) the precision values obtained for a given recall value are averaged over a number of search requests, and the resulting point is added to the recall-precision plot;
(e) the ten individual points on the plot are joined to produce an average recall-precision curve.

Averaged evaluation results are presented for three different document collections in Section 3.

C. Significance Computations

For each search request and each processing method, the evaluation procedure incorporated into the SMART system produces fourteen different statistics, including four global statistics (rank recall, log precision, normalized recall, and normalized precision) and ten local statistics (standard precision for ten recall levels). A problem then arises concerning the use of these fourteen statistics for the assessment of systems performance. In theory, comparisons between different processing methods are easy to make by contrasting, for example, the recall-precision plots obtained in each case. In practice, it is difficult to draw hard conclusions because the variation in performance between individual requests is large, because the fourteen measures have different ranges, and because it is unclear a priori whether the magnitude of a given recall or precision value is significant or not. In particular, given a specified recall or precision value, it is of interest to determine whether values as large, or larger, as the given one could be expected under random circumstances, or whether on the contrary the probability of obtaining a given specified value for an average system is very small.

Because of the large request variance and the differences in the range of the various parameters, the significance computations incorporated into the SMART system are based on *paired comparisons* between the request performance using processing method A, and the performance using method B. In particular, the difference in magnitude is computed for each of the fourteen pairs of statistics obtained for each request for each pair of processing methods. These differences are then averaged over many requests, and statistical computations are used to transform the averaged differences into probability measurements. Each of the fourteen values thus obtained represents the probability that if the performance level of the two methods A and B were in fact equally high for the given statistic (except for random variations in the test results), then a test value as large as the one actually observed would occur for a system. A probability value of 0.05 is usually taken as an upper bound in judging whether a deviation in test values is significant or not. Using this probability value as a limit, the corresponding test difference would in fact be significant nineteen times out of twenty, and only one time out of twenty would two equally effective systems be expected to produce as large a test difference.

Since it is difficult to judge systems performance by using fourteen different probability values, corresponding to the fourteen evaluation measures, an *aggregate probability value* is computed from the fourteen individual probabilities. The significance of this aggregate depends on the independence of the various significant tests.

Two separate testing procedures are incorporated into the SMART system. The first one uses the well-known *t-test* based on Student's *t*-distribution [13]. This test requires an underlying normal distribution of the data used in the test process, as well as the independence among the search requests processed against the document collections. The *t*-test process takes into account the actual magnitude of the differences for the statistics being calculated, and the resulting probabilities are considered to be reliable indicators of system differences.

A less demanding testing procedure is furnished by the *sign test*, where the magnitude of the differences in the statistics is not taken into account, but only the sign of the differences (that is, an indication of whether method A provides a larger test result than B, or vice versa) [14]. An attractive feature of the sign test is that normality of the input data is not required, and since this normality is generally hard to prove for statistics derived from a request-document correlation process, the sign test probabilities may provide a better indicator of system performance than the *t*-test.

The *t*-test computations are performed as follows: Let $m_{ij\mathrm{A}}$ be the value of statistic i for request j, using method A (for example, the value of the rank recall, or the normalized recall). Then, given two processing methods A and B, and a set of k requests, the averages of the differences for statistic i are computed. Specially,

$$d_{ij} = m_{ij\mathrm{A}} - m_{ij\mathrm{B}} \quad \text{and} \quad D_i = \frac{1}{k} \sum_{j=1}^{k} d_{ij}.$$

The difference computations for two statistics (rank recall and log precision) are shown in Table II. The average differences are then used to obtain the standard deviation of the differences $(SD)_i$ and the t-test values T_i, where $T_i = (D_i/(SD)_i) \cdot k$. The t-test values T_i are now converted to probabilities P_{ti} using Student's t-distribution with k degrees of freedom.

The probabilities derived from the fourteen statistics are then used to compute an aggregate probability by first converting the two-tailed t-test to a one-tailed test, changing each probability to χ^2, adding the χ^2 values, and finally reconverting to a probability P_t, using a χ^2 distribution with 28 degrees of freedom [13]. Specifically, let s be the sign of the sum of the differences D_i, or $s =$ sign $(\sum_i D_i)$. Then

$$\text{if sign } D_i = s \rightarrow P'_{ti} = \tfrac{1}{2}P_{ti};$$

alternatively

$$\text{if sign } D_i \neq s \rightarrow P'_{ti} = 1 - \tfrac{1}{2}P_{ti}.$$

The χ^2 of the sum is now obtained such that

$$\chi^2 = -\sum_{i=1}^{14} - 2 \log P'_{ti}.$$

Finally, the value is converted to the desired probability P_t.

The t-test computations are shown for two sample analysis methods A and B in Table III. The values in columns 2 and 3 of Table III represent averages over 17 search requests for each of the fourteen evaluation measures. The final probabilities P_{ti} range from a high of

0.107 for the standard precision at recall value 1, to a low of 0.0007 for the normalized precision. The final probability value P_t is smaller than 1.10^{-4}, thus indicating the combination algorithm concentrates on the significant tests, while ignoring the less significant ones. The validity of the process depends on an assumption of independence among the fourteen measures, which is true to a limited extent for the measures used.

The sign test uses the binomial instead of the t-distribution to produce a probability value. Specifically, given two processing methods for which the null hypothesis applies (that is, two equivalent methods), each d_{ij} has equal chances of being positive or negative; moreover, since the search requests are assumed unrelated (independent) and randomly distributed, the signs of the differences are unrelated. The number, say M, of positive signs is accordingly binominally distributed with p equal to one-half and k equal to the number of requests.

M can then serve as a statistic to test the null hypothesis by taking large values of M as significant evidence against the equivalence of the two methods tested. Obviously, a test based on rejecting the equivalence hypothesis for large values of M is equivalent to one based on rejection for small values of M', the number of negative signs. As before, a probability of 0.05 may be taken as an upper limit for rejecting the equivalence assumption.

Since the sign test does not depend on the magnitudes of the differences, the number of positive or negative signs can be cumulated directly. In particular, the number of requests preferring method A is summed over all measures, as well as the number of requests preferring

TABLE II

Computation of Recall and Precision Differences for Individual Requests
(Method A: stem concon; method B: thesaurus)

Request name	Rank recall			Log precision		
	Method A	Method B	Difference	Method A	Method B	Difference
AUTOMATA PHR	0.5238	0.9649	−0.4411	0.7126	0.9881	−0.2755
COMP SYSTEMS	0.0725	0.1228	−0.0503	0.3783	0.4806	−0.1023
COMPS-ASSEMB	0.3714	0.7428	−0.3714	0.8542	0.9453	−0.0911
CORE MEMORY	0.0691	0.1064	−0.0373	0.3157	0.3695	−0.0538
DIFFERNTL EQ	0.5298	0.7574	−0.2276	0.8620	0.9219	−0.0599
ERROR CONTRL	0.1460	0.1875	−0.0415	0.5342	0.5972	−0.0630
M10-COUNTERS	0.8182	0.7347	0.0835	0.8682	0.8599	0.0083
M2TRANSMIT	0.0522	0.0963	−0.0441	0.2819	0.4698	−0.1879
M3-INFORM	0.1968	0.3134	−0.1166	0.6300	0.7666	−0.1366
M8-STORAGE	0.0375	0.2763	−0.2388	0.2670	0.4666	−0.1996
MISSILE TRAK	1.0000	0.7500	0.2500	1.0000	0.6309	0.3691
MORSE CODE	1.0000	1.0000	0.0000	1.0000	1.0000	0.0000
PATTERN RECG	1.0000	1.0000	0.0000	1.0000	1.0000	0.0000
RANDOM NUMBS	0.0517	0.2000	−0.1483	0.1750	0.3408	−0.1658
SOLSTAT CIRC	0.2766	0.3402	−0.0636	0.6921	0.7912	−0.0991
SWITCH FUNCS	0.3529	0.4444	−0.0915	0.7416	0.8005	−0.0589
THIN FILMS	0.2157	0.8462	−0.6305	0.6294	0.9242	−0.2948
Total	6.7142	8.8833	−2.1691	10.9422	12.3531	−1.4109
Average value over 17 requests	0.3950	0.5225	−0.1276	0.6437	0.7267	−0.0830

TABLE III

t-TEST COMPUTATIONS FOR 14 DIFFERENT RECALL AND PRECISION MEASURES
(Averages over 17 requests, method A: stem concon; method B: thesaurus)

	Evaluation measure	Average value		Difference of average	Standard deviation	t-test value	Probability
		Method A	Method B				
1	Rank recall	0.3950	0.5225	−0.1276	2.07E-01	2.54E 00	0.0219
2	Log precision	0.6437	0.7267	−0.0830	1.47E-01	2.33E 00	0.0334
3	Normed recall	0.9233	0.9675	−0.0442	5.35E-02	3.41E 00	0.0036
4	Normed precision	0.7419	0.8639	−0.1219	1.20E-01	4.19E 00	0.0007
5	Recall-precision graph (precision for 10 recall levels) 0.1	0.7385	0.9735	−0.2351	2.88E-01	3.37E 00	0.0039
6	0.2	0.6544	0.8973	−0.2428	2.82E-01	3.55E 00	0.0026
7	0.3	0.5844	0.8245	−0.2401	2.51E-01	3.95E 00	0.0011
8	0.4	0.5326	0.7551	−0.2226	2.39E-01	3.84E 00	0.0014
9	0.5	0.5187	0.7146	−0.1959	2.00E-01	4.04E 00	0.0009
10	0.6	0.5035	0.6499	−0.1464	1.59E-01	3.79E 00	0.0016
11	0.7	0.4452	0.6012	−0.1561	1.79E-01	3.59E 00	0.0024
12	0.8	0.4091	0.5514	−0.1423	2.24E-01	2.62E 00	0.0184
13	0.9	0.3794	0.4973	−0.1179	2.29E-01	2.12E 00	0.0499
14	1.0	0.3106	0.4118	−0.1012	2.44E-01	1.71E 00	0.1070

Combined significance: Total χ^2, 1.67E 02
Total probability of B over A, 0.0000

method B. These totals are then subjected to the same testing process, as follows: Let t be a tolerance value, taken as 0.001 for the present test; further, for each statistic i, let k_{ai} be the number of $d_{ij}(j = 1, \cdots, k)$ exceeding $+t$, k_{bi}, the number of d_{ij} smaller than $-t$, and k_{ci}, the number of d_{ij} such that $|d_{ij}| \leq t$; where the number of requests $k = k_{ai} + k_{bi} + k_{ci}$.

The sign-test probability for statistic i is now computed as follows: Let $k_{vi} = k_{ai} + k_{bi}$ and $k_{wi} = \min(k_{ai}, k_{bi})$; then

$$P_{si} = \sum_{j=1}^{k_{wi}} \frac{k_{vi}!}{j!(k_{vi} - j)!} 2^{-k_{vi}+1}.$$

The overall probability, P_s, can be cumulated directly for the fourteen evaluation measures; specifically, if $k_a = \Sigma_i k_{ai}$, $k_b = \Sigma_i k_{bi}$, $k_v = k_a + k_b$, and $k_w = \min(k_a, k_b)$, then

$$P_s = \sum_{j=1}^{k_w} \frac{(k_v)!}{j!(k_v - j)!} 2^{-k_v+1}.$$

The sign-test computations are shown in Table IV for the same processing methods and search requests previously used as examples in Tables II and III. The individual probabilities P_{si} range in values from 0.0010 to 0.1185. The overall probability is again smaller than 1.10^{-4}; this is also reflected by the fact that method B is preferred 165 times, while A is superior only 26 times, with 47 ties.

Since the fourteen statistics used may not be fully independent, a question arises concerning the interpreta-

tion of the cumulated t-test probability P_t, and the cumulated sign test probability P_s. As a general rule, the equality hypothesis between two given methods A and B can safely be rejected when both probabilities P_s and P_t do not exceed 0.001 in magnitude, implying that most of the individual probabilities P_{si} and P_{ti} are smaller than 0.05, and when the same test results are obtained for all document collections being tested. If, on the other hand, the values of the final probabilities are larger, or if the test results differ from one collection to the next, additional tests would seem to be required before a decision can be made.

3. Experimental Results

A. Test Environment

The principal parameters controlling the test procedure are listed in Tables V, VI, and VII, respectively. The main properties of the document collections and search requests are shown in Table V. Specifically, results are given for three document collections in the following subject fields:

(a) Computer Science (IRE-3): a set of 780 abstracts of documents in the computer literature, published in 1959–1961, and used with 34 search requests;

(b) Documentation (ADI): a set of 82 short papers, each an average of 1380 words in length, presented at the 1963 Annual Meeting of the American Documentation Institute, and used with 35 search requests;

(c) Aerodynamics (CRAN-1): a set of 200 abstracts of documents used by the second ASLIB Cranfield Project [15], and used with 42 search requests.

TABLE IV

SIGN TEST COMPUTATIONS FOR 14 DIFFERENT RECALL AND PRECISION MEASURES
(Averages over 17 requests, method A: stem concon; method B: thesaurus)

Evaluation measure		Number of requests superior for method A	Number of requests superior for method B	Number of requests equal for A and B	Probability (B over A)
Rank recall		2	13	2	0.0074
Log precision		2	13	2	0.0074
Normed recall		2	13	2	0.0074
Normed precision		2	13	2	0.0074
	0.1	0	9	8	0.0039
	0.2	0	11	6	0.0010
	0.3	1	12	4	0.0034
	0.4	1	11	5	0.0036
	0.5	0	13	4	0.0002
Recall-precision graph	0.6	3	11	3	0.0574
	0.7	2	12	3	0.0129
	0.8	3	12	2	0.0352
	0.9	4	11	2	0.1185
	1.0	4	11	2	0.1185
Combined significance for 14 only measures		26	165	47	0.0000

Each of these collections belongs to a distinct subject area, thus permitting the comparison of the various analysis and search procedures in several contexts. The ADI collection in documentation is of particular interest because full papers are available rather than only document abstracts. The Cranfield collection, on the other hand, is the only one which is also manually indexed by trained indexers, thus making it possible to perform a comparison of the standard keyword search procedures with the automatic text processing methods.

The procedure used to collect relevance assessments and the related statistical information concerning the

TABLE V

DOCUMENT COLLECTION AND REQUEST CHARACTERISTICS

	Characteristics		IRE-3	CRAN-1	ADI
Document collection	Number of documents in collection		780	200	82
	Average number of words (all words) per document	Full text	—	—	1380
		Abstract	88	165	59
		Title	9	14	10
	Average number of words (common words deleted) per document	Full text	—	—	710
		Abstract	49	91	35
		Title	5	11	7
	Average number of concepts per analyzed document	Full text	—	—	369
		Abstract	40	65	25
		Title	5	9	6
Search requests	Number of search requests		34	42	35
	Average number of words per request (all words)		22	17	14
	Request preparation: (a) Short paragraphs prepared by staff members for test purposes		√		√
	(b) Short paragraphs prepared by subject experts previously submitted to operational system			√	

TABLE VI

Relevance Distribution and Assessment

Characteristics	IRE-3	CRAN-1	ADI
Preparation of relevance judgments:			
(a) Dichotomous prepared by staff experts based on abstracts using full relevance assessment	√		
(b) Dichotomous prepared by subject experts based on abstracts and full text (full relevance assessment)		√	
(c) Dichotomous prepared by staff experts based on full text using full relevance assessment			√
Number of relevant documents per request (all requests):			
(a) Range	2–65	1–12	1–33
(b) Mean	17.4	4.7	4.9
(c) Generality (mean divided by collection size)	22.2	23.6	59.2
Number of relevant documents per specific request:			
(a) Number of specific requests	17	21	17
(b) Mean number of relevant	7.5	3.0	2.1
Number of relevant documents per general request:			
(a) Number of general requests	17	21	18
(b) Mean number of relevant	25.8	6.4	7.4

average number of relevant documents per request are summarized in Table VI. Exhaustive procedures were used to assess the relevance of each document with respect to each search request. Only one person (the requester) was asked to collect the judgments for each request, and dichotomous assessments were made to declare each document as either relevant or not. In the words of a recent study on evaluation methodology, the process used consists of "multiple events of private relevance" [16].

Additional data concerning the user population and the number of search programs used are given in Table VII. In each case, the user population consisted of volunteers who were asked to help in the test process. Several hundred analysis and search methods incorporated into the SMART system were used with the three document collections. Results based on about sixty of these processing methods are exhibited in the present study.

The methods chosen are generally useful to answer a number of basic questions affecting the design of automatic information systems: for example, can automatic text processing methods be used effectively to replace a

TABLE VII

General Test Environment

Characteristics	IRE-3	CRAN-1	ADI
User population			
(a) 10 students and staff experts	√		√
(b) 42 subject experts		√	
Number of retrieved documents per request	All	All	All
Number of indexing and search programs used			
(a) Matching algorithms	2	2	2
(b) Term weight adjustment	2	2	2
(c) Document length variation	3	4	3
(d) Basic dictionaries (suffix "s," stem, thesaurus, stat. phrases, hierarchy, syntax)	6	5	5
(e) Concept-concept association dictionaries	2	3	1
(f) Total basic options	144	240	60

manual content analysis; if so, what part or parts of a document should be incorporated in the automatic procedure; is it necessary to provide vocabulary normalization methods to eliminate ambiguities caused by homographs and synonymous word groups; should such a normalization be handled by means of a specially constructed dictionary, or is it possible to replace thesauruses completely by statistical word association methods; what dictionaries can most effectively be used for vocabulary normalization; what should be the role of the user in formulating and controlling the search procedure. These and other questions are considered in the evaluation process described in the remainder of this section.

B. Document Length

A first variable of interest is the *length* of each document to be used for content analysis purposes. This fundamental question enters into many of the arguments between advocates of automatic systems, and others who hold that manual content analysis methods are essential, because in an automatic environment it is not normally possible to process the full text of all documents.

In Figure 2, three analysis systems based on document titles only are compared with systems based on the manipulation of complete document abstracts. In each case, weighted word stems, extracted either from the titles or from the abstracts of the documents, are matched with equivalent indicators from the search requests. Figure 2 exhibits recall-precision graphs, averaged, respectively, over 34, 42, and 35 search requests for the computer science, aerodynamics, and documentation collections. In every case, the abstract process is found to be superior to the "title only" option, particularly at the high-recall end of the curve, since the abstract curve comes closest to the upper right-hand corner of the graph where both recall and precision are equal to 1. (For an

ideal system which retrieves all relevant items before any irrelevant ones, the recall-precision curve shrinks to a single point with coordinates (1, 1).)

The significance output for the graphs shown in Figures 2–9 is collected in Table VIII. In each case, reference is made to the graphs being compared, and the combined probability values P_s and P_t are listed with an indicator specifying the preferred method. The superiority of the "abstract-stem" process of Figure 2 is reflected in the significance output of Table VIII. The probability of a correct null hypothesis is smaller than 1.10^{-4} for both the sign and the t-tests, thus showing that document titles are significantly inferior to document abstracts as a source of content indicators.

The ADI documentation collection was used to extend the analysis to longer document segments. The results of a comparison between document abstract processing (60 words) and full text processing (1400 words) show that the full text process is superior to the abstract process. The improvement in performance appears smaller than that shown in Figure 2 for the title-abstract comparison. In particular, the t-test probabilities for the abstract-full text comparisons are too large to permit an unequivocal rejection of the null hypothesis in this case.

To summarize: document abstracts are more effective for content analysis purposes than document titles alone; further improvements appear possible when abstracts are replaced by larger text portions; however, the increase in effectiveness is not large enough to reach the unequivocal conclusion that full text processing is always superior to abstract processing.

C. Matching Functions and Term Weights

It is easy in an automatic text processing environment to differentiate among individual content indicators by assigning weights to the indicators in proportion to their

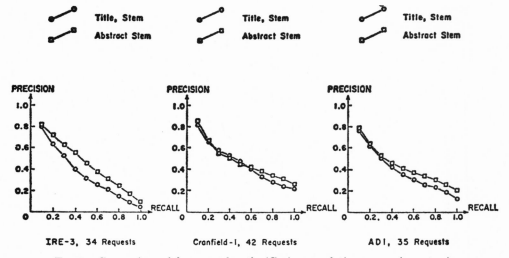

FIG. 2. Comparison of document length. (Cosine correlation; numeric vectors).

TABLE VIII

COMBINED SIGNIFICANCE OUTPUT

Retrieval methods being compared	Corresponding graph number	Document collection					
		IRE-3		CRAN-1		ADI	
		P_s	P_t	P_s	P_t	P_s	P_t
A. Title stem B. Abstract stem	Fig. 2	0.0000 (B > A)	0.0000 (B > A)	0.0000 (B > A)	0.0000 (B > A)	0.0000 (B > A)	0.0000 (B > A)
A. Abstract stem B. Full text stem		—	—	—	—	0.1420 (B > A)	0.0892 (B > A)
A. Abstract thesaurus B. Full text thesaurus		—	—	—	—	0.0064 (B > A)	0.0987 (B > A)
A. Numeric stem B. Logical stem	Fig. 3	0.0000 (A > B)	0.0000 (A > B)	0.0000 (A > B)	0.0000 (A > B)	0.3736 (A > B)	0.0040 (A > B)
A. Cosine logical stem B. Overlap logical stem	Fig. 4	0.0000 (A > B)	0.0000 (A > B)	0.0000 (A > B)	0.0000 (A > B)	0.0891 (A > B)	0.0148 (A > B)
A. Overlap numeric stem B. Overlap logical stem		—	—	0.3497 (B > A)	0.1427 (B > A)	—	—
A. Overlap numeric stem B. Cosine numeric stem		—	—	0.0000 (B > A)	0.0000 (B > A)	—	—
A. Word stem B. Suffix "s"		0.0000 (A > B)	0.0000 (A > B)	0.0000 (B > A)	0.0000 (B > A)	0.0000 (A > B)	0.0000 (A > B)
A. Thesaurus B. Word stem	Fig. 5	0.0000 (A > B)	0.0000 (A > B)	0.0020 (A > B)	0.1483 (A > B)	0.0000 (A > B)	0.0000 (A > B)
A. Old thesaurus B. New thesaurus	Fig. 6	0.0000 (B > A)	0.0000 (B > A)	0.0000 (B > A)	0.0000 (B > A)	—	—
A. Thesaurus B. Phrases, weight 1.0		1.0000 (A > B)	0.8645 (B > A)	0.0001 (A > B)	0.1120 (A > B)	0.0391 (B > A)	0.1171 (B > A)
A. Word stem B. Stem concon	Fig. 7	0.1948 (A > B)	0.0566 (A > B)	0.0086 (B > A)	0.0856 (B > A)	0.4420 (B > A)	0.6521 (B > A)
A. Thesaurus B. Stem concon		0.0000 (A > B)	0.0000 (A > B)	0.0175 (B > A)	0.6906 (B > A)	0.0000 (A > B)	0.0003 (A > B)
A. Concon all, 0.60 B. Concon 3–50, 0.60		—	—	0.0000 (B > A)	0.0525 (B > A)	—	—
A. Concon 3–50, 0.60 B. Concon 6–100, 0.45		—	—	0.0001 (B > A)	0.0991 (B > A)	—	—
A. Thesaurus B. Hierarchy parents	Fig. 8	0.1047 (A > B)	0.1676 (A > B)	—	—	—	—
A. Thesaurus B. Hierarchy brothers	Fig. 8	0.0000 (A > B)	0.0000 (A > B)	—	—	—	—
A. Thesaurus B. Hierarchy sons		0.0000 (A > B)	0.0000 (A > B)	—	—	—	—
A. Thesaurus B. Hierarchy cross-reference		0.0000 (A > B)	0.0000 (A > B)	—	—	—	—
A. Index stem B. Abstract stem	Fig. 9	—	—	0.0465 (A > B)	0.0415 (A > B)	—	—
A. Index stem B. Stem concon	Fig. 9	—	—	0.0020 (A > B)	0.0176 (A > B)	—	—
A. Index new thesaurus B. Abstract, new theaurus	Fig. 9	—	—	0.0019 (A > B)	0.0001 (A > B)	—	—

presumed importance. Such weights can be derived in part by using the frequency of occurrence of the original text words which give rise to the various indicators, and in part as a function of the various dictionary mapping procedures. Thus, ambiguous terms which in a synonym dictionary would normally correspond to many different thesaurus classes can be weighted less than unambiguous terms. The SMART system includes procedures for testing the effectiveness of such weighted (numeric) content indicators compared with nonweighted (logical) indicators, where all term weights are either 1 or 0 (1 if a given term is assigned to a given document and 0 if it is not).

The recall-precision graphs for the three collections previously used are shown in Figure 3 and the corresponding significance output is reproduced in Table VIII. In each case, weighted word stems extracted from document abstracts or full text are compared with nonweighted (logical) stems. The results are clearly in favor of the weighted process for all three collections, the largest performance differences being registered for the IRE collection in documentation. The recall-precision graph for the ADI collection also appears to show a considerable advantage for the weighted process, and this is reflected in the t-test probability of 0.0040. However, when the magnitudes of the results are disregarded, it is found that nearly as many evaluation parameters favor the nonweighted process as the weighted one for the documentation collection. The test results are therefore not wholly significant for that collection.

On the whole, it appears that weighted content indicators produce better retrieval results than nonweighted ones, and that binary term vectors should therefore be used only if no weighting system appears readily available.

Another variable affecting retrieval performance which can be easily incorporated into an automatic information system is the correlation coefficient used to determine the similarity between an analyzed search request and the analyzed documents. Two of the correlation measures which have been included in the SMART system are the cosine and overlap correlations, which are defined as follows:

$$\cos(\boldsymbol{q}, \boldsymbol{d}) = \frac{\sum\limits_{i=1}^{n} d_i q_i}{\left(\sum\limits_{i=1}^{n} (d_i)^2 \cdot \sum\limits_{i=1}^{n} (q_i)^2 \right)^{\frac{1}{2}}} \text{ and}$$

$$\mathrm{ovlap}(\boldsymbol{q}, \boldsymbol{d}) = \frac{\sum\limits_{i=1}^{n} \min (q_i, d_i)}{\min \left(\sum\limits_{i=1}^{n} q_i, \sum\limits_{i=1}^{n} d_i \right)},$$

where $\boldsymbol{q}$ and $\boldsymbol{d}$ are considered to be n-dimensional vectors of terms representing an analyzed query $\boldsymbol{q}$ and an analyzed document $\boldsymbol{d}$, respectively, in a space of n terms assignable as information identifiers.

Both the cosine and the overlap functions range from 0 for no match to 1 for perfect identity between the respective vectors. The cosine correlation is more sensitive to document length, that is, to the number of assigned terms, because of the factor in the denominator, and tends to produce greater variations in the correlations than the overlap measure.

A comparison of cosine and overlap matching functions is shown in the output of Figure 4. In each case logical (nonweighted) vectors are used with either of the two correlation methods. The results are clearly in favor of the cosine matching function for both the IRE and CRAN collections; for the ADI collection, the evidence is not sufficiently one-sided to reach a hard conclusion in that case.

The combined effect of parameter adjustments in both

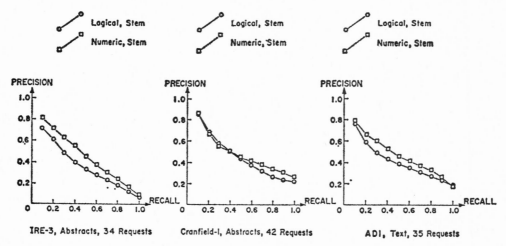

Fig. 3. Comparison of weighted (numeric) and unweighted (logical) concepts using the stem dictionary and cosine correlation.

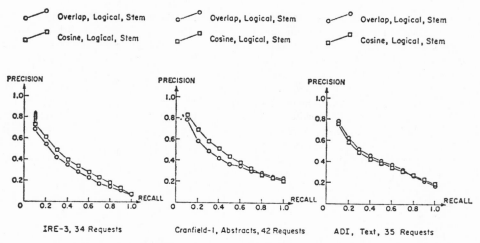

FIG. 4. Comparison of overlap and cosine matching functions.

the weighting and the correlation methods can be studied by combining the output of Figures 3 and 4, as reflected for the Cranfield collection in the significance output of Table VIII. The weakest method appears to be the combination of logical vectors with the overlap correlation, and the most satisfactory results are obtained with the numeric (weighted) term vectors and the cosine correlation.

It should be noted that the overlap-logical process corresponds to the standard keyword matching method used in almost all operational, semi-mechanized retrieval situations. In such cases, nonweighted keywords assigned to each document are compared with keywords attached to the search requests and a count is taken of the number of overlapping keywords; the resulting coefficient is then equivalent to a nonnormalized overlap function. It would appear from the results of Figures 3 and 4 that standard keyword matching systems can be improved by the simple device of using a better matching function and assigning weights to the keywords.

To summarize: weighted content identifiers are more effective for content description than nonweighted ones, and the cosine correlation function is more useful as a measure of document-request similarity than the overlap function; advantage can therefore be taken of the computational facilities incorporated into many mechanized information systems, and service can be improved by using more sophisticated request-document matching methods.

D. Language Normalization—The Suffix Process

If natural language texts are to form the basis for an automatic assignment of information identifiers to documents, then the question of language normalization is of primary concern. Indeed, there do not then exist human intermediaries who could resolve some of the ambiguities inherent in the natural language itself, or some of the inconsistencies introduced into written texts by the authors or writers responsible for the preparation of the documents.

A large number of experiments have therefore been conducted with the SMART system, using a variety of dictionaries for purposes of language normalization in each of the three subject fields under study. The performance of the following dictionaries is studied in particular:

(a) *suffix "s"* process, where words differing by the addition of a terminal "s" are recognized as equivalent (for example, the words "apple" and "apples" are assigned a common identifier, but not words "analyzer" and "analyzing");

(b) the *word-stem dictionary*, where all words which exhibit a common word stem are treated as equivalent; for example, "analysis," "analyzer," "analyst," and so on;

(c) the *synonym dictionary*, or thesaurus, where a set of synonymous, or closely related, terms are all placed into a common thesaurus class, thus ensuring that common identifiers are derived from all such terms;

(d) the *statistical phrase dictionary*, which makes it possible to recognize "phrases" consisting of the juxtaposition of several distinct concepts; thus if a given document contains the notion of "program," as well as the notion of "language," it could be tagged with the phrase "programming language"; the statistical phrase dictionary incorporated into the SMART system is manually constructed and contains a large variety of common noun phrases for each of the subject areas covered;

(e) the *concept association method*, in which concepts are grouped not by reference to a preconstructed dictionary, but by using statistical co-occurrence characteristics of the vocabulary under investigation.

A comparison of the suffix "s" dictionary with a complete word stem dictionary is illustrated in the output of Table VIII. In the former case, the texts of documents and search requests are looked up in a table of common words so as to delete function words and other text items not of immediate interest for content analysis purposes; the final "s" endings are then deleted so as to confound words which differ only by a final "s." In the latter case, a complete suffix dictionary is also consulted, and the original words are reduced to word-stem form before request identifiers are matched with document identifiers.

The results obtained from these experiments are contradictory, in the sense that for two of the collections used (IRE-3 and ADI) the more thorough normalization inherent in the word-stem process, compared with suffix "s" recognition alone, improves the search effectiveness; for the third collection (Cranfield), the reverse result appears to hold. For none of the collections is the improvement of one method over the other really dramatic, so that in practice either procedure might reasonably be used.

The discrepancy between the IRE and ADI results, on the one hand, and the Cranfield results, on the other, may be caused by differences in the respective vocabularies. Specifically, the Cranfield texts are substantially more technical in nature, and the collection is more homogeneous than is the case for the other collections. To be able to differentiate between the various document abstracts, it is then important to maintain finer distinctions for the Cranfield case than for ADI and IRE, and these finer differences are lost when several different words are combined into a unique class through the suffix cutoff process. The argument can be summarized by stating that dictionaries and word normalization procedures are most effective if the vocabulary is redundant and relatively nontechnical; in the reverse case, such procedures may not in fact result in processing advantages.

E. Synonym Recognition

One of the perennial problems in automatic language analysis is the question of language variability among authors, and the linguistic ambiguities which result. Several experiments have therefore been performed using a variety of synonym dictionaries for each of the three subject fields under study ("Harris 2" and "Harris 3" dictionaries for the computer literature, "Quasi-Synonym" or "QS" lists for aeronautical engineering, and regular thesaurus for documentation). Use of such a synonym dictionary permits the replacement of a variety of related terms by similar concept identifiers, thus ensuring the retrieval of documents dealing with the "manufacture of transistor diodes" when the query deals with the "production of solid-state rectifiers."

The output of Figure 5, which represents a comparison of the word-stem matching procedure with a process including a thesaurus look-up operation for the recognition of synonyms, shows that considerable improvements in performance are obtainable by means of suitably constructed synonym dictionaries. The improvement is again smallest for the Cranfield collection, in part for the reasons already stated in the last subsection, and in part because the dictionary available for this collection was not originally constructed to mesh in with the SMART retrieval programs. However, in the present case, the synonym recognition seems to benefit the Cranfield material also. The significance output for Figure 5 shows that all thesaurus improvements are fully significant, with the exception of the t-test for the Cranfield collection. Thus only for Cranfield can the null hypothesis not be rejected unequivocally.

The differences observed in the performance of the various synonym dictionaries suggest that not all dictionaries are equally useful for the improvement of retrieval effectiveness. The experiments conducted with the SMART system in fact lead to the following principles of dictionary construction [17]:

    (a) Very rare terms which occur in a representative sample document collection with insufficient fre-

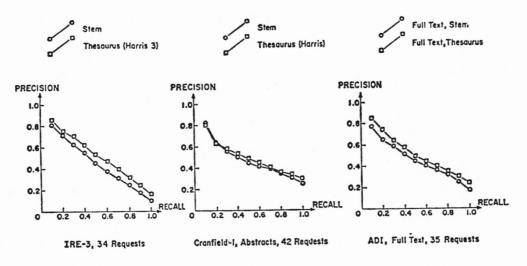

Fig. 5. Comparison of synonym recognition (thesaurus) with word-stem matching process.

quency should not be placed into separate categories in the dictionary, but should be combined if possible with other rare terms to form larger classes, since low-frequency categories provide few matches between stored items and the search requests.

(b) Very common high-frequency terms should either be eliminated since they provide little discrimination, or placed into synonym classes of their own, so that they cannot submerge other terms which would be grouped with them.

(c) Terms which have no special significance in a given technical subject area (such as "begin," "indicate," "system," "automatic," etc.) should not be included.

(d) Ambiguous terms (such as "base") should be coded only for those senses which are likely to occur in the subject area being considered.

(e) Each group of related terms should account for approximately the same total frequency of occurrence of the corresponding words in the document collection; this ensures that each identifier has approximately equal chance of being assigned to a given item.

These principles can be embodied into semiautomatic programs for the construction of synonym dictionaries, using word frequency lists and concordances derived from a representative sample document collection [17].

The differences in search effectiveness for two synonym dictionaries are shown in Figure 6. The less effective dictionaries (Harris-2 for the IRE collection, and Old Quasi-Synonym for the Cranfield) were in each case manually constructed by specialists using ad hoc procedures set up for the occasion. The other two dictionaries are improved versions obtained manually by using some of the dictionary construction principles previously listed. The significance output of Table VIII shows that fully significant improvements are obtained from one dictionary version to the next. It may be noted

in this connection that the synonym recognition results of the main Cranfield experiments [18] were obtained with the "old" less effective synonym dictionary, rather than with the new one.

To summarize: It appears that dictionaries providing synonym recognition produce statistically significant improvements in retrieval effectiveness compared with the word-stem matching process; the improvement is largest for dictionaries obeying certain principles with regard to the word groupings which are incorporated.

F. Phrase Recognition

The SMART system makes provision for the recognition of "phrases" to identify documents and search requests, rather than only individual concepts alone. Phrases can be generated using a variety of strategies: for example, a phrase can be assigned any time the specified components co-occur in a given document, or in a given sentence of a document; alternatively, more restrictive phrase generation methods can be used by incorporating into the phrase generation process a syntactic recognition routine to check the syntactic compatibility between the phrase components before a phrase is actually accepted [19].

In the SMART system, the normal phrase process uses a preconstructed dictionary of important phrases, and simple co-occurrence of phrase components, rather than syntactic criteria, are used to assign phrases to documents. Phrases seem to be particularly useful as a means of incorporating into a document representation, terms whose individual components are not always meaningful by themselves. For example, "computer" and "control" are reasonably nonspecific, while "computer control" has a much more definite meaning in a computer science collection.

The results of the phrase look-up procedure compared with the equivalent process using only a synonym dictionary indicate that for two of the collections the phrase

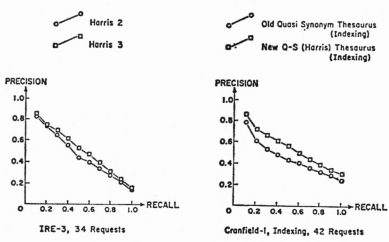

FIG. 6. Comparison of thesaurus dictionaries.

dictionary offers improvements in certain ranges of the recall and precision curve. The output of Table VIII shows, however, that the improvements are not significant, and on the whole the phrase dictionary does not appear to offer any real help in the middle recall range. Whether this result is due to the recognition of false phrases where phrase components are all present in the text but do not really belong together (such as in the phrase "solid state" in the sentence "people whose knowledge is solid state that computer processing is efficient") remains to be seen. The evidence available would seem to indicate that the presence of such false phrases is quite rare, and that a more serious deficiency is the small size of the statistical phrase dictionary from which many potentially useful phrases may be absent.

Phrases can also be recognized by using not a preconstructed dictionary of phrase components, but the statistical properties of the words in a text. Specifically, if two given terms co-occur in many of the documents of a collection, or in many sentences within a given document, a nonzero correlation coefficient can be computed as a function of the number of co-occurrences. If this coefficient is sufficiently high, the two terms can be grouped, and can be assigned jointly to documents and search requests. Associative methods are therefore comparable to thesaurus procedures except that the word associations reflect strictly the vocabulary statistics of a given collection, whereas a thesaurus grouping may have more general validity [20, 21].

Many possible methods exist for the generation of statistical word associations. Specifically, by suitably varying several parameters, a number of different types of term associations can be recognized; furthermore, once an association between term pairs is introduced, it is possible to assign to it a smaller or a greater weight. Two main parameters that can be used in this connection are the cutoff value K in the association coefficient below

which an association between terms is not recognized, and the frequency of occurrence of the terms being correlated. When all terms are correlated, no matter how low their frequency in the document collection, a great many spurious associations may be found; on the other hand, some correct associations may not be observable under any stricter conditions. Increasingly more restrictive association procedures, applied first only to words in the frequency range 3 to 50 and then in the frequency range 6 to 100, eliminate many spurious associations but also some correct ones.

Figure 7 shows a comparison of the word-stem matching process with the statistical term-term association method (labeled "stem concon" in Figure 7 to indicate a concept-concept association in which word stems are manipulated). The applicable frequency restrictions for the concept pairs and the cutoff values K are also included in Figure 7. The output of Figure 7 and the corresponding significance computations indicate that for the Cranfield collections in particular, the term associations provide some improvement over the word-stem process; local improvements for certain recall ranges are also noticeable for the ADI and IRE collections. Only for Cranfield does the sign test appear to be of some statistical significance, so that based on the present tests, no strong claims of overall effectiveness can be made for the association process.

This conclusion is reinforced by performing a comparison between the thesaurus look-up process and the word-stem association method. Table VIII shows that the advantage is clearly and significantly with the more powerful thesaurus method for both the ADI and IRE collections. For Cranfield, the advantage is still slightly with the word-stem association process, particularly at the high-recall end, where the more exhaustive indexing procedure represented by the stem associations supplies additional useful information identifiers, and serves there-

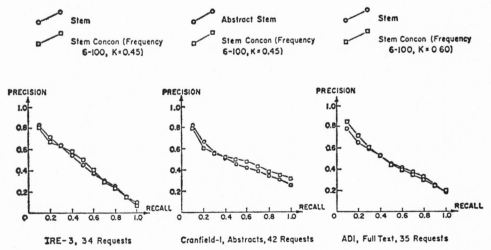

FIG. 7. Comparison of word-stem dictionary with addition of statistical word-word association (stem concon).

fore to maintain the finer distinctions among the Cranfield documents. However, the superiority of the association method is not statistically significant for Cranfield, so the conclusion previously reached must stand.

Table VIII also includes a comparison of various word-stem association strategies performed for the Cranfield collection. The output suggests that the more restrictive association processes are more effective as a retrieval aid than the more general ones. Specifically, as the number of generated association pairs grows, too many of them appear to become spurious, thus depressing the retrieval performance. In practice, limitations should thus be imposed on the number and types of associated terms actually used.

To summarize: the phrase generation methods, whether implemented by dictionary look-up or by statistical association processes, appear to offer improvements in retrieval effectiveness for some recall levels by introducing new associated information identifiers not originally available; the improvement is not, however, sufficiently general or substantial, when averages over many search requests are considered, to warrant incorporation into automatic information systems, except under special circumstances where suitable control procedures can be maintained.

G. Hierarchical Expansion

Hierarchical arrangements of subject identifiers are used in many standard library classification systems, and are also incorporated into many nonconventional information systems. Subject hierarchies are useful for the representation of generic inclusion relations between terms, and they also serve to broaden, or narrow, or otherwise "expand," a given content description by adding hierarchically related terms to those originally available. Specifically, given an entry point in the hierarchy, it is possible to find more general terms by going "up"

in the hierarchy (expansion by parents), and more specific ones by going "down" (expansion by sons); related terms which have the same parent can also be obtained (expansion by brothers), and finally any available cross-references between individual entries can be identified (expansion by cross-references).

A hierarchical arrangement of thesaurus entries was used with the IRE collection to evaluate the effectiveness of the hierarchical expansion procedures. In the test process carried out with the SMART system, the concepts present in both the document and request vectors were looked up in the hierarchy and appropriately related hierarchy entries were added to the original content identifiers. The expanded document vectors which resulted were then matched with the requests, and documents were arranged in decreasing correlation order as usual. A comparison of the standard thesaurus process with two of the four hierarchical expansions previously described is shown in Figure 8, and the corresponding significance output is included in Table VIII.

It is seen that in each case the standard thesaurus process alone is superior; moreover, the equality hypothesis can be rejected unequivocally for the expansions by brothers, sons, and cross-references. A question exists only for the expansion by parents, where more general terms are added to the original identifiers. Figure 8a shows, in particular, that this expansion process does in fact improve retrieval performance for certain recall levels.

There exist, of course, many alternative methods for using a hierarchy. It is possible, for example, to expand requests without expanding the documents, or vice versa; terms obtained from the hierarchy can also *replace* the original content identifiers instead of being added to them. In general, the expansions tend to produce large-scale disturbances in the information identifiers attached to documents and search requests. Occasionally, such a disturbance can serve to crystallize the meaning of a poorly stated request, particularly if the request is far

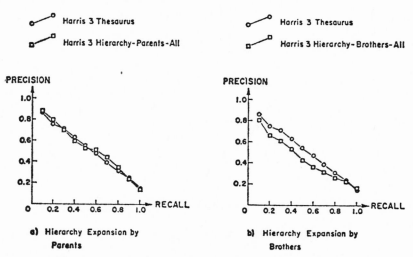

FIG. 8. Sample hierarchy procedures (IRE-3, 34 requests).

removed from the principal subjects covered by the document collection. More often, the change in direction specified by the hierarchy option is too violent, and the average performance of most hierarchy procedures does not appear to be sufficiently promising to advocate their immediate incorporation in an analysis system for automatic document retrieval.

H. Manual Indexing

The Cranfield collection was available for purposes of experimentation both in the form of abstracts and in the form of manually assigned index terms. The indexing performed by trained indexers is extremely detailed, consisting of an average of over 30 terms per document. As such, the indexing performance may be expected to be superior to the subject indexing normally used for large document collections. A meaningful comparison with standard manual keyword indexing systems may, therefore, not be possible. A comparison of index term performance with certain automatic procedures using document abstracts is represented in Figure 9, together with the corresponding significance output in Table VIII. Figures 9a and 9b show that the overall performance of a straight index term match is only slightly superior to a match of word stems abstracted from the document abstracts; for certain recall ranges, the automatic word-word association method in fact proves to be more effective than a manual index term match. In any case, Table VIII shows that the null hypothesis, postulating equivalence, cannot be rejected in that instance.

When the index terms are looked up in the thesaurus and a comparison is made with the thesaurus process for the document abstracts, a clearer advantage is apparent for the indexing; that is, the identification of synonyms and related terms, inherent in the thesaurus process, seems of greater benefit to the indexing than to the automatic abstract process. Even there, however, the advantage for the index term process is not fully significant.

Based on those results, it is therefore not possible to say that the automatic text processing is substantially inferior to the manual indexing method; indeed, one is tempted to say that the efforts of the trained indexers may well have been superfluous for the collection at hand, since equally effective results could be obtained by simple word matching techniques. Such a result appears even more probable in the case of larger or less homogeneous collections, where the manual indexing tends to be less effective because of the variabilities among indexers, and the difficulties of ensuring a uniform application of a given set of indexing rules to all documents. The computer process in such cases does not necessarily decay as the collections grow larger, and the evaluation output may then be even more favorable for the automatic procedures.

4. Concluding Comments

A summary of the main evaluation output is contained in Table IX, where eight processing methods are presented in order for the three document collections used. The measure used to rank the output is a combined coefficient consisting of the sum of the normalized recall and the normalized precision. The following principal conclusions can be drawn from the data of Table IX:

(a) The order of merit for the eight methods is generally the same for all three collections, with the possible exception of the suffix "s" method, which performs better than average for CRAN-1, and worse than average for ADI.

(b) The performance range of the methods used is smaller for the Cranfield collection than for the other two collections.

(c) The use of logical vectors (disregarding term weight), overlap correlation, and titles only is always less effective than the use of weighted terms, cosine correlations, and full document abstracts.

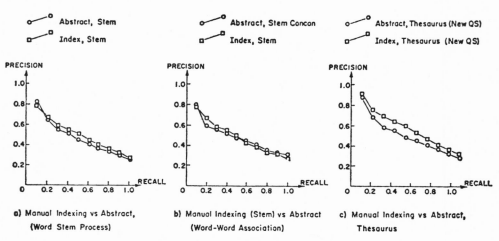

FIG. 9. Comparison of manual indexing with text processing (Cranfield-1, 42 requests).

TABLE IX

OVERALL MERIT FOR EIGHT PROCESSING METHODS USED WITH
THREE DOCUMENT COLLECTIONS

M: merit measure (normalized recall plus normalized precision);
D: dictionary used (D1: suffix "s," D2: word stem, D3: thesaurus,
D4: statistical phrase, D5: word-word association)

	IRE-3			CRAN-1			ADI		
Order	D	Method	M	D	Method	M	D	Method	M
1	D4	Stat. phrase	1.686	D3	Thesaurus	1.579	D4	Stat. phrase	1.456
2	D3	Thesaurus	1.665	D1	Suffix "s"	1.574	D3	Thesaurus	1.448
3	D2	Stems	1.570	D4	Stat. phrase	1.566	D5	Concon	1.367
4	D5	Concon	1.559	D5	Concon	1.556	D2	Stems	1.335
5	D1	Suffix "s"	1.530	D2	Stems	1.534	D2	No weights	1.294
6	D2	No weights	1.494	D2	No weights	1.477	D2	Title only	1.293
7	D2	Overlap	1.455	D2	Title only	1.430	D1	Suffix "s"	1.283
8	D3	Title only	1.369	D2	Overlap	1.407	D2	Overlap	1.241
Range		0.317			0.172			0.215	

(d) The thesaurus process involving synonym recognition always performs more effectively than the word-stem or suffix "s" methods when synonyms are not recognized.

(e) The thesaurus and statistical phrase methods are substantially equivalent; other dictionaries perform less well (with the exception of suffix "s" for Cranfield).

These results indicate that in automatic systems weighted terms should be used, derived from document excerpts whose length is at least equivalent to that of an abstract; furthermore, synonym dictionaries should be incorporated wherever available. Other, local improvements may be obtainable by incorporating phrases, hierarchies, and word-word association techniques. The Cranfield outputs shows that the better automatic text processing methods (abstracts — thesaurus) may not be substantially inferior to the performance obtained with manually assigned index terms.

A comparison of the test results obtained here with other related studies is difficult to perform. For the most part, only fragmentary results exist which do not lend themselves to a full analysis [16, 22]. The Cranfield project studies contain the only available extensive test results, including the performance of manually assigned index terms, phrases, and dictionary concepts together with a wide variety of "recall devices" (procedures that broaden or generalize the meaning of the terms), and "precision devices" (procedures that add discrimination and narrow the coverage of the terms) [18]. The principal conclusions reached by the Cranfield project are also borne out by the SMART studies: that phrase languages are not substantially superior to single terms as indexing devices, that synonym dictionaries improve performance, but that other dictionary types, such as hierarchies, are not as effective as expected.

Future experiments leading to the design of automatic information systems should be performed in different subject areas with larger document collections. Furthermore, it becomes increasingly important to evaluate also the search procedures likely to be used in an automatic system's environment, and particularly those real-time search methods where the user can control the search strategy to some extent by providing suitable feedback information. Work in this direction is continuing [7, 23, 24].

References

1. COMMITTEE ON SCIENTIFIC AND TECHNICAL INFORMATION (COSATI). Recommendations for national document handling systems. Rep. PB 168267, distributed by National Clearinghouse, Nov. 1965.

2. RUBINOFF, M. (Ed.). *Toward a National Information System.* Spartan Books, Washington, D.C., 1965.

3. SIMPSON, G. S., and FLANAGAN, C. Information centers and services. In *Annual Review of Information Science and Technology, Vol. 1,* C. Cuadra (Ed.), Wiley, New York, 1966, Chap. XII, pp. 305–335.

4. SALTON, G. A document retrieval system for man-machine interaction. Association for Computing Machinery, Proc. of the 19th National Conference, Philadelphia, Pa., Aug. 25–27, 1964, pp. L2.3-1–L2.3-20.

5. —— and LESK, M. E. The SMART automatic document retrieval system — an illustration. *Comm. ACM 8, 6* (June 1965), 391–398.

6. ——. Progress in automatic information retrieval. *IEEE Spectrum 2, 8* (Aug. 1965), 90–103.

7. ROCCHIO, J. J., and SALTON, G. Information search optimization and iterative retrieval techniques. Proc. AFIPS 1965 Fall Joint Comp. Conf., Vol. 27, pp. 293–305.

8. ——. Document retrieval systems — optimization and evaluation. Harvard U. doctoral thesis, Rep.

No. ISR-10 to the National Science Foundation, Harvard Computation Lab., March 1966.

9. CLEVERDON, C. W. The testing of index language devices. *ASLIB Proc. 15*, **4** (April 1963), 106–130.

10. SALTON, G. The evaluation of automatic retrieval procedures — selected test results using the SMART system. *Amer. Documentation 16*, **3** (July 1965), 209–222.

11. FAIRTHORNE, R. A. Basic parameters on retrieval tests. 1964 American Documentation Institute Annual Meeting, Philadelphia, Pa., Oct. 1964.

12. SALTON, G. Evaluation of computer-based retrieval systems. Proc. FID Congress 1965, Spartan Books, Washington, D.C., 1966.

13. FISHER, R. A. *Statistical Methods for Research Workers.* Hafner Publishing Co., New York, 1954.

14. HODGES, J. L., and LEHMANN, E. L. *Basic Concepts of Probability and Statistics.* Holden Day, San Francisco, 1964.

15. CLEVERDON, C. W., MILLS, J., and KEEN, M. *Factors Determining the Performance of Indexing Systems, Vol. 1 — Design; Part 1 — Text, Part 2 — Appendices.* ASLIB Cranfield Res. Proj., Cranfield, Bedford, England, 1966.

16. GIULIANO, V. E., and JONES, P. E. Study and test of a methodology for laboratory evaluation of message retrieval systems. Rep. ESD-TR-66-405 to the Electronics Systems Div., Arthur D. Little Co., Aug. 1966.

17. SALTON, G. Information dissemination and automatic information systems. *Proc. IEEE 54,* 12 (Dec. 1966), 1663–1678.

18. CLEVERDON, C., and KEEN, M. *Factors Determining the Performance of Indexing Systems, Vol. 2 — Test Results.* ASLIB Cranfield Res. Proj., Cranfield, Bedford, England, 1966.

19. SALTON, G. Automatic phrase matching. In *Readings in Automatic Language Processing,* D. Hays (Ed.), American Elsevier, New York, 1966, pp. 169–188.

20. DOYLE, L. B. Indexing and abstracting by association. *Amer. Documentation 13,* 4 (Oct. 1962), 378–390.

21. GIULIANO, V. E., and JONES, P. E. Linear associative information retrieval. In *Vistas in Information Handling, Vol. 1,* Howerton and Weeks (Eds.), Spartan Books, Washington, D.C., 1963, Chap. 2, pp. 30–46.

22. ALTMAN, B. A multiple testing of the natural language storage and retrieval ABC method: Preliminary analysis of test results. *Amer. Documentation 18,* **1** (Jan. 1967), 33–45.

23. KEEN, E. M. Semi-automatic user controlled search strategies. Fourth Annual National Colloquium on Information Retrieval, Philadelphia, Pa., 1967.

24. SALTON, G. Search strategy and the optimization of retrieval effectiveness. Rep. No. ISR-12 to the National Science Foundation, Cornell U., Dept. of Computer Science, 1967; also in Proc. of the FID/IFIP Conference on Mechanized Information Storage, Retrieval, and Dissemination, Rome, June 1967.

60 MEDLARS: Report on the Evaluation of Its Operating Efficiency

F. W. LANCASTER
American Documentation
Vol. 20, No. 2, April, 1969

1 MEDLARS: General Background

The Medical Literature Analysis and Retrieval System (MEDLARS) has been discussed in detail elsewhere (*1*). Only the most salient characteristics will be described here.

MEDLARS is a multipurpose system, a prime purpose being the production of *Index Medicus* and other recurring bibliographies. However, the present study concentrated on the evaluation of the *demand search* function (i.e., the conduct of retrospective literature searches in response to specific demands). The base of the retrospective search module consists of more than 800,000 citations to journal articles in the biomedical field input to the January 1964 and subsequent issues of the monthly *Index Medicus*. This data base is presently growing at the approximate rate of 200,000 citations annually Journal articles, of which roughly 45% are in languages other than English, are indexed at an average level of 6.7 terms per item, using a controlled vocabulary of *Medical Subject Headings* (MeSH). About 10,000 searches are now formulated annually in the United States; additional searches are handled at MEDLARS centers in the United Kingdom and in Sweden.

Approximately 2400 scientific journals are indexed regularly. About one-third of these are indexed *exhaustively* ("depth journals") at an average of 10 terms per article, and the remainder are indexed less exhaustively ("non-depth journals") at an average of slightly under four terms per article.

MeSH consists of about 7000 fairly conventional precoordinate type subject headings. A hierarchical classi-

fication ("tree structure") of these terms is available to the indexers and the search analysts. In January 1966, subheadings were introduced into the system. Subheadings, of which 53 were in use in 1966, are general concept terms (e.g., BIOSYNTHESIS, COMPLICATIONS) which can be affixed to main subject headings, thus effecting greater specificity through additional precoordination. Each subheading can only be used with main subject headings from specified MeSH categories. For example, the subheading ABNORMALITIES can only be used with Category A (anatomical) terms, while CONGENITAL is only applicable to Category C (disease) terms. These and other indexing conventions are spelled out in detail in a *MEDLARS Indexing Manual* revised annually.

A demand search is presently conducted, on a Honeywell 800 computer, by serial search of the index term profiles of the 800,000 citations on magnetic tape. This search is essentially a matching process: the index term profiles of journal articles are matched against a *search formulation*, which is a translation of a subject request into the controlled vocabulary of the system. Requests for demand searches are mostly received by mail at NLM, either embodied in a letter or on a "demand search request form"; a higher proportion of the requests processed by regional *MEDLARS* centers are made by personal visit to the center. The search formulations are prepared, by search analysts, in the form of Boolean combinations of main subject headings and subheadings. A generic search (known at NLM as an "explosion") can be conducted by means of the tree structure. An "explosion on A9.44.44" means that a search is conducted on the generic term RETINA (identified as A9.44.44 in the

Present affiliation: WESTAT Surveys, Inc., Bethesda, Maryland.

tree structure) and all the terms subordinate to it in the hierarchy, namely FUNDUS OCULI, MACULA LUTEA, and RODS AND CONES.

The final product of a MEDLARS search is a computer-printed *demand search bibliography,* in up to three sections of varying specificity, the citations usually appearing in alphabetical order by author within each section. Accompanying each bibliographic citation is a complete set of tracings (i.e., a record of all the index terms assigned to the article).

2 The MEDLARS Evaluation

Purpose

Planning of the MEDLARS evaluation began in December 1965, the principal objectives being:

1. To study the demand search requirements of MEDLARS users.
2. To determine how effectively and efficiently the present MEDLARS service is meeting these requirements.
3. To recognize factors adversely affecting performance.
4. To disclose ways in which the requirements of MEDLARS users may be satisfied more efficiently and/or economically. In particular, to suggest means whereby new generations of equipment and programs may be used most effectively.

The prime requirements of demand search users were presumed to relate to the following factors:

1. The *coverage* of MEDLARS (i.e., the proportion of the useful literature on a particular topic, within the time limits imposed, that is indexed into the system).
2. Its *recall* power (i.e., its ability to retrieve "relevant" documents, which, within the context of this evaluation, means documents of value in relation to an information need that prompted a request to MEDLARS).
3. Its *precision* power (i.e., its ability to hold back "non-relevant" documents).
4. The *response time* of the system (i.e., the time elapsing between receipt of a request at a MEDLARS center and delivery to the user of a printed bibliography).
5. The *format* in which search results are presented.
6. The amount of *effort* the user must personally expend in order to achieve a satisfactory response from the system (*2*).

The evaluation program was designed to establish user requirements and tolerances in relation to these various factors, and to determine the MEDLARS performance with regard to these requirements. In particular, we wanted to identify the principal causes of search failures, thus allowing corrective action to be taken to upgrade system performance.

The two most critical problems faced in the design of the evaluation were:

1. Ensuring that the body of test requests was, as far as possible, representative of the complete spectrum of "kinds" of requests processed.
2. Establishing methods for determining recall and precision performance figures.

The Test User Population

Through the detailed analysis of demand searches conducted at NLM in 1965, we established a list of twenty organizations that would form a suitable "test user group" for the purposes of the evaluation. The composition of this group was based upon the following considerations:

1. *Volume of requests.* Based on past performance these organizations were expected collectively to submit a minimum of 400 requests in the 12-month period allocated to the data gathering phase of the project. Based on a "pretest" conducted early in 1966, a return rate (of relevance assessments) of about 75% was anticipated. It was felt that the approximately 300 test searches that would thus be fully completed would be adequate to allow a meaningful study of major causes of system failure.

2. *Type of request.* Using as a guide the categories into which *Medical Subject Headings* are divided, we arrived at eight broad subject areas into which any MEDLARS request will tend to fall: *preclinical sciences, disease* (pathology), *technics* (surgical, diagnostic, analytical), *behavioral sciences, public health, drug/biology* (pharmacology), *drug/disease* (drug therapy), and *physics/biology* (effect of physical phenomena on the body). Judging from their 1965 requests, we expected that the test group would submit requests that would be representative of all these subject areas.

3. *Type of organization.* The group was selected to include representatives of the principal types of organization (clinical, research, academic, pharmaceutical, federal regulatory) making use of MEDLARS.

4. *Mode of user/system interaction.* The group was selected to include organizations whose members would, collectively, be likely to submit requests in all of the three possible modes: *personal* (the requester makes a visit to a MEDLARS center and negotiates his requirements directly with a search analyst), *no interaction* (the request comes directly by mail from the requester), and *local interaction* (the request comes by mail but is submitted by a librarian or information specialist on behalf of the requester).

The 20 major medical organizations thus selected to form the test user group were formally invited to participate in the evaluation program, and all agreed to do so. In addition, we decided to include in the evaluation a number of requests made, within the test period, by private practitioners.

Establishing the Performance Figures

The operating efficiency of MEDLARS was evaluated on the basis of its performance in relation to the demand search requests made, in a 12-month period, by individual physicians and other scientists affiliated with the 20 major medical organizations agreeing to cooperate in the study. While the organizations comprising the test user group had agreed to cooperate in the evaluation program (e.g., the dean of a medical school or the director of a research institute), the individual requesters knew nothing of the evaluation program until they submitted their requests. At that time they were asked to cooperate by allowing us to use their requests as "test requests." There is, then, no artificiality about the body of test requests. Each quite definitely represents an actual information need. For each of the test requests, a search was conducted and a computer printout of citations (*demand search bibliography*), which is the normal product of a MEDLARS search, was delivered to the requester. A duplicate copy of this printout was used in the extraction of a random sample of 25 to 30 of the retrieved citations. Photocopies of these sample articles were submitted to the requester for assessment, a second copy of each being retained for analysis purposes. This figure of 25 to 30 represents an upper bound on the number of articles for which we felt we could reasonably expect to obtain careful assessments. If the search retrieved a total of 30 articles or less, we normally submitted all for assessment.

We believe categorically that, within the environment of an operating retrieval system, where the performance of the entire system is being evaluated, a "relevant" document is nothing more nor less than a document of some value to the user in relation to the information need that prompted his request. In other words, in a real operating situation, a "relevance assessment" is a value judgement made on a retrieved document. We also believe that, to obtain valid precision figures and other data for analysis purposes, value judgments carefully made on a sample of a complete search output are of much greater value than less careful assessments made grossly on the complete output.

A *Form for Document Evaluation* was attached to each article submitted for assessment. This form ascertained whether or not the requester was previously aware of the retrieved item, and asked him to assess the article as of major, minor or no value *in relation to the information need that prompted his request to MEDLARS*. Most importantly, the requester was required to substantiate these judgments by indicating why particular items are of major value, others minor, and yet others of no value. These substantiations are of great utility in the analysis of search results. To get some idea of the serendipity value of searches, the requester was asked to indicate whether or not an article judged of no value in relation to the need that prompted his request was in fact of interest in relation to some other need or project. Finally, if the user was unable to assess the article because of inability to read the language (approximately 45% of the data base is not in English), the form determined whether or not he intended to obtain a complete or partial translation of its contents.

While precision figures for a MEDLARS search present no particular problem, it is extremely difficult to estimate the recall ratio for a "real-life" search in a file of over half a million citations. The only way to obtain a true recall figure is to have the requester examine and make assessments on each and every document in the file. While this is feasible in certain experimental situations, it is obviously out of the question for a collection of the MEDLARS size. The size of the base also rules out any hope of obtaining recall figures by conventional random sampling among the documents not retrieved by a particular search.

We therefore estimated the MEDLARS recall figure on the basis of retrieval performance in relation to a number of documents, judged relevant by the requester, *but found by means outside MEDLARS*. These documents could be, for example, (1) known to the requester at the time of his request, (2) found by his local librarian in non-NLM generated tools, (3) found by NLM in non-NLM-generated tools, (4) found by some other information center, or (5) known by authors of papers referred to by the requester.

For every test request we attempted to obtain a record of any articles within the time span of MEDLARS that the requester already knew to be relevant to the subject of his request. A form *Record of Known Relevant Documents* was completed by the requester after he had submitted his request but before he received the results of a MEDLARS search.

If the requester was able to supply a substantial quantity of citations not found by him in *Index Medicus* (citations found through direct search of *Index Medicus* should theoretically introduce a substantial bias into the recall estimate, since MEDLARS indexing is *Index Medicus* indexing plus), this was accepted as the recall base without further expansion. However, if the requester knew of no articles, or only one or two, an attempt was made to find additional potentially relevant items *by means outside the system*. These might be articles found by the librarian of the organization submitting the request, searching in tools not generated by the National Library of Medicine. Alternatively, they could be found by conventional manual literature searches conducted by members of the Evaluation Group in non-NLM generated tools held at the Library. In some cases, the one or two citations supplied by the requester would yield additional possibly relevant items, by means of a search in the *Science Citation Index*, or through direct contact with the authors of these known relevant papers. Occasionally it was possible to obtain additional items from a specialized information center such as the Parkinson's Disease Information and Research Center at Columbia University.

Although all these methods were tried, experience showed that conventional manual searching at NLM was the method most likely to expand the recall base with the minimum of effort. The documents found by

TABLE 1. Estimating recall ratio

Document Sources	Documents found outside of MEDLARS	Documents judged relevant
Requester	2	2
Local librarian	7	4
NLM staff		
Other center		
Authors of papers referred to by requester		
Totals	$\overline{9}$	$\overline{6}$

MEDLARS Retrieves 4/6.

Recall ratio for single request: $\frac{4}{6} \times 100 = 66\%$

these various methods extraneous to MEDLARS were considered no more than "possibly relevant." They were not incorporated into the *recall base* until the requester had examined them and judged them as of some value in relation to his information need. To achieve this, these additional items were interspersed with the *precision set* (i.e., the articles selected by random sampling from the MEDLARS search printout). The requester then assessed the enlarged set at one time.

Table 1 illustrates the way in which this method of obtaining a recall estimate works. In this instance, the requester is able to name two relevant documents, and his local librarian finds an additional seven which she believes to be relevant to the physician's request. The user, asked to make assessments of these seven documents, judges four to be relevant. We now have six known relevant documents upon which to base our recall figure. If all are in the MEDLARS data base, but only four are retrieved, we can say that the recall ratio for this search is 66%. This method works equally well, of course, whether the "possibly relevant" documents are discovered by the local librarian, NLM staff (in non-NLM tools), or by some other specialized information center, or are named by the author of a relevant paper referred to by the original requester.

Another way of considering this method of obtaining a recall estimate is illustrated by Figure 1.

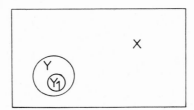

FIG. 1. Method used to compute recall estimate

TABLE 2.

	Major	Minor	No value	Not assessed
Known in advance	3	1		
Not known	1	5	8	5

The area X represents the entire MEDLARS collection. For any particular request made to the system, if the requester examined each and every item in the collection, he would be able to identify a subset, Y, of items which he considered of value in relation to his information need. All other items in the collection (X−Y) are of no value (i.e., "not relevant"). Unfortunately, except by complete examination of the collection, there is no foolproof method of establishing for any one request the exact subset Y of relevant items. However, we can establish a subset of the subset. That is, by methods outlined above, we can find some group, Y_1, of articles which the requester agrees to be relevant. We now establish the recall estimate on the basis of the performance of the system in relation to this particular group of relevant items. Thus, if we know 10 relevant articles within the data base, and MEDLARS retrieves seven of these, but misses three, we say that the MEDLARS recall ratio for this search is 70%, the assumption being that the "hit rate" for the group of documents Y_1 will approximate to the hit rate for the larger group Y.

Recall and precision figures are merely yardsticks by which we measure the effect of making certain changes in our system or in ways of operating the system. Although the recall estimate obtained by the present methodology may be slightly inflated or slightly deflated in relation to "true recall," since the method used to obtain the estimate was held constant throughout the evaluation program, the figures are still valid indicators of performance differences in various situations.

When the completed relevance assessment forms were returned, they were attached to the duplicate copies of the articles to which they related, and the recall and precision figures of the search were derived as illustrated in Table 1 and Table 2. In this case the requester was presented with a random sample of 25 articles, of which he assessed 20 (he could not assess the other five because they are in languages with which he is unfamiliar), judging 10 to be of value ("relevant") and 10 of no value. The *precision ratio* for this search is therefore $10/20 \times 100$, or 50%. The *novelty ratio* (proportion of the articles judged of value that were brought to the requester's attention for the first time by the MEDLARS search) is 6/10.

Analysis of Search Failures

Having derived the performance figures for a test search, the next step involved the detailed intellectual analysis of reasons why recall and precision failures occurred. The sample test results presented in Table 1 and Table 2 show that, in this particular search, we are faced with the analysis of (1) two *recall failures* (two of the six "known relevant" articles were not retrieved), and (2) ten *precision failures* (10 of the 20 articles assessed by the requester were judged of no value). The two recall failures and the 10 precision failures are not the only failures occurring in the search. They are the only ones that we know of, and as such they are accepted as exemplifying the complete recall and precision failures (i.e., they are symptomatic of problems occurring in this search).

The "hindsight" analysis of a search failure is the most challenging aspect of the evaluation process. It involves, for each "failure," an examination of the full text of the document; the indexing record for this document (i.e., the index terms assigned, which are obtained by printout from the magnetic tape record); the request statement; the search formulation upon which the search was conducted; the requester's completed assessment forms, particularly the reasons for articles being judged "of no value"; and any other information supplied by the requester. On the basis of all these records, a decision is made as to the prime cause or causes of the particular failure under review.

The MEDLARS Test Results

In the period from August 1966 to July 1967, 410 test requests were processed to the point of submitting photocopies of sample articles to requesters. From these, 317 sets of relevance assessments were returned (i.e., a 77% return rate), and 302 of these searches were completely analyzed.

For three of the 302 searches we were unable to obtain a recall base, but for the remaining 299 searches we have both a precision ratio and a recall ratio. When we take the individual performance ratios for the 299 test searches and average them, we arrive at the results displayed in Table 3. Over a substantial representative sample of MEDLARS requests, the system was found to be operating, on the average, at 57.7% recall and 50.4% precision. That is, on the average, over the 299 test

TABLE 3. Summary of average recall and precision ratios for 299 searches *

Overall precision ratio	50.4%
Precision ratio based on major value articles only	25.7%
Overall recall ratio (complete recall base)	57.7%
Recall ratio based on major value articles only (274 searches)	65.2%

* Omitting 3 that have no recall base. All figures in this table are calculated by averaging the individual ratios.

searches, MEDLARS retrieved a little less than 60% of the total of relevant literature within its base. At the same time, on the average, approximately 50% of the articles retrieved were of some value to requesters in relation to the information needs prompting their requests. Approximately 26% of the articles retrieved were judged of major value by the requesters. Alternatively, we can say that MEDLARS is retrieving about 65% of the major value articles, accompanied by around 50% irrelevancy.

In the 302 searches analyzed, there were 238 in which recall failures were known to have occurred, and we know of 797 cases of recall failure (i.e., 797 articles that should have been retrieved, because they were judged "of value" but were not retrieved) over these 238 searches. There were 278 searches in which precision faiures were known to have occurred, and we know of 3038 cases of precision failure (i.e., 3038 articles that were retrieved but judged "of no value"). All these failures were analyzed in detail. The results appear in Tables 4 and 5.

The figures quoted are not absolute figures for the total number of failures occurring. For example, in Table 5, the figure of 534 precision failures due to "lack of appropriate specific terms" is quoted. This does not mean that in 278 searches only 534 unwanted articles were retrieved because of lack of specificity in the vocabulary. We know of 534 and these exemplify a much larger number of failures of this type.[1] The meaningful figures are the percentages in this case; lack of specificity in the vocabulary contributed to 17.6% of all the precision failures, and affected the precision performance of 20.9% of all the 278 searches in which precision failures occurred.

3 Analyses of Failures: Explanatory Notes

We will now consider in detail the various factors contributing to recall and precision failures under the principal system components responsible: indexing, searching, index language, and the user-system interface. In these analyses, three terms appear that are given special meaning, and therefore require precise definition, namely *exhaustivity*, *specificity*, and *entry vocabulary*.

Exhaustivity and Specificity of Indexing

Exhaustivity and *specificity* are terms that apply both to the indexing of a document and to the preparation of a search formulation for a request. By *exhaustivity of indexing* we mean the extent to which the potentially indexable items of subject matter contained in a document are in fact recognized in the "conceptual analysis" stage of indexing and translated into the language of the system. For example, consider an article that discusses the use of radioisotope brain scanning in the localization of five

---

[1] In actual fact, over 4,000 precision failures in the 278 searches.

TABLE 4. Reasons for 797 recall failures in 238 of 302 searches examined

Source of failure	Number of missed articles	Percentage of total recall failures	Number of searches	Percentage of the 238 searches
Index Language				
Lack of appropriate specific terms	81	10.2	29	12.2
Searching				
Searcher did not cover all reasonable approaches to retrieval	171	21.5	80	33.6
Search formulation too exhaustive	67	8.4	31	13.0
Search formulation too specific	20	2.5	9	3.8
"Selective printout"	13	1.6	7	2.9
Use of "weighted" terms	2	0.2	1	0.4
Other searching failures due to sorting, screening, clerical error	6	0.8	5	2.1
Searching totals	279	35.0	133	55.9
Indexing				
Insufficiently specific	46	5.8	31	13.0
Insufficiently exhaustive	162	20.3	100	42.0
Exhaustive indexing (searches involving negations)	5	0.6	4	1.7
Indexer omitted important concept	78	9.8	61	25.6
Indexer used inappropriate term	7	0.9	7	2.9
Indexing totals	298	37.4	203	85.3
Computer Processing	11	1.4	7	2.9
Inadequate User-System Interaction	199	25.0	70	29.4
Total factors identified as contributing to 797 recall failures	868			

different types of lesions. If we completely omit to use an index term that would encompass one of these lesions, we are not indexing the subject matter of this document exhaustively. On the other hand, consider an article that presents case histories on, say, 20 patients. If the indexer includes terms to cover all diseases and abnormalities mentioned, all diagnostic techniques used, and all therapeutic procedures, including specific drugs employed, the subject matter of the document has been covered highly exhaustively.

A high level of exhaustivity of indexing will tend to result in a high recall performance for a retrieval system, but also in a low precision performance. Conversely, a low level of exhaustivity of indexing (i.e., inclusion of "most important" concepts only) will tend to produce a high precision, low recall performance. Exhaustivity of indexing is largely controlled by a policy decision of system management. At NLM, guidelines are given to indexers on the number of subject headings that may be applied to an article. This establishes a general exhaustivity level. Within this established level, the indexers choose terms to express what they consider to be the most important concepts discussed in an article. In the analyses, failure to retrieve a relevant document due to the fact that a particular concept was not indexed was called a recall failure due to lack of exhaustivity of indexing. Similarly, the retrieval of an unwanted document because of inclusion of minor importance concepts in indexing was called a precision failure due to exhaustivity of indexing. It is obvious that there is no "correct level" of exhaustivity in any absolute sense. There should, however, be an optimum level in relation to the types of request made of a particular retrieval system.

Specificity of indexing refers to the generic level at which a particular item of subject matter is recognized in indexing. For example, consider indexing the topic "tetrodotoxin." This could be expressed specifically by a single term TETRODOTOXIN, or we could deliberately

TABLE 5. Reasons for 3038 precision failures in 278 of 302 searches examined

Source of failure	Number of unwanted articles	Percentage of total precision failures	Number of searches	Percentage of the 278 searches
Index Language				
Lack of appropriate specific terms	534	17.6	58	20.9
False coordinations	344	11.3	108	38.8
Incorrect term relationships	207	6.8	84	30.2
Defect in hierarchical structure	9	0.3	5	1.8
Index Language totals	1094	36.0	255	91.7
Searching				
Search formulation not specific	462	15.2	87	31.3
Search formulation not exhaustive	356	11.7	62	22.3
Searcher used inappropriate terms or term combinations	132	4.3	31	11.2
Defect in search logic	33	1.1	6	2.2
Searching totals	983	32.4	186	67.0
Indexing				
Exhaustive indexing	350	11.5	137	49.3
Insufficiently exhaustive (searches involving negations)	5	0.2	2	0.7
Indexer omitted important concept (search involving negations)	1	0.0	1	0.4
Insufficiently specific	1	0.0	1	0.4
Indexer used inappropriate term	36	1.2	26	9.4
Indexing totals	393	12.9	167	60.1
Inadequate User-System Interaction				
Explicable	464	15.3	85	30.5
Inexplicable	39	1.3	26	9.4
Inadequate Interaction totals	503	16.6	111	39.9
Computer Processing	3	0.1	3	1.1
Value Judgment	71	2.3	40	14.4
"Inevitable" retrieval	4	0.1	4	1.4
Total factors identified as contributing to 3038 precision failures	3051			

choose to express this subject precisely by the joint use of two terms, TOXINS and PUFFER FISH (recording this decision in our *entry vocabulary* as: Tetrodotoxin *index under* TOXINS and PUFFER FISH). Alternatively, we could index this topic at a higher generic level (i.e., at the level of "toxins produced by fish") by the joint use of a term FISH and a term TOXINS. Climbing one level higher in the generic tree, we could index the topic under a term ANIMAL TOXINS, or ZOOTOXINS, or by the joint use of the term TOXINS and the term ANIMALS. We could, of course, choose to be even more general and index this specific toxin under the very broad term TOXINS.

Obviously, a high level of specificity in indexing will tend to produce a high precision capability in a retrieval system, whereas a low level of specificity will result in a low precision capability. This can be demonstrated by Figure 2. Unless we uniquely define that class of documents dealing with tetrodotoxin, we will never be able to retrieve documents on this subject except as part of a larger class of documents—in this case, as part of the class "fish toxins," the class "animal toxins," or the class "toxins." The greater the specificity of the indexing (i.e., the smaller the size of the document classes uniquely defined), the greater will be our precision capabilities.

Testing

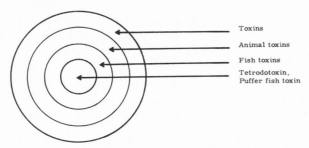

FIG. 2. Diagram of specificity in document classes

On the other hand, a high level of specificity in indexing will also tend to reduce recall. Reconsidering Figure 2, if we search only the class "tetrodotoxin" for a request on this subject, while those documents retrieved will tend to be highly relevant, we may well be missing some potentially useful items that have been assigned to the more general class "fish toxins" (for example, articles on tetrodotoxin not recognized by the indexer as being on this precise subject, or articles on fish toxins in general which contain substantial information relevant to the subject of puffer fish toxin).

To improve our recall, we can compensate for a high level of specificity in indexing by means of our searching strategies. That is, we can broaden the class of acceptable documents by searching at a higher generic level—in this case by accepting the entire class "fish toxins." However, no variations in searching strategy will ever be able to compensate for lack of specificity in indexing. If we subsume the class "tetrodotoxin" under the general class "animal toxins," there is no searching strategy that will allow us a very high-precision search on the subject of tetrodotoxin, since this class of documents is no longer uniquely defined.

Unlike exhaustivity (which is controlled in general by a policy decision of system management, and in particular by decisions made by individual indexers), specificity is governed by the index language. Although the degree of specificity in indexing is governed by properties of the index language, the indexer can in fact index a particular topic at a higher level of specificity than that allowed by the index language. This can either be a deliberate decision made by the indexer (e.g., he chooses to index an article on a number of pulmonary conditions under the term LUNG DISEASES rather than under terms for the specific diseases concerned) or it can be an indexing error (i.e., the indexer chooses a more general term because he is unaware of the existence of the specific term). In the analyses, failures due to lack of specificity in indexing (i.e., due to an indexer using a term of a higher generic level than that allowed by the index language) are distinguished from failures due to inherent lack of specificity in the index language.

Exhaustivity and Specificity in Searching

At the searching stage, the notions of exhaustivity and specificity are much less precise than they are in index-

ing; in fact, they tend to merge into one another. To take a very simple example, imagine a request for literature on oximetry applied to patients with pulmonary emphysema. This request involves only two facets or categories: the measurement technique facet and the disease facet. If we recognize both facets or categories, and demand their co-occurrence in our search formulation, we are being *exhaustive* in our formulation.

However, we can recognize each of these facets at any of several levels, as illustrated below:

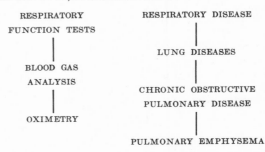

If we specify that both facets occur at exactly the level of specificity demanded in the request, i.e., we use terms defining the classes "oximetry" and "pulmonary emphysema," we are being fully exhaustive and fully specific in our search formulation for this request. We can, therefore, expect that the group of retrieved documents will, in the main, be highly relevant to the request (i.e., we will achieve a high precision search).

To improve our recall for this request, by pulling in a larger class of potentially relevant documents, we can move in one of two directions. Either we can reduce the exhaustivity of the formulation or we can reduce its specificity. We reduce specificity by moving up in one of the hierarchies, without omitting it entirely. For example, we could move to the more generic class "blood gas analysis" and demand that this co-occur with a term indicating "pulmonary emphysema." Or we could reduce specificity in the disease category and ask, as an example, for the co-occurrence of the class "lung diseases" and the class "oximetry." Of course, we can reduce specificity in more than one category simultaneously. For instance, we could demand co-occurrence of the class "blood gas analysis" and the class "lung diseases." Alternatively, we can broaden our search, with the object of improving recall, by reducing exhaustivity in the formulation (i.e., by omitting a category entirely). If we asked only for the class "oximetry," we would be searching at a low exhaustivity level for the stated request.

Both high level of exhaustivity and high level of specificity in searching, since they reduce the class of acceptable documents, make for high precision and low recall. Broadening the class of acceptable documents, by reducing specificity and/or exhaustivity in the formulation, will tend to improve recall and reduce precision.

In the analysis, failures to retrieve wanted documents because of a stringent search formulation were characterized as failures due to "formulation too exhaustive" or "formulation too specific." Conversely, failures to hold back unwanted documents due to a relaxed search requirement were characterized as failures due to "formulation not specific" or "formulation not exhaustive."

Obviously, there can be no such thing as a "correct level of exhaustivity" or a "correct level of specificity" in searching. Varying these levels, to widen or narrow the class of documents accepted in the search, is an essential part of searching strategy. The larger the class of documents retrieved, the greater we can expect to be our recall; the smaller the class of documents retrieved, the greater we can expect to be our precision (providing, obviously, that we are enlarging or reducing the class of acceptable documents in a sensible fashion).

Entry Vocabulary

The importance of an adequate entry vocabulary can be demonstrated by a reconsideration of Figure 2. We said earlier that the class of documents dealing with "tetrodotoxin" can be uniquely defined in the language of the system, or that the class can be subsumed under some larger class, thereby losing its separate identity. We also said that the precision performance of a system is directly controlled by the size of the document classes uniquely defined by the index language (i.e., by the level of specificity in indexing). However, from the point of view of recall, it matters little whether we uniquely define a class or subsume it under some larger class, *as long as we record the decision taken*. Thus, to return to our toxin example, we can uniquely define the class "tetrodotoxin," we can subsume it under "fish toxins," we can subsume it under "animal toxins," or we can subsume it under "toxins." Whichever decision we make, the class of documents relating to "tetrodotoxin" can be retrieved in subsequent searches, *providing we have an entry in our entry vocabulary* to tell us where this particular document class has been put, as:

Tetrodotoxin	index under FISH TOXINS
	or
Tetrodotoxin	index under ANIMAL TOXINS
	or
Tetrodotoxin	index under TOXINS

Obviously, the precision will deteriorate with the size of the document class retrieved. However, our entry vocabulary leads us to the group of wanted documents and allows us to retrieve it, however it has been subsumed.

An adequate entry vocabulary is essential to ensure that indexers and searchers consistently use the same terms, or term combinations, to describe identical items of subject matter. A rich entry vocabulary will include all words and phrases used in documents to describe notions that have been recognized in the conceptual analysis stage of indexing and translated into the language of the system. It will also include words and phrases used in requests to describe notions about which literature exists

in the system. The quality of an entry vocabulary can substantially affect the recall performance of an information retrieval system.

4 The Indexing Subsystem

From Tables 4 and 5, it can be seen that the indexing subsystem contributed to 37% of the recall failures and was in fact the largest contributor to this group of failures, but to only 13% of the precision failures. There are two distinct types of failure: (1) those due to indexer errors; and (2) those due to a policy decision governing the number of terms assigned to an article (i.e., the policy regarding *exhaustivity* of indexing).

Indexer errors are themselves of two types: (1) omission of a term or terms necessary to describe an important topic discussed in an article, and (2) use of a term that appears inappropriate to the subject matter of the article. Omissions will normally lead to recall failures, while use of an inappropriate term can cause either a precision failure (the searcher uses this term in a strategy and retrieves an irrelevant item) or a recall failure (the searcher uses the correct terms and a wanted document is missed because labeled with an incorrect term). Use of inappropriate terms (i.e., sheer misindexing) is negligible in MEDLARS, contributing to about 1% of the precision failures and 1% of the recall failures. The misindexings that do occur appear not to be errors of carelessness. Rather they appear due to the general misuse of a particular term at some point in time. For example RADIO-ISOTOPE SCANNING was used indiscriminately for any radioisotope monitoring operation, whether or not scanning was involved.

Indexer omissions, on the other hand, contribute significantly to almost 10% of all the recall failures, and were wholly or partly responsible for at least one missed article in 25% of all the searches in which recall failures occurred. These omissions are fairly gross errors and cannot be attributed primarily to a policy decision governing indexing exhaustivity. We have distinguished recall failures due to indexer omissions from recall failures due to lack of exhaustivity of indexing, as follows:

1. *Indexer omission.* A topic that appears central to the subject under discussion in the article is not covered at all in the indexing. It is felt that the omitted topic is so important that it should be covered even in "non-depth" indexing.

2. *Lack of exhaustivity.* An item of subject matter treated peripherally in the article is not covered in the indexing. The topic is not crucial to the article, and was presumably excluded in favor of other topics due to general policy regarding the average number of terms to be assigned, and perhaps also to the short time period allowed for indexing (an experienced indexer at NLM will index 40 to 50 articles per day).

The following are two examples of indexer omissions discovered in test searches:

Search 20. An article on the effect of visual deprivation on growth of the visual cortex in mice was indexed under CEREBRAL CORTEX and VISION and DARKNESS, but should also have been indexed under GROWTH and SENSORY DEPRIVATION. It is from a depth-indexed journal and was not retrieved in a search relating to growth in the nervous system, although it was regarded as of major value.

Search 39. A major value article on reversible sterility following discontinuance of medroxyprogesterone was not retrieved because the crucial term STERILITY, FEMALE was not applied. The search was on prolonged amenorrhea and infertility following discontinuance of oral contraceptives.

Although a certain number of indexing omissions are to be expected under the pressures of a tight production schedule, some of those occurring are difficult to excuse, particularly when a term appearing in the title of an article is omitted. For example, search #45 relates to electrical brain stimulation in elicitation of species-specific behavior. One of the missed articles, from a 1966 issue of *Behavior*, was not indexed under ELECTRIC STIMULATION even though entitled "Behavioral effects of electrical stimulation in the forebrain of the pigeon."

Some of these cases of indexer omission can be attributed to the fact that no MeSH term exists for the missed notion, and there is nothing in the entry vocabulary to say how the topic is to be indexed. As a result, the indexer either omits the topic entirely or indexes it much too generally. This type of failure was found, for example, in search #190, which relates to deiodination of thyroxine. A major value article, unretrieved, deals with flavin photo-deiodination of thyroxine. There is no MeSH term for "photodeiodination," or indeed for "deiodination," and there is nothing in the entry vocabulary to say how this concept is to be indexed. Consequently, the notion was completely ignored in indexing, although it might reasonably have been translated into IODINE. Similar, but much more drastic, failures occurred in other searches. Search #102 sought articles on hemodynamic analysis using Fourier series. Many major value articles (for example, on the Fourier analysis of vascular impedance) were missed. Despite the fact that "Fourier analysis" or "Fourier series" appeared prominently in these articles, this aspect was ignored by the indexers. Presumably these failures are due partly to lack of an adequate entry vocabulary. There is no specific term for Fourier series. Despite this, relevant articles could have been retrieved were there an entry in the entry vocabulary to tell indexers and searchers that "Fourier analysis" is to be subsumed under the broader term MATHEMATICS or whatever other term is chosen to express the topic. On the surface, it may appear strange that there should be so few instances of misindexing (that is, use of inappropriate terms) but so many cases of indexer omissions. The explanation may be simple. The work of the inexperienced indexers is scanned ("revised") by senior indexers. Usually the inappropriate terms will stand out quite clearly and are easily corrected in this revision process. However, omissions are not so readily detected by the reviser because this would involve a careful examination of the article. Consequently, errors of omission are more likely to creep through than examples of sheer misindexing.

Failures Due to Exhaustive Indexing or Lack of Exhaustivity

As previously mentioned, the more exhaustively we describe (by means of index terms) the subject matter of documents, the greater will be the recall potential of the system. Conversely, because of the inverse relationship between recall and precision, the more exhaustive the indexing, the more precision failures are likely to occur. This is partly attributable to the greater potential for false term coordinations, and partly to the fact that exhaustive indexing will cause retrieval of articles in response to requests to which they relate very weakly. In the operation of any retrieval system we are likely to find recall failures caused by indexing that is not sufficiently exhaustive. At the same time, we will discover precision failures due primarily to the fact that exhaustive indexing has brought out articles on topics for which they contain very little information.

This is exactly what happens in MEDLARS. Twenty percent of the recall failures are attributed to lack of exhaustivity of indexing, while 11.5% of the precision failures are caused largely by exhaustive indexing. Articles from "depth" journals (about one-third of all the 2400 journals regularly indexed) are presently indexed at an average of about 10 index terms per article, while the non-depth articles are indexed at an average of slightly less than four terms per article. The overall average for depth and non-depth is about 6.7 terms per item. In addition, some of the terms assigned to both depth and non-depth articles are chosen to be the headings under which entries for the articles will appear in *Index Medicus*. Only the terms representing the most important topics discussed in an article are chosen as *print* or *IM* terms. Thus, the *print* terms can function as *weighted index terms*. At present, there are approximately 2.6 print terms per article.

Recall Failures Due to Indexing of Insufficient Exhaustivity

One example is adequate to illustrate a typical recall failure due to indexing of insufficient exhaustivity. Search #535 relates to the transmission of viral hepatitis by parenteral inoculations of materials other than blood or blood products or during venipuncture. One major value article that was not retrieved deals with hepatic inflammation in narcotic addicts. The fact that viral hepatitis is transmitted by contaminated injection equipment was mentioned in the text but was not covered by the indexing.

Evaluation of Information Systems

Precision Failures Due to Exhaustive Indexing

Exhaustive indexing will contribute to a small proportion of the precision failures in certain searches and will be largely responsible for all the precision failures in others. For example, one of the irrelevant items retrieved in a search on the crystalline lens in vertebrates deals with the correlation between mast cells and the histamine content of the eye in cattle. It was indexed under LENS, CRYSTALLINE even though only one item of data on the lens is presented. Search #13, on blood or urinary steroids in human breast or prostatic neoplasms, retrieved two types of irrelevant article due to exhaustive indexing:

1. Articles in which the required neoplasm aspect is barely mentioned (for example, an article indexed under BREAST NEOPLASMS deals with plasma androgens in women and discusses a number of patients, only one of whom had breast cancer).
2. Articles in which the urinary aspect is very slight (PROSTATIC NEOPLASMS and URINE retrieved, for example, a single case report on prostatic cancer in which a urinary hormone assay value is presented in a table).

In other searches, exhaustive indexing had quite a drastic effect on precision. A search on the action of chloramphenicol retrieved 339 citations. In about 50% of the articles cited, the reference to chloramphenicol is very slender (e.g., it is used as an incubation medium in a bacterial study). The precision ratio for this search was only 20%.

Effect of Exhaustivity Levels

Seventy-three searches were selected for additional analysis to determine the effect of indexing exhaustivity on performance. This group of searches included 39 recall failures due to lack of exhaustivity and 69 precision failures due to exhaustive indexing. It was noted that the average number of index terms assigned to the 39 missed articles was 7.6, while the average number assigned to the 69 retrieved but unwanted items was 11.8.

It was also possible to derive figures indicative of performance variations caused by differences between depth and non-depth indexing. The combined random sample forming the overall precision base for the test searches consisted of 6491 articles, 4884 from depth journals and 1607 from non-depth. The overall precision ratios for these components, calculated by the *average of numbers,* was 2386/4672 (51.1%) for the depth articles and 533/1266 (43.7%) for non-depth.

The recall difference between depth and non-depth indexing was calculated on a sampling basis. Twenty searches having large requester-supplied recall bases were selected. The combined recall base consisted of 225 articles, 201 from depth journals and 24 from non-depth. The overall recall ratio for the depth journals, calculated by the *average of numbers* was 141/201 (70.1%). The overall recall ratio for non-depth was 13/24 (54.2%).

A further analysis was performed to determine what type of performance could be expected if the much lower level of exhaustivity adopted for *Index Medicus* (about 2.6 terms per article) was also the only level available in the retrospective search system. Because *print* terms are asterisked in the computer printout of index records (tracings), it was possible to determine the recall and precision results for a number of the test searches based only on these terms. The analysis simply involved the matching of tracings, for both recall and precision base documents, against the search formulation prepared for the request, and the counting of all articles that would have been retrieved had the indexing consisted only of the *print* terms. A total of 111 searches were analyzed. However, in the case of 23 of these searches the comparison was unreasonable because the search formulation used as a coordinate a term (a check tag such as HUMAN, or a technic term such as MICROSCOPY, ELECTRON) that would either never be used as a *print* term or would be used very rarely. Consequently, in nine of these searches no documents would have been retrieved on *print* terms only, while only a handful would have been retrieved in the other 14 searches. These 23 searches were therefore eliminated, all further analysis being conducted on the remaining 88.

The total combined recall base for these 88 searches comprised 633 articles. In the searches on the full MEDLARS indexing, 382 were retrieved, giving an overall recall ratio (by the *average of numbers*) of 60%. Only 280 of the articles would have been retrieved on the *print* terms however (i.e., a recall ratio of 44%). In other words, the much reduced exhaustivity of *Index Medicus* indexing led to the loss of one relevant document in every four.

The total combined precision base for the 88 searches consisted of 1716 documents, of which 890 were judged relevant (i.e., a precision ratio of 52%). Only 783 of these articles, of which 466 (60%) were relevant, would have been retrieved on the basis of the *print* terms only. In other words, searching on *Index Medicus* terms alone would have lost 344 of the 890 relevant documents (49%) with a compensatory gain in precision, because 509 of the 826 irrelevant items (61%) would also have been filtered out.

Summarized, the figures are as follows:

	Recall ratio %	Precision ratio %
Complete indexing	60	52
Index Medicus indexing only	44	60

These figures, of course, demonstrate the customary effect of variations in indexing exhaustivity: the more terms used, the greater will tend to be the recall but the lower the precision; the fewer, more selective the terms used, the lower will tend to be the recall and the higher the precision.

We can now look at this combined evidence relating to recall and precision performance as related to exhaustiv-

TABLE 6. Effect of indexing exhaustivity on retrieval performance in MEDLARS

Exhaustivity level	Recall ratio %	Precision ratio %
Depth indexing (10 terms approximately)	70	51
Non-depth indexing (4 terms approximately)	54	44
Index Medicus terms (2.6 terms approximately)	44	60

ity of indexing in MEDLARS. The data are presented in Table 6.

All other things being equal, we would expect that these results would show a strict inverse relationship between recall and precision. This is apparent in the relationship between the *Index Medicus* terms and the depth indexing. However, the results for the non-depth indexing do not correspond to the expected pattern: both recall and precision for the non-depth articles are lower than for depth articles. This is due to the fact that the non-depth articles are indexed not only with fewer terms, but also with more general terms. We will return to this matter, and discuss its implications, later.

Two small experiments were conducted to determine (1) whether re-indexing "in depth" of unretrieved non-depth articles would appreciably improve recall; and (2) whether re-indexing of nonretrieved depth articles, again in depth, would allow their retrieval. Eighteen non-depth articles that were unretrieved in a number of test searches (although the failure was not necessarily attributed primarily to non-exhaustive indexing) were re-indexed according to "depth" standards. Sixteen of the articles were indexed by three separate indexer-reviser pairs, and the other two articles were indexed by two separate indexer-reviser pairs. The average number of terms assigned in the original non-depth indexing was 5, while the average term assignment for the re-indexing was 11.2.

Seven of the 18 articles (38.9%) would have been retrieved on the basis of at least one out of three versions of the re-indexing, while 6 of the 18 (33.3%) would have been retrieved on the basis of at least two of the three versions.

The failure to retrieve 5 of the 18 articles was originally attributed to non-exhaustive indexing, and all 5 of these would have been retrieved by at least one of the three versions of the re-indexing, while 4/5 (80%) would have been retrieved on the basis of at least two of the three versions.

Thirteen of the failures were not originally attributed to nonexhaustive indexing, but two of these articles could in any case have been retrieved by the additional index terms assigned in the depth indexing. In other words, exhaustive indexing has a certain "fail-safe"

property which, under certain conditions, will compensate for other system failures, such as inadequate searching strategies.

The above experiment suggests that depth indexing of non-depth articles might allow retrieval of between 30% and 40% of the relevant non-depth articles that are presently unretrieved in MEDLARS searches.

The second small experiment involved the re-indexing of 13 articles from depth journals that were not retrieved because of indexing of insufficient exhaustivity. These articles were selected at random from all the recall failures of this type. It was not to be expected that this reindexing would have much effect on recall. The articles were originally indexed in depth at an average of 7.2 terms per item. The omitted topics are comparatively minor aspects of the articles, and only indexing at a substantially higher level of exhaustivity would be likely to affect recall significantly. The test confirmed this. The re-indexing was done by one experienced indexer at a slightly higher level of 9.1 terms per item, but the topic originally omitted from the indexing was added to only two of the 13 articles.

Failures Due to Lack of Specificity in Indexing

Only one precision failure was attributed to the failure of an indexer to use the most specific MeSH term available. However, 5.8% of all the recall failures were due to lack of specificity in indexing. In MEDLARS, lack of specificity and lack of exhaustivity of indexing are both closely related to policy regarding indexing depth (i.e., the average number of terms assigned). Articles from non-depth journals tend to be indexed in general terms. For example, search #64, on spina bifida and anencephalus, failed to retrieve a number of non-depth articles because they were indexed more generally under AB-NORMALITIES. In depth indexing, the specific malformations would have been indexed.

General Observations on Exhaustivity and Specificity of Indexing in MEDLARS

1. Indexing exhaustivity is, of course, a relative matter. We have already mentioned the article on mast cells and histamine content of the eye in cattle, which was retrieved on the term LENS, CRYSTALLINE although only one item of data was given on this topic. The requester regarded it as of no value in relation to his research on the crystalline lens in vertebrates. Therefore, we must say that exhaustive indexing was largely responsible for this precision failure and, judged in relation to this request, assignment of the term LENS, CRYSTALLINE was unjustified. Visualize, however, a second, much more specific request for articles presenting data on the histamine content of the crystalline lens. In response to this request, the above article is highly relevant and may in fact be one of the few articles in which measured values are quoted. Judged in relation to this request, the term LENS, CRYSTALLINE is completely justified.

2. On the whole it is better to err on the side of exhaustive indexing. It is difficult to retrieve an article on X if X has not been covered in the indexing of the item. On the other hand, within MEDLARS the searcher has a limited capability for reducing the exhaustivity by searching only on *Index Medicus* terms, and thus improving precision for any one search (although inevitably losing some recall). Alternatively, the searcher may use what is in effect a weighting device by demanding that the key term of a request (LENS, CRYSTALLINE in the above example) must be a *print* term, but not putting any such restriction on the coordinate terms. This procedure is likely to improve precision with rather less drastic effects on recall.

3. The artificial separation of all MEDLARS journals into depth and non-depth appears, from the detailed search analyses, to lead to indexing anomalies that can cause both recall and precision failures. Although many of the articles from non-depth journals seem somewhat superficial and repetitive, others are very substantial papers which, because of a general policy decision, are indexed completely inadequately. On the other hand, half-column letters in *Lancet* are sometimes assigned 15–20 terms and are thus retrieved in searches to which they contribute little or nothing. A policy of treating each article on its own merit, whatever journal it comes from, would reduce such seeming anomalies.

4. From the point of view of machine retrieval, the policy of indexing non-depth articles in general terms is indefensible. To quote but one example, in the analysis of search #531 an article from a non-depth journal (*Poultry Science*), entitled "Role of *streptococcus faecalis* in the antibiotic growth effect in chickens" was examined. Found by manual search, but missed by MEDLARS, it was indexed only under EXPERIMENTAL LAB STUDY, INTESTINAL MICROORGANISMS and POULTRY. Use of the general term INTESTINAL MICROORGANISMS for the specific organism implicated is inexcusable. On the basis of this indexing, one could not reasonably expect the article to be retrieved in response to a request on "streptococcus faecalis in poultry" or one on "effect of penicillin on steptococcus faecalis" or even one on "antibiotic growth effect in poultry," to all of which specific topics it is highly relevant. In fact, on the basis of the indexing one could only reasonably expect to retrieve it in a search on intestinal microorganisms of poultry, to which general subject it is indeed a slight contribution.

It is always a mistake to index specific topics under general terms. In the above example, use of the term STREPTOCOCCUS FAECALIS would allow retrieval of this item in response to a request involving this precise organism. On the other hand, the article could still be retrieved in a more general search relating to intestinal microorganisms, because the searcher is able to "explode" on all bacteria terms. The article could have been indexed very adequately under five terms: POULTRY, PENICILLIN, STREPTOCOCCUS FAECALIS, GROWTH, and EXPERIMENTAL

LAB STUDY. *As the article is presently indexed, it is difficult to visualize a single retrospective search in which it would be retrieved and judged of major value. In other words, this citation and others indexed in such general terms are merely occupying space on the citation file.*

5 The Searching Subsystem

Considering recall and precision failures together, the searching subsystem is the greatest contributor to all the MEDLARS failures, being at least partly responsible for 35% of the recall failures and 32% of the precision failures. We can distinguish three types of searching failure:

1. Recall failures due to the fact that the searcher did not cover all reasonable approaches to the retrieval of relevant articles.

2. Pure errors involving the use of inappropriate terms or the use of defective search logic.

3. Failures due to the levels of specificity and/or exhaustivity adopted in searching strategies.

Recall Losses Due to Failure to Cover All Reasonable Approaches to Retrieval

In the recall analysis, 21.5% of all the failures were attributed to the fact that the searcher did not cover all reasonable approaches to the retrieval of literature relevant to the request. In other words, 21.5% of the missed relevant articles could have been retrieved on terms or term combinations which, the author feels, the searcher might reasonably have been expected to use in the search formulation. This "failure to cover all reasonable approaches" in searching was a major contributor to recall losses in the 302 searches analyzed, being second only to failures of user-system interaction, which were responsible for 25% of the recall losses. There are really two categories of failures of this type:

1. Failure to use one particular relevant term, or term combination, in a formulation which otherwise reflects the complete interests stated in a request.

2. Failure to cover a complete aspect of the request as stated by the requester.

The first type has less drastic results than the second but nevertheless can substantially reduce the recall ratio for a search, as the following illustrate:

Search #19. In a search on nervous-tissue culture as affected by electrical stimulation, and certain other variables, the searcher did not explode on NERVOUS SYSTEM in coordination with TISSUE CULTURE and terms for the specific factors of interest. A directly related article could have been retrieved on CEREBRAL CORTEX *and* TISSUE CULTURE *and* ELECTRIC STIMULATION

Search #34. In a search on potassium shifts in isolated cell preparations, no use was made of the term CELL MEMBRANE PERMEABILITY. Used in conjunction with POTASSIUM CHLORIDE, it would have brought out several major value articles.

More drastic failures occur when the searcher omits a complete aspect of a topic that is explicitly stated in the request. This type of failure is particularly prone to occur with fairly long, multifaceted request statements. Whether the searcher overlooks the aspect through careless reading or deliberately ignores it is difficult to establish. An example of this type of failure occurred in search #174, which relates to testicular biopsy in cases of infertility. One aspect of interest (the effect of surgical and hormonal therapy on sperm count, testicular morphology, and fertility) was completely omitted from the formulation, contributing to the low recall ratio of 3/11 (27.3%).

Precision Failures Due to Searching on Inappropriate Terms or Term Combinations

Whereas omission of appropriate terms from a search formulation will lead to recall failures, use of inappropriate terms or term combinations will cause precision failures. The author attributes 4.3% of the precision failures to this cause. For example:

Search #47. In a search on computer recognition of cells, one strategy involved the coordination of CYBERNETICS with all cell terms. CYBERNETICS is inappropriate to a request on cell recognition, which is essentially a pattern recognition problem. It caused retrieval of articles on cells as cybernetic systems and was responsible for about one-third of the irrelevancy in this search.

Inappropriate *term combinations* tend to occur with fairly complex search formulations in which a list of terms in a logical sum (*or*) relation is *anded* with a second list of summed terms. While the overall strategy may appear sensible, some of the combinations resulting may be irrational in relation to the request.

Recall and Precision Failures Due to Variations in Exhaustivity of the Formulation

As previously mentioned, varying the exhaustivity and/or specificity of the formulation is an essential part of searching strategy. In fact, the central problem of searching is the decision as to the most appropriate level of specificity and exhaustivity to adopt for a particular request. The less specific and exhaustive the formulation, the more documents will be retrieved; recall will tend to increase and precision to decrease. The more specific and exhaustive the formulation, the fewer documents will be retrieved; recall will tend to deteriorate and precision to improve. For each particular request, we must decide in which direction to go. In other words, how near to 100% recall does the requester really want to approach, bearing in mind that the closer we get to this figure the more documents we are likely to retrieve and the lower is likely to be the precision of the search?

An *exhaustive* search formulation is one that demands the co-occurrence of all the notions asked for, in some relationship, by the requester (although not necessarily at the level of specificity stated in the request). Consider search #115, which concerns various specific intestinal microorganisms causing diarrhea or dysentery in cases of protein deficiency or kwashiorkor. This request involves a relationship between three separate notions: (1) certain specific intestinal microorganisms, (2) the disorder of diarrhea or dysentery, and (3) the disorder of protein deficiency or kwashiorkor.

The searcher was fully exhaustive in the formulation, allowing an article to be retrieved only if (1) it has been indexed under the term PROTEIN DEFICIENCY *or* the term KWASHIORKOR, and (2) it had been indexed under a term indicating the involvement of some microorganism, *and* (3) it had been indexed under a term indicating diarrhea or dysentery.

With an exhaustive formulation such as this, we can expect high precision. That is, most of the articles retrieved are likely to be relevant. On the other hand, our strategy may be too exhaustive; it may be asking too much to expect a relevant article to have been indexed under *all* of the notions demanded by the requester. This was exactly the case in search #115, which retrieved nothing, although relevant literature exists and some could have been retrieved with the less exhaustive strategy:

PROTEIN DEFICIENCY
           or   *and*   diarrhea terms
KWASHIORKOR

Exhaustivity of the search formulation is obviously related to the *coordination level* (i.e., the number of index terms required to co-occur before an article can be retrieved), but there is no strict one-to-one relationship between exhaustivity and coordination level. For example, PROTEIN DEFICIENCY *and* DYSENTERY *and* INTESTINAL MICROORGANISMS is a three-term coordination that is exhaustive in that it covers all the related notions demanded by the requester, but so also does PROTEIN DEFICIENCY *and* DYSENTERY, BACILLARY, which is a two-term coordination. Moreover, by varying the coordination level, we may be varying the *specificity* rather than the *exhaustivity* of the search.

For example, consider a request for "metastatic fat necrosis as a complication of pancreatitis." The formulation PANCREATITIS *and* NECROSIS is exhaustive in that it asks for the co-occurrence of the two notions specified. The three-term coordination PANCREATITIS *and* NECROSIS *and* ADIPOSE TISSUE is merely more specific in relation to the request.

Exhaustive search formulations were responsible for 8.4% of the recall failures, and nonexhaustive search formulations were responsible for 11.7% of the precision failures. Some further examples follow:

Exhaustive Formulations

Search #217. The request is for "influence of the styloid process on facial and head pains." The searcher required that some term indicating "face" or "head" be present, as well as a term indicating "pain" and the term for site of the "styloid process" (TEMPORAL BONE). This seems unnecessarily exhaustive because it is reasonable to assume that pain relating to the temporal bone would involve face or head. The simple, less exhaustive formulation TEMPORAL BONE *and* PAIN would materially have improved recall.

Search #460. This search concerned optical or spectral properties of malignant cells which would permit their detection with sufficient efficiency for counting. This request really boils down to "optical and spectral properties of malignant cells." However, in addition to requiring that a neoplasm term should co-occur with an optical property term, the searcher demanded that a "diagnosis" term should also be present. Recall was 76.5% but could have been 100% with a less exhaustive formulation.

Nonexhaustive Formulations

Search #9. The request relates to various aspects of induced hypothermia. This was searched on the single term HYPOTHERMIA, INDUCED. This retrieved 860 citations and predictably obtained 100% recall (25/25). However, the precision ratio was only 30%.

Search #18. In a search on "renal amyloidosis as a complication of tuberculosis," the strategy: amyloid term *and* tuberculosis term, omitting the requirement for kidney involvement, was responsible for most of the irrelevancy.

Recall and Precision Failures Due to Variations in Specificity of the Formulation

Only 2.5% of all the recall failures were attributed to the use of a specific search formulation. *This does not mean that reduction of searching specificity could not substantially have improved recall in many searches—*obviously it could. It merely means that only in the case of 20 missed documents, out of the total of 797 examined, could the blame be put primarily on a search formulation unnecessarily specific in relation to the stated request. On the other hand, 15.2% of all the precision failures could be attributed to lack of specificity in the search formulation. In the same way that reduction of exhaustivity in a formulation will tend to improve recall but reduce precision, so reduction in search specificity (if it involves logical generalization) will tend to improve recall but reduce precision. Some examples are given below:

Search #3. A request on "electron microscopy of lung or bronchi" was broadened to LUNG/CYTOLOGY, thus improving recall but inevitably losing precision.

Search #19. In a search on nervous tissue culture, the "tissue culture" was generalized to IN VITRO. This led to about 80% irrelevancy in the search.

Search #101. The ease with which an explosion can be conducted appears to have led the searcher into a very poor search. The request refers to various aspects of

personality in relation to choice of medical specialty. The searcher exploded on SPECIALISM and coordinated this set of terms with a group of behavioral terms. Unfortunately SPECIALISM brings out all the terms covering individual medical specialties (e.g., PATHOLOGY, PEDIATRICS, PSYCHIATRY, GERIATRICS). Coordinated with the behavioral terms, this retrieved 459 citations (e.g., on personality changes in aging, on doctor-patient relations in pediatrics) of which less than 20 are of any possible relevance.

Although it is terribly dangerous to generalize on the matter of searching strategy and the correct level of generality to adopt, a detailed study was undertaken to determine if any useful pointers could be derived to assist the searcher in deciding (a) when to broaden a search, (b) the best way to broaden, and (c) what type of search generalization is unwarranted. This study is presented in the full report of the project (3).

6 Joint Causes of System Failures

Now that both indexing failures and searching failures have been discussed, it is appropriate to re-emphasize the fact that not all failures are attributed to a single cause. Sometimes they are attributed jointly to two parts of the system. This is particularly true in the case of the relationship between indexing and searching. Occasionally we must say "if the indexer had included X, the document would have been retrieved, but it would also have been retrieved had the searcher used Y." This occurred, for example, in search #276, on keratinization of the gingiva. The search was conducted on

		GINGIVA
KERATIN	*and*	GINGIVAL DISEASES
		GINGIVAL HYPERPLASIA
		GINGIVAL HYPERTROPHY

One of the recall base articles, missed by the above strategy, could have been retrieved had the searcher also used KERATIN *and* GINGIVITIS. On the other hand, the indexer might well have applied the term GINGIVA to this article, as well as GINGIVITIS, because it deals with the effect of powered toothbrushing on gingival inflammation and keratinization. This is the type of failure which, in the analysis, was jointly attributed to both indexing and searching.

7 Recall and Precision Failures due to the Index Language

The quality of the index language is probably the most important single factor governing the performance of a retrieval system. Poor searching strategies and inadequate or inconsistent indexing can mar the performance of a system, but indexing and searching, however good, cannot compensate for an inadequate index language. In other words, indexers and searchers can perform only as well as the index language allows.

The index language contributed to 10.2% of the MEDLARS recall failures and to 36% of the precision failures. These failures are of two principal types: failures due to lack of specificity in the terms and failures due to ambiguous or spurious relationships between terms.

Lack of specificity in the index language can cause either recall failures or precision failures. In the present evaluation, it was responsible for 10.2% of all the recall failures and 17.6% of all the precision failures. Although an oversimplification, it is convenient to consider the index language of MEDLARS, or any other retrieval system, as comprising two vocabularies: (1) the controlled vocabulary of terms that indexers must use in describing the content of a document (i.e., the 7000 MeSH terms), and (2) the vocabulary of natural language words and phrases, occurring in documents and requests, that map onto the controlled vocabulary terms. This latter vocabulary we have described as an *entry vocabulary*. Within MEDLARS, the entry vocabulary is partly built into *Medical Subject Headings* through the use of references. For example, under CHARCOT-MARIE DISEASE in MeSH we find the instruction *see under* MUSCULAR ATROPHY. The former term is an *entry vocabulary* term: it does not uniquely define a class of documents in the system, because the class of "documents on Charcot-Marie Disease" is subsumed under the broader class of "documents on muscular atrophy," and thus has no separate identity. Within the Index Section at NLM is a further entry vocabulary, on 5″×3″ cards, of additional natural language terms that map onto MeSH terms. This entry vocabulary, known as the *authority file* consists of about 18,000 entries, of which approximately two-thirds relate to drugs and chemicals.

It is worthwhile returning to the earlier discussion on the matter of the entry vocabulary, and to the illustration given in Fig. 2. Consider articles on the subject of tetrodotoxin. We decide not to uniquely define this class of documents, but to subsume it under the more generic class "fish toxins," this topic being defined by the joint use of, say, a term ANIMAL TOXINS and a term FISH. Even though we do not uniquely define the class "tetrodotoxin," we must include it in our entry vocabulary, as a reference:

Tetrodotoxin *use* ANIMAL TOXINS *and* FISH

We must do this to:

1. Indicate that documents on this specific topic have been input to the system, and

2. Ensure that all indexers use the same term combination to enter articles on this precise topic into the system, and

3. Ensure that searchers use the right term combination to retrieve relevant literature.

Thus, although we do not uniquely define the class "tetrodotoxin," we should still be able to retrieve literature on this precise topic because our entry vocabulary tells us precisely where to look. That is, lack of specificity in the vocabulary will not cause recall failures in this case. However, we cannot retrieve articles on tetrodotoxin *alone*; we must retrieve the entire class of articles on fish toxins. Thus, lack of specificity will cause precision failures in a search on tetrodotoxin. In other words, if we do not uniquely define a particular class of documents, but still use our entry vocabulary to indicate how this class has been subsumed, we will get precision failures due to lack of specificity in the vocabulary, but not recall failures attributable to this cause. If we omit the notion even from our entry vocabulary, we will get both recall failures and precision failures. Some examples will help to illustrate this point:

Search #6. A search relating to aortic regurgitation had low precision because the 1963 and 1964 material was indexed under the more general term AORTIC VALVE DISEASES.

Search #70. A search on bacterial identification by computer achieved only 33.3% recall and 47.8% precision. There is no specific term for *bacterial identification* (speciation). The combination of bacteria terms *and* analysis or automation terms retrieved many articles on bacterial analysis (e.g., chromatographic purification) having nothing to do with species *identification*. Recall failures in this search can also be attributed to lack of specificity in the index language. "Bacterial identification by computer" is really "numerical taxonomy." There is no term for this, or for "numerical analysis," and nothing in the entry vocabulary to say how it is to be treated. This led to the complete omission of the topic in the indexing of several relevant articles.

Search #102. A search on the use of Fourier series in hemodynamic analysis achieved only 54.5% recall and 8% precision; 99 citations were retrieved. There is no specific term for "Fourier analysis" and nothing in the entry vocabulary to say how this notion is to be subsumed. Consequently, the concept was omitted in the indexing of several pertinent articles. Moreover, the searcher was forced into very general combinations (e.g., hemodynamics terms *and* MATHEMATICS or MODELS) which caused considerable irrelevancy.

Search #160. This search, on nephrogenic diabetes insipidus, clearly illustrates the importance of an adequate entry vocabulary. In an attempt to restrict the search to *nephrogenic* diabetes insipidus, the searcher coordinated DIABETES INSIPIDUS with kidney or kidney disease terms. This resulted in the low recall ratio of 1/9 (11.1%) because the topic is generally indexed only under DIABETES INSIPIDUS, with no co-occurring kidney term. However, the searcher had no way of knowing this because there is nothing in the entry vocabulary to say how this notion is to be indexed.

These examples illustrate overall index language deficiencies in MEDLARS and suggest areas (e.g., the behavioral sciences) in which the system is particularly weak. To pinpoint more precisely the subject areas in which the vocabulary is suspect, a breakdown by subject field was made for all the searches in which were found recall and/or precision failures due to lack of specificity in the index language.

Over one third of the searches falling in the general area of the behavioral sciences are marred because of lack of specificity in the vocabulary, while one-third (2/6) of the searches relating to public health are similarly affected. In the area of "technics," 27.6% of all the searches are affected by lack of specificity. On the whole, the language in this area is reasonably unambiguous. However, performance will depend upon the availability of specific terms. As already noted, there is no term covering high frequency radio therapy (diapulse) so that search #467 could operate at only 10.5% precision.

A quarter of the PHYSICS/BIOLOGY searches are affected by lack of specificity in the vocabulary (it is difficult to distinguish various types of radiation; e.g., ionizing from non-ionizing). About 23.6% of the searches falling into the DISEASE category are affected by lack of specificity, whereas only 17.6% of the PRECLINICAL SCIENCES searches are similarly affected. In other words, for the types of requests put to MEDLARS in the preclinical area, the vocabulary is shown to be reasonably adequate. The performance in the disease area will depend entirely upon whether or not terms for specific disease entities are available in either MeSH or the entry vocabulary. If we have no term for "colitis cystica profunda" we can hardly expect to achieve a satisfactory result in a search on this topic. On the whole, the search analyses have shown the MEDLARS vocabulary to be unexpectedly weak in the clinical area. Not only does it fail to express precisely a significant proportion of the pathological conditions occurring in requests, some of which are not particularly obscure (e.g., perforation of the gallbladder), but it is also deficient in its ability to express various *characteristics* of a disease. For example, we cannot indicate *extent* of pathological involvement (*diffuse* lesions of the lung, *solitary* pulmonary nodule). Nor can we readily distinguish *symptomatic* from *asymptomatic*; co-existent, unrelated conditions from true sequelae; or the situation of one disease simulating (masquerading as) another.

Again from the search analyses, the vocabulary appears weak in areas that impinge upon medicine. For example, in search #102, the terms MATHEMATICS, MODELS and COMPUTERS are as close as the searcher was able to get to the topic of "Fourier analysis." Similarly, in search #242, MICROWAVES was the only term available to express "masers."

Before leaving the matter of specificity in the vocabulary, it is worthwhile mentioning, or re-emphasising, the following:

1. There is a difference between failures due to lack of specificity in the vocabulary and failures due to lack of specificity in searching. In the former case, there is no specific term available so the searcher is obliged to use more general terms. In the second case, the searcher broadens the search even though more specific terms, of varying degrees of appropriateness to the request, exist in the vocabulary. As an example, we can consider a search on medicine in Somalia. Lack of a specific term before 1966 made it necessary for the searcher to include AFRICA, EASTERN in the formulation (*lack of specificity in the index language*), but the searcher went beyond the deficiency in the vocabulary by exploding on AFRICA, EASTERN, and thus bringing in articles indexed under ETHIOPIA and SUDAN (*lack of specificity in searching*). In some searches, although there was no specific MeSH term to cover a request topic (e.g., searches relating to ultrastructure), the author felt that the searcher generalized more than was necessary. In such cases, some of the failures were attributed to lack of specificity in the vocabulary, others to lack of specificity in searching.

2. To correct *precision failures* due to lack of specificity, requires that terms or term combinations *that uniquely define* the notion not presently covered specifically, be introduced into the vocabulary. To correct *recall failures*, we do not need a unique designation, but we must include the notion in our entry vocabulary.

3. The evaluation has shown the MEDLARS entry vocabulary to be very inadequate. Recall failures in the test searches could have been reduced by 10% if a satisfactory entry vocabulary had been available. Lack of an adequate entry vocabulary can lead to (1) indexer omissions, or lack of exhaustivity of indexing (the indexer does not know how to index a particular notion so leaves it out); (2) indexing inconsistencies; (3) recall failures; (4) precision failures (the searcher does not know how a particular notion has been treated, and is thus forced to use every possible term combination). Moreover, the fact that a term appears in an entry vocabulary indicates that literature on the topic exists in the system. Without such an entry, we have no assurance that MEDLARS even contains any articles on, say, some obscure syndrome. Consequently, we may willingly accept a negative result from the system when such a result is incorrect.

The value of the entry vocabulary is well illustrated by a search on "irradiation of mammalian oocytes." The searcher relied on OVUM *and* irradiation terms. The authority file contains an entry, dated July 31, 1966, which instructs "Oocytes *use* OVUM." But articles indexed before this date were indexed with no consistency (some were indexed under GERM CELLS), while this precise notion was omitted in various other articles (indexed only under CELL DIVISION).

5. Searching difficulties are caused by the fact that the vocabulary has been developed without consistency as to levels of specificity (degree of pre-coordination). Thus we have a specific term VAGOTOMY, for example, but we cannot express "pyloroplasty" except by PYLORIC STENOSIS *and* SURGERY, OPERATIVE, or by PYLORUS/SURGERY. Consequently, although we can say VAGOTOMY/ADVERSE EFFECTS, we have no precise way of expressing "adverse effects of pyloroplasty."

6. The MEDLARS index language is gradually becoming more specific. Not all of the failures attributed to lack of specificity indicate current inadequacies. That is, in some cases terminological changes have been made, but the searcher is still required to use nonspecific terms to retrieve material indexed before the specific terms were introduced. To discover what proportion of the failures, attributed to lack of specificity, represent terminological changes since rectified, and what proportion represent terminological deficiencies still existing, a special analysis of a sample of 100 searches was conducted. In this group of 100 searches, 24 contained recall and/or precision failures due to lack of specificity in the vocabulary. There were 25 separate terms involved, and 13 (52%) of these deficiencies no longer exist in MEDLARS (i.e., appropriate specific terms are now available). Note that the introduction of subheadings, in 1966, markedly increased the specificity of the vocabulary. It is now possible to express various notions (e.g., "epidemiology" and "etiology") which were not adequately covered in the vocabulary before the subheadings were introduced.

Failures Due to False Coordinations and Incorrect Term Relationships

Ambiguous and spurious relationships between terms accounted for approximately 18% of all the precision failures. In one sense, all terms assigned in the indexing of a particular article must be considered related in some way, even if it is only a proximity relationship (i.e., the terms are common to a particular index term profile). However, consider a search involving a simple two-term logical product relation, A *in relation to* B. Although all the articles retrieved by this coordination should be indexed under the term A and also under the term B, some of these articles may be irrelevant because the term A and the term B are not directly related in the article (a *false coordination*), while others may be irrelevant because, while A is related to B, the terms are not related in the way that the requester wants them (an *incorrect term relationship*).

To clarify the distinction between false coordinations and incorrect term relationships, consider a search relating to phosphate excretion. A term combination used in this search was PHOSPHATES *and* URINE. One of the articles retrieved by this combination discusses urinary excretion of Toxogonin, which is mentioned as being an antidote to alkyl-phosphate poisoning. Hence, the term URINE is not directly related to the term PHOSPHATE (i.e., it is a false coordination). The same terms retrieved a second article, not on excretion of phosphates, but on a phosphate precipitation method of determining magnesium in urine. This is an *incorrect term relationship:* URINE is related to PHOSPHATE, but not in the way that the requester wants these terms related.

False coordinations were responsible for 11.3% of the precision failures, *incorrect term relationships* for 6.8%. Some further examples follow.

False Coordinations

Search #71. In a search on mongolism occurring with leukemia, the combination LEUKEMIA *and* MONGOLISM retrieved a number of articles in which the two terms refer to different patients (e.g., general articles on sex-chromatic abnormalities). This type of failure is always likely to occur in MEDLARS when two disease terms are coordinated. In a search on the neuropathy of multiple myeloma, the coordination of MULTIPLE MYELOMA *and* neurological disease terms caused about 40% irrelevancy, while a search on ventricular septal defect in association with mitral stenosis or mitral insufficiency, achieved only 26% precision because in most of the retrieved articles the two terms are not related.

Search #96. LUNG *and* NYMPH NODES retrieved articles that do not deal with pulmonary lymphatics (the two are discussed separately).

Incorrect Term Relationships

Search #39. The search relates to cases of prolonged amenorrhea or infertility following discontinuance of oral contraceptives. But about a third of the articles retrieved deal with therapeutic use of contraceptive agents in the treatment of menstruation disorders, and not with side effects. This search illustrates the principal type of relational indicator needed by MEDLARS, namely an indicator of *sequence* or *cause-effect* relationship. The same type of failure is likely to occur in searches on radiation and drug effects, because it is sometimes difficult to distinguish therapy from adverse effects. For example, in search #95, on the effect of radiation on hair growth, HAIR REMOVAL *and* RADIOTHERAPY retrieved articles on therapeutic use of irradiation (e.g., in alopecia mucinosa) as well as articles on radiation *damage* to hair.

Search #67. In a search on lipids in annelids, the combinations CEPHALINS *and* LEECHES and CHOLESTEROL *and* NEMATODA retrieved a number of articles not on lipids of worms, but on the effect of lipids *on* worms (e.g., effect on leech muscle preparation).

Search #73. In a search on bovine leukosis, CATTLE *and* LEUKEMIA retrieved articles not on cattle leukosis but on the reaction of sera from human leukemia patients, or the reaction of mouse leukemia viruses, with bovine cell cultures.

Value of Subheadings

In the literature of documentation, the solution generally offered to the problem of false coordination is the *link*, while the solution generally offered to the problem of incorrect relationships is the *role indicator*. However, in the search analyses it was repeatedly discovered that both types of problem could now frequently be avoided by the use of subheadings. Moreover, failures of this type were found to be virtually nonexistent when indexer and searcher had both made correct use of subheadings.

This led the writer to undertake an investigation to determine just what proportion of all the failures of this type could be corrected by the use of subheadings (either existing subheadings or subheadings that could readily be devised.)

In 45 searches examined 20 examples of false coordinations and 22 examples of incorrect term relationships were encountered. A total of 16 (80%) of the false coordinations could have been prevented by subheadings, 12 of these by existing subheadings and 4 by suggested new subheadings. A total of 20 (90%) of the incorrect term relationships could be prevented by subheadings, 14 by existing subheadings and 6 by suggested new subheadings.

Full details of this analysis are given in the full report (3). It is sufficient to say that subheadings, properly used, are capable of solving 80–90% of the precision failures attributable to false coordinations and incorrect term relationships. The subheadings ADVERSE EFFECTS and THERAPEUTIC USE serve to distinguish articles on therapy from articles on side effects. ETIOLOGY is another subheading useful in obviating the sequential or cause-effect type of problem. The subheading COMPLICATIONS tends to tie two disease terms together and thus avoid some of the false coordinations that occur when we *and* these terms. That is, in an article indexed *disease A*/COMPLICATIONS and also *disease B*/COMPLICATIONS there is a high probability that both conditions co-exist in the same patient. However, the subheading COMPLICATIONS does not solve the sequential problem. Does condition A lead to condition B, or does B lead to A? It would be necessary to introduce a new subheading SEQUELAE to cope with this type of situation.

More freely available subheadings would tend to reduce problems stemming from variations in the specificity (by pre-coordination) of the vocabulary. We can now say BLOOD PRESERVATION, but we can only express "plasma preservation" by the coordination of BLOOD PRESERVATION and PLASMA, which leads to false coordinations. A generally applicable subheading PRESERVATION, in place of the pre-coordinations that exist in parts of the vocabulary, would solve this type of problem.

Of particular value within MEDLARS are *paired subheadings*. That is, subheadings that tend to tie two terms together and at the same time indicate the relationship between these terms. Such subheading pairs act simultaneously as links and as roles. They function in much the same way as the paired role indicators introduced by Western Reserve University (*property given* and *property given for*) and the Engineers Joint Council (causative agent, thing affected). For example the coordination of TOLBUTAMIDE *and* DIABETES MELLITUS, in a search on therapeutic use of oral hypoglycemic agents in diabetes, will retrieve irrelevant articles on the "tolbutamide tolerance test." But the coordination TOLBUTAMIDE/THERAPEUTIC USE *and* DIABETES MELLITUS/DRUG

THERAPY not only tends to tie the two terms together, but also shows their relationship.

8 Recall and Precision Failures due to User-System Interaction

Defective user-system interaction contributed to 25% of the recall failures and 16.6% of the precision failures in the present evaluation.

A recall failure due to defective interaction implies that the stated request is more specific than the actual area of information need. Articles of value to the requester in relation to his need are not retrieved because the searcher adheres to the stated request.

A precision failure due to defective interaction implies that the stated request is more general than the actual information need. Articles of no value to the requester are retrieved. These match his stated request but are of no value because of some additional limitation or requirement that was not given in the request statement.

In some searches there is a partial overlap between stated request and information need and in these cases it is likely that both recall and precision failures will result from inadequate interaction.

There appear to be basically two types of interaction failure (4).

1. The situation, long known to librarians, of the user who puts an imperfect request (i.e., a request that does not precisely match his information requirement), or the situation in which the information need is captured imperfectly by a librarian or search analyst.

2. The situation in which the user puts a request that is a fair reflection of his information need, but recall failures result from the fact that he is not fully aware of the types of article that exist and could be of use to him. This type of failure can only be solved by a browsing or *iterative* search. About 20% of the MEDLARS test searches involving inadequate interaction were judged to be of this type (i.e., the situation in which the requester could never precisely define his need except through some browsing in the literature).

In this evaluation program, a discrepancy between a stated request and an information need has been determined on the basis of:

1. The requester's relevance assessments, particularly the reasons given for judging certain articles of value and others of no value.

2. Revised request statements supplied by the requester in a covering letter to the Evaluator or on the test form *Revised Statement of MEDLARS Request*.

3. The requester's *Record of Known Relevant Documents*.

4. In a few cases, by telephone contact between the Evaluator and the requester.

Some examples of search failures attributed to defective interaction (i.e., failures due to request statements that imperfectly represent the area of information need) follow.

Search #5. The request is for "crossing of fatty acids through the placental barrier; normal fatty acid levels in placenta and fetus." Recall was only 25% because the requester is interested in the broader area of *lipid* transfer and also in lipid levels in the *newborn infant.*

Search #11. This search was a complete failure, retrieving 1167 articles of which only one was relevant. The request statement was "cancer in the fetus or newborn infant," but the area of need appears to the relationship between teratogenesis and oncogenesis at the cellular level.

Search #24. The request relates to the metabolism of steroids in liver or liver disease, but the requester did not indicate that animal studies were of no interest.

Search #32. This is an example of a request too specific in one aspect, insufficiently specific in another. The request is for "homonymous hemianopsia in visual aphasia," but the actual area of interest encompasses homonymous hemianopsia *and other visual field defects* in patients having aphasia *as a result of a tumor or cerebrovascular accident.*

Search #52. The request reads "skin grafts in monkeys." Only *homografts* are of interest.

In the design of the evaluation, we hypothesized that, of the modes of interaction presently used within MEDLARS, the most desirable would be the *personal interaction* mode (i.e., the situation in which the requester visits a MEDLARS center and discusses his needs personally with a search analyst). The other modes (mailed request direct to the system, and the request transmitted through a local librarian) would be likely to be less successful on the whole. This hypothesis was not supported by the test results. Table 7 presents the performance figures for 299 searches broken down by mode of interaction, from which it can be seen that the performance for the "no local interaction" group (i.e., request mailed directly to the system) is noticeably better than the performance for the other groups. Of course there are other variables that could be affecting the results in this table, including the variable of the MEDLARS center performing the search, the subject field, and the type of organization submitting the request. However, when each of these varia-

TABLE 7. Breakdown of MEDLARS performance figures by mode of interaction

Mode of interaction	Precision ratio %	Recall ratio %
Personal interaction (109 searches)	49.3	56.4
Local interaction (79 searches)	46.9	55.0
No local interaction (111 searches)	53.9	60.8

bles is held constant, and the results are tabulated by mode of interaction, the trend displayed in Table 7 is consistently maintained. Moreover, when we take the group of 134 searches in which, from the requester's relevance assessments, we know that interaction failures have occurred (i.e., failures due to request statements that do not closely correspond to the actual area of interest), we find that 37.8% of all the "no local interaction" searches contain failures attributed to inadequate interaction, whereas 46.8% of the "local interaction" searches and 50% of the personal interaction searches contain failures of this type.

From these results, and from the detailed search analyses, it appears that the best request statements (i.e., those that most closely reflect the actual area of information need) are those written down by the requester in his own natural-language narrative terms. When he comes to a librarian or search analyst, and discusses his need orally, a transformation takes place and, unfortunately, the request statement captured by the librarian or searcher is frequently a less perfect mirror of the information need then the one prepared by the requester himself in his own natural language terms. When the user writes down his request, he is forced to think of what exactly he is looking for. In this, he is not particularly influenced by the logical and linguistic constraints of the system. When making a personal visit to a MEDLARS center, if he has not gone through the discipline of recording his request, he has a less well formed idea of what he is seeking. When this somewhat imprecise need is discussed with a search analyst, in terms of *Medical Subject Headings,* it tends to become forced into the language and logic of the system.

Improving Request Statements

The large number of failures attributed to the area of user-system interaction prompted the conduct of a detailed analysis of the searches involved. This analysis was intended to determine what data, if it could have been collected from the requester, would have helped to define more exactly the area of his actual information requirement. Put differently, can we design a search request form that, without being too complex, will assist the requester in defining the exact scope of his need, and at the same time will give the searcher data adequate for a proper understanding of the requester's need?

The following observations resulted from this analysis:

1. Obviously, the prime requirement is a complete statement of what the requester is looking for. This should be a statement in the requester's own natural-language, narrative form. It must *not* be deliberately phrased in the language of the system. It must *not* be artificially structured in a form that the requester believes will approximate to a MEDLARS search strategy.

2. Knowing the *purpose* of a search would clearly

have helped, in a number of cases, to precisely define its scope. We only know of these cases because the requester has told us the reason for his search after it was completed. It is not unlikely that those data would have helped to define the scope of many of the other searches. For example, the request for search #11 came out as "cancer in the fetus or newborn infant," while the actual area of interest covers "the relationship between teratogenesis and oncogenesis at the cellular level." The search might have been successful had the requester informed us, as he did post facto, that he had been asked to write an article, for *Advances in Teratology,* on "some aspect of cell differentiation or malformations and how they are related to the cancer problem."

Knowing the purpose of a search may help to establish the recall and precision requirements and tolerances of users. A physician writing a book on "connective tissue in ocular disease," and asking for a search on this subject, will demand high recall and tolerate low precision. That is, he will be prepared to examine a comparatively large number of nonrelevant citations to assure himself that he is not missing any articles of prime importance. On the other hand, we have a requester who is preparing a seminar, for nurses, on kidney transplantation. He does not necessarily want everything, but would like to see a number of recent major surveys of the entire subject. The requirement is for high precision, and a low recall will be tolerable.

3. The titles of articles that the requester knows to be relevant at the time he makes his request (collected in the present evaluation program on the form *Record of Known Relevant Documents*) can be of great potential value in helping to define the scope of a search. For example, search #5 relates to "crossing of fatty acids through the placental barrier; normal fatty acid levels in placenta and fetus." The fact that the requester is really concerned with a broader topic (crossing of *lipids* through the placental barrier; normal *lipid* levels of placenta, fetus, or *newborn infant*) is well illustrated by the titles supplied in advance by him:

"Release of free fatty acids from adipose tissue obtained from newborn infants"

"Changes in the nucleic acid and phospholipid levels of the liver in the course of fetal and postnatal development"

"The amount of lipids and proteins in the foetus of rats and rabbits and in newborn infants"

Note that titles of "known relevant" articles will be most useful in indicating a request more specific than the actual information need. If the titles quoted are obviously outside the scope of the stated request, this is an indication of a request statement that is too precise.

On the other hand, if the titles supplied are more specific than the stated request, this does not really tell us very much—since they are included within the scope of the search as defined by the request statement.

Sometimes, however, the cited titles will relate to a topic *much more precise* than the general area covered by the request statement, and this will tend to identify a request that is probably too general in relation to the precise information need For example, the requester of search #11, on "cancer in fetus or newborn infant," could name only one known relevant paper before the search, namely: "Association of Wilm's tumor with aniridia, hemihypertrophy and other congenital malformations." The fact that the requester could name only one relevant article, and that so much more specific than the statement of his need, surely suggests that the request statement is much broader than it should be.

We are not, of course, advocating that search formulations be based on titles of known relevant papers rather than request statements. The two complement each other. The "known relevant" titles are most useful in signalling the fact that the request statement is probably imperfect and needs further clarification.

4. Occasionally, the requester's estimate of the volume of the relevant literature published on the subject of his request, within the time span of MEDLARS, will also signal a request statement that may either be too broad or too narrow. The danger here is that the requester may base his estimate on the request statement rather than on the volume of literature he expects on the *precise* topic of interest.

5. One of the problems is to get the requester to be sufficiently precise when he makes a narrative statement. We do not want him to omit any aspect of interest, but we would like to be able to eliminate certain categories of articles that will be of no possible use to the requester. In other words, we want to know what we can definitely exclude from a search. It is difficult usually for the requester to think in terms of exclusions when he prepares his narrative statement of need. Therefore we must help him to usefully delimit the scope of the search.

This could be done, for example, by incorporating into the request form a brief, carefully designed questionnaire relating to the previously recorded narrative statement. Certain types of exclusions, or limitations of scope, are applicable to many MEDLARS searches. For example, some requesters are interested only in humans, others are interested in both human and animal studies. Some requesters are interested only in particular sexes or age groups (e.g., "young, healthy, adult males"). Experimental studies are the sole concern of some requesters, while clinical case histories are all that is wanted by others. Some will accept all clinical studies, including single case reports, while others are only interested in "large series" of cases Again, one requester will be interested in a particular organ under normal physiological conditions, while another will be concerned with pathological conditions of the same organ, or in certain pathological conditions only (e.g., *not* neoplasms).

Such generally applicable limitations on a search could easily be incorporated into the demand search request form, either in the form of direct questions or by the use of check-off boxes (these would resemble the "check-tags" appearing on the MEDLARS indexing *Data Form* for generally applicable descriptors; e.g., age groups, sex, experimental animals, type of study). Very many request statements could have been made much more exact if the requester had been given this assistance in defining the scope of the search.

Having gone through this questionnaire approach, we should end up with a very precise statement of the requester's information need, including limitations that he would not think to include in his original request statement. We are now able, in our searching strategy, to eliminate a large segment of the data base (within the limitations of the vocabulary) that is of no interest to the requester, allowing us to undertake a broader search in the pertinent segment, while still obtaining a tolerable precision ratio.

6. The request form should also be designed to determine the recall and precision requirements and tolerances of the requester. At its simplest, the form could merely ascertain whether the requester would like all papers making some reference to the subject matter of interest, or whether he wants only papers in which the subject matter is treated centrally Alternatively, it could be made more complex by allowing the requester to choose from a number of alternatives. For example:

"Which would you prefer:

1. A search retrieving about 60% of the relevant articles within MEDLARS, but with about 50% irrelevancy in the search?
2. A search retrieving about 90% of the relevant articles within MEDLARS, but with about 80% irrelevancy in the search?"

9 Additional Analyses

The full report of the study contains additional analyses that can merely be mentioned here:

1. *Indexing coverage.* Collectively, the participating requesters knew 1054 relevant articles at the time they make their MEDLARS request, and 89.2% of these were found to be in the system at the time the various searches were conducted. An additional 6.1% of the articles were "not yet indexed." Assuming that these items in the indexing backlog would eventually get into the system, we can say that the ultimate MEDLARS coverage of the relevant journal literature, as known by requesters, was 95%.

2. *Use of foreign language literature.* Although 40-45% of the entire data base consists of foreign articles, the useful foreign language component in the 302 test searches was found to be no more than 16%. In 55 searches (18.2%) only English articles were requested. In an additional 35, some additional language restrictions (e.g., "English, French and German") was imposed. In the 212 searches without language restriction, MEDLARS

retrieves roughly in the proportion of 70% English to 30% foreign (English articles are indexed with more terms, on the average). Only 60% of the foreign articles retrieved in these searches could be assessed by the requesters and of these only 40% were judged of value.

3. *Journal usage factors.* It was possible to produce lists of both "depth" and "non-depth" journals ordered on the basis of the number of times each title appeared in the combined random sample of 6491 articles drawn from the 302 searches. From these tabulations it was possible to plot percentage of total retrievals against percentage of total journals cited. As expected, a comparatively small percentage of the journals contributed to a large percentage of the retrievals: the top 10 journals (0.7% of the 1387 separate journals represented in the 6491 retrievals) accounted for approximately 10% of the retrievals; 157 journals (11.3%) accounted for 50% of the retrievals.

4. *Effect of system response time.* Only 21 of the 302 searches (7.0%) were significantly reduced in value by processing delays.

5. *Serendipity value of MEDLARS searches.* Averaged over the 302 searches, it was discovered that requesters were glad to learn of the existence (because of other needs or projects) of 18% of the articles judged "of no value" in relation to the information needs prompting the MEDLARS requests. This, however, is undoubtedly an inflated estimate of the serendipity value of the machine search, because it is based on the requester's evaluation of actual articles spoonfed to him in photocopy form.

6. *Output screening.* Working from search printouts (titles and index terms), neither an M.D. on the staff of the Library (over 10 searches), nor an experienced search analyst (over 19 searches), were able to make "relevance predictions" that closely replicated the actual assessments made by requesters when seeing the articles themselves. On the basis of this performance, they would have screened out about 7% of the irrelevant material over the 29 searches, but at the same time they would have discarded about 8% of the articles subsequently judged relevant.

10 Conclusions

The test results have shown that the system is operating, on the average, at about 58% recall and 50% precision. On the average, it retrieves about 65% of the *major value* literature in its base at 50% precision. Averages, however, are somewhat misleading. A scatter diagram shows that few of the individual search results fall in the area bounded by the average ratios ± 5%. Some of the searches appear to have performed very well, with high recall accompanied by high precision. Others achieved completely unsatisfactory recall results. By a careful examination of a sample of searches at each end of the distribution, it has been possible to identify the most important factors governing the success or failure of a MEDLARS search.

We can take the average figures achieved in the test searches by each of the five MEDLARS processing centers and plot them as recall/precision points. By extrapolation from these points, we can hypothesize a generalized MEDLARS performance curve looking something like that of Fig. 3. The fact that, on the average, MEDLARS is operating at 58% recall and 50% precision indicates that, consciously or unconsciously the MEDLARS searchers choose to operate in this general area. It would be possible for MEDLARS to operate at a different performance point on the recall/precision curve of Fig. 3. By broadening of search strategies, the system could obtain a much higher average recall ratio, but this could only be achieved at a much lower average precision. From Fig. 3 it can be seen that there are differences in searching policies between the various centers, center E choosing to operate in a high precision mode, while center A appears to favor higher recall. The other centers use strategies that compromise more between recall and precision.

In operating at 58% recall and 50% precision, MEDLARS is retrieving an average of 175 citations per search. To operate at an average recall of 85–90% and an average precision ratio in the region of 20–25% implies that the system would need to retrieve an average of perhaps 500–600 citations per search. Are requesters willing to scan this many citations (75% of which will be completely irrelevant) in order to obtain a much higher level of recall? Clearly each individual has his own requirements in relation to the tradeoff between recall and precision. It is obviously important that we establish *for each request* the recall requirements and precision tolerances of the requester, thus allowing the

search analyst to prepare a strategy geared as required to high recall, high precision, or some compromise point in between.

The purpose of a comprehensive system evaluation, such as the one reported, is not simply to determine the present performance level but also to discover what needs to be done to upgrade the performance of the present system, i.e., what can be done to move the generalized performance curve of Figure 3 up and over to the right. On the basis of the diagnostic search analyses, it has been possible to make recommendations on actions designed to improve the overall operating efficiency of the system. Some of the more important of these are enumerated below:

1. Direct attention should be devoted to the improvement of user request statements because it is in this area that most immediate benefits in performance appear possible. The present search request form should be re-designed to demand greater participation from the user in making his precise requirements known to the system. All requesters should be required to complete this form personally, even in situations in which the requester makes a personal visit to a MEDLARS center or to his local library.

2. The search request form should record the recall and precision requirements and tolerances of the individual user, and search analysts should make use of this data in the formulation of appropriate strategies.

3. Consideration should be given to the possibility of establishing, and recording in machinable form, standard strategies for search elements likely to recur in a number of different searches.

4. The present distinction between "depth" and "non-depth" journals should be abandoned; each article should be treated on its own merit and sufficient terms assigned to index the extension and intension of its content. According to our best estimates, the present overall level of exhaustivity appears adequate to meet the type of demand currently being made of the system.

5. The further development of the MEDLARS vocabulary should be based primarily on continuous inputs from the indexing and searching operations. The entry vocabulary should be expanded and made readily available to every indexer and searcher.

6. The use of subheadings should be extended but additional precision devices, including links and role indicators, should not be incorporated into the system at the present time.

7. Steps should be taken to effect greater integration between the activities of indexing, searching and vocabulary control.

A large-scale study of the type that has been undertaken exposes the greatest weaknesses of a system, but, no matter how comprehensive, it cannot discover more than a small fraction of its specific (e.g., terminological) inadequacies. The Library is now investigating the feasibility of applying the procedures used in the present

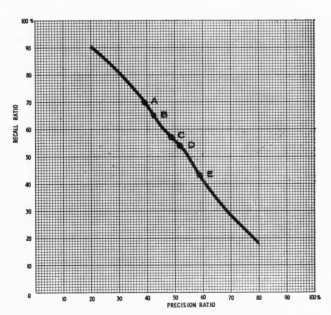

Fig. 3. MEDLARS extrapolated performance curve

evaluation to the continuous monitoring of MEDLARS performance. By these quality control procedures we will: (1) attempt to ensure that each search meets the performance needs of the individual MEDLARS user; and (2) collect necessary data to allow the continued improvement of indexing policies, searching strategies, vocabulary development, and modes of interaction with the user. Only by continuous self-appraisal can a large information system make itself responsive to the needs of the scientific community.

● Acknowledgments

The author wishes to acknowledge the assistance and encouragement given to him by members of the MEDLARS Evaluation Advisory Committee: Charles J. Austin, University of Colorado Medical Center; Julian Bigelow, Institute for Advanced Study, Princeton; Cyril Cleverdon, College of Aeronautics, Cranfield, England; W. D. Climenson, Central Intelligence Agency; Eugene Harris, National Institutes of Health; and Calvin Mooers, Rockford Research Institute. For their advice and criticism he is deeply indebted.

References

1. AUSTIN, C. J., *MEDLARS 1963–1967*, National Library of Medicine, Bethesda, Md., 1968.
2. CLEVERDON, C. W., J. MILLS, and M. KEEN, *Factors Determining the Performance of Indexing Systems, Vol. 1, Design,* ASLIB Cranfield Project, London, 1966.
3. LANCASTER, F. W., *Evaluation of the MEDLARS Demand Search Service,* National Library of Medicine, Bethesda, Md., 1968.
4. LANCASTER, F. W., *Information Retrieval Systems: Characteristics, Testing, and Evaluation,* Wiley, New York, 1968.

61 Selected Results from an Inquiry into Testing of Information Retrieval Systems

TEFKO SARACEVIC

1. On Testing

In the world of technology, engineering, and physical sciences, the testing of physical aspects of physical systems is a time-honored and studied tradition — an activity quite formalized with well-structured measures, instrumentation, and methodology. Unfortunately, testing social aspects of social systems, systems such as retrieval systems, libraries or educational institutions, is neither a time-honored nor a well-structured activity. A need for testing social systems exists as much as that for testing physical systems, and for the same reasons: complexity, competition, cost, and importance to society. A special impetus for testing social systems dealing with information came about with the utilization of sophisticated technology which attempted to interact with man's intellectual activity and decision-making and to cope with the profusion of printed paper. However, the problems encountered in testing such social systems as compared with testing physical systems are staggeringly different in nature — the hope for exactness in quantification is much smaller, the conduct of tests much more difficult, the complexity of testing is much greater and the limitations imposed on generalizations from results are much more stringent.

Given that we understand the notion of testing in a quantitative sense (where the performance of a system is related to its purpose and the variables affecting the performance are monitored), the following conclusion about testing of information retrieval systems was made at the end of this inquiry:

At present, real and productive testing of total retrieval systems, taking into account and controlling all inside and environmental factors is not feasible and not possible. At present it seems that generalizable, formal, quantified results of high validity and reliability on all or even on the majority of factors affecting the performance of retrieval systems cannot be attained.

The reasons seem fairly evident. There is an absence of a well-formulated theory which takes into account all or a majority of the factors operating within and upon retrieval systems. There is only an intuitive understanding of the objectives of retrieval systems within the communication processes in which systems operate — thus, the measures indicative of the achievement of objectives may not be comprehensive nor totally reflective of reality. There is an inadequate knowledge of processes involved within or outside the retrieval systems and, without a thorough understanding of processes, comprehensive testing is unattainable. There is a lack of standardized methodologies for experimentation, which precludes testing. Most importantly, there is an inadequate understanding of controls in experimentation with retrieval systems, and the controls are essential in monitoring the factors under consideration and in sorting out the factors contributing to the performance. There is a lack of effort to cumulate and synthesize existing knowledge of retrieval systems.

However, the picture is not as bleak and grim as it seems. On the contrary, the mere realization of all the above inadequacies is progress; the definition of problems is the most important aspect of their solution. The definition of problems associated with retrieval systems, in turn, is the major accomplishment of test activity such as conducted by Cleverdon (1) Salton (2) Lancaster (3) and reported in this Inquiry. Thus, although not achieving what it set out to do, the testing activity in the field of information retrieval can rightly claim these specific achievements:

a) uncovering the gross effects of a limited number of factors on the performance of retrieval systems;
b) discovering the main relationships between these factors;
c) generally observing how retrieval systems work;
d) introducing experimentation into the field of information retrieval;
e) eliminating dogmatic conclusions based on anecdotal evidence, and thus raising the level of discussion;
f) uncovering infinitely more problems than it solved — problems that are a challenge for additional work, which is being already conducted on a much higher level, and with greater rigor than the work performed at the outset of testing activity.

This inquiry is not exempt from the general deficiencies encountered in testing, and the results do not go beyond the limited achievements enumerated above. Although every attempt was made to achieve rigor and objective controls, human subjectivity was always encountered, it was at the root of all results. Again we demonstrated the self-evident fact that retrieval systems, in essence, are for the people and by the people, with some interference between the two. This interference is necessary, and nowadays unavoidable, in order to achieve a communication contact between the available literature (or information in general) and its users. The essential question is how we can optimize the contact while minimizing the interference. As in all other tests, the specific numerical results of this inquiry should be interpreted with a considerable plus-minus grain of salt; however, it

is believed that the general conclusions can help in providing some answers to the above question.

2. Aims and Approach

The results reported here were derived from a project entitled Comparative Systems Laboratory (*CSL*) conducted at the Center for Documentation and Communication Research, School of Library Science, Case Western Reserve University during a period of slightly over four years (1963–1968), and supported by a grant from the U.S. Public Health Service. The general aim of *CSL* was to inquire comprehensively into testing information retrieval systems. Specifically, the aims of CSL were to:

1. define the essential components of an information retrieval system and to construct a system model;
2. identify the varibles affecting the performance of the system;
3. design a methodology for experiments which would provide quantitative information concerning variation in system performance;
4. conduct experiments applying this methodology in relation to a limited specified number of variables;
5. gain a further understanding of variables and processes operating within retrieval systems and of methodologies needed for experimentation with such systems.

The general approach taken to achieve these aims was one in which a conscious effort was made to delineate and to distinguish between the various test- (experiment) related activities along with conducting them in a prescribed and interdependent order.

Activities in CSL may be divided into four distinct areas:

1. *Theory and General Methodology.* A general methodology for testing retrieval systems was developed; it included theoretical definitions, the model of an IR system, measures for evaluation of the system, and a general method of analysis. This methodology was fully specified by Goffman and Newill (4).
2. *Experimental Design and Operations.* On the basis of the general methodology, the experiments were designed and a selection was made of those components which were to be varied and those which were to be held constant; operational definitions and procedures were specified in relation to (a) development of components, and (b) comparative testing of components; actual operations followed.
3. *Controls.* Quality controls and controls against deviation and bias were attempted in every operation. The meaning of controls in information retrieval experimentation was investigated through a series of separate experiments.
4. *Analysis and Evaluation.* Analysis of quantitative

results led to evaluation and interpretation of performance of variables under experimentation.

A series of CSL technical reports issued by Case Western Reserve University presented various aspects of the inquiry. Two reports are of particular interest for a full understanding of the experiments: one presents the operational manuals used for constructing and operating various experimental components of a system (5), and the other is the Final Report which comprehensively presents the project as a whole with considerable attention paid to the control-related experiments conducted within CSL (6).

3. General Model, Measures, and Methodology

The approach taken in developing the testing methodology was first, to define the components in a manner that would permit their assembly into a retrieval system, i.e., to develop a model; second, to state measures in terms of which performance of a retrieval system might be evaluated; and third, to elaborate upon a general experimental method by which the measures could be utilized for comparative testing of retrieval systems.

3.1 Model

It was considered essential that, in the model of a retrieval system, both the purpose and function of the system be specified, because the performance can be evaluated only in terms of some functions of inputs and outputs in the system in relation to a given purpose. The basic purpose of a retrieval system was considered to be provision of relevant information to a group of users. This was to be accomplished by presenting the users with a set of documents containing relevant information in response to a query. The major components included in the information retrieval system under study were classified as being related either to purpose or to function. The *purpose components* included:

1. *the discipline,*
2. *the class of users,*
3. *the size of the file.*

The *function components* — those which are required in processing a query — were:

1. *Acquisition:* Policy determining the content of the file.
2. *Source of input:* Format of the document (such as title, abstract or full text) used for selecting index terms. (*Index term* is defined as a word or string of words connoting a concept and denoting a class).
3. *Indexing language:* Set of index terms together with a set of rules; the set of index terms is the vocabulary of the indexing language and is called *terminology.*
4. *Coding:* Symbolic representation of index terms.

5. *Organization of the file:* Order of the file contents.
6. *Question analysis:* Translation of query concepts into indexing language.
7. *Searching strategy:* Procedure used to search the file.
8. *Format of output:* Physical representation of documents provided to user (such as title, abstract, or full text) as an answer to query.

3.2 Measures

In order to define measures of a system's performance a distinction was made between (a) the system's assignment of relevance, i.e., documents included in the system's answer, and (b) user's assignment of relevance, i.e., user's evaluation of the system's answer. These correspond to relevance at the source and to relevance at the destination in a communication process.

The performance of the system may be evaluated in terms of measures indicating the degree of agreement between the two (system's and user's) assignments of relevance, where the user's assignment is the standard with which a system's assignment is compared. Specifically, the performance of a retrieval system was quantitatively indicated by the measures of Sensitivity (Se), Specificity (Sp), and Effectiveness (Es). *Sensitivity* measures the system's ability to provide a user with relevant (as a user would select) members of the file. *Specificity* measures the system's ability not to provide a user with nonrelevant members. *Effectiveness* is an additive combination of Se and Sp, indicating an overall performance.

Se and Sp can be expressed as conditional probabilities:

$$Se = P_R (A)$$
$$Sp = P_{R'} (A')$$
$$Es = Se + Sp - 1$$

i.e., Sensitivity is the probability that if given a document is relevant (R) it will be retrieved as an answer (A); Specificity is the probability that if given a document is not relevant (R') it will not be retrieved as an answer (A'); Effectiveness is as indicated. These measures may be approximated as follows:

$$Se = \frac{\text{number of relevant documents retrieved}}{\text{total number of relevant documents in the file}}$$

$$Sp = \frac{\text{number of nonrelevant documents not retrieved}}{\text{total number of nonrelevant documents in the file}}$$

Thus, Sensitivity as approximated above is the same as measure of recall, but Specificity is not the same as precision, since precision is:

$$Pr = \frac{\text{number of relevant documents retrieved}}{\text{total number of documents retrieved}}$$

3.3 General Methodology

The proposed solutions for deriving the approximation of the measures actually comprise the general methodology. The position was taken that comparison of performance of a variety of systems was meaningless, since, systems generally, have different purposes and functions. However, it is meaningful to evaluate performances of a variety of components which may make up a system, given a purpose and a function.

Thus, the methodology was devoted to accomplishing a comparative evaluation of a variety of components by measuring the variability in the system's performance caused by alternation of the components as variables of the system. The basic problem was the establishment of user's relevant sets which could serve as a standard for comparison. One way of establishing a user's relevant set may be by providing the user with the whole file and asking him to select the set of documents relevant to his query. This method was rejected as impractical — users refuse to wade through a whole file. Another method was developed: For each query, a user received a universal set of retrieved answers upon which he performed an evaluative selection of answers relevant to his query. A universal set can be defined as follows: Given a number of files which treated (e.g., indexed) the same documents in a different way and/or upon which a number of different searching procedures were applied, the *universal* set for a given query is a *union of outputs* obtained from searching all the different files and/or from all the different searching procedures. An evaluated universal set allows for a comparison between the performance of different files or searching procedures; that is, it enables a comparison between differently implemented components of a retrieval system.

It should be realized that the measures arrived at by the application of universal sets indicate a comparative but by no means an absolute performance. If a document that would be considered relevant by a user was not presented to the user within the universal set (union of outputs) it meant that the document was not retrieved by any of the files or searching procedures; thus, in the final comparison, all of the files or procedures would be penalized equivalently for not retrieving that document as an answer. The comparative performance will hold not only within the framework of a universal set but also will hold with respect to the compared files or searching procedures in general.

4. Experimental Design

The experimental design was completely governed by two factors: (a) the general model, measures, and methodology synthesized above, and (b) expediency, that is, availability of given users, material, operational facilities and personnel at the time. One aspect of the design was the operational definitions of components (summarized below), while another was the prescription of the experimental operations (summarized in Section 6). Components which were varied and which were kept constant are indicated.

I. Purpose Components (constant):
   1. *Discipline:*
      Tropical diseases, specifically, vector-borne diseases
   2. *Class of users:*
      Research investigators throughout the U.S., in the above discipline
   3. *Size of the file:*
      600 documents.

II. Function Components:
   1. *Acquisition* (constant):
      Random selection of documents from a year's volume of *Tropical Disease Bulletin* (*TDB*), London. (*TDB* is an abstracting and indexing service covering the world's literature in tropical diseases).
   2. *Source of input* (varied):
      (a) titles
      (b) abstracts from *TDB*
      (c) full texts
   3. *Indexing language* (varied):
      (a) *Telegraphic abstract* — a set of index terms, assigned without constraints, by indexers together, with a syntactic relationship indicated by the role indicators (roles) and a grouping of terms into levels (links) (indexed from all all three sources);
      (b) *Keywords selected by humans* — index terms contained in a given document (indexed from all three sources);
      (c) *Keywords selected by computer* — index terms selected on the basis of computer program instructions (indexed from titles only);
      (d) *Metalanguage* — an experimental indexing language with two sets of index terms: meta (general) terms that describe or indicate the action of the object (specific) terms (indexed from titles only);
      (e) *Tropical Diseases Bulletin* (*TDB*) *Index* — a set of subject headings and index terms as prepared for the Annual Index of the *TDB*. (The closest comparative sources are titles and abstracts).
   4. *Code* (*varied*):
      All index terms are represented in:
      (a) *English* — the English terms without terminology and relationship control;
      (b) *Medical coding scheme* (*MCS*) — a faceted-type thesaurus in symbolic language, which arranges the index terms by employing individual

classification for seven classes of terms: geographic and personal names; medical terms — anatomy; medical terms — diseases; organisms; chemicals; chemical and medical processes, techniques and operations; and general terms.

5. *File organization* (constant):

A sequential order of all index files handled by a set of computer programs.

6. *Question analysis* (varied):

Five types of question analysis that gradually increase the scope of the question; searches were done separately for each type:

Type A: enumeration of unit concepts (i.e., principal, searchable English terms describing the subject of a question) selected from the user-submitted question;

Type B: each of the Type A terms is expanded by locating generically, specifically, synonymously, and collaterally related terms through the MCS thesaurus only (i.e., QA Type A plus thesaurus);

Type C: Type A terms expanded through any other tool — reference works, dictionaries, personal knowledge — except the MCS thesaurus (i.e., Type A plus English);

Type D: Type C terms expanded further through using the MCS thesaurus (i.e., Type C plus thesaurus);

Type E: Type D terms verified through consultation with the user; if necessary, subsequent revisions — additions or deletions — were incorporated (Type D plus user).

7. *Searching strategy* (varied):

(a) *Question level (or narrow) search statement* is the statement that as completely and accurately as possible reflects the stated question for purposes of searching; that is, it incorporates *all* searchable terms (unit concepts) from the question regardless of their comparative importance; the search statements resulting from QA Type A to Type E are searched as narrow searches;

(b) *Broad search statement* is the statement that represents the question by only one general subject aspect (not necessarily one term) and all its expansions.

8. *Format of output* (varied)

(1) Bibliographic citation (including title)

(2) Abstract (as taken from *TDB*)

(3) Full text

On the basis of these definitions, a simple null-type hypothesis was formulated:

Variations in the sources of input, the indexing languages, methods of coding, question analysis, search strategies and/or formats of output do not significantly affect the performance of an information retrieval system in terms of sensitivity, specificity and effectiveness.

5. Experimental Operations

5.1 Acquisitions and Indexing

Six hundred documents randomly selected from the 1960 volume of *Tropical Diseases Bulletin* (*TDB*) were indexed in five indexing languages. (It is of interest to note that the file size of 600 documents in the field of tropical diseases represents a significant number of documents: nearly half the world's annual output in open periodical literature on tropical diseases as abstracted by *TDB*). For two of the index languages (Telegraphic Abstracts and Keywords), each document was indexed from three sources of input. Hence:

Index File	Indexing Language	Source of Input
A	Telegraphic Abstract	Title
B	Telegraphich Abstract	Abstract
C	Telegraphic Abstract	Full Text
D	Keywords by Indexers	Title
E	Keywords by Indexers	Abstract
F	Keywords by Indexers	Full Text
G	Keywords by Computers	Titles
H	Metalanguage	Titles
K	*TDB* Index Entries	Titles/Abstracts

In this way nine index files were formed which could be described in terms of two variables, the indexing language and the source of input employed. Each source of input produced indexes of different length, i.e., number of index terms. Thus, for the source of input, the length of indexes was actually the variable. The title-based files had indexes of approximately five to eight index terms, abstract-based files of approximately twenty-three to thirty index terms and full text-based files of approximately thirty-six to forty index terms. The *TDB Index* was approximately eleven index terms long, thus, it is not directly comparable to other abstract- or title-based files.

A manual for use in indexing each indexing language was developed. Seven indexers were utilized: three for the Telegraphic Abstracts, three for Keywords and one for Meta-language. An eighth indexer prepared the *Tropical Diseases Bulletin* original index slips for computer searching (the original *TDB Index* was intended for manual use). The indexers were selected on the bases of their biomedical educational background and previous experience in indexing. There was a three-week training period for all indexers to standardize their approach and indexing skills. No indexer indexed a document more than once and no indexer indexed in more than one indexing language. Separate control experiments indicated that the indexing obtained from the indexers was of high quality and consistency; thus, we were satsfied that we obtained, under the circumstances, the "best" indexing possible. The average intra-indexing consistency of the seven indexers was .71 and the inter-indexing consistency was .62, which means that even with the "best" indexing, there still remains considerable inconsistency. However, it should be realized that quality and consistency of indexing are not necessarily related.

5.2 Encoding and Thesaurus Construction

Each index term, for each language, was treated as an independent English term (i.e., no specified relation with other English terms) and as a coded entry in a faceted-type thesaurus (i.e., certain relations between index terms were specified). The thesaurus consisted only of terms identified in indexing the documents. The performance effect of coding (thesaurus vs. non-thesaurus free English terms) was then tested as a part of the question analysis procedure by enlarging the question terminology with and without the use of the thesaurus.

A manual for use in encoding (classifying) and in constructing the thesaurus was developed. Three coders were utilized: one for medical, one for chemical and one for general and geographic terms. The coders were selected on the basis of their extensive educational background in the appropriate subject disciplines and extensive information retrieval experience, especially in creation of similar thesauri. A constant review of procedures for encoding was presented. The coders were tested in a separate control experiment. The classifying (intra-coder) consistency of the medical-terms coder was .36, for the chemical-terms coder .86, and for the general-terms coder .93. Other coding tests indicated that the intra- and inter-consistency of classifying medical terms is usually as low as found above — the reasons could not be explained.

A master thesaurus was created containing all unique terms in all nine index files; in addition, for each file there was a thesaurus containing only the unique terms from that file. The thesaurus from title-based files contained approximately 1,700 unique index terms; from abstract-based files approximately 5,500 terms; and from full text-based files approximately 5,600 index terms. The master thesaurus contained some 11,000 terms; however, since keywords were also involved, many terms were simple grammatical variants of similar terms and many were compounds of single terms. Still, there was a considerable amount of symmetric differences between thesauri for different files, meaning that various thesauri for various files contained various terms. It is of interest to note that *thesauri* of abstract- and full text-based files were of similar length, although their *indexes* were not.

In general, it was found that the process of classification in construction of a thesaurus may be a subject of considerable human inconsistency, especially in classifying medical terms. However, it should be realized that quality and consistency of classification are not necessarily related.

5.3 Users and Question Asking

A volunteer group of twenty-five users was identified and recruited with the help of an Advisory Committee from the Communicable Disease Center in Atlanta, Georgia. Each user was a specialist in the field of tropical diseases and a senior worker in the institution of his primary affiliation. The users came from thirteen different institutions. Nineteen users have earned a Ph.D., five an M.D. and one a B.S. Eighteen users were primarily engaged in research, six in teaching and one in treatment. The specific subject interests most frequently cited were entomology, mycology, parasitology, microbiology, toxicology, bacteriology, and serology. The role of the users was to submit appropriate questions for searching; to discuss the question with the systems analyst, if necessary; to assess the relevance of system output submitted as answers to their questions; and to provide information about themselves and their activities within the experiment. In order to assist the users in performing their question formulating tasks, and in order to impose some control and standardization on this task, a guiding manual and forms for question-asking were developed and submitted to each user. In order to obtain realistic questions and ensure a realistic communication process between the users and CSL, the users were instructed to provide questions in relation to their current research interest. Accordingly, they were asked to describe their work. Later, questions were compared with the description of work to find if they matched. They did match for all queries. The text of queries is presented in Part III of the CSL Final Report (6).

In addition the users were instructed not to submit more than ten questions each. The users submitted 141 queries, of which 136 were searched and 124 included in the final analysis. Of the seventeen queries not included in the final analysis, five queries were rejected because they were on a subject outside of the file; for seven queries there was no output, and evaluation for five queries was not returned by the users. One user failed to return any evaluation of answers, thus, only twenty-four users were included in the final analysis. For the 24 users and 124 questions included in the final analysis, the range of the number of questions submitted by users was between 2 and 10, and the mean number of questions per user was 5. The questions were fairly evenly distributed across the total group of users, meaning that approximately fifty per cent of the questions were associated with some fifty per cent of the users.

5.4 Question Analysis and Searching

Each of the queries accepted from the users was prepared for searching by successively enlarging the scope of the query through formalized analyses. Terms were expanded, that is, related terms were added to a given term, with the searching restriction that all expanded terms had to be connected to each other and to the given term from which they were expanded by a logical "or." As previously defined, there were five types of question analyses, each building on the preceding one. The result of each analysis was a set of terms which were then combined into a search statement; the search statements resulting from question analysis Types A to E were considered to be on the narrow search strategy level (i.e., reflecting the question). A broad search strategy level and statement were established which resulted in searching only the primary subject concept requested in each question. Each search was transcribed for computer searching. Each question was searched over all index files in all question analysis types and on both search strategy levels. It was thus possible to run fifty-four searches per question.

A manual for question analysis and another for construction of search statements, were developed together with appropriate forms. Question analyses and searching were performed by four systems analysts, who were selected on the basis of their extensive educational background and experience in information retrieval. The background of analysts was as follows: Ph.D. in chemistry and information science; M.D.; B.S. in biology with an M.S. in library science; and B.S. in biology and chemistry. In order to achieve control in output, it was paramount that all question analyses and searches, especially for one given question, be consistent, otherwise they would not be comparable. To ensure maximum possible consistency, elaborate computer-aided and manual examinations were initiated, after all searches for the 124 questions were completed. Every search for every question was checked for consistency in scope and exhaustivity against other searches for that question, as well as for similarities in analysis with other questions. All errors were eventually corrected and, where necessary, new searches were initiated. It was surprising to find that, although every attempt was made to be consistent at the outset, a large number of inconsistencies were found and had to be corrected. Initially, there were 4091 search statements written for the 124 questions. After these search statements were checked, 2,590 had to be corrected and re-run, and 356 new search statements had to be run; thus, a total of 2,947 additional searches were run. At the end, 4,448 search statements were included as correct in the final analysis. This output control examination demonstrated that, even when considerable care is taken, question analysis and construction of search strategy may be subject to great human inconsistency.

5.5 Relevance Judgments

For each question the outputs (answers) from all searches were merged and a union of unique documents as answers was formed for submission to the user, thus establishing the univerisal set. The answers were presented to the user separately in three formats: titles, abstracts and full texts. He was not to proceed on judgment on the longer format unless he had finished all judgments on the shorter format. In the accompanying instructions, the user was asked to judge the relevance of each answer in relation to his query in accordance with a three point relevance scale: Relevant (R), Partially Relevant (P) and Nonrelevant (N). The following definitions were provided:

"A *relevant document* is any document which on the basis of the information it conveys, is considered to be related to your (user's) question even if the information is outdated or familiar to you.

A *partially relevant document* is any document which on the basis of the information it conveys is considered only somewhat or in some part related to your question or to any part of your question.

A *nonrelevant document* is any document which, on the basis of the information it conveys, is not at all related to your question."

A listing of document accession numbers for each format was provided; the user recorded his judgment on the listings and returned them to CSL. These relevance judgments, which established the user's relevant set for each query, served as a measuring instrument in comparing the performance of the variables within the system, and formed the basis for analysis of results. However, there were some unexpected restrictions on relevance judgments as explained below.

Although the CSL methodology and design called for all relevance judgments to be performed by the users, certain operational deficiencies prevented this. At the time users' questions were submitted, only three index files (A, B and C representing the indexing language Telegraphic Abstracts indexed respectively from titles, abstracts and full texts) were fully completed. The other six files were at various stages of completion, because the operational problems of indexing, encoding and compiling of dictionaries were more time consuming than expected. Under these circumstances it was decided not to wait for completion of the other six files, but to search comprehensively the available three files and submit the answers retrieved from those three files to users for evaluation. It was hoped that (a) there would be an insignificant number of additional (and therefore nonevaluated) documents retrieved from the other six files, and (b) whatever was retrieved in addition would not be relevant. The first assumption proved to be false and the second assumption was correct. Namely, after the six files were completed and searched, a considerable number of additional documents were retrieved. This was the situation:

1. In answer to *124 questions* posed by *24 users* the files A, B, and C retrieved *1,518 answers;* these were sent to *and* returned by the users;
2. After searching the other 6 index files an additional *1,108 answers* were retrieved; these answers were not evaluated by the users;
3. Thus, the total output at the source was *2,626 answers* of which *58% was evaluated* by the users.

The problem of what to do with the 1,108 non-evaluated documents presented itself. A method was developed by which an expert in biomedical communication (expert, by virtue of educational background and some 10 years of professional experience) interpolated the relevance judgments of the users with the non-evaluated answers; taking each query and the set of user's evaluations for that query as a standard, he interpolated what the user's judgment would be on the set of non-evaluated answers for that query. Furthermore, another independent method of interpolation was applied as a control: Textual similarities between the evaluated and nonevaluated answers for each query were studied and interpolations were made on the basis of the presence or absence of similarities; (the latter method is described by Gifford and Baumanis (7)). By both methods it was found that of the 1,108 non-evaluated answers, 6 were Relevant, 7 were Partially Relevant and 1,095 were Nonrelevant.

At the end, we were satisfied that we received an excellent approximation of user judgments through interpolation. Interestingly, the addition of different index files produced a magnitude of additional retrievals, almost all of which were nonrelevant. This demonstrates that the files basically responded equivalently in the retrieval of relevant answers, but there were large symmetric differences in the retrieval of nonrelevant answers. These differences, by and large, could be ascribed to the decisions of indexers to index or not to index peripheral terms from documents.

There was another operational problem associated with relevance judgments imposed by necessity. Three users who submitted twenty-five questions indicated a willingness to devote only a limited amount of their time to the evaluation of answers. In order to accommodate those users, only the full texts of documents were sent to them for evaluation. Since the final analysis was made from the full-text relevance judgments, this limitation had no effect on any of the variables except "format of output." Thus, data from 99 questions were used for analysis of the results of the variable "format of output" and data from 124 questions were used for all other variables.

5.6 *Answers*

There were altogether 2,626 answers retrieved (i.e., one question could have 15 answers, the other 30 answers, etc.; when all the answers were added over 124 questions,

2,626 answers were obtained). Of these, based on judgment from *full text,* there were:

249 Relevant (R)
139 Partially Relevant (P)
2,238 Not Relevant (N)

This is the standard against which the performance of all variables (except "format of output") was measured.

Of the 600 documents in the file, 540 documents (90% of the files) appeared or were retrieved as answers; in other words, the 2,626 answers were produced by 540 documents. The 388 relevant and partially relevant answers were produced by 209 documents (30% of the file). Thus, the answers were not associated with a small portion of the file, showing that questions and documents were diversified.

The distribution of the *total* (R + P + N) number of answers retrieved in relation to questions, was as follows:

31 questions had between 1 to   5 answers
23 questions had between 6 to 10 answers
34 questions had between 11 to 20 answers
18 questions had between 21 to 40 answers
12 questions had between 41 to 80 answers
 6 questions had between 81 to 160 answers

The distribution of the number of answers judged relevant (R) in relation to questions was as follows:

61 questions had no R answers
51 questions had between 1 to 5 R answers
 8 questions had between 6 to 10 R answers
 3 questions had between 11 to 20 R answers
 1 question had between 21 to 40 R answers

As can be seen, almost one-half of all questions had no relevant answers. Obviously with respect to these questions the system variables performed "badly", because no answers should have been retrieved — this is reflected in the analysis of results. Of the remaining questions, eighty per cent had between one and five relevant answers. This may indicate that the users, in general, were quite stringent in their judgment as specialists usually are, and that whatever was judged as relevant indeed was relevant.

5.7 *Control-Related Experiments*

A series of control-related experiments and studies were carried out in order to recognize source factors that substantially contribute to variations of results, and in order to learn more about the interaction among factors. For brevity these control-related experiments and studies are only enumerated here and not elaborated, although some results have been mentioned (e.g. indexers' and coders' consistency). A full description can be found in (6). The general conclusions at the end of this paper do take into account the results from these studies. The control experiments and studies included: a study of indexers and indexing consistency; an analysis of variations in length of indexes and thesauri; a study of coders and coding consistency; a study of characteristics of the *TDB* index and of the relation between indexes constructed for manual and machine searching; an analysis of the consistency of question analysis and of searching; a study on the reliability of relevance interpolation from users' judgments to a judgment by an expert; an analysis of sources of differences in results between index files; an analysis of index term frequencies; a study on the validation of a thesaurus; a study on the relation between text of questions and text of relevant and nonrelevant documents; an exploration of procedures for optimization of search strategies; and a study of the nature of questions obtained in relation to the nature of the file.

6. Results

6.1 Method of Analysis

The method of analysis was quite simple, and it followed the notion that comparative results were to be obtained. No statistical tests were employed, including taking of means, because it was felt that the data on hand did not satisfy the basic assumptions under which those kinds of tests are run — most notably, the independence of data, which is required for most interesting statistical tests, could not be assumed.

The method of analysis for *one* given question consisted of comparing the output (number of R, P, and N answers) obtained from each variable to the universal set for that question. The universal set was, as mentioned, the union of all outputs obtained for that question. In addition, outputs for some variables were combined in a union and compared to other combinations of variables or to the universal set. For example, the union of output for all title-based files was composed to the union of output for abstract-based files or to full-text based files; the union of output for all three Telegraphic Abstract Files was compared to the union of output for all three Keyword files; the union of output for all question analysis types was compared to the output for broad search, etc.

The method of analysis for *all* questions consisted of adding the output for individual variables or their combinations from each question and comparing that sum to the total output. As mentioned, the total output for 124 questoins was 2,626 answers, or 249 R, 139 P and 2,238 N answers. The measures were calculated after the sums for each variable were obtained; thus, the measures do not indicate means, but indicate proportions of the total output. In order to simplify the presentation of measures, the partially relevant answers are treated together with non-relevant ones. The standard for calculation of comparative measures then becomes:

249 Relevant answers
2377 Partially relevant and non-relevant answers (P + N)

Since these judgments were made from full texts, all the analysis are based on full-text judgments.

It should be noted that the total number of answers is also an extremely powerful indicator of the magnitude of retrieval caused by a variable. In the design of systems the magnitude of expected retrieval is an extremely important criterion affecting many design decisions. For the users the total size of output expected is also an important consideration. Moreover, this simple measure is an objective indication of quantitative performance, because it does not depend on relevance judgments; however, it certainly does not indicate the quality of performance.

6.2 Sources of Input

Table I compares the results obtained from title-, abstract- and full text-based index files which had indexes of previously stated lengths. In order to concentrate only on this one variable, the results from files based on identical sources were combined; thus, results for titles are from the union of outputs of the four title-based index files (A, D, G, H); for abstracts, from the union of files B, E, and K; and for full texts, from the union of files C and F. The results are shown as obtained from narrow searches (union of all question analysis types) and from the broad searches. The last row indicates the results from the union of output of all nine index files. (In reading the table note that the values for effectiveness were calculated from values of sensitivity and specificity *prior* to rounding them to the second decimal point; thus, on occasion the presented Es values may display a discrepancy from values which would have been obtained if Es were calculated from the rounded Se and Sp values.)

249 Relevant answers
2377 Partially relevant and non-relevant answers (P + N)

Some interesting observations and relations emerge. The ratio of *index lengths* between titles, abstracts, and full texts was approximately

$$1 : 4 : 6.$$

The ratio of the *total outputs* (T) between title-, abstract- and full text-based files was approximately

1 : 4 : 7 for narrow searches and
1 : 3 : 5 for broad searches.

The ratio of *Relevant + Partially Relevant answers* (R) for the same files was approximately

1 : 3 : 4 for both broad and narrow searches.

TABLE I

COMPARATIVE PERFORMANCE OF TITLE-, ABSTRACT-, AND
FULL TEXT-BASED FILES

Union of index files based on:	Narrow Searches			Broad Searches		
	Total	R,P,N	Se,Sp,Es	Total	R,P,N	Se,Sp,Es
Titles	113	51 11 51	.20 .97 .17	533	91 28 414	.37 .81 .17
Abstracts	503	147 56 300	.59 .85 .44	1666	199 98 1366	.80 .38 .18
Full Texts	754	181 70 503	.73 .76 .48	2322	238 125 1959	.96 .12 .07
All 9 Files	871	197 83 591	.79 .72 .50	2626	249 139 2238	1.00 0.00 0.00

Legend:

Narrow searches: union of all question analysis types.

Total: total number of answers retrieved.

R,P,N: respective numbers of relevant, partially relevant and non-relevant answers retrieved.

Se,Sp,Es: respective measures of Sensitivity, Specificity, and Effectiveness.

And the ratio of *Nonrelevant* answers (N) for the same files was approximately

$$1 : 6 : 10 \text{ for narrow searches and}$$
$$1 : 3 : 5 \text{ for broad searches.}$$

Thus, most interestingly, taking x as the length of indexes and an independent variable, all three values (T, R, and N) behaved in a remarkably linear fashion; T, R and N could be approximated by the simple equation,

$$y = ax + b$$

where a and b are constants and x is the length of indexes. In particular:

$$T = a_1 x + b_1$$
$$N = a_2 x + b_2$$
$$R = a_3 x + b_3$$

By using the data from this experiment it can be calculated that the constants, a_1, a_2, and a_3, are related approximately as:

$$a_1 \approx 1.5 a_2 \approx 3 a_3$$
$$\text{or, } a_1 \approx 3 a_3$$
$$a_2 \approx 2 a_3.$$

In general then it seems that a linear increase in the length of indexes provides a linear increase in the total number of answers, as well as in the number of relevant and nonrelevant answers from a retrieval system. However, the *coefficient* of increase is largest for the total output, somewhat smaller (approximately 1/3 smaller) for the nonrelevant answers, and considerably smaller (approximately 2/3 smaller) for the relevant answers. As indexes increase in length, we may say that N-times longer indexes will probably produce N-times larger outputs retrieved. Furthermore, it seems that the longer the indexes, the more relevant answers will be retrieved, but together with many more nonrelevant answers, too.

In relation to measures, it can be seen that *Sensitivity* rises for narrow searches from .20 (title-files) to .59 (abstract-files) to .73 (full text-files) and for the broad searches from .37 to .80 to .96, respectively a very significant increase throughout. At the same time for the same files, *Specificity* drops for narrow searches from .97 to .86 to .76 and for broad searches from .81 to .41 to .12 — a very significant decrease throughout. Thus, for the respective files *Effectiveness* increases for narrow searches from .17 to .45 to .48, and decreases for broad searches from .17 to .20 to a very low of .07. Over-all then, the abstract-based index files (between twenty-three and thirty index terms in length) were most effective.

In any case, even at a glance it can be seen that the variation in sources of input (i.e. length of indexes) produced a considerable variation in results. With respect to this variable, the null-hypothesis can be rejected.

6.3 Indexing Languages

Table II compares the results obtained from the four indexing languages in which titles have been indexed; Table III compares the three indexing languages in

TABLE II

COMPARATIVE PERFORMANCE OF THE FOUR INDEXING
LANGUAGES USED IN INDEXING OF TITLES

Indexing Language	Narrow Searches			Broad Searches		
	Total	R,P,N	Se,Sp,Es	Total	R,P,N	Se,Sp,Es
Telegraphic Abstracts (File A)	98	46 9 43	.18 .98 .16	507	87 26 394	.35 .82 .17
Keywords (File D)	96	42 9 45	.17 .98 .14	497	83 24 390	.33 .83 .15
Keywords by Computer (File G)	92	40 10 42	.16 .98 .13	491	78 25 388	.31 .83 .13
Meta Language (File H)	99	45 10 44	.18 .98 .15	499	87 25 387	.35 .83 .17

TABLE III

COMPARATIVE PERFORMANCE OF THE THREE INDEXING
LANGUAGES USED IN INDEXING OF ABSTRACTS

Indexing Language	Narrow Searches			Broad Searches		
	Total	R,P,N	Se,Sp,Es	Total	R,P,N	Se,Sp,Es
Telegraphic Abstracts (File B)	340	120 39 181	.48 .91 .38	1274	178 84 1012	.71 .54 .25
Keywords (File E)	419	130 46 243	.52 .88 .40	1464	186 82 1196	.75 .46 .20
Tropical Disease Bulletin Index (File K)	122	55 11 56	.22 .97 .19	653	101 32 520	.41 .77 .17

TABLE IV

COMPARATIVE PERFORMANCE OF THE TWO INDEXING
LANGUAGE USED IN INDEXING OF FULL TEXTS

Indexing Language	Narrow Searches			Broad Searches		
	Total	R,P,N	Se,Sp,Es	Total	R,P,N	Se,Sp,Es
Telegraphic Abstracts (File C)	547	169 63 315	.68 .84 .51	1863	228 120 1515	.92 .31 .22
Keywords (File F)	536	133 44 359	.53 .83 .36	1750	193 85 1472	.78 .34 .11

which abstracts have been indexed; Table IV compares the two indexing languages in which full texts have been indexed; Table V compares the union of output from the three files (A, B, C) representing Telegraphic Ab-

stracts as an indexing language with the union of output from the three files (D, E, F) representing Keywords by humans. The results are shown as obtained from narrow and from broad searches. For comparison

TABLE V

COMPARATIVE PERFORMANCE OF TWO INDEXING LANGUAGES:
TELEGRAPHIC ABSTRACTS AND KEYWORDS

Indexing language	Narrow Searches			Broad Searches		
	Total	R,P,N	Se,Sp,Es	Total	R,P,N	Se,Sp,Es
Telegraphic Abstracts (Union of files A, B, C)	625	187 72 368	.74 .81 .55	2080	243 134 1703	.98 .23 .20
Keywords (Union of files D, E, F)	673	163 61 449	.65 .79 .43	2113	221 104 1788	.89 .20 .09

between these outputs and the total output from all files see the last row of Table I, showing the results obtained from the union of all nine index files.

The results indicate that the four different indexing languages which were indexed from titles (Table II) showed remarkably equivalent performance. It seems that regardless of how titles are indexed the performance is the same. Of the three indexing languages indexed from abstracts (Table III), the first two (TA and KW) showed some slight differences in performance, where the Keywords performed higher, but the third language (*TDB Index*) was considerably lower. The explanation is simple: while the first two languages had indexes of approximately twenty-three to thirty terms, *TDB Index* had only eleven to twelve terms per index, and the results reflect this difference. The two indexing languages on full texts (TA and KW) performed differently, this time TA performed higher. For the same two languages the differences were much more pronounced from full texts than from abstracts and there were no differences from titles.

The overall performance of Telegraphic Abstracts and Keywords (Table V) did not differ very much, although of the two, the Telegraphic Abstracts performed somewhat better. However, from this slightly better performance we cannot conclude that it was due entirely to the ability of one indexing language over the other rather than to a combination of factors. It was seen that as the source of indexing lengthens the performance differences between languages increase; as a matter of fact, it can be seen that whatever differences occurred they stemmed from full texts as the source.

A separate analysis of factors contributing to differences in results between full-text files (File C, Telegraphic Abstracts, and File F, Keywords) was undertaken in order to illuminate the problem. Taking symmetric differences, it was found that File C retrieved forty-five relevant answers that were not retrieved by File F, and File F retrieved ten relevant answers that were not retrieved by File C. The causes for File F missing the forty-five relevant answers were studied. For each missing answer, the following were examined and compared, in the order of their listing: the text of the

question, both indexes (C and F), all related search statements for both files, and the text of documents. As far as the causes could be distinguished, the best assessment of them is as follows:

Cause of Non-Retrieval	Number of Incidents	Proportion of All Causes
a. Indexer did not index an important term	23	.51
b. Indexer did not index a term but could not have been clearly required to do so	14	.31
c. Question analyst did not search for a near synonym	5	.12
d. Ambiguous code and dictionary error	2	.04
e. Computer error	1	.02
	45	1.00

Thus, the majority (fifty-one percent) of incidents could be attributed entirely to the decision of the indexer not to index a term. A combination of indexers' decisions and limitations of the indexing language contributes approximately thirty-one percent to the causes for missing the documents. Thus, eighty-one percent of the misses is in one way or another attributable to indexers. With all the care that was taken in controlling question analysis, it still contributed to twelve percent of the misses. Thus, ninety-eight percent of the misses can be attributed to human decision-making at various stages and in various functions of the system.

A major disappointment was that Telegraphic Abstracts did not perform better in suppression of non-relevant answers, because the role indicators (roles) and levels (links) were built-in precisely for that purpose. An analysis revealed that this happened because the syntax of roles and links could not be utilized in searching — the questions are simply not asked that way. Role indicators were originally used in only 10 of the 124 questions; upon re-examination an additional 5 questions were found; they originally had not been used but clearly could have used some role indicators. Of the fifteen, only five questions produced answers with a significant suppression of nonrelevant answers. In general, when used, role indicators have a certain power to suppress nonrelevant answers, but they can be used quite rarely; furthermore, when used, there is a danger of simultaneous suppression of relevant answers.

Thus, the evidence gathered on indexing languages is not conclusive. However, it may be possible that the indexing languages, as defined, indeed do not make a substantial difference; whatever difference does exist seems to be a complex combination of a number of factors of which the indexing language is just one, and it seems to be a minor one at that.

6.4 Question Analysis and Search Strategy

Table VI presents the comparative performance of the five question analysis types which were searched as narrow searches and the broad search; various question analysis types are denoted by letters, and the union output from all question analysis types is denoted by U(QA).

the size of output. Again, it was observed that an almost linear relationship exists between the total output and the number of relevant and nonrelevant answers. It is interesting to note that when only the terms from the question were used without any elaboration (QA(A)) only approximately thirty-five percent of all relevant documents were retrieved and approximately every second document retrieved was nonrelevant. By using elaborate analysis procedures (QA(D)), we were able to approximately double the retrieval of relevant documents as compared to QA(A)), but then only every fourth document was relevant. The low performance of QA(A) suggests that questions need elaboration at all times.

The elaboration of questions by the use of the available thesaurus proved to be somewhat disappointing. Only when any other tool, including personal knowledge, was used for elaboration did the performance rise sharply. Thus, it seems that a question analysis should not depend only on the thesaurus of the type employed. Either more powerful thesauri are needed or a thesaurus-

TABLE VI

COMPARATIVE PERFORMANCE OF THE FIVE QUESTION ANALYSIS (QA) TYPES AS NARROW SEARCHES AND BROAD SEARCHES

| | Narrow Searches | | | | | | Broad Searches |
	QA(A)	QA(B)	QA(C)	QA(D)	QA(E)	U(QA)	
Total	261	369	768	853	755	871	2626
R	106	130	180	192	184	197	249
P	31	42	79	83	73	83	139
N	124	197	509	558	498	591	2238
Se	.43	.52	.72	.77	.74	.79	1.00
Sp	.93	.90	.75	.73	.76	.72	0.00
Es	.35	.42	.47	.50	.49	.50	0.00

Legend:
QA(A): question analysis Type A: terms from question only
QA(B): QA(A) plus expansion of terms through thesaurus
QA(C): QA(A) plus expansion through any other source but thesaurus
QA(D): QA(C) plus expansion through thesaurus
QA(E): Verification of all analysis by the user
U(QA): Union of output from all QA types

In itself, there was nothing significant in the particular method for or definition of question analysis types employed. They were thought of first, as being merely representative of many types of methods of analyses available, and second, as allowing for an orderly differentiation in results, especially in comparing the utilization of the available thesaurus. However, the magnitude of effects of different question analysis types employed was one of the surprising findings. For instance, the size of total output rose from QA(A) to the union of all question analysis types as 1 : 1.3 : 3 : 3.3 : 3 : 3.5. The rise is impressive: from the lowest 261 answers for QA(A), to the highest, 833 answers for QA(D). Sensitivity rose and Specificity fell in a direct relationship to

based analysis should always supplement personal knowledge and the utilization of other tools. Two aspects should be mentioned. First, only one function of a thesaurus was tested, namely its use in question analysis. Clearly a thesaurus has many other functions, especially in input, which were not tested. Second, the major single cost in time and effort in this experiment was the construction and maintenance of the thesaurus — the results should also be interpreted with this cost-factor in mind.

Another aspect tested was the validation of expanded terms by the users. Strangely enough, the contact with the users (QA(E)) evidently produced the dropping of some expanded terms from previous analysis types, and consequently fewer relevant documents were retrieved

— as carried out, the interview with users did not prove to be beneficial. However, this does not mean that a contact with users in general is not beneficial. It merely means that the way it was conducted was *not* successful.

Let us now turn to the effects of different search strategy levels. A somewhat disappointing finding was that, comparatively speaking, the number of *relevant* documents retrieved (and therefore also the measure of sensitivity) by any, even the most powerful, QA type (i.e. narrow search strategy level) did not come near to the number retrieved by the broad search. Regardless of how the question terms were elaborated upon, relevant documents were missed. We were confident that by judicious expansion of question terms we would be able to retrieve almost all relevant documents. However, by broadening the search in all instances a greater number of relevant documents was retrieved. This, of course, was achieved at a considerable price in retrieval of non-relevant documents. As a matter of fact, the price was found to be staggering: The broad searches retrieved approximately four times as many nonrelevant documents as the union of all QA types in order to retrieve approximately one-quarter to one-fifth more relevant documents than U(QA). Thus, there seems to be the following rule: As the retrieval of relevant answers works its way asymptotically to its maximum, the retrieval of nonrelevant ones soars almost exponentially. Completeness seems to exact a very high price. This also explains the source of the majority of nonrelevant answers in this experiment.

6.5 Relevance judgments on different formats of output

As mentioned previously, in analysis of results formats of output were treated separately from the other variables. Excluded from analysis of this variable are all the interpolated relevance judgments and obviously the questions for which only full texts of documents were sent to users. The analysis is performed on the data from ninety-nine questions submitted by twenty-two users. In response to these questions, users received 1,086 answers for judgment, receiving first titles, then abstracts, and finally full texts. Ability of users to recognize relevance from shorter formats in comparison to full-text judgment is analyzed — full text judgments are taken as the standard for comparison. Titles were submitted together with bibliographic citations; titles contained on the average some five to nine words. Abstracts were photocopies from *Tropical Disease Bulletin;* they included titles and bibliographic citations and on the average contained 250 to 400 words. Full texts were photocopies of original journal articles and on the average they contained 2,000 to 4,000 words.

It may be of interest to discuss the assumptions underlying the test of this particular variable. The full text provides the maximum length and maximum information available; thus the judgment of the full text was taken as final. If so, then the user's judgment of the shorter representations, titles and abstracts, can be expected to differ occasionally; in a sense, to "err" in two directions: leniency or strictness. Such "errors" seem to indicate an inability on the part of the user to determine final relevance from the shorter representations. This should not, however, be construed as a test of the user. Naturally, the user's ability is largely dependent upon the degree to which shorter formats accurately represent the content of the full text. In a sense, we may consider this as a user's performance on shorter formats.

The above reasoning rests on three additional assumptions: first, that a user does make the judgment on the text content of a shorter representation and not occasionally on some other clues, such as author, journal, date; second, that the judgment on each document in the set is entirely independent of judgments on other documents in the set; and third, that the manner of presentation of the sets of documents of differing formats made it possible for the judgments on one format to be independent of other formats, i.e., that the users followed the instructions fully.

The judgments were distributed over the three formats as follows:

| | No. of Answers | | | |
	Judged Relevant	Partially Relevant	Relevant	Total
Titles	167	157	762	1086
Abstracts	175	169	742	1086
Full Text	207	156	723	1086

These data, of course, do not provide a complete picture of the ability of the users to determine relevance from shorter formats, because they provide only the totals and do not indicate whether the actual membership of the set of answers judged relevant varies from format to format. Thus, for each pair of formats it was necessary to tabulate the changes of all possible relevance judgments as generally indicated by section A in Table VII; the entries in the cells represent the number of answers judged R(or P orN) on the shorter format that were judged R(or P or N) on the full text. For example: entry R-R denotes the number of answer judged relevant in full texts. The diagonal cells represent no change, and all other cells represent change of judgment from shorter to longer format. Section B of Table VII shows the changes in relevance judgments between titles and full texts and Section C between abstracts and full texts.

In order to express the data as proportions of full text judgments, we have chosen to express the users' ability to determine relevance or nonrelevance of answers by the same measures as used previously on systems performance:

Sensitivity measures the users' ability to recognize nonrelevant answers by their titles or abstracts in comparison with full texts (ratio of R-R and R on full text)

Specificity measures the users' ability to recognize nonrelevant answers by their titles or abstracts in comparison with full texts (ratio of N-N and N on full text)

Effectiveness = Se + Sp-1

In order to simplify the calculations, the partially relevant answers were counted together with nonrelevant ones. The results are as follows:

	Se	Sp	Es
Titles	.63	.96	.59
Abstracts	.77	.98	.75

TABLE VII

Changes of Relevance Judgment: A—Schematic Diagram of all Possible Changes Between a Shorter Format and Full Text Judgments. B—Changes Between Title and Full Text Judgments. C—Changes Between Abstract and Full Text Judgments

		Judgments on Full Texts (Final Judgment)		
		R	P	N
Judgments on Shorter	R	R-R	R-P	R-N
Representation	P	P-R	P-P	P-N
(or 1st Judgments)	N	N-R	N-P	N-N

		Full Text Judgments		
		207 R	156 P	723 N
Title Judgments	167 R	131	13	23
	157 P	33	95	29
	762 N	43	48	671

		Full Text Judgments		
		207 R	156 P	723 N
Abstract Judgments	175 R	160	3	12
	169 P	23	125	21
	742 N	24	28	690

An overall analysis revealed that of 1,086 answers judged, 843 or 78% had the same judgment (either R or P or N) on all three formats; 879 or 85% had the same judgment on titles as on full texts; and 975 or 90% had the same judgment on abstracts as on full texts. Thus, the answers that had different judgments on different formats constitute 22% of the total or 243 answers — over one-fifth of the output had different judgments on different formats.

However, the analysis of the measures used reveals an interesting and different picture: The judgment of what is relevant had a considerably lower percentage of agreement than of what is nonrelevant. Hence, the relatively high over-all agreement is more attributable to a high agreement of what is nonrelevant that of what is relevant. The measure of sensitivity reveals that the users recognized, in comparison with full texts, approximately two-thirds of relevant answers from titles and three-fourths from abstracts. At the same time they recognized ninety-six per cent of nonrelevant answers from titles and ninety-eight per cent from abstracts.

Let us now compare user and system performance on different document formats. This comparison may be intriguing because we can argue that it may be unreasonable to expect a system to perform any better than a user in determining relevance from a shorter format, but it might be desirable that a system perform as well as a user. In terms of specific data from this experiment, the sensitivity of users on titles was .63 and the highest sensitivity of title-based index files was .37 achieved by the broad search. The sensitivity of users on abstracts was .77 and the highest sensitivity of abstract-based files was .80. Thus, in recognition of relevant answers the users performed considerably better on titles than systems performed, probably because the users can read "to or from" the titles and accompanying bibliographic citation. It would be desirable to bring up the performance of title-based files to users' level. Both users and systems performed approximately the same on abstracts. Thus, the abstract-based files seemed to have reached their limit. But regarding specificity, or recognition of nonrelevant answers, users were considerably and significantly better than systems in all cases; essentially there was no contest. Obviously it would be highly desirable to bring the overall effectiveness of systems to that of users — at present, achievement of this goal seems highly unlikely.

Although not investigated in this experiment, cost consideration should be interpreted together with these results. It is clear that the cost of supplying titles or abstracts is so much lower than that of supplying full texts. Since the losses in false relevance judgments are really not that great, (approximately one-third on titles and one-fifth on abstracts) shorter formats may indeed be a desirable form of output, especially since we may expect that a large proportion of the output from a system to be nonrelevant anyway. The cost of throwing away nonrelevant titles or abstracts is much less than that of throwing away full text.

In conclusion, it seems evident that different formats significantly affect users' relevance judgments and, thus, the part of the null hypothesis dealing with formats of output can be rejected.

7. General Conclusions

The summary includes those conclusions made on the basis of selected results reported in this paper, as well as conclusions from other results presented in the Final Report of the Comparative Systems Laboratory:

1. The human factor, the variations introduced by human decision-making, seems to be the overwhelming variable, the major influencing factor affecting the performance of every and all components of an information retrieval (IR) system.

2. The output components — handling of questions, method of question analysis, and construction of logical statements for searching — seem to be as important in their effect on performance of IR systems, if not even more important, as input components; as a matter of fact, the output components can be termed the major components of a retrieval system.

3. The length of indexes (i.e., variation in number of index terms per index as produced from titles, abstracts, or full texts) seems to affect the performance considerably more than do the indexing languages; given the same length (often termed "depth") various indexing languages tend to perform at an equivalent level. Titles, regardless of how they are indexed by a system, seem to be quite inadequate beyond providing a general alerting service but quite adequate for relevance judgment by users.

4. The syntactic features of indexing languages (roles, links) do not reduce retrieval of nonrelevant answers over-all; in rare isolated and specific instances they may do so; however, for most questions they simply cannot be utilized in searching. The actual and transformational syntax of questions and the simplified syntax as specified by roles and links do not coincide to any great extent.

5. It seems that no expansion of question terms (by connecting any number of related terms by logical "or's" as done by various question analysis types) can insure retrieval from the file of all existing relevant answers.

6. It seems that all existing relevant answers can be retrieved only by broad searches, that is, by dropping of terms (or string of terms) connected by logical "and's"; however, the price in re-

trieval of nonrelevant answers in that case is considerable, almost unbearable.

7. Questions cannot be searched as stated — the performance is too low. Expansion of question terms is needed as a rule. Expansion through a thesaurus (as constructed in CSL) alone does not add a sufficient number of related terms. It seems that expansion is best achieved when every tool available is used, including personal knowledge, and then a thesaurus is used for further expansion. Construction of a thesaurus may be considered the single most costly aspect in the development of a retrieval system.

8. The contact with users (as conducted in CSL), in order to validate and expand on question terms, did not improve the system performance; as a matter of fact and quite surprisingly, it slightly decreased the performance.

9. It seems that there is a relatively close phraseological connection between the texts of questions and the texts of documents judged relevant by users, a connection which could not be found between questions and documents judged nonrelevant by users — even though the system retrieved both (relevant and nonrelevant) as answers; the system did not recognize these connections very well.

10. The format of output (e.g., titles, abstracts, full texts) seems to influence significantly the users' relevance judgment. Users can make a much higher estimate on what is relevant from titles than systems can in comparison to a full text relevance judgment.

11. It seems that the performance of retrieval systems could be optimized through judicious and complex work on search statements; however, and unfortunately, the method for optimization cannot be stated in general terms, but only described from question to question. An optimization seems to be possible, but a useful generalization as to what that optimization involves is elusive.

12. The handling of questions, i.e., elaboration of all related terms by which a concept could be expressed, and the construction of an adequate search statement, are costly, time-consuming, elaborate, tedious, error-prone but unmistakably necessary jobs. Without a doubt retrieval system needs to have designed into its operations elaborate procedures and adequate capacity in terms of people, cost, time, etc., for the handling of questions.

13. At present it seems that retrieval systems, regardless of their design, the claims of design, and technology involved, are able to perform only on a general level, failing to be at the same time specific and comprehensive; as a rule they produce

a tremendous amount of extraneous or nonrelevant material; their effectiveness is generally low. This is a fact of life that the researchers, designers, operators, users and funders should learn to live with, at least in the foreseeable future. The reasons for low effectiveness are not simple — they need thorough investigation. However, not all of the reasons are related to the system itself.

References

1. CLEVERDON, C., "The Cranfield Tests of Indexing Language Devices." *ASLIB Proceedings*, Vol. **19**, No. 6, pp. 173–194, 1967.

2. SALTON, G. and M. E. LESK, "Computer Evaluation of Indexing and Text Processing." *Journal of the Association for Computing Machinery*, Vol. **15**, No. 1, pp. 8–36 (1968).

3. LANCASTER, R. W. "MEDLARS: Report on the Evaluation of its Operating Efficiency." *American Documentation*, Vol. **20**, No. 2, pp. 119–142, 1969.

4. GOFFMAN, W. and V. A. NEWILL, "Methodology for Test and Evaluation of Information Retrieval Systems." *Information Storage and Retrieval*, Vol. **3**, No. 1, 19–25, 1966.

5. SARACEVIC, T. and L. ROTHENBERG, "Procedure." *Manuals for the Comparative Systems Laboratory Experiments*, CSL:TR-8, Center for Documentation and Communication Research, School of Library Science, Case Western Reserve University, Cleveland, Ohio 1967.

6. SARACEVIC, T. et al., *An Inquiry into Testing of Information Retrieval Systems*, CSL:Final Report, 3 Parts, Center for Documentation and Communication Research, School of Library Science, Case Western Reserve University, Cleveland, Ohio 1968.

7. GIFFORD, C. and G. J. BAUMANIS, "On Understanding User Choices: Textual Correlates of Relevance Judgments." *American Documentation*, Vol. **20**, No. 1, pp. 21–26, 1969.

62 Scientists Meet the KWIC Index

WILLIAM MANSFIELD ADAMS
LAURENCE C. LOCKLEY
American Documentation
Vol. 19, No. 1, January, 1968

1 Introduction

About 4 years ago, when the KWIC index devised by
Luhn (*2*) was being disseminated in the United States,
it was interesting to observe the response of scientists
exposed to this index for the first time. Some of the
scientists were exceptionally enthusiastic and lauded the
index—often before they even thoroughly understood its
use. At the other extreme, there were many who ad-
mitted their confusion when faced with the sorted and
assorted titles and phrases alleged to be an improved
index. There was wide disagreement concerning the
efficiency of the new index, but always there was agreement that it was different. As various denominations
and sects of indexers evolved, arose, and united, various
types of KWIC indexes came into existence, with so
many ramifications that it was sometimes a problem to
decide whether a given index was a standard subject index
or one of the new KWIC indexes. Thus in studying
KWIC indexes, not an insignificant problem is that of
defining the topics.

For our purposes, we consider a KWIC index to be a
presentation of titles ordered in such a fashion that

the title appears in the listing as many times as it has
significant words in the title. Its position in the listing
is alphabetical under each of the key words. This
alphabetical listing occurs in some formats about the
middle of the page, permitting those sections of the
title leading and following the significant word to be
presented to the user on the same line. The user is
directed to the item being indexed by a code word
terminating or preceding the line.

It is desirable to note that titles are sensitive to the
stage of the science covered by the journals being used.
For example, an older science must utilize many words
to delineate the narrow segment of the field upon which
work is being reported. In a youthful science, such as
seismology, it is not unusual to locate a paper with a
title as short as "The Earth's Mantle" (*3*). In an older
science, such as mathematics, it is not uncommon to
find a title as long as "On the Increase of Convergence
Rate of Relaxation Procedures for Elliptic Partial Differential Equations" (*4*).

There have been several motives for evaluating quantitatively the response of the scientist to this novel index.
It was amusing to see scientists, purportedly the epitome
of the "reasonably prudent man," become quite frustrated, confused, and emotional (sometimes almost

Hawaii Institute of Geophysics Contribution Nó. 210. This paper
is a condensation of a laboratory report (*1*).

violent) when faced with the new KWIC index—to such an extent had the format of the traditional subject index ingrained itself into their lives.

This paper describes the efforts to measure quantitatively the gradual evolution in attitudes of a group of scientists to the introduction of a KWIC index. For reasons of economy, and to provide a homogeneous population, a small society of scientists—defined by membership in the Seismological Society of America—has been utilized. The population of this Society number about 1,000.

Other features of the Seismological Society of America also made it favorable for study. One feature is that the Society is old, having been founded because of interests stimulated by the 1906 San Francisco earthquake. The journal of the Society, called the *Bulletin*, was begun in 1911. A history of the Society has recently been prepared by Perry Byerly (*5*), who served as secretary of the Society from 1931 to 1956.

Another favorable aspect of this group is that, in the entire 50-year publication history of the *Bulletin*, no index covering more than 1 year has ever been produced. Thus, any cumulative index developed in the course of the study would, as a "fringe benefit," supply the members with an index to their journal.

Yet another feature of the Society is the extremely high percentage of seismologists that are males. Indeed, in the entire world, there are probably less than 14 female earthquake seismologists. (Our apologies to the ladies, if we be wrong!)

The membership of the Society includes a significant percentage of persons not residing in the United States of America. These have been omitted from the study. The intent of the study was to limit the population to the male earthquake seismologists residing in the United States of America.

The difficulty of defining a KWIC index in general terms has already been mentioned. When one comes to grips with the problem of producing a KWIC index, then the number of details requiring specific decision becomes sizable. This aspect of the study was covered in a report entitled "A Comparison of Some Machine-Produced Indexes" (*6*).

2 Experimental Procedure

The experimental procedure used in this study consisted of introducing the scientists to the new type of index. Some time later, a poll was taken to determine the extent to which the scientists had become acquainted with the new index and the percentage of scientists preferring it to the standard subject index. (The same articles are reviewed in *Geophysical Abstracts* (*7*) which uses the traditional subject index method). This was followed two months later by an identical questionnaire requesting responses from those not responding to the earlier request. Shortly thereafter, one of the authors (Lockley) was the luncheon speaker at the annual meeting of the Society. His speech defined the information retrieval problem for the scientists and indicated the need for new tools. Six months after this "advertising," the KWIC index for the *Bulletin* of the Society was issued. A questionnaire was attached. This poll covered the same features as in the first poll.

On the basis of the sampling efforts just described, it is possible to determine the preference of the scientists for each of the two indexes—the traditional subject index and the KWIC index. Furthermore, it is possible to predict the percentage of scientists that will ultimately prefer the KWIC index, if all other factors remain constant. It is not possible to estimate the error of the prediction, however.

The experimental procedure (which has been outlined) will now be described in detail.

The problem that we are considering here is the change in attitude of a group of scientists towards a novel tool. It must be emphasized that "change" is the important aspect. This change occurs over time, so the study must involve samplings of attitude at various times. Consequently the experimental procedure has consisted of estimating the attitudes of the scientists at time intervals sufficiently great to allow attitudes to change significantly. Initially, the appropriate time interval must be estimated. Later it can be more suitably chosen, if necessary.

The *Bulletin* of the Society is a bimonthly publication, allowing the opportunity to sample with that frequency, at low cost. The convenience of sampling by inserting a postpaid questionnaire in the bimonthly *Bulletin* suggested that this time interval be used as the basic time interval.

For over 50 years it has been customary to publish an annual index to the contents of that year's *Bulletin*, in the last number of the year. To introduce the readers to the KWIC index, the 1963 annual index was made a KWIC index. (The index appeared in the December 1963 issue.) A description of the index and instructions on how to use it preceded the index.

It is important to note that the index code utilized in this KWIC index required that the user pass from a KWIC index to the bibliography index before going directly to the article itself. This is because the index code does not include the page number of the article. This is the only significant feature changed in the final cumulative KWIC index. In terms of the definitions of "preindex" and "postindex" given in an earlier paper (*8*), this KWIC index required the postindex of the bibliography index. It is not possible to exit directly from the KWIC index to the article.

No effort was made to bring this index to the attention of the members. It was listed in the table of contents by the page number; but no special costs were incurred to bring it before them. Indeed, the *Bulletin* had been printing computer listings directly by photo offset for several years so the reader was unlikely to even notice a stretch of several pages filled with reproductions of computer listings. Such reproductions have been used for earthquake catalogs and computation tables.

In 1964, a questionnaire was bound into the front of the February *Bulletin*. This was made noticeable by printing it on heavy-weight paper and placing it at the front. On this page was a note to the reader requesting his opinion of the annual index that had appeared 2 months earlier in the December issue as compared to earlier annual indexes of the traditional subject index type. The questionnaire included a postpaid card that could be torn out and answered by check marks. The only question requiring writing was that asking the reader in what other journals he had noticed the KWIC index. There was an additional space for remarks. A copy of the questionnaire is given as Fig. 1.

The response to this questionnaire was less than 10%

Bulletin of the
Seismological Society of America

EDITORIAL COMMITTEE

Wm. Mansfield Adams, Editor
John E. Nafe
Don Tocher

Dear Reader: Sometimes an editor needs the opinions of his readers for an important policy decision. I do now; will you please fill out this questionnaire, tear it out, and mail it back. No signature is required.

Sincerely,

Wm. Mansfield Adams
Editor

Did you look at the annual index which was included in the December, 1963 issue of the Bulletin of the Seismological Society of America? Yes........ No........ Don't know.........

Was it different from the indexes you are familiar with? Yes........ No........ Didn't notice.........

Do you think the index as it appeared in the December issue will be more convenient for your use than other types of indexes? More convenient........ Less convenient........ Can't say.........

The Bulletin of the Seismological Society of America will soon publish a 53-year cumulative index. Do you prefer that your copy be in the conventional form or in the new (KWIC) form? Prefer Conventional .... Prefer New Form........ No Preference.........

Did you have to go back and look at the December issue in order to answer the last question? Yes........ No.........

Have you published technical articles or papers? None........ One........ Two........ Three........ More than three.........

Have you noticed any other professional journals using the new (KWIC) form of index? Yes........ No.........

If yes, please list those you can remember...

....

....

....

Fig. 1. Form of questionnaire used in February 1964

but still much higher than the usual percentage (2%) for mail questionnaires. Seventy-two replies were received from the population. These results have been tabulated and are presented in matrix form as Table 1.

Notice that, of the questions used, the second serves to ascertain whether the index is actually novel to the member.

The most important question in the survey is that which concerns preference for the novel index. This is the third question. Notice that the fourth question serves to place material weight on the indicated preference. Thus, although as many people claim the KWIC index "more convenient" as claimed it "less convenient," more people expressed a desire to receive a convenient index rather than the KWIC form. It is assumed that the replies to question three may have been biased by a desire to "not disappoint the editor"!

The question devoted to inquiring the extent of publication of the members serves to separate the membership, in part, into innovators and followers. Unfortunately, no clear separation can be made between innovators and influencers, as was made by King (9) (see Discussion in this article). One may wish to assume that the innovators are influencers.

The last of the questions served to verify the second question. As has been emphasized by many students of preference surveys, it is important to know whether users are new users or repeat users. In the present case, it was expected that a large amount of education would be required to introduce the novel KWIC index.

In the following issue of the Bulletin (April) a post-paid return questionnaire was again inserted at the front. This requested the reader to return the questionnaire only if he had not replied earlier. The only method of separating these later questionnaires from the earlier ones was a change in the post office box number. It was thought that no member was likely to notice this change. Yet it permitted us to determine which questionnaire had been returned. The results were not numerous, and no use has been made of these data because of the next action.

In March of 1964, the annual meeting of the Seismological Society of America was held in Seattle, Washington. The results of the first survey, in February, were available and indicated that the study might stretch over an extensive period of time unless considerable education, equivalent to advertising, were done. As the annual meeting finds the dominant innovators and influencers together in one location, this opportunity to emphasize the value of studying the new index was exploited. This was done by two methods.

A survey was conducted with the help of two interviewers from the University of Washington, who were hired for the work. The purpose of the interviews was to force the discussion of indexes. The questions were ordered to go from a member's general professional interest in seismology to the specific number of the Bulletin that had appeared in February. The member was led to recall his own use of indexes and his need for convenient and thorough indexes. The interview then proceeded to a discussion comparing the traditional subject index and the novel KWIC index. The member was

TABLE 1. Table of results from February 1964 questionnaire

Answer No.	Q1 Yes	Q1 No	Q1 ?	Q2 Different Yes	Q2 No	Q2 ?	Q3 Conv. More	Q3 Less	Q3 ?	Q4 Prefer Conv.	Q4 New	Q4 ?	Q5 Yes	Q5 No	Q6 None	Q6 1	Q6 2	Q6 3	Q6 More	Q7 Yes	Q7 No
1 Yes	61	0	0	55	4	2	20	22	19	28	23	10	24	37	12	8	5	5	31	11	50
1 No		10	0	2	0	8	4	2	4	3	5	2	9	1	3	0	3	0	4	2	8
1 ?			1	0	0	1	0	0	1	1	0	0	0	1	1	0	0	0	0	0	1
2 Yes				57	0	0	20	23	14	28	23	6	25	32	12	8	4	5	28	9	48
2 No					4	0	1	0	3	0	1	3	0	4	0	0	1	0	3	2	2
2 ?						11	3	1	7	4	4	3	9	2	4	0	3	0	4	2	9
3 More							24	0	0	0	24	0	13	11	2	4	6	2	10	6	18
3 Less								24	0	24	0	0	9	15	7	2	2	0	13	3	21
3 ?									24	8	4	12	11	13	7	2	0	3	12	4	20
4 Conv.										32	0	0	12	20	9	3	2	0	18	4	28
4 New											28	0	16	12	3	5	6	3	11	6	22
4 ?												12	5	7	4	0	0	2	6	3	9
5 Yes													33	0	11	4	6	1	11	4	29
5 No														39	5	4	2	4	24	9	30
6 None															16	0	0	0	0	3	13
6 1																8	0	0	0	0	8
6 2																	8	0	0	2	6
6 3																		5	0	1	4
6 More																			35	7	28
7 Yes																				13	0
7 No																					59

finally asked to suggest both advantages and disadvantages of the novel index, using the subject index for comparison.

The last topics related to those on the earlier questionnaire postcard. The member was asked about his authorship of his professional articles and whether he had answered the questionnaire appearing in the February *Bulletin*.

The interview was conducted with the primary purpose of making the member realize his usage of indexes and the overall need for thinking about possible improvements in indexing.

The other action that was taken at the annual meeting to stimulate the interest of the members in indexes was a speech by Professor L. C. Lockley. At each annual meeting there is a luncheon meeting at which an invited speaker presents a talk on a subject of general interest. It was arranged for Professor Lockley to speak before the group at this time. In this talk, as in the interviews, the emphasis was on the need for scientists to improve indexes. The burgeoning of scientific publications and the size of the Library of Congress, among other things, were used as examples to emphasize the point. No preference for the novel index or the subject index was propounded, only the need for the scientist to be aware of the efforts being made, in his behalf, to facilitate his access to scientific literautre. The response of the membership to this talk was most enthusiastic and indicated that the point was well made.

The KWIC index was produced and issued to the membership in October 1964, as a special issue of the *Bulletin* (*10*). This time no author index, such as was presented in the annual index of December 1963, was included. It was thought that the bibliography index could be utilized satisfactorily. Now, however, the KWIC portion of the index did utilize a code which permitted direct exit from the KWIC index to the periodical of interest. As indicated in the illustration reproduced here as Fig. 2, the code on the right-hand side of the page gives the page number in the last four positions and the year of the volume (not the volume number) in the center of the code number between two hyphens. For example, the Los Angeles earthquake of July 16, 1920, the first article listed on the page illustrated, appeared in 1921 on page 63. Because the *Bulletin* was begun in 1911, it is very simple to determine the volume number from the year. The volume is obtained by subtracting 10 from the year. Thus, the volume that appeared in 1921 is Volume 11. The code utilized in the bibliography index of this 53-year cumulative index has the same code.

The KWIC index also included instructions on how to use the index. In particular, a list of references in which the reader could find alternative explanations on using such an index was given. It was even suggested that he might ask a colleague.

Another postpaid questionnaire was inserted at the front of the October issue of the *Bulletin*. This covered much the same aspects as the initial questionnaire. A copy of the form appears as Fig. 3 in this report. Notice that the request for a copy of an index in traditional form has been verified by a materialistically oriented question asking the amount that the member would pay. Again, the utilization of publications to separate innovators from followers has been used.

In reality, a subject index to the *Bulletin* already existed, as nearly every seismologist knew. The *Bulletin* is abstracted and included in the index of *Geophysical Abstracts*, which every seismologist had been using.

The results of this questionnaire are illustrated in Table 2 in the matrix format. In this matrix, there has been an additional category added for each question; it indicates no response. Consequently, all categories of a question should sum to the total number of responses.

From the responses to Question 2, it is immediately obvious that there has been a change in preference. This indication is verified by the responses to the third question. Additional confirmation, should such be deemed necessary, is also available from the fourth question. This question is related to materialistic aspects as opposed to the intellectual or emotional aspects of the other questions.

This section has described the procedures and presented the results of these investigations. Only qualitative interpretations have been given here; quantitative interpretations of the data presented here are given in the following section.

3 Analysis and Discussion

The problem we are considering here concerns human behavior. We are studying the response of a select group to a change in environment. The select group is the membership of the Seismological Society of America, and the change in environment is a novel index of the scientific literature. The conflict of the situation is in the selection of index to use. The member has a choice of using the traditional type index, such as *Geophysical Abstracts* (*7*), or of using the novel KWIC index.

For the purpose of studying the response of the group, the technical problem is to ascertain the ultimate preference of the group for each of the two types of indexes. This can be estimated by interrogating an individual member of the group at various times; hence, we conclude that a behavioral model is appropriate.

Mathematical models of a type suitable for the present situation have been developed for predicting the market performance of new products. A brief, nonmathematical review is given in Chapter 10, "Measuring and Predicting Marketing Behavior," of Buzzell (*11*). To apply such a theory, we consider the new type of index, the KWIC index, to be a new "product." The users of indexes (in the present experiment these are the members of the Seismological Society of America) are considered the "market." The market has been exposed heretofore, to other types of indexes.

Context	Keyword	Reference
THE	LOS-ANGELES EARTHQUAKES OF JULY 16, 1920	TABES -21-0063
Y OF EARTH MOVEMENTS IN	LOS-ANGELES HARBOR / PERIODICITY OF EARTH	LEYPH -38-0023
EVELS, 1919 TO 1927, IN	LOS-ANGELES HARBOR / VARIATIONS IN LEVELS	NICHGF-29-0200
OF COMPRESSION WAVES IN	LOSSY MEDIA / THE ATTENUATION OF COMPRESS	KNOPL -56-0047
H/ VELOCITIES OF MANTLE	LOVE AND RAYLEIGH WAVES OVER MULTIPLE PAT	TOKSMN-63-0741
S IN LAYER THICKNESS ON	LOVE WAVES / THE EFFECT OF VARIATIONS IN	DE-NJ -61-0227
NG AN INHOMO/ A NOTE ON	LOVE WAVES IN A HOMOGENEOUS CRUST OVERLYI	DEREH -62-0639
LLED POROUS SOLID.* II.	LOVE WAVES IN A POROUS LAYER / THE EFFECT	DEREH -61-0051
EARTHQUAKE OF AUGUST /	LOVE WAVES OF THE QUEEN CHARLOTTE ISLANDS	COULJ -52-0029
KE OF AUGUST 28, 1/ THE	LOVE WAVES OF THE SOUTH ATLANTIC EARTHQUA	WILSJT-40-0273
THE NORTH PACIFIC FROM	LOVE-WAVE DISPERSION / CRUSTAL STRUCTURE	DE-NJ -59-0331
THE PACIFIC BASIN	LOVE-WAVE DISPERSION AND THE STRUCTURE OF	EVERJF-54-0001
SHAW SEISMOGRAPH	LOW MAGNIFICATION ATTACHMENT FOR A MILNE-	PETEJH-39-0341
SOURCE IN A CYLINDRICAL	LOW VELOCITY MEDIUM / AZIMUTHAL ASYMMETRY	MEECWC-62-0139
THE LAYER OF RELATIVELY	LOW WAVE VELOCITY AT A DEPTH OF ABOUT 80	GUTEB -48-0121
ITH VISCOUS COUPLING/ A	LOW-COST VERTICAL-COMPONENT SEISMOGRAPH W	MCFAJ -41-0139
H-WAVE EVIDENCE FOR THE	LOW-VELOCITY ZONE IN THE MANTLE / RAYLEIG	TAKEH -59-0355
S)	LUMINOUS PHENOMENA OF EARTHQUAKES (LIGHT	BALLCM-13-0187
SOUTHERN CALIFORN/ THE	LUNAR TRIGGERING EFFECT ON EARTHQUAKES IN	ALLEMW-36-0147
PERSONAL RECORD OF ADA	M. TROTTER OF CERTAIN AFTERSHOCKS OF THE	LOUDGD-44-0199
ROGRAMS BY MEANS OF THE	M.I.T. DIFFERENTIAL ANALYZER / DETERMINAT	RUGEAC-43-0061
RTH CALCULATED FROM THE	MACELWANE P CURVE, 1933 / VELOCITY OF P W	DAHMCG-36-0001
ERIMENTS WITH A SHAKING	MACHINE / EXPERIMENTS WITH A SHAKING MACH	ROGEFJ-30-0147
S DIRECT FROM A SHAD/ A	MACHINE FOR REPRODUCING EARTHQUAKE MOTION	RUGEAC-36-0201
INTO FORCED VIBRATI/ A	MACHINE FOR SETTING STRUCTURES AND GROUND	BLUMJA-35-0361
DATA (COMPUTER)	MACHINE PROCESSING OF SEISMIC TRAVEL-TIME	BOLTBA-61-0259
ION OF FOCAL DEPTH FROM	MACROSEISMIC DATA / ON THE ESTIMATION OF	BLAKA -41-0225
ION OF FOCAL DEPTH FROM	MACROSEISMIC DATA / ON THE ESTIMATION OF	NEUBH -38-0259
ARTHQUAKES OF DECEMBER/	MACROSEISMIC STUDY OF THE NEW-HAMPSHIRE E	DEVLJJ-42-0067
S OF MARCH, 1937 A	MACROSEISMIC STUDY OF THE OHIO EARTHQUAKE	WESTAJ-40-0251
BER 1, 1930, IN THE NEW	MADRID REGION / THE EARTHQUAKES OF AUGUST	RAMIJE-31-0159
ION BETWEEN SEISMIC AND	MAGNETIC DISTURBANCES / THE RELATION BETW	HAZADL-18-0117
STATION AT THE HUANCAYO	MAGNETIC OBSERVATORY IN PERU / THE SEISMO	FLEMJA-32-0263
ISMIC AREAS AND SECULAR	MAGNETIC VARIATIONS / SEISMIC AREAS AND S	OMERGC-46-0021
STURBANCES ON SUSPENDED	MAGNETS / THE INFLUENCE OF EARTHQUAKE DIS	REIDHF-14-0204
SEISMOGRAPH LOW	MAGNIFICATION ATTACHMENT FOR A MILNE-SHAW	PETEJH-39-0341
RDING THRO/ NOTE ON THE	MAGNIFICATION CURVE OF A SEISMOGRAPH RECO	INGRRE-50-0021
FORMULA FOR THE DYNAMIC	MAGNIFICATION OF A MECHANICAL SEISMOGRAPH	KISSC -59-0267
	MAGNITUDE AND INTENSITY SCALES / MAGNITUD	ROBEEB-57-0013
TION IN BUILDINGS.* ITS	MAGNITUDE AND ITS IMPORTANCE IN LIMITING	WHITMP-41-0093
RTHQUAKES	MAGNITUDE DETERMINATION FOR DEEP-FOCUS EA	GUTEB -45-0117
DES OF P, PP, AND S AND	MAGNITUDE OF SHALLOW EARTHQUAKES / AMPLIT	GUTEB -45-0057
INSTRUMENTAL EARTHQUAKE	MAGNITUDE SCALE / AN INSTRUMENTAL EARTHQU	RICHCF-35-0001
RCEPTIBILIT/ EARTHQUAKE	MAGNITUDE, EFFICIENCY OF STATIONS, AND PE	JONEAE-44-0161
ATION EARTHQUAKE	MAGNITUDE, INTENSITY, ENERGY, AND ACCELER	GUTEB -42-0163
ATION (SECO/ EARTHQUAKE	MAGNITUDE, INTENSITY, ENERGY, AND ACCELER	GUTEB -56-0105
ES OF SURFACE WAVES AND	MAGNITUDES OF SHALLOW EARTHQUAKES / AMPLI	GUTEB -45-0003
ES FROM QUAR/ ENERGIES,	MAGNITUDES, AND AMPLITUDES OF SEISMIC WAV	BERGJW-61-0389
THQUAKE OF SOUTHEASTERN	MAINE / THE EARTHQUAKE OF SOUTHEASTERN MA	REIDHF-11-0044
ST)	MAJOR-CLARENCE-EDWARD DUTTON (SEISMOLOGI	DILLJS-11-0137
FEATURES IN MONO-C/ THE	MAMMOTH ,,EARTHQUAKE FAULT,, AND RELATED	BENIH -39-0333
STRUMENTAL STUDY OF THE	MANIX EARTHQUAKES CALIFORNIA / INSTRUMENT	RICHCF-51-0347
, 1947 THE	MANIX, CALIFORNIA, EARTHQUAKE OF APRIL 10	RICHCF-47-0171
IC WAVES IN THE EARTH/S	MANTLE / ATTENUATION OF SEISMIC WAVES IN	GUTEB -58-0269
OW-VELOCITY ZONE IN THE	MANTLE / RAYLEIGH-WAVE EVIDENCE FOR THE L	TAKEH -59-0355
VELOCITIES IN THE UPPER	MANTLE / THE TRAVEL TIMES OF THE LONGITUD	LEHMI -62-0519
ES IN THE EARTH/S UPPER	MANTLE AS INDICATED BY REFLECTED SEISMIC	HOFFJP-61-0017
STRIBUTION IN THE UPPER	MANTLE BY MANTLE RAYLEIGH WAVES / STUDY O	DORMJ -60-0087
PLE PATH/ VELOCITIES OF	MANTLE LOVE AND RAYLEIGH WAVES OVER MULTI	TOKSMN-63-0741
DISCONTINUITIES IN THE	MANTLE OF THE EARTH / ON SUPPOSED DISCONT	GUTEB -31-0216
AN INVESTIGATION OF	MANTLE RAYLEIGH WAVES / AN INVESTIGATION	EWINM -54-0127
IN THE UPPER MANTLE BY	MANTLE RAYLEIGH WAVES / STUDY OF THE SHEA	DORMJ -60-0087
EARTHQUAKE OF. NOVEMBER/	MANTLE RAYLEIGH WAVES FROM THE KAMCHATKA	EWINM -54-0471
GROUP VELOCITY CURVE OF	MANTLE RAYLEIGH WAVES WITH PERIODS ABOUT	TAKEH -59-0365
-TING SOFT LAYERS IN THE	MANTLE WITH RAYLEIGH WAVES / ON DETECTING	HARKDG-63-0539
REVIEW.* A	MANUAL OF SEISMOLOGY / REVIEW.* A MANUAL	TABES -22-0241
A FAULT	MAP OF CALIFORNIA / A FAULT MAP OF CALIFO	WILLB -23-0001
THE OHIO EARTHQUAKES OF	MARCH, 1937 / A MACROSEISMIC STUDY OF THE	WESTAJ-40-0251
NDAGRAPH (MICROSEISMS,	MAREGRAPH) / THE UNDAGRAPH (MICROSEISMS	KLOTO -13-0020
, AND ITS AFTERSHOCKS.*	MARICOPA SEED FARMS / AN ENGINEERING STUD	STEIKV-54-0390
FALL (MOUNT-PELEE, AND	MARTINIQUE) / EARTHQUAKES AND RAINFALL (	SAYLRW-13-0051
THE	MARVIN STRONG-MOTION SEISMOGRAPH / THE MA	DAVIEF-13-0195
ON OF THE RESISTANCE OF	MASONRY TO VIBRATION.* EFFECT OF EARTHQUA	BIERRW-11-0107
8 THE CHELMSFORD,	MASSACHUSETTS, EARTHQUAKE OF JUNE 23, 193	LINED -40-0099

FIG. 2. Page from a Keyword-in-Context index of a KWIC Index without postindex

Bulletin of the

Seismological Society of America

Dear Reader: Here is your copy of the 53-Year Cumulative Index in Key-Word-In-Context (KWIC) form. Please complete and return the card below. Postage is not required.

Sincerely,

Wm. Mansfield Adams

Editor

Do you understand the KWIC form?   Yes ....   No ....

Do you find the KWIC form is more useful than a traditional form index? Yes. ..... .   No ......   Same ... ..

Do you want a copy of the 53-Year Cumulative Index of the **Bulletin** in traditional form? Yes ....   No .....

How much would you pay for a traditional index?   Nothing ... .. ; $2.00 ....; $4.00.........; $6.00 . ;

$8.00.........;   more.........

Have you published technical articles or papers?   None ....;   One .. . ;   Two ....;   Three.........;

More than three...........

Did you return either one of the questionnaires in the Bulletin early this year? Yes ... ..   No.

Fig. 3. Form of a questionnaire used in October 1964

Any new index will evolve through the same sequence as a new product. Essentially, it *is* a new product. First, it must be noted that a study such as this usually extends over an extensive period of time. Indeed, Nielsen (*12*) has estimated that the median time required for determining the success of new products is from 19 to 24 months after completion of the full-scale launching of the product.

Another feature of such studies, which has been found to be of considerable importance, is the division of the market into three groups—innovators, influencers, and followers. This distinction was made by King (*9*). An "innovator" conceives and develops the novel feature; an "influencer" advertises and promulgates the novelty; and a "follower" consumes the product. Followers form the bulk of the market.

Mathematical analysis of user preference in brand

Evaluation of Information Systems

TABLE 2. Table of results from October 1964 questionnaire

Question No.

Answer No.		1			2				3			4							5						6		
		1	2	?	1	2	3	?	1	2	?	1	2	3	4	5	6	?	1	2	3	4	5	?	1	2	?
1 — 1	81	—	—	48	11	22	0	24	55	2	50	9	6	6	6	1	3	18	9	6	4	40	4	32	42	7
1 — 2	—	1	—	—	1	—	—	1	—	—	—	—	1	—	—	—	—	—	1	—	—	—	—	—	1	—
1 — ?	—	—	0	—	—	—	—	—	—	—	—	—	—	—	—	—	—	—	—	—	—	—	—	—	—	—
2 — 1				48	—	—	—	9	39	0	38	7	0	2	1	0	0	12	7	3	4	22	0	19	24	5
2 — 2				—	12	—	—	8	1	2	1	0	3	2	2	1	2	3	1	1	0	4	0	5	5	1
2 — 3				—	—	22	—	7	15	0	11	2	3	2	3	0	1	3	1	2	0	14	2	8	13	1
2 — ?				0	0	0	0	0	0	0	0	0	0	0	0	0	0	0	0	0	0	0	0	0	0	0
3 — 1								25	—	—	5	3	6	6	3	1	0	6	2	1	2	11	2	11	11	2
3 — 2								—	55	—	45	6	0	0	2	0	2	12	7	5	2	28	1	21	30	4
3 — ?								—	—	2	0	0	0	0	1	0	1	0	0	0	0	1	1	0	1	1
4 — 1											50	—	—	—	—	—	—	12	4	5	3	25	1	19	27	4
4 — 2											—	9	—	—	—	—	—	2	3	0	0	4	0	5	4	0
4 — 3											—	—	7	—	—	—	—	0	0	1	0	5	0	2	4	0
4 — 4											—	—	—	6	—	—	—	3	1	0	0	2	0	3	2	1
4 — 5											—	—	—	—	6	—	—	0	1	0	1	2	2	2	3	1
4 — 6											—	—	—	—	—	1	—	0	0	0	0	1	0	1	0	0
4 — ?											—	—	—	—	—	—	3	1	0	0	0	1	1	0	2	1
5 — 1																		18	—	—	—	—	—	3	13	2
5 — 2																		—	10	—	—	—	—	5	4	1
5 — 3																		—	—	6	—	—	—	5	1	0
5 — 4																		—	—	—	4	—	—	2	2	0
5 — 5																		—	—	—	—	40	—	17	21	2
5 — ?																		—	—	—	—	—	4	0	2	2
6 — 1																								32	—	—
6 — 2																								—	43	—
6 — ?																								—	—	7

choice has ranged from representation by simple Markov processes, such as propounded by Maffei (13), and affirmed by Lipstein (14), to recognition of the importance of the variation in user's rate probability (15) and inclusion of the effect of a variable use frequency (16). One of the most intriguing approaches is that of Kuehn (17, 18), which treats the user's choice procedure as a learning process.

Markov Process Model

The data have been analyzed by representing the use of indexes as a simple Markov process. This approach was the one initially planned (letter from Wm. Mansfield Adams to Allen J. Sprow of National Science Foundation, dated 18 December 1962). We present this approach now, following, in part, the notation of Maffei (13). Our interest is primarily in the transient conditions. (Those desiring an introduction to Markov processes are referred to Kemeny and Snell (19).)

We separate time into equal intervals. In any given interval, we assume a scientist uses predominantly one or the other index. The feature of interest is how the scientist varies his use of the KWIC index as a function of time.

Let:

p_{KK} be the probability that a scientist will prefer the KWIC index after having used that index in the preceding interval;

p_{KS} be the probability that a scientist will prefer the subject index after having used the KWIC index in the preceding interval;

p_{SK} be the probability that a scientist will prefer the KWIC index after having used the subject index in the preceding time interval; and

p_{SS} be the probability that a scientist will prefer the subject index after having used that index in the preceding interval.

We make the assumption that the transition probability of the seismologist does not change during any interval of this study. Therefore, the Markov process we use is the special case of a Markov chain.

Further, let:

$N(T)$ = the total percentage, 100% in our case.

$N_K(T)$ = estimate of the total percentage of scientists using the KWIC index during interval T.

$N_S(T)$ = estimate of the total percentage of scientists using the subject index during interval T.

$N_K(\infty)$ = estimate of the limiting, steady-state percentage of scientists that will prefer the KWIC index.

The transition probabilities are effectively constant over the time intervals if no other novel index is introduced or no promotion is done for the KWIC index. In fact, we believe the discussions and the lucheon talk at the annual meeting may have disrupted the time dependence despite our best efforts to be impartial. Consequently, replies from the April questionnaire were not used. Presumably any promotional effects in effect in April had become negligible by the October survey.

Now, from Eq. 5 of Maffei:

$$N_K(t + T) = s^T N_K(t) + p_{SK} N \sum_{i=0}^{T-1} s^i \qquad (1)$$

where $T = 1, 2, \ldots$

$$s = p_{KK} - p_{SK}$$

For our observations, we let $t = 0$. Since we are introducing the KWIC index as a novel item, $N_K(0) = 0$. Then the first questionnaire corresponds to the equations

$$N_K(1) = p_{SK} s^0 \qquad (2)$$

Since $s^0 = 1$, this is simply

$$N_K(1) = p_{SK} \qquad (3)$$

For the observation obtained from the second questionnaire, we have the equation

$$N_K(5) = N_K(1) \ (s^0 + s^1 + s^2 + s^3 + s^4) \qquad (4)$$

or

$$\frac{N_K(5) - N_K(1)}{N_K(1)} = s^1 + s^2 + s^3 + s^4 \qquad (5)$$

This is solvable (19, p. 218) by numerical techniques for s. Newton's method of approximation has been found to be suitable. Knowing s and p_{SK}, we have, from the definition of s,

$$p_{KK} = s + p_{SK} \qquad (6)$$

By definition:

$$1 = p_{KK} + p_{KS} \qquad (7)$$

and

$$1 = p_{SS} + p_{SK} \qquad (8)$$

so

$$p_{KS} = 1 - p_{KK} \qquad (9)$$

and

$$p_{SS} = 1 - p_{SK} \qquad (10)$$

Other properties of the two-state Markov chain have been derived and summarized in textbooks on the subject (20).

We now apply this theory to our observations. We assume a two-state case: a more elaborate model would be three-state, with the third state being that of indifference. However, such a model will not be used in this report.

From the first survey, we have, corresponding to Eq. 3,

$$P_{SK} = .33$$

It follows from Eq. 10 that $p_{SS} = .67$. From Eq. 5 and the data in Tables 1 and 2

$$s^4 + s^3 + s^2 + s = .85$$

Solving numerically, we have

$$s \simeq .50$$

Then, by Eq. 6

$$p_{KK} + .50 + .33 = .83$$

So, by Eq. 9

$$p_{KS} = .17$$

This gives us the complete transition matrix

$$\begin{matrix} .83 & .17 \\ .33 & .67 \end{matrix}$$

The limiting percentage of seismologists preferring the KWIC index is calculated with Eq. 5 of Maffei

$$N_K(\infty) \frac{p_{SK}}{p_{SK} + p_{KS}}$$

We find

$$N_K(\infty) = 66\%$$

These calculations have been based on all returns. The preponderance of authors among the respondents is outstanding. We will analyze the authors as a separate group. From the data given in Tables 1 and 2, we find, for the authors only, that

$$p_{SK} = .39$$

Hence

$$p_{SS} = .61$$

The data of Table 2 may now be used to formulate the following equation for authors

$$s^4 + s^3 + s^2 + s = .54$$

We find

$$s = .38$$

so

$$p_{KK} = .77$$

and

$$p_{KS} = .23$$

The transition matrix is

$$\begin{matrix} .77 & .23 \\ .39 & .61 \end{matrix}$$

The authors have the limit level of preference

$$N_K(\infty) = 63\%$$

(This analysis might be performed in a more elaborate manner as a three-state case. However, the two-state analyses presented here permit solution of the problem initiating this work.)

Birth and Death Model

Another approach is to determine the general functional form of the user response by experience with a large number of new products. Observations of the user acceptance for the particular new product being considered can then be used to evaluate the constants in the functional equation. This procedure has been reported by Fourt and Woodlock (21). The functional model selected is one in which the change in preference is proportional to the level of preference, corresponding to the usual exponential growth. This is the common birth and death model. For such a system, the level of preference is P and the limiting level of preference is P_o, so the rate of change in preference as a function of time is

$$\frac{d(P_o - P)}{dt} = R(P_o - P) \qquad (11)$$

This may be written as

$$\frac{d(P_o - P)}{(P_o - P)} + - R \, dt \qquad (12)$$

or

$$d \, ln \, (P_0 - P) = -R \, dt \qquad (13)$$

Hence, integrating

$$ln \, (P_0 - P) = -Rt + K \qquad (14)$$

The constants typifying any particular new product are R and K. (This derivation is somewhat different from that given by Fourt and Woodlock, however, it is equivalent.) This may be written as

$$P_0 - P = e^{-Rt+K} \qquad (15)$$
$$\text{At } t = o, \; P = o, \text{ so } P_0 = e^K \qquad (16)$$
$$P_0 - P = P_0 e^{-Rt} \qquad (17)$$
$$P = P_0(1 - e^{-Rt}) \qquad (18)$$

Then the membership size of those preferring the new product is

$$P = P_0(1 - e^{-Rt}) \qquad (19)$$

It is to this function that we wish to fit the observed data. For our situation, there are only two data points (corresponding to the two surveys and to both constants P_0 and R) to be estimated. Theoretically the solution is exact; however, we have used a numerical approximation in the computations.

Fourt and Woodlock have found that the most important indicator for predicting the ultimate success of innovation is the "first repeat ratio." This is defined to be the fraction of initial users who utilize the index a second time. Although no threshold value occurs, above which success can be guaranteed, it has been possible to determine a lower limit below which failure is almost certain. Fourt and Woodlock found that a new product for which less than 15 of every 100 triers repeat, almost always ends in commercial failure. As an indication of the upper limit, they do mention "some very successful items convert as many as half of all triers into repeat purchasers." This will be of value in interpreting the findings of this study.

In the introduction of a novel item, it is important to differentiate between preference and indifference. Two

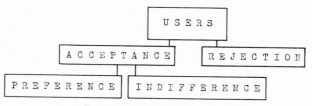

Fig. 4. Organization of users

levels of acceptance can be defined. We may say that active acceptance (preference) exists when the user wishes to utilize the novel item in place of all other possible items that could be used. Passive acceptance (indifference) exists when the user is indifferent to a choice between the novel and traditional items. Thus the acceptance group can be defined to be those who consider either of two items to be equally satisfactory or who prefer the novel item. The acceptance group includes the preference group as a subset. The complement of the acceptance group consists of those members who prefer the traditional subject index. This categorization is illustrated in Figure 4.

We treat the present situation as having an interval time of 2 months. Then the sequence of events described under experimental procedure may be graphed as in Fig. 5.

Following the method of Fourt and Woodlock, we make the analysis. For the first poll, we have the equation

$$RN = N_1 \qquad (20)$$

where R is the constant of proportionality,

      N is the ultimate percentage of scientists using KWIC index (an unknown)

and N_1 is the percentage of the scientists preferring the KWIC index during the first interval.

Note that we are using percentages instead of absolute numbers.

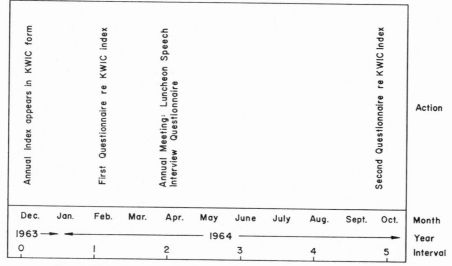

Fig. 5. Time sequence of the preference surveys in the present study

Testing

The other observation was made at the end of the fifth interval, so $t = 5$. The percentage of scientists at the end of the interval was observed—not the "increment in penetration" used by Fourt and Woodlock. For this observation, we have

$$RN [1 + (1 - R) + (1 - R)^2 + (1 - R)^3 + (1 - R)^4] = N_5 \quad (21)$$

where N_5 is the percentage of the scientists preferring the KWIC index during the fifth interval.

We eliminate the unknown N by dividing Equation (21) by (20), giving

$$1 + (1 - R) + (1 - R)^2 + (1 - R)^3 + (1 - R)^4 = \frac{N_5}{N_1} \quad (22)$$

This is one equation in one unknown: it may be solved by numerical iteration techniques.

In this study the observations have not been of each user. Instead, we have an estimate of the percentage of the population which is using the KWIC index. This estimate is at the end of each time interval of 2 months. We assume that the increment of users is satisfactorily estimated by taking the difference of the percentages observed.

Utilizing the calculation procedure just outlined, we find that the repeat ratio, assuming that all responders to the first survey responded to the second survey, is .43. This is based on data for the preference group. Thus we see that we are near to that level which would indicate the novel item to be "very successful." The limiting level of scientists preferring the KWIC index is found to be .75.

This analysis has been based on grouping all the respondents together, but it is also possible to separate out the authors. Authors constituted more than 60% of the respondents to the questionnaire: this is probably typical of the Society membership, but it seemed desirable to also consider the survey as being conducted among the authors of the membership, and not only the membership as a whole, because the authors are the innovators and influencers. Fortunately the form of the questionnaire permitted such an interpretation. This analysis of the authors is made here.

Because the percentage of authors among the respondents was greater than 60%, the number of questionnaires available for analysis from authors still permits a statistically significant result. These have been analyzed in a fashion similar to the data previously presented. The first repeat ratio, again assuming that respondents to the second questionnaire are the same as respondents to the first questionnaire, is .50. This time the limiting value of ultimate preference for the novel KWIC index is .80. This means that eventually the preference of authors for the KWIC index will attain approximately 80% of the authors.

These calculations are summarized in Table 3 to facilitate easy comparison.

Although these results make it apparent that the KWIC form of index probably has been quickly accepted by the members (especially the authors) of the Seismo-

TABLE 3. Table of results using the method of Fourt and Woodlock

	Repeat ratio (R)	Limiting level (P_0)
All respondents	.43	.75
Author respondents	.50	.80

logical Society of America, they do not indicate the true strength of the preference. In the second questionnaire, the last question asked whether the respondent had answered either of the earlier questionnaires. The number responding yes was only about half the number replying to the questionnaire. Therefore, it is probable that the first repeat ratio is actually much higher than indicated.

An attempt to apply the same analysis to nonauthors is impossible due to the small sample size remaining after the questionnaires of authors are removed.

In evaluating these findings, it is necessary to appreciate that the survey conducted is not identical with that described by Fourt and Woodlock. Observation of a user in each use would permit a statement of which user uses the novel product and when. In this study we did not consider it feasible to determine each time a member of the Society actually went to the index to use it. Instead, we have assumed that the rate of usage by an individual user is constant over time.

The assumption that each user's transition probability is constant does not necessarily means that the average transition probability is constant, as emphasized by Frank (15). Because of the limitation in our sampling ability, limiting us to averages only, we are making the additional assumption that average transition probabilities are constant.

This analysis following Fourt and Woodlock is not exactly equivalent to that made after Maffei. The Markov chain analysis has assumed that the number of transitions made during a time interval is a constant. The other analysis is of the "birth and death" type: in this type of process the transitions can occur at random times so the number of transitions during a time interval is also a random variable. The two methods of analysis are related, however. If the time interval becomes large, the transition probabilities will, in the limit, approach the corresponding probabilities of the Markov chain. This would not be true for short times, such as considered here in this study of transient behavior. Hence, the difference found between the two analyses is inherent in the difference between the models.

This study of the introduction of a novel KWIC index should be compared with studies conducted by Kraft (22), Ruhl (23), and Lancaster and Mills (24). All of these studies were primarily concerned with determining the similarity in the structure of the KWIC index and a subject index for the same articles. Although Kraft has a section entitled "Cost and User Acceptance," it does not deal with the user of the indexes but with the user of the KWIC code.

Both Ruhl and Kraft point out the probability that an author, knowing an article will be indexed by the KWIC system, will tend to choose words for the title that are adaptable to the KWIC system of indexing. As this feedback effect evolves, the value of a KWIC index to the user will increase.

4 Summary

This work was begun with the intention of determining which of two types of indexes is more useful to scientists. We assumed that the scientists would "prefer" the index which is more useful, so we studied the preference of scientists. We chose a group of scientists, the Seismological Society of America, and surveyed their preference —after an initial educational effort. The authors are the most important portion of the membership because they are the innovators and the influencers.

From our Markov-chain model we are able to conclude that those scientists in the Seismological Society of America that are authors will eventually approach a level of preference for the KWIC index of about 66%. Indeed, the group of authors seems to have already attained a *preference* level of 60% as of October 1964. If the group of authors that are indifferent to the KWIC index, and the subject index be added to those preferring the KWIC index, to form the acceptance group (see Fig. 4), then it becomes clear that the KWIC index is the index that will, in the long run, be rejected by the lowest percentage of seismologists.

A summary of the birth and death model is given in the abstract.

It is expected that many will be prompted to generalize this result to conclude that a scientific society should issue a KWIC index instead of a subject index to relevant literature. It must be remembered that the introduction of any novel item is likely to require education of the user.

Furthermore, what is a good index now may be a bad index by then.

We anticipate that the influx of KWIC indexes will cause authors to be more reflective in selecting titles. Already procedures are being developed for permitting (even requiring!) authors, reviewers, and editors to provide annotation words.

In the midst of this tempest of scientific literature, let us not forget: "Searchers want facts—not folios: retrieve data—not documents" (*24*).

• Acknowledgments

This work has extended over 4 years: the number of persons involved has been large. The need for the Society to have an index was first emphasized by Don Tocher. Dewitt Allen and Florence Sullivan of the University of California Lawrence Radiation Laboratory assisted one of these authors (Adams) in drafting the early proposals. At that time, discussions with George W. Housner, Perry Byerly, John H. Hodgson, and James T. Wilson were most stimulating. Additional technical guidance was provided by J. O. Parry, Jr., W. B. Heroy, Sr., and W. Rinehart.

The ultimate success of this work is due in great measure to the perseverance and counseling provided by Alan J. Sprow, Sarah N. Rhodes, and Helen L. Brownson of the National Science Foundation.

Production of the various indexes was made possible by correspondence with Richard D. Wadding of International Business Machines, William W. Youden of the National Bureau of Standards, W. E. Cossum of *Chemical Abstracts*, Robert R. Gulick and G. Miles Conrad of *Biological Abstracts*, and Ralph E. O'Dette. The operational analyses of the surveys, as well as the organization of index production, has been aided by Nancy L. Nuhn of Planetary Sciences, Inc., and Robert Rude and Thomas Gaffrey of International Business Machines.

The printing was executed under the guidance of Norwell Miller, III of Waverly Press, Inc. Data gathering and processing have been performed with the assistance of Marilyn E. Westin of Planetary Sciences Inc., Daniel Walker of the University of Hawaii, and the interviews, Claus Sinai and Dale Molander of the University of Washington.

Interpretation of the data has been made more interesting by discussions with John Wise of the University of Hawaii and John Tukey of Bell Telephone Laboratories. We remain responsible, however, for the analysis techniques selected and the opinions expressed. Any suggestions for improvement or correction would be heartily received.

> From the deep, dim, most distant past,
> A thousand thousand tomes we hold
> Of sacred texts and learned lore.
> Profound, abstruse, obscure and dark,
> Teachings diverse and manifold —
> Who can encompass such a store?
>
> Kūkai (774–835 A.D.)
> in Kōbō Daishi Zenshū I, 417–419

*   *   *

References

1. ADAMS, W. M., 1965, The Preference of Seismologists for the KWIC Index, *Hawaii Institute Geophysics. Report,* June, 65–12 (1965).
2. LUHN, H. P., *"Keyword-In-Context Index for Technical Literature (KWIC),"* International Business Machines Corp., Advanced Development Division, Yorktown Heights, New York, 1959.

3. LEET, L. D., and F. J. LEET, The Earth's Mantle, *Bulletin of Seismological Society of America*, 55:619 (1965).

4. JUNCOSA, M. L., On the Increase of Convergence Rate of Relaxation Procedures for Elliptic Partial Differential Equations, *Journal of the Association of Computing Machinery*, 29 (1960).

5. BYERLY, P., History of the Seismological Society of America," *Bulletin Seismological Society of America*, 54:1723–1742 (1964).

6. ADAMS, W. M., 1965, A Comparison of Some Machine-Produced Indexes, *Hawaii Institute Geophysics*. Report January, 65–1 (1965).

7. *Geophysical Abstracts*, 1929–to date, U. S. Geological Survey, United States Government Printing Office, Washington, D. C.

8. ADAMS, W. M., Relationship of Keywords in Titles to References Cited, *American Documentation*, 18:26–32 (1967).

9. KING, C., Product Adoption and Diffusion, A Summary of the Literature, unpublished research paper, Harvard Business School, 1962.

10. ADAMS, W. M., "53-year Cumulative Index," *Bulletin Seismological Society of America*, 54:1583–1722 (1964).

11. BUZZELL, R. D., Mathematical Models and Marketing Management, in *Measuring and Predicting Market Behavior*, Division Research, Graduate School Business Administration, Harvard University, Cambridge, 1964, Chap. 10, 205.

12. NIELSEN, A. C., JR., Consumer Product Acceptance Rates, L. H. Clark (Ed.), *Consumer Behavior*, Harper and Bros., New York, 1958.

13. MAFFEI, R. B., Brand Preferences and Simple Markov Processes, *Operations Research*, 7:210–218 (1960).

14. LIPSTEIN, B., Tests for Test Marketing, *Harvard Business Review*, 39:74–77 (1961).

15. FRANK, R., Brand choice as a Probability Process, *Journal of Business*, 35:43–56 (1962).

16. HERNITER, J. D., and R. HOWARD, Stochastic Marketing Models, Unpublished report, Arthur D. Little, Inc., 1963.

17. KUEHN, A. A., Consumer Brand Choice as a Learning Process, *Journal of Advertising Research*, 2:10–17 (1962).

18. KUEHN, A. A., "Consumer Brand Choice—a Learning Process," in *Qualitative Techniques in Marketing Analysis*, pp. 390–405, 1962a.

19. WILLERS, F. A., *Practical Analysis*, Dover Publications, Inc., New York, 1948.

20. KEMENY, J. G., and J. L. SNELL, *Finite Markov Chains*, D. Van Nostrand Co., Inc., New York, 1963.

21. FOURT, L. A., and J. W. WOODLOCK, Early Prediction of Market Success for New Grocery Products, *Journal of Marketing*, 25:31–38 (1960).

22. KRAFT, D. H., Comparison of Keyword-In-Context (KWIC) Indexing of Titles With a Subject Heading Classification System, *American Documentation*, 15:48–52 (1964).

23. RUHL, M. J., Chemical Documents and Their Titles: Human Concept Indexing vs. KWIC Machine Indexing, *American Documentation*, 15:136–141 (1964).

24. LANCASTER, F. W., and J. MILLS, Testing Indexes and Index Language Devices: The ASLIB Granfield Project, *American Documentation*, 15:4–13 (1964).

25. WALDO, W. H., Searchers Want Facts Not Folios—Retrieve Data Not Documents—The Needle is Dull—Sharpen It with Automation, *Automation and Scientific Communication*, 207–209 (1963).

Chapter Twelve
Economics
and
Growth

The basic economic problem in relation to communication in general and to information systems in particular is that no price tags can be attached to information and that no cost benefits can be derived, even though quite often information may have definite and considerable economic value. On the other hand, this inability to attach a price to information does not mean that information is not viewed as a commodity. It may be viewed as a necessity for survival of any modern social entity, in the same way that air is essential to life.

The creation, organization and dissemination of information may be, at times, inexpensive or even free of direct economic cost. But, as a rule, these propositions are extremely costly in the complex systems of today. That information systems are expensive must be accepted by users, management, funders, designers, operators and the general public. Information, in many diverse forms, as the products of these systems, might often be judged by users, funders, and management as not worth the price paid. But what remains questionable in comparison to the high price for information is what is the eventual price for no information or for inadequate information?

Investigations into the economics of information divide into two branches. On the one hand, there are theoretical works on the economic values of information and of communication within social entities and organizations. The work by Marschak (Article 63) is an example of such concern, bringing together the conceptual constructs necessary to analyze the economics of information. On the other hand, there are practical works dealing with the cost of designing, developing and operating information systems. Although there are thousands of information systems of various kinds operating, it is remarkable how little we know about their costs, how sparsely cost data exist. Another problem is that the existing data are not really comparable, because each set of computations is so idiosyncratic. In other words, the lack of similarity in approaches thwarts the efforts to cumulate knowledge about the internal economics of information systems. In turn, this could be attributed to the lack of generally accepted efficiency theories and methods for calculating costs. Rothenberg (Article 64) presents a formal efficiency model which can be used as a framework for calculating costs; furthermore, he proposes a function which combines the efficiency of an information system with its effectiveness. Extensive work on the economics of information systems clearly remains to be done.

The growth of information systems is indirectly related to economics and may be especially useful to economic planning. Libraries and information retrieval systems have observed definite patterns of growth. The significance of this behavior lies in the regularities observed in the growth, which could facilitate making predictions about it. Leimkuhler (Article 65) proposes an algorithm of growth and internal relationship for libraries, which can be utilized in systems studies of libraries and in other information systems. He isolates fundamental space-time relationships and develops models that show how acquisition, circulation, storage, loan period and duplication patterns interact over long segments of time. Studies of this type are basic to a systems approach to information systems. It is suggested here that there are many similarities among patterns of growth and behavior of literature to the patterns of growth and behavior of libraries and information retrieval systems. These similarities are of such a nature that they suggest regardless of other factors, libraries and information systems almost blindly follow and are governed by the behavior of literature. Again, this is an area open for investigation.

In conclusion, the questions of economics and of internal and external relationships are fundamental to the justification of information systems as these relate to funders, be they individual organizations, government agencies or the society. It has been said that it is the economics of information systems that either makes or breaks them. And it is essentially the willingness of social entities to support the information systems, mostly on faith and not on formal justification, that ensures their existence. It seems advisable to devote attention to formal justification; needless to say, for many individual systems, the faith ran out.

63 Economics of Inquiring, Communicating, Deciding

JACOB MARSCHAK
American Economic Review
Vol. 58, No. May 1968

We hear much of today's "informational revolution." We are also told of the rapid growth of the "knowledge industry." Informational revolution is exemplified by TV pictures of the moon surface and also by robotized stock market transactions and, hopefully, by computerized professors. Fritz Machlup defined the knowledge industry to include education and research as well as publishing and broadcasting. He estimated its share in the gross national product of 1958 at 23 percent to 29 percent, and its growth rate at about 10 percent, or twice that of the GNP. Projecting to the present, the share of the knowledge industry would then appear to straddle the 40 percent mark!

There is a suspicious overlap between these activities and those which Adam Smith and Karl Marx called "unproductive" and which include the work of kings and professors, none of whom add to the vendible and visible stocks of the nation. To be sure, recent analysis — for example, by T. W. Schultz and Carl V. Weizaecker — found it both convenient and feasible to define human capital and thus to consider education as investment. But the notable fact remains that professors and kings or the modern equivalent of kings — managers, both public and private — are strongly involved in those trends: informational revolution and growing knowledge industry.

Professors and managers, but also computers and TV sets, are involved in still another trend relevant to my talk. A growing proportion of both manhours and machine-hours is not employed for using large amounts of energy (muscular or otherwise) to transform or transport matter. Instead, so-called "brains" (human or otherwise) are employed to manipulate symbols. A sequence or network of such symbol manipulators uses up a minute amount of energy to eventually release, trigger-like, large amounts of energy through the more brutal medium of generators, muscles, and machine tools. In a modern assembly or disassembly plant (sawmill, meat packing), a growing majority of people, wearing white collars, or blue denims as well, do the brain work of inspecting, deciding, reporting — shunting, pushing buttons — and not the muscular work of shaping or carrying material masses; and a growing proportion of machines, called control mechanisms, are also busy with inspecting, reporting, deciding, and not with transforming or transporting matter and energy.

My topic is the economics of what I shall call the services of inquiring, communicating, deciding. Data are gathered. They are communicated to the decision-maker. He, on the basis of the message received, decides upon the action to be taken. A higher-order decision must have been made previously. Someone representing the interests of the economic unit considered — its head, leader, organizer — must have chosen a particular combination of these three services from all those available in their respective markets. The maker of this higher-order decision (the "meta-decider," sometimes called "the organizer") may happen to be the same person who will decide upon acting. Or more generally, the organizer will hire the services of the decision-maker — who, in appropriate cases, may be just a robot.

I might also call my topic the economics of the instruments, or devices, human or otherwise, for inquiring, communicating, and deciding. For it is not relevant, for my purposes, to distinguish between purchased instruments and hired services, provided the length of the hire contract is specified. In any case, I shall be concerned with symbol manipulators, human or otherwise, rather than with processors or transporters of matter or energy.

Here is what I plan to do. I shall present, in turn, from the user's point of view, the successive links in the sequence of symbol-manipulating services: inquiry, or data gathering; communication of messages; and deciding upon actions on the basis of messages received. It will turn out, in fact, that the link called "communication" must be broken into two distinct services: on the one hand, the service of "encoding and decoding" which, at the present state of arts and in the most numerous and socially most important cases, is best supplied by men; and on the other hand, the service of "transmission" which is best supplied by inanimate equipment. As to the supply conditions of services of inquiry, or data production, and of decision making, I shall be able to submit nothing but crude illustrations, I am afraid. As to the demand side, economists will not be surprised that to make an economical — that is, optimal, efficient — choice, the user must choose those links, or components, simultaneously (just as a manufacturer cannot choose between rail and road as means of bringing him fuel without making up his mind, at the same time, whether the fuel should be coal or oil). Hence, the jointness of demand for services of inquiry, communication, and decision.

To be sure, current engineering science finds it convenient to isolate a pure theory of communication — a theory of efficient coding and transmission alone, essentially created by Claude Shannon and streamlined by Jack Wolfowitz. At the other extreme, statistical decision theory culminating in the work of David Blackwell leaves out the communication component and only analyzes, from the point of view of a perfect decision-maker, the optimal choice of inquiry, or data producing, services, also called "experiments." I shall later state the implicit tacit assumptions made in each case. If they are not satisfied, the user guided by those subtheories will have suboptimized. This is not to say that we ought not to break up a complex problem into subproblems, assuming them independent as a provisional first approximation. Given our human limitations, this may even be the optimal research strategy. It just happens that the economist is aware of interdependencies: he calls them complementarity and substitutability of goods. He is also traditionally permitted — as is the philosopher — to attack complexities with ridiculously simple examples in order to get directly to the general and fundamental.

Let me, then, go ahead with a simple example. I must decide this Thursday night whether to fly West next Saturday morning. Visibility and winds along the airplane's route the day after tomorrow will determine whether, if I do fly, I shall arrive in time for an important appointment or shall be killed in a crash. If I don't fly, I miss the appointment. But I cannot know what the weather will be. Instead, I may look tonight at the hotel barometer; or I may rely on the radio reports of other, more numerous and accurate barometer readings; or I may rely on the *Farmer's Almanac*. If the cost of these various services were equal, I would choose the one which gives data most closely reflecting (in some sense) the actual event I am interested in: the weather on Saturday. But perfection is costly, and I shall choose a service that is known not to mislead too grossly or too frequently, yet will be relatively cheap.

Take another example. A store's profit will be influenced by its inventory policy, given the actual future demand for its merchandise. Lacking the knowledge of this demand, the firm will have to choose between various services of market forecasters differing in precision and accuracy but also in the fees charged.

So much about services that inquire; i.e., produce data. These data are not identical with, yet do reflect in some sense, the events that are relevant to the result of a decision. Now, the decision-maker may or may not be able to obtain such data directly. Another service called "communication" will bring to him, not those data, but a message possibly delayed or distorted, about those data. He must decide on the basis of such a message, which is now twice removed, in a sense, from the actual, result-relevant event: weather on Saturday, demand next month, and so on.

The inventory example illustrates also the nature of decision services. Inventory policy is a rule stating whether and how much to reorder when the stock at hand is at a given level and you have some — usually imperfect — knowledge related to the prospective demand of your customers. One policy is similar to the one you use when you decide whether to refill your car's oil tank up to a certain upper level (this you will do whenever oil is below a certain lower level) or to leave it alone. Except that in the inventory case the two critical levels themselves are not fixed but should depend on what the store has learned — however imperfectly — about future demand; that is, on the message it has received about the data produced by a market forecast. Such a decision rule or strategy — a rule of how to respond to the message — may require the sophisticated services of a specialist or a computer. Contrast with this a simple routine rule: to refill the inventory every Monday to a constant level. This can be handled by an unskilled clerk or a cheap robot. The more sophisticated, flexible, nonroutine rule would be preferable if it were not for its higher cost.

To state more precisely the problem facing the user of the data producing, communication, and decision services, it is convenient to represent each service as a transformer of inputs into outputs. (Transformer, transformation, and function mean essentially the same thing.) A data producing service such as a barometer is a transformer whose input is the result-relevant event (weather next Saturday) and whose output is an observed value, a datum (the barometer reading tonight). We say that the data service is both precise and reliable if to each result-relevant event corresponds one observation or datum, and conversely. But this perfection is almost never attained. Generally, each event may be reflected in various alternative observed values, with some alterna-

tives more likely than others. We have here the case of an "unreliable" (probabilistic, stochastic, noisy) transformer. For example, suppose that if Saturday's weather is going to be good, the chance that the barometer shows high pressure tonight is 80 percent. We say that the likelihood of the observation "high pressure," given the event "good weather," is 80 percent. Suppose the likelihood of low pressure if the weather is going to be dangerous is also 80 percent. Suppose that on a second barometer both these likelihoods are lower: 60 percent and 60 percent, say. If you have access to both barometers at the same cost or effort, you will prefer to be guided by the first one. For, in an obvious sense it is more reliable (more informative, in Blackwell's terminology). Indeed, in the case of perfect reliability the two likelihoods would be 100 percent and 100 percent; and clearly our first barometer (with 80 percent, 80 percent) comes to this perfection than the second (with 60 percent, 60 percent). In fact, the second comes closer than the first to the other extreme: likelihoods 50 percent, 50 percent, in which case the barometer would be useless.

Or consider a consumer survey conducted by a government agency. The success of the government decision to undertake one or another administrative action depends on the attitudes of all consumers. But only a cer-

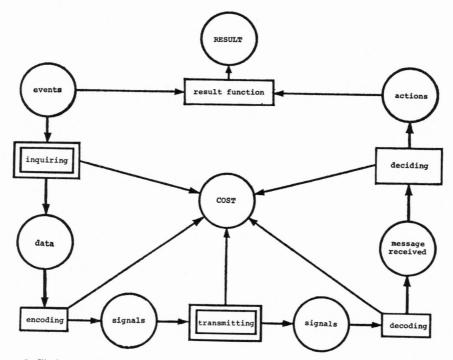

○ Circles = variables (generally random).

□ Boxes = transformers (noisy if double-framed). User maximizes average result minus cost (assuming additive utilities).

NOTE: In statistical theory, the lower row encoding → . . . → decoding is omitted so that messages received = data. In communication theory, data = events; action = messages received; and result = "bad" or "good" according as message is or is not identical with datum.

tain number are sampled. The larger the sample the more reliable is the estimate of people's attitude. But also the more expensive. It is not different with research into the laws of physics or biology. What I called "result-relevant events" the statisticians call "hypotheses." The data producing service (eg., a sampling) they call "experiment," and the data are called "observations."

Unfortunately, it is not always possible to compare two data producing services on the basis of the likelihoods only. How does our first barometer, with the 80 percent likelihood of high pressure given good weather, and 80 percent likelihood of low pressure given dangerous weather compare with the following one: if the weather is going to be good, the barometer will show high pressure for sure, i.e., with likelihood 100 percent; but given dangerous weather, it will show high or low pressure, not with 80:20 but with 50:50 chances. Thus, whenever the new barometer shows low pressure, it gives you absolute certainty that the weather cannot be good. But when it shows low pressure you are left guessing, and you might be better off with the original barometer. Which barometer should guide you?

Here I must remind you that, just as economists are Keynesians or non-Keynesians, the statisticians are Bayesians. The Bayesians, having given serious thought to our problem, tell me to consult two further items: (1) the approximate, so-called "prior," probabilities that I would assign to dangerous versus good weather for next Saturday — in the absence of any barometer, e.g., on the basis of my previous experience with December weather; (2) the utilities that I assign to various results of my actions and whose actuarial value I would like to be as high as possible. In our case, the best result is: surviving and making the appointment The second best is: surviving but missing the appointment. The worst is death. What matters is the ratio of the disadvantage of missing the appointment (but staying alive) to the disadvantage of death. Now, unless a barometer is useless, I would fly if it shows high pressure and not fly otherwise (or vice versa). The probabilities of these pressure readings depend on my prior probability of the two states of weather and on the likelihoods characterizing each of the two barometers. Therefore, those pressures will be read on the two barometers with different probabilities. Hence the aveage utility of the results of actions dictated by each barometer and weighted by the probabilities of its readings will differ as between the two barometers. I prefer the one whose dictation will yield, on the average, the higher utility.

Suppose, then, the prior probability of bad (i.e., deadly dangerous) weather is, in my judgment, about 10 percent. Should I use the "old" barometer (whose likelihoods are 80 percent and 80 percent) or the "new" barometer (whose likelihoods are 100 percent and 50 percent), still assuming that the costs are equal. It turns out that I should stick to the old barometer as long as I judge the disadvantage of missing the appointment (while staying alive) to be less than one-seventh of the disadvantage of death. This is surely my case!

I believe this business of assigning prior probabilities to events and of utilities to results is a headache familiar to cost-benefit analysts, certainly present in this very room! It surely requires some soul-searching to appraise and reappraise the subjective probabilities ("beliefs") and utilities ("goals," "values," "tastes") of your government agency. You will presumably try out various plausible assumptions and see whether your boss likes the decisions derived from them; and whether under repeated trials of this kind his choices reveal a consistency of his beliefs and of his tastes. Or perhaps such trials will gradually train him toward consistency — toward learning what he wants and believes.

So far, we have seen how the consistent user should choose between available inquiry services when their costs are equal. This has required, for some though not all pairs of such services, to take account of the user's utilities and prior probabilities in order to compute the average utility attainable on the basis of an inquiry. If costs are not equal, the knowledge of prior probabilities and utilities becomes necessary in all cases. For simplicity, a tacit assumption is made. One assumes, in terms of our example, that it is possible to represent the utility of, say, "having made the appointment and having my wealth diminished by the dollar cost of a particular inquiry" as a sum of two utilities. In other words, utility is assumed to be additive and to be commensurable with dollars. Under this assumption, one may call the average utility of results of actions guided by an inquiry simply its dollar value to the user, his demand price. He compares it with the dollar cost, which is the supply price. The additivity assumption is implicity made by statisticians. They assume in effect that the disutility of a result of action based on a sampling survey is measured by the size of the error of an estimate, and then vaguely compare its average with the dollar cost of the sampling survey. Engineers indulge in similar practices, as we shall see. Not so the economists. Sophisticated in matters of substitution, income elasticity, and risk aversion — all of which question the assumption of additive utility — they rase a warning finger. They do so at least when they talk theory and are not themselves engaged in the practical pursuits variously called "management science," "operations research," "system analysis," "cost-benefit analysis."

My barometer case — with just two alternative events, two possible observations, and two actions — is probably the simplest nontrivial problem in statistical decision theory. As I said before, this theory neglects the communication link. Result-relevant events, each having some prior probability, are transformed into data by a transformer called an "inquiry," or an "experiment" (like a barometer, or a sampling survey). Data flow directly into the transformer called "decision-maker," who applies a decision rule (e.g., "fly if barometer pressure high") and puts out actions. Finally, events and decisions are joint inputs of a transformer which may be called "result function": its output is a result. Assuming additive utility, a dollar amount can be attached to each result. And the probability of each result is determined by the prior probability of each event, by the array (characteristic of the data producing service) of the likelihoods of the data, given each event, and by the decision rule (characteristic of the given decision service) transforming data into actions. The probabilities of the results thus derived serve as weights to obtain the average of their utilities. This average may be called the "gross value," to a given user, of the given pair of data producing and decision-making services. It is the maximum demand price offered by their user. Their combined cost asked by the suppliers is the minimum supply price. The difference may be called "the net combined value of these two services to the user." He will choose the combination with highest net value.

This net value depends, then, on the one hand, on the choice of services made by their user. On the other hand, it depends on conditions outside of his control: viz., his utilities and prior probabilities and the costs of available services. His problem is to maximize the net value of the data producing and decision-making services, given those noncontrolled conditions.

Those familiar with what has been called "information theory" in the last two decades will have noticed that, so far, we have not used the concept of amount of information, measured in units called "bits." My uncertainty about a set of alternative events is the same as the amount of information that I would receive if that uncertainty were completely removed; that is, if I would know exactly which particular event does happen. Roughly speaking, this uncertainty is measured by the smallest average number of successive yes-and-no answers needed to completely remove uncertainty. This number depends roughly on the prior probabilities of events. Suppose, for example, that the following four events have equal probabilities (one-quarter each): the bride at the neighborhood church next Saturday will or won't wear a mini-dress, and her dress will or won't be white. To learn the color of the dress I need one yes-or-no question; so my uncertainty about color measures one bit. For the same reason, my uncertainty about both color and style is two bits since I need two yes-and-no answers to answer it. Thus the uncertainty, measured in bits, about those two mutually independent sets of events is the sum $(1 + 1 = 2)$ of the uncertainties about each of them. The number of bits is, in this sense, additive: a property that we require of every genuine measure, such as that of time, distance, volume, energy, dollar income, and dollar wealth.

If the four bridal events were not equally probable — for example, if the odds for a maxi-dress were not 1:1 but 9:1 (while a dress of each style were still as likely as not to be white) — the average necessary number of yes-

and-no questions and thus the number of information bits would be smaller in the long run, i.e., over a long sequence of such events: for we can then profitably identify the more probable sequences (i.e., those mostly consisting of maxi-dresses) by asking a few questions only — as any skilled player of the "20 questions game" knows. As before, the count of bits agrees remarkably with the intuitive use of the English word uncertainty: for when the odds are 9:1 I am almost certain, and with odds 1:1, I am fully ignorant, am I not?

Now suppose you have the choice between learning both the style and the color of the bride's dress and learning, with equal speed and for the same fee, the future price of your stocks. Suppose the price is as likely to rise as to fall. Depending on your selling or purchasing now, you may lose or double your fortune. A service that will tell you correctly whether the stock price will rise or fall conveys only one bit of information; whereas the service telling you correctly both the style and the color of the dress provides two bits. Yet you will prefer to learn about the stocks, not about the dress. There is, thus, no relation between the number of bits conveyed and the gross value of the data producing service. Nor does there seem to be a relation between the number of bits and the cost of a data producing service. For example, the cost of a sampling survey depends on its size, and this is not clearly related to the number of bits involved.

On the other hand, the number of yes-and-no symbols involved is clearly relevant to the performance and the cost of the transmission service regardless of whether these symbols refer to the length of the bridal skirt or to the trend of prices of your stock. To the economist, the contrast between production and transmission of data is strikingly analogous to the contrast between production and transportation of goods. A gallon of whiskey is more valuable than a gallon of gasoline: their costs to the producer and their values to the buyer are quite different. Yet to transport one gallon over one mile costs about the same for any liquid.

When, some twenty years ago, those elusive things labeled by the vague English words "uncertainty" and its negative, "information," were harnessed, subjected to genuine measurements (as was energy some hundred years ago, and mass and force much earlier), it was easy to understand the enthusiasm of people in elusive fields such as psychology. But also, to some extent, in statistics and in mathematics, where it was partly due to deep and beautiful theorems developed in this context. It is remarkable that C. Shannon who first proposed these theorems clearly limited their application to communications.

Statistical decision theory deals only with the choice of experiments and of decision rules; that is, with the choice of data producing and of deciding services. It omits the lower row of the chart reproduced above: encoding of data into signals, transmitting signals through a "communication channel," and decoding them back into messages that the decider would understand. In other words, for the statistician the decision is taken on the basis of a message which is simply the same thing as the data produced by the inquiry or experiment.

Not so with the communication engineer. His responsibility is to construct channels for the fast and reliable transmission of signals. (It all started in the telephone industry!) He is therefore also interested in devising appropriate codes which translate ordinary English into signals and signals back into English. But, to concentrate his mind on pure communication economics he makes, in effect, the following simplifying assumptions: First, events and data are identical, for he is not interested in the imperfections of the data producing service. Second, deciding is the same thing as decoding; so that action is simply the same thing as the message received. Third, as we have observed for the case of non-equiprobable events (which is, of course the usual case), the count of bits presupposes, in general, long sequences of events; and, as we shall see, such long sequences are also essential to make the crucial concept of "channel capacity" useful. Fourth, in most though not all[1] of their work, communication engineers assume an extremely simple result function. There are only two results: bad (say, minus one), when the decoded, received message is not identical with the datum sent; good (say, zero), when the two are identical. That is, all errors are equally important, have the same disutility, whether an inch is taken for a mile or merely a colon is taken for a semicolon. Finally, utility is assumed to be additive; i.e., it is conceived as the sum of certain measurable advantages and disadvantages, appropriately converted into dollars. We have seen that statisticians make the same assumption when they compare the sampling error with the dollar cost of the sample. The economist who detects and warns against this assumption is somewhat of a purist. The assumption is surely convenient for practical purposes and its removal is perhaps not that urgent.

Indeed this last assumption permits the engineer to ask the following economic question on behalf of the user of transmission channels and of coding services. Given the dollar costs of available channels, what is the best combination of the following evils: the probability of error (any error); the cost of the channel; the average time delay, which depends both on the length of signal sequences transmitted at a time and on the size of the code's vocabulary. That is, disutility is thought of, in effect, as a sum of dollars that buy a given channel; plus the dollar-equivalent of an error (any error); plus the dollar-equivalent, to a given user, of each time delay arising in the coding and transmission of a given datum. The user's problem is to choose that combination of channel and code which will minimize the sum of the averages of these amounts, weighted by appropriate probabilities. What do these probabilities depend on? On the uncertainty about data (= events); on the likelihood array characterizing the channel's reliability (the array of conditional probabilities of output symbols given an input symbol); and on the coding and decoding procedures.

Clearly, an appropriately redundant code can almost overcome the lack of reliability of the channel; that is, it can almost eliminate the occurrence of errors. For example, the encoder just lets every "yes" or "no" to be repeated many times, and the decoder takes "no" for the answer if he has received more "no's" than "yes's." "Don't! — repeat, don't! — repeat, don't shoot!" If I have heard two don'ts and only one do, I shan't shoot. However, we may need great redundancy of the code if the channel is very unreliable; and this will cause long delays if the channel is slow. But a channel that is fast and reliable is expensive.

If the user can afford to wait for a long sequence of data to flow in before they are encoded, the problem of choosing between channels is simplified, for their variety is reduced as follows. Instead of a whole array of likelihoods (of channel output symbols, given each input symbol) it becomes sufficient to use a single reliability measure (in bits per input symbol) which, multiplied by the channel's speed of transmission (in input symbols per time unit), gives the channel's "capacity," in bits per time unit.[2] Provided this capacity is larger than the number of bits per time unit that characterizes the uncertainty and speed of the flow of data, it has been shown that the user can achieve any desired probability of errors, however small, by using an appropriate, though redundant, code. Assuming that such codes have indeed been constructed (quite a difficult problem, solved only to a small part), it would be for the user to weigh against each other the disadvantages of errors, of time delays and of the high costs of high-capacity channels.

To avoid errors in our mutual understanding, let me be redundant, mindful of my low transmitting capacity and of your limited memory. I said a short time ago that engineers have isolated the pure communication problem by not concerning themselves with the services that produce data and that decide on acting; and also by usually refusing to distinguish between important and unimportant errors. I also pleaded, a longer time ago, on behalf of economists who emphasize that the demand for all services, all the transformers on my chart, is a joint one. Indeed, the user can improve the reliability of messages on which decisions are based by improving the communication service, but also by improving the data producing service which he is free to choose. Similarly, the user (the "meta-decider") is free to choose the deciding ser-

1. Not, in particular, in Claude E. Shannon's work on a "fidelity criterion," which does correspond to a general result function.

2. For example, two channels with equal transmission speeds and each characterized by the same array of likelihoods as, respectively, the old and the new barometer of our previous illustration have approximately equal capacities, in bits per second.

vice; for example, he may prefer not to burden the unskilled but inexpensive decider with messages written in a vocabulary that is too rich and fine. Moreover, depending on the user's result function, he may fear some errors of comunication but be indifferent to others. He may be indifferent to the music of the voice at the other end of the telephone; so he does not really need a high-fidelity telephone.

On the other hand, statisticians have isolated their problem, also essentially an economic one, by omitting the communication components. As I said before, this may be a good research strategy. I am told that in the early space vehicles rectangular pieces of equipment were used although the vehicles had circular cross-section. That is, the problem of building a good battery (say) was solved separately from, not jointly with, the problem of building a fast vehicle. Our problem-solving (decision-making) capacity is limited to only a few good solutions per manhour. To take up all problems at once is desirable but not cheap and perhaps not feasible. However, as time goes on the joint approach should be tried. Hence this economist's appeal to both statisticians and engineers.

I have just said that the limitation of the research capacity of all of us explains and possibly justifies the fact that engineers and statisticians have broken up the economics of symbol manipulation into separate sections, neglecting the essential complementarity of the several services from the point of view of the demand by the user.

However, this separation seems to be partly justified also by the economics of the services themselves; viz., by the supply side. I mean in particular the conditions for the production, and therefore for the supply, of inanimate transmission channels, such as telephones, the broadcasting apparatus, perhaps even the products of the old-fashioned printing press.

To be sure, you may not be anxious to learn about the bridal dress and be very much interested in the stock market. Yet your morning newspaper will bring you both a society page (which you will throw away) and a stock market page. Any page costs as much to print as any other page. The cost depends on the number of symbols on the page, and this corresponds to the number of bits transmitted by the printed messages. And the cost per bit turns out to be smaller if every subscriber receives both the social page and the stock market report and the sports page and the political news, regardless of his special tastes. Similarly, I am forced to subscribe to a high-fidelity telephone service although I am not interested in the music of the other person's voice. I suppose this is due to the economies of mass production. It is cheaper to produce instruments that will minimize the probability of transmission error — any error, however unimportant to me personally — than to custom-make instruments which would suit people's individual preferences. Remember that, in this country at least, with its large total demand for clothing and for food, consumers

do find it advantageous to buy ready-made suits and standardized groceries. To go to a Bond Street tailor or to buy fancy foods is slightly more satisfactory but so much more expensive!

The problem is familiar to operations researchers as that of optimal assortment. It is also known to social and economic statisticians, editors of census volumes, and makers of production indices. They call it "optimal aggregation." What indeed is the most economical way to break down a collection of items into groups, each to be treated as if it were homogeneous, when every detail suppressed involves some sacrifice, yet also saves cost?

Thus, it is just possible that, for the purposes of large markets (but not, I would think, for the purpose of building a particular satellite!) the isolated theory of transmission channels that minimize the probability of error — any error — is exactly what one needs. Yet, to be sure of this, we ought to have at least an approximate idea as to whether the services immediately complementing the transmission, that is, the services of coding, also exhibit advantages of mass production; and that the imperfections of available data producing and decision-making services are indeed negligible as to their economic effects.

Inanimate transmission channels do display the advantages of mass production. This makes it useful, when studying their supply conditions, to apply the pure theory of communication and to derive economically significant results from measuring information in bits. But what about other symbol-manipulating services: inquiry, coding, deciding? What can we say, in particular, about those supplied not by machines but by humans?

Before commenting on this most fascinating question, let us remind ourselves of the principles of the analysis of demand, supply, and the markets, and apply them, in particular, to the markets of symbol-manipulating services.

The demands of individual users are aggregated into the total demands for various data-providing services: total demands for weather forecasters and market prophets; for the output of research laboratories, for services of spies and detectives — given the prices of each of these services. Similarly with the total demands for various communication services — television, telephones, post office, newspapers, but also schools! — given, again, the prices of each. And so also with the demand for deciders — inventory clerks and vice-presidents for finance, and humble robots. Some of these services are substitutes for one another: for example, TV, radio and newspapers; telephone and mail. Some are mutual complements: the demand for weather data and for radio sets boosts each other.

Now, to explain the "given prices" in the markets and the kind and volume of transactions that actually come about, we need to know also the supply conditions. What does it cost to produce a market survey; to print a mass-circulation paper or a professional periodical; or to run a school? And to rear and train a vice-president or to build an automatic pilot? Again, the supply conditions are interrelated, although perhaps not as closely as the demand conditions. An automatic pilot combines the services of inquiring and of deciding, and it might be more costly to produce these services separately.

At any rate, the supply of a given service or a bundle of services — at given prices! — will depend on the costs of producing various kinds and amounts of them. Under competition the price will, then, equate demand and supply.

Is this not classroom economics? Yes indeed. But it should include the more advanced parts of it which allow for oligopoly, uncertainty, and other such things, mildly called "imperfections." Particularly important are the facts of indivisibility, or more precisely, the lack of homogeneity, of standardization of many of the symbol manipulators. There exist almost unique, irreplaceable research workers, teachers, administrators; just as there exist unique choice locations for plants and harbors. The problem of unique or imperfectly standardized goods is not peculiar to the economics of inquiring, communicating, and deciding. But it has been indeed neglected in the textbooks.

Let us return to the comparison of services supplied by men and by machines. The subject has seriously worried the most creatively imaginative pessimists of science fiction — from Karl Čapek to Ray Bradbury. It has also fascinated, and has led to some serious work of, psychologists and computer scientists. The results of this work, however tentative, are of great interest to us economists.

To begin with, humans are very poor transmission channels. "Indeed," says George Miller, a leading psycholinguist, "it is an act of charity to call a man a channel at all. Compared to telephone or television channels, man is better characterized as a bottleneck. Under optimal conditions it is possible for a skilled typist or piano player to transmit 25 bits per second. . . . We shall have to regard 25 bits per second as near the upper limit." More usually, the transmission capacity of an average person in our culture is only 10 bits or less, that is, we are unable to identify a stimulus without error when the stimulus is selected from more than 2^{10}, i.e., about a thousand equiprobable alternatives (that is, when the identification logically requires at least ten yes-or-no questions). As to the so-called "short memory," an important accessory of many transmission instruments, George Miller says that "no self-respecting photographic plate would even bother to sneer at us."

But what about the other symbol-manipulating services? Take coding. The lady who is typing the almost illegible manuscript of this lecture has an uncanny gift of recognizing the intended meaning of letters and words. I think she does this mostly by looking at the context of a whole sentence, or even of the whole paper itself. This we can interpret either by saying that she has the ability

of encoding almost without errors the data presented in longhand into the symbols of the typewriter alphabet; or that she decodes the longhand symbols given to her, into messages, and these into actions; viz., into pressing the keys, mostly in such a way that no error occurs. As you know, the computer industry has just begun to construct machines that may one day match the human ability to recognize simple visual patterns such as hand-written individual letters (not whole sentences!). But some people believe it will take a very long time (generations or centuries, Y. Bar-Hillel thinks) until a machine can conduct "intelligent conversation" with a man or with another machine. The key words are "heuristics" and "intuition." They are as vague as "pattern recognition," "Gestalt," and "context," and all these words are perhaps intended to have the same meaning. It is remarkable, in fact, in this very context, that you and I vaguely understand each other as to what the word "context' is intended to mean. We understand each other not letter by letter, not even word by word, but by grouping symbols into large chunks — letters (or, rather, phonemes) into words, and words into sentences, and even into larger entities, each including all sentences with the same so-called "meaning." The chunks forming the vocabulary of a human coder or decoder are of course much less numerous than the ensemble of all possible combinations of a given number of letters, say. The use of chunks diminishes therefore the flow of signals through the channel; it is more efficient, more economical. Consider the three letters C, O, W. They can be combined in six possible ways. But only one of the six combinations occurs in your vocabulary: cow. And, remarkably, it invokes not just the few properties listed by taxonomists who define a cow, but a whole image of shapes and sounds and colors and the tale waving the flies away. A most efficient, economical code — the living human language!

Most important, when you, a man, talk to a fellow human you adjust your code to the receptor, and keep readjusting it, sensitive to his feedback responses. Is this not what characterizes a good teacher? James Boswell, young and smug, wrote in his diary:

Health, youth, and gold sufficient I possess;
Where one has more, five hundred sure have less.

He could as well have said: my wealth is at the uppermost half per mill. This would be economical if you would address income statisticians: you would utilize a "subroutine" that has been educated into them! But when you address other people, better recite a poem.

Even the talking to computers is better done by men, at least today. The encoding, or programming, of a difficult problem for a computer is said to be an art, not a science. People who say this probably mean precisely this: the activity of programming cannot be delegated by men to machines, at least not in serious cases and not in the present state of technology. Hence the very large proportion (one-half, I understand) that the human activity of programming contributes to the value added by computing organizations.

To turn from coding to inquiring services. A biochemist (J. Lederberg) and a computer scientist (E. Feigenbaum) have told a computer how to generate the graphs of all imaginable organic compounds of a certain class, and also how to match them with certain empirically observed spectra. This was essentially a job of mathematical routine. But now comes the heuristics! The biochemist had accumulated enough experience and a flair to eliminate as unrealistic all but a few patterns from the thousands that the computer had produced. Yet the human being, a Nobel laureate, was not able to articulate his flair, although he did learn in this direction from the cooperation with the computer. Given the abilities and the technologies, there is some optimal way of allocating the tasks between men and machines — as economists have known long ago. And we must not be too hard on the computer: its hardware is certainly much less complex than the man's genetic endowment, and the computer's short babyhood is not rich in experience.

Finally, the service of decision making or problem solving. How to allocate tasks of this nature among executives and machines? A delicate problem! It involves all echelons of a corporation, up to, but of course not including, the president, who cannot fire himself. I had better skirt this subject!

But let me remind you of the distinction I have made earlier, between decision making and the higher-order activity of choosing who or what should provide a given service of decision making or of inquiring or of coding or transmitting. The man in charge was called the "leader" or "organizer." It is his judgment of prior probabilities and utilities, his "beliefs" and his "tastes" (or "values," in other words), that are used among the "givens" of the organizer's problem. He cannot delegate them, either to men or machines.

His problem may be, in fact, much, much larger than my chart suggests at first glance. The economic problem of organization is that of allocating numerous kinds of tasks, symbol manipulating as well as physical, to numerous transformers, arranged in a complex yet efficient network. And further complications, of a different kind, arise when a single organizer is replaced by several. Their beliefs and utilities are not the same. They engage in a nonconstant sum game. The economist's problem is then shifted from the search for optimality to the search for stability: he tries to explain, as does the biologist or anthropologist, why certain arrangements, certain allocations of tasks and incentives (rewards) have a greater chance to survive over a given period than other arrangements, and under what conditions.

The criterion of survival, viability and stability guides the social scientist who describes, and tries to explain, the existing institutions. Yet not everything that is stable is desirable. Some wicked dictatorships have been quite stable. Along with the stability criterion, the economist uses a weak collective optimality criterion, a modest common denominator on which people might agree in spite of their divergent utilities and beliefs: an arrangement of tasks and incentives is optimal in this modest sense if there is no feasible arrangement that would be better or at least not worse for all members of the organization.

What, then, if we consider the whole society as an organization? How should incentives and tasks be allocated in a way that is stable or is collectively optimal, or, if possible, both? Further, some of us cannot help but smuggle in our own values, in particular a high valuation of liberty and equity. I suppose "public policy," "public good," in our tradition, mean somehow to reconcile the criteria of stability and of collective optimality with those of liberty and equity. Though the economic theorist prefers to hide behind the technical term "welfare economics," he means not just Secretary Gardner's Department of Health, Education and Welfare, but much more, the whole public policy. Nor is our special concern only education, even if taken in the broad sense of the communication of what my chart calls "data," to the whole or some parts of the public. For research, inquiry has been also our concern here. Public policy problems in the field of symbol manipulation are crudely exemplified by questions such as, "When, if at all, should the government subsidize or protect research and teaching and the dissemination of news?"

As far as I know, welfare economics of symbol manipulation is at its beginning. Special problems, such as the theory of patents and of public versus private broadcasting and, most importantly, of the economics of education, have been studied and the names of Silberston, Coase, Gary Becker come to mind.

On the more abstract level, a basic distinction exists between the information about external facts and the information conveyed to a member of society about the doings of others. A preliminary analysis of economic policy of information about external facts has been made by my colleague Hirshleifer. If correct, his conclusions on teaching and research are quite relevant to the California battle of tuition fees, although Hirshleifer's analysis had to be based on some extreme, simplifying assumptions. To analyze the economics of information of people about other people is even harder. Game theorists have provided some building blocks. Ozga has worked on "imperfect markets through lack of knowledge" and Stigler on the information in the labor market. It is just one year ago that Leijonhufvud told this Association that Keynesian unemployment may be mostly due to lack of information. We know very little about the technology of such information; for example, about the optimal language. Indeed, many believe that the run on gold is dammed, not by verbal announcements in English or even in French, but by actually selling gold to all comers. And Radner has penetratingly pointed to the setup cost of information which makes for increasing returns to scale and makes it difficult to apply the classical theory of free markets, which reconciles optimality and stability.

All this discussion, mostly by young members of our Association, is very recent, very exciting, and, I believe, very important. The informational revolution is upon us, and the manipulation of symbols dominates our lives more and more. I do hope we shall soon understand how to harness and benefit from those trends in our culture.

64 An Efficiency Model and a Performance Function for an Information Retrieval System

DOUGLAS H. ROTHENBERG
Information Storage and Retrieval
Vol. 5, No. 3, October 1969

1. Introduction

The efficiency model and performance function presented below were constructed as devices for evaluation of a series of experimental information retrieval systems. These systems were studied rigorously within the Comparative Systems Laboratory (CSL), which formed a significant part of the activity summated under the Facility for the Health Sciences.

Although these functions were conceptualized specifically in terms of the CSL experiments, care was taken in their formulation to ensure generalization to a wider class of information retrieval systems. Thus, the variables of primary concern and the types of measures employed are widely applicable, and consequently, of considerable significance to persons engaged in the operation of information retrieval systems.

Previous work in the area of efficiency modeling and performance functions have included studies by Montague [1], Tell [2], Bourne and Ford [3], and Overmyer [4]. Montague's efficiency model calculated costs by task, whereas Bourne and Ford calculated costs by system use, and Overmyer calculated costs per search. Approximations of performance functions were implemented by Montague and Tell. Although this investigator recognizes the appropriateness of each of these earlier studies, he feels that they were significantly limited in their generalization to a number of operational cases.

The general efficiency model formulated below defines *efficiency* as the measure of the cost of operating a given information retrieval system. Thus, efficiency is a cost function of the number of units processed by the system as well as of the time the system is in operation. Subsequent to the formulation of the efficiency model, a performance function was constructed in order to compare the various information retrieval systems investigated within CSL, and the significant properties of this function also will be discussed. The performance function may be conceptualized as a combined measure of efficiency and of effectiveness — *effectiveness* being the ability of a system to retrieve relevant answers.

For these functions the terms cost and efficiency have been loosely equated. Strictly speaking, however, these terms express complementary concepts. That is, if the cost of a certain function is increasing, then its associate efficiency measure would be seen to decrease (all other factors held constant). Although economic studies are concerned with measures of efficiency, measures of cost are more easily obtained and may be seen to infer efficiency.

The representation of the efficiency model (also referred to at times as the cost function) is primarily personnel-oriented rather than task-oriented. That is, costs are calculated on personnel categories rather than on a task-by-task basis. This orientation was chosen in an attempt to generalize the model: personnel categories remain fairly constant from one project to another while task categories vary with the nature of the system. On the basis of this orientation, a static* model was formed for the efficiency measure. This model decomposes the entire retrieval process into an array of personnel cost coefficients and of increments of time required to operate the process. (For continuity all machine costs and time increments are treated in an analogous fashion.)

These functions were not actually implemented using data from CSL experiments, because record-keeping early in the project failed to provide valid and reliable data. (The necessary information might easily be obtained for other systems by implementing a set of simple bookkeeping practices as the system is developed and operationalized.) However, idealized cases are formulated and discussed.

The following discussion is divided into three sections: Section 2 dealing with the Efficiency Model, Section 3 dealing with the Performance Function, and Section 4 summarizing results.

2. The Formation of an Efficiency Model

This section discusses the formation of the efficiency model as it applies to an information retrieval process. The various costs associated with the total cost function are grouped according to their relative magnitudes and classification. The resulting model includes sufficient generality so as to be applicable to a broad class of studies while maintaining enough specificity to produce definite numerical results, given the necessary cost coefficients and data.

Section 2 is further subdivided into four cognate subsections: 2.1, Definition of terms; 2.2, Background and treatment of cost types; 2.3, Elements of the cost function; and 2.4, Final cost function.

2.1 Definition of terms

The following terms and variables are defined for use in this study (units for the variables are given within parentheses, following the definition):

v — efficiency, a cost function of time and quantity (dollars/unit time)

f_i — the ith subdivision of the fixed costs (dollars/unit time)

* By static model, it is implied that the parameters of the model, once obtained, are fixed over time, or at most, vary very slowly with respect to the operation of the process.

D — development costs, amortized as current costs (dollars/unit time)

C — general cost function (dollars/unit time/unit operation)

O — general operating costs function (dollars/unit time)

t — unit modulus of time (unit time)

c_j — the jth subdivision of the clerical costs coefficient (dollars/unit time/unit operation)

n — unit modulus of operation (unit operation)

m_k — the kth subdivision of the machine costs coefficient (dollars/unit time/unit operation)

z_q — the qth subdivision of the technical and clerical costs (dollars/unit time/unit operation)

$t_{c_j}, t_{m_k}, t_{z_q}$ — increment of time for clerical, machine, and technical operations respectively (unit time)

D_t — total development costs (dollars)

t_t — total expected life of the information retrieval process (units of time).

2.2 Background and treatment of cost types

"In the planning and execution of . . . projects it is frequently necessary to (compare or) select one of several alternatives, either on the basis of technical considerations or for reasons of economy. Frequently, such factors as technical feasibility, availability of capital, natural conditions, or the effects of diminishing returns, govern the choice of method. In many instances, however, the selection of an optimum alternative depends upon determination of the most economical choice." [5]

Thus it may be seen that the adequate treatment of the costs associated with a given program or project is important. In general, costs may be grouped into the following categories:

    a. Initial costs (development, etc.)
    b. Operating costs (personnel, updating, etc.)
    c. Fixed costs (rent, taxes, etc.)
    d. Operating returns (income for sale of products or by-products).

However, for purposes of this project, the operating returns factor will not be considered. In order to develop a general model with sufficient viability included to enable its application to produce numerical results, certain assumptions need to be made.

The first assumption concerns the linearity of the operating costs. All operating costs are assumed to appear in the final cost function linearly; e.g, if one unit of output (or operation) costs "x" dollars, then "n" units of output will cost $n \cdot x$ dollars. In reality, no process is entirely linear. However, in a practical situation, linearity can be assumed for at least a limited range of the quantity processed, n. Therefore, due to limited information concerning the process and conventional practice, operating costs will be considered to enter the efficiency model in a linear fashion.

The second assumption concerns the treatment of the cost of development of a given retrieval system. The development cost is defined to incorporate all expenses incurred through the actual development of a specific (retrieval) algorithm. Typical components of this cost include consultation fees, conferences and planning sessions, literature research, pilot studies, report compilations, etc. By the very nature of the manner in which the general costs are divided into different types, the development cost is a *once only* expense. A partial ambiguity arises concerning the development costs when one considers the chronological sequence of operations. It might be expected that these costs fit into the ordinary sequence of events: 1. Idea proposed; 2. Process developed, tested, etc.; 3. Process placed in operation. For most applications, the previous sequence it too restrictive. Many occasions arise during the operation of a particular process, after the development stage, when additional modifications and testing are necessary in order to insure proper operation. The ambiguity concerns whether to include the later costs into the development costs.* Since the particular process being discussed here is not considered to produce directly saleable products, liberty is taken by waiting until *all* costs are incurred before computing the various cost factors. Thus, development costs, no matter when they occurred, are grouped as development costs.

The third assumption concerns the type of amortization to be employed with respect to the development costs. It is exceedingly difficult to obtain or to predict the expected life of a specific information retrieval system. In the final analysis, anything obtained is only a very rough approximation. Thus, there is little justification to substantiate or suggest the employment of any sophisticated depreciation procedure. Consequently, the development cost per unit of time is given therefore by the following relationship:

$$D = \frac{D_t}{t_t} \qquad (2.1)$$

The fourth assumption concerns the availability of a digital computer capable of performing various integrated functions associated with the retrieval process. In this particular study it will be assumed that the desired machine will be available for use on an "actual time used" basis. This approach is in contrast with the case which considers that the machine has been obtained specifically for the given process. With present trends toward large networks of computer systems with centrally located processing units and remote data lines, the "actual time used" approach appears quite adequate.

* Usually development costs are computed when the process first is placed into operation, so that it can be amortized over the unts produced and thus be subsequently recovered.

Having made the preceding assumptions, the discussion will continue with a detailed study of the individual costs which eventually will compose the cost function in the efficiency model.

2.3 Elements of the cost function

As previously discussed, the costs are divided into three general categories: the cost of development (or initial cost), the operating cost, and the fixed costs.

The component parts of the development cost are enumerated below:

a. Designing — the cost of developing the product, technique, service, etc., including the associated planning and preliminary research.
b. Testing — the experimental verification of the theoretical concepts, investigation of alternative choices, or the gathering of additional information concerning certain properties or phenomena.
c. Evaluating — the cost of actively using and incorporating the results of "testing", both in a qualitative and quantitative manner.
d. Reporting — the costs associated with the preparation of suitable documentation sufficient to communicate the results, conclusions, knowledge, or experience gained by the research or development.

The specific development procedures vary considerably among projects and researchers. Thus, practices are employed during this stage which are not necessarily indicative of later operating practices. For this reason, the components of the development cost will not appear explicitly in the final cost function. Instead, a single term, D, will be assumed to represent the amortized development costs per unit of time.

The operating costs are defined to be those costs which are incurred during the actual operation of the process. Should the process be discontinued or shut down, these costs would reduce to zero during periods of inactivity. The component parts of the operating cost are given below. In contrast to the division of the development cost, the subdivision of the operating cost is a formal one. Each subdivision will appear explicitly in the final cost model.

i. *Clerical* (symbol: c)

1.	c_1	typist, salary category: 1
2.	c_2	typist, salary category: 2
.		
.		
.		
a.	c_a	typist, salary category: a
$a+1$.	c_{a+1}	file clerk, salary category: 1
.		
.		

$a + b.$ c_{a+b} file clerk, salary category: b

$a + b + 1.$ c_{a+b+1} key punch operator, salary category: 1

.

.

.

$a + b + c.$ c_{a+b+c} key punch operator, salary category: c

.

.

.

$J.$ c_J ...

ii. *Machine* (symbol: m)

   1. m_1 key punch, expense catgory: 1
   2. m_2 card verifier, expense category: 2
   3. m_3 card sorter, expense category: 3

.

.

.

$K.$ m_K digital computer, expense category: K

iii. *Technical, professional* (symbol: z)

   1. z_1 technical assistant (abstractor, checker, etc.), salary category: 1

.

.

.

$a.$ z_a technical assistant, salary category: a

$a + 1.$ z_{a+1} computer programmer, salary category: 1

.

.

.

$a + \beta.$ $z_{a+\beta}$ computer programmer, salary category: β

$a + \beta + 1.$ $z_{a+\beta+1}$ administrative assistant, salary category: 1

.

.

.

$a + \beta + \gamma.$ $z_{a+\beta+\gamma}$ administrative assistant, salary category: γ

.

.

.

$Q.$ z_Q principal investigator (developer), salary category: Q

The final cost type is the category of fixed costs. Normally, this includes all costs which are incurred by the process regardless of the quantity or amount processed or produced. Examples of these costs are rent, heat, light, taxes, etc. For convenience, the fixed cost are subdivided into "I" groups, each with a cost coefficient of "f_i".

In the next section the actual cost function will be formed. A detailed discussion of the properties of the function will follow.

2.4 *Final cost function*

The cost model, or cost function, will include the three types of costs previously discussed. Equation (2.2) below expresses these results.

$$v = C(t, n) = \sum_{i=1}^{I} f_i(t) + D(t) + O(t, n). \quad (2.2)$$

Expressing the operating costs in terms of its component parts, the resulting equation is given below.

$$O(t, n) = n \left\{ \sum_{j=1}^{J} c_j(t) t_{c_j} + \sum_{k=1}^{K} m_k(t) t_{m_k} + \sum_{q=1}^{Q} z_q(t) t_{z_q} \right\}. \quad (2.3)$$

Combining equations (2.2) and (2.3), the final cost function can be formed.

$$v = C(t, n) = \sum_{i=1}^{I} f_i(t) + D(t) + n$$
$$\left\{ \sum_{j=i}^{J} c_j(t) t_{c_j} + \sum_{k=1}^{K} m_k(t) t_{m_k} + \sum_{q=1}^{Q} z_q(t) t_{z_q} \right\}. \quad (2.4)$$

The cost function given by equation (2.4) is linear in n, the basic unit modulus of operation. The general shape of the cost function is shown in Fig. 1. The figure can be interpreted briefly as follows. If zero units of operation are performed during a unit period of time, the associated cost will be

$$v = C(t, 0) = \sum_{i=1}^{I} f_i(t) + D(t) \quad (2.5)$$

for as long as no output is required. Notice that $C(t, 0)$ is the v-intercept of Fig. 1. When output is desired, the cost (efficiency) increases linearly by the factor,

$$\sum_{i=1}^{J} c_j(t) t_{c_j} + \sum_{k=1}^{K} m_k(t) t_{m_k} + \sum_{q=1}^{Q} z_q(t) t_{z_q} \quad (2.6)$$

times the number of units, n. The factor above corresponds to the slope of the function in Fig. 1. The cost also can be expressed as a "cost per unit" and depicted as a function of the number of units. Figure 2 gives the function just described. The cost per unit decreases hyperbolically as the number of units increases. In the limit, as the number of units becomes very large, the cost per unit approaches the slope of the function given in Fig. 1.

In summary, this section has produced a model for the efficiency of an information retrieval system. Its properties have been briefly explained through the discussion of Figs. 1 and 2. The overall system performance

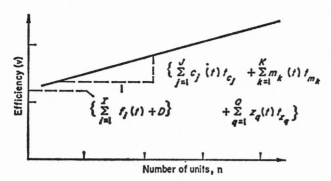

FIG. 1. Efficiency (cost) expressed as a function of the number of units produced.

can best be explained as a combination of its efficiency and its effectiveness. The following section discusses such a performance function.

3. System Performance

Two specific measures of system operation, effectiveness and efficiency, have been previously advanced. Consider the problem of comparing a number of separate systems by use of these two measures. For example, System A might operate very well mechanically (have a high effectiveness) and yet be very expensive (high efficiency = high cost). System B might have a substantially lower effectiveness and also operate at a significantly lower cost. Other systems, in addition could present various other combinations of their efficiency and effectiveness. Notice that the comparison between System A and System B is a very difficult one to make. The difficulty arises due to the fact that there are different attributes which must be simultaneously considered and compared.

One way of comparing the various systems would be to assume that one of the two attributes was very significant relative to the other. By doing this the problem has been reduced to the comparison of a single attribute. It is a simple matter to order the systems in a sequential order using this attribute as a measure. If the

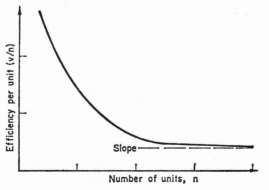

FIG. 2. Efficiency per unit produced expressed as a function of the number of units produced.

measure is a positive attribute* then one chooses the "best" system by selecting the one with the highest measure.

Clearly, the previous solution to the comparison dilemma is an extreme case. In actual experience it is usually not possible to reduce one attribute to insignificance. All the attributes are important, notwithstanding that some may be more important than others. The decision concerning the relative or comparative importance of various system attributes can be imbedded in a suitable performance function, a single measure — albeit composed of many complex elements — can be generated. Thus, a measure has been formed by which many systems can be ordered and compared each against the other.

The use of a performance function, however, is not magical. It possesses no supernatural power of decision-making or future forecasting. And so, its composure requires careful consideration and thought, in order that useful results be obtained. Thus, the performance function is in reality a formalization of one's objective, as well as subjective, conclusions concerning the relative importance of the various attributes or measures of the given systems.

As an example, consider the two systems, A and B, and the two measures, efficiency (v) and effectiveness (u). Consider also the following performance function,

$$P_s = \frac{v_s + u_s}{2} \tag{3.1}$$

where the subscript s refers to a general sth system. Equation (3.1) represents a performance function composed of the average of the effectiveness and efficiency. For systems A and B, we have

$$P_A = \frac{v_A + u_A}{2}, \qquad P_B = \frac{v_B + u_B}{2}.$$

If P_A is greater than P_B then system A is considered to be the preferable one; if P_B is greater than P_A then system B is considered preferable; and if $P_A = P_B$ then the two systems are considered to be equally satisfactory. Lest the impression be given by this example that if P_A is greater than P_B (P_B greater than P_A) for equation (3.1), the results hold for any performance function, a statement to the contrary will be made. The above results are true only for the given performance function. For the same two systems, if the performance function were changed, the results will not necessarily be the same.

Figure 3 depicts a very generalized information retrieval system. The terms used in the remaining text of this section will be defined in the next subsection.

* By positive attribute it is meant that the more of this attribute a given system possesses, the more desirable the system becomes.

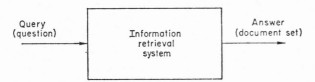

FIG. 3. The information retrieval process as an input/output system.

3.1 *Definition of terms*

The following terms and variables are defined below for use in this section. The units for the variables are given in parentheses following the definitions:

v — efficiency, a cost function of time and quantity produced (dollars/unit time)

u — effectiveness, a measure of an information retrieval system (dimensionless)

P — performance function, a function of v and u (not dimensioned)

$sgn(\cdot)$ — signum function, a function which has the value $+1$ if $(\cdot)$ is greater than or equal to zero: -1 otherwise (dimensionless)

$a, \beta, \bar{a}, \bar{\beta}$ — constants, positive in sign (dimensionless)

S_e — sensitivity, the measure of a system's ability to provide relevant answers to a user's query (dimensionless)

S_p — specificity, the measure of a system's ability to not provide non-relevant answers to a user's query (dimensionless)

a, b, c — constants, unrestricted in sign (dimensionless)

$1(u)$ — a function (dimensionless).

3.2 *Review of the effectiveness measure*

Recall that *effectiveness* is used as a measure of an information retrieval system's ability to perform the task for which it has been designed.

"The effectiveness measure must be an evaluation function that behaves in accordance with requirements imposed upon the system's performance.

" . . . effectiveness is defined [both] as a function of sensitivity and [of] specificity, where sensitivity measures the system's ability to provide the user with relevant members of the file and specificity measures the system's ability not to provide him with non-relevant members." [6]

Therefore, if sensitivity is defined to be,

$$S_e = \frac{\text{Number of documents retrieved that are relevant}}{\text{Total number of relevant documents}}$$

and specificity is defined to be,

$$S_p = \frac{\text{Number of documents not relevant and not retrieved}}{\text{Total number of not relevant documents}}$$

then effectiveness [7] can be defined to be,

$$v = \bar{a}(S_e) + \bar{\beta}(S_p - 1) \qquad (3.2)$$

where $\bar{a}, \bar{\beta} \geqq 0$.

3.3 *A performance function*

A performance function will be given in this subsection which measures a system's "quality" as a function of its effectiveness and efficiency. It is important to note that the performance function is not unique. There are conceivably large numbers of different performance functions which can be formed — they are limited only by the formulator's imagination and insight.

Consider the following function:

$$P = P(u, v) = u \cdot [au^2 - \beta(v - v_0)]^{[1.5 - 0.5\, sgn(u)]} \quad (3.3)$$
$$a, \beta > 0$$

where v_0 is the efficiency corresponding to $u = 0$.

The performance function given by equation (3.3) possesses the following useful properties:

1. The performance function is a positive attribute.
2. If $u < 0$ then P will always be less than zero (negative in sign).
3. If $u > 0$ then P is unconstrained in sign; e.g. may be positive or negative. This places primary emphasis upon whether the system is performing better than pure chance.
4. The performance, P, increases with (a) increasing values of effectiveness and (b) decreasing values of efficiency.
5. The relative magnitude of the effect between efficiency and effectiveness is governed by proper selection of the two parameters (or constants) a and β. Thus a and β are used to scale the two measures to the same relative order of magnitude as well as to emphasize one attribute over the remaining one, if desired.

Figure 4 depicts a structure for the implementation of the Performance Function to an information retrieval system. Thus, through the use of a performance function, the given retrieval system can be adjusted or adapted to perform in an optimal or "best" sense.

The arrow leaving the *performance* block and entering the *information retrieval system* block represents this adjustment. A few typical cases are given for the performance function in Fig. 5 for various values of a and β. Cases 1, 2 and 3 indicate in a qualitative manner the effects of an increasing emphasis of the effectiveness at the expense of the efficiency for a hypothetical system. Note that for each case, the experimental data — the observations on effectiveness and efficiency — remain fixed.

3.4 Optimality of performance function

In the preceding discussion a performance function has been advanced which will enable objective comparisons of information retrieval systems each of which may possess several attributes of interest. Therefore, given any number of retrieval systems and a suitable performance function, the systems can be ordered and the "best" determined. If a given system is in need of improvement, then all that is necessary is that another system be devised that performs better than its predecessor.

An inherent disadvantage of the previous line of action is the requirement of possessing that second system *in advance*. In other words, all that the performance function can do, for the present, is to compare different systems which are already in existence. We would like to be able to use the performance function to guide this search for a better system. The following discussion presents a method of at least predicting the characteristics of the optimal retrieval system.

In the discussion that follows, an illustrative example is presented in order to convey the potential of the approach. In this case, the knowledge of an optimal u may not be able to explicitly indicate the method by which this u may be achieved; however, it does offer an indicator as to the "best" results obtainable. Recall that a performance function is given by

$$P = P(u, v) = u \cdot [au^2 - \beta(v - v_0)]^{[1.5 - 0.5 sgn(u)]} \quad (3.3)$$

and that an empirical relationship (this can be determined from the data) between u and v can be formed for the given set of systems under study,

$$v = 1(u) = a + \tfrac{1}{2}bu + \tfrac{1}{3}cu^2. \quad (3.4)$$

Substituting equation (3.4) into equation (3.3), the result is,

$$P = u \cdot [au^2 - \beta(1(u) - v_0]^{[1.5 - 0.5\, sgn(u)]}. \quad (3.5)$$

For the moment, consider only the region for u greater than zero. A necessary condition for an optimal solution [7] to exist is that the derivative of P with respect to u vanish at the optimum.* Thus, find the u such that,

$$\frac{dP}{du} = 3au^2 - \beta \frac{d[1(u) - v_0] \cdot u}{du} = 0. \quad (3.6)$$

Note that $v_0 = a$, in this case.

Sufficient conditions for all u's satisfying equation (3.6) to be local maxima is that the second derivative of P with respect to u *exist* and that it be *negative* in sign. Consequently, the solution, u, of equation (3.6) and the equation given below,

$$\frac{d^2P}{du^2} = 6au - \beta \frac{d^2[1(u) - v_0] \cdot u}{du^2} < 0 \quad (3.7)$$

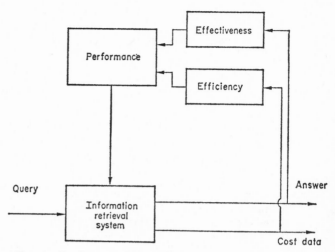

FIG. 4. Implementation of the performance function to an information retrieval system.

produce the optimal system for a given performance function and empirical data $[1(u)]$. The solution of equations (3.6) and (3.7) require the first and second derivatives of $[1(u) - v_0] \cdot u$. The first derivative of $[1(u) - v_0] \cdot u$ is given by,

$$\frac{d[1(u) - v_0] \cdot u}{du} = bu + cu^2 \quad (3.8)$$

and the second derivative is,

$$\frac{d^2[1(u) - v_0] \cdot u}{du} = b + 2ca. \quad (3.9)$$

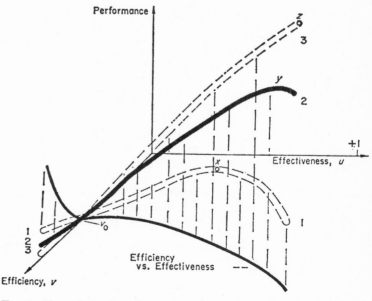

FIG. 5. Examples of performance functions based upon the same efficiency *vs.* effectiveness data.

Therefore, equation (3.6) becomes,

$$3au^2 - \beta(bu + cu^2) = 0 \qquad (3.6)'$$

and equation (3.7) becomes,

$$\frac{d^2P}{du^2} = 6au - \beta(b + 2cu) < 0. \qquad (3.7)'$$

The solution of equation (3.6)' is given by,

$$u^* = 0 \quad \text{and} \quad u^* = \frac{\beta b}{3a - \beta c} \qquad (3.10)$$
$$u > 0, \leqslant 1.$$

Incorporating the second derivative condition, if it exists, the optimal u will be found at u^* satisfying equation (3.10) and the following conditions:

$$\left.\frac{d^2P}{du^2}\right|_{u=u_*} = \beta b \qquad (3.11)$$

and thus we desire,

$$\beta b < 0 \qquad (3.12)$$

which in turn implies that the condition for u^* to be an optimal solution are met if,

$$b < 0$$

and

$$0 < u^* \leqslant 1.$$

As an example of the optimal value, refer again to Fig. 5. Notice that for each of the three cases there exists an optimal value of the performance function. For case 1 this maximum value occurs at point x; for case 2 the maximum is point y; and for case 3 the maximum is found at the endpoint corresponding to $u = 1$. The (u, v) coordinates for each of the optimal points x, y and z are different. This suggests that the best operating region for our system will be determined in a manner consistent with (and dependent upon) the predetermined emphasis upon u, the effectiveness, and v, the efficiency.

4. Summary and Conclusions

Previous investigators have structured the evaluation of information retrieval processes on the bases of two measures: namely, effectiveness and efficiency. This basis has been accepted as valid for the evaluative measures discussed here.

To summarize: A general efficiency model which allows calculation of specific costs data and a performance function based on Goffman's effectiveness model are con-

---

* This is true for any local optimum. A working definition of a local optimum is given to be any point (value of P) which is greater than (for positive attributes, less than for negative attributes) any other adjacent point. If P_0 is a local optimum then there exists an arbitrarily small ΔP such that

$$P_0 > P_0 \pm \Delta P$$

structed and discussed. These two measures permit the calculation of numerical data regarding the operation of given retrieval systems. Thus given a number of such systems, a table of values corresponding to the two measures — one pair for each system — may be produced. The problem of evaluating these pairs *vis-à-vis* each other, of ordering these pairs in regards to effectiveness and efficiency, and of choosing the "best" system for a given situation is handled by the performance function.

In essence, the performance function produces a single number representing the system's overall "performance" from the pair of numbers describing the efficiency and effectiveness of that system. The choice of the "best" system — i.e. that system with the most desirable properties — becomes a matter of selecting the system with the highest performance rating. Similarly, ordering systems according to their performance functions is achieved by arranging the systems in numerical order. The validity of this procedure depends largely upon the extent to which the efficiency and effectiveness measures embrace all criteria of primary concern to the evaluator.

An advantage inherent to this approach to evaluating system performance is the achievement of a tool helpful in measuring the evolution of retrieval systems. That is, the effects of the systematic variation of certain aspects of system's construction and implementation (both of subjective and objective origin) can be evaluated mathematically, and their effect upon the retrieval process measured. Hence we may consider the performance function as a metric in comparing information retrieval systems and in evaluating innovations.

References

1. B. A. MONTAGUE: Testing, comparison and evaluation of recall, relevance and cost of coordinate indexing with links and rolls, *Proc. Am. Docum. Inst.*, 1964, 357.
2. B. V. TELL: Auditing procedures for information retrieval systems, *Proc. Congr. Int. Federation for Documentation*, 1965, 119.
3. C. P. BOURNE and F. D. FORD: Cost analysis and simulation procedures for the evaluation of large information systems. *Am. Docum.*, 1964, **15**, 142.
4. L. OVERMYER: An analysis of output cost and procedure for an operational searching system, *Am. Docum.*, 1963, **14**, 123.
5. S. A. ROSENTHAL: *Engineering Economics and Practice.* MacMillan, New York (1964).
6. T. SARACEVIC and A. M. REES: Toward the identification and control of variables in information retrieval experimentation. *J. Docum.*, 1967, **23**, 7.
7. W. GOFFMAN and V. A. NEWILL: Methodology for test and evaluation of information retrieval systems, *Inf. Stor. Retr.*, 1966, **3**, 19.
8. G. HADLEY: *Non-Linear and Dynamic Programming.* Addison–Wesley, Reading, Mass. (1964).

65 Systems Analysis in University Libraries

FERDINAND F. LEIMKUHLER
College & Research Libraries
Vol. 27, No. 1, January 1966

This paper attempts to outline a fairly comprehensive, engineering approach to the functional design of a university library system. It is comprehensive in the sense that it considers both long-run and short-run patterns in library operations in an integrated manner. It is an engineering approach in that it attempts to isolate the fundamental space-time relationships that characterize a library and to treat them in an analytic manner.

Although a library is essentially a social institution steeped in human values of all kinds, it can be viewed as a complex communication system charged with the task of transferring information through space and time, and as such, it is particularly amenable to engineering analysis. The mathematical models which emerge from such an analysis may seem far removed from the librarian's view of the library, but they are almost certain to provide a much better basis for the design and operation of library systems than is now available.

The models developed below are the result of several years of discussions and joint research efforts by librarians and industrial engineers at Purdue University. There is no attempt here to make forced applications of industrial techniques, although the general methodology of operations research is readily applicable in the library

environment. The appropriate goal is neither the advent of total library automation nor the complete mathematical description of a library system. Rather, it is a search for reliable methods of measurement and analysis which are compatible with the established objectives of library administration.

In the remainder of the paper, models are developed to help to explain how acquisition, circulation, storage, loan period, and duplication policies and patterns interact over the long run. Circulation, as a measure of library activity, becomes the one factor related to all of the others. Total circulation is shown to depend on the size of the collection, its rate of growth, the usage of new acquisitions, and their obsolescence rate. The circulation of individual items is later seen to be closely bound up with the demand pattern, the loan period, and the availability of duplicate or substitute materials.

Availability can be increased by purchasing duplicate copies and maintaining branch libraries but with a consequent increase in the eventual accumulation of obsolete materials. Tighter control of acquisitions and loan policies is seen to reduce obsolescence to a limited extent, but eventually every library will have a considerable amount of inactive materials. Optimal selection rules for withdrawing these items from active storage, and optimal shelving rules for storing the selected materials are two promising methods for relieving the pressure on today's bulging libraries.

The models presented have been deliberately simplified in order to emphasize their contribution to an overview of the library as a system. Particular applications would require considerably more detail and complexity in the models. In their present state, however, they do serve to indicate some general trends, isolate the important factors associated with the trends, and indicate areas for further study.

The development is divided into three parts: (*a*) growth models, (*b*) storage models, and (*c*) availability models. The first involves a time-series analysis of acquisitions, holdings, and circulation. The second part considers several aspects of book storage in a manner that is analogous to modern inventory theory. The third part treats the library as a stochastic service system and applies some elementary queueing models to determine the availability and circulation of single and duplicate copies at central or branch libraries.

1. Acquisitions, Circulation, and Obsolescence

The twentieth-century explosion in knowledge is reflected in the growth of university libraries. A study of Danton's[1] figures for the holdings of the ten largest American universities indicates a fairly steady rate of growth of 4.5 percent per annum since the year 1850. This is the same rate Johnson[2] cites for the growth in scientific journals since the year 1700.

The history of the Purdue University libraries over the past forty years shows an amazingly steady increase of about 6 percent per annum in both acquisitions and holdings. The evidence suggests an elementary growth model of the form:

$$N_t = (1 + a) N_{t-1} = (1 + a)^t N_0 \qquad (1)$$

where N_t defines the size of the collection at the end of year t as a function of the annual growth rate, a, and the size t years ago, N_0. It follows that the acquisitions, A_t in year t are proportional to the size of the collection, since:

$$A_t = N_t - N_{t-1} = aN_{t-1} = \frac{a}{1+a} N_t. \qquad (2)$$

Circulation records are a measure of the service performed by a library, but such data has only recently been given the scrutiny it deserves. A forty-year record of circulation (home use) at the Purdue libraries suggests a long-run trend that parallels that of acquisitions and holdings, with some fluctuation both above and below the trend line. At all times, however, the total number of books checked out is considerably less than the total

holdings, with the implication that a large number of books in any one year are inactive and that the number of such volumes is increasing steadily (Fig. 1).

Studies by Fussler and Simon[3] at Chicago and by Jain[4] at Purdue have shown that the average circulation of library materials decreases consistently with the length of time since their publication or acquisition. A preliminary analysis of their data suggests that this decrease occurs at a fairly steady rate. Jain's data suggests a 6 percent annual decline since acquisition and a 4.5 percent rate since publication, but these estimates are based on a relatively small sample.

If the annual decrease in activity occurs at some constant "obsolescence" rate, β, then the circulation in year t of all books acquired in year t-j can be defined as follows:

$$C_t (A_{t-j}) = C_0 (1 - \beta)^j A_{t-j} \qquad (3)$$

where C_0 is their average circulation rate in the first year of acquisition. By combining equations (1), (2), and (3), the annual circulation of the entire collection can now be defined by:

$$C_t (N_t) = \frac{aC_0}{a + \beta} N_t + \frac{\beta C_0}{a + \beta} (1 - \beta)^t N_0. \qquad (4)$$

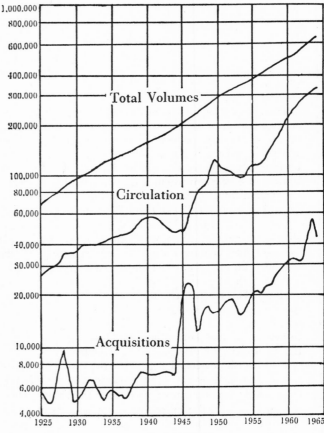

FIG. 1. Purdue libraries.

Here, the first term defines the long-run trend, since the second term disappears for large t. However, any change in a, β, or C_0 would cause an asymptotic shift in circulation to a new trend line.

2. Circulation, Storage, and Shelving

Many libraries are contemplating or practicing some form of depository storage of less active materials. Methods of selecting items for storage have been proposed by Fussler and Simon, Jain, and Trueswell,[5] all of which seek to minimize the anticipated circulation of the stored items as a collection, i.e. to select *least used* material for storage.

One such plan would be simply to relocate all items acquired more than d years ago, as is sometimes done with periodicals. The relative advantages of such a plan can be demonstrated with the use of equations (1) and (4). The proportion, n_d, of the total collection stored under this plan is found from equation (1) to be:

$$n_d = \frac{N_{t-d}}{N_t} = \frac{1}{(1+a)^d} . \tag{5}$$

From equation (4), the proportion of the total circulation which is due to the stored items is defined by:

$$c_d = \frac{C_t (N_t - d)}{C_t (N_t)} = \left(\frac{1-\beta}{1+a} \right)^d . \tag{6}$$

where a is the growth rate and β is the obsolescence rate as before.

Values of n_d and c_d are shown in Table I for a hypothetical library with $a = \beta = 0.06$. Such a library can expect to satisfy 95 percent of its circulation with its acquisitions of the past twenty-five years, or about 77 percent of the total collection. Acquisitions of the past twelve years alone account for half of the collection and 76 percent of the circulation.

Better utilization of shelf space can often be made in

TABLE I

Relative Use of Stored Items

Age, d, in Years, When Stored	Proportion of Collection in Storage*	Proportion of Circulation from Storage
5	0.75	0.55
10	.56	.30
12	.50	.24
15	.42	.17
20	.31	.09
25	.23	.05
30	.17	.03
35	.13	.02
40	.10	.01

* A 6 percent acquisition and obsolescence rate assumed.

TABLE II

Efficiency of Storage by Size

Number of Size Classes	Potential Capacity Increase	
	Storage by Height, Percent	Storage by Width, Percent
1	0	27
2	38	94
3	47	111
4	51	116
5	53	121
10	58	128

the storage of inactive materials. Leimkuhler and Cox[6] developed an exact method for evaluating the spatial efficiency of shelving books by size, and Cox[7] has extended the model to include various aspects of shelf construction. Raffel[8] has recently published a very efficient programing model for evaluating shelf storage by both height and width. These models are capable of specifying the best size classifications (shelf-heights) to use for any given collection.

Table II gives the results for shelving a representative sample of the Purdue collection at optimal shelf heights. It can be seen that the additional gain in capacity decreases quite rapidly as the number of size classes increases. The Purdue studies indicate that no more than three or four classes would ever be needed in a compact storage area. Further studies of shelving systems are needed especially with regard to their cost and compatibility in the total library context.

It is worth remembering that Dewey[9] recommended shelving by size. In general, subdivisions of large collections in various ways, by size, use, etc., permits more efficient operations on a suboptimal level. The bigger problem is to integrate the parts into a unified and effective system.

3. Availability, Circulation, and Duplication

Studies at Massachusetts Institute of Technology by Morse[10] and others have focused on the random nature of the demand for library services. This is a crucial element in the design of almost all kinds of service facilities and usually implies the need for considerable "over design" in the system or the provision of excess service capability. A well developed engineering treatment of this topic has evolved over the past fifty years within the telephone industry and recently has found wide application in such diverse places as supermarkets and superhighways. The theory is bound to play an increasingly important role in the future design of library systems.

As an elementary application, consider the circulation pattern of a single volume, which is requested randomly or independently in time but at a steady rate, R. (This is the pattern observed by Morse.) The average time interval between checkouts for the book can be divided into two parts: The mean loan interval, T_L, and the mean interval between checkin and checkout, T_R, which in the "random" case is equal to $1/R$. Thus, the mean circulation rate C_1 of the volume can be written:

$$C_1 = \frac{1}{T_R + T_L} = \frac{R}{1 + \dfrac{T_L}{T_R}} \qquad (7)$$

which indicates that the circulation rate is always less than the request rate.

The proportion of satisfied customers, C_1/R, is a useful measure of the availability of the book; and the fraction, T_L/T_r, is a measure of the service load on the book, commonly called "traffic intensity." Where $T_L = T_r$, the book is only available for 50 percent of the requests. As the request rate diminishes, availability increases but circulation decreases. If the request rate increases, circulation increases also, but availability falls off rapidly, so that the circulation increase is accompanied by a considerable rise in the number of disappointed customers.

Two common library responses to the demand for popular books are: (a) the shortened loan period, and (b) the acquisition of extra copies. Equation (7) can serve to evaluate the first of these strategies, since a reduction in T_L reduces the traffic intensity and increases both availability and circulation, assuming no change in demand. A 50 percent reduction in the loan period produces the same effect on availability that a 50 percent decrease in the request rate would produce. However, circulation is increased in the former case and reduced in the latter case.

The analysis of the effects of duplication on circulation and availability requires an extension of equation (7). The circulation rate, C_2, for two copies can be defined in terms of the rate, C_1, with one copy as follows:

$$C_2 = \frac{2C_1}{1 + \left(\dfrac{C_1}{R}\right)^2}. \qquad (8)$$

Since the availability with one copy C_1/R, is always less than unity, it can be seen immediately that two copies can never succeed in doubling circulation. For example, if the single copy was available only half of the time, duplication will increase total circulation for the two volumes only 60 percent above that of the single volume. Availability is increased in the same proportion, i.e. from 0.5 to 0.8.

What is even more significant for the long run is the fact that duplication always reduces the *average* circulation per volume. For the previous example, the circulation per volume was *reduced* 20 percent in order to increase availability. As the demand for a particular book diminishes, duplicate copies add less and less to the availability but contribute significantly to the apparent obsolescence of the collection.

The above models also shed some light on duplication among branch libraries, since this plan is analogous to the division of requests into two separate streams each serviced by its own copy. If loans between branches are not made, then it can be shown that the increase in circulation is always less than if the two copies are held at the same location.

The best that can be done under such circumstances is to divide the demand equally between the branches, which yields a total circulation of:

$$C_{2B} = \frac{2C_1}{1 + \dfrac{C_1}{R}}. \qquad (9)$$

For the above example, where $C_1/R = 0.5$, the total circulation is increased only 33 percent by the branch policy of duplication, and circulation per volume is decreased 33 percent. The availability at each branch would be 0.67 as contrasted to 0.5 for the single volume and 0.8 for two copies at a central point. With unequal division of demand between the branches the total circulation is increased even less and circulation per volume reduced even more.

These models serve to indicate the effects of various policy decisions. It is unlikely that they are precise estimators of actual performance because of the assumptions required in their development, as, for example, that the demand rate for a book is independent of its availability or the loan policy. Much more complex models would be required to account for such reader reactions as discouragement and impatience and the substitution of similar books. Such models can be or have been developed to varying degrees of perfection within the voluminous literature of queueing theory. The difficulties of adapting these theories to library practice should not be underestimated, but there is no question of the feasibility and eventual benefits of such an undertaking.

References

1. DANTON, J. P. *Book Selection and Collections: A Comparison of German and American Universities.* New York, Columbia, 1963.
2. JOHNSON, E. A. "The Crisis in Science and Technology and its Effect on Military Development." *Operations Research*, VI (No. 1, 1958), 11–34.
3. FUSSLER, H. H. & J. L. SIMON. *Patterns in the Use of Books in Large Research Libraries.* Chicago, University of Chicago Library, 1961.
4. JAIN, A. K. *A Sampled Data Study of Book Usage in the Purdue University Libraries.* Lafayette, Indiana, Purdue University, 1965.
5. TRUESWELL, R. W. "A Quantitative Measure of User Circulation Requirements and its Possible Effect

on Stack Thinning and Multiple Copy Determination." *American Documentation,* XVI (January, 1965), 20–25.

6. Leimkuhler, F. F. & J. G. Cox. "Compact Book Storage in Libraries." *Operations Research,* XII (May–June, 1964), 419–27.

7. Cox, J. G. *Optimum Storage of Library Materials.* Lafayette, Purdue University Libraries, 1964.

8. Raffel, L. J. "Compact Book Storage Models." (Master's thesis, Purdue University, 1965.)

9. Dewey, Melvil. "Library Shelving, Definitions and General Principles," *Library Notes,* II (September, 1887), 95–122.

10. Morse, P. M. "Probabilistic Models for Library Operations," Minutes of 63rd Meeting, Association of Research Libraries (Chicago, January, 1964), 9–13.

Part Four
A Unifying
Theory

Chapter Thirteen
A General
Theory
of
Communication

The nature, type, level, role and significance of a theory have been expounded in philosophy, in the philosophy of science and in individual sciences. Throughout the history of science, the values and impacts of a theory have been manifoldly demonstrated. Thus, these well-known aspects of a theory will be discussed only briefly.

A theory may be viewed as a symbolic construct, based on a judgment, conception, proposition, or on a coherent and systematic set of hypothetical, conceptual or pragmatic principles, which relates to the nature, cause, action, manifestation or origin of a phenomenon (or group of phenomena). A theory is formed by speculation, deduction, or abstraction and by generalization from facts or axioms. The structure of a theory is manifested by rational and comprehensive propositions, synthesized in succeeding, logical steps through reasoning. A theory may be said to be a device for interpreting, criticizing, and unifying established facts, laws, observations or axioms; it seems to demarcate the phenomena or axioms with which it deals by an explanatory shell or sphere.

As to the types of theories, Einstein (in Essays in Science) remarked:

"We can distinguish various kinds of theories in physics. Most of them are constructive. They attempt to build up a picture of the more complex phenomena out of the materials of a relatively simple formal scheme from which they start out . . . Along with this most important class of theories there exists a second, which I will call 'principle-theories.' These employ the analytic, not the synthetic, method. The elements which form their basis and starting point are not hypothetically constructed but empirically discovered ones, general characteristics of natural processes, principles that give rise to mathematically formulated criteria which the separate processes or the theoretical representations of them have to satisfy . . . The advantages of the constructive theory are completeness, adaptability and clearness, those of the principle theory are logical perfection and security of the foundations."

In relation to the role or function of a theory, Abraham Kaplan (in The Conduct of Inquiry, the basis of most of this discussion) views the function of a theory as: ". . . introducing order . . . systematization . . . simplification . . . providing meaning; . . . To make sense of what would otherwise be unscrutable or unmeaning empirical findings; . . . To integrate or organize into a single deductive system sets of empirical laws which previously were unrelated; . . . Theory may serve as a device to and in the formulation of further empirical laws."

Theories have been and should be utilized as a basis to stimulate, suggest and direct the course of experiments, especially when the direct object of a theory is to connect or coordinate apparently diverse phenomena. Thus, the significance of a theory lies in the activity that it may guide: forming concepts and laws, conducting experiments, measuring, providing explanations, and, quite importantly, yielding predictions.

The relation between one theory and other theories is explained by Kaplan as follows:

". . . The history of science is undeniably a history of the successive replacement of poor theories by better ones, but advances depend on the way in which each takes account of the achievements of its predecessors."

In relation to empirical laws, it may be said that laws are discovered, and theories are invented and constructed. And importantly, in relation to knowledge, theories also offer understanding, which may be valued for its own sake. J. B. Conant (in Modern Science and Modern Man) most aptly described the significance of theories and theory making: ". . . The history of science demonstrates beyond a doubt that the really revolutionary and significant advances come not from empiricism but from new theories."

The awareness of the nature, type, functions, relations and significance of theories in the sense discussed above, has not extensively penetrated the tradition and works in information science. On the one hand there remains a lack of accepted, formal, comprehensive theories which can serve as the basis for further inquiries. On the other hand, there is a proliferation of hypotheses, offered in isolation, which are used as quasi-theories. As a result, much of the experimental work, and especially developmental work, is done in its own vacuum, unconnected with other works. The cumulation of knowledge can hardly be accomplished in such an environment.

The final offering of this book is a comprehensive, mathematically oriented theory of communication. In the sense of Einstein's types of theories, this theory is a 'principle-theory,' employing the analytic method. By it, a diversity of previously unconnected phenomena are associated through the behavior, characteristics, and manifestations of the communication process with the structure of information systems and with the control of the processes involved. The theory's most interesting generalization is the analogy between the communication of ideas and the communication of diseases. The constructs in this theory could and did serve as a base for experimentation; more significantly, they could be utilized in the construction of further theories.

Even for those who are not mathematically oriented, this theory offers the basic definitions of the concepts involved and provides a foundation which could be the starting point of their own understanding and perhaps of the formulation of their own theories.

Information theory was the first unifying theory about the basic phenomenon, information, of interest in information science. That theory probably gave the impetus for the field to develop as a science, above and beyond the technology. However, information theory was primarily directed toward the physical transmission of signals and, as such, its limitation was recognized with regard to the overall complexities of human communication. This limitation does not in any way impugn the fundamental importance of information theory to information science. The implication is that more than information theory is needed, and that the theory offered here may fill a number of gaps.

A General Theory of Communication

WILLIAM GOFFMAN

1. Communication as an Epidemic Process

1.1 Introduction

Information science aims at being a unified scientific approach to the study of the various phenomena connected with the notion of information. These phenomena can be found in biological processes as well as in human existence and the machines created by human beings. Thus, the subject has evolved as a synthesis of methods drawn from the traditional disciplines for the purpose of studying the multivaried aspects of information flow within a population of objects be they human beings, micro-organisms or machines. Information science, therefore, is essentially concerned with the principles underlying communication processes and their associated information systems.

In general, a process is a time dependent phenomenon, i.e., a sequence of actions leading to some result. A communication process is thus a sequence of events resulting in the transmission of information from one object to another. The first object is called a source and the latter a destination. The mechanism by means of which a process is realized is called a system. More pre-cisely, a system is a collection of elements interacting to perform a specific function for a specific purpose. Systems whose function is the carrying out of communication processes are known as information systems. A system will thus take the information at the source and operate on it in some way to produce a signal suitable for transmission on some channel to a receiver at the destination. With every communication process there is associated a set of information systems, namely those systems capable of carrying out the particular process. Such systems need not be unique since a given process may be realized by a variety of mechanisms.

The major difficulty in any scientific treatment of communication processes arises from the fact that the concept of information although intuitively understood can be neither formally defined nor precisely measured. However, when considering processes whose outcomes are governed by the transmission of information, the information transmitted may be evaluated in terms of these outcomes. Hence, the study of communication processes and information systems may be approached in this way.

There seems to be three broad problem areas relating to the outcome of a communication process. These are:

1. *The behavioral problem* which deals with the success with which information conveyed from a source to a destination effects the desired outcome at the destination.
2. *The representation problem* which is concerned with all aspects of representing information to be conveyed so that it will be correctly understood at the destination.
3. *The technical problem* which is concerned with the accuracy of transmitting the information from the source to the destination.

Clearly, the three problem areas are not independent of each other because the question of behavior depends to some degree on the other two. In fact, it would seem that the representation and technical problems relate more directly to information systems, i.e., to the realization of communication processes rather than to such processes themselves. The mathematical theory of communication as developed by Claude Shannon and others[1,2] deals chiefly with the technical problem and although very profound is thereby limited. Hence, it is of little value in approaching the problems of communication from a general point of view.

The fundamental concept underlying the behavioral problem in communication is the notion of effective contact between the information source and the destination. For example, effective contact is clearly the governing factor in the outcomes of the two most familiar communication processes, namely the transmission of knowledge and the transmission of disease. It is thus not surprising to find a striking parallel between these two processes. An excellent detailed discussion of this analogy can be found in Siegfried[3]. In the case of disease we are dealing with infectious material which can be transported and transmitted while in the case of knowledge we are dealing with the transport and transmission of ideas, benevolent or malevolent depending on one's point of view. In either case, for diffusion to take place, there must be an individual who puts forth the infectious material or idea, a carrier who transfers it and receptive surroundings. The extent of diffusion in both instances is then a matter of effective contact between the agents transmitting the infectious material or ideas and those individuals coming in contact with them. The human being, in the case of ideas, is the propagating agent either by word of mouth or through the medium of books, articles, pamphlets and so forth just as he causes the spread of germs either directly or through intermediate hosts. Ideas, moreover, are propagated along the same routes as are the spreading of germs; in both cases the world's transportation routes. The routes of ancient caravans, for example, which provided the instrument of communication were also the routes travelled by disease. In fact, the vocabulary which normally comes to mind when dealing with diffusion of ideas is that of medicine. One often hears such expressions

as "that's a contagious idea" or "he's not too susceptible to that idea" and so forth.

Just as society fights against the invasion of disease, so it defends itself against subversive ideas. Its most decisive action is to destroy the germ or idea at its source. This is often difficult since, in both cases, one does not always know exactly where to find it. Another defense consists of suppressing the carrier or at least preventing him from entering the territory one wishes to preserve. The most prudent procedure is to take preventive measures. Censorship, police supervision and religious persecution are all examples of this approach. In the defense measures that human societies adopt against the attacks and penetrations of new ideas, mechanisms similar to immunization and vaccination likewise exist. A given reform, subtly inspired by the menace itself, will often prevent the new ideas from spreading when they appear locally. A healthy society has its own defenses against such infections which might endanger the integrity of its personality. On the other hand, an unhealthy society will catch all of the illnesses and will react to all infections. Rome, for example, was not able in its decline to defend itself against Christianity. As an example of the spread of ideas in the intellectual world consider the development of psychoanalysis in the early part of this century. Freud was no less host to the infectious material of the disease "psychoanalysis" than the person carrying the organism capable of transmitting a cold, nor are his writings less an intermediate host carrying infectious material than is the mosquito a carrier of the agent of malaria. Moreover, Abraham, Ferenczi, Jung and Jones were no less infected by the ideas of Freud than are those individuals infected by the agent transmitted by the cold carrier. After a certain period of time, Freud's disciples were themselves in a position to transmit infectious material to others. Jung might represent an example of acquired immunity to the disease while the resistance of the medical community of Vienna might represent innate immunity. The development of the psychoanalytic movement in the early part of the twentieth century was in its way no less an epidemic than was the outbreak of influenza in 1917 and 1918. It was also not surprising that the psychoanalytic epidemics took place in the Protestant countries which provided more receptive surroundings for the infectious material, i.e., Freud's ideas, than the Roman Catholic countries. Psychoanalysis is an example of an intellectual epidemic instigated by an individual. Such epidemics are not unusual in the world of scientific thought. One may cite many other well-known occurrences, e.g., Darwin and evolution, Cantor and set theory, Boole and symbolic logic, Newton and mechanics and so forth.

It is thus apparent that the process of transmitting infectious disease and the process of transmitting knowledge have many common characteristics. In fact, the primitive notions of knowledge, information and ideas stand in the same relation to each other in the one case as do the primitive notions of disease, agent and infectious material in the other. In the transmission of knowledge the idea plays the role of the infectious material; information corresponds to the agent by means of which the infectious material is transmitted and the interaction between an individual and an idea may or may not result in the accumulation of knowledge, just as the interaction between an individual and infectious material may or may not result in a case of disease.

Because the principles underlying the spread of infectious disease also govern the diffusion of information and the spread of knowledge, a communication process can be represented as an epidemic process. Consequently, epidemic processes can be used as models to develop our understanding of communication processes. That is, we can replace the study of communication processes by the study of epidemic processes for which a theory is known and which has certain important characteristics in common with the field under investigation.

1.2 The Epidemic Process

There are two elements necessary for the development of an epidemic process: a specific population and an exposure to infectious material. The members of the population may belong to one of three mutually exclusive classes at a given point in time:

1. *Infectives:* those members of the population who are host to the infectious material.
2. *Susceptibles:* those members of the population who can become infectives given effective contact with infectious material.
3. *Removals:* those members of the population who have been removed from circulation for a variety of reasons such as death or immunity. These members may have been either infectives or susceptibles at the time of their removal.

The entire process is time dependent, i.e., a sequence of events occurs which describes its behavior. An individual is exposed to infectious material either by direct contact with an infective or through some intermediate host. The exposed individual may either be resistant to the incoming organism, in which case the organism is rejected, or may be infected by it, in which case the invading organism proceeds on a course of development. The time interval in which this development takes place is called the latency period. The latency period is thus the time between receipt of infectious material by a susceptible and his ability to transmit infectious material to some other susceptible, i.e., the interval of time needed to transform a susceptible into an infective. When such a transition occurs, an effective contact between the susceptible and the infectious material transmitted by the infective is said to have taken place. The time interval between receipt of infectious material and the appearance

of symptoms is called the incubation period after which a manifest case of disease appears. The process itself may be in one of two states at a given point in time; namely

1. *Stable:* the change in the rate at which the number of infectives accrue with respect to time is equal to zero.
2. *Unstable:* the change in the rate at which the number of infectives accrue with respect to time is not equal to zero.

If the change in this rate is positive, then the process is said to be in an epidemic state. If the change in this rate is negative, then the process is said to be in a decreasing state.

Because epidemic processes can serve as models for communication processes, it follows that such processes can be defined in terms of a set N (population of objects) together with an agent i (information) which is conveying infectious material among the members of N. Consequently, the members of N pass through a set of states s (susceptible, infective and removal) and the entire process through a set of states S (stable and unstable) with respect to time. A communication process C can thus be formally expressed by

$$(1) \qquad C = <N, i, s, S:t>.$$

1.3 Mathematical Representation of Epidemic Processes

There has been an extensive development of a mathematical theory of epidemics which can now be of general use in studying communication processes. There are generally two types of mathematical representations of epidemic processes, namely deterministic and stochastic. The deterministic approach represents the process by a system of non-linear differential equations while the stochastic one describes it as a finite state Markov process of either discrete or continuous parameter depending upon the nature of the physical process. For example, if infectives occur in generations, then a Markov process of discrete parameter would constitute the appropriate representation. Although a complete mathematical theory of epidemics is still very far away, there has been considerable progress in this direction in recent years. An excellent survey of these developments can be found in Bailey[4] which also contains an essentially complete bibliography as well as an historical sketch of the development of mathematical and statistical theories of the spread of infectious disease.

Specifically, a mathematical representation of an epidemic process aims at establishing non-trivial stability conditions for the process, i.e., the circumstances, in terms of certain basic parameters, under which there will be an increase, decrease or no change in the number of infectives accrued with respect to time. The theory thus attempts to predict the future behavior of the process given a set of initial conditions. To solve these problems it is necessary to obtain a mathematical expression for the number of infectives as a function of time. The change in the number of infectives with respect to time is represented by the so called epidemic curve which traces the course of the epidemic process. If the epidemic curve is increasing then the process is in an epidemic state which reaches its peak point when the curve is maximum. We shall now look at a number of deterministic representations of epidemic processes of varying complexity with the aim of establishing stability conditions in each instance.

1.3.1 Deterministic Representations

The simplest type of mathematical representation of an epidemic process is one in which infection spreads by direct contact between the members of a population, but in which there is no removal from circulation by death, recovery or isolation. Consider a population of susceptibles into which infectious material is introduced. Let S and I be the numbers of susceptibles and infectives, respectively, at any point in time t. Thus $S + I = N$ is the total population which shall remain constant with time. Suppose that S, I and their derivatives are continuous functions of t and the population N is subject to homogeneous mixing, whence the number of new infections occurring in the time interval Δt is $aSI\Delta t$, where a is the rate of infection, i.e., the rate of effective contact between the members of S and I. Such a process is adequately described by the non-linear differential equation

$$(2) \qquad dI/dt = aSI = a[N - I]I = aNI - aI^2$$

with initial conditions

$$S = S_0; \; I = I_0.$$

The solution to (2) yields

$$(3) \qquad I = I_0 N e^{\alpha N t} / (S_0 + I_0 e^{\alpha N t}).$$

The epidemic curve which gives the rate at which infectives accrue is given by

$$(4) \qquad dI/dt = aS_0 I_0 N^2 e^{\alpha N t} / (S_0 + I_0 e^{\alpha N t})^2.$$

The epidemic reaches its peak when (4) attains its maximum. This occurs when

$$d^2 I/dt^2 = a^2 S_0 I_0 N^3 e^{\alpha N t} [(S_0 - I_0) e^{\alpha N t}] / (S_0 + I_0 e^{\alpha N t})^3 = 0$$

whence

$$t = \log (S_0/I_0)/aN.$$

Thus, at the peak point $I = N/2$ and at the limit $I = N$. That is, as one would expect of a process of this nature,

one half of the population will be infected at the peak point while the total population will be infected after the epidemic has spent itself.

We shall now consider a more general mathematical representation of an epidemic process, namely one in which removal from circulation takes place. As in the simpler case, it is assumed that the spread of infection is propagated by direct contact between members of the population. It is further assumed that there is a susceptible population of size S, an infective population of size I and a removed population R where removal can occur only via the infective state, i.e., either by death due to the disease or the development of permanent immunity to it. Hence removal constitutes an absorbing state. Suppose that the total population, $N = S + I + R$, remains constant with time, that there is homogeneous mixing among the circulating members of N and that latency and incubation periods are equal to zero. Infections thus occur continuously in time and a susceptible becomes an infective as well as a manifest case at the time of effective contact. This process can be represented by the system of differential equations

$$(5) \qquad \begin{aligned} dS/dt &= -aSI \\ dI/dt &= aSI - \gamma I \\ dR/dt &= \gamma I \end{aligned}$$

where a is the rate of infection, γ the rate of removal and S, I and R together with their derivatives are continuous functions of time t. Hence, in time t, the number of new infections will equal $aSI\Delta t$ while $\gamma I\Delta t$ infectives will be removed. Assume initial conditions of $S_0 + I_0 = N$ at time t_0. For the process (5) to enter an epidemic state at t_0 it is necessary that the rate of change of the number of infectives be positive in the neighborhood of that point. Hence, it follows from (5) that

$$aS_0 I_0 - \gamma I_0 > 0$$

whence

$$S_0 > \gamma/a = p.$$

Thus, an epidemic can develop from time t_0 only if the number of susceptibles at that point exceeds the threshold ρ. On the other hand, for the process to remain stable $d^2 I/dt^2$ must equal zero. Consequently,

$$d^2 I/dt^2 = a[SdI/dt + IdS/dt] - \gamma dI/dt = 0$$

whence

$$Id^2 S/dt^2 + 2(dS/dt)(dI/dt) = 0$$

and

$$d^2 S/dS + 2dI/I = 0$$

the solution to which yields relation

$$(6) \qquad I^2 dS = k \quad \text{whence} \quad d^2 S = -2k dI/I^3$$

where k is some constant. But, from the relation, $N = S + I + R$ it follows that

$$d^2S = -\gamma dI$$

for $d^2I/dt^2 = 0$. Substituting this expression for d^2S into (6) leads to the conclusion that $d^2I/dt^2 = 0$ implies that I is constant and $d^2S/dt^2 = 0$. Hence, if $dI/dt > 0$ then $d^2I/dt^2 > 0$. In other words, for the epidemic process described by equations (5), $dI/dt > 0$ is both a necessary and sufficient condition for an epidemic outbreak to take place.

Unfortunately, the system of equations (5) is not subject to an exact solution, hence the course of the epidemic cannot be predicted from these equations. However, by introducing a new parameter, namely the agents carrying the infectious material being transmitted among the members of the population N, such a solution can be obtained.

Let M be the number of agents carrying the infectious material transmitted by the infective population I. M and its derivatives are assumed to be continuous functions of time t. The change in M can be thus expressed by

$$(7) \qquad dM/dt = -aM - bM(S + I) + cI$$

where a is the rate at which agents are removed from circulation before establishing contact with members of N; b is the rate at which agents penetrate members of N; and c is the rate at which agents are transmitted by the infective population I. If we assume that penetration of a susceptible by an agent is tantamount to effective contact then, from (7), the number of new infections in time Δt is expressed by $bMS\Delta t$. But, the number of new infections can also be expressed, from equations (5), by $aSI\Delta t$. Hence,

$$(8) \qquad aI = bM.$$

By substituting into equation (7) the expressions for M from (8) and S from the second equation of (5), we obtain

$$(9) \qquad dI/dt = uI - vI^2$$

where
$$u = (cb - \gamma b - aa)/(a + b)$$
$$v = ab/(a + b).$$

Integrating (9) yields

$$(10) \qquad I = ue^{ut}/(k + ve^{ut}) \; ; \; k = (u - vI_0)/I_0.$$

The epidemic curve is thus given by

$$(11) \qquad dI/dt = ku^2e^{ut}/(k + ve^{ut})^2$$

and the peak point at which

$$d^2I/dt^2 = ku^3e^{ut}(k - ve^{ut})/(k + ve^{ut})^3 = 0$$

occurs when

$$t = \log(k/v)/u.$$

For the process to enter an epidemic state, from (11), k must be greater than zero from which it follows that

$$u > vI_0$$
whence

$$c > (\gamma b + aa + abI_0)/b = r.$$

Thus, the rate at which agents carrying the infectious material are transmitted by the members of the infective population must exceed r in order for an epidemic outbreak to occur.

Substituting the expressions for I and its derivative from (10) into the second equation of (5) yields the following expression for S as a function of t.

$$S = ku/a(k + ve^{ut}) + \gamma/a$$

Thus, at the peak point, i.e., when $t = \log(k/v)/u$,

$$I = u/2v$$

while

$$\lim_{t \to \infty} I = u/v \; ; \; \lim_{t \to \infty} S = \gamma/a.$$

Hence, the process will converge to a stable state in which the number of infectives is twice that at the peak point. Moreover, the density of susceptibles at this point will be precisely at the threshold ρ. Consequently, any slightly unfavorable change in conditions could trigger another epidemic outburst.

In summary, the epidemic process represented by the system of equations (5) will enter an epidemic state if and only if $k > 0$. In this event, the process will peak and enter a decreasing state at time $t = \log(k/v)/u$ from which it converges to a stable state with $I = u/v$. The number of infectives remaining in the population will depend upon the value of u, the closer u is to zero the smaller the number of infectives. In order for this number to be zero, u must be less than or equal to zero, from which it follows that

$$c \leqslant (\gamma b + aa)/b = r' < r.$$

Thus, there exist two threshold conditions. The first states that c, the rate at which agents are transmitted by the infective population must be less than or equal to some number r to insure against an epidemic outbreak. The second condition states that c must be even smaller, namely less than or equal to $r' < r$ in order to rid the population of infectives.

Because N is a closed population, i.e., constant with time, a process of the type described by equations (5) must always return to a stable state following the occurrence of an epidemic outbreak. In fact this is one of the principles underlying the effectiveness of quarantine as a control mechanism. In a more realistic representation of an epidemic process the population N is open, i.e., it is not assumed to be constant. In such a process new supplies of susceptibles and infectives are introduced into the population as the process proceeds on its course of development. In this case, we again consider a population N consisting of S susceptibles, I infectives and R removals in which infectious material is communicated by direct contact. N, S, I, R and their derivatives are all continuous functions of time t and susceptibles and infectives are introduced into the population N at constant rates. If homogeneous mixing and zero latency and incubation periods are assumed, the process can be represented by

$$(12) \quad \begin{aligned} dS/dt &= -aSI - \delta S + \mu \\ dI/dt &= aSI - \gamma I + v \\ dR/dt &= \delta S + \gamma I \end{aligned}$$

Here a is the rate of infection, δ and γ are the respective rates at which susceptibles and infectives are removed from circulation and μ and v the respective rates at which new susceptibles and infectives are introduced into the population N. Assume initial conditions of

$$N_0 = S_0 + 1.$$

That is, at time t_0, the population N_0 consists of S_0 susceptibles and a single infective.* A threshold density of susceptibles can be obtained as follows: if $dI/dt > 0$ then

$$S_0 > (\gamma - v)/a = \rho'.$$

Thus, the process can enter an epidemic state at time t_0 only if the number of susceptibles at that time exceeds ρ'.

On the other hand, the process will be stable if and only if $d^2I/dt^2 = 0$. In this event, from the second equation of (12), it follows that

$$I^2 dS = k \text{ whence } d^2S = -2k dI/I^3$$

k being some constant. Thus, because μ is constant, the identical relation holds for stability of the process described by (12) as for the one described by (5). Since dN/dt is also constant, it follows from the relation

$$S + I + R = N$$

that

$$d^2S = -d^2R = -\delta dS - \gamma dI$$

*There is no loss in generality by assuming a single initial infective.

whence

$$d^2S + dS = k'$$

a solution to which is

$$dS = K \text{ and } d^2S = 0$$

k' and K being constants. Hence, I must be constant. Thus,

THEOREM 1: An epidemic process in a constant or linearly increasing population will enter an epidemic state if and only if $dI/dt > 0$.

Consequently, for populations which are constant or linearly increasing, changes in the number of infectives accrued occur either exponentially or not at all. Hence, in such a process, stability is equivalent to equilibrium, i.e., the number of infectives remain constant in a stable state.

As was the case for the system of equations (5), an expression for I as a function of t can be obtained by introducing the variable M representing the agents carrying the infectious material transmitted by the infective population I. Thus, from equation (7), by substitution of the expressions for M from (8) and S from the second equation of (12), we obtain

$$(13) \qquad dI/dt = -n + mI - gI^2$$

where $n = bv(a + b)$; $m = (cb - aa - \gamma b)/(a + b)$; $g = ba/(a + b)$.

Integration of (13) yields

$$(14) \quad I = [(m + Q)ke^{Qt} - (m - Q)1/2g(ke^{Qt} - 1); \\ Q = (m^2 - 4ng)^{1/2} \text{ and } k = [2gI_0 + (Q - m)]/[2gI_0 - (Q + m)].$$

The epidemic curve is given by

$$(15) \qquad dI/dt = -4gkQ^2e^{Qt}/[2g(ke^{Qt} - 1)]^2$$

which attains a maximum when

$$d^2I/dt^2 = kQ^3e^{Qt}(ke^{Qt} + 1)/q(ke^{Qt} - 1)^3 = 0.$$

Whence,

$$t = \log(-1/k)/Q$$

is the point in time when the epidemic reaches a peak and enters a decreasing state.

From (15), the process can enter an epidemic state only if $k < 0$, whence

$$c > [2b(ba)^{1/2} + \gamma b + aa]/b = r$$

For the number of infectives to be at a level less than or equal to ν after the epidemic has spent itself, it follows from

$$\lim_{t \to \infty} I = (m + Q)/2g$$

that

$$c \leqslant (b + ab\nu + aa + \gamma b)/b = r' < r.$$

Substituting the expressions for I and dI/dt from (14) and (15) into the second equation of (12) yields

$$S = - [2k0^2 e^{Qt} + \nu]/a[(m + Q)ke^{Qt} \\ - (m - Q)] [ke^{Qt} - 1] + \gamma/a$$

whence,

$$\lim_{t \to \infty} S = \gamma/a.$$

But, $dI/dt > 0$ only if $S > (\gamma - \nu/I)/a$ which is approximately equal to γ/a as $t \to \infty$. Hence, the entire process converges to a state of stability approximately at the threshold.

In summary, the introduction of a variable population, namely one which is is linearly increasing, does not essentially alter the stability conditions of the epidemic process. As was the case for a constant population, there are two threshold conditions. The first says that the rate at which agents are transmitted by the members of the infective population must be less than or equal to some number, to insure against an epidemic outbreak. On the other hand, to reduce the number of infectives contained in the population this rate must be yet smaller. Moreover, if an epidemic does occur and conditions remain unaltered, the process will converge to a stable state in which the number of susceptibles is approximately at the threshold. Hence, any slightly unfavorable change in conditions could result in another epidemic outbreak.

The mathematical theory of epidemics has generally been concerned with the study of epidemic processes developing within a distinct population. In such representations, as those given above, the population N is said to consist of S susceptibles, I infectives and R removals; members of N who are removed from circulation for whatever the reason are lumped into a single subpopulation of N and fresh supplies of susceptibles and infectives are considered to be arriving from some unspecified source outside of N. It would seem more realistic to consider epidemic processes as developing within some population N which is made up of n distinct subpopulations each of which is interacting with the others, i.e., migrations occur among the n subpopulations of N. These migrations may be either the actual physical transference of individuals from one population to another or may simply reflect contacts among the members of the different populations.

Consider an epidemic process developing within a population N consisting of two distinct populations N_1

and N_2. Assume that migrations may occur, i.e., susceptibles and infectives may migrate from N_1 to N_2 and vice versa. Moreover, susceptibles in N_1 may be infected as a result of effective contacts with infectives in N_2 and susceptibles in N_2 may be infected by infectives in N_1. A process of this type can be represented a follows

$$(16) \quad \begin{aligned} dS_1/dt &= - S_1(a_1 I_1 + a_2 I_2) - \delta_1 S_1 + \delta_2 S_2 \\ dI_1/dt &= S_1(a_1 I_1 + a_2 I_2) - \gamma_1 I_1 + \gamma_2 I_2 \\ dS_2/dt &= - S_2(\beta_1 I_1 + \beta_2 I_2) - \delta_2 S_2 + \delta_1 S_1 \\ dI_2/dt &= S_2(\beta_1 I_1 + \beta_2 I_2) - \gamma_2 I_2 + \gamma_1 I_1 \end{aligned}$$

where

1) S_1 and S_2 represent the respective susceptible populations in N_1 and N_2.
2) I_1 and I_2 represent the respective infective populations in N_1 and N_2.
3) δ_1 and δ_2 are the respective rates of migration of susceptibles from N_1 to N_2 and vice versa.
4) γ_1 and γ_2 are the respective rates of migration of infectives from N_1 to N_2 and vice versa.
5) a_1 and a_2 are the respective rates of effective contact between susceptibles in N_1 and infectives in N_1 and N_2.
6) β_1 and β_2 are the respective rates of effective contact between susceptibles in N_2 and infectives in N_1 and N_2.
7) S_1, S_2, I_1, I_2 and their derivatives are continuous functions of time t.

An epidemic process will be stable in a population N if the change in the rate at which susceptibles and infectives accrue with respect to time is zero. It therefore follows that

$$- \delta_1 dS_1/dt + \delta_2 dS_2/dt - \gamma_1 dI_1/dt + \gamma_2 dI_2/dt = 0$$

whence

$$(\delta_2 S_2 + \gamma_2 I_2) - (\delta_1 S_1 + \gamma_1 I_1) = k$$

k being some constant, is a sufficient condition for the stability of (16) in either population N_1 or N_2. Thus, the epidemic process (16) will be stable in N_1 and N_2 if their rates of change of migration differ only by a constant.

In the general case, we consider n interacting subpopulations N_i, $i = 1, 2, \ldots n$, of N. An epidemic process developing in an arbitrary population N_n* can be represented by

$$(17) \quad \begin{aligned} dS_n/dt &= - S_n \left(\sum_{i=1}^{n} a_i I_i\right) + \sum_{i=1}^{n-1} \delta_i S^i - \sum_{i=1}^{n-1} \delta^i S_n \\ dI_n/dt &= S_n \left(\sum_{i=1}^{n} a_i I_i\right) + \sum_{i=1}^{n-1} \gamma_i I^i - \sum_{i=1}^{n-1} \gamma^i I_n \end{aligned}$$

*Since the sequence of populations is of no importance, we take the arbitrary population as N_n to simplify the notation.

where

1) a_i is the rate of effective contact between susceptibles in N_n and infectives in the N_i population, $i = 1, 2, \ldots, n$.
2) δ_i is the rate at which susceptibles migrate to N_n from the N_i population, $i = 1, 2, \ldots, n-1$.
3) δ^i is the rate at which susceptibles migrate from N_n to the N_i population, $i = 1, 2, \ldots, n-1$.
4) γ_i is the rate at which infectives migrate to N_n from the N_i population, $i = 1, 2, \ldots, n-1$.
5) γ^i is the rate at which infectives migrate from N_n to the N_i population, $i = 1, 2, \ldots, n-1$.
6) S_i, I_i and their derivatives, $i = 1, 2, \ldots, n$, are continuous functions of time t.

From $d^2(S + I)/dt = 0$, it follows that

$$\sum_{i=1}^{n-1} \delta_i dS_i/dt + \sum_{i=1}^{n-1} \gamma_i dI/dt - \sum_{i=1}^{n-1} \delta^i dS_n/dt - \sum_{i=1}^{n-1} \gamma^i dI_n/dt = 0$$

whence

$$(18) \qquad \sum_{i=1}^{n-1} (\delta_i S_i + \gamma_i I_i) - \sum_{i=1}^{n-1} (\delta^i S_n + \gamma^i I_n) = k$$

where k is a constant. Thus,

THEOREM 2: The epidemic process (17) will be stable in the nth population of N if the difference in the rate of change of migrations from N_n and migrations to N_n is constant.

We have concerned ourselves up to this point with epidemic processes in which the agent carrying infectious material is communicated by direct contact between infectives and susceptibles. Let us now examine an epidemic process involving an intermediate host, i.e., a process where the agent is transmitted indirectly through an intermediary from infective to susceptible. In treating such a process, the basic approach is as follows. Suppose that there are two populations, one the definitive host and the other the intermediate host. The numbers of susceptibles, infectives and removals in the former population are denoted by S, I and R respectively; the corresponding quantities in the latter population by S', I' and R' respectively, S, I, R, S', I', R' and their derivatives being continuous functions of the time parameter t. Because susceptibles in the definitive host population acquire the infection by way of infectives in the intermediate host population and vice versa, the number of new infections in the time interval Δt is given by $aSI'\Delta t$ for the definitive host and $a'S'I\Delta t$ for the intermediate host, where a and a' are the respective rates of effective contact. The epidemic process is thus represented by

(19)

$$
\begin{array}{ll}
dS/dt = -aSI' - \delta S + \mu \; ; & dS'/dt = -a'S'I - \delta'S' + \mu' \\
dI/dt = aSI' - \gamma I & ; \quad dI'/dt = a'S'I - \gamma'I' \\
dR/dt = \delta S + \gamma I & ; \quad dR'/dt = \delta'S' + \gamma'I'.
\end{array}
$$

Here, δ and γ denote the rates at which susceptibles and infectives are respectively removed from the definitive host population. Similarly, δ' and γ' denote the respective rates of removal of susceptibles and infectives from the intermediate host population, while the influx of new susceptibles in each population is denoted by μ and μ' respectively.

For the process described by (19) to enter an epidemic state, it is necessary that

$$dI/dt > 0 \text{ and } dI'/dt > 0$$

whence

$$SS' > \gamma\gamma'/aa' = \rho\rho'.$$

Hence, no epidemic can occur unless the product of susceptibles in both the definitive host and intermediate host populations exceeds the threshold $\rho\rho'$.

Let M be the number of agents carrying infectious material transmitted by the infective population I of the definitive host. If a is the rate at which agents are removed from circulation before making contact with members of the intermediate host population, b the rate at which agents penetrate members of the intermediate host population and c the rate at which agents are transmitted by the infective population of the definitive host, the change in M with respect to time is given by

$$(20) \qquad dM/dt = -aM - bM(S' + I') + cI$$

Similarly, the rate of change of agents transmitted by the infective population of the intermediate host is given by

$$(21) \qquad dM'/dt = -a' - b'M'(S + I) + c'I'$$

where M' denotes the number of agents carrying infectious material transmitted by the infective population I', b' the rate at which they penetrate the members of the definitive host population, a' the rate at which agents are removed from circulation before coming into contact with members of the definitive host and c' the rate at which they are transmitted. If we assume that penetration of a susceptible by an agent is tantamount to effective contact, then from (20) and (21), the number of new infections in the definitive host and intermediate host in the time interval Δt is expressed by $b'M'S\Delta t$ and $bMS'\Delta t$ respectively. But, the numbers of new infections in these populations can also be expressed from (19) by $aSI'\Delta t$ and $a'S'I\Delta t$. Hence,

$$
(22) \qquad
\begin{array}{l}
I = bM/a' \\
I' = b'M'/a.
\end{array}
$$

Substituting into equations (20) and (21) the expressions for I and I' from (22) and S and S' from the second equations of (19) yields

$$(23) \qquad u\,dM/dt - \nu M = u'\,dM'/dt - \nu'M'$$

where

$$u = a - b \quad ; \quad u' = a' - b'$$
$$\nu = -aa + \gamma b + cba/a' \quad ; \quad \nu' = a'a' + \gamma'b' + a'c'b'/a.$$

However, a, a', b and b' are very small numbers. Hence, u and u' are approximately equal to zero, whence

$$(24) \qquad \begin{aligned} M' &\simeq pM \\ p &= \nu/\nu'. \end{aligned}$$

By substituting into equation (20) the expressions for S' from the second equation of (19), I' from (22), M' from (24) and I from (22) we obtain

$$(25) \qquad dM/dt = mM - nM^2$$

where

$$m = (acb - aa'a - \gamma'b'a'p)/(a + b'p)a'$$
$$n = bb'p/(a + b'p).$$

Integrating (25) yields

$$(26) \qquad M = me^{mt}/(k + ne^{mt})$$

whence, from (22),

$$(27) \qquad \begin{aligned} I &= bme^{mt}/(k + ne^{mt})a'; \\ k &= (bm - a'I_0 n)/a'I_0, \end{aligned}$$

I_0 being the initial number of infectives in the definitive host population. The epidemic curve is given by

$$(28) \qquad dI/dt = bkm^2 e^{mt}/(k + ne^{mt})^2 a'$$

and the peak point at which

$$(29) \qquad d^2I/dt^2 = bkm^3 e^{mt}(k - ne^{mt})/a'(k + ne^{mt})^3 = 0$$

is reached when

$$(30) \qquad t = \log(k/n)/m.$$

For the process (19) to enter an epidemic state, it follows from (29) that k must be positive, whence

$$(31) \qquad c > (b'pI_0 a' + \gamma'b'p + aa)a'/ab = R.$$

Thus, the rate at which agents are transmitted by the

infective population I of the definitive host must exceed R in order for an epidemic outbreak to take place.

From (22) and (24) it follows that

$$(32) \qquad I' = b'pme^{mt}/a(k + ne^{mt}).$$

Substituting the expressions for I, I', and their derivatives from (27) and (32) into the second equations of (19) yields the following expressions for S and S' as functions of t,

$$(33) \qquad \begin{aligned} S &= bkm/b'a'p(k + ne^{mt}) + \gamma b/b'a'p \\ S' &= b'kp^m/ba(k + ne^{mt}) + \gamma'b'p/ab. \end{aligned}$$

The limits of I, I', S and S' as t goes to infinity are

$$\begin{aligned} \lim I &= bm/a'n \quad ; \quad \lim I' = b'pm/an \\ \lim S &= \gamma b/b'a'p \quad ; \quad \lim S' = \gamma'b'p/ab. \end{aligned}$$

Hence, the process converges to an endemic state where the numbers of infectives remaining will depend upon the value of m, i.e., the closer m is to zero the smaller the number of infectives. Moreover,

$$(\lim S)(\lim S') = \gamma\gamma'/aa'.$$

Thus, at the limit, the product of the densities of susceptibles is precisely at the threshold. Hence, any slightly unfavorable change in conditions could trigger another epidemic outbreak. If, however, the constant k could be kept at a value less than or equal to zero, no epidemic would occur since c would be less than or equal to R. On the other hand, in order that the number of infectives in the definitive host population be zero, m must be less than or equal to zero from which it follows that

$$(34) \qquad c \leqslant a'(aa + \gamma'b'p)/ab = R' < R.$$

Consequently, in order to insure against an epidemic outbreak, it is necessary that the rate at which agents are transmitted by the members of the infective population I of the definitive host be less than or equal to some constant R. This condition, however, is not sufficient to rid the population of infectives which requires that this rate be yet smaller, namely less than or equal to R'.

Let us now consider a simplified case of this representation, i.e., one in which the number of susceptibles and infectives in the intermediate host population, $N' = S' + I'$, is constant with respect to time. In this case, substitution of the expressions for I, I' and dI'/dt from (22) into the second equation on the right side of (19) yields the differential equation

$$(35) \qquad dM/dt = gM - bM^2$$

a solution to which is

$$M = g e^{gt} / (h + b e^{gt})$$
$$\text{where } g = (b_a N' - \gamma' b' p) / b' p$$
$$h = (g - b M_0) / M_0,$$

M_0 being the initial number of agents transmitted by the infective population I_0 at time $t = 0$. Thus,

(36)
$$I = b g e^{gt} / a' (h + b e^{gt})$$
$$I' = b' g e^{gt} / a (h + b e^{gt}).$$

The epidemic curve is expressed by

(37)
$$dI / dt = b h g^2 e^{gt} / a' (h + b e^{gt})^2$$

and

$$d^2 I / dt^2 = b h g^3 e^{gt} (h - b e^{gt}) / a' (h + b e^{gt})^3 = 0$$

at

$$t = \log (h/b) / g$$

which constitutes the peak point of the process. For $dI / dt > 0$, h must be positive. Hence,

$$N' > b' p (M_0 b + \gamma') / ab = (b_a I'_0 + b' p \gamma') / ab$$

whence,

(38)
$$S'_0 = N' - I'_0 > b' p \gamma' / ab = \tau.$$

Thus, the introduction of infection into the definitive host population at time $t = 0$ can give rise to an epidemic only if S'_0 the number of susceptibles in the intermediate host population, exceeds τ. In this event, the epidemic will reach its peak at time $t = \log (h/b) / g$. As in the general case, the process converges to an endemic state with:

$$\lim I = g / a' \quad ; \quad \lim I' = g b' p / ab$$
$$\lim S = \gamma b / a' b' p \quad ; \quad \lim S' = \gamma' b' p / ab.$$

Because S' converges to the threshold τ, any minutely unfavorable change in conditions may result in another outbreak. To insure against such an occurrence, S' must remain less than or equal to τ. For I to be positive, g must be positive implying that $N' > \tau$. Consequently, for the number of infectives in the definitive host to be zero, it is necessary that the intermediate host population N' be less than or equal to τ.

It is interesting to note that the number of susceptibles in both definitive and intermediate host populations converge to the same values as in the general case, i.e., where N' is not constant. Thus, any variation in the intermediate host population will have no effect on the outcome of the process once its numbers exceeds the threshold. This threshold moreover, has been reduced to a simpler form in that it now involves only the inter-

mediate host population. Thus, control of the process may be achieved by control of the intermediate host.

1.3.2 Stochastic Representations

When dealing with large populations, deterministic representations of epidemic processes are appropriate. However, it is more realistic to treat processes involving small populations probabilistically, i.e., as stochastic processes. In general, a stochastic process is a family of random variables (x_t) where t is a member of some index set T. Usually t is interpreted as a time parameter and x_t represents an observation at time t. If T is a sequence then the stochastic process (x_t) is called a process of discrete parameter. If T is an interval then the stochastic process (x_t) is said to be of continuous parameter.

The most important type of stochastic process is a Markov process named after the Russian mathematician A. A. Markov. Such a process possesses the so-called Markov property, namely that knowledge of the present state of the process uniquely determines its subsequent behavior. Thus, the behavior of a Markov process is completely determined by (i) its set of possible states, (ii) its initial probability distribution and (iii) the conditional probabilities of state transitions.

An epidemic process can be represented as a finite state Markov process of either discrete or continuous parameter depending upon the nature of the process. For example if infectives occur in generations then a discrete time parameter would be applicable. The stochastic approach to epidemic processes is given extensive coverage in both Bailey[4] and Bartlett[5]. However, we shall give a simple example of an epidemic process as a stochastic process.

Suppose that an infective enters a population at time t_0. This infective gives rise to fresh infectives by establishing effective contact with susceptibles in the population who in turn establish effective contact with other susceptibles independently of each other and so forth. Let the random variable x_t denote the number of infectives in the population at time t. We say that the population is in the state E_n at time t if the number of infectives at time t is $x_t = n$. Assume that the probability that an infective gives rise to another infective in the population in the time interval $[t, t + \Delta t]$ is equal to $\bar{a} \Delta t + o(\Delta t)$. Assume, further, that the probability that an infective will be removed from circulation in the time interval $[t, t + \Delta t]$ is equal to $\bar{\gamma} t + o(\Delta t)$. Let $x_0 = 1$, i.e., a single infective enters the population at time t_0, and let $P_n(t)$ denote the probability of n infectives at time t. The process (x_t) is a homogeneous Markov process for which

$$dP_n(t) / dt = - n(\bar{a} + \bar{\gamma}) P_n(t) +$$
$$(n - 1) \bar{a} P_{n-1}(t) + (n + 1) \bar{\gamma} P_{n+1}(t)$$

with initial conditions

$$P_n(0) = \begin{cases} 1 & \text{if } n = 1 \\ 0 & \text{if } n \neq 1. \end{cases}$$

We introduce the generating function,

$$U(t,z) = \sum_{n=0}^{\infty} P_n(t) z^n$$

which satisfies the partial differential equation,

$$(39) \qquad \partial U / \partial t = (\bar{a}z - \bar{\gamma})(z - 1)\, \partial U / \partial z$$

with the initial condition $U(0,z) = z$. The solution to (39) is

$$U(z) = \{\bar{\gamma}\theta + z[1 - (\bar{a} + \bar{\gamma})\theta]\} / (1 - z\bar{a}\theta)$$

where

$$\theta = \begin{cases} [1 - e(\bar{a} + \bar{\gamma})t(\bar{a} + \bar{\gamma})t] / [\bar{\gamma} - \bar{a}e\ ]; & \text{if } \bar{a} \neq \bar{\gamma}, \\ t / (1 + \bar{\gamma}t) & ; \text{if } \bar{a} = \bar{\gamma}. \end{cases}$$

Hence,

$$P_0(t) = \bar{\gamma}\theta$$
$$P_n(t) = (1 - \bar{a}\theta)(1 - \bar{\gamma}\theta)(\bar{a}\theta)^{n-1} \ ; \ n = 1, 2, \ldots\ldots$$

Whence, the probability of extinction,

$$\lim P_0(t) = \begin{cases} 1 & \text{if } \bar{\gamma} \geqq \bar{a} \\ \bar{\gamma} / \bar{a} & \text{if } \bar{\gamma} \leqq \bar{a}. \end{cases}$$

In the stochastic representation the coefficients correspond to the rates of effective contact and removal in the deterministic representation. The probability of extinction in the stochastic case is thus equal to the threshold in the corresponding deterministic case.

Although, in general, stochastic representations are more precise, deterministic representations are more usefull since the mathematics is less complicated and solutions can be more readily obtained. In either case, the ultimate usefulness of any mathematical representation depends largely upon obtaining reliable estimates of the basic parameters of the process from statistical data. Naturally, different physical situations call for representations with specific properties which reflect the particular physical process under study. An excellent example of such a special case is the theory of rumors recently developed by Daley and Kendall[6]. For applications of the epidemic theory to the transmission of ideas as represented by a subject literature see[7,8].

2. Information Retrieval Processes

2.1. Introduction

As was pointed out in the previous sections, the crucial factor in the development of an epidemic process, hence a communication process, is the establishment of effective contact. No epidemic can develop unless there is transmission of the appropriate infectious material from infectives to susceptibles. Thus, there is imbedded within an epidemic process a subprocess which acts as the instrument for providing the agents (information) which carry the appropriate infectious material. We shall call such a process an information retrieval process.

Therefore, an information retrieval process can, in general, be characterized in terms of two sets and a relation between their members. One set stands for a susceptible population S the other for an infective population I and the relation R is such that if a susceptible $s \varepsilon S$ stands in the relation R to an infective $x \varepsilon I$, then an effective contact, i.e., a case of "disease," will result when s comes into contact with x. The result of an effective contact between a susceptible and an infective in the transmission of ideas is the acquisition of knowledge. The result in the transmission of an infectious disease is a case of disease. In terms of the transmission of ideas a susceptible can be thought of an an individual searching for ideas and an infective as an individual conveying information. Similarly, in the infectious disease case the susceptible can be thought of as searching for an infectious agent, albeit not willingly.

Thus, a susceptible is in essence posing a query and an infective is conveying an agent (information) which may or may not carry the appropriate infectious material (idea or fact). Hence, with every susceptible we can associate a query and with every infective an agent carrying infectious material. These infectives shall be called documents, since the word document in its broadest sense denotes an object which conveys information. So, instead of talking about susceptibles and infectives in an information retrieval process, we can talk about queries and documents. Thus we can consider the process as an interrogation procedure. The set of documents interrogated shall be called a file and a subset of the file shall be called an answer if those infectives and only those infectives represented by the subset will infect the susceptible, represented by the query, given a contact between them. The property which assigns members of the file to the answer is called relevance. Relevance is, thus, a measure of effective contact between infectives and susceptibles.

More precisely, given a set of susceptibles (queries) S and a set of infectives (documents) I, there is a mapping R of $s \varepsilon S$ into $M(I)$, the power set of I. The function R is called the relevance function and $X = R(s)$ states that $X \varepsilon M(I)$ is that subset of the file I which contains those members and only those members of I that are relevant to s.

Since an information retrieval process consists of a population N (queries and documents), infectious material i (information*), and a set of states s (determined

* Information is used in a general sense, as any agent in which infectious material is imbedded.

by a relevance relation R), the process can be formally denoted as

$$\sqcap = <N, i, s>$$

Therefore a communication process can be denoted as

$$C = <\sqcap, S : t>$$

i.e., it can be characterized as an epidemic process consisting of an information retrieval process $\sqcap$ with a set of external states S.

2.2 Mathematical Representation

The simplest mathematical respresentation of an information retrieval process is the so-called Boolean model. In the Boolean model queries are represented by propositional functions, and the file of documents by a finite set. Since both the algebra of sets and the propositional calculus are Boolean algebras, there is a unique subset of the file which corresponds to each propositional function. This subset represents the answer to the query which is represented by the propositional function. For example, suppose every document in a file I is completely described by a set of attributes. Then a query can be represented by a propositional function of attributes constructed in the usual manner by conjunctions, disjunctions, and negations; and with every proposition there is associated a unique subset $X \subseteq I$ of documents which possess the appropriate attributes. Because of the Boolean property, the set X can be obtained by taking unions, intersections, and complements of those sets corresponding to the propositional variables, i.e., attributes, which appear respectively as disjunctions, conjunctions, and negations in the propositional function.

The usefulness of the Boolean model is based on the assumption that the appropriate subsets of the file can be constructed on the basis of the property of relevance. In the theory of sets the formation of subsets of a given set is guaranteed by the axiom of separation.[9] This axiom states that given a set M and a property Ψ there exists a set N each of whose members are in M and that every member of N possesses the property Ψ while every member of M not in N does not possess this property. Formally this axiom can be stated as follows:

$$(40) \qquad (\exists N)\, (\forall x)\, ((x \varepsilon N \equiv x \varepsilon M) \wedge \Psi(x)).$$

In a strict sense (40) is not an axiom but what is usually called an axiom schema since an infinite number of axioms can be generated from (40) depending upon the nature of the property Ψ. For example, if M were the set of positive integers less than 10 and $\Psi(x)$ the property that the positive integer $x \varepsilon M$ is odd, the subset N is precisely defined by (40) as $N = (1, 3, 5, 7, 9)$. If $\Psi(x)$ were the property that x is prime, then N is precisely defined as $N = (2, 3, 5, 7)$.

However, the property of relevance of a document to a query does not possess the definiteness required by (40) for the construction of subsets as do the properties of odd or prime in the case of the positive integers. Hence a document cannot be thought of as being definitely relevant or definitely non-relevant to a given query but can only be thought of in terms of its degree of relevance to the query. Thus a more general relevance measure must be introduced. There is no loss in generality if this measure is taken to be a probability.

In a probabilistic representation of an information retrieval process it is initially assumed that every query $s \varepsilon S$ defines a probability function on the file I. Then

$$\xi = F_s(x)$$

is the probability that document x in I is relevant to query s. Hence ξ represents a measure of effective contact or degree of susceptibility between the susceptible s and the members of the file I.

Secondly we assume that there exists a function E whose job it is to evaluate or recognize the relevancy of the members of I relative to some given s. Such a function must be a function of the probability measure ξ. Hence we define

$$(41) \qquad E(X) = \sum_{x \epsilon X} G_s(\xi) = \sum_{x \epsilon X} V_s(x)$$

where the function $V_s(x)$ is monotonic increasing on $[0, 1]$.

The optimal answer $R(s)$ will then consist of that set X for which $E(X)$ is maximal. Finding this set in terms of the probability measure F is not too difficult since $E(X)$ will increase only for $x \epsilon I$ such that $V(x) > \xi_0$ where $G(\xi_0) = 0$. Hence ξ_0 which we call the critical probability determines the mapping $R(s)$ by acting as the point of truncation of the sequence of documents $I(\xi)$ ordered according to decreasing probabilities. Then the optimal answer $A = R(s)$ will consist of all members $x \epsilon I$ such that $F_s(x) > \xi_0$. The critical probability ξ_0 thus acts as a threshold for s relative to $x \epsilon I$.

The mapping $A = R(s)$ assumes, however, that the process is static. That is, it only considers the process at a given point in time and not as it moves through time. In effect this assumes that the effectiveness of infectious material transmitted by each of the documents in the file I and therefore in the set A is independent of the other members.

But the information transmitted by one document may either inhibit or enhance the effectiveness of the information transmitted by the others. That is, the power of an agent to infect a susceptible may depend upon previous exposures. In other words, the measure of an effective contact, i.e., the degree of susceptibility, may either increase or decrease as a result of previous contacts. This notion reflects the fact that any measure of information conveyed must depend upon what is already known.

Therefore, it is necessary to introduce a time dependency relation among the members of I, relative to s, namely the notion of conditional probabilities of relevance. We shall only consider the case where dependency is restricted to pairs of documents. That is, if an individual is exposed to information in some arbitrary order, then the relevance of a given element can be influenced only by its immediate predecessor in the sequence of exposure. The results can easily be extended to the general case. Thus

Given a set I and a query s

Definition 1: p_{ij} is the conditional probability that x_j in I is relevant to s if x_i is relevant to s: $p_{ii} = 1$.

Definition 2: r_{ij} is the conditional probability that x_j is relevant to s if x_i is not relevant to s: $r_{ii} = 0$.

Clearly, $r_{ij} = F_s(x_j)$ for $i \neq j$ for if x_i is not relevant to s then the conditional probability of x_j being relevant is just its initial probability since the effect of x_i is zero.

Consider the subset $A = R(s)$, i.e., all members $a \varepsilon I$ for which $F_s(a) > \xi_0$. Assume that the members of A are encountered by s in some arbitrary order. Thus s is exposed to the information transmitted by the members $a \varepsilon A$ in the arbitrary sequence

$$A = (a_0, a_1, \ldots, a_j, \ldots).$$

Let $P_s(a)$ be the probability that $a \varepsilon A$ is relevant to s. Then $P_s(a_j)$ can be defined recursively as follows:

$$P_s(a_0) = F_s(a_0) = r_{01}$$
$$P_s(a_1) = p_{01}P_s(a_0) + r_{01}[1 - P_s(a_0)] = r_{01} + \lambda_{01}P_s(a_0)$$
$$P_s(a_j) = p_{j-1,j} + r_{j-1,j}[1 - P_s(a_{j-1})] =$$
$$r_{j-1,j} + \lambda_{j-1,j}P_s(a_{j-1})$$

where

$$\lambda_{j-1,j} = p_{j-1,j} - r_{j-1,j}.$$

Theorem 3: A necessary and sufficient condition that $P_s(a_j) > \xi_0$ for every $a_j \varepsilon A$, irrespective of their order, is that $\lambda_{ij} \geqq 0$ for every a_i and a_j in A.

Proof: $P_s(a_j) > \xi_0$ implies that

$$r_{j-1,j} + \lambda_{j-1,j}P_s(a_{j-1}) > \xi_0$$

or

$$\lambda_{j-1,j} > \frac{\xi_0 - r_{ij}}{P_s(a_{j-1})}$$

Since a_{j-1} is an arbitrary element in A, the inequality must hold for every a_i and a_j in A. Therefore

$$\lambda_{ij} \geqq \text{Sup}\left[\frac{\xi_0 - r_{ij}}{P_s(a_i)}\right] = 0$$

since Inf $r_{ij} = \xi_0$. Hence, it follows that $P_s(a_j) > \xi_0$ for every $a_j \varepsilon A$, independent of order, only if

$$\lambda_{ij} \geqq 0 \qquad \text{for every } a_i \text{ and } a_j \text{ in } A.$$

Sufficiency shall be established by induction. Suppose that A contains a single element a_i. In this event $p_{ii} = 1$,

$r_{ii} = 0$ and $F_s(a_i) > \xi_0$. Hence $\lambda_{ij} \geqq 0$ and $P_s(a_i) = F_s(a_i) > \xi_0$.

Therefore the conditions hold for the unit set in A. Suppose that A contains n members such that $\lambda_{ij} \geqq 0$ for every a_i and a_j in A. We now introduce an $n + 1$ element a_{n+1} which possesses the required properties, namely that $F_s(a_{n+1}) > \xi_0$ and $\lambda_{j,n+1} \geqq 0$ and $\lambda_{n+1,j} \geqq 0$ for every $a_j \varepsilon A$. Let T be an arbitrary sequence of the $n + 1$ members of A and let a_{n+1} occupy some arbitrary position in T, say the kth place. Then

$$P_s(a_k) = p_{k-1,k}P_s(a_{k-1}) + r_{k-1,k}[1 - P_s(a_{k-1})] =$$
$$r_{k-1,k} + \lambda_{k-1,k}P_s(a_{k-1})$$

where a_{k-1} is the immediate predecessor of a_k in T. Since $\lambda_{k-1,k} \geqq 0$ it follows that

$$P_s(a_k) \geqq r_{k-1,k} > \xi_0.$$

On the other hand let a_{k+1} be the immediate successor to a_k in T. Then

$$P_s(a_{k+1}) = r_{k,k+1} + \lambda_{k,k+1}P_s(a_k) \geqq r_{k,k+1} > \xi_0.$$

Thus the information transmitted by members of the set A will be relevant to s, irrespective of the order of transmission, if and only if $\lambda_{ij} \geqq 0$ and $\lambda_{ji} \geqq 0$ for every pair of documents a_i and a_j in A.

Definition 3: If the members of a subset $X \subseteq I$ have the property that $P_s(x) > \xi_0$ for every $x \varepsilon X$, irrespective of their order, then X is called an informational set. The information relation is denoted by $x_1 \Longleftrightarrow x_j$ and an informational set by $\overset{\star}{X}$.

Definition 4: A subset $X \subseteq I$ is said to be informationally closed if for every $y \notin X$, there exists an $x \varepsilon X$ such that X is not informational with y.

Definition 5: A closed informational set X is called the closure of each of its elements and is denoted by $\overline{X}$.

Theorem 4: The closure of a given element is not unique.

Proof: Let $\overline{X}_i$ be the closure of an element $x_i \varepsilon I$. Then $x_i \Longleftrightarrow x_j$ for every $x_j \notin \overline{X}_i$. There can exist an element x_k in $I - \overline{X}_i$ such that $x_i \Longleftrightarrow x_k$ and $x_k \Longleftrightarrow x$ for every $x \varepsilon \overline{X}_i$ except one, say x_t. Then the set $\overset{\star}{X}_i = \{(\overline{X}_i - x_t) + x_k\}$ is an informational set containing x_i. If $\overset{\star}{X}_i$ is closed, then it constitutes a closure of x_i different from $\overline{X}_i$. If not then there exists an informational set $\overset{\star}{X}$ in $I - \overset{\star}{X}_i$ such that $\overset{\star}{X}_i + \overset{\star}{X}$ is closed and informational. Hence $\overline{X} = \overset{\star}{X}_i + \overset{\star}{X}$ is a closure of x_i not equal to $\overline{X}_i$.

Clearly every member of the set A belongs to at least one informational set. Hence there is a set of closures associated with every a_j in A. Therefore the set A is covered by a family of closures of its elements, i.e., sets of type $\overline{A}$. Thus there is a one to many mapping $\overline{R}(s) = \{\overline{A}\}$ of s into $M(I)$. That is, there exists a multiplicity of not necessarily disjoint subsets of I, namely any one of the $\bar{A}$, whose members are relevant to s, independent of order, i.e., irrespective of the order in which the information is transmitted from the members of $\bar{A}$ to s.

In the event that the members of A are independent of each other, then $\bar{R}(s) = A$. On the other extreme if $\lambda_{ij} < 0$ for every a_i and a_j in A, then $\bar{R}(s) = \{a_j\}$, i.e., the family of closures covering A consists of the unit sets in A.

Definition 6: A set of documents all of whose members are relevant to a query s is called a compatible set and its members are said to be compatible with respect to s.

The members of an informational set are obviously compatible. The question now arises whether there exist informational sets other than those of type $\bar{A}$, i.e., subsets of A.

Consider an arbitrary subset $B \subseteq (I - A)$. Then

$$P_s(b_j) = p_{ij} P_s(b_i) + r_{ij}[1 - P_s(b_i)]$$

for arbitrary b_i and b_j in B.

$$P_s(b_j) > \xi_0 \text{ implies that } \lambda_{ij} > \frac{\xi_0 - r_{ij}}{P_s(b_i)}.$$

Hence $P_s(b_j) > \xi_0$ for every $b_j \varepsilon B$, irrespective of their order, implies that

$$\lambda_{ij} \geqq \text{Sup}\left[\frac{\xi_0 - r_{ij}}{P_s(b_i)}\right] = \left[\frac{\xi_0 - \text{Inf } r_{ij}}{\xi_0}\right] = \epsilon,$$

$\xi_0 \neq 0$. Thus a necessary condition for $P_s(b_j) > \xi_0$, independent of its position in the sequence of transmission, is that

$$\lambda_{ij} \geqq \epsilon > 0$$

for every b_i and b_j in B.

Clearly this condition is not sufficient since the conclusion does not follow for the case where $B = \{b_j\}$ is a unit set in B since $F_s(b_j) \leqq \xi_0$ for every $b_j \varepsilon B$. However, given an arbitrary element $a \varepsilon A$, the condition would be sufficient provided that every sequence of exposures to the elements of B follows an exposure to a. For suppose B contains a single element b_j preceded by some a_i in A, with $\lambda_{ij} \geqq \epsilon$. Then $P_s(a_i) = F_s(a_i) > \xi_0$ and

$$P_s(b_j) = r_{ij} + \lambda_{ij} P_s(a_i) \geqq r_{ij} + \epsilon P_s(a_i) > \\ r_{ij} + \xi_0 - \text{Inf } r_{ij} > \xi_0$$

Sufficiency follows by induction, hence

Theorem 5: Necessary and sufficient conditions that $P_s(b_j) > \xi_0$ for every $b_j \varepsilon B$, $B \subseteq (I - A)$, irrespective of their order, are that

(1) B is preceded by an informational set $\tilde{A}$ in A.

(2) $\lambda_{ij} \geqq \epsilon$ for every $a_i \varepsilon \tilde{A}$ and $b_j \varepsilon B$

(3) $\lambda_{ij} \geqq \epsilon$ for every b_i and b_j in B

where

$$\epsilon = \frac{\xi_0 - \text{Inf } r_{ij}}{\xi_0}.$$

Thus a set B whose members were not initially relevant to s can become relevant if it follows the appropriate set. Denote a subset of $(I - A)$ for which the conditions of theorem 5 are satisfied by $\tilde{B}$. Such a set is called conditionally informational. If a conditionally informational subset of $(I - A)$ is also closed it is denoted by $\bar{B}$ which is called the closure of its elements. Clearly, as in the case of the $\bar{A}$, the closure of an element need not be unique. Moreover, $U(\bar{B})$, the union of all $\bar{B} \subseteq (I - A)$ does not necessarily exhaust the membership of $(I - A)$ for $U(\bar{B})$ contains only those elements $b_j \varepsilon (I - A)$ for which $\lambda_{ij} \geqq \epsilon$, $b_j \varepsilon B$ and $a_i \varepsilon A$. Hence the set $\{(I - A) - U(\bar{B})\}$ need not be empty and there can exist sets $\bar{E}$ which stand in the same relation to the $\bar{B}$ as the $\bar{B}$ stand to the $\bar{A}$ and so forth. Hence an ordered set of the form

$$\bar{I} = \langle \bar{A} + \bar{B} + \bar{E} + \ldots + \bar{K} \rangle$$

where each of the disjoint set $\bar{A}, \bar{B}, \ldots, \bar{K}$ are informational constitutes a compatible set. Thus a susceptible s, as a result of information obtained from an $\bar{A}$, is placed in a position to accept infectious material transmitted by the members of $\bar{B}$ and so on.

Such a situation occurs, for example, in the case of rheumatic fever which cannot become manifest unless a certain streptococcus strain has been present. In the intellectual world such a process is commonplace since the reaction to an idea is predicated on the existence or absence of a certain body of knowledge.

Since the informational relation is not transitive, i.e., from $x_i \Longleftrightarrow x_j$ and $x_j \Longleftrightarrow x_k$ it does not generally follow that $x_i \Longleftrightarrow x_k$, it is not an equivalence relation. Hence informationality does not partition the members of the file I into equivalence classes each one of which consists of all of the closures of a given element.

Definition 7: Two elements x_i and x_j in I such that $p_{ij} > \xi_0$ and $p_{ji} > \xi_0$ are said to be conversant. This relation is denoted by $x_i \longleftrightarrow x_j$ and a set all of whose members are conversant with each other is called a conversant set.

Clearly every set of type $\bar{A}$ is a subset of a conversant set. However, conversance is not an equivalence relation since it too is not transitive.

Definition 8: A sequence of elements in I from x_i to x_j such that $x_i \longleftrightarrow x_{i+1} \longleftrightarrow \ldots \longleftrightarrow x_j$ is called a chain from x_i to x_j.

Definition 9: If two elements x_i and x_j in I belong to a chain, then they are said to communicate with each other. Communication is denoted by $x_i \longleftrightarrow\!\circ\!\longrightarrow x_j$.

Theorem 6: Communication is an equivalence relation.

Proof: 1) $x_i \longleftrightarrow\!\circ\!\longrightarrow x_i$ since an element communicates with itself.

2) If $x_i \longleftrightarrow\!\circ\!\longrightarrow x_j$ then $x_j \longleftrightarrow\!\circ\!\longrightarrow x_i$ for if there is a chain from x_i to x_j there is a chain from x_j to x_i.

3) If $x_i \longleftrightarrow\!\circ\!\longrightarrow x_j$ and $x_j \longleftrightarrow\!\circ\!\longrightarrow x_k$, then $x_i \longleftrightarrow\!\circ\!\longrightarrow x_k$ since if there is a chain from x_i to x_j and a chain from x_j to x_k, then there is a chain from x_i to x_k, namely the sum of both chains.

Theorem 7: If two elements in I are informational then they communicate.

Proof: The conclusion is trivial for $a_i \Longleftrightarrow a_j$, a_i and a_j in A, since $\lambda_{ij} \geq 0$ implies that $p_{ij} \geq r_{ij} > \xi_0$. Now consider two arbitrary elements of $(I\text{-}A)$ such that $x_i \Longleftrightarrow x_j$. Then $r_{ij} \leq \xi_0$. Since $x_i \Longleftrightarrow x_j$, $p_{ij} \geq r_{ij} + \epsilon$ and $p_{ij} \geq r_{ij} + \epsilon$. Suppose that $p_{ij} \leq \xi_0$, then

$$\xi_0 \geq r_{ij} + \xi = r_{ij} + \frac{\xi_0 - \text{Inf } r_{jj}}{\xi_0}$$

or

$$\xi_0(\xi_0 - r_{ij}) \geq (\xi_0 - \text{Inf } r_{ij})$$

and $\xi_0 \geq 1$. But this is impossible, hence $p_{ij} > \xi_0$. Similarly $p_{ji} > \xi_0$. Thus $x_i \longleftrightarrow\!\circ\!\longrightarrow x_j$ and therefore x_i and x_j communicate. Hence the file I can be partitioned into equivalence classes

$$I = \sum_{i=1}^{m} C_i$$

where every closure of a given element $x \varepsilon I$ belongs to one and only one communication class C_i.

Definition 10: Two elements x_i and x_j in I are said to be semi-informational, denoted by $x_i \Rightarrow x_j$ if

(1) $\lambda_{ij} \geq 0$ for $x_j \varepsilon A$
(2) $\lambda_{ij} \geq \epsilon$ for $x_j \notin A$

Theorem 8: The members of a subset $X \subseteq I$ are compatible if there exists a sequence of X such that

(1) the initial element $x_0 \varepsilon A$
(2) $x_j \Rightarrow x_{j+1}$ for every $x_j \varepsilon X$

Proof: Assume that there exists a sequence T of the members of X which satisfies conditions (1) and (2). Assume further that there is an element $x_j \varepsilon X$ which is not compatible with the other members. Then $P_s(x_j) \leq \xi_0$. Suppose that x_j is the initial member of T. Then $F_s(x_j) \leq \xi_0$ and $x_j \notin A$ as is required by condition 1). Suppose that x_j occupies some arbitrary position in T, say the kth place. Then

$$P_s(x_k) = r_{k-1,k} + \lambda_{k-1,\,k} P_s(x_{k-1}) \leq \xi_0$$

If $x_k \varepsilon A$, then $\lambda_{k-1,k} \geq 0$ and $r_{k-1,k} \leq \xi_0$ which contradicts the fact that $x_k \varepsilon A$. Hence $x_k \notin A$ and

$$\xi_0 \geq r_{k-1,k} + \varepsilon P_s(x_{k-1}) = r_{k-1,k} + \left(\frac{\xi_0 - \text{Inf } r_{k-1,k}}{\xi_0}\right) P_s(x_{k-1})$$

or

$$\xi_0(\xi_0 - r_{k-1,k}) \geq (\xi_0 - \text{Inf } r_{k-1}) P_s(x_{k-1})$$

and

$$\xi_0 \geq P_s(x_{k-1})$$

Continuing this process it follows that

$$P_s(x_{k-2}) \leq \xi_0$$
$$P_s(x_{k-3}) \leq \xi_0$$
$$\vdots$$
$$P_s(x_0) \leq \xi_0$$

Hence $x_0 \notin A$ which is contrary to hypothesis that $x_0 \varepsilon A$.

In summary, any closed compatible set, relative to a susceptible s, constitutes an answer to the query associated with s. The answer is not necessarily unique for there can exist a number of, not necessarily disjoint, closed compatible sets. The information transmitted by each of the elements of the answer augments the information conveyed to the susceptible by the others while the totality of information conveyed by one closed compatible set inhibits the effectiveness of the information transmitted by another. The specific membership of a particular answer in practice is determined by the accessibility to the susceptible of those infectives (documents) which can form closed compatible sets.

3. Information Retrieval Systems

3.1. Systems

In the introduction it was pointed out that systems are mechanisms by means of which processes are carried out. Thus information retrieval processes are realized by information retrieval systems. In this section we shall be concerned with such systems particularly with those features which relate to 1) their design and 2) the evaluation of their performance.

Systems may be either natural or artificial. For example, biological processes are generally carried out by natural systems. Artificial systems are usually developed for the purpose of producing a process when the desired results are not obtainable by natural means. Thus artificial systems are designed to simulate natural ones. Such systems may be very complex or relatively simple and may attempt to generate a total process or only a small part of one. To illustrate, an artificial system may be introduced in order to activate a natural system in the realization of some process. Such is the case when a vaccine is used to instigate a natural biological system to carry out an immunization process. Similarly, a telephone system places its users in a position for a natural flow of information to occur between them. In each case the system activates the development of a natural process. On the other hand an artificial system may serve to eliminate a bottleneck somewhere along the course of development of a process. Such is the case when insulin injections are used in the treatment of diabetes. Naturally, in any given physical situation the desired results may be accomplished in various ways. Finding the optimal way constitutes the fundamental problem of systems theory. This problem shall be discussed more fully in the sequel.

A system was previously defined as a collection of elements interacting in the performance of a specific function for a specific purpose. The important terms in this definition are (1) elements, (2) purpose, and (3) function. The elements of a system which are called its components may either be things or operations: that is, the elements may consist of tangible objects such as gears or relays or intangibles such as arithmetical operations or chemical reactions. The purpose of a system is associated with the requirements placed upon it by its users, while its function deals with the procedure employed by the system for satisfying these requirements. It is essential that a system have both a purpose and a function, for evaluation of its performance depends upon both. The reason for this is that a system is intended to optimize a certain performance function of its inputs and outputs as related to its user requirements. For example, the function of a vaccine is the prevention of the occurrence of some disease. Its purpose, let us say, is the betterment of mankind. Clearly the vaccine cannot be adequately evaluated without considering both its purpose and function.

The function of an information retrieval system is to carry out an information retrieval process, i.e., to put susceptibles and infectives of a given population into effective contact with each other. The fact that a communication system puts a susceptible in contact with an infective does not guarantee that a specific result, namely an infection, will result. In fact the system's users may not require that this occur. Such is the case with the users of a telephone system. They do not hold the system responsible for any particular piece of information which may be conveyed; they expect only that a contact take place. On the other hand the user of an information retrieval system requires that the contact effected by the system lead to a specific result. We call such a contact an effective contact. An effective contact may lead, for example, to the acquisition of knowledge or to a case of disease.

Thus the output of an information retrieval system consists of information (agents) containing those ideas or facts (infectious material) which are relevant (capable of infecting) to a query (susceptible). In reality it is by no means necessary that the system be instigated by its users, for the system may volunteer or disseminate the information (agents) to its users (susceptibles). In this event, since its purpose is only served by satisfying certain requirements of its users, it is essential that the system not transmit information out of self-satisfaction. Thus a system which disseminates information voluntarily can be said to be enacting for the user by formulating the query which appropriately corresponds to his requirement. Hence the voluntary system is theoretically equivalent to the system activated directly by the user.

It should be noted that the purpose of a system need not be constructive nor need its users necessarily desire to avail themselves of its services. Optimization of such a system from the user point of view would consist of minimizing rather than maximizing the performance function of its inputs and outputs.

3.2. Systems Design

The first step in the design of any system is the definition of its purpose and function. Once it has been decided what functions must be performed by the system in order to satisfy its users' requirements, trial solutions can be attempted. The system can consist of many components which contribute to its performance. The designer's task is to organize these components in such a way that the inputs will optimally produce the desired outputs. In this endeavor he may have a choice of a number of alternative combinations of components.

The first set of trial solutions involves the so-called single thread performance. By this is meant the solution of the engineering problem of performing the function at all, considering the requirements which must be satisfied. Usually there are techniques available from former experience for accomplishing this task. Often, however, it is necessary for new methods to be devised.

The second set of trial solutions takes into consideration the fact that some of the system's functions must be performed many times. This step is sometimes called the solution for high traffic density. Here the designer may encounter problems which do not exist in the single thread solution. Typical high traffic density problems are concerned with such things as waiting time and occupancy. Solution of such problems is very important, for example in the operation of a telephone system. Often the single thread solution must be scrapped in order to accomodate high traffic.

The third set of solutions is that of competitive design. This phase is necessary only if the system is to operate in an hostile environment. The design of an immunization system, for example, requires that the competitive nature of its environment be taken into account. For it may be that the system performs very well when in an isolated surrounding but breaks down completely when confronted with the real environment in which it must perform its function.

An extremely important concept in the design of systems is the notion of trade-offs. Basically trade-offs consist of a series of decisions in which the system designer gives up something in return for something else. The basis underlying the necessity of having trade-offs is that 1) a system generally must serve many users, and 2) a given system cannot satisfy the requirements of every one of its potential users.

As an illustration, consider an airline ticketing system which provides satisfaction to the airline's customers ninety-eight percent of the time. Suppose that in order to accommodate the remaining two percent the cost of operation and maintenance is tripled. The designer must decide whether to trade off two percent of unhappy customers for an increased economy and efficiency in the system's operation.

Another example which is more pertinent to our subject is concerned with the development of an artificial immunization system. As is well known there are two types of vaccines which may be used namely, the inactive or the attenuated virus types. Assuming that it is physically possible to arrive at a solution with either system, e.g., the Salk and Sabin polio vaccines, the researcher must decide, for example, whether the greater antibody concentration achieved by the attenuated virus vaccine is worth the risk of inducing the disease. We have only presented a very superficial outline of some of the problems of system analysis. For a comprehensive treatment see Goode-Machol[10] or Hall.[11]

3.3 Components of Information Retrieval Systems

Since information retrieval is a communication process, there must exist a channel so that the system can transmit information from one object to another, i.e., from infective to susceptible. This communication is accomplished by means of a language.

Although it is beyond the scope of this short paper to launch into any detailed discussion of language, it is expedient to point out certain of its more prominent features. First of all, it is not necessary to describe the language employed by an information retrieval system. All that is needed is that is must contain certain conventions which are generally understood. Secondly, the language must be specific, i.e., given a choice of languages, at most one is used. This language should contain the technical terminology and linguistic devices which are required by the members of the population for understanding. Thus the language employed by an information retrieval system may be a natural language, as, in the communication of ideas, language of chemistry as in the communication of a disease or a genetic property, or some artificial language as in the communication between man and machine, or among machines.

In its most general sense a language is defined in terms of a certain set of objects called its alphabet and a set of rules for specifying how to form certain combinations of these objects, called letters, into meaningful expressions called words and sentences. A language is not static but is in a continuous process of development. In this way it becomes more precise. The problems of languages are well-known and there is an enormous literature dealing with them from many different points of view. We cite the following references as most pertinent to this discussion.[12, 13, 14]

A given language may be represented in any one of a number of different symbolic forms or codes. Thus, once the system designer has selected a language, he must decide upon an appropriate means for representing it. The problem of coding in communication systems is very basic and there exists a very elaborate theory deal-with it. This is of course the information theory initiated by Shannon and already developed into a highly specialized discipline. For an excellent treatment of the fundamentals of this theory see Wolfwitz.[15]

An information retrieval system must provide effective contact between its information source (its file) and its users. Therefore it is not sufficient for it to provide the user with "any old" information. It must provide relevant information. Hence the system must have built into it a selection procedure for recognizing the relevant material contained in the file. That is, it must be able to adequately approximate the recognition function $E(X)$. Moreover, it must be able to select this material in a very efficient manner. That is, the system must have its information source organized in a fashion which allows for the location of the desired material in minimum time. We shall call this operation a searching procedure, since it involves in terms of the process a search of the file I for an answer with respect to a query s.

It should be noted that sources of information, as well as resistance and susceptibility, are not static but in constant flux. This is true of the members of any population, whether they be cells, human beings or machines. Thus an information retrieval system should have the property of being self-organizing and error-adjusting. This property requires that the system possess certain automatic feedback loops in order to maintain optimal functioning under varying circumstances. We shall not go into this property here, except simply to point out that the design of an information retrieval system requires the consideration of this problem.

In summary, the essential components of an information retrieval system are: a language, a code, a searching procedure, and a series of automatic feedback loops. Each of these components may themselves be made up of other components and so-forth. There are various ways in which a set of components can be organized into a system for the purpose of carrying out a given process. The designer must determine which set of components should be assembled in order to perform the assigned task. That is, given certain classes of components, which assembly of these into a system will provide the optimum performance relative to the specified purpose and function? The answer to this question requires a means of evaluating a system's performance.

3.4 Performance Measures for IR Systems

The perfomance M of an information retrieval system can be measured in terms of a function of two variables,

$$M = f(u, v)$$

where u is a measure of the system's effectiveness and v is a measure of the system's efficiency.

Informally, effectiveness u is defined as a measure of the system's ability to perform the task for which it was designed, while efficiency v is a measure of the cost or speed of performing this task.

Effectiveness of a system is measured by a function u which should behave in accordance with the requirements imposed upon the system's performance. The system is expected to transmit that information contained in its file and only that information which is relevant to the user's query. In other words, the system is expected to provide the user with that part of the infectious material at its disposal which will result in an effective contact when transmitted to a susceptible.

The effectiveness of an information retrieval system can be measured in the same way as the effectiveness of a diagnostic test. A diagnosis is an evaluation of the result of a communication process. Thus a diagnostic test is simply a method for determining whether an effective contact has occurred. Hence the evaluation of a diagnostic test is a special case of the evaluation of an information retrieval system. In the diagnostic case the problem is to determine whether a screening test can correctly identify an effective contact between a susceptible and the infectious material of a given disease. In the general case the problem is to determine whether an information retrieval system can correctly select the relevant material namely those agents and only those agents which will lead to an effective contact when transmitted to the user.

In the evaluation of a screening test for a given disease, the physician is concerned with two measures which are called sensitivity and specificity.[16, 17] Sensitivity is defined as the "ability" of the test to classify as positive those who have the condition being screened for." In other words, sensitivity is a measure of how well a test correctly identifies those individuals who have a certain disease. Specificity is defined as "the ability of the test to classify as negative those who do not have the condition." Thus specificity is a measure of how well a test correctly identifies those persons who do not have the disease. Failure of the test to identify a case of disease is

called a false negative. If the test incorrectly identifies an individual as a case of the disease, this is labeled a false positive.

Just as a diagnostic test is expected to identify every case of disease within a given population, so an information retrieval system is expected to retrieve that material and only that material contained in its file (information source) which is relevant to the user's request, i.e., that will result in an effective contact. Borrowing the terminology from medicine we define effectiveness as a function of sensitivity and specificity, where sensitivity measures the system's ability to transmit to the user the relevant members of the file and specificity measures the system's ability not to transmit the non-relevant members.

Hence sensitivity can be represented by the conditional probability that a member x of the file I will be transmitted to the user s given that x is relevant to s. Thus

$$S_e = P_A(X)$$

where X represents the system output and A the set of relevant members contained in I.

The measure of specificity can be represented as the conditional probability that a member y of I will not be transmitted by the system given that y is not relevant to s. Thus

$$S_P = P_{A'}(X')$$

where X' is the complement of the system's output X and A' is the set of non-relevant members of I.

We shall define the measure of effectiveness of an information retrieval system as

(42) $$u = P_A(X) + P_{A'}(X') - 1$$

and show that this function possesses the essential properties expected of such a measure.

First, we observe that the values of the function u can range from -1 to $+1$. The maximum value of $+1$ is attained if and only if

$$P_A(X) = 1 \text{ and } P_{A'}(X') = 1$$

This is precisely the case where the system transmits all members and only those members of the file which are relevant.

On the other hand u achieves its minimum value of -1 if and only if

$$P_A(X) = 0 \text{ and } P_{A'}(X') = 0$$

This is exactly the case where the system transmits all members and only those members of the file which are non-relevant.

Since

$$P_{A'}(X) = 1 - P_{A'}(X')$$

(42) can be expressed as

$$(43) \qquad u = P_A(X) - P_{A'}(X)$$

From (43) it can be seen that u = 0 if and only if the conditional probability that information will be transmitted by the system given that it is relevant is equal to the conditional probability that information will be transmitted given that it is non-relevant. In this event the system is operating in a random fashion. Positive values of u indicate that the system's chances of transmitting information which leads to an effective contact are better than not, while negative values of u indicate the converse.

The random performance is the worst possible, since the system under such circumstances is making no contribution to the communication process. A negative contribution in certain instances may be very desirable, i.e., in those cases where the results of a communication process are to be minimized rather than maximized, e.g., in the transmission of a disease.

The efficiency v is measured by some function which can be considered as a function of time

$$v = C(t).$$

Thus the performance of an information system may in general be measured in terms of its effectiveness per unit of time.

$$M = u(t).$$

Clearly the performance of an information retrieval system can provide a control over the outcome of a communication process. General methods for dealing with this problem shall be the topic of the next section.

4. Communication as a Control Process

4.1 Optimal Control Processes

Physical processes which occur either in nature or technology are often controllable. That is, they may be carried out by various means depending upon the will of man. The basic problem is that of determining the best way or the optimal control of the process.

Optimization of a process may be thought of in several senses, e.g., shortest length of time, minimal cost, least expenditure of energy and so forth. Problems of this type have been studied in a general sense by a group of Soviet mathematicians led by Academician L. S. Portryagin. The results of these studies which appeared in a recent monograph[18] provide a very powerful tool for handling optimal control problems. In this short section we shall very briefly outline the fundamental problem, its solution

and indicate how this work could be useful in the study of communication processes. Since the mathematics is quite sophisticated we shall not give too much detail but refer the interested reader to the literature[18] in which the subject is treated with mathematical rigor.

Consider a process which is describable by a system of ordinary differential equations

$$\frac{dx}{dt} i = f_i(x_1, x_2, \ldots x_n) \quad i = 1, 2, \ldots n$$

where the x_i represents the variables which characterize the process. These variables are called phase coordinates and are usually functions of time t. Since the behavior of the process at any given instant in time is given by the n real numbers $x_1, x_2, \ldots x_n$, i.e., by the vector $\bar{x} = (x_1, x_2, \ldots, x_n)$ then the vector space $\bar{X}$ of vectors $\bar{x}$ constitutes a phase space of the process.

If we assume that the process is controllable then there exists controls u which determine the course of the process. These controls can be represented as points in a control region U of a space of control parameters $u_1, u_2, \ldots, u_m$. The control region U is thus a bounded region in an m dimensional Euclidean space. The region is bounded because it is physically realistic to assume that the control parameters are bounded, i.e., that they are physically restricted. Generally the region is taken to be an m dimensional cube. Thus

$$|\bar{u}_i| = r \qquad i = 1, 2, \ldots, m$$

where r is an arbitrary positive real number. If we consider the process to be passing through a certain time interval $[t_0, t_1]$, then a control is a function $u = u(t)$ defined for values of t on the interval $[t_0, t_1]$ where the range is the control region U. Since U is imbedded in a vector space of control parameters, each control is a vector function

$$\bar{u}(t) = (u_1(t), u_2(t), \ldots, u_m(t))$$

with range in U.

In given physical situations controls may have to satisfy certain conditions, e.g., continuity, differentiability, etc. Controls which satisfy the constraints placed upon them are called admissible controls.

Hence a control process can be characterized in vector form by

$$(44) \qquad \frac{d\bar{x}}{dt} = f(\bar{x}, \bar{u})$$

where $\bar{u}$ is an admissible control.

For any initial condition $\bar{x}_0 = \bar{x}(t_0)$ the development of the process is uniquely determined given the selection of a certain admissible control $\bar{u}(t)$. In other words the solution $\bar{x} = \bar{x}(t)$ to equation (44) defines the realization of the process corresponding to the control $\bar{u}(t)$ with initial conditions $\bar{x}_0 = \bar{x}(t_0)$.

The control $\bar{u}(t)$ is said to move the process from the position $\bar{x}_0$ to the position $\bar{x}_1$ if the solution $\bar{x} = \bar{x}(t)$ is defined for all values of t on the interval $[t_0, t_1]$ and passes through $\bar{x}_1$ at time t_1.

The fundamental problem of optimal control theory can now be formulated as follows:

Given two points $\bar{x}_0$ and $\bar{x}_1$ in the phase space $\bar{X}$, then from among all admissible controls which transfer the process from $\bar{x}_0$ to $\bar{x}_1$ find the one for which

$$(45) \qquad \int_{t_0}^{t_1} f(x(t)), u(t) dt$$

is minimal. $f(\bar{x}, \bar{u})$ is assumed to be continuous in $\bar{x}$ and $\bar{u}$, i.e., it is defined and continuous on the product space $X \cdot U$ and $\bar{x}(t)$ is a solution to equation (44) with initial conditions $\bar{x}_0 = \bar{x}(t_0)$.

Note that t_0 and t_1 are not constant for fixed $\bar{x}_0$ and $\bar{x}_1$ but depend upon the choice of the control which makes the transfer. That is, the time required for the process to move from $\bar{x}_0$ to $\bar{x}_1$ is not constant but depends upon the control which is selected.

The control $\bar{u}(t)$ which yields the minimal solution to the integral (45) is called the optimal control. The corresponding path $\bar{x}(t)$ taken by the process in its course of development is called the optimal trajectory. Hence the fundamental problem consists of finding the optimal control and optimal trajectory.

An extremely important special case of the optimal control problem is the one for which $f(\bar{x}, \bar{u}) \equiv 1$. In this case the integral (45) takes the form

$$\int_{t_0}^{t_1} dt = t_1 - t_0$$

Hence the optimal control $\bar{u}(t)$ in this instance stands for a transition from $\bar{x}_0$ to $\bar{x}_1$ in minimal time.

The solution to the fundamental problem is given by Pontryagin's maximum principle. The maximum principle is a theorem which gives the necessary conditions for a control to be optimal.

It says that if $\bar{u}(t)$, $t_0 \leqq t \leqq t_1$ is an admissable control which moves a process from $\bar{x}_0$ to $\bar{x}_1$, then $\bar{u}(t)$ will be optimal if

(a) there exists a non zero continuous vector function $\psi(t) = [\psi_0(t), \psi_1(t), \ldots, \psi_n(t)]$ corresponding to $\bar{u}(t)$ and its trajectory $\bar{x}(t)$ and

(b) a function $H(\psi, \bar{x}, \bar{u}) = \sum_{\alpha=1}^{n} \psi_\alpha f^\alpha(\bar{x}, \bar{u})$

which for fixed $\psi(t)$, $\bar{x}(t)$ is a function of $\bar{u}_{\epsilon\nu}$ such that

(c) $H(\psi(t), \bar{x}(t), \bar{u})$ reaches its maximum at $\bar{u} = \bar{u}(t)$ with least upper bound greater or equal to zero at the terminal point t_1.

4.2 Epidemics as Optimal Control Processes

Since systems are the mechanisms by which processes are realized, it follows that the answer to the optimization question in the physical sense can be found in the manipulation of systems or rather the components of systems. That is, the control over the development of a process can be said to rest in the performance of the system which was designed to carry it out. The components of the system then represent the control parameters. Thus optimal control theory seems to be directly applicable to the problem in which we are interested.

It was established in section 1 that every communication process can be studied in terms of an epidemic process. It was also established that an epidemic process can be characterized in terms of a system of differential equations

$$\frac{d\bar{x}_i}{dt} = f_i(x_1, \ldots x_n) \qquad i = 1, \ldots, m$$

where the x_i represents the variables of the process namely susceptibles, infectives and removals. Thus in the case of a direct contact model $n = 3$ and in the case of a process involving an intermediary host $n = 6$.

The system of equations describing the epidemic process could be characterized as a vector space W, which represents the phase space of the communication process.

Effective contact between susceptibles and infectives in the population in which the process is developing is brought about by means of an information retrieval process which is realized by an information retrieval system. Thus the effectiveness of the IR system is the control u which determines the course of the process while its components are the control parameters. Hence there exists a control region U in which points represent the effectiveness measures

$$u = (u_i) \qquad i = 1, \ldots, k$$

of the various systems which act as admissible controls. An admissible control in this case is simply an admissible system.

The region U is bounded and is in fact the unit k dimensional cube since

$$|u_k| \leqq 1.$$

The maximum principle gives the necessary conditions for any one of these systems to be optimal. Thus we are able to separate from among all of the trajectories which move the process from a position $\bar{x}_0$ to a position $\bar{x}_1$ the ones which accomplish this task optimally.

The mathematical theory of optimal control processes also contains methods for handling a process which is represented stochastically as a Markov process. Thus it would seem that this theory can be profitably applied to the study of communication processes and in fact could be a very powerful tool in the design of IR systems whose function is to optimize either minimally or maximally the epidemic property of a communication process.

4.3 Stability of Epidemic Processes

The problem of stability in the study of epidemic processes is a very important one. Generally speaking stability in physical processes is concerned with the question of whether or not the initial state or position of the process remains constant with time. In the real case it is impossible to control the initial state exactly since physical processes are subject to disturbances. Hence the problem of stability is more precisely concerned with whether or not the initial state of the process remains within a certain region of its phase space. In other words a process will follow a certain course of development under certain initial conditions. The question concerns the effect of slight disturbances in the initial conditions upon the development of the process.

The stability problem has been studied mathematically as a part of the theory of differential equations, notably by the Russian mathematician A. M. Lyapunov. Thus the stability theory of Lyapunov[19] can be of use in the study of a physical process which can be represented by systems of differential equations.

Consider a system of differential equations written in vector form

(46) $$\frac{d\bar{x}}{dt} = f(\bar{x}) \qquad \bar{x} = (x_1, x_2, \ldots x_n).$$

Suppose that in the system (46) the phase coordinates have reached the fixed point $\bar{a} = (a_1, a_2, \ldots, a_n)$. Then $f(\bar{a}) = 0$ and $\bar{x} = \bar{a}$ is called a state of equilibrium of the process. If $\bar{a}$ is taken to be the initial state of the process represented by the system (46) then the question of stability asks whether or not the process will remain near $\bar{a}$ under a slight disturbance. That is do the trajectories g^* which start near $\bar{a}$ stay near the trajectory g emanating from $\bar{a}$ or do they drift away from g. In the first case the state $\bar{a}$ is said to be stable while in the second case unstable.

It is convenient to take the initial state $\bar{a}$ as the origin of the phase space $\bar{X}$. This is easily accomplished by means of a transformation of coordinates. By doing this we are dealing with a process for which

$$f(0) = 0$$

and thus our concern is with the stability of the origin of the phase space $\bar{X}$ of equations which characterize the process under study.

The origin of a process is said to be stable in the sense of Lyapunov if: given the initial state $\bar{a}$, there exists a spherical region $S(R)$ of radius R about the origin $\bar{a}$ such that for $r \leqq R$ a trajectory g^* starting at the point $\bar{x}_0$ in the region $S(r)$ will remain in the region $S(R)$.

The origin is said to be unstable if for any r no matter how small the trajectory reaches the boundary of the sphere $S(R)$.

The methods of Lyapunov reduce these considerations to the study of the properties of a special type of function called a Lyapunov function. A function $V(x)$ is a Lyapunov function if

(1) $V(x)$ together with its partial derivatives are continuous in a open region about the origin

(2) $V(0) = 0$

(3) $V(x)$ is positive everywhere in Ω except at the origin

(4) $\dfrac{dV}{dt} = 0$

Lyapunov's stability theorem then states that the origin in stable if there exists a Lyapunov function $V(x)$ in some neighborhood Ω about the origin.

A general epidemic process can be described by a system of type (46) with phase coordinates $S, I, R,$ representing the number of susceptibles, infectives and removals in the population N at a given point in time.

Theorem (2) states that a general epidemic process in an open population will be stable if the difference in the rate of change of migrations to and from the population is constant. Denote this difference by dM/dt. We shall show that $dM/dt = k$, k a constant, is a Lyapunov function, hence its existence in the region of the origin of the process guarantees its stability.

Let $\bar{x}_0 = (S_0, 1, 0)$ be the initial state of the epidemic process. By translation of coordinates the initial state $\bar{x}_0$ can be taken as the origin of the phase space $\bar{X}$. Clearly

(1) $\dfrac{dM}{dt} = V(S, I)$ together with its first partial derivatives are continuous in a region surrounding the origin.

(2) $V(0) = 0$

(3) $\dfrac{dM}{dt}$ is positive everywhere in this region except at the origin and

(4) $\dfrac{dV}{dt} = 0$ since $\dfrac{dM}{dt} = k$

Hence $\dfrac{dM}{dt}$ is a Lyapunov function.

Earlier it was pointed out that an epidemic process can be represented as a control process by the system of differential equations

$$\frac{d\bar{x}}{dt} = f(\bar{x}, \bar{u})$$

$\bar{x} = (x_1, x_2, \ldots, x_n)$ and $\bar{u} = (u_1, u_2, \ldots, u_m)$ where the x_i as before are the phase coordinates which characterize the state of the process and the u_i are the control parameters.

A system of differential equations always has an infinite number of solutions. In order to obtain a definite solution the initial state together with a particular control must be specified. From the definition of stability it would seem that the phase space of a system of differential equations which describes an epidemic process can be decomposed into two domains. One domain would represent stable solutions while the other would represent unstable ones. It then would be possible given certain initial conditions to select all controls for which the process attains a state of stability, or instability if that is desired. One could then apply Pontryagin's maximum principle in order to determine which control produces the desired state optimally.

References

1. Shannon, C. E. "The Mathematical Theory of Communication." Bell System Technical Journal, Vol. 27, pp. 379–423; pp. 623–656 (1948).
2. Khinchin, A. I. "Mathematical Foundations of Information Theory." Dover, New York (1957).
3. Siegfried, A. "Germs and Ideas." Oliver & Boyd, London (1965).
4. Bailey, N. T. J. "The Mathematical Theory of Epidemics." Griffin, London (1960).
5. Bartlett, M. S. "Stochastic Population Models in Ecology and Epidemiology." Wiley, New York (1960).
6. Daley, D. J. and D. G. Kendal. "Stochastic Rumours." J. Inst. Maths. Applics., Vol. 1, pp. 42–55 (1965).
7. Goffman, W. and V. A. Newill. "Generalization of Epidemic Theory." Nature, Vol. 204, p. 225 (1964).
8. Goffman, W. "Mathematical Approach to the Spread of Ideas — the History of Mast Cell Research." Nature, Vol. 212, pp. 449–452 (1966).
9. Fraenkel, A. A. "Abstract Set Theory," North-Holland, Amsterdam, (1961).
10. Goode, H. H. and R. E. Machol. "Systems Engineering." McGraw-Hill, New York (1957).
11. Hall A.D., "A Methodology for Systems Engineering." McGraw-Hill, New York (1957).
12. Carnap, R. "The Logical Syntax of Language," Harcourt-Brace & Co., New York (1937).
13. Harris, Z. S. "Methods in Structural Linguistics," University of Chicago Press, Chicago (1951).
14. Chomsky, N. "Syntactic Structures," Mouton & Co., The Hague (1964).
15. Wolfowitz, J. "Coding Theorems of Information Theory," Springer, Berlin (1961).
16. Kurlander, A. B., A. P. Iskrant and M. E. Kent. "Screening Tests for Diabetes: A Study of Specificity and Sensitivity." Diabetes, Vol. 3, p. 213, (1954).
17. Remein, Q. R. and H. L. C. Wilkerson. "The Efficiency of Screening Tests for Diabetes." J. Chr. Dis., Vol. 13, p. 6, (1961).
18. Pontryagin, L. S., et al. "The Mathematical Theory of Optimal Control Processes." John Wiley & Sons, New York (1963).
19. LaSalle, J. and S. Lefschetz. "Stability by Lyapunov's Direct Method," Academic Press, New York (1961).

Index